AUTOMOTIVE HANDBOOK

BOSCH

Imprint

Published by:
© Robert Bosch GmbH, 1993
Postfach 30 02 20, D-70442 Stuttgart.
Automotive Equipment Business Sector,
Department for Technical Information
(KH/VDT).

Editor-in-Chief:
Dipl.-Ing.(FH) Ulrich Adler
Editors:
Dipl.-Ing.(FH) Horst Bauer,
Ing.(grad.) Arne Cypra,
Folkhart Dinkler,
Dipl.-Ing. Peter Künne,
Dipl.-Phys. Johannes Röder
Production management:
Günter Berger
Layout:
Dipl.-Ing.(FH) Ulrich Adler,
Günter Berger

Translation:
Editor-in-chief:
Peter Girling
Translated by:
Ingenieurbüro für Technische und
Wissenschaftliche Übersetzungen
Dr. W.-D. Haehl GmbH, Stuttgart
Member of the ALPNET Services Group
William D. Lyon
Technical graphics:
Bauer & Partner GmbH, Stuttgart
Design, cover, front matter:
Zweckwerbung, Kirchheim u.T.
Joint production:
Walter Wirtz Druck & Verlag, Speyer

Worldwide distribution, 3rd Edition:
SAE Society of Automotive Engineers
400 Commonwealth Drive
Warrendale, PA 15096-001 USA
ISBN 1-56091-372-X.

Approved Editions under license:

Robert Bentley, Publishers
1000 Massachusetts Avenue
Cambridge, MA 02138
1-800-423-4595 USA
ISBN 0-8376-0330-7.

VDI-Verlag GmbH
Verlag des Vereins Deutscher Ingenieure
Graf-Recke-Str.85
D-40239 Düsseldorf, Germany
ISBN 3-1-419115-X.

The following companies placed picture matter, diagrams and other informative material at our disposal:

Audi AG, Ingolstadt;
Bayerische Motoren Werke AG, Munich;
Behr GmbH & Co, Stuttgart;
Continental AG, Hannover;
Eberspächer KG, Eßlingen;
Filterwerk Mann und Hummel, Ludwigsburg;
Ford-Werke AG, Cologne;
Aktiengesellschaft Kühnle, Kopp und Kausch, Frankental;
Mannesmann Kienzle GmbH, Villingen-Schwenningen;
Mercedes-Benz AG, Stuttgart;
Pierburg GmbH, Neuss;
RWE Energie AG, Essen;
Volkswagen AG, Wolfsburg;
Zahnradfabrik Friedrichshafen AG, Friedrichshafen.

Printed in Germany.
Imprimé en Allemagne.

Editorial closing: 15.9.1993

Foreword to the 3rd Edition

The "Automotive Handbook" is a handy, concise, pocket-sized technical reference work. Its primary purpose is to provide the automotive engineer, the mechanic, the student, and all those interested in technical matters, with a wealth of reliable technical data as well as an insight into present-day state-of-the-art automotive technology in Germany. With this assignment in mind, the scope of the theoretical chapters dealing with **passenger cars and commercial vehicles**, as well as the remaining contents, has been kept to the practical and necessary level.

With the framework of a pocket-sized handbook, it is impossible to present a detailed coverage of individual technical subjects. On the other hand, with the very wide range of users in mind, we did not want to dispense with generally applicable topics and data.

We recommend their you leaf through this Automotive Handbook before attempting to use it, this will prove to be a valuable help when you actually want to refer to a particular point at a later date.

The addition of new technical subjects and the expansion and up-dating of existing material are reflected in the fact that this 3rd Edition is 140 pages longer than its predecessor.

This 3rd English Edition was revised and up-dated by specialists from the Bosch Group, as were the two previous editions. For certain chapters, other firms also made contributions. At this point, we would like to express our appreciation to all concerned.

The editors

For your information:

Compared to the 2nd Edition, we have up-dated the following subjects:

Oscillations: Modal analysis
Electronics: Solar cells, PC-board techniques, micromechanics, mechatronics, A/D conversion
Technical optics: Laser engineering, beam waveguides
Materials: Automotive paints
Motor-vehicle dynamics: Driving dynamics (as per ISO)
Exhaust systems: Catalytic converters, soot filters
Engine management (spark-ignition (SI) engines): Electronic engine-power control (EMS), electronic boost-pressure control, variable-length intake manifold, evaporative-emissions control, exhaust-gas recirculation (EGR), alcohol/hydrogen-powered engines
Engine management (diesel engines): In-line control-sleeve fuel-injection pump, unit injectors (PDE), exhaust-gas analyzers
Drivetrain: Traction control (ASR)
Suspension: Suspension systems, active suspensions
Tires: Traction
Steering: Power-assisted steering, rear-wheel steering
Braking systems: Antilock braking systems (ABS), Electronically controlled commercial-vehicle braking systems (ELB)
Lighting: PES headlamps, Litronic
Safety systems: Seat-belt tighteners, airbags, rollover protection, tire-pressure monitoring system
Comfort systems: Central locking systems
Vehicle electrical systems: Compact alternators, CAN, EMC

And we have introduced the following subjects:

Sensors, Actuators, Quality, Reliability, Automotive data-processing, Bonding techniques / Sheet-metal processing, Tribology / Wear, Park-Pilot, Navigation systems, Mobile telephone, Driver information systems

Contents

Physics, basics
Quantities and units 10
Conversion tables 17
Oscillations 39
Mechanics 44
Strength of materials 52
Acoustics 60
Heat 66
Electrical engineering 70
Electronics 86
Sensors 102
Actuators 116
Electric machines 123
Technical optics 128

Mathematics, methods
Mathematical signs, symbols 136
Trigonometry 138
Volumes and surface areas 142
Quality 144
Engineering statistics, measuring techniques 150
Reliability 158
Data processing in motor vehicles 160
Control engineering 164

Materials science
Chemical elements 168
Terminology and parameters 172
Material groups 174
Material properties 178
Lubricants 218
Fuels 226
Chemicals 236
Corrosion/corrosion protection 242
Heat treatment 252
Hardness 258

Machine elements
Tolerances 263
Sliding and rolling bearings 268
Spring calculation 276
Threaded fasteners 282
Gears and gear teeth 292
Belt drives 302

Bonding and joining techniques
Welding 306
Soldering 308
Adhesives 309
Riveting 310
Pressurized clinching 311

Sheet-metal processing
Deep-drawing techniques 312
Laser techniques 314

Tribology, wear 315

Motor-vehicle dynamics
Road-going vehicle requirements 320
Fuel requirements 321
Dynamics of linear motion 324
Dynamics of lateral motion 336
Operating behavior (as per ISO) 340
Operating dynamics, comm. vehicles 345
Agricultural-tractor requirements 348
Environmental stress 350

Internal-combustion (IC) engines
Principle of operation and classification 352
Thermodynamic cycles 353
Reciprocating-piston engine with internal combustion 355
  Spark-ignition (SI) engine 358
  Diesel engine 362
  Hybrid processes 367
  Gas exchange 368
  Supercharging/Turbocharging 372
  Power transmission 376
  Cooling, lubrication 392
  Values and data for calculations 394
Reciprocating-piston engine with external combustion (Stirling engine) 406
Wankel rotary engines 408
Gas turbines 410

Engine cooling
Air cooling 412
Water cooling 412
Charge-air cooling 414
Oil cooling 415

Intake air, exhaust systems
Air filters 416
Superchargers and turbochargers 418
Exhaust systems 424

Engine management, spark-ignition (SI) engines
Parameters, operation 428

Fuel management 430
Carburetors 431
Single-point electronic fuel-injection systems (TBI) 436
  Mono-Jetronic 436
Multipoint electronic fuel-injection systems (MPI) 438
  K-Jetronic 438
  KE-Jetronic 440
  L-Jetronic 442
  LH-Jetronic 444

Ignition
Basics 446
Components
  Ignition coils 449
  Spark plugs 450
Ignition systems
  Conventional coil ignition (CI) 455
  Transistorized ignition (TCI) 458
  Capacitor-discharge ignition (CDI) 460
  Electronic ignition (EI) 461
  Distributorless electronic ignition (DLI) 463
Knock control 464

Further engine-management functions
Idle-speed control 466
Electronic engine-power control (EMS) 467
Electronic boost-pressure control 468
Variable-length intake manifolds 469
Evaporative-emissions control 470
Exhaust-gas recirculation (EGR) 470

Integrated engine-management systems, Motronic
Detection and processing of measured variables 472
Motronic system 473
System configuration 475
Competition and racing 475

Engine test technology 476

Exhaust emissions, spark-ignition (SI) engines
Combustion products 478
Exhaust-gas control 479
Lambda closed-loop control 482
Testing exhaust and evaporative emissions 483
Exhaust-gas limits 485
Exhaust-gas analyzers 489

Internal-combustion (IC) engines for alternative fuels
LPG operation 490
Alcohol operation 492
Hydrogen operation 493

Engine management (diesel engines)
Fuel metering 494
Fuel-injection systems 494
Fuel-injection pumps, in-line 496
Fuel-injection pumps, control-sleeve type 502
Fuel-injection pumps, distributor type 502
Unit injectors (PDE) 505
Fuel filters 506
Nozzles and nozzle holders 506
Fuel-injection pump test benches 511

Exhaust emissions (diesel engines)
Combustion products 512
Exhaust-gas control 512
Exhaust-gas testing 513
Exhaust-gas limits 515
Exhaust-gas analyzers 518

Auxiliary starting devices for diesel engines
Sheathed-element glow plugs 520
Flame plugs 521
Heater plugs 521
Glow control unit 521

Starting systems 523

Alternative drive systems
Electric drives 527
Hybrid drives 533

Drivetrain
Basics 536
Clutches 538
Transmissions and gearboxes 541
Final drives 551
Differentials 553
All-wheel drive (AWD) 555
Traction control/acceleration slip regulation (ASR) 555
  ASR for passenger cars 556
  ASR for commercial vehicles 558

Chassis systems
Suspension 560
Suspension linkage 568
Wheels 572
Tires 576
Steering 586

Braking systems
Definitions and principles 594
Legal regulations 598
Braking-system classification 603
Braking-system configuration 604
Braking systems for passenger cars and light commercial vehicles 606
  Control devices 606
  Wheel brakes 608
Antilock braking systems (ABS) for passenger cars 610
Braking systems for commercial vehicles 620
  Classification and configuration 620
  Braking-force metering 621

Wheel brakes 624
Parking-brake systems 628
Retarder braking systems 628
Compressed-air braking-system components 633
Antilock braking systems (ABS) for commercial vehicles 638
Electronically controlled commercial-vehicle braking systems (ELB) 642
Brake analyzers 644

Road-vehicle systematics 646

Vehicle bodies, passenger-car
Main dimensions 648
Body structure 652
Body materials 563
Body surface 564
Body finishing components 654
Safety 656
Calculations 660

Vehicle bodies, commercial-vehicle
Commercial vehicles 662
Delivery trucks and vans 662
Medium and heavy-duty trucks and tractor vehicles 663
Buses 664
Passive safety 666
Commercial-vehicle noise reduction 667

Lighting
Legal regulations 668
Headlamps 670
Lamps 682
Lamp bulbs 687
Headlamp aiming devices 689

Signaling and alarm systems
Visual signaling systems 690
Acoustic signaling devicess 691
Theft-deterrent systems (Car Alarm) 692

Windshield, rear-window and headlamp cleaning systems, windshield and window glass
Windshield wipers 694
Rear-window wipers 695
Headlamp wash-wipe systems 696
Windshield and window glass 698

Heating, ventilation, and air-conditioning (HVAC)
Engine-dependent heating systems 700
Air-conditioning systems 701
Engine-independent heating systems 703

Communication and information systems
Car radio 704
Check control 707
Trip computer 708
Park-Pilot 709
Trip recorder 710
Navigation systems 712
Mobile radio, mobile telephone 714
Board Information Terminal (BIT) 716

Safety systems
Seat-belt tightener 717
Air bag 718
Rollover protection system 720
Tire-pressure monitoring system (RKS) 721

Comfort and convenience systems
Power windows 722
Power sunroof 723
Seat and steering-column adjustment, electrical 724
Central locking systems 724

Automotive hydraulics
Basics 726
Pumps, motors 727
Valves 730
Cylinders 733
Tractor hydraulics 734
Hydraulic accumulators 737
Hydrostatic fan drive 738
Hydrostatic drives 740

Automotive pneumatics
Door operation 742
Radiator louvers 743

Electrical system and power supply
Symbols 744
Circuit diagrams 752
Conductor-size calculations 756
Electrical power supply 758
Starter batteries 763
Battery chargers 767
Alternators 768
Controller Area Network (CAN) 776
Electromagnetic compatibility (EMC) and interference suppression 779

Passenger-car specifications 784
Specifications of German and foreign passenger cars

Road traffic legislation 814

Miscellaneous
Alphabets and numbers 822

Index of Headings 823

Authors of the 3rd Edition[1])

Quantities and Units
Dipl.-Ing. G. Brüggen
Dipl.-Ing. W. Bazlen †
Oscillations/Vibrations
Dipl.-Ing. J. Bohrer,
Dr.rer.nat. M. Hillen
Mechanics
Dipl.-Ing. G. Brüggen
Strength of materials
Dipl.-Ing. J. Huhnen
Acoustics
Dr.rer.nat. W. Keiper
Heat
Dipl.-Ing. E. Ungerer

Electrical engineering
Dr.rer.nat. W. Draxler,
Dipl.-Ing. B. Wörner
Electronics
Dr.rer.nat. G. Matthäi, Dr.rer.nat. P. Egelhaaf, Dr.-Ing. R. Kasper, Dr.rer.nat. R. Schmid, Dr.-Ing. F. Piwonka, Dr.-Ing. J. Marek, Dipl.-Ing. F. Raichle
Sensors
Dr.-Ing. E. Zabler
Actuators
Dr.-Ing. G. Keuper, Dr.-Ing. C. Kramer
Electric machines
Dr.-Ing. K. Harms
Technical optics
Dr.-Ing. F. Prinzhausen,
Dr.rer.nat. H. Sautter

Mathematics
Dipl.-Ing. G. Brüggen
Quality
Dipl.-Ing. M. Graf
Engineering statistics, measurement
Dipl.-Math. R. Lang
Reliability
Dr.rer.nat. E. Dilger,
Dr.rer.nat. H. Weiler
Automotive data processing
Dr.rer.nat. S. Dais
Control engineering
Dipl.-Ing. R. Karrelmeyer

[1]) Unless otherwise stated, the authors are employees of Robert Bosch GmbH

Materials science
Dr.rer.nat. M. Gaiser; Dr.rer.nat. W. Draxler; Dr.-Ing. D. Wicke; Dipl.-Ing. D. Weidemann, Mercedes-Benz AG, Sindelfingen; Dr.rer.nat. H.-J. Spranger; Dr.rer.nat. H. P. Koch; Dipl.-Ing. R. Mayer; Dipl.-Ing. G. Lindemann; Dr.rer.nat. K. Müller; Dipl.-Ing. H. Schneider; Dr.rer.nat. K. Kinberger, BASF, Münster; Dieter Herbst, BASF, Münster; Dr.rer.nat. G. Dornhöfer; Dr.rer.nat. B. Blaich; Dr.phil.nat. B. Peters
Hardness, heat treatment
Dr.-Ing. D. Liedtke
Corrosion
Dr.rer.nat. H. Jahnke,
Dr.rer.nat. M. Schönborn

Tolerances
Ing. (grad.) Jürgen Pfänder
Sliding and rolling bearings
Dr.-Ing. R. Heinz
Springs
Dipl.-Ing. O. Krickau
Threaded fasteners
Dipl.-Ing. J. Huhnen,
Dipl.-Ing. M. Nöcker
Gears
Dipl.-Ing. P.-I. Pladek
Belt drives
Dipl.-Ing. D. Pfitzenmaier

Bonding techniques
Dr.-Ing. M. Witt, Volkswagen AG, Wolfsburg

Sheet-metal processing
Ing. W. Gertler, Volkswagen AG, Wolfsburg; Dr.-Ing. M. Witt, Volkswagen AG, Wolfsburg

Tribology, wear
Dipl.-Ing. H. Schorr

Road-vehicle requirements
Dr.-Ing. H. Hiereth, Mercedes-Benz AG Stuttgart; Dipl.-Ing. E. Siegert, Mercedes-Benz AG, Stuttgart

Motor-vehicle dynamics
Dipl.-Ing. E. Siegert, Mercedes-Benz AG, Stuttgart; Dr.-Ing. E.-C. v. Glasner, Mercedes-Benz AG, Stuttgart; Dipl.-Ing. H. Geißler, Mercedes-Benz AG, Stuttgart; Dr.-Ing. H. Steinkampf, Institut für Betriebstechnik der FAL, Braunschweig

Environmental stresses
Dipl.-Ing. G. Adalbert

Combustion engines
Dr.-Ing. H. Hiereth, Mercedes-Benz AG, Stuttgart

Engine cooling
Dipl.-Ing. S. Jenz, Behr GmbH & Co, Stuttgart; Dipl.-Ing. H. Martin, Behr GmbH & Co, Stuttgart

Filters
Dr.-Ing. O. Parr, Filterwerk Mann und Hummel, Ludwigsburg
Superchargers and turbochargers
Dipl.-Ing. A. Förster, Aktiengesellschaft Kühnle, Kopp und Kausch, Frankental
Exhaust systems
Dipl.-Ing. W. Steinle, Eberspächer KG, Eßlingen

Engine management, spark-ignition (SI) engines
Dr.rer.nat. H. Schwarz, Dipl.-Ing. G. Felger, Dipl.-Ing. M. Lembke, Dr.rer.nat. W. Huber, Ing. (grad.) L. Seebald, Dipl.-Ing. (FH) U. Steinbrenner, Dr.-Ing. W. Richter
Carburetors
Dr.-Ing. D. Großmann, Pierburg GmbH, Neuss
Gasoline fuel-injection systems
Dipl.-Ing. G. Felger, Dipl.-Ing. M. Lembke, Ing. (grad.) L. Seebald
Ignition
Dipl.-Ing. R. Schleupen, Dipl.-Ing. D. Betz, Dr.-Ing. K.-D. Pohl
Integrated engine-management systems, Motronic
Dipl.-Ing. (FH) U. Steinbrenner
Exhaust emissions, spark-ignition (SI) engines
Dipl.-Ing. G. Felger, Dr.-Ing. W. Grözinger

Internal-combustion (IC) engines for alternative fuels
J. van der Weide, TNO Road-Vehicles Research Institute, Delft, Netherlands; Ing. (grad.) L. Seebald; Dipl.-Ing. E. Schnaibel

Engine management (diesel engines)
Dipl.-Ing. (FH) E. Ritter, Dipl.-Ing.(FH) K. Dahlmeier, Dipl.-Ing. (FH) W. Wessel

Auxiliary starting devices
Dipl.-Ing. B. Kaczynski, Dr.rer.nat. H.-P. Bauer
Exhaust emissions, diesel engines
Dr.-Ing. W. Polach, Dipl.-Ing. V. Schneider

Starting systems
Dr.-Ing. K. Bolenz

Electric drives
Dr. Ing. B. Sporckmann, RWE Energie AG, Essen; Dipl.-Ing. E. Zander, RWE Energie AG, Essen
Hybrid drives
Dr.-Ing. C. Bader, Mercedes-Benz AG, Stuttgart

Drivetrain
Dipl.-Ing. K. Lorenz, Bayerische Motoren Werke AG, München; Dipl.-Ing. P. Köpf, Zahnradfabrik Friedrichshafen AG; Dr.rer.nat. M. Schwab, Zahnradfabrik Friedrichshafen AG; Dipl.-Ing. A. Czinczel; Dr.-Ing. H. Schramm

Steering
Dr.-Ing. J. Duminy, Zahnradfabrik Friedrichshafen AG, Schwäbisch Gmünd; Ing. (grad.) D. Elser, Zahnradfabrik Friedrichshafen AG, Schwäbisch Gmünd; Dipl.-Ing. (FH) W. Rieger, Zahnradfabrik Friedrichshafen AG, Schwäbisch Gmünd; Dr.-Ing. W. Schleuter

Suspension, suspension linkage
Dr.-Ing. H. Wallentowitz, Bayerische Motoren Werke AG, München

Wheels
Dipl.-Ing. R. Braun, Mercedes-Benz AG, Stuttgart; Dr.-Ing. E.-C. v. Glasner, Mercedes-Benz AG, Stuttgart

Tires
Dipl.-Ing. B. Meiß, Continental AG, Hannover; Dr.-Ing. H. Meyer, Continental AG, Hannover; Dr.-Ing. E.-C. v. Glasner, Mercedes-Benz AG, Stuttgart

Braking systems
Dipl.-Ing. (FH) L. Steinke; Dr.-Ing. E.-C. v. Glasner, Mercedes-Benz AG, Stuttgart; Dipl.-Ing. W. Kruse, Mercedes-Benz AG, Stuttgart; Dipl.-Ing. A. Czinczel; Dipl.-Ing. I. Grauel; Dr.-Ing. H. Schramm

Road-vehicle systematics
Dipl.-Ing. D. Weidemann, Mercedes-Benz AG, Sindelfingen

Vehicle bodies, passenger-car
Dipl.-Ing. D. Weidemann, Mercedes-Benz AG, Sindelfingen
Vehicle bodies, commercial-vehicle
Dipl.-Ing. H. Geißler, Mercedes-Benz AG, Stuttgart

Lighting
Dipl.-Ing. G. Lindae, Dipl.-Ing. B. Wörner

Signaling and alarm systems
Ing. (grad.) W. Hofer

Windshield, rear-window and headlamp cleaning systems
Dr.-Ing. J.-G. Dietrich

Heating, ventilation, and air-conditioning (HVAC)
Dr.-Ing. K. Molt, Behr GmbH & Co, Stuttgart; Dipl.-Ing. G. Schweizer, Behr GmbH & Co, Stuttgart

Car radio
Blaupunkt-Werke, Presse- und Information, Hildesheim

Check control, trip computer, Park-Pilot
Ing. (grad.) D. Meyer

Trip recorders
Mannesmann Kienzle GmbH, PR-Abteilung, Villingen-Schwenningen

Navigation systems
Dipl.-Ing. E. P. Neukirchner
Mobile radio
Dr.-Ing. J. Wazeck
Board Information Terminal (BIT)
Dr.rer.nat. D. Elke

Safety systems
Dipl.-Ing. B. Mattes, Dr.-Ing. H.-D. Schmid

Comfort and convenience systems
Ing. (grad.) E. Ursel

Automotive hydraulics
Ing. (grad.) W. Dworak; Dipl.-Ing. K.-H. Müller; Dipl.-Ing. G. Nonnenmacher; Dipl.-Ing. W. Kötter; Dipl.-Ing. H. Lödige; Dipl.-Ing. B. Killing, Hägglunds Denison GmbH, Hilden; Ing. (grad.) H. Walter

Automotive pneumatics
Dipl.-Ing. S. Straub

Symbols, conductor-size calculations
Dipl.-Ing. (FH) H. Bauer

Electrical power supply
Dipl.-Ing. (FH) F. Meyer

Starter batteries, battery chargers
Dr.-Ing. G. Richter, Ing. (grad) T. Meyer-Staufenbiel

Alternators
Dr.-Ing. K. G. Bürger

Controller Area Network (CAN)
Dr.rer.nat. J. Unruh

Electromagnetic compatibility (EMC)
Dr.-Ing. H. Neu

Testing
Dipl.-Ing. (FH) W. Dieter

Passenger-car specifications
D. Baer

Road traffic legislation
Dipl.-Ing. K. Haffner, Technischer Überwachungs-Verein Südwest, Stuttgart

Quantities and units

SI units

SI denotes "Systéme International d'Unités" The system is laid down in ISO 31 and ISO 1000 (ISO: International Organization for Standardization), and for Germany in DIN 1301 (DIN = Deutsches Institut für Normung – German Institute for Standardization).

SI units comprise the seven base SI units and coherent units derived from these base SI units using a numerical factor of 1.

Base SI units

Base quantity and symbols		Base SI unit Name	Symbol
Length	l	meter	m
Mass	m	kilogram	kg
Time	t	second	s
Electric current	I	ampere	A
Thermodynamic temperature	T	kelvin	K
Amount of substance	n	mole	mol
Luminous intensity	I	candela	cd

All other quantities and units are derived from the base quantities and base units. The international unit of force is thus obtained by applying Newton's Law:

force = mass × acceleration

$F = m \cdot a$

where m = 1 kg and a = 1 m/s².
thus F = 1 kg · 1 m/s² =
1 kg m/s² = 1 N (newton).

Definitions of the base SI units

1 meter is defined as the distance which light travels in a vacuum in 1/299,792,458 seconds (17th CGPM, 1983[1]). The meter is therefore defined using the speed of light in a vacuum, c = 299,792,458 m/s, and no longer by the wavelength of the radiation emitted by the krypton nuclide ^{86}Kr. The meter was originally defined as the forty-millionth part of a terrestrial meridian (standard meter, Paris, 1875).

1 kilogram is the mass of the international prototype kilogram (1st CGPM, 1889 and 3rd CGPM, 1901[1]).

1 second is defined as the duration of 9,192,631,770 periods of the radiation corresponding to the transition between the two hyperfine levels of the ground state of atoms of the ^{133}Cs nuclide (13th CGPM, 1967[1]).

1 ampere is defined as that constant electric current which, if maintained in two straight parallel conductors of infinite length, of negligible circular cross-sections, and placed 1 meter apart in a vacuum will produce between these conductors a force equal to 2×10^{-7} N per meter of length (9th CGPM, 1948[1]).

1 kelvin is defined as the fraction 1/1273.16 of the thermodynamic temperature of the triple point[2]) of water (13th CGPM, 1967[1]).

1 mole is defined as the amount of substance of a system which contains as many elementary entities as there are atoms in 0.012 kilogram of the carbon nuclide ^{12}C. When the mole is used, the elementary entities must be specified and may be atoms, molecules, ions, electrons, other particles, or specified groups of such particles. 14th CGPM[1]), 1971.

1 candela is defined as the luminous intensity in a given direction of a source which emits monochromatic radiation of frequency 540×10^{12} hertz and of which the radiant intensity in that direction is 1/683 watt per steradian. 16th CGPM[1]), 1979.

---

[1]) CGPM: Conférence Générale des Poids et Mesures (General Conference on Weights and Measures)

[2]) Fixed point on the international temperature scale. The triple point is the only point at which all three phases of water (solid, liquid and gaseous) are in equilibrium (at a pressure of 1013.25 hPa). This temperature of 273.16 K is 0.01 K above the freezing point of water (273.15 K).

Decimal multiples and fractions of SI units

Decimal multiples and fractions of units are denoted by prefixes before the name of the unit or by prefix symbols before the unit symbol. The prefix symbol is placed immediately in front of the unit symbol to form a coherent unit, such as the milligram (mg). Multiple prefixes, such as microkilogram (µkg), may **not** be used.

Prefixes are not to be used before the units angular degree, minute and second, the time units minute, hour, day and year, and the temperature unit degree Celsius.

Prefix	Prefix symbol	Power of ten	Name
atto	a	10^{-18}	trillionth
femto	f	10^{-15}	thousand billionth
pico	p	10^{-12}	billionth
nano	n	10^{-9}	thousand millionth
micro	µ	10^{-6}	millionth
milli	m	10^{-3}	thousandth
centi	c	10^{-2}	hundredth
deci	d	10^{-1}	tenth
deca	da	10^{1}	ten
hecto	h	10^{2}	hundred
kilo	k	10^{3}	thousand
mega	M	10^{6}	million
giga	G	10^{9}	milliard[1])
tera	T	10^{12}	billion[1])
peta	P	10^{15}	thousand billion
exa	E	10^{18}	trillion

Legal units

The Law on Units in Metrology of 2 July 1969 and the related implementing order of 26 June 1970 specify the use of "legal units" in business and official transactions in Germany[2]).

Legal units are

- the SI units
- decimal multiples and submultiples of the SI units.
- other legal units; see the tables on the following pages.

Legal units are used in the Bosch Automotive Handbook. In many sections, values are also given in units of the technical system of units (e.g., in parenthesis) to the extent considered necessary.

Systems of units not to be used

The physical system of units

Like the SI system of units, the physical system of units used the base quantities length, mass and time. However, the base units used for these quantities were the centimeter (cm), gram (g), and second (s) (CGS System).

The technical system of units

The technical system of units used the following base quantities and base units:

Base quantity	Base SI unit Name	Symbol
Length	meter	m
Force	kilopond	kp
Time	second	s

Newton's Law, $F = m \cdot a$, provides the link between the international system of units and the technical system of units, whereby weight G is substituted for F and acceleration of free fall g is substituted for a.

In contrast to mass, acceleration of free fall, and therefore of force due to weight, depend upon location. The standard value of acceleration of free fall is defined as $g_n = 9.80665$ m/s^2 (DIN 1305). The approximate value $g = 9.81$ m/s^2 is generally acceptable for technical calculations.

1 kp is the force with which a mass of 1 kg exerts pressure on the surface beneath it at a place on the earth. Since $G = m \cdot g$,

1 kp = 1 kg·9.81 m/s^2 = 9.81 N.

[1]) In the USA: 10^9 = 1 billion, 10^{12} = 1 trillion

[2]) Also valid: "Gesetz zur Änderung des Gesetzes über Einheiten im Meßwesen" dated 6 July 1973; "Verordnung zur Änderung der Ausführungsverordnung ..." dated 27 November 1973; "Zweite Verordnung zur Änderung der Ausführungsverordnung ..." dated 12 December 1977.

Selected quantities and units

(From DIN 1301)

The following table gives a survey of the most important physical quantities and their standardized symbols, and includes a selection of the legal units specified for these quantities. Additional legal units can be formed by adding prefixes (see p. 11). For this reason, the column "other units" only gives the decimal multiples and submultiples of the SI units which have their own names. Units which are not to be used are given in the last column together with their conversion formulas. Page numbers refer to conversion tables.

Quantity and symbol	Legal units SI	Others	Name	Relationship	Units not to be used and their conversion
1. Length, area, volume (p. 17–23)					
Length l	m		meter		1 µ (micron) = 1 µm 1 Å (Ångström) = 10^{-10} m 1 X.E. (X-unit) ≈ 10^{-13} m 1 p (point: printer's) measure = 0.376 mm
		sm	international nautical mile	1 sm = 1852 m	
Area A	m^2		square meter		
		a	are	1 a = 100 m^2	
		ha	hektar	1 ha = 100 a = 10^4 m^2	
Volume V	m^3		cubic meter		
		l, L	liter	1 l = 1 dm^3	
2. Angle (p. 22)					
(Plane) angle α, β etc.	rad[1])		radian	$1\ \text{rad} = \frac{1\ \text{m arc}}{1\ \text{m radius}}$	1 ∟ (right angle) = 90° = (π/2) rad = 100 gon 1^g (grade or centesimal degree) = 1 gon 1^c (centesimal minute) = 1 cgon 1^{cc} (centesimal second) = 0.1 mgon
		°	degree	1 rad = 180°/π = 57.296° ≈ 57.3° 1° = 0,017453 rad 1° = 60′ = 3600″ 1 gon = (π/200) rad	
		′	minute		
		″	second		
		gon	gon		
Solid angle Ω	sr		steradian	$1\ \text{sr} = \frac{1\ \text{m}^2\ \text{spherical surface}}{1\ \text{m}^2\ \text{sphere radius}^2}$	
3. Mass (p. 24–27)					
Mass (weight)[2]) m	kg		kilogramm		1 γ (gamma) = 1 µg 1 dz (Doppelzentner) = 100 kg 1 Kt = 0.2 g
		g	gramm		
		t	metric ton	1 t = 1 Mg = 10^3 kg	

[1]) The unit rad (p. 22) can be replaced by the numeral 1 in calculations.
[2]) The term "weight" is ambiguous in everyday usage; it is used to denote mass as well as weight (DIN 1305).

Quantity and symbol	Legal units SI	Others	Name	Relationship	Units not to be used and their conversion
Density ϱ	kg/m^3			1 kg/dm^3 = 1 kg/l = 1 g/cm^3 = 1000 kg/m^3	Weight per unit volume γ (kp/dm^3 or p/cm^3). Conversion: The numerical value of the weight per unit volume in kp/dm^3 is equal to the numerical value of the density in kg/dm^3
		$\frac{kg}{dm^3}$			
		kg/l			
		g/cm^3			
Moment of inertia (Second moment of mass) J	$kg \cdot m^2$			$J = m \cdot i^2$ i = Radius of gyration	Flywheel effect $G \cdot D^2$, Conversion: The numerical value of $G \cdot D^2$ in $kp \cdot m^2$ = 4 × the numerical value of J in $kg \cdot m^2$

4. Time quantities (pp. 35–37)

Quantity and symbol	SI	Others	Name	Relationship	Units not to be used and their conversion
Time, duration, interval t	s		second[1]		In power economics, 1 year = 8760 hours
		min	minute[1]	1 min = 60 s	
		h	hour[1]	1 h = 60 min	
		d	day	1 d = 24 h	
		a	year	1 a = 365 d = 8760 h	
Frequency f	Hz		hertz	1 Hz = 1/s	
Rotational frequency (frequency of rotation) n	s^{-1}			1 s^{-1} = 1/s	rpm and r/min (rotations per minute) is still permissible for expressing rotational speed, however it should be replaced by min^{-1} (1 rpm = 1 r/min = 1 min^{-1})
		min^{-1} 1/min		1 min^{-1} = 1/min = (1/60) s^{-1}	
Angular frequency $\omega = 2\pi f$ ω	s^{-1}				
Velocity v	m/s	km/h		1 km/h = (1/3.6) m/s	
		kn	knot	1 kn = 1 sm/h = 1.852 km/h	
Acceleration a	m/s^2			see p. 11 for acceleration of free fall g	
Angular velocity ω	rad/s[2]				
Angular acceleration α	rad/s^2[2]				

5. Force, energy, power (pp. 28–31)

Quantity and symbol	SI	Others	Name	Relationship	Units not to be used and their conversion
Force F weight G	N N		newton	1 N = 1 $kg \cdot m/s^2$	1 p (pond) = 9.80665 mN 1 kp (kilopond) = 9.80665 N ≈ 10 N 1 dyn (dyne) = 10^{-5} N

1) Clock time: h, m, s written as superscripts; example: $3^h 25^m 6^s$.
2) The unit rad can be replaced by the numeral 1 in calculations.

Quantity and symbol	Legal units SI	Others	Name	Relationship	Units not to be used and their conversion
Pressure, gen. p	Pa		pascal	1 Pa = 1 N/m^2	1 at (technical atmosphere) = 1 kp/cm^2 = 0.980665 bar ≈ 1 bar 1 atm (physical atmosphere) = 1.01325 bar[1] 1 mm H_2O (water column) = 1 kp/m^2 = 0.0980665 hPa ≈ 0.1 hPa 1 torr = 1 mm Hg (mercury column) = 1.33322 hPa 1 dyn/cm^2 = 1 μbar
Absolute pressure p_{abs} Atmospheric pressure p_{amb}		bar	bar	1 bar = 10^5 Pa = 10 N/cm^2 1 μbar = 0,1 Pa 1 mbar = 1 hPa	
Gauge pressure p_e $p_e = p_{abs} - p_{amb}$	Gauge pressure etc., is no longer denoted by a unit symbol, but rather by a formula symbol. Negative pressure is given as negative gauge pressure. Examples: previously — now 3 atg, — p_e = 2.94 bar ≈ 3 bar 10 ata, — p_{abs} = 9.81 bar ≈ 10 bar 0.4 atu, — p_e = −0.39 bar ≈ −0.4 bar.				
Mechanical stress σ, τ	N/m^2			1 N/m^2 = 1 Pa	1 kp/mm^2 = 9.81 N/mm^2 ≈ 10 N/mm^2 1 kp/cm^2 ≈ 0.1 N/mm^2
		N/mm^2		1 N/mm^2 = 1 MPa	
Hardness (p. 248)	Brinell and Vickers hardness is no longer given in kp/mm^2. Rather, an abbreviation of the hardness scale used is written as the unit after the numerical value used previously (including an indication of the test force, etc. where applicable).				Example: previously — now HB = 350 kp/mm^2 — 350 HB HV30 = 720 kp/mm^2 — 720 HV30 HRC = 60 — 60 HRC
Energy, work E, W	J		joule	1 J = 1 N·m = 1 W·s = 1 kg·m^2/s^2	1 kp·m (kilopondmeter) = 9.81 J ≈ 10 J 1 PS·h (metric horsepower hour) = 0.7355 kW·h ≈ 0.74 kW·h 1 erg (erg) = 10^{-7} J 1 kcal (kilocalorie) = 4.1868 kJ ≈ 4,2 kJ 1 cal (calorie) = 4.1868 J ≈ 4,2 J
Heat, Quantity of heat Q (pp. 30, 31)		W·s	watt-second		
		kW·h	kilowatt-hour	1 kW·h = 3.6 MJ	
		eV	electron-volt	1 eV = 1.60219·10^{-19} J	
Moment of force M	N·m		newton-meter		1 kp·m (kilopondmeter) = 9.81 N·m ≈ 10 N·m
Power P Heat flow rate Q, Φ (pp. 30, 31)	W		watt	1 W = 1 J/s = 1 N·m/s	1 kp·m/s = 9.81 W ≈ 10 W 1 PS[2] = 0.7355 kW ≈ 0.74 kW 1 kcal/s = 4.1868 kW ≈ 4.2 kW 1 kcal/h = 1.163 W

6. Viscosimetric quantities (p. 34)

Dynamic viscosity η	Pa·s		pascal-second	1 Pa·s = 1 N·s/m^2 = 1 kg/(s·m)	1 P (poise) = 0.1 Pa·s 1 cP (centipoise) = 1 mPa·s
Kinematic viscosity ν	m^2/s			1 m^2/s = 1 Pa·s/(kg/m^3)	1 St (stokes) = 10^{-4} m^2/s = 1 cm^2/s 1 cSt (centistokes) = 1 mm^2/s

[1]) 1.01325 bar = 1013.25 hPa = 760 mm mercury column is the standard value for air pressure.
[2]) PS = Pferdestärke = metric horsepower; 1 hp = 1.0139 PS = 0.7457 kW

Quantity and symbol		Legal units SI	Others	Name	Relationship	Units not to be used and their conversion

7. Temperature and heat (pp. 32, 33)

Quantity and symbol		SI	Others	Name	Relationship	Units not to be used and their conversion
Temperature	T	K		kelvin	$t = (T - 273.15\,\text{K})\,\frac{°\text{C}}{\text{K}}$	
	t		°C	degree Celsius		
Temperature difference	ΔT	K		kelvin	1 K = 1 °C	
	Δt		°C	degree Celsius		
		In the case of composite units, express temperature differences in K, e.g., kJ/(m·h·K); tolerances for temperatures in degree Celsius, for example, are written as follows: $t = (40 \pm 2)$ °C or $t = 40\,°\text{C} \pm 2\,°\text{C}$ or $t = 40\,°\text{C} \pm 2\,\text{K}$.				

See under 5. for quantity of heat and heat flow rate.

Quantity and symbol		SI	Others	Name	Relationship	Units not to be used and their conversion
Specific heat capacity (spec. heat).	c	$\frac{\text{J}}{\text{kg}\cdot\text{K}}$				1 kcal/(kg · grd) = 4.187 kJ/(kg · K) ≈ 4.2 kJ/(kg · K)
Thermal conductivity	λ	$\frac{\text{W}}{\text{m}\cdot\text{K}}$				1 kcal/(m·h·grd) = 1.163 W/(m · K) ≈ 1.2 W/(m · K) 1 cal/(cm·s·grd) = 4.187 W/(cm · K) 1 W/(m · K) = 3.6 kJ/(m·h·K)

8. Electrical quantities (p. 70)

Quantity and symbol		SI	Others	Name	Relationship	Units not to be used and their conversion
Electric current	I	A		ampere		
Electric potential	U	V		volt	1 V = 1 W/A	
Electric conductance	G	S		siemens	1 S = 1 A/V = 1/Ω	
Electric resistance	R	Ω		ohm	1 Ω = 1/S = 1 V/A	
Quantity of electricity, electric charge	Q	C		coulomb	1 C = 1 A · s	
			A · h	ampere-hour	1 A · h = 3600 C	
Electric capacitance	C	F		farad	1 F = 1 C/V	
Electric flux density, displacement	D	C/m²				
Electric field strength	E	V/m				

Quantity and symbol	Legal Units SI	Others	Name	Relationship	Units not be used and their conversion
9. Magnetic quantities (p. 70)					
Magnetic flux Φ	Wb		weber	1 Wb = 1 V · s	1 M (maxwell) $= 10^{-8}$ Wb
Magnetic flux density, Magnetic induction B	T		tesla	1 T = 1 Wb/m²	1 G (gauss) $= 10^{-4}$ T
Inductance L	H		henry	1 H = 1 Wb/A	
Magnetic field strength H	A/m			1 A/m = 1 N/Wb	1 Oe (oersted) $= 10^3/(4\pi)$ A/m = 79.58 A/m
10. Quantities used in illumination engineering (p. 131)					
Luminuous intensity I	cd		candela[1])		
Luminance L	cd/m²				1 sb (stilb) $= 10^4$ cd/m² 1 asb (apostilb) $= 1/\pi$ cd/m²
Luminuous flux Φ	lm		lumen	1 lm = 1 cd · sr (sr = steradian)	
Illumi-nance E	lx		lux	1 lx = 1 lm/m²	
11. Quantities used in nuclear physics and other fields					
Energy W		eV	electron volt	1 eV = 1,60219 · 10^{-19} J 1 MeV = 10^6 eV	
Activity of a radioactive substance A	Bq		becquerel	1 Bq = 1 s^{-1}	1 Ci (curie) = 3.7 · 10^{10} s^{-1}
Absorbed dose D	Gy		gray	1 Gy = 1 J/kg	1 rd (rad) = 10^{-2} J/kg
Dose equivalent Dq	SV		sievert	1 Sv = 1 J/kg	1 rem (rem) = 10^{-2} Sv
Absorbed dose rate $\dot{D}$				1 Gy/s = 1 W/kg	
Ion dose J	C/kg				1 R (röntgen) = 258 · 10^{-6} C/kg
Ion dose rate $\dot{J}$	A/kg				
Amount of substance n	mol		mol		

References for pp. 10—16: DIN 1301: Units, Parts 1 to 3. Feb. 1978, DIN 1304: General formula symbols. Feb. 1978. Haeder, W.; Gärtner, E.: Die gesetzlichen Einheiten in der Technik. (Legal Units in Engineering), 5th edition. Deutsches Institut für Normung e.V., Berlin 1980. Beuth-Verlag GmbH

[1]) The second syllable is accented: can<u>de</u>la.

Conversion tables

Units of length

See conversion tables on pages 18, 19 for figures printed in bold type.
For conversion tables for velocity, see page 36.

Unit		X.U.	pm	Å	nm	μm	mm	cm	dm	m	km
1 X.E.	≈	1	10^{-1}	10^{-3}	10^{-4}	10^{-7}	10^{-10}	10^{-11}	10^{-12}	10^{-13}	–
1 pm	=	10	1	10^{-2}	10^{-3}	10^{-6}	10^{-9}	10^{-10}	10^{-11}	10^{-12}	–
1 Å	=	10^{3}	10^{2}	1	10^{-1}	10^{-4}	10^{-7}	10^{-8}	10^{-9}	10^{-10}	–
1 nm	=	10^{4}	10^{3}	10	1	10^{-3}	10^{-6}	10^{-7}	10^{-8}	10^{-9}	10^{-12}
1 μm	=	10^{7}	10^{6}	10^{4}	10^{3}	1	10^{-3}	10^{-4}	10^{-5}	10^{-6}	10^{-9}
1 mm	=	10^{10}	10^{9}	10^{7}	10^{6}	10^{3}	1	10^{-1}	10^{-2}	10^{-3}	10^{-6}
1 cm	=	10^{11}	10^{10}	10^{8}	10^{7}	10^{4}	10	1	10^{-1}	10^{-2}	10^{-5}
1 dm	=	10^{12}	10^{11}	10^{9}	10^{8}	10^{5}	10^{2}	10	1	10^{-1}	10^{-4}
1 m	=	–	10^{12}	10^{10}	10^{9}	10^{6}	10^{3}	10^{2}	10	1	10^{-3}
1 km	=	–	–	–	10^{12}	10^{9}	10^{6}	10^{5}	10^{4}	10^{3}	1

Do not use X.U. (X-unit) and Å (Ångström)

Unit		in	ft	yd	mile	n mile	mm	m	km
1 in	=	1	0.08333	0.02778	–	–	**25.4**	**0.0254**	–
1 ft	=	12	1	0.33333	–	–	304.8	**0.3048**	–
1 yd	=	36	3	1	–	–	914.4	**0.9144**	–
1 mile	=	63 360	5280	1760	1	0.86898	–	1609.34	**1.609**
1 n mile[1]	=	72 913	6076.1	2025.4	1.1508	1	–	1852	**1.852**
1 mm	=	**0.03937**	$3.281 \cdot 10^{-3}$	$1.094 \cdot 10^{-3}$	–	–	1	0.001	10^{-6}
1 m	=	39.3701	**3.2808**	**1.0936**	–	–	1000	1	0.001
1 km	=	39 370	3280.8	1093.6	**0.62137**	**0.53996**	10^{6}	1000	1

in = inch, ft = foot, yd = yard, mile = statute mile, n mile = nautical mile

Other British and American units of length

1 μin (microinch) = 0.0254 μm
1 mil (milliinch) = 0.0254 mm
1 link = 201.17 mm
1 rod = 1 pole = 1 perch = 5.5 yd = 5.0292 m
1 chain = 22 yd = 20.1168 m
1 furlong = 220 yd = 201.168 m
1 fathom = 2 yd = 1.8288 m

Astronomical units

1 L.y. (light year) $= 9.46053 \cdot 10^{15}$ m (the distance travelled by electromagnetic waves in free space in 1 year)
1 AU (astronomical unit) $= 1.496 \cdot 10^{11}$ m (mean distance of the earth from the sun)
1 pc (parsec, parallax second) $= 206\,265$ AE $= 3.0857 \cdot 10^{16}$ m (1 pc is the distance at which 1 AU subtends an angle of 1 second of arc)

Do not use

1 line (horology) = 2.256 mm
1 p (printer's point) = 0.376 mm
1 German mile = 7500 m
1 geographical mile = 7420.4 m (≈ 4 minutes of arc of the equator)

[1]) 1 n mile = 1 sm (seamile) = 1 international nautical mile ≈ 1 minute of arc of the degree of longitude. In Great Britain 1 n mile (UK) = 6080 ft ≈ 1853 m. 1 knot = 1 n mile/h = 1 n mile/h = 1.853 km/h.

Units of length

Conversion from	in to m	ft to m	yd to m	mile to km	sm to km	m to ft	m to yd	km to mile	km to sm
1.0	0.0254	0.305	0.914	1.609	1.852	3.281	1.094	0.621	0.540
1.1	0.0279	0.335	1.006	1.770	2.037	3.609	1.203	0.684	0.594
1.2	0.0305	0.366	1.097	1.931	2.222	3.937	1.312	0.746	0.648
1.3	0.0330	0.396	1.189	2.092	2.408	4.265	1.422	0.808	0.702
1.4	0.0356	0.427	1.280	2.253	2.593	4.593	1.531	0.870	0.756
1.5	0.0381	0.457	1.372	2.413	2.778	4.921	1.640	0.932	0.810
1.6	0.0406	0.488	1.463	2.574	2.963	5.249	1.750	0.994	0.864
1.7	0.0432	0.518	1.554	2.735	3.148	5.577	1.859	1.06	0.918
1.8	0.0457	0.549	1.646	2.896	3.334	5.905	1.968	1.12	0.972
1.9	0.0483	0.579	1.737	3.057	3.519	6.234	2.078	1.18	1.03
2.0	0.0508	0.610	1.829	3.218	3.704	6.562	2.187	1.24	1.08
2.1	0.0533	0.640	1.920	3.379	3.889	6.890	2.297	1.30	1.13
2.2	0.0559	0.671	2.012	3.540	4.074	7.218	2.406	1.37	1.19
2.3	0.0584	0.701	2.103	3.701	4.260	7.546	2.515	1.43	1.24
2.4	0.0610	0.732	2.195	3.862	4.445	7.874	2.625	1.49	1.30
2.5	0.0635	0.762	2.286	4.022	4.630	8.202	2.734	1.55	1.35
2.6	0.0660	0.792	2.377	4.183	4.815	8.530	2.843	1.62	1.40
2.7	0.0686	0.823	2.469	4.344	5.000	8.858	2.953	1.68	1.46
2.8	0.0711	0.853	2.560	4.505	5.186	9.186	3.062	1.74	1.51
2.9	0.0737	0.884	2.652	4.666	5.371	9.514	3.171	1.80	1.57
3.0	0.0762	0.914	2.743	4.827	5.556	9.842	3.281	1.86	1.62
3.2	0.0813	0.975	2.926	5.149	5.926	10.50	3.500	1.99	1.73
3.4	0.0864	1.036	3.109	5.471	6.297	11.15	3.718	2.11	1.84
3.6	0.0914	1.097	3.292	5.792	6.667	11.81	3.937	2.24	1.94
3.8	0.0965	1.158	3.475	6.114	7.038	12.47	4.156	2.36	2.05
4.0	0.1016	1.219	3.658	6.436	7.408	13.12	4.374	2.49	2.16
4.2	0.1067	1.280	3.840	6.758	7.778	13.78	4.593	2.61	2.27
4.4	0.1118	1.341	4.023	7.080	8.149	14.44	4.812	2.73	2.38
4.6	0.1168	1.402	4.206	7.401	8.519	15.09	5.031	2.86	2.48
4.8	0.1219	1.463	4.389	7.723	8.890	15.75	5.249	2.98	2.59
5.0	0.1270	1.524	4.572	8.045	9.260	16.40	5.468	3.11	2.70
5.2	0.1321	1.585	4.755	8.367	9.630	17.06	6.687	3.23	2.81
5.4	0.1372	1.646	4.938	8.689	10.00	17.72	5.905	3.36	2.92
5.6	0.1422	1.707	5.121	9.010	10.37	18.37	6.124	3.48	3.02
5.8	0.1473	1.768	5.304	9.332	10.74	19.03	6.343	3.60	3.13
6.0	0.1524	1.829	5.486	9.654	11.11	19.68	6.562	3.73	3.24
6.2	0.1575	1.890	5.669	9.976	11.48	20.34	6.780	3.85	3.35
6.4	0.1626	1.951	5.852	10.30	11.85	21.00	6.999	3.98	3.46
6.6	0.1676	2.012	6.035	10.62	12.22	21.65	7.218	4.10	3.56
6.8	0.1727	2.073	6.218	10.94	12.59	22.31	7.436	4.23	3.67
7.0	0.1778	2.134	6.401	11.26	12.96	22.97	7.655	4.35	3.78
7.5	0.1905	2.286	6.858	12.07	13.89	24.61	8.202	4.66	4.05
8.0	0.2032	2.438	7.315	12.87	14.82	26.25	8.749	4.97	4.32
8.5	0.2159	2.591	7.772	13.68	15.74	27.89	9.296	5.28	4.59
9.0	0.2236	2.743	8.230	14.48	16.67	29.53	9.842	5.59	4.86
9.5	0.2413	2.896	8.687	15.29	17.59	31.17	10.39	5.90	5.13

Examples: 1 ft = 0.305 m; 7.5 yd = 6.858 m.

Inch — Millimeter

based on 1 inch = 25.4 mm

inch		0	1	2	3	inch		0	1	2	3
	—	—	**25.40**	**50.80**	**76.20**	**1/2**	0.5	12.700	38.10	63.50	88.90
1/64	0.015 625	0.397	25.80	51.20	76.60	**33/64**	0.515 625	13.097	38.50	63.90	89.30
1/32	0.031 25	0.794	26.19	51.59	76.99	**17/32**	0.531 25	13.494	38.89	64.29	89.69
3/64	0.046 875	1.191	26.59	51.99	77.39	**35/64**	0.546 875	13.891	39.29	64.69	90.09
1/16	0.062 5	1.588	26.99	52.39	77.79	**9/16**	0.562 5	14.288	39.69	65.09	90.49
5/64	0.078 125	1.984	27.38	52.78	78.18	**37/64**	0.578 125	14.684	40.08	65.48	90.88
3/32	0.093 75	2.381	27.78	53.18	78.58	**19/32**	0.593 75	15.081	40.48	65.88	91.28
7/64	0.109 375	2.778	28.18	53.58	78.98	**39/64**	0.609 375	15.478	40.88	66.28	91.68
1/8	0.125	3.175	28.58	53.98	79.38	**5/8**	0.625	15.875	41.28	66.68	92.08
9/64	0.140 625	3.572	28.97	54.37	79.77	**41/64**	0.640 625	16.272	41.67	67.07	92.47
5/32	0.156 25	3.969	29.37	54.77	80.17	**21/32**	0.656 25	16.669	42.07	67.47	92.87
11/64	0.171 875	4.366	29.77	55.17	80.57	**43/64**	0.671 875	17.066	42.47	67.87	93.27
3/16	0.187 5	4.763	30.16	55.56	80.96	**11/16**	0.687 5	17.463	42.86	68.26	93.66
13/64	0.203 125	5.159	30.56	55.96	81.36	**45/64**	0.703 125	17.859	43.26	68.66	94.06
7/32	0.218 75	5.556	30.96	56.36	81.76	**23/32**	0.718 75	18.256	43.66	69.06	94.46
15/64	0.234 375	5.953	31.35	56.75	82.15	**47/64**	0.734 375	18.653	44.05	69.45	94.85
1/4	0.25	6.350	31.75	57.15	82.55	**3/4**	0.75	19.050	44.45	69.85	95.25
17/64	0.265 625	6.747	32.15	57.55	82.95	**49/64**	0.765 625	19.447	44.85	70.25	95.65
9/32	0.281 25	7.144	32.54	57.94	83.34	**25/32**	0.781 25	19.844	45.24	70.64	96.04
19/64	0.296 875	7.541	32.94	58.34	83.74	**51/64**	0.796 875	20.241	45.64	71.04	96.44
5/16	0.312 5	7.938	33.34	58.74	84.14	**13/16**	0.812 5	20.638	46.04	71.44	96.84
21/64	0.328 125	8.334	33.73	59.13	84.53	**53/64**	0.828 125	21.034	46.43	71.83	97.23
11/32	0.343 75	8.731	34.13	59.53	84.93	**27/32**	0.843 75	21.431	46.83	72.23	97.63
23/64	0.359 375	9.128	34.53	59.93	85.33	**55/64**	0.859 375	21.828	47.23	72.63	98.03
3/8	0.375	9.525	34.93	60.33	85.73	**7/8**	0.875	22.225	47.63	73.03	98.43
25/64	0.390 625	9.922	35.32	60.72	86.12	**57/64**	0.890 625	22.622	48.02	73.42	98.82
13/32	0.406 25	10.319	35.72	61.12	86.52	**29/32**	0.906 25	23.019	48.42	73.82	99.22
27/64	0.421 875	10.716	36.12	61.52	86.92	**59/64**	0.921 875	23.416	48.82	74.22	99.62
7/16	0.437 5	11.113	36.51	61.91	87.31	**15/16**	0.937 5	23.813	49.21	74.61	100.01
29/64	0.453 125	11.509	36.91	62.31	87.71	**61/64**	0.953 125	24.209	49.61	75.01	100.41
15/32	0.468 75	11.906	37.31	62.71	88.11	**31/32**	0.968 75	24.606	50.01	75.41	100.81
31/64	0.484 375	12.303	37.70	63.10	88.50	**63/64**	0.984 375	25.003	50.40	75.80	101.20

Values of 1 inch and more are rounded off to one hundredth of a millimeter.

Units of area

See conversion table on page 21 for figures printed in bold type

Unit		in^2	ft^2	yd^2	$mile^2$	cm^2	dm^2	m^2	a	ha	km^2
1 in^2	=	1	—	—	—	**6.4516**	0.06452	—	—	—	—
1 ft^2	=	144	1	0,1111	—	929	9.29	**0.0929**	—	—	—
1 yd^2	=	1296	9	1	—	8361	83.61	**0.8361**	—	—	—
1 $mile^2$	=	—	—	—	1	—	—	—	—	259	**2.59**
1 cm^2	=	**0.155**	—	—	—	1	0.01	—	—	—	—
1 dm^2	=	15.5	0.1076	0.01196	—	100	1	0.01	—	—	—
1 m^2	=	1550	**10.76**	**1.196**	—	10000	100	1	0.01	—	—
1 a	=	—	1076	119.6	—	—	10000	100	1	0.01	—
1 ha	=	—	—	—	—	—	—	10000	100	1	0.01
1 km^2	=	—	—	—	**0.3861**	—	—	—	10000	100	1

in^2 = square inch (sq in),
ft^2 = square foot (sq ft),
yd^2 = square yard (sq yd),
$mile^2$ = square mile (sq mile)

Other British and American units of area

1 mil^2 (square mil) = 10^{-6} in^2
= 0.0006452 mm^2

1 cir mil (circular mil) = $\frac{\pi}{4}$ mil^2
= 0.0005067 mm^2
(Area of circle with diameter of 1 mil)

1 cir in (circular inch) = $\frac{\pi}{4}$ in^2 = 5.067 cm^2
(Area of circle with diameter of 1 in)

1 $line^2$ (square line) = 0.01 in^2
= 6.452 mm^2

1 rod^2 (square rod) = 1 $pole^2$ (square pole) = 1 $perch^2$ (square perch)
= 25.29 m^2

1 $chain^2$ (square chain) = 16 rod^2
= 404.684 m^2

1 rood = 40 rod^2 = 1011.71 m^2

1 acre = 4840 yd^2 = 4046.86 m^2
= **40.4686 a**

1 section (US) = 1 $mile^2$ = 2.59 km^2

1 township (US) = 36 $mile^2$ = 93.24 km^2

Old German measures of land

(do not use)

1 Baden Morgen = 36 a
1 Bavarian Tagwerk = 34.07 a
1 Prussian Morgen = 25.53 a
1 Württemberg Morgen = 31.52 a

Paper sizes

(DIN 476)

Dimensions in mm

A 0	841 × 1189	**A 6**	105 × 148
A 1	594 × 841	**A 7**	74 × 105
A 2	420 × 594	**A 8**	52 × 74
A 3	297 × 420	**A 9**	37 × 52
A 4	210 × 297[1])	**A 10**	26 × 37
A 5	148 × 210		

[1]) USA: 216 × 279

Units of area

	Conversion from								
	in²	**ft²**	**yd²**	**acre**	**mile²**	**cm²**	**m²**	**m²**	**km²**
↓	to cm²	to m²	to m²	to a	to km²	to in²	to ft²	to yd²	to mile²
1,0	6.45	0.0929	0.836	40.5	2.59	0.155	10.8	1.20	0.386
1.1	7.10	0.102	0.920	44.5	2.85	0.171	11.8	1.32	0.425
1.2	7.74	0.111	1.00	48.6	3.11	0.186	12.9	1.44	0.463
1.3	8.39	0.121	1.09	52.6	3.37	0.202	14.0	1.55	0.502
1.4	9.03	0.130	1.17	56.7	3.63	0.217	15.1	1.67	0.541
1.5	9.68	0.139	1.25	60.7	3.89	0.233	16.1	1.79	0.579
1.6	10.3	0.149	1.34	64.7	4.14	0.248	17.2	1.91	0.618
1.7	11.0	0.158	1.42	68.8	4.40	0.264	18.3	2.03	0.656
1.8	11.6	0.167	1.50	72.8	4.66	0.279	19.4	2.15	0.695
1.9	12.3	0.177	1.59	76.9	4.92	0.295	20.5	2.27	0.734
2.0	12.9	0.186	1.67	80.9	5.18	0.310	21.5	2.39	0.772
2.1	13.5	0.195	1.76	85.0	5.44	0.326	22.6	2.51	0.811
2.2	14.2	0.204	1.84	89.0	5.70	0.341	23.7	2.63	0.849
2.3	14.8	0.214	1.92	93.1	5.96	0.357	24.8	2.75	0.888
2.4	15.5	0.223	2.01	97.1	6.22	0.372	25.8	2.87	0.927
2.5	16.1	0.232	2.09	101	6.47	0.388	26.9	2.99	0.965
2.6	16.8	0.242	2.17	105	6.73	0.403	28.0	3.11	1.00
2.7	17.4	0.251	2.26	109	6.99	0.419	29.1	3.23	1.04
2.8	18.1	0.260	2.34	113	7.25	0.434	30.1	3.35	1.08
2.9	18.7	0.269	2.42	117	7.51	0.450	31.2	3.47	1.12
3.0	19.4	0.279	2.51	121	7.77	0.465	32.3	3.59	1.16
3.2	20.6	0.297	2.68	129	8.29	0.496	34.4	3.83	1.24
3.4	21.9	0.316	2.84	138	8.81	0.527	36.6	4.07	1.31
3.6	23.2	0.334	3.01	146	9.32	0.558	38.8	4.31	1.39
3.8	24.5	0.353	3.18	154	9.84	0.589	40.9	4.54	1.47
4.0	25.8	0.372	3.34	162	10.4	0.620	43.1	4.78	1.54
4.2	27.1	0.390	3.51	170	10.9	0.651	45.2	5.02	1.62
4.4	28.4	0.409	3.68	178	11.4	0.682	47.4	5.26	1.70
4.6	29.7	0.427	3.85	186	11.9	0.713	49.5	5.50	1.78
4.8	31.0	0.446	4.01	194	12.4	0.744	51.7	5.74	1.85
5.0	32.3	0.465	4.18	202	12.9	0.775	53.8	5.98	1.93
5.2	33.5	0.483	4.35	210	13.5	0.806	56.0	6.22	2.01
5.4	34.8	0.502	4.51	219	14.0	0.837	58.1	6.46	2.08
5.6	36.1	0.520	4.68	227	14.5	0.868	60.3	6.70	2.16
5.8	37.4	0.539	4.85	235	15.0	0.899	62.4	6.94	2.24
6.0	38.7	0.557	5.02	243	15.5	0.930	64.6	7.18	2.32
6.2	40.0	0.576	5.18	251	16.1	0.961	66.7	7.42	2.39
6.4	41.3	0.595	5.35	259	16.6	0.992	68.9	7.65	2.47
6.6	42.6	0.613	5.52	267	17.1	1.02	71.0	7.89	2.55
6.8	43.9	0.632	5.69	275	17.6	1.05	73.2	8.13	2.63
7.0	45.2	0.650	5.85	283	18.1	1.09	75.3	8.37	2.70
7.5	48.4	0.697	6.27	304	19.4	1.16	80.7	8.97	2.90
8.0	51.6	0.743	6.69	324	20.7	1.24	86.1	9.57	3.09
8.5	54.8	0.790	7.11	344	22.0	1.32	91.5	10.2	3.28
9.0	58.1	0.836	7.52	364	23.3	1.40	96.9	10.8	3.47
9.5	61.3	0.883	7.94	384	24.6	1.47	102	11.4	3.67

The above table also applies to decimal multiples and submultiples.
Example: 1 in² = 6.45 cm²; 5.8 yd² = 4.85 m²; 58 yd² = 48.5 m²

Units of angle

See p. 12 for names of units

Unit[1])		°	′	″	rad	gon	cgon	mgon
1°	=	1	60	3600	0.017453	1.1111	111.11	1111.11
1′	=	0.016667	1	60	–	0.018518	1.85185	18.5185
1″	=	0.0002778	0.016667	1	–	0.0003086	0.030864	0.30864
1 rad[2])	=	57.2958	3437.75	206265	1	63.662	6366.2	63662
1 gon	=	0.9	54	3240	0.015708	1	100	1000
1 cgon	=	0.009	0.54	32.4	–	0.01	1	10
1 mgon	=	0.0009	0.054	3.24	–	0.001	0.1	1

Units of volume

See conversion table on page 23 for figures printed in bold type

Unit		in^3	ft^3	yd^3	gal (UK)	gal (US)	cm^3	dm^3 (l)	m^3
1 in^3	=	1	–	–	–	–	**16.3871**	0.01639	–
1 ft^3	=	1728	1	0.03704	6.229	7.481	–	**28.3168**	0.02832
1 yd^3	=	46656	27	1	168.18	201.97	–	764.555	**0.76456**
1 gal (UK)	=	277.42	0.16054	–	1	1.20095	4546.09	**4.54609**	–
1 gal (US)	=	231	0.13368	–	0.83267	1	3785.41	**3.78541**	–
1 cm^3	=	0.06102	–	–	–	–	1	0.001	–
1 dm^3 (l)	=	61.0236	0.03531	0.00131	0.21997	0.26417	1000	1	0.001
1 m^3	=	61023.6	35.315	1.30795	219.969	264.172	10^6	1000	1

in^3 = cubic inch (cu in), ft^3 = cubic foot (cu ft), yd^3 = cubic yard (cu yd), gal = gallon

Other British and American units of volume
Volume of ships
1 RT (register ton) = 100 ft^3 = 2.832 m^3; GRT (gross RT) = total shipping space, net register ton = cargo space of a ship.
GTI (gross tonnage index) = total volume of ship (shell) in m^3.
1 ocean ton = 40 ft^3 = 1.1327 m^3.

Great Britain (UK)
1 min (minim) = 0.059194 cm^3
1 fluid drachm = 60 min = 3.5516 cm^3
1 fl oz (fluid ounce) = 8 fl drachm = 0.028413 l
1 gill = 5 fl oz = 0.14207 l
1 pt (pint) = 4 gills = **0.56826** l
1 qt (quart) = 2 pt = 1.13652 l
1 gal (gallon) = 4 qt = **4.5461** l
1 bbl (barrel) = 36 gal = 163.6 l

Units of dry measure:
1 pk (peck) = 2 gal = 9.0922 l
1 bu (bushel) = 8 gal = 36.369 l
1 qr (quarter) = 8 bu = 290.95 l

United States (US)
1 min (minim) = 0.061612 cm^3
1 fluid dram = 60 min = 3.6967 cm^3
1 fl oz (fluid ounce) = 8 fl dram = 0.029574 l
1 gill = 4 fl oz = 0.11829 l
1 liq pt (liquid pint) = 4 gills = **0.47318** l
1 liq quart = 2 liq pt = 0.94635 l
1 gal (gallon) = 231 in^3 = 4 liq quarts = **3.7854** l
1 liq bbl (liquid barrel) = 119.24 l
1 barrel petroleum[3]) = 42 gal = **158.99** l

Units of dry measure:
1 dry pint = 0.55061 dm^3
1 dry quart = 2 dry pints = 1.1012 dm^3
1 peck = 8 dry quarts = 8.8098 dm^3
1 bushel = 4 pecks = 35.239 dm^3
1 dry bbl (dry barrel) = 7056 in^3 = 115.63 dm^3

[1]) It is better to indicate angles by using only one of the units given above, i.e. not 33° 17′ 27.6″, but rather = 33.291° or 1997.46′ or 119.847.6″.
[2]) In calculations, the unit rad is replaced by the number 1.
[3]) For crude oil.

Units of volume, flow rates

	Conversion from								
	in^3	ft^3	yd^3	pt (UK)	liq pt (US)	gal (UK)	gal (US)	barrel petrol.	ft^3/min cfm
↓	to cm^3	to l	to m^3	to l	to l	to l	to l	to l	to m^3/h
1.0	16.4	28.3	0.765	0.568	0.473	4.55	3.79	159	1.70
1.1	18.0	31.1	0.841	0.625	0.520	5.00	4.16	175	1.87
1.2	19.7	34.0	0.917	0.682	0.568	5.46	4.54	191	2.04
1.3	21.3	36.8	0.994	0.739	0.615	5.91	4.92	207	2.21
1.4	22.9	39.6	1.07	0.796	0.662	6.36	5.30	223	2.38
1.5	24.6	42.5	1.15	0.852	0.710	6.82	5.68	238	2.55
1.6	26.2	45.3	1.22	0.909	0.757	7.27	6.06	254	2.72
1.7	27.9	48.1	1.30	0.966	0.804	7.73	6.44	270	2.89
1.8	29.5	51.0	1.38	1.02	0.852	8.18	6.81	286	3.06
1.9	31.1	53.8	1.45	1.08	0.899	8.64	7.19	302	3.23
2.0	32.8	56.6	1.53	1.14	0.946	9.09	7.57	318	3.40
2.1	34.4	59.5	1.61	1.19	0.994	9.55	7.95	334	3.57
2.2	36.1	62.3	1.68	1.25	1.04	10.0	8.33	350	3.74
2.3	37.7	65.1	1.76	1.31	1.09	10.5	8.71	366	3.91
2.4	39.3	68.0	1.83	1.36	1.14	10.9	9.08	382	4.08
2.5	41.0	70.8	1.91	1.42	1.18	11.4	9.46	397	4.25
2.6	42.6	73.6	1.99	1.48	1.23	11.8	9.84	413	4.42
2.7	44.2	76.5	2.06	1.53	1.28	12.3	10.2	429	4.59
2.8	45.9	79.3	2.14	1.59	1.32	12.7	10.6	445	4.76
2.9	47.5	82.1	2.22	1.65	1.37	13.2	11.0	461	4.93
3.0	49.2	85.0	2.29	1.70	1.42	13.6	11.4	477	5.10
3.2	52.4	90.6	2.45	1.82	1.51	14.5	12.1	509	5.44
3.4	55.7	96.3	2.60	1.93	1.61	15.5	12.9	541	5.78
3.6	59.0	102	2.75	2.05	1.70	16.4	13.6	572	6.12
3.8	62.3	108	2.91	2.16	1.80	17.3	14.4	604	6.46
4.0	65.5	113	3.06	2.27	1.89	18.2	15.1	636	6.80
4.2	68.8	119	3.21	2.39	1.99	19.1	15.9	668	7.14
4.4	72.1	125	3.36	2.50	2.08	20.0	16.7	700	7.48
4.6	75.4	130	3.52	2.61	2.18	20.9	17.4	731	7.82
4.8	78.7	136	3.67	2.73	2.27	21.8	18.2	763	8.16
5.0	81.9	142	3.82	2.84	2.37	22.7	18.9	795	8.50
5.2	85.2	147	3.98	2.95	2.46	23.6	19.7	827	8.83
5.4	88.5	153	4.13	3.07	2.56	24.5	20.4	859	9.17
5.6	91.8	159	4.28	3.18	2.65	25.5	21.2	890	9.51
5.8	95.0	164	4.43	3.30	2.74	26.4	22.0	922	9.85
6.0	98.3	170	4.59	3.41	2.84	27.3	22.7	954	10.2
6.2	102	176	4.74	3.52	2.93	28.2	23.5	986	10.5
6.4	105	181	4.89	3.64	3.03	29.1	24.2	1018	10.9
6.6	108	187	5.05	3.75	3.12	30.0	25.0	1049	11.2
6.8	111	193	5.20	3.86	3.22	30.9	25.7	1081	11.6
7.0	115	198	5.35	3.98	3.31	31.8	26.5	1113	11.9
7.5	123	212	5.73	4.26	3.55	34.1	28.4	1192	12.7
8.0	131	227	6.12	4.55	3.79	36.4	30.3	1272	13.6
8.5	139	241	6.50	4.83	4.02	38.6	32.2	1351	14.4
9.0	147	255	6.88	5.11	4.26	40.9	34.1	1431	15.3
9.5	156	269	7.26	5.40	4.50	43.2	36.0	1510	16.1

The above table also applies to decimal multiples and submultiples.
Examples: 1 in^3 = 16.4 cm^3; 3 gal (UK) = 13.6 l; 30 gal (UK) = 136 l

Units of mass

(Colloquially also called "units of weight")

See conversion table on page 26 for figures printed in bold type

Avoirdupois-system (commercial weights in general use in the UK and USA)

Unit		gr	dram	oz	lb	cwt (UK)	cwt (US)	ton (UK)	ton (US)	g	kg	t
1 gr	=	1	0.03657	0.00229	1/7000	–	–	–	–	**0.064799**	–	–
1 dram	=	27.344	1	0.0625	0.00391	–	–	–	–	**1.77184**	–	–
1 oz	=	437.5	16	1	0.0625	–	–	–	–	**28.3495**	–	–
1 lb	=	7000	256	16	1	0.00893	0.01	–	0.0005	453.592	**0.45359**	–
1 cwt (UK)[1]	=	–	–	–	112	1	1.12	0.05	–	–	**50.8023**	–
1 cwt (US)[2]	=	–	–	–	100	0.8929	1	0.04464	0.05	–	**45.3592**	–
1 ton (UK)[3]	=	–	–	–	2240	20	22.4	1	1.12	–	1016.05	**1.01605**
1 ton (US)[4]	=	–	–	–	2000	17.857	20	0.8929	1	–	907.185	**0.90718**
1 g	=	15.432	0.5644	0.03527	–	–	–	–	–	1	0.001	–
1 kg	=	–	–	35.274	2.2046	0.01968	0.02205	–	–	1000	1	0.001
1 t	=	–	–	–	2204.6	19.684	22.046	0.9842	1.1023	10^6	1000	1

UK = United Kingdom, US = USA.

gr = grain, oz = ounce, lb = pound, cwt = hundredweight

1 slug = 14.5939 kg = mass, accelerated at 1 ft/s^2 by a force of 1 lbf
1 st (stone) = 14 lb = 6.35 kg (UK only)
1 qr (quarter) = 28 lb = 12.7006 kg (UK only, seldom used)
1 quintal = 100 lb = 1 short cwt = 45.3592 kg
1 tdw (ton dead weight) = 1 long ton = 1.016 t.
The tonnage of dry cargo ships (cargo + ballast + fuel + supplies) is given in tdw.

[1]) also called "long cwt (cwt l)"
[2]) also called "short cwt (cwt sh)"
[3]) also called "long ton (tn l)"
[4]) also called "short ton (tn sh)"

Troy system used in the UK and USA for gemstones and precious metals) and **Apothecaries' system** (used in the UK and USA for drugs)

Unit		gr	s ap	dwt	dr ap	oz t = oz ap	lb t = lb ap	Kt	g
1 gr	=	1	0.05	0.04167	0.01667	–	–	0.324	**0.064799**
1 s ap	=	20	1	0.8333	0.3333	–	–	–	1.296
1 dwt	=	24	1.2	1	0.4	0.05	–	–	1.5552
1 dr ap	=	60	3	2.5	1	0.125	–	–	3.8879
1 oz t = 1 oz ap	=	480	24	20	8	1	0.08333	–	31.1035
1 lb t = 1 lb ap	=	5760	288	240	96	12	1	–	373.24
1 Kt	=	3.086	–	–	–	–	–	1	0.2000
1 g	=	15.432	0.7716	0.643	0.2572	0.03215	0.002679	5	1

gr = grain,
s ap = apothecaries' scruple,
dwt = pennyweight,
dr ap = apothecaries' drachm (US: apothecaries' dram),
oz t (UK: oz tr) = troy ounce,
oz ap (UK: oz apoth) = apothecaries' ounce,
lb t = troy pound,
lb ap = apothecaries' pound (not a legal unit in the UK),
Kt = metric carat, used only for gemstones[1])

Mass per unit length
SI-unit: kg/m
1 lb/ft = **1.48816** kg/m , 1 lb/yd = **0.49605** kg/m
Legal units in the textile industry (DIN 60905 and 60910):
1 tex = 1 g/km, 1 mtex = 1 mg/km,
1 dtex = 1 dg/km, 1 ktex = 1 kg/km
Former unit (do not use):
1 den (denier) = 1 g/9 km = 0.1111 tex, 1 tex = 9 den

Density
SI-unit: kg/m^3
1 kg/dm^3 = 1 kg/l = 1 g/cm^3 = 1000 kg/m^3
1 lb/ft^3 = **16.018** kg/m^3 = 0.016018 kg/l
1 lb/gal (UK) = **0.099776** kg/l, 1 lb/gal (US) = **0.11983** kg/l

[1]) The term "carat" was formerly used with a different meaning in connection with gold alloys to denote the gold content: pure gold (fine gold) = 24 carat; 14-carat gold has 14/24 = 585/1000 parts by weight of fine gold.

Units of mass (weights)

	Conversion from							
↓	grain	dram	oz	lb	cwt (UK)	cwt (US)	ton (UK)	ton (US)
	to g	to g	to g	to kg	to kg	to kg	to t	to t
1.0	0.0648	1.77	28.3	0.454	50.8	45.4	1.02	0.907
1.1	0.0713	1.95	31.2	0.499	55.9	49.9	1.12	0.998
1.2	0.0778	2.13	34.0	0.544	61.0	54.4	1.22	1.09
1.3	0.0842	2.30	36.9	0.590	66.0	59.0	1.32	1.18
1.4	0.0907	2.48	39.7	0.635	71.1	63.5	1.42	1.27
1.5	0.0972	2.66	42.5	0.680	76.2	68.0	1.52	1.36
1.6	0.104	2.83	45.4	0.726	81.3	72.6	1.63	1.45
1.7	0.110	3.01	48.2	0.771	86.4	77.1	1.73	1.54
1.8	0.117	3.19	51.0	0.816	91.4	81.6	1.83	1.63
1.9	0.123	3.37	53.9	0.862	96.5	86.2	1.93	1.72
2.0	0.130	3.54	56.7	0.907	102	90.7	2.03	1.81
2.1	0.136	3.72	59.5	0.953	107	95.3	2.13	1.91
2.2	0.143	3.90	62.4	0.998	112	99.8	2.24	2.00
2.3	0.149	4.08	65.2	1.04	117	104	2.34	2.09
2.4	0.156	4.25	68.0	1.09	122	109	2.44	2.18
2.5	0.162	4.43	70.9	1.13	127	113	2.54	2.27
2.6	0.168	4.61	73.7	1.18	132	118	2.64	2.36
2.7	0.175	4.78	76.5	1.22	137	122	2.74	2.45
2.8	0.181	4.96	79.4	1.27	142	127	2.84	2.54
2.9	0.188	5.14	82.2	1.32	147	132	2.95	2.63
3.0	0.194	5.32	85.0	1.36	152	136	3.05	2.72
3.2	0.207	5.67	90.7	1.45	163	145	3.25	2.90
3.4	0.220	6.02	96.4	1.54	173	154	3.45	3.08
3.6	0.233	6.38	102	1.63	183	163	3.66	3.27
3.8	0.246	6.73	108	1.72	193	172	3.86	3.45
4.0	0.259	7.09	113	1.81	203	181	4.06	3.63
4.2	0.272	7.44	119	1.91	213	191	4.27	3.81
4.4	0.285	7.80	125	2.00	224	200	4.47	3.99
4.6	0.298	8.15	130	2.09	234	209	4.67	4.17
4.8	0.311	8.50	136	2.18	244	218	4.88	4.35
5.0	0.324	8.86	142	2.27	254	227	5.08	4.54
5.2	0.337	9.21	147	2.36	264	236	5.28	4.72
5.4	0.350	9.57	153	2.45	274	245	5.49	4.90
5.6	0.363	9.92	159	2.54	284	254	5.69	5.08
5.8	0.376	10.3	164	2.63	295	263	5.89	5.26
6.0	0.389	10.6	170	2.72	305	272	6.10	5.44
6.5	0.421	11.5	184	2.95	330	295	6.60	5.90
7.0	0.454	12.4	198	3.18	356	318	7.11	6.35
7.5	0.486	13.3	213	3.40	381	340	7.62	6.80
8.0	0.518	14.2	227	3.63	406	363	8.13	7.26
8.5	0.551	15.1	241	3.86	432	386	8.64	7.71
9.0	0.583	15.9	255	4.08	457	408	9.14	8.16
9.5	0.616	16.8	269	4.31	483	431	9.65	8.62

The above table also applies to decimal multiples and submultiples.

Examples: 1 lb = 0.454 kg; 5 ton (UK) = 5.08 t; 42 oz = 1190 g.

Mass per unit length and density

↓	lb/ft to kg/m	lb/yd to kg/m	lb/ft^3 to kg/m^3	lb/gal (UK) to kg/l	lb/gal (US) to kg/l
1.0	1.49	0.496	16.0	0.0998	0.120
1.1	1.64	0.546	17.6	0.110	0.132
1.2	1.79	0.595	19.2	0.120	0.144
1.3	1.93	0.645	20.8	0.130	0.156
1.4	2.08	0.694	22.4	0.140	0.168
1.5	2.23	0.744	24.0	0.150	0.180
1.6	2.38	0.794	25.6	0.160	0.192
1.7	2.53	0.843	27.2	0.170	0.204
1.8	2.68	0.893	28.8	0.180	0.216
1.9	2.83	0.943	30.4	0.190	0.228
2.0	2.98	0.992	32.0	0.200	0.240
2.1	3.13	1.04	33.6	0.210	0.252
2.2	3.27	1.09	35.2	0.220	0.264
2.3	3.42	1.14	36.8	0.229	0.276
2.4	3.57	1.19	38.4	0.239	0.288
2.5	3.72	1.24	40.0	0.249	0.300
2.6	3.87	1.29	41.6	0.259	0.312
2.7	4.02	1.34	43.2	0.269	0.324
2.8	4.17	1.39	44.9	0.279	0.336
2.9	4.32	1.44	46.5	0.289	0.348
3.0	4.46	1.49	48.1	0.299	0.359
3.2	4.76	1.59	51.3	0.319	0.383
3.4	5.06	1.69	54.5	0.339	0.407
3.6	5.36	1.79	57.7	0.359	0.431
3.8	5.66	1.89	60.9	0.379	0.455
4.0	5.95	1.98	64.1	0.399	0.479
4.2	6.25	2.08	67.3	0.419	0.503
4.4	6.55	2.18	70.5	0.439	0.527
4.6	6.85	2.28	73.7	0.459	0.551
4.8	7.14	2.38	76.9	0.479	0.575
5.0	7.44	2.48	80.1	0.499	0.599
5.2	7.74	2.58	83.3	0.519	0.623
5.4	8.04	2.68	86.5	0.539	0.647
5.6	8.33	2.78	89.7	0.559	0.671
5.8	8.63	2.88	92.9	0.579	0.695
6.0	8.93	2.98	96.1	0.599	0.719
6.5	9.67	3.22	104	0.649	0.779
7.0	10.4	3.47	112	0.698	0.839
7.5	11.2	3.72	120	0.748	0.899
8.0	11.9	3.97	128	0.798	0.959
8.5	12.6	4.22	136	0.848	1.02
9.0	13.4	4.46	144	0.898	1.08

The above table also applies to decimal multiples and submultiples.

↓	+ °Bé to kg/l	− °Bé to kg/l	°API to kg/l
0	1.000	1.000	1.076
2	1.014	0.986	1.060
4	1.029	0.973	1.044
6	1.043	0.960	1.029
8	1.059	0.947	1.014
10	1.074	0.935	1.000
12	1.091	0.923	0.986
14	1.107	0.912	0.973
16	1.125	0.900	0.959
18	1.143	0.889	0.946
20	1.161	0.878	0.934
22	1.180	0.868	0.922
24	1.200	0.857	0.910
26	1.220	0.847	0.898
28	1.241	0.837	0.887
30	1.262	0.828	0.876
32	1.285	0.818	0.865
34	1.308	0.809	0.855
36	1.332	0.800	0.845
38	1.357	0.792	0.835
40	1.384	0.783	0.825
45	1.453	0.762	0.802
50	1.530	0.743	0.780
55	1.616	0.724	0.759
60	1.712	0.706	0.739
65	1.820	0.689	0.720
70	1.942	0.673	0.702

°Bé (degrees Baumé) is a measure of the density of liquids which are heavier (+ °Bé) or lighter (− °Bé) than water (at 15°C). The unit °Bé is no longer to be used.

$\varrho = 144.3/(144.3 \pm n)$

ϱ Density is expressed in kg/l, and hydrometer degrees n in °Bé.

°API (American Petroleum Institute) is used in the USA to indicate the density of fuels and oils.

$\varrho = 141.5/(131.5 + n)$

ϱ Density is expressed in kg/l, hydrometer degrees n in °API.

Examples: 7 lb/gallon (US) = 0.839 kg/l; −30°Bé = 0.828 kg/l

Units of force

See conversion table on page 29 for figures printed in bold type

Unit		N	kp	lbf
1 N (newton)	=	1	0.101972	0.224809
Do not use 1 kp (kilopond)	=	**9.80665**	1	2.204615
1 lbf (pound-force)	=	**4.44822**	0.453594	1

1 pdl (poundal) = 0.138255 N = force which accelerates a mass of 1 lb by 1 ft/s².
1 sn (sthène)* = 10³ N

Units of pressure and stress

See conversion table on page 29 for figures printed in bold type.

Unit[1])		Pa	μbar	hPa	bar	N/mm²	kp/mm²	at	kp/m²	Torr	atm	lbf/in²	lbf/ft²	tonf/in²
1 Pa = 1 N/m²	=	1	10	0.01	10^{-5}	10^{-6}	–	–	0.10197	0.0075	–	–	–	–
1 μbar	=	0.1	1	0.001	10^{-6}	10^{-7}	–	–	0.0102	–	–	–	–	–
1 hPa = 1 mbar	=	100	1000	1	0,001	0.0001	–	–	10.197	0.7501	–	0.0145	2.0886	–
1 bar	=	10^5	10^6	1000	1	0.1	0.0102	1.0197	10197	750.06	0.9869	14.5037	2088.6	–
1 N/mm²	=	10^6	10^7	10000	10	1	0.10197	10.197	101972	7501	9.8692	145.037	20886	0.06475
Do not use														
1 kp/mm²	=	–	–	98066.5	98.0665	**9.80665**	1	100	10^6	73556	96.784	1422.33	–	0.63497
1 at = 1 kp/cm²	=	98066.5	–	980.665	**0.98066**	0.0981	0.01	1	10000	735.56	0.96784	14.2233	2048.16	–
1 kp/m² = 1 mmWS	=	9.80665	98.0665	0.0981	–	–	10^{-6}	10^{-4}	1	–	–	–	0.2048	–
1 Torr = 1 mmHg	=	133.322	1333.22	**1.33322**	–	–	–	0.00136	13.5951	1	0.00132	0.01934	2.7845	–
1 atm	=	101325	–	1013.25	**1.01325**	–	–	1.03323	10332.3	760	1	14.695	2116.1	–
British and American units														
1 lbf/in²	=	6894.76	68948	68.948	**0.0689**	0.00689	–	0.07031	703.07	51.715	0.06805	1	144	–
1 lbf/ft²	=	**47.8803**	478.8	0.4788	–	–	–	–	4.8824	0.35913	–	–	1	–
1 tonf/in²	=	–	–	–	154.443	**15.4443**	1.57488	157.488	–	–	152.42	2240	–	1

lbf/in² = pound-force per square inch (psi), lbf/ft² = pound-force per square foot (psf), tonf/in² = ton-force (UK) per square inch
1 pdl/ft² (poundal per square foot) = 1.48816 Pa
1 barye* = 1μbar; 1 pz (pièce) = 1 sn/m² (sthène/m²)* = 10³ Pa

[1]) See pp. 13 and 14 for names of units. * French units.

Units of force, pressure and stress

	Conversion from kp/mm² [1]) to N/mm²	at to bar	atm to bar	Torr to hPa	lbf to N	lbf/in² to bar	tonf/in² to N/mm²	lbf/ft² to Pa
1.0	9.807	0.9807	1.013	1.333	4.448	0.0689	15.44	47.88
1.1	10.79	1.079	1.115	1.467	4.893	0.0758	16.99	52.67
1.2	11.77	1.177	1.216	1.600	5.338	0.0827	18.53	57.46
1.3	12.75	1.275	1.317	1.733	5.783	0.0896	20.08	62.24
1.4	13.73	1.373	1.419	1.867	6.228	0.0965	21.62	67.03
1.5	14.71	1.471	1.520	2.000	6.672	0.103	23.17	71.82
1.6	15.69	1.569	1.621	2.133	7.117	0.110	24.71	76.61
1.7	16.67	1.667	1.723	2.266	7.562	0.117	26.26	81.40
1.8	17.65	1.765	1.824	2.400	8.007	0.124	27.80	86.18
1.9	18.63	1.863	1.925	2.533	8.452	0.131	29.34	90.97
2.0	19.61	1.961	2.026	2.666	8.896	0.138	30.89	95.76
2.1	20.59	2.059	2.128	2.800	9.341	0.145	32.43	100.5
2.2	21.57	2.157	2.229	2.933	9.786	0.152	33.98	105.3
2.3	22.56	2.256	2.330	3.066	10.23	0.158	35.52	110.1
2.4	23.54	2.354	2.432	3.200	10.68	0.165	37.07	114.9
2.5	24.52	2.452	2.533	3.333	11.12	0.172	38.61	119.7
2.6	25.50	2.550	2.634	3.466	11.57	0.179	40.16	124.5
2.7	26.48	2.648	2.736	3.600	12.01	0.186	41.70	129.3
2.8	27.46	2.746	2.837	3.733	12.46	0.193	43.24	134.1
2.9	28.44	2.844	2.938	3.866	12.90	0.200	44.79	138.9
3.0	29.42	2.942	3.040	4.000	13.34	0.207	46.33	143.6
3.2	31.38	3.138	3.242	4.266	14.23	0.220	49.42	153.2
3.4	33.34	3.334	3.445	4.533	15.12	0.234	52.51	162.8
3.6	35.30	3.530	3.648	4.800	16.01	0.248	55.60	172.4
3.8	37.27	3.727	3.850	5.066	16.90	0.262	58.69	181.9
4.0	39.23	3.923	4.053	5.333	17.79	0.276	61.78	191.6
4.2	41.19	4.119	4.256	5.600	18.68	0.289	64.87	201.1
4.4	43.15	4.315	4.458	5.866	19.57	0.303	67.95	210.7
4.6	45.11	4.511	4.661	6.133	20.46	0.317	71.04	220.2
4.8	47.07	4.707	4.864	6.399	21.35	0.331	74.13	229.8
5.0	49.03	4.903	5.066	6.666	22.24	0.345	77.22	239.4
5.2	50.99	5.099	5.269	6.933	23.13	0.358	80.31	249.0
5.4	52.96	5.296	5.472	7.199	24.02	0.372	83.40	258.6
5.6	54.92	5.492	5.674	7.466	24.91	0.386	86.49	268.1
5.8	56.88	5.688	5.877	7.733	25.80	0.400	89.58	277.7
6.0	58.84	5.884	6.079	7.999	26.69	0.413	92.67	287.3
6.5	63.74	6.374	6.586	8.666	28.91	0.448	100.4	311.2
7.0	68.65	6.865	7.093	9.333	31.14	0.482	108.1	335.2
7.5	73.55	7.355	7.599	9.999	33.36	0.517	115.8	359.1
8.0	78.45	7.845	8.106	10.67	35.59	0.551	123.6	383.0
8.5	83.36	8.336	8.613	11.33	37.81	0.586	131.3	407.0
9.0	88.26	8.826	9.119	12.00	40.03	0.620	139.0	430.9
9.5	93.16	9.316	9.626	12.67	42.26	0.655	146.7	454.9

The above table also applies to decimal multiples and submultiples.
Example: 260 lbf/in² = 17.9 bar

[1]) also valid for conversion from kp to N.

Units of energy

(Units of work) See conversion table on page 31 for figures printed in bold type

Units[1])	J	kW · h	kp · m	PS · h	kcal	ft · lbf	Btu
1 J =	1	$277.8 \cdot 10^{-9}$	0.10197	$377.67 \cdot 10^{-9}$	$\mathbf{238.85 \cdot 10^{-6}}$	0.73756	$947.8 \cdot 10^{-6}$
1 kW · h =	$3.6 \cdot 10^6$	1	367098	**1.35962**	859.85	$2.6552 \cdot 10^6$	3412.13
Do not use							
1 kp · m =	**9.80665**	$2.7243 \cdot 10^{-6}$	1	$3.704 \cdot 10^{-6}$	$2.342 \cdot 10^{-3}$	7.2330	$9.295 \cdot 10^{-3}$
1 PS · h =	$2.6478 \cdot 10^6$	**0.735499**	270000	1	632.369	$1.9529 \cdot 10^6$	2509.6
1 kcal[2]) =	**4186.8**	$1.163 \cdot 10^{-3}$	426.935	$1.581 \cdot 10^{-3}$	1	3088	3.9683
British and American units							
1 ft · lbf =	**1.35582**	$376.6 \cdot 10^{-9}$	0.13826	$512.1 \cdot 10^{-9}$	$323.8 \cdot 10^{-6}$	1	$1.285 \cdot 10^{-3}$
1 Btu[3]) =	**1055.06**	$293.1 \cdot 10^{-6}$	107.59	$398.5 \cdot 10^{-6}$	0.2520	778.17	1

ft lbf = foot pound-force, Btu = British thermal unit
1 in ozf (inch ounce-force) = 0.007062 J, 1 in lbf (inch pound-force) = **0.112985** J,
1 ft pdl (foot poundal) = 0.04214 J,
1 hph (horsepower hour) = $2.685 \cdot 10^6$ J = **0.7457** kW · h,
1 thermie (France) = 1000 frigories (France) = 1000 kcal = 4.1868 MJ,
1 kg C.E. (coal equivalent kilogram)[4]) = 29.3076 MJ = 8.141 kWh
1 t C.E. (coal equivalent ton)[4]) = 1000 kg C.E. = 29.3076 GJ = 8.141 MWh

Units of power

See conversion table on page 31 for figures printed in bold type

Units[1])	W	kW	kp · m/s	PS*	kcal/s	hp	Btu/s
1 W =	1	0.001	0.10197	$1.3596 \cdot 10^{-3}$	$238.8 \cdot 10^{-6}$	$1.341 \cdot 10^{-3}$	$947.8 \cdot 10^{-6}$
1 kW =	1000	1	101.97	**1.35962**	$\mathbf{238.8 \cdot 10^{-3}}$	1.34102	$947.8 \cdot 10^{-3}$
Do not use							
1 kp · m/s =	**9.80665**	$9.807 \cdot 10^{-3}$	1	$13.33 \cdot 10^{-3}$	$2.342 \cdot 10^{-3}$	$13.15 \cdot 10^{-3}$	$9.295 \cdot 10^{-3}$
1 PS =	735.499	0.735499	75	1	0.17567	0.98632	0.69712
1 kcal/s =	4186.8	**4.1868**	426.935	5.6925	1	5.6146	3.9683
British and American units							
1 hp =	745.70	**0.74570**	76.0402	1.0139	0.17811	1	0.70678
1 Btu/s =	1055.06	**1.05506**	107.586	1.4345	0.2520	1.4149	1

hp = horsepower
1 ft · lbf/s = **1.35582** W
1 ch (cheval vapeur) (France) = 1 PS = 0.7355 kW,
1 poncelet (France) = 100 kp · m/s = 0.981 kW
Continuous human power generation ≈ 0.1 kW

Standards: DIN 66 035 Calorie – Joule, Joule – Calorie Conversion Tables
DIN 66 036 Metric Horsepower – Kilowatt, Kilowatt – Horsepower Conversion Tables
DIN 66 039 Kilocalorie – Watt-Hour, Watt-Hour – Kilocalorie Conversion Tables

[1]) See p. 14 and below the tables for the names of the units.
[2]) 1 kcal ≈ quantity of heat required to raise the temperature of 1 kg of water at 15 °C by 1 °C.
[3]) 1 Btu ≈ quantity of heat required to raise the temperature of 1 lb of water 1 °F. 1 therm = 10^5 Btu
[4]) The units of energy kg C.E. and t C.E. were based on a specific calorific value H_u of 7000 kcal/kg of coal.

* PS = Pferdestärke = metric horsepower

Units of energy and power

	Conversion from								
	kp · m *kp · m/s*	**PS · h** *PS*	**kW · h** *kW*	**kcal** *kcal/s*	**kJ** *kW*	**ft · lbf** *ft · lbf/s*	**in · lbf** *in · lbf/s*	**hp · h** *hp*	**Btu** *Btu/s*
↓	to J *W*	to kW · h *kW*	to PS · h *PS*	to kJ *kW*	to kcal *kcal/s*	to J *W*	to J *W*	to kW · h *kW*	to kJ *kW*
1.0	9.807	0.7355	1.360	4.187	0.2388	1.356	0.1130	0.7457	1.055
1.1	10.79	0.8090	1.496	4.605	0.2627	1.491	0.1243	0.8203	1.161
1.2	11.77	0.8826	1.632	5.024	0.2866	1.627	0.1356	0.8948	1.266
1.3	12.75	0.9561	1.767	5.443	0.3105	1.763	0.1469	0.9694	1.372
1.4	13.73	1.030	1.903	5.862	0.3344	1.898	0.1582	1.044	1.477
1.5	14.71	1.103	2.039	6.280	0.3583	2.034	0.1695	1.119	1.583
1.6	15.69	1.177	2.175	6.699	0.3822	2.169	0.1808	1.193	1.688
1.7	16.67	1.250	2.311	7.118	0.4060	2.305	0.1921	1.268	1.794
1.8	17.65	1.324	2.447	7.536	0.4299	2.440	0.2034	1.342	1.899
1.9	18.63	1.397	2.583	7.955	0.4538	2.576	0.2147	1.417	2.005
2.0	19.61	1.471	2.719	8.374	0.4777	2.712	0.2260	1.491	2.110
2.1	20.59	1.545	2.855	8.792	0.5016	2.847	0.2373	1.566	2.216
2.2	21.57	1.618	2.991	9.211	0.5255	2.983	0.2486	1.641	2.321
2.3	22.56	1.692	3.127	9.630	0.5493	3.118	0.2599	1.715	2.427
2.4	23.54	1.765	3.263	10.05	0.5732	3.254	0.2712	1.790	2.532
2.5	24.52	1.839	3.399	10.47	0.5971	3.390	0.2825	1.864	2.638
2.6	25.50	1.912	3.535	10.89	0.6210	3.525	0.2938	1.939	2.743
2.7	26.48	1.986	3.671	11.30	0.6449	3.661	0.3051	2.013	2.849
2.8	27.46	2.059	3.807	11.72	0.6688	3.796	0.3164	2.088	2.954
2.9	28.44	2.133	3.943	12.14	0.6927	3.932	0.3277	2.163	3.060
3.0	29.42	2.206	4.079	12.56	0.7165	4.067	0.3390	2.237	3.165
3.2	31.38	2.354	4.351	13.40	0.7643	4.339	0.3616	2.386	3.376
3.4	33.34	2.501	4.623	14.24	0.8121	4.610	0.3841	2.535	3.587
3.6	35.30	2.648	4.895	15.07	0.8598	4.881	0.4067	2.685	3.798
3.8	37.27	2.795	5.167	15.91	0.9076	5.152	0.4293	2.834	4.009
4.0	39.23	2.942	5.438	16.75	0.9554	5.423	0.4519	2.983	4.220
4.2	41.19	3.089	5.710	17.58	1.003	5.694	0.4745	3.132	4.431
4.4	43.15	3.236	5.982	18.42	1.051	5.966	0.4971	3.281	4.642
4.6	45.11	3.383	6.254	19.26	1.099	6.237	0.5197	3.430	4.853
4.8	47.07	3.530	6.526	20.10	1.146	6.508	0.5423	3.579	5.064
5.0	49.03	3.677	6.798	20.93	1.194	6.779	0.5649	3.728	5.275
5.5	53.94	4.045	7.478	23.03	1.314	7.457	0.6214	4.101	5.803
6.0	58.84	4.413	8.158	25.12	1.433	8.135	0.6779	4.474	6.330
6.5	63.74	4.781	8.838	27.21	1.552	8.813	0.7344	4.847	6.858
7.0	68.65	5.148	9.517	29.31	1.672	9.491	0.7909	5.220	7.385
7.5	73.55	5.516	10.20	31.40	1.791	10.17	0.8474	5.593	7.913
8.0	78.45	5.884	10.88	33.49	1.911	10.85	0.9039	5.966	8.440
8.5	83.36	6.252	11.56	35.59	2.030	11.52	0.9604	6.338	8.968
9.0	88.26	6.619	12.24	37.68	2.150	12.20	1.017	6.711	9.496
9.5	93.16	6.987	12.92	39.77	2.269	12.88	1.073	7.084	10.02

The above table also applies to decimal multiples and submultiples.
Example: 3.8 PS* = 2.795 kW; 38 PS* = 27.95 kW
* PS = Pferdestärke = metric horsepower

Heat engineering units

Conversion from ↓	kcal/(kg·K) [1]; Btu/(lb·°R) [1] to kJ/(kg·K)	kcal/(m·h·K) [2][4] to W/(m·K)	Btu/(s·ft·°R) [2] to kW/(m·K)	Btu/(s·ft²·°R) [3] to kW/(m²·K)	Btu/ft² to kJ/m²	Btu/lb to kJ/kg	Btu/ft³ to kJ/m³
1.0	4.1868	1.1630	6.2306	20.442	11.357	2.3260	37.259
1.1	4.605	1.279	6.854	22.49	12.49	2.559	40.98
1.2	5.024	1.396	7.477	24.53	13.63	2.791	44.71
1.3	5.443	1.512	8.100	26.57	14.76	3.024	48.44
1.4	5.862	1.628	8.723	28.62	15.90	3.256	52.16
1.5	6.280	1.744	9.346	30.66	17.03	3.489	55.89
1.6	6.699	1.861	9.969	32.71	18.17	3.722	59.61
1.7	7.118	1.977	10.59	34.75	19.31	3.954	63.34
1.8	7.536	2.093	11.22	36.80	20.44	4.187	67.07
1.9	7.955	2.210	11.84	38.84	21.58	4.419	70.79
2.0	8.374	2.326	12.46	40.88	22.71	4.652	74.52
2.1	8.792	2.442	13.08	42.93	23.85	4.885	78.24
2.2	9.211	2.559	13.71	44.97	24.98	5.117	81.96
2.3	9.630	2.675	14.33	47.02	26.12	5.350	85.70
2.4	10.05	2.791	14.95	49.06	27.26	5.582	89.42
2.5	10.47	2.907	15.58	51.10	28.39	5.815	93.15
2.6	10.89	3.024	16.20	53.15	29.53	6.048	96.87
2.7	11.30	3.140	16.82	55.19	30.66	6.280	100.6
2.8	11.72	3.256	17.45	57.24	31.80	6.513	104.3
2.9	12.14	3.373	18.07	59.28	32.93	6.745	108.1
3.0	12.56	3.489	18.69	61.33	34.07	6.978	111.8
3.2	13.40	3.722	19.94	65.41	36.34	7.443	119.2
3.4	14.24	3.954	21.18	69.50	38.61	7.908	126.7
3.6	15.07	4.187	22.43	73.59	40.88	8.374	134.1
3.8	15.91	4.419	23.68	77.68	43.16	8.839	141.6
4.0	16.75	4.652	24.92	81.77	45.43	9.304	149.0
4.2	17.58	4.885	26.17	85.86	47.70	9.796	156.5
4.4	18.42	5.117	27.41	89.94	49.97	10.23	163.9
4.6	19.26	5.350	28.66	94.03	52.24	10.70	171.4
4.8	20.10	5.582	29.91	98.12	54.51	11.16	178.8
5.0	20.93	5.815	31.15	102.2	56.78	11.63	186.3
5.5	23.03	6.396	34.27	112.4	62.46	12.79	204.9
6.0	25.12	6.978	37.38	122.7	68.14	13.96	223.6
6.5	27.21	7.559	40.50	132.9	73.82	15.12	242.2
7.0	29.31	8.141	43.61	143.1	79.50	16.28	260.8
7.5	31.40	8.722	46.73	153.3	85.17	17.44	279.4
8.0	33.49	9.304	49.85	163.5	90.85	18.61	298.1
8.5	35.59	9.885	52.96	173.8	96.53	19.77	316.7
9.0	37.68	10.47	56.08	184.0	102.2	20.93	335.3
9.5	39.77	11.05	59.19	194.2	107.9	22.10	354.0

The above table also applies to decimal multiples and submultiples.
Examples: 2.9 kcal/(m · h · K) = 3.373 W/(m · K), 1.2 Btu/lb = 2.791 kJ/kg

[1] Specific heat capacity
[2] Thermal conductivity
[3] Heat transfer coefficient
[4] 1 cal/(cm · s · K) = 360 kcal/(m · h · K) = 418.68 W/(m · K).

Temperature units

°C = degree Celsius, K = kelvin,
°F = degree Fahrenheit,
°R = degree Rankine

Temperature conversion

$$T_K = (273.15°C + t_C)\,\frac{K}{°C} = \frac{5}{9}\,T_R$$

$$T_R = (459.67°F + t_F)\,\frac{°R}{°F} = 1.8\,T_K$$

$$t_C = \frac{5}{9}(t_F - 32°F)\,\frac{°C}{°F} = (T_K - 273.15\,K)\,\frac{°C}{K}$$

$$t_F = (1.8\,t_C + 32°C)\,\frac{°F}{°C} = (T_R - 459.67°R)\,\frac{°F}{°R}$$

t_C, t_F, T_K and T_R denote the numerical values of a temperature in in °C, °F, K and °R.

Temperature difference
1 K = 1 °C = 1.8 °F = 1.8 °R

Zero points: 0°C ≙ 32°F, 0°F ≙ −17.78°C
Absolute zero:
0 K ≙ −273.15°C ≙ 0°R ≙ −459.67°F

International practical temperature scale:
Boiling point of oxygen: −182.97°C, triple point of water: 0.01°C[1]), boiling point of water 100°C, boiling point of sulfur (sulfur point): 444.6°C, setting point of silver (silver point): 960.8°C, setting point of gold: 1063°C.

[1]) That temperature of pure water at which ice, water and water vapour occur together in equilibrium (at 1013.25 hPa). See also footnote [2]) on p. 10.

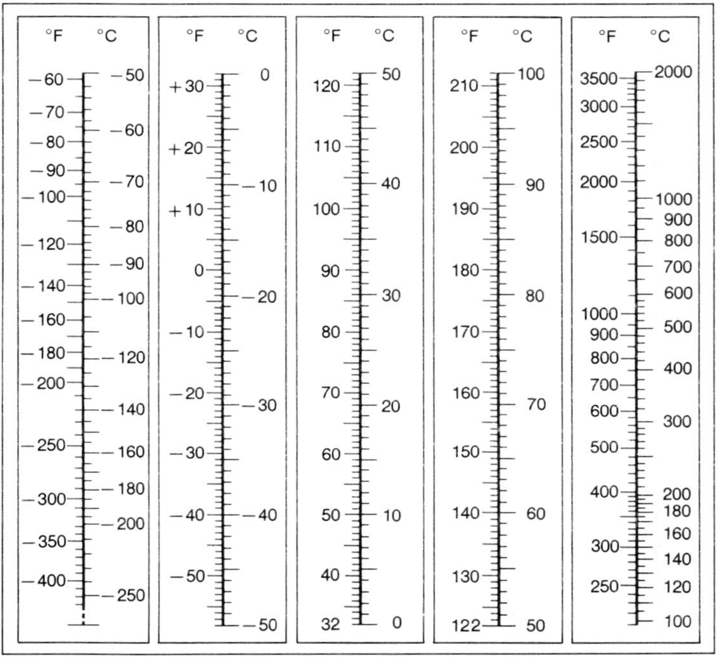

Viscosity units

Legal units of kinematic viscosity ν
1 m²/s = 1 Pa·s/(kg/m³) = 10^4 cm²/s = 10^6 mm²/s

British and American units:
1 ft²/s = 0.092903 m²/s
RI seconds = efflux time from Redwood I viscometer (UK)
SU seconds = efflux time from Saybolt Universal viscometer (US)

Do not use:
St (Stokes) = cm²/s, cSt = mm²/s

Conventional units
E (Engler degree) = relative efflux time from Engler apparatus (DIN 51 560)
For $\nu > 60$ mm²/s is 1 mm²/s = 0.132 E

At values below 3 E, Engler degrees do not give a true indication of the variation of viscosity; for example, a fluid with 2 E does not have twice the kinematic viscosity of a fluid with 1 E, but rather 12 times that value.

A-seconds = efflux time from flow cup (DIN 53 211)

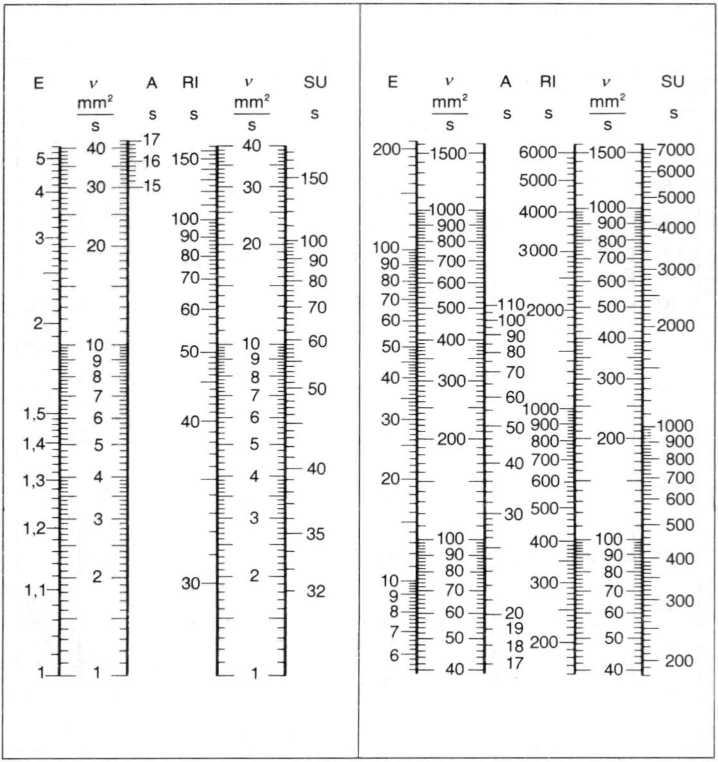

Units of time

Unit[1])		s	min	h	d
1 s[2]) (second)	=	1	0.01667	0.2778×10^{-3}	11.574×10^{-6}
1 min (minute)	=	60	1	0.01667	0.6944×10^{-3}
1 h (hour)	=	3600	60	1	0.041667
1 d (day)	=	86 400	1440	24	1

1 civil year = 365 (or 366) days = 8760 (8784) hours (for calculation of interest in banking, 1 year = 360 days)
1 solar year[3]) = 365.2422 mean solar days = 365 d 5 h 48 min 46 s
1 sidereal year[4]) = 365.2564 mean solar days

Conversion from decimal fractions of hours and angles to minutes and seconds

h (°)	0.00	0.01	0.02	0.03	0.04	0.05	0.06	0.07	0.08	0.09
					min (′) and s (″)					
0.0	0′00″	0′36″	1′12″	1′48″	2′24″	3′00″	3′36″	4′12″	4′48″	5′24″
0.1	6′00″	6′36″	7′12″	7′48″	8′24″	9′00″	9′36″	10′12″	10′48″	11′24″
0.2	12′00″	12′36″	13′12″	13′48″	14′24″	15′00″	15′36″	16′12″	16′48″	17′24″
0.3	18′00″	18′36″	19′12″	19′48″	20′24″	21′00″	21′36″	22′12″	22′48″	23′24″
0.4	24′00″	24′36″	25′12″	25′48″	26′24″	27′00″	27′36″	28′12″	28′48″	29′24″
0.5	30′00″	30′36″	31′12″	31′48″	32′24″	33′00″	33′36″	34′12″	34′48″	35′24″
0.6	36′00″	36′36″	37′12″	37′48″	38′24″	39′00″	39′36″	40′12″	40′48″	41′24″
0.7	42′00″	42′36″	43′12″	43′48″	44′24″	45′00″	45′36″	46′12″	46′48″	47′24″
0.8	48′00″	48′36″	49′12″	49′48″	50′24″	51′00″	51′36″	52′12″	52′48″	53′24″
0.9	54′00″	54′36″	55′12″	55′48″	56′24″	57′00″	57′36″	58′12″	58′48″	59′24″
1.0	60′00″									

Examples: 0.58 h = 34 min 48 s; 0.58° = 34′48″; 12.46° = 12°27′36″

Conversion from minutes to decimal fractions of hours or degrees (or of seconds to decimal fractions of minutes)

min	0	1	2	3	4	5	6	7	8	9
					h or °					
0	–	0.017	0.033	0.050	0.067	0.083	0.100	0.117	0.133	0.150
10	0.167	0.183	0.200	0.217	0.233	0.250	0.267	0.283	0.300	0.317
20	0.333	0.350	0.367	0.383	0.400	0.417	0.433	0.450	0.467	0.483
30	0.500	0.517	0.533	0.550	0.567	0.583	0.600	0.617	0.633	0.650
40	0.667	0.683	0.700	0.717	0.733	0.750	0.767	0.783	0.800	0.817
50	0.833	0.850	0.867	0.883	0.900	0.917	0.933	0.950	0.967	0.983
60	1.000									

Conversion from seconds to decimal fractions of hours or degrees

s (″)	5	10	15	20	25	30	35	40	45	50	55	60
h (°)	0.001	0.003	0.004	0.006	0.007	0.008	0.010	0.011	0.012	0.014	0.015	0.017

Examples: 32 min = 0.533 h or 0.533°; 14 min 45 s = 0.233 + 0.012 h = 0.245 h or 0.245°

---

[1]) See also p. 13.
[2]) Base SI unit; see p. 10 for definition.
[3]) Time between two successive passages of the earth through the vernal equinox.
[4]) True time of revolution of the earth about the sun.

Velocities

1 km/h = 0.27778 m/s
1 mile/h = 1.60934 km/h
1 kn (knot) = 1.852 km/h
1 ft/min = 0.3048 m/min

1 m/s = 3.6 km/h
1 km/h = 0.62137 mile/h
1 km/h = 0.53996 kn
1 m/min = 3.28084 ft/min

x km/h $\triangleq \frac{60}{x}$ min/km $\triangleq \frac{3600}{x}$ s/km

x mile/h $\triangleq \frac{37.2824}{x}$ min/km $\triangleq \frac{2236.9}{x}$ s/km

x s/km $\triangleq \frac{3600}{x}$ km/h (see table on next page)

	Conversion from								
	km/h	m/s	km/h	mile/h (mph)	kn	ft/min	km/h	mile/h (mph)	km/h
↓	to m/s	to km/h	to mile/h	to km/h	to km/h	to m/min	to time/km	to time/km	to time/100 km
10	2.78	36.0	6.21	16.1	18.52	3.05	6 min	3 min 44 s	10 h
20	5.56	72.0	12.4	32.2	37.04	6.10	3 min	1 min 52 s	5 h
30	8.33	108	18.6	48.3	55.56	9.14	2 min	1 min 15 s	3 h 20 min
40	11.1	144	24.9	64.4	74.08	12.2	1 min 30 s	55.9 s	2 h 30 min
50	13.9	180	31.1	80.5	92.60	15.2	1 min 12 s	44.7 s	2 h
60	16.7	216	37.3	96.6	111	18.3	1 min	37.3 s	1 h 40 min
70	19.4	252	43.5	113	130	21.3	51.4 s	32.0 s	1 h 26 min
80	22.2	288	49.7	129	148	24.4	45 s	28.0 s	1 h 15 min
90	25.0	324	55.9	145	167	27.4	40 s	24.9 s	1 h 6.7 min
100	27.8	360	62.1	161	185	30.5	36 s	22.4 s	1 h
110	30.6	396	68.4	177	–	33.5	32.7 s	20.3 s	54 min 33 s
120	33.3	432	74.6	193	–	36.6	30 s	18.6 s	50 min
130	36.1	468	80.8	209	–	39.6	27.7 s	17.2 s	46 min 9 s
140	38.9	504	87.0	225	–	42.7	25.7 s	16.0 s	42 min 51 s
150	41.7	540	93.2	241	–	45.7	24 s	14.9 s	40 min
160	44.4	576	99.4	257	–	48.8	22.5 s	14.0 s	37 min 30 s
170	47.2	612	106	274	–	51.8	21.2 s	13.2 s	35 min 18 s
180	50.0	648	112	290	–	54.9	20.0 s	12.4 s	33 min 20 s
190	52.8	684	118	306	–	57.9	18.9 s	11.8 s	31 min 35 s
200	55.6	720	124	322	–	61.0	18 s	11.2 s	30 min
250	69.4	900	155	402	–	76.2	14.4 s	8.9 s	24 min
300	83.3	1080	186	483	–	91.4	12 s	7.5 s	20 min
400	111	1440	249	644	–	122	9 s	5.6 s	15 min
500	139	1800	311	805	–	152	7.2 s	4.5 s	12 min
600	167	2160	373	966	–	183	6 s	3.7 s	10 min
800	222	2880	497	1287	–	244	4.5 s	2.8 s	7 min 30 s
1000	278	3600	621	1609	–	305	3.6 s	2.2 s	6 min
1200	333[1]	–	746	–	–	366	3 s	–	5 min
1400	389	–	870	–	–	427	2.6 s	–	4 min 17 s

The **Mach number** Ma indicates the ratio of the speed of a body to the speed of sound. Ma = 1.3 therefore denotes 1.3 times the speed of sound.

[1]) Approximately the speed of sound in air.

Conversion of elapsed time for 1 km (s/km) to speed (km/h)

s/km	0	1	2	3	4	5	6	7	8	9
	Speed in km/h									
10	360	327	300	277	257	240	225	212	200	189
20	180	171	164	157	150	144	138	133	129	124
30	120	116	113	109	106	103	100	97	95	92
40	90	88	86	84	82	80	78	77	75	73
50	72	71	69	68	67	65	64	63	62	61
60	60	59	58	57	56	55	55	54	53	52
70	51	51	50	49	49	48	47	47	46	46
80	45	44	44	43	43	42	42	41	41	40
90	40	40	39	39	38	38	38	37	37	36

Example: An elapsed time of 41 s/km corresponds to a speed of 88 km/h.

Clock times

The clock times listed for the following time zones are based on 12 hours CET (Central European Time)[1]:

Clock time	Meridian of the time zone	Countries (examples)
	West longitude	
0100	150°	Alaska
0300	120°	West coast of Canada and USA
0400	105°	Western central zone of Canada and USA
0500	90°	Central zone of Canada and USA, Mexico, Central America
0600	75°	Canada between 68° and 90° Eastern USA, Equador, Columbia, Panama, Peru
0700	60°	Canada east of 68°, Bolivia, Chile, Venezuela
0800	45°	Argentina, Brazil, Greenland, Paraguay, Uruguay
1100	0°	**Greenwich Mean Time (GMT)**[2]: Great Britain, Ireland, Canary Islands, Portugal, West Africa

Clock time	Meridian of the time zone	Countries (examples)
	East longitude	
1200	15°	**Central European Time (CET):** Austria, Belgium, Czechoslovakia, Denmark, Germany, France, Italy, Jugoslavia, Luxembourg, Netherlands, Norway, Sweden, Switzerland, Spain, Hungary; Algeria, Israel, Libya, Nigeria, Tunesia, Zaire
1300	30°	**Eastern European Time (EET):** Bulgaria, Finland, Greece, Rumania; Egypt, Lebanon, Jordan, Sudan, South Africa, Syria
1400	45°	Western states of the former USSR, Turkey, Iraq, Saudi Arabia, Eastern Africa
1430	52.5°	Iran
1630	82.5°	India, Sri Lanka.
1800	105°	Indonesia, Cambodia, Laos, Thailand, Vietnam
1900	120°	Chinese coast, Phillipines, Western Australia
2000	135°	Japan, Korea
2030	142.5°	North and South Australia
2100	150°	Eastern Australia

[1]) During the summer months in countries in which daylight saving time is observed, clocks are set ahead by 1 hour (from approximately April to September north of the equator and October to March south of the equator).

[2]) = UT (Universal Time), mean solar time at the 0° meridian of Greenwich, or UTC (Coordinated Universal Time), defined by the invariable second of the International System of Units (see p. 10) Because the period of rotation of the earth about the sun is gradually becoming longer, UTC is adjusted to UT from time to time by the addition of a leap second (a leap second was last added on 1 July 1983).

Fuel consumption

1 g/PS · h = 1.3596 g/kW · h*
1 lb/hp · h = 608.277 g/kW · h
1 liq pt/hp · h = 634.545 cm^3/kW · h
1 pt (UK)/hp · h = 762.049 cm^3/kW · h

x mile/gal (US) $\triangleq \frac{235.21}{x}$ l/100 km

x mile/gal (UK) $\triangleq \frac{282.48}{x}$ l/100 km

1 g/kW · h* = 0.7355 g/PS · h
1 g/kW · h = 0.001644 lb/hp · h
1 cm^3/kW · h = 0.001576 liq pt/hp · h
1 cm^3/kW · h = 0.001312 pt (UK)/hp · h

x l/100 km $\triangleq \frac{235.21}{x}$ mile/gal (US)

x l/100 km $\triangleq \frac{282.48}{x}$ mile/gal (UK)

See pp. 22 and 30 for the names of British and American units.

↓	Conversion from g/PS · h to g/kW · h	Conversion from g/kW · h to g/PS · h
100	136.0	73.55
120	163.2	88.26
140	190.3	103.0
160	217.5	117.7
180	244.7	132.4
200	271.9	147.1
220	299.1	161.8
240	326.3	176.5
260	353.5	191.2
280	380.7	205.9
300	407.9	220.6
320	435.1	235.4
340	462.3	250.1
360	489.5	264.8
380	516.6	279.5
400	543.8	294.2
420	571.0	308.9
440	598.2	323.6
460	625.4	338.3
480	652.6	353.0
500	679.8	367.7
520	707.0	382.5
540	734.2	397.2
560	761.4	411.9
580	788.6	426.6
600	815.8	441.3
650	883.7	478.1
700	951.7	514.8
750	1020	551.6
800	1088	588.4
900	1224	661.9

Example: 240 g/PS · h* = 326.3 g/kW · h

↓	Conversion from lb/hp · h to g/kW · h	Conversion from liq pt/hp · h to cm^3/kW · h	Conversion from pt (UK)/hp · h to cm^3/kW · h
0.10	60.83	63.45	76.20
0.15	91.24	95.18	114.3
0.20	121.7	126.9	152.4
0.25	152.1	158.6	190.5
0.30	182.5	190.4	228.6
0.32	194.6	203.1	243.9
0.34	206.8	215.7	259.1
0.36	219.0	228.4	274.3
0.38	231.1	241.1	289.6
0.40	243.3	253.8	304.8
0.42	255.5	266.5	320.1
0.44	267.6	279.2	335.3
0.46	279.8	291.9	350.5
0.48	292.0	304.6	365.8
0.50	304.1	317.3	381.0
0.52	316.3	330.0	396.3
0.54	328.5	342.7	411.5
0.56	340.6	355.3	426.7
0.58	352.8	368.0	442.0
0.60	365.0	380.7	457.2
0.62	377.1	393.4	472.5
0.64	389.3	406.1	487.7
0.66	401.5	418.8	503.0
0.68	413.6	431.5	518.2
0.70	425.8	444.2	533.4
0.75	456.2	475.9	571.5
0.80	486.6	507.6	609.6
0.85	517.0	539.4	647.7
0.90	547.4	571.1	685.8
0.95	577.9	602.8	723.9

Example: 0,68 liq pt/hp · h = 431.5 cm^3/kW · h

↓	Conversion from mile/gal (US) to l/100 km	Conversion from mile/gal (UK) to l/100 km
10	23.5	28.2
11	21.4	25.7
12	19.6	23.5
13	18.1	21.7
14	16.8	20.2
15	15.7	18.8
16	14.7	17.7
17	13.8	16.6
18	13.1	15.7
19	12.4	14.9
20	11.8	14.1
22	10.7	12.8
24	9.80	11.8
26	9.05	10.9
28	8.40	10.1
30	7.84	9.42
32	7.35	8.83
34	6.92	8.31
36	6.53	7.85
38	6.19	7.43
40	5.88	7.06
42	5.60	6.73
44	5.35	6.42
46	5.11	6.14
48	4.90	5.88
50	4.70	5.65
55	4.28	5.14
60	3.92	4.71
70	3.36	4.04
80	2.94	3.53
90	2.61	3.14

Example: 18 mile/gal (US) = 13.1 l/100 km

* PS = Pferdestärke = metric horsepower

Vibration and oscillation

Symbols and units

Quantity		Unit
a	Storage coefficient	
b	Damping coefficient	
c	Storage coefficient	
c	Spring constant	N/m
c_α	Torsional rigidity	N · m/rad
C	Capacity	F
f	Frequency	Hz
f_g	Resonant frequency	Hz
Δf	Half-value width	Hz
F	Force	N
F_Q	Excitation function	
I	Current	A
J	Moment of inertia	kg · m²
L	Self-inductance	H
m	Mass	kg
M	Torque	N · m
n	Rotational speed	1/min ($\min^{-1}$)
Q	Charge	C
Q	Resonance sharpness	
r	Damping factor	N · s/m
r_α	Rotational damping coefficient	N · s · m
R	Ohmic resistance	Ω
t	Time	s
T	Period	s
U	Voltage	V
v	Particle velocity	m/s
x	Travel/Displacement	
y	Instantaneous value	
$\hat{y}$	Amplitude	
$\dot{y}$ ($\ddot{y}$)	Single (double) derivative with respect to time	
y_{rec}	Rectified value	
y_{rms}	Effective value	
α	Angle	rad
δ	Decay coefficient	1/s
Λ	Logarithmic decrement	
ω	Angular velocity	rad/s
ω	Angular frequency	1/s
Ω	Exciter circuit frequency	1/s
ϑ	Damping ratio	
ϑ_{opt}	Optimum damping ratio	

Subscripts:	
0	Undamped natural oscillation
d	Damped natural oscillation
T	Absorber
U	Base support
G	Machine

Definitions

(See also DIN 1311)

Vibrations and oscillations

Vibrations and oscillations are the terms used to denote changes in a physical quantity which repeat at more or less regular time intervals and whose direction changes with similar regularity.

Period

The period is the time taken for one complete cycle of a single vibration (period)

Amplitude

Amplitude is the maximum instantaneous value (peak value) of a sinusoidally oscillating physical quantity.

Frequency

Frequency is the number of vibrations in one second, the reciprocal value of the period of oscillation T.

Angular frequency

Angular frequency is 2π times the frequency.

Particle velocity

Particle velocity is the instantaneous value of the alternating velocity of a vibrating particle in its direction of vibration. It must not be confused with the velocity of propagation of a traveling wave (e.g., the velocity of sound).

Fourier series

Every periodic function, which is piecewise monotonic and smooth, can be expressed as the sum of sinusoidal harmonic components.

Beats

Beats occur when two sinusoidal oscillations, whose frequencies do not differ greatly, are superposed. They are periodic. Their basic frequency is the difference between the frequencies of the super posed sinusoidal oscillations.

Natural oscillations

The frequency of natural oscillations (natural frequency) is dependent only on the properties of the oscillating system.

Damping

Damping is a measure of the energy losses in an oscillatory system when one form of energy is converted into another.

Logarithmic decrement
Natural logarithm of the relationship between two extreme values of a natural oscillation which are separated by one period.

Damping ratio
Basis for calculation of damping.

Forced oscillations
Forced oscillations arise under the influence of an external physical force (excitation), which does not change the properties of the oscillator. The frequency of forced oscillations is determined by the frequency of the excitation.

Transfer function
The transfer function is the quotient of amplitude of the observed variable divided by the amplitude of excitation, plotted against the exciter frequency.

Resonance
Resonance occurs when the transfer function produces very large values as the exciter frequency approaches the natural frequency.

Resonant frequency
Resonant frequency is the exciter frequency at which the oscillator variable attains its maximum value.

Half-value width
The half-value width is the difference between the frequencies at which the level of the variable has dropped to $1/\sqrt{2} \approx 0.707$ of the maximum value.

Resonance sharpness
Resonance sharpness, or the quality factor (Q-factor), is the maximum value of the transfer function.

Coupling
If two oscillatory systems are coupled together – mechanically by mass or elasticity, electrically by inductance or capacitance – a periodic exchange of energy between the systems takes place.

Wave
Spatial and temporal change of state of a continuum, which can be expressed as a unidirectional transfer of location of a certain state over a period of time. There are transverse waves (e.g., waves in rope and water) and longitudinal waves (e.g., sound waves in air).

Interference
The principle of undisturbed superposition of waves. At every point in space the instantaneous value of the resulting wave is equal to the sum of the instantaneous values of the individual waves.

Standing waves
Standing waves occur as a result of interference between two waves of equal frequency, wavelength and amplitude traveling in opposite directions. In contrast to a propagating wave, the amplitude of the standing wave is constant at every point; nodes (zero amplitude) and antinodes (maximum amplitude) occur. Standing waves occur by reflection of a wave back on itself if the characteristic impedance of the medium differs greatly from the impedance of the reflector.

Rectification value
Arithmetic mean value, linear in time, of the values of a periodic signal.

$$y_{rec} = (1/T) \int_0^T |y| \, dt$$

For a sine curve:

$$y_{rec} = 2\hat{y}/\pi \approx 0.637\,\hat{y}.$$

Effective value
Quadratic mean value in time of a periodic signal.

$$y_{rms} = \sqrt{(1/T) \int_0^T y^2 \, dt}$$

For a sine curve:

$$y_{rms} = \hat{y}/\sqrt{2} \approx 0.707\,\hat{y}.$$

Sinusoidal oscillation

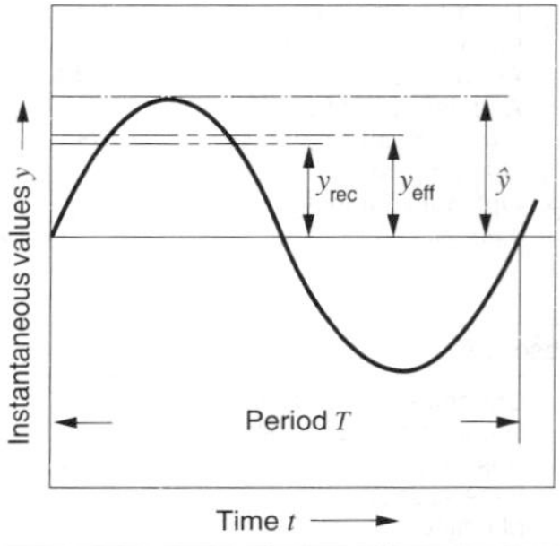

Form factor = y_{rms}/y_{rec}
For a sine curve:

$y_{rms}/y_{rec} \approx 1.111$.

Peak factor = $\hat{y}/y_{rms}$
For a sine curve:
$\hat{y}/y_{rms} = \sqrt{2} \approx 1.414$.

Equations
The equations apply for the following simple oscillators if the general quantity designations in the formulas are replaced by the relevant physical quantities.

Simple oscillatory systems

	Mechanical		Electrical
	Translat-ional	Rotational	
	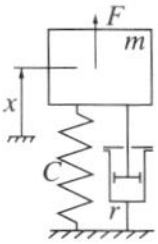	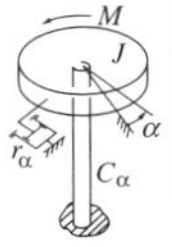	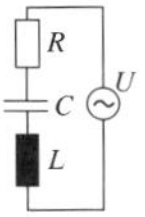
Gen. desig-nation	Physical quantity		
y	x	α	Q
$\dot{y}$	$\dot{x} = v$	$\dot{\alpha} = \omega$	$\dot{Q} = I$
$\ddot{y}$	$\ddot{x} = \dot{v}$	$\ddot{\alpha} = \dot{\omega}$	$\ddot{Q} = \dot{I}$
F_Q	F	M	U
a	m	J	L
b	r	r_α	R
c	c	c_α	$1/C$

Differential equations

$a\ddot{y} + b\dot{y} + cy = F_Q(t) = \hat{F}_Q \sin \Omega t$

Period $T = 1/f$

Angular frequency $\omega = 2\pi f$

Sinusoidal oscillation
(e.g., vibration displacement) $y = \hat{y} \sin \omega t$

1st derivative
(e.g., particle velocity)

$\dot{y} = dy/dt = \omega\hat{y} \cos \omega t = \omega \hat{y} \sin (\omega t + \pi/2)$

2nd derivative
(e.g., particle acceleration)

$\ddot{y} = d^2y/dt^2$

$= -\omega^2\hat{y} \sin \omega t = \omega^2\hat{y} \sin (\omega t + \pi)$

Free oscillations ($F_Q = 0$)

Logarithmic decrement

$\Lambda = \ln(y_n/y_{n+1}) = \pi b/\sqrt{ca - b^2/4}$

Decay coefficient $\delta = b/(2a)$

Damping ratio $\vartheta = \delta/\omega_0 = b/(2\sqrt{ca})$

$\vartheta = \Lambda/\sqrt{\Lambda^2 + 4\pi^2} \approx \Lambda/(2\pi)$
(low level of damping)

Angular frequency of the undamped oscillation ($\vartheta = 0$) $\omega_0 = \sqrt{c/a}$

Angular frequency of the damped oscillation $0 < \vartheta < 1$) $\omega_d = \omega_0\sqrt{1 - \vartheta^2}$

For $\vartheta \geq 1$ no oscillations, but creepage.

Forced oscillations

Quantity of transfer function

$\hat{y}/\hat{F}_Q = 1/\sqrt{(c - a\,\Omega^2)^2 + (b\,\Omega)^2}$

$= (1/c)/\sqrt{(1 - (\Omega/\omega_0)^2)^2 + (2\vartheta\Omega/\omega_0)^2}$

Resonant frequency $f_g = f_0\sqrt{1 - 2\vartheta^2} < f_0$

Resonance
sharpness $Q = 1/\ (2\vartheta\sqrt{1 - \vartheta^2})$

Oscillator with low level of damping ($\theta \leq 0.1$):

Resonant frequency $f_g \approx f_0$

Sharpness of resonance $Q \approx 1/(2\vartheta)$

Half-value width $\Delta f = 2\,\vartheta f_0 = f_0/Q$

Free oscillation and damping

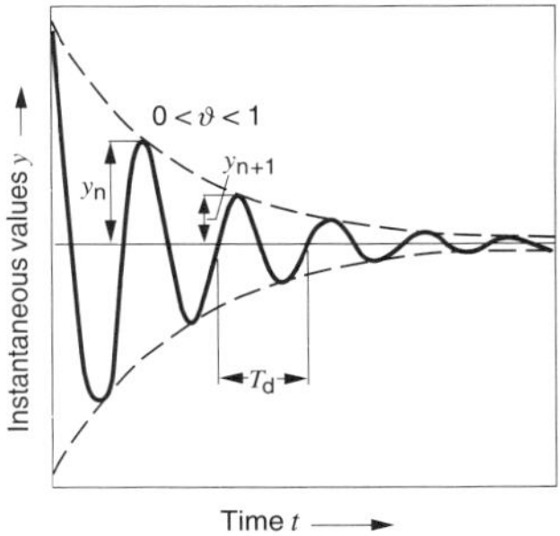

Vibration reduction

Vibration isolation

Active vibration isolation
Machines are to be mounted so that the forces transmitted to the base support (carrier) are small. One measure to be taken: The bearing point should be set below resonance, so that the natural frequency lies below the lowest exciter frequency. Damping impedes insulation. However, too-low values may lead to difficulties caused by resonance during running-up.

Passive vibration insulation
Machines are to be mounted so that vibration and shaking reaching the base support are only transmitted to the machines to a minor degree. The same measures as in the case of active insulation are to be taken. If damping can only be carried out between the machine and a quiescent point, the damping must be at a high level (see Transmission function $\hat{X}_G/\hat{X}_U$ in forced oscillations).

In many cases flexible suspension or extreme damping is not practicable. So that no resonance can arise, the machine attachment should be so rigid that the natural frequency is far enough in excess of the highest exciter frequency which can occur.

Vibration absorption

Absorber with fixed natural frequency
By tuning the natural frequency ω_T (absorber frequency) of an absorption mass with a flexible, loss-free coupling to the excitation frequency, the vibration of the main mass is completely absorbed. Only the absorption mass still vibrates. The effectiveness of the absorption decreases as the exciter frequency changes. The effectiveness is determined by the characteristic of the main mass transfer function (steepness, proximity to the resonance frequencies). The transfer functions of the main and absorption masses are dependent on the type of absorber tuning (mass, spring constant).

Damping prevents complete absorption. However, appropriate tuning of the absorber frequency and an optimum damping ratio produce broadband vibration reduction, which remains effective when the exciter frequency changes.

Absorber with changeable natural frequency
Rotational oscillations with exciter frequencies proportional to the rotational speed (harmonics) of variable-speed motors can be absorbed by absorbers with natural frequencies proportional to the rotational speed (pendulum in the centrifugal force field). The absorption is effective at all rotational speeds.

Absorption is also possible for oscillators with several degrees of freedom and interrelationships, as well as by the use of several absorption bodies.

Standardized transfer function

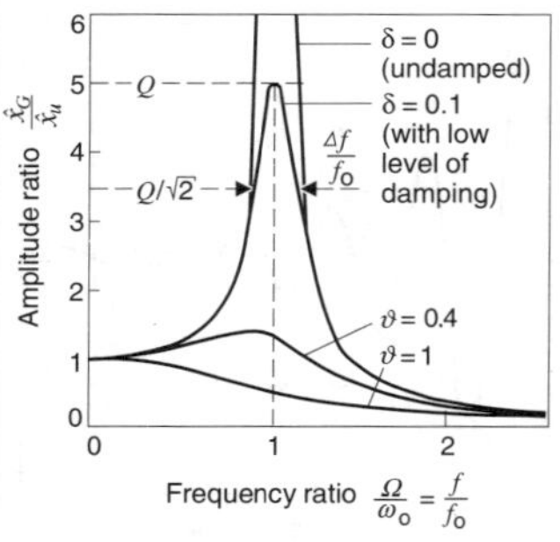

Vibration isolation

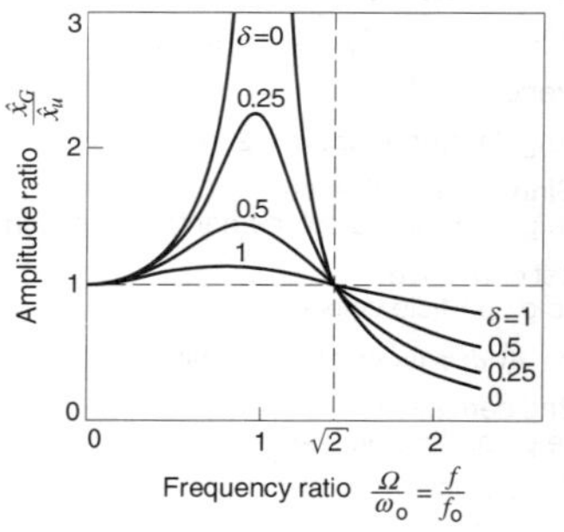

Vibration absorption
Transmission function of the main mass.

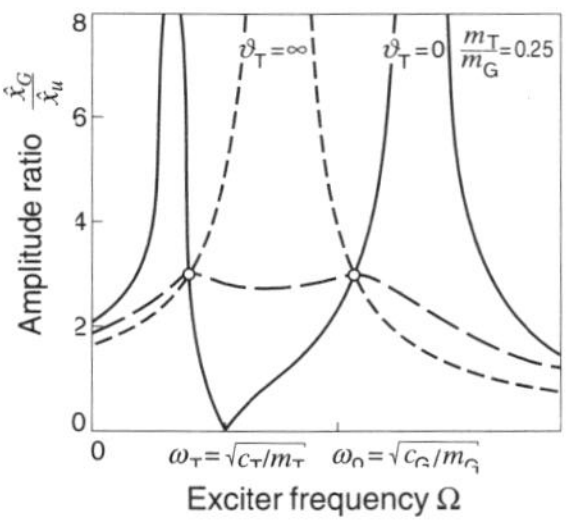

Modal analysis

The dynamic behavior (oscillatory characteristics) of a mechanical structure can be predicted with the aid of a mathematical model. By means of modal analysis, the model parameters of one of the possible models (the modal model) are ascertained. A time-invariant and linear-elastic structure is a prerequisite. The oscillations are only observed at a limited number of points in the possible oscillation directions (degrees of freedom) and at defined frequency intervals. In modal analysis the continuous structure is then replaced in a clearly-defined manner by a finite number of single-mass oscillators. Each single-mass oscillator is comprehensively and clearly defined by a characteristic vector and a characteristic value. The characteristic vector (mode form, natural oscillation form) describes the relative amplitudes and phases of all degrees of freedom, the characteristic value describes the behavior in terms of time (damped harmonic oscillation). Every oscillation of the structure can be artificially recreated from the characteristic vectors and values ascertained. The modal model not only describes the actual state of the dynamic behavior, but also forms the basis for simulation calculations: In response calculation, the response of the structure to a defined excitation, corresponding, for instance, to test laboratory conditions, is calculated. By means of structure modifications (changes in mass, damping or stiffness) the dynamic behavior can be optimized to the level required by operating conditions. The even more detailed substructure coupling process collates modal models of various structures, for example, into one overall model. The modal model can be constructed analytically or experimentally. The basis in each case is a model which is an equivalent model to the modal model. Analytical and experimental modal analysis are mutually complementary. When the modal models produced by both processes are compared with each other, the modal model resulting from an analytical modal analysis is more accurate than that from an experimental modal analysis as a result of the greater number of degrees of freedom in the analytical process. This particularly applies to simulation calculations based on the model.

Analytical modal analysis

For analytical modal analysis the geometry, material data and marginal conditions must be known. Depending on the structure, for instance, a multibody system or a finite element model can be produced from the analytical modal analysis. A linear differential equation system of the second order describes the corresponding motion model. Converted into a characteristic problem, it provides characteristic vectors and values. Analytical modal analysis requires no specimen sample, and can therefore be applied at an early stage of development. However, it is often the case that precise knowledge concerning the structure's fundamental properties (damping, marginal conditions) are lacking, which means that the modal model can be very inaccurate. As well as this, the error is unidentified.

Experimental modal analysis

Experimental modal analysis is based on measurements. Information concerning the structure is not necessary, but specimen and accessible measuring points are required. Then, for instance, the transfer functions in the frequency range in question are measured from one excitation point to a number of response points, and vice versa. The modal model is derived from the matrix of the transfer functions (which define the response model). It describes the dynamic behavior of the structure with sufficient accuracy, despite having relatively few degrees of freedom.

Basic equations used in mechanics

See pp. 12–16 for names of units

Symbol	Quantity	SI-Unit
A	Area	m^2
a	Acceleration	m/s^2
a_{cf}	Centrifugal acceleration	m/s^2
d	Diameter	m
E	Energy	J
E_k	Kinetic energy	J
E_p	Potential energy	J
F	Force	N
F_{cf}	Centrifugal force	N
G	Weight	N
g	Acceleration of free fall (g = 9.81 m/s^2, see. p. 11)	m/s^2
h	Height	m
i	Radius of gyration	m
J	Moment of inertia (second moment of mass)	$kg \cdot m^2$
L	Angular momentum	$N \cdot s \cdot m$
l	Length	m
M	Moment of force/Torque	$N \cdot m$

Symbol	Quantity	SI-Unit
m	Mass (weight)	kg
n	Rotational frequency	s^{-1}
P	Power	W
p	Linear momentum	$N \cdot s$
r	Radius	m
s	Length of path	m
T	Period, time of one revolution	s
t	Time	s
V	Volume	m^3
v	Velocity	m/s
	v_1 Initial velocity	
	v_2 Final velocity	
	v_m Mean velocity	
W	Work, energy	J
α	Angular acceleration	rad/s^2 [1]
ε	Wrap angle	rad [1]
μ	Coefficient of friction	–
ϱ	Density	kg/m^3
φ	Angle of rotation	rad [1]
ω	Angular velocity	rad/s [1]

Relationships between quantities, numbers

If not otherwise specified, the following relationships are relationships between quantities, i. e. the quantities can be inserted using any units (e. g., the SI units given above). The unit of the quantity to be calculated is obtained from the units chosen for the terms of the equation.

In some cases, additional numerical relationships are given for customary units (e. g., time in s, but speed in km/h). These relationships are identified by the word "numerical relationship", and are only valid if the units given for the relationship are used.

Rectilinear motion

Uniform rectilinear motion

Velocity
$v = s/t$

Uniform rectilinear acceleration

Mean velocity
$v_m = (v_1 + v_2)/2$

Acceleration
$a = (v_2 - v_1)/t = (v_2^2 - v_1^2)/(2s)$

Numerical relationship:
$a = (v_2 - v_1)/(3.6\,t)$
a in m/s^2, v_2 und v_1 in km/h, t in s

Distance covered after time t
$s = v_m \cdot t = v_1 \cdot t + (a \cdot t^2)/2$
$= (v_2^2 - v_1^2)/(2a)$

Final velocity
$v_2 = v_1 + a \cdot t = \sqrt{v_1^2 + 2a \cdot s}$

Initial velocity
$v_1 = v_2 - a \cdot t = \sqrt{v_2^2 - 2a \cdot s}$

For uniformly retarded motion (v_2 smaller than v_1), a is negative.

For acceleration from rest, substitute $v_1 = 0$. For retardation to rest, substitute $v_2 = 0$.

[1] The unit rad (= m/m) can be replaced by the number 1.

Force
$F = m \cdot a$

Work, energy
$W = F \cdot s = m \cdot a \cdot s = P \cdot t$

Potential energy
$E_p = G \cdot h = m \cdot g \cdot h$

Kinetic energy
$E_k = m \cdot v^2/2$

Power
$P = W/t = F \cdot v$

Lifting power
$P = m \cdot g \cdot v$

Linear momentum
$p = m \cdot v$

Rotary motion

Uniform rotary motion

Peripheral velocity
$v = r \cdot \omega$
Numerical relationship:
$v = \pi \cdot d \cdot n/60$
v in m/s, d in m, n in min^{-1}
$v = 6 \cdot \pi \cdot d \cdot n/100$
v in km/h, d in m, n in min^{-1}

Angular velocity
$\omega = \varphi/t = v/r = 2\pi \cdot n$
Numerical relationship:
$\omega = \pi \cdot n/30$
ω in s^{-1}, n in min^{-1}

Uniform angular acceleration

Angular acceleration
$\alpha = (\omega_2 - \omega_1)/t$
Numerical relationship:
$\alpha = \pi (n_2 - n_1)/(30\,t)$
α in $1/\text{s}^2$, n_1 and n_2 in min^{-1}, t in s

Final angular velocity
$\omega_2 = \omega_1 + \alpha \cdot t$

Initial angular velocity
$\omega_1 = \omega_2 - \alpha \cdot t$

For uniformly retarded rotary motion (ω_2 is smaller than ω_1), α is negative.

Centrifugal force
$F_{cf} = m \cdot r \cdot \omega^2 = m \cdot v^2/r$

Centrifugal acceleration
$a_{cf} = r \cdot \omega^2$

Moment of force/Torque
$M = F \cdot r = P/\omega$
Numerical relationship:
$M = 9550 \cdot P/n$
M in N · m, P in kW, n in min^{-1}

Moment of inertia (see p. 48)
$J = m \cdot i^2$

Work
$W = M \cdot \varphi = P \cdot t$

Power
$P = M \cdot \omega = M \cdot 2\pi \cdot n$
Numerical relationship:
$P = M \cdot n/9550$ (see graph, p. 50)
P in kW, M in N · m (= W · s),
n in min^{-1}

Energy of rotation
$E_{rot} = J \cdot \omega_2/2 = J \cdot 2\pi^2 \cdot n^2$
Numerical relationship:
$E_{rot} = J \cdot n^2/182.4$
E_{rot} in J (= N · m), J in kg m²,
n in min^{-1}

Angular momentum
$L = J \cdot \omega = J \cdot 2\pi \cdot n$
Numerical relationship:
$L = J \cdot \pi \cdot n/30 = 0.1047\ J \cdot n$
L in N · s · m, J in kg · m², n in min^{-1}

Pendulum motion

(Mathematical pendulum, i. e. a point-size mass suspended from a thread of zero mass)

Plane pendulum

Period of oscillation (time for one complete swing back and forth)
$T = 2\pi \cdot \sqrt{l/g}$
The above equation is only accurate for small excursions α from the rest position (for $\alpha = 10°$, the error is approximately 0.2%).

Conical pendulum

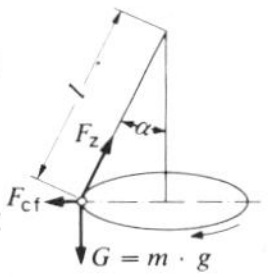

Time for one revolution:
$T = 2\pi \cdot \sqrt{(l \cos \alpha)/g}$
Centrifugal force
$F_{cf} = m \cdot g \cdot \tan \alpha$
Force pulling on thread:
$F_z = m \cdot g/\cos \alpha$

Throwing and falling

(See p. 44 for equation symbols)

Body thrown vertically upward (neglecting air resistance). Uniform retardation. Retardation: $a = g = 9.81\ m/s^2$	Upward velocity	$v = v_1 - g \cdot t = v_1 - \sqrt{2g \cdot h}$
	Height reached	$h = v_1 \cdot t - 0.5 g \cdot t^2$
	Time of upward travel	$t = \frac{v_1 - v}{g} = \frac{v_1 - \sqrt{v_1^2 - 2g \cdot h}}{g}$
	At highest point	$v_2 = 0;\ h_2 = \frac{v_1^2}{2g};\ t_2 = \frac{v_1}{g}$
Body thrown obliquely upward (neglecting air resistance). Angle of throw α; superposition of uniform rectilinear motion and free fall	Range of throw (maximum value at $\alpha = 45°$)	$s = \frac{v_1^2 \cdot \sin 2\alpha}{g}$
	Duration of throw	$t = \frac{s}{v_1 \cdot \cos\alpha} = \frac{2 v_1 \cdot \sin\alpha}{g}$
	Height of throw	$h = \frac{v_1^2 \cdot \sin^2\alpha}{2g}$
	Energy of throw	$E = G \cdot h = m \cdot g \cdot h$
Free fall (neglecting air resistance). Uniform acceleration; acceleration: $a = g = 9.81\ m/s^2$	Velocity of fall	$v = g \cdot t = \sqrt{2g \cdot h}$
	Height of fall	$h = \frac{g \cdot t^2}{2} = \frac{v^2}{2g} = \frac{v \cdot t}{2}$
	Time of fall	$t = \frac{2h}{v} = \frac{v}{g} = \sqrt{\frac{2h}{g}}$
Fall with allowance for air resistance Non-uniform acceleration; initial acceleration: $a_1 = g = 9.81\ m/s^2$, final acceleration $a_2 = 0$	The velocity of fall approaches a limiting velocity v_0 at which the air resistance $F_A = \varrho \cdot c_W \cdot A \cdot v_0^2/2$ is as great as the weight $G = m \cdot g$ of the falling body, thus:	
	Limiting velocity	$v_0 = \sqrt{2m \cdot g/(\varrho \cdot c_W \cdot A)}$ (ϱ air density, c_W coefficient of drag, A cross-sectional area of the body).
	Velocity of fall	$v = v_0 \cdot \sqrt{1 - 1/\varkappa^2}$ The following abbreviated term is substituted: $\varkappa = e^{g\,h/v_0^2};\ e = 2.718$
	Height of fall	$h = \frac{v_0^2}{2g} \ln \frac{v_0^2}{v_0^2 - v^2}$
	Time of fall	$t = \frac{v_0}{g} \ln (\varkappa + \sqrt{\varkappa^2 - 1})$

Example: A heavy body (mass m = 1000 kg, cross-sectional area $A = 1\ m^2$, coefficient of drag $c_W = 0.9$) falls from a great height. The air density $\varrho = 1.293\ kg/m^3$ and the acceleration of free fall $g = 9.81\ m/s^2$ are assumed to be the same over the entire range as at ground level.

Height of fall	Neglecting air resistance, values at end of fall from indicated height would be			Allowing for air resistance, values at end of fall from indicated height are		
	Time of fall	Velocity of fall	Energy	Time of fall	Velocity of fall	Energy
m	s	m/s	kJ	s	m/s	kJ
10	1.43	14.0	98	1.43	13.97	97
50	3.19	31.3	490	3.2	30.8	475
100	4.52	44.3	980	4.6	43	925
500	10.1	99	4900	10.6	86.2	3690
1000	14.3	140	9800	15.7	108	5850
5000	31.9	313	49 000	47.6	130	8410
10 000	45.2	443	98 000	86.1	130	8410

Drag coefficients c_W

Body shape		c_W
	Disc, plate	1.1
	Open dish, parachute	1.4
	Sphere $Re < 200\,000$ $Re > 250\,000$	 0.45 0.20
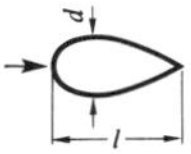	Slender rotating body $l:d = 6$	0.05

Body shape		c_W
	Long cylinder $Re < 200\,000$ $Re > 450\,000$	 1.0 0.35
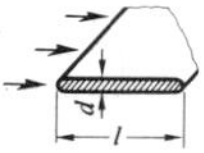	Long plate $l:d = 30$ $Re \approx 500\,000$ $Re \approx 200\,000$	 0.78 0.66
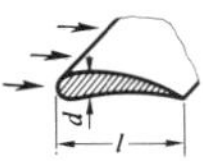	Long airfoil $l:d = 18$ } $Re \approx 10^6$ $l:d = 8$ } $Re \approx 10^6$ $l:d = 5$ } $Re \approx 10^6$ $l:d = 2$ $Re \approx 2 \cdot 10^5$	 0.2 0.1 0.08 0.2

Reynolds number

$Re = (v + v_0) \cdot l/\nu$

v Velocity of body in m/s,
v_0 Velocity of air in m/s,
l Length of body in m (in direction of flow),
d Thickness of body in m,
ν Kinematic viscosity in m/s^2.

For air with $v = 14 \cdot 10^{-6}$ m^2/s (annual mean 200 m above sea level)

$Re \approx 72{,}000\,(v + v_0) \cdot l$ with v and v_0 in m/s
$Re \approx 20{,}000\,(v + v_0) \cdot l$ with v and v_0 in km/h

The results of flow measurements on two geometrically similar bodies of different sizes are comparable only if the Reynolds number is of equal magnitude in both cases (this is important in tests on models).

Discharge of air from nozzles

The curves below only give approximate values. In addition to pressure and nozzle cross section, the air discharge rate depends upon the surface and length of the nozzle bore, the supply line and the rounding of the edges of the discharge port.

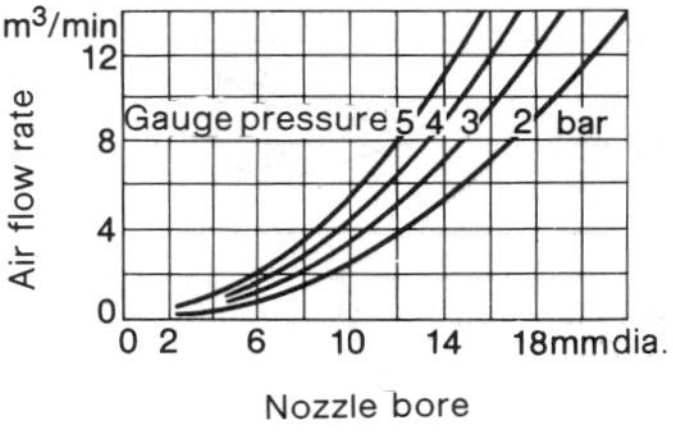

Gravitation

Force of attraction between two masses:

$F = f\,(m_1 \cdot m_2)/r^2$

r Distance between centers of mass
f Gravitation constant $= 6.67 \times 10^{-11}$ N·m^2/kg^2

Lever law

$F_1 \cdot r_1 = F_2 \cdot r_2$

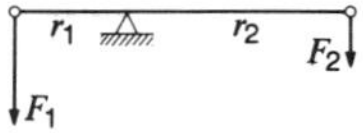

Moments of inertia

See p. 44 for symbols, mass $m = V \cdot \varrho$, p. 143 for volumes of solids V, pp. 13, 178 for density ϱ, and p. 59 for second moments of area.

Type of body		Moments of inertia J_x about the x-axis[1]), J_y about the y-axis[1])	
Right parallelepiped, cuboid	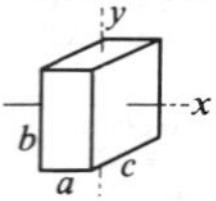	$J_x = m\,\frac{b^2+c^2}{12}$ $J_y = m\,\frac{a^2+c^2}{12}$	Cube with side length a: $J_x = J_y = m\,\frac{a^2}{6}$
Circular cylinder	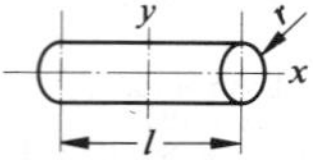	$J_x = m\,\frac{r^2}{2}$ $J_y = m\,\frac{3\,r^2+l^2}{12}$	
Hollow circular cylinder	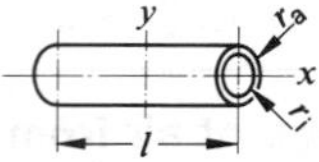	$J_x = m\,\frac{r_a^2+r_i^2}{2}$ $J_y = m\,\frac{r_a^2+r_i^2+l^2/3}{4}$	
Right circular cone	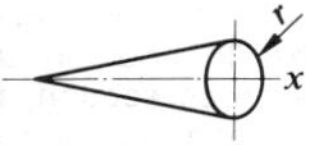	$J_x = m\,\frac{3\,r^2}{10}$ Surface of cone (excluding end base) $J_x = m\,\frac{r^2}{2}$	
Frustum of right circular cone	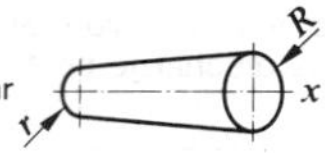	$J_x = m\,\frac{3\,(R^5-r^5)}{10\,(R^3-r^3)}$ Surface of cone (excluding end faces) $J_x = m\,\frac{R^2+r^2}{2}$	
Pyramid	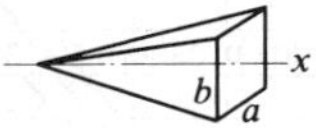	$J_x = m\,\frac{a^2+b^2}{20}$	
Sphere and hemisphere	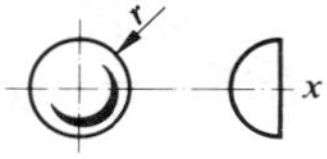	$J_x = m\,\frac{2\,r^2}{5}$ Surface area of sphere $J_x = m\,\frac{2\,r^2}{3}$	
Hollow sphere	r_a outer sphere radius r_i inner sphere radius	$J_x = m\,\frac{2\,(r_a^5-r_i^5)}{5\,(r_a^3-r_i^3)}$	
Torus	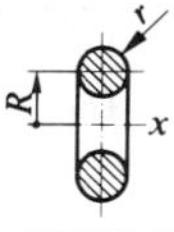	$J_x = m\left(R^2+\frac{3}{4}\,r^2\right)$	

[1]) The moment of inertia for an axis parallel to the x-axis or y-axis at a distance a is $J_A = J_x + m \cdot a^2$ or $J_A = J_y + m \cdot a^2$.

Friction

(See below for coefficients of friction μ)

On a horizontal plane
Frictional force (frictional resistance):
$F_R = \mu \cdot m \cdot g$

On an inclined plane
Frictional force (frictional resistance):
$F_R = \mu \cdot F_N = \mu \cdot m \cdot g \cdot \cos\alpha$

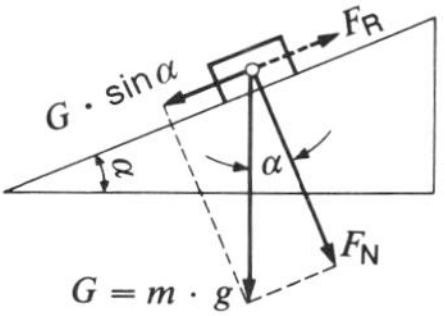

Force parallel to an inclined plane[1])
$F = G \cdot \sin\alpha - F_R = m \cdot g(\sin\alpha - \mu \cdot \cos\alpha)$

Acceleration parallel to an inclined plane[1])
$a = g(\sin\alpha - \mu \cdot \cos\alpha)$

Velocity after distance
s (for height $h = s \cdot \sin\alpha$)
$v = \sqrt{2g \cdot h(1 - \mu \cdot \cot\alpha)}$

[1]) A body at rest remains at rest if ($\sin\alpha - \mu \cdot \cos\alpha$) is negative or zero.

Belt-wrap friction
Tension forces:
$F_1 = F_2 \cdot e^{\mu\varepsilon}$

Transmissible peripheral force:
$F_u = F_1 - F_2 = F_1(1 - e^{-\mu\varepsilon}) = F_2(e^{\mu\varepsilon} - 1)$
$e = 2.718$ (base of natural logarithms)

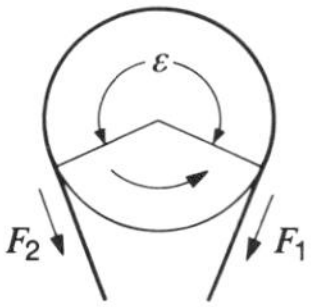

Coefficients of friction

Materials	Kinetic coefficient of friction (sliding friction) μ dry	lubricated	Static coefficient of friction (static friction) μ_r dry	lubricated
Steel on steel	0.12	0.08	0.15	0.12
Steel on bronze or gray cast iron	0.18	0.06	0.2	0.1
Steel on ice	0.014	–	0.03	–
Steel on wood	0.5	0.1	0.6	0.12
Gray cast iron on gray cast iron	0.28	0.08	0.3	0.2
Gray cast iron on bronze	0.2	0.08	0.3	0.2
Leather on metal	0.48	0.15	0.6	–
Leather on wood	0.4	–	0.5	–
Rubber on metal	0.5	–	–	–
Brake lining on steel	0.5	–	–	–
Stone on stone	0.65	–	0.7	–
Wood on wood	0.5	–	0.6	–

Static friction is usually somewhat greater than sliding friction.

Power and torque

See p. 45 for equations.

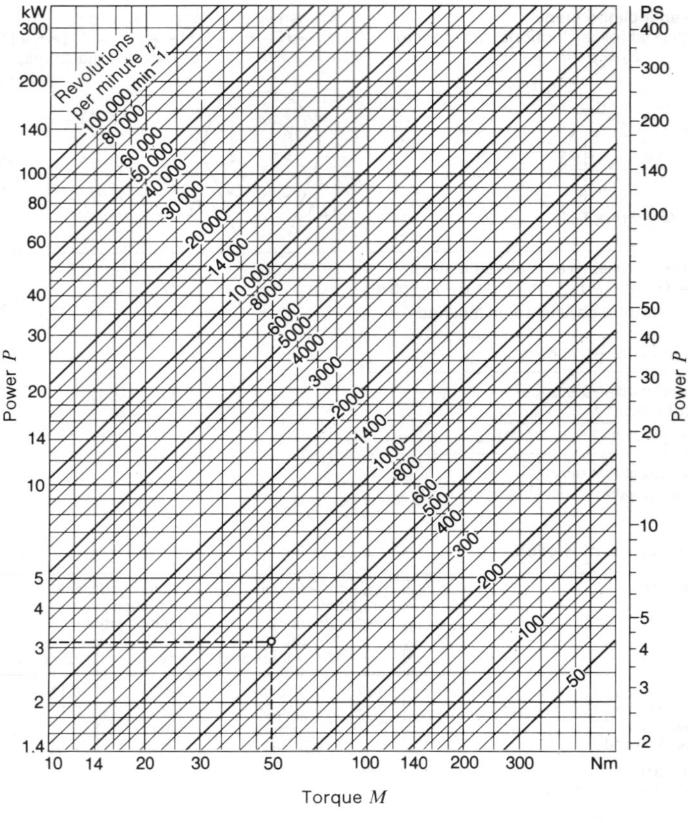

A multiple of P corresponds to the same multiple of M or n.

Examples: For $M =$ 50 N·m and $n =$ 600 min^{-1}, $P =$ 3.15 kW (4.3 PS*)
For $M =$ 5 N·m and $n =$ 600 min^{-1}, $P =$ 0.315 kW (0.43 PS*)
For $M =$ 5000 N·m and $n =$ 60 min^{-1}, $P =$ 31.5 kW (43 PS*)

* PS = Pferdestärke = metric horsepower

Fluid mechanics

Symbol	Quantity	SI-Unit
A	Cross-sectional area	m^2
A_b	Area of base	m^2
A_s	Area of side	m^2
F	Force	N[1]
F_a	Buoyancy force	N
F_b	Force acting on bottom	N
F_s	Force acting on sides	N
G	Weight	N
g	Acceleration of free fall $g = 9.81\ m/s^2$	m/s^2
h	Depth of fluid	m

Symbol	Quantity	SI-Unit
m	Mass	kg
p	Fluid pressure	Pa[2]
	$p_1 - p_2$ differential pressure	Pa
p_e	Gauge pressure	Pa
	Flow rate	
Q	Volume	m^3/s
V	Flow velocity	m^3
v	Density	m/s
ϱ	Density of water[3]) $\varrho_W = 1\ kg/dm^3 = 1000\ kg/m^3$	kg/m^3

Fluid at rest in an open container

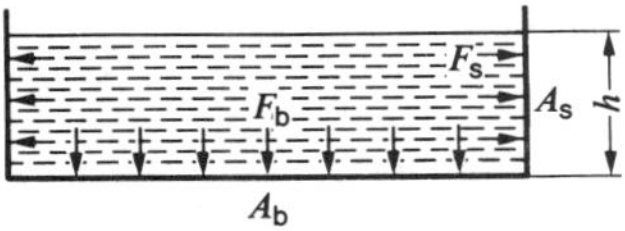

Force acting on bottom $F_b = A_b \cdot h \cdot \varrho \cdot g$

Force acting on sides $F_s = 0.5\, A_s \cdot h \cdot \varrho \cdot g$

Buoyancy force $Fa = V \cdot \varrho \cdot g$

= weight of displaced volume of fluid.

A body will float if $F_a \geq G$

Hydrostatic press

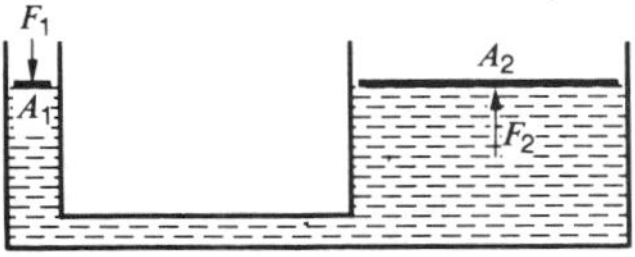

Fluid pressure $p = \dfrac{F_1}{A_1} = \dfrac{F_2}{A_2}$

Piston forces $F_1 = p \cdot A_1 = F_2 \dfrac{A_1}{A_2}$

$F_2 = p \cdot A_2 = F_1 \dfrac{A_2}{A_1}$

Flow with change in cross section

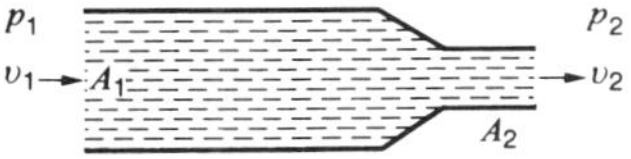

Flow rate

$$Q = A_1 \cdot v_1 = A_2 \cdot v_2 = \sqrt{\frac{2}{\varrho} \cdot \frac{p_1 - p_2}{1/A_2^2 - 1/A_1^2}}$$

Discharge from vessels

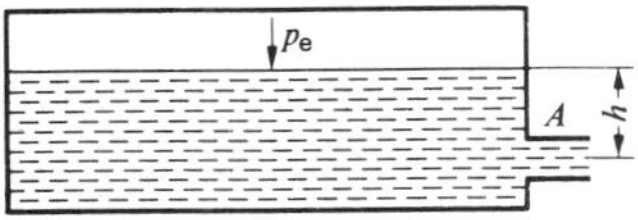

Discharge velocity

$v_a = \psi \cdot \sqrt{2g \cdot h + 2p_e/\varrho}$

Discharge rate

$Q_a = \varkappa \cdot A \cdot v_a$

$= \varkappa \cdot \psi \cdot A \cdot \sqrt{2g \cdot h + 2p_e/\varrho}$

Coefficient of contraction $\varkappa$ with sharp edge: 0.62 ... 0.64; for slightly broken edge: 0.7 ... 0.8; for slightly rounded edge: 0.9; for heavily rounded, smooth edge, 0.99.

Discharge coefficient ψ = 0.97...0.998.

[1]) 1 N = 1 kg m/s² (see p. 10)

[2]) 1 Pa = 1 N/m²; 1 bar = 10^5 Pa; 1 at (= 1 kp/cm²) = 0.981 bar ≈ 1 bar (see p. 28 for units of pressure).

[3]) See p. 182 for densities of other fluids.

Strength of materials

Symbols and units (See pp. 12–14)

Quantity		Unit
A	Cross-sectional area	mm^2
E	Modulus of elasticity (Young's modulus)	N/mm^2
F	Force, load	N
G	Modulus of elasticity in shear	N/mm^2
I_a	Axial moment of inertia (of plane areas) (see p. 59)	mm^4
I_p	Polar moment of inertia (of plane areas) (see p. 59)	mm^4
l	Length	mm
M_b	Bending moment	N mm
M_t	Torque; turning moment	N mm
R	Radius of curvature at neutral axis (N.A.)	–
S	Factor of safety	–
s	Maximum deflection	mm
W_b	Section modulus under bending (see p. 59)	mm^3
W_t	Section modulus under torsion (see p. 59)	mm^3
α_k	Stress concentration factor	–
β_k	Fatigue strength reduction factor	–
γ	Elastic shear	rad
δ	Elongation at fracture[1])	%
ε	Elastic elongation or compression, strain	%
σ	Stress	N/mm^2
$\sigma_{0.2}$	0.2-yield strength[1])[2])	N/mm^2
σ_{gr}	Limit stress	N/mm^2
σ_B	Tensile strength[1])	N/mm^2
σ_D	Endurance limit = fatigue limit	N/mm^2
σ_S	Yield point[1])	N/mm^2
σ_W	Fatigue limit under reversed stresses	N/mm^2
σ_a	Stress amplitude	N/mm^2
σ_{bB}	Bending strength	N/mm^2
σ_{bF}	Elastic limit under bending	N/mm^2
σ_{bW}	Fatigue limit under reversed bending stresses	N/mm^2
τ	Torsional (shear) stress	N/mm^2
τ_{gr}	Torsional stress limit	N/mm^2
τ_B	Torsional strength	N/mm^2
τ_F	Elastic limit under torsion	N/mm^2
τ_W	Fatigue limit under reversed torsional stress	N/mm^2
ψ	Angle of rotation	rad

The equations in this section are general equations of quantities, i.e. they also are applicable if other units are chosen, except equations for buckling and the formula for shearing resistance on p. 55.

Mechanical stresses

Tension and compression
(normal to surface)

Tensile (compression) stress $\sigma = \dfrac{F}{A}$

Strain $\varepsilon = \dfrac{\Delta l}{l}$

Δl Increase (or decrease) in length
l Original length

Modulus of elasticity $E = \dfrac{\sigma}{\varepsilon}$[3])

Long, thin bars subjected to compressive loads must also be investigated with regard to their buckling strength.

Bending

The effects of a transverse force can be neglected in the case of long beams subjected to bending stress. In calculating bending stresses (resulting from bending moments without transverse force) it can therefore be assumed for reasons of symmetry (the axis of the beam becomes circular) that plane cross sections remain plane. With these assumptions as given, the neutral axis passes through the center of gravity of every conceivable cross section.
The following equation thus applies:

$$M_b = \frac{E \cdot I}{R}$$

Edge stress $\sigma_b = \dfrac{M_b}{I} \cdot e_1 = \dfrac{M_b}{W}$,

if $W = \dfrac{I}{e_1}$.

I Moment of inertia (of plane areas): the sum of the products of all cross-sectional elements by the squares of their distances from the neutral axis.
W Section modulus of a cross section: indicates, for the edge stress 1, the inner moment with which the cross section can resist an external bending load.
Q Transverse force: the sum of all forces acting vertically on the beam to the left or right of a given cross section. Q subjects the beam to shearing stress.
e_1 Distance between the neutral-axis zone and the outer-surface zone.

Table 1. Loading cases under bending

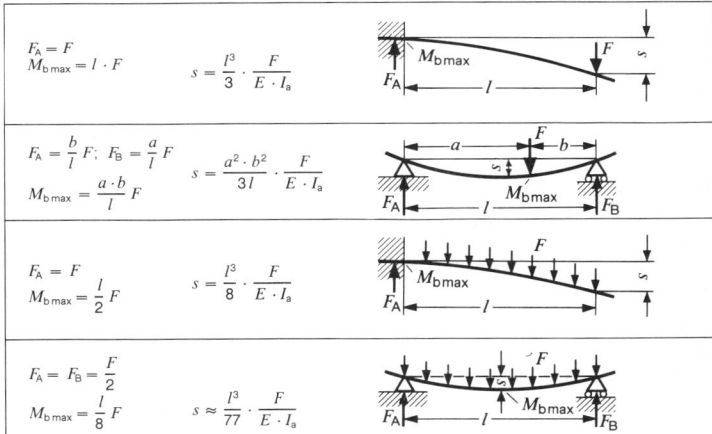

$F_A = F$ $M_{b\,max} = l \cdot F$	$s = \frac{l^3}{3} \cdot \frac{F}{E \cdot I_a}$	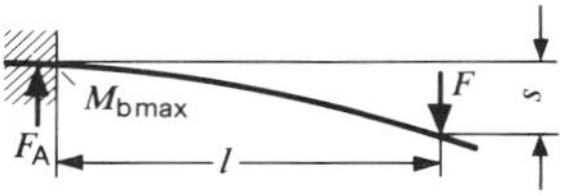
$F_A = \frac{b}{l} F$; $F_B = \frac{a}{l} F$ $M_{b\,max} = \frac{a \cdot b}{l} F$	$s = \frac{a^2 \cdot b^2}{3l} \cdot \frac{F}{E \cdot I_a}$	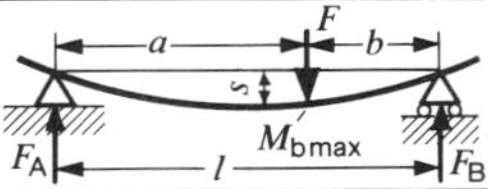
$F_A = F$ $M_{b\,max} = \frac{l}{2} F$	$s = \frac{l^3}{8} \cdot \frac{F}{E \cdot I_a}$	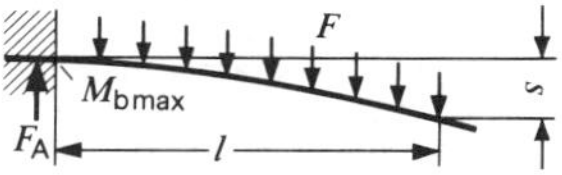
$F_A = F_B = \frac{F}{2}$ $M_{b\,max} = \frac{l}{8} F$	$s \approx \frac{l^3}{77} \cdot \frac{F}{E \cdot I_a}$	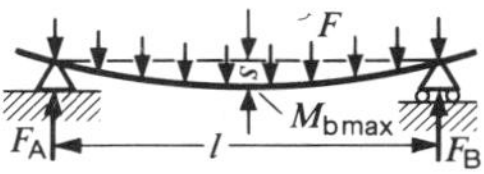

Buckling

In bars which are subjected to compression, the compressive stress $\sigma = F/A$ must always be less than the permissible buckling stress

$\sigma_{k\,perm} = \sigma_k / S$,

otherwise the bar will buckle.

Depending upon the centricity of the applied force, a factor of safety $S \geq 3 \ldots \geq 6$ must be selected.

Slenderness ratio $\lambda = l_k / \sqrt{I_a / A}$

l_k Free buckling length (see diagram)

Buckling stress $\sigma_k = \pi^2 \frac{E}{\lambda^2} \approx 10 \frac{E \cdot I_a}{l_k^2 A}$

The above equation for σ_k (Euler's formula) only applies to slender bars with the following slenderness ratios:

$\lambda \geq 100$ for St 37 steel,

$\lambda \geq \pi \sqrt{E \sigma_S}$ for steels whose σ_s values are different from that of St 37,

$\lambda \geq 80$ for GG 25 gray cast iron,

$\lambda \geq 100$ for coniferous wood.

According to Tetmajer, the following is valid for lower values of λ:

for St 37 steel $\sigma_k = (284 - 0.8\,\lambda)$ N/mm^2,

for St 52 steel $\sigma_k = (578 - 3.74\,\lambda)$ N/mm^2, for GG 25 gray cast iron $\sigma_k = (760 - 12\,\lambda + 0.05\,\lambda^2)$ N/mm^2, for coniferous wood $\sigma_k = (29 - 0.19\,\lambda)$ N/mm^2.

Loading cases under buckling

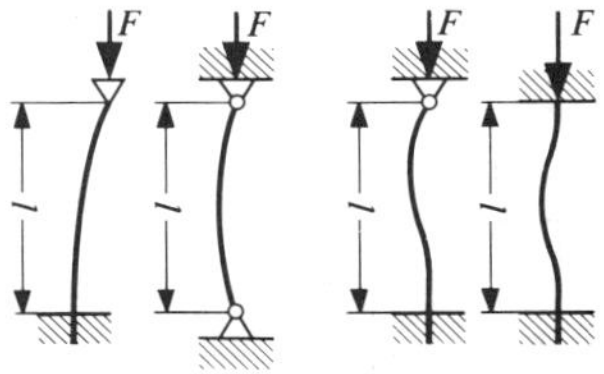

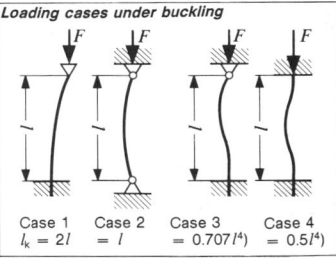

Case 1	Case 2	Case 3	Case 4
$l_k = 2l$	$= l$	$= 0.707\,l$[4]	$= 0.5\,l$[4]

[1]) According to the new international standard, σ_B, $\sigma_{0.2}$, ϱ_s and δ_5 are replaced by R_m, $R_{p0.2}$, R_e and A_5, respectively. Because A and R are also the international symbols for area and radius, the symbols σ_B, $\sigma_{0.2}$, σ_S and δ have been retained here.

[2]) 0.2 % yield strength: that stress which causes permanent deformation of 0.2 %.

[3]) Hook's Law applies only to elastic deformation, i.e. in practice approximately up to the elastic limit (yield point, elastic limit under bending, elastic limit under torsion; see also p. 55).

[4]) Applies to ideal clamping point, without eccentricity of the top fixing points. Calculation in accordance with Case 2 is more reliable.

Shear
Shearing stress $\tau = F/A$.
τ = shearing force per unit area of the cross section of a beam or body. The stress acts in the direction of the plane of the cross section. Shear strain γ is the angular deformation of the beam as a result of shearing stress.
Shear modulus (modulus of rigidity)
$G = \tau/\gamma$[1][2])

Torsion (twisting)
Torsional stress $\tau = M_t/W_t$
See p. 59 for section moduli W_t.
Torque M_t = torsional force × lever arm. The torque generates the illustrated shearing-stress distribution in every cross-sectional plane on every diameter.

Angle of rotation $\psi = \frac{l \cdot M_t}{G \cdot I_p} = \frac{l \cdot W_t \cdot \tau}{I_p \cdot G}$

The angle of rotation ψ is the angle of twist in rad of a bar of length l (Conversion: 1 rad ≈ 57.3°; see p. 22). See p. 59 for polar moments of inertia of plane areas I_p.

Shear

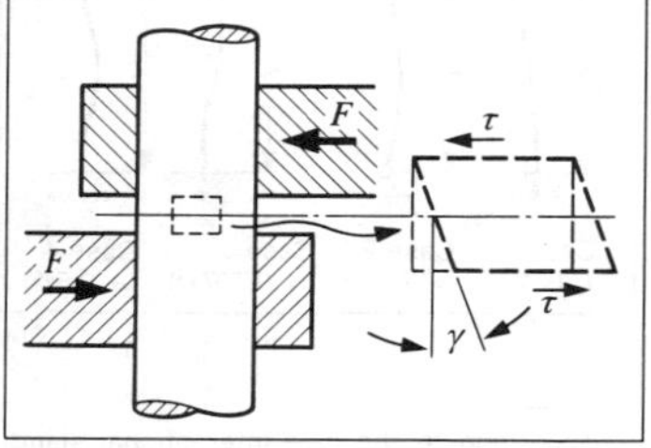

Torsion

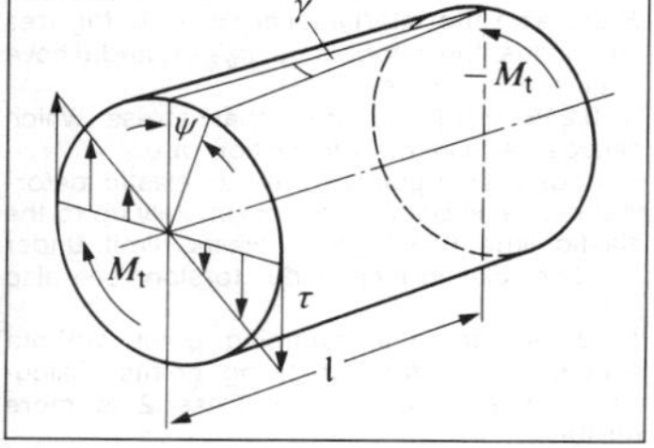

Notch effect

The equations cited above apply to smooth rods and bars; if notches are present, these equations yield the following nominal stresses (referred to the residual cross section):

$\sigma_n = F/A$ under tension (see diagram)
$\sigma_n = M_b/W_b$ under bending
$\tau_n = M_t/W_t$ under torsion.

Notches (such as grooves and holes) and changes in cross section (shoulders and offsets) as well as various clamping methods give rise to stress concentrations (σ_{max}) which are usually far in excess of the nominal stresses:

$\sigma_{max} = \alpha_k \cdot \sigma_n$.

See p. 58 for the stress concentration factor α_k.

Notches reduce the endurance strength and fatigue limit (see p. 57, Fatigue strength of structure), as well as the impact strength of brittle materials; in the case of tough materials, the first permanent (plastic) deformation occurs earlier. The stress concentration factor α_k increases with the sharpness and depth of the notch (V-notches, hairline cracks, poorly machined, "picked" surfaces). This also holds true, the more sharp-edged the changes in cross section are.

[1]) See footnote 3, p. 53.
[2]) The relationship between the shear modulus G and the modulus of elasticity E for metallic materials is: $G \approx 0.385\ E$; see p. 185 ff. for values of E.

Notch effect caused by grooves and holes

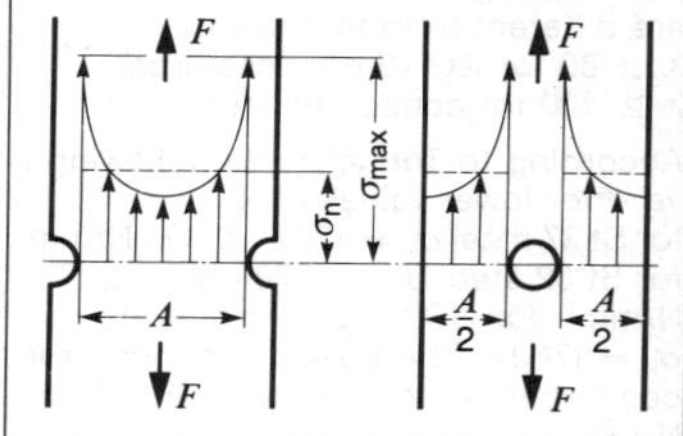

Permissible loading

The equations in the sections "Mechanical stresses" and "Notch effect" (p. 52 and p. 54), apply only to the elastic range; in practice they permit calculations approximately up to the elastic limit or up to 0.2 % yield strength (see footnote 2, p. 53). The permissible loading in each case is determined by materials testing and the science of the strength of materials, and is governed by the material itself, the nature of the material (tough, brittle) and the type of loading (static, alternating).

σ_B Tensile strength. For steel up to ≈ 600 HV, σ_B (in N/mm²) ≈ 3.3 times the HV value; see p. 185 ff. and p. 261.

σ_F Stress at the elastic limit (under tension this σ_S is the yield point)

δ (Plastic) elongation at fracture.

Table 2. Limit stresses σ_{gr}, τ_{gr} under static loading

Generally speaking, the limit stresses σ_{gr} and τ_{gr}, at which failure of the material occurs (permanent deformation or fracture), should not be reached in practice (s. below and p. 56). Depending upon the accuracy of the loading calculation, the material, and type of stress, and possible damage in the event of failure, allowance must be made for a safety factor $S = \sigma_{gr}/\sigma_{perm}$ (σ_{perm} is the maximum permissible stress in service). For tough materials, S should be 1.2 ... 2 (... 4), and for brittle materials (1.2 ...) 2 ... 4, 2 ... 4 (... 10). σ_{max} must be less than or equal to σ_{perm} (σ_{max} is the maximum stress (stress peak) in service).

Limit stress	Tough materials	Brittle materials
Under tension	σ_{gr} = yield point σ_S (≈ limit of elastic elongation). For steel up to approx. σ_B = 600 N/mm² and cold-rolled metals, σ_S = 0.6 ... 0.8 σ_B. σ_{gr} = 0.2 % yield strength $\sigma_{0.2}$ (see footnote 2, p. 53). For metals without a marked yield point such as steels with $\sigma_B \geq$ 600 N/mm² and Cu and Al.	σ_{gr} = tensile strength σ_B
Under compression	σ_{gr} = compressive yield point σ_{dF} (limit of elastic compression, roughly corresponding to σ_S.	σ_{gr} = compression strength σ_{dB}
Under bending	σ_{gr} = elastic limit under bending σ_{bF} (limit of elastic deflection). σ_{bF} is usually higher than the yield point under tension, depending upon the material and cross-sectional shape. Permanent curvature occurs if σ_{bF} is exceeded.	σ_{gr} = bending strength $\sigma_{bB} \approx \sigma_B$. For gray cast iron up to GG 40, however, σ_{bB} = 1.4 ... 2.0 σ_B, since $\varepsilon = \sigma/E$ does not apply because the neutral axis is displaced.
Under torsion	τ_{gr} = elastic limit under torsion τ_{tF} (limit of elastic twist), torsional limit $\tau_{tF} \approx$ 0.5 ... 0.6 σ_S. If exceeded, twist becomes permanent deformation.	τ_{gr} = torsional strength τ_{tB}. τ_{tB} = 0.5 ... 0.8 σ_B, however for gray cast iron up to GG 25 τ_{tB} = 1 ... 1.3 σ_B.
Under shear	τ_{gr} = elastic limit under shear $\tau_{sF} \approx$ 0.5 σ_S	τ_{gr} = shear strength τ_{sB}
During shearing	Shear strength τ_{aB} represents the stress required for shearing. $\tau_{aB} \approx 150 + 0.55\ \sigma_B$ (up to σ_B = 1800 N/mm²).	

It is possible to extend the loads on tough materials beyond the limits of elastic compression and deflection in applications where minimal plastic deformations can be accepted. The internal areas of the cross section are then stressed up to their yield point while they provide support for the surface-layer zone. The bending force applied to an angular bar can be increased by a maximum factor of 1.5; the maximum increase in torsional force applied to a round torsion bar is 1.33.

Limit stresses under pulsating loads
If the load alternates between two stress values, different (lower) stress limits σ_{gr} are valid: the largest stress amplitude, alternating about a given mean stress, which can be withstood "infinitely", often without fracture and impermissible distortion, is called the fatigue limit or endurance limit σ_D. It is determined experimentally by applying a pulsating load to test specimens until fracture occurs, whereby with the reduced load the number of cycles to fracture increases and yields the so-called "Wöhler curve". This is also termed the S–N curve. The Wöhler curve is nearly horizontal after 2 ... 10 million load cycles for steel, and after roughly 100 million cycles for non-ferrous metals; oscillation stress = fatique limit in such cases.

If no additional factors are present in operation (wear, corrosion, multiple overloads, etc.), fracture does not occur after this "ultimate number of cycles". It should be noted that $S \cdot \sigma_a \leq \sigma_W$, and $S \cdot \sigma_a \leq \sigma_A$ in the case of increased mean stresses; factor of safety $S = 1.25$ to ≥ 3 (stress values have small-letter subscripts, and fatigue strength values have capital-letter subscripts). A fatigue fracture generally does not exhibit permanent deformation. For plastics, it is not always possible to give an ultimate number of cycles.

Fatigue limit diagram
The greatest "infinitely often" endurable stress amplitude can be determined from the fatigue limit diagram (at right) for any minimum stress σ_u or mean stress σ_m. The diagram is produced using several Wöhler curves with various mean stress factors.

Special cases of fatigue limit

Fatigue limit under completely reversed stress:
The stress alternates between two opposite limit values of the same magnitude; the mean stress is zero.

Fatigue diagram

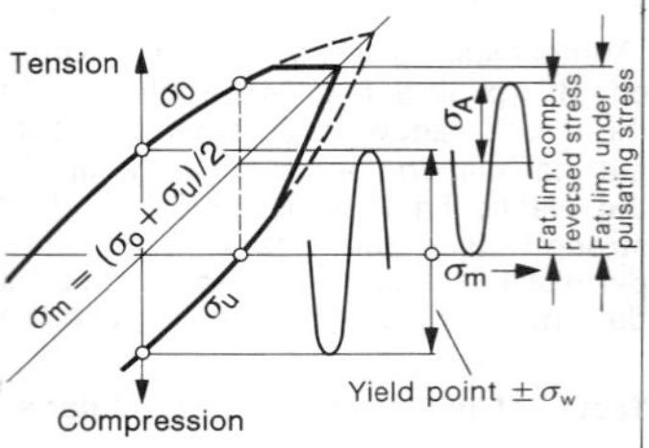

Effect of surface quality finish on fatigue limit during bending and tension-compression stresses

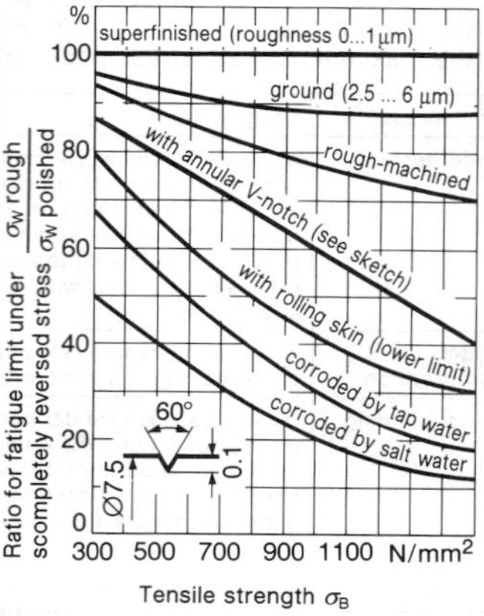

The fatigue limit σ_W is approximately

Load	Steel	Non-ferrous metals
Tension-compression	0.30 ... 0.45 σ_B	0.2 ... 0.4 σ_B
Bending	0.40 ... 0.55 σ_B	0.3 ... 0.5 σ_B

Fatigue limit under pulsating stress:
The stress alternates between zero or nearly zero and a positive (or negative) limiting value.

$$\sigma_{puls} = \sigma_m \pm \sigma_A, \text{ where } \sigma_m \geq \sigma_A$$

Table 3. Relaxation for various materials

Material	Part	σ_B N/mm²	Initial stress N/mm²	Temperature °C	Time h	Relaxation %
GD-Zn Al4 Cu1	Thread	280	150[1]	20	500	30
GD-Mg Al8 Zn1	Compression test specimen	157	60	150	500	63
GD-Al Si12 (Cu)		207	60	150	500	3.3
Cq35	Bolt	800	540	160	500	11
40Cr Mo V47	Bar under tension	850	372	300	1000	12

Permissible alternating loading of notched machine parts
The fatigue limit of notched parts is usually higher than that calculated using stress concentration factor α_k (see p. 58). Also, the sensitivity of materials to the effect of a notch in case of (alternating) fatigue loading varies, e.g., spring steels, highly quenched and tempered structural steels, and high-strength bronzes are more sensitive than cast iron, stainless steel and precipitation-hardened aluminum alloys. For (alternating) fatigue loading, fatigue-strength reduction factor β_k applies instead of α_k, so that at $\sigma_m = 0$, for example, the effective stress amplitude on the structural member is $\sigma_{wn}\,\beta_k$ (σ_{wn} is the nominal alternating stress referred to the residual cross section). The following must hold true:

$$\sigma_{wn}\,\beta_k \leq \sigma_{w\,perm} = \sigma_w/S$$

Attempts have been made to derive β_k from α_k. Thum, introduced notch sensitivity η_k, and established that:

$$\beta_k = 1 + (\alpha_k - 1)\,\eta_k$$

However η_k is not a material constant, and it also depends upon the state of heat treatment and type of loading (e.g., alternating or dynamic).

Fatigue limit values under reversed stress
σ_W for various materials can be found on pp. 185 and 190.

Stress concentration factors
α_k for different notch configurations are given on p. 58.

[1]) In the stress area of a steel bolt.

Fatigue strength of structure
For many machine parts it is difficult or even impossible to determine the stress concentration factor α_k and thus the fatigue-strength reduction factor β_k. In this case the fatigue limit of the entire part (fatigue strength of structural member, e.g., pulsating loads in N or moment of oscillation in Nm) must be determined experimentally and compared with test results given in literature.

Creep behavior
If materials are subjected to loads at **high temperatures** and/or under **high stresses** for **long periods of time,** creep or relaxation may occur. If resulting deformations (generally very small) are not acceptable, allowance must be made for the material "creep behaviour".

Creep:
Permanent deformation under constant load, and (at least approximately) constant stress (example: turbine blades).

Relaxation:
Diminution of the applied load and stresses, whereby the initially applied (usually purely elastic) deformation remains constant (see Table 3 for examples).

In the case of alternating loads (where $\sigma_a \geq 0.1\,\sigma_B$) and maximum stresses and temperatures such as are encountered in static relaxation tests, the same deformations and losses of force only occur after a period of load which is approximately 10 times (or more) as long as that of the static relaxation tests.

Stress concentration factor α_k for various notch configurations

Stress concentration factors for flat bars

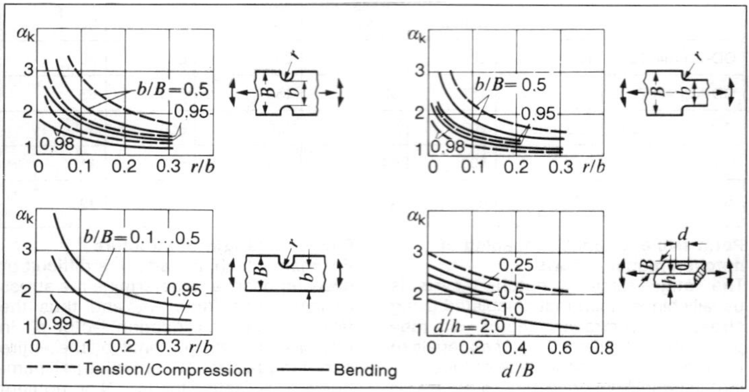

Stress concentration factors for rods

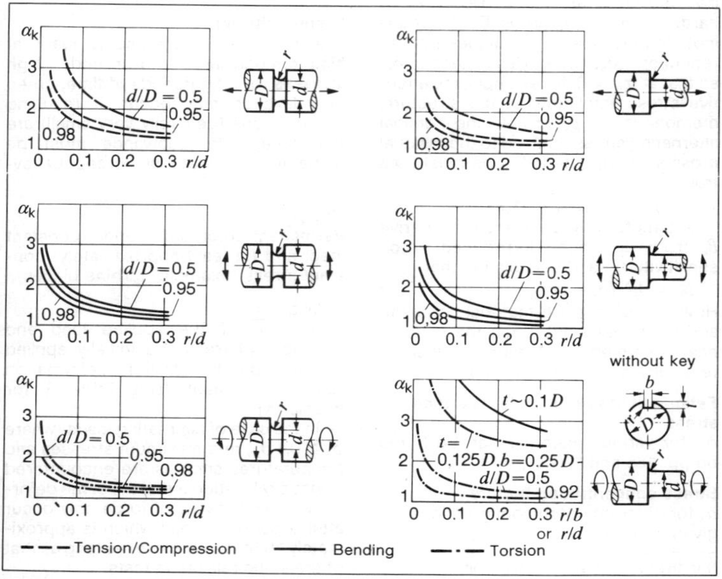

Section moduli and moments of inertia of plane areas

NL = "neutral axis"

See p. 48 for moments of inertia of mass.

	Section modulus W_b under bending W_t under torsion	Moment of inertia of plane areas I_a axial, referred to NL I_p polar, referred to center of gravity
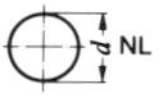	$W_b = 0.098\ d^3$ $W_t = 0.196\ d^3$	$I_a = 0.049\ d^4$ $I_p = 0.098\ d^4$
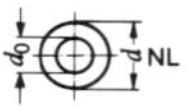	$W_b = 0.098\ (d^4 - d_0^4)/d$ $W_t = 0.196\ (d^4 - d_0^4)/d$	$I_a = 0.049\ (d^4 - d_0^4)$ $I_p = 0.098\ (d^4 - d_0^4)$
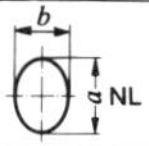	$W_b = 0.098\ a^2 \cdot b$ $W_t = 0.196\ a \cdot b^2$	$I_a = 0.049\ d^3 \cdot b$ $I_p = 0.196\ \dfrac{a^3 \cdot b^3}{a^2 + b^2}$
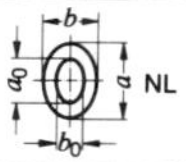	$W_b = 0.098\ (a^3 \cdot b - a_0^3 \cdot b_0)/a$ $W_t = 0.196\ (a \cdot b^3 - a_0 \cdot b_0^3)/b$	$I_a = 0.049\ (a^3 \cdot b - a_0^3 \cdot b_0)$ $I_p = 0.196\ \dfrac{n^3\,(b^4 - b_0^4)}{n^2 + 1}$

for $\dfrac{a_0}{b_0} = \dfrac{a}{b} = n \geq 1$

	$W_b = 0.118\ a^3$ $W_t = 0.208\ a^3$	$I_a = 0.083\ a^4$ $I_p = 0.140\ a^4$
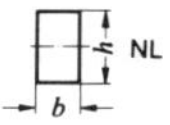	$W_b = 0.167\ b \cdot h^2$ $W_t = x \cdot b^2 \cdot h$	$I_a = 0.083\ b \cdot h^3$ $I_p = \eta \cdot b^3 \cdot h$

$h:b$	x	η
1	0,208	0,140
1,5	0,231	0,196
2	0,246	0,229
3	0,267	0,263
4	0,282	0,281

(In the case of torsion, the initially plane cross sections of a rod do not remain plane)

	$W_b = 0.104\ d^3$ $W_t = 0.188\ d^3$	$I_a = 0.060\ d^4$ $I_p = 0.115\ d^4$
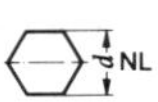	$W_b = 0.120\ d^3$ $W_t = 0.188\ d^3$	$I_a = 0.060\ d^4$ $I_p = 0.115\ d^4$
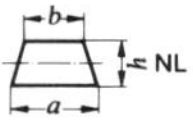	$W_b = \dfrac{h^2\,(a^2 + 4a \cdot b + b^2)}{12\,(2a + b)}$	$I_a = \dfrac{h^3\,(a^2 + 4a \cdot b + b^2)}{36\,(a + b)}$
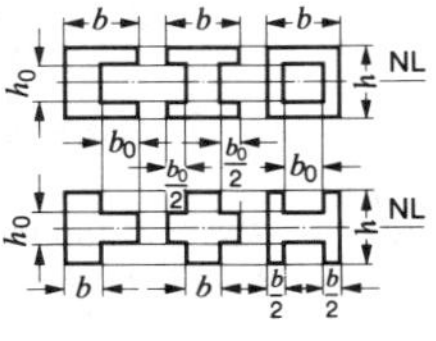	$W_b = \dfrac{b \cdot h^3 - b_0 \cdot h_0^3}{6\,h}$	$I_a = \dfrac{b \cdot h^3 - b_0 \cdot h_0^3}{12}$
	$W_b = \dfrac{b \cdot h^3 + b_0 \cdot h_0^3}{6\,h}$	$I_a = \dfrac{b \cdot h^3 + b_0 \cdot h_0^3}{12}$

Acoustics

Symbols and units
(see also DIN 1332)

Quantity		SI Unit
c	Velocity of sound	m/s
f	Frequency	Hz
I	Sound intensity	W/m²
L_I	Sound intensity level	dB
L_{Aeq}	Equivalent continuous sound level, A-weighted	dB (A)
L_{pA}	Sound pressure level, A-weighted	dB (A)
L_r	Rating sound level	dB (A)
L_{WA}	Sound power level, A-weighted	dB (A)
P	Sound power	W
p	Sound pressure	Pa
S	Surface area	m²
T	Reverberation time	s
υ	Particle velocity	m/s
Z	Specific acoustic impedance	Pa·s/m
α	Sound absorption coefficient	1
λ	Wavelength	m
ϱ	Density	kg/m³
ω	Angular frequency ($= 2\,\pi f$)	1/s

General terminology
(see also DIN 1320)

Sound
Mechanical vibrations and waves in an elastic medium, particularly in the audible frequency range (16 to 20,000 Hz).

Ultrasound
Mechanical vibrations above the frequency range of human hearing.

Propagation of sound
In general, sound propagates spherically from its source. In a free sound field, the sound pressure decreases by 6 dB each time the distance from the sound source is doubled. Reflecting objects influence the sound field, and the rate at which the sound level is reduced as a function of the distance from the sound source is lower.

Velocity of sound c
The velocity of sound is the velocity of propagation of a sound wave.

Sound velocities and wavelengths in different materials

Material or medium	Sound velocity c m/s	Wavelength λ m at 1000 Hz
Air, 20 °C, 1014 hPa	343	0.343
Water, 10 °C	1440	1.44
Rubber (according to hardness)	60 ... 1500	0.06 ... 1.5
Aluminum (rod)	5100	5.1
Steel (rod)	5000	5.0

Wavelength $\lambda = c/f = 2\,\pi\,c/\omega$

Particle velocity υ
Particle velocity is the alternating velocity of a vibrating particle. In a free sound field: $\upsilon = p/Z$. At low frequencies, perceived vibration is approximately proportional to the particle velocity.

Sound pressure p
Sound pressure is the alternating pressure generated in a medium by the vibration of sound. In a free sound field, this pressure equals $p = \upsilon \cdot Z$. It is usually measured as the RMS value.

Specific acoustic impedance Z
Specific acoustic impedance is a measure of the ability of a medium to transmit sound waves. $Z = p/\upsilon = \varrho \cdot c$. $Z = 415$ N·s/m³ for air at 20 °C and 1013 hPa (760 torr), and $1.44 \cdot 10^6$ Ns/m³ $= 1.44 \cdot 10^6$ Pa·s/m for water at 10 °C.

Sound power P
Sound power is the power emitted by a sound source. Sound power of some sound sources:

Normal conversation, average	$7 \cdot 10^{-6}$ W
Violin, fortissimo	$1 \cdot 10^{-3}$ W
Peak power of the human voice	$2 \cdot 10^{-3}$ W
Piano, trumpet	0.2 ... 0.3 W
Organ	1 ... 10 W
Kettle drum	10 W
Orchestra (75 musicians)	up to 65 W

Sound intensity I
Sound intensity $I = P/S$, i.e. sound power through a plane normal to the direction of propagation. In a sound field, $I = p^2/\varrho \cdot c = \upsilon^2 \cdot \varrho \cdot c$.

Doppler effect
For moving sound sources: If the distance between the source and the observer decreases, the perceived pitch (f') is higher than the actual pitch (f); as the distance increases, the perceived pitch falls. The following relationship holds true if the observer and the sound force are moving along the same line:

$$f'/f = (c-u')/(c-u).$$

where:
c = velocity of sound, u' = velocity of observer, u = velocity of sound source.

Interval
The interval is the ratio of the frequencies of two tones. In the equal temperament tuning system of our musical instruments (introduced by J. S. Bach), the octave (interval 2:1) is divided into 12 equal semitones with a ratio of $\sqrt[12]{2}$ = 1.0595, i.e. a series of any number of tempered intervals always leads back to a tempered interval. In the case of "pure pitch", on the other hand, a sequence of pure intervals usually does not lead to a pure interval. (Pure pitch has the intervals 1, 16/15, 9/8, 6/5, 5/4, 4/3, 7/5, 3/2, 8/5, 5/3, 9/5, 15/8, 2.)

Sound spectrum
The sound spectrum, generated by means of frequency analysis, is used to show the relationship between the sound pressure level (airborne or structure-borne sound) and frequency.

Octave band spectrum
The sound levels are determined and represented in terms of octave bandwidth. Octave: frequency ranges with fundamental frequencies in a ratio of 1:2. The mean octave frequency $f_m = \sqrt{f_1 \cdot f_2}$. Recommended center frequencies: 31.5, 63, 125, 250, 500, 1000, 2000, 4000, 8000 Hz.

Third-octave band spectrum
Sound levels are determined and represented in terms of third-octave bandwidth. The bandwidth referred to the center frequency is relatively constant, as in the case of the octave band spectrum.

Sound insulation
Sound insulation is the reduction of the effect of a sound source by interposing a reflecting (insulating) wall between the source and the impact location.

Sound absorption
Loss of sound energy when reflected on peripheries, but also for the propagation in a medium.

Sound absorption coefficient α
The sound absorption coefficient is the ratio of the non-reflected sound energy to the incident sound energy. With total reflection, $\alpha = 0$; with total absorption, $\alpha = 1$.

Noise reduction
Attenuation of acoustic emissions:
Reduction in the primary mechanical or electrodynamic generation of structure-borne noise and flow noises; damping and modification of sympathetic vibrations; reduction of the effective radiation surface; encapsulation.

Low-noise design
Application of simulation techniques (modal analysis, modal variation, finite-element analysis, analysis of coupling effects of airborne noise) for advance calculation and optimization of the acoustic properties of new designs.

Quantities for noise emission measurement

Sound field quantities are normally measured as RMS values, and are expressed in terms of frequency-dependent weighting (A-weighting). This is indicated by the subscript A next to the corresponding symbol.

Sound power level L_W
The sound power of a sound source is described by the sound power level L_W. The sound power level is equal to ten times the logarithm to the base 10 of the ratio of the calculated sound power to the reference sound power $P_0 = 10^{-12}$ W. Sound power cannot be measured directly. It is calculated based on quantities of the sound field which surrounds the source. Measurements are usually also made of the sound pres-

sure level L_p at specific points around the source (see DIN 45 635). L_w can also be calculated based on sound intensity levels L_I measured at various points on the surface of an imaginary envelope surrounding the sound source. If noise is emitted uniformly through a surface of $S_0 = 1\ m^2$, the sound pressure level L_p and the sound intensity level L_I at this surface have the same value as the sound power level L_w.

Sound pressure level L_p
The sound pressure level is ten times the logarithm to the base 10 of the ratio of the square of the RMS sound pressure to the square of the reference sound pressure

$p_0 = 20\ \mu Pa$. $L_p = 10 \log p^2/p_0^2$

or

$L_p = 20 \log p/p_0$.

The sound pressure level is given in decibels (dB).

The frequency-dependent, A-weighted sound pressure level L_{pA} as measured at a distance of $d = 1$ m is frequently used to characterize sound sources.

Sound intensity level L_I
The sound intensity level is equal to ten times the logarithm to the base ten of the ratio of sound intensity to reference sound intensity

$I_0 = 10^{-12}\ W/m^2$. $L_I = 10 \log I/I_0$.

Interaction of two or more sound sources
If two independent sound fields are superimposed, their sound intensities or the squares of their sound pressures must be added. The overall sound level is then determined from the individual sound levels as follows:

Difference between 2 individual sound levels	Overall sound level = higher individual sound level + allowance of:
0 dB	3 dB
1 dB	2.5 dB
2 dB	2.1 dB
3 dB	1.8 dB
4 dB	1.5 dB
6 dB	1 dB
8 dB	0.6 dB
10 dB	0.4 dB

Motor-vehicle noise measurements and limits

The noise measurements employed to monitor compliance with legal requirements are concerned exclusively with external noise levels. Testing procedures and limit values for stationary and moving vehicles were defined in 1981 with the promulgation of EC Guideline 81/334.

Noise emissions from moving vehicles
The vehicle approaches line AA, which is located 10 m from the microphone plane, at a constant velocity. Upon reaching line AA, the vehicle continues under full acceleration as far as line BB (also placed 10 m from the microphone plane), which serves as the end of the test section. The noise-emissions level is the maximum sound level as recorded by the microphone 7.5 m from the middle of the lane.

Passenger cars with manual transmission and a maximum of 4 forward gears are tested in 2nd gear. Consecutive readings in 2nd and 3rd gear are employed for vehicles with more than 4 forward gears, with the noise emissions level being defined as the arithmetic mean of the two maxima.

Separate procedures are prescribed for vehicles with automatic transmissions.

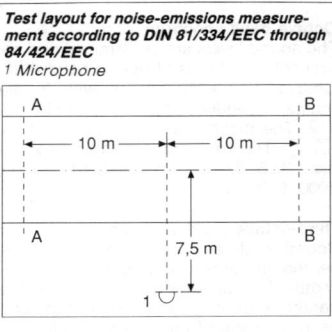

Test layout for noise-emissions measurement according to DIN 81/334/EEC through 84/424/EEC
1 Microphone

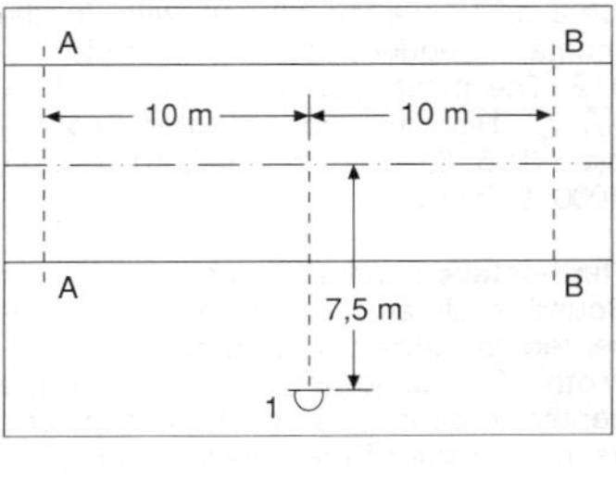

Limits and tolerances in dB(A) for noise emissions from motor vehicles

Vehicle category	Germany 84/424/EEC	Germany Para. 49/3 StVZO* Low-noise trucks	Switzer-land	Austria Phase II (0 toler-ance)
Passenger cars with spark-ignition or diesel engine	77+1	–	75+1	77
– with direct-injection diesel engine	78+1	–	–	–
Trucks and tractor-trailers Max. permissible fully loaded weight below 2 t	78+1	–	77+1	79
– with direct-injection diesel engine	79+1	–	–	–
Tractor-trailers Max. permissible fully loaded weight 2 t ... 3.5 t	79+1	–	77+1	79
– with direct-injection diesel engine	80+1	–	–	–
Max. permissible fully loaded weight above 3.5 t – engine output up to 150 kW	80+1	–	80+1	80
– engine output above 150 kW	83+1	–	82+1	83
Trucks Max. permissible fully loaded weight 2 t ... 3.5 t	79+1	77/78	77+1	79
– with direct-injection diesel engine	80+1	–	–	–
Max. permissible fully loaded weight above 3.5 t (StVZO: above 2.8 t) – engine output up to 75 kW	81+1	77+1	80+1	–
– engine output up to 150 kW	83+1	78+1	82+1	83
– engine output above 150 kW	84+1	80+1	84+1	84

Higher limits are valid for off-road and 4WD vehicles.
Supplementary noise limits apply for engine brakes and pneumatic equipment.
* StVZO = FMVSS/CUR

Noise emissions from stationary vehicles

Measurements are taken in the vicinity of the exhaust muffler in order to facilitate subsequent testing of motor-vehicle noise levels. Measurements are carried out with the engine running at 3/4 the speed at which it develops its rated power output. Once the engine speed levels off, the throttle valve is quickly returned to its idle position. During this procedure, the maximum A-weighted sound-pressure level is monitored with a microphone located 50 cm distant from the tailpipe at a horizontal angle of 45 ± 10° to the direction of exhaust flow. The recorded level is entered in the vehicle documentation in dB(A) with the suffix "P" (making it possible to distinguish between this figure and levels derived using earlier test procedures). No legal maxima have been specified for standing noise levels.

Interior noise level

There are no legal requirements for interior noise levels. The A-weighted sound pressure level can be measured at constant speed or when gradually accelerating, for example, beginning at

60 km/h or 40 % of the maximum speed (the lower of the two). These sound pressure level measurements are then plotted as a function of speed. One series of measurements is always to be made at the driver's seat; other measurement locations are selected in accordance with the passenger seating arrangement inside the vehicle. There are no plans to introduce a single value for indicating inside noise levels.

Quantities for noise immission measurement

Rating sound level L_r
The effect of noise on the human being is evaluated using the rating sound level L_r (see DIN 45645). This is a measure of the mean noise immission during a period of time (e.g., 8 working hours); with noises which fluctuate over time, it is measured directly using integrating measurement equipment or is calculated using individual sound pressure level measurements and the corresponding periods of time in which the individual noise effects are observed (see DIN 45641). Noise immission parameters such as pulsation and tonal quality can be taken into account through level allowances (see Table below for reference values).

Equivalent continuous sound level L_{Aeq}
In the case of noises which fluctuate in time, the mean A-weighted sound pressure level resulting from the individual sound pressure levels and the individual exposure times, equals the equivalent continuous sound level if it describes the mean sound energy over the entire assessment time period (see DIN 45641). The equivalent continuous sound level in accordance with the German "Aircraft Noise Abatement Law" is arrived at in a different manner (see DIN 45643).

The following guideline values for the rating sound level (Germany; Technical Instructions on Noise Abatement, 16 July 1968) are measured outside the nearest residential building (0.5 m in front of an open window):

	Day	Night
Purely industrial areas	70 dB (A)	70 dB (A)
Areas with predominantly industrial premises	65 dB (A)	50 dB (A)
Mixed areas	60 dB (A)	45 dB (A)
Areas with mainly residential buildings	55 dB (A)	45 dB (A)
Purely residential areas	50 dB (A)	35 dB (A)
Health resorts, hospitals, etc.	45 dB (A)	35 dB (A)

Perceived noise levels

The human ear can distinguish approximately 300 levels of acoustic intensity and 3000 ... 4000 different frequencies (pitch levels) in rapid temporal succession and evaluate them according to complex patterns. Thus there is not necessarily any direct correspondence between perceived noise levels and (energy-oriented) technically-defined sound levels. A rough approximation of subjective sound-level perception is provided by A-weighted sound levels, which take into account variations in the human ear's sensitivity as a function of frequency, the phon unit and the definition of loudness in sone. Sound-level measurements alone do not suffice to define the nuisance and disturbance potential of noise emanating from machinery and equipment. A hardly-perceptible ticking noise can thus be perceived as extremely disturbing, even in an otherwise loud environment.

Loudness level L_s
The loudness level is a comparative measure of the intensity of sound perception measured in phon. The loudness level of a sound (pure tone or noise) is the sound pressure level of a standard pure tone which, under standard listening conditions, is judged by a normal observer to be equally loud. The standard pure tone is a plane sound wave with a frequency of 1000 Hz impinging on the observer's head from the front. A difference 8 to 10 phon is perceived as twice or half as loud.

Phon
The standard pure tone judged as being equally loud has a specific sound pressure level in dB. This value is given as the loudness level of the tested sound, and has the designation "phon". Because human perception of sound is frequency-dependent, the dB values of the tested sound for notes, for example, do not agree with the dB values of the standard pure tone (with the exception of the 1000 Hz reference frequency), however the phon figures do agree. See the graph below for curves of equal loudness level according to Fletcher-Munson.

Loudness S in sone
The sone is the unit employed to define subjective noise levels. The starting point for defining the sone was: How much higher or lower is the perceived level of a particular sound relative to a specific standard.

Definition: The sound level $L_s = 40$ phon corresponds to the loudness $S = 1$ sone. Doubling or halving the loudness level is equivalent to a variation in sound level of approximately 10 phon.

There exists an ISO standard for calculating stationary sound using tertiary levels (Zwicker method). The procedure is scaled for frequency and screening effects in hearing.

Pitch, sharpness
The spectrum of perceptible sound can be divided into 24 hearing-oriented frequency groups (bark). The groups define perceived pitch levels. The loudness/pitch distribution (analogous to the tertiary spectrum) can be used to quantify other subjective aural impressions, such as the sharpness of a noise.

Acoustic quality control
This is the evaluation of noise and interference levels, and the classification of operating defects based on audible sound or structure-borne noise as part of the production process. Applications include testing electric motors during initial run-up; human testers are generally used. Automated test devices are used for specialized applications, but they are at present still unable to achieve human levels of flexibility, selectivity and learning ability.

***Assignment of sounds** to objective and subjective scales, curves of equal loudness level, weighting curve A of the sound-level meter.*

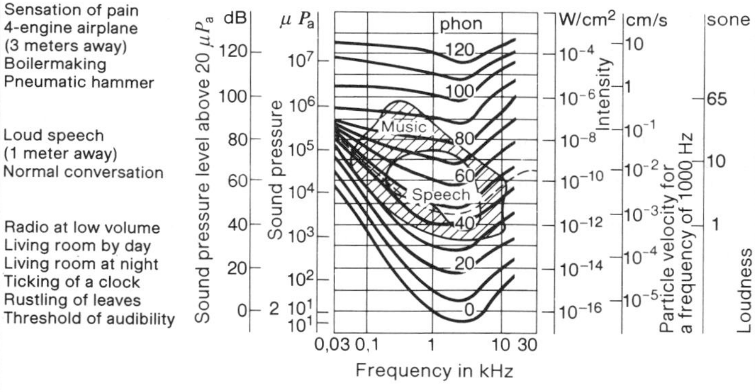

Heat

Symbols and units

See pp. 10 ... 16 for names of units, pp. 32, 33 for conversion of heat units, and p. 172 for thermal expansion, heat of fusion, and heat of evaporation.

Quantity		SI Unit
A	Area, cross-section	m^2
c	Specific heat c_p Isobaric (constant pressure) c_v Isochoric (constant volume)	J/(kg · K)
k	Heat transmission coefficient	W/(m^2 · K)
m	Mass	kg
p	Pressure	N/m^2
H	Enthalpy (heat content)	J
Q	Quantity of heat	J
$\dot{Q}$	Heat flow = Q/z	W
R	Molar gas constant = 8.314 J/mol K (same for all gases)	J/(mol · K)
R_i	Special gas constant $R_i = R/M$ (M = molecular weight)	J/(kg · K)
S	Entropy	J/K
s	Distance	m
T	Thermodynamic temperature $T = t + 273$ T_1 higher, T_2 lower	K
ΔT	Temperature difference $= T_1 - T_2 = t_1 - t_2$	K
t	Celsius temperature t_1 higher, t_2 lower	°C
V	Volume	m^3
v	Specific volume	m^3/kg
W	Work	J
z	Time	s
a	Heat transfer coefficient a_e external, a_i internal	W/(m^2 · K)
ε	Emissivity	
λ	Thermoconductivity (see p. 15 for values)	W/(m · K)
ϱ	Density	kg/m^3

Conversion from outdated units

(see also pp. 14 and 15)

1 kcal (kilocalorie) = 4186.8 J
≈ 4200 J = 4.2 kJ

1 kcal/(m · h · grd) = 1.163 W/(m · K)

Enthalpy (heat content)

$$H = m \cdot c \cdot T$$

The enthalpy difference (ΔH) is the quantity of heat released (Q) as a result of a change in temperature

$$(\Delta T = T_1 - T_2)$$

$$\Delta H = H_1 - H_2 = Q$$
$$= m \cdot c \cdot \Delta T = V \cdot \varrho \cdot c \cdot \Delta T$$

Heat transfer

Heat is transferred in three different ways:

Thermal conduction: Heat is conveyed inside a solid, liquid or gaseous substance by contact among the particles.

Convection: Heat is conveyed by the particles of a moving liquid or gaseous substance. In natural or free convection, the state of motion is brought about by the effect of buoyancy; in forced convection, however, the motion is maintained artificially.

Radiation: Heat is transferred from one body to another by electromagnetic waves without a material carrier.

Thermal conduction

The heat flow in a body of constant cross section A between two parallel transverse planes separated by a distance s, given a temperature difference ΔT is:

$$\dot{Q} = \frac{\lambda}{s} A \cdot \Delta T$$

Thermal radiation

Empty space and air are pervious to thermal radiation. Solid bodies and most liquids are impervious to thermal radiation, as are various gases to certain wavelengths.

The thermal radiation emitted by area A at temperature T is

$$\dot{Q} = \varepsilon \cdot \sigma \cdot A \cdot T^4$$

where $\sigma = 5.67 \times 10^{-8}$ W/$m^2 \cdot K^4$ is the radiation constant of a black-body radiator, and ε is the emissivity of the surface (see table on opposite page).

Emissivity ε
up to a temperature of 300°C (573 K)

Black body radiator[1])	1
Aluminum, unmachined	0.07
Aluminum, polished	0.04
Brass, matt	0.22
Brass, polished	0.05
Bricks	0.93
Cast iron, rough, oxidized	0.94
Cast iron, turned	0.44
Copper, oxidized	0.64
Copper, polished	0.05
Enamel paint, white	0.91
Glass	0.93
Ice	0.9
Lime mortar, rough, white	0.93
Nickel, polished	0.07
Oil	0.82
Paper	0.80
Porcelain, glazed	0.92
Silver, polished	0.02
Soot	0.93
Steel, matt, oxidized	0.96
Steel, polished, oiled	0.40
Steel, polished, oil-free	0.06
Tin, polished	0.06
Water	0.92
Wood, smooth	0.9
Zinc, matt	0.23
Zinc, polished	0.05

Transmission of heat through a wall
The heat flow through a wall of area A and thickness s, given a temperature difference ΔT, is:

$$\dot{Q} = k \cdot A \cdot \Delta T$$

The heat transmission coefficient k is calculated as follows:

$$1/k = 1/\alpha_i + s/\lambda + 1/\alpha_a$$

Thermal resistance
Thermal resistance is composed of the thermal resistance of the individual layers of the wall:

$$s/\lambda = s_1/\lambda_1 + s_2/\lambda_2 + \dots$$

See p. 178 for the thermal conductivity λ of various materials.

[1]) A black-body radiator completely absorbs all incident light and heat radiation directed against it; and therefore when heated radiates the maximum amount of light which can be emitted by a body. An example of a black body radiator is the opening in a carbon tube.

Heat transfer coefficients α
(convection + radiation)

Type of material, wall surface, etc.	α_i or α_a W/m²·K
Natural air movement	
in a closed room:	
Wall surfaces, interior windows	8
Exterior windows	11
Floors, ceilings	
upwards	8
downwards	6
Forced air movement	
on a flat wall	
Mean wind velocity	
$w = 2$ m/s	15
Mean wind velocity	
$w > 5$ m/s	$6.4 \cdot w^{0.75}$
Water on a flat wall	
Still	500 ... 2000
Moving	2000 ... 4000
Boiling	2000 ... 6000

Thermal resistance of air layers s/λ
(conduction + convection + radiation)

Position of air layer	Thickness of air layer mm	Thermal resistance s/λ m² K/W
Vertical air layer	10	0.14
	20	0.16
	50	0.18
	100	0.17
	150	0.16
Horizontal air layer Upward heat flow	10	0.14
	20	0.15
	50	0.16
Downward heat flow	10	0.15
	20	0.18
	50	0.21

Heat required to heat dwellings
50 to 60 W is required to heat each 1 m² of living area.

Engineering temperature measurement

(VDE/VDI Guideline 3511)

Measurement system	Measure-ment range	Method of operation	Examples of application
Liquid-in-glass thermometer	−200 ... 1000 °C	Thermal expansion of the liquid is visible in a narrow glass tube. Liquid: Pentane (−200 ... 30 °C) Alcohol (−100 ...210 °C) Toluene (−90 ... 100 °C) Mercury (−38 ... 600 °C) Gallium (... 1000 °C)	For liquids and gases, for monitoring steam, heating and drying systems; refrigeration equipment; media flowing through pipes.
Pressure-spring thermometer	−50 ... 500 °C	A liquid in an immersion vessel actuates a pointer or a recording instrument via a Bourdon tube due to its expansion pressure (mercury, toluene) or vapor pressure (ether, hexane, toluene, xylene).	For monitoring and recording temperatures (including remote applications up to 35 m) in power plants, factories, heating plants, cold rooms.
Rod expansion thermometer	0 ... 1000 °C	Different thermal expansion of two metals (rod in tube).	Temperature regulators.
Bimetallic strip thermometer	−50 ... 400 °C	Curvature of a strip consisting of two different metals.	Temperature regulators.
Resistance thermometer	−220 ... 850 °C	Change in resistance caused by change in temperature. Platinum wires −220 ... 850 °C, Nickel wires −60 ... 150 °C, Copper wires −50 ... 150 °C, Semiconductors −40 ... 180 °C,	Temperature measurements on machines, windings, refrigeration equipment. Remote transmission possible.
Thermistors	0 ... 500 °C (2200 °)	Sharp drop in electrical resistance as the temperature increases.	Measurement of minor temperature differences due to high sensitivity.
Thermocouples	−200 ... 3000 °C	Thermoelectromotive force of two metals whose junctions are at different temperatures.	Temperature measurements on and in machines, engines, etc. Remote transmission possible.
Radiation thermometer (pyrometer, infrared camera, high-speed pyrometer)	>600 °C (special design also as low as −40 °C)	The radiation emitted by a body is an indicator of its temperature. It is sensed by using either thermocouples or photocells, or by comparing luminance values. Emissions level must be observed.	Melting and annealing furnaces. Surface temperatures. Moving objects, thermogravimetry, extremely rapid response.
Temperature indicating lacquers and crayons	40 ... 1350 °C	Color changes when specific temperatures are exceeded. Lacquers and crayons are available with one or more color changes (up to 4). The new color remains after cooling.	Temperature measurements on rotating parts, in inaccessible places, in machining processes; warning of excessive temperature; material testing (cracks).
Suction thermometers, pyrometers	1800 ... 2800 °C	Gas is extracted from the flame.	Measurement of flame temperature (delayed display).

Other temperature measurement methods include spectroscopy, interferometry, quartz thermometry, noise thermometry, liquid crystals, acoustic and magnetic thermometers.

Thermodynamics

First law of thermodynamics:
Energy can be neither created nor destroyed. Only the form in which energy exists can be changed, e.g., heat can be transformed into mechanical energy.

Second law of thermodynamics:
Heat cannot be completely converted to another form of energy, e.g., mechanical work. All natural and synthetic energy transformation processes are irreversible and occur in a preferred direction (according to the probable state). On its own, heat passes only from warmer to colder bodies; the reverse is possible only if energy is supplied.

Entropy S is a measure of the thermal energy in a system which is no longer capable of performing work. That proportion of energy available for work is also referred to as exergy.

For reversible processes, the sum of the entropy changes is equal to zero.

The greatest efficiency in the conversion of heat to mechanical work is achieved in a reversible process. The following then applies:
Thermal efficiency:

$$\eta_{th} = (Q_1 - Q_2)/Q_1 = (T_1 - T_2)/T_1$$

Work in one cycle:

$$W = Q_1(T_1 - T_2)/T_1$$

(Carnot cycle)

Changes of state for gases

(general equation of state: $p \cdot v = R_i \cdot T$)

Change of state	Characteristics	Specific heat capacity[1])	Equations (k, K are constants)[1])	Examples
Isobaric	Constant pressure	c_p	$p = k$ $v = K \cdot T$	"Constant pressure" combustion in diesel engines; heating or cooling in once-through boilers.
Isochoric	Constant volume	c_v	$v = k$ $p = K \cdot T$	"Constant volume" combustion in spark-ignition engines; heating or cooling in closed boilers
Isothermal	Constant temperature	–	$T = k$ $p \cdot v = K$	Slow change of state (heat flows through partitions).
Adiabatic	Heat neither dissipated nor supplied	–	$P \cdot v^{\varkappa} = k$ $T \cdot v^{\varkappa-1} = k$	Compression or expansion stroke without cooling losses (the ideal condition which is virtually achieved in high-speed machines).
Isentropic	Adiabatic with no friction losses (reversible)	–	$T^{K} \cdot p^{1-\varkappa} = k$	Theoretically optimum attainable comparison processes.
Polytropic	General change of state	$c = \dfrac{c(n-\varkappa)}{n-1}$	$P \cdot v^{n-1} = K$ $T - v^{n-1} = K$ $T^{n} \cdot P^{1-n} = K$	Compression and power strokes in internal-combustion engines, steam engines (n = 1.2 ... 1.4).

[1]) c_p, c_v and $\varkappa = c_p/c_v$ see p. 184, $n = \dfrac{\lg p_2 - \lg p_1}{\lg v_1 - \lg v_2}$

Electrical engineering

Quantities and units

Quantity		SI Unit
A	Area	m^2
a	Distance	m
B	Magnetic flux density, induction	$T = Wb/m^2 = V \cdot s/m^2$
C	Capacitance	F = C/V
D	Dielectric displacement	C/m^2
E	Electric field strength	V/m
F	Force	N
f	Frequency	Hz
G	Conductance	$S = 1/\Omega$
H	Magnetic field strength	A/m
I	Current	A
J	Magnetic polarization	T
k	Electrochemical equivalent[1])	kg/C
L	Inductance	$H = Wb/A = V \cdot s/A$
l	Length	m
M	Electric polarization	C/m^2
P	Power	$W = V \cdot A$
P_s	Apparent power[2])	$V \cdot A$
P_q	Reactive power[3])	var
Q	Quantity of electricity, electric charge	$C = A \cdot s$
q	Cross-sectional area	m^2
R	Electrical resistance	$\Omega = V/A$
r	Radius	m
t	Time	s
U	Electric voltage	V
V	Magnetic voltage	A
W	Work, energy	$J = W \cdot s$
w	Number of turns in winding	–
X	Reactance	Ω
Z	Impedance	Ω
ε	Dielectric constant	$F/m = C/(V \cdot m)$
ε_0	Electric field constant $= 8.854 \times 10^{-12}$ F/m	
ε_r	Relative permittivity	–
Θ	Electric flux	A
μ	Permeability	$H/m = V \cdot s/(A \cdot m)$
μ_0	Magnetic field constant $= 1.257 \cdot 10^{-6}$ H/m	
μ_r	Relative permeability	–
ϱ	Resistivity[4])	$\Omega \cdot m$
σ	Conductivity ($= 1/\varrho$)	$1/(\Omega \cdot m)$
Φ	Magnetic flux	$Wb = V \cdot s$
φ	Angle of phase difference (phase angle)	° (degress)
φ(P)	Potential at point P	V
ω	Angular frequency ($= 2 \cdot \pi \cdot f$)	Hz

Additional symbols and units are given in the text.

Conversion of obsolete units (see also p. 15):

– magnetic field strength H:
1 Oe (oersted) = 79.577 A/m

– magnetic flux density B:
1 G (gauss) = 10^{-4} T

– magnetic flux Φ:
1 M (maxwell) = 10^{-8} Wb

Electromagnetic fields

Electrical engineering deals with electromagnetic fields and their effects. These fields are produced by electric charges which are integral multiples of the elementary charge. Static charges produce an electric field, whereas moving charges give rise to a magnetic field as well. The relationship between these two fields is described by Maxwell's equations. The presence of these fields is indicated by the effects of their forces on other electric charges. The force of attraction or repulsion between two charges concentrated at two points Q_1 and Q_2 is described by:

---

[1]) The unit in common use is g/C.

[2]) Apparent power is usually given in $V \cdot A$ rather than in W.

[3]) Reactive power is usually given in var (volt-ampere reactive) rather than in W.

[4]) The unit in common use is $\Omega\,mm^2/m$, with the wire cross section given in mm^2 and the wire length given in m; conversion formula: $1\,\Omega mm^2/m = 10^{-6}\,\Omega m = 1\,\mu\Omega m$.

Coulomb's Law:

$F = Q_1 \cdot Q_2/(4\pi \cdot \varepsilon_0 \cdot a^2)$

The force acting on a moving charge in a magnetic field is expressed by the Lorentz force equation:

$F = Q \cdot \upsilon \cdot B \cdot \sin\alpha$

ε_0 = Electric constant, Q_1 and Q_2 = Charges, a = Distance between Q_1 and Q_2, υ = Velocity of charge Q, B = Magnetic induction, α = Angle between the direction of motion and the magnetic field.

Electric field

An electric field can be described by the following quantities:

Electric potential φ(P) and voltage U

The electric potential φ (P) at point P is a measure of the work required to move the charge Q from a reference point to point P:

$\varphi\,(P) = W\,(P)/Q$

The voltage U is the potential difference (using the same reference point) between two points P_1 and P_2:

$U = \varphi\,(P_2) - \varphi\,(P_1)$

Electric field strength E

The electric field strength at point P depends on the location P and its surrounding charges. It describes the maximum slope of the potential gradient at point P. The following equation describes the field strength at a distance a from a point charge Q:

$E = Q/(4\pi \cdot \varepsilon_0 \cdot a^2)$

Force $F = Q \cdot E$ acts on a charge Q at point P.

Electric field and matter

Electric polarization M and dielectric displacement D

In a material which can be polarized (dielectric), an electric field generates electric dipoles (positive and negative charges at a distance a; $Q \cdot a$ is called the dipole moment). The dipole moment per unit volume is called the polarization M.

The dielectric displacement density D indicates the density of the electric displacement flux, and is defined as follows:

$D = \varepsilon \cdot E = \varepsilon_r \cdot \varepsilon_0 \cdot E = \varepsilon_0 \cdot E + M$

where:

ε: Dielectric constant of the material; $\varepsilon = \varepsilon_r \cdot \varepsilon_0$

ε_0: Electric field constant (dielectric constant of a vacuum)

ε_r: Relative permittivity (relative dielectric constant); $\varepsilon_r = 1$, for air, see p. 207 and 208 for materials.

Capacitance C of some conductor arrangements in Farad (F)

Plate capacitor with n parallel plates	$C = (n-1)\dfrac{\varepsilon_r \cdot \varepsilon_0 \cdot A}{a}$	ε_r, ε_0 n A a	See above Number of plates Surface area of one plate in m^2 Distance between plates in m
Parallel conductors (twin conductors)	$C = \dfrac{\pi \varepsilon_r \cdot \varepsilon_0 \cdot l}{\ln\left(\dfrac{a-r}{r}\right)}$	l a r	Length of twin conductors in m Distance between conductors in m Conductor radius in m
Coaxial conductor (cylindrical capacitor)	$C = \dfrac{2\pi \cdot \varepsilon_r \cdot \varepsilon_0 \cdot l}{\ln(r_2/r_1)}$	l r_1, r_2	Length of conductor in m Conductor radius in m where $r_2 > r_1$
Conductor to ground	$C = \dfrac{2\pi \cdot \varepsilon_r \cdot \varepsilon_0 \cdot l}{\ln(2a/r)}$	l a r	Length of conductor in m Distance from conductor to ground in m Conductor radius in m
Sphere with respect to distant surface	$C = 4\pi \cdot \varepsilon_r \cdot \varepsilon_0 \cdot r$	r	Sphere radius in m

Capacitor
Two electrodes separated by a dielectric form a capacitor. When a voltage is applied to the capacitor, the two electrodes receive equal but opposite charges. The charge Q received by the capacitor conforms to the following equation:

$$Q = C \cdot U.$$

C is the capacitance of the capacitor. It depends on the geometry of the electrodes, the distance by which they are separated and the dielectric constant of the dielectric.
Energy content of charged capacitor:

$$W = Q \cdot U/2 = Q^2/(2C) = C \cdot U^2/2.$$

The force of attraction between two parallel plates (surface area A) at a distance of a is:

$$F = E \cdot D \cdot A/2 = \varepsilon_r \cdot \varepsilon_0 \cdot U^2 \cdot A/(2a^2).$$

Direct current

Moving charges give rise to a current I whose strength is measured in amperes. The direction of flow and magnitude of direct current are independent of time.

Direction of current flow and measurement
Current flowing from positive pole to negative pole outside the current source is designated as positive (in reality, the electrons travel from the negative to the positive pole). An ammeter (A) in the current path measures current flow; voltage is measured by a voltmeter (V) connected in shunt.

Current and voltage measurement
R Load, A Ammeter in circuit,
V Parallel-connected voltmeter.

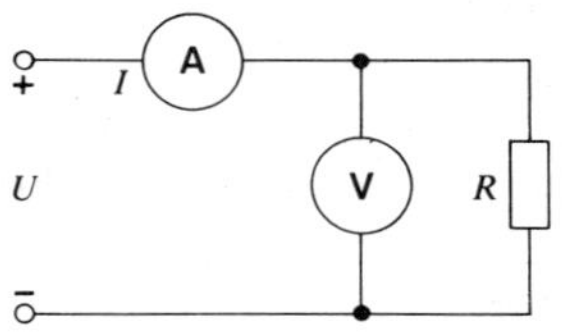

Ohm's Law
Ohm's law describes the relationship between voltage and current in solid and liquid conductors.

$$U = R \cdot I$$

The constant of proportionality R is called ohmic resistance, and is given in ohms (Ω). The reciprocal of resistance is called conductance G:

$$G = 1/R.$$

Ohmic resistance[1]
Ohmic resistance depends upon the material and its dimensions.
Round wire: $R = \varrho \cdot l/q = l/(q \cdot \sigma)$
Waveguide: $R = \ln(r_2/r_1)/(2\pi \cdot l \cdot \sigma)$
ϱ Resistivity in $\Omega mm^2/m$,
$\sigma = 1/\varrho$ Conductivity,
l = Wire length in m,
q = Wire cross section in mm^2,
r_2 and r_1 = Wire radii where $r_2 > r_1$,
In the case of metals, resistance increases with temperature:

$$R_\vartheta = R_{20}[1 + \alpha(\vartheta - 20°C)]$$

R_ϑ = Resistance at ϑ°C
R_{20} = Resistance at 20°C
α = Temperature coefficient[2] in 1/K (= 1/°C),
ϑ Temperature in °C.

Near absolute zero (−273°C) the resistance of many metals approaches zero (superconductivity).

Work and power
The following two equations represent the amount of work (or amount of heat generated) and power produced in a resistor through which a current flows:
Work: $W = U \cdot I \cdot t = R \cdot I^2 \cdot t$
Power: $P = U \cdot I = R \cdot I^2$.

Kirchhoff's Laws
First Law
The current flowing to each junction in a circuit is equal to the current flowing away from that point.

Second Law
The algebraic sum of the voltage drops in any closed path in a circuit is equal to the algebraic sum of the electromotive forces in that path.

[1]) See p. 205 for wire table, p. 204 for ϱ values.
[2]) See p. 204 for α values.

Direct-current circuits

Circuit with load

$U = (R_a + R_l) \cdot I$

R_a = Load

R_l = Line resistance

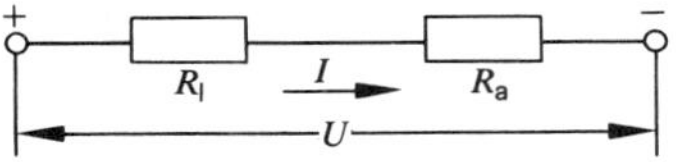

Battery-charging circuit

$U - U_0 = (R_v + R_i) \cdot I$

U = Line voltage, U_0 = Battery open-circuit voltage[1], R_v = Series resistance, R_i = Battery internal resistance. To charge the battery, the charging voltage must exceed the battery open-circuit voltage.

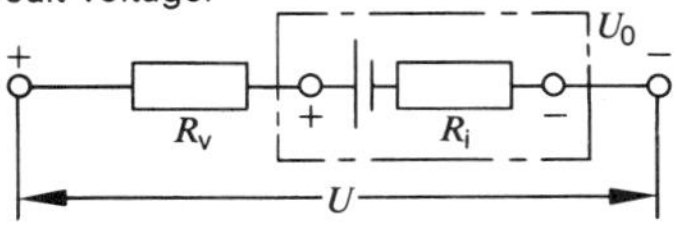

Charging and discharging a capacitor

The time constant $\tau = R \cdot C$ is the decisive factor in the charging and discharging of a capacitor.

Charging

$I = U/R \cdot \exp(-t/\tau)$

$U_C = U[1 - \exp(-t/\tau)]$

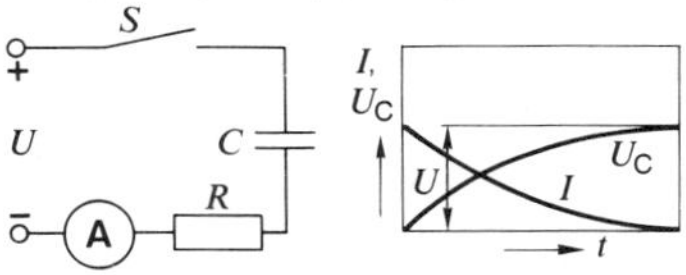

Circuit diagram, voltage and current curves

Discharging

$I = I_0 \cdot \exp(-t/\tau)$

$U_C = U_0 \cdot \exp(-t/\tau)$

U = Charging voltage, I = Charging current, U_C = Capacitor voltage, I_0 = Initial current, U_0 = Voltage at commencement of discharge.

[1]) Formerly called emf (electromotive force).

Series connection of resistors

$R_{total} = R_1 + R_2 + ...$

$U = U_1 + U_2 + ...$

The current is the same in all resistors.

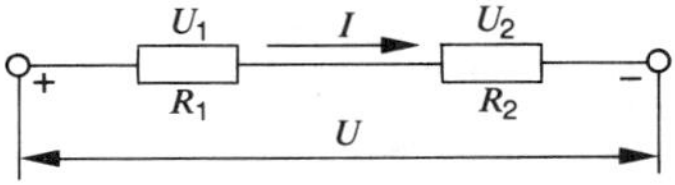

Parallel connection of resistors

$1/R_{total} = 1/R_1 + 1/R_2$ or

$G = G_1 + G_2$

$I = I_1 + I_2$; $I_1/I_2 = R_2/R_1$

The voltage is the same across all resistors (Kirchhoff's second law).

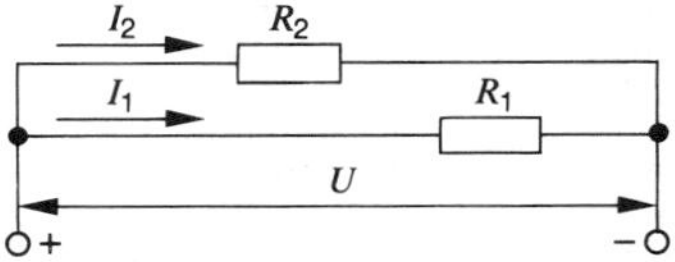

Measurement of a resistance

A resistance can be measured by measuring current and voltage, by using a direct-reading ohmmeter or a bridge circuit, e.g., Wheatstone bridge. If sliding contact D is set so that Wheatstone bridge galvanometer A reads zero, the following equations apply:

$I_1 \cdot R_x = I_2 \cdot \varrho \cdot a/q$

$I_1 \cdot R = I_2 \cdot \varrho \cdot b/q$

thus: $R_x = R \cdot a/b$

Wheatstone bridge circuit

R_x Unknown resistance, R Known resistance, AB Homogeneous slide wire (whose resistivity is ϱ) with the same cross section q at every point, A Galvanometer, D Sliding contact.

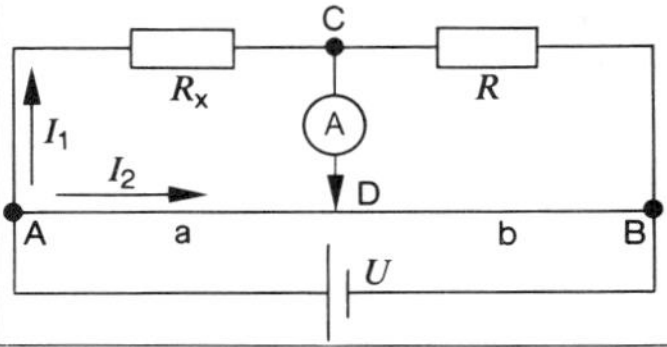

Electrolytic conduction

Substances whose solutions or melts (salts, acids, bases) conduct current are called electrolytes. In contrast to conduction in metals, electrolytic conduction involves chemical decomposition at the electrodes. This decomposition is called electrolysis, and the electrodes are termed anode (positive pole) and cathode (negative pole).

When dissolved, the electrolyte dissociates into various ions which move freely. When voltage is applied, the positive ions (cations) migrate toward the cathode and the negative ions (anions) migrate toward the anode. In addition to all metal ions, cations include ammonium ions (NH_4^+) and hydrogen ions (H^+). Anions comprise the ions of the non-metals, oxygen, halogens, acid radical ions and OH ions (see p. 763 for use in batteries).

The ions are neutralized at the electrodes and precipitate out of solution. Faraday's laws describe the relationship between the amount of precipitated material and the transported charge:

1. The amount of precipitate is proportional to the current and time

$$m = k \cdot I \cdot t$$

m = Mass in g, I = Current in A, t = Time in s, k = Electrochemical equivalent in g/C. The electrochemical equivalent k indicates how many g of ions are precipitated by 1 coulomb:

$$k = A/(F \cdot w) = 1.036 \times 10^{-5} A/w$$

A = Atomic weight; see p. 168, w = Valence (see Table), F = Faraday (Faraday constant) equal to 96,485 C/g equivalent. The g-equivalent is the mass in g which corresponds to the equivalent weight A/w.

2. When the same quantity of electricity is passed through different electrolytes, the masses of the precipitates are proportional to their equivalent weights.

Electrochemical equivalent k

Substance	Valence w	Electrochemical equivalent k 10^{-3} g/C
Cations		
Aluminum Al	3	0.0932
Lead Pb	2	1.0735
Chromium Cr	3	0.1796
Cadmium Cd	2	0.5824
Copper Cu	1	0.6588
	2	0.3294
Sodium Na	1	0.2384
Nickel Ni	2	0.3041
	3	0.2027
Silver Ag	1	1.1180
Hydrogen H	1	0.01044
Zinc Zn	2	0.3387
Anions		
Chlorine Cl	1	0.3675
Oxygen O	2	0.0829
Hydroxyl OH	1	0.1763
Chlorate ClO_3	1	0.8649
Chromate CrO_4	2	0.6011
Carbonate CO_3	2	0.3109
Manganate MnO_4	2	0.6163
Permanganate MnO_4	1	1.2325
Nitrate NO_3	1	0.6426
Phosphate PO_4	3	0.3280
Sulfate SO_4	2	0.4978

Electrolytic polarization

Ohm's law is also essentially applicable with electrolysis. In electrolysis, however, the so-called unconstant elements precipitate out at the electrodes creating a voltage U_z which is opposite in polarity to the applied voltage. The following equation describes the current in a cell with resistance R:

$$I = (U - U_z)/R.$$

The change in the electrodes is called galvanic or electrolytic polarization. It can be largely avoided through the use of oxidizing chemicals (called depolarisers), e.g., manganese dioxide to prevent the formation of H_2.

Galvanic cells
Galvanic cells convert chemical energy to electrical energy. They consist of two different metals in one or two electrolytic solutions. The open-circuit voltage of the cell depends upon the electrode materials and the substance used as the electrolyte. Examples:

Weston normal cell
Electrodes: Cd + Hg(−) and Hg_2SO_4 + Hg(+)
Electrolyte: $CdSO_4$
Voltage: 1.0187 V at 20°C

Leclanché cell (dry cells)
Electrodes: Zn(−) and C(+)
Depolariser: MnO_2
Electrolyte: NH_4Cl
Voltage: 1.5 V

Storage battery (see p. 763)

Alternating-current diagram
T Duration of one complete cycle (period) in s, f Frequency in Hz (f = 1/T), $\hat{i}$ Peak value (amplitude of current), $\hat{u}$ Peak value (amplitude) of voltage, ω Angular frequency in 1/s (ω = 2π · f), φ Phase angle between current and voltage (out of phase means that the current and voltage reach their peak values or cross the zero axis at different times).

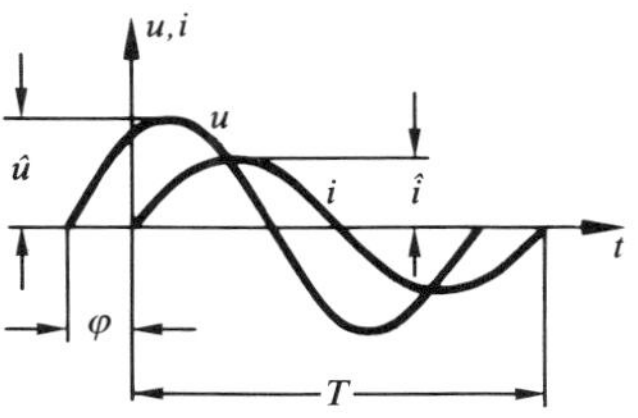

Alternating current

Alternating current is a current whose magnitude and direction vary periodically (often sinusoidally). Its value lies in the fact that it is well suited to remote energy transmission because it can be stepped up to high voltages by means of transformers.

Standard frequencies for alternating-current power lines:
Africa: 50 Hz; most of Asia: 50 Hz; Australia: 50 Hz; Europe: 50 Hz; North America: 60 Hz; South America: 50/60 Hz.
Railroad power lines: Austria, Germany, Norway, Sweden, Switzerland: 16 2/3 Hz; USA: 20 Hz.

Electrolytic (galvanic) mean of sinusoidal alternating current. This value is the arithmetic mean, i.e.

$I_{galv} = 2\hat{i}/\pi = 0.64\,\hat{i}$

$U_{galv} = 2\,\hat{u}/\pi = 0.64\,\hat{u}$

and has the same electrolytic effect as a direct current of this magnitude.

Root-mean-square value of sinusoidal alternating current:

$I\,(= I_{rms}) = \hat{i}/\sqrt{2} = 0.71\,\hat{i}$

$U\,(= U_{rms}) = \hat{u}/\sqrt{2} = 0.71\,\hat{u}$.

These equations indicate the magnitude of direct current which will generate the same amount of heat.

There are three kinds of power in an alternating-current circuit:

Active power $P = U \cdot I \cdot \cos\varphi$
Reactive power $P_q = U \cdot I \cdot \sin\varphi$
Apparent power $P_s = U \cdot I$

The power factor $\cos\varphi$ indicates what percentage of the apparent power is useful as actual power. The remainder, called reactive power, is useless, and oscillates between the source and the load, and loads the lines.

In order to reduce the necessary size of the lines, the phase-difference angle φ is kept as small as possible, usually by using phase changers (e.g., capacitors).

Alternating-current circuits

Alternating-current circuit with coils
A coil of inductance L (see p. 83) acts like a resistor of size $R_L = \omega \cdot L$ (inductive resistance). Because it consumes no energy, it is also called a reactance. The induced countervoltage U_L (see p. 82 for law of induction) lags the current by 90°, which in turn lags the voltage by 90°.

$$U = U_L = \omega \cdot L \cdot I$$

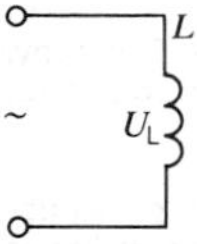

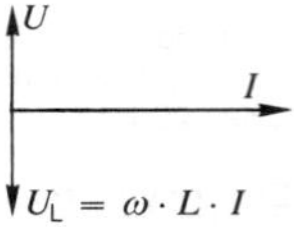

Inductance of coils connected in series and parallel:

Coils connected in series

$$L_{total} = L_1 + L_2 + \ldots$$

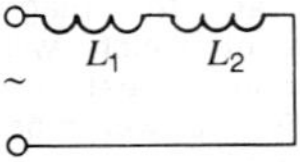

Coils connected in parallel

$$\frac{1}{L_{total}} = \frac{1}{L_1} + \frac{1}{L_2} + \ldots$$

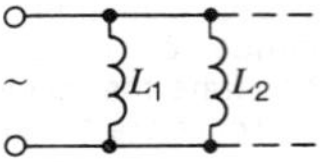

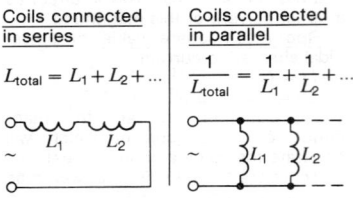

Alternating-current circuit with capacitor
A capacitor of capacitance C acts as a resistance of magnitude $R_C = 1/(\omega \cdot C)$ (capacitive reactance); it also consumes no power (reactance). The countervoltage U_C across the capacitor leads the current by 90°, which in turn leads the applied voltage U by 90°.

$$U = U_c = I/(\omega \cdot C)$$

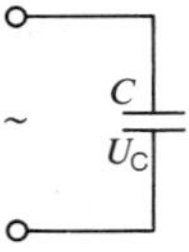

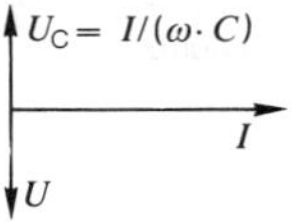

Capacitance of capacitors connected in series and parallel:

Capacitor connected in series

$$1/C_{total} = 1/C_1 + 1/C_2 + \ldots$$

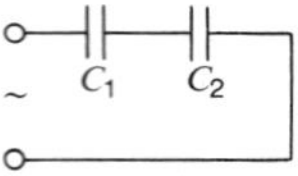

Capacitors connected in parallel

$$1/C_{total} = C_1 + C_2 + \ldots$$

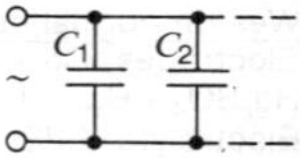

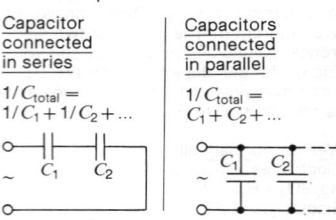

Ohm's Law for alternating current
In an alternating-current circuit with ohmic resistance (R), coil (inductance L) and capacitor (capacitance C), the same laws apply to the electrical parameters resistance, voltage and current as in a direct-current circuit.

In calculating the total resistance, the voltage and the current in the circuit, however, phase must also be considered, i.e. the vectors of the values must be added together. Vector diagrams are often used for this purpose.

Series connection

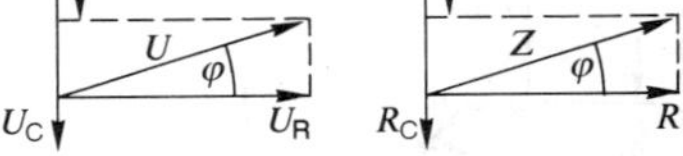

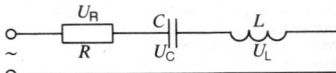

Vector diagrams for determining U, Z and φ.

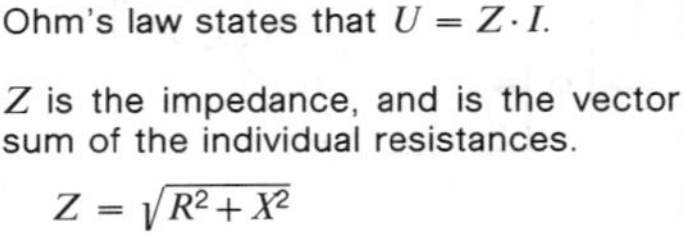

Ohm's law states that $U = Z \cdot I$.

Z is the impedance, and is the vector sum of the individual resistances.

$$Z = \sqrt{R^2 + X^2}$$

R = Ohmic resistance, X = Reactance.

$X = \omega \cdot L - 1/(\omega \cdot C)$

$\omega \cdot L$ is the inductive component of reactance, and $1/(\omega \cdot C)$ is the capacitive component of reactance.

The following equation describes the phase difference φ between the current and the voltage:

$$\tan \varphi = [\omega \cdot L - 1/(\omega \cdot C)]/R.$$

The maximum possible current flows when the circuit resonates ($I = U/R$). The circuit will resonate if:

$$\omega^2 \cdot L \cdot C = 1; \text{ (i.e. } X = 0)$$

Parallel connection

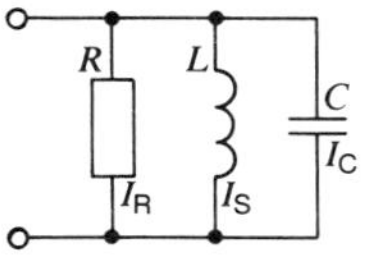

Vector diagrams for determining I, Y and φ.

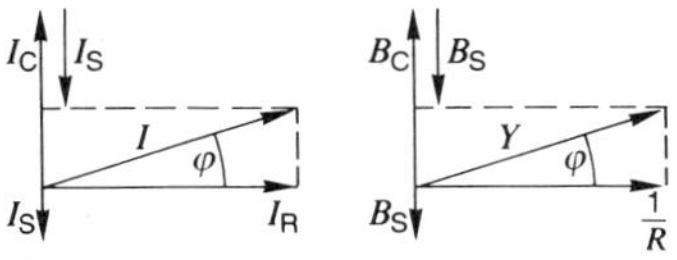

Current is determined by the following equation (Ohm's law):

$I = U \cdot Y$

Y is the complex admittance,

$Y = \sqrt{G^2 + B^2}$

$G (= 1/R)$ is the conductance and $B [= \omega \cdot C - 1/(\omega \cdot L)]$ is the susceptance.

The following equation describes the phase-difference φ between the current and the voltage:

$$\tan \varphi = R \cdot [\omega \cdot C - 1/(\omega \cdot L)].$$

As in the case of series connection, the circuit will resonate (minimum current flows in the main winding) if:

$$\omega^2 \cdot L \cdot C = 1 \text{ (i.e. } B = 0).$$

Three-phase current

Three-phase alternating current in which the phases differ by 120° is called three-phase current. Three-phase current is generated by three-phase generators which have three mutually independent windings which are displaced relative to one another by two-thirds of a pole pitch (120°).

The number of conductors carrying voltage is reduced from six to either three or four by linking the component voltages; customary conductor configurations are the star (Y) and delta connections.

Star (Y) connection

$I = I_p$
$U = \sqrt{3} \cdot U_p$

Delta connection

$I = \sqrt{3} \cdot I_p$
$U = U_p$

I = Line current, I_p = Phase current,
U = Line voltage, U_p = Phase voltage.

The transmitted power is independent of the type of connection, and is determined by the following equations:

Apparent power:

$$P_s = \sqrt{3} \cdot U \cdot I = 3\, U_p \cdot I_p$$

True power:

$$P = P_s \cdot \cos \varphi = \sqrt{3} \cdot U \cdot I \cdot \cos \varphi.$$

Star (Y) connection

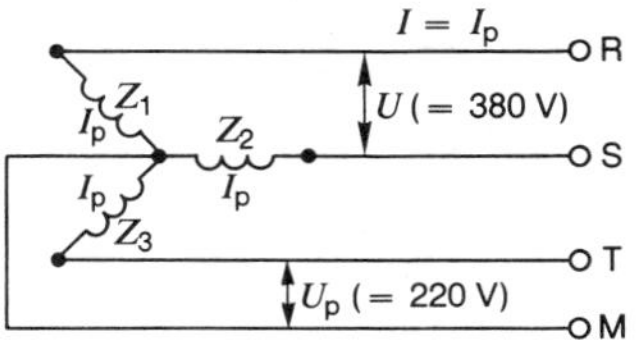

Delta connection

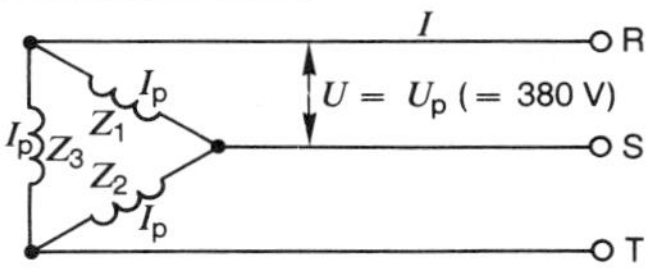

Magnetic field

Magnetic fields are produced by moving electric charges, current-carrying conductors, magnetized bodies or by an alternating electric field.

They can be detected by their effect on moving electric charges (Lorentz force) or magnetic dipoles (like poles repel, and unlike poles attract).

Magnetic fields are characterized by the vector of the magnetic flux density B (magnetic induction). This vector can be determined by measuring either force or voltage, because a voltage is induced in a loop of wire by a changing magnetic field (see p. 82 for law of induction):

$$U = \Delta (B \cdot q)/t.$$

$\Delta(B \cdot q)$ = Change in the product of magnetic induction (in T) and cross-sectional area of the loop (in m^2), t = Time (in s).

The following equations show the relationships between induction B and the other field parameters:

Magnetic flux Φ

$$\Phi = B \cdot q$$

q = Cross-sectional area in m^2.

Magnetic field strength H

In a vacuum:

$$B = \mu_0 \cdot H$$

$\mu_0 = 1.257 \times 10^{-6}$ H/m, magnetic field constant.

Magnetic field and matter

In matter, induction B theoretically consists of two components. One component comes from the applied field ($\mu_0 \cdot H$), and the other from the material (J) (see also the relationship between electric displacement density and electric field strength).

$$B = \mu_0 \cdot H + J.$$

J is the magnetic polarization and describes that component of flux density contributed by the material. In physical terms, J is the magnetic dipole moment per unit volume, and is generally a function of field strength H.

$J \ll \mu_0 \cdot H$ for many materials, and is proportional to H, so that:

$$B = \mu_r \cdot \mu_0 \cdot H$$

μ_r = Relative permeability; $\mu_r = 1$ in a vacuum.

Materials are divided into 3 groups according to their relative permeability values:

Diamagnetic materials ($\mu_r < 1$)

(e.g., Ag, Au, Cd, Cu, Hg, Pb, Zn, water, organic materials, gases)

μ_r is independent of magnetic field strength and smaller than 1, and lies in the range

$$(1 - 10^{-11}) > \mu_r > (1 - 10^{-5}).$$

Paramagnetic materials ($\mu_r > 1$)

(e.g., O_2, Al, Pt, Ti)

μ_r is independent of magnetic field strength and greater than 1, and lies in the range

$$(1 + 4 \cdot 10^{-4}) > \mu_r > (1 + 10^{-8}).$$

Ferromagnetic materials ($\mu_r \gg 1$)

(e.g., Fe, Co, Ni, ferrites)

The magnetic polarization in these materials is very high, and its change as a function of the field strength H is non-linear; it is also dependent upon hysteresis. Nevertheless, if (as is usual in electrical engineering) use is made of the relationship $B = \mu_r \cdot \mu_0 \cdot H$, then μ_r is a function of H and exhibits hysteresis; the values for μ_r lie in the range $5 \cdot 10^5 > \mu_r > 10^2$.

The hysteresis loop, which illustrates the relationship between B and H as well as J and H, is explained as follows:

If the material is in the unmagnetized state ($B = J = H = 0$) when a magnetic field H is applied, the magnetization of the material follows the rise path (1). At a specific field strength, and when all magnetic dipoles are aligned, J reaches the (material-dependent) saturation polarization which can no longer be increased. If H is now reduced, J decreases along section 2 of the curve and at $H = 0$ intersects the B or J axis at the remanence point B_r or J_r (in which case $B_r = J_r$).

Hysteresis loop *(e.g., hard ferrite)*

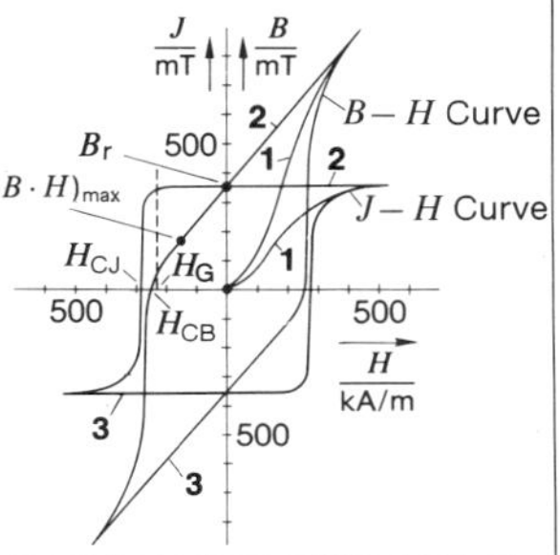

The most important parameters of the hysteresis loop are:

– Saturation polarization J_s,

– Remanence B_r (residual induction for $H = 0$),

– Coercive field strength H_{cB} (demagnetizing field strength where B becomes equal to 0) or

– Coercive field strength H_{cJ} (demagnetizing field strength where J becomes equal to 0; of significance only for permanent magnets),

– Limiting field strength H_G (a permanent magnet remains stable up to this field strength),

– μ_{max} (maximum slope of the rise path; significant only for soft magnetic materials),

– Hysteresis loss (energy loss in the material during one remagnetizing cycle; corresponds to the area under the $B - H$ hysteresis loop, and is significant only for soft magnetic materials).

The flux density and polarization drop to zero only upon the application of an opposing field whose field strength is H_{cB} or H_{cJ}; this field strength is called the coercive field strength. As the field strength is further increased, saturation polarization in the opposite direction is reached. If the field strength is again reduced and the field reversed, curve (3), which is symmetrical to curve section 2, is traversed.

Ferromagnetic materials[1])

Permanent-magnet materials

Permanent-magnet materials have high coercive field strengths; the values lie in the range

$$H_{cJ} > 1\,\frac{\text{kA}}{\text{m}}.$$

Thus high demagnetizing fields H can occur without the material losing its magnetic polarization. The magnetic state and operating range of a permanent magnet lie in the second quadrant of the hysteresis loop, on the so-called demagnetization curve. In practice, the operating point of a permanent magnet never coincides with the remanence point because a demagnetizing field is always present due to the self-demagnetization of the magnet which shifts the operating point to the left.

The point on the demagnetization curve at which the product $B \cdot H$ reaches its maximum value, $(B \cdot H)_{max}$, is a measure for the maximum attainable air-gap energy. In addition to the remanence and the coercive field strength, $(B \cdot H)_{max}$ is a further important parameter for the characterization of permanent magnets.

AlNiCo, ferrite, FeNdB (REFe), and SeCo magnets are currently the most important types of permanent magnets in terms of technical applications; their demagnetization curves exhibit characteristics typical of the individual magnet types.

(See p. 199 for characteristics of permanent-magnet materials).

Soft magnetic materials

Soft magnetic materials have a low coercive field strength ($H_c < 1000$ A/m), i.e. a narrow hysteresis loop. The flux density is high (high μ_r values) even at low field strengths, such that in customary applications $J \gg \mu_0 \cdot H$, i.e. in practice, no differentiation need be made between the $B(H)$ and $J(H)$ curves.

[1]) In the future, ferromagnetic materials are to be subdivided into three groups:
– soft-magnetic substances, $H_C \leq 1$ kA/m
– magnetic half-hard substances $1\text{ kA/m} < H_C \leq 30$ kA/m
– hard-magnetic substances $H_C > 30$ kA/m

Due to their high induction at low field strengths, soft magnetic materials are used as conductors of magnetic flux.

Because they exhibit minimal magnetic loss (hysteresis), materials with low coercive field strengths are particularly well-suited for application in alternating magnetic fields.

The characteristics of soft magnetic materials depend essentially upon their pretreatment. Machining increases the coercive field strength, i.e. the hysteresis loop becomes broader. The coercive field strength can be subsequently reduced to its initial value through material-specific annealing at high temperatures (magnetic final annealing). The magnetization curves, i.e. the $B-H$ relationships, are shown below for several important magnetically soft materials.

Remagnetization losses

In the table below, P1 and P1.5 represent the remagnetization losses for inductions of 1 and 1.5 tesla respectively, in a 50 Hz field at 20 °C. These losses are composed of hysteresis losses and eddy-current losses. The eddy-current losses are caused by voltages which are induced (law of induction) in the magnetically soft circuit components as a result of changes in flux during alternating-field magnetization. Eddy-current losses can be kept low if electric conductivity is reduced by:

— lamination of the core,
— use of alloyed materials (e.g., silicon iron),
— division into insulated powder particles (powdered cores) in the higher frequency range,
— use of ceramic materials (ferrites).

Type of steel sheet	Nominal thickness mm	Total loss in W/kg P 1	P 1.5	B (for H = 10 kA/m) T
V 270—35 A	0.35	1.1	2.7	1.70
V 330—35 A	0.35	1.3	3.3	1.70
V 400—50 A	0.5	1.7	4.0	1.71
V 530—50 A	0.5	2.3	5.3	1.74
V 800—50 A	0.5	3.6	8.1	1.77

Magnetization curves for soft magnetic materials

1 Pure iron
2 78 NiFe (Permalloy)
3 36 NiFe
4 Ni-Zn Ferrite
5 50 CoFe
6 V360-50A (magnetic steel sheet)
7 Structural steel
8 Cast iron
9 Powdered-iron core

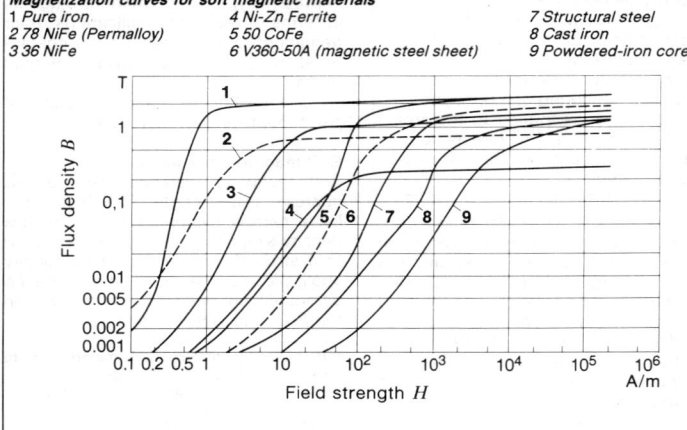

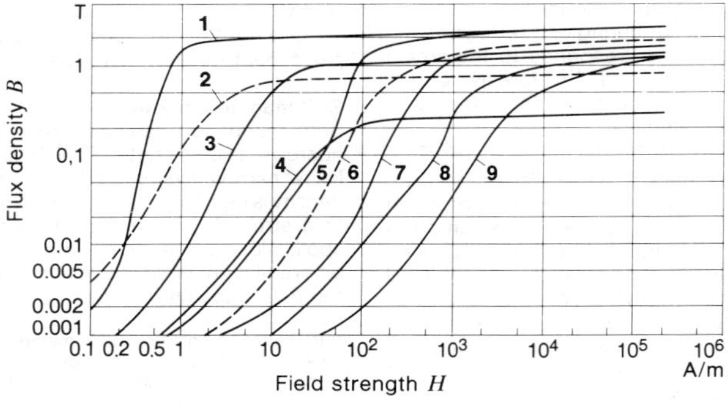

Demagnetization curves for various permanent-magnet materials

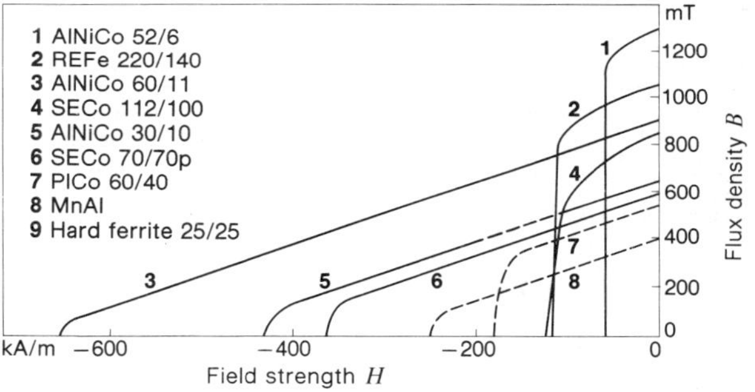

The magnetic circuit

In addition to material equations, the following equations also determine the design of magnetic circuits:

1. The law of ampere turns (equation of magnetic voltage). The following equation holds true for a closed magnetic circuit:

$\sum_i H_i \cdot l_i = V_1 + V_2 + \ldots + V_i = I \cdot w$ or 0,

depending upon whether or not the circuit includes a power source.

$I \cdot w = \Theta$ ampere turns

$H_i \cdot l_i = V_i$ magnetic voltage ($H_i \cdot l_i$ is to be calculated for circuit components in which H_i is constant).

2. The law of continuity (equation of magnetic flux)

The same magnetic flux $\Phi (= B \cdot A)$ flows in the individual components of the circuit:

$\Phi =$ const. or $\Phi_1 = \Phi_2 = \ldots = \Phi_i$.

The Φ of a circuit is determined by the amount of flux available in the air gap. This flux is called useful flux; the ratio of useful flux to total flux (flux of the permanent magnet or electromagnet) is called the leakage coefficient σ (practical values for σ lie between 0.2 and 0.9). The leakage flux – the difference between the total flux and the useful flux – does not pass through the air gap and does not add to the power of the magnetic circuit.

Magnetic field and electric current

Moving charges generate a magnetic field, i.e. conductors through which current flows are surrounded by a magnetic field. The direction in which the current flows (⊗ current flow into the page, ⊙ current flow out of the page) and the direction of the magnetic lines of force form a right-handed screw. See the table on page 83 for the magnetic field H of various conductor configurations.

Two parallel conductors through which current flows in the same direction attract each other; if the current flows in opposite directions, they repel each other. The force acting between two conductors of length l, separated by distance a and carrying currents I_1 and I_2 is governed by the equation:

$$F = \frac{\mu_0 \cdot \mu_r \cdot I_1 \cdot I_2 \cdot l}{2\pi \cdot a}\ ^{1)}$$

In air, the approximate force is given by the equation:

$F \approx 0.2 \cdot 10^{-6} \cdot I_1 \cdot I_2 \cdot l/a.$[1)]

In a magnetic field B, a force is exerted on a current-carrying conductor (current I) of length l; if the conductor and the magnetic field form an angle of α

[1)] Force F in N, current I_1, I_2 and I in A, length l and a in m; inductance B in T.

Current-carrying conductors and their magnetic fields *(H)*
a) A single current-carrying conductor with magnetic field.
b) Parallel conductors attract each other if current flows in the same direction.
c) Parallel conductors repel each other if current flows in opposite directions.
d) A magnetic field (B) exerts a force on a current-carrying conductor. The direction in which force is exerted is determined using the right-hand rule.

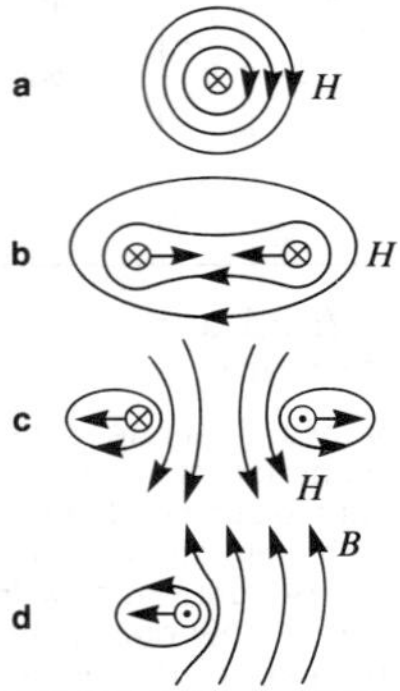

In air, the approximate force is given by the equation:

$$F \approx 0.2 \cdot 10^{-6} \cdot I_1 \cdot I_2 \cdot l/a.^1)$$

In a magnetic field B, a force is exerted on a current-carrying conductor (current I) of length l; if the conductor and the magnetic field form an angle of α with respect to one another, the force acting on the conductor is:

$$F = B \cdot I \cdot l \sin \alpha.^1)$$

The direction of this force can be determined using the right-hand rule (when the thumb is pointed in the direction of current flow, and the index finger in the direction of the magnetic field, the middle finger indicates the direction of force).

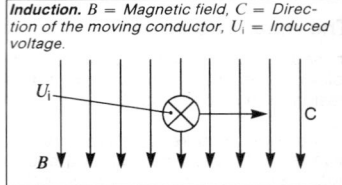

Induction. *B = Magnetic field, C = Direction of the moving conductor, U_i = Induced voltage.*

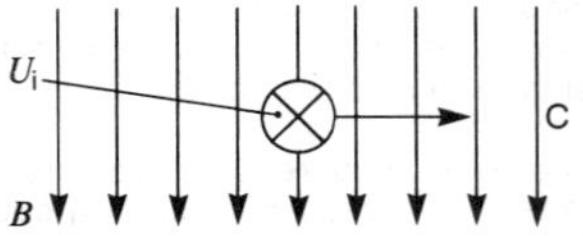

[1]) Force F in N, current I_1, I_2 and I in A, length l and a in m; inductance B in T.

Field strength H of several conductor configurations

Circular conductor	$H = I/(2\,a)$ at the center of the circle	H Field strength in A/m I Current in A a Radius of circular conductor in m
Long, straight conductor	$H = I/(2\pi \cdot a)$ outside the conductor $H = I \cdot a/(2\pi \cdot r^2)$ inside the conductor	a Distance from conductor axis in m r Conductor radius in m
Solenoid	$H = I \cdot w/l$	w Number of turns on coil l Length of coil in m

Inductance L of several conductor configurations

Solenoid	$L = \frac{1.257\,\mu_r}{10^6} \cdot \frac{w^2 \cdot q}{l}$	L Inductance in H μ_r Relative permeability w Number of turns in winding q Coil cross section in m^2 l Coil length in m
Twin conductor (in air, $\mu_r = 1$)	$L = \frac{4\,l}{10^7} \ln (a/r)$	l Length of conductors in m a Distance between conductors in m r Conductor radius in m
Conductor to ground (in air, $\mu_r = 1$)	$L = \frac{2\,l}{10^7} \ln (2\,a/r)$	l Length of conductor in m a Distance from conductor to ground in m r Conductor radius in m

Law of induction
Change in the magnetic flux Φ around which there is a conducting loop, caused by movement of the loop or changes in field strength, for example, induces voltage U_i in the loop. A voltage U_i going into the page is induced in a conductor moving in the direction C through a magnetic field:

$$U_i = B \cdot l \cdot v.$$

U_i in V, B in T, l = Conductor length in m, v = Velocity in m/s.

In a direct-current machine

$$U_i = p \cdot n \cdot z \cdot \Phi / (60\,a)$$

U_i in V, Φ Magnetic flux generated by the excitation winding (field winding) in Wb, p = Number of pole pairs, n = Rotational speed in min^{-1}, z = Number of wires on the armature surface, a = Half the number of parallel armature winding paths.

In an alternating-current machine

$$U_i = 2.22\,f \cdot z \cdot \Phi$$

U_i in V, Φ = Magnetic flux generated by the excitation winding in Wb, f = Frequency of the alternating current in Hz = $p \cdot n/60$, p = Number of pole pairs, n = Rotational speed in min^{-1}, z = Number of wires on the armature surface.

In a transformer

$$U_i = 4.44\,f \cdot w \cdot \Phi$$

U_i in V, Φ = Magnetic flux in Wb, f = Frequency in Hz, w = Number of coil windings on the coil which surrounds the magnetic flux Φ.

The terminal voltage U is smaller (generator) or larger (motor) than U_i by the amount of the ohmic voltage drop in the winding (approx. 5 %). In the case of alternating voltage, U_i is the rms value.

Self-induction
The magnetic field of a current-carrying conductor or a coil changes with the conductor current. A voltage proportional to the change in current is induced in the conductor itself and counteracts the current change producing it:

$$U_s = -L \frac{dJ}{dt}$$

The inductance L depends upon the relative permeability μ_r, which is constant and practically equal to 1 for most materials with the exception of ferromagnetic materials (see p. 78). In the case of iron-core coils therefore, L is highly dependent upon the operating conditions.

Energy of the magnetic field

$$W = L \cdot I^2/2$$

Electric effects in metallic conductors

Contact potential between conductors
Contact potential occurs in conductors, and is analogous to the triboelectricity or contact emf in insulators (e.g., glass/hard rubber). If two dissimilar metals (at the same temperature) are joined to make metal-to-metal contact with one another and are then separated, a contact-potential difference occurs between them. This is caused by the different work functions of the two metals. The magnitude of contact potential depends upon the element positions in the electrode-potential series. If more than two conductors are so joined, the resulting contact potential is the sum of the individual contact potential values.

Contact potential values

Material pair	Contact potential
Zn/Pb	0.39 V
Pb/Sn	0.06 V
Sn/Fe	0.30 V
Fe/Cu	0.14 V
Cu/Ag	0.08 V
Ag/Pt	0.12 V
Pt/C	0.13 V
Zn/Pb/Sn/Fe	0.75 V
Zn/Fe	0.75 V
Zn/Pb/Sn/Fe/Cu/Ag	0.97 V
Zn/Ag	0.97 V
Sn/Cu	0.44 V
Fe/Ag	0.30 V
Ag/Au	−0.07 V
Au/Cu	−0.09 V

Thermoelectricity
A potential difference, the Galvani potential, forms at the junction of two conductors due to their dissimilar work functions. The sum of all Galvani potentials is zero in a closed conductor loop

(in which the temperature is the same at all points). Measurement of these potentials is only possible by indirect means as a function of temperature (thermoelectric effect, Seebeck effect). The thermoelectric potential values are highly dependent upon impurities and material pretreatment. The following equation gives an approximate value for thermoelectric potential in the case of small temperature differences:

$$U_{th} = \Delta T \cdot a + \Delta T^2 \cdot b/2 + \Delta T^3 \cdot c/3$$

where

U_{th} = Thermoelectric potential
$\Delta T = T_1 - T_2$ Temperature difference
a, b, c = Material constants

The thermoelectric series gives the thermoelectromotive forces referred to a reference metal (usually platinum, copper or lead). At the hot junction, current flows from the conductor with the lower differential thermoelectromotive force to that with the higher force. The thermoelectromotive force η of any couple (thermocouple) equals the difference of the differential thermoelectromotive forces.

Thermoelectric series
(referred to platinum)

Material	Thermoelectric potential 10^{-6} V/°C
Selenium	1003
Tellurium	500
Silicon	448
Germanium	303
Antimony	47 ... 48.6
Nickel-chromium	22
Iron	18.7 ... 18.9
Molybdenum	11.6 ... 13.1
Cerium	10.3
Cadmium	8.5 ... 9.2
Steel (V2A)	7.7
Copper	7.2 ... 7.7
Silver	6.7 ... 7.9
Tungsten	6.5 ... 9.0
Iridum	6.5 ... 6.8
Rhodium	6.5
Zinc	6.0 ... 7.9
Manganin	5.7 ... 8.2
Gold	5.6 ... 8.0
Tin	4.1 ... 4.6
Lead	4.0 ... 4.4
Magnesium	4.0 ... 4.3
Aluminum	3.7 ... 4.1
Platinum	±0
Mercury	−0.1
Sodium	−2.1
Potassium	−9.4
Nickel	−19.4 ... −12.0
Cobalt	−19.9 ... −15.2
Constantan	−34.7 ... −30.4
Bismuth ⊥ axis	−52
Bismuth ∥ axis	−77

Thermocouples in common use[1])

Material pair	Temperature
Copper/constantan	up to 600°C
Iron/constantan	up to 900°C
Nickel-chromium/constantan	up to 900°C
Nickel-chromium/nickel	up to 1200°C
Platinum-rhodium/platinum	up to 1600°C
Platinum-rhodium/ platinum-rhodium	up to 1800°C
Iridium/iridium-rhodium	up to 2300°C
Tungsten/tungsten-molybdenum[2])	up to 2600°C
Tungsten/tantalum[2])	up to 3000°C

[1]) In addition to their use for measuring temperature, thermocouples are used as thermal converters. Efficiencies of approx. 10 % have already been achieved (in satellites).
[2]) In reducing atmosphere.

The reciprocal of the Seebeck effect is the Peltier effect, in which electrical energy produces a temperature difference (heat pump). If current flows through an A-B-A sequence of conductors, one thermojunction absorbs heat

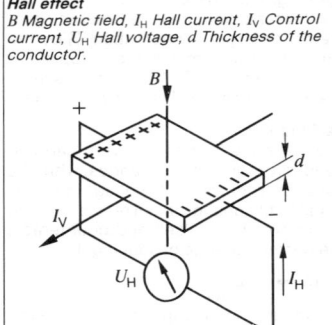

Hall effect
B Magnetic field, I_H Hall current, I_V Control current, U_H Hall voltage, d Thickness of the conductor.

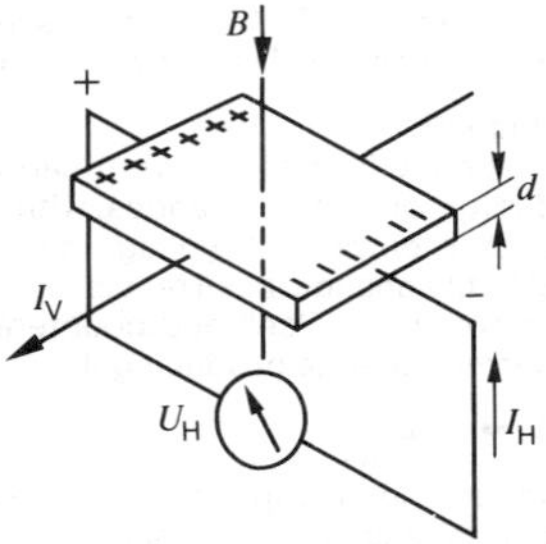

while the other produces more heat than can be accounted for by the Joule effect. The amount of heat produced is governed by the equation:

$$\Delta Q = \pi \cdot I \cdot \Delta t$$

π = Peltier coefficient, I = Current, Δt = Time interval.

The relationship between Peltier coefficient π and the thermoelectromotive force η is as follows:

$$\pi = \eta \cdot T$$

where T = temperature.

Current flowing through a homogeneous conductor will also generate heat if a temperature gradient $\Delta T/l$ is maintained in the conductor (Thomson effect). Whereas the power developed by the Joule effect is proportional to I^2, the power developed by Thomson effect is as follows:

$$P = -\sigma \cdot I \cdot \Delta T$$

σ = Thomson coefficient, I = Current, ΔT = Temperature difference.

The reciprocal of the Thomson effect is called the Benedicks effect, in which an electric potential is produced as a result of asymmetrical temperature distribution (particularly at points where there is a significant change in cross-sectional area).

Galvanomagnetic and thermomagnetic effects

Such effects are understood to be changes caused by a magnetic field in the flow of electricity or heat within a conductor. There are 12 different recognized effects which fall into this category, the most well-known of which are the Hall, Ettingshausen, Righi-Leduc and Nernst effects.

The Hall effect is of particular significance in technical applications (see p. 106 for a discussion of the Hall generator). If a voltage is applied to a conductor located in a magnetic field perpendicular to the direction of applied voltage, a voltage is produced which is perpendicular to both the flow of current and the magnetic field. This voltage is called the Hall voltage U_H:

$$U_H = R \cdot I_V \cdot B/d.$$

R = Hall constant, I_V = Control current, B = Magnetic field, d = Thickness of the conductor

The Hall constant can be used to determine particle density and movement of electrons and holes. In ferromagnetic materials the Hall voltage is a function of magnetization (hysteresis).

Gas discharge

Gas discharge describes the process that occurs when electric current travels through a space containing a gas or vapor atmosphere; the process is generally characterized by emission of heat, light and sound.

The free charge carriers present in the gas accelerate within the field between the two charged electrodes, producing charge-carrier cascades through impact-ionization. This, in turn, results in the actual current discharge, which ignites with voltages of up to 100 million volts (atmospheric lightning), depending upon the type of gas, the pressure and the gap between electrodes. Self-discharge occurs when the excitation energy from the discharge frees electrons at the cathodes; the current flow is then maintained at sharply reduced arc voltages. Glow discharge generally takes places in low-pressure gas atmospheres.

The characteristic radiation of light is determined by the transport and reaction zones produced by field forces and ionic diffusion at low current densities. At higher currents, thermal ionization in the plasma concentrates the current flow – the current lines contract.

Thermal emission of electrodes at the cathode is followed by a transition to arc discharge. The current increases (limited by the external circuit). At temperatures of up to 10^4 K, intense light is then emitted around the electrodes and from the bow-shaped (due to convection) plasma column lying between them; the arc voltage drops to just a few volts. The discharge is terminated when voltage drops below the characteristic extinction potential for the specific momentary condition.

Technical applications: Spark-discharge gap as switching element, arc welding, spark ignition for combustion of gases, discharge lamps, high-pressure arc lamps.

Electronics

Fundamentals of semiconductor technology

Electrical conductivity in solid bodies

An individual material's capacity for conducting electricity is determined by the number and mobility of the free charge carriers which it contains. The disparities in the electrical conductivities displayed by various solid bodies at room temperature extend through a range defined by 10 to the 24th power. Materials are accordingly divided into three electrical classes (examples):

Conductors, metals	Semi-conductors	Non-conductors, insulators
Silver Copper Aluminum	Germanium Silicon Gallium-arsenide	Teflon Quartz glass Aluminum-oxide

Metals, insulators, semiconductors

Solid bodies contain approximately 10^{22} atoms per cm^3; these are held together by electrical forces.

In metals the number of free charge carriers is extremely high (one free electron per atom). The free carriers are characterized by moderate mobility and extremely high conductivity. Conducting capacity of a good conductor: 10^6 siemens/cm. The number of free charge carriers found in insulators is practically nil, resulting in negligible electrical conductivity. A good insulator exhibits a conductivity of 10^{-18} siemens/cm.

Semiconductors assume an intermediate position between metals and insulators in electrical conductivity. The conductivity response of the semiconductor varies from that of metals and insulators in being extremely sensitive to factors such as variations in pressure (affects the mobility of the charge carriers), temperature fluctuations (number and mobility of the charge carriers), variations in illumination intensity (number of charge carriers), and the presence of additives (number and type of charge carriers).

Because they respond to changes in pressure, temperature and light intensity, semiconductors are suitable for application in sensors.

Doping (controlled addition of electrically active foreign substances to the base material) makes it possible to define and localize the semiconductor's electrical conductivity; it is this procedure which lies at the heart of present-day semiconductor technology. Doping can be employed for technically assured production of silicon-based semiconductors with conducting capacities ranging from 10^4 to 10^{-2} siemens/cm.

Electrical conductivity of semiconductors

The following discussion focuses on the silicon-based semiconductor. In its solid state, silicon assumes the form of a crystal lattice with four equidistant contiguous atoms. Each silicon atom possesses 4 valence electrons, with two shared electrons forming the valence bond between each pair of silicon atoms. In this ideal state silicon has no free charge carriers; thus it is not conductive. The situation changes dramatically with the addition of appropriate additives and the application of energy.

N-doping: Because only four electrons are required for bonding in a silicon lattice, the introduction of foreign atoms with 5 valence electrons (e.g., phosphorus) results in the presence of free electrons. Thus each additional phosphorus atom will provide a free, negatively-charged electron. The silicon is transformed into an n-type semiconductor.

P-doping: This process entails the introduction of foreign atoms with 3 valence electrons (e.g., boron) to produce the electron gaps ("holes") which result from the fact that the boron atom has one electron too few for complete bonding in the silicon lattice. This gap in the bonding pattern is also called a positive, or mobile hole.

As the latter designation indicates, these holes remain in motion within the silicon; in an electric field, they migrate in a direction opposite to that of the electrons. The holes exhibit the properties of a free positive charge carrier. Thus every additional boron atom provides a free, positively-charged electron gap (positive hole). The silicon is transformed into a p-type semiconductor.

Intrinsic conduction
Heat and light also generate free mobile charge carriers in untreated silicon; the resulting electron-hole pairs produce intrinsic conduction in the semiconductor material. This conductivity is generally modest in comparison with that achieved through doping. Increases in temperature induce an exponential rise in the number of electron-hole pairs, ultimately obviating the electrical differences between the p and n regions produced by the doping procedure. This phenomenon defines the maximum operating temperatures to which semiconductor components may be subjected:

Germanium	90...100 °C
Silicon	150...200 °C
Gallium arsenide	300...350 °C

A small number of opposite-polarity charge carriers is always present in both n-type and p-type semiconductors. These minority carriers exert an influence on the operating characteristics of virtually all semiconductor devices.

The pn-junction in the semiconductor
The area of transition between a p-type and an n-type zone within a single semiconductor crystal is referred to as the pn-junction. The properties of this area exercise a major influence on the operating properties of most semiconductor components.

pn-junction without external voltage
The p-type zone is characterized by the presence of numerous holes (O), while the n-type zone possesses very few. Meanwhile, a large number of electrons (●) is present in the n-type zone; the number in the p-type area is extremely limited. Each type of mobile charge carrier tends to move across the concentration gradient, diffusing into the opposed zone (diffusion currents).

The loss of holes on the p-type side results in a negative charge in this area, while electron depletion in the n-type zone produces a positive charge in this region.

The pn-junction with external voltage
1 Reverse-biased, 2 Forward-biased.

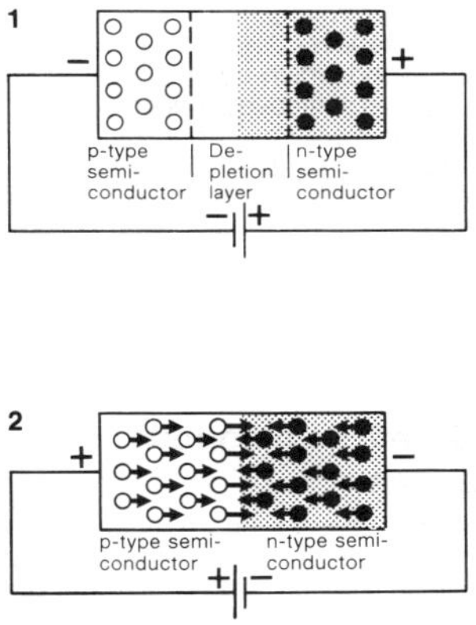

The result is an electrical potential (diffusion potential) between the p and n-type zones. This potential opposes the respective migration tendencies of the charge carriers, ultimately bringing the exchange of holes and electrons to a halt.

Result: An area deficient in mobile charge carriers is produced at the pn-junction. This area, the space-charge region or depletion layer, is characterized by both severely attenuated electrical conductivity and the presence of a strong electrical field.

pn-junction with external voltage
Reverse state: If the negative pole is connected to the p-type zone, and the positive pole to the n-type zone, an extension of the space-charge region will be the result. Under these conditions the flow of current is interrupted except for a minimal residual current (reverse, or back current) which is maintained by the minority carriers.

Forward state:
When the positive pole is connected to the p-type zone with the negative pole at the n-type region, charge carriers permeate

the pn-junction, resulting in a large current flow in the normal direction of conductance.

Breakdown voltage:
This is the level of reverse-direction voltage beyond which a minimal increase in voltage will suffice to produce a sharp rise in reverse blocking current.

Cause: Separation of bonded electrons from the crystal lattice, either by high field strength (Zener breakdown), or due to mutual impacts between accelerated electrons, resulting in rupture of the valence bonds of other electrons, ultimately producing a dramatic rise in the number of charge carriers (avalanche breakdown).

Discrete semiconductor devices

The properties of the pn junction and of combinations of several pn junctions in a single semiconductor-crystal wafer (chip) provide the basis for a steadily increasing array of inexpensive, reliable, compact semiconductor devices.

A single pn junction forms a diode, two pn junctions are used for transistors, and three or more pn junctions make up a thyristor. The planar technique makes it possible to combine numerous operating elements on a single chip to form the extremely important component group known as integrated semiconductor circuits, which combine the device and the circuitry in a single unit.

Semiconductor chips measure no more than several cubic millimeters and are usually installed in standardized housings (metal, ceramic, plastic).

Diodes

The diode is a semiconductor device incorporating a single pn junction. An individual diode's specific properties are determined by the distribution pattern of the dopant in the crystal. Diodes which conduct currents in excess of 1 A in the forward direction are referred to as power diodes.

Rectifier diode
The rectifier diode acts as a kind of current valve; it is therefore ideally suited for rectifying alternating current. The current in the reverse direction (reverse current) can be approximately 10^7 times lower than the forward current. It rises rapidly in response to increases in temperature.

Rectifiers for high reverse voltages
At least one zone with low conductivity is required for high reverse voltages (high resistance in forward direction results in generation of excessive heat). The insertion of a weakly-doped zone (I) between the highly-doped p-type and n-type zones produces a PIN rectifier. This type of unit is characterized by a combination of high reverse voltage and low forward-flow resistance (conductivity modulation).

Switching diode
These devices are generally employed for rapid switching between high and low impedances. More rapid switching response can be achieved by diffusing gold into the material (promotes the recombination of electrons and holes).

Zener diode
This is a semiconductor diode which, once a specific initial level of reverse voltage is reached, responds to further increases with a sharp rise in current flow. This phenomenon is a result of a Zener and/or avalanche breakdown. Zener diodes are designed for continuous operation in this breakdown range.

Varactor (variable-capacitance diode)
The space-charge zone at the pn-junction functions as a capacitor; the dielectric element is represented by the semiconductor material in which no charge carriers are present. Increasing the applied voltage extends the depletion layer and reduces the capacitance, while reducing the voltage increases the capacitance.

Schottky barrier diode (Schottky diode)
A semiconductor diode featuring a metal-to-semiconductor junction. Because the electrons move more freely from the n-type silicon into the metal layer than in the opposite direction, an electron-depleted region results in the semiconductor material; this is the Schottky barrier. Charges are carried exclusively by the electrons, a factor which results in extremely rapid switching, as the minority carriers do not perform any charge storage function.

Photodiode
This is a semiconductor diode designed to exploit the photovoltaic effect. Reverse voltage is present at the pn-junction. Incident light releases electrons from their lattice bonds to produce additional free electrons and holes. These increase the reverse current (photovoltaic current) in direct proportion to the intensity of the light.

Photovoltaic cell
(See Solar cell)

LED (Light-emitting diode)
See "Technical optics", p. 135.

Transistors

Two contiguous pn-junctions produce the transistor effect, a feature employed in the design of components used to amplify electrical signals and to assume switching duties.

Bipolar transistors
Bipolar transistors consist of three zones of varying conductivity, the configuration being either pnp or npn. The zones (and their terminals) are called the emitter (E), the base (B) and the collector (C).

Transistors carry various designations, depending upon the specific individual application. Classifications include the small-signal transistor (power dissipation up to 1 watt), power transistor, switching transistor, low-frequency transistor, high-frequency transistor, microwave transistor, and phototransistor. They are called bipolar because both classes of charge carrier (holes and electrons) are active. In the npn transistor, the base current's positive charge carriers (holes) control roughly 100 times their number in negative charge carriers (electrons) flowing from the emitter to the collector.

Operation of the bipolar transistor
(explanation based on the npn transistor)
The emitter-base junction (EB) is forward biased. This causes electrons to be injected into the base region.

The base-collector junction (BC) is reverse biased, inducing the formation of a space-charge region with a strong electrical field. Significant coupling (transistor effect) occurs if the two pn junctions lie in close mutual proximity (in silicon approx. 10 μm).

Bipolar npn transistor *(diagram)*

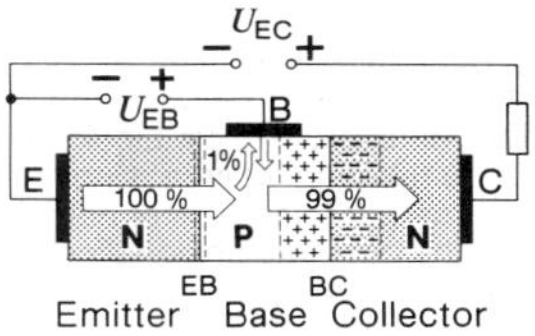

Junction field-effect transistor *(diagram)*

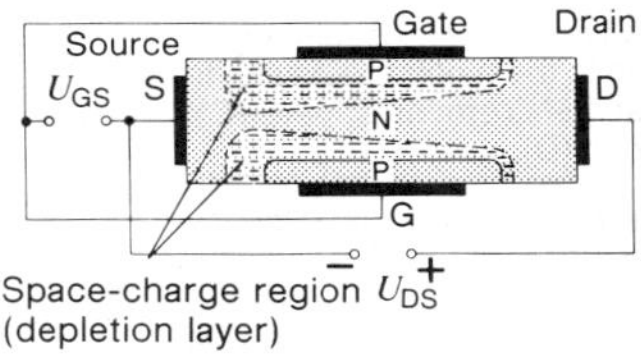

The electrons injected at the EB then diffuse through the base to the collector. Upon entering the BC's electrical field, they are accelerated into the collector region, whence they continue to flow in the form of collector current. Thus the concentration gradient in the base is retained, and additional electrons continue to migrate from the emitter to the collector. In standard transistors 99% or more of all the electrons emanating from the emitter reach the space-charge region and become collector current. The few missing electrons are caught in the electron gaps while traversing the p-doped base. Left to their own devices, these electrons would produce a negative charge in the base; almost immediately (50 ns), the repulsive forces would prevent the flow of additional electrons. A small base current comprised of positive charge carriers (holes) provides partial or complete compensation for this negative charge in the transistor. Small variations in the base current produce substantial changes in the emitter-collector current. The npn transistor is a bipolar, current-controlled semiconductor amplifier.

Field-effect transistors (FET)
In these devices, primary control of the current flow in a conductive path is exercised by an electric field. The field, in turn, is generated with voltage applied at the control electrode, or gate. Field-effect transistors differ from their bipolar counterparts in utilizing only a single type of charge carrier (electrons or holes), giving rise to the alternate designation "unipolar transistor". Various classifications include:
– Junction field-effect transitors (junction FET, JFET).
– Insulated-gate field-effect transistors, especially MOS field-effect transistors (MOSFET), or MOS transistors for short.

MOS transistors are well suited for application in highly-integrated circuitry. The power FET represents a genuine alternative to the bipolar transistor in many applications. Terminals: gate (G), source (S), drain (D).

Operation of the depletion layer (or junction) FET (based on the n-channel FET)
DC voltage is present at the ends of an n-type crystal. Electrons flow from the source to the drain. The width of the channel is defined by two laterally diffused p-type zones and by the negative voltage present within them. Raising the negative gate voltage causes the space-charge regions to extend further into the channel, thereby constricting the current path. Thus the current flow between the source (S) and drain (D) is governed by the voltage applied at the control electrode (or gate, G). The FET only requires charge carriers of a single polarity in order to operate, while the power necessary for controlling the current is virtually nil. Thus the depletion layer FET is a unipolar, voltage-controlled component.

Operation of the MOS transistor (based on p-channel enhancement device)
MOS represents the standard layer configuration: Metal Oxide Semiconductor. If no voltage is applied at the gate electrode, then no current will flow between the source and the drain: the pn-junctions remain in the blocking mode. The application of negative voltage at the gate causes the electrons in the adjacent n-type region to be displaced toward the interior of the

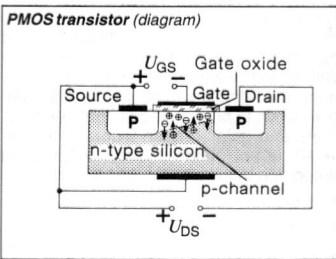

PMOS transistor *(diagram)*

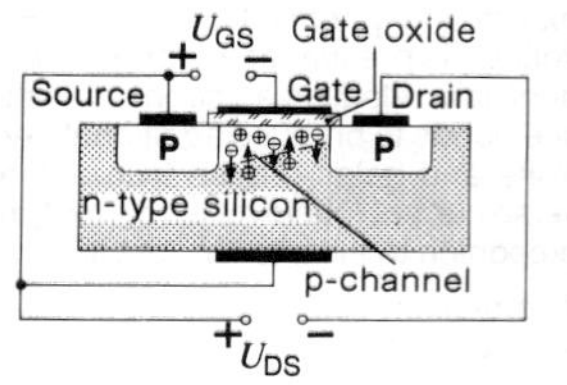

CMOS transistor pair *(diagram)*

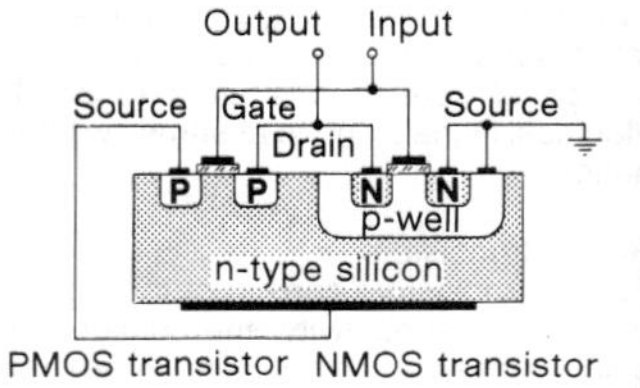

crystal, while holes – which are always present in n-type silicon in the form of minority charge carriers – are pulled to the surface. A narrow p-type layer – the p-channel - forms beneath the surface. Current can now flow between the two p-type regions (source and drain). This current consists exclusively of holes. Because the gate voltage is exercised through an insulating oxide layer, no current flows in the control circuit: no power is required for the control function. In summary, the MOS transistor is a unipolar, voltage-controlled component.

PMOS, NMOS, CMOS transistors
If a p-channel MOS transistor (PMOS transistor) is doped with a donor impurity rather than an acceptor impurity, it becomes an NMOS transistor. Because the electrons in the NMOS transistor are more mobile, it operates more rapidly than the PMOS device, although the latter was the first to become available due to the fact that it is physically easier to manufacture.

It is also possible to employ complementary MOS technology to pair

PMOS and NMOS transistors in a single silicon chip; the resulting devices are called complementary MOS, or CMOS transistors. The specific advantages of the CMOS transistor: extremely low power dissipation, a high degree of immunity to interference, relative insensitivity to varying supply voltages, suitability for analog signal processing and highly-integrated applications.

Thyristors

Three consecutive pn junctions provide the thyristor effect, which is applied for components which act as snap switches when triggered by an electrical signal. The term "thyristor" is the generic designation for all devices which can be switched from the forward (conducting) state to the reverse (blocking) state (or vice versa). Applications in power electronics: Control of frequency and rpm; rectification and frequency conversion; switching. In specialized usage, "thyristor" is understood to mean a reverse-blocking triode thyristor.

Four-layer diode

DIN definition: A reverse-blocking diode thyristor. It is a semiconductor device featuring two terminals (anode A, cathode K) which operates as a switch. It is composed of four doped layers of alternating conductivity types. This device's electrical response is best understood by visualizing the four-layer structure as representing two transistor paths T_1 and T_2. Increasing the current between A and K induces a rise in the reverse currents of both transistors. However, the reverse current of T_1 is the base current of T_2, while the reverse current of T_2 represents the base current of T_1. Once the switching voltage U_{AK} reaches a specific level, the reverse current of the one transistor increases to such a degree that it begins to exert a slight bias effect on the other transistor, resulting in conduction. Meanwhile, the second transistor operates in the same fashion. The mutual bias effect exerted by the two transistor units reaches such an intensity that the four-layer diode begins to act as a conductor; this is the thyristor effect.

The four-layer diode cannot revert to its high-resistance state until the current I falls below a specific minimum level, referred to as the holding point.

Thyristor with control terminal

DIN definition: Triode thyristor (also SCR, silicon controlled rectifier), a controllable device with switching characteristics. It consists of four zones of alternating conductivity type. Like the four-layer diode, it has two stable states (high resistance and low resistance). The switching operations between the respective states are governed via the control terminal (gate) G.

GTO thyristor

DIN definition: Gate turn-off (acronym: GTO) switch activated by positive control voltage, with deactivation via a negative control impulse at the same gate.

Triac

DIN definition: Bidirectional triode thyristor (triac = triode alternating current switch), a

Four-layer diode and thyristor effect
1 Four-layer structure,
2 Separated into two transistor paths.

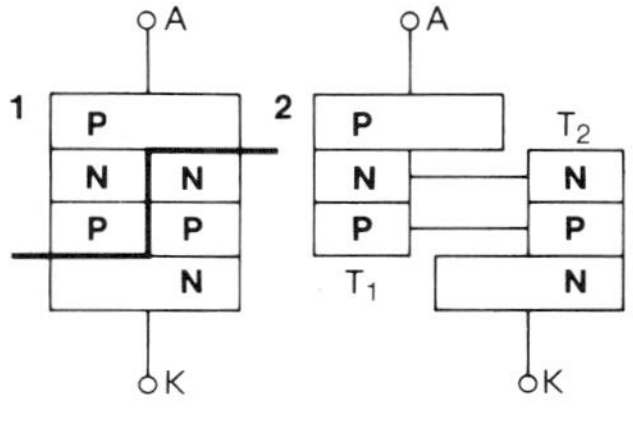

Solar cell
1 Light, 2 Electrical field, 3 Metal contact.

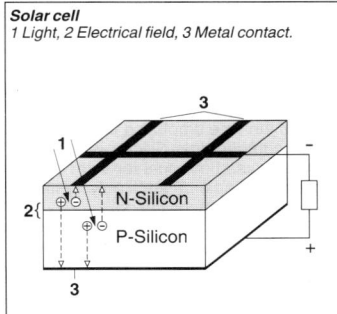

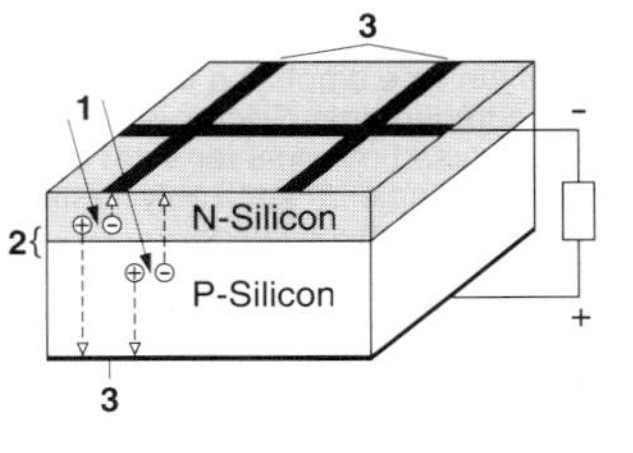

controllable thyristor with three terminals. It maintains essentially identical switching properties in both of its two switching directions.

Photovoltaic solar cells

The photovoltaic effect is applied to convert light energy directly into electrical energy.

Solar cells, consisting largely of semiconductor materials, represent the basic elements of photovoltaic technology. Exposure to light results in the creation of free charge carriers (electron-hole pairs) in the semiconductor material (photo-electric effect). If the semiconductor incorporates a pn junction, then the charge carriers separate in its electric field before proceeding to the metal contacts on the semiconductor's surface. DC voltage (photo-electric voltage) is produced between the contacts; the electrical potential ranges between 0.5 and 1.2 V, depending on the semiconductor material being used. Connection of a load resistor results in a current flow (photo-electric current), e.g., 2.8 A for a 100 cm^2 Si-solar cell at 0.58 V.

The efficiency level with which radiated light energy is converted into electrical energy (indicated in percent) depends both upon how well the semiconductor material is suited to the spectral distribution, and the efficiency with which the free charge carriers which are produced can be isolated and conducted to the appropriate surface contacts.

The paths within the semiconductor should be short (thin layers from several µm to 300 µm) to prevent the free charge carriers from recombining. The structure of the crystal lattices in the material must be as perfect as possible, while the material itself must be free of impurities. The manufacturing processes include procedures of the type employed for microelectronics components. Silicon is the most commonly used material for solar cells. It is used in single-crystal, polycrystalline and amorphous modification.

Typical efficiency levels achieved under laboratory conditions include:

Silicon	– single crystal	24%
	– polycrystalline	16%
	– amorphous	12%
CdS/Cu_2S		9%
$CuInSe_2$		14%
GaAs[1])		26%
Si/GaAs tandem[1])		37%.

[1]) Concentrated sunlight.

The efficiency levels obtained from mass-produced solar cells are approximately one third lower on average.

The "tandem cells" achieve their high efficiency by incorporating two solar cells - made of different materials - in consecutive layers; the unit is thus capable of converting light from various spectral ranges into charge carriers.

The single solar cells are interconnected within a circuit to form solar modules. The product always assumes the form of DC voltage; an inverter can be used for the conversion to AC (e.g., for discharge into mains electrical supply). The module's essential specifications are its output voltage and its power output at full solar exposure (approx. 1000 W/m^2).

The ultimate objective is to develop inexpensive processes allowing the manufacture of large-area solar cells. Proven procedures include extracting crystals from molten mass, or cutting cast crystals into individual wafers and blocks. Research is now extending into new areas such as strip pulling, foil casting and separation of thin semiconductor layers. Although the energy generated by photovoltaic processes is still more expensive than that provided by convential power stations, improvements in cell manufacturing techniques, increases in efficiency and large-scale production will combine to cause further reductions in cost. For applications involving isolated systems (consumers without external electrical connections) and minimal power requirements (watches, pocket calculators), photovoltaics already represents the best solution.

Monolithic integrated circuits

Monolithic integration

Oxidizing silicon wafers is a relatively simple matter, while the speed with which dopants penetrate into silicon is exponentially greater than that with which they enter the oxide - doping only occurs at those locations where openings are present in the oxide layer. These characteristics provide the basis for planar technology. The specific design requirements of the individual integrated circuit determine the precise geometric configuration, which is applied to the wafer in a photolithographic process. All processing procedures (oxidizing, etching, doping and separation) progress consecutively from the surface plane (planar).

Planar technology makes it possible to manufacture all circuit componentry (resistors, capacitors, diodes, transistors, thyristors) and the associated conductor strips on a single silicon chip in a unified manufacturing process. The semiconductor devices are combined to produce mono-lithic integrated circuits: IC = Integrated Circuit.

This integrated element is generally employed as a subsystem within the electronic circuit; in some cases it represents the entire system (system-on-chip).

Integration level

Either the number of individual functional elements, the number of transistors, or the number of gates on a single chip. The following classifications relate to the level of integration (and chip surface):

SSI Small Scale Integration
Extends to approximately
100 functional elements per chip,
mean chip surface area 3 mm^2.

MSI Medium Scale Integration
Roughly 100 to 1000 functional
elements per chip,
mean chip surface area 8 mm^2.

LSI Large Scale Integration
Less than 100,000 functional
elements per chip, mean chip
surface area 20 mm^2.

VLSI Very Large Scale Integration
More than 100,000 functional
elements per chip,
mean chip surface area 30 mm^2.

ULSI Ultra Large Scale Integration
More than 1 million functional
elements per chip.

Computer-supported simulation and design methods (CAE/CAD) are essential elements in the manufacture of the more complex integrated circuits (exception: SSI).

Classifications for integrated circuitry

- According to transistor technology: Bipolar – MOS – Combined (bipolar/MOS),
- According to circuit type: Analog – Digital – Combined (analog/digital),
- According to component types: Analog – Logic – Memory – Microcomponents,
- According to application: Standard IC – Application-specific IC (ASIC)

Integrated analog circuits

Basic structures: Stabilized-voltage supply, stabilized-current supply, differential amplifier components, switching elements, potential shift, output stages.

Application classes: Operation amplifiers (OP), voltage regulators, comparators, clocks, converters, interface circuits (p. 100).

Basic monolithic integrated circuit (bipolar)
Circuit and configuration. 1...5 terminals.

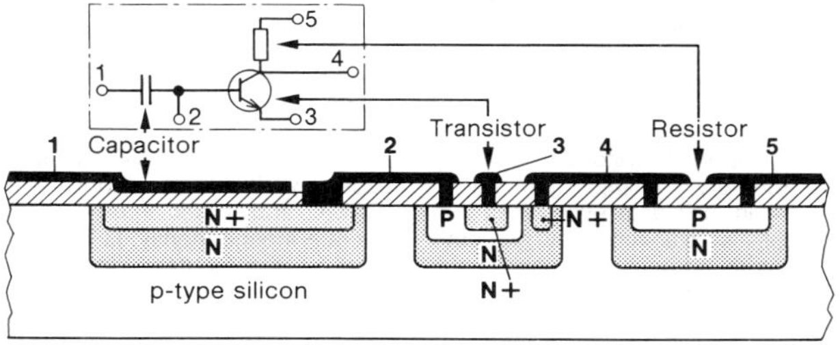

Special analog IC's: Voltage references, wideband amplifiers, analog multipliers, function generators, phase-lock circuits, analog filters, analog switches.

Integrated digital circuits

The scale extends from SSI (logic chip) to LSI/VLSI (memory, microprocessors, microcontrollers).

Several conditions must be met before logic chips can be combined within a single system: The voltage supply, logic level, the circuit speed and the signal-propagation delay must all be identical. This requirement is met within the respective circuit families. The most important are:

- Standard TTL (Transistor – Transistor – Logic),
- Schottky TTL,
- Low-power Schottky TTL,
- ECL (Emitter Coupled Logic),
- I^2L (Integrated Injection Logic),
- MOS logic, esp. CMOS logic.

Semiconductor memories

Data storage includes the following operations: Recording (writing, entering), storage (data storage in the narrow sense), retrieval and readout. The memory operates by exploiting physical properties that facilitate unambiguous production and recognition of two opposed states (binary information). In semiconductor memory chips, the conditions produced are "conductive/non-conductive" or "charged/discharged". The latter state relies on special properties in the silicon/silicon oxide or silicon nitride/metal junction.

Semiconductor storage elements are divided into the two main categories of volatile and non-volatile memory. Volatile memory chips (temporary memory) can be read out and written over an unlimited number of times, and are thus referred to as RAMs (Random Access Memory). The data which they contain is lost as soon as the voltage supply is switched off. Non-volatile memory chips (permanent memory) retain their data even when the power supply is removed; they are employed to store permanent, non-variable data (ROM = Read-Only Memory). The chart shows the relationships and classification of the most common types of memory.

Microprocessors and microcomputers

A microprocessor is an integrated central processing unit in a single chip. Microprocessor design seeks to avoid individualization in the face of large-scale integration, and the units can be programmed to meet the numerous and variegated requirements associated with specific operating conditions. The microprocessor cannot operate by itself. It always acts as part of a microcomputer.

The microcomputer consists of:

– The microprocessor serving as CPU (central processing unit). The microprocessor contains the controller, and the logic and arithmetic unit. The logic and arithmetic unit performs the operations indicated by its name, while the controller ensures implementation of the commands stored in the program memory.

– Input/Output (IO) circuitry controls data communications with peripheral devices.

– Program memory provides permanent storage for the operating program (user program). As a non-volatile memory is required, the data are stored in ROMs, PROMs or EPROMs.

– Data memory for the data being run at any given time. These data change continually; thus the storage medium for this application is the RAM.

– Clock generator and power supply.

The bus circuitry forms the junction between the individual elements in the computer. A clock generator provides the time frame or rhythm for all of the operations carried out in the microcomputer. The auxiliary logic consists of the special-application chips, such as those for program interrupt, insertion of intermediate programs, etc. Input/output devices and external memory are referred to as peripherals.

The microcomputer's main elements are either combined in a circuit on a printed-circuit board, or integrated within a single silicon wafer. A component which integrates CPU, read-only memory (as ROM, EPROM or EEPROM), input/output capability (I/O) and read/write memory (RAM), and which has the ability to operate independently, is called: Single-chip microcomputer, single-chip computer, or microcontroller.

The transputer is a special type of microprocessor which is especially useful for

Overview of semiconductor memory devices

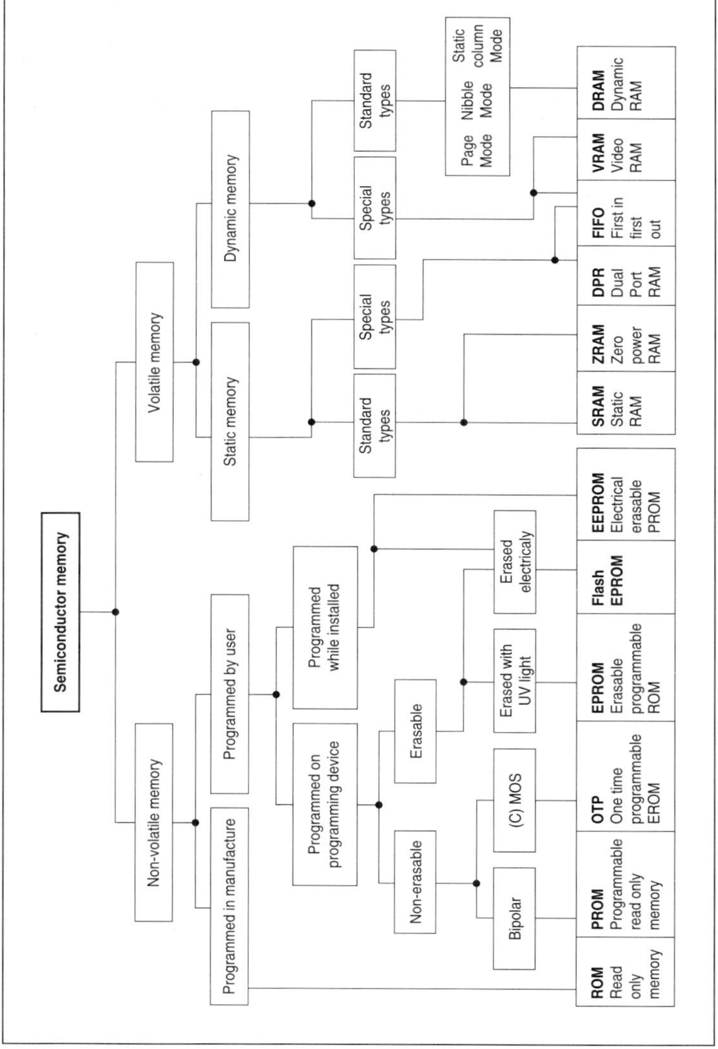

building parallel networks. In addition to the standard microprocessor components, the chip is also equipped with communications and processing hardware.

It has four bidirectional serial transmission channels (links) allowing extremely rapid communications (20 Mbit/s per link) with other transputers. Because communications are completely asynchronous, distributed networks do not require a common clock circuit. Each link has its own DMA controller; once initialized by the CPU, it can process data transmission on its own. Thus processing and communications are essentially parallel operations. Particular advantages include the extremely brief turnaround and interrupt-response times of approx. 1 s. The transputer achieves these without a real-time operating system; the required processing commands are contained in its command set.

The transputer operates as a communications node within the parallel network, meaning that it serves as both computer and communications interface. The transputer can therefore be employed to avoid one of the gravest liabilities of many parallel systems, which is the inherent need to share a common bus.

Application-specific IC's

Application-specific IC's (ASIC – Application-Specific Integrated Circuits) differ from standard IC's in that they are conceived to fulfill a single purpose. They represent the result of a fruitful cooperation between users, with their specialized system experience, and the manufacturers, who enjoy access to the requisite technology. The essential advantages of ASIC: Reduced number of components, lower system costs, reliability, enhanced security against copying.

The ASIC family is generally classified according to the development method which has been selected: Chip-mounted circuitry, composed of single functional elements (full-custom IC) provides the best results as measured in operation and packaging density. It is, however, only suited for large-series applications (time and expense). Standardized basic circuit functions (developed and tested in advance) represent one means of rationalizing the development process. The circuits are incorporated in elements of varying sizes (ROM, RAM, computer core, or individualized, user-specific circuitry). Depending upon the number of available user-specific elements, this method can be employed to obtain shorter development times while maintaining efficient exploitation of the chip surface.

The next stage is the use of standardized, relatively complex basic functions. These are developed in advance, in the form of elements of single height and variable width, which remain available in the form of cell libraries. These standard cells are automatically collated and combined with polysilicon and aluminum conductors. A dual-layer metallic coating can be applied to achieve even better utilization of the surface area.

Overview of ASIC devices
1 Programmable logic (PLD), 2 Gate arrays, 3 Standard cells (CBIC, cell-based IC), 4 User-specific cells, 5 Individual elements (full-custom IC).

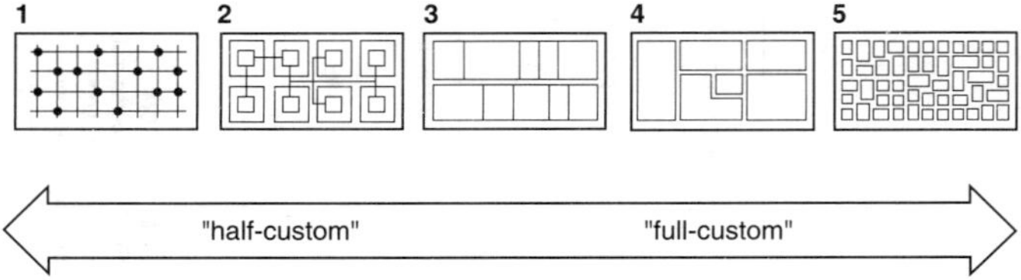

Gate arrays are predeveloped as far as the transistor/gate connection, and are manufactured in advance, leaving only the final masking operations for later completion. The connection with the user-specific circuitry is then automatic. Rationalization is achieved by providing standard circuits for frequent basic computer functions (similar to a cell library). Special gate arrays designed for specific applications display particular advantages (e.g., computer-oriented digital circuitry for application in standard environments).

Programmable logic devices (PLD's) are preassembled transistor arrays. The user programs them for the specific application in a process analogous to that employed with PROM's. The PLD thus provides system developers with the option of producing silicon breadboard circuits within a short period of time. The production of complex systems in silicon is becoming increasingly important, as it allows the production of practical working models in the development phase.

Smart-power IC's

Automotive and industrial systems incorporate electronics in which numerous final-control elements and other loads must be controlled electronically. The power switches must be capable of assuming auxiliary functions extending beyond the control of circuit power: Driver circuits for controlling transistor switches; protective circuits for excess voltage, current and temperature; error monitoring in case of operating faults. This kind of power-IC generally incorporates bipolar or MOS technology, and carries the generic designation smart-power IC.

Film and hybrid integrated circuits

Film circuits

The integrated film circuit features passive circuit elements - these include capacitors and inductors, as well as conductor tracks, insulators and resistors. An integrated film circuit is produced by applying the layers which contain these elements to a substrate carrier. The terms "thin-film" and "thick-film" circuit derive from the fact that the film thickness was originally the determining factor for tailoring to specific performance characteristics; present technology employs a variety of manufacturing techniques to achieve the same end.

Thin-film circuits
Integrated film circuits on which the individual layers are applied to glass or ceramic substrata in a vacuum coating process. Advantages: Fine structures (to approx. 10 µm) provide high circuit-element density, extremely good HF characteristics and low-noise resistor elements. On the minus side are the relatively high manufacturing costs.

Thick-film circuits
Integrated film circuits in which the layers are usually applied to ceramic carriers in a silk-screening process before being fused on. Advantages: Multi-layer construction provides high circuit-element density and good HF characteristics. A high degree of manufacturing automation is possible for large-scale production.

Hybrid circuits

Integrated film circuits incorporating additional discrete components, such as capacitors and integrated semiconductor circuits (IC). These circuits are manufactured by soldering or bonding. A high component density is achieved by using unencapsulated semiconductor chips, connected to the circuit via bonding, or SMD components (SMD – Surface-Mounted Device). Advantages: The good thermal dissipation allows high installation temperatures, while compact construction provides good vibration resistance; good HF behaviour. Hybrid circuits are especially well-suited for application in motor vehicles and in telecommunications.

SMT Circuit board technology

The circuitry for an individual electronic system can basically be subdivided into the categories semiconductor technology, hybrid technology and circuit-board technology; the selection is contingent upon such factors as economy (cost, number of units in the series), time (development time and service life) and the environmen-

Circuit-board technology – Design options
a) Insertion mounting (conventional),
b) SMD mounting on ceramic substrate (hybrid technology), c) Combined mounting.
1 Wired devices, 2 Circuit board, 3 Chips,
4 Ceramic base, 5 Bonding material.

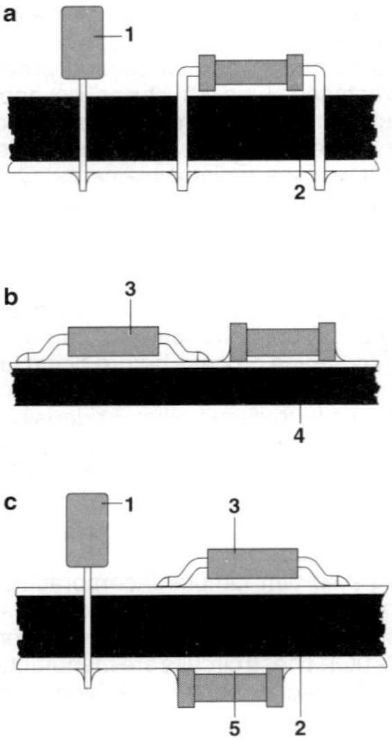

tal conditions (electrical, thermal, physical).

Circuit boards represent the classical form for producing an electrical circuit. On the most basic type of circuit board, the electronic components are mounted on a fiberboard or fiberglass-reinforced synthetic-resin carrier. A printing process may be employed to apply the conductor tracks (copper foil) to the board (thus: printed circuit).

An alternative is to etch the circuit from a copper-plated board. The components' contact pins are inserted through holes in the board and soldered into position.

Increasing integration of the integrated circuits resulted in a commensurate rapid increase in the number of pins to be connected. This development initiated the transition from conventional insertion-mounting to SMT, or surface-mounting technology. In the meantime, the number of devices suitable for surface mounting (SMD or Surface Mounted Devices) has proliferated to embrace a wide range of components which can be soldered to the circuit board's surface. The SMD's and their housing configuration (SOT, SO, PLCC, Flat Pack, etc.) are especially suitable for mounting with automated equipment.

The most important application advantages provided by surface-mounting technology include:
– rationalized production of assemblies (high installation speed and reliability),
– low surface requirement with no operational sacrifices,
– standard circuit boards can be used (e.g., FR4 epoxy-fiberglass weave),
– the number of holes per board is reduced, or the holes become entirely redundant,
– can be used in combination with wired components,
– reduced number of connections provides improved reliability,
– facilitates improved circuit design and coupling, as well as consistency,
– better HF characteristics.

Surface-mounting technology is much more sensitive to the combination of processing techniques than is conventional insertion mounting. The advantages to be garnered from SMT are directly proportional to the care with which componentry, circuit-board layout, automatic mounting, joining techniques, testing, repair, etc., are mutually adapted for optimal performance.

Micromechanics

The term "micromechanics" is employed to designate the production of mechanical components using semiconductors (generally silicon) and semiconductor technology. This type of application exploits both the semiconductive and the mechanical properties of silicon. The first micromechanical silicon pressure sensors were installed in motor vehicles at the beginning of the '80s. Typical mechanical dimensions are in the micrometer range.

Physical characteristic	Unit	Silicon	Steel (max.)	Stainless steel
Tensile load	10^5 N/cm^2	7.0	4.2	2.1
Knoop-hardness	kg/mm^2	850	1500	660
Young's modulus	10^7 N/cm^2	1.9	2.1	2.0
Density	g/cm^3	2.3	7.9	7.9
Thermal conduction	W/cm · K	1.57	0.97	0.33
Thermal expansion	10^{-6}/K	2.3	12.0	17.3

The mechanical characteristics of silicon (e.g., strength, hardness and Young's modulus, see Table) can be compared to those of steel. However, silicon is lighter and has greater thermal conductivity. Single-crystal Si wafers with almost perfect physical response characteristics are used: Hysteresis and surface diffusion are negligible. Due to the brittleness of the single-crystal material, the stress-strain curve does not display a plastic range; the material ruptures when the elastic range is exceeded.

In the manufacture of micromechanical structures, conventional processes of semiconductor technology are supplemented by special anisotropic etching, both with and without etch stop, and anodic and direct bonding. The anisotropic process displays substantial variations in the etching effect produced by the alkaline hydroxides, depending upon the orientation of the crystals. Thus the variations in etching resistance can reach a factor of 200 between a given crystal direction and another crystal layer with a higher etching rate.

The pressure sensor can serve as an example of the manufacturing stages involved in the production of micromechanical devices (see illustration). Micro-electronic procedures are employed to produce resistors and the attendant electrical connections on the surface of the wafer. A lithographic process is used to position the hole on the back; this opening allows the anisotropic etching medium to attack the silicon. The horizontal crystal layers are etched rapidly, while the lateral crystals remain largely immune due to the characteristic angle of the silicon crystal. The structure is etched out in three dimensions according to the lithographic definition. The electrochemical etch stop at the surface brings the etching process to a halt at the pn junction, producing a diaphragm with a typical thickness of 5 ... 50 μm.

Maximum physical expansion occurs adjacent to the loading edge, where any pressure differential in the diaphragm will affect the resistor elements implanted there. This phenomenon, based on the piezoresistive effect (variations in resistance induced by physical expansion), can be picked up at the external contact in the form of an electrical signal. The typical dimensions of a micromechanical device in the form of a suction-pressure sensor are 3 x 3 x 3 mm^3.

Micro-electronic processes can be employed to produce not only resistors, but also transistors and entire circuits on the surface of the wafer, making it possible to combine signal amplification and calibration on the same device. The combination of micromechanics and micro-electronics is called microsystems technology.

Micromechanical pressure sensor
1 El. terminal, 2 Conductor (low impedance), 3 Si diaphragm, 4 Piezo-electric resistor, 5 Al conductor track.

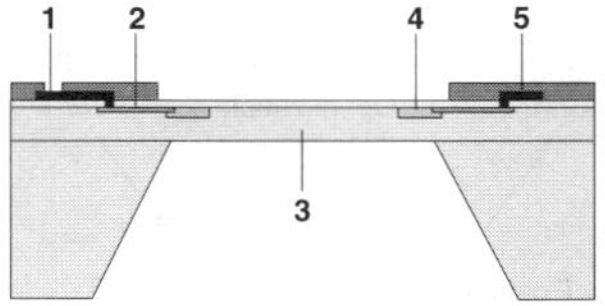

Mechatronics

"Mechatronics" is a branch of engineering which seeks to enhance the functionality of technical systems by means of thorough mutual integration of mechanical, electronic and data-processing components. Mechatronic systems are becoming increasingly significant in the guise of complex control structures (especially in automotive and production technology). Examples: Engine-management systems for spark-ignition and diesel engines, ABS, ASR, ride-control and steering systems, CNC machine tools and robotics. The mechanical components in these systems are frequently characterized by both non-linear response and broad transmission bands.

A synergistic, interdisciplinary approach is crucial in the development of mechatronic systems. Modern software engineering plays a decisive role. The classical analysis and design processes of design technology are being supplemented and partially replaced by real-time simulations, identification and parameter optimization, in which actual components are also included (hardware in the loop).

The objective of microsystems technology is to miniaturize mechatronic systems by integrating micro-electronics and micromechanics.

Interrelationships in mechatronics

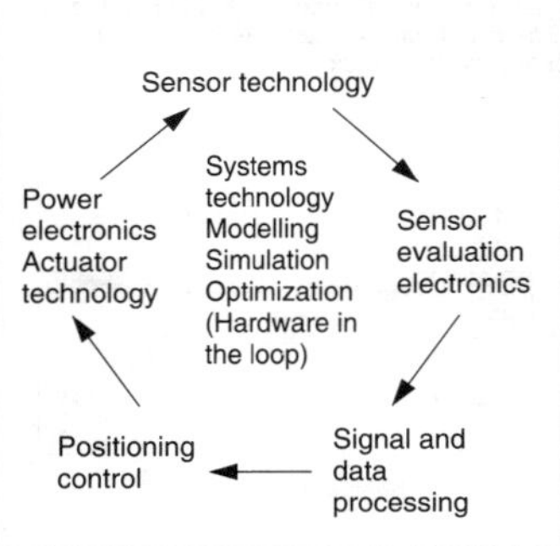

Analog/Digital converters

Analog signals are electrical quantities whose amplitude, frequency and phase convey information on physical variables or technical processes. Data registration is continuous in both time and quantity; within certain limits, analog signals can reflect any number of quantitative variations at any given point in time. Analog technology provides means for processing these signals. Initial processing, consisting of filtering and amplification, can be supplemented by mathematical operations such as addition and multiplication, as well as integration over time, etc. The operational amplifier (OP) is an integrated circuit of extreme importance in analog technology. Under ideal conditions, a relatively simple external circuit is sufficient for determining its operating characteristics (infinite amplification, no input current).

Analog units also display several disadvantages: The characteristic response curves of the various components alter with age, temperature fluctuations influence precision, and the manufacturing process must generally be supplemented by subsequent calibration.

Conversion to digital signals entails a transition to discrete monitoring of both time and intensity, i.e., the analog signal is sampled with specific periodicity (scan spots). The sampled values are assigned a numeric expression in which the number of possible values and thus the resolution are limited (quantification).

Instead of using the decimal system, digital technology recognizes the computer's preferences by employing the binary system to represent the values.
Example: 101 (dual) =
$1 \cdot 2^2 + 0 \cdot 2^1 + 1 \cdot 2^0 = 5$ (decimal).

The bit (position) with the greatest value is described as the MSB (Most Significant Bit), the lowest as the LSB (Least Significant Bit). When represented as a two's compliment, the MSB provides the prefix for the decimal number ($1 \triangleq$ negative, $0 \triangleq$ positive). Values ranging from -4 to $+3$ can be represented with a 3-bit word.
Example: 101 =
$-1 \cdot 2^2 + 0 \cdot 2^1 + 1 \cdot 2^0 = -3$

A word of n bits in length is able to represent 2^n different values. This is 256

Operational amplifier (OP)
a) Inversion amplifier,
b) Differential amplifier.

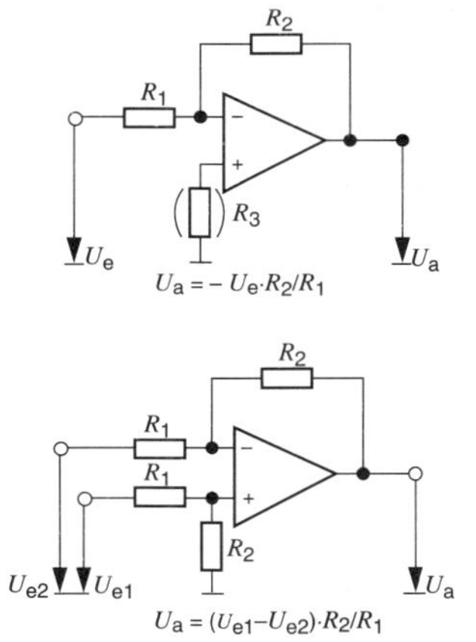

Digital conversion of analog signal
F Filter, S/H Sample-and-hold element,
A/D Analog/digital converter.

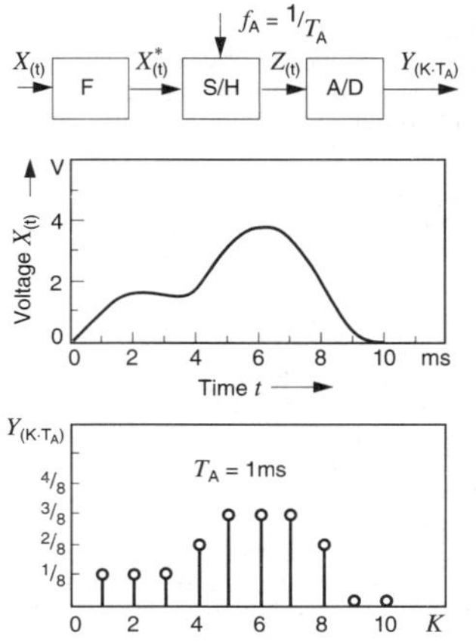

for 8 bits, for 16 bits it is 65,536. An analog input voltage of ± 5 V (FSR – Full Scale Range) results in a resolution (LSB value) of 39 mV with 8 bits and 0.15 mV with 16 bits.

It is necessary to limit the bandwidth of the signal being scanned (anti-aliasing filter). The highest signal frequency f_g must be less than half the scan frequency f_A ($f_A > 2 \cdot f_g$). When a sample-and-hold scanning arrangement is employed, the maximum allowable variation in input voltage during the A/D converter's conversion period (aperture point) is one LSB.

The transfer function illustrates how a single digital value is assigned to various input voltages. The maximum amplitude of the quantification error is $Q/2$ (rounding-off error) at Q = FSR/(2^n) $\triangleq$ LSB.

The quantification process results in an overlay of quantification noise contaminating the actual data signal. If a sinus-curve signal is employed for full modulation in the A/D converter, the result is a signal-to-noise ratio which increases by about 6 dB for each additional bit of resolution. Actual A/D converters display deviations from the ideal transfer curve. These are caused by offset, amplification and linearity errors (static errors) as well as aperture inconsistency and finite settling times (dynamic error).

Transfer function of an ideal 3-bit A/D converter

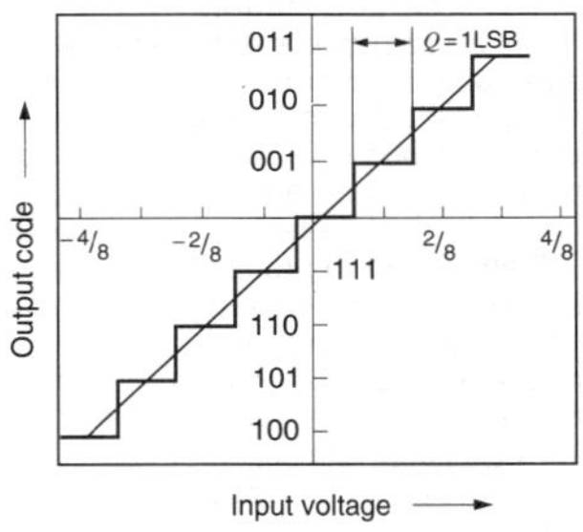

Sensors

Basics

Purpose

Sensors convert a physical (usually non-electrical) quantity into an electrical quantity (a non-electrical intermediate stage may be employed).

Classifications

1. Purpose and application
– Function (open-loop and closed-loop control circuits),
– Safety and back-up,
– Monitoring and information.

2. Types of characteristic curve
– Continuous linear: Control applications across a broad measurement range,
– Continuous non-linear: Control of a parameter within a narrow measurement range,
– Discontinuous multi-stage: Monitoring in applications where a punctual signal is required when a limit value is reached,
– Discontinuous dual-stage (with hysteresis in some cases): Monitoring of limits in cases where corrective measures are required, either when the limit value is reached or subsequently.

3. Type of output signal
Output signal proportional to:
– Current/voltage, amplitude,
– Frequency/periodicity,
– Impulse length/Pulse duty factor.
Discrete output signal:
– Dual stage (binary),
– Multi-stage (irregular graduation),
– Multi-stage (equidistant) or digital.

Motor-vehicle application

Sensors and actuators represent the peripheral communications link between the vehicle, with its complex drive, braking, chassis and body-component operations (including guidance and navigation), and the (usually digital-electronic) control unit (ECU) employed for processing. An adapter circuit is generally used to convert the sensor's signals into the standardized form (measuring chain, measured-data registration system) required by the control unit. In addition, sensor information from other processing elements can also influence the process, as can the driver by means of simple operating switches. Display elements provide the driver with information on the static and dynamic status of the vehicle as a synergistic process.

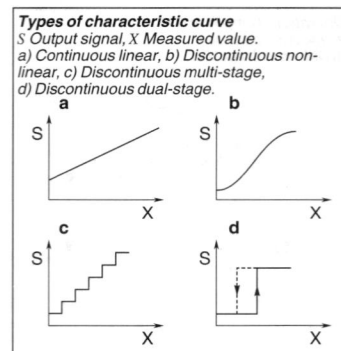

Types of characteristic curve
S Output signal, X Measured value.
a) Continuous linear, b) Discontinuous non-linear, c) Discontinuous multi-stage, d) Discontinuous dual-stage.

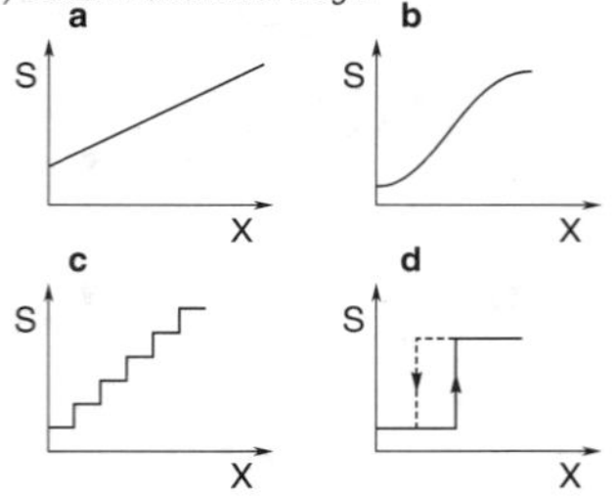

***Signal shapes** (Examples)*
Output signal U: a) Frequency f, b) Impulse length T_P.

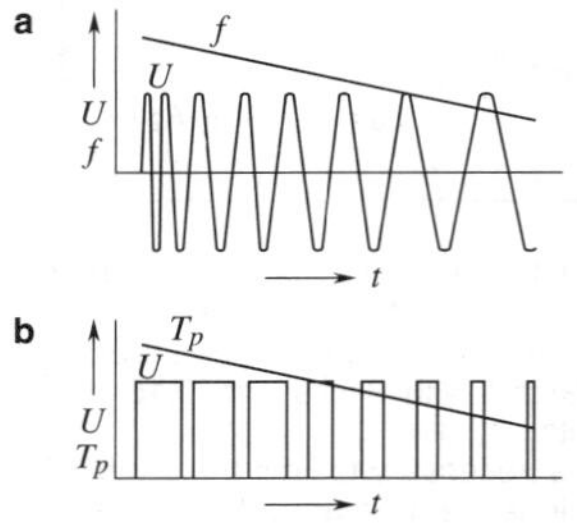

Requirement priorities, trends

The degree of stress to which the sensor is subjected is determined by the operating conditions (mechanical, climatic, chemical, electromagnetic influences) present at the installation location (for standard degrees of protection, see DIN 40 050, Sheet 9).

According to application and requirements, motor-vehicle sensors are assigned to one of three reliability classes:
Level 1: Steering, brakes, passenger protection,

Level 2: Engine, drivetrain, chassis, tires,
Level 3: Comfort, information and diagnosis, anti-theft.

Rationalized production methods and high-volume production are both necessary for achieving low costs.

Miniaturization procedures make it possible to achieve compact unit dimensions:
- Substrate and hybrid technology (pressure and temperature sensors),
- Semiconductor technology (monitoring rotational speed, e.g., with Hall vane switch),
- Micromechanics (pressure and acceleration sensors),
- Microsystem technology (combination of micromechanics, micro-electronics, can also include micro-optics).

Automotive sensors

Φ Physical quantity, E Electrical quantity, Z Interference factors, AK Actuator, AZ Display, SA Switch, SE Sensor(s), SG Control unit, 1 Measurement recorder, 2 Adapter circuit, 3 Driver, 4 Servo components.

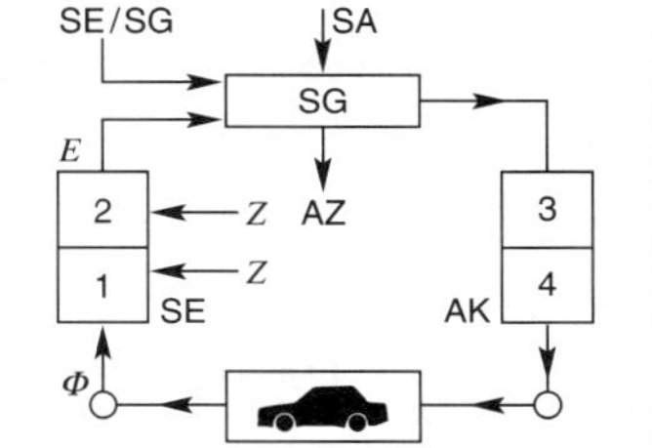

Integrated "intelligent" sensors

Systems ranging from hybrid and monolithic integration of sensors and signal electronics at the sensor location all the way to complex digital circuitry, such as A/D converters and microcomputers (mechatronics), which fully exploit the sensor's inherent precision and offer the following possibilities:
- Reduction of load on the control unit,
- Uniform, flexible, bus-compatible communications links,
- Multiple application of sensors,
- Multi-sensor designs,
- Processing of low-intensity and HF signals (amplification, demodulation),
- Storage of individual correction factors in a PROM in order to facilitate correction of sensor deviations at the sensor location and to provide integrated balance adjustment and compensation for sensor and circuit.

Fiber-optic sensors

Due to their specific advantages, fiber-optic sensors will acquire increasing significance for motor-vehicle applications in the coming years.

Various physical factors can be employed to modify the intensity, phase (coherent laser light) and polarization of the light conducted in the optical fibers. Fiber-optic sensors are impervious to electromagnetic interference; they are, however, sensi-

Sensor integration levels

SE Sensor(s), SA Signal processing (analog), A/D Analog-digital converter, SG Control unit (digital), MC Microcomputer.

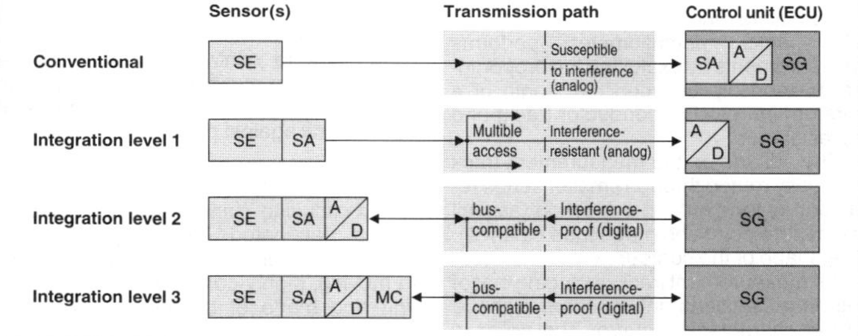

tive to physical pressure (intensity-modulated sensors), and, to some degree, to contamination and aging. Inexpensive plastic fibers are still not suitable for application throughout the temperature range found in motor vehicles.

Extrinsic sensors: The optical conductor generally conducts the light to an end point; it must emerge from the conductor to exert an effect.

Intrinsic sensors: The measurement effect occurs internally within the fibers.

Sensor types

Position sensors (displacement/angle)
Position sensors employ both contact wipers and contactless designs to register displacement and angle.
Directly monitored variable quantities:
- Throttle-valve position,
- Gas-pedal position,
- Seat and mirror position,
- Control-rod travel and position,
- Fuel level.

Indirectly monitored variable quantities:
- Sensor-flap deflection angle (flow rate),
- Deflection angle of a spring-mass system (acceleration),
- Diaphragm deflection angle (pressure),
- Compression travel (headlamp vertical-aim adjustment),
- Torsion angle (torque).

New applications:
- Distance, vehicle-to-vehicle, obstruction
- Steering-wheel angle
- Steering angle,
- Tilt angle,
- Vehicle-course angle.

Wiper potentiometers
The wiper potentiometer performs measurements by exploiting the proportional relationship between the length of a wire or film resistor (conductor track) and its resistance.

The voltage on the measurement track is usually routed through smaller series resistors R_V for overload protection (as well as for zero point and magnitude balance). The shape of the contour across the width of the measurement track (including that of individual sections) influences the shape of the characteristic curve. The wiper is

Wiper potentiometer
1 Wiper, 2 Resistor track, 3 Contact track, U_0 Supply voltage, U_A Measurement voltage, R Resistor, α Wiper angle.

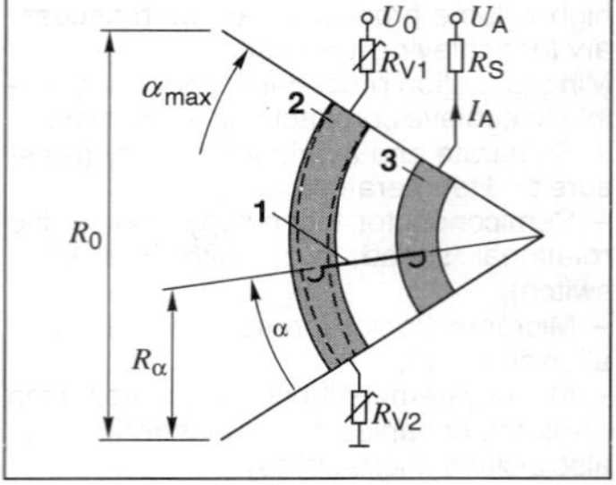

Short-circuiting ring sensor
1 Short-circuiting ring (moving), 2 Soft magnetic core, 3 Coil. I Current, I_W Eddy current, $L(x)$ Inductance / $\Phi(x)$ Magnetic flux at travel x.

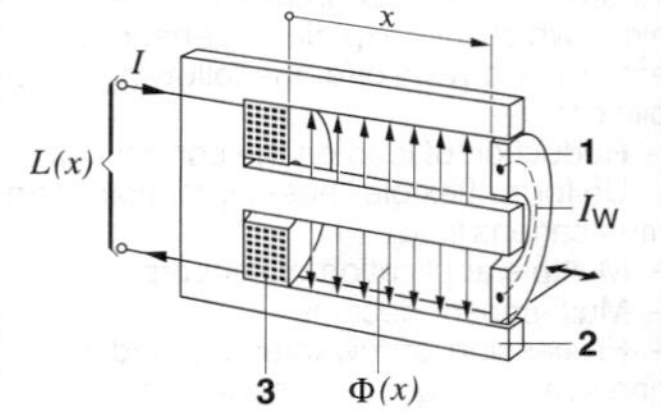

generally connected via a second contact track with the same surface material, but with a substrate of low-resistance conductor material.

Wear and measurement distortions (e.g., due to contact resistance at the wiper) can be avoided by minimizing the current at the pick-up ($I_A < 1$ mA) and sealing the unit against dust.

Short-circuiting ring sensors
Short-circuiting ring sensors consist of a laminated soft-magnetic core (straight/curved U or E-shape), a coil and a moving, highly-conductive short-circuiting ring made of copper or aluminum. They represent a variable inductance.

Even with uncritical tolerances in the short-circuiting ring, the eddy currents in the ring limit the expansion of the magnetic field to the area between the coil and the short-circuiting ring. Virtually the entire length of the sensor can be utilized for measurements. Varying leg contours can be employed to influence the shape of the characteristic curve: Reducing the distance between the legs toward the measuring-range end further enhances the good natural linearity. Operation is generally in the 5 ... 50 kHz range, depending on material and shape.

Half-differential sensors employ a moving measuring ring and a stationary reference short-circuiting ring to meet exacting demands for precision (rod-travel sensor for in-line fuel-injection pumps on diesels); they measure by acting as
– inductive voltage dividers (processing L_1 / L_2 or $(L_1 - L_2) / (L_1 + L_2)$), or as
– frequency-determining element in an oscillating circuit, producing a signal which is proportional to the frequency (excellent interference resistance, easy digital conversion).

The measuring effect is fairly substantial, typically $L_{max} / L_{min} = 4$.

Short-circuiting disk sensor
Instead of using a short-circuiting ring, the short-circuiting disk sensor employs a highly-conductive short-circuiting plate (no mechanical contact) which can be guided to various depths between the core legs (E or U-shaped). These sensors produce a somewhat less pronounced measuring effect. The shape of the short-circuiting disks or plates affects the characteristic response curve. Example: A differential deflection-angle sensor using two spiral plates with opposed rotational directions produces a characteristic curve with a saw-tooth pattern.

Further sensors
Solenoid plunger, differential-throttle and differential-transformer sensors are based on the variation in the inductance of an individual coil and the proportional relationship of voltage dividers (supplied either directly or via inductive coupling) with moving cores. The length of the unit is often substantially greater than that of the travel being measured.

Hall-effect sensors are suitable for measuring small distances.

Half-differential sensor
1 Reference (fixed), 2 Short-circuiting ring (moving), A/D Analog-digital converter, SA Signal processing, SG Control unit (ECU).

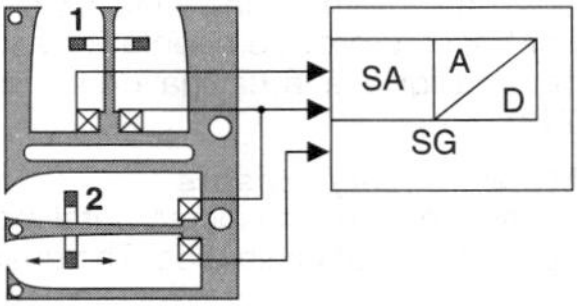

Future sensors
HF eddy-current sensors (electronics at the measuring point), e.g., for contactless monitoring of the throttle-valve angle.

Magneto-resistive NiFe thin-film resistors (permalloy sensors, as variation: "barber-shop pole").

Thermal, hydrostatic and ultrasonic methods (for fuel tanks with irregular shapes) will be replacing conventional fuel-level monitoring with potentiometric sensors in the future.

For vehicle collision-avoidance devices, ultrasonic transit-time methods (short-range 0.5 ... 5 m), transit time and triangulation procedures with short-range infrared

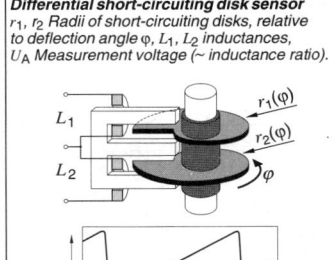

Differential short-circuiting disk sensor
r_1, r_2 Radii of short-circuiting disks, relative to deflection angle φ, L_1, L_2 inductances, U_A Measurement voltage (~ inductance ratio).

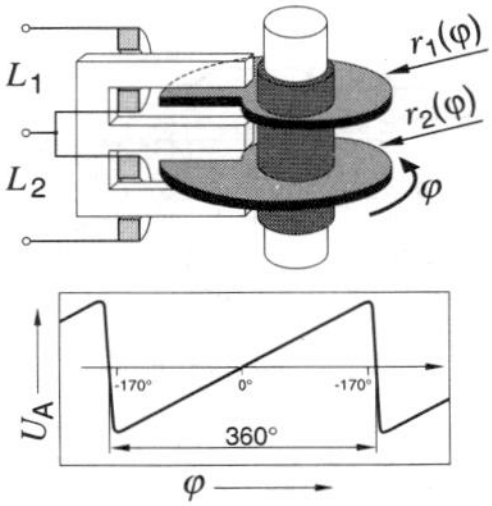

light (Lidar: Middle-range up to 50 m) and electromagnetic radar (long-range, up to 150 m) are suitable.

Magnetic-field sensors (saturation-core probes) can determine the vehicle's direction of travel to provide orientation assistance, and for use in navigation systems (p. 712).

RPM and velocity sensors

These sensors provide incremental monitoring of gear rotating speeds. The quantities measured include, for instance, crankshaft rpm/position, camshaft rpm, wheel rpm (ABS/ASR), rpm at diesel injection pumps.

New applications:

– Linear velocity,

– Vehicle rotation rate (vehicle-dynamics control systems).

Inductive sensors

The inductive sensor consists of a bar magnet with a soft-magnetic pole pin supporting an induction coil with two connections. When a ferro-magnetic ring gear (or a rotor of similar design) rotates past this sensor, it produces a voltage in the coil which is directly proportional to the periodic variation in the magnetic flux. A uniform tooth pattern produces a sinusoidal voltage curve. The rotational speed is determined according to the periodicity between zero transitions for the voltage; at the same time, the amplitude is also proportional to rotating speed.

The air gap and the tooth dimensions are important factors in determining the (exponential) signal amplitude. Air gaps measuring one half or one third of tooth interval can be detected without difficulty. Air gaps of up to 0.8 and 1.5 mm are covered with conventional crankshafts and the toothed impulse wheel for the ABS wheel-speed sensors. The reference point for the ignition timing is obtained by either omitting a tooth or by closing a gap between teeth. This is then recognized through the additional distance between zero transitions, and produces (due to the apparently larger tooth) a substantially greater signal voltage.

Hall sensors/Hall-effect vane switches

Semiconductor sensors utilize the Hall effect (p. 85) by employing Hall-effect vane switches, e.g., as ignition triggering sensors in ignition distributors (p. 458). The probe and the electronic circuitry for supply and signal processing are integrated on the sensor chip. This "Hall-IC" (with bipolar technology for continuous temperatures of up to 150 °C and direct connection to the vehicle electrical system) is located within an almost completely closed magnetic circuit consisting of permanent magnet and pole pieces. A soft-magnetic vane rotor (e.g., camshaft-driven) travels through the remaining air gap. The vane interrupts the magnetic field (that is, it conducts it past the sensor), while the gap in the vane rotor allows it to travel through the sensor unimpeded.

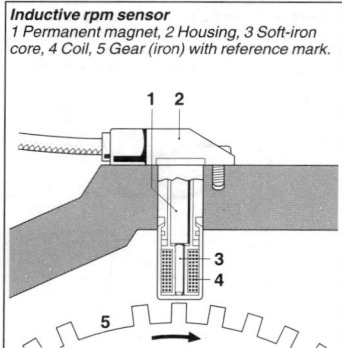

Inductive rpm sensor

1 Permanent magnet, 2 Housing, 3 Soft-iron core, 4 Coil, 5 Gear (iron) with reference mark.

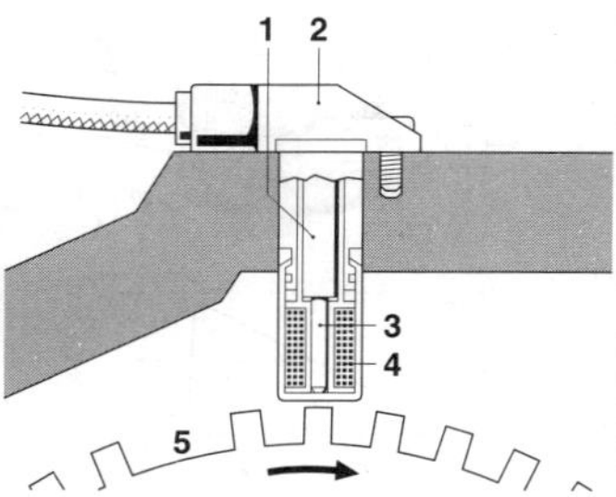

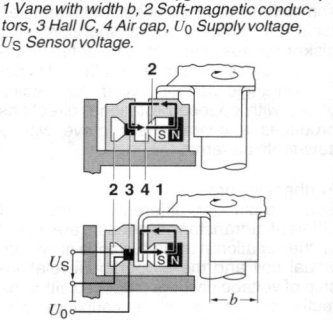

Hall-effect vane switch (ignition distributor)

1 Vane with width b, 2 Soft-magnetic conductors, 3 Hall IC, 4 Air gap, U_0 Supply voltage, U_S Sensor voltage.

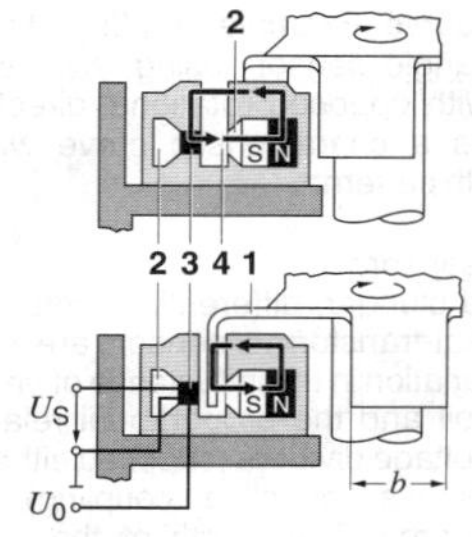

Future sensors
The objectives for future sensors include realization of the following characteristics: static monitoring (e.g., zero rpm), larger air gaps, insensitivity to air-gap deviations, temperature range up to 200 °C.

Gradient sensors
Gradient sensors (e.g., based on Hall differential or differential magnetoresistor sensors) incorporate a permanent magnet on which the pole surface facing the gear is homogenized with a thin ferro-magnetic wafer. Two galvanomagnetic elements (generic term for Hall sensors and magnetoresistors) are located on each of these on the sensor tip, at a distance of roughly one half a tooth interval. Thus one of the elements is always opposite a gap between teeth when the other is opposite a tooth. The sensor measures the difference in the intensity of the field at two contiguous locations on the circumference. The output signal is approximately proportional to the diversion/reduction of field strength as a function of the angle at the circumference; polarity is therefore independent of the air gap.

Gauss-effect magnetoresistors are magnetically-controllable, dual-pole semiconductor resistors (indium-antimonide) with a design similar to that of the Hall sensor. Within the application range their resistance is essentially proportional to the square of the field strength. The differential sensor's two resistors assume the function of voltage dividers in the electrical circuit and compensate largely for the amount of temperature fluctuation. The substantial measurement effect makes it possible to dispense with electronic amplifiers at the measuring point (output signal 0.1 ... 1 V). Magnetoresistors for automotive applications withstand temperatures ≤ 170 °C (brief peaks ≤ 200 °C).

Differential magnetoresistor sensor
1 Magnetoresistor R_1,R_2, 2 Soft-magnetic substrate, 3 Permanent magnet, 4 Gear or toothed wheel, U_0 Supply voltage, $U_A(\varphi)$ Measurement voltage at rotational angle φ.

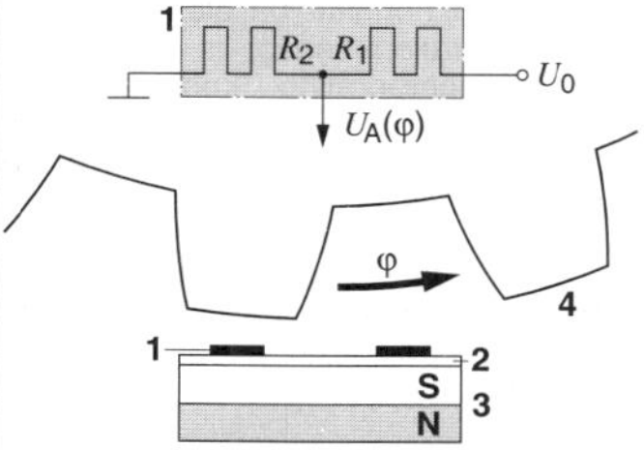

Oscillation gyrometers
Oscillation gyrometers measure absolute rates of rotation, e.g., along the vertical axis of the vehicle (yaw axis) in systems for controlling a vehicle's dynamic behavior (skid stabilization) and for navigation. In principle, these are mechanical gyroscopes; for measurement purposes they employ the Coriolis acceleration attendant upon oscillating motion.

Radar sensors
For the "vehicle speed" measurement variable, research is being conducted with, e.g., simple (low-cost) Doppler radar systems.

Acceleration and vibration sensors

These sensors can be employed to trigger passenger-protection systems (airbag, seatbelt tightener, rollover bar), for knock-control on internal-combustion engines, and to record lateral acceleration and velocity variations in four-wheel drive vehicles equipped with ABS.
Examples of typical acceleration rates in vehicles:

Application	Range
Knock-control	1 ... 10 g
Passenger-protection	
Airbag, belt-tightener	50 g
Rollover bar	4 g
Seatbelt retention	0.4 g
ABS	0.8 ... 1.2 g
Ride control	
Body	1 g
Axle	10 g

Thin-film sensors (DMS)
The acceleration (50 g range) is recorded by a semi-elliptic spring which is provided with a seismic mass for additional inertia. Thin-film strain-gauge resistors (2 active and 2 passive resistors in a bridge circuit) measure the spring's acceleration-induced deflection. The sensor, encapsula-

Thin-film acceleration sensor
1 Contacts, 2 Spring, 3 Insulation with bridge circuit, 4 Inertial mass, a Acceleration.

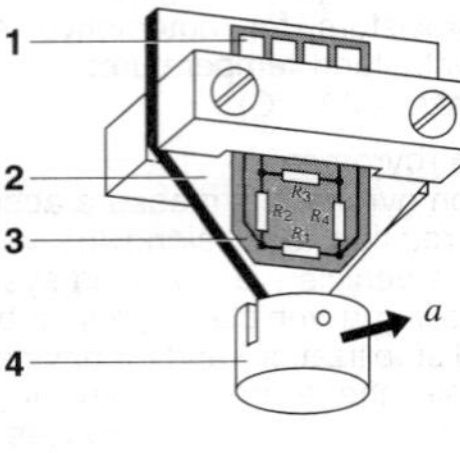

Piezoelectric sensor
a) At rest, b) under acceleration a.
1 Piezo-ceramic bimorphous spring element, U_A measurement voltage.

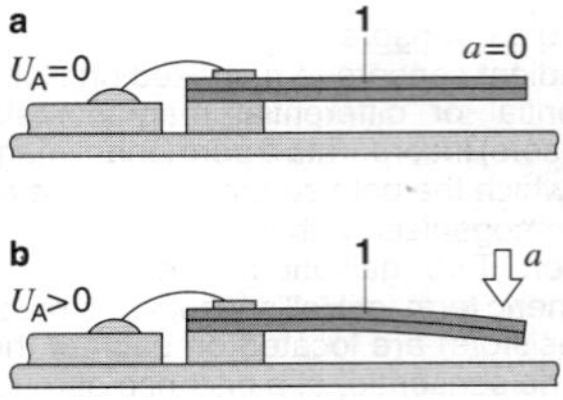

ted within a metallic casing, is installed directly in the control unit, and requires no internal signal pre-amplification or EMC protective circuitry despite its low signal voltage (1 ... 2 mV). A silicone-oil damper inhibits self-oscillation.

Similar sensors record vertical body and axle-acceleration rates (Range: 1 g and 10 g) for the ride-control system's electronic damping regulation. To meet the particularly stringent requirements, this sensor is equipped with electro-dynamic damping: A highly-conductive Cu strip, solidly connected to the sensor's spring-mass system, protrudes into the narrow gap of a high-inductance permanent-magnetic circuit. The motion accompanying deflection of the measurement system is inhibited in direct proportion to velocity by eddy currents in the Cu strip. Although these sensors are inherently static – and thus also suited for measurement of constant acceleration – in the cited application, the circuitry only amplifies AC-voltage signals (1 Hz as lower frequency limit).

Hall-effect acceleration sensor

In ABS-equipped vehicles with four-wheel drive, the wheel-speed sensors are supplemented by a Hall-effect acceleration sensor to monitor slippage. The deflection of the spring-mass system used in this application is recorded with a superimposed permanent magnet and a Hall sensor (Range: 1 g). The sensor is designed for a narrow sensitivity range (several Hz) and is equipped with electro-dynamic damping.

Piezoelectric sensors

Piezoelectric bimorphous spring elements

(Two-layer piezoceramics), for applications such as triggering seatbelt tighteners, airbags and rollover bars (p. 717). Due to their intrinsic inertial mass, these deflect under acceleration to provide a dynamic (not DC voltage) signal which is well-suited for processing (10 Hz is the typical frequency limit).

The sensor element is located in a sealed housing together with the initial signal-amplification stage. It is sometimes encased in gell for physical protection.

The sensor's actuating principle can also be inverted: An additional actuator electrode makes it easy to check the sensor (on-board diagnosis).

Knock sensor (longitudinal element)

This acceleration sensor is for ignition systems incorporating knock control (p. 464). It measures (with low directional selectivity) the structure-borne noise at the engine block (measurement range approx. 10 g at typical vibration frequency of 5 ... 15 kHz). An unencapsulated, annular piezoelectric element measures the inertial forces exerted upon a homogeneous seismic mass.

Capacitive ceramic acceleration sensor
1. Upper/lower electrode, 2. Support arms, 3 Center electrode/seismic mass, 4 Spacer ring. a Acceleration.

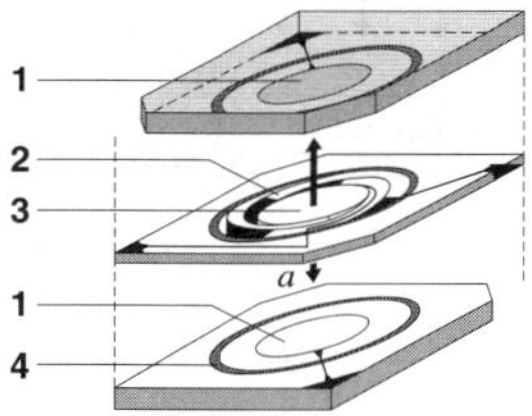

Pressure measurement
a) Direct pressure-sensitive resistor (3), b) With force sensor (1), c) With diaphragm distortion/DMS (2). p Pressure

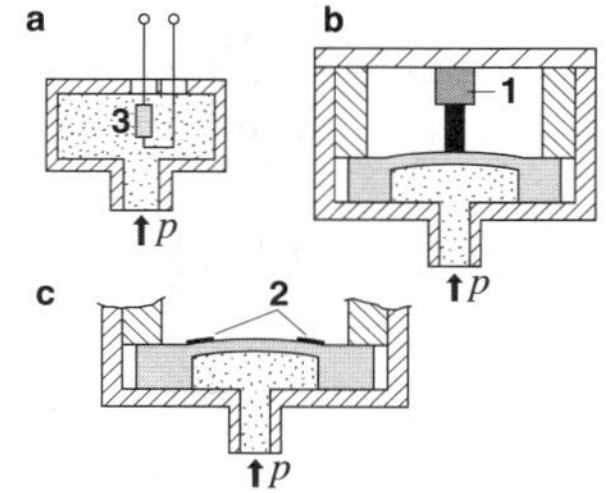

New measurement principles

Capacitive ceramic acceleration sensors

The motion of a ceramic sheet (seismic mass), 200 µm thick with a metal coating on both sides and flexible spiral-shaped support arms, produces a damping air current in extremely small gaps (low sensitivity to temperature). Its deflection under acceleration is monitored at the counterelectrodes by means of thicker ceramic base plates, which act as differential capacitors. Signal-processing electronics are mounted directly on the upper cover plate (possible integration in a single chip in future micromechanical Si sensors of similar design).

Pressure sensors

Pressure measurement is direct, with diaphragm deflection or force sensor.

Sample applications:

– Intake-manifold pressure (1 ... 5 bar),

New applications:

– Brake pressure (10 bar), electro-pneumatic brakes,

– Suspension air pressure (16 bar), for vehicles with pneumatic suspension,

– Tire pressure (5 bar absolute), for monitoring and/or adjusting tire pressure,

– Hydraulic reservoir pressure (approx. 200 bar), ABS, power steering,

– Shock-absorber differential pressure (± 200 bar), ride-control system,

– Refrigerant pressure (35 bar), air-conditioning systems,

– Modulator pressure (35 bar), automatic transmissions,

– Brake pressure in master and wheel cylinders (200 bar), automatic yaw compensation,

– Positive/vacuum pressure in fuel tank (0.5 bar), on-board diagnosis,

– Combustion-chamber pressure (100 bar, dynamic, 600 °C), ignition miss and knock sensing,

– Diesel pump-element pressure (1000 bar, dynamic), electronic diesel injection.

Thick-film pressure sensors

The measurement diaphragm and its strain-gauge resistors, both incorporating thick-film technology, measure absolute pressures of up to approx. 20 bar with a K factor (relative variation in resistance/expansion) of approx. 12 ... 15.

When the respective coefficients of expansion for the ceramic substrate and the ceramic cover film are correct, the

Thick-film pressure sensor
1 Piezoresistive measurement bridge, 2 Thick-film diaphragm, 3 Reference-pressure chamber ("bubble"), 4 Ceramic substrate, p Pressure.

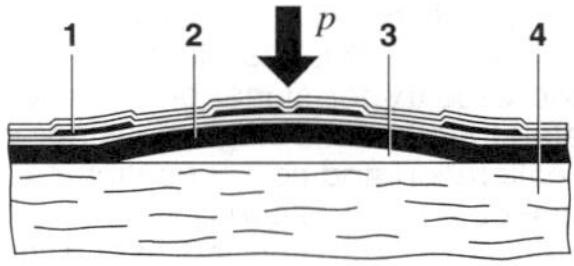

Semiconductor pressure sensor
1 Silicon, 2 Vacuum, 3 Glass (Pyrex), p Pressure, U_0 Supply voltage, U_A Measurement voltage, Strain-gauge resistors R_1 (expanded) and R_2 (deflected) in bridge circuit.

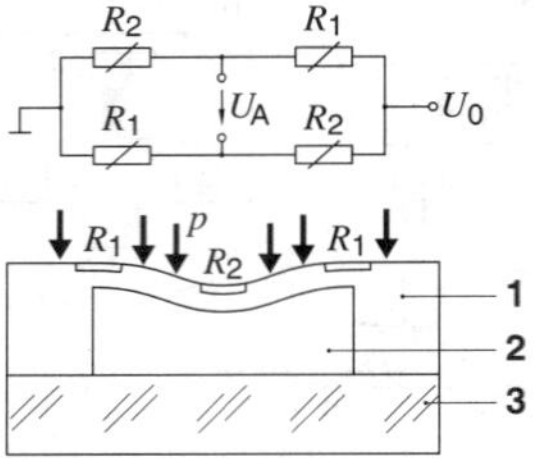

Piezoelectric pressure sensor
1 Metallic coating, 2 Piezoelectric disk, 3 Insulation, 4 Housing, p Pressure, U_A Measurement current.

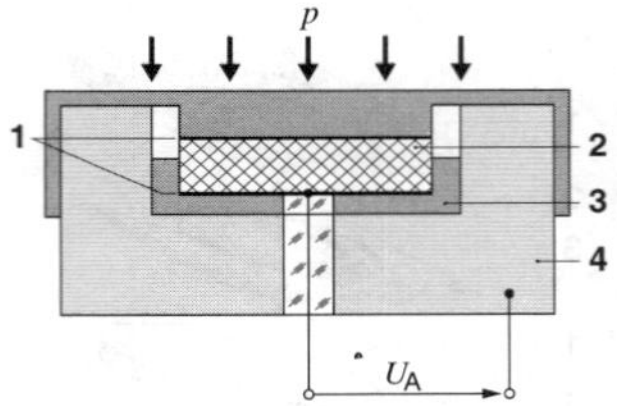

diaphragm will form a dome-shaped bubble upon cooling after being bonded-on during manufacture. The result is a hollow chamber ("bubble") of approx. 100 µm in height, with a diameter of 3 ... 5 mm. After the application of additional thick-film strain-gauge resistors, the unit is hermetically sealed with another ceramic glass coating. The residual gas which remains in the "bubble" compensates for temperature changes in the sensor.

The signal-amplification and correction components are separate from the measurement medium, but are located directly adjacent to the sensor on the same substrate.

The "bubble sensor" principle is not suitable for extremely high or low pressures; versions for these applications should generally incorporate flat ceramic diaphragms.

Semiconductor pressure sensors

The pressure is exerted against a Si diaphragm incorporating pressure-sensitive resistors, manufactured using micromechanics technology. The K factor of the resistors which are diffused into the monocristalline silicon is especially high, typically K = approx. 100. The sensor and the hybrid circuitry for signal processing are located together in a single housing. Sensor calibration and compensation can be continuous or in stages, and are performed either on an ancillary hybrid chip (a second Si chip providing signal amplification and correction: 2-chip concept) or on the sensor chip (1-chip concept). In the future, the values for parameters such as zero point and magnitude correction will be stored in digital form in a PROM.

These sensors will also be available for application in tire-pressure monitoring systems. Measurement will be continuous and contactless (transformer).

New sensor technology

Piezoelectric sensors

Piezoelectric sensors provide dynamic pressure measurement. For example: The pressure in a combustion chamber can be transmitted as a force through a pressure diaphragm mounted flush with the combustion chamber. The force travels through a plunger and on to a "cooler zone" (≤ 150 °C), where it acts upon a pellet which produces a voltage proportional to the pressure; this pellet is constructed of piezoceramic material and is usually cylindrical in shape. Deviations which may occur due to hysteresis and temperature fluctuation are relatively insignificant in applications with limited precision requirements (recording ignition miss, knocking, pressure maxima). Piezoresistive thick-film pressure sensors are also suitable for this type of dynamic measurement. With these, the forces acting upon the diaphragm are transferred to the pressure-sensitive (conductive plastic or Cermet) resistors at right angles to their surfaces.

Magnetoelastic bearing-pin sensors
1 Primary winding (feed), 2 Secondary winding (measurement signal), 3 Primary pole surface, 4 Secondary pole surface.

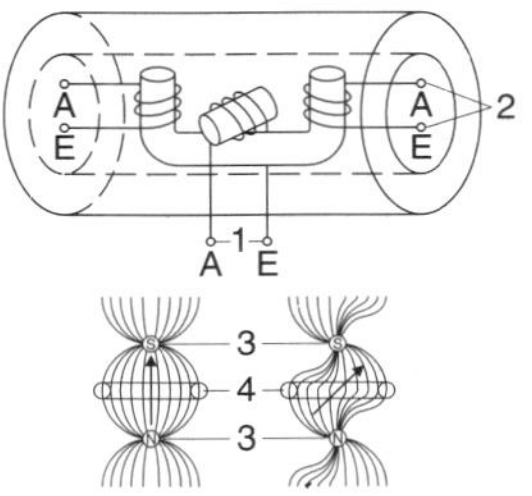

Force and moment sensors

Application:
Bearing-pin sensors on tractors.

Magnetoelastic bearing-pin sensors
The bearing-pin sensors are based on the magnetoelastic pinciple. The hollow coupling pin contains a magnetic field coil. Positioned at a 90° angle to this is a measuring coil to which no magnetic flux is applied when no forces are present. However, when the ferromagnetic material in the pin becomes anisotropic under force, a flux which is proportional to the force permeates the measuring coil, where it induces electrical voltage. The electronics for supply and amplification are also located inside the pin.

New sensor technology
– Eddy-current principle: Eddy-current torsional-force sensor, radial torsion-measurement spring, radial and axial slotted-disk and coil configuration.
– Measurement with strain-gauge resistors (DMS principle): Pressed-in and welded-in sensors.
– Force-measurement ring using thick-film technology: Force measurement using pressure-sensitive resistors with orthogonal loading.
– Hydrostatic pressure measurement in plunger-loaded hydrostatic cylinders, generally charged with rubber or gum elastic (no danger of leakage).
– Microbending effect: Fiber-optic pressure tension sensor.

New applications:
– Measuring coupling forces between the tractor and the trailer on commercial vehicles to provide controlled braking.
– Measuring damping forces for electronic ride-control systems.
– Measuring axle load for electronically-controlled braking-force distribution on commercial vehicles.
– Measurement of pedal force on electronically-controlled brake systems.
– Contactless measurement of drive and braking forces.
– Contactless measurement of steering and power-steering forces.
– Finger-protection for electrically-operated window lifts and sunroofs.

Flow meters

Flow quantities in automotive applications:
– Amount of fuel actually consumed by the engine, measured according to the difference between the supply and return quantities. On spark-ignition engines featuring electronically-controlled fuel-metering systems which monitor air-flow or air quantity, this figure is already available in the form of a calculated metering value; thus measurement for control of the combustion process would be redundant. However, fuel-flow measurement is required for determination and display of fuel consumption on engines which are not equipped with electronic control systems.
– Air flow in the engine intake manifold:
The mass relationships are the salient factors in the chemical process of combustion, thus the actual objective is to measure the mass flow of the intake or charge air, although procedures employing volume and dynamic pressure are also applied. The maximum air-mass flow to be monitored lies within a range of 400 ... 1000 kg/h, depending upon engine output. As a result of the modest idle requirements of modern engines, the ratio between minimum and maximum air flow is 1:90 ... 1:100.

Flow measurement
A medium with uniform density ρ flows through a tube with the constant diameter A at the velocity v which is essentially uniform at all points of the tube's diameter ("turbulent" flow). The resulting conditions are defined as:

– Volume flow rate $Q_V = v \cdot A$ (e.g., in m^3/h)
– Mass flow rate $Q_M = \rho \cdot v \cdot A$ (e.g., in kg/h).
– If a measurement flap is then installed in the duct, forming a restriction, this will result in a pressure differential as defined in Bernoulli's Equation. This differential is an intermediate quantity between the flow rate for mass and that for volume:
$\Delta p = \text{const} \cdot \sqrt{p} \cdot v = \text{const} \cdot \sqrt{Q_V \cdot Q_M}$

Fixed-position flaps can only cover measurement variables within a range of 1 : 10; variable flaps are able to monitor variations through a substantially greater ratio range.

Volume flow sensors
According to the principle of the Karman vortex path, whirls and eddies separate from the air stream behind an obstruction. Their periodicity – as measured (e.g., monitoring of pressure, temperature or acoustic waves) at their periphery (tube wall) provides an eddy frequency in the form of a signal ratio: $f = 1 / T = \text{const} \cdot Q_V$. Disadvantage: Pulsation in the flow can result in measuring errors.

The ultrasonic flow-measurement procedure can be employed to monitor the transit time t of an acoustic wave as it travels through the medium to be measured (e.g., air) at angle α (see Fig. at top right). One measurement is taken upstream and one downstream using the same measurement path l. The resulting transit-time differential is essentially proportional to the volume flow rate.

Pitot-tube air-flow sensors
Pivoting, variable-position pressure flaps leave a variable section of the flow diameter unobstructed, with the size of the free diameter being dependent upon the flow rate. A potentiometer monitors the characteristic flap position for the respective flow rate. The physical and electrical design of the air-flow sensor, e.g., for the L-Jetronic (p. 442), are such as to ensure a logarithmic relationship between flow rate and output signal (at low flow rates the incremental voltage variations are substantially greater than at higher flow rates). Other types of automotive air-flow sensors are designed to provide a linear characteristic (KE-Jetronic). Measuring errors can occur

Ultrasonic air-flow measurement
1,2 Transmitter/Receiver 1 and 2, l Measurement section, S Transmit command, t Transit period, Q_V Volume flow, α Angle.

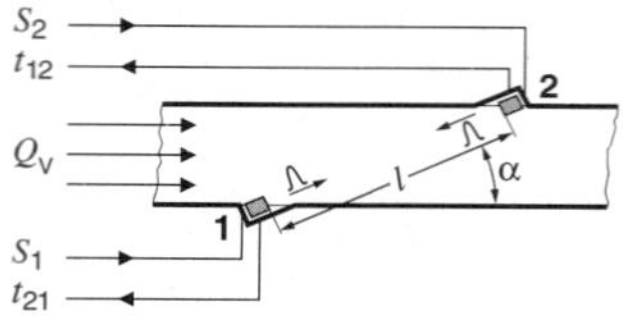

Pitot-tube air-flow sensor
1 Pressure flap, 2 Compensation flap, 3 Compression volume, Q Flow.

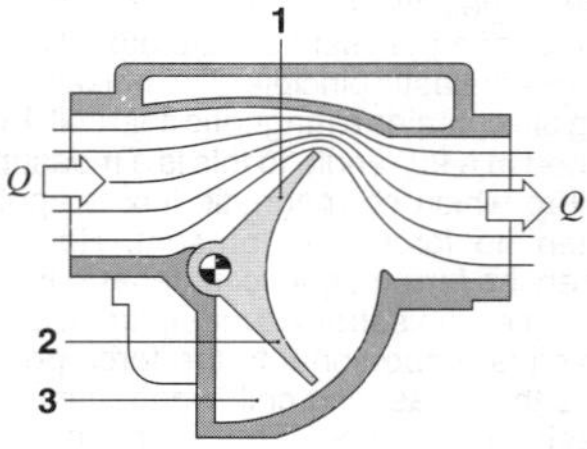

Hot-wire air-mass flow sensor
Q_M Mass flow, U_m Measurement voltage, R_H Hot-wire resistor, R_K Temperature-compensator resistor, R_M Precision resistor, R_1 Balancing resistor.

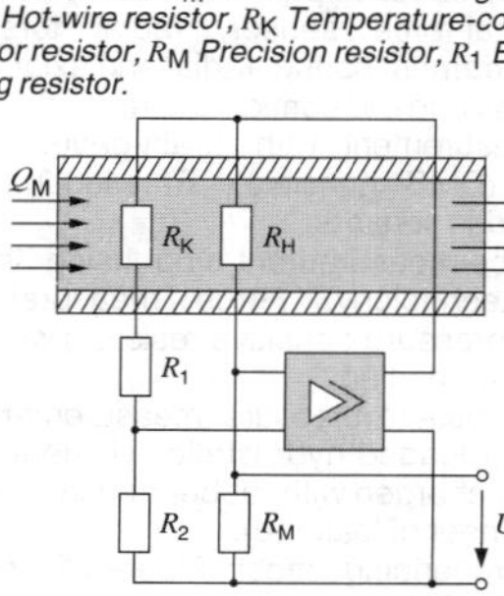

Lambda Sensor
1 Sensor ceramic, 2 Electrodes, 3 Contact, 4 Housing contacts, 5 Exhaust pipe, 6 Protective ceramic coating (porous), U_S *Sensor voltage.*

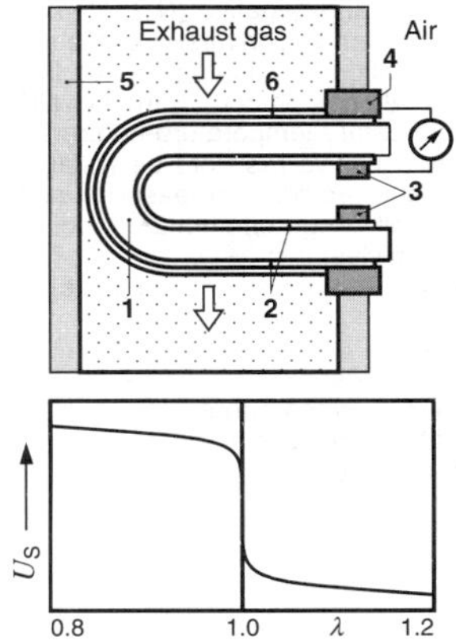

in cases where the flap's mechanical inertia prevents it from keeping pace with a rapidly pulsating air current (full-load condition at high engine speeds).

Air-mass flow sensors
Air-mass flow sensors (meters) operate according to the hot-wire or hot-film principle and include no mechanically-actuated components. The closed-loop control circuit in the sensor's housing maintains a fine platinum wire or thick-film resistor at a constant temperature exceeding that of the ambient air. The current required for heating provides an extremely precise – although extremely non-linear – indication of the air-mass throughput. The associated control unit generally converts the signals into linear form, as well as assuming other signal-processing duties. Due to its closed-loop design, this type of air-flow sensor can keep pace with changes in flow rate in the millisecond range.

The platinum wire in the hot-wire air-mass flow sensor functions both as the heating element and as the heating element's temperature sensor.

The hot-film air-mass flow sensor combines all measuring elements and the control electronics on a single substrate. In current versions, the heating resistor is located on the back of the base wafer, with the corresponding temperature sensor on the front. This results in somewhat more pronounced time-delay than that associated with the hot-wire sensor. The temperature-compensation sensor (R_k) and the heating element are thermally decoupled by means of a saw-cut in the ceramic substrate.

It is likely that micromechanical air-mass sensors operating on the thermal principle will see use in automotive applications.

Oxygen-concentration sensor (Lambda sensor)

The fuel-metering system employs the residual-oxygen content of the exhaust gas for exact regulation of the combustible air-fuel mixture, which is then adjusted to precisely the ratio required to achieve the excess-air factor λ (Lambda) = 1 (stoichiometric ratio, p. 428). It employs a solid-state electrolyte made of ZrO ceramic material. At high temperatures, this electrolyte displays electrical conductivity which generates a characteristic galvanic voltage at the sensor connections; this varies according to the oxygen content of the exhaust gas relative to the surrounding atmosphere. The maximum variation occurs at $\lambda = 1$.

Electrically-heated sensors are especially well-suited for measurements in the lean range, and already begin operating in the warm-up phase. Both smaller, flat "wafer sensors" and sensors with curves extending far into the lean range (for Diesel engines) will appear in the future.

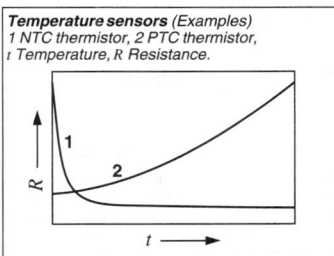

Temperature sensors *(Examples)*
1 NTC thermistor, 2 PTC thermistor, t *Temperature,* R *Resistance.*

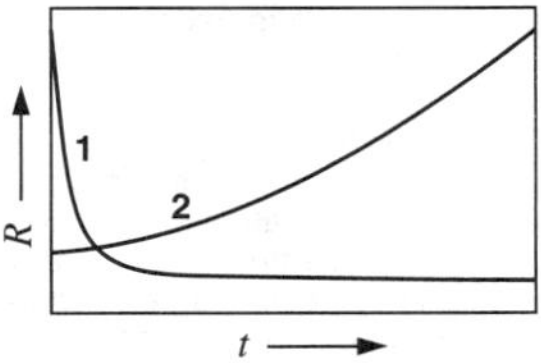

Temperature sensors

Temperature measurements in vehicles are conducted almost entirely using the sensitivity to temperature variation which characterizes electrical resistors with positive (PTC) and negative (NTC) temperature coefficients. Conversion of the resistance variation into analog voltage is performed almost entirely with the aid of supplementary temperature-neutral or inversely-sensitive resistors as voltage dividers (also providing increased linearity).

The following temperatures occur in motor vehicles:

Location	Range °C
Intake air	–40 ... 170
Outside atmosphere	–40 ... 60
Passenger compartment	–20 ... 80
Ventilation & heating air	–20 ... 60
Evaporator (AC)	–10 ... 50
Engine coolant	–40 ... 130
Engine oil	–40 ... 170
Battery	–40 ... 100
Fuel	–40 ... 120
Tire pressure	–40 ... 120
Exhaust gas	100 ... 1000
Brake calipers	–40 ... 2000

At many locations, temperature is also monitored as a secondary variable for providing compensation should it cause a fault to occur, or act as an undesirable influencing factor.

Sintered-ceramic resistors (NTC)

Sintered-ceramic resistors (heat conductors, thermistors) made of heavy-metal oxides and oxidized mixed crystals (sintered in pearl or plate-form) are included among the semiconducting materials which display an inverted exponential response curve. The high sensitivity to temperature means that applications are restricted to a "window" of approx. 200 K; however, the exact range can be selected from an overall range extending from – 40 °C to approx. 850 °C.

Thin-film metallic resistors (PTC)

Thin-film metallic resistors, integrated upon a single substrate wafer together with two supplementary, temperature-neutral balancing resistors, are characterized by extreme precision, as they can be manufactured and then "trimmed" with lasers to maintain exact response-curve tolerances over long periods of time.

Metallic-film resistor

1 Auxiliary contact, 2 Bridge, R_{Ni} Nickel-plated resistor, $R(t)$ Resistance relative to temperature t, R_1,R_2 Temperature-dependent resistors.

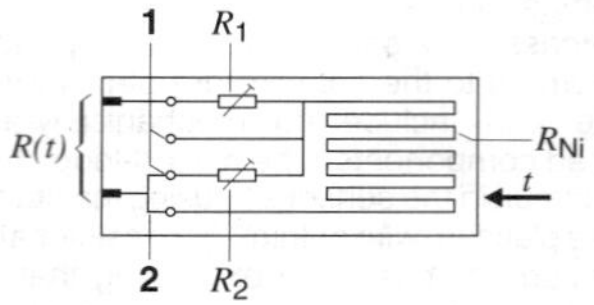

The use of layer technology makes it possible to adapt the base material (ceramic, glass, plastic) and the upper layers (plastic molding or paint, sealed foil, glass and ceramic coatings) to the respective application, and thus provide protection against the measuring-medium. Metallic resistors, manufactured using thick-film technology, cover a substantially larger area, as the achievable conductor-track length/width is approximately 10 times greater.

Although metallic layers are less sensitive to temperature change than oxide-ceramic semiconductor resistors, they do display better linearity and consistency:

Sensor-material	Temperature-coefficient TC	Measurement range
Ni	$5.1 \cdot 10^{-3}$/K	– 60 ... 320 °C
Cu	$4.1 \cdot 10^{-3}$/K	– 50 ... 200 °C
Pt	$3.5 \cdot 10^{-3}$/K	–220 ... 850 °C

At TC = $[R(100\ °C) - R(0\ °C)] / [R(0\ °C) \cdot 100\ K]$

Thick-film resistors (PTC/NTC)

Thick-film pastes with both high specific resistance (low surface-area requirement) and positive and negative temperature coefficients are generally employed as temperature sensors for compensation purposes. They have non-linear response characteristics (without, however, the extreme variations of the massive NTC resistor) and can be laser-trimmed. The measurement effect can be enhanced by using NTC and PTC materials to form voltage-divider circuits.

Si semiconductor resistor (Spreading-resistance principle)
1 Contacts, 2 Passivation (nitride, oxide), 3 Si substrate, 4 Unconnected counter-electrode, R(t) Temperature-dependent resistors.

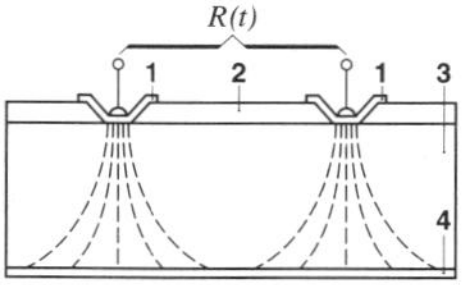

Monocrystalline Si-semiconductor resistors (PTC)

When monocrystalline semiconductor materials such as Si are used to manufacture the temperature sensor, it is possible to integrate additional active and passive circuitry on the sensor chip (initial signal processing can be performed directly at the measuring point).

Due to the closer tolerancing which is possible, these are manufactured according to the spreading-resistance principle. The current flows through the measuring resistor and through a surface-point contact before arriving at the Si bulk material. It then proceeds, widely distributed, to a counterelectrode covering the base of the sensor chip. The high current density behind the contact point (high precision achieved through photolithographic manufacture), together with the extremely high reproducibility of the material constants, is basically the essential factor determining the resistance value of the sensor.

The sensitivity is virtually twice that of a Pt resistor (TC = $7.73 \cdot 10^{-3}$/K). However, the temperature-response curve is less linear than that of a metallic sensor.

Sensors for other applications

Contamination sensors

The sensor measures the level of contamination on the headlamp lens. This is the prerequisite for automatic lens cleaning.

The sensor's photoelectric reflected-light barrier consists of a light source (LED) and a light receiver (phototransistor). It is positioned on the inside of the lens, within the cleansed area, but not directly in the light beam's path. When the lens is clean, or covered with rain droplets, the infrared measurement beam emitted by the unit passes through the lens without being obstructed. Only a minuscule part is reflected back to the light receiver. However, if it encounters dirt particles on the outside surface of the lens, then it is reflected back to the receiver in an intensity which is directly proportional to the degree of contamination. If the headlamps are switched on, the headlamp washer unit will be activated automatically when a specific contamination level is reached or exceeded.

Contamination sensor
1 Lens, 2 Dirt particles, 3 Sensor element, 4 Transmitter, 5 Receiver.

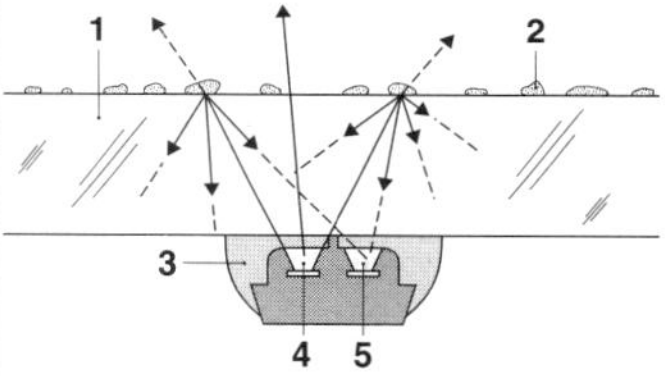

Rain sensors

The rain sensor recognizes rain droplets on the windshield, making it possible to trigger the windshield wipers automatically.

The sensor consists of an optical transmission and reception path (similar to the contamination sensor). However, here the light is directed into the windshield at an angle and the dry outer surface reflects (total reflection) it back to the receiver, which is also mounted at an angle. When water droplets are present on the outer surface, a substantial amount of the light is refracted outward, thus weakening the received signal. Above a certain signal level, the windshield wiper is switched on automatically. Contamination also reduces the intensity of the received signal.

Future measurement applications:

- Earth-field sensor (navigation),
- Moisture sensor (to monitor pneumatic brake systems, black or road-ice warning, climate in passenger compartment),
- CO sensor (climate in passenger compartment),
- Soot sensor (to monitor diesel exhaust),
- Fuel-Flex sensor (to recognize fuel types).

Actuators (final-controlling elements)

Quantities and units

Quantity		Unit
A	Pole face/Piston-face area	mm^2
B	Magnetic induction	T
F	Force	N
I	Electric current	A
l	Length of conductor in field	mm
M	Torque	N·m
p	Pressure	Pa
Q	Volume flow	l/min
Q_{Heat}	Heat flow	W
s	Distance, piston travel	mm
V	Volume	mm^3
V_{th}	Displaced volume per rotation	mm^3
α	Angle between current flow direction and magnetic lines of force	°
δ	Gap length	mm
μ_0	Permeability constant	
φ	Rotation angle	°

Final-controlling elements form the junction between the electronic signal processor (data processing) and the actual process (mechanics). They convert the low-power signals conveying the positioning information into operating signals of an energy level adequate for process control. Signal converters are combined with amplifier elements to exploit the physical transformation principles governing the interrelationships between various forms of energy (electrical – mechanical – fluid – thermal). The final-controlling elements are operated either directly or as components in a closed-loop control system. The qualitative criteria for the evaluation of signal transformation are efficiency, linearity and dynamic response (minimum delay).

Electromechanical actuators

This type of energy conversion represents one option for classifying electromechanical actuators. The energy emanating from the source is transformed into magnetic or electrical field energy, or converted to thermal energy (see illustration). The particular force-generation principle is determined by the form of energy, and bases upon either field forces or certain specific material characteristics. Magnetostrictive materials make it possible to design actuators for application in the micropositioning range; piezoelectric actuators also belong to this category. Thermal actuators depend exclusively upon the exploitation of characteristics of specific materials.

Automotive actuators are generally electro-magnetic mechanical actuators, from which are derived the electric actuator motors, and translational and rotational magnetic actuators. An exception is the pyrotechnical airbag inflation system (p. 718). The magnetic actuators can themselves be the final-controlling element, or they can serve as the controlling element for a force-amplification device (e.g., mechanical-hydraulic).

Force generation in the magnetic field

The distinction between the electrodynamic and the electromagnetic actuation principles stems from the manner in which forces are generated in the magnetic field. Common to both principles is the magnetic circuit with soft-magnetic material and the coil for excitation of the magnetic field. A major difference lies in the force which can be extracted from the unit under technically-feasible conditions. Under identical conditions, the force produced through application of the electromagnetic principle is greater by a factor of 40. The electrical time constant for this type of actuator is comparable to the mechanical time constants. Both force-generation principles

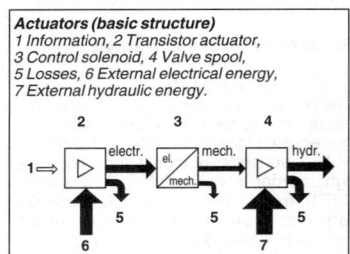

Actuators (basic structure)
1 Information, 2 Transistor actuator, 3 Control solenoid, 4 Valve spool, 5 Losses, 6 External electrical energy, 7 External hydraulic energy.

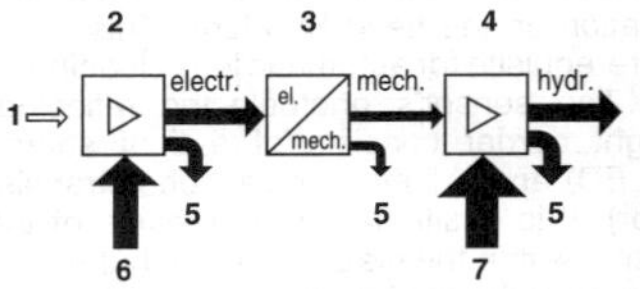

Electromechanical actuators (system)

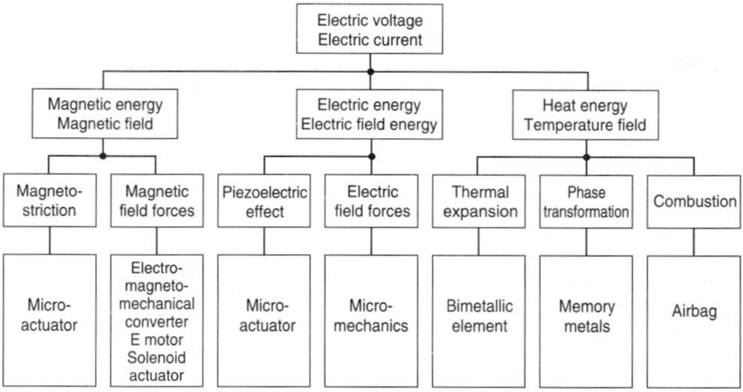

are applied in linear and rotary drive mechanisms.

The electrodynamic principle bases upon the force exerted on charges in motion or on conductors under current within the magnetic field (Lorentz force). An excitation coil or a permanent magnet generates a constant magnetic field. The electrical energy which is to be converted is applied to the moving armature coil (plunger or immersion coil). A high degree of actuator precision is achieved by designing the armature coil with low mass and low inductivity. The two accumulator elements (one on the fixed and one on the moving component) produce two active force directions via current-direction reversal in the armature and excitation coils. The permanent magnets (ferrite, SmCo, etc.), which are usually employed to generate the excitation field, display permeability approximating that of empty space (μ_0). Thus the secondary field produced by the armature's current flows in an open magnetic circuit, diminishing the effects of saturation. Approximately speaking, the force (torque) exerted by an electrodynamic actuator over its operating range is proportional to current and insensitive to travel.

The electromagnetic principle exploits the mutual attraction displayed by soft ferrous materials in a magnetic field. The electromagnetic actuator is equipped with only one coil, which generates both field energy and the energy to be transformed. In accordance with the operating principles, the excitation coil is equipped with

Electrodynamic and electromagnetic transformers

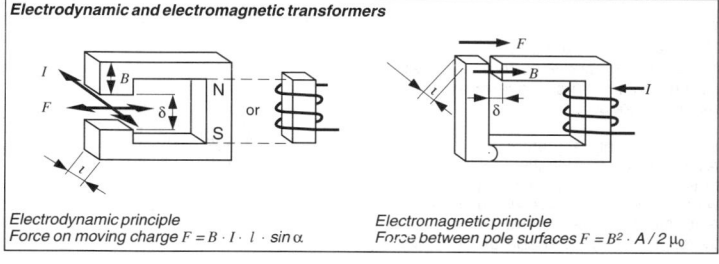

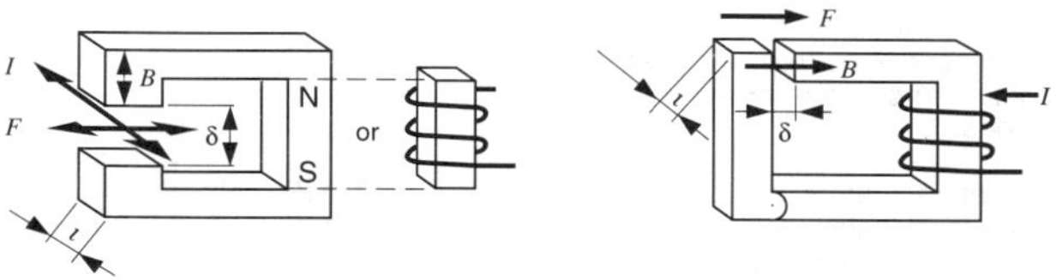

Electrodynamic principle
Force on moving charge $F = B \cdot I \cdot l \cdot \sin\alpha$

Electromagnetic principle
Force between pole surfaces $F = B^2 \cdot A / 2\,\mu_0$

an iron core to provide higher inductance. However, as the force is proportional to the square of the density of the magnetic flux, the unit is operative in but a single direction. The electromagnetic actuator thus requires a return element (such as a mechanical spring or a magnetic return mechanism).

Dynamic response

The dynamic or switching response of an electromechanical actuator is described by the differential equation for the electrical circuit and Maxwell's equations for dynamics, which define the forces according to current and position.

The most basic electrical circuit consists of an inductor with an ohmic resistor. One means of enhancing the dynamics is over-excitation at the instant of activation, while the switching-off process can be accelerated with a Z-diode. In any case, enhancement of the electrical circuit's dynamic response is always achieved at the price of additional expenditure and increased losses in the actuator's triggering electronics.

Field diffusion is a delay effect which is difficult to influence in actuators with high dynamic response. Rapid switching operations are accompanied by high-frequency field fluctuations in the soft-magnetic material in the actuator's magnetic circuit. These fluctuations, in turn, induce eddy currents, which counteract their cause (build-up and decay of the magnetic field). The resultant delay in the build-up or reduction of forces can only be diminished through the selection of appropriate materials featuring low electrical conductivity and permeability.

Design

The design is essentially determined by the operating conditions (e.g., installation space, required force-travel curve and dynamic response).

Electromagnetic actuators

A typical form for translational electromagnetic actuators is the switching solenoid with a force/travel curve which drops off as a function of the square of positioning travel. The precise shape of the curve is

Switching solenoid
1 Armature, 2 Coil, 3 Magnetic yoke

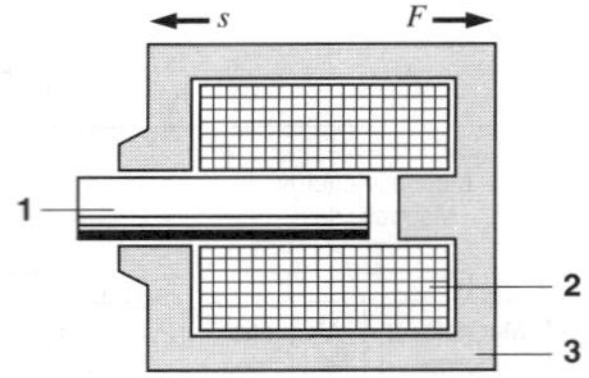

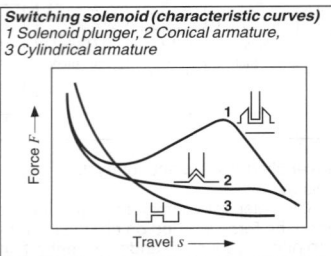

Switching solenoid (characteristic curves)
1 Solenoid plunger, 2 Conical armature, 3 Cylindrical armature

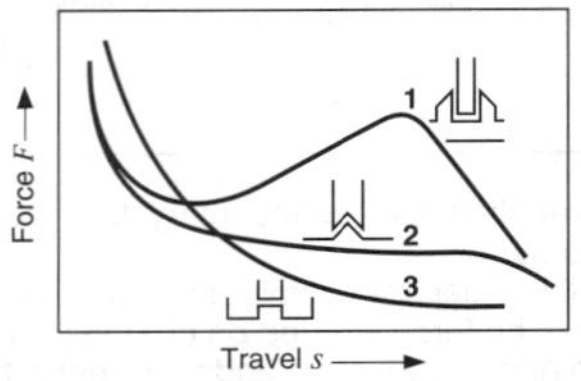

Electromagnetic single-winding rotary actuator
1 Winding, 2 Stator, 3 Armature

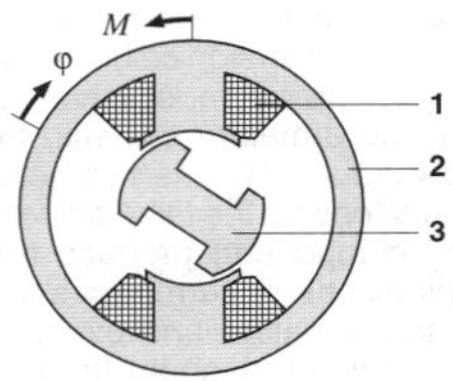

Torque motor
1 Magnets, 2 Armature, 3 Control windings

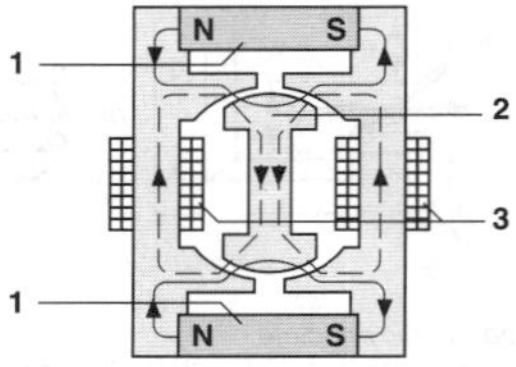

determined by the type of working gap (e.g., conical or immersion armature).

Rotational electromagnetic actuators are characterized by a defined pole arrangement in stator and rotor. If current flows in one of the coils, the rotor and stator poles respond with mutual attraction, and in doing so generate a torque.

The single-winding rotary actuator incorporates a pair of poles in each of the two main sections, as well as a coil in the stator. Its maximum positioning range is approx. 45°.

The torque motor is a bidirectional electromagnetic rotary actuator featuring a stable working point and without counterforces. The rotor is maintained in a stable position by the excitation field of the permanent magnet in the stator. The magnetic field generated by one or two stator windings produces torque and provides unilateral compensation for the excitation field. This type of layout is suitable for applications in which substantial forces over small angles are required. The relationship between the applied current and the torque motor's force is roughly linear. The torque-motor principle is also employed in translational actuators.

Electrodynamic actuators

The pot magnet (immersion-coil actuator) operates when a cylindrical immersion coil (armature winding) is set in motion in a working gap. The positioning range is limited by the axial length of the armature winding and by the gap.

The short-stroke linear motor is an actuator with a virtually round disk coil.

A distinction is made between rotational actuators which incorporate a single winding and those employing a dual winding. Both types include a permanent magnet within the rotor and one or two stator windings. The rotor magnet is magnetized at both ends to produce magnetic flux in the rotary magnet's working gap, which combines with the armature current to produce a torque. In the position illustrated, the positioning range is less than ±45°. In addition, the positioning range of the single-winding rotary actuator is dependent upon both the torque requirement and the angle range in which the necessary flux density can be provided.

Electromagnetic rotary actuator
(characteristic curves)
1 Single-winding rotary actuator,
2 Torque motor

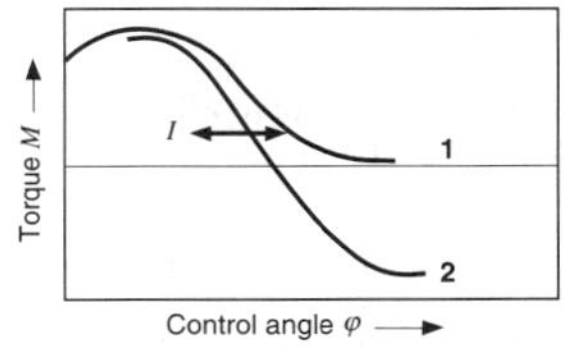

Electrodynamic immersion-coil actuator
1 Immersion coil, 2 Permanent magnet,
3 Magnetic yoke

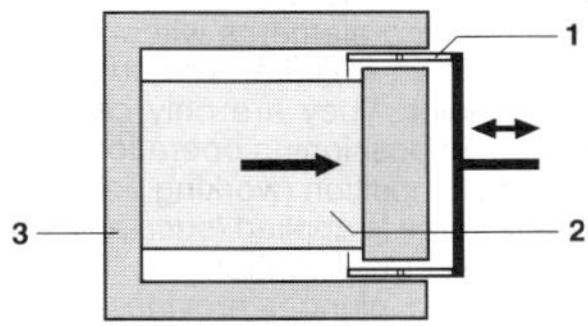

Electrodynamic short-stroke linear motor
1. Coil, 2 Permanent magnet, 3 Magnetic yoke

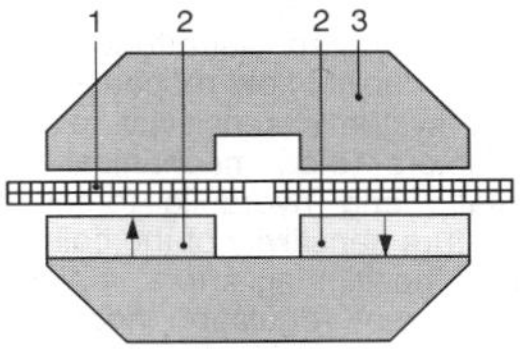

Electrodynamic rotary actuator
a) Single-winding rotary actuator,
b) Dual-winding rotary actuator
1 Coil 1, 2 Coil 2, 3 Stator,
4 Permanent magnet, 5 Shaft.

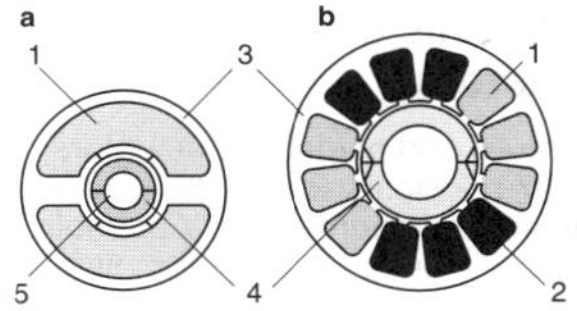

The dual-winding rotary actuator can be described as a combination of two single-winding rotary actuators, being staggered at 90° at the periphery and producing opposite torque flows. A stable working point is achieved at the zero transition point on the resulting torque curve without auxiliary counteracting forces.

Applications

Electromechanical actuators are direct-action control elements; they convert the energy of the electrical control signal into a mechanical positioning factor/work with no intermediate ratio-conversion mechanism. Typical applications include positioning of flaps, sliders and valves. The majority of the described actuators are final controlling elements without internal return mechanisms, i.e., without a stable working point. They are only capable of carrying out positioning operations from a stable initial position (working point) when a counterforce is applied (such as a return spring or electrical control).

A solenoid plunger provides a stable static bias point when its force-travel curve is synchronized with the characteristic response of a return spring. Variations in the current flow through the winding shift the working point; basic positioning is achieved by regulating the current flow. Points requiring special attention are the non-linear current/flow response and the actuator system's sensitivity to interference factors (e.g., mechanical friction, pneumatic and hydraulic forces). The temperature sensitivity of the coil resistor results in positioning errors, making corrective current regulation necessary. A high-precision positioning system with good dynamic response must incorporate a position sensor and a controller.

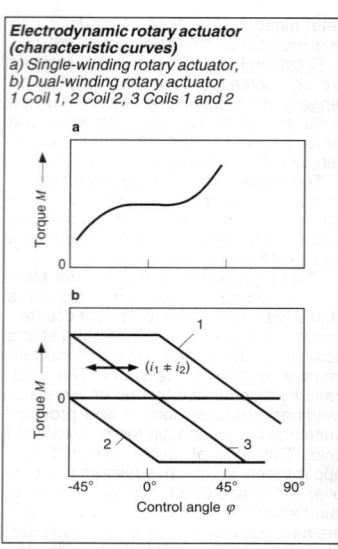

Electrodynamic rotary actuator (characteristic curves)

a) Single-winding rotary actuator,
b) Dual-winding rotary actuator
1 Coil 1, 2 Coil 2, 3 Coils 1 and 2

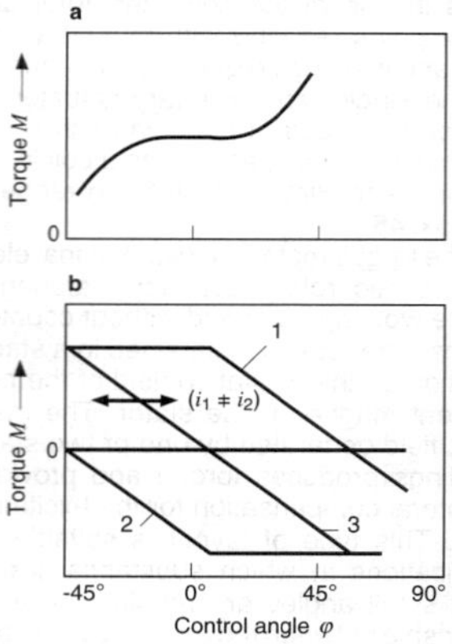

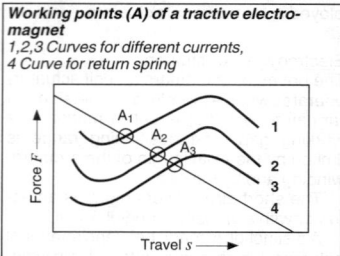

Working points (A) of a tractive electromagnet

1,2,3 Curves for different currents,
4 Curve for return spring

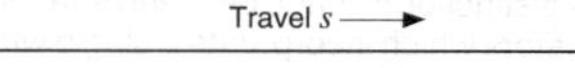

Fluid-mechanical actuators (hydraulic and pneumatic actuators)

Hydraulic and pneumatic actuators utilize similar principles for the conversion and regulation of energy (see "Automotive hydraulic systems" and "Automotive pneumatic systems"). The table shows the differences in characteristics and applications.

In most applications, fluid-mechanical actuator drives assume the form of hydrostatic energy transformers. These operate according to the displacement principle, converting the pressure energy of the fluid medium into mechanical work and vice versa.

In contrast, hydrodynamic transformers operate by converting flow energy (kinetic energy of the moving fluid) into mechanical work (Example: hydrodynamic coup-

	Hydraulic actuator	Pneumatic actuator
Medium	– Fluid, usually hydraulic oil – Supply from tank, oil pan – Virtually incompressible – Self-lubricating – Viscosity extremely temperature-sensitive	– Gas, usually air – Supply from surrounding air – Compressible – Auxiliary lubrication required – Viscosity fluctuations virtually irrelevant
Pressure range	– to approx. 30 MPa	– to approx. 1 MPa (more than approx. 0.05 MPa for vacuum actuators)
Line connections	– Supply and return lines (leakage line optional)	– Pressure connection only Return direct to environment
Applications	– Positioning applications with high load rigidity, demanding requirements for synchronization and positioning precision within closed-loop control system	– Actuators with limited force requirements, positioning via mechanical contact, operation in open control loop

ling, p. 539).

Losses in energy conversion stem from leakage and friction. Fluid-thermal losses are caused by flow resistance, in which throttle action transforms the fluid energy into heat.

A portion of this heat is dissipated into the environment, and some of it is absorbed and carried away by the fluid medium.

$$Q_{Heat} = Q_1 \cdot p_1 - Q_2 \cdot p_2$$

With incompressible fluids

$$Q_{Heat} = Q \cdot (p_1 - p_2)$$

Turbulence forms where the flow passes through restrictions (such as throttles). The medium's flow rate is then largely independent of viscosity. On the other hand, viscosity does play a role with laminar flow in narrow pipes and apertures (see "Automotive hydraulic systems").

Fluid-mechanical amplifiers control the transition of energy between fluid and mechanical states. The energy required to control the regulating mechanism is only a small proportion of the energy flow intended for ultimate control.

Switching valves open and close the flow orifice governing the flow to and from a fluid-mechanical energy converter.

Provided that the control-element opens sufficiently, the throttling losses remain negligible. Pulse-width-modulated opening and closing can be applied to achieve quasi-continuous control of the fluid-mechanical conversion process with virtually no losses. In actual practice, however, pressure fluctuations and the mechnical contact between valve components produce undesirable noise and vibration.

Flow resistance

The flow of energy is throttled by flow resistors featuring either graduated or continuosly-variable control. The hydraulic energy is transformed into heat according to the degree of throttling.

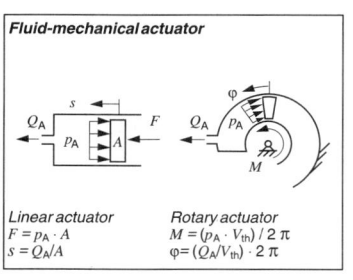

Fluid-mechanical actuator

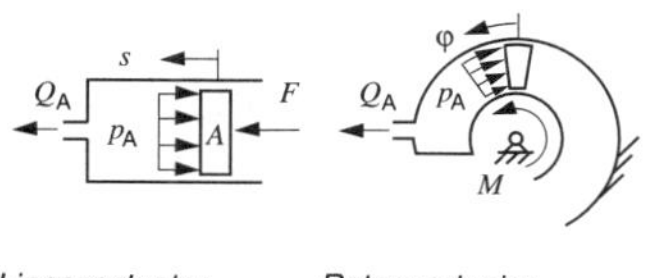

Linear actuator
$F = p_A \cdot A$
$s = Q_A / A$

Rotary actuator
$M = (p_A \cdot V_{th}) / 2\pi$
$\varphi = (Q_A / V_{th}) \cdot 2\pi$

Energy regulation with 2/2 directional-control valves

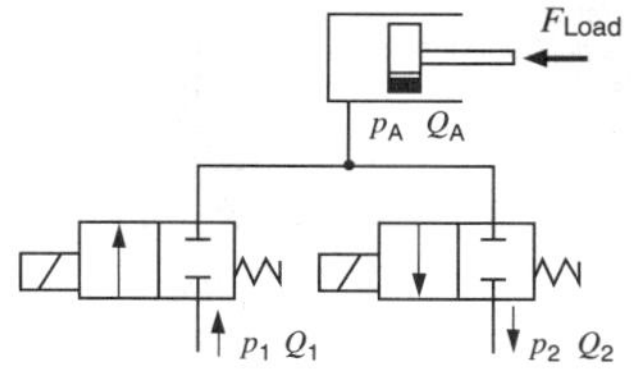

Variable flow resistors have a variety of forms, including mechanically-adjustable flow restrictors, variable flow-orifice geometry or variation of the viscosity of the fluid in the aperture, achieved through local heating or exploitation of electro-rheological effects.

Hydraulic half-bridges

Continuously-variable fluid resistors are generally combined to form a pressure-divider circuit in an arrangement analogous to that found in electrical half-bridge circuits. At least one variable resistor is employed to produce three different circuit variations.

Assuming that the variable resistors can be adjusted between 0 and ∞, p_A can be assigned any value between p_1 and p_2. If the geometry of the variable resistors remains constant, then variant a will provide flow volume and pressure amplification twice as great as those derived from b and c. The operating direction of c is the inverse of that of b.

Hydraulic half bridge
a) Two opposed variable resistors,
b) Variable input resistor,
c) Variable output resistor

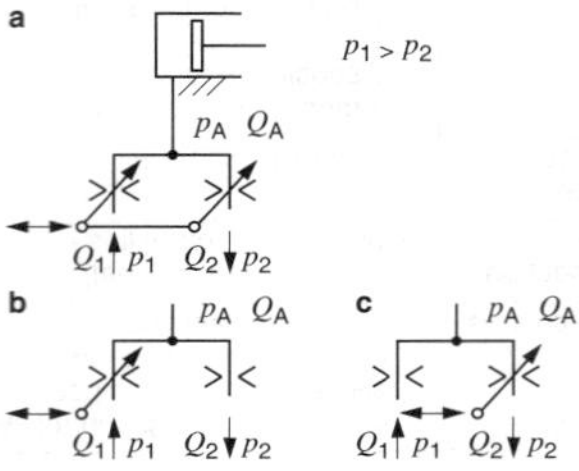

Flapper-nozzle system

This system, employed frequently for mechanical-fluid converters, features two type-c half-bridges combined to form a full bridge. Opposed outlet orifices represent the variable resistors; their resistance value increases as a function of the flapper's proximity.

The pressure differential between the central taps of the two half bridges is usually employed as a control system for a downstream valve.

Nozzle and flapper system

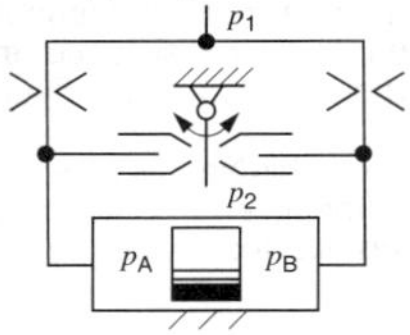

Jet diversion systems

A nozzle directs a jet stream of fluid against a flapper plate, whereupon its kinetic impulses are transformed into static pressure. A bell-shaped pressure pattern is formed at the flapper plate with maximum pressure occurring at the center of the stream's contact area. It is possible to vary the position of the jet tube to shift the pressure contact area, thus changing the pressure differential between the two control orifices in the flapper plate. Jet dividers and jet diverters use the same basic principle.

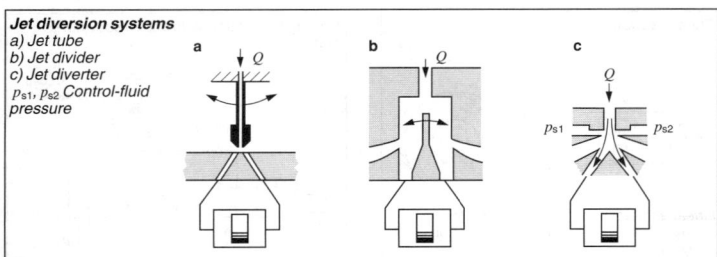

Jet diversion systems
a) Jet tube
b) Jet divider
c) Jet diverter
p_{s1}, p_{s2} Control-fluid pressure

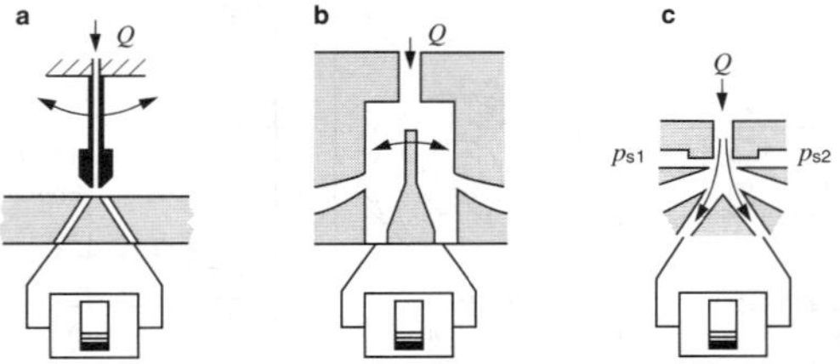

Electric machines

Principal of operation

Electric machines are used to convert electrical and mechanical energy. An electric motor converts electrical energy into mechanical energy; a generator converts energy in the opposite direction. Electric machines consist of a stationary component (the stator) and a rotating component (the rotor). There are special designs which depart from this configuration such as linear machines which produce linear motion. Permanent magnets or several coils (windings) are used to produce magnetic fields in the stator and rotor which cause torque to develop between these two machine components. Electric machines have iron stators and rotors in order to control the magnetic fields. Because the magnetic fluxes change over time, stators and rotors must consist of stacks of individual laminations which are insulated with respect to one another. The spatial arrangement of the coils and the type of current used (direct current, alternating current or three-phase current) permit a number of different electric-machine designs. They differ from one another in the way they operate, and therefore have different applications.

Direct-current machines

The stator of a direct-current machine contains salient poles which are magnetized by the direct-current field windings. In the rotor (here also called the armature), the coils are distributed among slots in the laminated stack and connected to a commutator. Carbon brushes in the stator frame wipe against the commutator as it rotates, thereby transferring direct current to the armature coils. The rotation of the commutator causes a reversal in the direction of current flow in the coils. The different ways in which the field winding and armature can be connected result in different rotational speed vs. torque characteristics:

Series-wound machine

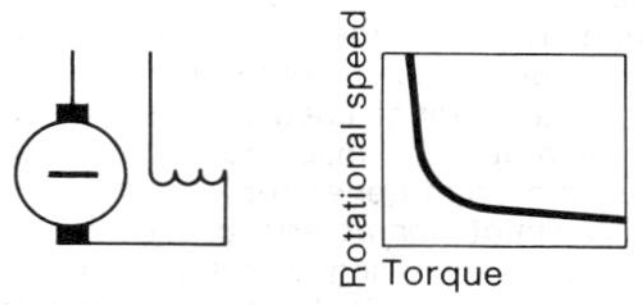

Shunt-wound machine

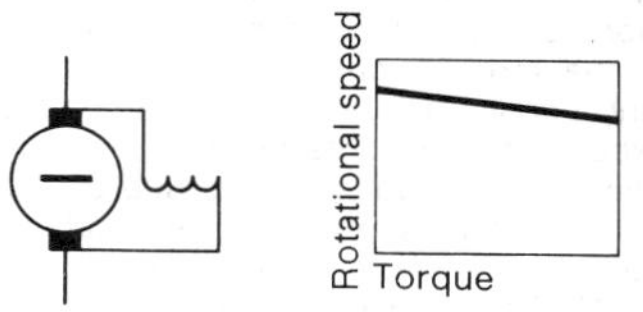

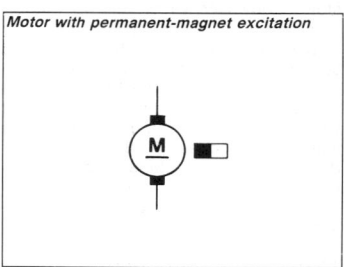

Motor with permanent-magnet excitation

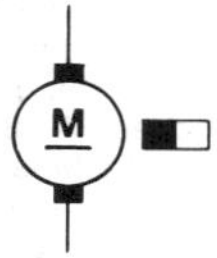

Series connection (series characteristic)
Rotational speed is highly dependent upon load; high starting torque; "racing" of the machine if the load is suddenly removed, therefore load must be rigidly coupled; direction of rotation changed by reversing the direction of current in the armature or field winding; used, among other things, as motor-vehicle drive motor and starter motor for internal-combustion engines.

Parallel (shunt) connection (shunt characteristic)
Rotational speed remains largely constant regardless of load; direction of rotation is changed by reversing the direction of the current in the armature or field winding; used for instance, as drive motor for machine tools and as direct-current generator.

A shunt characteristic can also be obtained by using a separate power supply for the field winding (separate excitation) or by using permanent-magnet poles in the stator. Uses for motors with permanent-magnet excitation in the motor vehicle: starter motors, windshield wiper motors and fractional-horsepower motors for various drives. If the motor incorporates both series and parallel field windings (compound-wound motor), intermediate levels in the rotational speed vs. torque characteristic can be obtained; applications: large starter motors for instance.

All direct-current machines are easily capable of speed control over a wide range. If the machine incorporates a static converter which allows adjustment of the armature voltage, the torque and therefore the rotational speed is infinitely variable. The rotational speed can be further increased by reducing the field current (field weakening) when the rated armature voltage is reached. A disadvantage of direct-current machines is carbon brush and commutator wear which makes regular maintenance necessary.

Three-phase machines

A three-phase winding is distributed among the stator slots in a three-phase machine. The three phases of current produce a magnetic field which rotates (rotating field). The speed n_0 (in min^{-1}) of the rotating field is calculated as follows:

$n_0 = 60 \cdot f/p$.

f frequency (in Hz), p number of pole pairs

Three-phase machines are either synchronous or asynchronous, depending upon rotor design.

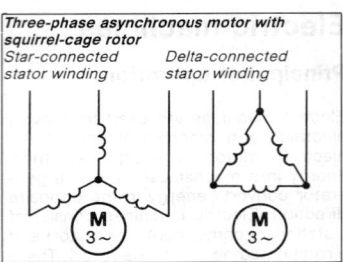

Three-phase asynchronous motor with squirrel-cage rotor

Star-connected stator winding *Delta-connected stator winding*

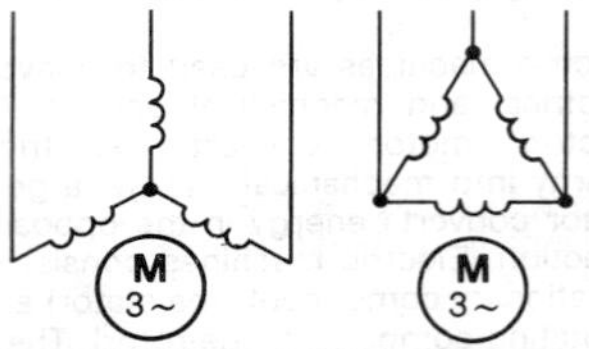

Asynchronous machines
The laminated rotor contains either a three-phase winding, as in the stator, or a bar winding. The three-phase winding is connected to slip rings which are short-circuited either directly or via external resistances. In the case of the bar winding, the bars are connected to one another by two short-circuiting rings (squirrel-cage rotor). As long as the rotational speed of the rotor deviates from n_0, the rotating stator field induces current in the rotor windings, thereby generating torque. Deviation of the rotational speed of the rotor n from n_0 is termed slip s:

$s = (n_0 - n)/n_0$.

Continuous operation is only economical in the vicinity of n_0, because losses increase as slip increases (nominal slip $\leq 5\%$). In this range the asynchronous machine has a shunt characteristic. The machine operates as a motor when $n < n_0$, and as a generator when $n > n_0$. The direction of rotation is changed by reversing two of the phases.

The asynchronous machine is the most frequently used electric motor in the field of drive engineering. With a

Examples of rotating field speeds

Number of poles	Frequency 50 Hz	150 Hz	200 Hz
	Rotating field speed in min^{-1}		
2	3000	9000	12000
4	1500	4500	6000
6	1000	3000	4000
8	750	2250	3000
10	600	1800	2400
12	500	1500	2000

squirrel-cage rotor it is easy to operate, and requires little maintenance.

Sychronous machines
In the rotor (here also called the inductor), the poles are magnetized by direct-current coils. The magnetizing current is usually transferred via two slip rings to the rotor. The inductor can be made of solid steel, because the magnetic flux remains constant over time.

Constant torque is generated as long as the rotor rotates at a speed of n_0. At other speeds, the torque fluctuates periodically between a positive and a negative maximum value, and excessively high current is produced.

For this reason, a synchronous machine is not self-starting. The synchronous machine also differs from the asynchronous machine in that the reactive power absorption and generation are adjustable. The synchronous machine is most frequently used as a generator in electric power plants. Synchronous motors are used in cases where constant motor speed based on constant line frequency is desired, or where a reactive power demand exists. The motor vehicle three-phase alternator is a special type of synchronous machine.

The rotational speed of all three-phase machines is determined by the stator frequency. Such machines can operate over a wide range of speeds if used in conjunction with static converters which vary the frequency.

EC Motors
The "electronically-commutated direct-current" or "EC" motor is becoming increasingly popular. It is essentially a permanently-excited synchronous machine, and thus dispenses with a slip ring. The EC motor is equipped with a rotor-position sensor, and is connected to the DC power source through its control and power electronics. The electronic transfer circuit switches the current in the stator winding according to rotor position — the magnets which induce the excitation current are attached to the rotor — to provide the interdependence between rotational speed and torque which is normally

Star-connected three-phase synchronous generator
Slip-ring rotor with field winding.

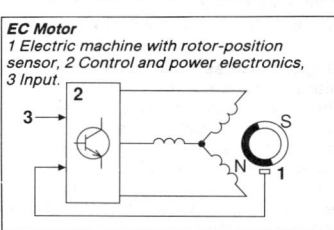

EC Motor
1 Electric machine with rotor-position sensor, 2 Control and power electronics, 3 Input.

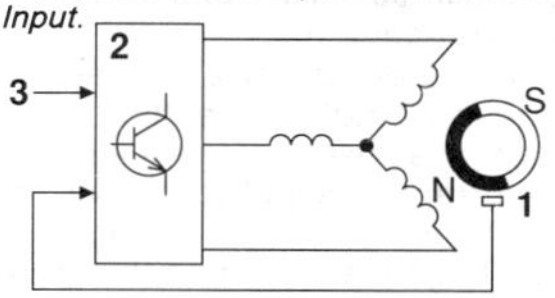

associated with an externally-excited DC unit. The respective magnetic functions of the stator and rotor are the opposite of what they would be in a classical direct-current machine.

The EC motor's potential applications are a result of the advantages which this drive principle provides: Commutator and carbon brushes are replaced by electronic circuitry, dispensing with both brush noise and wear. EC motors are maintenance-free (long service life) and can be constructed to meet high degrees of protection (s. below). The electronic control feature makes it easy for drive units with EC motors to incorporate auxiliary functions such as infinitely-variable speed adjustment, direction reversal, gradual starts and lock-up protection.

The main areas of automotive application are for climate control and ventilation, pumps and servo units. In the area of production machinery, EC motors are chiefly employed as precision drive units for feed-control in machine tools. Here the deciding advantages are freedom from maintenance, favorable dynamic properties and consistent torque output with minimal ripple.

Single-phase alternating-current machines

Universal motors

The direct-current series-wound motor can be operated on alternating current if a laminated rather than a solid iron stator is used. It is then called a universal motor.

When operated on alternating current, a torque component at twice the frequency of the current is superposed on the constant torque component.

Single-phase asynchronous motors with squirrel-cage rotor

The simplest design of a single-phase asynchronous motor is a three-phase asynchronous machine in which alternating current is supplied to only two stator phases. Although its operation remains largely the same, the power and the maximum torque are reduced. In addition, the single-phase asynchronous machine is not self-starting.

Machines which are intended only for single-phase operation have only a single-phase main winding in the stator, as well as auxiliary starting circuits. The stator also contains an auxiliary winding connected in parallel with the main winding for this purpose. The necessary phase shift of the auxiliary winding current can be achieved through increased winding resistance (low breakaway torque) or by means of a capacitor connected in series with the auxiliary winding (somewhat greater starting torque).

The auxiliary winding is switched off after the motor starts. The direction of rotation of the motor is changed by reversing the two auxiliary or main winding connections. A motor which has a capacitor in series with the auxiliary winding is called a capacitor motor. Capacitor motors with a starting and running capacitor also operate continuously with capacitor and auxiliary winding. Optimum operation is achieved by correctly choosing the capacitor for a specific working point. An additional capacitor is often used in order to increase the starting torque; this capacitor is then disconnected after the motor starts.

Two-value capacitor motor

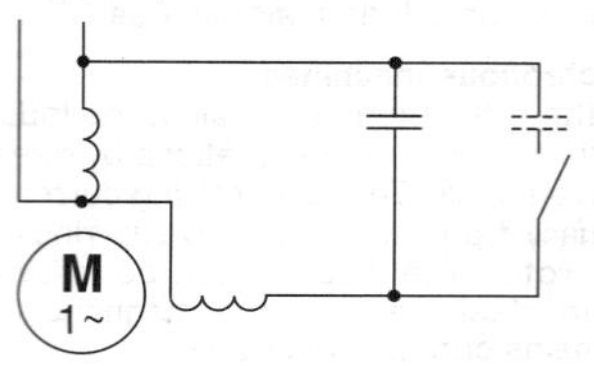

Duty-type ratings for electric machines

(VDE 0530)

S 1: Continuous-running duty
Operation under constant load (rated output) of sufficient duration for thermal equilibrium to be reached.

S 2: Short-time duty
Operation under constant load is so brief that thermal equilibrium is not reached. The rest period is so long that the machine is able to cool down to the temperature of the coolant.

Recommended short-time duty periods: 10, 30, 60 and 90 min.

S 3 to S 5: Intermittent duty
Continuous alternating sequence of load and idle periods. Thermal equilibrium is not reached during the load period or during the cooling period of one duty cycle.

S 3 Intermittent duty without influence of starting on temperature.

S 4 Intermittent duty with influence of starting on temperature.

S 5 Intermittent duty with influence of starting and braking on temperature.

S 6: Continuous operation with intermittent loading
Operation with intermittent loading. Continuous alternating sequence of load periods and no-load periods, otherwise as S 3.

S 7: Uninterrupted duty
Operation with starting and braking.

S 8: Uninterrupted duty
Operation with pole changing.

For S 3 and S 6, the duty cycle time is 10 min unless otherwise agreed; recommended values for cyclic duration factor: 15, 25, 40 and 60%. For S 2, S 3 and S 6, the operating time or cycle time and the cyclic duration factor are to be specified following the rating. The duty cycle time is only to be specified if it is other than 10 min. Example: S 2—60 min, S 3—25 %.

Cyclic duration factor
The cyclic duration factor is the ratio of the loading period including starting and braking to the cycle time.

Winding temperature
The mean temperature t_2 of the windings of an electric machine can be determined by measuring the resistance (R_2) and referring it to an initial temperature R_1 at a temperature t_1:

$$t_2 = \frac{R_2 - R_1}{R_1}\ (\tau + t_1) + t_1$$

where

$$\tau = \frac{1}{\alpha} - 20\,\mathrm{K}$$

α = Temperature coefficient.

Degrees of protection of electric machines

(DIN 40050)

Degree of protection IP 00
No protection against accidental contact, no protection against solid bodies, no protection against water.

Degree of protection IP 11
Protection against large-area contact by the hand, protection against large solid bodies, protection against dripping water.

Degree of protection IP 23
Protection against contact by the fingers, protection against medium-size-solid bodies, protection against water sprayed vertically and obliquely up to an angle of 60° to the vertical.

Degree of protection IP 44
Protection against contact by tools or the like, protection against small solid bodies, protection against splash water from all directions.

Degree of protection IP 67
Total protection against contact, dustproof. Protection against entry of dangerous quantities of water when immersed in water under conditions of defined pressure and for a defined period of time.

Explosion protection Ex
(VDE 0170/0171)
Symbol d: flameproof enclosure; symbol f: forced ventilation; symbol e: increased safety; symbol s: special protection, e.g., for machines operating in flammable liquids.

Technical optics

Electromagnetic radiation

Electromagnetic radiation is propagated at the velocity of light in the form of waves. It is not deflected by electrical or magnetic fields. Wavelength: $\lambda = c/f$; where c = velocity of light $\approx 3 \times 10^8$ m/s ($\approx$ 300 000 km/s) and f = frequency in Hz.

Type of radiation	Wavelength range	Causes/sources	Examples of application
Cosmic radiation	< 0.1 pm	Bombardment of earth's atmosphere by elementary cosmic particles	Experiments in nuclear physics
Gamma radiation	0.1 ... 10 pm	Radioactive decay	Nuclear physics, isotope technology
X-radiation	10 pm ... 10 nm	X-ray tube (bombardment of anticathode by high-energy electrons)	Materials tests, medical diagnosis
Ultraviolet radiation	10 ... 380 nm	Gaseous-discharge lamps, lasers.	Epidermal therapy, photolithography in IC fabrication
Visible radiation	380 ... 780 nm	Gaseous-discharge lamps, incandescent lamps (lamp bulbs), lasers	Technical optics, photography
Infrared radiation	780 nm ... 1 nm	Thermal radiators, infrared-emitting diodes, lasers	Therapy, motor-vehicle distance measurement
EHF-waves	1 mm ... 1 cm	Travelling-wave tubes, Resonant circuits, Quartz oscillators	Satellite communications, microwave heating, road traffic radar, televison and radio brodcasting, radio dispatching services
SHF-waves	1 ... 10 cm		
UHF-waves	10 cm ... 1 m		
VHF-waves	1 ... 10 m		
HF-waves	10 ... 100 m		
MF-waves	100 m ... 1 km		
LF-waves	1 ... 10 km		
VLF-waves			

Geometrical Optics

In many cases, the geometrical dimensions of the media in which optical radiation propagates are large in comparsion to the wavelength of the radiation. In such cases, the propagation of radiation can be explained in terms of "light rays", and can be described by simple geometrical laws.

An incident beam of light is split into a refracted beam and a reflected beam at the interface between two media.

The law of refraction applies to the refracted beam:

$n_1 \cdot \sin \varepsilon_1 = n_2 \cdot \sin \varepsilon_2$

The indices of refraction n_1 and n_2 of a vacuum and the so-called dielectric media (air, glass and plastics, but not metallic materials) are real numbers; for other media they are complex numbers. For this reason, application of the law

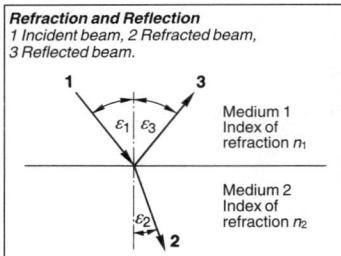

Refraction and Reflection
1 Incident beam, 2 Refracted beam, 3 Reflected beam.

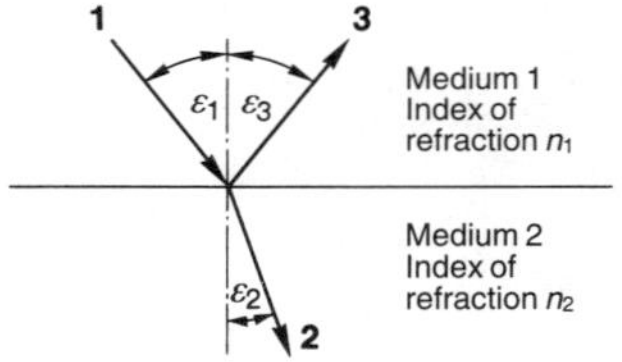

of refraction is practical only for a vacuum and dielectric media.

The indices of refraction of media are a function of the wavelength (dispersion). In most cases, they decrease as the wavelength increases.

The reflected beam behaves according to the following equation:

$\varepsilon_3 = \varepsilon_1$

The ratio of the intensity of the reflected beam to the intensity of the incident beam (degree of reflection) depends upon the incident angle and the indices of refraction of the adjacent media. In the case of a beam of light passing through air (n_1 = 1.00) into glass (n_2 = 1.52) at an angle of 90° (ε_1 = 0), 4.3% of the energy of the beam is reflected.

If the beam emanates from the optically denser medium ($n_1 > n_2$), total reflection occurs if the angle of incidence ε_1 is equal to or exceeds the limiting angel of total reflection $\varepsilon_{1\,max}$. According to the law of refraction:

$\sin \varepsilon_{1max} = n_2/n_1$

Indices of refraction n_D (for yellow sodium light; wavelength: λ= 589.3nm):

Vacuum, air	1.00
Ice (± 0 °C)	1.31
Water (+ 20 °C)	1.33
Fluorite	1.43
Silica glass	1.46
Standard glass for optics (BK 7)	1.51673
Window glass, glass used for headlamp lenses	1.52
Crown glass	1.58
Flint glass	1.6 ... 1.9
Polymethyl methacrylate	1.49
Polyvinyl chloride	1.54
Polycarbonate	1.58
Polystyrene	1.59
Epoxy resin	1.60
Gallium arsenide (according to doping level)	approx. 3.5

Degree of reflection of some materials:

Silver, polished	93%
Aluminum, vacuum-evaporated	89%
Evaporated, corrosion-protected, vapor-deposited aluminum (reflector)	86%
Aluminum, polished	65 ... 80%
Magnesium oxide, white	95%
Road surface, light	20 ... 30%
Road surface, dark	5 ... 15%

Components

Cylindrical lenses

Parallel rays are made to converge in a focal line by a cylindrical lens.

Prisms

Prismatic elements are used for the purpose of deflecting a beam of light by a desired angle. Parallel rays remain parallel after deflection by a prism. In the motor-vehicle headlamp, cylindrical lenses and prismatic elements are used in order to more favorably direct the light emanating from the reflector.

Reflectors

The function of motor-vehicle lamp reflectors is to reflect as much light as possible from the headlamp bulb, to achieve as great a range as possible, and to influence the distribution of light on the road in such a way that the requirements of legislation are met. Additional demands are placed on the headlamps as a result of the design (for instance, when fitted into the bumper).

Whereas in the past paraboloids were almost exclusively used as reflectors, the above-mentioned requirements, which are in some cases mutually contradictory, can today only be met by the use of stepped reflectors, free-formed areas or new headlamp designs (PES = Polyellipsoid System, see p. 672).

In general, the larger the area of aperture, the greater a headlamp's range.

Cylindrical lens element of a headlamp lens

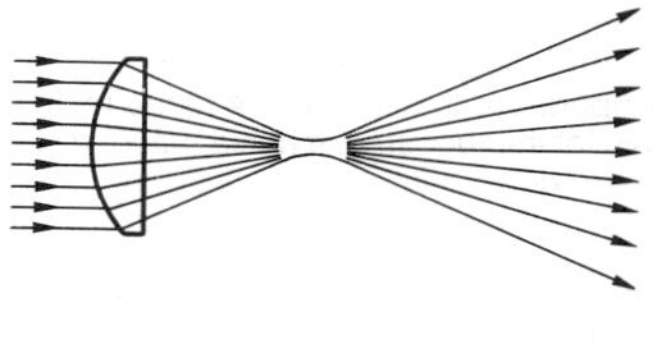

On the other hand, the greater the solid angle achieved by the reflector, the greater the luminous efficiency.

Color filters

Motor-vehicle lamps must meet precise specifications with regard to chromaticity coordinates depending upon their intended functions (turn-signal lamps, stop lamps). These specifications can be met through the use of color filters which weaken the light emitted in certain parts of the visible spectrum.

Light sources

The outer electron shells of atoms can absorb varying levels of energy. The tranition from higher to lower levels may lead to the emission of electromagnetic wave trains.

The various types of light source can fundamentally be distinguished by the kind of energy addition providing the stimulus.

Thermal radiators

In the case of this light source, the energy level is increased by the addition of heat energy. The emission is continuous across a broad wavelength range. The total radiation capacity is proportional to the power of 4 of the absolute temperature (Stephan Boltzmann's Law) and the distribution curve maximum is displaced to shorter wavelengths as the temperature increases (Wien's Displacement Law).

Incandescent lamps, with tungsten glow filament (melting temperature 3660 K), are also thermal radiators. The evaporation of the tungsten and the consequent unavoidable blackening of the bulb restrict the service life of this type of lamp.

The halogen lamp allows the filament temperature to rise to close to the melting point of the tungsten. It has a halogen filler gas (iodine or bromine). Close to the hot bulb wall the evaporated tungsten combines with the filler gas to form tungsten halide. This is gaseous, conductive for light beams and stable in the temperature range 500 K to 1700 K. It reaches the filament by means of convection, decomposes as a result of the high filament temperature, and forms an even tungsten deposit on the filament. In order to maintain this cyclic process, an external bulb temperature of approx. 300 °C is necessary. To achieve this the bulb, made of silica glass, must closely surround the filament. A further advantage of this measure is that higher filling pressure can be used, thereby providing additional resistance to tungsten evaporation.

Gaseous-discharge lamps

In these types of lamp a gas discharge is maintained in an enclosed, gas-filled bulb by applying a voltage between two electrodes. The excitation of the atoms of the emitted gas is effected by impulses. In low-pressure lamps, the resonance radiation (return from the excited state to the initial state) is used, and in high-pressure lamps the transition between two states of excitation is used.

Examples of gaseous-discharge lamps are fluorescent lamps (interior illumination), sodium-vapor lamps (street lighting) and motor-vehicle headlamps ("Litronic", page 673).

Relative spectral sensitivity V ***(υ) of the light-adapted eye.***

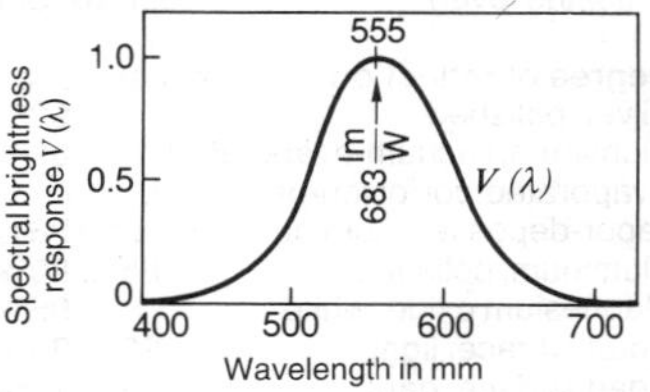

Photometric quantities and units

See p. 16 for names of units.

Quantity		SI-Unit
A	Area A_1 radiating area (surface) A_2 irradiated area (surface)	m^2
E	Illuminance	$lx = lm/m^2$
I	Luminous intensity	cd
L	Luminance	cd/m^2
M	Luminous emittance	lm/m^2
P	Power	W
Q	Luminous energy	lm · s
r	Distance	m

Quantity		SI-Unit
t	Time	s
ε_1	Incident angle of radiation (with respect to surface normal)	°
ε_2	Angle of refraction	°
ε_3	Angle of reflection	°
η	Luminous efficiency	lm/W
Φ	Luminous flux	lm
Ω	Solid angle	sr
λ	Wavelength	nm

Light and the physiology of vision

Because the range of sensitivity to visible radiation varies from person to person, a general brightness sensitivity function has been established for photometric calculation an measurements and is contained, in tabular form for example, in DIN 5031, Part 3. This function is called the spectral brightness response for photopic vision $V(\lambda)$. This function allows unambiguous values for illumination engineering quantites to be obtained by calculation from objective physical values.

Definition of photometric quantities and units:

Luminous flux Φ
luminous flux is the radiant power emitted by a source of light assessed on the basis of spectral brightness sensitivity.

$$\Phi = K_m \cdot \int P\lambda \cdot V(\lambda)\, d\lambda$$

K_m= 683 lm/W (maximum luminous effiacy)
$V(\lambda)$ = Spectral brightness response for a 2° field of visoin in accord ance with DIN 5031, Part 3
P_λ = Spectral distribution of radiant energy

Luminous energy Q
The luminous energy is the spectral radiation energy assessed on the basis of $V(\lambda)$. The follwing equation applies for temporarily constant luminous flux:

$$Q = \Phi \cdot t$$

Luminous intensity I
The luminous intensity is the ratio of the luminous flux to the irradiated solid angle.

$$I = \Phi / \Omega$$

Illuminance E
Illuminance is the ratio of the incident luminous flux to the area of the illuminated surface

$$E = \Phi / A_2$$

Luminance L
Luminance is the ratio of the lumious intensity to the apparent (projected) area of the surface from ehich it is emitted.

$$L = I / (A_1 \cdot \cos\alpha).$$

where α is the angle between the axis of the surface normal.

Luminous emittance M
Luminous emittance is the ratio of the luminous flux emitted by a luminous surface to thr area of that surface.

$$M = \Phi / A_1.$$

Luminous efficiency η
Luminous efficiency is the ratio of the emitted luminous flux to the power absorbed.

$$\eta = \Phi / P.$$

Luminous efficiency can never exceed the maximum lumious efficacy value K_m = 683 lm/W at a wavelength of λ = 555 nm.

Solid angle Ω
A solid angle is the ratio of the irradiated portion of the surface of a sphere concentric with the source of light to the square of the radius of the sphere.
The total solid angle is

$$\Omega = 4\pi \cdot sr = 12.56 \cdot sr$$

sr = steradians.

Contrast
Contrast is the ratio of the luminance values of two adjacent surfaces.

Photometric requirements in a motor vehicle

Coping with complex situations, such as in traffic, requires the employment of as many as possible of the following basic sensations inherent in human vision:

- Sensitivity to brightness
- Sensitivity to space
- Color perception
- Perception of motion
- Perception of differences in luminance
- Color comparison
- Sharpness of vision
- Perception of shapes and objects.

Good lighting supports these sensations, or indeed makes them possible. For that reason stringent photometric requirements are made of motor-vehicle headlamps, and compliance with these requirements must be proven by means of measurements. In the regulations, both minimum illuminance values in order to achieve good road illumination and maximum values to avoid glare are stipulated. In the diagram below a measurement specification for low-beam and high-beam headlamps is shown.

Perspective diagram with measurement points for illuminance in accordance with ECE Regulation 20

The specified values are given in lx for headlamps with H4 bulbs at a distance of 25 m.

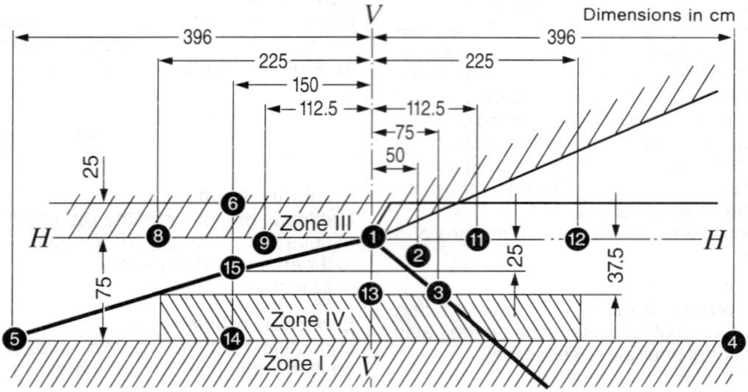

Lower beam			
Measurement points	Specified lx values	Measurement points	Specified lx values
1. E_{HV}	≤ 0.7	Max. value in Zone I	≤ 2 E_{50R}
2. E_{75R}	≥ 12	Max. value in Zone III	≤ 0.7
3. E_{50R}	≥ 12	Min. value in Zone IV	≥ 3
4. E_{25R}	≥ 2	13. E_{50V}	≥ 6
5. E_{25L}	≥ 2	14. E_{50L}	≤ 15
6. E_{B50L}	≤ 0.4	15. E_{75L}	≤ 12

Upper beam	
Measurement points	Specified lx values
7. E_{max}	> 48 < 16 × E_{75R} (< 240)
8. $E_{H-5.15°}$	≥ 6
9. $E_{H-2.55°}$	≥ 24
10. E_{HV}	≥ 0.8 E_{max}
11. $E_{H+2.55°}$	≥ 24
12. $E_{H+5.15°}$	≥ 6

Laser technology

The laser has the following characteristic properties in comparison with other light sources:
- High luminance, concentration of radiation on a diameter of few light wavelengths,
- Low beam expansion,
- Monochromatic radiation,
- Usable for coherent metrology (high radiation coherence length),
- High power (20 kW in laser tools).

Light generation in the laser is effected by induced emission in a specific laser material which is brought to a state of excitation by the addition of energy (usually light). A resonator influences the beam geometry as required. The laser radiation emerges at the end of a resonator, via a semitransparent mirror.

Examples of lasers in common use are:

Type of laser	Wave-length	Example of application
Helium-neon laser	633 nm	Measuring technology
CO2 laser	10.6 μm	Material processing
YAG laser	1064 nm	Material processing
Solid-state laser	e.g. 670 nm e.g. 1300 nm	Measuring technology Telecommunications

Laser principle
1 Pumping light source, 2 Resonator mirror, 3 Laser-active material, 4 Semitransparent mirror, 5 Laser beam.

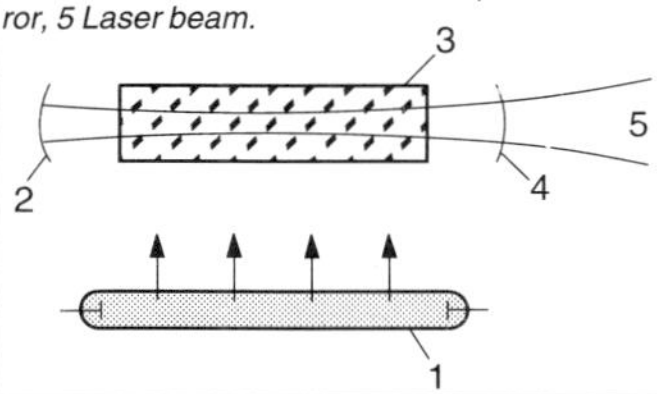

With laser measuring technology the non-contact, non-interacting testing of production tolerances of precision-machined surfaces (e.g., fuel-injection valves) is possible. With interferometric methods resolutions in the nm range are achieved.
Further laser applications in technology are holography, automatic character recognition (bar codes), information scanning (compact disc) and material processing.
Specific regulations are to be observed when handling laser products. Laser products are classified according to potential hazard. For details see DIN/VDE 0837, "Radiation Safety of Laser Products".

Optical fibers

(optical waveguides)

Structure

Optical fibers transmit electromagnetic waves in the ultraviolet (UV), visible and infrared (IR) ranges of the spectrum. They are made of quartz, glass or polymers, usually in the form of fibers with a core of which the index of refraction is higher than that of the cladding. Thus incident light entering the core zone is retained in that area by means of refraction or reflection. Depending on the refractive index profile, a distinction is made between three types of fiber (see diagram):

- The step-index optical fiber, with a sharply-defined border between the core and the cladding,
- The graded-index optical fiber, with parabolic refractive index curve form in the core zone,
- The monomode fiber with a very small core diameter.

Step-index and graded-index fibers are multimode fibers, that is, lightwaves can be propagated in them at varying trajectories, generally at an oblique angle to the fiber axis. In the monomode fiber, propagation is only possible in the principal mode. Polymer fibers are always step-index fibers.

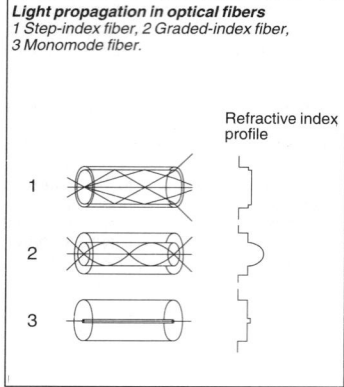

Light propagation in optical fibers
1 Step-index fiber, 2 Graded-index fiber, 3 Monomode fiber.

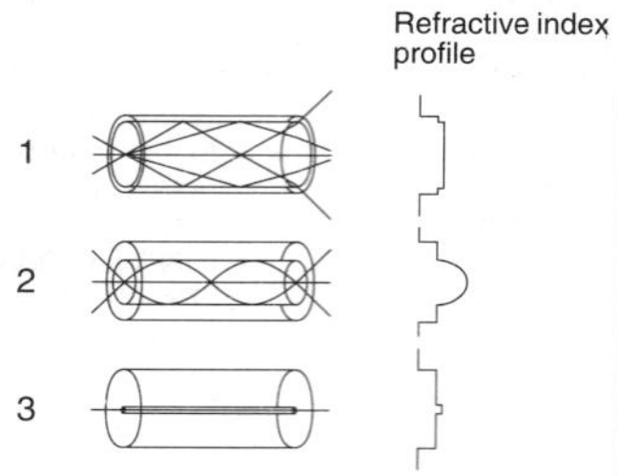

Properties
Optical fibers can only absorb light from a restricted angular range θ. The numerical aperture NA = SIN (θ/2) serves as a basis for calculating this range (see Table).
Conductivity is restricted in the UV range by Rayleigh scattering, and in the IR range by molecular absorption. Glass optical fibers have a high degree of transparency in the range UV to IR. Attenuation is particularly low at the wavelengths 0.85 μm, 1.3 μm and 1.55 μm. Synthetic fibers absorb above 0.85 μm and below 0.45 μm.
The differences in dispersion and propagation time of the various modes cause an increasing widening of light pulses as the length of the fiber increases, and thus restrict the bandwidth.
Optical fibers can be used in the temperature range – 40 °C to 135 °C; special versions can be used up to 800 °C.

Areas of application
The main area of application is data transmission. Synthetic fibers are preferred for use in the LAN (Local Area Network) field. Graded-index fibers are the most suitable for medium ranges. Only monomode fibers are used for long-distance data transmission.

Optical fibers are becoming more and more significant in the field of sensor technology. Fiber-optic sensors generate neither stray fields nor sparks, and are themselves non-sensitive to that kind of disturbance. They are currently primarily employed in potentially explosive environments, in medicine and in the military field.

In the area of material processing with laser beams, in microsurgery and in lighting engineering, the energy transport problem is of primary importance.

Holography

In conventional image recording (photography, video cameras) a three-dimensional image is reduced to a two-dimensional representation. The spatial information contained in the image is lost when the image is stored. Spatial impressions gained when looking at the picture are based on sensory illusions.

With holography, three-dimensional information can be stored and also reproduced. For recording, coherent lightwave trains are necessary.

In hologram imaging, a beam splitter divides the laser beam into object and reference beams. The resulting object and reference waves form an interference pattern on the recording medium (hologram

Characteristics of optical fibers (optical waveguides)

Fiber type		Diameter Core μm	Cladding μm	Wave-length nm	NA	Attenu-ation dB / km	Bandwidth MHz · km
Step-index fiber	Quartz Glass	50 ... 1000	70 ... 1000	250 ... 1550	0.2 ... 0.87	5 ... 10	10
	Polymer	200 ...>1000	250 ... 2000	450 ... 850	0.2 ... 0.6	100 ... 500	< 10
Graded-index fiber		50 ... 150	100 ... 500	450 ... 1550	0.2 ... 0.3	3 ... 5	200 ... 1000
Monomode fiber		3 ... 10	100 ... 500	850 ... 1550	0.12 ... 0.21	0.5 ... 1	2500 ... 15000

plate), where the pattern is stored as a diffraction grating.

The expanded beam of a laser illuminates the hologram plate and reconstructs the hologram. The diffraction grating on the hologram deforms the laser wave to such an extent that the observer has the impression that the holographically captured object is present behind the hologram plate.

Examples of application:
– Registering of minute path deviations,
– Measurement of deformations and vibration amplitudes far below the wavelength of light by means of holographic interferometry,
– Holographic measuring and testing methods in precision manufacturing (e.g., fuel-injection technology components),
– Production of forgery-proof documents,
– Use of holographic elements for illustration purposes.

Display elements

The most important optical information displays are liquid crystal and light-emitting diode displays.

Liquid Crystal Display

The liquid crystal display, or LCD, is a passive display element. The contrast differences created are made visible by additional illumination. The most widely used type of LCD is the twisted nematic cell, or TN cell.

The liquid crystal substance is held between two glass plates. In the area of the display segments these glass plates are covered with a transparent conducting layer, between which an electric field can be applied. An additional orientation layer causes the plane of polarization of light passing through the cell to be rotated by 90°. When polarizers acting at right angles to one another are added to both outside surfaces, the cell is initially transparent. In the area of the two opposed electrodes the liquid crystal molecules are aligned in the direction of the electric field by applying voltage. Rotation of the plane of polarization is now suppressed and the display area becomes opaque.

Numbers, letters and symbols can be displayed by incorporating a number of independently controlled liquid crystal segments into the display device.

Light-Emitting Diodes

The light-emitting diode, or LED, display is an active (self-luminous) display. It consists of a semiconductor element with PN junction. During operation in forward direction the charge carriers (free electrons and holes) recombine. The resulting energy released is converted into electromagnetic radiation energy when certain semiconductor materials are used.
Frequently used semiconductor materials are: gallium arsenide (infrared), gallium arsenide phosphide (red to yellow) and gallium phosphide (green).

Hologram reproduction
1 Reconstruction wave, 2 Hologram, 3 Deformed wave, 4 Observer, 5 Virtual image.

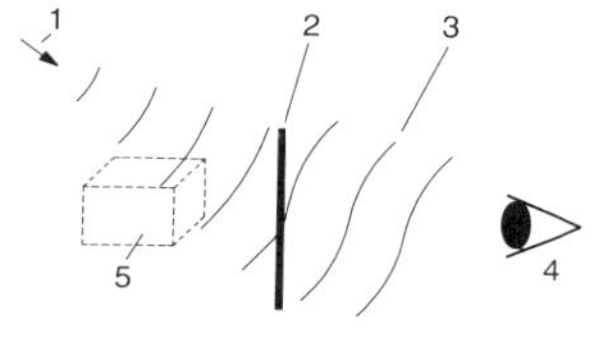

Principle of operation of a liquid crystal display (nematic cell).
1 Polarizer, 2 Glass, 3 Orientation and insulation layer, 4 Electode, 5 Polarizer (and reflector), a Segment area.

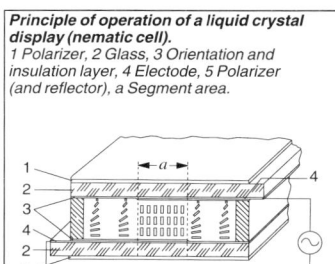

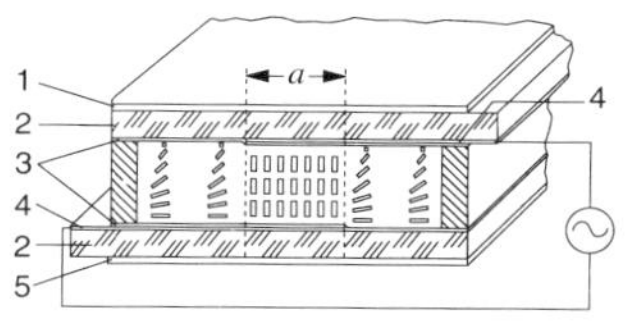

Mathematics

Mathematical signs and symbols

$\approx$	Approximately equal to
$\ll$	Much less than
$\gg$	Much greater than
$\triangleq$	Corresponds to
...	and so forth, to
$=$	Equals
$\neq$	Not equal to
$<$	Less than
$\leq$	Less than or equal to
$>$	Greater than
$\geq$	Greater than or equal to
$+$	Plus
$-$	Minus
$\cdot$ or $\star$ or $\times$	Times
— or / or :	Divided by
Σ	Summation of
Π	Product
$\sim$	Proportional
$\sqrt{\ }$	Radical ($\sqrt[n]{n}$-th root of)
$n!$	n factorial (e. g. $3! = 1 \cdot 2 \cdot 3 = 6$)
$\lvert x \rvert$	Absolute value of x
$\rightarrow$	Approaches
∞	Infinity
i or j	Imaginary number; $i^2 = -1$
$\perp$	Perpendicular to
$\parallel$	Parallel to
$\sphericalangle$	Angle
$\triangle$	Triangle
lim	Limit
Δ	Delta (difference between two values)
d	Total differential
δ	Partial differential
$\int$	Integral
ln	Logarithm to base e[1]
lg	Logarithm to base 10

Useful numbers

e	= 2.718282[1]	$\sqrt{\pi}$	= 1.77245
e^2	= 7.389056	$1/\pi$	= 0.31831
1/e	= 0.367879	π^2	= 9.86960
lg e	= 0.434294	$180/\pi$	= 57.29578
$\sqrt{e}$	= 1.648721	$\pi/180$	= 0.017453
1/lg e	= 2.302585	$\sqrt{2}$	= 1.41421
ln 10	= 2.302585	$1/\sqrt{2}$	= 0.70711
1/ln 10	= 0.434294	$\sqrt{3}$	= 1.73205
π	= 3.14159		

Number systems

Number systems are employed to form numerals in cases where the number of digits is to be less than the quantity of individual units being described. This type of notation requires the use of a single symbol (digit) for collective representation of more than one element.

Today's standard position or place system differs from former additive systems in employing groups which increase in uniform increments. The position of the digit within the numeral corresponds to the size of the unit (place value). The number at which the first new unit is formed is the base number of the place system; it is equal to the maximum number of individual digits which are available.

Most frequently used is the decimal or base 10 systems. The dual system (base 2), using the digits 0 and 1, and the hexadecimal (base 16) system, using the digits 0 through 9 and A through F, are frequently employed for data processing.

The real number a is represented in the place system by:

$$a = \pm \sum_{i=-\infty}^{\infty} Z_i \cdot B^i$$

i Position, B Base, Z_i natural numbers ($0 \leq Z_i < B$) at position i

Roman number system (Additive system)	Decimal system (Base 10)	Dual system (Base 2)
I	1	1
X	10	1010
C	100	1100100
M	1000	1111100110
II	2	10
V	5	101
L	50	110010
D	500	111110010
MCMLXXVII	1977	11110111001

(In the Roman system, a smaller numeral is subtracted from a larger subsequent numeral when it directly precedes it.)

[1]) e = 1 + 1/1! + 1/2! + 1/3! + ...
(Base of natural logarithms).

Preferred numbers

Preferred numbers are rounded-off terms in geometric series whose increments (the ratio of a term to its predecessor) are as follows:

Series	R 5	R 10	R 20	R 40
Increment	$\sqrt[5]{10}$	$\sqrt[10]{10}$	$\sqrt[20]{10}$	$\sqrt[40]{10}$

They are used for selecting preferred size and dimension increments. In addition to the principal series, DIN 323 also contains the exceptional series R 80 as well as series of rounded numbers.

Electrical components such as resistors and capacitors are rated in increments in accordance with the E Series:

Series	E 6	E 12	E 24
Increment	$\sqrt[6]{10}$	$\sqrt[12]{10}$	$\sqrt[24]{10}$

Preferred numbers (DIN 323)

Principal series				Exact values	
R 5	**R 10**	**R 20**	**R 40**		lg
1.00	**1.00**	**1.00**	1.00	1.0000	0.0
			1.06	1.0593	0.025
		1.12	1.12	1.1220	0.05
			1.18	1.1885	0.075
	1.25	**1.25**	1.25	1.2589	0.1
			1.32	1.3335	0.125
		1.40	1.40	1.4125	0.15
			1.50	1.4962	0.175
1.60	**1.60**	**1.60**	1.60	1.5849	0.2
			1.70	1.6788	0.225
		1.80	1.80	1.7783	0.25
			1.90	1.8836	0.275
	2.00	**2.00**	2.00	1.9953	0.3
			2.12	2.1135	0.325
		2.24	2.24	2.2387	0.35
			2.36	2.3714	0.375
2.50	**2.50**	**2.50**	2.50	2.5119	0.4
			2.65	2.6607	0.425
		2.80	2.80	2.8184	0.45
			3.00	2.9854	0.475
	3.15	**3.15**	3.15	3.1623	0.5
			3.35	3.3497	0.525
		3.55	3.55	3.5481	0.55
			3.75	3.7584	0.575
4.00	**4.00**	**4.00**	4.00	3.9811	0.6
			4.25	4.2170	0.625
		4.50	4.50	4.4668	0.65
			4.75	4.7315	0.675
	5.00	**5.00**	5.00	5.0119	0.7
			5.30	5.3088	0.725
		5.60	5.60	5.6234	0.75
			6.00	5.9566	0.775
6.30	**6.30**	**6.30**	6.30	6.3096	0.8
			6.70	6.6834	0.825
		7.10	7.10	7.0795	0.85
			7.50	7.4989	0.875
	8.00	**8.00**	8.00	7.9433	0.9
			8.50	8.4140	0.925
		9.00	9.00	8.9125	0.95
			9.50	9.4409	0.975
10.0	**10.0**	**10.0**	10.0	10.0000	1.0

E Series (DIN 41 426)

E 6	**E 12**	**E 24**
1.0	1.0	1.0
		1.1
	1.2	1.2
		1.3
1.5	1.5	1.5
		1.6
	1.8	1.8
		2.0
2.2	2.2	2.2
		2.4
	2.7	2.7
		3.0
3.3	3.3	3.3
		3.6
	3.9	3.9
		4.3
4.7	4.7	4.7
		5.1
	5.6	5.6
		6.2
6.8	6.8	6.8
		7.5
	8.2	8.2
		9.1
10.0	10.0	10.0

Trigonometric functions

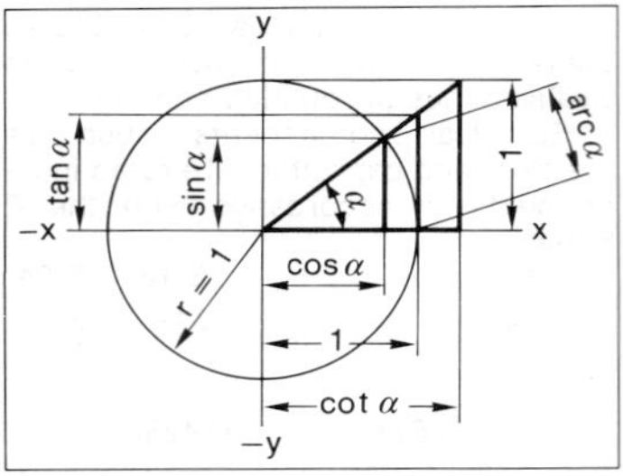

$\sin 0° = \cos 90° = 0$
$\cos 0° = \sin 90° = 1$
$\tan 0° = \cot 90° = 0$
$\cot 0° = \tan 90° = \infty$
$\sin 30° = \cos 60° = 0.5$
$\cos 30° = \sin 60° = 0.5\sqrt{3}$
$\tan 30° = \cot 60° = \sqrt{3}/3$
$\cot 30° = \tan 60° = \sqrt{3}$

$$\widehat{\alpha} = \text{arc}\,\alpha = \frac{\pi \cdot \alpha}{180°}\,\text{rad}^{1)} = \frac{\alpha}{57.3°}$$

$$\widehat{1}° = \text{arc}\,1° = \frac{\pi}{180} = 0.017453$$

$\text{arc}\,57.3° = 1$

$$\cos^2\alpha + \sin^2\alpha = 1$$

$$\tan\alpha = \frac{\sin\alpha}{\cos\alpha} = \frac{1}{\cot\alpha}$$

$$1 + \tan^2\alpha = \frac{1}{\cos^2\alpha}$$

$$1 + \cot^2\alpha = \frac{1}{\sin^2\alpha}$$

$$\sin\alpha \approx \widehat{\alpha} - \frac{\widehat{\alpha}^3}{6}$$

error < 1 % bei $\alpha < 58°$

$$\sin\alpha \approx \widehat{\alpha}$$

error < 1 % at $\alpha < 14°$

$$\cos\alpha \approx 1 - \frac{\widehat{\alpha}^2}{2}$$

error < 1 % at $\alpha < 37°$

$$\cos\alpha \approx 1$$

error < 1 % at $\alpha < 8°$

$\varphi =$	$\pm\alpha$	$90 \pm \alpha$	$180 \pm \alpha$	$270 \pm \alpha$
$\sin\varphi =$	$\pm\sin\alpha$	$\cos\alpha$	$\mp\sin\alpha$	$-\cos\alpha$
$\cos\varphi =$	$+\cos\alpha$	$\mp\sin\alpha$	$-\cos\alpha$	$\pm\sin\alpha$
$\tan\varphi =$	$\pm\tan\alpha$	$\mp\cot\alpha$	$\pm\tan\alpha$	$\mp\cot\alpha$
$\cot\varphi =$	$\pm\cot\alpha$	$\mp\tan\alpha$	$\pm\cot\alpha$	$\mp\tan\alpha$

Sine α = side opposite to α/hypotenuse
Cosine α = side adjacent to α/hypotenuse
Tangent α = side opposite to α/side adjacent to α
Cotangent α = side adjacent to α/side opposite to α
Arc $\alpha = \widehat{\alpha}$ = radian measure in a circle whose radius is 1

$\sin 2\alpha = 2\sin\alpha \cdot \cos\alpha$
$\cos 2\alpha = \cos^2\alpha - \sin^2\alpha$
$\tan 2\alpha = 2/(\cot\alpha - \tan\alpha)$
$\cot 2\alpha = (\cot\alpha - \tan\alpha)/2$
$\sin 3\alpha = 3\sin\alpha - 4\sin^3\alpha$
$\cos 3\alpha = 4\cos^3\alpha - 3\cos\alpha$

$$\sin(\alpha \pm \beta) = \sin\alpha \cdot \cos\beta \pm \cos\alpha \cdot \sin\beta$$

$$\cos(\alpha \pm \beta) = \cos\alpha \cdot \cos\beta \mp \sin\alpha \cdot \sin\beta$$

$$\tan(\alpha \pm \beta) = \frac{\tan\alpha \pm \tan\beta}{1 \mp \tan\alpha \tan\beta}$$

$$\cot(\alpha \pm \beta) = \frac{\cot\alpha \cdot \cot\beta \mp 1}{\cot\beta \pm \cot\alpha}$$

$$\sin\alpha \pm \sin\beta = 2\sin\frac{\alpha \pm \beta}{2} \cdot \cos\frac{\alpha \mp \beta}{2}$$

$$\cos\alpha + \cos\beta = 2\cos\frac{\alpha + \beta}{2} \cdot \cos\frac{\alpha - \beta}{2}$$

$$\cos\alpha - \cos\beta = -2\sin\frac{\alpha + \beta}{2} \cdot \sin\frac{\alpha - \beta}{2}$$

$$\tan\alpha \pm \tan\beta = \frac{\sin(\alpha \pm \beta)}{\cos\alpha \cdot \cos\beta}$$

$$\cot\alpha \pm \cot\beta = \frac{\sin(\beta \pm \alpha)}{\sin\alpha \cdot \sin\beta}$$

Euler's Formula
(Basis of symbolic method):

$$e^{\pm ix} = \cos x \pm i\sin x$$

$$\sin x = \frac{e^{ix} - e^{-ix}}{2i}; \quad \cos x = \frac{e^{ix} + e^{-ix}}{2}$$

with $i = \sqrt{-1}$

Trigonometric functions

°	arc α	sin α	tan α	cot α	inv α[1]	cos α	—	—
0	0.0000	0.0000	0.0000	∞	0.00000	1.0000	1.5708	**90**
1	175	175	175	57.290	00	0.9998	533	**89**
2	349	349	349	28.636	01	94	359	**88**
3	524	523	524	19.081	05	86	184	**87**
4	698	698	699	14.301	11	76	010	**86**
5	873	872	875	11.430	22	62	1.4835	**85**
6	0.1047	0.1045	0.1051	9.514	38	45	661	**84**
7	222	219	228	8.144	61	25	486	**83**
8	396	392	405	7.115	91	03	312	**82**
9	571	564	584	6.314	0.00130	0.9877	137	**81**
10	745	736	763	5.671	79	48	1.3963	**80**
11	920	908	944	5.145	0.00239	16	788	**79**
12	0.2094	0.2079	0.2126	4.705	0.00312	0.9781	614	**78**
13	269	250	309	4.331	97	44	439	**77**
14	443	419	493	4.011	0.00498	03	265	**76**
15	618	588	679	3.732	615	659	090	**75**
16	793	756	867	487	749	613	1.2915	**74**
17	967	924	0.3057	271	902	563	741	**73**
18	0.3142	0.3090	249	078	0.01076	511	566	**72**
19	316	256	443	2.904	271	455	392	**71**
20	491	420	640	747	490	397	217	**70**
21	665	584	839	605	734	336	043	**69**
22	840	746	0.4040	475	0.02005	272	1.1868	**68**
23	0.4014	907	245	356	305	205	694	**67**
24	189	0.4067	452	246	635	135	519	**66**
25	363	226	663	145	998	063	345	**65**
26	538	384	877	050	0.03395	0.8988	170	**64**
27	712	540	0.5095	1.963	829	910	1.0996	**63**
28	887	695	317	881	0.04302	829	821	**62**
29	0.5061	848	543	804	816	746	647	**61**
30	236	0.5000	774	732	0.05375	660	472	**60**
31	411	150	0.6009	664	981	572	297	**59**
32	585	299	249	600	0.06636	480	123	**58**
33	760	446	494	540	0.07345	387	0.9948	**57**
34	934	592	745	483	0.08110	290	774	**56**
35	0.6109	736	0.7002	428	934	192	599	**55**
36	283	878	265	376	0.09822	090	425	**54**
37	458	0.6018	536	327	0.1078	0.7986	250	**53**
38	632	157	813	280	181	880	076	**52**
39	807	293	0.8098	235	291	771	0.8901	**51**
40	981	428	391	192	410	660	727	**50**
41	0.7156	561	693	150	537	547	552	**49**
42	330	691	0.9004	111	674	431	378	**48**
43	505	820	325	072	820	314	203	**47**
44	679	947	657	036	977	193	029	**46**
45	854	0.7071	1.0000	1.000	0.2146	071	0.7854	**45**
—	—	cos α	cot α	tan α	—	sin α	arc α	°

[1]) Involute function $\text{inv}\,\alpha = \tan\alpha - \text{arc}\,\alpha$.

Equations for plane and spherical triangles

Plane triangle

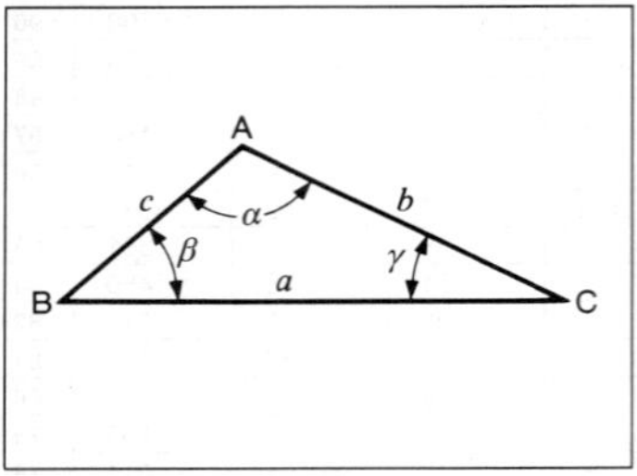

$\alpha + \beta + \gamma = 180°$

Law of Sines

$a : b : c = \sin\alpha : \sin\beta : \sin\gamma$

Pythagorean Theorem (Law of Cosines)

$a^2 = b^2 + c^2 - 2bc\cos\alpha$

for a right triangle

$a^2 = b^2 + c^2$

Spherical triangle

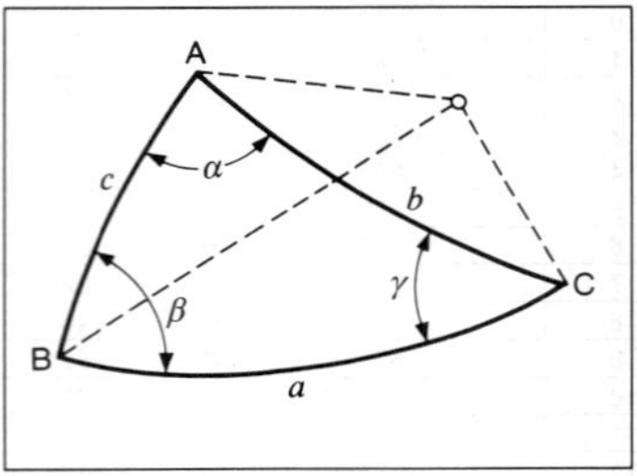

Law of Sines

$\sin a : \sin b : \sin c = \sin\alpha : \sin\beta : \sin\gamma$

Law of Cosines for the sides

$\cos a = \cos b \cos c + \sin b \sin c \cos\alpha$

Law of Cosines for the angles

$\cos\alpha = -\cos\beta\cos\gamma + \sin\beta\sin\gamma\cos a$

Often used equations

Solution of the quadratic equation

$ax^2 + bx + c = 0$

$$x = \frac{-b \pm \sqrt{b^2 - 4ac}}{2a}$$

Golden section (continuous division)

$1 : x = x : (1 - x)$, from which $x = 0.618$

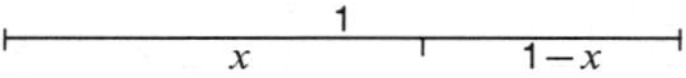

Conversion of logarithms

$\lg N = 0.434294 \cdot \ln N$

$\ln N = 2.302585 \cdot \lg N$

Geometric Series

$a + aq + aq^2 + aq^3 + \ldots$

nth member $= aq^{n-1}$

for $q > 1$: $\sum_n = a(q^n - 1)/(q - 1)$

for $q < 1$: $\sum_n = a(1 - q^n)/(1 - q)$

for $n \to \infty$ wird $q^n = 0$

$\sum_{n\to\infty} = a/(1 - q)$

Arithmetic Series

$a + (a + d) + (a + 2d) + (a + 3d) + \ldots$

nth member $= a + (n - 1)d$

$$\sum_n = \frac{n}{2}[2a + (n - 1)d]$$

Powers, circumference and area of circles, natural logarithms

n	n^2	n^3	ln n	πn	$\pi n^2/4$	n	n^2	n^3	ln n	πn	$\pi n^2/4$
1	1	1	0.000	3.142	0.785	**51**	2601	132651	3.932	160.2	2043
2	4	8	0.693	6.283	3.142	**52**	2704	140608	3.951	163.4	2124
3	9	27	1.099	9.425	7.069	**53**	2809	148877	3.970	166.5	2206
4	16	64	1.386	12.57	12.57	**54**	2916	157464	3.989	169.6	2290
5	25	125	1.609	15.71	19.63	**55**	3025	166375	4.007	172.8	2376
6	36	216	1.792	18.85	28.27	**56**	3136	175616	4.025	175.9	2463
7	49	343	1.946	21.99	38.48	**57**	3249	185193	4.043	179.1	2552
8	64	512	2.079	25.13	50.27	**58**	3364	195112	4.060	182.2	2642
9	81	729	2.197	28.27	63.62	**59**	3481	205379	4.078	185.4	2734
10	100	1000	2.303	31.42	78.54	**60**	3600	216000	4.094	188.5	2827
11	121	1331	2.398	34.56	95.03	**61**	3721	226981	4.111	191.6	2922
12	144	1728	2.485	37.70	113.1	**62**	3844	238328	4.127	194.8	3019
13	169	2197	2.565	40.84	132.7	**63**	3969	250047	4.143	197.9	3117
14	196	2744	2.639	43.98	153.9	**64**	4096	262144	4.159	201.1	3217
15	225	3375	2.708	47.12	176.7	**65**	4225	274625	4.174	204.2	3318
16	256	4096	2.773	50.27	201.1	**66**	4356	287496	4.190	207.3	3421
17	289	4913	2.833	53.41	227.0	**67**	4489	300763	4.205	210.5	3526
18	324	5832	2.890	56.55	254.5	**68**	4624	314432	4.220	213.6	3632
19	361	6859	2.944	59.69	283.5	**69**	4761	328509	4.234	216.8	3739
20	400	8000	2.996	62.83	314.2	**70**	4900	343000	4.248	219.9	3848
21	441	9261	3.044	65.97	346.4	**71**	5041	357911	4.263	223.1	3959
22	484	10648	3.091	69.11	380.1	**72**	5184	373248	4.277	226.2	4072
23	529	12167	3.135	72.26	415.5	**73**	5329	389017	4.290	229.3	4185
24	576	13824	3.178	75.40	452.4	**74**	5476	405224	4.304	232.5	4301
25	625	15625	3.219	78.54	490.9	**75**	5625	421875	4.317	235.6	4418
26	676	17576	3.258	81.68	530.9	**76**	5776	438976	4.331	238.8	4536
27	729	19683	3.296	84.82	572.6	**77**	5929	456533	4.344	241.9	4657
28	784	21952	3.332	87.96	615.8	**78**	6084	474552	4.357	245.0	4778
29	841	24389	3.367	91.11	660.5	**79**	6241	493039	4.369	248.2	4902
30	900	27000	3.401	94.25	706.9	**80**	6400	512000	4.382	251.3	5027
31	961	29791	3.434	97.39	754.8	**81**	6561	531441	4.394	254.5	5153
32	1024	32768	3.466	100.5	804.2	**82**	6724	551368	4.407	257.6	5281
33	1089	35937	3.497	103.7	855.3	**83**	6889	571787	4.419	260.8	5411
34	1156	39304	3.526	106.8	907.9	**84**	7056	592704	4.431	263.9	5542
35	1225	42875	3.555	110.0	962.1	**85**	7225	614125	4.443	267.0	5675
36	1296	46656	3.584	113.1	1018	**86**	7396	636056	4.454	270.2	5809
37	1369	50653	3.611	116.2	1075	**87**	7569	658503	4.466	273.3	5945
38	1444	54872	3.638	119.4	1134	**88**	7744	681472	4.477	276.5	6082
39	1521	59319	3.664	122.5	1195	**89**	7921	704969	4.489	279.6	6221
40	1600	64000	3.689	125.7	1257	**90**	8100	729000	4.500	282.7	6362
41	1681	68921	3.714	128.8	1320	**91**	8281	753571	4.511	285.9	6504
42	1764	74088	3.738	131.9	1385	**92**	8464	778688	4.522	289.0	6648
43	1849	79507	3.761	135.1	1452	**93**	8649	804357	4.533	292.2	6793
44	1936	85184	3.784	138.2	1521	**94**	8836	830584	4.543	295.3	6940
45	2025	91125	3.807	141.4	1590	**95**	9025	857375	4.554	298.5	7088
46	2116	97336	3.829	144.5	1662	**96**	9216	884736	4.564	301.6	7238
47	2209	103823	3.850	147.7	1735	**97**	9409	912673	4.575	304.7	7390
48	2304	110592	3.871	150.8	1810	**98**	9604	941192	4.585	307.9	7543
49	2401	117649	3.892	153.9	1886	**99**	9801	970299	4.595	311.0	7698
50	2500	125000	3.912	157.1	1963	**100**	10000	1000000	4.605	314.2	7854

Areas of plane surfaces

Type of surface	Area A $\pi = 3.1416$
Triangle 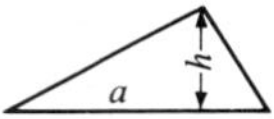	$A = \frac{a \cdot h}{2}$
Trapezoid 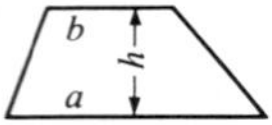	$A = \frac{a + b}{2}\, h$
Parallelo-gramm 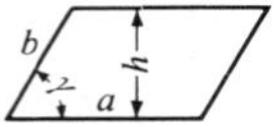	$A = a \cdot h = a \cdot b \cdot \sin\gamma$
Circle 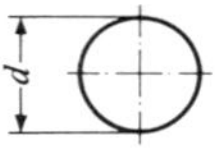	$A = \frac{\pi \cdot d^2}{4} = 0.785\, d^2$ Circumference $U = \pi \cdot d$ See table on p. 141
Annulus 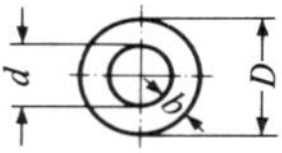	$A = \frac{\pi}{4}(D^2 - d^2) = \frac{\pi}{2}(D + d)\, b$
Sector 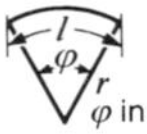 φ in degree	$A = \frac{\pi \cdot r^2 \cdot \varphi}{360°} = 8.73 \cdot 10^{-3} \cdot r^2 \cdot \varphi$ Lengh of arc $l = \frac{\pi \cdot r \cdot \varphi}{180°} = 1.75 \cdot 10^{-2} \cdot r \cdot \varphi$
Segment 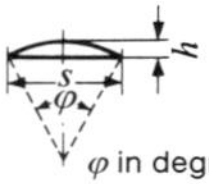 φ in degree	$A = \frac{r^2}{2}\left(\frac{\pi \cdot \varphi}{180°} - \sin\varphi\right) \approx h \cdot s \left[0.667 + 0.5 \left(\frac{h}{s}\right)^2\right]$ Length of chord $s = 2\, r \cdot \sin\frac{\varphi}{2}$ Arc height $h = r\left(1 - \cos\frac{\varphi}{2}\right) = \frac{s}{2}\tan\frac{\varphi}{4} = 2\, r \cdot \sin^2\frac{\varphi}{4}$
Hexagon 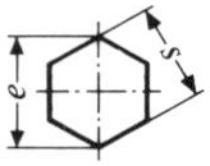	$A = \frac{\sqrt{3}}{2}\, s^2 = 0.866\, s^2$ Width across corners $e = \frac{2\, s}{\sqrt{3}} = 1.155\, s$
Ellipse 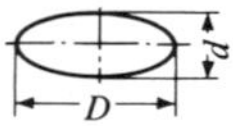	$A = \pi \cdot D \cdot d/4 = 0.785\, D \cdot d$ Perimeter $U \approx 0.75\, \pi\, (D + d) - 0.5\, \pi \sqrt{D \cdot d}$
Guldin's Rule for plane surfaces 	The area of a surface of revolution is equal to the length l of the generatrix times the distance travelled by the centroid: $A = 2\pi \cdot r \cdot l.$

Volume and surface area of solids

Type of solid		Volume V, surface S, lateral area M $\pi = 3.1416$
Regular cylinder	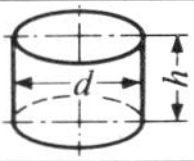	$V = \frac{\pi \cdot d^2}{4} h = 0.785\, d^2 \cdot h$ $M = \pi \cdot d \cdot h,\ S = \pi \cdot d\,(d/2 + h)$
Pyramid A Area of base h Height	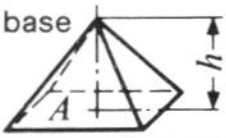	$V = \frac{1}{3} A \cdot h$
Circular cone	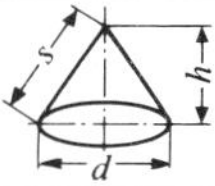	$V = \frac{\pi \cdot d^2 \cdot h}{12} = 0.262\, d^2 \cdot \mathrm{h}$ $\mathrm{M} = \frac{\pi \cdot d \cdot s}{2} = \frac{\pi \cdot d}{4}\sqrt{d^2 + 4h^2} = 0.785\, d \cdot \sqrt{d^2 + 4h^2}$
Frustum	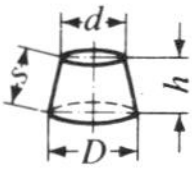	$V = \frac{\pi \cdot h}{12}(D^2 + D \cdot d + d^2) = 0.262\, h\,(D^2 + D \cdot d + d^2)$ $M = \frac{\pi\,(D + d)\, s}{2} \quad s = \sqrt{\frac{(D-d)^2}{4} + h^2}$
Sphere	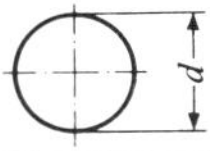	$V = \frac{\pi \cdot d^3}{6} = 0.524\, d^3$ $S = \pi \cdot d^2$
Spherical segment of one base	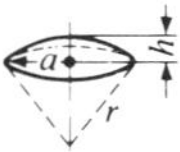	$V = \frac{\pi \cdot h}{6}(3a^2 + h^2) = \frac{\pi \cdot h^2}{3}(3r - h)$ $M = 2\pi \cdot r \cdot h = \pi\,(a^2 + h^2)$
Spherical sector	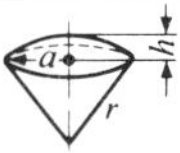	$V = \frac{2\pi \cdot r^2 \cdot h}{3} = 2.094\, r^2 \cdot h$ $S = \pi \cdot r\,(2h + a)$
Spherical segment of two bases	 r Radius of sphere	$V = \frac{\pi \cdot h}{6}(3a^2 + 3b^2 + h^2)$ $M = 2\pi \cdot r \cdot h$
Torus	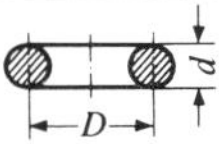	$V = \frac{\pi^2}{4} D \cdot d^2 = 2.467\, D \cdot d^2$ $S = \pi^2 \cdot D \cdot d = 9.870\, D \cdot d$
Ellipsoid	d_1, d_2, d_3 Length of axes	$V = \frac{\pi}{6} d_1 \cdot d_2 \cdot d_3 = 0.524\, d_1 \cdot d_2 \cdot d_3$
Circular cask	D Diameter at bung d Diameter at base h Distance between bases	$V \approx \frac{\pi \cdot h}{12}(2D^2 + d^2) \approx 0.26\, h\,(2D^2 + d^2)$
Guldin's rule for solids	Centroid 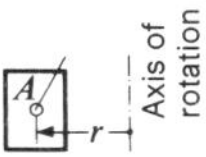	The volume of a solid of revolution is equal to the generating area A times the distance travelled by the centroid: $V = 2\pi \cdot r \cdot A$.

Quality

Quality is defined as the extent to which the customer expectations are fulfilled or exceeded; the quality requirement is determined by the customer. With his demands and expectations, he determines what quality is – in both products and service. Because competition leads to increased customer expectations, quality remains a dynamic quantity. Quality is defined through product and service-related factors which are susceptible to quantitative or qualitative analysis. The preconditions for achieving high quality are:
Quality policies: The company commitment to quality as a top-priority business objective,
Leadership: Employee-motivation measures
Quality assurance.

Quality assurance

Quality-assurance system

All elements in a quality-assurance program and all quality-assurance procedures must be systematically planned. The individual assignments and the areas of competence and responsibility are to be defined in writing (Quality-Assurance Handbook). Quality-assurance systems are also described in international standards, such as DIN ISO 9001 - 9004.

Increased requirements for defect-free products (target of zero defects) and economic considerations (defect prevention in place of sorting and reworking, or scrapping) make it imperative that preventative quality-assurance procedures be applied.
These serve the following objectives:
– To develop products that are insensitive to production fluctuations.
– To establish production processes to ensure that quality requirements are maintained within the specified limits.
– To apply methods which identify the sources of defects at an early stage, and can be applied to rectify the production process in good time.

Three types of audit are employed in the periodic monitoring of all elements in a quality-assurance system:
– System audit: Evaluation of the effectiveness of the quality-assurance system concentrating on its comprehensiveness and on the practical application of the individual elements.
– Process audit: Evaluation of the effectiveness of the elements in the quality-assurance program, confirmation of quality capability, of adherence to and suitability of particular procedures, and the determination of specific measures for improvement.
– Product audit: Evaluation of the effectiveness of quality-assurance elements performed by examining the final products or their components.

Quality assurance in development

At the outset, each of the new products which is to fulfill the customer's quality and reliability demands is assigned a project specifications manual.

As early as the definition phase, its contents are to serve as the basis for the planning of all sample and endurance testing required to verify the product's operation and reliability.

Quality evaluation

At the conclusion of specific development stages, all the available data regarding quality and reliability are subjected to a quality evaluation procedure, leading to initiation of the required corrective measures. Responsible for the quality evaluation are staff members from development, preproduction and quality control; these, in turn, receive support from specialists from the specific departments.

Failure Mode and Effects Analysis

This cost-reduction and risk-prevention procedure is suitable for investigating the types of defects which can occur in system components and their effects on the system (for details see "Reliability," page 158).

Quality assurance and suppliers

This aspect must extend beyond the delivery inspection; it must comprise an entire system. This system must ensure that the components acquired from subcontractors contribute to the reliable fulfillment of the Technical Specifications defined for the final product.

Example for application of Failure Mode and Effects Analysis (FMEA)

QUALITY ASSURANCE		FMEA Actuator 9 319 150 342 Part 6: Parts production and assembly of bushing						DEPT. FMEA PAGE DATE		FVB 75 1289940001 10 10.10.88		
NO.	COMPONENT PROCESS	FUNCTION PURPOSE	FAULT TYPE	FAULT EFFECT	FAULT CAUSES	FAULT PREVENTION	FAULT DETECTION	S S	– A	E E	SxE RZ	MEASURES V:/T:
1110	Assemble bushing	Prepare parts for soldering	Damaged sealing surfaces	Actuator leaks to the sur-roundings → Gasoline vapor in engine compart-ment	Swarf in assembly device	Wash before assembly, clean tool regularly	100% visual inspection of soldering; surface check; 100% visual inspection of before packing	10	2	1	20	
1180	Solder bushing	Hold parts together	Parts not soldered		Solder missing	Scan solder feed	100% visual inspection of soldering; surface check; 100% seal-tight test	10 (10	2 2	2 1	40 20)	100% seal-tight test of the bushing sub-assembly V: FVB2 T: 01.89
		Ensure leak-tightness	Part leaks (cavities)		Insufficient solder	Scan Solder feed	100% visual inspection of soldering	10 (10	4 3	6 2	240 60)	100% seal-tight test V: FVB2 T: 01.89 + Design improvements at soldering point V: EVA3 T: 03.89

S = Severity of fault
V = Responsibility
A = Probability of occurrence
T = Deadline for introduction
E = Probability of detection
RZ = Risk number = S x A x E

It is imperative that the subcontractor's quality capability be supported by modern, preventive techniques of assuring quality (e.g., SPC statistical process control, or FMEA). All individual requirements for the product must be specified in a clear and unambiguous manner in order to allow the subcontractor to achieve and competently evaluate comprehensive compliance with the quality requirements for the product. These guidelines generally are in the form of drawings, order specifications, standards, formulas, etc.

For example, the initial sample inspection can be performed by the subcontractor who manufactures the product. This inspection must be reproduced by the purchaser when the product is received (with particular emphasis on the interrelationships involving manufacturing processes and the final product), and confirmed by means of a delivery inspection.

The subcontractor's final or shipping inspection can take the place of the purchaser's delivery inspection in those cases where the subcontractor possesses special knowledge and/or the technical equipment necessary for carrying out specific kinds of testing. The subcontractor confirms the appropriate product quality examinations in quality-test certificates in accordance with DIN 55 350, or material test certificates according to DIN 50 049. The test results must be forwarded to the purchaser.

Quality assurance in the preproduction phase

The conditions for supplying reliable quality are established in the production-planning phase. Compliance with the following conditions is required:

- Planning of the production process and material flow.
- Planning of requirements for production material.
- Selection and acquisition of suitable production methods and production equipment, as well as the requisite test stands (e.g., for SPC).
- Examination of production procedures, production equipment and machines to determine equipment and process capability.
- Documentation of the production procedure in the production plan.
- Determination of the necessary level of employee qualification.
- Preparation of technical drawings and parts lists.

The Process FMEA provides a means of anticipating potential faults in the production process and of evaluating their effects on the quality of the attribute or the product. The Process FMEA is employed to discover the sources of defects, and to avoid the defects or minimize their effects. This makes it possible to initiate the necessary production and monitoring procedures required for defect avoidance.

FMEA work group

Area of operation	Product FMEA	Process FMEA	FMEA contribution
FMEA moderator		■	Coordination Methods
Construction (Ⓥ = Responsibility)	□ Ⓥ	■	Construction
Testing	□	■	Functionality
Endurance testing	□		Durability Climate resistance
Technical marketing	□		Project specifications
Customer service	□	■	Customer service
Pre-production (Ⓥ = Responsibility)	□	■ Ⓥ	Manufacturing verifiability procecedures
Quality services	□ □	■	Quality and reliability assurance
Production	□	■	Production
Materials		■	Subcontractor supply
Miscellaneous			

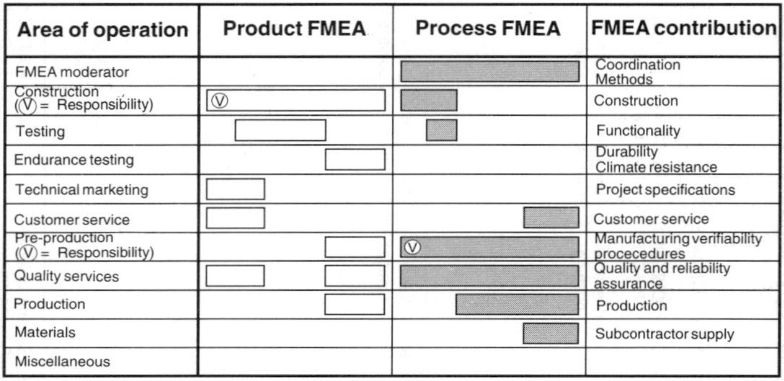

Inspection planning comprises the following points:
– Analysis of the operations to be evaluated.
– Determination of the test criteria.
– Selection of suitable means and methods for testing.
– Determination of the test content and frequency.
– Documentation of the test procedure in the inspection plan.
– Planning for compiling and recording of data on quality (e.g., in quality-control cards for SPC).
– Planning for monitoring of test equipment.
– Planning for quality-data documentation.

The specified inspection criteria must always include all essential characteristics of the finished products.

Suitable means for compilation and interpretation of the inspection results are to be specified for evaluating the quality of products and their components, and for controlling production processes. Test results are to be processed in such a manner as to be suitable for application in open-loop and closed-loop process-control systems, fault analysis and fault rectification.

Machine and process capability

The evaluation of machine capability is to confirm performance potential in the following two areas:
– The machine under examination must operate with verifiable consistency. When indicated, this consistency is to be defined with the aid of statistical quantities, e.g., as a normal (Gaussian) distribution factor with mean value $\bar{x}$ and mean square deviation *s*.
– The machine must be able to maintaining production within specified tolerances. This can only be confirmed using the quantification of consistency indicated above.

Testing of machine capability is restricted to a limited period, and to the investigation of the equipment-related effects on the production process. However, it should be noted that equipment-related and non-equipment-related factors (e.g., effects of material or procedures) cannot usually be separated completely. Individual tests are designed to determine whether:
– unusual process results are recognized,
– mean values and scatter range remain stable within the test series (the verification limits of statistical process control are employed for this examination).

If no unusual process results are present, and the mean and the scatter range are stable, then the process is considered to be fully controlled; the suitability of the equipment is then described using the familiar statistical parameters c_m and c_{mk}. The value for c_m only reflects the scatter range for the machine; it is calculated with the following equation:

$$c_m = (OGW - UGW)/(6 \cdot \hat{\sigma})$$

On the other hand, the value for c_{mk} reflects not only the machine's scatter range, but also the position of the mean within the tolerance range. It is essential that it be calculated for the production machinery on which adjustments are either imprecise or impossible. It is calculated as follows:

$$c_{mk} = (\bar{\bar{x}} - UGW)/(3 \cdot \hat{\sigma}) \text{ or}$$
$$c_{mk} = (OGW - \bar{\bar{x}})/(3 \cdot \hat{\sigma})$$

with the lesser value being valid. The definitions are:

$\bar{\bar{x}}$ Total mean value
UGW Lower tolerance-range limit
OGW Upper tolerance-range limit
$\hat{\sigma}$ Estimated process scatter range

Bosch only designates production equipment as capable of ensuring that manufacture will result in the required product attributes when c_{mk} is at least 1.67.

Unusual process results, or an instable mean or scatter range indicate that the process is not fully controlled. This means that non-random influences (interference factors) are affecting the process. These must be rectified either through removal or compensation; after this the equipment's performance potential is tested again.

If the result of the machine-capability test is positive, it is followed by an examination of the process capability. This is intended to ensure that the production process is capable of consistently meeting the quality requirements placed upon it.

The examination of process capability extends over a longer period of time. All changes in the process (e.g., different material, tooling changes or modification of methods) are reflected in the examination procedure, where they are considered in determining the extent and frequency of sample testing.

Once compiled, the data are subjected to a statistical analysis comparable to that employed for determining equipment performance potentials. Particular attention is devoted to ascertaining whether the process mean and process control are stable, i.e., whether the process is fully controlled. If the process is fully controlled, then the process performance potential is confirmed using the familiar statistical values c_p and c_{pk}. These values are calculated in the same manner as c_m and c_{mk}; the values for $\bar{\bar{x}}$ and $\hat{\sigma}$ must be derived from the process examination.

If the process is not fully controlled, then c_p and c_{pk} are not to be calculated. In this case the causes of the instability in the process must be dealt with through removal or compensation. The examination of process performance potential is then repeated.

Bosch designates a process as ensuring the required product attributes only in cases where c_{pk} is at least 1.33.

Machinery and processes must be tested before SPC is applied. However, both investigations are also important for processes which are not controlled by SPC, as the required potential must be confirmed for each type of process.

Statistical Process Control (SPC)
SPC is a process-control system intended to assist in the prevention of errors and their associated costs. SPC is employed in production, being applied for attributes which are vital to operation (for details, see "Technical Statistics", page 154).

Test equipment
The test equipment must be able to demonstrate whether the test attributes of the finished product conform to the prescribed specifications. Test equipment must be monitored, calibrated and maintained. Measuring error is to be considered when using test equipment. It must be minimal relative to the tolerance range for the attribute being tested. With test equipment, attention is to be paid to:
– Determining the measurements to be performed, the required precision and the suitable test equipment.
– Ensuring that the test equipment meets precision requirements, i.e., the measuring error is generally not to exceed 10 % of the tolerance range.
– All test equipment and gauges used for product quality-assurance are to be

Process-control system

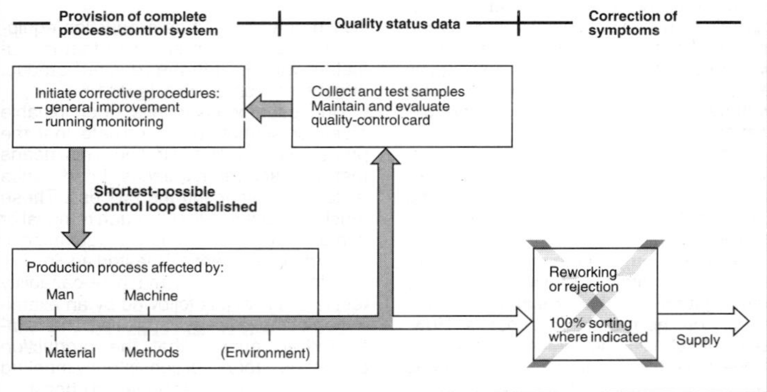

specified in an inspection plan; they must be labeled, and are to be calibrated and adjusted at prescribed intervals.

– Calibration procedures must be specified. These must comprise individual data on the type of unit, its identification, application area and calibration intervals, and are also to include the steps to be taken in case of unstatisfactory results.

– Test devices are to be provided with labels indicating their calibration status.

– Calibration records (histories) are to be maintained.

– The appropriate environmental conditions for calibrating, testing and measurement must be maintained.

– Test equipment is to be carefully stored and protected against contamination in order to maintain consistent levels of precision and suitability for use.

– The test equipment and the software are to be protected against any influences which might invalidate their calibration.

Test-equipment monitoring – Scope and procedures

Satisfactory arrangements for monitoring test equipment embrace all measuring devices employed in development, production, assembly and in customer service. This category includes calipers, unit standards, instruments, recording devices, and special test equipment along with its ancillary computer software. In addition, the equipment, mounts and clamps, and instruments employed for process control are also monitored.

Procedures which extend to include the equipment and the abilities of the operator are employed in evaluating whether a test process is controlled. Measurement deviations are compared with the quality specifications. Appropriate corrective measures are to be initiated when the requirements for precision and function in test equipment are no longer satisfied.

Calibration requirements and measuring devices

German legal requirements on weights and measures stipulate that calibration of measuring devices which are for use in "business transactions" be officially certified in those cases where the results of their measurements are employed to determine the price of goods or energy. This category includes equipment for measuring length, surface area, volume and mass, and thermal and electrical energy. If these conditions apply, then the calibration of the measuring devices in question must be officially-certified. Continuing compliance must then be minitored by an official or an officially approved agency.

Relationship between test results, statistical analysis and process capability

Process	← Tolerance T →	Status	Process capability
Individual values	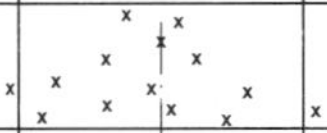	Unsure	Not calculated
Statistical analyis	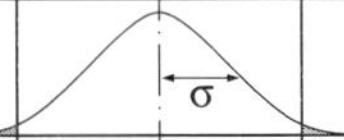	Result negative due to excessive dispersion	$C_p = \frac{T}{6\sigma} = 0.67$ Outside T by 4.6%
Minimum requirement	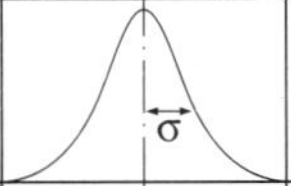	Result positive Low dispersion Mean value maintained	$C_p = 1.33$ Outside T by 630 ppm
Mean tolerance value displaced	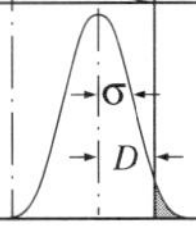	Result negative despite low dispersion	$C_p = 2.0$ but $C_{pk} = \frac{D}{3\sigma} = 0.67$ i.e., outside T by 2.3%

Engineering statistics

Purpose of statistics

1. To describe sets of items with specific, different characteristics using stistical parameters which allow objective comparisons and evaluations.
2. To provide informationon the statistical parameters of larger sets (populations) based on relatively few individual data (samples).

Bacause such statements are based on the laws of change and probabilty, their validity is always subject to a certain level of confidence, usually 95% in the field of engineering.

Examples of populations:

– All products of the same type produced under constant manufacturing conditions.
– All possible values resulting from measurement of a variable under unchanging conditions.

There are two different types of characteristics:

– Quantitative characteristics usually physical quantities (referred to as "measured values"),
– Attributes, e.g. "OK" or "Defective" etc. (referred to as "test results").

Statistical analysis provides valuable assistance for ensuring and improving quality standards in industrial products. Today's levels of vehicle reliability would be impossible without it.

Presentation of measured values

N Population size: the number of all items which form the basis of the statistical analysis

n Sample size: number of items in the sample

P_A Confidence level

x Individual measured value

R Range: $R = x_{max} - x_{min}$

k Number of classes into which R is divided $k = \sqrt{n}$ (min. 5)

w Class interval

i Ordinal number of the measured values (as subscript)

j Ordinal number of the classes (as subscript)

x_j Center of the jth class

n_j Absolute frequency of the jth class: the number of measured values in the jth class

h_j Relative frequency in the fth class: $h_j = n/n$

h_j/w Frequency density

G_j Cumulative absolute frequency: absolute frequency summed up to a certain class

$$G_j = \sum_{r=1}^{j} n_r$$

H_j Cumulative relative frequency = G_j/n

$F(x)$ Distribution function: probability for values $\leq x$

$f(x)$ Probability density function $\frac{dF(x)}{dx}$

μ Arithmetic mean of the population

$\overline{x}$ Arithmetic mean of the sample

$$\overline{x} = \sum_{i=1}^{n} x_i/n$$

$\overline{\overline{x}}$ Mean of several $\overline{x}$ values

σ Standard deviation of the population; (a measure for the average deviation of the individual values from the mean)

s Standard deviation of the sample

$$s = \sqrt{\sum_{i=1}^{n} (x_i - \overline{x})^2 / (n-1)}$$

V Variation coefficient $V = s/x$

u Standardized normal deviate

Histogramm and cumulative frequency Curve of an empirical distribution

The simplest way of clearly presenting a large number of measured values is to plot them in classes in a histogram (frequency diagram). A histogram consists of rectangles whose areas are proportional to the frequencies, and whose bases equal the class interval. The heights of these rectangles are thus proportional to the frequencies densities. The cumulative frequency curve is obtained by plotting the cumulative frequencies Hj versus the corresponding upper class limit.

With smaller samples, $H_i = (i - 0.5)/n$ is entered above the individual values for xi, which are entered in a progressive sequence.

The advantage of the cumulative frequency curve over the histogram is that

Empirical distribution

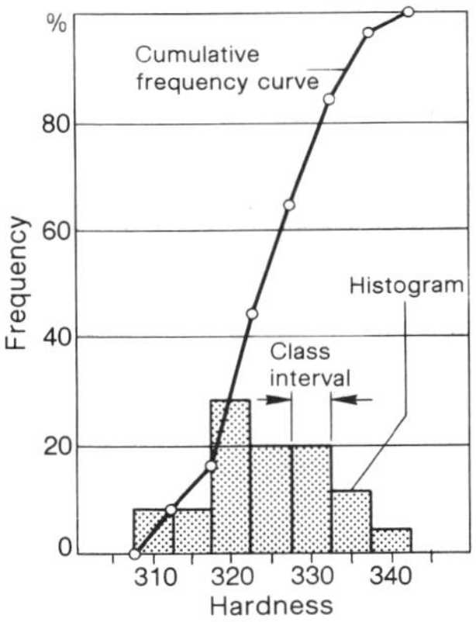

Normal distribution

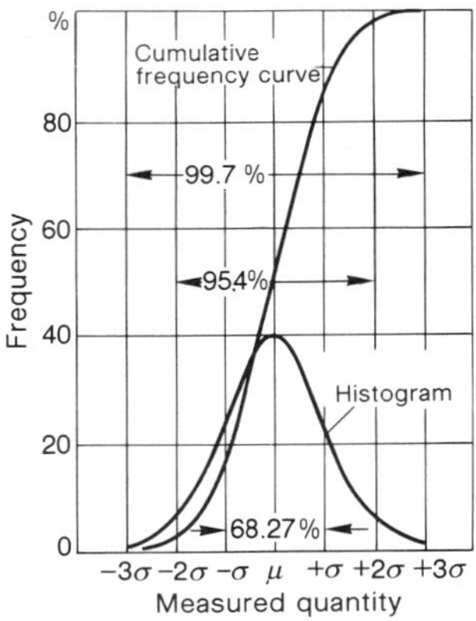

the percentage of measured values in any interval can easily be read off (estimate of out-of tolerance percentages).

Distributors and statistical parameters

A random varaible x is characteristized by its distribution. The distribution function $F(x)$ describes the relationship between x and the cumulative frequency or the probability of values $\leq x$. In empirical distributions, this function corresponds to the cumulative frequency curve. The histogram is described by the frequency density function.

The most important parameters of a distribution are μ and σ.

μ Mean of the x values
σ Variance of th x values
(= mean quadratic deviation from μ)

μ and σ in empirical distributions are represented by $\bar{x}$ and s (see p. 153 for formulas).

The normal distribution

The normal, or Gaussian, distribution is the mathematically ideal distribution which always results when many mutually independent random effects are added together. The probability density function of the Gaussian distribution forms a bell-shaped symmetrical curve.

The total area under the bell-shaped curve corresponds to 1 = 100 %. The standard deviation σ and its multiples allow the delimination of specific areas with boundaries $\mu \pm u\sigma$in which P% of the permissible values fall (see Table 1). The percentage $\alpha = (100 - P)/2$ lie outside these areas on either side.

Table 1. Normal distribution probabilty P within $\pm u\sigma$, α below or above $\pm u\sigma$

u	1.00	1.28	1.64	1.96	2.00	2.33	2.58	3.00	3.29
P%	68.27	80	90	95	95.4	98	99	99.7	99.9
α%	15.86	10	5	2.5	2.3	1	0.5	0.15	0.05

Normally probability paper

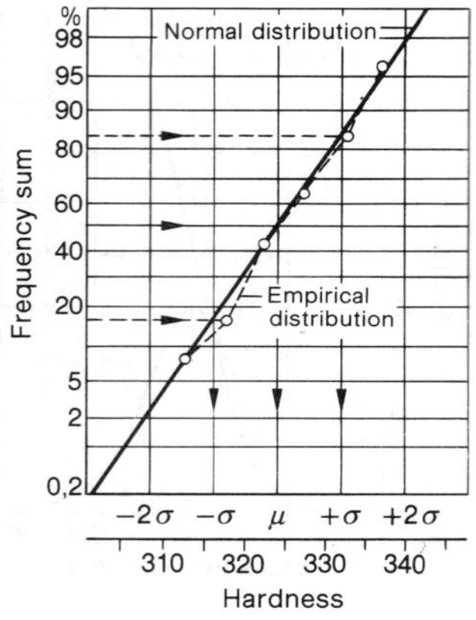

Empirical distribution and normal distribution plotted on normal probability paper

Normal probability paper distorts the ordinate in such a way that the S-shaped cumulative frequency curve is transformed into a straight line.

Determination of μ and σ using normal probability paper:

1. Read off μ at 50% frequency sum.
2. Read off the values on the abscissa at 16% and 84%.

The difference corresponds to $2\,\sigma$.

Law of quadratic error sum

The mean and standard deviation of a random variable $z = a \cdot x + b \cdot y$, generated by the linear combination of 2 independently distributed random variables x and y are:

$$\mu_z = a \cdot \mu_x + b \cdot \mu_y$$
$$\sigma_z^2 = a^2 \cdot \sigma_x^2 + b^2 \cdot \sigma_y^2$$

Typical applications

1. Fits. Hole diameter: x. Shaft diameter: y. Clearance: $z = x - y$.
For $\sigma_x = \sigma_y$, the following applies:
$\sigma_z^2 = 2 \cdot \sigma_x^2$
2. Combined dimension. If the individual dimensions are statistically independently distributed about their mean tolerances, the tolerance for the combined dimension can be calculated by quadratic addition (cf. DIN 7186).

Evaluation of series measurements

Random of intervals for $\bar{x}$ and s

Quantity	Random interval Lower limit	Upper limit
$\bar{x}$	$\mu - u\dfrac{s}{\sqrt{n}}$	$\mu + u\dfrac{\sigma}{\sqrt{n}}$
S	$D_u \cdot \sigma$	$D_o \cdot \sigma$
R	$D_u \cdot \sigma \cdot d_n$	$D_o \cdot \sigma \cdot d_n$

D_u and D_o as a function of n from Tables 1 and 2.

Random Intervals for $\bar{x}$ und s

If many samples each containing n values are taken from the same population with a mean of μ and a standard deviation of σ, the mean values $\bar{x}_1, \bar{x}_2 \ldots$ of the samples are dispersed with the standard deviation

$$\sigma_{\bar{x}} = \frac{\sigma}{\sqrt{n}} \text{ about the trule value } \mu.$$

(cf. Law of quadratic error sum)

Similarly, random intervals can be defined for s and R.

Table 2. Auxiliary constants for evaluation of series of measurements

n	d_n	t-values for $P =$ 90%	95%	99%	D_u for P = 95%	D_o
2	1.13	6.31	12.7	63.7	0.03	2.24
3	1.69	2.92	4.30	9.92	0.16	1.92
5	2.33	2.13	2.78	4.60	0.35	1.67
10	3.08	1.83	2.26	3.25	0.55	1.45
20	3.74	1.73	2.09	2.86	0.68	1.32
50	–	1.68	2.01	2.68	0.80	1.20
∞	–	1.65	1.96	2.58	1.00	1.00

Confidence intervals for μ and σ

(a posteriori)

If only x and s for the samples are known, the mean value μ to be anticipated as the result of an infinite number of measurements can be indicated using a confidence interval; the probability that μ lies within this range will be P_A%. The same holds true for σ.

Quantity	Confidence interval Lower limit	Upper limit
μ	$\overline{x} - t \frac{s}{\sqrt{n}}$	$\overline{x} + t \frac{s}{\sqrt{n}}$
σ	$\frac{s}{D_o}$	$\frac{s}{D_u}$

t, D_o and D_u from Table 2

Comparison of mean values

Given 2 random samples (n_i, x_i, s_i), let $s_1 = s_2$.

The confidence interval for the difference $\mu_1 - \mu_2$ is:

$(\overline{x}_1 - \overline{x}_2) \pm t \cdot s_A \cdot \sqrt{1/n_1 + 1/n_2}$ with

with $n' = n_1 + n_2 - 1$.

Select t value for n' from Table 2.

Estimation of fraction of defectives

The percentage of parts lying outside the tolerance limit a is to be estimated based on the measured values $\overline{x}$, s from a sample series.

Calculation procedure:

If μ and s are known, then the percentage outside a in Table 1 or in the Figure "Confidence limits for fraction of defectives" ("best estimate" or "most likely value" curve) is determined with:

$$u = | a - \mu | / \sigma.$$

A value of e.g. $\mu = 1.65$ corresponds to a fraction of 5 %. Usually, however, only $\overline{x}$ and s from the random sample are known. As these values are random, the fraction of defectives can only be specified in terms of a confidence range, in which it will lie with the indicated probability.

In the figure, the confidence limits can be determined as a function of $| a - \overline{x} | / s$; with a probability of being exceeded of only 5 %. Separate analyses are required for each of the two tolerance limits.

Confidence limits for fraction of defectives

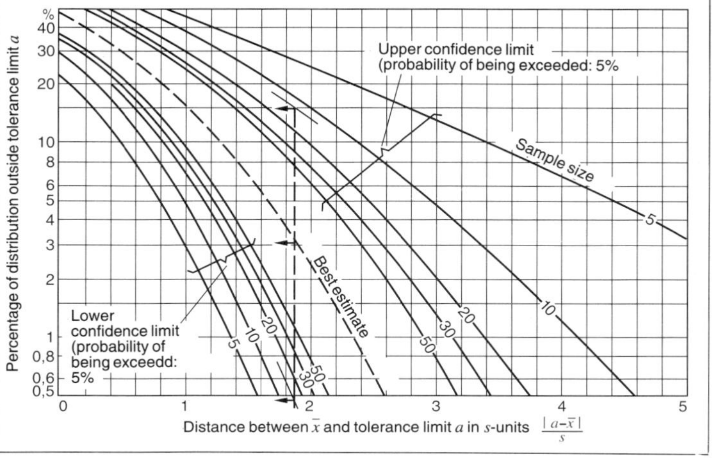

Example:
Prescribed tolerance for ground rollers $14^{-0.016}_{-0.043}$
Tested are 14 parts of 13.961 to 13.983 mm. x = 13.972 mm; R = 0.022 mm.

Estimated value for s from R with d_n from Table 2:
s = 0.022/3.5=0.0063

Upper tolerance limit exceeded:

$$\frac{|a-\bar{x}|}{s} = \frac{13.984-13.972}{0.0063} = \frac{0.012}{0.0063} = 1.9$$

Referring to the figure:
Upper confidence limit ≈ 15%
Most likely value ≈ 3.1%
Lowest confidence limit < 0.5%

Lower tolerance limit exceeded:

$$\frac{|a-\bar{x}|}{s} = \frac{|13.957-13.972|}{0.0063} = \frac{0.015}{0.0063} = 2.38$$

Referring to the illustration:
Upper confidence limit ≈ 9 %
Most likely value ≈ 1 %
Lowest confidence limit < 0.5%

Statistical Process Control (SPC)
Quality-control charts are employed to ensure consistent quality in manufacturing processes. Random samples are tested at specified intervals; For test results, the measured values $\bar{x}$ and R are entered, while the defects are noted for attribute testing.
T_l, T_u Lower and upper tolerance limits,
T Difference between the lower and upper tolerance limit (tolerance range),
$T = T_l - T_u$, $T_m = (T_l + T_u)/2$,
$\bar{x}$, R Values obtained from ≥ 20 random samples,
$\sigma = R/d_n$ = Standard deviation,
$c_p = T/(6 \times \sigma)$ = Capability index
A process is considered to be "controlled" if
1) $C_p > 1$ (better: $c_p \geq 1.33$),
2) The curve displays no unusual variations (no trends, etc.),
3) $\bar{x}$ and R lie within the "action limits" of the corresponding random intervals.

Table 3 shows the approximate values for action limits as a percent of T. The calculation is based upon the assumptions that values are:
99.7% random intervals and c_p = 1.

Table 3. Action limits as % of T

n	3	4	5	6	7	8	10	12	15
$R/T<5$	72	78	82	84	86	88	91	93	95
$(\bar{x}-T_m)<5\%$	29	25	22	20	19	18	16	14	13

Evaluation of an endurance test involving n = 19 switches in the Weibull probability paper

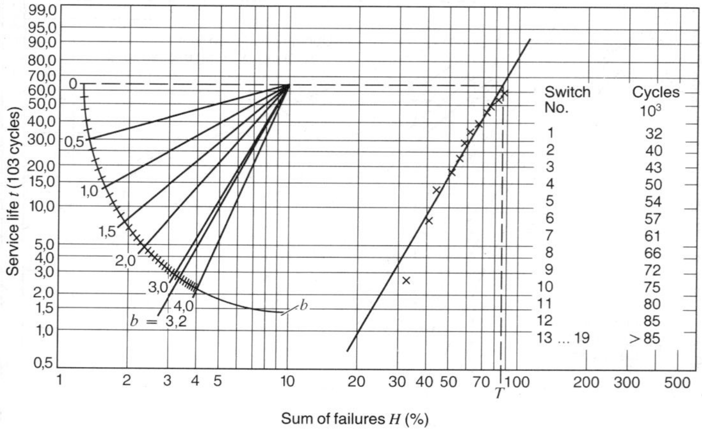

The Weibull distribution

The Weibull Distribution has gained acceptance as the standard in the investigation of the service lives of technical products. Its distribution function (probability of service lives $\leq t$) is:

$$F(t) = 1 - e^{-(t/T)^b}$$

Survival probability (Reliability function):

$$R(t) = 1 - F(t)$$

Failure rate (failures per unit time referred to remaining products)

$$\lambda(t) = f(t)/R(t)$$

where

T Characteristic service life, corresponding sum of failures: 63.2%

b Failure steepness:
- $b < 1$: falling (early failures)
- $b = 1$: constant (random failures)
- $b > 1$: rising (wear)

$F(t)$ becomes a straight line in the Weibull probability paper with $\ln t$ as the abscissa and $\ln(-\ln R[t])$ as the ordinate.

Evaluation of an endurance test involving n test specimens:

The Figure on p. 154 shows the evaluation of an endurance test involving $n = 19$ switches, of which $r = 12$ have failed. The service lives t are arranged according to length in cycles; the composite failure rate is plotted as:

$H = (i - 0.5)/n$.

The result is:

$T = 83 \cdot 10^3$ Cycles
$b = 3.2$ (wear)

T and b are random values like $\bar{x}$ and s. Approximate confidence limits ($n \geq 50$) for the "true values" are provided by the formulae:

$T \pm (u/\sqrt{n})\ (T/b)$

$b - 0.5 \cdot (u/\sqrt{n'}) \cdot b \ldots b + (u/\sqrt{n'}) \cdot b$

u from Table 1.

For incomplete observations ($r < n$):

$n' \approx r \cdot (1 + (r/n))/2$

T, b are thus less precisely defined at r failures at ($r < n$) than at $r = n$. The proportion exceeding a specific life expectancy is estimated in the following section.

Statistical evaluation of inspection by attributes

N Size of the population: number of parts in the production lot. An attribute divides the lot into two classes, e.g., "failed" and "OK".
n Sample size
I Defective parts or number of defects in the lot
i Defective parts or number of defects in the sample
p Particular value in the sample $p = i/n$
p' Particular value in the lot $p' = I/N$

Distribution of the defective fraction p in random samples

The number of defectives i within the sample is a random variable. Larger lots ($N > 10 \cdot n$) are characterized by binomial distribution, with anticipated result: $E(i) = n \cdot p'$,
Standard deviation:
$\sigma_i = \sqrt{n \cdot p' (1 - p')}$.
Random ranges for p (p' known) and confidence intervales for p' (p known), relative to n are provided by the figure on page 156 with a probability = 10% that any specific limit will be exceeded.

In the $p' < 5\%$ range, frequently encountered in practice, Poisson's law of infrequent events, which depends exclusively on $n \cdot p'$, with $E(i) = n \cdot p'$, $\sigma_i = \sqrt{n \cdot p'}$, is used instead of the binomial distribution.

Table 4. Confidence limits for infrequent events

Obs. no. of def. parts i	Lower limit $n\,p'_u$		Upper limit $n\,p'_o$	
	Probability a of being exceeded			
	2.5%	10%	10%	2.5%
0	–	–	2.30	3.69
1	0.225	0.105	3.89	5.57
2	0.242	0.532	5.32	7.22
3	0.619	1.10	6.68	8.77
4	1.09	1.74	8.00	10.24
5	1.62	2.43	9.27	11.67
6	2.20	3.15	10.53	13.06
7	2.81	3.89	11.77	14.42
8	3.45	4.66	12.99	15.76
9	4.12	5.43	14.21	17.08
10	4.80	6.22	15.41	18.39
u	−1.96	−1.28	+1.28	−1.96
k	+1.0	+0.2	1.2	+2.0

Examples:

1. Binomial distribution

In durability testing with $n = 20$ units, $i = 2$ units have failed after extended usage.

What percentage p' of the series will not achieve the corresponding service life T?

Percentage in the random sample $p = 2/20 = 10\%$.
At $p = 10\%$, $n = 20$, the family of curves below provides the following figures:
$p'_u = 2.8\%$, $p'_o = 24\%$.

At a constant quality, the percentage of units with a service life $< T$ will lie within this range.

2. Poisson distribution (Table 4)

During delivery inspection, a random sampling of $n = 500$ parts found $i = 1$ part which was out of tolerance.

What is the maximum percentage of out-of-tolerance parts in the lot as expressed with 90 % probability?
At $i = 1$, $a = 10\%$, Table 4 indicates:
$np'_o = 3.89$
$p'_o = 3.89/500 = 7.78$ ‰

Approximation formula for Poisson distribution

The approximate value for $i > 10$ can be derived using:
$n \cdot p' = i + u \cdot \sqrt{i + k}$
(see Table 4 for u, k).

Random and confidence limits for fractions defective *(Binominal distribution)*
Probability of each limit being exceeded: a = 10%.

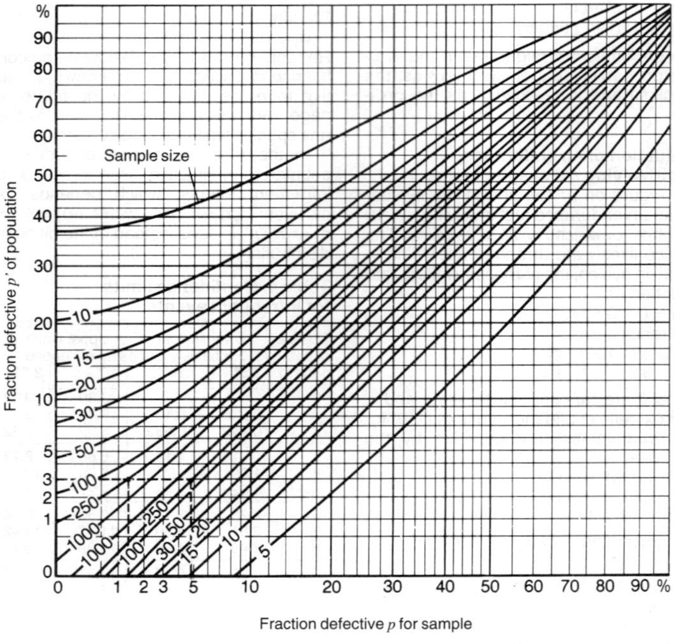

Example for Poisson approximation:
In a preproduction series consisting of n= 10,000 units, there were k= 17 warranty claims. With 97.5% probability, what is the limit for warranty claims which will not be exceeded in normal series production if identical conditions are maintained?

Inserting the values from Table 4 into the approximation formula given above provides the following:

$np'_0 = 17 + 1.96\ \sqrt{17} + 2 = 27.08$
$n \cdot p' = 27.08/10{,}000 = 2.7\ ^0/_{00}$

Measurement: basic terms

Measurements can only be only used as the basis for responsible decisions if their limits of error are known. Here, statistical terms are used.

Definition of terms (as per DIN1319):
Measured variable
Physical variable which is measured (length, density, etc.).

Measured value
Particular value of the measured variables, e.g. 3 m.

Measurement result
Special value of the measured variables, e.g. 3 m.

Measurement error $F = x_a - x_r$
x_a indicated measured value; x_r "correct" measured value. Causes: measured object, measurement equipment, measurement procedure, environment, observer.

Relative measurement error
Normally: F/x_r
F/x_e when characterizing measurement devices, where x_e is the full-scale value of measurement device.

Systemeatic measurement errors
Measurement errors which, under the same conditions, have the same magnitude and sign.

Those systematic errors which can be detected are to be corrected, $B = -F$ otherwise the measurement result is incorrect. Systematic errors which cannot be detected are to be estimated (f).

Random measurement errors
Measurement errors whose magnitudes and signs are randomly dispersed. These errors are to be estimated using the standard deviation s.

Result of a series of measurements
If n measured values x_i are measured under the same conditions, the measurement results are shown as follows:
$y = \overline{x}_E \pm u$ Confidence limits for correct measured value, where:
$\overline{x}_E = \overline{x} + B$ Corrected mean
$u = t \cdot s/\sqrt{n} + |f|$ Measurement uncertainty.
Calculation of s, p. 150.
Table 2 for t, p. 152.
f = Non-detected systematic errors.

Separation of measurement and manufacturing accuracy
On each of n products, a characteristic x_i with measurement error f_{ik} is measured twice:

$y_{ik} = x_i + f_{ik}\ \ (i = 1, \ldots n;\ \ k = 1, 2)$

The differences between the 2 measured values on the same product contain 2 measurement errors:

$$z_i = y_{i1} - y_{i2} = f_{i1} - f_{i2}$$

$$\sigma_z^2 = 2\ \sigma_f^2$$

$$\sigma_y^2 = \sigma_x^2 + \sigma_f^2$$

The last two relationships can be used to determine the standard deviation σ_f of the measurement errors and the corrected standard deviation σ_x of product characteristic x.

Standards
DIN 55 303 Statistical Evaluation of Data
DIN 53 804 Statistical Evaluation
DIN 55 350 Quality Assurance and Statistics Terms
DIN 40 080 Specifications and Tables for Attributive Sampling
DIN 7186 Statistical Tolerances
DIN/ISO 9000 Quality-Assurance Systems
DGQ-11-04 Quality-Assurance Terms and Formulas (Beuth)

Literature
Graf, Henning, Stange: Formeln und Tabellen der Statistik (Formulas and tables for statistics). Springer-Verlag, Berlin, 1966;
Rauhut: Berechnung der Lebensdauerverteilung (Calculation of service life distribution). Glückauf-Verlag, Essen, 1982.

Reliability

According to DIN 40041, reliability is the sum total of those characteristics in the unit under investigation which exert an effect on the unit's ability to achieve specified requirements under given conditions during a specified period of time. Reliability is one of the constituent elements of quality; it is quantified in terms of availability, which, in turn, is defined as the probability that at any given time a system will prove to be fully operational.

Failure rate

The failure rate is the relative probability density of a component failing before time $t + dt$ once it has survived beyond t. The failure rate is generally described by what, with reference to its shape, is referred to as the "bathtub curve" and can be defined by an overlay of three Weibull distributions with varying failure components b (see "Technical Statistics").

Reliability analysis

Mutually supplementary analysis methods are applied to determine the potential failure risk associated with a product, i.e., to discover all possible effects of operational and internal failure, as well as external interference factors (such as incorrect operator input). These methods include FMEA, FTA, failure process analysis, block diagrams and Markov models. Simulations are also employed.

FMEA (DIN 25448, IEC 812)
FMEA (Failure Mode and Effects Analysis) is a "bottom-up" analysis, proceeding from the lowest level of the system hierarchy (in construction FMEA this is generally the individual component, while system FMEA's start with single function blocks, and the process FMEA's basic units are individual operations). The analysis investigates the proliferation of the failure throughout higher levels. It provides a rough evaluation of a failure's significance, and is able to detect all those critical system conditions which result from individual failures.

FMEA can be applied in various stages of development and production.

Design FMEA
Precondition: Parts have been manufactured according to specification. Products and components are examined for conformity between design and initial project specifications in order to avoid errors in system design and to facilitate recognition of field risks.

Process FMEA
Precondition: Specifications correct. The production process is examined to avoid manufacturing errors in the finished products.

System FMEA
The investigation concentrates on mutually complementary operation of the system components and their interconnections. It seeks to ensure satisfactory operation and to avoid failures due to incorrect system design, and to recognize field risks.

Fault-tree analysis (DIN 25424)
Fault-tree analysis (FTA) is a "top-down" procedure. A failure effect (top event, undesirable occurrence) is analyzed to determine its origin; the analyis registers all potential instigators (including cumulative individual failures) of the undesirable event. When the probability factors for the individual failures are known, it is possible to calculate the likelihood of a specific undesirable event occuring.

Reliability planning

The Reliability Growth management procedure (RG, Mil Hdbk 189) for development of components and systems is employed to ensure that newly developed products conform to reliability requirements from the first day of production.

If the cumulative operating time (total test time for all products) is plotted against the momentary MTTF (Mean Time to Failure, expected service life; here: Total test time of all samples divided by the number of failed samples) in double logarithmic scale, experience indicates that the momentary MTTF will increase in a straight line at a rate α; this lies between 0.35 and 0.5, depending upon the product and the associated testing effort. Under favorable conditions, the procedure can permit total test time to be reduced by a factor of $1 - \alpha$.

Testing according to an RG plan must be accompanied by measures to be implemented in response to the evaluation results. As the RG program progresses, intermediate reliability goals, specified in advance, must also be met. The test program must be planned to strike an acceptable balance in terms of time and testing effort. It must also be based upon a realistic estimate of the potential gains.

Reliability in automotive electronic systems

Electronics in open and closed-loop control systems are being employed to regulate vehicular processes in ever-greater profusion. Once this was the province of analogue electronics; today, digital, microcomputer-controlled systems are becoming the norm. They represent the only available means for realizing the requirements for comfort, cleanlinesss, vehicle economy, and, not least important, the increasing safety expectations.

Prediction of system reliability

Failure in electronic components is generally spontaneous, with no advance indication of impending defects. This condition is described by an exponential distribution (constant failure rate, middle section of the "bathtub curve"). Neither quality control procedures nor preventative maintenance can keep these failures from occurring. This category does not include failures due to factors such as incorrect component selection, excessive loads or abuse, or faulty manufacturing; such defects are generally found in the initial section of the bathtub curve.

If no additional measures are implemented (redundancy measures) then the availability factor of an electronic system decreases as a direct function of the increase in the number of components. Components and systems installed in motor vehicles are subjected to extreme thermal, physical and climatic stresses, as well as to electromagnetic interference. In addition, the electronic system's inherent complexity makes it difficult to maintain the reliability standards achieved by more conventional systems.

In taking these extraneous influences into account, compilations of component-reliability data such as the Mil Hdbk 217E, and SAE 870050 permit fairly useful reliability projections for the system.

Purely electronic components, such as transistors, integrated circuits and microprocessors, are responsible for only 10 % of the failures encountered in electronic systems. The proportion of failures from defective sensors and final-control elements is 30 %, and 60 % are caused by faults in the connections between various components, or between the components and the outside world.

Enhancing system reliability

System reliability can always be improved by avoiding errors or narrowing tolerances. One preventative measure is to select more reliable components; another method is to reduce the number of individual components, and thus the number of connections, by increasing the degree of integration. If preventative measures do not prove sufficient, then failure-tolerance measures (e.g., multi-channel circuitry, self-monitoring) must be implemented in order to mask the effects of a defect.

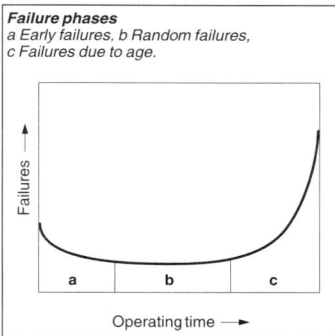

Failure phases
a Early failures, b Random failures, c Failures due to age.

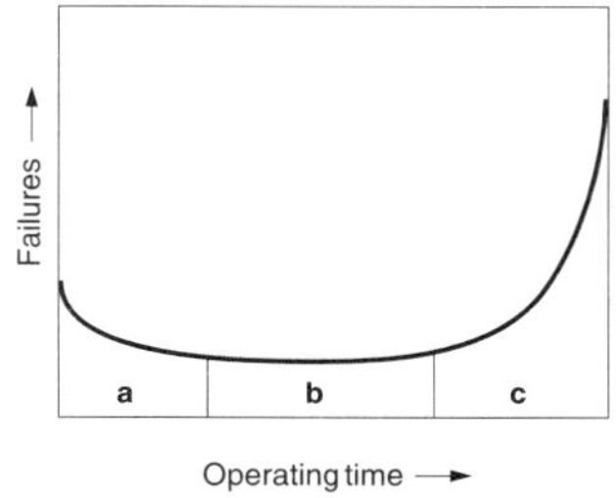

Data processing in motor vehicles

Requirements

Highly sophisticated state-of-the-art open-loop and closed-loop control concepts are essential for meeting the demands for function, safety, environmental compatibility and comfort associated with the wide range of automotive subsystems installed in modern-day vehicles. Sensors monitor reference and controlled variables, which an electronic control unit (ECU) then converts into the signals required to adjust the final-controlling elements/actuators. The signals can be analogue (e.g., pressure, temperature), digital (e.g., switch position) or pulse-shaped (that is, information generated with specific periodicity, e.g., engine-speed limitation signal); these signals undergo initial conditioning (filtering, amplification, pulse formation, analogue/digital conversion) before further processing in the ECU. Digital signal-processing methods are generally employed.

Thanks to modern semiconductor technology, powerful computer units, with their ancillary program and data memories, and special peripheral circuitry, designed specifically for real-time applications, can all be integrated on a limited number of chips.

Modern vehicles are equipped with numerous digital ECU's for systems such as ignition/fuel injection, ABS and transmission control. Improved performance and additional functions are obtained by synchronizing the processes controlled by the individual ECU's and by mutual real-time adaptation of the respective parameters. The ECU for traction control (ASR), which reduces the drive torque when the drive wheels show a tendency to spin, provides an example of this type of function.

Up to now, the flow of data between the ECU's (in the example cited above, ABS/ASR and the engine power control) has been conducted exclusively through separate individual circuits. However, this type of point-to-point connection is only suitable for a limited number of signals. The data-transmission potential between the individual ECU's can be enhanced by using a simple network topology designed specifically for serial data transmission in automotive applications.

Microcomputers

The microcomputer comprises both the central processing unit (CPU) for processing arithmetic operations and logical relationships, and special function modules to monitor external signals and to generate the control signals for external servo elements. These peripheral modules are largely capable of assuming complete control of real-time operations; the program-controlled central processor could only discharge these at the price of both additional complication and curtailment in the number of functions (e.g., determining the moment at which an event occurred).

Computing power

The computing capability of the CPU is determined by the following factors: the product of internal clock frequency and the average number of clock pulses required per instruction, the architecture (e.g., accumulator, register-storage organization), and the word size (4 ... 32 bit):
- Clock frequency: 1 ... 20 MHz (typical),
- Clock pulses per instruction: 1 ... 32 pulses (standard), depending upon the CPU's architecture and the instruction (e.g., 6 pulses for addition, 32 pulses for multiplication).

Electronic control unit (ECU)

Digital input signals

Digital input signals register a switch position or digital signals from sensors (e.g., rotational-speed pulses from a Hall-type sensor).
Voltage range: 0 V to battery voltage

Analogue input signals

Signals from analogue sensors (Lambda sensor, pressure sensors, potentiometers).
Voltage range: Several mV up to 5 V.

Microcomputer

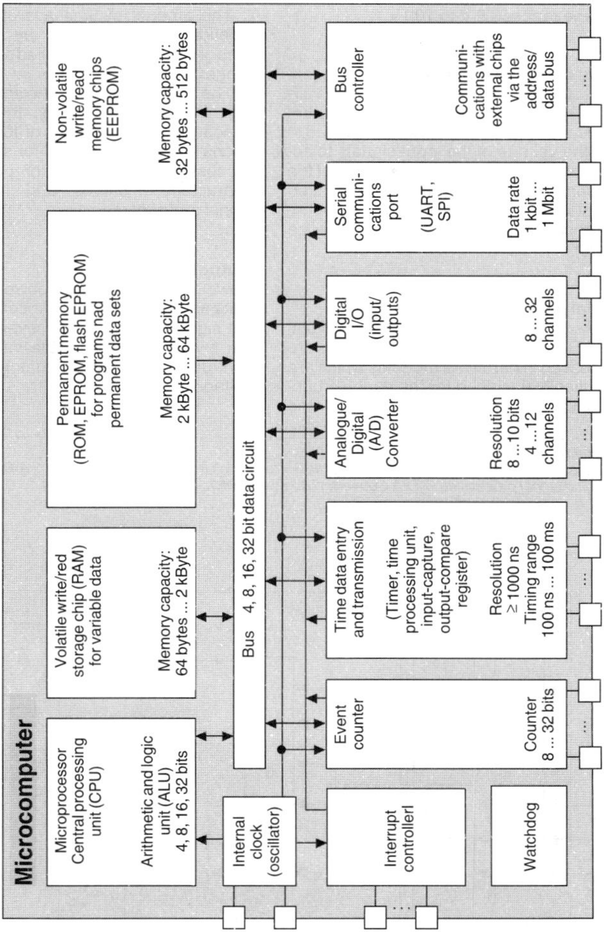
Microcomputer
Microprocessor Central processing unit (CPU)
Arithmetic and logic unit (ALU) 4, 8, 16, 32 bits
Volatile write/red storage chip (RAM) for variable data
Memory capacity: 64 bytes ... 2 kByte
Permanent memory (ROM, EPROM, flash EPROM) for programs nad permanent data sets
Memory capacity: 2 kByte ... 64 kByte
Non-volatile write/read memory chips (EEPROM)
Memory capacity: 32 bytes ... 512 bytes
Bus 4, 8, 16, 32 bit data circuit
Internal clock (oscillator)
Interrupt controllerl
Watchdog
Event counter
Counter 8 ... 32 bits
Time data entry and transmission
(Timer, time processing unit, input-capture, output-compare register)
Resolution ≥ 1000 ns
Timing range 100 ns ... 100 ms
Analogue/ Digital (A/D) Converter
Resolution 8 ...10 bits
4 ...12 channels
Digital I/O (input/ outputs)
8 ... 32 channels
Serial communi- cations port
(UART, SPI)
Data rate 1 kbit ... 1 Mbit
Bus controller
Communi- cations with external chips via the address/ data bus

Pulse-shaped input signals
Signals from inductive rpm sensors; these are converted to digital form before further processing.
Voltage range: 0.5 V to 100 V.

Initial conditioning of input signals
Protection circuits (Passive: R and R/C circuits. Active: special overvoltage-resistant semiconductor elements) are employed to limit the voltage of the input signals to acceptable levels. Filters remove most of the superimposed noise from the transmitted signals, which are then amplified to the microprocessor's input voltage. Voltage range: 0 V to 5 V.

Signal processing
ECU's generally process signals in digital form. Rapid, periodic, real-time signals are processed in hardware modules which are specifically designed for the various functions. Data such as the clock count or the time of a particular event are transmitted to the CPU for further processing in registers. This substantially reduces the CPU's interrupt-response requirements (μs-range).

The amount of time available for calculations is determined by the open-loop or closed-loop controlled system (ms-range).

The software contains the actual control algorithms. Depending on the data, an almost unlimited number of logical operations can be established for storage and processing in the form of parameters, characteristic curves and multidimensional program maps.

Output signals
Power switches and power-gain circuits amplify the microprocessor's output signals (0 to 5 V, several mA) to the levels required by the various final-controlling elements/actuators (battery voltage, several A).

Signal processing in the ECU
1 Digital input signal, 2 Analogue input signal, 3 Protective circuit, 4 Amplifier, Filter, 5 A/D Converter, 6 Digital signal processing, 7 D/A Converter, 8 Power switch, 9 Power-gain amplifier.

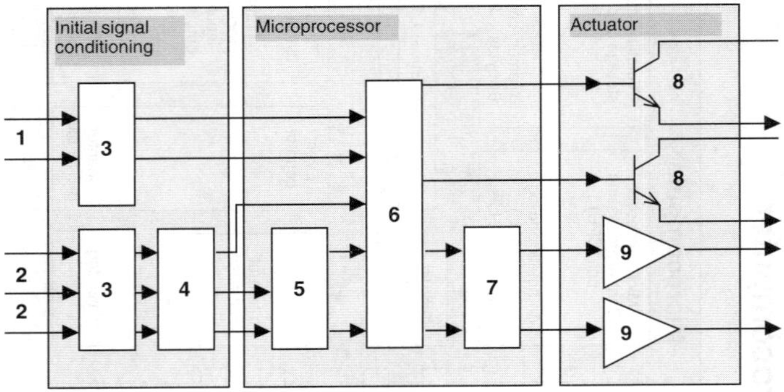

Network

Logistical concept (Cartronic)

The concept divides the total automotive electrical system into conveniently-dimensioned subsystems. Units with closely-related functions (units with a high rate of mutual data exchange) are combined in a sub-network. This logistical concept results in sub-networks with varying requirements for transmission capacity, while data transmission remains compatible.

Topology

At the logical level, all of the known communications systems developed especially for automotive applications are based on a single serial network for the ECU. The physical layout employs one-wire or differential two-wire interfaces in bus form to connect the appropriate control units with one another.

Protocol

The protocol consists of a specific collection of execution statements which are used to control data communications between the individual ECU's units. The codes for bus access, message structure, bit and data codes, error recognition and response and the identification of faulty bus users (CAN, p. 776) have already been standardized.

Transmission speed

Multiplex bus: 10 kbits/s ...125 kbits/s
Drivetrain bus: 125 kbits/s ...1 Mbit/s
Telecommunications bus:
10 kbit/s ...125 kbit/s.

Latency time

The period that elapses between the transmitter's send request and the target station's receipt of the error-free message.
Multiplex bus: 0.5 ms ...100 ms
Drivetrain bus: 5.0 µs ...10 ms
Telecommunications bus:
0.5 ms ...100 ms.

Bus interfaces
1 Control unit, 2 Bus controller, 3 Gataway.

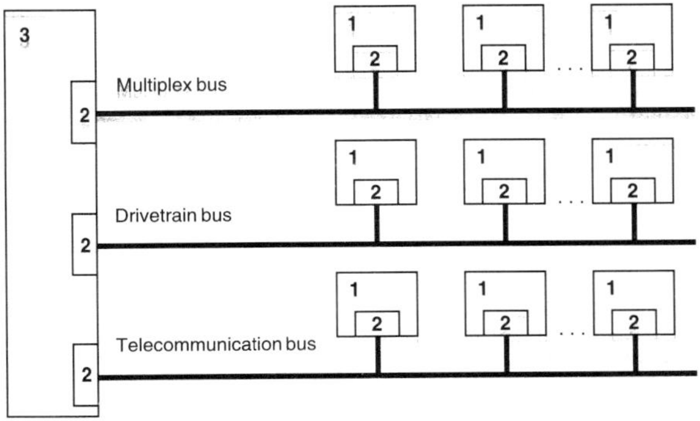

Control engineering

Terms and definitions (in accordance with DIN 19 226)

Closed-loop control	Open-loop control
Closed-loop control Closed-loop control is a process by which a variable, the directly controlled variable (directly controlled variable x), is continuously measured, compared with another variable, the reference variable w_1, and changed as a result of this comparison in such a sense that deviation from the reference variable is reduced. This action takes place in a closed loop. The purpose of the closed-loop control is to bring the value of the directly controlled variable as close as possible to the value specified by the reference variable in spite of disturbances, even if conditions do not allow for a perfect match between the command and control variables.	**Open-loop control** Open-loop control systems feature processes in which one or several input variables are employed for adjustments to one or several output variables. The precise nature of the adjustment depends upon the system's specific control characteristics. This type of control system is characterized by open-loop action via an individual transfer element or the open control loop. The term "control" is often used not only to mean the control process itself but also the entire system which performs the control function.
Closed control loop The closed control loop comprises all of the elements which interact in the closed-loop control process. This type of control system is a closed system which acts in one direction. The directly controlled variable x is fed back to the control system and acts on itself. **In contrast to an open-loop control system, a closed-loop control system acts to offset the effect of all disturbances (z_1, z_2) in the closed control loop.** The closed control loop comprises the controlled system and the controlling system.	**Open control loop** An open control loop is a series of elements (systems) which act on one another as links in a chain. An open control loop can be a subordinate part of another system, and can interact in any fashion with other systems. In an open control loop, only the effect of the disturbance as measured by the control unit can be addressed (z_1 in Fig. 2); the open loop has no effect on other disturbances (such as z_2). The open control loop comprises the controlling system and the controlled system.

Open- and closed-loop controlling systems
The open-loop or closed-loop controlling system is that part of the control loop which acts on the controlled system via the final-controlling element as determined by the control parameters.

System boundaries
The open-loop and closed-loop controlling systems include all those devices and elements which act directly to produce the desired condition within the control circuit.

Fig. 1: Closed control loop

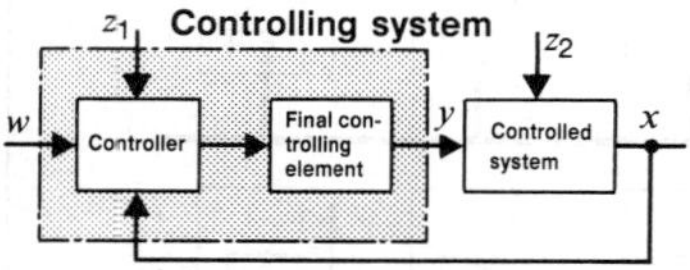

Input variables and output variable of the closed-loop controlling system
The input variables to the controlling system are the directly controlled variable x, the reference variable w and the disturbances z_1. The output variable from the controlling system is the manipulated variable y.

Fig. 2: Open control loop

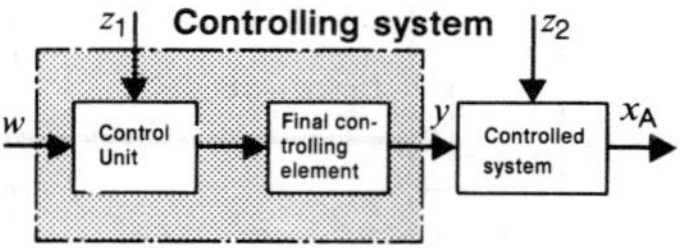

Input variables and output variable of the open-loop controlling system
The input variables to the controlling system are the reference variable w and the disturbances z_1. The output variable from the controlling system is the manipulated variable y.

Closed-loop control	Open-loop control

Controlled system (open- and closed-loop)
The controlled system in an open- or closed-loop control is that part of the control loop which is acted on by the controlling system in accordance with the control parameters.

Closed-loop control	Open-loop control
Input and output variables of the closed-loop controlled system The input variables to the closed-loop controlled system are the manipulated variables y and the disturbances z_2. The output variable from the controlled system is the directly controlled variable x.	**Input and output variables of the open-loop controlled system** The input variable is the manipulated variable y. The output variable is the indirectly controlled variable x_A or an output variable which manipulates the indirectly controlled variable in accordance with the control parameters.

Transfer elements and system elements
Open- and closed-loop controls can be subdivided into elements along the control loop.

In terms of equipment design and function these are called system elements and transfer elements, respectively.

In terms of closed- or open-loop control function, only the relationship between the variables and their values which act upon one another in the system are described.

Loop, direction of control action
Both the open control loop and the closed control loop comprise individual elements (or systems) which are connected together to form a loop.

The loop is that path along which open- or closed-loop control takes place. The direction of control action is the direction in which the control function operates.

The loop and the direction of control action need not necessarily coincide with the path and the direction of corresponding energy and mass flows.

Final controlling element, control point
The final controlling element is that element which is located at the upstream end of the controlled system, and which directly affects the flow of mass or energy. The location at which this action takes place is called the control point.

Disturbance point
The disturbance point is the location at which a variable not controlled by the system acts on the loop, thereby adversely affecting the condition which the control is designed to maintain.

Manipulated variable y, correcting range Y_h
The manipulated variable y is both the output variable of the controlling system and the input variable of the controlled system. It transfers the action of the controlling system to the controlled system.

The correcting range Y_h is the range within which the manipulated variable may lie.

Reference variable w, reference variable range W_h
The reference variable w of an open- or closed-loop control is a variable which is not acted on directly by the control; it is input to the loop from outside the control, and is that variable whose value is to be reflected by the output variable in accordance with the control parameters.

The reference variable range W_h is that range within which the reference variable w of an open- or closed-loop control may lie.

Disturbances z, disturbance range Z_h
Disturbances z in open- and closed-loop controls are all variables acting from outside the control which adversely affect the action of the control. In many cases, the most important disturbance is the load or the throughput through the system. The disturbance range Z_h is that range within which the disturbance may lie without adversely affecting the operation of the control.

Desired value x_A, desired-value range X_{Ah}
The indirectly controlled variable x_A of an open- or closed-loop control is that variable which the control is intended to influence.

The indirectly controlled variable range X_{Ah} of an open- or closed-loop control is that range within which the indirectly controlled variable may lie, with full functional capability of the control.

Controller design, transfer elements

A series of analytical and synthesizing processes are available for application in control engineering. Many of the problems posed by the requirements of control engineering can be solved by using certain controller types. These, in turn, rely essentially on the four following basic elements:

– *P* element (proportional-action transfer element),
– *I* element (integrated-action transfer element),
– *D* element (differentiating transfer element),
– T_1 element (1st order time-delay element).

	Transient response	Equation
P	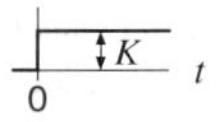	$F = K$
I	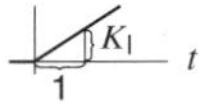	$F = \frac{K_I}{p}$
D		$F = K_D p$
T_1	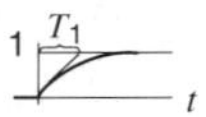	$F = \frac{1}{1+T_1 p}$

Parallel circuitry on the input side, addition of the output variables from the three relay elements *P, I, D* and downstream location of the T_1 element can be used to generate the controller types *P, I, PI, PP, PD, PID, PPD*. See DIN 19226 for specifications and system performance characteristics.

Digital control

Microprocessors can only be employed when a distinction is made between the following types of closed-loop control circuit:

Continuous-time control

Continuous-time control systems monitor controlled variables and compare these with the reference variables in an uninterrupted process. This comparison provides the basis for continuous generation of the controlled variable.

Discrete-time control

With discrete-time control, the controlled variable is monitored and continuously compared with the reference variable only at the sampling instants. When the result of the comparison is processed, and the controlled variable is generated in digital form, this type of regulation is referred to as digital control.

The control algorithm is implemented via a software program. A/D and D/A converters convert the analogue controlled variables into digital values, and transform the digital manipulated variable into analogue form.

Process schematic of a digital-control circuit
*T Sampling time, * Digital signal*

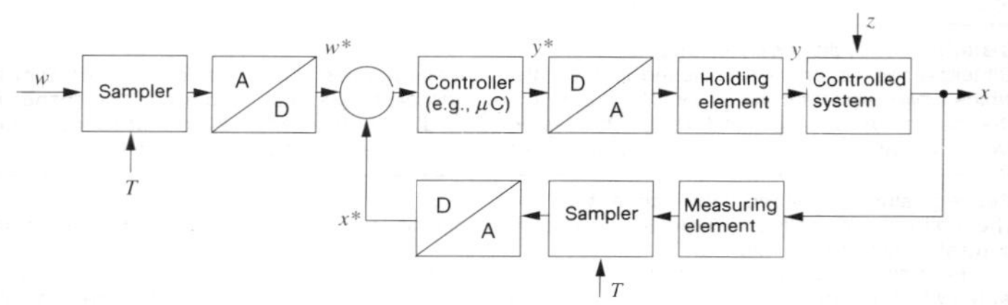

Motor vehicle closed-loop control systems (simplified examples)

Closed-loop control system	Variables: Indirectly controlled variable (x_A)	Directly controlled variable (x)	Reference variable (w)	Manipulated variable (y)	Disturbances (z)	Elements: Controlling system	Final controlling element	Controlled system
Lambda closed-loop control	Air/fuel ratio (λ)	O_2 content of exhaust gas	$\lambda = 1.0$ (fixed command control)	Quantity of injected fuel	Inexact pilot control, leaks, crankcase ventilation	Lambda control unit and lambda sensor	Injectors	Combustion chamber; part of intake system and exhaust system up to λ sensor
Rotational-speed governing in diesel engines	Engine speed		Theoretical speed (follow-up control)	Quantity of injected fuel	Load	Governor	Fuel-injection pump	Mixture formation area in engine
Antilock braking system (ABS)	Wheel slip	Wheel slip	Wheel-slip threshold (adaptive control)	Braking pressure	Road condition	Controller in ABS control unit	Pressure-control valve	Tires/road
Temperature control (cabin)	Cabin temperature	Cabin, heater output and outside air temperature	Set temperature (follow-up control)	Hot water flow rate or hot/cold air mixture ratio	Engine temp., outside air temp.; incident heat; driving speed; engine speed	Temperature regulator and temperature sensor	Electro-magnetic heating valve or air flap	Cabin

Open-loop engine control systems (examples)

Open-loop control system	Variables: Indirectly controlled variable (x_A)	Reference variables (w)	Control system input variables	Disturbances (z)	Manipulated variable (y)	Elements: Controlling system	Final controlling element	Controlled system
Jetronic fuel-injection system	Air/fuel ratio	Air/fuel ratio (setpoint)	Engine speed, engine temperature, battery voltage, air mass, air temperature, throttle-valve	Fuel temperature, deposits on manifold walls	Injection duration	Jetronic control unit with various measuring elements	Injectors	Mixture formation area
Electronic ignition systems	Ignition point	Ignition point (setpoint)	Engine speed, crankshaft position, intake-manifold pressure, throttle-valve position, engine temperature, battery voltage	Spark-plug condition, air/fuel ratio, fuel quality, mechanical tolerances	Ignition point	Ignition control unit and triggering system	Ignition output stage	Combustion chamber in engine

Chemical elements

Element	Symbol	Type[1])	Atomic number	Atomic weight	Valence	Year of Discovery	Discoverers
Actinium	Ac	m	89	227	3	1899	Debierne
Aluminum	Al	m	13	26.98	3	1827	Wöhler
Americium[2])	Am	m	95	243	3; 4; 5; 6	1945	Seaborg, Morgan
Antimony	Sb	m	51	121.75	3; 5	ancient	
Argon	Ar	g	18	39.95	0	1894	Ramsay, Rayleigh
Arsenic	As	n	33	74.92	3; 5	1649	Schröder
Astatine	At	n	85	210	1; 3; 5; 7	1940	Carson et al.
Barium	Ba	m	56	137.34	2	1808	Davy
Berkelium[2])	Bk	m	97	245	3; 4	1950	Seaborg
Beryllium	Be	m	4	9.01	2	1827	Wöhler
Bismuth	Bi	m	83	208.9	3; 5	1546	Agricola
Boron	B	n	5	10.81	3	1808	Gay-Lussac, Thénard
Bromine	Br	n	35	79.91	1; 5	1826	Balard
Cadmium	Cd	m	48	112.4	2	1818	Strohmeyer
Calcium	Ca	m	20	40.08	2	1808	Davy
Californium[2])	Cf	m	98	246	2; 3; 4	1950	Seaborg
Carbon	C	n	6	12.01	2; 4	ancient	
Cerium	Ce	m	58	140.12	3; 4	1814	Berzelius
Cesium	Cs	m	55	132.9	1	1860	Bunsen, Kirchhoff
Chlorine	Cl	g	17	35.46	1; 3; 5; 7	1774	Scheele
Chromium	Cr	m	24	52.00	2; 3; 6	1797	Vauquelin
Cobalt	Co	m	27	58.93	2; 3	1735	Brandt
Copper	Cu	m	29	63.54	1; 2	ancient	
Curium[2])	Cm	m	96	243	3; 4; 5; 6	1945	Seaborg and James
Dysprosium	Dy	m	66	162.5	3	1886	Lecoq de Boisbaudran
Einsteinium[2])	Es		99	246	3	1955	Seaborg et al.
Erbium	Er	m	68	167.26	3	1843	Mosander
Europium	Eu	m	63	151.96	3	1892	Lecoq de Boisbaudran
Fermium[2])	Fm		100	250	1; 2; 3	1955	Seaborg et al.
Fluorine	F	g	9	19.00	1	1887	Moissan
Francium	Fr	m	87	223	1	1939	Perey
Gadolinium	Gd	m	64	157.25	3	1880	Marignac
Gallium	Ga	m	31	69.72	2; 3	1875	Lecoq de Boisbaudran
Germanium	Ge	m	32	72.59	2; 4	1886	Winkler
Gold	Au	m	79	196.97	1; 3	ancient	
Hafnium	Hf	m	72	178.49	4	1923	Hevesy and Coster
Hahnium[2])	Ha	m	105			1970	USA
Helium	He	g	2	4.003	0	1894	Ramsay, Rayleigh
Holmium	Ho	m	67	164.93	3	1911	Holmberg
Hydrogen	H	g	1	1.008	1	1766	Cavendish
Indium	In	m	49	114.82	3	1863	Reich and Richter
Iron	Fe	m	26	55.85	2; 3; 6	ancient	
Iridium	Ir	m	77	192.2	3; 4	1803	Tennant
Iodine	J	n	53	126.9	1; 3; 5; 7	1811	Courtois

Note: Isotopes of the elements with Atomic Numbers 104 through 109 have been produced artificially, but to date have not been allocated standard unified designations.

[1]) m metal, n nonmetal, g gas.
[2]) Artificially produced; does not occur in nature.
[3]) Called joliotium (Jo) in the former USSR.

Element	Symbol	Type[1])	Atomic number	Atomic weight	Valence	Year of discovery	Discoverers
Krypton	Kr	g	36	83.80	0	1898	Ramsay
Lanthanum	La	m	57	138.91	3	1839	Mosander
Lawrencium[2])	Lr	m	103	257	3	1961	Ghiorso et al.
Lead	Pb	m	82	207.19	2; 4	ancient	
Lithium	Li	m	3	6.94	1	1817	Arfvedson
Lutetium	Lu	m	71	174.97	3	1905	Auer v. Welsbach
Magnesium	Mg	m	12	24.31	2	1808	Davy
Manganese	Mn	m	25	54.94	2; 3; 4; 6; 7	1780	Gahn, Scheele
Mendelevium[2])	Md		101	256	1; 2; 3	1955	Seaborg
Mercury	Hg	m	80	200.59	1; 2	ancient	
Molybdenum	Mo	m	42	95.94	3; 4; 6	1782	Hjelm
Neodymium	Nd	m	60	144.24	3	1885	Auer v. Welsbach
Neon	Ne	g	10	20.18	0	1898	Ramsay, Travers
Neptunium[2])	Np	m	93	237	3; 4; 5; 6	1938	Fermi, Hahn, Millan
Nickel	Ni	m	28	58.71	2; 3	1751	Cronstedt, Bergmann
Niobium	Nb	m	41	92.91	2; 3; 5	1801	Hatchett
Nitrogen	N	g	7	14.01	3; 5	1772	Rutherford, Scheele
Nobelium[2])[3])	No	m	102	254		1957	Sweishu and English group
Osmium	Os	m	76	190.2	2; 3; 4; 8	1803	Tennant
Oxygen	O	g	8	16.00	2	1774	Priestley, Scheele
Palladium	Pd	m	46	106.4	2; 4	1803	Wollaston
Phosphorus	P	n	15	30.97	3; 5	1669	Brandt
Platinum	Pt	m	78	195.1	2; 4	1748	Ulloa
Plutonium[2])	Pu	m	94	242	3; 4; 5; 6	1940	Seaborg
Polonium	Po	m	84	210	6	1898	P. and M. Curie
Potassium	K	m	19	39.10	1	1807	Davy
Praseodymium	Pm	m	61	145	3	1926	Hopkins, Yntema
Protactinium	Pa	m	91	231	5	1917	Hahn and Meitner
Radium	Ra	m	88	226.0	2	1898	Curie
Radon	Rn	g	86	222	0	1900	Dorn
Rhenium	Re	m	75	186.2	3; 4; 5; 6; 7	1925	Noddack
Rhodium	Rh	m	45	102.9	3	1803	Wollaston
Rubidium	Rb	m	37	85.47	1	1860	Bunsen, Kirchhoff
Ruthenium	Ru	m	44	101.07	4; 8	1848	Klaus
Samarium	Sm	m	62	150.35	3	1879	Lecoq de Boisbaudran
Scandium	Sc	m	21	44.96	3	1879	Nilson
Selenium	Se	n	34	78.96	2; 4; 6	1817	Berzelius
Silicon	Si	n	14	28.09	4	1823	Berzelius
Silver	Ag	m	47	107.87	1; 2	ancient	
Sodium	Na	m	11	22.99	1	1807	Davy
Strontium	Sr	n	38	87.62	2	1808	Davy
Sulphur	S	m	16	32.08	2; 4; 6	ancient	

→

Chemical elements (continued)

Element	Symbol	Type[1])	Atomic number	Atomic weight	Valence	Year of discovery	Discoverers
Tantalum	Ta	m	73	180.95	5	1802	Eckeberg
Technetium	Tc	m	43	99	7	1937	Perrier, Segré, Wu
Tellurium	Te	m	52	127.6	2; 4; 6	1789	Klaproth
Terbium	Tb	m	65	158.92	3	1842	Mosander
Thalium	Tl	m	81	204.37	1; 3	1861	Crookes
Thorium	Th	m	90	232.04	4	1828	Berzelius
Thulium	Tm	m	69	168.93	3	1879	Cleve
Tin	Sn	m	50	118.69	2; 4	ancient	
Titanium	Ti	m	22	47.90	2; 3; 4	1791	Gregor
Tungsten	W	m	74	183.85	2; 3; 4; 5; 6	1785	Elhuyar
Uranium	U	m	92	238.03	3; 4; 5; 6	1786	Klaproth
Vanadium	V	m	23	50.94	2; 3; 4; 5	1830	Sefström
Xenon	Xe	g	54	131.3	0	1898	Ramsay
Ytterbium	Yb	m	70	173.04	3	1907	Auer v. Welsbach
Yttrium	Y	m	39	88.90	3	1843	Mosander
Zinc	Zn	m	30	65.37	2	ancient	
Zirconium	Zr	m	40	91,22	4	1824	Berzelius

[1]) m metal, n nonmetal, g gas.

Periodic system of elements

In the periodic system (periodic table, L. Meyer, D. Mendelejeff, 1869), all of the chemical elements are arranged in the order of increasing atomic number (rows = "periods") and periodically recurring chemical properties (columns = "groups"). Beginning with the N period, the groups are divided into a and b series. (In some scientific literature these two series designations are reversed.) The groups contain elements with similar chemical and physical properties. In the periods, the elements are arranged according to increasing atomic number. This number, and the number of elements within a period, are related to the atomic structure. At the end of each period, in Group 0, there is an inert gas with a valence of 0. The 14 lanthanides (rare-earth elements) and the transuranic elements have similar atomic structures. Elements 19, 37, 43, 61, 62, 71 and from 84 upward are naturally radioactive. Elements with even atomic numbers are more abundant in nature than those with odd atomic numbers.

Period	Number of elements in each period	Group I		Group II		Group III		Group IV		Group V		Group VI		Group VII		Group VIII	Group 0
		a	b	a	b	a	b	a	b	a	b	a	b	a	b		
K	$2 \cdot 1^2 = 2$	1 **H**															2 **He**
L	$2 \cdot 2^2 = 8$	3 **Li**		4 **Be**		5 **B**			6 **C**		7 **N**		8 **O**		9 **F**		10 **Ne**
M	$2 \cdot 2^2 = 8$	11 **Na**		12 **Mg**		13 **Al**			14 **Si**		15 **P**		16 **S**		17 **Cl**		18 **Ar**
N	$2 \cdot 3^2 = 18$	19 **K**	29 **Cu**	20 **Ca**	30 **Zn**	21 **Sc**	31 **Ga**	22 **Ti**	32 **Ge**	23 **V**	33 **As**	24 **Cr**	34 **Se**	25 **Mn**	35 **Br**	26 **Fe** 27 **Co** 28 **Ni**	36 **Kr**
O	$2 \cdot 3^2 = 18$	37 **Rb**	47 **Ag**	38 **Sr**	48 **Cd**	39 **Y**	49 **In**	40 **Zr**	50 **Sn**	41 **Nb**	51 **Sb**	42 **Mo**	52 **Te**	43 **Tc**	53 **J**	44 **Ru** 45 **Rh** 46 **Pd**	54 **Xe**
P	$2 \cdot 4^2 = 32$	55 **Cs**	79 **Au**	56 **Ba**	80 **Hg**	57 **La**[1])	81 **Tl**	72 **Hf**	82 **Pb**	73 **Ta**	83 **Bi**	74 **W**	84 **Po**	75 **Re**	85 **At**	76 **Os** 77 **Ir** 78 **Pt**	86 **Rn**
Q		87 **Fr**		88 **Ra**		89 **Ac**		90 **Th**		91 **Pa**		92 **U**[2])					

[1]) Elements 58 ... 71 "lanthanides": 58 **Ce**, 59 **Pr**, 60 **Nd**, 61 **Pm**, 62 **Sm**, 63 **Eu**, 64 **Gd**, 65 **Tb**, 66 **Dy**, 67 **Ho**, 68 **Er**, 69 **Tm**, 70 **Yb**, 71 **Lu**.

[2]) Elements 90 ... 103 "Actinides": 90 **Th**, 91 **Pa**, 92 **U**, 93 **Np**, 94 **Pu**, 95 **Am**, 96 **Cm**, 97 **Bk**, 98 **Cf**, 99 **Es**, 100 **Fm**, 101 **Md**, 102 **No**, 103 **Lr**. The (artificially-produced) elements from number 93 onward are also described as the „transuranic elements"; there are still no standard unified designations for elements 104 through 109.

Material terminology[1)]

State of aggregation
There are three classical states of aggregation depending upon the arrangement of the elementary particles (atoms, molecules, ions): solid, liquid and gaseous. Plasma (ionized gas which has high electrical conductivity) is often considered as a fourth state of aggregation.

Solution
A solution is a homogeneous mixture of different materials which are distributed at the atomic or molecular level.

Compound
A compound is the union of two or more chemical elements whose masses are always in the same ratio with respect to one another. Compounds which have metallic characteristics are called intermetallic compounds.

Dispersion
A dispersion or disperse system consists of at least two materials; one material, called the disperse phase, is finely distributed in the other material, called the dispersion medium.

Suspension
A suspension is a disperse system in which solid particles are distributed in a liquid. Examples: graphite in oil, clay in water.

Emulsion
An emulsion is a disperse system in which droplets of one liquid are distributed in a second liquid. Examples: drilling oil, butterfat in milk.

Colloid
A colloid is a disperse system in which the particles of the disperse phase have linear dimensions ranging from about 10^{-9} to 10^{-6} m. Examples: smoke, latex, gold-ruby glass.

1) The following is a list of the most important materials terms and parameters which appear in subsequent materials tables and are not defined elsewhere.

Materials parameters[1)]

Density
Density is the ratio of the mass to the volume of a specific amount of substance.

See DIN 1306, 1984 edition, for special density terms.

Radial crushing strength
Radial crushing strength is a strength parameter which is specified in particular for sinter (PM) metal used for plain bearings. It is determined by the amount of pressure required to crush a hollow cylinder. For additional information see "Technical Conditions of Delivery for PM Parts (Sint. 03)", Aug. 1981 edition.

Yield strength (0.2 %)
The 0.2 % yield strength is that tensile stress which causes permanent (plastic) elongation of 0.2 % in a solid body. The monotonic 0.2 % yield strength is taken from the $\sigma-\varepsilon$ curve of the standard tensile test.

Cyclic loading of a test specimen by tensile/compressive stresses with increasing amplitude yields the cyclic $\sigma-\varepsilon$ curve, from which the cyclic 0.2 % yield strength can be determined. When compared with the monotonic 0.2 % yield strength, this value is a measure of possible softening or hardening brought about by cyclic overstressing.

The yield strength ratio γ is the ratio of the cyclic to the monotonic 0.2 % yield strength. $\gamma > 1$ indicates cyclic hardening, and $\gamma < 1$ indicates cyclic softening.

Fracture toughness
Fracture toughness, or the K_{Ic} factor, is a material parameter which deals with fracture mechanics. The K_{Ic} factor is that stress intensity ahead of a crack tip which leads to unstable crack propagation, and therefore to the fracture of the structural part. If the K_{Ic} factor of a material is known, the critical fracture load can be determined from crack length, or critical crack length can be determined from the given external loading value.

Specific heat capacity
Specific heat capacity is the quantity of heat in J required to raise the temperature of 1 kg of a substance by 1 K. Specific heat capacity is a function of temperature.

In the case of gases, it is necessary to differentiate between specific heat capacity at constant pressure and at constant volume (symbols: c_p and c_v, respectively). This difference is usually negligible in the case of solid and liquid substances.

Specific heat of fusion
The specific heat of fusion of a solid is the quantity of heat in J required to transform 1 kg of a substance at fusion temperature from the solid to the liquid state.

Specific heat of evaporation
The specific heat of evaporation of a liquid is the quantity of heat in J required to evaporate 1 kg of a liquid at boiling temperature. The specific heat of evaporation is highly dependent upon pressure.

Thermal conductivity
Thermal conductivity is the quantity of heat in J which flows in one second through a material sample which has a surface area of 1 m^2 and a thickness of 1 m if the temperatures of the two end surfaces of the sample differ by 1 K.

In the case of liquids and gases, thermal conductivity is often highly dependent upon temperature, whereas temperature is generally not significant in the case of solids.

Coefficient of thermal expansion
The linear coefficient of expansion α indicates the relative change in length of a material caused by a change in temperature of 1 K. The linear change of length Δl for a temperature variation ΔT is defined as $\Delta l = l \cdot \alpha \cdot \Delta T$. The same applies to the volume coefficient of expansion. The volume coefficient of expansion for gases is roughly 1/273. For solids, it is roughly three times as large as the linear coefficient of expansion.

Permeability
Permeability μ or relative permeability μ_r describes the relationship between magnetic induction and the applied field.

$$B = \mu_r \cdot \mu_0 \cdot H$$

Depending upon the application in which the magnetic material is used, various types of permeability (around 15) are defined, and are dependent upon the modulation range and the type of loading (direct-current or alternating-current field loading). Examples:

Initial permeability μ_a
Initial permeability is the slope of the normal induction curve for $H \rightarrow 0$. In most cases the slope for a specific field strength (in mA/cm) is specified rather than this limit value. Example: μ_4 is the slope of the virgin magnetization curve for $H = 4$ mA/cm.

Maximum permeability μ_{max}
Maximum permeability is the maximum slope of the virgin magnetization curve.

Permanent permeability μ_p or μ_{rec}
Permanent permeability is the average slope of a retrograde magnetic hysteresis loop whose lowest point usually lies on the demagnetization curve.

$$\mu_p = \Delta B / (\Delta H \cdot \mu_0)$$

Temperature coefficient of magnetic polarization $TK\,(J_s)$
This temperature coefficient indicates the relative change in saturation polarization as the temperature changes, it is given in % per kelvin.

Temperature coefficient of coercive field strength $TK\,(H_c)$
This temperature coefficient indicates the relative change in coercive field strength as the temperature changes; it is given in % per kelvin.

Curie point (Curie temperature) T_c
The Curie point is that temperature at which the magnetization of ferromagnetic and ferrimagnetic materials is zero, and at which they behave like paramagnetic materials (sometimes defined differently; see characteristic values of soft ferrites on p. 198).

Material groups[1])

Materials used in industrial techniques today can be broken down into 4 material groups; these groups, in turn, can be broken down further into subgroups:

– Metal:
Wrought, rolled, cast etc. metals, sinter (PM) metals
– Nonmetallic inorganic material:
Ceramic materials, glasses
– Nonmetallic organic material:
Natural materials, plastics and elastomers
– Composite materials

Magnetic materials form an important material group with special characteristics, and will be described separately.

Sinter (PM) metals

Generally, sinter (PM) metals are formed by pressing powder, or by the injection-molding of mixtures composed of metal-powder and plastic. Following the removal of parting agents and plasticizers, the parts are then sintered to give them their characteristic properties. Sintering is a type of heat treatment in the range 800...1300 °C. In addition to its chemical composition, the sintered part's properties and application are to a large extent determined by its degree of porosity.

Sinter (PM) metal structural parts with complicated shapes can often be made very economically, requiring little or no finishing.

Metals

Metals generally exhibit a crystalline structure. Their atoms are arranged in a regular crystal lattice. The valence electrons of the atoms are not bound to a special atom, but rather are able to move freely within the metal lattice (metallic bond).

This metal lattice structure explains the characteristic properties of metals: high electrical conductivity which decreases as temperature increases; good thermal conductivity; low transparency to light; high optical reflectivity (metallic luster); ductility and the resulting high degree of formability. Alloys are metals which consist of two or more components, of which at least one is a metal.

Wrought, rolled, cast etc. metals

Apart from small flaws such as shrinkholes and nonmetallic inclusions, such metals contain no voids. Components are either cast directly (e.g., gray cast iron diecast aluminum), or are manufactured from semifinished products which are machined or formed.

Nonmetallic inorganic materials

These materials are characterized by ion bonds (e.g., ceramic materials), mixed (heteropolar/homopolar) bonds (e.g., glass) or homopolar bonds (e.g., carbon). These kinds of bonds, in turn, are responsible for several characteristic properties: generally poor thermal and electrical conductivity (the latter increases with temperature), poor reflectivity, and brittleness, making them almost completely unsuited to cold forming.

Ceramics

Ceramics are at least 30 % crystalline in nature; most ceramics also contain amorphous components and pores. Their manufacture is similar to that of sinter (PM) metals however nonmetallic powders or powder mixtures are used; sintering at temperatures generally higher than 1000 °C gives ceramics their characteristic properties. Ceramic structural parts are sometimes also manufactured at high temperatures or even by a melting process, with subsequent crystallization.

Glasses
Glasses are viewed as under-cooled, frozen liquids. Their atoms are only in a short-range order. They are regarded as amorphous. Molten glass turns to solid glass at a temperature called the transformation (or vitrification) temperature T_g (T_g is derived from the former designation "glass formation temperature"). T_g ist determined by several parameters, and can therefore not be exactly defined, so that it is better to speak of a transformation range.

Nonmetallic organic materials

These materials consist mainly of compounds of the elements carbon and hydrogen, whereby nitrogen, oxygen and other elements are also often included in the structure. In general, these materials exhibit low thermal and electrical conductivity, and are combustible.

Natural materials
The best-known natural materials are wood, leather, resin, natural rubber, and fibers made of wool, cotton, flax, hemp and silk. Most natural materials are used in processed or refined from, or serve as raw materials in the manufacture of plastics.

Plastics transformation
A significant characteristic of plastics is their macromolecular structure. There are three different types of plastics: thermoplastics, thermosets (sometimes also called thermosetting plastics) and elastomers. The transformation temperature T_E for thermoplastics and thermosets lies above the temperature of application; the reverse is true for elastomers. T_E (comparable to the transformation temperature T_g of glasses) is understood to mean that temperature, below which intrinsic molecular motion ceases.

The major importance of thermoplastics and thermosets lies in the fact that they can be shaped and molded without machining.

Thermoplastics
Thermoplastics soften and lose their dimensional stability at temperatures above T_E. Their physical properties are highly temperature-dependent. The effect of temperature can be somewhat reduced by using mixtures of thermoplastic polymers.

Thermosets
Thermosets retain their dimensional stability up to temperatures almost as high as the processing temperature due to closely-spaced cross-linking. Their mechanical properties are less temperature-dependent than those of thermoplastics. Fillers are usually added to thermosetting resins to counteract their inherent brittleness.

Elastomers
Elastomers are useful in many applications because of their elasticity, which is only present at temperatures above T_E. Elastomers are vulcanized (widely-spaced cross-linking) in order to stabilize their molecular bonds.

Composite materials

Composite materials consist of at least two physically or chemically different components which must be tightly bound together at a defined interface. The formation of the interface must have no negative affect on any of the bound components. Under these two conditions it is possible to bond many materials together. Composite materials exhibit combinations of properties which none of the components alone possesses. Different classes of composite materials are:
Particle composite materials
(e.g., powder-filled resins, hard metals, plastic-bonded magnets, cermets),
Laminated composite materials
(e.g., composite or sandwich panels, resin-bonded fabric),
Fiber composite materials
(e.g., glass-fiber, carbon-fiber, and cotton-fiber-reinforced plastics).

Magnetic materials

Materials which have ferromagnetic or ferrimagnetic characteristics are called magnetic materials, and belong to one of two groups; metals or nonmetallic, inorganic materials. They are characterized by their ability to store magnetic energy (permanent magnets), or by their good magnetic flux conductivity (soft magnets). In addition to ferromagnets and ferrimagnets, diamagnetic, paramagnetic and antiferromagnetic materials also exist. They differ from each other regarding their permeability μ (p. 78) or the temperature-dependence of their susceptibility $\varkappa$.[1])

$$\mu_r = 1 + \varkappa$$

Diamagnets: Susceptibility $\varkappa_{Dia}$ is independent of temperature. See p. 78 for examples.

Paramagnets: Susceptibility $\varkappa_{Para}$ drops as temperature increases. Curie's law:

$$\varkappa_{Para} = C/T$$

C Curie constant, T Temperature in K. See p. 78 for examples.

Ferromagnets and ferrimagnets: Both types exhibit spontaneous magnetization which disappears at the Curie point (Curie temperature T_c). At temperatures above the Curie temperature, they behave like paramagnets. For $T > T_c$, the Curie-Weiss law describes the susceptibility $\varkappa$:

$$\varkappa = C/(T - T_c)$$

The saturation induction of ferromagnets is higher than it is for ferrimagnets, because all magnetic moments are aligned in parallel. In the case of ferrimagnets, on the other hand, the magnetic moments of the two sublattices are aligned antiparallel to one another. These materials are nevertheless magnetic, because the magnetic moments of the two sublattices have different magnitudes.

Antiferromagnets:
Examples: MnO, MnS, $FeCl_2$, FeO, NiO, Cr, V_2O_3, V_2O_4.

As in the case of ferrimagnets, adjacent magnetic moments are aligned antiparallel with respect to one another. Because they are of equal magnitude, the effective magneticism of the material is zero.

At temperatures above the Néel point (Néel temperature T_N), they behave like paramagnets. For $T > T_N$, the susceptibility $\varkappa$ is described by the following equation:

$$\varkappa = C/(T + \Theta)$$

Θ Asymptotic Curie Temperature

Soft magnetic materials

The figures given have been taken from the appropriate DIN Standards.

Magnetic Sheet Steel and Steel Strip (DIN 46 400)
Designations:
a) Code letter:
V Cold-rolled, not grain-oriented, finish-annealed (DIN 46400, Part 1)
VH Cold-rolled, not grain-oriented, not finish-annealed (DIN 46400, Part 2; non-alloy steels)
VM Grain-oriented (DIN 46 400, Part 3)
VE Cold-rolled, not grain-oriented, not finish-annealed (DIN 46400, Part 4; alloy steels)
b) One hundred times the maximum specific total loss at a magnetic-flux density of 1.5/1.7 Tesla (P 1.5/P 1.7) in W/kg
c) One hundred times the product's nominal thickness in mm
d) Supplementary code letter for sheet steels with code letter V or VM
A Finish-annealed version (V-, VM-sheet steels)
N – Standard specific total losses
S – Limited specific total losses
P – Low specific total losses
For material properties, see p. 194.

Materials for transformers (DIN 41301)
Definition: Material permeability μ_x:

$$\mu_x = \hat{B}/(\hat{H} \cdot \mu_0)$$

where $\hat{B}$ = peak value of the fundamental component of the induction
$\hat{H}$ = Peak value of the sinusoidal field strength
The subscript x indicates the measured field strength in A/cm.
See p. 195 for material properties.

[1]) Susceptibility is the ratio of the magnetization of the substance to the magnetic field strength or excitation.

Materials for direct-current relays
(DIN 17405); see p. 196 for material properties.
Designation:
a) Identifying letter R (relay material)
b) Identifying letters for the characteristic alloying constituents:
  Fe unalloyed
  Si silicon steels
  Ni nickel steels or nickel alloys
c) Identifying number for maximum coercive field strength
d) Identifying letter for desired condition as supplied:
  U untreated
  GB preannealed, bendable
  GT preannealed for deep-drawing
  GF final-annealed

Sintered metals for soft magnetic components
Material specification sheets for sintered materials, DIN 30910.
See p. 197 for material properties.

Soft magnetic ferrite cores
DIN 41280)
Soft magnetic ferrites are formed parts made of a sintered material with the general formula $MO \cdot Fe_2O_3$ whereby M is one or more of the bivalent metals Cd, Co, Ca, Mg, Mn, Ni, Zn.
Designation:
The various types of magnetically soft ferrites are classified in groups according to nominal initial permeability, and are designated by capital letters. Additional numbers may be used to further subdivide them into subgroups; these numbers have no bearing on material quality.

The coercive field strength of soft ferrites normally lies in the range 4 A/m $< H_c <$ 500 A/m. Their induction lies in the range 350 mT $< B <$ 470 mT, given a field strength of 3000 A/m.
See p. 198 for material properties.

Permanent-magnet materials
(DIN 17410, IEC 404-8-1)
If chemical symbols are used in the abbreviated names of the materials, they refer to the primary alloying constituents of the materials. The numbers to the left of the diagonal line indicate the $(B-H)_{max}$-value in kJ/m^3, and those to the right of the diagonal line are one tenth of the $_JH_c$ value in kA/m (rounded values). Permanent magnets with binders are indicated by a final p.

Schematic representation of the magnetic dipoles in ferromagnets, ferrimagnets and antiferromagnets for $T < T_c$ and $T < T_N$.

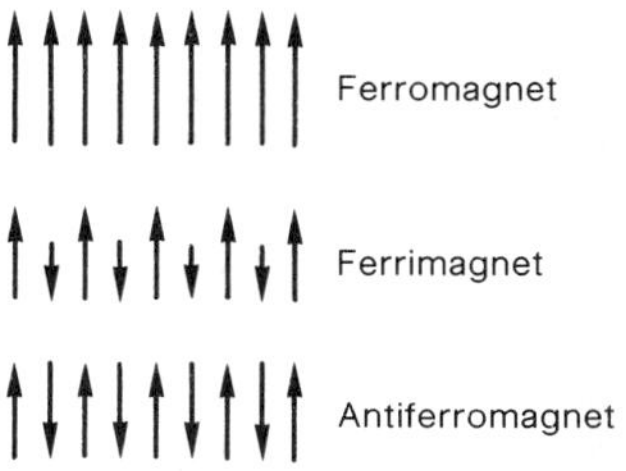

Designation by abbreviated name or material number

DIN	IEC
Material number as per DIN 17 007, Part 2 and Part 4	Explanation of material numbers: Identifying letter: R – Metallic permanent-magnet materials S – Ceramic permanent-magnet materials 1st Digit – Type of material, e.g., 1-AlNiCo, 5 RECo 2nd Digit – 0: Isotropic material 1: Anisotropic material 2: Isotropic material with binder 3: Anisotropic material with binder 3rd Digit – Quality grade

See p. 199 for material properties.

Properties of solids[7])

Substance		Density g/cm³	Melting point[1]) °C	Boiling point[1]) °C	Thermal conductivity[2]) W/(m·K)	Mean-specific heat[3]) kJ/(kg·K)	Specific heat of fusion[4]) kJ/kg	Coefficient of linear expansion[3]) x10⁻⁶/K
Aluminum	Al	2,70	660	2270	204	0.94	356	23.9
Aluminum alloys		2.60 ... 2.85	480 ... 655	–	70 ... 240	–	–	21 ... 24
Antimony	Sb	6.69	630.5	1635	22	0.21	163	–
Arsenic	As	5.72	–	–	–	0.35	–	–
Asbestos		2.1 ... 2.8	≈ 1300	–	–	0.81	–	–
Asphalt		1.1 ... 1.4	80 ... 100	≈ 300	0.70	0.92	–	–
Barium	Ba	3.59	704	1700	–	0.29	–	–
Barium chloride		3.10	955	1600	–	0.38	–	–
Basalt		2.6 ... 3.3	–	–	1.67	0.86	–	–
Amber		1.0 ... 1.1	≈ 300	Decomp.	–	–	–	–
Beryllium	Be	1.85	1280	≈ 3000	165	1.02	–	–
Concrete		1.8 ... 2.2	–	–	≈ 1.0	0.88	–	–
Bitumen		1.05	≈ 90	–	0.17	1.78	–	–
Lead	Pb	11.3	327.4	1740	34.7	0.13	24.3	29
Lead monoxide	PbO	9.3	880	1480	–	0.22	–	–
Boron	B	2.34	2500	> 3800	–	1.05	–	–
Borax		1.72	740	–	–	1.00	–	–
Bronze CuSn 6		8.8	910	2300	64	0.37	–	17.5
Cadmium	Cd	8.64	321	765	91	0.23	54	30
Calcium	Ca	1.54	850	1400	–	0.66	–	–
Cellulose acetate		1.3	–	–	0.26	1.47	–	100...160
Calcium chloride		2.2	774	–	–	0.69	–	–
Chromium	Cr	7.1	1800	2700	69	0.46	–	8.4
Chromium oxide	Cr_2O_3	5.2	2300	–	0.42 (powder)	0.75	–	–
Roofing felt		1.1	–	–	0.19	–	–	–
Diamond	C	3.5	–	–	–	0.52	–	1.1
Thermosetting plastics								
Phenolic resin without filler		1.3	–	–	0.20	1.47	–	80
Phenolic resin with asbestos fibers		1.8	–	–	0.70	1.25	–	15 ... 30
Phenolic resin with wood flour		1.4	–	–	0.35	1.47	–	30 ... 50
Phenolic resin with fabric shreds		1.4	–	–	0.35	1.47	–	15 ... 30
Melamine resin with cellulose fibers		1.5	–	–	0.35	–	–	≈ 60
Ice (0°C)		0.92	0	100	2.33[5])	2.09[5])	–	51[6])
Iron, pure	Fe	7.87	1530	3070	81	0.47	–	12
Germanium	Ge	5.3	936	2700	55	0.31	–	6.1
Gypsum		2.3	1200	–	0.45	1.09	–	–
Glass, window		2.4 ... 2.7	≈ 700	–	0.81	0.83	–	≈ 8
Glass, quartz		–	–	–	–	–	–	0.5
Mica		2.6 ... 2.9	Decomp. at 700°C		0.35	0.87	–	3
Gold	Au	19.29	1063	2960	310	0.13	67	14.2
Granite		2.7	–	–	3.49	0.83	–	–
Graphite, pure	C	2.24	≈ 3800	≈ 4200	168	0.71	–	7.8
Gray cast iron		7.25	1200	2500	58	0.50	125	10.5

[1]) At 1.013 bar. [2]) At 20°C. [3]) At 0 ... 100°C, see also p. 173. [4]) At the melting point and 1.013 bar. [5]) At −20 ... 0°C. [6]) At −20 ... −1°C. [7]) Materials, pp. 185–215.

Properties of materials[9])

Substance		Density g/cm³	Melting point[1]) °C	Boiling point[1]) °C	Thermal conductivity[2]) W/(m·K)	Mean-specific heat[3]) kJ/(kg·K)	Specific heat of fusion[4]) kJ/kg	Coefficient of linear expansion[3]) x10⁻⁶/K
Fabric-base laminate		1.3 ... 1.4	–	–	0.23	1.47	–	10 ... 25[8])
Hard rubber (ebonite)		1.2 ... 1.5	–	–	0.16	1.42	–	50 ... 90[8])
Hard alloy K 20		14.8	>2000	≈ 4000	81.4	0.80	–	5 ... 7
Rigid plastic foam, air-filled[5])		0.015 ... 0.06	–	–	0.036 ... 0.06	–	–	–
freon-filled		0.015 ... 0.06	–	–	0.02 ... 0.03	–	–	–
Heating-element alloy NiCr 8020		8.3	1400	2350	14.6	0.50[6])	–	–
Wood[7]) Maple		0.62	–	–	0.16	2.1...2.9	–	In the direction of the fibers: 3...4; transverse to the fibers: 22...43
Balsa		0.20	–	–	0.06		–	
Birch		0.63	–	–	0.14		–	
Beech		0.72	–	–	0.17		–	
Oak		0.69	–	–	0.17		–	
Ash		0.72	–	–	0.16		–	
Spruce, fir		0.45	–	–	0.14		–	
Pine		0.52	–	–	0.14		–	
Walnut		0.65	–	–	0.15		–	
Poplar		0.50	–	–	0.12		–	
Charcoal		0.3 ... 0.5	–	–	0.084	1.0	–	–
Wood-wall building slabs		0.36...0.57	–	–	0.093	–	–	–
Indium	In	7.3	156	2000	24.4	0.23	–	–
Iridium	Ir	22.5	2454	>4800	59	0.13	–	–
Iodine	J	5.0	113.6	183	0.44	0.23	–	–
Potassium	K	0.86	63.6	760	110	0.78	65	–
Rubber, raw		0.92	125	–	0.15	–	–	–
Boiler scale		≈ 2.5	≈ 1200	–	0.12...2.3	0.80	–	–
Cobalt	Co	8.8	1490	3100	69.1	0.43	268	–
Table salt		2.15	802	1440	–	0.92	–	–
Coke		1.6 ... 1.9	–	–	0.18	0.83	–	–
Rosin (colophony)		1.08	100 ... 130	Decomp.	0.32	1.21	–	–
Cork		0.1 ... 0.3	–	–	0.04...0.06	1.7 ... 2.1	–	–
Chalk		1.8 ... 2.6	Decomposes into CaO and CO_2		0.92	0.84	–	–
Copper	Cu	8.93	1083	≈ 2500	384	0.39	213	17
Leather, dry		0.86 ... 1	–	–	0.14... 0.16	≈ 1.5	–	–
Linoleum		1.2	–	–	0.19	–	–	–
Lithium	Li	0.534	180	1370	65	3.6	–	–
Magnesium	Mg	1.74	650	1110	172	1.04	368	–
Magnesium alloys		≈ 1.8	≈ 630	1500	46 ... 139	–	–	24.5
Manganese	Mn	7.43	1244	2100	21	0.48	–	–
Marble	$CaCO_3$	2.6...2.8	Decomposes into CaO and CO_2		2.8	0.84	–	–
Red lead (minium)	Pb_3O_4	8.6...9.1	Forms PbO		0.70	0.092	–	–

[1] At 1.013 bar. [2]) At 20°C. [3]) At 0 ... 100°C. [4]) At the melting point and 1.013 bar. [5]) Phenolic-resin rigid foam, polystyrene rigid foam, polyethylene rigid foams, etc. Values depend on cell diameter and filling gas. [6]) At 0 ... 1000°C. [7]) Mean values for air-dried wood (moisture content: approx. 12%). Thermal conductivity: figures given result from radial measurements. Figures for axial conductivity are about twice as high. [8]) At 20 ... 50°C. [9]) Materials, see p. 185 ... 215.

Substance		Density g/cm³	Melting point[1]) °C	Boiling point[1]) °C	Thermal conductivity[2]) W/(m·K)	Mean specific heat[3]) kJ/(kg·K)	Specific heat of fusion[4]) kJ/kg	Coefficient of linear expansion[3]) $\times 10^{-6}$/K
Brass CuZn 37		8.4	900	1110	113	0.38	167	18.5
Molybdenum	Mo	10.2	2600	5500	145	0.26	–	5.2
Monel metal		8.8	1240... 1330	–	19.7	0.43	–	–
Mortar (lime)		1.6 ... 1.8	–	–	0.87	–	–	–
Mortar (cement)		1.6 ... 1.8	–	–	1.40	–	–	–
Sodium	Na	0.97	97.8	883	126	1.3	113	–
Nickel silver CuNi12Zn24		8.7	1020	–	48	0.40	–	18
Nickel	Ni	8.9	1452	2730	59	0.45	306	13
Niobium	Nb	8.6	2415	2900	53	0.27	–	–
Osmium	Os	22.5	2500	>5300	–	0.13	–	–
Palladium	Pd	12.0	1555	2930	71	0.23	–	–
Paper		0.7 ... 1.2	–	–	0.14	1.34	–	–
Paraffin		0.9	52	300	0.26	3.27	–	–
Pitch		1.25	–	–	0.13	–	–	–
Phosphorus (yellow)	P	1.82	44	280	–	0.80	21	–
Platinum	Pt	21.5	1773	4400	70	0.13	113	9
Plutonium	Pu	17.6	640	>3300	–	0.16	–	–
Polyamide		1.1	–	–	0.31	–	–	70...150
Polyethylene		0.94	–	–	0.41	2.1	–	200
Polycarbonate		1.2	–	–	0.20	1.17	–	–
Polystyrene		1.05	–	–	0.17	1.3	–	70
Polyvinyl chloride		1.4	–	–	0.16	–	–	70...150
Porcelain		2.3...2.5	≈ 1600	–	1.6[5])	1.2[5])	–	4...5
Quartz		2.1...2.5	1480	2230	9.9	0.80	–	8[6])/14.6[7])
Radium	Ra	5	960	1140	–	–	–	–
Rhenium	Re	21	3180	≈ 5500	71	0.14	–	–
Red bronze CuSn5ZnPb		8.8	950	2300	38	0.67	–	–
Rubidium	Rb	1.52	39	701	58	0.33	–	–
Soot (carbon black)		1.7 ... 1.8	–	–	0.07	0.84	–	–
Sand, quartz (dry)		1.5 ... 1.7	≈ 1500	2230	0.58	0.80	–	–
Sandstone		2 ... 2.5	≈ 1500	–	2.3	0.71	–	–
Fireclay		1.7 ... 2.4	≈ 2000	–	1.4	0.80	–	–
Sponge rubber		0.06 ... 0.25	–	–	0.04 ... 0.06	–	–	–
Slag (blast furnace)		2.5 ... 3	1300... 1400	–	0.14	0.84	–	–
Sulphur	S	1.96 ... 2.06	115	444.6	0.20	0.70	46	–
Selenium	Se	4.4	220	688	0.20	0.33	–	–
Silver	Ag	10.5	960.5	2170	407	0.23	105	19.7
Silicon	Si	2.33	1420	2600	83	0.75	–	4.2
Silicon carbide		2.4	Decomposes above 3000°C		9[8])	1.05[8])	–	–
Sillimanite		2.4	1820	–	1.51	1.0	–	–
Steel, sintered		–	–	–	–	–	–	11.5
Corundum, sintered		–	–	–	–	–	–	6.5[9])

[1]) At 1.013 bar. [2]) At 20°C. [3]) At 0 ... 100°C. [4]) At the melting point and 1.013 bar. [5]) At 800°C. [6]) Parallel to the crystal axis. [7]) Perpendicular to the crystal axis. [8]) At 1000°C. [9]) At 20 ... 1000°C.

Substance		Density g/cm³	Melting point[1]) °C	Boiling point[1]) °C	Thermal conductivity[2]) W/(m·K)	Mean-specific heat[3]) kJ/(kg·K)	Specific heat of fusion[4]) kJ/kg	Coefficient of linear expansion[3]) x10⁻⁶/K
Steel, unalloyed and low-alloy		7.9	1460	2500	48 ... 58	0.49	205	11.5
Steel, stainless (18Cr, 8Ni)		7.9	1450	–	14	0.51	–	16
Steel, tungsten steel (18W)		8.7	1450	–	26	0.42	–	–
Steel, chromium steel		–	–	–	–	–	–	11
Steel, electrical sheet steel		–	–	–	–	–	–	12
Steel, magnet steel AlNiCo 12/6		–	–	–	–	–	–	11.5
Steel, high-speed steel		–	–	–	–	–	–	11.5
Steel, nickel steel 36% Ni (Invar)		–	–	–	–	–	–	1.5
Steatite		2.6 ... 2.7	≈ 1520	–	1.6[6])	0.83	–	8 ... 9[5])
Hard coal (anthracite)		1.35	–	–	0.24	1.02	–	–
Beef tallow		0.9 ... 0.97	40 ... 50	≈ 350	–	0.87	–	–
Tantalum	Ta	16.6	2990	4100	54	0.14	–	–
Tellurum	Te	6.24	455	1300	4.9	0.20	–	–
Thorium	Th	11.7	≈ 1700	≈ 4000	38	0.14	–	–
Titanium	Ti	4.5	1670	3200	15.5	0.47	–	8.2
Tombac CuZn20		8.65	1000	≈ 1300	159	0.38	–	–
Clay, dry		1.5 ... 1.8	≈ 1600	–	0.9 ... 1.3	0.88	–	–
Peat dust (mull), air-dried		0.19	–	–	0.081	–	–	
Uranium	U	19.1	1133	≈ 3800	28	0.12	–	–
Vanadium	V	6.1	1890	≈ 3300	31.4	0.50	–	–
Vulcanized fiber		1.28	–	–	0.21	1.26	–	–
Wax		0.96	60	–	0.084	3.4	–	–
Cotton wadding		0.01	–	–	0.04	–	–	–
Rubber		1.08	–	–	0.14 ... 0.24	–	–	–
Resistance alloy CuNi 44		8.9	1280	≈ 2400	22.6	0.41	–	15.2
Bismuth	Bi	9.8	271	1560	8.1	0.12	59	12.1
Tungsten	W	19.2	3410	5900	130	0.13	–	4.5
Cement, set		2 ... 2.2	–	–	0.9 ... 1.2	1.13	–	–
Brick, factory		> 1.9	–	–	1.0	0.9	–	–
Zinc	Zn	7.14	419.5	906	113	0.40	101	29
Tin	Sn	7.28	231.9	2500	65.7	0.24	59	23
Zirconium	Zr	6.5	1852	≈ 3600	22	0.29	–	–

[1]) At 1.013 bar. [2]) At 20 °C. [3]) At 0 ... 100 °C. [4]) At the melting point and 1.013 bar.
[5]) At 20 ... 1000 °C. [6]) At 100 ... 200 °C.

Properties of liquids

Substance		Density[2]) g/cm³	Melting point[1]) °C	Boiling point[1]) °C	Thermal conductivity[2]) W/(m·K)	Specific heat[2]) kJ/(kg·K)	Specific heat of fusion[3]) kJ/kg	Specific heat of evaporation[4]) kJ/kg	Volume expansion coefficient x 10^{-3}/K
Acetone	$(CH_3)_2CO$	0.79	−95	56	0.16	2.21	–	523	–
Ethanol (ethyl alcohol)	C_2H_5OH	0.79	−114	78	0.17	2.43	–	904	1.1
Ethyl ether	$(C_2H_5)_2O$	0.71	−116	35	0.13	2.28	–	377	1.6
Ethyl chloride	C_2H_5Cl	0.90	−139	12.5	0.11[5])	1.54[5])	–	–	–
Ethylene glycol		1.114	−12	197	0.25	2.40	–	–	–
Gasoline (IC-engine)		0.72 ... 0.75	−30 ... −50	25 ... 210	0.13	2.02	–	–	1.0
Benzene	C_6H_6	0.88	+5.5[6])	80	0.15	1.70	127	394	1.25
Diesel fuel		0.81 ... 0.85	−30	150 ... 360	0.15	2.05	–	–	–
Antifreeze-water mixture									
23% by vol.		1.03	−12	101	0.53	3.94	–	–	–
38% by vol.		1.04	−25	103	0.45	3.68	–	–	–
54% by vol.		1.06	−46	105	0.40	3.43	–	–	–
Glycerin	$C_3H_5(OH)_3$	1.26	+19	290	0.29	2.37	200	–	0,5
Heating oil, extra-light		≈ 0.83	−10	> 175	0.14	2.07	–	–	–
Table salt solution (20%)		1.15	−18	109	0.58	3.43	–	–	–
Linseed oil		0.93	−15	316	0.17	1.88	–	–	–
Methanol (methyl alcohol)	CH_3OH	0.79	−98	65	0.20	2.51	–	1109	–
Methyl chloride	CH_3Cl	0.99[7])	−92	−24	0.16	1.38	–	406	–
m-Xylene		–	–	–	–	–	–	339	–
Paraffin oil		–	–	–	–	–	–	–	0.764
Petroleum ethyl		0.66	−160	> 40	0.14	1.76	–	–	–
Kerosene		0.76 ... 0.86	−70	> 150	0.13	2.16	–	–	1.0
Mercury[8])	Hg	13.5	−39	357	10	0.14	11.3	285	0.18
Raps oil		0.91	±0	300	0.17	1.97	–	–	–

[1]) At 1.013 bar. [2]) At 20°C. [3]) At the melting point and 1.013 bar. [4]) At the boiling point and 1.013 bar. [5]) At 0°C. [6]) Congealing point 0°C. [7]) At −24°C.
[8]) For conversion of Torr to Pa, use 13.5951 g/cm³ (at 0°C).

Substance		Density[2]) g/cm³	Melting point[1]) °C	Boiling point[1]) °C	Thermal conductivity[2]) W/(m·K)	Specific heat[2]) kJ/(kg·K)	Specific heat of fusion[3]) kJ/kg	Specific heat of evaporation[4]) kJ/kg	Volume expansion coefficient x 10^{-3}/K
Nitric acid, concentrated	HNO_3	1.51	−41	84	0.26	1.72	–	–	–
Hydrochlorid acid, 10%	HCl	1.05	−14	102	0.50	3.14	–	–	–
Lubricating oil		0.91	−20	>300	0.13	2.09	–	–	–
Sulphuric acid, concentrated	H_2SO_4	1.83	+10.5[5])	338	0.47	1.42	–	–	0.55
Silicone oil		0.76 ... 0.98	–	–	0.13	1.09	–	–	–
Rectified spirit 95%[6])		0.81	−114	78	0.17	2.43	–	–	–
Coke-oven tar		1.2	−15	300	0.19	1.56	–		–
Turpentine		0.86	−10	160	0.11	1.80	–	293	1.0
Toluene[3])	C_7H_8	0.87	−95	110	0.14	1.67	–	364	–
Transformer oil		0.88	−30	170	0.13	1.88	–	–	–
Trichloroethylene	C_2HCl_3	1.47	−86	87	0.12	0.93	–	–	1.19
Water		1.00[7])	±0	100	0.60	4.18	332	2256	0.18[8])

Water vapor

Absolute pressure bar	Boiling point °C	Specific heat of evaporation kJ/kg[2])
0.1233	50	2382
0.3855	75	2321
1.0133	100	2256
2.3216	125	2187
4.760	150	2113
8.925	175	2031
15.55	200	1941

Absolute pressure bar	Boiling point °C	Specific heat of evaporation kJ/kg[2])
25.50	225	1837
39.78	250	1716
59.49	275	1573
85.92	300	1403
120.5	325	1189
165.4	350	892
221.1	374.2	0

1) At 1.013 bar.
2) At 20°C.
3) At the melting point and 1.013 bar.
4) At the boiling point and 1.013 bar.
5) Freezing point: 0°C.
6) Denatured ethanol.
7) At 4°C.
8) Volume expansion on freezing: 9%.

Properties of gases

Substance		Density[1])	Melting point[2])	Boiling point[2])	Thermal conductivity[3])	Specific heat kJ/(kg·K)		c_p/c_v	Spec. heat of evaporation[2])
		kg/m³	°C	°C	W/(m·K)	c_p	c_v		kJ/kg
Acetylene	C_2H_2	1.17	−84	−81	0.021	1.64	1.33	1.23	–
Ammonia	NH_3	0.77	−78	−33	0.024	2.06	1.56	1.32	1369
Argon	Ar	1.78	−189	−186	0.018	0.52	0.31	1.67	–
Ethane	C_2H_6	1.36	−183	−88	0.021	1.66	1.36	1.22	–
Ethanol vapor		2.04	−114	+78	0.015	–	–	1.13	–
Ethylene	C_2H_4	1.26	−169	−103	0.020	1.47	1.18	1.24	–
n-Butane	C_4H_{10}	2.70	−135	+0,5	0.016	–	–	–	–
i-Butane	C_4H_{10}	2.67	−145	−10,2	0.016	–	–	1.11	–
Chlorine	Cl_2	3.22	−102	−34	0.010	0.50	0.37	1.34	–
Hydrogen chloride	HCl	1.64	−114	−85	0.014	0.81	0.57	1.42	–
Cyanogen (Dicyan)	$(CN)_2$	2.33	−34	−21	–	1.72	1.35	1.27	–
Difluordichloromethane (freon)	CF_2Cl_2	5.51	−140	−30	0.010	–	–	1.14	–
Natural gas		≈ 0.83	–	−162	–	–	–	–	–
Fluorine	F_2	1.69	−220	−188	0.026	–	–	–	–
Blast-furnace gas		1.28	−210	−170	0.024	1.05	0.75	1.40	–
Helium	He	0.18	−272	−269	0.15	5.23	3.15	1.66	–
Carbon monoxide	CO	1.25	−205	−191	0.025	1.05	0.75	1.40	–
Carbon dioxide	CO_2	1.98	−57[4])	−78	0.016	0.82	0.63	1.30	368
Krypton	Kr	3.74	−157	−153	0.0095	0.25	0.15	1.67	–
Air		1.293	−220	−191	0.026	1.005	0.716	1.40	209
Methane	CH_4	0.72	−183	−162	0.033	2.19	1.68	1.30	–
Methyl chloride	CH_3Cl	2.31	−92	−24	–	0.74	0.57	1.29	–
Neon	Ne	0.90	−249	−246	0.049	1.03	0.62	1.67	–
Ozone	O_3	2.14	−251	−112	0.019	–	–	1.29	–
Propane	C_3H_8	2.00	−190	−43	0.018	–	–	1.14	–
Propylene	C_3H_6	1.91	−185	−47	0.017	–	–	–	–
Oxygen	O_2	1.43	−219	−183	0.026	0.91	0.65	1.40	214
Sulphur dioxide	SO_2	2.93	−75	−10	0.010	0.64	0.46	1.40	402
Carbon disulphide	CS_2	3.41	−112	+46	0.0073	0.67	0.56	1.19	–
Hydrogen sulphide	H_2S	1.54	−86	−60	–	0.96	0.72	1.34	553
Municipal gas		0.56...0.61	−230	−210	0.064	2.14	1.59	1.35	–
Nitrogen	N_2	1.25	−210	−196	0.026	1.04	0.74	1.40	201
Steam at 100°C[5])		0.60	±0	+100	0.025	2.01	1.52	1.32	–
Hydrogen	H_2	0.09	−259	−253	0.18	14.24	10.10	1.41	461
Xenon	X	5.89	−112	−108	0.0055	0.16	0.096	1.67	–

[1]) At 0°C and 1.013 bar.
[2]) At 1.013 bar.
[3]) At 20°C and 1.013 bar.
[4]) At 5.3 bar.
[5]) At saturation and 1.013 bar; see also the table entitled "Properties of liquids".

Properties of metallic materials

Material	DIN	Codes of selected types	Primary alloying constituents, mean values in % by wt.	R_m[1]) N/mm²	R_e[2]) N/mm²	A_5[3]) %	σ_{bw}[4]) Ref. value N/mm²	test bar ϕ[5]) mm	Notes
Cast iron and malleable cast iron[6]) E[7]) in 10^3 N/mm²: GG 78 .. 143[8]); GGG 160 ... 180; GTW and GTS 175 ... 195									
Cast iron with flake graphite (gray cast iron)	1691	GG-25	3.3 C; 2.0 Si; 0.8 Mn; <0.3 P	250 ... 350	–	–	120	30	Brittle, good machinability
Modular cast iron	1693	GGG-40	3.6 C; 2.2 Si; 0.4 Mn; 0.05 Mg	≥400	≥250	≥15	200	25	More ductile than gray cast iron, good machinability
Malleable cast iron	1692								
White-heart malleable (cast) iron		GTW-40-05	3.1 C; 0.6 Si; 0.4 Mn; 0.2 S	≥400	≥220	≥5 (A_3)	160	12	Ductility similar to CGG, good machinability
Black-heart malleable (cast) iron		GTS-35-10	2.5 C; 1.3 Si; 0.4 Mn; 0.1 S	≥350	≥200	≥10 (A_3)	140	12	
Cast steel E[7]) as steel	1681	GS-45	≤0,25 C; 0,6 Si	≥450	≥230	≥22	210	–	Heat-treatable
Steel E[7]) in 10^3 N/mm²: Unalloyed and low-alloy steel 212, austenic steels ≥190, high-alloy tool steels ≤230									
Untreated structural steel (ϕ ≤ 40 mm)	17 100	St 37-2 St 60-2	≤0.17 C 0.40 C	340 ... 510 570 ... 770	≤225 ≤325	≥24 ≥14	≥170 ≥280	– –	Low-stressed parts Higher-stressed parts
Strip and sheet of mild unalloyed steels	1623	St 14	≤0.08 C	270 ... 350	≤210	≥38 (A_{80})		–	Difficult deep-drawn parts
Hot galvanized strip and sheet	17 162 P. 1	St 05 Z	≤0.08 C	270 ... 380	≤260	≥30 (A_{80})		–	Corrosion-stressed, difficult deep-drawn parts
Free-cutting steel (ϕ 16 ... 40 mm)	1651	9 SMn 28 K 35 S 20 K	≤ 0.14 C; 1.1 Mn; 0.28 S 0.35 C; 0.7 Mn; 0.2 S	460 ... 710 540 ... 740	≥375 ≥315	≥8 ≥8	– –	– –	Soft free-cutting steel Free-cutting heat-treatable steel

Steel (continued)

Material	DIN	Codes of selected types	Primary alloying constituents, mean values in % by wt.	R_m[1]) N/mm²	R_e[2]) N/mm²	A_5[3]) %	σ_{bW}[4]) Ref. value N/mm²	test bar ϕ[5]) mm	Notes
Heat-treatable steel heat-treated (ϕ ≤ 16 mm)	17 200	Ck 45 34 Cr 4 42 CrMo 4 30 CrNiMo 8	0.45 C 0.34 C; 1.1 Cr 0.42 C; 1 Cr; 0.2 Mo 0.3 C; 2 Cr; 0.4 Mo; 2 Ni	700 ... 850 900 ...1100 1100 ...1300 1250 ...1450	≥ 14 ≥ 700 ≥ 900 ≥ 1050	≥ 14 ≥ 11 ≥ 10 ≥ 9	≥ 280 ≥ 360 ≥ 440 ≥ 500	– – – –	Increasing hardenability ↓
				Hardness HV (ref. value) Surface	Core				
Case-depth steel case-hardened and core-hardened (ϕ ≤ 11 mm)	17 210	Ck 15 16 MnCr 5 15 CrNi 6 17 CrNiMo 6	0.15 C; 0.16 C; 1 Cr 0.15 C; 1.5 C; 1.5 Ni 0.17 C; 1.6 Cr; 1.5 Ni; 0.3 Mo	700 700 700 700	– 450 450 450	In the case of hard steels – hardened anc core-hardened, case-hardened, nitrided etc. – the material characteristic values measured in the tensile test are unsuitable for dimensioning of the hard components.			High wear-resistance, high vibrostability ↓ Inreasing harden-ability
Nitriding steel heat-treated and nitrided	17 211	31 CrMoV 9 34 CrAlMo 5	0.30 C; 2.5 Cr; 0.2 Mo; 0.15 V 0.35 C; 1 Al; 1.15 Cr; 0.2 Mo	700 ... 850 850 ...1100	250 ... 350 250 ... 350				High wear-resistance, high vibrostability
Rolling bearing steel hardened and core-hardened	17 230	100 Cr 6	1 C; 1.5 Cr	Hardness ≥ 59 HRC					High wear-restistance
Tool steel Unalloyed cold work steel, hardened and core-hardened	17 350	C 80 W 1	0.8 C	Usual hardness 60 ... 63 HRC					Water-hardening steel
Alloyed cold work steel, hardened and core-hardened	17 350	115 CrV 3 90 MnCrV 8 x 155 CrVMo 121	1.15 C; 0.7 Cr; 0.1 V 0.9 C; 2 Mn; 0.1 V 1.55 C; 12 Cr; 1.0 V; 0.7 Mo	60 ... 63 HCR 60 ... 63 HRC 60 ... 63 HRC					Water/oil-hardening steel Oil-hardening steel Very high wear-resistance

Hot work steel hardened and core-hardened	17 350	X40 CrMoV51	0.4 C; 5 Cr; 1 Mo; 1 V	43 ... 45 HRC		In the case of hard steels – hardened and core-hardened, case-hardened, nitrided etc. – the material characteristic values measured in the tensile test are unsuitable for dimensioning of the hard components.			
High-speed steel hardened and core-hardened	17 350	S-6-5-2	0.8 C; 6 W; 5 Mo; 2 V	61 ... 65 HRC					Wear-resistant at high temperature
Stainless steel Ferritic steel annealed	17 440	X 6 Cr 17	≤ 0.08 C; 17 Cr	450 ... 600 Hardness < 185 HV	≥ 270	≥ 20			Non-hardenable
Martensitic steel hardened and core-hardened	17 440 17 440 (SEW-400)	X 20 CrNi 17 2 X 46 Cr 13 X 90 CrMoV 18	0.20 C; 17 Cr; 2 Ni 0,46 C; 13 Cr 0,9 C; 18 Cr; 1.1 Mo; 0,1 V	Hardness approx. 40 HRC Hardness approx. 50 HRC Hardness ≥ 57 HRC					Increasing wear resistance ↓
Austenic steel chilled	17 440	X 5 CrNi 18 10	≤ 0,07 C; 18 Cr; 9.5 Ni	500 ... 700	≥ 195	≥ 45	–	–	Non-magnetic, non-hardenable
Hard metals E = 440 000 ... 550 000	–	–	W (Ti, Ta)-Karbid + Co	800 ... 1900 HV			Sinter materials, extremely resistant to pressure and wear, but brittle; machining, cutting and forming tools.		
Extremely heavy metals E = 320 000 ... 380 000	–	–	> 90 W; Ni e.g.	≥ 650 240 ... 450 HV	≥ 560	≥ 2	Density 17 ... 18.5 g/cm^3, governor flyweights, centrifugal and balance masses.		

[1]) Tensile strength
[2]) Yield point (or $R_{p0.2}$).
[3]) Elongation at fracture.
[4]) Fatigue limit under reversed bending stress.
[5]) The fatigue limits given apply to the separately cast test bar.
[6]) The fatigue limits of all types of cast iron are dependent on the weight and section thickness of the cast pieces.
[7]) Modulus of elasticity.
[8]) For gray cast iron, E decreases with increasing tensile stress and remains almost constant with increasing compression stress.

Steel (continued)

Spring steel

Materials	DIN	Primary alloying constituents, approx. in % by wt.; E and G in N/mm²	Diameter mm	R_m[1]) min. N/mm²	Z[2]) %	σ_b[3]) N/mm²	τ_{kh}[4]) N/mm²	τ_{perm}[5]) N/mm²	Characteristic properties, applications
Spring steel wire D patented and springy drawn[6])	17 223 Sheet 1	0.8 C; 0.6 Mn; < 0.35 Si $E = 206\,000$ $G = 81\,500$	1 3 10	2230 1840 1350	40 40 30	1590 1280 930	380[7]) 360[7]) 320	1115 920 675	For high maximum stresses (see page 280).
Stainless-steel spring wire	17 224	< 0.12 C; 17 Cr; 7.5 Ni $E = 185\,000$ $G = 73\,000$	1 3	2000 1600	40 40	1400 1130	– –	1000 800	Stainless-steel springs.
Oil-tempered valve-spring steel wire[6])	17 223 Sheet 2	0.65 C; 0.7 Mn; < 0.30 Si $E = 206\,000$ $G = 80\,000$	1 3 8	1720 1480 1390	45 45 38	1200 1040 930	380[8]) 380[8]) 360[8])	860 740 690	For severe fatigue loading.
Oil-tempered, alloyed valve-spring steel wire VD Si Cr[6])	–	0.55 C; 0.7 Mn; 0.65 Cr; 1.4 Si $E = 200\,000$ $G = 79\,000$	1 3 8	2060 1920 1720	50 50 40	– – –	430[8]) 430[8]) 380[8])	1030 960 860	For most severe fatigue loading and high temperatures.
Oil-tempered, alloyed valve-spring steel wire VD Cr V[6])	–	0.7 C; 0.7 Mn; 0.5 Cr; 0.15 V; ≤ 0.30 Si $E = 200\,000$ $G = 79\,000$	1 3 8	1860 1670 1420	45 45 40	– – –	470[8]) 470[8]) 400[8])	930 835 710	For severe fatigue loading.
Spring steel strip Ck 85	17 222	0.85 C; 0.55 Mn; 0.25 Si $E = 206\,000$	h ≤ 2.5	1470	–	1270	σ_{bh} = 640	–	Highly-stressed leaf springs.
Stainless-steel spring strip	17 224	< 0.12 C; 17 Cr; 7.5 Ni $E = 185\,000$	h ≤ 1	1370	–	1230	σ_{bh} = 590	–	Stainless steel leaf springs.

[1]) Tensile strength. [2]) Reduction of area at fracture. [3]) Permissible bending stress. [4]) Permissible lift stress for stress cycles endured $N \geq 10^7$.
[5]) Permissible maximum stress for temperatures to approx. 30 °C and 1 ... 2 % relaxation in 10 hrs.; for higher temperatures see page 280.
[6]) See pages 280 and 281 for fatigue-strength diagrams. [7]) 400 N/mm² for peened springs. [8]) Approx. 40 % higher for peened springs.

Vehicle-body sheet metal

Abbreviated material name	Standard material thickness mm	$R_{p0.2}$[1]) N/mm²	R_m[2]) N/mm²	A_{80}[3]) %	Properties, typical appplications
St 12	0.6 ... 2.5	≈ 280	≈ 270 ... 410	≈ 28	For simple drawn metal parts
St 13		≈ 250	≈ 270 ... 370	≈ 32	For complicated drawn metal parts
St 14		≈ 240	≈ 270 ... 350	≈ 38	For very complex deep drawn parts, outer body parts (roof, doors, fenders, etc.; 0.75 ... 1.0 mm); see also DIN 1623
ZE 260	0.75 ... 2.0	260 ... 340	≈ 370	≈ 28	For highly-stressed, load-bearing beams whose forming is not too complicated
ZE 340		340 ... 420	≈ 420	≈ 24	
ZE 420		420 ... 500	≈ 490	≈ 20	
AlMg 0.4 Si 1.2	0.8 ... 2.5	≈ 140	≈ 250	≈ 28	For outer body parts such as front fenders, doors, hood, trunk lid, etc.; usually 1.25 mm; see DIN 1745
AlMg 4.5 Mn 0.3	0.5 ... 3.5	≈ 130	≈ 270	≈ 28	For inner reinforcements of hinged covers; for parts which are not visible; stretcher strains are acceptable

[1]) Proof stress (non-proportional elongation).
[2]) Tensile strength.
[3]) Percentage elongation at fracture.

Nonferrous metals

Material	DIN	Designation	Nominal composition, mean values % by wt.	E[1]) N/mm²	R_m[2]) min. N/mm²	$R_{p0.2}$[3]) min. N/mm²	σ_{bW}[4]) min. N/mm²	Properties, typical applications
Heavy metals								
High-conductivity copper	1787	E-Cu 57 F 20	99.90 Cu	128×10^3	200	120[5])	70	Very good electrical conductivity
Brass	17 660	CuZn 28 F 35	72 Cu; 28 Zn	114×10^3	350	200	120	Deep-drawn parts
		CuZn 37 F 44	63 Cu; 37 Zn	110×10^3	440	370	140	Good cold-formability
		CuZn 39 Pb 3 F 43	58 Cu; 39 Zn; 3 Pb	96×10^3	430	250	150	Free-cutting brass
Nickel silver	17 663	CuNi 12 Zn 24 F 43	64,5 Cu; 23,5 Zn; 12 Ni	125×10^3	430	230	–	Corrosion-resistant
Tin bronze	17 662	CuSn 6 F 41	94 Cu; 6 Sn	118×10^3	410	300	175	Good antifriction features; bearing bushes, springs
Cast tin bronze	1705	G-CuSn 12	86 Cu; 12 Sn	100×10^3	260[6])	140[6])	90	Corrosion-resistant, wear-resistant; gears
Red brass	1705	GC-CuSn 7 ZnPb	85 Cu; 7 Sn; 4 Zn; 6 Pb	85×10^3	270	120	80	Corrosion-resistant
Commercial lead	1719		99,9 Pb	17×10^3	10	–	2	Soft, acid-resistant; seals
Hard lead	17 641	PbSb 5	94 Pb; 6 Sb		30	–	–	Acid-resistant; fittings, battery plates
Lead diecastings	1741	GD-Pb 87 Sb	87 Pb; 13 Sb		60	–	–	Dimensionally accurate centrifugal and balance weights
Tin alloy	4381	SnSb 12 Cu 6 Pb	80 Sn; 12 Sb; 6 Cu; 2 Pb	30×10^3	–	60[7])	28	Plain bearings
Zinc diecastings	1743	GD-ZnAl 4 Cu 1	96 Zn; 4 Al	130×10^3	280[6])	200[6])	80	Dimensionally accurate castings
Heating-element alloy	17 470	NiCr 80 20	80 Ni; 20 Cr	–	650	–	–	High electrical resistance (See p. 204).
	17 743	NiCu 30 Al F 62	64 Ni; 31 Cu; 3 Al; 1 Fe; 1 Ti	–	620	270	–	
Resistance alloy	17 471	CuNi 44	55 Cu; 44 Ni; 1 Mn	–	420	–	–	
		CuNi 30 Mn	67 Cu; 30 Ni; 3 Mn	–	400	–	–	
		CuMn 12 NiAl	82 Cu; 12 Mn; 5 Ni; 1 Al	–	400	–	–	

[1]) Modulus of elasticity, reference values. [2]) Tensile strength. [3]) Yield strength (0.2% offset). [4]) Bending fatigue strength. [5]) Maximum. [6]) For separately cast test rod. [7]) Approx.

Light metals

Material	Nominal composition, mean values % by wt.	R_m[1]) min. N/mm²	$R_{p0.2}$[2]) min. N/mm²	σ_{bW}[3]) min. N/mm²	Properties, typical applications
Wrought aluminum alloys (DIN 1712, 1725, 1745 ... 1749, 40501), modulus of elasticity $E = 65{,}000$ to 73,000 N/mm²					
Al 99.5 W 7	99.5 Al	65	55[4])	40	Soft, good conductor, can be anodized/polished;
AlMg 2 Mn 0.8 W 19	97 Al; 2 Mg; 0.8 Mn	190	80	90	Resistant to sea water, can be anodized
AlMgSi 1 F 28	97 Al; 0.9 Mg; 1 Si; 0.7 Mn	275	200	90	Precipitation hardened, resistant to sea water
AlCuMg 1 F 40	94 Al; 4 Cu; 0.7 Mg; 0.7 Mn; 0.5 Si	395	265	120	Precipitation hardened, good creep properties
AlZnMgCu 1.5 F 53	90 Al; 6 Zn; 2 Mg; 2 Cu; 0.2 Cr	530	450	140	Maximum strength
Cast-aluminum alloys[5]) (DIN 1725, Part 2), modulus of elasticity $E = 68{,}000$ to 75,000 N/mm²					
GK-AlSi 12	88 Al; 12 Si; 0,2 Mn	180	80	70	Thin-walled parts with good fatigue strength
GK-AlMg 5 Si	94 Al; 5 Mg; 1 Si; 0.2 Mn; 0.1 Ti	180	110	70	Sea-water resistant; can be anodized/polished
GK-AlSi 10 Mg wa	89 Al; 10 Si; 0.4 Mg; 0.2 Mn	240	210	80	Precipitation hardened; highly-stressed parts with good fatigue strength
GK-AlSi 6 Cu 4	89 Al; 6 Si; 4 Cu; 0.3 Mn; 0.3 Mg	180	120	60	Precipitation hardened; highly-stressed parts
GK-AlCu 4 Ti wa	95 Al; 5 Cu; 0.2 Ti	330	220	90	Precipitation hardened; simple parts to meet maximum strength and toughness requirements
GD-AlSi 9 Cu 3	87 Al; 9 Si; 3 Cu; 0.3 Mn; 0.3 Mg	240	140	70[6])	Good thermal strength; complex diecastings
GD-AlMg 9	90 Al; 9 Mg; 1 Si; 0.4 Mn	200	140	60[6])	Sea-water resistant; medium-stressed parts.
Magnesium alloys (DIN 1729, 9715), modulus of elasticity $E = 45{,}000$ N/mm²					
MgAl 6 Zn F 27	93 Mg; 6 Al; 1 Zn; 0.3 Mn	270	195	–	Parts subject to medium to high stress (Chips are combustible)
GK-MgAl 9 Zn 1 wa	90 Mg; 9 Al; 0.6 Zn; 0.2 Mn	240	150	80	Precipitation hardened (Chips are combustible)
GD-MgAl 9 Zn 1	90 Mg; 9 Al; 0.6 Zn; 0.2 Mn	200	150	50	Complex diecastings (Chips are combustible)
Titanium alloys (DIN 17850, 17851, 17860 ... 17864), modulus of elasticity $E = 110{,}000$ N/mm²					
Annealed titanium	99.7 Ti	290	180	–	Corrosion-resistant
TiAl 6 V 4 F 89	90 Ti; 6 Al; 4 V	890	820	–	Corrosion-resistant, maximum strength

[1]) Tensile strength. [2]) Yield strength (0.2 % offset). [3]) Rotating bending fatigue strength. [4]) Maximum. [5]) Strength values apply to permanent mold castings and die-castings for separately cast test rods. Sand castings have slightly lower values than permanent mold castings. [6]) Flat bending fatigue strength.

Sinter (PM) metals 1) for plain bearings

	Permissible ranges						Representative examples					
Material	Material code Sint-	Density ρ g/cm³	Porosity $\Delta V/V$ %	Chemical composition % (by mass)	Radial crushing strength K²) N/mm²	Hardness HB	Density ρ g/cm³	Chemical composition % (by mass)	Radial crushing strength K²) N/mm²	Compressive yield point $\delta_{d\,0.2}$ N/mm²	Hardness HB²)	Thermal conductivity λ W/mK
PM iron	A 00 B 00 C 00	5.6 ... 6.0 6.0 ... 6.4 6.4 ... 6.8	25 ± 2.5 20 ± 2.5 15 ± 2.5	< 0.3 C; < 1.0 Cu; < 2 others; rest Fe	> 150 > 180 > 220	> 25 > 30 > 40	5.9 6.3 6.7	< 0.2 others; rest Fe	160 190 230	130 160 180	30 40 50	37 43 48
PM steel containing Cu	A 10 B 10 C 10	5.6 ... 6.0 6.0 ... 6.4 6.4 ... 6.8	25 ± 2.5 20 ± 2.5 15 ± 2.5	< 0.3 C; 1 ... 5 Cu; < 2 others; rest Fe	> 160 > 190 > 230	> 35 > 40 > 55	5.9 6.3 6.7	2.0 Cu < 0.2 others; rest Fe	170 200 240	150 170 200	40 50 65	36 37 42
PM steel containing Cu and C	B 11	6.0...6.4	20 ± 2.5	0.4 ... 1.0 C; 1 ... 5 Cu < 2 others; rest Fe	> 270	> 70	6.3	0.6 C; 2.0 Cu; < 0.2 others; rest Fe	280	160	80	28
PM steel containing high percentage of Cu	A 20 B 20	5.8...6.2 6.2...6.6	25 ± 2.5 20 ± 2.5	< 0.3 C; 15 ... 25 Cu; < 2 others; rest Fe	> 180 > 200	> 30 > 45	6.0 6.4	20 Cu; < 0.2 others; rest Fe	200 220	140 160	40 50	41 47
PM steel containing high percentage of Cu and C	A 22 B 22	5.5...6.0 6.0...6.5	25 ± 2.5 20 ± 2.5	0.5...2.0 C; 15 ... 25 Cu < 2 others; rest Fe	> 120 > 140	> 20 > 25	5.7 6.1	2.0 C³); 20 Cu < 0.2 others; rest Fe	125 145	100 120	25 30	30 37
PM bronze	A 50 B 50 C 50	6.4...6.8 6.8...7.2 7.2...7.7	25 ± 2.5 20 ± 2.5 15 ± 2.5	< 0.2 C; 9 ... 11 Sn; < 2 others; rest Cu	> 120 > 170 > 200	> 25 > 30 > 35	6.6 7.0 7.4	10 Sn; < 0.2 others; rest Cu	140 180 210	100 130 160	30 35 45	27 32 37
PM bronze containing graphite⁴)	A 51 B 51 C 51	6.0...6.5 6.5...7.0 7.0...7.5	25 ± 2.5 20 ± 2.5 15 ± 2.5	0.5 ... 2.0 C; 9 ... 11 Sn; < 2 others; rest Cu	> 100 > 150 > 170	> 20 > 25 > 30	6.3 6.7 7.1	1.5 C⁴); 10 Sn; < 0.2 others; rest Cu	120 155 175	80 100 120	20 30 35	20 26 32

1) According to "Material Specification Sheets for Sinter (PM) Materials": DIN 30910, 1990 Edition.
2) Measured on calibrated bearings 10/16 ∅ · 10. 3) C is mainly present as free graphite.
4) C is present as free graphite.

Sinter (PM) metals[1]) for structural parts

Material	Material code Sint-	Density ρ g/cm³	Porosity Δ V/V %	Chemical composition % (by mass)	Hardness HB	Density ρ g/cm³	Chemical composition % (by mass)	Tensile strength R_m N/mm²	Compressive yield point $R_{p\,0.1}$ N/mm²	Elongation after fracture A %	Hardness HB	E modulus $E \cdot 10^3$ N/mm²
	Permissible ranges					Representative examples						
PM iron	C 00 D 00 E 00	6.4 ... 6.8 6.8 ... 7.2 > 7.2	15 ± 2.5 10 ± 2.5 < 7.5	< 0.3 C; < 1.0 Cu; < 2 others; rest Fe	> 35 > 45 > 60	6.6 6.9 7.3	< 0.5 others; rest Fe	130 190 260	60 90 130	4 10 18	40 50 65	100 130 160
PM steel containing C	C 01 D 01	6.4 ... 6.8 6.8 ... 7.2	15 ± 2.5 10 ± 2.5	0.3...0.6 C; < 1.0 Cu; < 2 others; rest Fe	> 70 > 90	6.6 6.9	0.5 C; < 0.5 others; rest Fe	260 320	180 210	3 3	80 100	100 130
PM steel containing Cu	C 10 D 10 E 10	6.4 ... 6.8 6.8 ... 7.2 > 7.2	15 ± 2.5 10 ± 2.5 < 7.5	< 0.3 C; 1...5 Cu; < 2 others; rest Fe	> 40 > 50 > 80	6.6 6.9 7.3	1.5 Cu; < 0.5 others; rest Fe	230 300 400	160 210 290	3 6 12	55 85 120	100 130 160
PM steel containing Cu and C	C 11 D 11	6.4 ... 6.8 6.8 ... 7.2	15 ± 2.5 10 ± 2.5	0.4...1.5 C; 1...5 Cu; < 2 others; rest Fe	> 80 > 95	6.6 6.9	0.6 C; 1.5 Cu; < 0.5 others; rest Fe	460 570	320 400	2 2	125 150	100 130
	C 11	6.4 ... 6.8	15 ± 2.5	0.4...1.5 C; 5...10 Cu; < 2 others; rest Fe	> 105	6.6	0.8 C; 6 Cu; < 0.5 others; rest Fe	530	410	< 1	150	100
PM steel containing Cu, Ni and Mo	C 30 D 30 E 30	6.4 ... 6.8 6.8 ... 7.2 > 7.2	15 ± 2.5 10 ± 2.5 < 7.5	< 0.3 C; 1...5 Cu; 1...5 Ni; < 0.8 Mo; < 2 others; rest Fe	> 55 > 60 > 90	6.6 6.9 7.3	0.3 C; 1.5 Cu; 4.0 Ni. 0.5 Mo; < 0.5 others; rest Fe	390 510 680	310 370 440	2 3 5	105 130 170	100 130 160
PM steel containing P	C 35 D 35	6.4 ... 6.8 6.8 ... 7.2	15 ± 2.5 10 ± 2.5	< 0.3 C; < 1.0 Cu; 0.3...0.6 P; < 2 others; rest Fe	> 70 > 80	6.6 6.9	0.45 P; < 0.5 others; rest Fe	310 330	200 230	11 12	85 90	100 130
PM steel containing Cu and P	C 36 D 36	6.4 ... 6.8 6.8 ... 7.2	15 ± 2.5 10 ± 2.5	< 0.3 C; 1...5 Cu; 0.3...0.6 P; < 2 others; rest Fe	> 80 > 90	6.6 6.9	2.0 Cu; 0.45 P; < 0.5 others; rest Fe	360 380	290 320	5 6	100 105	100 130
PM steel containing Cu, Ni, Mo and C	C 39 D 39	6.4 ... 6.8 6.8 ... 7.2	15 ± 2.5 10 ± 2.5	0.3...0.6 C; 1...3 Cu; 1...5 Ni; < 0.8 Mo < 2 others; rest Fe	> 90 > 120	6.6 6.9	0.5 C; 1.5 Cu; 4.0 Ni; 0.5 Mo; < 0.5 others; rest Fe	520 600	370 420	1 2	150 180	100 130
PM bronze	C 50 D 50	7.2...7.7 7.7...8.1	15 ± 2.5 10 ± 2.5	9...11 Sn; < 2 others; rest Cu	> 35 > 45	7.4 7.9	10 Sn; < 0.5 others; rest Cu	150 220	90 120	4 6	40 55	50 70

[1]) According to "Material Specification Sheets for Sinter (PM) Materials": DIN 30910, 1990 Edition.

Soft magnetic materials

Magnetic steel sheet and strip

Type of sheet or strip: Abbreviated name	Material number	Nominal thickness mm	Density ϱ g/cm³	Max. specific total loss (at 50 Hz) W/kg when magnetic flux density is: P 1.0	P 1.5	P 1.7	Min. magnetic induction T (Tesla) with field strength H in A/m: 2500 (B 25)	5000 (B 50)	10 000 (B 100)	Static coercive field strength A/m	Permeability μ_{max}	Characteristic property, applications
V270 – 35 A	1.0801	0.35	7.60	1.10	2.70	–	1.49	1.60	1.70			Magnetic hysteresis loss.
V330 – 35 A	1.0804	0.35	7.65	1.30	3.30	–	1.49	1.60	1.70			Design of magnetic circuits with alternating-current field magnetization (e.g. motors).
V330 – 50 A	1.0809	0.50	7.60	1.35	3.30	–	1.49	1.60	1.70			
V530 – 50 A	1.0813	0.50	7.70	2.30	5.30	–	1.54	1.64	1.74			
V800 – 50 A	1.0816	0.50	7.80	3.60	8.00	–	1.58	1.68	1.77			
V400 – 65 A	1.0821	0.65	7.65	1.70	4.00	–	1.50	1.60	1.70	≈ 100 ... 300	≈ 5000	
V940 – 65 A	1.0828	0.65	7.80	4.20	9.40	–	1.58	1.68	1.77			
VH 660 – 50	1.0361	0.50	–	2.80	6.60	–	1.62	1.70	1.79			
VH 1050 – 50	1.0363	0.50	–	4.30	10.50	–	1.58	1.65	1.77			
VH 800 – 65	1.0364	0.65	–	3.30	8.00	–	1.62	1.70	1.79			
VH 1200 – 65	1.0366	0.65	–	5.00	12.00	–	1.58	1.65	1.77			
							With field strength in H in A/m 800 (B 8)					
VM 97 – 30 N	1.0861	0.30	–	–	0.97	1.50	1.75					
VM 140 – 30 S	1.0862	0.30	–	–	–	1.40	1.78			≈ 1	≈ 30 000	
VM 111 – 30 P	1.0881	0.30	–	–	–	1.11	1.85					
VE 340 – 50	1.0841	0.50	7.65	1.40	3.40	–	1.52	1.62	1.73			
VE 560 – 50	1.0844	0.50	7.80	2.40	5.60	–	1.56	1.66	1.77	≈ 100 ... 300	≈ 5000	
VE 390 – 65	1.0846	0.65	7.65	1.60	3.90	–	1.52	1.62	1.73			
VE 630 – 65	1.0849	0.65	7.80	2.70	6.30	–	1.56	1.66	1.77			

Materials for transformers

Material type: Abbreviated name	Material type: Material number	Chemical composition	Thickness mm	Density ϱ g/cm³	Specif. elec. resistance[1] $\Omega \cdot mm^2/m$	Static coercive field strength[1] A/m	Saturation induction[1] T (Tesla)	Curie temperature[1] °C	Material permeability[1] μ_{16}	Material permeability[1] μ_4	Specific total loss at 50 Hz W/kg	Characteristic property, applications
A 0	1.3850	Steel with ≈ 2.5 ... 4.5 % Si	0.5 0.35	7.7	0.40	100	2.03	750	450	–	–	Permeability at low field strengths
A 2	1.3852		0.35	7.63	0.55	60	2.0	750	900	–		
A 3	1.3853		0.35 0.20	7.57	0.68	35	1.92	750	900 750	– –		
C 2	1.3856	Steel with ≈ 3.5 ... 4.5 % Si	0.35	7.55	0.5	30	2.0	750	1300	–	P 1.5: ≈ 1	
C 5	1.3859		0.35	7.65	0.45	15	2.0	750	Depending upon the rolling direction			
D 1a	1.3915	Steel with ≈ 36 ... 40% Ni	0.35 0.05	8.15	0.75	50	1.3	250	2400 2300	– –	P 1.0: ≈ 0.5 ... 1	Manufacturing of transformers in communications technology
			0.35 0.1						2200	–		
D 3	1.3916		0.35 0.05	8.15	0.75	15	1.3	250	2900 2500	– –		
E 3	2.4591	Ni-Fe alloy with ≈ 75 % Ni, additional additives	0.35 0.05	8.6	0.5	2	0.7 – 0.8	400	– –	20 000 16 000	P 0.5: ≈ 0.03	
E 4	2.4592		0.35 0.05	8.7	0.55	1	0.6 – 0.8	270 400	– –	35 000 30 000		
F 3	1.3922	Ni-Fe alloy with ≈ 50% Ni	0.35 0.05	8.25	0.45	10	1.5	470	–	4000	P 1,0: ≈ 0.3	

[1]) Standard values.

Materials for DC relays

Material type: Abreviated Name	Material Number	Alloying constituents % by mass	Density[1]) ϱ g/cm³	Hardness[1]) HV	Remanence[1]) T (Tesla)	Permeability[1]) μ_{max}	Specific elec. resistance[1]) $\frac{\Omega \cdot mm^2}{m}$	Coercive field strength A/m max.	Min. magnetic induction T (Tesla) with field strength H in A/m: 20	50	100	200	300	500	1000	4000	Characteristic properties, applications
Unalloyed steels																	
RFe 160	1.1011				–	–	0.15	160	–	–	–	–	1.15	1.30	–	1.60	Low coercive field strength
RFe 80	1.1014				1.10	–	0.15	80	–	–	–	1.10	1.20	1.30	1.45	1.60	
RFe 60	1.1015	–	7.85	max. 150	1.20	–	0.12	60	–	–	–	1.15	1.25	1.35	1.45	1.60	
RFe 20	1.1017				1.20	≈ 20 000	0.10	20	–	–	1.15	1.25	1.30	1.40	1.45	1.60	
RFe 12	1.1018				1.20		0.10	12	–	–	1.15	1.25	1.30	1.40	1.45	1.60	
Silicon steels																	DC relays and similar applications
RSi 48	1.3840	2.5	7.55	130	0.50	–	0.42	48	–	–	0.60	–	1.10	1.20	–	1.50	
RSi 24	1.3843	–	–	–	1.00	≈ 20 000	–	24	–	–	1.20	–	1.30	1.35	–	1.50	
RSi 12	1.3845	4 Si	7.75	200	1.00	≈ 10 000	0.60	12	–	–	1.20	–	1.30	1.35	–	1.50	
Nickel steels and nickel alloys																	
RNi 24	1.3911	≈ 36 Ni	8.2	130...180	0.45	≈ 5000	0.75	24	0.20	0.45	0.70	–	0.90	1.00	–	1.18	
RNi 12	1.3926	≈ 50 Ni	8.3	130...180	0.60	≈ 30 000	0.45	12	0.50	0.90	1.10	–	1.25	1.35	–	1.45	
RNi 8	1.3927	≈ 50 Ni	8.3	130...180	0.60	30000...100000	0.45	8	0.50	0.90	1.10	–	1.25	1.35	–	1.45	
RNi 5	2.4596	70 ... 80 Ni Small quanties of Cu, Cr, Mo	8.7	120...170	0.30	≈ 40 000	0.55	5	0.50	0.65	0.70	–	–	–	–	0.75	
RNi 2	2.4595		8.7	120...170	0.30	≈ 100 000	0.55	2	0.50	0.65	0.70	–	–	–	–	0.75	

[1]) Standard values.

Sintered metals for magnetically soft components

Designation	Density ϱ g/cm³	Porosity %	Chemical composition % by mass: C	others	Fe	Coercive field strength[1] A/m max.	Magnetic induction[1] T (Tesla) min.	Permeability[1] μ_{max} min.	Hysteresis loss[1][4] $P_{H1,0}$ W/kg	Eddy current loss[1][4] $P_{W1,0}$ W/kg	Applications
Sint-C 02	6.4 ... 6.8	15 ± 2.5	0 ... 0.1	< 0.5	Remainder	175	1.1[2]	2900	125	23	Magnetic circuit components
Sint-D 02	6.8 ... 7.2	10 ± 2.5				170	1.3[2]	3800	100	20	
Sint-E 02	7.2 ... 7.5	6 ± 1.5				165	1.45[2]	4400	75	18	
Bosch grades (not standardized)											
Fe special	7.0 ... 7.2	8 ... 10	0 ... 0.05	< 0,2	Remainder	100	1.4[3]	4000	6	45	
Fe-P	7.0 ... 7.2		0 ... 0.05	0.45 P	Remainder	120	1.4[3]	4000	8	30	
Fe-P special	7.0 ... 7.2		0 ... 0.05	0.45 P	Remainder	50	1.4[3]	8500	2	33	
Fe-P-Si	7.0 ... 7.2		0 ... 0.05	2 Si, 0.45 P	Remainder	120	1.35[3]	3800	4	16	

[1]) Measured in sintered or soft-annealed condition.
[2]) At field strength $H = 5000$ A/m (B_{50}).
[3]) At field strength $H = 13{,}500$ A/m (B_{135}).
[4]) Standard values at $\hat{B} = 1.0$ T and 50 Hz.

Soft magnetic ferrites

Ferrite type	Initial permeability[1]) μ_i ±25 %	Referenced loss factor $\tan\delta/\mu_i$[2]) 10^{-6}	MHz	Referenced power loss[3]) mW/g	Amplitude permeability[4]) μ_a	Curie Temperature[5])[6]) Θ_c °C	Frequency for $0.8 \cdot \mu_i$[6]) MHz	Characteristic properties, applications
Materials in largely open magnetic circuits								
C 1/12	12	350	100	–	–	> 500	400	Initial permeability. High specific resistance (10^{0} ... $10^{5}\,\Omega\cdot$m) compared to metals (10^{-7} ... $10^{-6}\,\Omega\cdot$m), therefore low eddy-current losses. Communications technology (coils, transformers).
D 1/50	50	120	10	–	–	> 400	90	
F 1/250	250	100	3	–	–	> 250	22	
G 2/600	600	40	1	–	–	> 170	6	
H 1/1200	1200	20	0,3	–	–	> 150	2	
Materials in largely closed magnetic circuits								
E 2	60 ... 160	80	10	–	–	> 400	50	
G 3	400 ... 1200	25	1	–	–	> 180	6	
J 4	1600 ... 2500	5	0.1	–	–	> 150	1.5	
M 1	3000 ... 5000	5	0.03	–	–	> 125	0.4	
P 1	5000 ... 7000	3	0.01	–	–	> 125	0.3	
Materials for power applications								
W 1	1000 ... 3000	–	–	45	1200	> 180	–	
W 2	1000 ... 3000	–	–	25	1500	> 180	–	

[1]) Nominal values.
[2]) $\tan\delta/\mu_i$ denotes the frequency-dependent material losses at a low flux density ($B < 0.1$ mT).
[3]) Losses at high flux density. Measured preferably at: $f = 25$ kHz, $B = 200$ mT, $\Theta = 100$ °C.
[4]) Permeability when subjected to a strong sinusoidal magnetic field. Measured at: $f \leq 25$ kHz, $\hat{B} = 320$ mT, $\Theta = 100$ °C.
[5]) Curie temperature Θ_c in this table is that temperature at which the initial permeability μ_i drops to below 10% of its value at 25 °C.
[6]) Standard values.

Permanent-magnet materials

Material: Abbreviated name	Material number DIN	IEC	Chemical composition[1]) % by wt. Al	Co	Cu	Nb	Ni	Ti	Fe	Density ϱ[1]) g/cm³	$(BH)_{max}$[2]) kJ/m³	Remanence B_r[2]) mT	Coercive field strength[2]) of the flux density $_BH_c$ kA/m	Coercive field strength[2]) of the polarization $_JH_c$ kA/m	Rel. permanent permeability[1]) μ_p	Curie temp.[1]) T_c K	Temp. coeff. of polar. $TK(J_s)$ [1])[3]) %/K	Temp. coeff. of coerciv. $TK(H_c)$ [1])[3]) %/K	Manufacturing, processing, applications
Metallic magnets																			
Isotropic																			
AlNiCo 9/5	1.3728	R 1-0-3	11...13	0...5	2...4	–	21...28	0...1	Re-	6.8	9.0	550	44	47	4.0...5.0	1030		+0.03	
AlNiCo 18/9	1.3756	–	6...8	24...34	3...6	–	13...19	5...9	main-	7.2	18.0	600	80	86	3.0...4.0	...	–0.02	...	
AlNiCo 7/8p	1.3715	R 1-2-3	6...8	24...34	3...6	–	13...19	5...9	der	5.5	7.0	340	72	84	2.0...3.0	1180		–0.07	
Anisotropic																			
AlNiCo 35/5	1.3761	–	8...9	23...26	3...4	0...1	13...16	–	Re-	7.2	35.0	1120	47	48	3.0...4.5				Manufacture: Casting or sintering. Magnets with binders are pressed or injection-molded. Processing: Grinding. Max. temperature of application 400...500 °C.
AlNiCo 44/5	1.3757	R 1-1-2	8...9	23...26	3...4	0...1	13...16	–	main-	7.2	44.0	1200	52	53	2.5...4.0	1030		+0.03	
AlNiCo 52/6	1.3759	–	8...9	23...26	3...4	0...1	13...16	–	der	7.2	52.0	1250	55	56	1.5...3.0	...	–0.02	...	
AlNiCo 60/11	1.3763	R 1-1-6	6...8	35...39	2...4	0...1	13...15	4...6		7.2	60.0	900	110	112	1.5...2.5	1180		–0.07	
AlNiCo 30/14	1.3765	–	6...8	38...42	2...4	0...1	13...15	7...9		7.2	30.0	680	136	144	1.5...2.5				
			V	Co	Cr	Fe													
FeCoVCr 11/2	2.4570	R 3-1-3	8...15	51...54	0...4	Re-				–	11.0	800	24	24	2.0...8.0				
FeCoVCr 4/1	2.4571	–	3...15	51...54	0...6	main-der				–	4.0	1000	5	5	9.0...25.0	1000	–0.01	≈ 0	
RECo 80/80	–	R 5-1-1								8.1	80	650	500	800					
RECo 120/96	–	R 5-1-2								8.1	120	770	590	960	1.05	1000	–0.05	–0.3	
RECo 160/80	–	R 5-1-3								8.1	160	900	640	800					
RECo 48/60p	–	R 5-3-1								5.2	48	500	360	600					
CrFeCo 12/4	–	R 6-0-1								7.6	12	800	40	42	5.5...6.5	1125	–0.03	–0.04	
CrFeCo 28/5	–	R 6-1-1								7.6	28	1000	45	46	3...4	1125	–0.03	–0.04	
REFe 165/170[4])	–	R 7-1-1								7.4	165	940	700	1700	1.07	583	–0.1	–0.8	
REFe 220/140[4])	–	R 7-1-6								7.4	220	1090	800	1400	1.05	583	–0.1	–0.8	
REFe 260/80[4])	–	R 7-1-8								7.4	260	1180	750	800	1.05	583	–0.1	–0.8	

[1]) Standard values. [2]) Minimum values. [3]) In the range of 273...373 K. [4]) Not yet standardized.

Permanent magnet materials (continued)

Material Abbreviated name	Material number DIN	IEC	Density[1]) ϱ g/cm³	$(BH)_{max}$[2]) kJ/m³	Remanence[2]) B_r mT	Coercive field strength[2]) of the flux density $_BH_c$ kA/m	of the polarization $_JH_c$ kA/m	Permanent permeability[1]) μ_p	Curie temp.[1]) T_c K	Temp. coeff. of polar.[1]) $TK(J_s)$ %/K	Temp. coeff. of coerciv.[1]) $TK(H_c)$ %/K	Manufacturing, processing,
Ceramic magnets												
Isotropic												
Hard ferrite 7/21	1.3641	S 1-0-1	4.9	6.5	190	125	210	1.2	723	−0,2	0,2 ... 0,5	
Hard ferrite 3/18p	1.3614	S 1-2-2	3.9	3.2	135	85	175	1.1				
Anisotropic												
Hard ferrite 20/19	1.3643	S 1-1-1	4.8	20.0	320	170	190	1.1	723	−0.2	0.2 ... 0.5	Manufacture: Sintering. Plastic-bound magnets are manufactured by rolling and extruding. Processing: Grinding.
Hard ferrite 20/28	1.3645	S 1-1-2	4.6	20.0	320	220	280	1.1				
Hard ferrite 24/23	1.3647	S 1-1-3	4.8	24.0	350	215	230	1.1				
Hard ferrite 25/25	1.3651	S 1-1-5	4.8	25.0	370	230	250	1.1				
Hard ferrite 9/19p	1.3616	S 1-3-1	3.4	9.0	220	145	190	1.1				
Hard ferrite 10/22p	–	S 1-3-2	3.5	10.0	230	165	225	1.1				
Bosch grades (not standardized)												
RBX HC 375			4.7 ... 4.9	23	350	260	360					
RBX 370				25	360	240	260					
RBX 380K				27	380	280	300					
RBX 380				27	380	255	260					
RBX HC 400				32	400	250	260					
RBX 410K				32	405	290	300					
RBX 420				35	420	255	260					
RBX HC 410				30	395	290	340					

[1]) Standard values.
[2]) Minimum values.

Solders and filler materials

Type of alloy	Material code	Primary alloying constituents, mean values % (by mass)	Melting range of alloy °C	Minimum workpiece temperature °C	Properties Primary applications
Soft solders (selection from DIN 1707)					
Lead-base, tin-base soft solders	L-PbSn 20 Sb 3	20 Sn; max. 3 Sb; Rest Pb	186 ... 270	270	Soft soldering in motor-vehicle body construction
	L-PbSn 12 Sb	12 Sn; max. 0.7 Sb; Rest Pb	250 ... 295	295	Soft soldering of copper in radiator construction
	L-PbSn 40 (Sb)	40 Sn; max. 0.5 Sb; Rest Pb	183 ... 235	235	Tin plating; soft soldering of sheet-metal parts
	L-PbSn 8 (Sb)	8 Sn; max. 0.5 Sb; Rest Pb	280 ... 305	305	Soft soldering; electric motors, radiator construction
Tin-base, lead-base soft solders	L-Sn 63 Pb	63 Sn; Rest Pb	183	183	Wave soldering of printed-circuit boards
	L-Sn 60 Pb	60 Sn; Rest Pb	183 ... 190	190	Tin plating of copper and copper alloys in the electrical industry
Tin-base, lead-base soft solders with Ag. Cu or P added	L-Sn 63 PbAg	63 Sn; max. 1.5 Ag; Rest Pb	178	178	Wave soldering of printed-circuit boards
	L-Sn 60 PbCu 2	60 Sn; max. 2 Cu; Rest Pb	183 ... 190	190	Soldering (using an iron) of copper and copper alloys in the electrical industry
	L-Sn 60 PbCuP	60 Sn; max. 0.2 Cu; max. 0.004 P; Rest Pb	183 ... 190	190	Dip soldering of copper and copper alloys in the electrical industry
Special soft solders	Wood's alloy	25 Pb; 12.5 Sn; 12.5 Cd; Rest Bi	69 ... 71	71	Soft soldering of heat-sensitive components; fuses
	L-SnIn 50	50 Sn; Rest In	117 ... 125	125	Soft soldering of glass/metal
	L-SnAg 5	max. 5 Ag; Rest Sn	221 ... 240	240	Soft soldering of copper in the electrical industry and in the installation of water pipes
	L-SnSb 5	max. 5.5 Sb; Rest Sn	230 ... 240	240	Soft soldering of copper in refrigeration engineering and in the installation of water pipes
	L-SnCu 3	max. 3.5 Cu; Rest Sn	230 ... 250	250	Soft soldering of copper for water-pipe installation
	L-SnZn 10	max. 15 Zn; Rest Sn	200 ... 250	250	Ultrasonic soft soldering of aluminum and copper without flux
	L-ZnAl 5	max. 6 Al; Rest Zn	380 ... 390	390	

Type of alloy	Material code	Primary alloying constituents, mean values % (by mass)	Melting range of alloy °C	Minimum workpiece temperature °C	Properties Primary applications
Filler metals for brazing and high-temperature brazing (selection from DIN 8513 and ISO 3677)					
Aluminum-base filler metals	L-AlSi 12 L-AlSi 10 L-AlSi 7.5	12 Si; Rest Al 10 Si; Rest Al 7.5 Si; Rest Al	575 ... 590 575 ... 595 575 ... 615	590 595 615	Brazing of Al and Al alloys with a sufficiently high melting point.
Silver-bearing filler metals Ag < 20 %	BCu 75AgP 643 L-Ag 15 P	18 Ag; 7.25 P; Rest Cu 15 Ag; 5 P; Rest Cu	643 650 ... 800	650 710	Brazing of Cu/Cu without flux.
	L-Ag 5	5 Ag; 55 Cu; 0.2 Si; Rest Zn	820 ... 870	860	Brazing of steel, Cu, Ni and Ni alloys with flux.
Silver-bearing filler metals Ag ≥ 20 %	L-Ag40Cd L-Ag55Sn L-Ag44	40 Ag; 20 Cd; 19 Cu; Rest Zn 55 Ag; 22 Cu; 5 Sn; Rest Zn 44 Ag; 30 Cu; Rest Zn	595 ... 630 620 ... 660 675 ... 735	610 650 730	Brazing of steel, Cu and Cu alloys, Ni and Ni alloys with flux.
	L-Ag49	49 Ag; 16 Cu; 7.5 Mn; 4.5 Ni; Rest Zn	625 ... 705	690	Brazing of hard metal, steel, W, Mo and Ta with flux.
	BAg 60 CuIn 605-710 BAg 60 CuSn 600-700 L-Ag 72 BCu 58 AgNi 780-900	60 Ag; 13 In; Rest Cu 60 Ag; 10 Sn; Rest Cu 72 Ag; Rest Cu 40 Ag; 2 Ni; Rest Cu	605 ... 710 600 ... 720 780 780 ... 900	710 720 780 900	Brazing of Cu, Ni, steel in a vacuum or under shielding gas.
	BAg 68 CuPd 807-810 BAg 54 PdCu 901-950 BAg 95 Pd 970-1010 BAg 64 PdMn 1180-1200	68 Ag; 5 Pd; Rest Cu 54 Ag; 21 Pd; Rest Cu 95 Ag; Rest Pd; 64 Ag; 3 Mn; Rest Pd	807 ... 810 901 ... 950 970 ... 1010 1180 ... 1200	810 950 1010 1200	Brazing of steel, Ni and Co alloys, Mo, W, Ti in a vacuum or under shielding gas.
	L-Ag 56 InNi L-Ag 85	56 Ag; 14 In; 4 Ni; Rest Cu 85 Ag; Rest Mn	620 ... 730 960 ... 970	730 960	Brazing of Cr and Cr/Ni steels in a vacuum or under shielding gas.
Copper-base filler metals	BCu 86 SnP 650-700	6.75 P; 7 Sn; Rest Cu	650 ... 700	690	Brazing of Cu and Cu alloys with flux. Not for Fe and Ni alloys or media containing S.

[1]) Depending on the process.

Filler metals for brazing and high-temperature brazing (continued)

Type of alloy	Material code	Primary alloying constituents, mean values % (by mass)	Melting range of alloy °C	Minimum workpiece temperature °C	Properties Primary applications
Copper-base filler metals (contd.)	L-CuP 8	8 P; Rest Cu	710 ... 740	710	Brazing of Cu/Cu without flux. Not for Fe and Ni alloys or media containing S.
	L-CuZn 40	60 Cu; 0.2 Si; Rest Zn	890 ... 900	900	Brazing of steel, Cu, Ni and Ni alloys with flux.
	L-CuSn 6 L-SFCu	6 Sn max; 0.4 P; Rest Cu 100 Cu	910 ... 1040 1083	1040 1100	Brazing of steel in a vacuum or under shielding gas.
	BCu 86 MnNi 970-990 BCu 87 MnCo 980-1030 BCu 96.9 NiSi 1090-1100	2 Ni; 12 Mn; Rest Cu 3 Co; 10 Mn; Rest Cu 0.6 Si; 2.5 Ni; Rest Cu	970 ... 990 980 ... 1030 1090 ... 1100	990 1020 1100	Brazing of hard metal, steel, W, Mo, Ta in a vacuum with partial shielding-gas pressure.
Nickel-base filler metals	L-Ni6 L-Ni1 L-Ni5	11 P; Rest Ni 3 B; 14 Cr; 4.5 Fe; 4.5 Si; Rest Ni 19 Cr; 10 Si; Rest Ni	880 980 ... 1040 1080 ... 1135	925 1065 1150	Brazing of Ni, Co and their alloys, unalloyed, low- and high-alloy steels in a vacuum or hydrogen shielding gas.
Gold-base filler metals	BAu 80 Cu 910	20 Cu; Rest Au	910	910	Brazing of Cu, Ni, steel in a vacuum or under shielding gas.
	BAu 82 Ni 950	18 Ni; Rest Au	950	950	Brazing of W, Mo, Co, Ni, steels in a vacuum or under shielding gas.
Active filler metals containing titanium	– – –	72.5 Ag; 19.5 Cu; 5 In; Rest Ti 70.5 Ag; 26.5 Cu; Rest Ti 96 Ag; Rest Ti	730 ... 760 780 ... 805 970	850 850 1000	Direct brazing of non-metallized ceramics with each other or combined with steel in a vacuum or under argon shielding gas.

[1]) Depending on the process.

Electrical properties

Electrical resistivity at 20 °C
(Resistance of a wire 1 m long with a cross section of 1 mm^2)

Resistivity is highly dependent upon the purity of the metal concerned. The mean temperature coefficient α refers to temperatures between 0 and 100 °C wherever possible. Resistivity at a temperature t °C is $\varrho_t = \varrho_{20}\,[1+\alpha(t-20\,°C)]$. See p. 127 for the calculation of the temperature of a winding based on the increase in resistance.

$1\,\Omega mm^2/m = 1\,\mu\Omega m$, $1\,S\,m/mm^2 = 1\,MS/m$ (S = Siemens)

Material	Electrical resistivity ϱ µΩm	Electrical conductivity $\gamma = 1/\varrho$ MS/m	Mean temperature coefficient $\alpha \times 10^{-3}$ 1/°C	Maximum operating temperature about °C
Aluminum, Al 99.5 (soft)	0.0286	35	3.8	–
Aluminum alloy E-AlMgSi	< 0.0328	> 30.5	3.8	–
Lead Pb 99.94	0.207	4.8	4	–
Bronze CuBe 0.5, age-hardened	0.04 ... 0.05	20 ... 25	–	300
Cadmium	0.077	13	–	–
Magnetic steel sheet I	0.21	4.76	–	–
Magnetic steel sheet IV	0.56	1.79	–	–
Gold (fine gold)	0.022	45	4	–
Gold-chromium alloy Cr 2.05	0.33	3.03	± 0.001	–
Gray cast iron	0.6 ... 1.6	0.62 ... 1.67	1.9	–
Heating-element alloy[1]) CrAl 20 5	1.37	0.73	0.05	1200
NiCr 30 20	1.04	0.96	0.35	1100
NiCr 60 15	1.13	0.88	0.15	1150
NiCr 80 20	1.12	0.89	0.05	1200
Carbon brushes, unfilled	10 ... 200	0.1 ... 0.05	–	–
metal-filled	0.05 ... 30	20 ... 0.03	–	–
Copper, soft	0.01754	57	3.9	–
hard (cold-stretched)	0.01786	56	3.9	–
Brass CuZn 39 Pb 3	0.0667	15	2.33	–
CuZn 20	0.0525	19	1.60	–
Molybdenum	0.054	18.5	4.7	1600[3])
Nickel silver CuNi 12 Zn 24	0.232	4.3	–	–
Nickel Ni 99.6	0.095	10.5	5.5	–
Platinum	0.0981	10.2	3.923	–
Mercury	0.964	1.0386	0.9	–
Silver (fine silver)	0.015	66.5	4.056	–
Steel C 15	0.14 ... 0.16	7.15	–	–
Tantalum	0.124	8.06	3.82	–
Resistance alloy[2]) CuMn 12 Ni	0.43	2.33	± 0.01	140
CuNi 30 Mn	0.40	2.50	0.14	500
CuNi 44	0.49	2.04	± 0.04	600
Bismuth	1.25	0.8	4.54	–
Tungsten	0.0548	18.2	4.82	–
Zinc	0.06	16.67	4.17	–
Tin	0.114	8.82	4.4	–

[1]) DIN 17 470. [2]) DIN 17 471. [3]) Under shielding gas or in a vacuum.

Round copper wire
with single (1 L) and double (2 L) varnish insulation (from DIN 46435)

Diameter, bare		Direct-current resistance at 20 °C			Outside diameter			
					Single insulation		Double insulation	
	Tolerance	Rated value[1]	Minimum value[2]	Maximum value[3]	Minimum dimension	Maximum dimension	Minimum dimension	Maximum dimension
mm	mm	Ω/m	Ω/m	Ω/m	mm	mm	mm	mm
0.063	[4]	5.531	5.196	5.848	0.068	0.078	0.077	0.085
0.071		4.355	4.104	4.610	0.076	0.088	0.087	0.095
0.08		3.430	3.235	3.625	0.088	0.098	0.099	0.105
0.09		2.710	2.556	2.864	0.098	0.110	0.109	0.117
0.1		2.195	2.072	2.318	0.109	0.121	0.121	0.129
0.112	±0.003	1.74	1.646	1.864	0.122	0.134	0.135	0.143
0.125		1.405	1.328	1.488	0.135	0.149	0.147	0.159
0.14		1.120	1.064	1.180	0.152	0.166	0.164	0.176
0.16		0.8575	0.8192	0.8983	0.173	0.187	0.185	0.199
0.18		0.6775	0.6499	0.7068	0.195	0.209	0.206	0.222
0.2		0.5488	0.5282	0.5706	0.216	0.230	0.227	0.245
0.224		0.4375	0.4224	0.4534	0.242	0.256	0.252	0.272
0.25	±0.004	0.3512	0.3374	0.3659	0.268	0.284	0.279	0.301
0.28		0.2800	0.2698	0.2907	0.301	0.315	0.310	0.334
0.315		0.2212	0.2139	0.2289	0.336	0.352	0.349	0.371
0.355		0.1742	0.1689	0.1797	0.377	0.395	0.392	0.414
0.4	±0.005	0.1372	0.1327	0.1419	0.424	0.442	0.438	0.462
0.45		0.1084	0.1051	0.1118	0.475	0.495	0.490	0.516
0.5		0.08781	0.08534	0.09037	0.526	0.548	0.543	0.569
0.56	±0.006	0.07000	0.06794	0.07215	0.578	0.611	0.606	0.632
0.63		0.05531	0.05381	0.05687	0.658	0.684	0.678	0.706
0.71	±0.007	0.04355	0.04234	0.04481	0.739	0.767	0.762	0.790
0.75	±0.008	0.03903	0.03788	0.04022	0.779	0.809	0.802	0.832
0.8		0.03430	0.03334	0.03530	0.829	0.861	0.853	0.885
0.85	±0.009	0.03038	0.02950	0.03131	0.879	0.913	0.905	0.937
0,9		0.02710	0.02634	0.02789	0.929	0.965	0.956	0.990
0.95	±0.010	0.02432	0.02362	0.02506	0.979	1.017	1.007	1.041
1		0.02195	0.02134	0.02259	1.030	1.068	1.059	1.093
1.06	±0.011	0.01953			1.090	1.130	1.121	1.153
1.12		0.01750			1.150	1.192	1.181	1.217
1.18	±0.012	0.01576			1.210	1.254	1.241	1.279
1.25	±0.013	0.01405			1.281	1.325	1.313	1.351
1.32		0.01259			1.351	1.397	1.385	1.423
1.4	±0.014	0.01120			1.433	1.479	1.466	1.506
1.5	±0.015	0.009757			1.533	1.581	1.568	1.608
1.6	±0.016	0.008575			1.633	1.683	1.669	1.711
1.7	±0.017	0.007596			1.733	1.785	1.771	1.813
1.8	±0.018	0.006775			1.832	1.888	1.870	1.916
1.9	±0.019	0.006081			1.932	1.990	1.972	2.018
2	±0.020	0.005488			2.032	2.092	2.074	2.120

[1]) Calculated with 1/58 ≈ 0.0172 μΩ m (Ω mm^2/m). [2]) Calculated with 1/58.5 ≈ 0.0171 μΩ m.
[3]) Calculated with 1/57.5 ≈ 0.0174 μΩ m. [4]) Not specified; resistance values compulsory.

Electrical properties of insulating materials

The properties of insulating materials are highly dependent upon the purity, homogeneity, processing and aging of the materials, as well as on moisture content and temperature. The following values are given as a guideline for non-aged test specimens at room temperature with average moisture content; 1 min test voltage at 50 Hz; specimen thickness: 3 mm.
Loss factor $\tan\delta$ = Active power/reactive power; in the USA loss factor = $\varepsilon_r \cdot \tan\delta$.

Insulating material	Relative permittivity at 800 Hz (air = 1) ε_r	Loss factor $\tan\delta$ at 800 Hz $\times 10^{-3}$	at 10^6 Hz $\times 10^{-3}$	Volume resistivity $10^n\ \Omega$ m Values of n	Dielectric strength kV_{rms}/mm	Tracking resistance according to DIN 53 480; degree:
Cellulose acetates	4.7 ... 5.8	17 ... 24	48 ... 66	11 ... 13	32	–
Epoxy casting resins and molding compounds	3.2 ... 5	2 ... 30	2 ... 60	10 ... 15	6 ... 15	KA 3b, KA 3c
Hard porcelain	5 ... 6.5	≈ 15	6 ... 12	>9	30 ... 40	KA 3c
Mica	5 ... 8	0,1 ... 1	0,2	13 ... 15	60	KA 3c
Paraffin waxes	1.9 ... 2.3	<0.3	<0.3	13 ... 16	10 ... 30	–
Phenolic resin molding compounds with inorganic filler	5 ... 30	30 ... 400	50 ... 200	6 ... 11	5 ... 30	KA 1
Phenolic resin molding compounds with organic filler	4 ... 9	50 ... 500	50 ... 200	6 ... 10	5 ... 20	KA 1
Polyamides	8 ... 14	20 ... 200	20 ... 200	6 ... 12	10 ... 50	KA 3b, KA 3c
Polycarbonates	3	1.0	10	14 ... 16	25	KA 1
Polyester casting resin and molding compounds	3 ... 7	3 ... 100	6 ... 60	8 ... 14	6 ... 25	KA 3c
Polyethylene	2.3	0.2 ... 0.6	0.2 ... 0.6	>15	≈ 80	KA 3c
Polymethyl methacrylate	3.1 ... 3.4	40	20	>13	30	KA 3c
Polypropylene	2.3	<0.5	<0.5	>15	–	KA 3b
Polystyrene	2.5	0.1	0.1	14	40	KA 2, KA 1
Polytetrafluorethylene	2	0.1 ... 0.5	0.1 ... 0.5	13 ... 15	50	KA 3c
Polyvinyl chloride	3.3 ... 6.5	15 ... 150	10 ... 100	10 ... 14	15 ... 50	KA 3b
Quartz glass	3.5 ... 4.2	0.5	0.2	14 ... 16	25 ... 40	KA 3c
Rubber	2 ... 14	≈ 4	–	2 ... 14	15 ... 30	KA 1 ... KA 3c
Silicones	5 ... 8	0.2 ... 100	≈ 4	10 ... 14	20 ... 60	KA 3c
Steatite	5.5 ... 6.5	1 ... 3	0.3 ... 2	10 ... 12	20 ... 45	KA 3c
Titanicum ceramic	12 ... 10 000	–	0.05 ... 100	–	2 ... 30	–
Transformer oil, dry	2 ... 2.7	≈ 1	≈ 10	11 ... 12	5 ... 30	–

Properties of non-metallic materials

Ceramics

Material	Composition	ϱ[1] g/cm^3	σ_{bB}[2] N/mm^2	σ_{dB}[3] N/mm^2	E[4] N/mm^2	α_t[5] K^{-1}	λ[6] W/m·K	c[7] kJ/kg·K	ϱ_D[8] Ω·cm	ε_r[9]	tan δ[10] 10^{-4}
Aluminum nitride	AlN >97 %	3.3	250 ... 350	1100	320 ... 350	5.1	100 ... 220	0.8	$>10^{14}$	8.5 ... 9.0	3 ... 10
Aluminum oxide	Al_2O_3 >99 %	3.9 ... 4.0	300 ... 500	3000 ... 4000	380 ... 400	7.2 ... 8.6	20 ... 40	0.8 ... 0.9	$>10^{11}$	8 ... 10	2
Aluminum titanate	$Al_2O_3 \cdot TiO_2$	3.0 ... 3.2	20 ... 40	450 ... 550	10 ... 20	0.5 ... 1.5	<2	0.7	$>10^{11}$	–	–
Beryllium oxide	BeO >99 %	2.9 ... 3.0	250 ... 320	1500	300 ... 340	8,5 ... 9,0	240 ... 280	1.0	$>10^{14}$	6.5	3 ... 5
Boron carbide	B_4C	2.5	300 ... 500	2800	450	5.0	30 ... 60	–	10^{-1} ... 10^2	–	–
Cordierite e.g. KER 410, 520	$2MgO \cdot 2Al_2O_3 \cdot 5SiO_2$	1.6 ... 2.1	40 ... 200	300	70 ... 100	2.0 ... 5.0	1.3 ... 2.3	0.8	$>10^{11}$	5.0	70
Graphite	C >99.7 %	1.5 ... 1.8	5 ... 30	20 ... 50	5 ... 15	1.6 ... 4.0	100 ... 180	–	10^{-3}	–	–
Porcelain e.g. KER 110–2 (non-glazed)	Al_2O_3 30 ... 35 % balance SiO_2 glassy phase	2.2 ... 2.4	45 ... 60	500 ... 550	50	4.0 ... 6.5	1.2 ... 2.6	0.8	10^{11}	6	120
Silicon carbide pressureless-sintered SSiC	SiC >98 %	3.1 ... 3.2	400 ... 450	>1200	400	4.0 ... 4.5	90 ... 120	0.8	10^3	–	–
Silicon carbide hot-pressed HPSiC	SiC >99 %	3.1 ... 3.2	450 ... 650	>1500	420	4.0 ... 4.5	100 ... 120	0.8	10^3	–	–
Silicon carbide reaction-sintered SiSiC	SiC >90 % + Si	3.0 ... 3.1	300 ... 400	>2200	380	4.2 ... 4.3	100 ... 140	0.8	10 ... 100	–	–
Silicon nitride sintered SSN	Si_3N_4 >90 %	3.2	400 ... 700	>2500	300	3.2 ... 3.5	30 ... 40	0.7	10^{12}	–	–

See p. 208 for explanations and footnotes.

Ceramic materials (continued)

Material	Composition	ϱ[1]) g/cm^3	σ_{bB}[2]) N/mm^2	σ_{dB}[3]) N/mm^2	E[4]) N/mm^2	α_t[5]) K^{-1}/K	λ[6]) W/m·K	c[7]) kJ/kg·K	ϱ_D[8]) Ω·cm	ε_r[9])	tan δ[10]) 10^{-4}
Silicon nitride hot-pressed HPSN	Si_3N_4 >95 %	3.2	600 ... 900	>3000	310	3.2 ... 3.5	30 ... 40	0.7	10^{12}	–	–
Silicon nitride reaction-sintered RBSN	Si_3N_4 >99 %	2.4 ... 2.6	200 ... 300	–	140 ... 160	2.9 ... 3.0	15 ... 20	0.7	10^{14}	–	–
Steatite e.g. KER 220, 221	SiO_2 55 ... 65 % MgO 25 ... 35 % Al_2O_3 2 ... 6 % Alk. oxide <1.5 %	2.6 ... 2.9	120 ... 140	850 ... 1000	80 ... 100	7.0 ... 9.0	2.3 ... 2.8	0.7 ... 0.9	>10^{11}	6	10 ... 20
Titanium carbide	TiC	4.9	–	–	320	7.4	30	–	$7 \cdot 10^{-5}$	–	–
Titanium nitride	TiN	5.4	–	–	260	9.4	40	–	$3 \cdot 10^{-5}$	–	–
Titanium dioxide	TiO_2	3.5 ... 3.9	90 ... 120	300	–	6.0 ... 8.0	3 ... 4	0.7 ... 0.9	–	40 ... 100	8
Zirconium dioxide partially stabilized	ZrO_2 >90 % Rest Y_2O_3, MgO	5.7 ... 6.0	500 ... 800	1800 ... 2100	200	9.0 ... 11.0	2 ... 3	0.4	10^8	–	–
Standards		DIN 51 065 DIN 40 685/ VDE 0335 DIN 1306	DIN 40 685/ VDE 0335 DIN 51 221	DKG Fach-aus-schuß Bericht Nr. 22	DIN 40 685/ VDE 0335	DIN 40 685/ VDE 0335	DIN 40 685/ VDE 0335	DIN 40 685/ VDE 0335	DIN 40 685 / VDE 0335 VDE 0303 VDE 0446 VDE 0560 VDE 0674		

The characteristic values for each material can vary widely, depending on raw material, composition and manufacturing process. The material data relate to the information provided by various manufacturers.
The designation "KER" corresponds to DIN 40 685, Part 1.

1) Density.
2) 3-point bending strength; for definition, see DKG Fachausschußbericht No. 22.
3) Compressive strength; for definition, see DKG Fachausschußbericht No. 22.
4) Modulus of elasticity.
5) Coefficient of thermal expansion RT ... 1000 °C.
6) Thermal conductivity at 20 °C.
7) Specific heat.
8) Electrical resistivity at 20 °C and 50 Hz.
9) Relative permittivity.
10) Dielectric loss factor at 25 °C and 10 MHz.

Laminates

Type	Type of resin	Filler	ϑ_G [1] °C	σ_{bB} [2] min. N/mm²	$a_{k\,10}$ [3] min. kJ/m²	CTI [4] min. grade	Properties, typical applications
Paper-base laminates (DIN 7735, Part 2 / VDE 0318, Part 2)							
Hp 2061	Phenolic resin	Paper web	120	150	5	CTI 100	For mechanical loading
Hp 2062.8	Phenolic resin	Paper web	120	80	2.5	CTI 100	Low water absorption, tropicalized
Hp 2063	Phenolic resin	Paper web	120	80	2.5	CTI 100	For electrical loading; base material FR 2 for printed-circuit boards
Hp 2262	Melamine resin	Paper web	90	100	–	CTI 600	Particularly resistant to tracking; decorative laminates
Hp 2361.1	Epoxy resin	Paper web	90	120	2	CTI 100	Good electrical and mechanical properties, flame-resistant; base material FR 3 for printed-circuit boards
Fabric-base laminates (DIN 7735, Part 2 / VDE 0318, Part 2)							
Hgw 2072	Phenolic resin	Glass-fiber fabric	130	200	40	CTI 100	High mechanical, electrical and thermal strength
Hgw 2082	Phenolic resin	Fine-weave cotton fabric	110	130	10	CTI 100	Good workability, good sliding and
Hgw 2083	Phenolic resin	Fine-weave cotton fabric	110	150	12	CTI 100	wear behavior; especially good material for gears and bearings
Hgw 2372.1	Epoxy resin	Very-fine-weave cotton fabric	120	350	50	CTI 200	Optimum chemical and electrical properties, base material FR 4 for printed-circuit boards
Hgw 2572	Silicone resin	Very-fine-weave cotton fabric	180	125	25	CTI 400	For high service temperature
Glass-mat-base laminates (DIN 7735, Part 2 / VDE 0318, Part 2)							
Hm 2472	Unsaturated polyester resin	Glass-fiber mat	130	200	60	CTI 500	Good mechanical and electrical properties, particularly resistant to tracking

[1]) Limit temperature according to VDE 0304, Part 2, for service life of 25,000 h.
[2]) Flexural strength according to DIN 53 452.
[3]) Notched impact strength in accordance with DIN 53 453.
[4]) Tracking resistance according to DIN IEC 112, Comparative Tracking Index (CTI).

Plastic molding compounds

Chemical name	Material code (ISO 1043/ DIN 7728)	t_G[1]) °C	E[2]) N/mm²	$a_{k\,10}$[3]) min. kJ/m²	Resistance at 20°C to[4]) Gas-oline	Ben-zene	Die-sel fuel	Alco-hol	Min-eral oil	Other properties, typical applications
Thermoplastics (Selection from DIN 7740 ... 7749; DIN 16771 ... 16779)										
Acrylnitrile-butadien-styrene	ABS	80	2000	5 ... 10	0	–	×	+	+	High gloss, some types transparent; tough housings
Cellulose acetate	CA	120/80	2000	5	×	0	+	0	+	Transparent: molded parts, panels, films
Cellulose acetate butyrate	CAB	60/50	1500	2	+	–	+	–	+	Impact-resistant even at low temperatures
Fluorinated hydrocarbons	PFEP[7]) PFA[7])	250/205 260	600 650	[6]) [6])	+ +	+ +	+ +	+ +	+ +	Extreme reduction in rigidity as temperature increases, resistant to chemicals; used for coatings, sliding parts and seals
Polyamide 11, 12	PA 11, 12	140/120	1500	18	+	+	+	0	+	Tough, hard and resistant to abrasion, low coefficient of friction, good attentuation of sound, approx. 1 ... 3 % water absorption required for good toughness, PA 11/12 have much lower water absorption
Polyamide 6	PA 6	170/120	2000	15	+	+	+	×	+	
Polyamide 66	PA 66	190/120	2500	10	+	+	+	×	+	
Polyamide 6 + GF[5])	PA 6-GF	190/120	7000	8 ... 14	+	+	+	×	+	Impact-resistant machine housings
Polyamid 66 + GF[5])	PA 66-GF	200/120	7000	6 ... 12	+	+	+	×	+	
Polybutylene terephthalate	PBT	160/120	1700	2 ... 4	+	+	+	+	+	Wear-resistant, chemically resistant, rigidity decreases above 60 °C, hydrolysis above 70 °C in water
Polybutylene terephthalate + GF[5])	PBT-GF	180/120	4500	5 ... 9	+	+	+	+	+	Higher rigidity than PBT without GF
Polycarbonate	PC	130/125	2500	20	+	–	+	0	+	Uniform toughness and rigidity over wide temperature range, transparent
Polycarbonate + GF[5])	PC-GF	130	4000	6 ... 7	+	–	+	0	+	Very rigid structural parts
Polyethylene	PE	80	1000	[6])	×	0	+	+	+	Acid-resistant containers and pipes, films
Polyethylene terephthalate	PETP	180/120	2000	2 ... 7	+	+	+	+	+	Wear-resistant, chemically resistant, rigidity decreases above 60 °C, hydrolysis above 70 °C in water

Polyethylene terephthalate + GF[5])	PETP-GF	200/120	7000	5 ... 12	+	+	+	+	+	Higher rigidity than PETP without GF
Polymethyl-methacrylate	PMMA	80	3000	1,5 ...2,5	+	–	×	0	+	Clear and in all colors, weatherproof; diffuser screen, lenses
Polyoxymethylene	POM	120	2000	5 ... 7	+	0	+	+	+	Sensitive to acid-induced stress cracking; precision moldings
Polyoxymethylene + GF	POM-GF	135	6000	3 ... 5	+	0	+	+	+	
Polyphenylene ether + SB[7])	(PPE+S/B)	120/100	2500	4 ... 14	0	–	0	0	+	Resistant to hot water, flame-retardant
Polyphenylene sulfide + GF	PPS-GF	270/240	13 000	1.4...1.4	+	+	+	+	+	High resistance to heat, parts under the engine hood
Polypropylene	PP	130/110	2000	6	×	0	+	+	+	Household articles, battery cases, cover hoods
Polypropylene + GF[5])	PP-GF	130/110	3000	4 ... 8	×	0	+	+	+	Fan pulleys
Polystyrene	PS	80	2500	2	–	–	0	+	+	Molded parts; transparent and coated in all colors
Polyvinyl chloride, plasticized	PVC	80/70	200	[6])	–	–	0	0	+	Synthetic leather, flexible caps, cable insulation, tubing and hosing, seals
Polyvinyl chloride, unplasticized	PVC	70/60	3000	2 ... 30	+	–	+	+	+	Weatherproof exterior parts, pipes, parts for galvanotechnical equipment
Polyurethane, hard	PUR	150/130	900	2.5	+	+	+	0	+	Shore D = 80; used for slide and wear parts
Polyurethane, soft	PUR	120/100	40	[6])	+	0	+	0	+	Shore A = 90; diaphragms, insulation
Styrene-acrylonitrile	SAN	90	3000	1.5 ... 2.5	0	–	×	0	+	Molded parts; good chem. resist., also transp.
Styrene-butadiene	SB	60	1500	4 ... 14	–	–	–	+	+	Tough housings for many applications
Non cross-linked plastics which can be processed only by molding and sintering:										
Polyimide	PI	320/290	3100	2	+	+	+	+	+	High resistance to heat and radiation, hard
Polytetrafluorethylene	PTFE	300/240	400	13 ... 15	+	+	+	+	+	Extreme reduction in rigidity as temp. rises; high resistance to heat, aging and chemicals; low coefficient of friction; for sliding parts

[1]) Maximum service temperature, short-term (1 h)/long-term (5000 h).
[2]) Modulus of elasticity, approx. standard values.
[3]) Notched impact strength in accordance with DIN 53 453.
[2] and [3]) Polyamides, saturated by air humidity at 23 °C and 25 % rel. humidity.
[4]) + good resistance, × limited resistance, 0 low resistance, – no resistance.
[5]) GF Glass fiber (25 ... 35 % by wt.).
[6]) No fracture.
[7]) Polymer mixture of polyphenylene ether and styrene/butadiene.

Type	Type of resin	Filler	t_G[1]) °C	σ_{bB}[2]) min. N/mm²	a_n[3]) min. kJ/m²	CTI[4]) min. grade	Properties, typical applications
Thermosetting plastics (selection from DIN 7708, 16911, 16912)							
11.5	Phenol-cresol	Rock flour	180/130	50	3.5	CTI 150	High resistance to glow heat, good heat dissipation, little dimensional change in humid atmosphere; used for thermally stressed parts. Good electrical properties for Type 11.5 and 13.5.
12[13])		Asbestos fibers	200/140	50	3.5	CTI 150	
13.5[13])		Mica	180/130	50	3.0	CTI 150	
16		Asbestos cord	200/140	70	15	CTI 150	
30.5		Wood flour	140/100	60	5	CTI 125	Types 30.5 and 31.5 for parts with high electrical loads.
31 and 31.5		Wood flour	140/100	70	6	CTI 125	
51		Cellulose[5])	140/100	60	5	CTI 150	Somewhat greater water absorption than Types 11 ... 16. For parts with good insulating properties in low-voltage range. Type 74 has high impact strength.
71		Cotton fibers[5])	140/100	60	6	CTI 150	
74		Cotton fabric shreds[5])	140/100	60	12	CTI 150	
83		Cotton fibers[6])	140/100	60	5	CTI 150	Tougher than Type 31.
–		Glass fibers, short	180/140	80	6	CTI 150	High mechanical strength, resistent to glow heat.
150	Melamine	Wood flour	120/80	70	6	CTI 600	Resistant to glow heat, high-grade electrical properties, high shrinkage factor.
181	Melamine-phenol	Cellulose	120/80	80	7	CTI 250	For parts subject to electrical and mech. stress.
801 and 803	Polyester	Glass fibers, inorganic fillers	170/130	60	22	CTI 600	Types 801 + 804: low molding pressure (large-area parts manufacture), 803 + 804 glow-heat resistant.
802 and 804			170/130	55	4.5	CTI 600	
870	Epoxy	Rock flour	180/130	50	5	CTI 500	Types 870 and 871 as low-pressure plastics for encapsulating metal parts and electronic components. Low softening temperatures, low shrinkage factor.
871		Glass fibers, short	180/130	80	8	CTI 500	
872		Glass fibers, long	180/130	90	15	CTI 500	
–	Silicone	Glass fibers, short	340/180	55	2	CTI 600	High temp. resist., high-grade electr. properties.
–	Bismaleinimide	Glass fibers, long	320/170	200	25	CTI 150	High strength even at high temperatures, for sliding parts and bearings exposed to high temperatures.
–		Graphite	290/160	65	4	–	

Material	Code[7]	Range of application[8] °C	Shore A hardness	Tensile strength[9] N/mm²	Ultimate Elongation[9] %	Resistance to[11] Weathering	Ozone	Gasoline	Diesel fuel	Mineral oil	Highly inflammable hydraulic fluids HF[12] A	B	C	D
Rubbers														
Butyl rubber	IIR	−40 ... +125	40 ... 85	7 ... 17	300 ... 600	× [10]	× [10]	–	–	–	–	–	+	×
Chlorinated polyethylene	CM	−30 ... +140	50 ... 95	10 ... 20	100 ...700	+	+	0	0	×	×	×	+	–
Chloroprene rubber	CR	−40 ... +110	20 ... 90	7 ... 25	100 ... 800	×	× [10]	×	×	×	0	0	+	–
Chlorosulphonated polyethylene	CSM	−30 ... +140	50 ... 85	15 ... 25	200 ... 500	+	+	–	0	0	×	×	+	–
Epichlorohydrin rubber	ECO	−40 ... +135	50 ... 90	6 ... 15	150 ... 500	+	+	×	×	+	×	×	–	–
Ethylene acrylate rubber	EAM	−40 ... +135	50 ... 90	6 ... 15	150 ... 500	+	+	×	×	+	×	×	–	–
Ethylene propylene rubber	EPDM	−50 ... +150	20 ... 85	7 ... 17	150 ... 500	+	+	–	–	–	–	–	+	+
Fluorcarbon rubber	FPM	−25 ... +250	40 ... 90	7 ... 17	100 ... 350	+	+	+	+	+	+	+	–	+
Fluorsilicons	MFQ	−60 ... +200	40 ... 70	4 ... 9	100 ... 400	+	+	×	+	+	+	+	–	+
Hydrogenated nitrile rubber	HNBR	−20 ... +150	45 ... 90	15 ... 35	100 ... 600	+	+	×	+	+	+	+	+	–
Natural rubber	NR	−55 ... +90	20 ... 100	15 ... 30	100 ... 800	0 [10]	– [10]	–	–	–	–	–	+	–
Nitrile butadiene rubber	NBR	−30 ... +120	35 ... 100	10 ... 25	100 ... 700	× [10]	– [10]	×	×	+	×	×	+	–
Polyacrylate rubber	ACM	−20 ... +150	55 ... 90	5 ... 13	100 ... 350	×	+	–	×	+	+	×	×	–
Polyurethane elastomers	AU/EU	−25 ... +80	50 ... 98	20 ... 50	300 ... 700	×	×	–	–	0	–	–	–	–
Silicone rubber	MVQ	−60 ... +200	20 ... 80	4 ... 9	100 ... 400	+	+	–	0	×	+	+	+	+
Styrene butadiene rubber	SBR	−50 ... +110	30 ... 100	7 ... 30	100 ... 800	0 [10]	– [10]	–	–	–	–	–	+	–

[1]) Maximum service temperature, short-term (100 h)/continuous (20,000 h).
[2]) Flexing strength.
[3]) Impact strength.
[4]) Tracking resistance according to DIN IEC 112, Comparative Tracking Index (CTI).
[5]) With or without addition of other organic fillers.
[6]) And/or wood flour.
[7]) DIN ISO 1629.
[8]) Not continuous-service temperature.
[9]) Depending upon composition of compound.
[10]) Can be improved by adding protective agents.
[11]) + Good resistance, × limited resistance, 0 low resistance, – no resistance.
[12]) A oil-in-water emulsion, B water-in-oil emulsion; C polyglycol-water solution, D synthetic liquids.
[13]) Not used in new parts (asbestos ban).

Plastics abbreviations with chemical names and trade names[3])

Code	Chemical name	Trade names
ABS	Acrylonitrile butadiene styrene	Cycolac, Novodur, Ronfalin, Terluran
ACM	Polyacrylate rubber	Cyanacryl, Hycar
EAM	Ethylene acrylate rubber	Vamac
APE[1])	Ethylene propylene rubber	Arylef
Aramid	Aromatic polyester corresponds to aromatic polyamide	Kevlar, Nomex
ASA	Acrylate styrene acrylonitrile	Luran S
AU	Polyurethane elastomers	Urepan
CA	Cellulose acetate	Cellidor
CAB	Cellulose acetate butyrate	
CM	Chlorinated polyethylene	Bayer CM, CPE
CR	Chloroprene rubber	Baypren, Neoprene
CSM	Chlorosulphonated polyethylene	Hypalon
ECO	Epichlorohydrin rubber	Herclor, Hydrin
EP	Epoxy	Araldit
EPDM	Ethylene propylene rubber	Buna AP, Dutral, Keltan, Nordel, Vistalon
EU	Polyurethane elastomers	Adiprene C
FPM	Fluorcarbon rubber	DAI-EL, Fluorel, Tecnoflon, Viton
HNBR	Hydrogenated nitrile rubber	Therban, Zetpol
IR	Isoprene rubber	Cariflex IR, Natsyn
MF	Melamine-formaldehyde	Bakelite, Resinol, Supraplast, Resopal
MPF	Melamine/phenol-formaldehyde	Supraplast, Resiplast
MVQ	Silicone rubber	Rhodorsil, Silastic, Silopren
NBR	Nitrile butadiene rubber	Buna N, Chemigum, Hycar, Perbunan
PA 46[1])	Polyamide 46	Stanyl
PA 6-3-T	Amorphous polyamide	Trogamid T
PA 6	Polyamide 6 (polymers of caprolactam	Durethan B, Grilon, Perlon, Renyl, Sniamid, Technyl, Ultramid B, Wellamid
PA 66	Polyamide 66 (polymers of hexamethylene diamide and adipic acid)	Akulon, Durethan A, Minlon, Nylon, Sniamid, Technyl, Ultramid A, Wellamid, Zytel
PA 6/6 T	Partially aromatic polyamide	Ultramid T
PA 11	Polyamide 11 (polymers of 11-aminoundecanoic acid)	Rilsan B
PA 12	Polyamide 12 (polymers of 12-dodecalactam)	Grilamid, Rilsan A, Vestamid
PAI	Polyamide imide	Torlon
PAN	Polyacrylonitrile	Dralon, Orlon
PBTP	Polybutylene terephthalate	Crastin, Pocan, Ultradur, Vestodur
PC	Polycarbonate	Makrolon, Orgalan, Sinvet, Lexan

Code	Chemical name	Trade names
(PC + ABS)	Blend of polycarbonate + ABS	Bayblend T, Cycoloy
(PC + ASA)	Blend of polycarbonate + ASA	Terblend S
(PC-PBT)	–	Makroblend PR, Xenoy
PE	Polyethylene	Hostalen, Lupolen, Stamylan, Vestolen
PEEK[1])	Polyether ether ketone	Victrex „PEEK"
PEBA[1])	Polyether blockamide	Pebax
PEI	Polyether imide	Ultem
PES	Polyether sulphone	Victrex „PES"
PETFE[1])	Ethylene tetrafluorethylene copolymer	Hostaflon ET, Tefzel
PETP	Polyethylene terephthalate	Arnite, Crastin, Mylar, Rynite, Trevira
PF	Phenol-formaldehyde	Bakelite, Supraplast, Vyncolite
PFA	Perfluoralkoxyethylene	Teflon PFA
PFEP[1])	Fluorinated ethylene-propylene copolymer	Teflon FEP
PI	Polyimide	Kapton, Kerimid, Kinel, Vespel
PMMA	Polymethyl methacrylate	Degalan, Diakon, Perspex, Plexiglas, Resarit, Vedril
POM	Acetal (polyoxymethylene)	Delrin, Hostaform C, Ultraform
PP	Polypropylene	Daplen, Hostalen PP, Moplen, Stamylan P, Starpylen, Vestolen
(PPE + SB)	Blend of polyphenylene ether + SB	Noryl, Luranyl
(PPE + PA)	Blend of polyphenylene ether + PA	Noryl GTX, Ultranyl, Vestoblend
PPS	Polyphenylene sulphide	Ryton
PS	Polystyrene	Edistir, Hostyren, Lustrex
PSU	Polysulphone	Udel
PTFE	Polytetrafluorethylene	Fluon, Hostaflon, Teflon
PUR	Polyurethane	Desmopan, Elastollan, Lycra, Vulkollan
PVC-P	Polyvinyl chloride, plasticized	Trosiplast, Vestolit, Vinoflex
PVC-U	Polyvinyl chloride, unplasticized	Trovidur, Hostalit, Vinidur, Vestolid
PVDF	Polyvinylidene fluoride	Dyflor, Kynar, Solef
PVF	Polyvinyl fluoride	Tedlar
SAN	Styrene acrylnitrile	Kostil, Luran, Tyril
SB	Styrene butadiene	Hostyren, Lustrex
SBR	Styrene butadiene rubber	Buna Hüls, Buna S, Cariflex S
TPE-E[1])	TPE[2]) polyester base	Arnitel, Hytrel, Riteflex
TPE-O[1])	TPE[2]) olefin base	Leraflex, Santoprene
TPE-S[1])	TPE[2]) styrene base	Cariflex, Evoprene, Kraton
UF	Urea-formaldehyde	Bakelite, Pollopas
UP	Unsaturated polyester	Keripol, Leguval, Palatal

[1]) Material code not yet standardized.
[2]) TPE – Thermoplastic rubber.
[3]) ISO 1043/DIN 7728 (Thermoplastics, thermosetting plastics), ISO 1629 (Rubbers)

OEM automotive paints

Structure of solid-color coatings

Layer	Layer thickness in µm	Structure	Compositon Binders	Solvents	Pigments	Extenders	Additives and SC	Application
1a	20 ... 25	KTL	Epoxy resins, Polyurethane	Water, small amounts of water-soluble organic solvents	Anorganic (organic)	Anorganic extenders	Surface-active substances, anti-crater agents, 20% SC	ET
1b	30 ... 35	DS-KTL						
2a	approx. 35	Primer surface	Polyester, melamine, urea & epoxy resins	Aromatic compounds, alcohols	Anorganic & organic	Anorganic solids	e.g., wetting agents, surface-active substances (no silicones) 58 ... 62% SC	PZ ESTA-HR
2b	approx. 35	Waterborne primer surface	Water-soluble polyester & melamine resins	Water, small amounts of water-soluble organic solvents				ESTA-HR
3a	40 ... 50	Solid-color top coat	Alkyd & melamine resins	Esters, aromatic compounds, alcohols		–	e.g., leveling & wetting agents	PZ ESTA-HR
3b	9 ... 30 (depends on color)	Waterborne solid-color base coat	Water-soluble polyester, polyurethane & melamine resins	–		–	Silicone-free wetting agents	PZ ESTA-HR
4a	40 ... 50	Conv. clear coat	Acrylic & melamine resin	Aromatic compounds, alcohols, esters	–	–	e.g., leveling agents and light stabilizers, 45% SC	PZ ESTA-HR
4b	40...50	2K-HS	HS Acrylate resin polyisocyanates	Esters, aromatic compounds	–	–	e.g., leveling agents and light stabilizers, 58% SC	

Acronyms: DS High film build; ESTA-HR Electrostatic high rotation; ET Electrophoretic coating, SC (FK) Solids content or non-volatiles, KTL Cathodic deposition, PZ Pneumatic spray, 2K-HS 2-component high-solid (high levels of non-volatile matter).

Structure of metallic coatings

Layer	Layer thickness in µm	Structure	Compositon					
			Binders	Solvents	Pigments	Extenders	Additives and SC	Application
1a	20 ... 25	KTL	Epoxy resins, Polyurethane	Water, small amounts of water-soluble organic solvents	Anorganic (organic)	Anorganic extenders	Surface-active substances, anti-crater agents, 20% SC	ET
1b	30 ... 35	DS-KTL						
2a	approx. 35	Primer surfaces Melamine, urea & epoxy resins	Polyesters, alcohols	Aromatic compounds, alcohols	Anorganic & organic	Anorganic extenders	e.g., wetting agents, surface-active substances (no silicones) 58 ... 62% SC	PZ ESTA-HR
2b	appox. 35	Water-based primer surfaces	Water-soluble polyester & melamine resins	Water, small amounts of water-soluble organic solvents				ESTA-HR
3a	10 ... 15	Metallic base coat	CAB Polyester & melamine resins	Esters, aromatic compounds	Aluminum particles	–	15% SC	PZ ESTA-HR
3b	10 ... 15	Water-soluble metallic base coat	Water-soluble polyester, polyurethane & melamine resins	–	Aluminum and mica particles, organic & anorganic pigments	–	Silicone-free wetting agents	PZ ESTA-HR
4a	40 ... 50	Conv. clear coat	Acrylic & melamine resin	Aromatic compounds, alcohol, esters	–	–	e.g., leveling agents & light stabilizers, 45% SC	PZ ESTA-HR
4b	40 ... 50	2K-HS	HS Acrylate resin Polyisocyanates	Esters, aromatic compounds	–	–	e.g., leveling agents & light stabilizers, 58% SC	

Acronyms: DS Top coat; ESTA-HR Electrostatic high rotation; ET Electrophoretic coating, SC (FK) Solids content or non-volatiles, KTL Cathodic deposition, PZ Pneumatic spray, 2K-HS 2-component high-solid (high levels of non-volatile matter).

Lubricants

Terms and definitions

Lubricants are agents which serve to separate two bodies in a state of relative motion. The lubricant's function is to prevent direct contact between these bodies, thereby reducing friction and wear. It can also serve as a coolant and sealant; it can inhibit corrosion and reduce operating noise. Lubricants can be solid, consistent, liquid or gaseous in form. The appropriate lubricant is selected according to the design characteristics, the combination of materials, the operating environment and the stresses at the friction surface.

Additives
Additives are substances which are added to the lubricant in order to improve specific properties. These substances modify either the physical properties of the lubricant (e.g., VI* improvers, pour-point depressors) or its chemical properties (e.g., oxidation inhibitors, corrosion inhibitors). In addition, the properties of the friction surfaces themselves can be modified with additives which change the friction characteristics (friction modifiers), protect against wear (anti-wear agents), or provide protection against scoring and seizure (extreme-pressure additives). Extreme care must be exercised in the selection of additives in order to ensure that no mutually antagonistic effects occur between them, or between an additive and the base lubricant.
* VI = Viscosity Index

Ash (DIN 51575, 51803)
The mineral residue which remains after oxide and sulphate incineration.

ATF (Automatic Transmission Fluid)
Special-purpose lubricants which are specifically formulated to meet the severe demands of automatic transmissions.

Bingham bodies
Materials whose flow characteristics differ from those of Newtonian liquids.

Bleeding
(Oil separation, DIN 51817)
Separation of the base oil and the thickener in lubricating grease.

Cloud point (DIN ISO 3015)
The temperature at which mineral oil becomes opaque due to the formation of paraffin crystals or the precipitation of other solids.

Consistency (DIN ISO 2137)
A measure of the ease with which lubricating greases and pastes can be deformed by a cone.

Doped lubricants
Lubricants containing additives for improving specific properties (e.g., aging stability, wear protection, corrosion protection, viscosity-temperature characteristics).

Dropping point (DIN ISO 2176)
The temperature at which a lubricating grease achieves certain flow properties under specific test conditions.

EP Lubricants (Extreme Pressure)
See high-pressure lubricants.

Fire point/Flash point
(DIN ISO 2592)
The lowest temperature (at 1013 hPa) at which a gaseous mineral product initially flashes (fire point), or continues to burn for at least 5 sec. (burning point).

Flow pressure (DIN 51805)
According to Kesternich, the pressure required to press a consistent lubricant through a standardized test nozzle. The flow pressure provides information on a lubricant's flow characteristics, particularly at low temperatures.

Friction modifiers
Polar lubricant additives which reduce the friction in the mixed-friction range and increase bearing capacity by means of adsorption on the surface of the metal. They also inhibit the occurrence of stick-slip behavior.

Gel-type greases
Inorganic gelling agents instead of soap (e.g., Bentonites, Aerosiles, silica gels).

Graphite
Solid lubricant with layer-lattice structure. Graphite provides excellent lubrication when combined with water (e.g., high at-

mospheric humidity) and in carbon-dioxide atmospheres. It does not inhibit friction in a vacuum.

High-pressure lubricants
Contain additives to enhance load-bearing capacity, and to reduce wear and scoring.

Induction period
The period which elapses before substantial changes occur in a lubricant (e.g., aging of an oil containing an oxidation inhibitor).

Inhibitors
Additives which protect lubricant and surface (e.g., oxidation and corrosion inhibitors).

Low-temperature sludge
Products of oil degradation which form in the engine crankcase as a result of incomplete combustion and condensation at low engine load. Low-temperature sludge increases wear and can cause engine damage. Modern high-quality engine oils inhibit its formation.

Metal soaps
Reaction products from metals or from their compounds with fatty acids. They are used as thickeners for grease and as friction modifiers.

Mineral oils
Mineral oils are distillates or raffinates produced from petroleum or from coal. They consist of numerous hydrocarbons in various chemical combinations. According to which components predominate, we refer to
– paraffin-based oils (chain-shaped saturated hydrocarbons),
– naphthene-based oils (closed-chain saturated hydrocarbons, generally with 5 or 6 carbon atoms per ring)
– aromatic oils (e.g., alkylbenzene).
These differ from one another in various respects, including major differences in their chemical-physical properties.

Molybdenum disulphide (MoS_2)
A solid lubricant with layer-lattice structure. Only low cohesive forces are present between the individual layers, making it possible to slide the layers relative to each other through the application of relatively low shear forces. A reduction in friction is only obtained when MoS_2 is applied in suitable form to the surface of the metal (e.g., in combination with a binder (MoS_2 sliding lacquer)).

Multigrade oils
Engine and transmission oils with good resistance to viscosity-temperature change (high viscosity index VI). These oils are formulated for year-round use in motor vehicles; their viscosity ratings extend through several SAE grades.

Penetration (DIN ISO 2137)
Depth (in 10^{-1} mm) to which a standardized cone penetrates into a consistent lubricant within a defined period and at a specified temperature. The larger the number, the softer the lubricant.

Polar substances
Dipolar molecules are easily adsorbed onto metal surfaces. They enhance adhesion and bearing capacity, thus reducing friction and wear. This category includes e.g., esters, ethers, polyglycols and fatty acids.

Pour point (DIN ISO 3016)
The temperature at which an oil just barely continues to flow when cooled under defined conditions.

Total acid number (TAN) (DIN 51809)
The TAN provides information on the acidic and alkaline components contained in lubricating greases. The TAN is the amount of potassium hydroxide (in mg) which is required to neutralize 1 g of the acids contained in the grease, or which is equivalent to the alkaline component.

Yield point (DIN 13342)
The minimum shear stress at which a substance begins to flow. Above the yield point, the rheological characteristics of plastic substances are the same as those of liquids.

Rheology

Science dealing with the flow characteristics of materials. These are generally represented in the shape of flow curves.
Coordinate plotting:
Shear stress $\tau = F/A$ (N/m²)
F force, A surface area
against
Shear rate $D = v/y$ (s⁻¹)
(linear shear rate)
v velocity
y thickness of lubricating film

Dilatant flow behavior
Increase in viscosity with increasing shear rate.

Dynamic viscosity
$\eta = \tau / D$ (Pa · s)
The formerly-employed "centipoise" (cP) unit is equal to the unit (mPa · s).

Intrinsically viscous flow behavior
Decrease in viscosity with increasing velocity slope (e.g., liquid grease, multigrade oil with VI-improvers).

Kinematic viscosity
$\nu = \eta / \rho$ (mm²/s)
ρ density (kg/m³).
The formerly-employed "centistokes" (cSt) unit is equal to the unit (mm²/s).

Newtonian fluids
These display a linear relationship between τ and D in the shape of a straight line through zero, with the slope increasing proportionally to viscosity.

All materials which are not characterized by this kind of flow behavior are classified as non-Newtonian fluids.

Plastic flow behavior
Characteristic of the intrinsic viscosity of fluids with yield value (e.g., lubricating greases).

Rheopexy
A characteristic of those non-Newtonian fluids which are characterized by an increase in viscosity proportional to shear time, and which only gradually recover their original viscosity once shearing has ceased.

Thixotropy
A characteristic of those non-Newtonian fluids which are characterized by a reduction in viscosity depending on shear time, and which only gradually recover their original viscosity once shearing has ceased.

Stribeck curve

Portrays the friction between two lubricated bodies in mutual sliding contact (e.g., plain or roller bearings) as a function of sliding speed.

Hydrodynamics
Complete separation between basic and counter-body (wear-free condition).

Flow curves
1 Rheopex, 2 Thixotrope, 3 Newtonian, 4 Plastic, 5 Dilatant, 6 Intrinsically viscous, 7 Yield value.

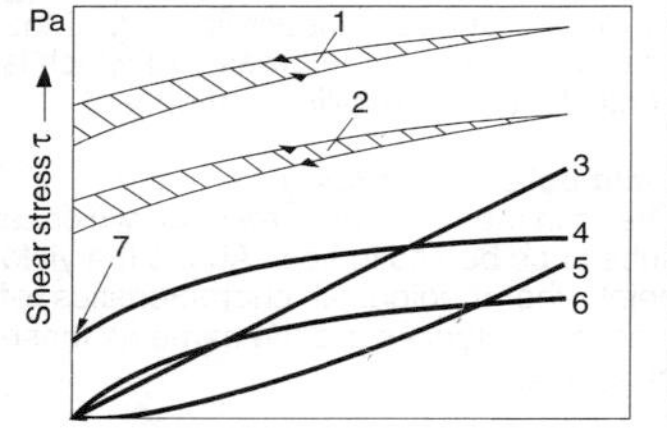

Stribeck curve
R Surface roughness,
d Distance between basic and counter-body.
Area a – Solid friction, high wear
Area b – Mixed friction, low wear,
Area c – Hydrodynamics, no wear.

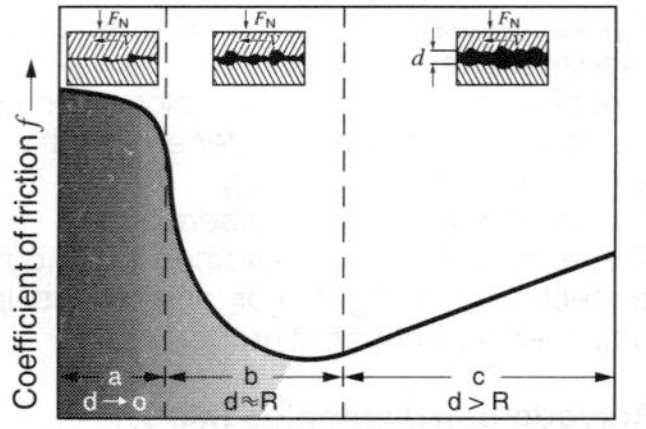

Mixed friction
The height of the lubricant layer is approximately equal to surface roughness.

Solid friction
The height of the lubricant layer is lower than that of the surface roughness of the material.

Viscosity (DIN 1342, DIN 51550)
Expresses the internal friction of substances. It indicates the degree of resistance (internal friction) with which the substance's molecules oppose displacement forces (see Rheology).

Viscosity classification
Classification of oils in specific viscosity ranges. ISO viscosity classifications (DIN 51519, see Table 1).
SAE viscosity grades (DIN 51511, SAE J300, SAE J306, see Tables 2 and 3).

Table 1. ISO viscosity classification (DIN 51519)

ISO viscosity classification	Viscosity at 40 °C mm^2/s	Kinematic viscosity limits at 40 °C mm^2/s min.	max.
ISO VG 2	2.2	1.98	2.42
ISO VG 3	3.2	2.88	3.52
ISO VG 5	4.6	4.14	5.06
ISO VG 7	6.8	6.12	7.48
ISO VG 10	10	9.00	11.0
ISO VG 15	15	13.5	16.5
ISO VG 22	22	19.8	24.2
ISO VG 32	32	28.8	35.2
ISO VG 46	46	41.4	50.6
ISO VG 68	68	61.2	74.8
ISO VG 100	100	90.0	110
ISO VG 150	150	135	165
ISO VG 220	220	198	242
ISO VG 320	320	288	352
ISO VG 460	460	414	506
ISO VG 680	680	612	748
ISO VG 1000	1000	900	1100
ISO VG 1500	1500	1350	1650

Viscosity index (VI) (DIN ISO 2909)
The viscosity index VI is a mathematically-derived number expressing the change in a mineral-oil product's viscosity relative to temperature. The greater the VI, the lower the effect of temperature on the viscosity.

Worked penetration (DIN ISO 2137)
Penetration of a grease sample after it is warmed to 25 °C and processed in a grease kneader.

Table 2. SAE viscosity grades for engine oils (SAE J300, Feb. 1991)

SAE viscosity grade	Max. low-temperature viscosities, cranking in mPa · s at °C	Low-temperature viscosities, pumping (Max. with no-yield stress)	Min. viscosity in mm^2/s at 100 °C min.	max.
0 W	3250/–30	30 000 at –35	3.8	–
5 W	3500/–25	30 000 at –30	3.8	–
10 W	3500/–20	30 000 at –25	4.1	–
15 W	3500/–15	30 000 at –20	5.6	–
20 W	4500/–10	30 000 at –15	5.6	–
25 W	6000/– 5	30 000 at –10	9.3	–
20	–	–	5.6	9.3
30	–	–	9.3	12.5
40	–	–	12.5	16.3
50	–	–	16.3	21.9
60	–	–	21.9	26.1

Table 3. SAE viscosity grades for transmission lubricants (SAE J 306, March 1985).

SAE viscosity grade	Maximum temperature in °C for viscosity of 150.000 mPa · s	Kinemac viscosity in mm^2/s at 100 °C min.	max.
70 W	–55	4.1	–
75 W	–40	4.1	–
80 W	–26	7.0	–
85 W	–12	11.0	–
90 W	–	13.5	24.0
140 W	–	24.0	41.0
250 W	–	41.0	–

Engine oils

Engine oils are employed to lubricate contiguous components in the internal-combustion engine which are in a state of relative motion. The most common motor oils are mineral oils which have been treated with additives. Fully and semi-synthetic oils, such as hydro-crack oils, are also being employed due to the increasing stresses to which oil is subjected and the extended oil-change intervals. The quality of a motor oil is determined by its origin, the refining of the mineral oil (except in the case of synthetic oils) and the additives.

We distinguish between the following types of additives according to their respective functions:
- Viscosity-index (VI) improvers,
- Pour-point depressors,
- Oxidation and corrosion-inhibitors,
- Detergent and dispersant additives,
- Extreme-pressure (EP) additives,
- Friction modifiers,
- Anti-foaming agents.

Oil is subjected to considerable thermal and mechanical stresses in the IC engine. The data on the oils' physical properties provide information on their operating range without any indication of their other performance characteristics.

There thus exist several different procedures for evaluating engine oils (see comparison of engine-oil performance categories):
- CCMC Standard (Committee of Common Market Automobile Constructors). This standard considers the performance requirements of European engines with low displacement and high specific output. CCMC no longer exists, the successor organization of European automotive manufacturers is ACEA (Association des Constructeurs Européens d'Automobiles). CCMC test sequences are still valid.
- API Classifications (American Petroleum Institute),
- MIL Specifications.

The approval criteria include the following:
- Sulfate-ash content,
- Zinc content,
- Engine type (diesel or spark-ignition engine, naturally-aspirated or forced-induction engines),
- Load on power-transmission components and bearings,
- Wear-protection properties,
- Oil operating temperature (temperature in oil pan),
- Combustion residue and chemical stress exerted upon the oil by acidic combustion products,
- Detergent and residue-scavenging properties,
- Minimum interaction with elastomeric seal materials.

CCMC Specifications
- G: Oils for SI engines (gasoline).
- D: Oils for diesel engines,
- PD: Oils for diesel engines in passenger cars (Passenger Diesel).
- G4: Exceeds API SF standards and conforms to most of the SG requirements. Special requirements for aging resistance, evaporative loss, high-temperature residue formation, wear and anti-sludge protection.
- G5: High-lubricity engine oils of the 5W-X and 10W-X viscosity classes. Relative to G4, characterized by more stringent demands on aging resistance, shear resistance and anti-sludge protection.
- D4: Exceeds API CD and CE requirements. D4 is for engine oils used in naturally-aspirated diesel engines under extreme operating conditions, and for turbocharged diesels in normal operation.
- D5: Specifies SHPD oils (Super High-

Viscosity/Temperature curves of single-grade and multigrade engine oils

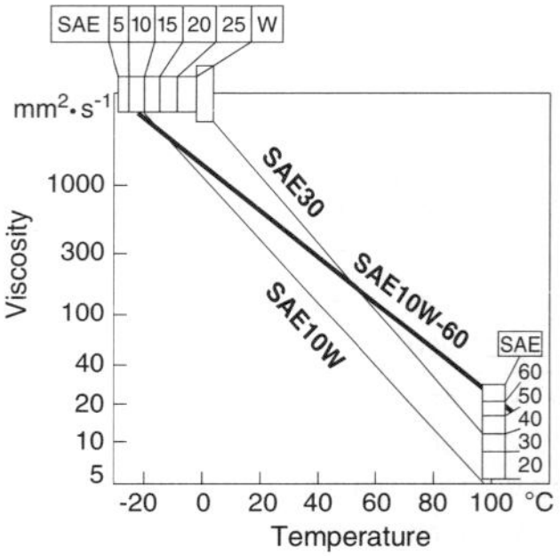

Performance Diesel) for diesel engines in commercial vehicles. There is no directly comparable API classification. Extreme demands for piston cleanlines, resistance to scoring, and wear to cylinders and camshafts.
– PD2: New classification for moderate-displacement diesels with naturally aspirated or turbocharged engines. Higher performance level than CD. Test conditions similar to those of D4.

API Classifications
S Classes (Service) for SI engines.
C Classes (Commercial) for diesel engines.
– SE: For engines up to approx. 1979.
– SF: For engines produced in the 80's.
– SG: Most recent specification, existing since 1988, with more stringent requirements for oxidation stability and sludge protection.
– CC: Engine oils for non-turbocharged diesel engines
– CD: Engine oils for non-turbocharged and turbocharged diesels
– CE: Oils with CD performance characteristics which absolve supplementary test operation in American Mack and Cummins engines.

MIL Specifications
– L-46152 B/C: Oils for spark-ignition and non-turbocharged diesel engines. Corresponds to API SF/CC.

Comparison of engine oil classifications
The bars indicate comparable performance specifications; these are not always identical.

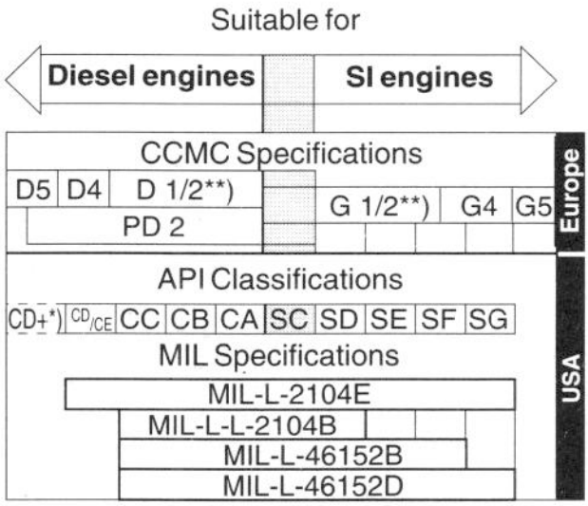

*) SHPD Super-High-Performance-Diesel-Oil
**) G1, G2, D1, D2 invalid as of 1990

– L-46152 D: Similar to L-46152 B/C, but with more stringent requirements for anti-sludge and oxidation testing. Corresponds to API SG.
– L-2104 C: Oils for spark-ignition engines, and for naturally aspirated and turbocharged diesel engines. No longer significant for extended oil-change intervals in European turbocharged engines in commercial applications.
– L-2104 D: Oils meeting the demands of L-2104 C with supplementary American test procedures.
– L-2104 E: Oils corresponding to the requirements defined in L-2104 D, but with more demanding testing in SI engines.

SAE Viscosity grades
(DIN 51511, SAE J300, SAE J306)
The SAE (Society of Automotive Engineers) classifications are the internationally-accepted standard for defining viscosity. The standard provides no information on the quality of the oil. A distinction is drawn between single-grade and multigrade oils, with multigrade being the type which is generally used today.

Two series are employed for the designation (see Table 2) with the letter "W" (Winter) being used to define specific cold-flow properties. The viscosity grades including the letter "W" are rated according to maximum low-temperature viscosity, maximum viscosity pumping temperature and the minimum viscosity at 100 °C. Viscosity grades without the "W" are rated only according to viscosity at 100 °C.

Multigrade oils
Multigrade oils are characterized by a less pronounced proportional relationship between temperature and viscosity. They reduce friction and wear, can be used year round, and provide rapid lubrication for all engine components in cold starts.

A good multigrade oil extends through several SAE grades, e.g., SAE 10W-60.

High-lubricity oils
Lubricating oils with multigrade properties, low viscosity at low temperatures, and special anti-friction additives. Extremely low friction under all engine operating conditions results in reduced fuel consumption.

Transmission lubricants

The quality of the transmission lubricant is determined according to the type of transmission and the stresses to which it is subjected under all operating conditions. The requirements (high pressure resistance, high viscosity stability relative to temperature, good anti-foaming properties, compatibility with gaskets and seals) can only be satisfied by lubricants to which additives have been added. The use of unsuitable and qualitatively inferior oils typically leads to damage to bearings and gear-tooth flanks.

The viscosity must also be suited to the respective application. For motor vehicle transmissions, the viscosity grade is defined in DIN 51512 and SAE J 306 (see Table 3).

Synthesized oils are being increasingly used to meet special requirements (e.g., poly-α-olefins). These are characterized by superior temperature-viscosity properties and increased aging resistance.

API Classifications for transmission lubricants

– GL1-GL3: no particular practical significance.

– GL4: Transmission lubricants for moderately-stressed hypoid-gear transmissions and for transmissions which operate at extreme speeds and impact loads, high rotational speeds and low torques, or low rotational speeds and high torques. Comparable to MIL-L-2105.

– GL5: Transmission lubricants for highly-stressed hypoid-gear transmissions in passenger cars and in other vehicles where they are exposed to impact loads at high rotational speeds, and at high rotational speeds and low torque, or low rotational speeds and high torque. Comparable to MIL-L-2105B/C/D.

Lubricants for automatic transmissions

(ATF = Automatic Transmission Fluid)
Automatic transmissions differ from their manually shifted counterparts in that they do not transmit forces by hydrodynamic and positive mechanical means exclusively; they also employ friction coupling arrangements. Thus the frictional behavior of automatic transmission fluids is extremely important. The applications are basically classified according to the friction characteristics:

ATF Type	Specification
ATF-A	Type A Suffix A
ATF-B	Dexron IB
ATF-D	Dexron IID
ATF-F	Ford M2C33G
ATF-E	Dexron IIE (new classification featuring improved low-temperature properties)

Lubricating greases

Lubricating greases are thickened lubricating oils. A great advantage that greases enjoy over oil is that they do not drain from the contact location. Thus complicated measures designed to seal them in place are unnecessary (e.g., application in wheel bearings and moving systems such as ABS, alternators, ignition distributors, windshield-wiper motors, servomotors). Table 4 provides a general description of the components in a consistent lubricating grease as blended from three base components - base oils, thickeners and additives.

Mineral oils are usually employed as the base component, although fully-synthetic oils have recently become more common as a replacement (due to more stringent requirements in aging resistance, cold-flow properties, viscosity-temperature characteristics).

The thickener is used as a binder for the base oil; here metal soaps are generally employed. They bind the oil in a sponge-like soap structure (micelle) via occlusion and Van der Waals forces. The higher the proportion of thickener in the grease (depends upon the type of thickener), the greater the grease's consistency and NLGI classification (see Table 5).

The additives serve to modify physical and chemical properties of the grease to achieve specific objectives (such as improvement of anti-oxidation properties, increased load-carrying ability (EP additives), and reduction of friction and wear). Solid lubricants (e.g., MoS_2) are also added to lubricating greases (for instance, for lubricating constant-velocity joints in motor vehicles).

Specific lubricating greases are selected with reference to their physical characteristics and their effects upon the sliding surface, and to minimize interaction between the grease and the contact materials.

Example:
Antagonistic effects with plastics:
- Formation of stress cracks,
- Consistency changes
- Polymer degradation,
- Swelling, shrinkage, brittleness.

Thus, for example, mineral-oil greases and greases based on synthetic hydrocarbons should not come into contact with elastomers that are employed together with brake fluid (polyglycol base), as this could result in substantial swelling.

In addition, greases with varying compositions should not be mixed (changes in physical properties, grease liquification due to drop-point reduction).

The selection of the correct lubricating grease makes it possible to substantially enhance the performance capabilities of products with sliding contact-surfaces (e.g., transmissions, friction roller bearings, servo systems).

Table 5. Consistency classifications for lubricating greases (DIN 51 818)

NLGI-Klasse	Worked penetration as per DIN ISO 2137 in tenths of a millimeter (0.1 mm)
000	445 ... 475
00	400 ... 430
0	355 ... 385
1	310 ... 340
2	265 ... 295
3	220 ... 250
4	175 ... 205
5	130 ... 160
6	85 ... 115

Table 4. Composition of lubricating greases

Base oils

- Mineral oils
  - Paraffinic
  - Naphthenic
  - Aromatic
- Synthetic oils
  - Olefin polymers
  - Alkyl aromatics
  - Esters
  - Alcohols
  - Ethers
  - Silicones
  - Fluorinated hydrocarbons
  - Perfluoropolyethers

Thickeners

- Soaps (Li, Na, Ca, Ba, Al)
  - Standard
  - Hydroxi
  - Complex
- Organic thickeners (soap-free)
  - Polyureas
  - PTFE (Teflon)
  - PE (polyethylene)
- Inorganic thickeners
  - Betonites (aluminum oxide)
  - Aerosiles (SiO_2)

Additives

- Extreme-pressure additives
- Wear-protection additives
- Friction modifiers (anti-friction agents)
- Adhesion improvers
- Oxidation inhibitors
- Corrosion inhibitors
- Solid lubricants
  - Molybdenum disulfide
  - Graphite

Fuels

Characteristics

Net and gross calorific values

The specific values for the net (formerly: lower) and gross (formerly: higher, or combustion) calorific values, or H_u and H_o respectively, provide an index for the energy content of fuels. Only the net calorific value H_u (combustion vapor) is significant when dealing with fuels with which water is produced as a byproduct of combustion.

When fuels (such as methanol) with a lower calorific value than their hydrocarbon counterparts are used, greater quantities will be required to achieve comparable engine output.

Calorific value of air-fuel mixture

The calorific value of the combustible air-fuel mixture determines the engine's output. Assuming a constant stoichiometric ratio, this figure remains roughly the same for all liquid gases and fuels (approx. 3500 ... 3700 kJ/m^3).

Vaporization heat

The air-fuel mixture cools as the fuel vapor vaporizes. In cool, damp weather (approx. 2 ... 8 °C, rel. humidity > 65 %), this phenomenon can result in ice forming on the throttle valve (carburetor icing), leading to impaired engine operation.

Cold intake air does not contain enough heat to support complete evaporation of fuels (such as methanol) with a high vaporization heat. Proper mixture formation is not possible under these circumstances, and supplementary measures are required (e.g., preheated intake air).

Fuels for spark-ignition engines (gasoline/petrol)

The minimum requirements for these types of fuels are specified in various national standards. European Standard 228 defines the unleaded fuels which have been introduced within Europe ("Euro-Super"). The corresponding German specifications are contained in DIN 51 600 (leaded gasoline) and DIN 51 607 (unleaded gasoline). These define fuels for spark-ignition engines as hydrocarbon compounds which may contain supplements in the form of oxygenous organic components or other additives to improve performance.

A distinction is made between regular and premium (super-grade) gasolines. Premium gasoline has higher knock-resistance and is for use in high-compression engines. There are also different volatility ratings for summer and winter fuels.

Unleaded gasoline (DIN 51 607)
Unleaded fuel is indispensible for vehicles which employ catalytic converters to treat exhaust gases, as lead would damage the layers of noble metals in the catalytic converter thus rendering it inoperative. Platinum and rhodium are the noble metals which are most effective as catalysts.

Unleaded fuels are a special mixture of high-grade, high-octane components (especially platformates, alkylates and isomerisates, with a high proportion of aromatic compounds and isoparaffins). Resistance to pre-ignition can be effectively increased with nonmetallic additives such as methyl tertiary butyl ether (MTBE) in concentrations of 3 ... 15 %, and alcohol mixtures (methanol 2 ... 3 %, and higher alcohols). The maximum lead content is limited to 13 mg/l.

Leaded gasoline (DIN 51 600)
Environmental considerations dictate that the use of leaded fuels be restricted to those vehicles whose exhaust valves require the combustion products of the lead-alkyl compounds for lubrication. Generally, this only applies to a relatively small number of older vehicles. Sales of leaded fuels are decreasing steadily. The "Super Plus" which is now available on the German market has the same antiknock qualities as leaded gasoline. In most European countries the lead content is legally restricted to a maximum of 0.15 g/l.

Density (DIN 51 757)
Varying density ranges are approved for regular and premium fuels. Because premium fuels generally include a higher proportion of aromatic compounds, they are denser than regular gasoline, and also have a slightly higher calorific value.

Table 1: Minimum standards for unleaded gasoline
(Excerpt from DIN 51 607, August 1989)

Requirements		Super Plus (D)	Premium Summer	Premium Winter	Regular Summer	Regular Winter	Test Standard
Knocking resistance	ROZ MOZ	≥ 98.0 ≥ 88.0	≥ 95.0 ≥ 85.0		≥ 91.0 ≥ 82.5		DIN 51 756 Part 1+2
Lead content Mass concentration of Pb	g/l	as for premium	≤ 0.013				DIN 51 769 Part 1+8 or 11
Evaporation residue (washed) Mass concentration	mg/(100 ml)		≤ 5				DIN EN 5
Density at 15 °C	g/ml		0.735...0.785		0.720...0.770		DIN 51 757
Boiling curve: Total evaporated volume ... 70 °C	%		15...42	20...47	15...42	20...47	DIN 51 751
... 100 °C	%		40...65	42...70	40...65	42...70	
... 180 °C	%		≥ 85	≥ 85	≥ 85	≥ 85	
Final boiling point	°C		≤ 215				DIN 51 751
Reid vapor pressure	hPa		450 ...700	600 ...900	450 ...700	600 ...900	DIN 51 754
Oxidation stability			≥ 360				DIN 51 780

Maximum contents for benzene (5 % vol.): Sulfur (0.1 % by weight) and oxygenous components (methanol 3 % vol., ethanol 5 % vol., ether and MTBE 15 % vol., total oxygen 2.8 % by weight).

Knocking-resistance (octane rating)
The octane rating defines the gasoline's antiknock quality, in other words its resistance to pre-ignition. The higher the octane rating, the greater the resistance to engine knock. Two differing procedures are in international use for determining the octane rating; these are the Research Method and the Motor Method (DIN 51 756; ASTM D 2699 and ASTM D 2700).

RON, MON
The number determined in testing according to the Research Method is the Research Octane Number, or RON. It can be regarded as the essential index of acceleration knock.

The Motor Octane Number, or MON, is derived in testing according to the Motor Method. The MON basically provides an indication of the tendency to knock at high-speeds.

The Motor Method differs from the Research Method by using preheated mixtures, higher engine speeds and variable ignition timing, thereby placing more stringent thermal demands on the fuel under examination. MON figures are lower than those for RON.

Octane numbers up to 100 indicate the volumetric content in percent of C_8H_{18} iso-octane (trimethyl pentane) contained in a mixture with C_7H_{16} n-heptane, at the point where the mixture's knock-resistance in a test engine is identical to that of the fuel being tested. Iso-octane, which is extremely knock-resistant, is assigned the octane number 100 (100 RON and MON), while n-heptane, with low-resistance to pre-ignition, is assigned the number 0.

Increasing the antiknock quality
Normal (untreated) straight-run gasoline displays little resistance to knock. Various knock-resistant refinery components must be added to obtain a fuel with adequate knock resistance. The highest-possible octane level must also be maintained throughout the entire boiling range. Cyclic hydrocarbons (aromatics) and branched chains (isoparaffins) provide greater knock resistance than straight-chain molecules (n-paraffins).

Additives based on oxygenous components (methanol, ethanol, methyl tertiary butyl ether) have a positive effect on the octane number, but can lead to difficulties in other areas (alcohols raise the volatility level and can damage materials).

Knock inhibitors
The most effective knock inhibitors are organic lead compounds (lead-alkyl compounds; tetraethylene lead (TEL) and tetramethylene lead (TML). These can raise the octane number by several points, with the exact amount of improvement depending upon the specific hydrocarbon structure. Both DIN 51 600 and most European national standards limit the maximum lead content to 150 mg per liter of fuel.

Environmental concerns, and as a result the increasing numbers of vehicles equipped with catalytic converters, have led to a steady reduction in the amounts of lead alkyls in fuels.

Volatility

Fuels for SI engines must conform with stringent specifications regarding their volatility characteristics to ensure satisfactory operation. The fuel must contain a large enough proportion of highly volatile components for good cold starts, but the volatility must not be so high as to impair operation (vapor lock) and starting when the engine is hot.

In addition, environmental considerations demand that evaporative losses be held low. Volatility is defined in various ways.

Boiling curve
There are three areas on the boiling curve which exercise a particularly pronounced effect on operating behaviour. They can be defined according to fuel evaporation at three temperatures (see Table 1). The volume which evaporates up to 70 °C must be adequate to ensure good cold starting, but not so large as to cause vapor locks when the engine is hot. The vaporized volume at 180 °C should be high enough to minimize dilution of the engine's lubricating oil, with particular emphasis on cold engines. The percentage of fuel which evaporates at 100 °C determines the engine's warm-up qualities, as well as it's acceleration and response characteristics once it has reached normal operating temperature.

Vapor pressure
DIN 51 600 and DIN 51 607 limit the vapor pressure of fuels at 38 °C to 0.7 bar in summer and 0.9 bar in winter. The actual vapor-pressure/temperature curves for specific gasolines are largely determined by their individual compositions. The curves for fuels containing alcohol, for instance, are much steeper than those for pure hydrocarbon mixtures. The result is that fuels with alcohol display a greater tendency to vaporize and form vapor locks thus impairing operation at higher temperatures.

Vapor/liquid ratio
This specification provides an index of a fuel's tendency to form vapor bubbles (vapor locks). It is based on the volume of vapor generated by a specific quantity of fuel at a set temperature. The counter-pressure exerted by the atmosphere is significant: Assuming a constant temperature, a larger volume of vapor will form at low pressures (i.e., at high altitudes) than at higher pressures (such as at sea level). This phenomenon can lead to vapor-lock problems when driving in mountainous areas. The addition of alcohols – and methanol in particular – raises the vapor/liquid ratio.

Additives

Along with the structure of the hydrocarbons (refinery components), it is the additives which determine the ultimate quality of a fuel. Additives are generally combined in packages containing individual components with various attributes.

Extreme care and precision are required both in the testing of additives and in determining their optimal concentrations, and they must produce no undesirable side-effects. Mixing-in the additives is thus a task for the fuel manufacturer.

Anti-aging additives
Such agents are added to fuels to improve their stability during storage, and are particularly important when the fuel also contains cracked components. They inhibit oxidation from atmospheric oxygen (phenolic and aminic components) and prevent catalytic reactions with metal ions (metal deactivators).

Intake-system contamination inhibitors
Freedom from deposits throughout the intake system (carburetor, throttle valve, injectors, intake valves) is essential for ensuring trouble-free operation and minimal exhaust emissions. To achieve this end, effective detergent agents should be added to the fuel.

Corrosion protection
Moisture in the fuel can lead to corrosion in the fuel system. An extremely effective remedy is afforded by anti-corrosion additives which form a protective layer below the film of water.

Icing protection
Appropriate additives are designed to prevent the throttle valve from icing up. As an example, alcohols dissolve ice crystals, while other agents inhibit the formation of ice deposits on the throttle valve.

Diesel fuels

Diesel fuels contain a multiplicity of individual hydrocarbons with boiling points ranging from roughly 180 °C to 360 °C. They are the product of graduated distillation of crude oil. The refineries are also adding increasing amounts of conversion products to the diesel fuel; these "cracked components" are extracted from heavy oil by breaking up (cracking) large molecules. The requirements for diesel fuels are defined in national standards, with DIN 51 601 being applicable in Germany. The most important specifications in this standard are:

Ignition quality and cetane number
Because the diesel engine dispenses with an externally-generated ignition spark, the fuel must ignite spontaneously and with minimal delay (ignition lag) upon being injected into the hot, compressed air in the combustion chamber. The cetane number (CN) expresses the fuel's ignition quality (suitability for spontaneous self-ignition in a diesel engine). The higher the cetane number, the greater the fuel's tendency to support self-ignition. The cetane number 100 is assigned to n-hexadecane (cetane), which ignites very easily, while methyl naphthalene, with a low ignition quality, carries the cetane number 0. The cetane number is determined using a test engine. DIN 51 601 prescribes a cetane number of 45 as the minimum for diesel fuels, but higher ratings of around 50 are desirable for optimal operation in modern engines (smooth operation, particulate emissions). High-quality diesel fuels contain a high proportion of paraffins with elevated CN ratings. Conversely, the aromatic compounds found in cracked components have a detrimental effect on ignition quality.

Yet another indication of ignition quality is provided by the cetane index, which is based on density and the 50 % point on the boiling curve. In contrast to the cetane number, this index does not reflect the positive influence of ignition improvers on ignition response.

Cold-flow properties, filtration properties

The precipitation of paraffin crystals at low temperatures can result in fuel-filter blockages, ultimately leading to interruption of the fuel flow. Under unfavorable conditions paraffin particles can start to form at temperatures as high as 0 °C. Special selection and manufacturing procedures are thus necessary for winter diesel fuels in order to ensure trouble-free operation in cold weather. Normally, flow-improvers are added to the fuel at the refinery. These do not actually prevent paraffin precipitation, but they do limit the growth of the crystals, which remain small enough to pass through the pores in the filter material. Other additives can be used to maintain the crystals in a state of suspension, extending the filtration limit downward to below –22 °C. According to DIN 51 601, this limit should extend down to at least –15 °C.

Another option is to add kerosine to the fuel, while regular gasoline also acts to inhibit crystalization. It must, however, be remembered that this method reduces the fuel's ignitability while simultaneously lowering the flash point by a substantial amount (fuels for SI engines have extremely low cetane numbers).

Flash point

The flash point is the temperature at which the quantities of vapor which a combustible fluid emits into the adjoining atmosphere are sufficient to allow a spark to ignite the vapor-air mixture above the fluid. Safety considerations (transport, storage) dictate that diesel fuels must meet the requirements for Class A III Hazardous Materials, i.e., the flash point should lie above 55 °C. Less than 3 % gasoline in the diesel fuel is sufficient to reduce the flash point temperature to such an extent that ignition is possible at room temperature.

Boiling range
The boiling range affects several parameters which are of major importance in determining a diesel fuel's operating characteristics. Extending the boiling range downward to embrace lower temperatures improves the fuel's cold-operation properties, but at the price of a reduction in the cetane number. Particularly critical is the negative effect on the fuel's lubrication properties, as it increases the risk of wear in the injection-system components. In contrast, raising the final temperature at the upper end of the boiling range, although being desirable for more efficient crude-oil utilization, also results in soot emissions as well as carbon deposits (combustion residue) at the injection nozzles.

Density
There is a reasonably constant correspondence between a diesel fuel's calorific value and its density; higher densities have a higher calorific value. Assuming constant injection-pump settings, and thus in our example constant injection volume, then the use of fuels with widely differing densities in a given system will be accompanied by variations in mixture ratios which are due to the fluctuations in calorific value. Higher densities provoke increased particulate emissions.

Viscosity
The diesel fuel's viscosity must be adequate for ensuring proper hydrodynamic lubrication of the injection-pump assembly. At the same time, excessive viscosity can impair fuel-spray dispersion at the injection nozzles.

Sulfur
Diesel fuels contain chemically bonded sulfur, with the actual quantities depending upon the quality of the crude petroleum and the components which are added at the refinery. Cracked components are characterized by especially high sulfur contents, but these can be reduced with hydrogen treatment at the refinery. During combustion, sulfur is converted to sulfur dioxide (SO_2) which is environmentally incompatible due to its acidic reactions. For this reason, legal limits were placed on diesel-fuel sulfur content which during the past years have been progressively tightened. The currently-applicable regulation in Germany stipulates a maximum of 0.2 % by weight.

Sulfur also increases the particulate content of the exhaust emissions, diminishing the effectiveness of the catalytic converters employed to control soot emissions.

Carbon deposits
The carbon-deposit index indicates a fuel's tendency to form residues on the injection nozzles. The mechanisms of deposit formation are complex and not easily described.

The components which the diesel fuel contains at the end of vaporization exercise a not inconsiderable influence on deposit formation.

Additives
Additives, which had long been employed in fuels for SI engines, have attained increasing significance as quality improvers for diesel fuels. The various agents are generally combined in additive packages to achieve a variety of objectives. As the total concentration of the additives generally lies below 0.1 %, the fuel's physical characteristics – such as density, viscosity and boiling range – remain unchanged.

Flow improvers
Flow improvers are polymers whose application is generally restricted to winter (see Cold-flow properties).

Cetane improvers
Cetane improvers are added to promote good ignition response; they are in the form of alcohol-derived esters of azotic acid. These agents improve the fuel's combustion properties, with positive effects upon noise and particulate emissions.

Table 2: Minimum standards for diesel fuels
(Excerpt from DIN 51 601, February 1986)

Requirements				Test Standard
Density at 15 °C		g/ml	0.820...0.860	DIN 51 757
Boiling curve: ... 250 °C – Quantity vaporized ... 350 °C – Quantity vaporized	 maximum minimum	 % vol. % vol.	 65 85	DIN 51 751
Kinematic viscosity at 20 °C		mm^2/s (cSt)	2...8	DIN 51 561 DIN 51 562
Flash point	to exceed	°C	55	DIN 51 755
Flow properties: Filtration limits Summer Winter	 maximum maximum	 °C °C	 0 –15	DIN 51 428
Sulfur content	maximum	% by weight	0.3[1])	DIN EN 41 DIN 51 400
Ignition quality (cetane no.)	minimum	CN	45	DIN 51 773

[1]) According to Federal Emissions Law (Germany): 0.2%.

Detergent additives
Detergent additives inhibit the formation of deposits on the injection nozzles.

Corrosion inhibitors
Corrosion inhibitors resist corrosion on metallic components (when moisture penetrates into the fuel system).

Anti-foaming agents
Anti-foaming agents facilitate the refueling process.

Alternative fuels

Coal liquification

The essential raw materials are coal and coke. These emerge from initial processing in the form of water gas (H_2 + CO), while subsequent catalytic conversion produces hydrocarbons. These, in turn, provide the basic materials for the production of gasoline and diesel fuel. The byproducts are liquified petroleum gas (LPG) and paraffin. The Fischer-Tropsch synthesis has acquired particular significance in South Africa, where it is in large-scale use.

Liquified Petroleum Gas (LPG)

The two major components of LPG are butane and propane. It is in limited application as a fuel for motor vehicles. LPG is a byproduct of the petroleum-refining process, and can be liquified under pressure. LPG has a high octane number (RON > 100).

Alcohol fuels

Methanol, ethanol, and their various byproducts (e.g., ether) are the main contenders as alternative fuels for SI engines, being the focus of both discussion and actual application. Methanol can be derived from the plentiful hydrocarbon reserves represented by coal, natural gas, and heavy oils. In certain countries (such as Brazil), biomass (sugar cane, wheat) is distilled to produce ethanol for use as an engine fuel.

Small volumetric concentrations of ethanol are also found in the hybrid fuels which appear on the market from time to time, while fuels with higher concentrations (15 ... 85 %) are currently being subjected to large-scale testing. The use of alcohol, either pure or in mixtures, is associated with a range of specific problems, and definitive solutions have not yet been found for all of them. Their calorific value, and other characteristics which differ from conventional SI-engine fuels, mean that specific modification and adaptation are sometimes required on the vehicle.

The attention being focused upon LPG and alcohol derives not only from their potential as substitutes for liquid hydrocarbons, but also from their beneficial effect on exhaust emissions.

Properties of liquid fuels and hydrocarbons

Substance	Density kg/l	Main constituents % by weight	Boiling points °C	Latent heat of vaporization kJ/kg[1]	Specific calorific value MJ/kg[1]	Ignition temperature °C	Theoretical air requirement kg/kg	Ignition limit Lower %by vol. of gas in air	Ignition limit upper %by vol. of gas in air
Spark-ignition engine fuel									
Regular gasoline	0.715 ... 0.765	86 C, 14 H	25 ... 215	380 ... 500	42.7	≈ 300	14.8	≈ 0.6	≈ 8
Premium gasoline	0.730 ... 0.780	86 C, 14 H	25 ... 215	–	43.5	≈ 400	14.7	–	–
Aviation gasoline	0.720	85 C, 15 H	40 ... 180	–	43.5	≈ 500	–	≈ 0.7	≈ 8
Kerosene	0.77 ... 0.83	87 C, 13 H	170 ... 260	–	43	≈ 250	14.5	≈ 0.6	≈ 7.5
Diesel fuel	0.815 ... 0.855	86 C, 13 H	180 ... 360	≈ 250	42.5	≈ 250	14.5	≈ 0.6	≈ 7.5
Crude oil	0.70 ... 1.0	80 ... 83 C, 10 ... 14 H	25 ... 360	222 ... 352	39.8 ... 46.1	≈ 220	–	≈ 0.6	≈ 6.5
Lignite tar oil	0.850 ... 0.90	84 C, 11 H	200 ... 360	–	40.2 ... 41.9	–	13.5	–	–
Bituminous coal oil	1.0 ... 1.10	89 C, 7 H	170 ... 330	–	36.4 ... 38.5	–	–	–	–
Pentane C_5H_{12}	0.63	83 C, 17 H	36	352	45.4	285	15.4	1.4	7.8
Hexane C_6H_{14}	0.66	84 C, 16 H	69	331	44.7	240	15.2	1.2	7.4
n-Heptane C_7H_{16}	0.68	84 C, 16 H	98	310	44.4	220	15.2	1.1	6.7
Isooctane C_8H_{18}	0.69	84 C, 16 H	99	297	44.6	410	15.2	1	6
Benzene C_6H_6	0.88	92 C, 8 H	80	394	40.2	550	13.3	1.2	8
Toluene C_7H_8	0.87	91 C, 9 H	110	364	40.6	530	13.4	1.2	7
Xylene C_8H_{11}	0.88	91 C, 9 H	144	339	40.6	460	13.7	1	7.6
Ether $(C_2H_5)_2O$	0.72	64 C, 14 H, 22 O	35	377	34.3	170	7.7	1.7	36
Acetone $(CH_3)_2CO$	0.79	62 C, 10 C, 28 O	56	523	28.5	540	9.4	2.5	13
Ethanol C_2H_5OH	0.79	52 C, 13 H, 35 O	78	904	26.8	420	9	3.5	15
Methanol CH_3OH	0.79	38 C, 12 H, 50 O	65	1110	19.7	450	6.4	5.5	26

Viscosity at 20 °C in mm²/s (= cSt, p. 34): Gasoline ≈ 0.6; Diesel fuel ≈ 4; ethanol ≈ 1.5; methanol ≈ 0.75.

[1]) Values per l = values per kg x density in kg/l. See pp. 30 ... 32 for conversion tables.

Properties of gaseous fuels and hydrocarbons

Substance		Density at 0 °C and 1013 mbar	Main constituents	Boiling point at 1013 mbar	Specific calorific value Fuel	Specific calorific value Air-fuel mixture	Ignition temperature	Theoretical air requirement	Ignition limit Lower	Ignition limit Upper
		kg/m³	% by weight	°C	MJ/kg[1]	MJ/m³ [1]	°C	kg/kg	%by vol. of gas in air	
Liquefied gas		2.25[2]	C_3H_8, C_4H_{10}	–30	46.1	3.39	≈ 400	15.5	1.5	15
Municipal gas		0.56 ... 0.61	50 H, 8 CO, 30 CH_4	–210	≈ 30	≈ 3.25	≈ 560	10	4	40
Natural gas		≈ 0.83	76 C, 24 H	–162	47.7	–	–	–	–	–
Water gas		0.71	50 H, 38 CO	–	15.1	3.10	≈ 600	4.3	6	72
Blast-furnace gas		1.28	28 CO, 59 N, 12 CO_2	–170	3.20	1.88	≈ 600	0.75	≈ 30	≈ 75
Sewage gas [3]		–	46 CH4, 54 CO2	–	27.2[3]	3.22	–	–	–	–
Hydrogen	H_2	0.090	100 H	–253	120.0	2.97	560	34	4	77
Carbon monoxide	CO	1.25	100 CO	–191	10.05	3.48	605	2.5	12.5	75
Methane	CH_4	0.72	75 C, 25 H	–162	50.0	3.22	650	17.2	5	15
Acetylene	C_2H_2	1.17	93 C, 7 H	–81	48.1	4.38	305	13.25	1.5	80
Ethane	C_2H_6	1.36	80 C, 20 H	–88	47.5	–	515	17.3	3	14
Ethene	C_2H_4	1.26	86 C, 14 H	–102	14.1	–	425	14.7	2.75	34
Propane	C_3H_8	2.0[2]	82 C, 18 H	–43	46.3	3.35	470	15.6	1.9	9.5
Propene	C_3H_6	1.92	86 C, 14 H	–47	45.8	–	450	14.7	2	11
Butane	C_4H_{10}	2.7[2]	83 C, 17 H	–10; +1[4]	45.6	3.39	365	15.4	1.5	8.5
Butene	C_4H_8	2.5	86 C, 14 H	–5; +1[4]	45.2	–	–	14.8	1.7	9

[1]) Values per m³ = values per kg x density in kg/m³. See pp. 30 ... 32 for conversion tables..
[2]) Density of liquified gas 0.54 kg/l; density of liquified propane 0.51 kg/l; density of liquified butane 0.58 kg/l.
[3]) Purified sewage gas contains 95% CH_4 (methane) and has a heating value of 37.7 MJ/kg.
[4]) First value for isobutane, second value for n-butane or n-butene.

Hydraulic fluids

Brake fluids

Brake fluid is the hydraulic medium employed for transmitting force within the braking system. Stringent requirements must be complied with in order to guarantee reliable braking-system operation. These requirements are defined in various standards of similar content (SAE J 1703, FMVSS 116, ISO 4925). The performance data contained in FMVSS 116 (Federal Motor Vehicle Safety Standard), legally binding in the US, also serve as an international reference. The US Department of Transportation (DOT) has defined specific ratings for salient characteristics (Table: "Brake fluids").

Requirements

Equilibrium boiling point
The equilibrium boiling point provides an index of the brake fluid's resistance to thermal stress. The heat encountered in the wheel cylinders (with the highest temperatures in the entire braking system) can be especially critical. Vapor bubbles form at temperatures above the brake fluid's momentary boiling point, resulting in brake failure.

Wet boiling point
The wet boiling point is the equilibrium boiling point of the fluid after it has absorbed moisture under specified conditions. Hygroscopic (glycol-based) fluids in particular, are marked by a sharp drop in the boiling-point. This means that in case of repeated heavy braking, the brake fluid boils sooner and braking efficiency is impaired earlier than would otherwise be the case.

Testing of the wet boiling point is directed toward determining the characteristics of used brake fluid. Brake fluid can absorb moisture through the system's hoses, mostly through diffusion. This is the main reason for it having to be replaced every 1 ... 2 years.

Viscosity
The viscosity must be such as to display minimal sensitivity to temperature so that reliability is ensured throughout the braking system's wide operating range (–40 °C ... +100 °C). Maintenance of the lowest possible viscosity at very low temperatures is especially significant in ABS-equipped vehicles.

Compressibility
The fluid should consistently maintain a low level of compression with minimal temperature sensitivity.

Corrosion protection
FMVSS 116 stipulates that brake fluids will exercise no corrosive effect on those metals which are generally employed in a braking system. The required corrosion protection can only be achieved by the use of additives.

Elastomer swelling
The elastomers employed in the brake system must be able to adapt to the type of brake fluid being used. Although a small amount of swelling is desirable, it is imperative that it not exceed 16%. Above this figure, the brake fluid has a negative effect on the strength of the elastomer components. Even minute levels of mineral-oil contamination (mineral-oil-based brake fluid, solvents) in glycol-based brake fluid can lead to destruction of rubber components (such as seals), with braking-system failure as the final result.

Chemical composition

Glycol-ether fluids
Glycol-ether fluids are the type most commonly employed as brake fluids. These generally consist of monoethers of low polyethelene glycols. Although these components can be used to produce a brake fluid which conforms to the DOT 3 requirements, their undesirable hygroscopic properties cause the fluid to absorb moisture at a relatively rapid rate, with an attendant rapid reduction in the boiling point.

If the free OH (Hydroxyl) groups are partially esterified with boric acid, this results in components which can be used to produce substantially better DOT 4 fluids (chemically reactive with water and thus capable of neutralizing the effects of moisture). As the DOT 4 brake fluid's boiling point drops much more slowly than that of a DOT 3 fluid, its service life is longer.

Table: Brake fluids

Reference standard for testing		FMVSS 116			SAE J 1703
Requirements/Date		DOT 3	DOT 4	DOT 5	Nov.1983
Dry boiling point	min. °C	205	230	260	205
Wet boiling point	min. °C	140	155	180	140
Cold viscosity at –40 °C	mm^2/s	1500	1800	900	1800

Mineral-oil fluids (ISO 7308)

The great advantage of mineral-oil-based fluids is the fact that they are not hygroscopic. In other words, they are not subject to variations in boiling point due to absorption of moisture. The mineral and synthetic oils to be employed must be selected with utmost care. Viscosity-index improvers are generally added in order to achieve the desired relationship between viscosity and temperature. There are also numerous other additives available from the oil industry for the improvement of further brake-fluid properties. It should be noted that braking systems designed for glycol ether should never be topped-up with mineral-oil-based brake fluids (or vice versa), as this destroys the elastomers.

Silicone fluids

Because silicone fluids – like mineral oils – do not absorb moisture, they were sometimes used as brake fluid in the past. The disadvantages associated with these products include palpably higher compressibility and less satisfactory lubrication properties. These factors also reduce their suitability for use as hydraulic fluid in many systems.

A critical factor for brake fluids based on silicone or mineral oils is the absorption of free water in a fluid state, as the water forms vapor bubbles when it heats up to more than 100 °C and freezes when it cools to less than 0 °C.

Hydraulic fluids

Group	Fluid
Hydraulic fluids with mineral-oil base	
H	No additives
HL	Contains additives for enhanced aging resistance and corrosion protection
HLP	Contains additives for reducing wear and/or for increasing loadability
HLP-D	Contains additives for cleaning and lubricating sliding surfaces (avoidance of stick-slip effects, such as at piston-rod seals and guides at low speeds)
Flame-resistant hydraulic fluids for special applications (e.g., mining, aeronautics, pressure diecasting and rolling mills, with increasing use for transfer lines in the automotive industry)	
HF-A	Oil-in-oil emulsions (2 ... 20 % emulsifiable concentrate, rest water)
HF-B	Water-in-oil emulsions (40 % water, 60 % oil; seldom used in Germany)
HF-C	Aqeous solutions (essentially solutions of water and polyalkylene glycol; 35 ... 55 % water)
HF-D	Anhydrous fluids (synthetic; usually phosphoric esters or mixtures of phosphoric esters and chlorated hydrocarbons. For environmental reasons, use within Germany is restricted to closed systems for coal mining. In addition, substances employed for special applications include silicones, diesters, polyphenyl ethers, polyglycols, silicates and fluorocarbons)

Names of chemicals

Commercial name English	German	French	Chemical name / explanations	Chemical formula
Acetic ether; vinegar naphtha	Essigester; Essigäther	Éther acétique	Ethylacetate	$CH_3COOC_2H_5$
Aerosil; fumed silica	Aerosil®	Aerosil®	Silicon dioxide in extremely fine particles	SiO_2
Almond oil bitter	Bittermandelöl	Essence d'amandes	Benzaldehyde	C_6H_5CHO
Alum (potash alum)	Alaun (Kalialaun)	Alun de potassium	Potassium aluminum sulfate	$KA1(SO_4)_2 \cdot 12H_2O$
Ammonia liquor	Salmiakgeist	Ammoniaque	Aqueous solution of ammonium hydroxide	NH_4CH
Anon; pimelic ketone	Anon	Cyclohexanone	Cyclohexanone	$C_6H_{10}O$
Aqua fortis	Scheidewasser	Eau-forte	Nitric acid	HNO_3
Aqua regia	Königwasser	Eau régale	Mixture of nitric acid and hydro-chloric acid	$HNO_3 + HCl\ (1 + 3)$
Baking soda; Vichy salt	Natron; Natriumbikarbonat	Sel de Vichy	Sodium hydrogen carbonate	$NaHCO_3$
Bleaching powder; chlorinated lime	Chlorkalk	(Chlorure de chaux)	Calciumchloride-hypochlorite	$Ca(OC1)Cl$
Blue vitriol	Kupfervitriol	Vitriol bleu	Copper sulfate pentahydrate	$CuSO_4 \cdot 5H_2O$
Borax; tincal	Borax; Tinkal	Borax, tincal	Sodium tetraborate	$Na_2B_4O_7 \cdot 10H_2O$
Brimstone		Cristal de soufre	Sulfur	S
Burnt lime	Ätzkalk; gebrannter Kalk	Chaux vive	Calcium oxide	CaO
Butoxyl	Butoxyl®	Butoxyl®	3-methoxybutyl acetate	$CH_3COO(CH_2)_2CH(OCH_3)CH_3$
Butter of tin	Zinnbutter	Beurre d' étain	Tin(IV)chloride hydrate	$SnCl_4 \cdot 5H_2O$

Calomel	Kalomel	Calomel	Mercury(I)chloride	Hg_2Cl_2
Carbide	Karbid	Carbure	Calciumcarbide	CaC_2
Carbitol®[1] (-solvent)	Carbitol®[1] Dioxytol®	Carbitol®[1]	Diethylenglycol mono-ethylether	$HO(CH_2)_2O(CH_2)_2OC_2H_5$
Carbitol acetate®[1]	Carbitolacetat®[1]	Acétate de Carbitol®[1]	Diethylenglycol ethylether acetate	$CH_3COO(CH_2)_2O(CH_2)_2OC_2H_5$
Carbolic acid	Karbolsäure	Acide carbolique	Phenol	C_6H_5OH
Carbolic acid gas	Kohlensäure	Gaz carbonique	Carbon dioxide	CO2
Caustic potash	Ätzkali	Potasse caustique	Potassium hydroxide	KOH
Caustic soda	Ätznatron	Soude caustique	Sodium hydroxide	NaOH
Cellosolve®[1] (-solvent)	Cellosolve®[1] Oxitol®	Cellosolve®[1] (solvant)	Ethylenglycol monoethylether	$HO(CH_2)_2OC_2H_5$
Cellosolve acetate®[1]	Cellosolveacetat®[1]	Acétate de Cellosolve®[1]	Ethylenglycol ethylether acetate	$CH_3COO(CH_2)_2OC_2H_5$
Chloral	Chloral	Chloral	Trichloro acetaldehyde	Cl_3CCHO
Chloramine-T	Chloramin T	Chloramine T	Sodium salt of the p-toluenesulfonic acid chloroamide	$CH_3C_6H_4SO_2NClNa \cdot 3H_2O$
Chloroprene	Chloropren	Chloroprène	2-chloro butadiene-1.3	$CH_2{=}CCl{-}CH_2{=}CH_2$
Chlorothene	Chlorothene®; 1.1.1	Chlorothène®; 1.1.1	1.1.1-trichloroethane	CH_3CCl_3
Chromic anhydride	Chromsäure	Anhydride chromique	Chromium trioxide	CrO_3
Cinnabar	Zinnober	Cinabre, vermillon	Mercury(II)sulfide	HgS
Colophony; silvic acid	Kolophonium	Colophane	Naturally occurring abietic acid	$C_{19}H_{29}COOH$
Cryolite	Kryolith	Cryolite	Sodium hexafluoroaluminate	$Na_3[AlF_6]$

[1]) methyl-, propyl-, i-propyl-, butyl- c.: names for analogous ethers containing the above mentioned groups instead of ethyl -

Names of chemicals (continued)

Commercial name English	German	French	Chemical name / explanations	Chemical formula
Decalin	Dekalin	Décaline	Decahydro naphthalene	$C_{10}H_{18}$
Diane	Bisphenol A; Diphenylolpropan	Bisphénol A	4.4-dihydroxyphenyl-propane-2.2	$(CH_3)_2C(C_6H_4(OH)\text{-}4)_2$
Diglyme			Diethylene glycol dimethyl ether	$CH_3O(CH_2)_2O(CH_2)_2OCH_3$
Diisobutylene	Diisobutylen	Diisobutylène	2.2.4-trimethyl pentenes -1 and -2	$(CH_3)_3CCH_2C(CH_3){=}CH_2$ + $(CH_3)_3C{=}CH(CH_3)_2$
DMF	DMF	DMF	N,N-dimethyl formamide	$HCON(CH_3)_2$
DMSO	DMSO	DMSO	Dimethyl sulfoxide	$(CH_3)_2SO$
Dry ice	Trockeneis	Carboglace	(solid) carbon dioxide	CO_2
English red	Polierrot	Rouge d'Angleterre	Iron(III)oxide	FE_2O_3
Epsom salt	Bittersalz; Magnesiumvitriol	Sel d'Epsom	Magnesium sulfate	$MgSO_4 \cdot 7H_2O$
Fixing salt; hypo	Fixiersalz; "Antichlor"	Sel fixateur	Sodium thiosulfate	$Na_2S_2O_3 \cdot 5H_2O$
Fluorspar; fluorite	Flußspat; Fluorit	Spath fluor; fluorine	Calcium fluoride	CaF_2
Formalin	Formalin®	Formol	Aqueous solution of formaldehyde	H_2CO
Freon (s)®	Freon(e)®; Frigen(e)®	Fréon(s)®; Frigène(s)	Compounds of C, H, F, C1 (Br)	Numerical characterization (2)

Glacial acetic acid	Eisessig (Essigessenz)	Acide acétique	Acetic acid	CH_3COOH
Glauber's salt; mirabilite	Glaubersalz	Sel de Glauber	Sodium sulfate	$Na_2SO_4 \cdot 10H_2O$
Golden antimony sulphide	Goldschwefel	Soufre doré d'antimoine	Antimony pentasulfide	Sb_2S_5
Green vitriol	Eisenvitriol	Vitriol vert; couperose verte	Iron(II)sulfate	$FeSO_4 \cdot 7H_2O$
Halon®	Halon®	Halon®	Polymer from tetrafluoroethylene	$(C_2F_4)_n$
Halone(s)	Halon(e)	Halon(s)	Compounds of C, F, C1, Br	Numerical characterization [3]
Halothane	Halothan		1.1.1-trifluorochlorobromoethane	$F_3CCHBrC1$
Hartshorn salt	Hirschhornsalz	Levure chimique	Ammonium hydrogencarbonate + ammonium carbaminate	$NH_4HCO_3 + NH_2COONH_4$
Hexalin	Hexalin®	Hexaline®	Cyclohexanol (also: hexahydronaphtalene)	$C_6H_{11}OH$ $(C_{10}H_{14})$
Hexone	Hexon; MIBK		4-methyl pentanone-2 (methyl isobutyl ketone)	$(CH_3)_2CHCH_2COCH_3$
Laughing gas	Lachgas; Stickoxydul	Gaz hilarant	Nitrous oxide	N2O
Lead vinegar	Bleiessig	Eau blanche; vinaigre de plomb	Aqueous solution of lead acetate and lead hydroxide	$(CH_3COO)_2Pb + Pb(OH)_2$
Libavius' fuming spirit	Spiritus fumans	Chlorure stannique	Tin tetrachloride	$SnCl_4$
Lime nitrogen; nitrolim	Kalkstickstoff	Chaux azotée	Techn. calcium cyanamide	$CaCN_2$
Lime salpeter	Kalksalpeter; Norgesalpeter	Salpêtre	Calcium nitrate	$Ca(NO_3)_2 \cdot 2H_2O$
Liquid gas	Flüssiggas	Gaz liquéfié	Propane, isobutane, n-butane	$C_3H_8 + C_4H_{10}$
Lunar caustic	Höllenstein	Pierre infernale	Silver nitrate	$AgNO_3$

Names of chemicals (continued)

Commercial name English	German	French	Chemical name / explanations	Chemical formula
Marble	Marmor	Marbre	Calcium carbonate	$CaCO_3$
Methylchloroform	Methylchloroform; 1.1.1	Trichloro-éthane 1.1.1	1.1.1-trichloroethane	CH_3CCl_3
Microcosmic salt	Phosphorsalz	Sel de phosphore	Sodium ammonium hydrogenphosphate	$NH_4NaHPO_3 \cdot 4H_2O$
Mine gas	Grubengas; Sumpfgas	Grisou, gaz des marais	Methane	CH_4
Minium	Mennige	Minium	Lead(II)orthoplumbate	Pb_3O_4 (Pb_2PbO_4)
Mohr's salt	Mor' sches Salz	Sel de Mohr	Iron(II)ammonium sulfate	$(NH_4)_2Fe(SO_4) \cdot 6H_4O$
Monoglyme			Ethylene glycol dimethylether	$CH_3O(C_2H_4)OCH_3$
Mordant rouge	Essigsaure Tonerde	Mordant	Basic aluminum acetate	$(CH_3COO)_2A10H$
Mota, Meta®	Meta®; Hartspiritus	Méta®	Tetramethyl tetroxacyclooctane (metaldehyde)	$(CHCH_3)_4O_4$
Muthmann's liquid	Muthmann's Flüssigkeit		1.1.2.2-tetrabromoethane	$Br_2CHCHBr_2$
Nitroglycerin	Nitroglyzerin	Nitroglycérine	Glycerol trinitrate	$CHONO_2(CH_2ONO_2)_2$
Norway saltpeter	Ammonsalpeter	Nitrate d'ammonium	Ammonium nitrate	NH_4NO_3
Oleum	Oleum; "Vitriolöl"	Oléum	Sulfuric acid + disulfuric acid	$H_2SO_4 + H_2S_2O_7$
Phosgene gas	Phosgen	Phosgène	Carbonic acid dichloride	$COCl_2$
Phosphine	Phosphin	Phosphine	Hydrogen phosphide	PH_3
Picric acid	Pikrinsäure	Acide pricrique	2.4.6-trinitro phenoi	$C_6H_2(NO_2)_3OH$
Potash	Pottasche	Potasse	Potassium carbonate	K_2CO_3
Potassium metabisulphite	Kaliummetabisulfit	Métabisulfite de potassium	Potassium disulfite	$K_2S_2O_5$
Pyrolusite	Braunstein	Pyrolusite	Manganese dioxide	MnO_2
Red prussiate of potash	Rotes Blutlaugensalz	Ferricyanure	Potassium hexacyano-ferrate (III)	$K_3[Fe(CN)_6]$
Rochelle salt; salt of Seignette	Seignettesalz	Sel de Seignette	Potassium sodium tartrate	$(CHOH)_2COOKCOONa$

Sal ammoniac	Salmiak	Sel ammoniaque	Ammonium chloride	NH_4C1
Salt of sorrel; potassium bioxalate	Kleesalz; Sauerkleesalz	Sel d'oseille	Potassium hydrogenoxalate-oxalic acid-double salt	$(COOHCOOK) \cdot (COOH)_2 \cdot 2H_2O$
Salt of tin	Zinnsalz	Sel d'étain	Tin(II)chloride	$SnCl_2 \cdot 2H_2O$
Saltpeter	(Kali-)Salpeter	Salpêtre	Potassium nitrate	KNO_3
Slaked lime	Gelöschter Kalk	Chaux éteinte	Calcium hydroxide	$Ca(OH)_2$
Soda crystals	(Kristall-)Soda	(cristaux de) soude	Sodium carbonate	$Na_2CO_3 \cdot 10H_2O$
Soda niter; Chile saltpeter	Chile Salpeter; Natronsalpeter	Salpêtre du Chili	Sodium nitrate	$NaNO_3$
Sugar of lead	Bleizucker	Sel de Saturne	Lead acetate	$(CH_3COO)_2Pb$
Sulphuric ether	Schwefeläther	Éther sulfurique	Diethyl ether	$C_2H_5OC_2H_5$
Tetralin	Tetralin	Tétraline	Tetra hydro naphthalene	$C_{10}H_{12}$
TNT; trotyl	TNT	TNT; tolite	2.4.6-trinitro toluene	$C_6H_2(NO_2)_3CH_3$
Urea	Harnstoff	Urée	Carbonic acid diamide	$CO(NH_2)_2$
Urotropine; hexamin	Urotropin	Urotropine	Hexamethylene tetramine	$(CH_2)_6N_4$
Water glass	Wasserglas	Verre soluble	Aqueous solution of sodium- (or potassium-) silicates	$M_2SiO_3 + M_2Si_2O_5$ ($M_2 = Na_2$ [or K_2])
Yellow prussiate of potash	Gelbes Blutlaugensalz	Ferrocyanure	Potassium hexacyanoferrate(II)	$K_2[Fe(C)_6]$

2) Numerical codes for freons (fluorine-chlorine derivatives of methane and ethane, CH_4 and C_2H_6):
number in hundreds column = number of carbon atoms - 1
number in tens column = number of hydrogen atoms + 1
number in ones column = number of fluorine atoms
the missing atoms for valence saturation are chlorine atoms.
Examples: freon 113 = $C_2F_3Cl_3$; freon 21 = $CHFCl_2$

3) numerical codes for halones (fully halogenated hydrocarbons):
number in thousends column = number of C atoms
number in hundreds column = number of F atoms
number in tens column = number of Cl atoms
number in ones column = number of Br atoms
Examples: halone 1211 = CF_2ClBr; halone 2402 = $C_2F_4Br_2$

Corrosion and corrosion protection

Corrosion is the attrition of metal beginning at the surface as a result of electrochemical reactions with components in the environment. Metal atoms are oxidized and form nonmetallic compounds. In thermodynamic terms, this process can be viewed as the transition from an ordered, high-energy state, into a state which is less ordered, of lower energy, and therefore more stable.

Corrosion processes are always interphase reactions. An example of this type of reaction is the scaling of metals, i. e. oxidation in hot gases. The following deals exclusively with corrosion which occurs at the phase limit between the metal and aqueous phases, generally referred to as electrochemical corrosion.

Corrosive attack

Two basically different reactions occur in every corrosive attack: In the anodic subprocess, the directly visible corrosive effect, the metal is oxidized as a result of the potential difference in accordance with the reaction equation

$$Me \rightarrow Me^{n+} + ne^-,$$

leaving behind an equivalent number of electrons. The metal ions thus formed can either be dissolved in the electrolyte, or can precipitate out on the metal after reacting with constituents of the attacking medium.

This anodic subprocess can continue only as long as the electrons formed by the process are consumed in a second process. This second subprocess is a cathodic partial reaction in which oxygen is reduced to hydroxyl ions in neutral or alkaline media in accordance with the reduction equation

$$O_2 + 2\,H_2O + 4\,e^- \rightarrow 4\,OH^-.$$

The hydroxyl ions, in turn, are able to react with the metal ions, whereas in acidic media the hydrogen ions are reduced via the formation of free hydrogen which escapes as a gas according to the following formula:

$$2\,H^+ + 2\,e^- \rightarrow H_2.$$

If two different metals wetted by the same fluid are in electrical contact with one another, the cathodic subprocess takes place at the more noble metal and the anodic subprocess takes place at the more base metal. This is called contact corrosion.

However, it is also possible for both reactions to occur on the same metal. In this case the process is termed "free corrosion". Anodic and cathodic subprocesses can alternate continuously at the metal/solution interface with statistically random time and location distributions of the individual subprocesses.

Each of the individual partial reactions corresponds to an anodic and cathodic partial current/voltage curve. The total current is the sum of the two currents I_a and I_c:

$$I_{total} = I_a + I_c.$$

The two partial current/voltage curves are added together to produce the cumulative current/voltage curve.

Free corrosion at the metal/corrosive liquid phase limit

In an aggressive fluid, oxygen is reduced at the corroding metal and corrosion products are simultaneously formed.

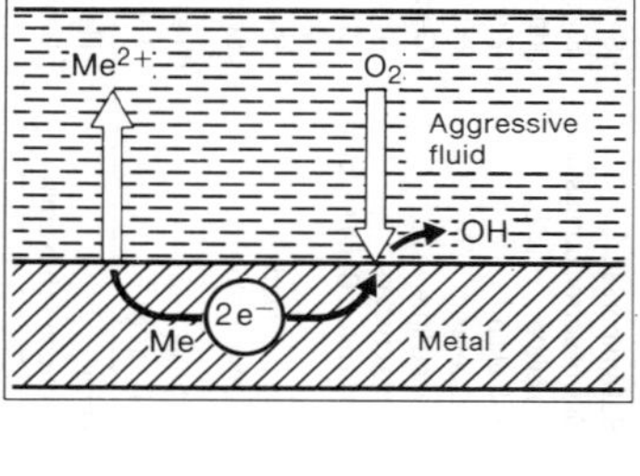

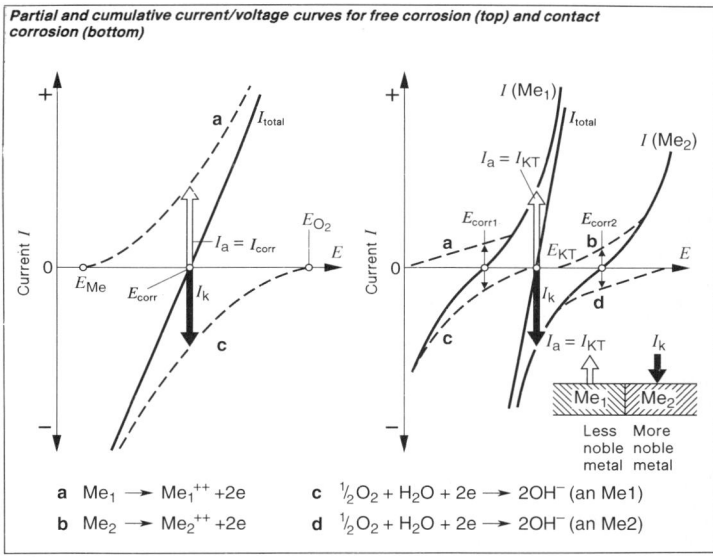

Partial and cumulative current/voltage curves for free corrosion (top) and contact corrosion (bottom)

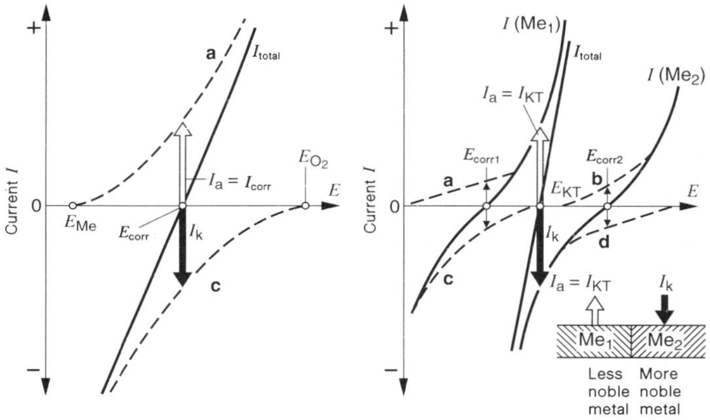

a $Me_1 \rightarrow Me_1^{++} + 2e$ **c** $\frac{1}{2}O_2 + H_2O + 2e \rightarrow 2OH^-$ (an Me1)

b $Me_2 \rightarrow Me_2^{++} + 2e$ **d** $\frac{1}{2}O_2 + H_2O + 2e \rightarrow 2OH^-$ (an Me2)

If no voltage is supplied externally, i.e. in the case of free corrosion, the system assumes that state in which the anodic and cathodic partial currents exactly compensate for one another.

$$I_a = -I_c = I_{corr}.$$

In this case, the anodic current is called the corrosion current I_{corr}. The corresponding potential at which this current compensation occurs is called the "open-circuit potential", E_{corr}. The open-circuit potential is a mixed potential in which there is no equilibrium, as matter is continuously being converted in accordance with the following general equation:

$$O_2 + 2H_2O + \frac{4}{n}Me \rightarrow \frac{4}{n}Me^{n+} + 4\,OH^-$$

The above also applies in general to contact corrosion, however, here the interrelationships are more complicated: In addition to pairs of partial current/voltage curves for each of the two metals and the resulting two cumulative current/voltage curves, the resultant total current/voltage curve for the entire system must be considered as a value which can be measured externally.

Electrochemical series of metals

Metals are often ranked in the "electrochemical series of metals" according to the increasing values of their "standard potentials". Here, the term "standard potential" indicates that the values given apply to standard conditions, especially to the activities (the electrochemically active part of the concentration) of the dissolved metal ions and hydrogen as given in a concentration of 1 mol/l at a hydrogen pressure of 1 bar at 25 °C. Such conditions are seldom found in practice; in fact, most solutions are practically free of ions of the metal in question.

It must be emphasized that the table on the preceding page gives purely thermodynamic values, and does not take into account the effect of corrosion kinetics due to the formation of protective films, for example. For instance, lead is shown as a base metal and as such should dissolve in sulphuric acid. Although the "practical" or "technical" electrochemical series of metals do not have this disadvantage, they are nevertheless only very limited in their practical applicability. On the other hand, electrochemical corrosion measurements provide conclusive results.

As a point of reference, the following relationships between potential and susceptibility to corrosion can be given for levels to which no external voltage is applied, provided that the behavior of the metals is not affected by secondary reactions such as complexing reactions or the formation of protective films:

Very base metals (potential below −0.4 V) e.g., Na, Mg, Be, Al, Ti and Fe, corrode in neutral aqueous solutions, even in the absence of oxygen.

Standard electrode potentials of the metals

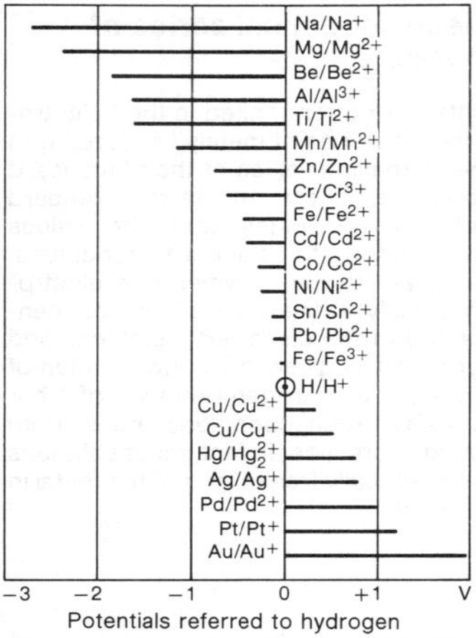

Base metals (potential between −0.5 and 0 V), e.g., Cd, Co, Ni, Sn and Pb, corrode in neutral aqueous solutions in the presence of oxygen, and corrode in acids giving off hydrogen even in the absence of oxygen.

Semi-noble metals (potential between 0 and +0.7 V), e.g., Cu, Hg and Ag, corrode in all solutions only if oxygen is present.

Noble metals (potentials above +0.7 V), e.g., Pd, Pt and Au, are generally stable.

If an external voltage is applied to the metals in question, they may behave quite differently than indicated above. This phenomenon is used to advantage in the field of electrochemical corrosion protection (see the section entitled "Electrochemical Corrosion Protection").

Types of corrosion

General corrosion

Uniform removal of material over the entire material/attacking medium interface. A very frequent type of corrosion in which the thickness of removed material can be calculated per unit of time on the basis of the corrosion current.

Pitting corrosion

Extremely localized attack by the corrosive medium which forms holes, or pits, in the material whose depth is almost always greater than their diameter. Practically no material is removed from the surface outside the pitted areas. Pitting corrosion is frequently caused by halogenide ions.

Crevice corrosion

Corrosive attack which primarily takes place in narrow crevices, and is caused by concentration differences in the corrosive medium, e.g., as a result of long oxygen diffusion paths. This type of corrosion causes potential differences to occur between the beginning and the end of the crevice, which in turn cause intensified corrosion in more poorly ventilated areas.

Stress corrosion cracking

Corrosion which occurs as a result of the simultaneous effect of a corrosive medium and mechanical tensile stress which can also take the form of internal stress in the workpiece. Intercrystalline or transcrystalline cracks form, in many cases without the appearance of visible corrosion products.

Vibration corrosion cracking

Corrosion caused by the simultaneous effect of a corrosive medium and mechanical fatigue stress, e.g., caused by vibrations. Transcrystalline cracks are formed, often without visible deformations.

Fretting corrosion

Corrosion caused by the simultaneous effect of a corrosive medium and mechanical friction; sometimes called frictional oxidation.

Intercrystalline and transcrystalline corrosion

Types of corrosion in which corrosion forms selectively along the grain boundaries or approximately parallel to the direction of deformation through the grain interior.

Dezincification

Selective removal of zinc from brass, leaving behind a porous copper structure. Denickelification and dealuminification are analogous processes.

Rust formation

The formation of ferriferous oxide and hydroxide corrosion products on iron and steel.

Corrosion testing

Electrochemical corrosion testing procedures (DIN 50918)

In electrochemical corrosion testing, the corrosion currents are determined in addition to the potential-dependence of the corroding materials during the corrosion reaction. These corrosion currents can be used to precisely calculate the loss of weight and thickness per unit of time in the case of uniform general corrosion. Table 2 gives the corresponding conversion factors.

Electrochemical processes are thus a valuable supplement to non-electrochemical methods.

In the case of free corrosion, the degree of corrosion is measured by the polarization resistance method, which is the slope of the current/voltage curve at the open-circuit potential, and which can be determined via small anodic and cathodic pulses which are imparted alternately to the metal.

In measuring contact corrosion, the current which flows between the two metals concerned is measured when both are immersed in the same corrosive medium.

The corrosion rates determined through electrochemical measurements are very close to those achieved in field tests. In addition to the short amount of time required for testing (1 day) and the small amount of corrosive medium required (several tenths of a litre), electrochemical procedures have the advantage over non-electrochemical procedures in that they provide quantitative corrosion rates.

Non-electrochemical corrosion testing procedures

In non-electrochemical test procedures, either the weight loss is measured by weighing or the degree of rust is determined. DIN 53210 defines 5 different degrees of rust indicated by rust-covered or rust-perforated surfaces (Table 3).

Table 1. Selected standardized non-electrochemical corrosion testing procedures

Standard	Type of corrosion testing procedure
DIN 50 016	Alternating climate with humid heat
DIN 50 017	Alternating climate with humid heat and condensate
DIN 50 018	Test in alternating climate with SO_2 atmosphere (Kesternich test)
DIN 50 113	Metallic materials test (rotating bending fatigue test)
DIN 50 142	Metallic materials test (flat bending fatigue test)
DIN 50 900	Definitions for corrosion testing
DIN 50 905	Corrosion of metals – Basics (research on chemical corrosion)
DIN 50 911	Testing of copper alloys (mercury nitrate test)
DIN 50 914	Testing intercrystalline corrosion in rust-resistant steels (copper sulfate – sulphuric acid test; Strauss test)
DIN 50 915	Testing intercrystalline stress corrosion in non-alloy and low-alloy steels
DIN 50 917	Testing under natural conditions (outside exposure) Testing under natural conditions (sea water)
DIN 50 919	Testing contact corrosion in electrolyte solutions
DIN 50 920	Testing corrosion in flowing liquids
DIN 50 922	Testing resistance of metallic materials against stress corrosion cracking
DIN 50 928	Testing and evaluating protection of coated metallic materials against aqueous corrosives
DIN 51 213	Testing metallic wire coatings (tin, zinc)
ASTM B 380	Methods for corrosion testing of chrome-plated motor-vehicle parts by the Corrodcote procedure
ASTM B 117	Salt spray (fog) testing
ASTM G 48–76	Ferric-chloride test for pitting and crevice corrosion on stainless steels and related alloys

Table 2. Loss of mass and thickness due to general corrosion of various metals with a corrosion current density of 1 μA/cm².

Metal	Atomic weight	Density g/cm³	Loss of mass mg/(cm²· year)	Loss of thickness μm/year
Fe	55.9	7.87	9.13	11.6
Cu	63.5	8.93	10.4	11.6
Cd	112.4	8.64	18.4	21.0
Ni	58.7	8.90	9.59	10.8
Zn	65.4	7.14	10.7	15.0
Al	26.9	2.70	2.94	10.9
Sn	118.7	7.28	19.4	26.6
Pb	207.2	11.3	33.9	30.0

Table 3. Conversion between DIN rust-degree scale and European rust-degree scale.

Rust degree as per DIN 53 210	Rust degree as per European rust-degree scale
R_i0	R_e0
R_i1	R_e1
R_i2	R_e2
R_i3	R_e3
–	R_e4
R_i4	R_e5
–	R_e6
R_i5	R_e7
–	R_e8
–	R_e9

The corresponding corrosion tests have been established based on requirements in practice. In addition to DIN or ASTM standardized corrosion-testing procedures (Table 1, p. 246), testing procedures have become established in practice which are specially adapted to specific requirements, e.g., motor-vehicle testing (outdoor weathering under driving conditions, splash-water tests of air-fuel mixture systems), and which provide reliable indications of service life in actual operation as a result of exposure to harsher conditions over a shorter period of time.

Corrosion protection

Electrochemical processes

The schematic current/voltage curves of a metal which can be passivated show how these processes work. The current-density values arranged in ascending order on the y-axis represent anodic currents which correspond to a corrosion reaction according to the equation

$$Me \rightarrow Me^{+} + ne^{-}.$$

The current-density values entered in descending order, on the other hand, represent cathodic currents for which the reaction equation is to be read from right to left. From the schematic it can be seen how the application of an external voltage can suppress corrosion. There are two principal ways of doing this:

In cathodic protection the potential is shifted so far toward the left that no anodic currents flow, i.e. it becomes $U < U_a$. In addition to the application of an external voltage, this potential shift can also be brought about by introducing a base metal, which then becomes a reactive anode.

The potential of the electrode to be protected, however, can also be shifted into the passive range, i.e. into the potential range between U_p and U_d.

This is called anodic protection. The anodic currents which flow in the passive range are 3 to 6 orders of magnitude below the currents which flow in the active range, depending upon the type of metal and the corrosive medium, thereby achieving a high degree of protection. However, the potential must not be greater than U_d, otherwise oxygen would be produced

Schematic current/voltage curve of a metal which can be passivated
U_a Free corrosion potential of the metal in an active state,
U_p Passivating potential,
U_d Breakthrough potential.

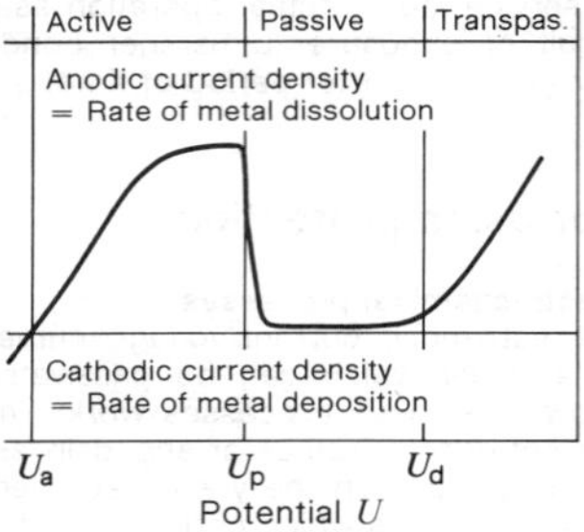

in this transpassive range, and under certain circumstances additional metal would be oxidized. Both of these effects would cause the current to increase.

The shape of the current/voltage curve can also be influenced by the addition of inhibitors. Inhibitors are substances which are added in low concentrations (up to a maximum of several hundred ppm) to the attacking medium, and are absorbed chemically at the surface of the metal to be protected, thereby drastically reducing the rate of corrosion by blocking either the anodic or the cathodic subprocess (frequently blocking both subprocesses simultaneously). Organic amines and amides of organic acids are most often used as inhibitors. In the motor vehicle, for example, inhibitors are constituents of fuel additives; they are also added to antifreeze in order to inhibit corrosion damage in the coolant circuit.

Coatings

Coatings inhibit corrosion by forming protective films which are applied directly to the metal to be protected, where they resist attack by corrosive media. These protective coatings must not be porous, must not conduct, and must be of sufficient thickness. Their use is therefore frequently problematic in systems which require close dimensional tolerances.

Inorganic nonmetallic coatings
Protective coatings can be formed interactively with the material to be protected. The formation of stable oxide covering layers can be improved in the case of many metals, for example, if they are alloyed with small amounts of foreign metals, such as silicon with cast iron, or molybdenum with chrome-nickel steels. Covering layers can also form in the presence of phosphates, chromates or silicates. Use of these substances is frequently made, for example, in the motor vehicle industry for chassis ("phosphatizing") and in cooling systems.

Diffusion process
Surface treatment can be selectively combined with surface hardening by using the diffusion process to thermochemically carburize, carbonitride or chromize the metal, or treat it with boron or vanadium. The metal can also be oxidized, nitrided or sulphided without hardening.

Browning
Browning is used to produce covering layers which offer a certain degree of protection over a short period of time. A ferrous material is browned by dipping it in hot concentrated sodium hydroxide containing $NaNO_2$.

Anodizing
The anodizing process pertains only to aluminum. This anodic oxidation process in electrolytes which contain sulphuric, chromic, or oxidic acids usually produces very resistant covering layers, which in turn can be further stabilized and given different colors by chromizing. Cadmium and magnesium surfaces can also be chromized.

Enameling
Enameling provides a high degree of corrosion protection, particularly when applied to unalloyed steel. On the other hand, however, enamel coatings are brittle and therefore particularly sus-

ceptible to impact loads and thermal shocks. In addition, they always exhibit internal compressive stresses, because tensile stresses (e.g., when the yielding point of the carrier material is exceeded) lead to cracks in the enamel due to insufficient toughness. To improve enamel bond during manufacturing, an intermediate layer consisting of a base material is first fused to the metal; this intermediate layer is then covered with the actual silica-based protective coating.

Glass ceramics
The newly developed glass ceramics do not display the disadvantages of enamel under mechanical or thermal loading. They are applied to the material in the form of a semicrystalline coating through controlled crystallization of thermodynamically unstable glasses. Subsequent heat treatment establishes roughly 50 % crystallinity.

Metallic coatings
There are many different ways of applying foreign metals or metal compounds to the base material. In many cases, corrosion protection is combined with protection against wear or with the formation of decorative surfaces. The standard procedure, suitable metals and their ranges of application are compiled in Table 4.

It should be noted that not every metal is suitable for every type of protection (e.g., molten aluminum which is thermally sprayed onto the base material provides no protection against wear).

Electroplating
In electrolytic plating, metals suspended in ionized metallic-salt solutions are deposited on conductive bases in a cathodic reaction. Appropriate conditions make it possible to produce alloys and dispersion coatings (layers of finely dispersed additives) of a type not amenable to duplication in fusion processes. Most metals are deposited from aqueous solutions. In contrast, aluminum — an extremely base metal — can only be applied from suspension in water-free organic solutions or molten salt.

Table 4. Uses of inorganic protective coatings

Method of application	Type of metal	Primarily used for
Chemical deposition	Ni (NiB, NiP, NiPCu), Cu, dispersion coatings (NiB + SiC, NiP + SiC).	Corrosion protection, protection against wear, decorative surfaces
Evaporation	Al, Au, Ta	Corrosion protection
Electroplating (external power source)	Ag, Al, Au, Cd, Cr, Ni, Sn, Zn, ZnNi, ZnNiP	Corrosion protection, decorative surfaces
Cladding	Al, Cu, Ni, Pb, Ti, Zr and their alloys, stainless steels	Corrosion protection
Hot dipping (including "hot-dip galvanizing")	Al, Pb, Sn, Zn.	Corrosion protection
Thermal spraying	Al and alloys, Cr, Ni, NiCr, NiCrBSi, Ti, borides, carbides, oxides	Corrosion protection, protection against wear

Chemical deposition
In principle this process is the same as the electroplating process, however, the electrons required for reduction do not come from an external power source, but rather from an added reducing agent, usually sodium hypophosphite or sodium boranate. For this reason, the elements phosphorus and boron are present in most nickel coatings.

Hot dipping
The most common hot-dipping process is the hot-dip galvanizing of iron and steel; this process is also the one most frequently used in the automobile industry. In this process, the material to be dipped is pretreated (pickled and wetted with flux), and dipped in the molten coating metal such that alloying layers are produced at the phase limit in accordance with solubility conditions of the phase diagrams; these alloying layers promote the bonding of the covering metal to the base material. In this manner, much thicker layers can be achieved than are possible using the electroplating process.

Evaporation
Due to its high cost, the evaporation process is only used for special applications, particularly for applying thin coatings to small-area objects. In many cases, thin evaporated coatings must in turn be protected by an inorganic or organic coating (example: headlamp reflectors). The coating material is heated by an electric current and evaporated in a high vacuum.

Thermal spraying
In thermal spraying, the coating material (which is usually in powdered form) is melted by a plasma ("plasma spraying") or an arc as it leaves the spray gun. A certain amount of inhomogeneity and porosity in the coating are characteristic of the process, and require that thick coating layers be applied (150 to 200 µm) in order to achieve good corrosion protection.

Cladding
Cladding is the joining of two or more metal layers at high temperature and/or under high pressure. Separation of the metal layers is not possible under normal stress. Cladding processes include roll cladding, explosion cladding and mechanical cladding. The cladding metal and the base material interlock mechanically, or by means of diffusion processes combined with the formation of alloys. Cladding materials are several millimeters thick.

Organic coatings
Thermoplastics, elastomers and duromers are the primary types of organic protective coatings. They are also used in the automobile industry in the form of paints, whirl-sintered compounds, interior coatings, fiber-reinforced resins and fillers. How well these coatings protect the underlying material depends not only on the type of plastic, but also on the binder, anti-aging agent, UV stabilizers and the type of filler and pigment used. Organic coatings can either be used by themselves or in conjunction with one of the inorganic coatings mentioned above.

Painting
According to requirements, paints can be applied by conventional brushing, by rollers, as compressed-air or high-pressure sprays, by dipping (also making use of electrophoresis) and by electrostatic spray painting. An adhesion-promoting primer coat is applied to the pretreated metal surface, and the actual protective coating is applied on top of the primer. A closed film forms by solvent evaporation or absorption of oxygen.

Powder coating
Powdered plastics, which at room temperature are very difficult to transform into a liquid phase, can be applied by the powder coating process. The powder can either be fused onto the preheated parts, flame-sprayed or electrostatically sprayed. If necessary, the coatings can be made homogeneous and impervious by heat treatment. Powder coating pro-

cesses are usually more economical and environmentally less hazardous than painting processes, and require less stringent safety measures.

Internal rubber and plastic coating
Rubber coatings and plastic coatings are frequently used to protect the insides of transport and storage tanks, vessels and pipes. Natural and synthetic-rubber cross-linked films as well as pretreated thermoplastic films in conjunction with cross-linking adhesives are used; final cross-linking takes place either catalytically or by applying heat after the coatings have been applied to the bare carrier materials.

Plasma polymerisation
Plasma polymerisation provides new ways of coating materials. In this process, organic monomers are polymerized on the material to be coated under the influence of a gas-discharge plasma. All metals can be coated with a polymer film produced in this manner. The result is a bubble-free, organic film which does not contain the customary volatile components that are frequently found in solid polymers.

Other types of corrosion protection

It is often possible to reduce the rate of corrosion of a part by using a design which is inherently less susceptible to corrosion. Gaps and restrictions should therefore be avoided, and designs with smooth surfaces should be used wherever possible. In the design of systems which may contain two liquid phases (e.g., gasoline/water), of which only one (water) is corrosive, care should be taken to ensure that critical metal parts are not wetted by the corrosive phase during non-operative periods. This can be accomplished by using only one metal in each area which is exposed to the environment. If this is not possible for design reasons, the two metals should be electrically isolated from one another. In terms of corrosion protection, it is better to apply a coating to the more noble of the two metals.

Vapor-phase inhibitors

Vapor-phase inhibitors provide temporary protection during storage and transport of metallic products.

Vapor-phase inhibitors (VPI), or volatile corrosion inhibitors (VCI) as they are commonly known, are organic substances of moderate vapor pressure. The are frequently found in special packing materials or in liquid or oily solutions. The inhibitors evaporate or sublimate over the course of time, and are adsorbed in monomolecular configuration on the metal, where they inhibit either anodic or cathodic corrosion reactions, or both at once (typical example: dicyclohexylamin nitrite).

In order for these inhibitors to be effective, the substance must have the largest possible surface and the coating should be sealed. This is why they are also used in packing materials such as special paper or polyethylene foil. An air-tight edge seal is not required; the packing can be opened briefly for inspection of contents. The duration of the packing's effectiveness depends on the tightness of the seal and the temperature (normally approx. 2 years, but less at temperatures well above normal room temperature).

Standard commercial vapor-phase inhibitors are generally a combination of numerous components capable of providing simultaneous protection for several metals or alloys, exceptions being cadmium, lead, tungsten and magnesium.

Heat treatment of metallic materials

Heat treatment is employed to endow metallic tools and components with the specific qualities required either for subsequent manufacturing processes or for actual operation. The heat-treating process includes one or several time and temperature cycles. First, the parts to be treated are heated to the required temperature, where they are maintained for a specific period before being cooled back down to room temperature (or below in some processes) at a rate calculated to achieve the desired results.

The process modifies the microstructure to achieve the hardness, strength, ductility, wear resistance, etc., required to withstand the stresses associated with static and dynamic loads. The most significant industrial processes are summarized in Table 1 (see DIN 17 014, Part 1, for terminology).

Hardening

Hardening procedures produce a martensitic microstructure of extreme hardness and strength in ferrous materials such as steel and cast iron.

The parts being treated are heated to the austenitizing, or hardening temperature, at which they are maintained until an austenitic structure emerges, and until an adequate quantity of carbon (released in the decay of carbides, such as graphite in cast iron) is dissolved in the treated material. The material is then quenched or otherwise cooled back to room temperature as quickly as possible in order to obtain a maximum degree of conversion to a martensitic microstructure (the time-temperature transformation chart for the specific steel in question contains the reference figures for the necessary cooling rate).

Table 2. Standard austenitizing temperatures

Type of steel	Quality specification DIN	Austenitizing temperature °C
Unalloyed and low-alloyed steels < 0.8% by mass of C	17 200 17 211 17 212	780 ... 950
≥ 0.8% by mass of C	–	780 ... 820
Cold and hot-working tool steels	17 350	950 ... 1100
High-speed steels		1150 ... 1230
Cast iron	–	850 ... 900

The austenitizing temperature varies according to the composition of the material in question (for specific data, consult the DIN Technical Requirements for Steels). Table 2 above furnishes reference data. See DIN 17 022, Parts 1 and 2, for practical information on hardening procedures for tools and components.

Table 1. Summary of heat-treatment processes

Hardening	Austempering	Tempering	Annealing	Thermo-chemical treatment	Precipitation hardening
Through hardening Surface hardening Hardening of carburized parts (case-hardening)	Isothermic transformation to bainite	Tempering of hardened materials Hardening and tempering above 550 °C	Stress-relief Spheroidizing of cementite Recrystallization annealing Normalizing Homogenizing	Nitrogen case hardening Nitrogen carburizing Carburizing Carbonitriding Boron treatment Chromizing	Solution treatment and aging

Not all types of steel and cast iron are suitable for hardening. The following equation describes the hardening potential for alloyed and unalloyed steels with mass carbon contents of between 0.15 ... 0.60 %, and can be applied to estimate the hardness levels achievable with a completely martensitic microstructure:

Max. hardness = 35 + 50 · (%C) $\pm$ 2 HRC

If the microstructure does not consist entirely of martensite, then the maximum hardness will not be reached.

When the carbon content exceeds 0.6 % by mass, it may be assumed that the material's structure contains untransformed austenite (residual austenite) in addition to the martensite. This condition prevents the maximum hardness from being achieved, and the wear resistance will be lower. In addition, residual austenite is metastable, i.e., there exists a potential for subsequent transformation to martensite at temperatures below room temperature or under stress, with changes in specific volume and internal stress as the possible results. Low-temperature follow-up procedures or tempering operations at over 230 °C can be useful in cases where residual austenite is an unavoidable product of the hardening procedure.

The surface and core hardnesses remain virtually identical with material thicknesses of up to approx. 10 mm. Beyond this point the core hardness is lower; there is a hardness progression or gradient. The rate of the progression depends upon the hardening response (testing described in DIN 50 191), which is a function of the material's composition (Mo, Mn, Cr). This factor requires particular attention with parts which do not cool well (thick parts and/or slow or graduated cooling processes designed to minimize the risk of cracks and/or distortion).

DIN 50 150 defines the method for using hardness as the basis for estimating tensile strength R_m; this method can only be applied in cases where the surface and core hardnesses are virtually identical:

$R_m \approx$ (34 ... 37.7) · Rockwell C hardness number in N/mm², or

$R_m \approx$ (3.2..3.35) · Vickers hardness number in N/mm².

The specific volume of the martensitic microstructure is approximately 1 % greater than that of the original material. In addition, stresses result from the rearrangement of the microstructure and from contraction during cooling. As the latter phenomenon does not take place at a uniform rate in all sections of the part, it produces variations in shape and dimensions; tensile stresses near the surface and pressure tension at the core are the common result.

Surface hardening

The process is especially suited for integration within large-scale manufacturing operations, and can be adapted to fit the rhythm of the production-line.

Heating and hardening are restricted to the surface, thereby minimizing alterations in shape and dimensions. Heating is generally provided by high or medium-frequency alternating current (inductive hardening) or by a gas burner (flame hardening). Friction (friction hardening) and high-energy beams (e.g., electron or laser beams) can also provide the heat required for austenitizing. Table 3 provides a summary of the specific heat energies for the individual procedures.

These methods can be used to treat both linear and flat surfaces, meaning that the parts can be heated either while stationary or in motion. The heat

Table 3. Comparison of the power density when heating with different sources, and the effective depth in the case of inductive heating (heating time 1 ... 100 ms)

Heat source	Power density
Laser beam	10 ... 10^8 MW/cm²
Induction heating	≈ 15 kW/cm²
Plasma beam	≈ 10 kW/cm²
Flame heating	≈ 1.0 kW/cm²
Convection in molten salt	≈ 20 W/cm²
Convection with air or inert gas	≈ 0.5 W/cm²
Frequency range	**Effective depth**
HF pulse approx. 27 MHz	0.05 ... 0.5 mm
HF pulse 400 ... 2500 kHz	1.0 ... 0.4 mm
MF pulse 3 ... 10 kHz	8.0 ... 5.0 mm

source itself can also be moved. Rotation is the best way of dealing with radially symmetrical parts, as it ensures concentric hardening. Either immersion or spraying arrangements can be applied for quenching.

The temperatures must be 50 ... 100 °C above those used in oven heating to provide the extremely rapid warming which is required. The procedure is generally employed with low-alloy or unalloyed steels with mass carbon contents of 0.35 ... 0.60% (consult DIN 17 212 for list of suitable steels). However, surface-hardening processes can also be applied with alloyed steels, cast iron and rolling-bearing steels. The parts can be heat-treated to provide a combination of improved base strength and high surface = hardness, making them suitable for high-stress applications (recessed edges, bearing surfaces, cross-sectional transitions).

Surface hardening generally results in internal compression stresses along the edge. In particular with fluctuating vibrating stresses this leads to increased fatigue resistance, especially on notched parts. (Refer to the illustration.)

The relationship defined above can be employed to estimate the potential surface hardness. There is a substantial reduction in hardness between the surface and the unhardened core region. The hardening depth *Rht* – the depth at which 80 % of the Vickers hardness at the surface is found – can be derived from the hardness progression curve (see DIN 50 190, Part 2).

Austempering

The object of this process is to achieve a bainite microstructure. This microstructure is not as hard as martensite, but does display greater ductility as well as smaller changes in specific volume.

After austenitizing (see hardening), the parts for austempering are first cooled to a temperature of 200 ... 350 °C (depending upon the exact composition of the material) at the required rate. The parts are then held at this temperature until the microstructure's transformation into bainite has been completed. The parts can then be cooled to room temperature (no special procedure required).

Cyclically alternating stress according to surface-layer hardening
+ σ Tensile stress, – σ Compression; 1 Case layer, 2 Bending stress, 3 Reduction of tensile stress, 4 Resulting tension, 5 Intrinsic stress, 6 Increase in compression stress.

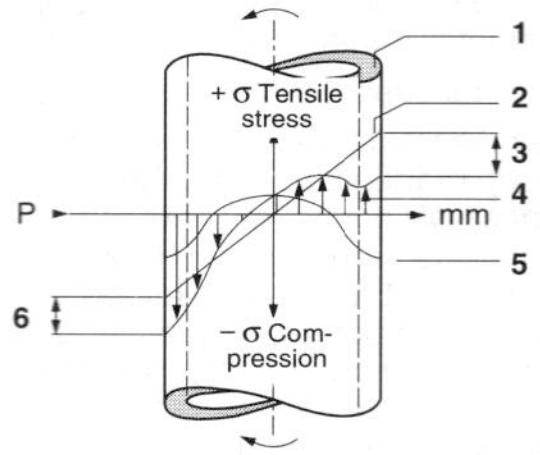

Austempering is an excellent alternative for parts whose sensitive geometrical configuration makes them sensitive to distortion and/or cracks, or in which high ductility is required together with high hardness.

Draw tempering

Parts emerge from the hardening process in a brittle state; they must be tempered to increase their ductility in order to reduce the risk of damage associated with excessive internal tension, such as delayed cracking after hardening or splintering during grinding. This tempering process is based on the elimination of carbides, a phenomenon accompanied by an increase in ductility, albeit at the price of reductions in hardness.

The parts are heated in the draw to a temperature of between 180 ... 650 °C; they are then held there for at least one hour before being allowed to cool to room temperature. Depending upon the specific composition of the material, tempering at temperatures in excess of 230 °C may result in any residual austenite being transformed into bainite and/or martensite.

Tempering at temperatures as low as 180 °C is enough to reduce the hardness of unalloyed and low-alloy steels by approx. 1 ... 5 HRC. The individual materials respond to higher temperatures with specific characteristic hardness loss. The graph at the right shows a characteristic tempering curve for typical types of steel. The graph illustrates the fact that the hardness of high-alloy steels remains constant until the temperature exceeds 550 °C.

The mutual relationships between tempering temperature on the one side, and hardness, strength, yield point, fracture contraction and ductility on the other, can be taken from the tempering diagrams for the various steels (see DIN 17 200).

Tempering of hardened parts is accompanied by a reduction in specific volume. In some cases, tempering can also induce changes in the progressive variation in internal tension at different depths in the parts.

It must be remembered that steels alloyed with manganese, chromium, manganese and chromium, chrome-vanadium, and chromium and nickel should not be tempered at temperatures of 350 ... 500 °C, as brittleness could result. When these types of materials are cooled from higher tempering temperatures, the transition through this critical range should also be effected as rapidly as possible (see DIN 17 022, Parts 1 and 2 for additional information).

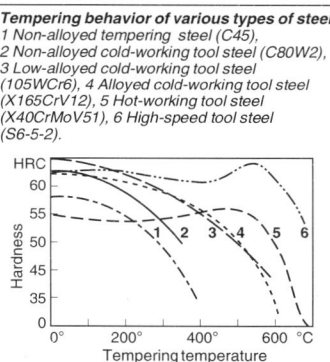

Tempering behavior of various types of steel
1 Non-alloyed tempering steel (C45), 2 Non-alloyed cold-working tool steel (C80W2), 3 Low-alloyed cold-working tool steel (105WCr6), 4 Alloyed cold-working tool steel (X165CrV12), 5 Hot-working tool steel (X40CrMoV51), 6 High-speed tool steel (S6-5-2).

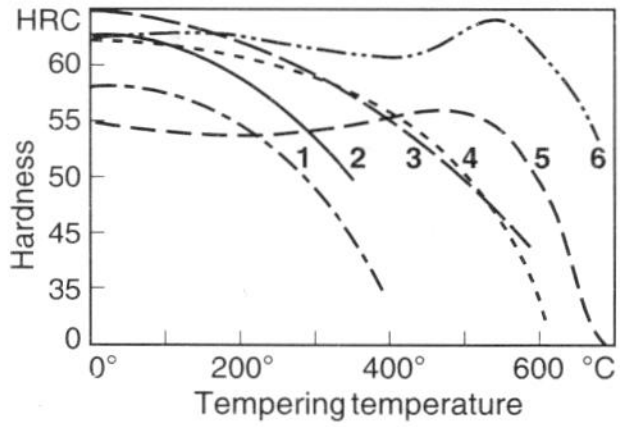

Quench and draw

This type of quench and draw process combines hardening and tempering at temperatures above 500 °C. This procedure is designed to achieve an optimal relationship between strength and ductility. It is applied in cases where extreme ductility or malleability are required.

Particular care must be devoted to avoiding brittleness in the quench and draw operation.

Thermochemical treatment

In thermochemical treatment, the parts are soaked in agents which emit specific elements. When these elements diffuse into the surface layer of the parts being treated, they modify the structure to produce specific properties. Of particular importance for this process are the elements carbon, nitrogen and boron.

Carburizing, carbonitriding, case hardening

Carburizing increases the carbon content in the surface layer, while carbonitriding supplements the carbon enrichment with nitrogen. This process is generally carried out in salt baths, granulate, or gas atmospheres at temperatures ranging from 850 ... 1000 °C. The actual hardening is performed subsequently, either by quenching directly from the carburizing/carbonitriding temperature (direct hardening), or by allowing the parts to cool to room temperature (single hardening), or by allowing them to cool to a suitable intermediate temperature prior to reheating (hardening after isothermic conversion, e.g., at 620 °C) to the hardening temperature. This process produces a martensitic surface layer, while the degree of martensite at the core is a function of hardening temperature, hardenability and part thickness.

Specific temperatures can be selected for either surface hardening in the upper layers with higher carbon content (case refining), or for the non-carburized core (core refining) (see DIN 17 022, Part 3).

Carburizing and carbonitriding produce a characteristic carbon declivity, with levels dropping as the distance from the surface increases (carbon curve). The distance between the surface and the point at which the mass carbon content is still 0.35 % is normally defined as the carburization depth At.

The length of the carburizing or carbonitriding process depends upon the required carburization depth, the temperature and the atmosphere's carbon-diffusion properties. A reasonable approximation is possible:

$$At = K \cdot \sqrt{t} - D/\beta \text{ in mm}$$

Depending upon temperature and carbon levels, K lies between 0.3 ... 0.6 during carburizing in, e.g., a gas atmosphere; the correction factor D/β generally is 0.1 ... 0.3 mm; the time t in h must be inserted.

Generally, the objective is to achieve a carbon gradient with a concentration of at least 0.60 % mass carbon content, the ultimate goal being a surface hardness of 750 HV (corresponding to 65 HRC). Higher concentrations of carbon can lead to residual austenite and/or carbide diffusion, which could have negative effects on the part's performance in actual use. Control of the atmosphere's carbon level, and thus the part's ultimate carbon content, is thus extremely important.

The gradient defining the relationship between hardness and depth corresponds to the slope for carbon concentration. The hardness gradient is used to define the case depth Eht. DIN 50 190, Part 1 defines this as the maximum distance from the surface before the hardness drops below 550 HV.

The case-hardened part generally exhibits compression tension at the surface, and tensile stresses at the core. As with surface-hardened materials, this distribution pattern provides enhanced resistance to vibration loads.

In carbonitriding, nitrogen is also absorbed; it serves to improve the material's tempering properties, increase its durability and enhance its wear resistance. The positive effects are especially pronounced with non-alloyed steels. For additional, more detailed information on case-hardening procedures consult DIN 17 022, Part 3, and Information Sheet 452 of the Steel Information Center, Düsseldorf.

Nitriding and nitrocarburizing

Nitriding is a thermal treatment process (temperature range: 500 ... 600 °C) which can be used to enrich the surface layer of virtually any ferrous material with nitrogen. In nitrocarburizing, a certain amount of carbon is diffused into the material at the same time.

The nitrogen enrichment is accompanied by precipitation hardening. This strengthens the surface layer, enhancing the material's resistance to wear, corrosion and alternating cyclic stress.

Because the process employs relatively low temperatures, there are no volumetric changes of the kind associated with transformations in the microstructure; changes in dimensions and shape are minute.

The nitrided region consists of an outer layer, several millimeters in depth, and a transitional white layer, the hardness of which may be anywhere from 700 to over 1200 HV, depending upon the composition of the material. Still deeper is a softer diffusion layer extending several tenths of a millimeter. The thickness of the individual layers is determined by the temperature and duration of the treatment process. The process produces a hardness gradient (similar to that which results from surface and case-hardening); this gradient furnishes the basis for determining the nitriding depth Nht. DIN 50 190, Part 3 defines this as the depth from the surface at which the hardness is still 50 HV above the core hardness.

The material's resistance to wear and corrosion is essentially determined by the white layer, which contains up to 10 mass components of nitrogen in %. The nitriding depth and the surface hardness determine the material's resistance to alternating cyclic stress (for additional details, see Information Sheet 447 from the Steel Information Center, Düsseldorf).

Boron treatment

This is a thermochemical treatment method which employs boron to enrich the surface layer of ferrous materials. Depending upon duration and temperature (normally 850 ... 1000 °C), an iron-boron white layer of 30 µm ... 0.2 mm in depth and with a hardness of 2000 ... 2500 HV is produced.

Boron treatment is particularly effective as a means of protecting against abrasive wear. However, the comparitively high process temperature leads to relatively large changes in shape and dimension, meaning that this treatment is only suitable for applications in which large tolerances can be accepted.

Annealing

Annealing can be applied to optimize parts both for subsequent manufacturing processes or for actual operation. With this method, the parts are heated to the required temperature and maintained there for an adequate period before being cooled to room temperature. Table 1 lists the various processes used in specific individual applications.

Stress-relief

Depending upon the precise composition of the parts, this operation is carried out at temperatures ranging from 450 ... 650 °C. The object is to achieve the maximum possible reduction in internal stress in components, tools and castings by inducing physical deformation.

After an oven time of 0.5 ... 1 h, the parts are cooled back to room temperature; this cooling should be as gradual as possible to prevent new stresses from forming.

Recrystallization annealing

Recrystallization annealing is applied with parts that have been formed using non-cutting procedures. The goal is to restructure the grain pattern in order to prevent increased hardening, thereby facilitating subsequent machining work.

The temperature requirement depends upon the composition of the material and the degree of deformation: it lies between 550 ... 730 °C for steel.

Soft annealing

Soft annealing is intended to facilitate the machining and/or shaping of workpieces which have become hard due to cold-forming, age, or other heat treatment.

The temperature requirement is determined by the material's composition. It is in a range of 650 ... 720 °C for steel, and lower for non-ferrous materials.

Spheroidizing of cementite is applied when a microstructure with a granular carbide pattern is desired. If the initial structure is martensite or bainite, the result will be an especially homogeneous carbide distribution.

Normalizing

Normalizing is carried out by heating the parts to austenitizing temperature and then allowing them to gradually cool to room temperature. In low-alloy and non-alloyed steels, the result is a structure consisting of ferrite and perlite. This process is essentially employed to reduce grain size, reduce the formation of coarse grain patterns in parts with limited reshaping, and to provide maximum homogeneity in the distribution of ferrite and perlite.

Precipitation hardening treatment

This process combines solution treatment with aging at ambient temperature. The parts are heated and then maintained at temperature to bring precipitated structural constituents into a solid solution, and quenched at room temperature to form a supersaturated solution. The aging process comprises one or several cycles in which the material is heated and held at above-ambient temperatures (hot aging). In this process, one or several phases, i.e., metallic bonds between certain base alloys, are formed and precipitated in the matrix.

The precipitated particles enhance the hardness and strength of the base microstructure. The actual characteristics are determined by the temperature and duration of the aging process (option of mutual substitution); exceeding a certain maximum will usually reduce the strength and hardness of the final product.

Precipitation hardening is mostly applied for non-ferrous alloys, but some steels (maraging steels) can also be hardened.

Hardness

Hardness tests

Hardness is a property of solid materials and is defined as the material's resistance to deformation. In metallic materials the hardness is also used to assess mechanical properties such as strength, machinability, plasticity, or wear resistance. In accordance with DIN 50 150, measured hardness can be converted to tensile strength. Measurement is almost entirely non-destructive.

In order to obtain a characteristic value, the indentation created by deformation with a defined test indenter under a defined load is measured.

A distinction is made between static and dynamic testing. In static testing, the permanent impression left by the indenter is measured. Standard or widely-used hardness tests are the Rockwell, Vickers and Brinell test methods. In dynamic testing, the rebound of an indenter from the flat surface of the test specimen is measured.

A further possibility is deformation by scratching with a hard indenter and measurement of the score width as the basis for calculating hardness. The table (right) shows a comparison between the areas of application of the Rockwell, Vickers and Brinell hardness tests.

Rockwell hardness (DIN 50 103)

This method is particularly well suited to large-scale testing of metallic workpieces. The steel or diamond indenter is positioned vertically on the surface of the workpiece to be tested and a specified minor load is applied. A specified major load is then applied for at least 30 s. The major load is then removed and the depth of permanent penetration e in mm gives the Rockwell hardness value (see Table 1).

The test surface should be smooth (depending on hardness range, $R_{max} \leq 1.2 \ldots 3.4\ \mu m$) and as flat as possible. If the radius of curvature of the specimen is less than 20 mm the measurement value must be corrected dependent on the hardness.

The applicability of the test methods shown in Table 1 depends on the thickness of the specimen, or of the "hard" surface layer (cf. fig. 3 in DIN 50 103). The abbreviation of the method used must be given in the hardness notation after the numerical value, e.g., 65 HRC, 76 HR 45 N etc. Measurement inaccuracy in the Rockwell C test method is approx. ± 1 HRC.

An advantage of the Rockwell test method is shown to be that preparation of the specimen consumes little time and the measurement can be carried out quickly and fully automatically.

Table 1. Rockwell test methods

Abbreviation	Indenter	Minor load N	Total test load N	Hardness number (e indenter penetration depth)	
HRC	Diamond pyramid	98 ± 2	1471 ± 9	$100 - e / 0.002$	20 ... 70
HRA			588 ± 5		60 ... 881
HRB	Steel ball		980 ± 6.5	$130 - e / 0.002$	35 ... 100
HRF			588 ± 5		60 ... 100
HR15N HR30N HR45N	Diamond pyramid	29.4 ± 0.6	147 ± 1 294 ± 2 441 ± 3	$100 - e / 0.001$	66 ... 92 39 ... 84 17 ... 75
HR15T HR30T HR45T	Steel ball	3 ± 0.06	15 ± 0.1 30 ± 0.2 45 ± 0.3		50 ... 94 10 ... 84 0 ... 75

Bumping of the test machine, shifting of the specimen and the indenter during the test, positioning of the specimen on an uneven surface or damage to the diamond indenter may lead to erroneous measurements.

Brinell hardness (DIN 50 351)

The method is used for metallic materials of low to medium hardness. A hard metal or hardened steel ball is used to test the specimen. It is applied to the surface of the test specimen with varying load F for at least 15 s[1]). The diameter d of the impression remaining after the ball is removed is measured with a hand microscope and used as the basis for calculation of Brinell hardness, which can be read from tables or calculated as follows:

$$\text{Brinell hardness} = \frac{0.204 \cdot F}{\pi \cdot D \cdot (D - \sqrt{D^2 - d^2})} \text{ HB}$$

F Load in N
D Ball diameter in mm
d Diameter of impression in mm

The applied loads cover a range of 9.81 to 29,420 N. The results obtained by using balls of different diameters can only be compared with each other if they were

[1]) at least 30 s for lead, zinc etc.

Comparison of the hardness ranges covered by the various test methods
The numbers at the upper and lower limits of each range are hardness values for the corresponding method. HB test methods with the following load-diameter ratios: 30(1); 10(2); 5(3); 2.5(3); und 1(4).

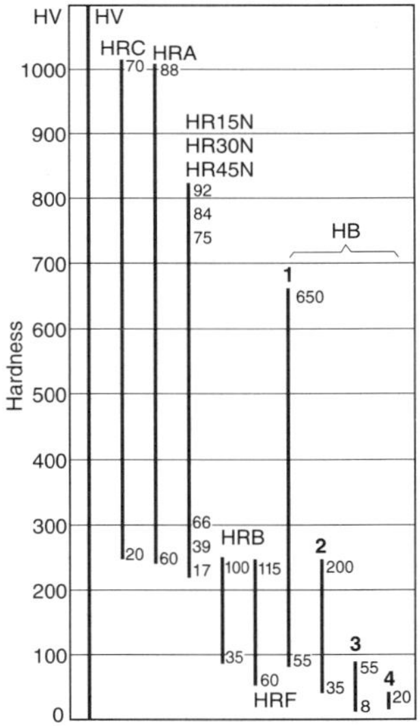

Table 2. Application of the Brinell hardness test

Ball diameter D	Applied load F N for load-diameter ratio				
mm	30	10	5	2.5	1
10	29 420	9807	4903	2452	980.7
5	7 355	2452	1226	612.9	345.2
2.5	1 839	612.9	306.5	153.2	61.3
1	294.2	98.1	49.0	24.5	9.81
Hardness range (HB) covered	55 ... 650	35 ... 200	< 55	8 ... 55	3 ... 20
Application for:	Steel, gray cast iron, copper, copper alloys, light metals and their alloys	Gray cast iron, copper alloys, light metals and their alloys	Copper, copper alloys, light metals and their alloys	Light metals and their alloys	Lead, tin

measured with the same load-diameter ratio. The largest possible diameter of ball should be used and the load-diameter ratio should be selected such that the diameter of the impression lies in the range of (0.24 ... 0.6) $\cdot D$. Table 2 shows the hardness range covered for various materials in accordance with DIN 50 351.

The abbreviation for the method used, the ball material (W for hard metal, S for steel), the ball diameter and the applied test load in N multiplied by a factor of 0.102 are to be appended to the numerical value for Brinell hardness, e.g., 250 HBW 2.5/187.5.

Above 45 HB the measurement may only be carried out with a hard metal ball, in order to exclude the possibility of erroneous measurements resulting from ball deformation during measuring.

At high test loads relatively large impressions can be created, so that inhomogenous materials can also be tested. It is advantageous that the correlation between the Brinell hardness and tensile strength of steel is relatively high.

The range of application of the Brinell test method is limited by the thickness of the test specimen (cf. DIN 50 351) and by the ball material. Preparation and measurement is more time-consuming than is the case in the Rockwell Test method. The necessity of visual measuring of the impression diagonals, as well as unevenness of impressions, may lead to erroneous measurements.

Vickers hardness (DIN 50 133)

This test method can be used for all metallic materials, regardless of hardness, for unusually small and thin parts, and in particular for skin- and case-hardened, nitrided or nitrocarburized workpieces.

A square-based diamond pyramid with an apical angle of 136° is used as the indenter, and is applied to the surface of the test specimen with varying load F.

The diagonal d of the rhombic impression left after removing the indentor is measured using a hand microscope, and is a basis for the calculation of Vickers hardness, which can be read from tables or calculated as follows:

Vickers hardness = $0.189 \cdot F/d^2$ HV

F Applied load in N
d Diagonal of impression in mm

The load increments given in Table 3 are specified in DIN 50 133.

The abbreviation HV, the load in N multiplied by a factor of 0.102 and, separated by a slash, the time for which load is applied if deviating from the standard (15 s) in s are appended to the numerical value for Vickers hardness, e.g.: 750 HV 10/25.

The test specimen surface should be smooth ($R_{max} \leq 0.005 \cdot d$) and flat. The influence of arched surfaces on the measurement value is to be compensated with a correction value as per DIN 50 133. The applied test load is determined in accordance with the thickness of the test specimen, or of the "hard" surface layer (cf. fig. 2 in DIN 50 133). Practical experience shows that measurement inaccuracy is about ± 25 HV. Although the hardness values are geometrically similar, they are dependent on the applied load.

A major advantage of the test method is its almost unlimited applicability on thin parts or layers. The hardness of individual macrostructural constituents can also be determined at very low load. Correlation between Brinell and Vickers numbers exists up to approximately 350 HV.

However, in order to avoid erroneous measurements the surface of the test specimen must be sufficiently smoothed. In terms of accuracy, the same basic aspects apply as for the Brinell test method, although the measurement is extremely sensitive to bumping of the test

Table 3. Vickers hardness load increment

Designation	HV0.2	HV0.3	HV0.5	HV1	HV2	HV3	HV5	HV10	HV20	HV30	HV50	HV100
Applied load N	1.96	2.94	4.9	9.8	19.6	29.4	49	98	196	294	490	980

Correlation between hardness and strength in accordance with DIN 50 150

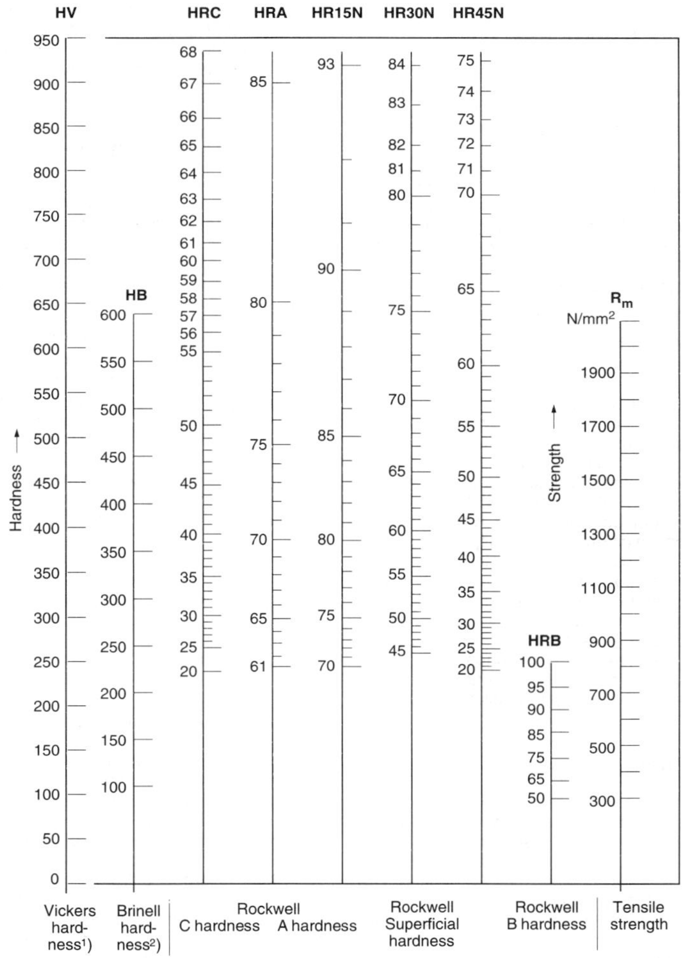

[1]) Applied load ≥ 98 N. [2]) Load-diameter ratio 30.

machine. The indenters are more expensive than the balls used in the Brinell test method.

Knoop hardness

This method is very similar to the Vickers hardness test method. It is particularly common in the English-speaking countries for hardness testing of thin layers.

The indenter is shaped such that it leaves an impression in the form of a narrow rhombus. The long diagonal d is seven times longer than the short diagonal, and only the long diagonal is measured. The applied load is less than 9.8 N. The hardness value is read from a table or calculated as follows:

Knoop hardness = $1.451 \cdot F/d^2$ HK

F Applied load in N
d Long diagonal in mm

The diagonal, which is roughly 2.8 times longer than in the Vickers method, can be visually measured with greater accuracy. The penetration depth is 1/3 less than in the Vickers method, so that the surface hardness of thin parts or layers can be ascertained. By making Knoop impressions in different directions, even material anisotropies can be detected.

A disadvantage of this method is that the surface of the specimen must be aligned very carefully and vertical to the load axis. The method is not standardized in Germany and only loads up to 9.8 N can be used. Test results cannot be correlated with those of the Vickers test.

Shore hardness

This method is primarily used for the hardness testing of rubber and soft plastics. The indenter is a steel pin with 1.25 mm diameter, which is forced against the surface of the test specimen by a spring. The resulting change in the spring length (spring travel) is used as a basis for the calculation of the Shore hardness number.

In the Shore D method a preloaded spring exerts a force of 0.55 N.; the tip of the steel pin has the shape of a frustrum (testing of hard rubber). The spring rate c is 4 N/mm.

In the Shore A method, the measurement is carried out with a conical steel pin with a rounded tip without the spring being preloaded. The spring rate is 17.8 N/mm. Each 0.025 mm of spring travel corresponds to 100 Shore units.

Ball impression hardness
(DIN 53 456)

This method is the one most often used for hardness testing of thermosetting plastics, but also of hard rubber. The indenter is a 5 mm diameter hardened steel ball, and a minor load of 9.81 N is used to force it against the surface of the test specimen, which must be at least 4 mm thick. A major load of 49, 132, 358 or 961 N is then applied, and after 30 s the penetration depth is measured and indicated on an analog display. The test load F should be selected such that the penetration depths h lie between 0.15 and 0.35 mm.

Ball impression hardness is defined as the ratio of the applied load to the surface area of the impression measured. It can be read from tables or calculated as follows:

$$\text{Ball impression hardness} = \frac{0.21 \cdot F}{1.25 \cdot \pi \cdot (h - 0.04)} \ \text{N/mm}^2$$

F Applied load in N
h Penetration depth in mm

Scleroscope hardness

This is a dynamic measurement method, designed specially for large, heavy workpieces. The procedure is based on the measurement of the rebound height (energy of impact) of a steel indenter (hammer) with a diamond or hard metal tip, which is dropped from a stipulated height onto the surface of the specimen under test. This measurement is taken as the basis for calculating the hardness.

The method is not standardized and there are no correlations to other hardness testing methods.

Tolerances

Correlations

In drawings based on DIN standards relating to tolerances and fits, and in which no differing definitions are contained (e.g., Independence Principle in accordance with ISO 8015), the envelope condition applies for all individual form elements. The basis of the envelope condition is the Taylor gauge test. This specifies that the geometric envelope of the maximum material dimension of the dimensional tolerance must not be exceeded.

It is not possible to produce geometrically ideal workpieces; therefore dimensions, limits (dimensional tolerances) are set down for production.

In accordance with DIN 7167, all tolerances of form as well as tolerances of parallelism, position and run-out are within the dimensional tolerances. The tolerance of form may lie anywhere within the dimensional tolerance (see diagram).

For the following tolerances of position the envelope dimension at maximum material dimension is not defined:

Tolerances of perpendicularity, slope, symmetry, coaxiality and true running. For these tolerances of position either direct specifications on the drawing or the general tolerances are necessary.

ISO **I**nternational **O**rganization for **S**tandardization

Tolerance position
1 Actual form
a Form tolerance, b Dimensional tolerance.

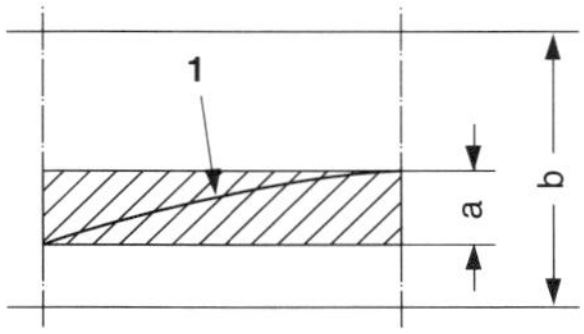

ISO system for limit allowances and fits

The ISO tolerance classes are indicated by letters (for basic allowances) and numbers (for basic tolerance grades).

The **letters** A to Z indicate the position of the tolerance field relative to the zero line; small letters for shafts; capital letters for holes.

The **numbers** 01 to 18 indicate the size of the tolerance grade.

The ISO tolerance fields for shafts and holes can be combined as desired to give fits, however the basic hole and basic shaft systems of fits are preferred.

Basic hole: The basic allowances for all holes are identical, and different fits are obtained by appropriately choosing the allowances for the shafts.

Basic shaft: The basic allowances for all shafts are identical, and different fits are obtained by appropriately choosing the allowances for the holes.

The most common clearance, transition and interference fits can be formed using the following selection of ISO tolerances from ISO 286.

Example for tolerance class: H7
Basic allowance
Tolerance grade

Tolerances of form and position

Tolerances of form and position should only be prescribed when necessary (e.g., as a result of functional requirements, interchangeability and possible production circumstances).

A tolerance of form and position of an element defines a zone within which that element must be located (surface, axis or generating line).

Within the tolerance zone the toleranced element may have any desired form or face in any desired direction. The tolerance applies to the entire length or surface of the toleranced element.

The tolerances are entered on the drawing by means of symbols (see table).

Symbols for toleranced properties

Properties		Symbols
Straightness	[1]	⏤
Flatness		▱
Roundness (circularity)		○
Cylindricity		⌭
Profile of any line		⌒
Profile of any surface		⌓
Parallelism	[2]	//
Perpendicularity		⊥
Slope		∠
Position	[3]	⌖
Concentricity, coaxiality		◎
Symmetry		⌯
Running	[4]	↗
Total running		⌰

[1]) Tolerances of form, [2]) Tolerances of direction,
[3]) Tolerances of location, [4]) Running tolerances.

Additional symbols

Description		Symbols
Identification of the toleranced element	direct	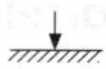
	with letter	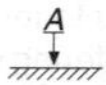
Identification of the reference	direct	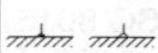
	with letter	
Reference point		Ø2 A1
Theoretically precise dimension		50
Projected tolerance zone		Ⓟ
Maximum material condition		Ⓜ

System for ordering deviations of form (DIN 4760)

Deviation of form (shown as exaggerated surface profile)	Examples of deviation	Typical causes
1st order: Deviation of form 	Deviation from straightness, flatness, roundness	Faulty machine-tool guides, deflection of machine or workpiece, workpiece held incorrectly
2nd order: Waviness 	Waves (see DIN 4761)	Workpiece held off-center, deviations in form or true running of milling cutter, vibrations
3rd order: Roughness 	Grooves (see DIN 4761)	Form of tool, feed or approach of tool
4th order: Roughness 	Score marks, flaking proruberances (see DIN 4761)	Chip formation process, material deformation due to sand blasting, formation of buds due to electroplating
5th order: Roughness (not easily illustrated)	Structure	Crystalization processes, chemical action (e.g., pickling) corrosion processes
6th order: (not easily illustrated)	Lattice structure of material	–

Deviations of form

The deviations of form are set out in an ordering system (see table). In the case of deviations of the 1st order the total actual surface of a form element is observed. The 2nd to 5th order deviations are assessed on the basis of a surface profile. Roughness refers to 3rd to 5th order deviations of form.

There is no generally valid correlation between dimensional tolerance and peak-to-valley height (standard value $R_z \leq 0.5 \cdot T$).

Roughness parameters

In cases where there are no particular requirements, indication of the permissible R_z values in accordance with DIN 4768 is usually sufficient for the tolerancing of roughness.

If particular requirements are made, e.g., high unit loads, high density, uniform and low friction, long service life, low noise, porous surfaces, it is often no longer sufficient to indicate the R_z value alone, but further or other roughness parameters must be given.

Average peak-to-valley height

The average peak-to-valley height R_z (DIN 4768) is the arithmetic average of the individual peak-to-valley heights z_1 to z_5 of the filtered profile.

Maximum peak-to-valley height

The maximum peak-to-valley height R_{max} (DIN 4768) is the greatest individual peak-to-valley height z_1 to z_5 of values obtained within the entire measurement section l_m of the filtered profile.

Roughness average

The roughness average R_a (DIN 4768) is the arithmetic average of the absolute values of all profile measurements within the entire measurement section l_m.

$R_a = 1/l_m \; | \; y(x) \; | \; dx$

Core roughness

The core roughness R_k (DIN 4776) is the peak-to-valley height of the roughness profile excluding protruding peaks and deep score marks.

Maximum and average peak-to-valley height
l_e Individual measurement sections,
l_m Total measurement section,
R_{max} Maximum peak-to-valley height,
$z_1 \ldots z_5$ Individual peak-to-valley heights.

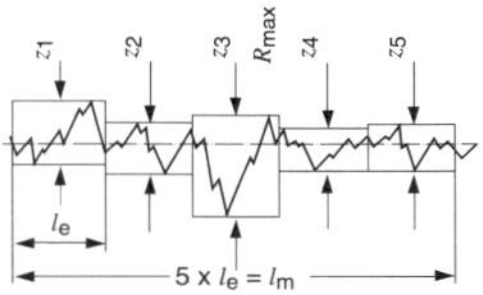

Roughness average
l_m Evaluation length
R_a Average roughness height.

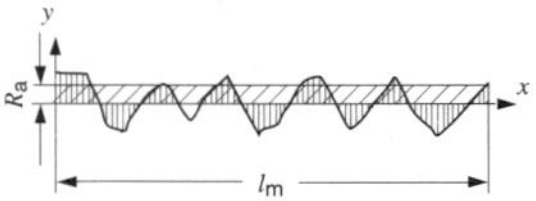

Core roughness
R_k Core roughness, R_{pk} Reduced peak height,
R_{vk} Reduced score depth.,

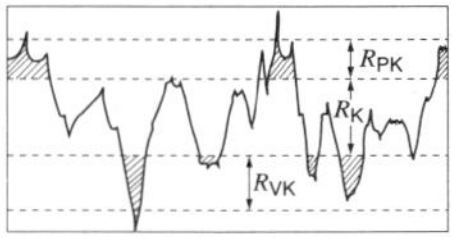

Profile height
l Reference section, P_t Profile height.

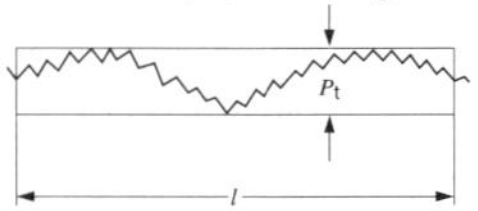

Reduced peak height

The reduced peak height R_{pk} (DIN 4776) indicates the proportion of protruding profile peaks (run-in).

Reduced score depth

The reduced score depth R_{vk} (DIN 4776) indicates the proportion of score marks which penetrate into the material.

Profile peak-to-valley height

The profile peak-to-valley height P_t (DIN 4771) is the peak-to-valley height of the unfiltered profile within the reference measurement section l.

ISO-Allowances

Selection (for explanation see p. 263)

Nominal size mm over	to	**Exterior dimensions** (shafts) z 6	u 6	u 8	s 6	r 6	p 6	n 6	k 6	j 6	h 6	h 8	h 9	h 11	g 6
1	**3**	+ 32	+ 24	+ 34	+ 20	+ 16	+ 12	+ 12	+ 6	+ 4	0	0	0	0	− 2
		+ 26	+ 18	+ 20	+ 14	+ 10	+ 6	+ 4	0	− 2	− 6	− 14	− 25	− 60	− 8
3	**6**	+ 43	+ 31	+ 46	+ 27	+ 23	+ 20	+ 16	+ 9	+ 6	0	0	0	0	− 4
		+ 35	+ 23	+ 28	+ 19	+ 15	+ 12	+ 8	+ 1	− 2	− 8	− 18	− 30	− 75	− 2
6	**10**	+ 51	+ 37	+ 56	+ 32	+ 28	+ 24	+ 19	+ 10	+ 7	0	0	0	0	− 5
		+ 42	+ 28	+ 34	+ 23	+ 19	+ 15	+ 10	+ 1	− 2	− 9	− 22	− 36	− 90	− 14
10	**14**	+ 61		+ 67											
		+ 50	+ 44	+ 40	+ 39	+ 34	+ 29	+ 23	+ 12	+ 8	0	0	0	0	− 6
14	**18**	+ 71	+ 33	+ 72	+ 28	+ 23	+ 18	+ 12	+ 1	− 3	− 11	− 27	− 43	− 110	− 17
		+ 60		+ 45											
18	**24**	+ 86	+ 54	+ 87											
		+ 73	+ 41	+ 54	+ 48	+ 42	+ 35	+ 28	+ 15	+ 9	0	0	0	0	− 7
24	**30**	+ 101	+ 61	+ 81	+ 35	+ 21	+ 22	+ 15	+ 2	− 4	− 13	− 33	− 52	− 130	− 20
		+ 88	+ 48	+ 48											
30	**40**	+ 128	+ 76	+ 99											
		+ 112	+ 60	+ 60	+ 59	+ 50	+ 42	+ 33	+ 18	+ 11	0	0	0	0	− 9
40	**50**	−	+ 86	+ 109	+ 43	+ 34	+ 26	+ 17	+ 2	− 5	− 16	− 39	− 62	− 160	− 25
		−	+ 70	+ 70											
50	**65**	−	+ 106	+ 133	+ 72	+ 60									
		−	+ 87	+ 87	+ 53	+ 41	+ 51	+ 39	+ 21	+ 12	0	0	0	0	− 10
65	**80**	−	+ 121	+ 148	+ 78	+ 62	+ 32	+ 20	+ 2	− 7	− 19	− 46	+ 74	− 190	− 29
		−	+ 102	+ 102	+ 59	+ 43									
80	**100**	−	+ 146	+ 178	+ 93	+ 73									
		−	+ 124	+ 124	+ 71	+ 51	+ 59	+ 45	+ 25	+ 13	0	0	0	0	− 12
100	**120**	−	+ 166	+ 198	+ 101	+ 76	+ 37	+ 23	+ 3	− 9	− 22	− 54	− 87	− 220	− 34
		−	+ 144	+ 144	+ 79	+ 54									
120	**140**	−	+ 195	+ 233	+ 117	+ 88									
		−	+ 170	+ 170	+ 92	+ 63									
140	**160**	−	+ 215	+ 253	+ 125	+ 90	+ 68	+ 52	+ 28	+ 14	0	0	0	0	− 14
		−	+ 190	+ 190	+ 100	+ 65	+ 43	+ 27	+ 3	− 11	− 25	− 63	− 100	− 250	− 39
160	**180**	−	+ 235	+ 273	+ 133	+ 93									
		−	+ 210	+ 210	+ 108	+ 68									
180	**200**	−	+ 265	+ 308	+ 151	+ 106									
		−	+ 236	+ 236	+ 122	+ 77									
200	**225**	−	+ 287	+ 330	+ 159	+ 109	+ 79	+ 60	+ 33	+ 16	0	0	0	0	− 15
		−	+ 258	+ 258	+ 130	+ 80	+ 50	+ 31	+ 4	− 13	− 29	− 72	− 115	− 290	− 44
225	**250**	−	+ 313	+ 356	+ 169	+ 113									
		−	+ 284	+ 284	+ 140	+ 84									
250	**280**	−	+ 347	+ 396	+ 190	+ 126									
		−	+ 315	+ 315	+ 158	+ 94	+ 88	+ 66	+ 36	+ 16	0	0	0	0	− 17
280	**315**	−	+ 382	+ 431	+ 202	+ 130	+ 56	+ 34	+ 4	− 16	− 32	− 81	− 130	− 320	− 49
		−	+ 350	+ 350	+ 170	+ 98									
315	**355**	−	+ 426	+ 479	+ 226	+ 144									
		−	+ 390	+ 390	+ 190	+ 108	+ 98	+ 73	+ 40	+ 18	0	0	0	0	− 18
355	**400**	−	+ 471	+ 524	+ 244	+ 150	+ 62	+ 37	+ 4	− 18	− 36	− 89	− 140	− 360	− 54
		−	+ 435	+ 435	+ 208	+ 114									

Allowances in μm = 1/1000 mm

							Internal dimensions (holes)								
f 7	f 8	e 8	e 9	d 9	c 11	a 11	H 7	H 8	H 11	G 7	F 8	E 9	D 10	C 11	A 11
-6	-6	-14	-14	-20	-60	-270	+10	+14	+60	+12	+20	+39	+60	+120	+330
-16	-20	-28	-39	-45	-120	-330	0	0	0	+2	+6	+14	+20	+60	+270
-10	-10	-20	-20	-30	-70	-270	+12	+18	+75	+16	+28	+50	+78	+145	+345
-22	-28	-38	-50	-60	-145	-345	0	0	0	+4	+10	+20	+30	+70	+270
-13	-13	-25	-25	-40	-80	-280	+15	+22	+90	+20	+35	+61	+98	+170	+370
-28	-35	-47	-61	-70	-170	-370	0	0	0	+5	+13	+25	+40	+80	+280
-16	-16	-32	-32	-50	-95	-290	+18	+27	+110	+24	+43	+75	+120	+205	+400
-34	-43	-59	-75	-93	-205	-400	0	0	0	+6	+16	+32	+50	+95	+290
-20	-20	-40	-40	-65	-110	-300	+21	+33	+130	+28	+53	+92	+149	+240	+430
-41	-53	-73	-92	-117	-240	-430	0	0	0	+7	+20	+40	+65	+110	+300
					-120	-310								+280	+470
-25	-20	-50	-50	-80	-280	-470	+25	+39	+160	+34	+64	+112	+180	+120	+310
-50	-64	-89	-112	-142	-130	-320	0	0	0	+9	+25	+50	+80	+290	+480
					-290	-480								+130	+320
					-140	-340								+330	+530
-30	-30	-60	-60	-100	-330	-530	+30	+46	+190	+40	+76	+134	+220	+140	+340
-60	-76	-106	-134	-174	-150	-360	0	0	0	+10	+30	+60	+100	+340	+550
					-340	-550								+150	+360
					-170	-380								+390	+600
-36	-36	-72	-72	-120	-390	-600	+35	+54	+220	+47	+90	+159	+260	+170	+380
-71	-90	-126	-159	-207	-180	-410	0	0	0	+12	+36	+72	+120	+400	+630
					-400	-630								+180	+410
					-200	-460								+450	+710
					-450	-710								+200	+460
-43	-43	-85	-85	-145	-210	-520	+40	+63	+250	+54	+106	+185	+305	+460	+770
-83	-106	-148	-185	-245	-460	-770	0	0	0	+14	+43	+85	+145	+210	+520
					-230	-580								+480	+830
					-480	-830								+230	+580
					-240	-660								+530	+950
					-530	-950								+240	+660
-50	-50	-100	-100	-170	-260	-740	+46	+72	+290	+61	+122	+215	+355	+550	+1030
-96	-122	-172	-215	-285	-550	-1030	0	0	0	+15	+50	+100	+170	+260	+740
					-280	-820								+570	+1110
					-570	-1110								+280	+820
					-300	-920								+620	+1240
-56	-56	-110	-110	-190	-620	-1240	+52	+81	+320	+69	+137	+240	+400	+300	+920
-108	-137	-191	-240	-320	-330	-1050	0	0	0	+17	+56	+110	+190	+650	+1370
					-650	-1370								+330	+1050
					-360	-1200								+720	+1560
-62	-62	-125	-125	-210	-720	-1560	+57	+89	+360	+75	+151	+265	+440	+360	+1200
-119	-151	-214	-265	-350	-400	-1350	0	0	0	+18	+62	+125	+210	+760	+1710
					-760	-1710								+400	+1350

Sliding-bearings and rolling bearings

Sliding bearings

Different types of sliding bearings range from bearings with usually complete separation of the sliding surfaces by a lubrication film (fluid friction), through self-lubricating bearings, most of which exhibit mixed friction (i.e. some of the bearing load is transformed to solid contact between the sliding surfaces), to dry sliding-contact bearings which exhibit dry friction (i.e. completely without an effective fluid lubricating film), but which nevertheless have an adequate service life.

Most of the hydrodynamic sliding bearing types used in automotive applications are circular cylindrical radial-sleeve bearings (often with oval clearance) for holding the crankshaft and camshaft, and turbocharger bearings. Thrust bearings are usually used only as axial locators, and are not subjected to large forces.

Hydrodynamic sliding bearings

Symbols (DIN 31 652)

Quantity	Symbol	Unit
Axial bearing length	B	m
Inside bearing diameter (journal diameter)	D	m
Shaft diameter (nominal diameter)	d	m
Journal eccentricity (distance between shaft and bearing centers)	e	m
Load	F	N
Minimum film thickness	h_0	m
Local film pressure	p	$\mathrm{Pa} = \mathrm{N/m^2}$
Specific load $\overline{p} = F/(B \cdot D)$	$\overline{p}$	Pa
Bearing clearance $s = (D - d)$	s	m
Sommerfeld number	So	–
Relative eccentricity $2e/s$	ε	–
Effective dynamic viscosity of the lubricant	η_{eff}	Pa·s
Relative bearing clearance $\psi = s/D$	ψ	–
Displacement angle	β	°
Hydrodynamically effective angular velocity	ω_{eff}	s^{-1}

A hydrodynamic sliding bearing is reliable in service if it remains sufficiently unaffected by the following:
– Wear (sufficient separation of the contact surfaces by the lubricant),
– Mechanical stress (bearing material of sufficient strength),
– Thermal loading (observance of thermal stability of bearing material and viscosity/temperature behavior of lubricant).

The dimensionless Sommerfeld number So is used to determine load-ability, i.e. to assess the formation of the lubricating film:

$$So = F \cdot \psi^2 / (D \cdot B - \eta_{\text{eff}} \cdot \omega_{\text{eff}})$$

As the Sommerfeld number So increases, relative eccentricity ε increases and minimum lubricating-film thickness h_0 drops.

$$h_0 = (D - d)/2 - e = 0.5\,D \cdot \psi \cdot (1 - \varepsilon)$$

With relative eccentricity

$$\varepsilon = 2\,e/(D - d)$$

Table 1. Orders of magnitude of the coefficients of friction for different types of friction

The coefficients of friction given below are approximate values, and are intended solely for comparison of the different types of fricition.

Type of friction	Coefficient of friction f
Dry friction	0.1 ... > 1
Mixed friction	0.01 ... 0.1
Fluid friction	0.01
Friction in rolling bearings	0.001

Table 2. Empirical values for maximum permissible specific bearing load

Bearing materials	Maximum specific bearing load $\overline{P}_{\text{lim}}$ in $\mathrm{N/mm^2}$
Pb and Sn alloys (babbit metals)	5 ... 15
Bronze, high-lead	7 ... 20
Bronze, tin	7 ... 25
AlSn alloys	7 ... 18
AlZn alloys	7 ... 20

The Sommerfeld number is also used to determine the coefficient of friction in the bearing, and thus for calculation of frictional power and thermal stress (cf. DIN 31 652, VDI Guideline 2204).

Because hydrodynamic bearings also operate with mixed friction a certain amount of the time, they must accommodate a certain amount of contamination without loss of function, and are additionally subjected to high dynamic and thermal stress (particulary in piston engines), the bearing material must meet a number of requirements, some of which are opposed to one another.

– Comformability (compensation of misalignment without shortening service life),
– Wettability by lubricant,
– Embeddability (ability of the bearing surface to absorb particles of dirt without increasing bearing or shaft wear),
– Wear resistance (in the case of mixed friction),
– Seizure resistance (bearing material must not weld to shaft material, even under high compressive load and high sliding velocity),
– Anti-seizure performance (resistance to welding),
– Run-in performance (a combination of compatibility, resistance to wear and embeddability),
– Mechanical loadability,
– Fatigue strength (under fatigue loading, particularly with high thermal stress).

If a bearing (e.g., piston-pin bushings) is to be simultaneously subjected to high loads and low sliding velocities, high fatigue strength and wear resistance should take precedence over resistance to seizing. Bearing materials used in such cases are hard bronzes, e.g., leaded tin bronzes (Table 3).

Connecting-rod and crankshaft bearings in internal-combustion engines must fulfill a number of different requirements, because they are subjected to high dynamic loads with high sliding velocities. In these applications, **multilayer bearings**, above all **trimetal bearings**, have performed well.

The service life of crankshaft bearings can be further increased through the use of **grooved sliding bearings**. In these bearings, fine grooves have been machined into the surface in the sliding direction, and filled with a liner made of soft material (an electroplated liner similar to that found in trimetal bearings). These contact areas are separated from one another by a harder light-alloy metal.

These bearings achieve low rates of wear, and exhibit high fatigue strength with good embeddability properties with respect to lubricant impurities.

Multi-layer bearing
(Design of a trimetal bearing)
1 Steel backing shell, 2 Cast lead bronze (0.4 mm), 3 Nickel barrier between lead bronze and babbit-metal (1 ... 2 μm), 4 Electroplated babbit-metal liner (overlay, e.g., 20 μm.

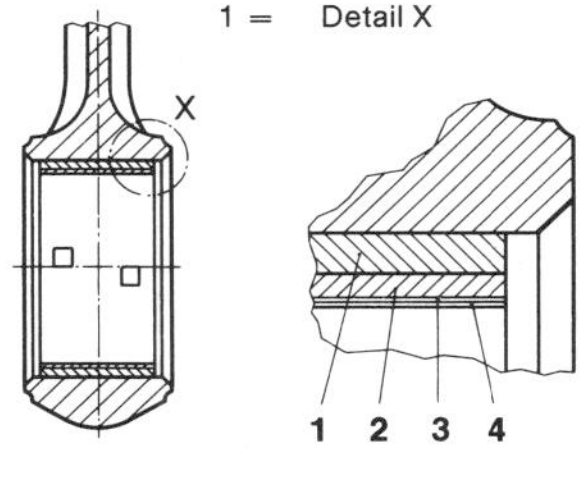

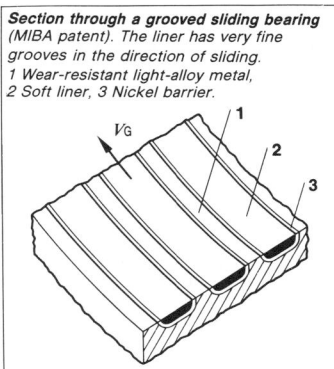

Section through a grooved sliding bearing *(MIBA patent). The liner has very fine grooves in the direction of sliding.*
1 Wear-resistant light-alloy metal,
2 Soft liner, 3 Nickel barrier.

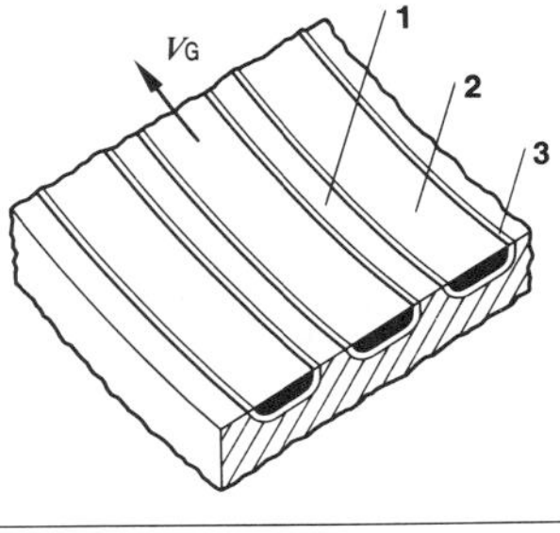

Table 3. Selection of materials for hydrodynamic sliding bearings

Material	Chemical alloy designation	Composition in %	HB Hardness 20°C	HB Hardness 100°C	Remarks Application examples
Tin-base babbit metal	LgPbSn 80 (WM 80)	80 Sn; 12 Sb; 6 Cu; 2 Pb	27	10	Very soft, good conformance of contact surfaces to off-axis operation, excellent anti-seizure performance.
Lead-base babbit metal	LgPbSn 10 (WM 10)	73 Pb; 16 Sb; 10 Sn; 1 Cu	23	9	Reinforcement necessary, e.g., as composite steel casting or with intermediate nickel layer on lead bronze
Lead-base bronze	G-CuPb 25	74 Cu; 25 Pb; 1 Sn	50	47	Very soft, excellent anti-seizure performance, less resistant to wear.
	G-CUPb 22	70 Cu; 22 Pb; 6 Sn; 3 Ni	86	79	
Lead-tin-base bronze	G-CuPb 10 Sn 10	80 Cu; 10 Pb; 10 Sn	75	67	Improved anti-seizure performance by alloying with Pb. More resistant to off-axis operation than pure tin bronzes, therefore leaded bronzes are preferable for use as crankshaft bearings. Composite bearings used in internal-combustion engine manufacture, piston-pin bushings. $\overline{p}$ up to 100 N/mm^2.
	G-CuPb 23 Sn	76 Cu; 23 Pb; 1 Sn	55	53	Composite casting for low-load bearings (70 N/mm^2). Also thick-wall bearing shells. Very good anti-seizure performance. Crankshaft and camshaft bearings, connecting-rod bearings.
Tin-base bronze	G-CuSn 10 Zn	88 Cu; 10 Sn; 2 Zn	85		Hard material. Sliding bearing shells can be subjected to moderate loads at low sliding velocities. Worm gears.
	CuSn 8	92 Cu; 8 Sn	80 ... 220		High-grade wrought alloy. Good performance under high loads and in absence of sufficient lubrication. Steering knuckle bearings. Particularly well suited for use as thin-wall sliding bearing bushings.
Red brass	G-CuSn 7 ZnPb	83 Cu; 6 Pb; 7 Sn; 4 Zn	75	65	Tin partially replaced with zinc and lead. Can be used in place of tin bronze, but only for moderate loads (40 N/mm^2). General sliding bearings for machinery. Piston pins, bushings, crankshaft and toggle-lever bearings.

Material	Chemical alloy designation	Composition in %	HB Hardness 20°	100°C	Remarks Application examples
Brass	CuZn 31 Si	68 Cu; 31 Zn; 1 Si	90 ... 200		Zn content is disadvantageous at high bearing temperatures. Can be used in place of tin bronze; low loads.
Aluminum bronze	CuAl 9 Mn	88 Cu; 9 Al; 3 Mn	110 ... 190		Thermal expansion comparable to that of light alloys. Suitable for use as interference-fit bearing in light-alloy housings. Greater wear resistance than tin bronze, but increased friction.
Aluminum alloy	AlSi 12 Cu NiMn	1 Cu; 85 Al; 12 Si; 1 Ni; 1 Mn	110	100	Piston alloy for low sliding velocities.
Rolled aluminum cladding	AlSn 6	1 Cu; 6 Sn; 90 Al; 3 Si	40	30	Liquated tin stretched by rolling, therefore high loadability and good anti-friction properties. Improved by electroplated layer.
Electroplated liners	PbSn 10 Cu	2 Cu; 88 Pb; 10 Sn	50 ... 60		Used in modern trimetal bearings, electroplated to thickness of 10 to 30 μm, very fine grain. Intermediate nickel layer on bearing metal.

For materials, see also DIN 1703, 1705, 1716, 17 660, 17 662, 17 665, 1494, 1725, 1743.
ISO 4381, 4382, 4383.

Table 4. Sintered-metal bearing materials
Sint-B indicates 20 % P (porosity) (Sint-A: 25 % P; Sint-C: 15 % P).

Material group	Designation Sint-...	Composition	Remarks
Sintered iron	B 00	Fe	Standard material which meets moderate load and noise requirements.
Sintered steel, containing Cu	B 10	< 0.3 C 1 ... 5 Cu Rest Fe	Good resistance to wear, can be subjected to higher loads than pure Fe bearings.
Sintered steel, higher Cu content	B 20	20 Cu Rest Fe	More favorably priced than sintered bronze, good noise behavior and P values.
Sintered bronze	B 50	< 0.2 C 9 ... 10 Sn Rest Cu	Standard Cu-Sn-base material, good noise behavior.

Sintered-metal sliding bearings

Sintered-metal sliding bearings consist of sintered metals which are porous and impregnated with liquid lubricants. For many small motors in automotive applications, this type of bearing is a good compromise in terms of precision, installation, freedom from maintenance, service life and cost. They are primarily used in motors with shaft diameters from 1.5 ...12 mm. Sintered-iron bearings and sintered-steel bearings (inexpensive, less likely to interact with the lubricant) are preferable to sintered-bronze bearings for use in the motor vehicle (Table 4). The advantages of sintered-bronze bearings are greater loadability, lower noise and lower coefficients of friction (this type of bearing is used in phonograph equipment, office equipment, data systems and cameras). The performance of sintered bearings over long periods of service is closely related to the use of optimum lubricants.

Mineral oils: Good mechanical loadability, but pronounced tendency toward evaporation.

Synthetic oils (e.g., esters, poly-α olefins): High degree of resistance to thermal stresses and to evaporation.

Synthetic greases (poly-α olefins, polyglycol): Low starting friction.

Dry sliding bearings

(see Table 5, p. 274)

Plastic bearings made of thermoplastics

Advantages: Economically-priced, no danger of seizure with metals.

Disadvantages: Low thermal conductivity, relatively low operating temperatures, possible swelling due to humidity, low loadability, high coefficient of thermal expansion.

The most frequently used polymer materials are: Polyvinylacetal (POM, POM-C), polyamide (PA), polyethylene and polybutylene terephthalate (PETP, PBTP), polyetheretherketone (PEEK).

The tribological and mechanical properties can be varied over a wide range by incorporating lubricants and reinforcements in the thermoplastic base material.

Lubricant additives: polytetrafluoroethylene (PTFE), graphite (C), silicone oil and other liquid lubricants.

Reinforcement additives: glass fibers, carbon fibers.

Application examples: windshield wiper bearings (PA and fiberglass, idle-position actuators (PEEK and carbon fiber, PTFE and other additives).

Polymer bearings made of duroplastics and elastomers

These materials, which exhibit high intrinsic friction, are seldom used as bearing materials in the motor vehicle. Duroplastics include: phenol resins (high friction, e.g., Resitex), epoxy resins (require the addition of PTFE or C in order to reduce their high intrinsic brittleness, reinforcement necessary usually by fibers), polyimides (high thermal and mechanical loadability).

Application examples: polyimide axial stop in wiper motor.

Metal-backed composite bearings

Composite bearings are combinations of polymer materials, fibers and metals. Depending upon bearing structure, they provide advantages over pure or filled polymer sliding bearings in terms of loadability, bearing clearance, thermal conductivity and installation (suitable for use with oscillating motion).

Example of bearing structure: Tin-plated or copper-clad steel backing (several millimeters thick), onto which is sintered an 0.2 ... 0.35 mm thick porous bronze layer with a porosity of 30 ... 40 %. A low-friction polymer material is rolled into this bronze layer as a liner made of

a) acetal resin, either impregnated with oil or containing lubricating recesses, or

b) PTFE + Pb or MoS_2 additive.

Metal-backed composite bearings are available in a number of different shapes and compositions. Metal-backed composite bearings with woven PTFE fiber inserts exhibit unusually high loadability and are suitable for use in ball-and-socket joints.

Some motor-vehicle applications for this type of bearing are: Shock-absorber-piston bearings, release-lever bearings for clutch pressure plates, brake-shoe bearings in drum brakes, ball-and-socket bearings, door-hinge bearings, bearings for seat-belt rewinding shafts, steering-knuckle bearings, gear-pump bearings.

Carbon-graphite bearings

Carbon-graphite bearings are members of the ceramic bearing family due to their method of manufacture and material properties. The base materials are powdered carbon; tar or synthetic resins are used as binders.

Advantages: Heat-resistant up to 350°C (hard-burnt carbon) or 500°C (electrographite), good antifriction properties, good corrosion resistance, good thermal conductivity, good thermal shock resistance. They are highly brittle, however.

Examples of carbon-graphite bearing applications: Fuel-pump bearings, bearings in drying ovens, adjustable blades in turbochargers.

Metal-ceramic bearings

Metal-ceramic bearings consist of material manufactured by powder metallurgy processes; in addition to the metallic matrix, the bearing material also contains finely distributed solid lubricant particles.

Matrix: e.g., bronze, iron, nickel.

Lubricant: e.g., graphite, MoS_2.

These materials are suitable for use under extremely high loads, and are at the same time self-lubricating.

Application example: Steering-knuckle bearings.

Section through a metal-backed composite bearing

1 Polymer liner, 2 Porous bronze layer, 3 Copper layer, 4 Steel backing, 5 Tin layer

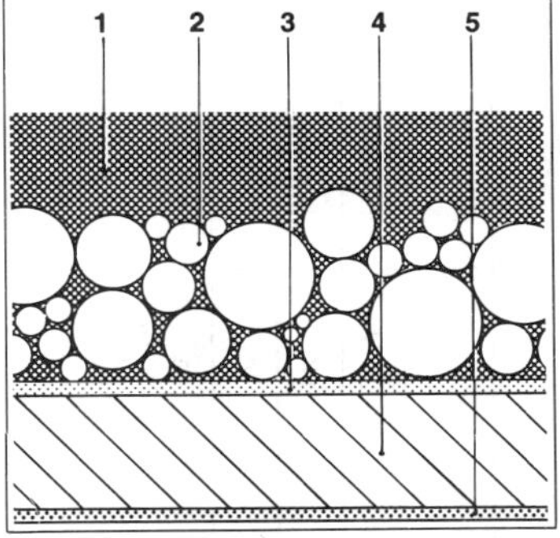

Metal-backed composite bearing with fabric insert made of PTFE and fiberglass

1 PTFE fiber fabric, 2 Adhesive fibers, 3 Resin, 4 Fiberglass backing, 5 Adhesive, 6 Steel backing.

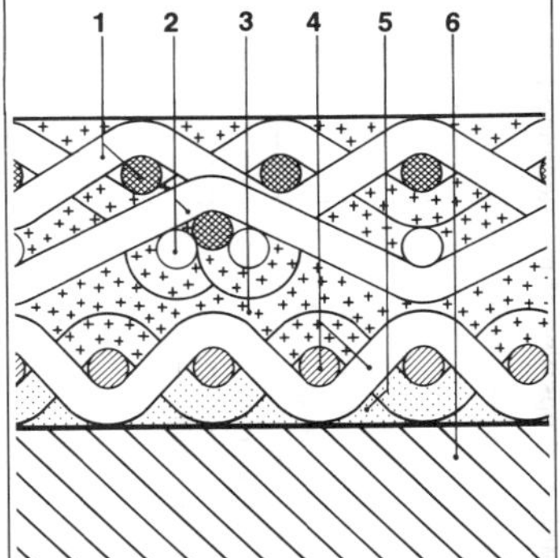

Table 5. Properties of maintenance-free, self-lubricating bearings.

	Oil-impregnated sintered bearings		Polymer bearings		Metal-backed composite bearings Liner		Synthetic carbons
	Sintered iron	Sintered bronze	Thermoplastic polyamide	Duroplastic polyimide	PTFE + additive	Acetal resin	
Comp. strength N/mm²	80 ... 180		70	110	250	250	100 ... 200
Max. sliding velocity m/s	10	20	2	8	2	3	10
Typical load N/mm²	1 ... 4 (10)		15	50 (at 50°C) 10 (at 200°C)	20 ... 50	20 ... 50	50
Permissible operating temperature °C Short-term	−60 ... 180 (depends on oil) 200		−130 ... 100 120	−100 ... 250 300	−200 ... 280	−40 ... 100 130	−200 ... 350 500
Coefficient of friction without lubrication	with lubrication 0.04 ... 0.2		0.2 ... 0.35	0.2 ... 0.5 (unfilled) 0.1 ... 0.4 (filled)	0.04 ... 0.2	0.07[1]) ... 0.2 [1]) PTFE filled	0.1 ... 0.35
Thermal conductivity W/(m · K)	20 ... 40		0.3	0.4 ... 1	46	2	10 ... 65
Corrosion resistance	poor	good	very good		good	good	very good
Chemical resistance	no		very good		conditional	conditional	good
max. $p \cdot v$ (N/mm²) · (m/s)	20		0.05	0.2	1.5 ... 2		0.4 ... 1.8
Embeddability of dirt and abraded material	poor		good	good	poor	good	poor

Rolling bearings

In rolling bearings, forces are transmitted by rolling elements (balls or rollers). In rolling bearings a microslip (i.e. sliding) nearly always occurs in addition to the pure rolling movement. In the case of mixed friction, this sliding movement leads to increased wear.

Advantages:
Low static coefficient of friction (0.001 ... 0.002), therefore particularly well suited to applications in which starting occurs frequently,
Low maintenance,
Suited to permanent lubrication,
Low lubricant consumption,
Small bearing width,
High precision.

Disadvantages:
Sensitive to impact loads,
Sensitive to dirt,
Bearing noise is too high for many applications,
Standard bearings are only 1-piece bearings.

Bearing materials
Bearing races and rolling elements are made of a special chromium-alloy steel (100 Cr6H) which has a high degree of purity and a hardness in the range of 58 ... 65 HRC.

Depending upon application, the cages are made of stamped sheet steel or brass. Cages made of polymer materials have come into recent use due to their ease of manufacture, improved adaptability to bearing geometry and other tribological advantages (e.g., antifriction properties). Polymer materials made of fiberglass-reinforced polyamide 66 can withstand continuous operating temperatures of up to 120° C, and can be operated for brief periods at temperatures up to 140° C.

Static loadability (ISO 76-1987)
The static load rating Co is used as a measure of the loadability of very slow-moving or static rolling bearings. Co is that load at which total permanent deformation of rolling elements and races at the most highly-loaded contact point amounts to 0.0001 of the diameter of the rolling element. A load equal to this load rating Co generates a maximum compressive stress of 4000 N/mm² in the center of the most highly-loaded rolling element.

Dynamic loadability
The basic load rating C is used for calculating the service life of a rotating rolling bearing. C indicates that bearing load at which bearing service life is 1 million revolutions. In accordance with ISO 281:

Service life equation $L_{10} = \left(\frac{C}{P}\right)^p$

L_{10} Nominal service life in millions of revolutions achieved or exceeded by 90 % of a large number of identical bearings,
C Basic load rating in N (determined empirically),
P Equivalent dynamic bearing load in N,
p Empirical exponent of the service life equation: for ball bearings, $p = 3$, for roller bearings, $p = 10/3$

Modified nominal service life

$$L_{na} = a_1 \cdot a_2 \cdot a_3 \cdot \left(\frac{C}{P}\right)^p$$

L_{na} modified nominal service life in millions of revolutions,
a_1 Factor for survival probability, e.g., 90 %: $a_1 = 1$: 95 %: $a_1 = 0.62$,
a_2 Material coefficient of friction
a_3 Coefficient of friction for operating conditions (bearing lubrication)

As the frictional coefficients a_2 and a_3 are not mutually independent, the combined coefficient a_{23} ist employed.

According to the latest research, a fatigue-stress is included in the calculation of service life, together with other influencing parameters, such as contamination (see catalogs from roller-bearing manufacturers).

Spring calculations

See pp. 12 ... 14 for names of units

Quantity	Unit
b Width of spring leaf	mm
c Spring rate (spring constant): spring, increase in spring force per mm of spring deflection	N/mm
for torsion bar springs, coiled torsion springs and flat spiral springs, increase in spring moment per degree of rotation	N · mm/°
d Wire diameter	mm
D Mean coil diameter	mm
E Modulus of elasticity (Young's modulus) for spring steel = 206,000 N/mm², for other materials see p. [4]... see p. 188	N/mm²

Quantity	Unit
F Spring force	N
G Shear modulus: for got-formed springs $G \approx 78{,}500$ N/mm²; for cold-formed springs $G \approx 81{,}400$ N/mm²	N/mm³
h Height of spring leaf	mm
n Number of active coils	—
M Spring moment	N · mm
s Spring deflection	mm
α Angle of rotation	°
σ_b Bending stress	N/mm²
τ Torsional stress	N/mm²

Conversion of no longer permissible units:
1 kp = 9.81 N ≈ 10 N, 1 kp/mm ≈ 10 N/mm, 1 kp mm ≈ 10 N mm,
1 kp mm/° ≈ 10 N mm/°, 1 kp/mm² ≈ 10 N/mm²:

Springs subjected to bending stress

Type	Bending stress	Spring rate
Rectangular cantilever spring (Constant cross section) 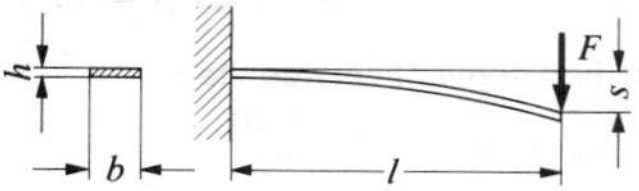	$\sigma_b = \dfrac{6\,l}{b \cdot h^2} F$ See fatigue limit diagram on p. 277.	$c = \dfrac{F}{s} = \dfrac{E \cdot b \cdot h^3}{4 \cdot l^3}$
Single-leaf spring, rolled out parabolically (Vehicle spring) 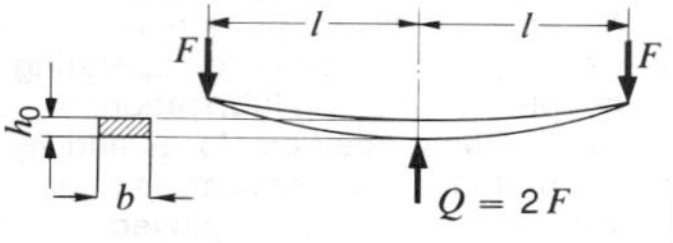	$\sigma_b = \dfrac{3\,l}{b \cdot h_0^2} Q$	$c = \dfrac{Q}{s} = \dfrac{E \cdot b \cdot h_0^3}{4 \cdot l^3}$
Multi-leaf spring, Constant cross-section of the leaves (Vehicle spring) 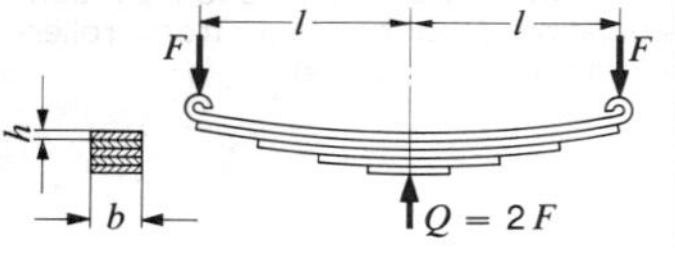	$\sigma_b = \dfrac{3\,l}{n \cdot b \cdot h^2} Q$ n = number of leaves n' = number of leaves at ends of spring	$c = \dfrac{(2 + n'/n)\, E \cdot n \cdot b \cdot h^3}{6 \cdot l^3}$

Type of spring	Bending stress	Spring rate
Torsion spring (DIN 2088) 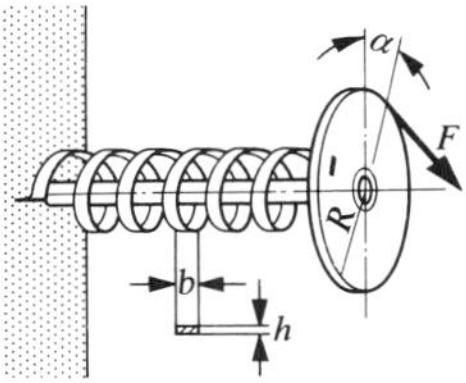	Rectangular cross section $\sigma_b = \frac{6}{b \cdot h^2} M$ Circular section $\sigma_b = \frac{32}{\pi \cdot d^3} M$ where $M = F \cdot R$ l = straight length of spring material = $2 \cdot \pi \cdot r \cdot n$ (r mean coil radius) Under a pulsating load the stress increase due to curvature must be taken into consideration.	 $c = \frac{M}{\alpha} = \frac{E \cdot b \cdot h^3}{57.3 \cdot 12 \cdot l}$ $c = \frac{M}{\alpha} = \frac{E \cdot \pi \cdot d^4}{57.3 \cdot 64 \cdot l}$
Spiral torsion spring (both ends clamped) 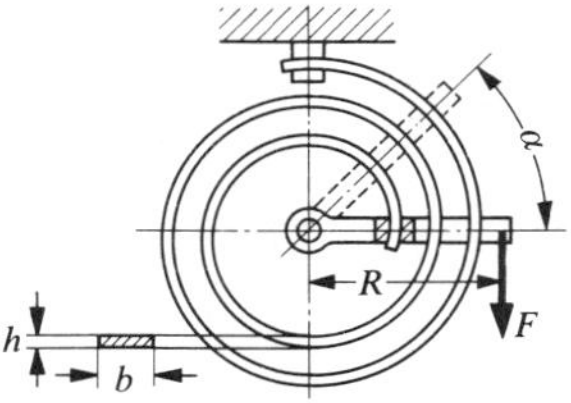	Equations as for torsion spring (see above)	

Fatigue-limit diagram

For polished spring-steel strip (not for vehicle springs) in accordance with DIN 17 222 Ck 75 and Ck 85, hardened and tempered to 430 ... 500 HV[1]), and Ck 85 and Ck 101, hardened and tempered to 500 ... 580 HV.

Example (broken line in diagram):
For a leaf spring with a hardness of 430 . . . 500 HV, assuming a minimum stress of,

$\sigma_u = 600 \text{ N/mm}^2$

the permissible stress range is

$\sigma_{hperm} = 480 \text{ N/mm}^2$

and the overstress is

$\sigma_0 = \sigma_u + \sigma_{hperm} = 1080 \text{ N/mm}^2$.

For reasons of safety, the stress range selected should be approximately 30 % lower. Surface damage (corrosion pits, score marks) drastically reduces the fatigue limit.

Bending

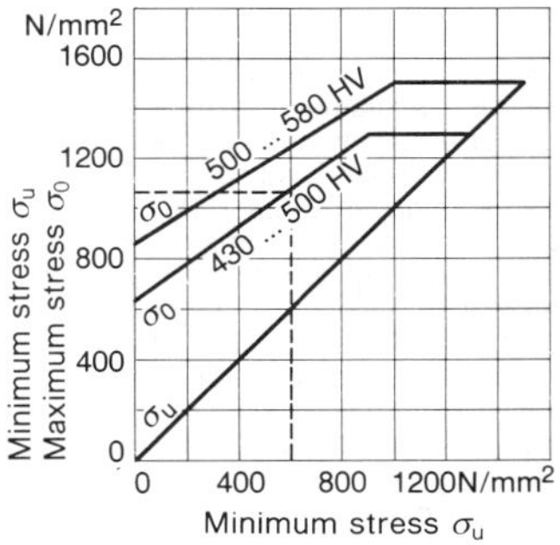

1) Vickers hardness; see p. 260.

Springs subjected to torsional stress

Type of spring	Torsional stress	Spring rate
Torsion-bar spring of circular cross section (DIN 2091) 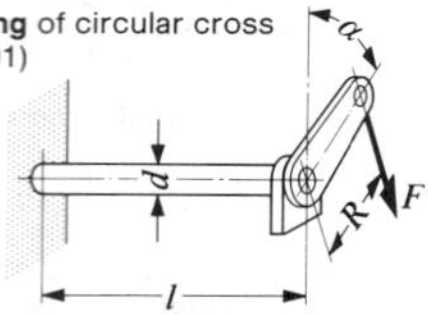	$\tau = \frac{16}{\pi \cdot d^3} M$	$c = \frac{M}{\alpha} = \frac{G \cdot \pi \cdot d^4}{57.3 \cdot 32 \cdot l}$
	where $M = F \cdot R$	

Helical springs made of round wire (DIN 2089)

Compression spring

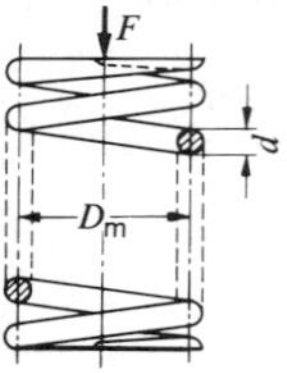

Extension spring

Above: half "German" loop, Below: hifo hook (see. p. 231)

Torsional stress:

a) In the case of a static or infrequently alternating load, allowance need not be made for the effect of the wire curvature:

$$\tau_i = \frac{8 \cdot D}{\pi \cdot d_3} F$$

b) In the case of a pulsating load, the non-uniform distribution of torsional stresses must be taken into consideration:

$$\tau_k = k \cdot \tau = \frac{8\, k \cdot D}{\pi \cdot d^3} F$$

Spring rate:

$$c = \frac{F}{s} = \frac{G \cdot d^4}{8 \cdot n \cdot D^3}$$

In the case of compression springs with 1 ... 3 coils, the load deflection curve is no longer a straight line; the spring rate c is initially smaller and then larger than the calculated amount.

The curvature correction factor k depends upon the spring index D/d

D/d	3	4	6	8	10	20
k	1.55	1.38	1.24	1.17	1.13	1.06

Avoid $D/d < 3$ and > 20.

The maximum permissible stresses τ_{ko} for various wire diameters at temperatures up to approximately 40 °C can be taken from the vertical boundary lines of the RDZ diagrams on pages 280 and 281 (RDZ = relaxation, fatigue limit, fatigue strength for finite life). Interpolation is to be used for intermediate values. At higher temperatures, the relaxation curves (loss of load) must be considered. After 300 h, relaxation values are approximately 1.5 times as great as after 10 h. Values for other materials are given on p. 188.

In the case of extension springs with initial tension, maximum permissible stress values must be reduced to 90 % of the values indicated in the diagrams because so-called setting is not possible here.

Explanation of the nomogram on the following page

The nomogram applies to cilindrical helical extension and compression springs made of round steel wire (shear modulus G = 81,400 N/mm²). In the case of materials with a different shear modulus G' spring deflection must be multiplied by G/G'.

The nomogram indicates the deflection s' of one coil. Total deflection s is obtained by multiplying (s') by the number of active coils $n : s = n \cdot s'$.

Nomogram for helical spring calculation

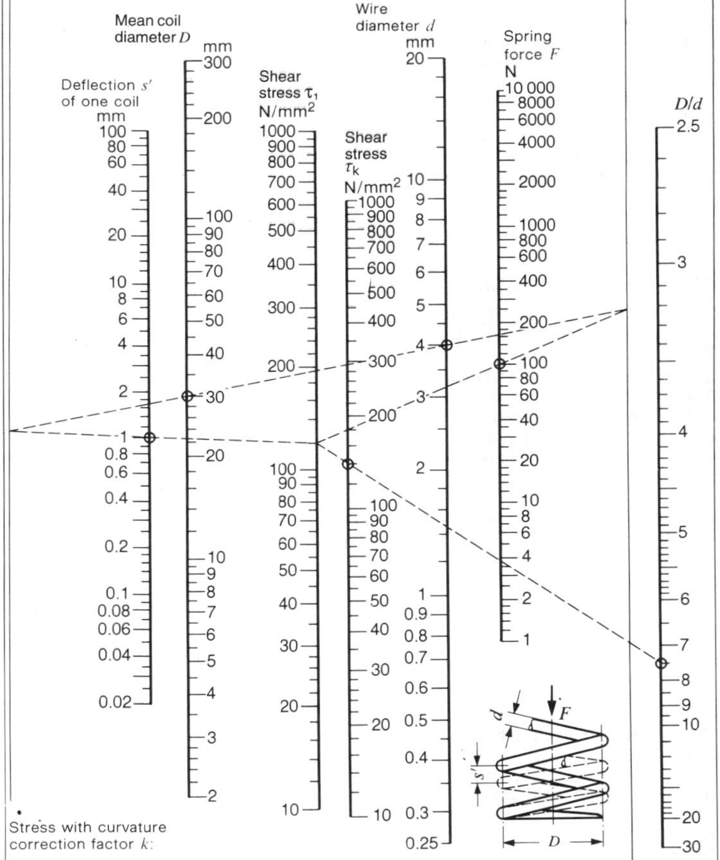

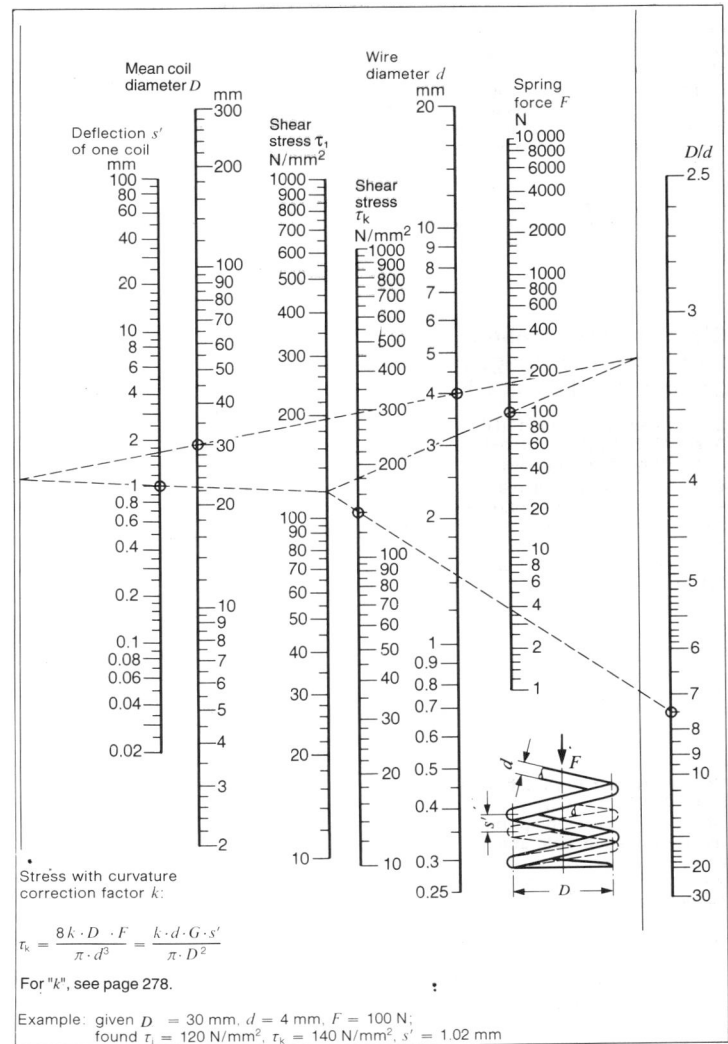

Stress with curvature correction factor k:

$$\tau_k = \frac{8k \cdot D \cdot F}{\pi \cdot d^3} = \frac{k \cdot d \cdot G \cdot s'}{\pi \cdot D^2}$$

For "k", see page 278.

Example: given $D = 30$ mm, $d = 4$ mm, $F = 100$ N;
found $\tau_i = 120$ N/mm², $\tau_k = 140$ N/mm², $s' = 1.02$ mm

Fatigue-limit diagram for torsion springs

Spring-steel wire, type C (DIN 17 223, Sheet 1).Torison springs not shot-peened.

Example (broken line in diagram):
For a torsion spring with a wire diameter of $d = 2$ mm, the permissible stress range to which the spring can be subjected for 10^7 load cycles and more without fracture is $\sigma_{bh} = 500$ N/mm² at a minimum stress σ_u of 800 N/mm².
The maximum stress is then

$$\sigma_0 = \sigma_u + \sigma_{bh} = 1300\,\text{N/mm}^2$$

Bending, Type C

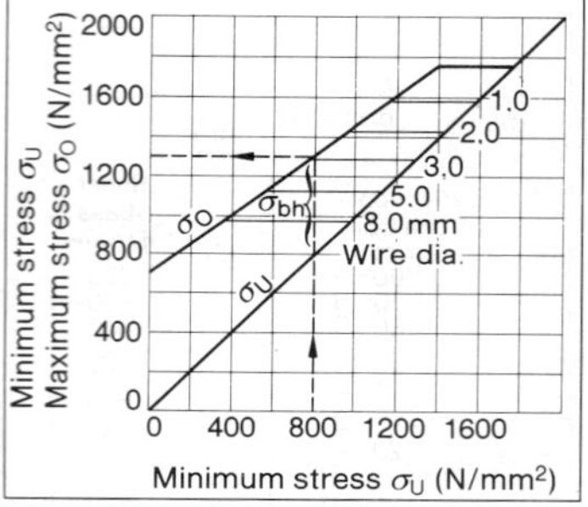

Diagrams of relaxation fatigue limit and fatigue Strength for finite life (RDZ)

Spring-steel wire, type C (DIN 17 223, Sheet 1). Helical compression springs not shot-peened, cold-set.

Example (broken line in diagram):
A helical compression spring with a wire diameter of 3 mm and a maximum stress of $\tau_{ko} = 900$ N/mm² at an operating temperature of 80 °C, has a loss of load after 10 h of

$$\Delta F_{10} = 5.5\,\%.$$

Given 4 x 10^5 load cycles to fracture, the stress range would be

$$\tau_{kh} = \tau_{ko} - \tau_{ku} = 900 - 480 = 420\,\text{N/mm}^2$$

Bending, Type C
Loss of load ΔF_{10} (%) at t = 80 °C

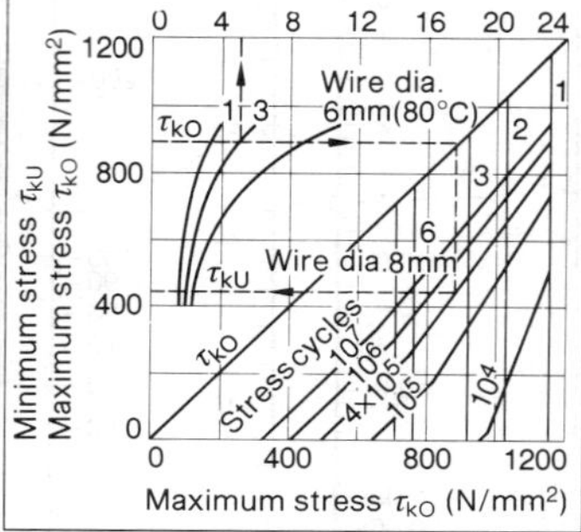

Valve-spring steel wire, type VD (DIN 17 223, Sheet 2).
Helical compression springs not shot-peened, cold-set.

Example (broken line in diagram):
A helical compression spring with a wire diameter of 3 mm and a maximum stress of τ_{ko} = 700 N/mm² at an operating temperature of 80 °C, has a loss of load after 10h of $\Delta F_{10} = 5$ %.

For an infinite number of load cycles (> 10^7), a stress range of

$$\tau_{kh} = 700 - 320 = 380\ \text{N/mm2}$$

is permissible.

Torsion, Type VD
Loss of load ΔF_{10} (%) at t = 80 °C

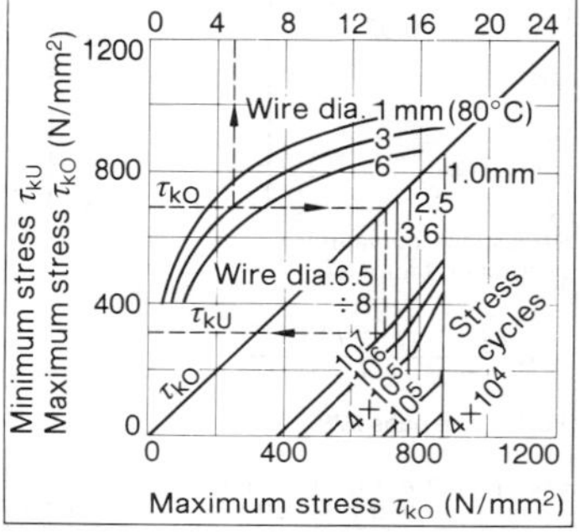

Valve-spring steel wire, VD CrV.[1]
Helical compression springs, not shot-peened, cold-set.
Example (broken line in diagram):
A helical compression spring with a wire diameter of 3 mm and a maximum stress of τ_{kO} = 700 N/mm² at an operating temperature of 160°C, has a loss of load after 10 h of ΔF_{10} = 6 %.

For an infinite number of load cycles (> 10^7), a stress range of

τ_{kh} = 700 − 240 = 460 N/mm²

is permissible.

Valve-spring steel wire, VD SiCr.[1]
Helical-compression springs, not shot-peened, cold-set.
Example (broken line in diagram):
A helical compression spring with a wire diameter of 3 mm and a maximum stress τ_{kO} = 900 N/mm² at an operating temperature of 160°C, has a loss of load after 10h of ΔF_{10} = 3.5 %.

For an infinite number of load cycles (> 10^7), a stress range of

τ_{kh} = 900 − 510 = 390 N/mm²

is permissible.

If the danger of natural oscillation or other additional loads is present, reduce the selected stress range by approximately 30 %. Shot peening increases the permissible stress range by approximately 30 %.

In the case of **compression springs**, force eccentricity is reduced as far as possible by winding the spring such that the wire end at each end of the spring touches the adjoining coil (closed ends). Each end of the spring is then ground flat perpendicular to the axis of the spring (wire end ≈ $d/4$). The following values then apply:
Total number of coils $n_t = n+2$.
The solid length from coil to coil $\leq (n+2)\,d$.

Helical extension springs are overstressed by roughly 50 % at standard hooks and loops when the body of the spring is subjected to permissible stress ranges. Hifo® hooks (German Patent, and others) exhibit infinite fatigue strength due to internal high initial force F_o.

[1]) According to DIN 17 223, Part 2.

Torsion, VD CrV
Loss of load ΔF_{10} (%) at t = 160 °C

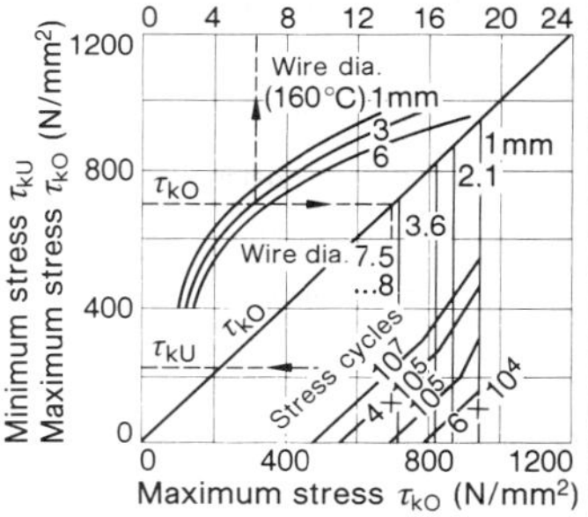

Torsion, VD SiCr
Loss of load ΔF_{10} (%) at t = 160 °C

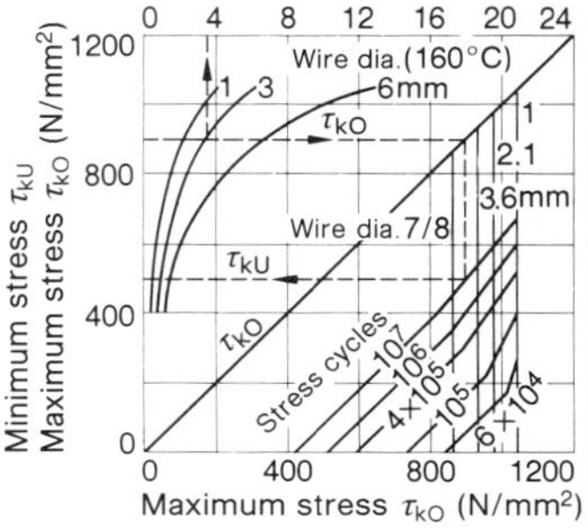

Due to their favorable internal stresses, twist-wound extension springs can be subjected to stresses as high as those to which compression springs are subjected, and exhibit smaller relaxation than the latter. For high initial forces F_o (= hifo), these springs can be up to 50 % shorter at F_1 than standard extension springs.

Basic principles of threaded fasteners

Quantities and units

Quantity		Unit
A_S	Stress area of thread (see p. 284)	mm^2
D_{Km}	Acting diameter for determining the friction torque at the fastener head or nut bearing face	mm
F_M	Tension force in the fastener after completed mounting (general)	N
F_{sp}	Axial installation tension of threaded fastener at 90 % of yield strength	N
M_M	Tightening torque for mounting	N·m
M_{sp}	Tightening torque required to load a threaded fastener to F_{sp})	N·m
P	Thread pitch	mm
d	Fastener diameter (major diameter of the thread)	mm
d_2	Mean flank diameter of thread ≈ Pitch diameter	mm
d_3	Minor diameter of thread	mm
μ_G	Coefficient of thread friction (Friction factor, coefficient of friction)	mm
μ_{tot}	Mean coefficient of friction for thread, fastener head and nut bearing faces	–
μ_K	Coefficient of friction for the fastener head or nut bearing faces	–
$\sigma_{0.2}$	0.2 % yield strength of the fastener material (for low-strength fasteners, the yield point σ_s applies instead; see footnote[1]) on p. 53)	N/ mm^2

Basic rules

Threaded fastener (screws, bolts, nuts) should clamp parts together with a force great enough to hold them in contact with one another without dislocation in spite of all applied operating forces. Bolts must not be subjected to shear.

A correctly preloaded fastener needs itself only to absorb a fraction of those operating forces which are applied roughly parallel to the bolt axis and which are usually dynamic in nature. The lowest fastener fatigue loading is achieved by using elastic fasteners (viz. long and reduced in the body to d_3) of property classes 8.8 to 12.9 with optimum tension force, and parts to be joined which are themselves as rigid as possible; highly stressed joints are also the best provision against subsequent setting of the joint and self-acting unscrewing. As a rule of thumb, setting of the joint reduces the installed tension force of a joint using 8.8-fasteners by 10 ... 20 % if the maximum temperature is 100°C and the parts so joined are metals with a tensile strength of at least 300 N/mm^2.

The tensioned section of the threaded fastener should have a minimum threaded length of 0.5 d, the object being to achieve 1.0 d whenever possible.

The spring force of installed locking devices (spring lock washers and the like) should be as great as the tension force of the fastener! Spring lock washers are usually disadvantageous when used with screws of property classes ≥ 8.8, grip lengths > 2.5 d and metallic components (because $F \ll F_{sp}$, and joint setting in the bearing faces additionally occurs). In the case of 4.8 and 5.6/5.8 fasteners, spring lock washers are generally superfluous if grip lengths are ≥ 5 d.

The compressive load per unit area under fastener heads and nuts must not exceed the crushing yield point (corresponds to at least the 0.2 % permanent elongation limit or yield strength) of the material of the joint parts (if required, use large washers or flanged hex screws).

Flange mountings using four bolts are considerably more reliable than such joints which use 3 bolts in a 120° arrangement (in the latter case, failure of one bolt leads to failure of the entire bolted joint).

Property classes

The designation system for threaded fasteners consists of two numbers separated by a decimal point. The first number represents ≈ 1/100 of the minimum tensile strength in N/mm^2, while the second number is 10 times the ratio of the minimum yield point (or 0.2 % yield strength) to the minimum tensile strength.

Table 1. Threaded fasteners: Mechanical strength properties and designations
Fasteners made of steels alloyed with boron which have a low carbon content are indicated by a solid line below the numerical designation, e.g., 10.9 (see also DIN-ISO 898, Part 1).

Property class		3.6	4.6	4.8	5.6	5.8	6.8	8.8	10.9	12.9
Tensile strength σ_B N/mm²	min	330	400	420	500	520	600	800	1040	1220
	max ≈	490	550		700		800	1000	1200	1400
Yield point σ_s N/mm², 0.2 % yield strength $\sigma_{0.2}$	min	180	240	320	300	400	480	–	–	–
	min	–	–	–	–	–	–	640	900	1080
Vickers hardness HV 30	min	95	120	130	155	160	190	250	320	385
	max	220					250	320	380	435
Color identification of the package		–	–		–		–	red	blue	yellow

The property classes of standard nuts (with nominal heights $\geq 0.8\,d$ and width across flats $\geq 1.45\,d$) are indicated by a number which corresponds to 1/100 of the stress under proof load in N/mm², this stress corresponds to the minimum tensile strength of a fastener in the same property class. The ability of a nut to withstand the stress under proof load is determined using a bolt thread of greater strength (min. 45 HRC); after the stress is relieved, the nut must still be movable on the thread.

Property classes for nuts:

4	5	6	8	10	12

For nuts with limited loadability:

04	06

(e.g., flat nuts)

For thread diameters of 5 mm and larger,
– Fasteners in property class 6.6 and greater, as well as
– Nuts in property class 8 and greater must be marked with the property class on the fastener head or nut face (if the bolts are small, the decimal point between the two numbers can be omitted; for nuts, a code system can also be used, whereby the chamfers of the nuts are marked with notches and dots).

Table 2. Yield strength for threaded fasteners made of other materials

Material	Designation	Thread	0.2% yield strength N/mm²
X5CrNi 1911	A2-70	≤ M20	450
CuZn37	Cu2	≤ M6	340
		M8 ... M39	250
CuSn6	Cu4	≤ M12	340
		M14 ... M39	200
AlMg5	Al2	≤ M14	205
AlMgSi1	Al3	≤ M39	250

The fatigue limit σ_D of cold-formed steel fasteners of sizes up to M12 is $\sigma_m \pm 50 \ldots 60$ N/mm² (referred to the root cross section), and applies up to a mean stress of $\sigma_m = 0.6\,\sigma_{0.2}$ and for all property classes from 4.8 to 12.9. Bolts of sizes up to M8 whose threads are rolled after hardening and tempering can achieve σ_D values of 450 ± 100 N/mm², whereas with gray cast iron and aluminum nuts, fasteners can achieve values of 450 ± 120 N/mm².

Tightening of threaded fasteners

Sufficient tightening torque for threaded fasteners can be realized by hand using a screwdriver up to sizes M5 – 8.8, using a 6-point socket up to a maximum of M8 – 10.9, and using a ring wrench or box-end wrench up to a maximum of M12 – 10.9 (provided that $\mu = \mu_G = \mu_K = 0.14$).

When fasteners are tightened using (conventional) torque measurement, variations in tension force occur in a ratio of approx. 1:2, and are caused by

– Variations in the coefficients of friction μ_K and μ_G (for screw head or nut and thread),

– Variations in the tightening torque (when tightened by hand and using power screwdrivers). For $\mu_G = \mu_K = 0.1$, the effective torque to produce the tension force is 17 % of the complete tightening torque. For $\mu_G = \mu_K = 0.2$, the effective torque is only 9.5 % of the tightening torque.

The highest possible clamping forces with very small variations can be achieved with threaded fasteners using the angular tightening method and the yield-point-controlled tightening method! It must be noted that these procedures – employed to greatest advantages with grades 8.8 and above – necessitate the use of precalculations and empirical testing and/or special electronically-controlled wrenches. In addition, the angular tightening method is in most cases only suitable for use with waisted-shank fasteners; if the yield-point-controlled tightening method is used, the grip (total thickness of the bolted parts without female thread) should be at least as thick as the nominal diameter of the bolt.

Basic formulas for tightening with torque measurement

The maximum permissible tension force in the fastener is limited by the effective stress (tension and torsion) which is equal to 0.9 times the minimum yield strength; this installed force is designated F_{sp}. The effective stress for the stress area is calculated according to the formula

$$A_s = \frac{\pi}{4} \cdot \left(\frac{d_2 + d_3}{2}\right)^2$$

with which the static axial tensile stresses and the torsional stresses (generated by thread friction) can be viewed as if the fastener were a smooth part (A_s is greater than the minor cross section due to the fact that the threads inhibit deformation). Thus

$$F_{sp} = \frac{0.196\,(d_2 + d_3)^2 \cdot 0.9 \cdot \sigma_{0.2}}{\sqrt{1 + 4.86 \left(\frac{P + \mu_G \cdot 3.63\, d_2}{d_2 + d_3}\right)^2}}$$

The values given in Table 5 on Page 287 for the installed tension forces F_{sp} were calculated for various coefficients of thread friction μ_G using the above formula.

In determining tightening torque it was formally customary to assume that $\mu_G = \mu_K = \mu_{tot}$ in order to arrive at the simplified formula

$$M_{sp} = F_{sp}\left[0.16\,P + \mu_{tot}\left(0.58\,d_2 + \frac{D_{Km}}{2}\right)\right]$$

and corresponding graphs. In the case of differing fastener head and thread coefficients of friction (see example on Page 288), however, this formula cannot be used to correctly determine the necessary tightening torque (see also the explanation above Table 4).

A simple, practical way of calculating tightening torque in the case of differing coefficients of friction μ_G and μ_K is the K-method (proposed by Gill, used in the USA and contained in VDI Recommendations 2230, 1977 Edition):

According to this method, the installed tightening torque is

$$M_M = K \cdot F_M \cdot d$$

and

$$M_{sp} = \mathrm{K} \cdot \mathrm{F}_{sp} \cdot d$$

for tightening to 90 % of the yield strength where

$$K = \frac{0.16 \cdot P + \mu_G \cdot 0.58 \cdot d_2 + \mu_K \cdot D_{Km}/2}{d}$$

For differing coefficients of friction μ_G and μ_K and a wide range of fastener dimensions, K can be given independently of d in tabular form (see Table 4).

Coefficients of friction

Using table 3 below, both the coefficient of friction for fastener head or nut (μ_K) and thread friction (μ_G) are determined separately and one after the other.

These coefficients of friction are significantly increased by the use of self-locking screws, washers with sharp, roughly radial edges and lock nuts; connections using these fastening devices must be tightened according to special specifications.

Tightening threaded-fastener connections

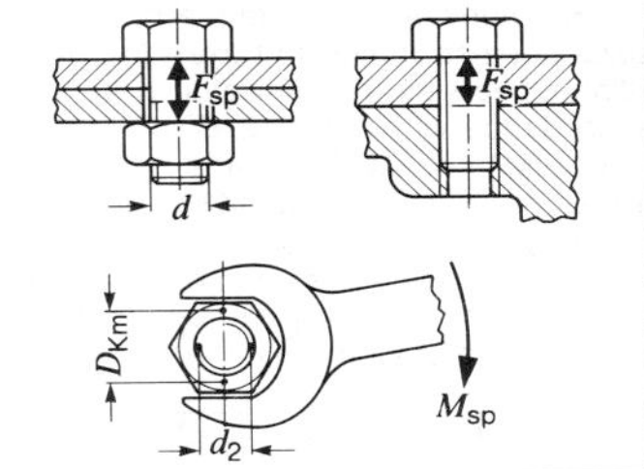

Table 3.
Coefficients of friction μ_K and μ_G for various surface and lubrication conditions
$\mu_{G\,min}$ (lower value in Table 3) is used to determine tension force F_{sp} in Table 5.

Surfaces on mating party: Bearing face on part (μ_K) or *nut thread* (μ_G)	Lubrication condition	Fastener surfaces: Bearing face of fastener head or bottom surface of nut (μ_K) or *fastener thread* (μ_G) — Steel, oil-quenched or zinc-phosphated: pressed, rolled	Steel, oil-quenched or zinc-phosphated: turned, cut	Steel: zinc-electroplated 6 µm
Steel, rolled	Lightly oiled	0.13 ... 0.19	0.10 ... 0.18	0.10 ... 0.18
Steel, planed, milled, turned, cut	Lightly oiled	0.10 ... 0.18	–	0.10 ... 0.18
Steel, ground	Lightly oiled	0.16 ... 0.22	0.10 ... 0.18	0.10 ... 0.18
Gray cast iron, planed, milled, turned, cut	Lightly oiled	0.10 ... 0.18	–	0.10 ... 0.18
All-black malleable iron, ground	Lightly oiled	0.16 ... 0.22	0.10 ... 0.18	0.10 ... 0.18
Steel, cadmium-electroplated, 6 µm	Lightly oiled	0.08 ... 0.16	0.08 ... 0.16	–
Steel, zinc-electroplated, 6 µm	Lightly oiled	0.10 ... 0.18	0.10 ... 0.16	0.16 ... 0.20
Steel, zinc-electroplated female threads	Lightly oiled	–	–	0.10 ... 0.18
Steel, ground, rolled, phosphated	Lightly oiled	0.12 ... 0.20	–	–
Steel, machined, phosphated	Lightly oiled	0.10 ... 0.18	–	–
Al-Mg alloys, processed, cut	Lightly oiled	0.08 ... 0.20	–	–
Steel, cadmium-electroplated, 6 µm	Dry	0.08 ... 0.16	–	–
Steel, cadmium-electroplated, female threads	Dry	0.08 ... 0.14	–	–
Steel, zinc-electroplated, 6 µm	Dry	0.10 ... 0.18	–	0.20 ... 0.30
Steel, zinc-electroplated, female threads	Dry	0.08 ... 0.16	–	0.12 ... 0.20

Table 4. K-Values

The K-values apply to standard threads of sizes M1.4 to M42 and bolt head and nut sizes corresponding to hexagon bolts and screws in accordance with DIN 931, 933; fillister-head slotted screws in accordance with DIN 84, hexagon cap screws in accordance with DIN 912, 6912, 7984; nuts in accordance with DIN 934.

For M16 to M42 threads, the K-value is to be reduced by 5 %, because the transition from M14 to M16 represents a significant jump in the courseness of thread pitch d/P.

Intermediate values can be interpolated with sufficient accuracy. Note: In special cases where only μ_{tot} has been determined previously, the K-value is determined for the case in which $\mu_K = \mu_G = \mu_{tot}$ (see also p. 284).

Coefficient of friction for threads μ_G	Coefficient of friction for fastener head and nut bearing face μ_K										
	0.04	0.06	0.08	0.10	0.12	0.14	0.16	0.18	0.20	0.24	0.28
0.008	0.094	0.108	0.120	0.134	0.148	0.162	0.176	0.190	0.204	0.232	0.260
0.10	0.104	0.118	0.132	0.146	0.158	0.172	0.186	0.200	0.214	0.242	0.270
0.12	0.114	0.128	0.142	0.156	0.170	0.184	0.196	0.210	0.224	0.252	0.280
0.14	0.124	0.138	0.152	0.166	0.180	0.194	0.208	0.222	0.234	0.262	0.290
0.16	0.134	0.148	0.162	0.176	0.190	0.204	0.218	0.232	0.246	0.272	0.300
0.18	0.146	0.160	0.172	0.186	0.200	0.214	0.228	0.242	0.256	2.284	0.312
0.20	0.156	0.170	0.184	0.198	0.210	0.224	0.238	0.252	0.266	0.294	0.322
0.24	0.176	0.190	0.204	0.218	0.232	0.246	0.260	0.274	0.286	0.314	0.342
0.28	0.198	0.212	0.224	0.238	0.252	0.266	0.280	0.294	0.308	0.336	0.362

Axial clamping forces of bolted joints

Scope of Table 5 for installed tension forces F_{sp}

Table 5 applies only to

- Bolts with standard thread and

$$\frac{\text{shank diameter } d_1}{\text{minor diameter } d_3} \geq 1.05$$

- Correct mating of nut and bolt, or female thread in machine parts, with respect to material strength;
- Nut height at least 0.8 × thread diameter and sufficient depth of thread in housings and the like.

Correction factors for tension forces and coefficients of friction (selection)

Flat nuts with a height of $0.5 \cdot d$ and the same hardness as the bolts allow a tension force of only 80 % of the values given in the table; in the case of low-strength flat nuts (04) on 12.9 bolts, only 33 % of F_{sp} is permissible.

In the case of fastener heads and nuts with smaller or larger bearing faces as well as adjusting screws and locating screws which do not have contact at their heads, the μ_K-value must be reduced or increased by the same ratio as the ratio of the mean friction diameter of their bearing faces to the mean friction diameter of the above-mentioned standard hexagon bolts, etc. and hexagon nuts. It is this corrected hypothetical μ_K-value which is used to determine the K-value (for this reason, Table 4 gives μ_K-values beginning with 0.04). In the case of countersunk head screws, allowance must be additionally made for the conical effect of the countersink angle as well as the greater elasticity of the outer edge of the head; thus the μ_K-value hypothetically increases by a factor of 1.25 in the case of standard countersunk screws (countersink angle: 90°).

Table 5. Tension forces F_{sp} in 10^3 N for standard threads and coefficients of friction μ_G in the threads (for 90% utilization of $\sigma_{0.2}$ or σ_s).

Dimension (Pitch)	Property class	F_{sp} (10^3 N) for coefficients of friction μ_G in the threads 0.06	0.08	0.10	0.12	0.14	0.16	0.18	0.20	0.24	0.28
M 4	4.8	2.3	2.2	2.1	2.0	1.9	1.9	1.8	1.7	1.6	1.4
	5.8	2.8	2.7	2.6	2.5	2.4	2.3	2.2	2.1	2.0	1.8
	8.8	4.5	4.4	4.2	4.1	3.9	3.7	3.6	3.4	3.2	2.9
	10.9	6.4	6.2	5.9	5.7	5.5	5.3	5.0	4.8	4.4	4.1
(0.7)	12.9	7.7	7.4	7.1	6.9	6.6	6.3	6.0	5.8	5.3	4.9
M 5	4.8	3.7	3.6	3.5	3.3	3.2	3.1	2.9	2.8	2.6	2.4
	5.8	4.6	4.5	4.3	4.2	4.0	3.8	3.6	3.5	3.2	3.0
	8.8	7.4	7.2	6.9	6.6	6.4	6.1	5.9	5.6	5.2	4.8
	10.9	10.4	10.1	9.7	9.4	9.0	8.6	8.3	7.9	7.3	6.7
(0.8)	12.9	12.5	12.1	11.7	11.2	10.8	10.3	9.9	9.5	8.7	8.1
M 6	4.8	5.2	5.1	4.9	4.7	4.5	4.3	4.1	4.0	3.7	3.4
	5.8	6.6	6.3	6.1	5.9	5.6	5.4	5.2	5.0	4.6	4.2
	8.8	10.5	10.1	9.8	9.4	9.0	8.6	8.3	7.9	7.3	6.7
	10.9	14.7	14.2	13.7	13.2	12.7	12.1	11.7	11.2	10.3	9.5
(1.0)	12.9	17.7	17.1	16.5	15.8	15.2	14.6	14.0	13.4	12.3	11.4
M 8	4.8	9.6	9.3	8.9	8.6	8.3	7.9	7.6	7.3	6.7	6.2
	5.8	12.0	11.6	11.2	10.8	10.3	9.9	9.5	9.1	8.4	7.7
	8.8	19.2	18.6	17.9	17.2	16.5	15.7	15.2	14.6	13.4	12.4
	10.9	27.0	26.1	25.2	24.2	23.2	22.3	21.4	20.5	18.9	17.4
(1.25)	12.9	32.4	31.3	30.2	29.0	27.9	26.8	25.7	24.6	22.6	20.9
M 10	4.8	15.3	14.8	14.2	13.7	13.2	12.6	12.1	11.6	10.7	9.9
	5.8	19.0	18.5	17.8	17.1	16.5	15.9	15.1	14.5	13.4	12.3
	8.8	30.5	29.5	28.5	27.4	26.3	25.3	24.2	23.2	21.4	19.7
	10.9	42.9	41.5	40.1	38.5	37.0	35.5	34.1	32.7	30.1	27.7
(1.5)	12.9	51.5	49.8	48.1	46.2	44.4	42.6	40.1	39.2	36.1	33.2
M 12	4.8	22.2	21.5	20.8	20.0	19.2	18.4	17.7	16.9	15.6	14.4
	5.8	27.8	26.9	25.9	25.0	24.0	23.0	22.1	21.2	19.5	18.0
	8.8	44.5	43.0	41.5	40.0	38.4	36.8	35.3	33.9	31.2	28.7
	10.9	62.5	60.5	58.4	56.2	54.0	51.8	49.7	47.7	43.8	40.4
(1.75)	12.9	75.0	72.6	70.0	67.4	64.8	62.2	59.6	57.2	52.6	48.5
M 14	4.8	30.5	29.6	28.5	27.4	26.4	25.3	24.3	23.3	21.4	19.7
	5.8	38.1	36.9	35.6	34.3	32.9	31.6	30.3	29.1	26.8	24.7
	8.8	61.0	59.1	57.0	54.9	52.7	50.6	48.5	46.5	42.8	39.5
	10.9	85.8	83.1	80.1	77.1	74.1	71.2	68.3	65.5	60.2	55.5
(2.0)	12.9	103	99.7	96.2	92.6	89.0	85.4	81.9	78.5	72.3	66.6
M 16	4.8	41.8	40.5	39.2	37.7	36.3	34.8	33.4	32.1	29.5	27.2
	5.8	52.3	50.7	48.9	47.2	45.4	43.6	41.8	40.1	36.9	34.0
	8.8	83.6	81.1	78.3	75.5	72.3	69.7	66.9	64.2	59.0	54.4
	10.9	118	114	110	106	102	98.0	94.1	90.2	83.0	76.5
(2.0)	12.9	141	137	132	127	122	118	113	108	99.6	91.9
M 20	4.8	65.3	63.3	61.2	59.0	56.7	54.5	52.2	50.1	46.1	42.5
	5.8	81.7	79.2	76.5	73.7	70.9	68.1	65.3	62.7	57.7	53.2
	8.8	131	127	122	118	113	109	105	100	92.3	85.1
	10.9	184	178	172	166	159	153	147	141	130	120
(2.5)	12.9	220	214	206	199	191	184	176	169	156	144

In contrast to 5.8 bolts, the tension forces F_{sp} for bolts in other (including non-ferrous) property classes must be converted based on their yield points or their yield strengths; e.g. for an M6-Cu2 bolt with $\mu_G = 0.10$, $F_{sp} = (340/400) \cdot 6.1 \cdot 10^3 \approx 5.2 \cdot 10^3$ N.

Advantages of the K-method over previously used methods of determining tightening torque

– Easily takes into account the different coefficients of friction μ_K and μ_G. The K-method therefore allows for more reliable design and greater minimum installed tension force (if the example below were calculated using $\mu_{tot} = \mu_K$, the maximum tension force would be impermissibly high, reaching a value just below the yield point. If the calculation were made using $\mu_{tot} = \mu_G$ instead, the tightening torques would be lower and the minimum tension force would be only 68 % of 14,800 N).

– In order to express the values listed in Table 3 as μ_{tot} values, more comprehensive tabular information would be required. Table 3 requires only a fraction of this information.

– The K-method is used to precisely determine the tightening torques when tightening threaded fasteners using a torque wrench, and is an advantageous replacement for previous tables and somewhat complicated graphs.

– Using yield point or angle-controlled tightening methods, better utilization factors can still be achieved at threaded-fastener connections (see p. 284).

Determination of tension forces and tightening torques

The maximum attainable installed tension force $F_{sp\,max}$ is determined using the smallest coefficient of friction in the threads μ_G and Table 5. (Most of the torque applied to the screw shank is used to overcome thread friction, while only the remainder is converted to tension force by the thread pitch; the maximum permissible tension force must not be exceeded even when this residual torque reaches its maximum value and μ_G its minimum value.)

The maximum permissible installed tightening torque $M_{sp\,max}$ is calculated using the K-value for the lowest values for μ_K and μ_G (because the maximum permissible clamping force must not be exceeded even when maximum tightening torque coincides with the smallest coefficients of friction).

$$M_{sp\,max} = K_{min} \cdot F_{sp\,max} \cdot d$$

The lowest installed tightening torque $M_{sp\,min}$ is a result of the quality of the tightening process and the equipment used. If good power screwdrivers are used or the tightening process is carefully performed by hand using torque wrenches, the nominal torque can usually be achieved within a variation ±10 %. The lowest installed tightening torque is then

$$M_{sp\,min} \approx 0.8 \cdot M_{sp\,max}$$

The lowest installed clamping force $F_{sp\,min}$ which then may occur is calculated using the K-value for the maximum values of the two coefficients of friction μ_K and μ_G as follows:

$$F_{sp\,min} = M_{sp\,min}/(K_{max} \cdot d)$$

Example: *An M 10-8.8 bolt or screw (pressed and rolled, phosphated) is used to fasten a ground steel part to an AlMg housing with blind threaded holes; the parts are lightly oiled.*

From Table 3: $\mu_K = 0.16 \ldots 0.22$; $\mu_G = 0.08 \ldots 0.20$ → in accordance with Table 3: for $\mu_G = 0.08$, $F_{sp\,max} = 29{,}500$ N

From Table 4: $K_{min} = 0.176$ | $K_{max} = 0.280$

→ $M_{sp\,max} = 0.176 \cdot 29{,}500 \cdot 0.010 = 51.9$ N·m

$M_{sp\,min} = 0.8 \cdot M_{sp\,max} = 41.5$ N·m

→ $F_{sp\,min} = 41.5/(0.280 \cdot 0.010) = 14{,}800$ N

(with d in m)

Threads (Selection)

ISO metric screw threads

(DIN 13); basic dimensions

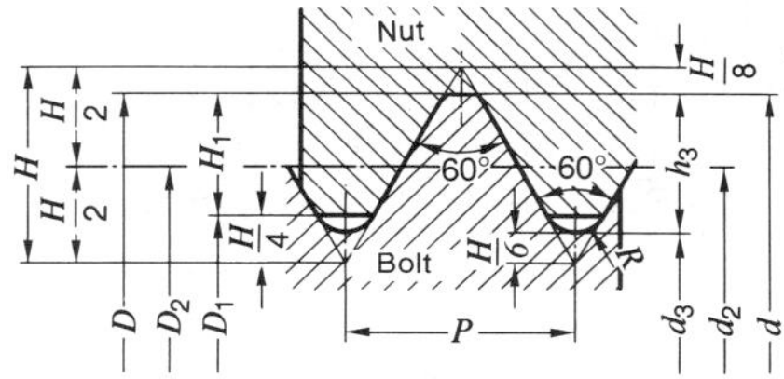

Metric standard thread

Example of designation: M 8 (nominal thread diameter: 8 mm)

Nominal thread dia. $d = D$	Pitch P	Pitch dia. $d_2 = D_2$	Minor dia. d_3	Minor dia. D_1	Thread depth h_3	Thread depth H_1	Tensile stress area A_s in mm²
3	0.5	2.675	2.387	2.459	0.307	0.271	5.03
4	0.7	3.545	3.141	3.242	0.429	0.379	8.78
5	0.8	4.480	4.019	4.134	0.491	0.433	14.2
6	1	5.350	4.773	4.917	0.631	0.541	20.1
8	1.25	7.188	6.466	6.647	0.767	0.677	36.6
10	1.5	9.026	8.160	8.376	0.920	0.812	58.0
12	1.75	10.863	9.853	10.106	1.074	0.947	84.3
16	2	14.701	13.546	13.835	1.227	1.083	157
20	2.5	18.376	16.933	17.294	1.534	1.353	245
24	3	22.051	20.319	20.752	1.840	1.624	353

Metric fine thread

Example of designation: M8 × 1 (Nominal thread diameter: 8 mm; pitch: 1 mm)

Nominal thread dia. $d = D$	Pitch P	Pitch dia. $d_2 = D_2$	Minor dia. d_3	Minor dia. D_1	Thread depth h_3	Thread depth H_1	Tensile stress area A_s in mm²
8	1	7.350	6.773	6.917	0.613	0.541	39.2
10	1.25	9.188	8.466	8.647	0.767	0.677	61.2
10	1	9.350	8.773	8.917	0.613	0.541	64.5
12	1.5	11.026	10.160	10.376	0.920	0.812	88.1
12	1.25	11.188	10.466	10.647	0.767	0.677	92.1
16	1.5	15.026	14.160	14.376	0.920	0.812	167
18	1.5	17.026	16.160	16.376	0.920	0.812	216
20	2	18.701	17.546	17.835	1.227	1.083	258
20	1.5	19.026	18.160	18.376	0.920	0.812	272
22	1.5	21.026	20.160	20.376	0.920	0.812	333
24	2	22.701	21.546	21.835	1.227	1.083	384
24	1.5	23.026	22.160	22.376	0.920	0.812	401

UST (Unified screw threads): Basic dimensions

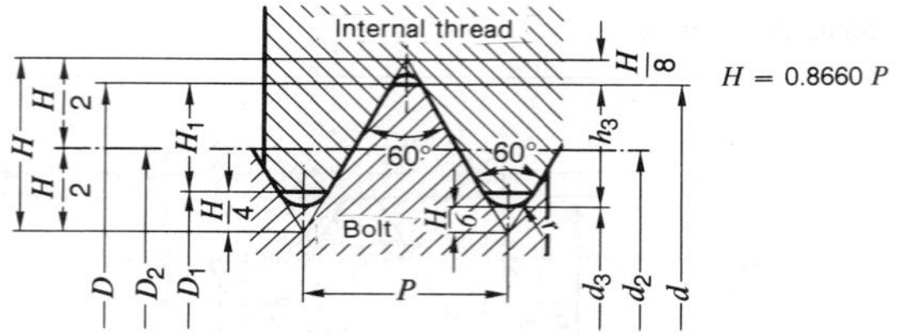

UNC (Coarse thread)

Example of designation: 1/4-20 UNC (nominal thread diameter: 1/4 inch; 20 threads/inch)

Nominal thread dia. inch	Major thread dia. $d = D$ mm	Number of threads per 1 inch	Pitch P mm	Pitch dia. $d_2 = D_2$ mm	Minor dia. d_3 mm	Minor dia. D_1 mm	Tensile stress area A_s mm²
1/4	6.35	20	1.270	5.524	4.839	4.976	20.5
5/16	7.94	18	1.411	7.021	6.258	6.411	33.8
3/8	9.53	16	1.588	8.494	7.633	7.805	50.0
7/16	11.11	14	1.814	9.934	8.953	9.149	68.6
1/2	12.70	13	1.954	11.430	10.373	10.584	91.5
9/16	14.29	12	2.117	12.913	11.768	11.996	117
5/8	15.88	11	2.309	14.376	13.127	13.376	146
3/4	19.05	10	2.540	17.399	16.025	16.299	215
7/8	22.23	9	2.822	20.391	18.864	19.169	298
1	25.40	8	3.175	23.338	21.620	21.963	391

UNF (Fine thread)

Example of designation: 1/4-28 UNF (nominal thread diameter: 1/4 inch; 28 threads/inch)

Nominal thread dia. inch	Major thread dia. $d = D$ mm	Number of threads per 1 inch	Pitch P mm	Pitch dia. $d_2 = D_2$ mm	Minor dia. d_3 mm	Minor dia. D_1 mm	Tensile stress area A_s mm²
1/4	6.35	28	0.907	5.761	5.268	5.367	23.5
5/16	7.94	24	1.058	7.249	6.678	6.792	37.4
3/8[1])	9.53	24	1.058	8.837	8.265	8.379	56.6
7/16	11.11	20	1.270	10.287	9.601	9.738	76.6
1/2[1])	12.70	20	1.270	11.874	11.189	11.326	103
9/16	14.29	18	1.411	13.371	12.608	12.761	131
5/8	15.88	18	1.411	14.958	14.196	14.348	165
3/4	19.05	16	1.588	18.019	17.178	17.330	241
7/8	22.23	14	1.814	21.046	20.066	20.262	328
1	25.40	12	2.117	24.026	22.862	23.109	428

[1]) These American threads are also used as mounting threads for drill chucks.

Pipe threads for non self-sealing joints

(DIN ISO 228, Part 1); Parallel external and internal threads; basic dimensions

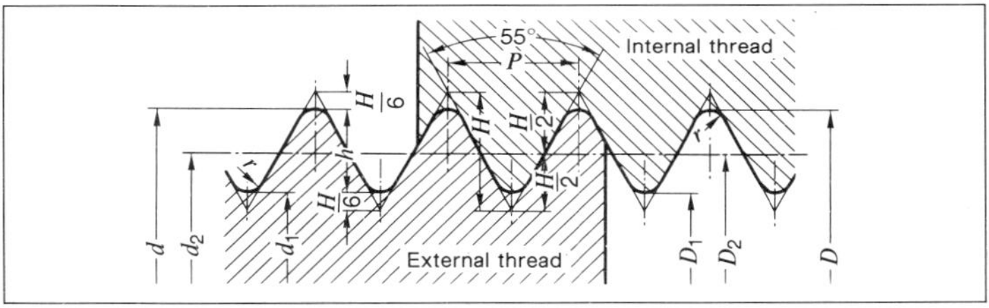

Example of designation: G 1/2 (nominal thread size 1/2 inch)

Nominal thread size	Number of threads per 1 inch	Pitch P mm	Thread depth h mm	Major diameter $d = D$ mm	Pitch diameter $d_2 = D_2$ mm	Minor diameter $d_1 = D_1$ mm
1/4	19	1.337	0.856	13.157	12.301	11.445
3/8	19	1.337	0.856	16.662	15.806	14.950
1/2	14	1.814	1.162	20.955	19.793	18.631
3/4	14	1.814	1.162	26.441	25.279	24.117
1	11	2.309	1.479	33.249	31.770	30.291

Whitworth pipe threads for threaded pipes and fittings

(DIN 2999); Parallel internal threads and taper external threads; basic dimensions (mm)

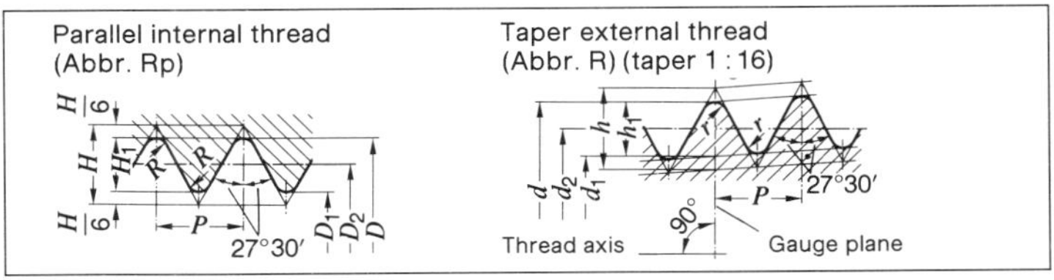

Designations		Major diameter	Pitch diameter	Minor diameter	Pitch	Number of threads per 1 inch
External thread	Internal thread	$d = D$	$d_2 = D_2$	$d_1 = D_1$	P	Z
R 1/4	**Rp 1/4**	13.157	12.301	11.445	1.337	19
R 3/8	**Rp 3/8**	16.662	15.806	14.950	1.337	19
R 1/2	**Rp 1/2**	20.955	19.793	18.631	1.814	14
R 3/4	**Rp 3/4**	26.441	25.279	24.117	1.814	14
R 1	**Rp 1**	33.249	31.770	30.291	2.309	11

Areas of application: For joining pipes with parallel internal threads to valves, fittings, threaded flanges, etc. which have taper external threads.

Gears and tooth systems

(with involute flanks)

Quantities and units (DIN 3960)

Quantity	Unit
a Center distance	mm
b Face width	mm
c Bottom clearance	
d Reference diameter	mm
d_a Outside diameter	mm
d_b Base circle diameter	mm
d_f Root diameter	mm
h_a Addendum $= m \cdot h^*_{aP}$	mm
h_f Dedendum $= m \cdot h^*_{fP}$	mm
j_n Normal backlash	
m Module $m = d/z$	mm
n Rotational speed	min^{-1}
p Pitch $p = \pi \cdot m$	mm
s Tooth thickness (circular)	mm
W Span measurement	mm
x Addendum modification coefficient	–
z Number of teeth	–

Quantity	Unit
α Pressure angle	°
β Helix angle	°
ε Contact ratio	°
* Specific value, to be multiplied by m	
Indices	
1 referred to gear 1	
2 referred to gear 2	
a referred to tooth tip	
b referred to base circle	
f referred to root	
n referred to normal profile	
t referred to transverse profile	
w referred to operating pitch circle	
F referred to root tooth load	
P referred to basic rack	
W referred to contact pressure	

Gear type and shape are determined by the position of the shafts which are joined by the gears in order to transmit forces or movements.

Cycloidal teeth: Cycloidal teeth are used primarily in the watch and clock industry. They permit small numbers of teeth without cutter interference (undercut). They are characterized by low contact pressure, but are sensitive to variations in the distance between centers.

Involute teeth: Involute teeth, on the other hand, are not sensitive to variations in the distance between centers. They can be produced with relatively simple tools using the generating method. The automobile industry uses involute teeth almost exclusively, therefore the following information is limited to this type of gear system.

All spur gears with the same module (and the same pressure angle) can be produced using the same generating tool, regardless of the number of teeth and addendum modification. A number of modules have been standardized in

***Effect of addendum modification as shown on an 8-tooth gear** ($\alpha = 20°$)*

1 without addendum modification, 2 with addendum modification

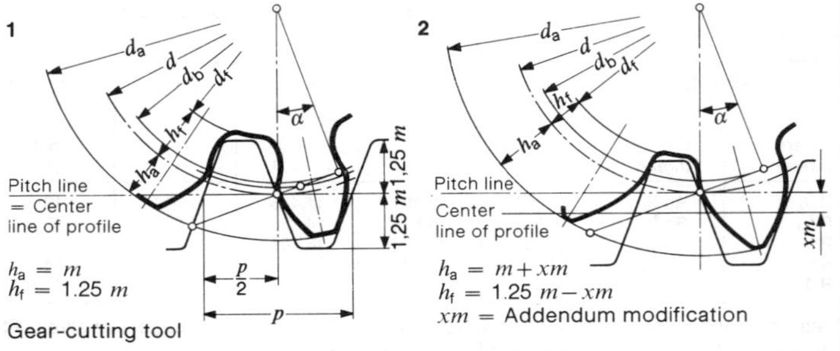

Definitions

Gear types

Position of shafts	Gear type	Properties	Examples of application in automotive engineering
Parallel	External or internal spur-gear pair with straight or helical teeth	Helical teeth run more smoothly, but are subject to axial thrust	Manual transmissions
Intersecting	Bevel-gear pair with straight, helical or curved teeth		Differentials
Crossed	Offset bevel-gear pair with helical or curved teeth		Rear-axle drive
	Crossed helical-gear pair	For small loads	Distributor drives
	Worm-gear pair	High-ratio, single-stage transmission	Windshield-wiper drives
Coaxial	Toothed shaft and hub	Sliding shaft coupling	Starting motors
	Coarse-thread shaft and hub		

order to limit the number of such tools and the number of master gears required for gear testing:
Module for cylindrical and bevel gears: DIN 780 (see table on p. 295); module for worms and worm gears: DIN 780; module for toothed shafts and hubs: DIN 5480.

The module in the normal profile for crossed helical gears is also selected in conformance with DIN 780 in most cases. A series of modules suited to the manufacturing process is generally used for curved-tooth bevel gears.

Tooth shape
Basic rack for spur gears: DIN 867, DIN 58 400; basic rack for bevel gears: DIN 3971; basic rack for worms and worm gears: DIN 3975; basic rack for toothed shafts and hubs: DIN 5480.

The tooth shape for crossed helical gears can also be designed in conformance with the basic rack as per DIN 867. In addition to the standardized pressure angles (20° for running gears and 30° for toothed shafts and hubs), pressure angles of 12°, 14° 30′, 15°, 17° 30′, 22° 30′ and 25° are used.

Addendum modification
Addendum modification (see diagram) is used to avoid undercut when the number of teeth is small, to increase tooth root strength and to achieve a specific distance between centers.

Gear pair with reference center distance
With a gear pair at reference center distance, the addendum modifications to the gear and pinion are equal but opposite, such that the distance between centers does not change. This design is preferred for crossed helical and bevel gear pairs.

Gear pair with modified center distance
The addendum modifications to the gear and pinion do not cancel each other, therefore the distance between centers varies.

Terms and errors
Terms and errors are explained in detail in the following standards: DIN 3960, DIN 58 405 (spur gears), DIN 3971 (bevel gears) and DIN 3975 (worms and worm gears).

Basic equations for spur gears

Designation	Straight gear ($\beta = 0$)	Helical gear ($\beta = 0$)
Pitch diameter	$d = z \cdot m$ See p. 292 for module m	$d = \frac{z \cdot m_n}{\cos\beta}$ See p.292 for module m_n
	The negative value of z_2 is to be used for internal teeth; center distance a becomes negative.	
Base circle diameter	$d_b = d \cdot \cos\alpha_n$	$d_b = d \cdot \cos\alpha_t$ α_t from $\tan\alpha_t = \frac{\tan\alpha_n}{\cos\beta}$
Center distance, no backlash if normal backlash $j_n = 0$	$a = m \frac{z_1 + z_2}{2} \cdot \frac{\cos\alpha}{\cos\alpha_w} = \frac{d_{b1} + d_{b2}}{2 \cdot \cos\alpha_w}$ $\alpha = 20^\circ$ as per DIN 867 α_w from: $\mathrm{inv}\alpha_w = \frac{2(x_1+x_2)\sin\alpha + j_n/m}{(z_1+z_2)\cos\alpha} + \mathrm{inv}\alpha$	$a = m_t \frac{z_1 + z_2}{2} \cdot \frac{\cos\alpha_t}{\cos\alpha_{wt}} = \frac{d_{b1} + d_{b2}}{2 \cdot \cos\alpha_{wt}}$ $m_t = \frac{m_n}{\cos\beta}$ $\cos\beta_b = \frac{\sin\alpha}{\sin\alpha_t}$ $\mathrm{inv}\alpha_{wt} = \frac{m_n \cdot 2(x_1+x_2)\sin\alpha_n + j_n/\cos\beta_b}{m_t(z_1+z_2)\cos\alpha_t} + \mathrm{inv}\alpha_t$
Involute	$\mathrm{inv}\alpha = \tan\alpha - \hat{\alpha}$ p. 139, inv. $\alpha = 0.014904$ when $\alpha = 20^\circ$	
Operating pitch diameter	$d_w = d_b/\cos\alpha_w$	$d_w = d_b/\cos\alpha_{wt}$
Root diameter	$d_f = d + 2xm - 2h^*_{fP} \cdot m$	$d_f = d + 2xm_n - 2h^*_{fP} \cdot m_n$
	with dedendum $h^*_{fP} \cdot m$ ($h^*_{fP} = 1.167$ or 1.25 as per DIN 3972)	
Outside diameter	$d_a + d + 2xm + 2h^*_{aP} \cdot m$	$d_a = d + 2xm_n + 2h^*_{aP} \cdot m_n$
	with addendum $h^*_{aP} \cdot m$ ($h^*_{aP} = 1.0$ as per DIN 867)	
Bottom clearance	$c_1 = a_{min} - d_{a1}/2 - d_{f2}/2$; $c_2 = a_{min} - d_{a2}/2 - d_{f1}/2$ $c \geqq 0.15\, m_n$	
Tooth thickness in pitch circle (circular)	$s = m(\pi/2 + 2x \cdot \tan\alpha)$	Normal profile $s_n = m_n(\pi/2 + 2x\tan\alpha_n)$ Transverse profile $s_t = s_n/\cos\beta = m_t(\pi/2 + 2 \cdot x \cdot \tan\alpha_n)$
Ideal number of teeth	$z_i = z$	$z_i = z\frac{\mathrm{inv}\,\alpha_t}{\mathrm{inv}\,\alpha_n}$
Number of teeth spanned	$z' \approx z_i \frac{\alpha_{nx}}{180} + 0.5$ α_{nx} from $\cos\alpha_{nx} \approx \frac{z_i}{z_i + 2x}\cos\alpha_n$ for z' take next whole number	
Base tangent length over z' teeth	$W_{z'} = \{[(z' - 0.5)\pi + z_i\,\mathrm{inv}\alpha_n]\cos\alpha_n + 2x \cdot \sin\alpha_n\}\, m_n$	
Transverse contact ratio for gears without allowance for cutter interference	$\varepsilon_\alpha = \frac{\sqrt{d_{a1}^2 - d_{b1}^2} + \frac{z_2}{\lvert z_2 \rvert}\sqrt{d_{a2}^2 - d_{b2}^2} - (d_{b1} + d_{b2})\tan\alpha_w}{2 \cdot \pi \cdot m \cdot \cos\alpha}$ (straight teeth) $\varepsilon_\alpha = \frac{\sqrt{d_{a1}^2 - d_{b1}^2} + \frac{z_2}{\lvert z_2 \rvert}\sqrt{d_{a2}^2 - d_{b2}^2} - (d_{b1} + d_{b2})\tan\alpha_{wt}}{2 \cdot \pi \cdot m_t \cdot \cos\alpha_t}$ (helical teeth)	
Overlap ratio	–	$\varepsilon_\beta = \frac{b \cdot \sin\lvert\beta\rvert}{m_n \cdot \pi}$
Total contact ratio	$\varepsilon_\gamma = \varepsilon_\alpha > 1$	$\varepsilon_\gamma = \varepsilon_\alpha + \varepsilon_\beta$
	Apply only if: $\varepsilon_\gamma > 1$ for $d_{a\,min}$ and a_{max}	

Inserting $j_n = 0$ in the preceding formulas results in gearing with zero backlash. The tooth thickness and span measurement deviations required to produce backlash can be specified in accordance with DIN 3967 and DIN 58 405, taking into consideration the quality of the gears. It is necessary to ensure that the minimum backlash is great enough to compensate for tooth error (such as total composite error, alignment deviation, center-to-center distance error, etc.) without reducing the backlash to zero, and without leading to gear jamming. Other parameters for which the tolerances must be determined (with reference to the tooth errors given above in parantheses) are those for (two-flank) total composite error and (two-flank) tooth-to-tooth composite error (DIN 3963, DIN 58 405), alignment deviation (DIN 3962 T2, DIN 3967, DIN 58 405) and distance between centers (DIN 3964, DIN 58 405).

Module series for spur and bevel gears in mm (excerpt from DIN 780)

0.3	**1**	**3**	**10**	**32**
0.35	1.125	3.5	11	36
0.4	**1.25**	**4**	**12**	**40**
0.45	1.375	4.5	14	45
0.5	1.5	**5**	**16**	**50**
0.55	1.75	5.5	18	55
0.6	**2**	**6**	**20**	**60**
0.65	2.25	7	22	70
0.7	**2.5**	**8**	**25**	
0.75	2.75	9	28	
0.8				
0.85				
0.9				
0.95				

Modules given in bold type are preferred.

DIN gear qualities (DIN 3961 to DIN 3964)

Quality	Examples of applications	Manufacture
2	Primary-standard master gears	Form grinding (50 ... 60 % scrap rate)
3	Master gears for the inspection department	Form grinding and generative grinding
4	Master gears for the workshop, measuring mechanisms	
5	Drives for machine tools, turbines, measuring equipment	
6	As 5, also highest gears of passenger-car and bus transmissions	
7	Motor-vehicle transmissions (highest gears), machine tools, rail vehicles, hoisting and handling equipment, turbines, office machines	Non-hardened gears (carefully manufactured) by hobbing, generative shaping and planing (subsequent shaving desirable); additional grinding is required for hardened gears
8 and 9	Transmissions for motor vehicles (middle and lower gears), rail vehicles, tools and office machines	Hobbing, generative shaping and planing (non-ground but hardened gears)
10	Transmissions for farm tractors, agricultural machinery, subordinate gear units in general mechanical equipment, hoisting equipment	All of the usual processes apply, additionally extrusion and sintering, injection molding for plastic gears
11 and 12	General agricultural machinery	

Addendum modification coefficient x

For straight teeth, $\alpha = 20°$, Basic rack I as per DIN 3972 ($h_{fP} = 1.167 \cdot m$)

1	2	3	4
Number of teeth z, for helical teeth z_i	Tooth free from undercut if $x \geq$	Top land width $0.2 \cdot m$, if $x \approx$	Tooth pointed if $x \geq$
7	+0.47	–	+0.49
8	+0.45	–	+0.56
9	+0.4	+0.4	+0.63
10	+0.35	+0.45	+0.70
11	+0.3	+0.5	+0.76
12	+0.25	+0.56	+0.82
13	+0.2	+0.62	+0.87
14	+0.15	+0.68	+0.93
15	+0.1	+0.72	+0.98
16	0	+0.76	+1.03

If addendum modification is used to increase strength, to maintain a specific distance between centers, etc., x must never exceed the value given in column 3 (use column 4 for case-hardened gears if necessary, however in this case tip relief is required) and must never be smaller than the value given in column 2, or, in the case of large numbers of teeth, never smaller than

$x = (16 - z)/17$,

for helical teeth

$x = (16 - z_i)/17$.

Starter tooth design

The system of tolerances for gears "Standard distance between centers" as specified in DIN 3961, which is customary in mechanical engineering and by which the required backlash is produced by negative tooth thickness tolerances, cannot be used for starters. Starter gear teeth require far more backlash than constant-mesh gears due to the starter engagement process. Such backlash is best achieved by increasing the distance between centers.

The high torque required for starting necessitates a high transmission ratio ($i = 10$ to 20). For this reason, the starter pinion has a small number of teeth ($z = 9$, 10 or 11). The pinion generally has positive addendum modification. In the case of pitch gears, this addendum modification is expressed using the following notation outside Germany: Number of teeth = 9/10 for instance.

This means that only 9 teeth are cut on a gear blank with a diameter for 10 teeth; this corresponds to an addendum modification coefficient of +0.5. Slight deviations from $x = +0.5$ are quite common, and do not affect the above-mentioned notation method: Number of teeth = 9/10. (This notation is not to be confused with the notation P 8/10, see below and next page.)

Customary starter gearing

Module m mm	Diametral pitch P 1/inch	Pressure angle of basic rack	American standard	European draft standard
2.1167	12/14	12°	SAE J 543 c	ISO/DIS 8123.2
2.5	–	15°		ISO/DIS 9457-1
2.54	10/12	20°	SAE J 543 c	ISO/DIS 8123.2
3	–	15°		ISO/DIS 9457-1
3.175	8/10	20°	SAE J 543 c	ISO/DIS 8123.2
3.5	–	15°		ISO/DIS 9457-1
4.233	6/8	20°	SAE J 543 c	ISO/DIS 8123.2

American gear standards

Instead of the module, in the USA standardization is based on the number of teeth on 1 inch of pitch diameter = diametral pitch (P).

$P = z/d$

The conversion is as follows: Module $m = 25.4\ \text{mm}/P$

The tooth spacing in the pitch circle is called circular pitch (CP):

$$CP = \frac{1\ \text{inch}}{P} \cdot \pi$$

Pitch $t = 25.4\ \text{mm} \cdot CP$

Full-depth teeth
Full-depth teeth have an addendum $h_a = m$ as in German standards, however the dedendum is frequently somewhat different.

Stub teeth
The formulas are the same as for full-depth teeth, however calculation of the addendum is based on a different module from that used for the other dimensions. Notation (example):

P 5/7 —— P 7 for calculation of the addendum
└—— P 5 for calculation of all other dimensions

Notation and conversions:

Outside diameter:
$OD = d_a$

Pitch diameter:
$PD = z/P = d$ in inches

Root diameter:
$RD = d_f$

Layout diameter:
$LD = (z+2x)/P$ in inches
$LD = (z+2x) \cdot m$ in mm
$LD \approx d_w$
d_w = Pitch circle diameter

Measurement over D_M-pins:
M_d = measurement over D_M-pins

Back-calculation of addendum modification coefficient x from the span measurement W_k over k teeth.

$$x = \frac{(W/m_n) - [(k-0.5) \cdot \pi + z_i \cdot \text{inv}\,\alpha_n] \cdot \cos\alpha_n}{2 \cdot \sin\alpha_n}$$

Diametral pitches P and modules derived therefrom

Diametral pitch P 1/inch	Corresponds to module m mm	Diametral pitch P 1/inch	Corresponds to module m mm	Diametral pitch P 1/inch	Corresponds to module m mm
20	1.27000	**6**	4.23333	**2**	12.70000
18	1.41111	5.5	4.61818	1.75	14.51429
16	1.58750	**5**	5.08000	**1.5**	16.93333
14	1.81429	4.5	5.64444	**1.25**	20.32000
12	2.11667	**4**	6.35000	**1**	25.40000
11	2.30909	3.5	7.25714	0.875	29.02857
10	2.54000	**3**	8.46667	**0.75**	33.86667
9	2.82222	2.75	9.23636	**0.625**	40.64000
8	3.17500	**2.5**	10.16000	**0.5**	50.80000
7	3.62857	2.25	11.28889		

Calculation of load-bearing capacity

The following can be employed for rough estimations as an alternative to DIN 3990 "Calculation of load-bearing capacity of spur bevel gears". It applies to 2-gear pairs in a stationary transmission unit. The quantities which appear in the following formulas are to be entered in the units given below:

Symbol	Term	Unit
P	Power	kW
P_{PS}	Metric horse-power	PS*
M	Torque	N · m
n	Rotational speed	min^{-1}
F	Peripheral force	N
u	Gear ratio	—

Symbol	Term	Unit
φ	Life factor	—
HB	Brinell hardness	
HRC	Rockwell hardness	
b_N	Useful face width	mm
k	Contact pressure	N/mm^2
L_h	Service life	h

Power		$P = 0.736 \cdot P_{PS}$ $P = M \cdot n/9549$ $P = F_t \cdot d \cdot n/(19.1 \cdot 10^6)$
Peripheral force	in operating pitch circle	$F_{tw} = 2000 \cdot M/d_w = 19.1 \cdot 10^6 \cdot P/(d_w \cdot n)$
	in generated pitch circle	$F_t = 2000 \cdot M/d = 19.1 \cdot 10^6 \cdot P/(d \cdot n)$
Gear ratio		$u = z_2/z_1 = n_1/n_2$ for pairs of internal gears $u < -1$
Life factor		$\varphi = \sqrt[6]{5000/L_h}$ or from the table on p. 299
Contact pressure	for the small gear	$k_{perm} = \dfrac{(HB)^2}{2560 \cdot \sqrt[6]{n}} = \dfrac{(HRC)^2}{23.1 \cdot \sqrt[6]{n}}$ or from the table on p. 299
	Straight teeth	$k_{actual} = \dfrac{F_{tw}}{b_N \cdot d_{w1}} \cdot \dfrac{4(u+1)}{u \cdot \sin 2\alpha_w}$
	Helical teeth	$k_{actual} = \dfrac{F_{tw}}{b_N \cdot d_{w1}} \cdot \dfrac{4(u+1) \cdot \cos^2\beta}{u \sin 2\alpha_{wt}}$ $\cos^2\beta$ only for full contact, otherwise = 1
Resistance to pitting		$S_w = \varphi \cdot k_{perm}/k_{actual} \geq 1$

Resistance to pitting and wear due to excessive contact pressure is provided if the equations for S_w for the smaller gear (gear 1) yields a value equal to or greater than 1. In the case of gear pairs where $z_1 < 20$, select $S_w \geq 1.2 \ldots 1.5$ due to the greater contact pressure at the inside single engagement point. Because the contact pressure k is equal in magnitude for both gears of the pair, for k_{perm} a material can be selected for gear 2 from the table which has at least the same contact pressure as gear 1 at rotational speed n_2.

* PS = Pferdestärke = metric HP

The k_{perm}-values in the table below apply when both gears are made of steel. For cast iron on steel or bronze on steel, the values should be roughly 1.5 times higher; for cast iron on cast iron or bronze on bronze, they should be approximately 1.8 times higher. For the gear with non-hardened surfaces, 20 % higher k_{perm}-values are permissible if the other gear of the pair has hardened tooth flanks. The values in the table apply to a service life L_h of 5000 hours. A different service life L_h is allowed for in the equation for resistance to pitting S_w by means of the life factor φ.

Permissible contact pressure k_{perm} in N/mm² for a service life L_h of 5000 h.

Hardness of teeth		Rotational speed min⁻¹ (for 1 load change per revolution)											
HB	HRC	10	25	50	100	250	500	750	1000	1500	2500	5000	10000
90		2.2	1.9	1.7	1.5	1.3	1.1	1.05	1.0	0.94	0.86	0.77	0.68
100		2.7	2.3	2.0	1.8	1.6	1.4	1.3	1.2	1.15	1.06	0.94	0.84
120		3.8	3.3	2.9	2.6	2.2	2.0	1.9	1.8	1.66	1.53	1.36	1.21
140		5.2	4.5	4.0	3.6	3.0	2.7	2.5	2.4	2.26	2.08	1.85	1.65
170		7.7	6.6	5.9	5.2	4.5	4.0	3.75	3.6	3.34	3.06	2.73	2.43
200		10.7	9.1	8.1	7.3	6.2	5.6	5.2	4.9	4.6	4.24	3.78	3.37
230		14.1	12.1	10.8	9.6	8.2	7.3	6.9	6.5	6.1	5.61	5.0	4.45
260		18.0	15.4	13.8	12.2	10.5	9.4	8.8	8.4	7.8	7.17	6.39	5.69
280		20.9	17.9	16.0	14.2	12.2	10.9	10.2	9.7	9.0	8.31	7.41	6.6
300		24.0	20.6	18.3	16.3	14.0	12.5	11.7	11.1	10.4	9.54	8.5	7.6
330		29.0	24.9	22.2	19.8	17.0	15.1	14.1	13.5	12.6	11.6	10.3	9.2
400		42.6	36.6	32.6	29.0	24.9	22.2	20.7	19.8	18.5	17.0	15.1	13.5
	57	96.0	82.3	73.3	65.3	56.0	49.9	46.7	44.5	41.6	38.2	34.0	30.3
	≥62	112	96.5	86.0	76.6	65.8	58.6	54.8	52.2	48.8	44.8	39.9	35.6

Corresponding materials are given in the table "Strength values" on p. 301.

Life factor φ

The life factor is used to convert the values in the table (referred to a service life L_h of 5000 hours) to values which correspond to a different service life period.

Service life in hours of operation L_h	10	50	150	312	625	1200	2500	5000	10.000	40.000	80.000	150.000
Life factor φ	2.82	2.15	1.79	1.59	1.41	1.27	1.12	1	0.89	0.71	0.63	0.57

Guidelines for selection of service life: Drives in continuous operation at full load: 40,000 ... 150,000 hours of operation; drives run intermittently at full load or only intermittently: 50 ... 5000 hours of operation.

Teeth calculations for bending and tooth fracture

Peripheral velocity $v_1 = v_2$ m/s	$v_1 = \frac{\pi \cdot d_1 \cdot n_1}{60{,}000}$ d_1 in mm, n_1 in min^{-1}, $\pi = 3.1416$	
Velocity factor f_v	Take from table below, or calculate.	
Perm. root stress $\sigma_{F\,perm}$ N/mm²	Take $\sigma_{F\,lim}$ and Y_{NT} from table on p. 301; estimate intermediate values. $\sigma_{F\,perm} = \sigma_{F\,lim} \cdot Y_{NT} \cdot Y_L$ $Y_L = 1$ for pulsating loads. $Y_L = 0.7$ for alternating loads.	
Tooth profile factor Y_{Fa}	Take from graph below.	
Root stress of tooth $\sigma_{F\,actual}$ N/mm²	For straight teeth: $\sigma_{F\,actual} = \frac{F_t}{b \cdot m} \cdot \frac{Y_{Fa}}{f_v \cdot \varepsilon_\alpha}$ See p. 294 for ε_α. See p. 298 for m, m_n, b in mm, F_t in N	For helical teeth: $\sigma_{F\,actual} = \frac{F_t}{b \cdot m_n} \cdot \frac{Y_{Fa}}{f_v \cdot \varepsilon_\alpha} \left(1 - \frac{\varepsilon_\beta \cdot \beta}{120°}\right)$ where $(1 - \varepsilon_\beta \cdot \beta/120°)$ must be ≥ 0.75. See p. 294 for ε_β, β in °.
Resistance to tooth fracture S_F	$S_F = \sigma_{F\,perm}/\sigma_{F\,actual} \geq 1$	

Resistance to tooth fracture is provided if the equations for S_F for the smaller gear (gear 1) yield a value greater than or equal to 1.

If a better material is selected for gear 1 than for gear 2, the calculation for bending must also be made for gear 2.

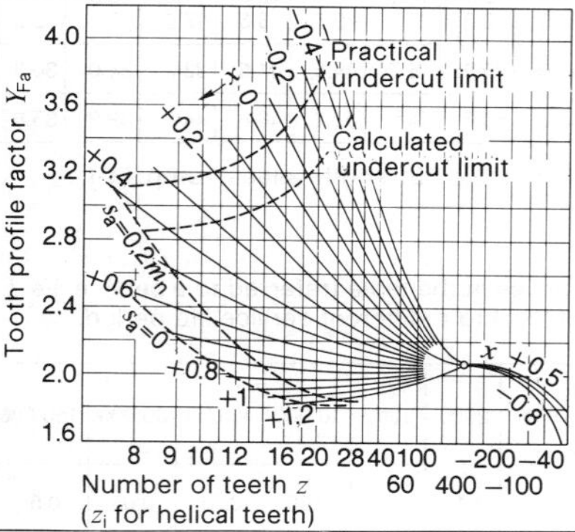

Tooth profile factor *Y_{Fa} ($\alpha = 20°$) is a function of the number of teeth z and the addendum modification coefficient x. In the case of internal teeth, $Y_{Fa} \leq 2.07$ (see graph).*

$$Y_{Fa} = \frac{6 \cdot h_{Fa} \cdot \cos\alpha_{Fan}/m_n}{(s_{Fn}/m_n)^2 \cdot \cos\alpha_n}$$

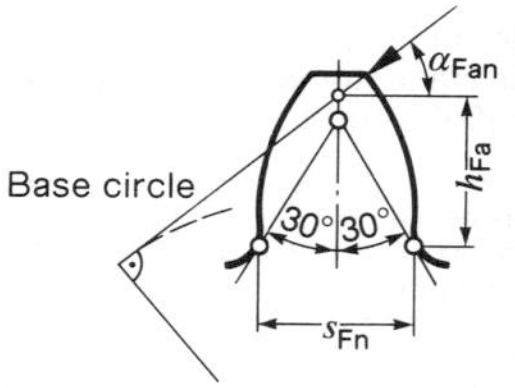

Velocity factor f_v

Materials	Peripheral velocity v m/s 0.25	0.5	1	2	3	5	10	Basic equation
Steel and other metals	Velocity factor f_v 0.96	0.93	0.86	0.75	0.67	0.55	0.38	$f_v = \frac{A}{A + v}$ [1]
Fabric-base laminates and other non-metals	0.85	0.75	0.62	0.5	0.44	0.37	0.32	$f_v = \frac{0.75}{1 + v} + 0.25$

Gear materials

	Material	Condition	Tensile strength R_m N/mm² min.	Fatigue strength f. reversed bending stress σ_{bw} N/mm² min.	Hardness HB or HRC min.	Perm. root stress²) $\sigma_{F\,lim}$ N/mm²	Life factor Y_{NT}³) at number of load changes $N_L = L_h \cdot 60 \cdot n$ $\geq 3 \times 10^6$	10^6	10^5	10^4	10^3
Heat-treatable steel	St 60-2, C 45	annealed	590	255	170 HB	160	1	1.25	1.75	2.5	2.5
		heat-treat.	685	295	200 HB	185					
		heat-treat.	980	410	280 HB	245					
	St 70-2, C 60	annealed	685	295	200 HB	185					
		heat-treat.	785	335	230 HB	209					
		heat-treat.	980	410	280 HB	245					
	50 Cr V 4	annealed	685	335	200 HB	185					
		heat-treat.	1130	550	330 HB	294					
		heat-treat.	1370	665	400 HB	344					
	37 Mn Si 5	annealed	590	285	170 HB	160					
		heat-treat.	785	355	230 HB	200					
		heat-treat.	1030	490	300 HB	270					
Case-hardening steel	RSt 34-2, C 15	annealed	335	175	100 HB	110	1	1.25	1.75	2.5	2.5
		surface-hardened	590	255	57 HRC	160	1	1.2	1.5	1.9	2.5
	16 Mn Cr 5	annealed	800	–	150 HB	–	–	–	–	–	–
		surface-hardened	1100	–	57 HRC	300	1	1.2	1.5	1.9	2.5
	20 Mn Cr 5	annealed	590	275	170 HB	172	–	–	–	–	–
		surface-hardened	1180	590	57 HRC	330	1	1.2	1.5	1.9	2.5
	18 Cr Ni 8	annealed	640	315	190 HB	200	–	–	–	–	–
		surface-hardened	1370	590	57 HRC	370	1	1.2	1.5	1.9	2.5
Castings	Gray iron GG-18	–	175		200 HB	50	1	1.1	1.25	1.4	1.6
	Steel GS-52.1	–	510		140 HB	110	1	1.25	1.75	2.5	2.5
	Tin bronze G-SnBz 14	–	195		90 HB	100	1	1.25	1.75	2.5	2.5
	Polyamide PA 66	at 60°C	–	40	–	27	1	1.2	1.75	–	–
	PA 66 + 30% fiberglass		140	43	–	29					
	Fabric-base laminate fine		–	–	–	75	1	1.15	1.4	1.65	2.0
	Fabric-base laminate coarse		–	–	–	50	1	1.2	1.6	2.1	2.8

For the heat-treatable steels, two values are given in each case for the heat-treated condition. For smaller gears up to roughly module 3, the larger of the two values can be specified. With very large gears, however, only the smaller value can be achieved with certainty.

¹) Values are valid for $A = 6$ (average tooth quality). With cast gears and high-precision gears, $A = 3$ and 10 respectively. ²) For pulsating loads with a material fatigue strength $N_L \geq 3 \times 10^6$. In the case of alternating loads (idler gears), take into account the alternating load factor Y_L. ³) Within fatigue strength of finite life, root bending stress is multiplied by the factor Y_{NT}, depending upon the number of load changes $N_L = L_h \cdot 60 \cdot n$.

Belt drives

Friction belt drives

Quantities and units

Quantity	Unit
A Belt cross section	mm^2
F Contact force	N
F_1 Belt force in load side	N
F_2 Belt force in slack side	N
F_F Centrifugal force of belt	N
F_f Centrifugal force per side	N
F_R Frictional force	N
F_u Peripheral force	N
F_v Pretensioning force	N
F_w Tensioning force of shaft	N
P Required power transmission	kW
k_1 Pretension factor, with reference to operating conditions and wrap angle	—
k_2 Factor for centrifugal force	—
v Belt speed	m/s
z Number of belts (V-belt drives) or ribs (V-ribbed belts)	—
α Groove angle	°
β Wrap angle	°
μ Coefficient of friction	—
μ' Wedge coefficient of friction	—
ρ Mean density of belt material	g/cm^3

Transmission of force

The general equation for friction

$$F_R = \mu \cdot F$$

yields the following equation for V-belt pulleys (see illustration)

$$F_R = \mu \cdot 2 \cdot F'$$

or $F_R = \mu' \cdot F$

where $\mu' = \mu/\sin(\alpha/2)$

The Eytelwein equation describes the transition from static friction to sliding friction:

$$F_1/F_2 = e^{\mu'\beta}$$

where $\mu' \approx 0.5 \pm 0.15$

according to the specifications of the V-belt manufacturers with the incorporation of various safety factors.

V-Belt forces

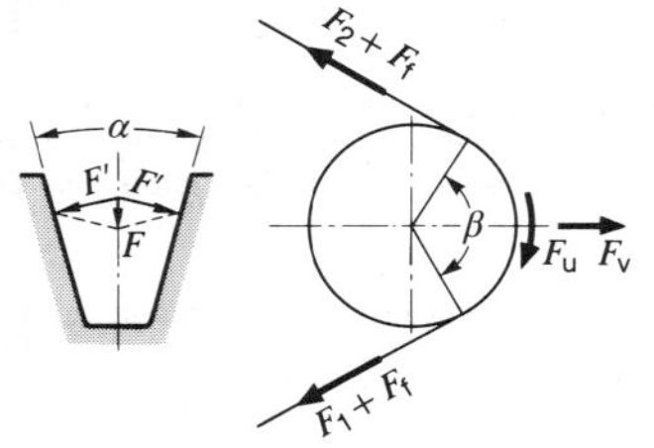

As long as the ratio of forces on the two belt sides is

$$F_1/F_2 \leq e^{\mu'\beta}$$

the belt will not slip during transmission of the peripheral force

$$F_u = F_1 - F_2 = P \cdot 1020/v.$$

A pretensioning force F_v is required in order to transmit the peripheral force F_u; at high rotational speeds, the centrifugal force constituent F_F of the belt must be taken into consideration.

The pretensioning force is

$$F_v = F_w + F_F$$

where

$$F_w = F_u \cdot [(e^{\mu'\beta}+1)/(e^{\mu'\beta}-1)] \cdot \sin(\beta/2)$$

$$F_F = 2 \cdot z \cdot F_f \cdot \sin(\beta/2)$$

$$F_f = \varrho \cdot A \cdot v^2 \cdot 10^{-3}$$

or in simplified form:

$$F_F = 2 \cdot z \cdot k_2 \cdot v^2 \cdot \sin(\beta/2)$$

In practice, the following approximation process[1]) is frequently sufficient for calculating the pretensioning force:

$$F_v = (k_1 \cdot F_u + z \cdot k_2 \cdot v^2) \cdot \sin(\beta/2).$$

The following rule of thumb can often be used for drives with 2 pulleys:

$$F_v = (1.5 \ldots 2) \cdot F_u.$$

In order to check belt pretensioning, the static force applied to each side of each belt

$$F_s = F_v/(2z \cdot \sin(\beta/2))$$

is compared with the value obtained by measuring belt deflection.

Belt drive calculations are performed in accordance with DIN 2218, or inaccordance with the specifications supplied by the belt manufacturers. Manufacturer's belt performance specifications are based on a theoretical service life of 25,000 h. Computer programs are used to perform service life calculations. In properly designed drives, belt creep is less than 1 %, and belt efficiency is 94 ... 97 %.

Belt service life is shortened if the maximum permissible belt speed and bending frequency are exceeded, if the belt pulleys are smaller than the minimum permissible pulley diameter or, in the case of V-belts, belt tensioners are used to apply force to the back of the belt.

1) According to Continental Gummi-Werke AG.

Determination of the static force F_s of the side of the belt by means of belt deflection t_e, produced by a test force F_e

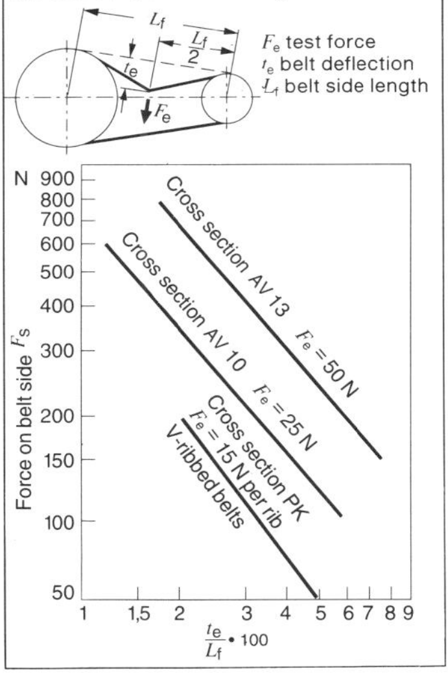

Standard V-belts (classical V-belts)
In accordance with DIN 2215, for home appliances, agricultural machinery, heavy machinery. Ratio of top width to height: 1.6 : 1. Belt designs which use corded caable and bundled fibers as the tension members transmit considerably less power than equally wide narrow V-belts. Due to their high tensile strength and transverse stiffness, they are suitable for use under rough operating conditions with sudden load changes. Belt velocities up to 30 m/s and bending frequencies up to 40 s^{-1} are permissible. See DIN 2217 for corresponding pulley dimension

V-belt types
1 Wrapped standard V-belt
2 Wrapped narrow V-belt
3 Raw-edge narrow V-belt

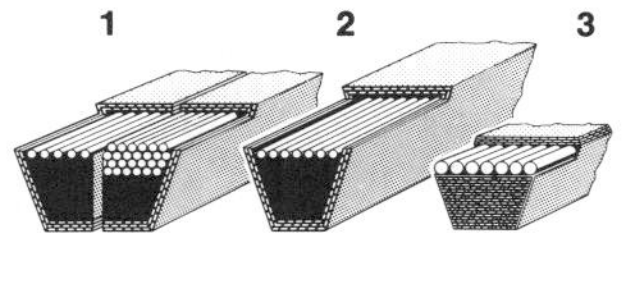

Pretension factor k_1				
Belt	β	Drive		
		Light constant loads	Moderate loads	Heavy shock loads
V-belts	180°	1.5	1.7	1.9
	90°	2.6	2.8	3.0
V-ribbed belts	180°	1.8	2.0	2.2
	90°	3.3	3.5	3.7

Intermediate values for other wrap angles may be interpolated.

Belt	Cross section	Centrifugal factor k_2
V-belt	SPZ	0.07
	SPA	0.12
V-ribbed belts	K	0.02

Narrow V-belts
In accordance with DIN 7753, Part 1; machine construction, motor vehicles built in the 1960s and 1970s. Ratio of top width to height: 1.2 : 1. The narrow V-belt is a modified version of the standard V-belt in which the central section, which in any case transmitted only limited forces, has been omitted. Higher capacity than standard V-belts of equal width. Toothed version exhibits less creep when bending around small pulleys. Belt velocities up to 42 m/s and bending frequencies up to 100 s^{-1} are permissible. (See DIN 2211 for corresponding pulley dimensions).

Raw-edge V-belts
Raw-edge standard V-belts in accordance with DIN 2215, and raw-edge narrow V-belts for motor vehicles in accordance with DIN 7753, Part 3 (draft). Sub-surface belt fibers perpendicular to the direction of belt motion provide a high degree of flexibility while at the same time giving extreme transverse stiffness and high wear resistance. They also provide excellent support for the specially treated tension member. Particularly with small-diameter pulleys, this design increases belt capacity and provides a longer service life than wrapped narrow V-belts.

Further developments
The latest development are V-belts with tension members made of Kevlar. Kevlar has very high tensile strength with a very small degree of elongation, and is more highly temperature-resistant.

V-ribbed belts (poly-grooved belts)
In accordance with DIN 7867. Very flexible; the back of the belt may also be used to transmit power. This capability makes it possible for one such belt to be used to drive several vehicle accessories simultaneously (alternator, fan, water pump, air-conditioner compressor, power-steering pump, etc.) if the wrap angle around each driven pulley is sufficiently large. Optional cross sections include the PH, PJ, PK, PL, and PM, of which the PK cross section has been widely used in motor vehicles in recent years. This allows use of narrower pulley diameters ($d_{b\ min} \approx 34$ mm) than those possible with narrow V-belts (cross section: AVX 10). A pretension approximately 20% greater than that employed on a narrow V-belt is recommended to provide the same force-transmission capabilities.

V-ribbed belts (poly-grooved belts)

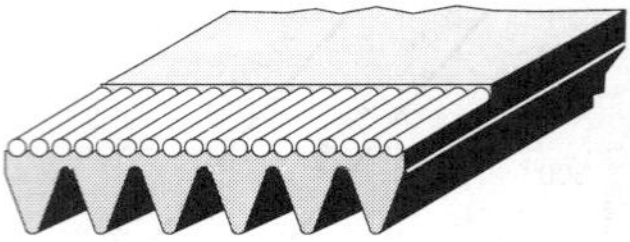

Narrow V-belts for motor vehicles in accordance with DIN 7753, Part 3
Example of designation: narrow V-belt DIN 7753 AVX 10 x 750 La
Raw-edge, toothed with belt cross-section code AVX 10 L_a = 750 mm

Narrow V-belt			Wrapped (U)		Raw-edge: Solid cross section (V)		Raw-edge: Toothed (G)	
Belt cross section	Code		9.5	12.5	AVP10	AVP 13	AVX10	AVX13
	ISO Code		AV 10	AV 13	AV 10	AV 13	AV 10	AV 13
Top width		$b_0 \approx$	10	13	10	13	10	13
Belt height		$h \approx$	8	10	7.5	8.5	8	9
Eff. line differential		h_b	1.8	2.6	0.9			
Belt runout		$h_{a\ max}$	–		2.4			
Effective length		L_a	500 to 2550: in increments of 25 mm					

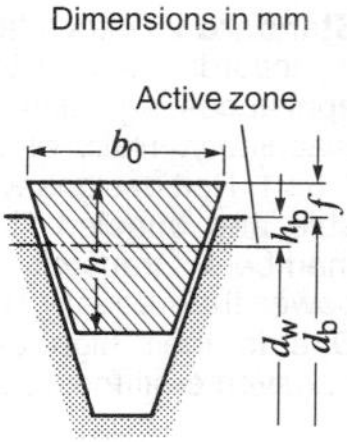

Groove cross section		AV 10		AV 13	
Effective diameter	d_b	< 57	≥ 57	< 70	≥ 70
Groove angle	$\alpha \pm 0.5°$	34°	36°	34°	36°
Effective width	b_b	9.7		12.7	
Groove depth	t_{min}	11		14	
Radius of curvature	r	0.8			
Distance between grooves	ε_{min}	12.6		16	

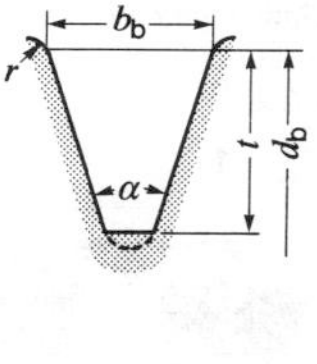

Positive belt drives

Synchronous drive belts
inaccordance with DIN/ISO 5296

Toothed belts are used in motor vehicles as camshaft drives, and in some cases as ignition distributor drives.

Synchronous drive belts with trapezoidal or rounded teeth combine the advantages of a belt drive (any desired distance between pulley centers, quiet operation, low maintenance) with the advantages of a positive transmission (synchronous operation, low bearing stress due to low shaft load). Synchronous drive belts must be guided on both sides to prevent them from running off. This is accomplished by using either a toothed pulley with two flanges or two toothed pulleys with one flange each on opposite sides.

See DIN/ISO 5294 for corresponding toothed-pulley dimension

Synchronous drive belts
1 with trapeoidal teeth
2 with rounded teeth

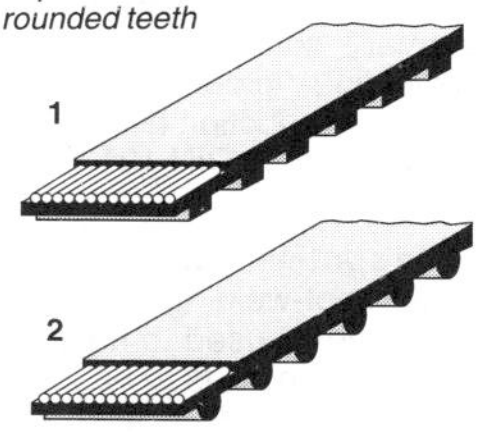

V-ribbed belts and pulleys as per DIN 7867

Designation for a 6-ribbed V-belt, cross-section code PK and reference length 800 mm: V-ribbed belt DIN 7867-6 PK 800

Designation for corresponding V-belt pulley with 90 mm reference diameter: V-ribbed belt pulley DIN 7867-6 Kx 90

Dimensions in mm	Belt	Groove profile
Cross-section code	PK	K
Rib or groove spacing s or e	3.56	3.56
Deviation tolerance for s or e	±0.2	±0.05
Sum of deviation tolerances for s or e	±0.4	±0.30
Groove angle α		40° ±0.5°
r_k at rib / r_a at groove head	0.50	0.25
r_{rg} at rib / r_i at groove seat	0.25	0.50
Belt height h	6	
Nominal dia. of test pin d_s		2.50
$2 \cdot h_s$ nominal dimension		0.99
$2 \cdot \delta$ (s. illustration)		2.06
f (s. illustration)		2.5

Belt cross section

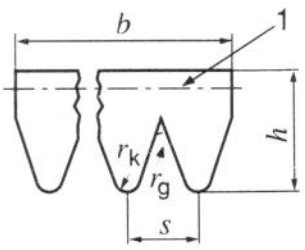

Groove cross section

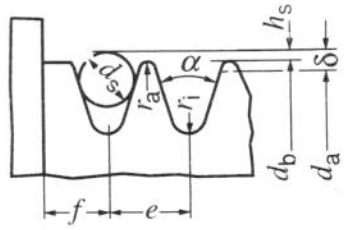

Determining effective diameter

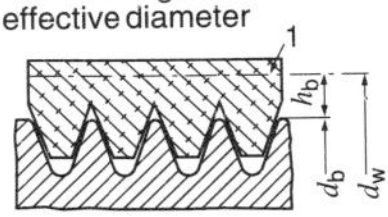

Belt width $b = n \cdot s$
with number of rib $s = n$

Effective diameter $d_w = d_b + 2\,h_b$
for K cross section $h_b = 1.6$ mm

Bonding techniques

Welding

Automotive components and subassemblies are joined using a wide and highly-variegated range of welding and bonding techniques. Resistance-pressure welding and fusion welding are among the most commonly applied welding techniques. This summary concentrates on the resistance-welding methods which are commonly used in production (Processes and symbols according to DIN 1910, Part 5).

Resistance spot-welding

In resistance spot-welding, locally-applied electrical current is used to melt the contact surfaces of the parts to be joined into a soft or fluid state; the parts are then joined together under pressure. The contact-point electrodes which conduct the welding current, simultaneously convey the electrode force to the parts. The amount of heat required to form the welding joint is determined according to $Q = I^2 \cdot R \cdot t$ (Joule's Law).
The precise amount of heat required is a function of current, resistance and time. The following factors should be coordinated in order to achieve a good weld of adequate point diameter d_1:
- Welding current I
- Electrode force F, and
- Welding time t.

According to the manner in which the current is conducted, a distinction is drawn between:
- bilateral direct resistance spot-welding, and
- unilateral indirect resistance spot-welding.

The electrode for a specific spot-welding operation is selected with reference to shape, outside diameter and point diameter. Before welding, the parts must always be completely free of scaling, oxides, paint, grease and oil; they thus receive appropriate surface treatment prior to welding (where indicated).

Projection welding

Projection welding is a process in which electrodes with a large surface area are employed to conduct the welding current and the electrode force to the workpiece. The projections, which are generally incorporated in the thicker of the workpieces, cause the current to concentrate at the contact surfaces. Meanwhile, the electrode force compresses the projections partially or completely during the welding process. A permanent, inseparable joint is produced at the contact

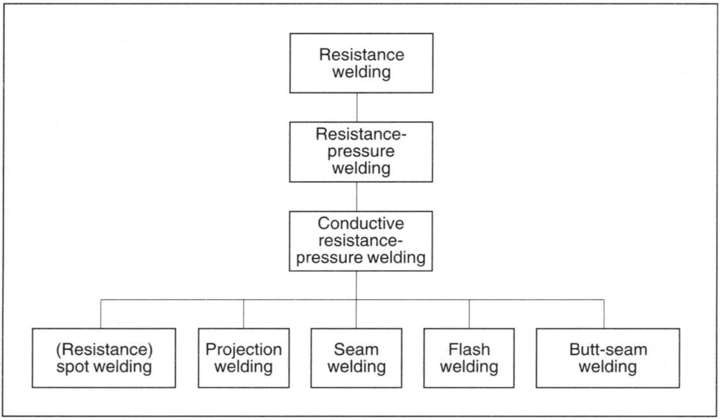

points along the welding seam. Either one or several projections may be welded simultaneously, depending upon the type of projection (round or annular) and the power available from the welding unit. Depending upon the number of connections which are made, a distinction is drawn between:
– Single-projection welding, and
– Multiple-projection welding.

The process requires that high welding currents be applied for a short period of time. Applications:
– Joining materials of varying thicknesses,
– Welding several projections in a single process.

Seam welding
In this process, roller electrodes replace the spot-welding electrodes used in resistance spot-welding. Contact between the roller pair and the workpiece is limited to an extremely small surface area. The roller electrodes conduct the welding current and electrode force, while their rotation is coordinated with the movement of the part.

Application:
Production of sealed welds or seam spot welds (e.g., fuel tanks).

Flash welding
In flash welding, the butt ends of the workpieces are joined under moderate pressure while the flow of current at the contact surfaces produces localized heat and melting (high current density). The metal's vapor pressure drives molten material from the contact patches (burn-off) while force is applied to form an upset butt weld. The butt ends should be parallel to each other and at right angles to the direction in which the force is applied (or virtually so). A smooth surface is not required. A certain amount of extra length must be factored in to compensate for the losses incurred in the flash-welding process. Result: A weld with the characteristic projecting seam (burr).

Welding processes
a) Bilateral resistance spot-welding, b) Unilateral resistance spot-welding, c) Projection welding, d) Seam welding, e) Flash welding, f) Pressure welding.

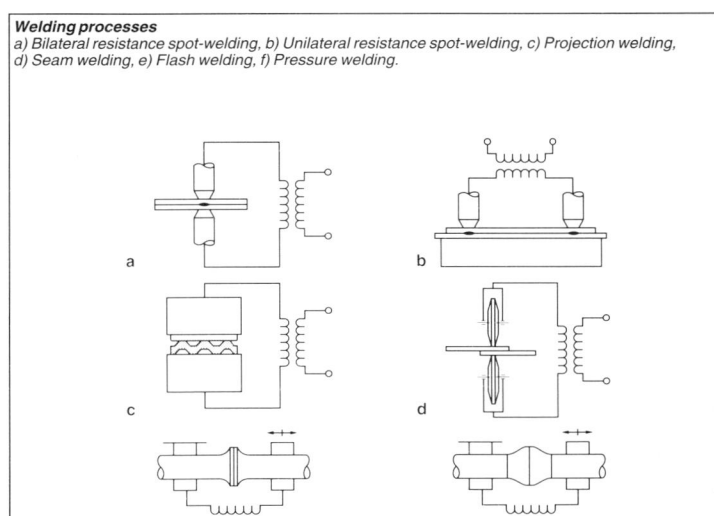

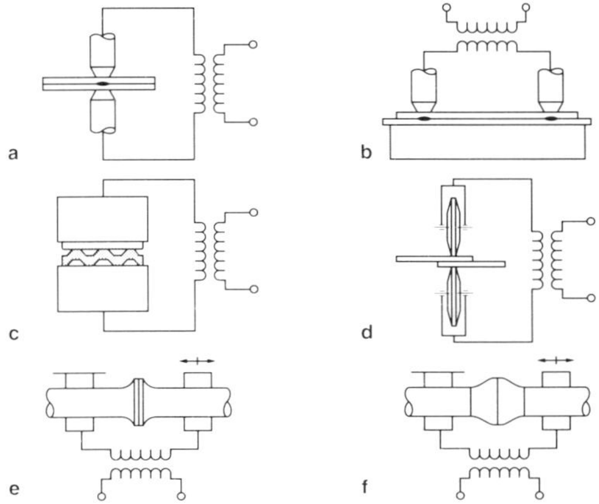

Butt-seam welding
This process employs copper jaws to conduct the welding current to the ends of the workpieces which are to be joined. When the welding temperature is reached, the current switches off. Constant pressure is maintained and the workpieces then weld together (Requirement: properly machined contact surfaces). The result is a burr-free seam. The process does not completely displace any contamination that may be present at the butt ends.

Fusion welding
The term "fusion welding" describes a procedure employing limited local application of heat to melt and join the parts; no pressure is used.

Shielded (inert gas) arc welding is a type of fusion welding. The electrical arc extending between the electrode and the workpiece serves as the heat source. Meanwhile, a layer of inert gas shields the arc and the melted area from the atmosphere. The type of electrode depends upon which of the following procedures is being applied:

Tungsten inert-gas welding
In this process, an arc is maintained between the workpiece and a stable, non-melting tungsten electrode. The shielding (inert) gas is argon or helium. Additional material is supplied from the side (as in gas fusion welding).

Gas-shielded metal-arc welding
In this process, the arc ignites between the melting end of the wire electrode (material feed) and the workpiece. The welding current flows to the wire electrode via sliding contacts in the torch holder. Inert-gas metal-arc welding uses inert gases (slowly-reacting and noble gases such as argon, helium or combinations of the two) as protective gas. Active-gas metal-arc welding, on the other hand, employs reactive gases (e.g., CO_2 and mixed gases containing CO_2, argon, and sometimes oxygen), and is frequently referred to as CO_2 welding.

This procedure is employed in welding non-alloy and mild-alloy steels.

In addition, the following welding techniques are also applied by the automobile industry:

- Electron-beam welding,
- Friction welding,
- Arc pressure welding (stud welding),
- Stored-energy welding (pulse welding).

Soldering

In soldering, a supplementary material (solder) is melted onto two or more parts of similar or varying metallic composition in order to produce a permanent connection between them. Flux and/or protective gas may also be used. The melting temperature of the solder lies below that of the parts being joined. The solder is distributed along the joint to produce the connection without the parts themselves being melted.

Soldering processes are classified according to working temperature. This is defined as the lowest surface temperature, at the connection between the workpieces to be joined, at which the solder can be melted and distributed to form a joint.

Soft soldering
Soft soldering is employed to form permanent solder joints at melting temperatures below 450 °C (as with soldering tin). Soft solders which melt at temperatures of 200 °C and below are also known as quick solders.

Hard soldering
Hard soldering is used to form permanent solder joints at melting temperatures above 450 °C (as with copper/zinc, combined copper/zinc and silver alloys, e.g, silver brazing filler). Further data on soldering materials is contained in DIN Sheets 1707, 8512, 8513 and 8516.

Fluxing agents (non-metallic materials) are applied to remove any film (oxidation) remaining on the surface of the parts after cleaning and to prevent a new film from forming: This makes it possible to apply a consistent coat of solder to the joint surfaces. Information on fluxing agents can be found in DIN 8511.

The strength of a soldered joint can be equal to that of the base material itself. This phenomenon is due to the fact that the more rigid adjoining materials limit the solder's deformation potential.

The method used for heating provides yet another criterium for the classification of soldering processes. The two standard types are: Open-flame and iron soldering.

Open-flame soldering

A hand-held burner or a gas-warmed unit provides the heat. Depending upon the specific soldering operation, either oxy-acetylene burners (familiar from gas welding) or soldering lamps are employed.

Iron soldering

The heat is provided by a manually or mechanically guided soldering iron. The soldering iron can also be used for work on pretinned joint surfaces.

Further processes include: Oven, salt-bath, submersion, resistance and induction soldering.

Adhesive technologies

Organic or anorganic adhesives are employed to form permanent rigid connections between two metallic or non-metallic materials. The adhesive is applied under pressure, either at room temperature or with moderate heat. The actual connection bases upon adhesion, i.e., physical and chemical bonding forces operate at the molecular level to bond the surfaces. Depending upon the type of packaging, a distinction is drawn between single and dual-component adhesives.

Single-component adhesives

These are adhesives which already contain all the components necessary to form a bond.

Dual-component adhesives

With this type of adhesive, the other component is a separate hardener suitable for initiating the interlacing process. An accelerator component may be added to the hardener. Metal adhesives are generally dual-component adhesives. The hardening (interlacing) process is in the form of polymerisation, polycondensation or polyaddition under the influence of temperature and/or time. Spatially interlaced molecules are the result. Depending upon the hardening temperature, we distinguish between cold adhesives (harden at room temperature, relatively easy to apply) and hot adhesives (harden at 100 ... 200 °C).

Adhesive connections should be designed to ensure that the bond is subjected to tensile shear loads exclusively. Overlapping connections are practically the only application for adhesives. Butt ends which will be subjected to tensile or sliding forces should be avoided.

Metal adhesives can be employed in combination with spot welding. The adhesive prevents premature swelling in the plates between the resistance-welded points. This method is also suitable for reducing voltage peaks at the welding-spot edges, and for limiting the number of welding spots needed. Such constructions display enhanced structural integrity, rigidity and damping when exposed to dynamic loads. The welding process is carried out while the adhesive is still soft; otherwise the adhesive will act as an insulator.

Among the most significant metal adhesives are: epoxy, polyester, and acrylic resin, vinyl acetate, metal cement.

Automotive applications

Adhesive-bonding has become a standard automotive joining technique. The individual areas of application can be classified as follows:

- Body shell: Raised-seam and brace bonding for attached components.
- Paint line: Attachment of stiffeners.
- Assembly line: Attaching insulating material, appliques, side strips, mirror-support bracket to windshield.
- Component production: Bonding brake pads, laminated safety glass (LSG), rubber-to-metal connections to absorb vibration.

Riveting

Riveting is used to produce a permanent fixed connection between two or more components made of either identical or different materials. Depending upon the particular method and its specific application, riveted connections are divided into the following categories:
– Permanent rigid connections (force joints, e.g., in mechanical and plant engineering),
– Permanent, rigid, sealed connections (e.g., boilers and pressurized tanks),
– Extremely tight seals (e.g., pipes, vacuum equipment).

In some areas, such as mechanical engineering in general and in tank manufacture, riveting has largely been displaced by welding. A distinction is made between cold and hot riveting, depending upon the temperature used. Cold riveting is employed for rivet joints of up to 10 mm in diameter with steel, copper, copper alloys, aluminum and such. Rivets with a diameter of more than 10 mm are applied hot.

The most common types of rivet are mushroom head, countersunk, tallow-drop, hollow, and tubular. There are also standardized rivets for specialized applications, such as explosive and blind rivets. The blind type is a hollow rivet which is driven into place with a drift punch or similar instrument. The types of rivet and the corresponding materials applications are defined in DIN bulletins, while structural integrity and chemical composition are specified in DIN 17 111. In order to avoid the danger of electrochemical corrosion, the rivet material and the material of the part being joined should be as similar as possible.

Advantages/disadvantages compared to other joining techniques

– Unlike welding, riveting exerts no effects such as hardening or molecular change on the material,
– No distortion of the components,
– Suitable for joining dissimilar materials,
– Riveting weakens the components,
– Butt-end joints are not possible,
– Riveting is generally more expensive than welding when performed outside the factory.

Automotive applications

– Riveting joint pins (window winders, windshield-wiper linkages),
– Riveting reinforcement plates (in the course of repairs).

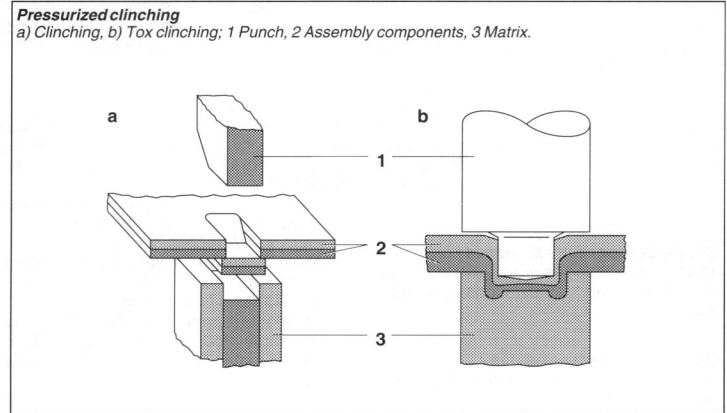

Pressurized clinching
a) Clinching, b) Tox clinching; 1 Punch, 2 Assembly components, 3 Matrix.

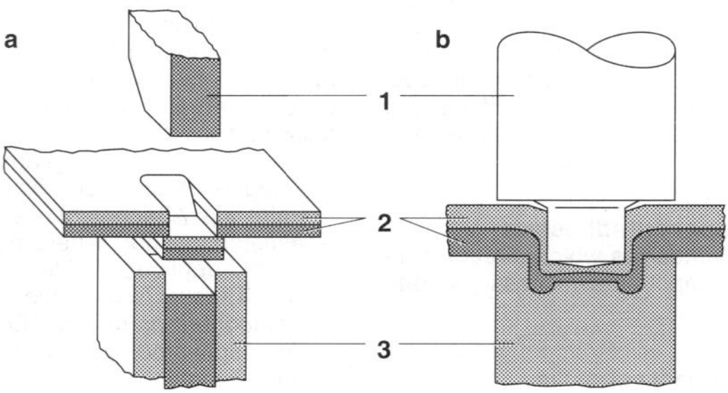

Punch-force/punch-travel curve
A Combined indentation and melding
B Upsetting and expansion
C Filling upper contour of mold
D Filling annular canal
E Cup extrusion

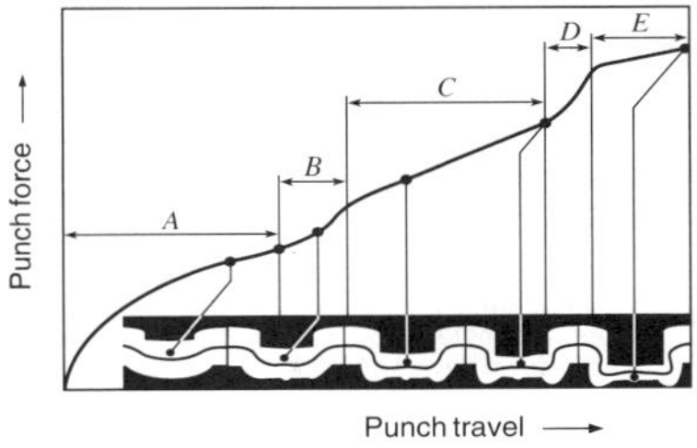

Bonding and joining technology (Pressurized clinching)

Pressurized clinching is a mechanical process for penetration assembly of different layers. It combines cutting, penetration and cold upsetting in a single continuous joining operation without it being necessary to apply additional heat. The basic principle is one of joining through reshaping. The first reference to this process as a means of joining sheet-metal panels through deformation is found in DIN 8593, Part 5, from September, 1985.

The past few years have marked the advent of tox clinching as yet another joining procedure. It resembles penetration clinching, but does not include a cutting operation. The tools employed for tox clinching are relatively small. The diameter can be varied to suit the specific application. At present, pressurized clinching can be used to join panels of up to 3 mm, whereby the total thickness of both sheets should not exceed 5 mm. The panel materials being joined can be of the same type (e.g., steel to steel) or they can be mutually dissimilar (e.g., steel to non-ferrous metals). In addition, pressurized clinching can be used to process coated metals and painted parts as well as components to which adhesives have been applied. Multiple clinching can be used to produce numerous pressure-assembly elements (up to 50) in a single process (one stroke of the press). A typical curve for press force relative to press distance can be divided into five characteristic phases (A ... E).

Advantages/disadvantages of pressurized clinching

- Obviates the requirement for noise-protection encapsulation,
- Tox clinching does not damage corrosion protection,
- When combined with a cutting operation there is a partial loss of corrosion protection,
- No heat distortion,
- Painted, protected (oil, wax) and glued panels can be processed,
- Panels of different materials (e.g., steel to plastic) can be joined together,
- Energy savings, no power supply required for welding and no cooling water,
- One side of the workpiece displays a projection similar to that of a rivet head, while the opposite side has a corresponding depression.

Automotive applications

- Windshield wiper bracket,
- Fastening of door interior panels,
- Positioning of individual components.

Sheet-metal processing

Deep-drawing technology

Quantities and units

Quantities		Units
D	Section diameter	mm
d_B	Support diameter of hold-down device	mm
d_1	Stamping diameter 1st draw	mm
d_2	Stamping diameter 2nd draw	mm
F	Total deep-drawing force	kN
F_B	Hold-down force	kN
F_Z	Deep-draw force	kN
p	Pressure of hold-down device	N/mm²
R_m	Tensile strength	N/mm²
s	Sheetmetal thickness	mm
β_1, β_2	Individual drawing ratio	
β_{max}	Maximum possible drawing ratio	

Drawing methods

The drawing procedure employs a drawing die, punch and sheet-metal retaining device to reshape flat sections, blanks and round plates.

The variables exercising an influence on the deep-drawing of three-dimensional bodywork components are exceedingly complex; rough calculations thus do not provide a suitable basis for their definition. At present, the finite-element method (FEM), in which powerful computers employ numerical procedures from continuum mechanics, promises to become the most effective method for calculating deep-drawing processes. Software development must take into account specific parameters affecting the deep-drawing process, including the influence of friction, of bilateral contact, of material values which vary according to rolling direction, and additional factors. The required research is continuing.

Deep-drawing process

The drawing process reshapes a flat blank into a concave section. A punch, surrounded by a retaining mechanism (holding-down clamp, blank holder), pulls the sheet metal into the matrix. The clamp applies the previously determined force to the sheet and prevents creases from forming, thus making the application of tensile force possible.

The maximum possible drawing ratio is determined by various factors:
- Resistance of the material,
- Tool dimensions and sheet-metal thickness,
- Hold-down force,
- Friction,
- Lubrication,
- Material and surface of the workpiece.

Drawing with single-action presses

This category includes all crank presses in which the ram represents the only moving component.

Deep drawing
a) With single-action press, b) With double-action press; 1 Ram, 2 Air cushion, 3 Hold-down device, 4 Matrix, 5 Punch, 6 Air pins, 7 Matrix insert, 8 Hold-down ram.

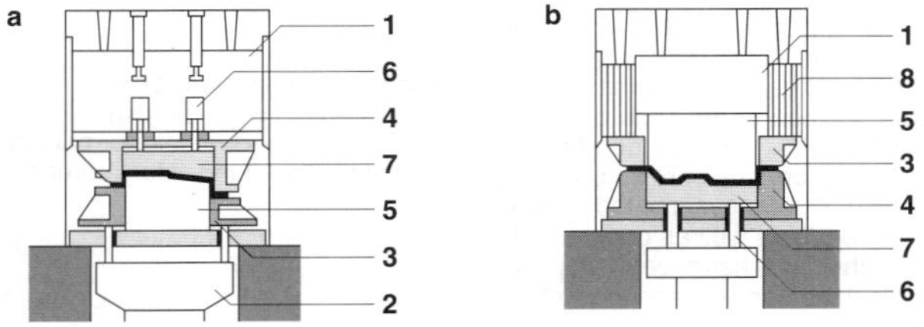

Applications: For deep-drawing flat workpieces in uncomplicated reshaping operations to produce edge pieces, arches, supports.

Drawing on double-action presses
Double-action drawing presses employ separate rams to retain the metal and to pull it. The hold-down ram is actuated mechanically via disk or toggle, or hydraulically.

Calculations for the drawing process

$$F_Z = \pi \cdot (d_1 + s) \cdot s \cdot R_m$$
$$F_B = \frac{\pi}{4} \cdot (D^2 - d_B^2) \cdot p$$
$$F = F_Z + F_B$$
$$\beta_1 = D/d_1;\ \beta_2 = d_1/d_2.$$

Example
D = 210 mm; d_B = 160 mm; d_1 = 140 mm; p = 2.5 N/mm²; R_m = 380 N/mm²; s = 1 mm; β_{max} = 1.9.

Result
Drawing ratio β_1 = 1.5; Deep-drawing force F_Z = 112.2 kN; Hold-down force F_B = 36.3 kN; Total deep-drawing force F = 148.5 kN.

The diagram shows the motions performed by the drawing ram and the hold-down ram in the course of one cycle. The rams have differing strokes. The drawing ram, with its longer stroke, is set in motion first, while the shorter-stroke hold-down ram starts second, but is first to achieve contact.

Material	β_1 max.	β_2 max.	Pressure of hold down device p N/mm²
St 10	1.7	1.2	
St 12	1.8	1.2	2.5
St 13	1.9	1.25	
St 14	2.0	1.3	
Kupfer	2.1	1.3	
CuZn 37 w	2.1	1.4	2.0...2.4
CuZn 37 h	1.9	1.2	
CuSn 6 w	1.5	–	
Al 99.5 w	2.1	1.6	
AlMg 1 w	1.85	1.3	1.2...1.5
AlCuMg 1 pl w	2.0	1.5	
AlCuMg 1 pl ka	1.8	1.3	

[1]) Valid to d_1/s = 300; specified for d_1 = 100 mm, s = 1 mm. Different sheet thicknesses and punch diameters result in minor deviations from the figures given.

Forces during drawing

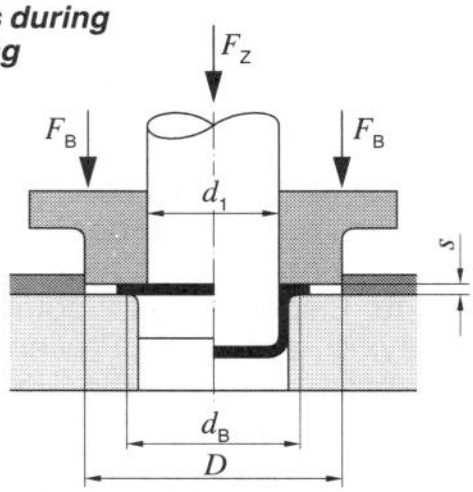

Time-distance diagram for a double-action drawing press
1 Curve for drawing ram, 2 Curve for hold-down ram;
h_Z Stroke of drawing ram, h_B Stroke of hold-down ram, z_{max} max. drawing depth,
t_Z Duration of drawing process, t_{HB} Retaining time of hold-down ram,
a Initial-approach travel of drawing ram.

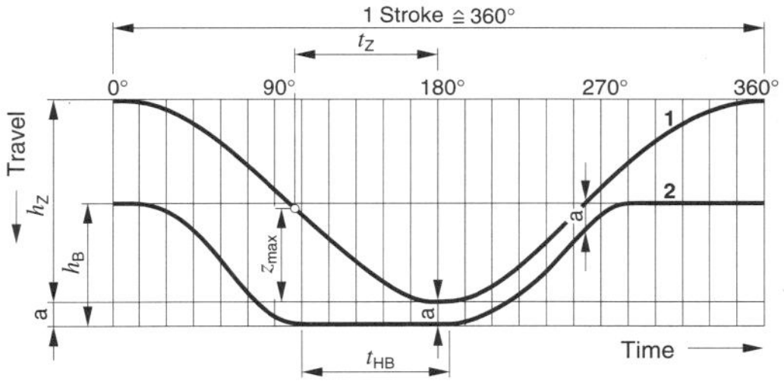

Laser technology

Deviation mirrors are used to deflect the coherent light beam generated by the laser for concentration in a focusing device. At the focal point the laser beam has a diameter of approx. 0.3 ... 0.5 mm, meaning that intensities exceeding 10^6 ... 10^8 W/cm^2 can be achieved. The workpiece melts and vaporizes in milliseconds if the focal point is in its immediate vicinity, an effect which can be exploited in laser-based processing operations. According to the physical condition of the active medium, the device is classified as a solid-state, gas, semiconductor or liquid laser. The following are applied in industrial metal processing:

Solid-state laser (Nd:YAG)
Neodynium (Nd) is an element of the rare-earth group, while YAG stands for yttrium-aluminum-garnet ($Y_5Al_5O_{12}$). The crystal exhibits mechanical and thermal stability equal to that of the ruby.

The Nd:YAG laser emits light in the infrared range of the spectrum, with a wavelength of 1.06 µm. The essential advantage of the Nd:YAG laser lies in the fact that the generated beam can be transmitted using optical fibers, making it possible to dispense with complicated beam-relaying systems. Present laser power ratings are in the range of 400 ... 1200 W; pulse-mode operation is generally employed. The foremost application for solid-state lasers is in welding parts with high requirements for precision, e.g., in precision mechanics. Welding depths depend on power and welding speed, and are in the range of tenths of a millimeter.

Gas laser (CO_2)
The CO_2 laser is among the most important gas-laser devices. Molecular gas serves as the active medium. Radiation emissions are in the medium infrared range, with wavelengths spread across a number of spectral lines between 9.2 and 10.9 µm; the mean is 10.6 µm. This type of laser is generally used in continuous operation, with standard laser power ratings of between 2 and 5 kW. Laboratory units with up to 20 kW have already been installed.

Characteristics of the laser cutter
– Clean, burr-free edges,
– High dimensional/manufacturing precision (no further processing necessary),
– Minimal thermal and mechanical stresses on the workpiece during the cutting process,
– Uncomplicated clamping device,
– Sheet metal of up to 10 mm can be cut (1 kW), rapid cutting (10 m/min with metal 1 mm thick).

Characteristics of laser welding
– High depth/width ratio (e.g., approx. 1 mm seam width at 5 mm seam depth),
– Minimal base-material thermal stress results in narrow heat-affected zone (HAZ),
– Minimal distortion,
– Welding in protective-gas atmosphere,
– Joining gaps must be virtually zero,
– Additional materials can be used for welding (for bridging gaps or to achieve specific metallurgical effects at the welding joint),
– A high level of clamping and equipment technology is required.

Applications in machine tool and automotive engineering
– Cutting and welding bodywork sheet metal,
– Welding (joining) blanks of various thicknesses,
– Welding (joining) of rotationally symmetrical parts (transmission components, tappets, automotive components),
– Boring and perforation,
– Surface hardening, such as that used for treating valve seats, etc.,
– Providing surfaces with upgraded finishes, e.g., structural transformation around cylinder liners.

Overview of laser techniques

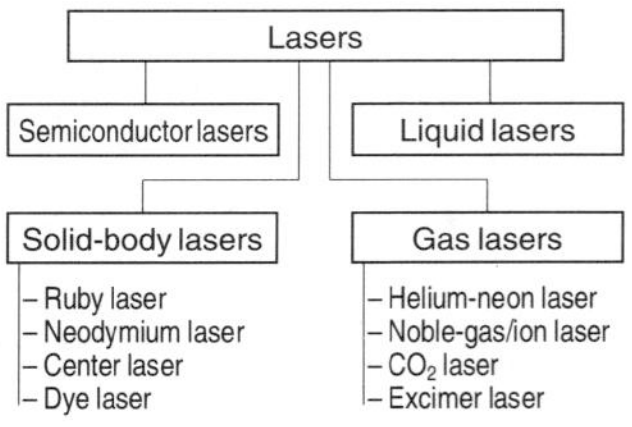

Tribology

Purpose and goals

Tribology is defined as "The study of the phenomena and mechanisms of friction, lubrication, and wear of surfaces in relative motion". Industrial application is directed toward gathering information for use in extending the service lives of products and maximizing utilization of resources. The specific activities are as follows:
- Analysis of friction and wear,
- Analysis and evaluation of tribological damage,
- Provision of technical recommendations on materials, lubricants and design (for damage control and in the design of new components and products),
- Quality assurance,
- Assistance in providing optimal performance,
- Service-life assessment,
- Development and selection of new materials and lubricants.

The complexity of the task makes a synergetic approach essential. The disciplines involved include materials science, physics, chemistry and mechanical engineering.

Definitions

Friction (DIN 50281)
Friction is physical resistance to relative motion at two or more surfaces in a state of mutual contact. The most significant physical parameters for describing friction are:
Friction force: The amount of force with which a motion is resisted.
Coefficient of friction (or friction factor): Friction force relative to normal force.
Friction power: Friction force x sliding speed.
Classification of friction:
1. According to condition of friction (type of contact),
2. According to type of motion.

Condition of friction (type of contact)
Gas friction: A gas layer completely separates the base object and the opposed body from one another, thereby assuming the entire load.
Fluid friction (hydrodynamic and hydrostatic friction): A fluid layer completely separates the base object and opposed body from one another, thereby assuming the entire load.
Combination friction: The base object and the opposed body are in mutual contact at surface peaks. The load is shared by the fluid/lubricating film and by the objects in contact.
Dry or boundary friction: The lubricating film no longer performs any support function, but residue from previously absorbed lubricants continues to exercise a tribological effect.
Solid-body friction: Direct contact between the opposed surfaces.

Types of motion
Possible types of moving contact include sliding friction, rolling friction, and combinations of the two.

In many cases the effects which friction produces in machine components are undesirable, as there are negative consequences for energy consumption and/or associated temperature increases and/or changes to the material. In other cases, friction can make a necessary contribution to proper operation. This is the case with self-locking transmission devices, where the lubricant must furnish a specific coefficient of friction, and in some types of clutches in which defined levels of friction are also required.

Tribology (DIN 50323)
Tribology embraces the science and associated technology devoted to the interaction of surfaces in mutually opposed states of motion. It focuses on the entire range of friction, wear and lubrication, and also includes the effects at the contact surfaces of solids as well as those between solids and gases.

Tribo-technology (DIN 50323)
This branch is devoted to the actual technical application of tribology.

Tribological stress (DIN 50320)
The stress which results at a solid body from contact with, and the relative motion of, an opposed body in solid, fluid or gaseous form.
Tribological damage
Damage resulting from tribological stress.

This contrasts with the concepts of wear and wear damage as defined in DIN 50320. Here, the term "tribological damage" extends to embrace both numerous tribologically-induced changes to the material's surface, as well as reductions in operational efficacy which according to DIN 50320 are not regarded as wear.

Wear (DIN 50320)
Progressive loss of material from the surface of a solid body, caused by tribological stress. Wear is characterized by the presence of abraded particles, as well as changes in both the material and structure of the surface which is exposed to tribological stress. This type of wear is generally undesirable, and impairs functionality (exception: "running-in" processes). Thus any such procedures which enhance the object's operational value are not considered as wear.

Tribological system

Wear can be regarded as a system characteristic. There exists no specific material value for "wear-resistance" as such, corresponding to, say, tensile strength in materials science. The tribological system for the contact surfaces which are the focus of the present discussion consists of:
- The material "A elements": base object, opposed body, intermediate material and surrounding medium,
- The properties P of the elements A,
- The reciprocal influence R between the elements A (see illustration below).

The elements, their properties and their reciprocal effects all combine to form the structure of the tribological system. As the composite stress factor (comprising forces, motion, temperature) acts upon this structure, it is transformed into useful quantities and loss quantities. The latter include friction and wear.

Because tribological stresses are surface stresses, the previously-mentioned P properties must also be viewed as surface characteristics. In technical applications, there frequently exists a substantial discrepancy between the material values measured for the base material and those actually found upon examination of the surfaces.

Manufacturing procedures, cleaning processes, and the operating environment can all cause changes in the surface layer, provoking attendant variations in the tribological response of the material.

Types of wear

Wear processes can be classified according to the type of stress and the materials involved (system structure), a classification from which the following types of wear emerge:
Sliding → Sliding wear,
Rolling → Rolling wear,
Oscillation → Vibration wear.

Tribological system

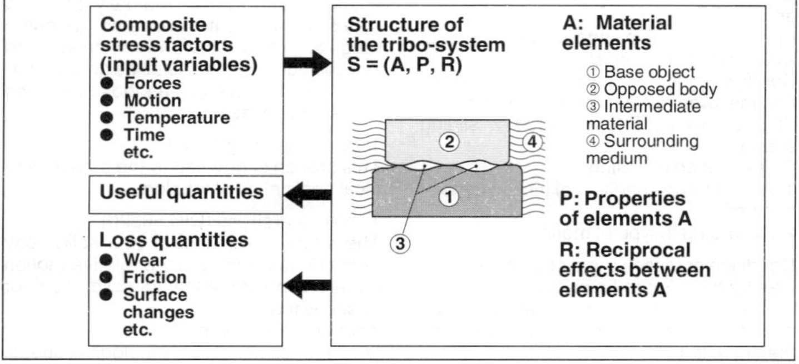

Table 1. Classification of wear according to type of tribological stress (reference: DIN 50320).

System structure	Tribological stress Symbols	Type of wear	Effective mechanisms (single or combined) Adhesion	Abrasion	Surface scraping	Tribochemical reactions
Solid body – Intermediate material (compl. layer separation) – Solid body	Sliding Rolling Revolving Bounce Impact	–	–	–	x	x
Solid body – Solid body (solid-body friction, boundary friction, mixed friction)	Sliding	Sliding wear	x	x	x	x
	Rolling Revolving	Rolling wear Revolving wear	x	x	x	x
	Bounce Impact	Bounce wear Impact wear	x	x	x	x
	Oscillation	Vibration wear	x	x	x	x
Solid body – Solid body and particle	Sliding	Scoring wear	–	x	–	–
	Sliding	Grain-sliding wear	–	x	–	–
	Rolling	Grain-rolling wear	–	x	–	–
Solid body – Fluid with particles	Flow	Scouring (Erosion wear)	–	x	x	x
Solid body – Gas with particles	Flow	Blasting attrition (Erosion wear)	–	x	x	x
	Bounce	Direct & offset bounce wear	–	x	x	x
Solid body – Fluid	Flow Oscillation	Material cavitation, cavitation-erosion	–	–	x	x
	Impact	Impingement	–	–	x	x

Manifestations of wear

The manifestations of wear as defined by DIN 50 320 apply to the surface changes resulting from abrasion, as well as to the type and shape of the resulting particles.

Wear mechanisms

Adhesion
Formation and separation of (molecular) surface bonds. There is a transfer of material when the separation deviates from the original boundary between the base object and the opposed body. The adhesion process starts at the molecular level, but can expand until damage on a massive scale occurs (seizing).

Abrasion
Scraping stress and microscopic scraping action, performed by the base object, the opposed body, reaction products or solid particles in the intermediate medium.

Surface fatigue
Alternating tribological loads (e.g., impact, rolling, sliding stress, cavitation) cause mechanical stresses. The resulting fissures lead to material separation (separation of wear particles).

Tribo-chemical reactions
Reaction of the base and/or opposed object with the intermediate material (and surrounding medium), caused by tribological stress.

Wear quantities

Rates of wear are defined by the so-called wear quantites. These provide direct or indirect indices of the variations in the shape or in the mass of a body which are traceable to wear (definitions based on DIN 50 321).

Coefficient of wear
The quantities by which wear is defined can only be indicated as system-specific quantities. The wear coefficient k facilitates comparison of wear rates at varying surface pressures and speeds:

$k = W_V/(F \cdot s)$ in mm^3 / (N·m)

F Force, W_V Volumetric wear, s Sliding distance.

Tribological damage analysis

In cases where operation of a component results in damage or changes of a kind which could be expected to affect the component's functional integrity, DIN 50320 indicates that all stresses and characteristics occurring at the points of tribological contact should be investigated (DIN 50320, Appendix A).

The topographical and material analyses of tribological contact (base object, opposed body, intermediate material) provide information on the mechanisms causing the damage and/or wear (adhesion, abrasion, surface fatigue, tribo-chemical reactions). These investigations also provide data on accompanying phenomena and on changes in the lubricant. The analysis must be based on the following information:

Surface structure, material composition of the surface, microstructure, microhardness, intrinsic tension, material composition and chemical/physical changes in the lubricant.

Material layers subject to tribological stress at surface

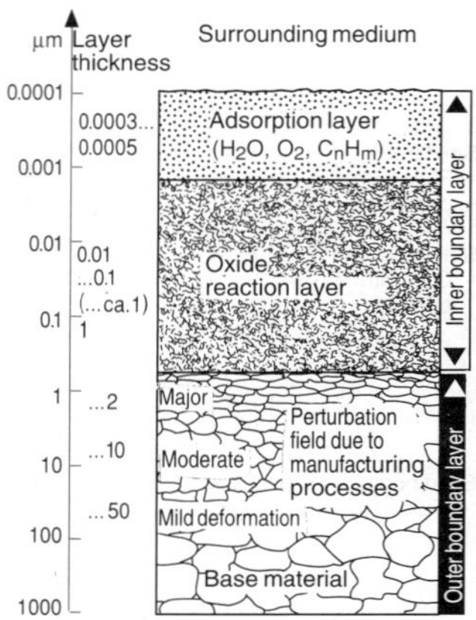

Tribological test procedures

DIN 50 322 divides wear testing into 6 categories:
Category I: Operational testing.
Category II: Test-stand procedure with complete machine.
Category III: Test-stand procedure with assembly or entire unit.
Category IV: Testing with unmodified component or reduced assembly.
Category V: Simulated operational stress with test specimens.
Category VI: Model test with simple test specimens.

The original production assembly is employed for testing according to categories I through III, while the structure of the system is modified substantially from Category IV onward.

It is highly advisable to integrate the tribological examinations of essential and safety-related products into a tribological test series extending from model testing all the way to testing of the actual product:
- Model testing (e.g., pin and sphere, plate for sliding and vibration wear),
- Component testing,
- Product testing.

Model tests (with simple test specimens), although frequently employed in basic research, are no longer used for examining complex tribological systems. Of the various elements in the sequence of tribological tests, it is examination of the actual product itself that provides the most reliable information. This type of testing is applied at the end of product development. Modern research procedures (such as radio-nuclide testing) make it possible to garner precise data on wear as a function of composite stress.

For radio-nuclide testing (RNT), the parts to be examined are marked radioactively. The abraded particles can then be detected "on-line" by gamma-ray measurement.

Inhibiting wear

Variations in design, materials and lubricants can all be employed to improve tribological properties.

Design

The design options include:
- Improving the surface topography,
- Reduction of surface pressures by raising the contact-surface ratio,
- Surface reinforcement,
- Improving lubrication efficiency.

Material

The materials options include:
- Skin-layer hardening,
- Skin-layer remelting,
- Skin-layer remelt alloying,
- Thermochemical processes,
- Electrical and chemical plating,
- Resurface welding,
- Thermal spraying,
- Metal coating,
- PVD/CVD layers (physical/chemical vapor deposition, e.g., TiN, TiC),
- Ion-beam treatment (e.g., ion implantation, ion-beam mixing, and ion-beam supported coating),
- Diamond-like carbon coatings (metallic),
- Anti-friction paints,
- Penetration coatings (soft metals prevent high local surface pressures).

There exist a multiplicity of surface treatment and coating processes. The process parameters can frequently be adjusted to focus on specific kinds of wear. The result is a wide potential field of options for applying tribology to assist products in meeting numerous requirements.

Lubricants

In many cases, selection of the appropriate lubricant (p. 218) and optimal lubrication-system design will exercise a dramatic effect on the tribological properties – the potential is frequently greater than that represented by a change in materials. The choice of lubricant is the initial response when dealing with unsatisfactory operating characteristics.

Basic requirements for road-going vehicles

Driveability
The vehicle must be capable of effecting the transition from a stationary to a mobile state. Once in motion, it must be able to ascend gradients and accelerate to the desired cruising speed with a reasonable degree of alacrity. With a given power P, ideal correspondence with these requirements is achieved when force M and the engine speed n can be varied according to the formula $P = M \cdot n$ at all points on the operating curve. Under these conditions, the limits on the potential field of operation are defined by $P_{Nominal}$, resulting in an inverse relationship between available force and vehicle speed (limit curve defined by tractive-force hyperbola).

Power density and storage density
Both the power density (W/kg) and the energy-storage density (Wh/kg) of the combined engine/energy-storage system must be high if the size of the vehicle – and with it the mass to be accelerated – are to be maintained at a modest level. Low density factors for power and energy storage would increase vehicle size and mass, with attendant escalations in the power and energy consumption which would be needed to achieve the desired performance (acceleration, speed).

Discharge or operating time of the energy-storage device
The vehicle's operating time – and thus the operating range which can be covered before the energy-storage device must be replenished (renewed/refilled/recharged) – is a function of the energy-storage density, the power requirement, and the vehicle weight; the latter, in turn, is influenced by

Power and energy-storage densities for various propulsion concepts
(Engine/motor and storage unit)[1])
1 Gas turbine, 2 Internal-combustion engine, 3 External-combustion engine, 4 Electric motor with fuel cell, 5 Lithium-chloride battery, 6 Zinc-air battery, 7 Nickel-cadmium battery, 8 Lead-acid battery.

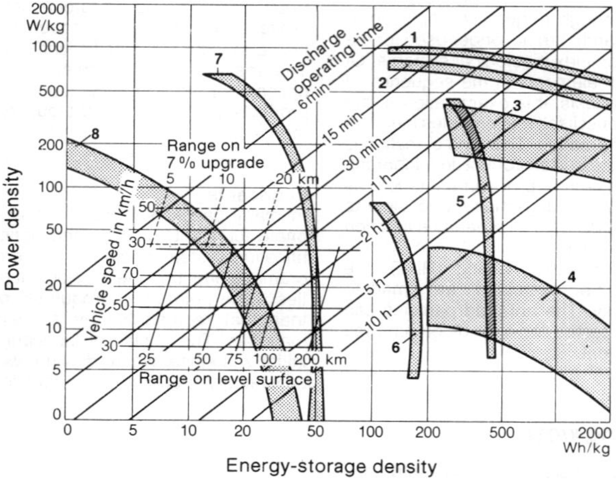

[1]) From "The Automobile and Air Pollution" US Department of Commerce (Morse Report); Mahle "Kolben-Handbuch" (Piston Handbook).

the power-to-weight ratio of the drive system.

The drive and energy-storage configuration employed for a specific application determines the relationship between power density/energy-storage density and operating time; it also exerts a decisive influence on the shape of the torque curve. Auspicious power-to-weight ratios combine with high energy-storage densities (period of operation per tank of fuel) to make internal-combustion engines particularly suitable for vehicular applications. However, the torque curves provided by the standard piston powerplants (diesel and spark-ignition engines) are less satisfactory. Thus a transmission unit is required for both the transfer and the conversion of torque. The unit must be capable of transmitting torque in the slip range (for starting off) while incorporating various torque-conversion ratios (for ascending gradients and selecting different speed ranges). Electric and steam-driven powerplants also need a transmission due to the limitations imposed by the respective maxima for current and steam pressure.

Relative torques for various power units
1 Reference point: Gas-turbine base point, Piston engine n_{max}, 2 Steam engine, 3 Electric motor, 4 Limit curve for max. pressure/max. current, 5 Dual-shaft gas turbine, 6 Gasoline (SI) engine, 7 Diesel engine, 8 Single-shaft gas turbine.

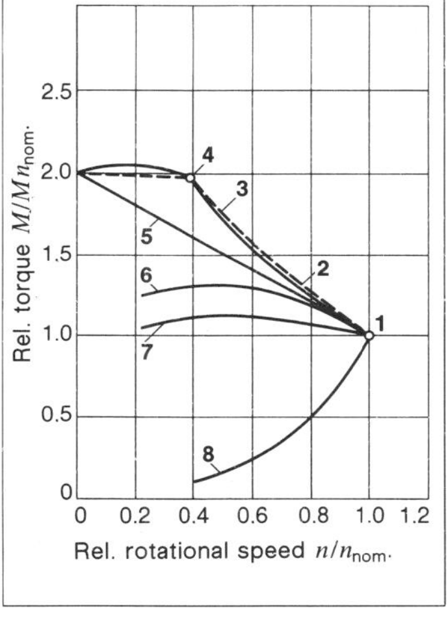

In addition to fulfilling the basic requirements enumerated above, the powerplant and energy-storage system must also meet the following demands:

Economy, characterized by minimal fuel consumption, low manufacturing and maintenance costs, long service life;

Environmental compatibility with low emissions levels for both pollutants and noise, sparing use of raw materials;

Flexibility in operation, including good starting from −30° C to +50° C, operation unaffected by climate and altitude, good drive-off, acceleration and braking characteristics.

Internal-combustion (IC) engines are thus the most favorable option for independent self-contained vehicles, whereby the priority assigned to the individual factors in the above list will vary according to application. Examples:

Passenger cars: High power density, low exhaust and noise emissions, low manufacturing costs,

Trucks and buses: Maximum economy and long service life, and conformity with all emissions requirements.

Special drive systems, such as those relying exclusively on electric motors, or hybrids (dual-system buses, p. 533 ff.) can represent the best, or indeed only, option for special applications and/or under certain operating conditions.

Basic requirements for fuels

Engines featuring external combustion place the least exacting demands on fuel quality, as their combustion and working gases are not identical and remain isolated from each other. In contrast, the fuel used in internal-combustion engines must burn rapidly and virtually without residue.

Engine fuel-consumption graph

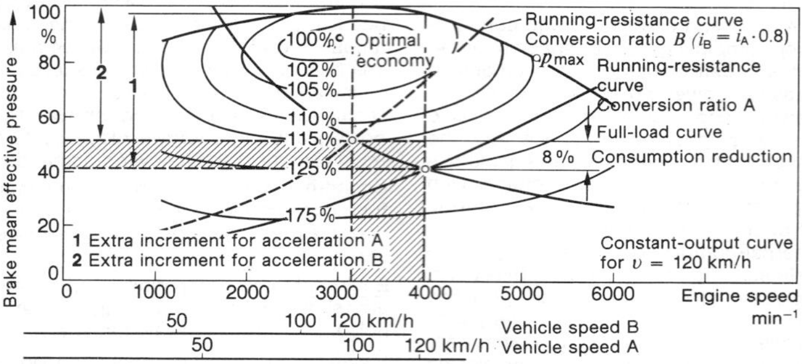

Determining fuel consumption

(as prescribed by DIN 70 030)

Procedure for passenger cars

The procedure prescribed for determining fuel consumption consists of three parts: one driving cycle simulates urban operation (p. 486, 487), while the other two are carried out at constant speeds of 90 km/h and 120 km/h, respectively.

The urban driving cycle is simulated on a chassis dynamometer, while the constant-speed consumption levels can be measured on either a dynamometer or on the road. The test distance must be at least 2 km, and the track may not deviate from the horizontal by more than ±2 %.

During the urban driving cycle, the vehicle must be loaded to the weight prescribed for exhaust-emissions testing, while the load factor for the constant-speed highway tests must be half the vehicle's payload, or at least 180 kg.

Fuel consumption

In the USA, fuel consumption (fuel economy) is expressed in miles per gallon or kilometers per liter. In Germany, in accordance with the above DIN Standard, fuel consumption C is expressed in liters per 100 km.

Gravimetric measurement:

$$C = \frac{m}{\varrho_r \cdot s} \cdot 100 \quad \text{l/100 km}$$

m Weight of fuel consumed in kg, ϱ_r Density of fuel under standard conditions in kg/l, s Distance covered in km.

Volumetric measurement:

$$C = \frac{V(1 + \alpha\,(20° - t_k))}{s} \cdot 100 \quad \text{l/100 km}$$

V Volume of fuel consumed in liters,
α Expansion coefficient of fuel (≈ 0.001/°C),
t_k Temperature of fuel in °C.

Procedure for vehicles in general

(excluding pass. cars and truck tractors) Fuel consumption is measured in both directions on a level track (±1.5 % slope) of approx. 10 km in length. The vehicle is held as steady as possible at ³/₄ its top speed throughout the test distance. The maximum test speed for two-wheeled vehicles is 110 km/h. With other vehicles, the maximum permissible speed is defined in the StVZO Road Licensing Regulations (FMVSS/CUR).

The vehicle is to carry 50 % of its specified payload. Two-wheeled vehicles carry a driver weighing approx. 65 kg.

Fuel consumption

In the USA fuel consumption (fuel economy) is stated in miles per gallon or kilometers per liter. In Germany, in accordance with standards, fuel consumption C is stated in liters per 100 km.

$$C = 1.1 \cdot \frac{V}{s} \cdot 100 \quad \text{l/100 km}$$

V Volume of fuel consumed in liters,
s Distance covered in km,
1.1 Correction factor to compensate for detrimental influences encountered during normal highway operation.

Effect of vehicle design on fuel consumption

Consumption per unit of distance ← Fuel consumption →

Drivetrain ← Running resistance →

Engine | Rolling resistances | Aerodynamic drag | Acceleration resistance | Climbing resistance | Braking resistance

$$B_e = \frac{\int b_e \cdot \frac{1}{\eta_{ü}} \left[\left(m \cdot f \cdot g \cdot \cos\alpha + \frac{\varrho}{2} \cdot c_W \cdot A \cdot v^2\right) + m\,(a + g \cdot \sin\alpha) + B_r\right] \cdot v \cdot \mathrm{d}t}{\int v \cdot \mathrm{d}t}$$

Distance

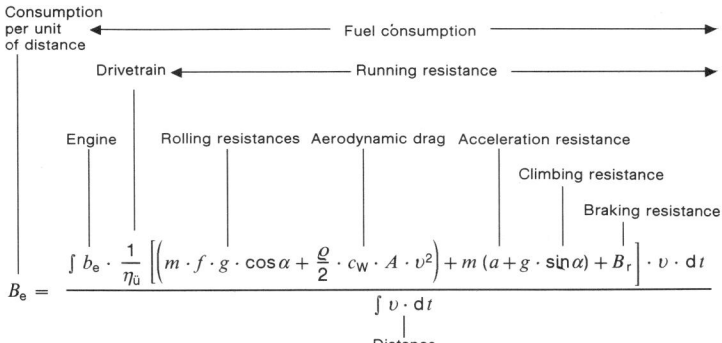

Symbol		Unit
B_e	Consumption per unit of distance	g/m
$n_{ü}$	Transmission efficiency of drivetrain	–
m	Vehicle mass	kg
f	Coefficient of rolling resistance	–
g	Gravitational acceleration	m/s^2
α	Angle of ascent	°
ϱ	Air density	kg/m^3
c_w	Drag coefficient	–
A	Frontal area	m^2
v	Vehicle speed	m/s
a	Acceleration	m/s^2
B_r	Braking resistance	N
t	Time	s
b_e	Specific fuel consumption	g/kWh

The consumption equation distinguishes between three distinct groups of factors:
- Engine (p. 401),
- Transmission, and
- External resistance factors.

Transmission
The influence of the transmission is determined by both the power-transmission losses and the transmission (gear) ratios selected for the application. The former should be kept as low as possible; the latter determine the correspondence between vehicle speed and specific points on the engine's fuel-consumption curve. "Long" gearing will generally move a specific operating state onto a point on the curve corresponding to lower fuel consumption (see illustration), albeit at the expense of reduced acceleration.

External resistance factors
Outside resistance to motion can be counteracted by measures such as weight reduction, improved aerodynamics and lower rolling resistance.

On an average production vehicle, 10 % reductions in weight, aerodynamic drag and in rolling resistance result in fuel-economy improvements of roughly 6 %, 3 % and 2 %, respectively.

The cited formula distinguishes between acceleration resistance and braking resistance, thereby illustrating with particular clarity the fact that losses in fuel economy associated with acceleration largely stem from subsequent application of the brakes. If the brakes are not applied, then the vehicle's kinetic energy is exploited to impel it forward (retardation = negative acceleration), with attendant reductions in overall fuel consumption.

Vehicle dynamics

Dynamics of linear motion

Symbol		Unit
A	Maximum vehicle cross section[1])	m²
a	Acceleration, deceleration	m/s²
c_w	Drag coefficient	—
F	Motive force	N
F_{cf}	Centrifugal force	N
F_L	Aerodynamic drag	N
F_{Ro}	Rolling resistance	N
F_{St}	Climbing resistance	N
F_W	Running resistance	N
f	Coefficient of rolling resistance	—
G	Weight $= m \cdot g$	N
G_B	Sum of wheel forces on driven or braked wheels	N
g	Gravitational acceleration $= 9.81\ m/s^2 \approx 10\ m/s^2$	m/s²
i	Gear or transmission ratio between engine and drive wheels	N

Symbol		Unit
M	Engine torque	N·m
m	Vehicle mass (weight)	kg
n	Engine speed	rpm
P	Power	W
P_W	Motive power	W
p	Gradient (= 100 tan α)	%
r	Dynamic radius of tire	m
s	Traversed distance	m
t	Time	s
v	Vehicle speed	m/s
v_0	Headwind speed	m/s
W	Work	J
α	Gradient angle	°
μ_r	Coefficient of static friction	—

Additional symbols and units in text.

[1]) On passenger cars, $A \approx 0.9 \times \text{Track} \times \text{Height}$.

Total running resistance
The running resistance is calculated as:

$$F_W = F_{Ro} + F_L + F_{St}$$

from which is derived the

Running-resistance power
The power which must be transmitted through the drive wheels to overcome running resistance is:

$$P_W = F_W \cdot v$$

or

$$P_W = \frac{F_W \cdot v}{3600}$$

with P_W in kW, F_W in N, v in km/h.

Rolling resistance
The rolling resistance F_{Ro} is the product of deformation processes which occur at the contact patch between tire and road surface.

$$F_{Ro} = f \cdot G = f \cdot m \cdot g$$

An approximate calculation of the rolling resistance can be made using the coefficients provided in the following table and in the diagram on page 325.

The increase in the coefficient of rolling resistance f is directly proportional to the level of deformation, and

Running resistance

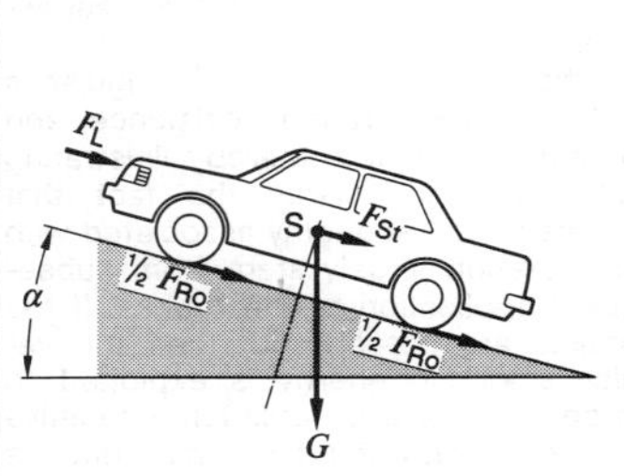

Road surface	Coefficient of rolling resistance f
Pneumatic car tires on	
Large sett pavement	0.015
Small sett pavement	0.015
Concrete, asphalt	0.013
Rolled gravel	0.02
Tarmacadam	0.025
Unpaved road	0.05
Field	0.1 ... 0.35
Pneumatic truck tires on concrete, asphalt	0.006 ... 0.01
Strake wheels in field	0.14 ... 0.24
Track-type tractor in field	0.07 ... 0.12
Wheel on rail	0.001 ... 0.002

inversely proportional to the radius of the tire. The coefficient will thus increase in response to greater loads, higher speeds and lower tire pressure.

During cornering, the rolling resistance is augmented by the cornering resistance

$F_K = f_K \cdot G$

The coefficient of cornering resistance f_K is a function of vehicle speed, curve radius, suspension geometry, tires, tire pressure, and the vehicle's response under lateral acceleration.

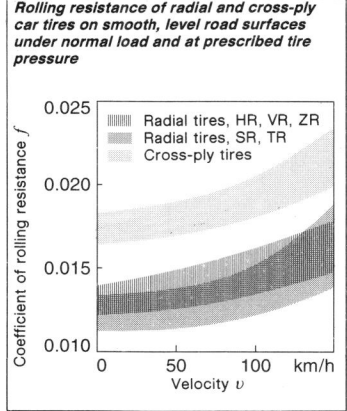

Rolling resistance of radial and cross-ply car tires on smooth, level road surfaces under normal load and at prescribed tire pressure

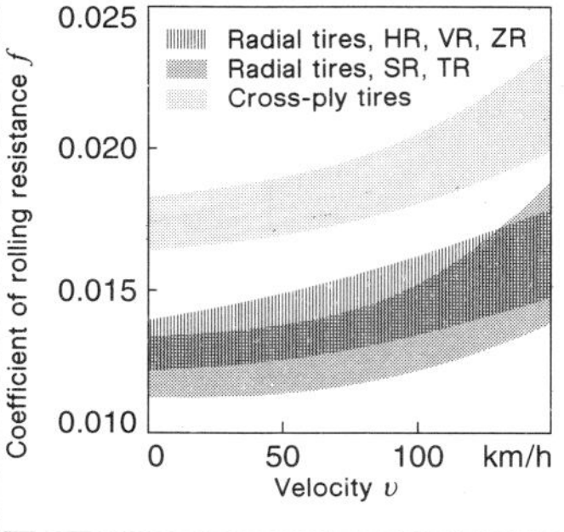

Aerodynamic Drag

Aerodynamic drag is calculated as:

$F_L = 0.5 \cdot \varrho \cdot c_w \cdot A\,(\upsilon + \upsilon_0)^2$

With υ in km/h:

$F_L = 0.0386 \cdot \varrho \cdot c_w \cdot A \cdot (\upsilon + \upsilon_0)^2$

Air density ϱ

(at 200 m altitude $\varrho = 1.202$ kg/m^3),

Drag coefficient c_w, pp. 47 and 326.

Aerodynamic drag in kW

$P_L = F_L \cdot \upsilon = 0.5 \cdot \varrho \cdot c_w \cdot A \cdot \upsilon \cdot (\upsilon + \upsilon_0)^2$

or

$P_L = 12.9 \cdot 10^{-6} \cdot c_w \cdot A \cdot \upsilon \cdot (\upsilon + \upsilon_0)^2$

with P_L in kW, F_L in N, υ and υ_0 in km/h, A in m^2, $\varrho = 1.202$ kg/m^3.

Empirical determination of coefficients for aerodynamic drag and rolling resistance

Allow vehicle to coast down in neutral under windless conditions on a level road surface. The time that elapses while the vehicle coasts down by a specific increment of speed is measured from two initial velocities, υ_1 (high speed) and υ_2 (low speed). This information is used to calculate the mean deceleration rates a_1 and a_2. See following table for formulas and example.

The example is based on a vehicle weighing $m = 1450$ kg with a cross section $A = 2.2$ m^2.

The method is suitable for application at vehicle speeds of less than 100 km/h.

	1st Trial (high speed)	2nd Trial (low speed)
Initial velocity Terminal velocity Interval between υ_a and υ_b	$\upsilon_{a1} = 60$ km/h $\upsilon_{b1} = 55$ km/h $t_1 = 6.5$ s	$\upsilon_{a2} = 15$ km/h $\upsilon_{b2} = 10$ km/h $t_2 = 10.5$ s
Mean velocity	$\upsilon_1 = \frac{\upsilon_{a1} + \upsilon_{b1}}{2} = 57.5$ km/h	$\upsilon_2 = \frac{\upsilon_{a2} + \upsilon_{b2}}{2} = 12.5$ km/h
Mean deceleration	$a_1 = \frac{\upsilon_{a1} - \upsilon_{b1}}{t_1} = 0.77 \frac{\text{km/h}}{\text{s}}$	$a_2 = \frac{\upsilon_{a2} - \upsilon_{b2}}{t_2} = 0.48 \frac{\text{km/h}}{\text{s}}$
Drag coefficient	$c_w = \frac{6\,m \cdot (a_1 - a_2)}{A \cdot (\upsilon_1^2 - \upsilon_2^2)} = 0.36$	
Coefficient of rolling resistance	$f = \frac{28.2\,(a_2 \cdot \upsilon_1^2 - a_1 \cdot \upsilon_2^2)}{10^3 \cdot (\upsilon_1^2 - \upsilon_2^2)} = 0.013$	

Drag coefficient and associated power requirements for various body configurations

	Drag coefficient c_w	Drag power in kW, average values for $A = 2\ m^2$ at various speeds[1]) 40 km/h	80 km/h	120 km/h	160 km/h
 Open convertible	0.5 ... 0.7	1	7.9	27	63
 Station wagon (2-box)	0.5 ... 0.6	0.91	7.2	24	58
 Conventional form (3-box)	0.4 ... 0.55	0.78	6.3	21	50
 Wedge shape, headlights & bumbers integrated in body, wheels covered, underbody covered, optimized flow of cooling flow.	0.3 ... 0.4	0.58	4.6	16	37
 Headlights and all wheels enclosed within body, underbody cover	0.2 ... 0.25	0.37	3.0	10	24
 K-shape (minimal cross section at tail)	0.23	0.38	3.0	10	24
 Optimum streamlining	0.15 ... 0.20	0.29	2.3	7.8	18
Trucks, combinations	0.8 ... 1.5	–	–	–	–
Motorcycles	0.6 ... 0.7	–	–	–	–
Buses	0.6 ... 0.7	–	–	–	–
Streamlined buses	0.3 ... 0.4	–	–	–	–

[1]) No headwind ($v_0 = 0$).

Climbing resistance and downgrade force

The climbing resistance (F_{St} with positive operational sign) and the downgrade force (F_{St} with negative operational sign) are calculated as:

$$F_{St} = G \cdot \sin\alpha$$
$$= m \cdot g \cdot \sin\alpha$$

or, for a working approximation:

$$F_{St} \approx 0.01 \cdot m \cdot g \cdot p$$

valid for gradients of up to $p = 20\,\%$, as $\sin\alpha = \tan\alpha$ at small angles (less than 2 % error).

The climbing power is calculated as:

$$P_{St} = F_{St} \cdot v$$

With P_{St} in kW, F_{St} in N, v in km/h:

$$P_{St} = \frac{F_{St} \cdot v}{3600} = \frac{m \cdot g \cdot v \cdot \sin\alpha}{3600}$$

or, for a working approximation:

$$P_{St} \approx \frac{m \cdot g \cdot p \cdot v}{360{,}000}$$

The gradient is:

$$p = (h/l) \cdot 100\,\%, \text{ or}$$
$$p = (\tan\alpha) \cdot 100\,\%$$

with h as the height of the projected distance l. In the English-speaking countries, calculations are based on the *gradient*.

Conversion: *Gradient* 1 in 100/p.

Example: 1 in 2 grade.

Gradient angle α	Incline p %	Incline *Gradient*	Climbing resistance at m = 1000 kg N

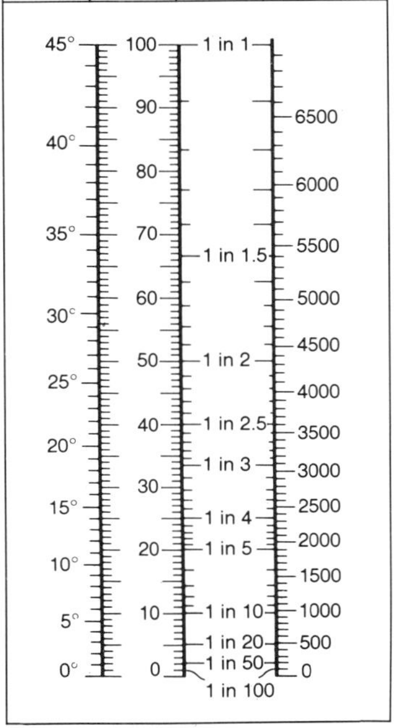

Values at m = 1000 kg

Climbing resistance F_{St} N	Climbing power P_{St} in kW at various speeds 20 km/h	30 km/h	40 km/h	50 km/h	60 km/h
6500	36	54	72	–	–
6000	33	50	67	–	–
5500	31	46	61	–	–
5000	28	42	56	69	–
4500	25	37	50	62	–
4000	22	33	44	56	67
3500	19	29	39	49	58
3000	17	25	33	42	50
2500	14	21	28	35	42
2000	11	17	22	28	33
1500	8.3	12	17	21	25
1000	5.6	8.3	11	14	17
500	2.3	4.2	5.6	6.9	8.3
0	0	0	0	0	0

Example: To climb a hill with a gradient of $p = 18\,\%$, a vehicle weighing 1500 kg will require approximately $1.5 \cdot 1700$ N = 2550 N motive force and, at v = 40 km/h, roughly $1.5 \cdot 19$ kW = 28.5 kW climbing power.

Motive force

The motive force F available at the drive wheels increases along with increasing engine torque M and overall transmission ratio between engine and driven wheels i. It decreases in response to higher power-transmission losses:

$$F = \frac{M \cdot i}{r} \cdot \eta \text{ or } F = \frac{P \cdot \eta}{\upsilon}$$

η Drivetrain efficiency level
(lengthways engine $\eta \approx$ 0.88 ... 0.92)
(transverse engine $\eta \approx$ 0.91 ... 0.95)

The motive force F is partially consumed in overcoming the running resistance F_W. Numerically higher transmission ratios are applied to deal with the substantially increased running resistance encountered on gradients (gearbox).

Vehicle and engine speeds

$$n = \frac{60 \cdot \upsilon \cdot i}{2 \cdot \pi \cdot r}$$

or with υ in km/h:

$$n = \frac{1000 \cdot \upsilon \cdot i}{2 \cdot \pi \cdot 60 \cdot r}$$

Acceleration

The surplus force $F - F_W$ accelerates the vehicle (or retards it when F_W exceeds F).

$$a = \frac{F - F_W}{k_m \cdot m} \text{ or } a = \frac{P \cdot \eta - P_W}{\upsilon \cdot k_m \cdot m}$$

Determining the rotational inertia coefficient k_m

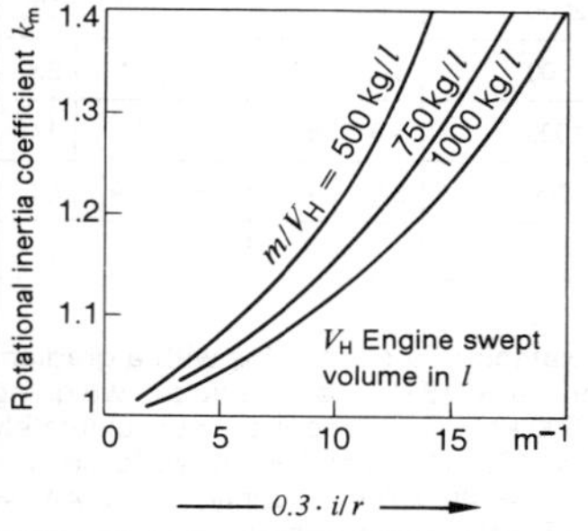

Hydrodynamic converter
1 Power, 2 Turbine, 3 Pump, 4 Stator, 5 One-way clutch, 6 Output.

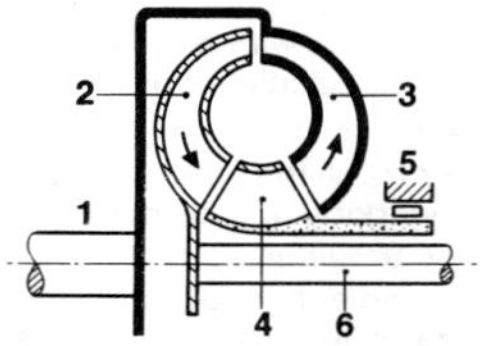

The rotational inertia coefficient k_m compensates for the apparent increase in vehicle mass due to the rotating masses (wheels, flywheel, crankshaft, etc.).

Motive force and road speed on vehicles with automatic transmissions

When the formula for motive force is applied to automatic transmissions with hydrodynamic torque converters or hydrodynamic clutches, the engine torque M is replaced by the torque at the converter turbine, while the rotational speed of the converter turbine is used in the formula for engine speed.

The relationship between $M_{Turb} = f(n_{Turb})$ and the engine curve $M_{Eng} = f(n_{Eng})$ is determined using the performance curve of the hydrodynamic converter (p. 540).

Running diagram for car with automatic transmission and hydrodynamic Trilok converter under full throttle

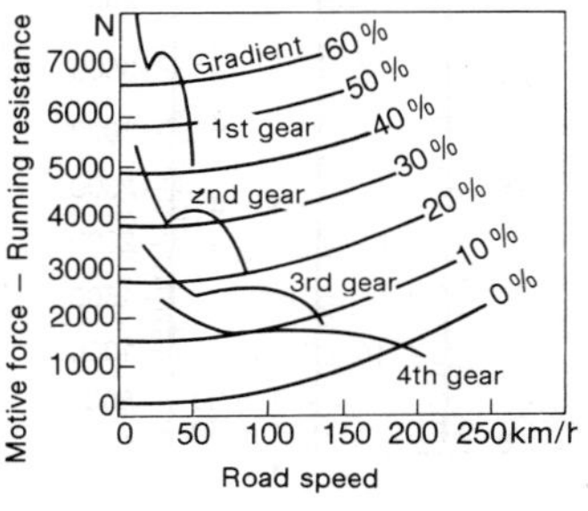

Adhesion to road surface

Coefficients of static friction for pneumatic tires on various surfaces

Vehicle speed	Tire condition	Road condition Dry	Wet Water approx. 0.2 mm deep	Heavy rainfall Water approx. 1 mm deep	Puddles Water approx. 2 mm deep	Ice (Black ice)
		Coefficient of static friction μ_r				
50	new	0.85	0.65	0.55	0.5	0.1 and less
	worn[1])	1	0.5	0.4	0.25	
90	new	0.8	0.6	0.3	0.05	
	worn[1])	0.95	0.2	0.1	0.05	
130	new	0.75	0.55	0.2	0	
	worn[1])	0.9	0.2	0.1	0	

The static coefficient of friction (between the tires and the road surface), also known as the tire-road-interface friction coefficient, is determined by the vehicle's speed, the condition of the tires and the state of the road surface (see table above). The figures cited apply for concrete and tarmacadam road surfaces in good condition. The coefficients of sliding friction (with wheel locked) are usually lower than the coefficients of static friction.

Special rubber compounds providing friction coefficients of up to 1.8 are employed in racing tires.

The maxima for acceleration and uphill driving, and for retardation and downhill braking, are provided on page 331.

Aquaplaning

Aquaplaning, has a particularly dramatic influence on the contact between tire and road surface. It describes the state in which a layer of water separates the tire and the (wet) road surface. The phenomenon occurs when a wedge of water forces its way underneath the tire's contact patch and lifts it from the road. The tendency to aquaplane is dependent upon such factors as the depth of the water on the road surface, the vehicle's speed, the tread pattern, the tread wear, and the load pressing the tire against the road surface. Wide tires are particularly susceptible to aquaplaning. It is not possible to steer or brake an aquaplaning vehicle, as its front wheels will have ceased to rotate, meaning that neither steering inputs nor braking forces can be transmitted to the road surface.

Aquaplaning
1 Tires, 2 Wedge of water, 3 Road surface.

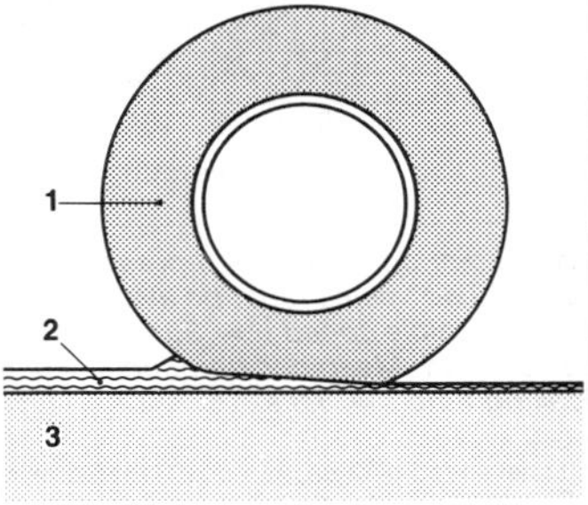

[1]) Worn to tread depth of 1 mm (minimum allowed under Paragraph 36.2, StVZO).

Accelerating and braking

The vehicle is regarded as accelerating or braking (decelerating) at a constant rate when a remains constant. The following equations apply to an initial or final speed of 0:

	Equations for v in m/s	Equations for v in km/h
Acceleration or braking (deceleration) in m/s²	$a = \frac{v^2}{2 \cdot s} = \frac{v}{t} = \frac{2 \cdot s}{t^2}$	$a = \frac{v^2}{26 \cdot s} = \frac{v}{3.6 \cdot t} = \frac{2 \cdot s}{t^2}$
Accelerating or braking time in s	$t = \frac{v}{a} = \frac{2 \cdot s}{v} = \sqrt{\frac{2 \cdot s}{a}}$	$t = \frac{v}{3.6 \cdot a} = \frac{7.2 \cdot s}{v} = \sqrt{\frac{2 \cdot s}{a}}$
Accelerating or braking distance¹) in m	$s = \frac{v^2}{2 \cdot a} = \frac{v \cdot t}{2} = \frac{a \cdot t^2}{2}$	$s = \frac{v^2}{26 \cdot a} = \frac{v \cdot t}{7.2} = \frac{a \cdot t^2}{2}$

Stopping distance, p. 332.
Symbols and units, p. 13.

Constant rates of acceleration and deceleration

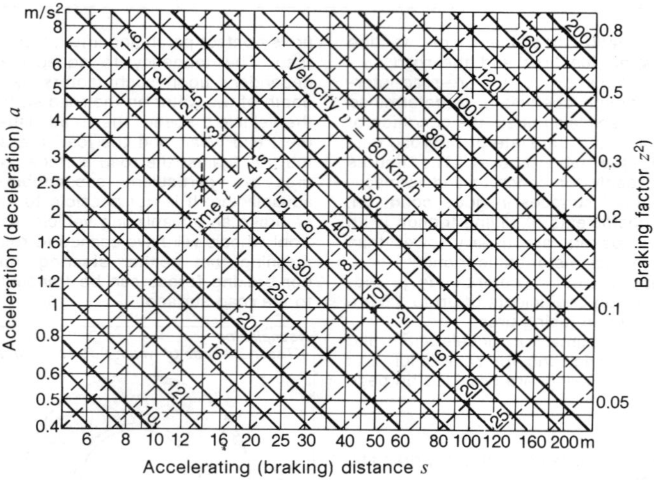

Every point on the graph represents a particular relationship between v, a or z²), s and t. Two values must be available for all values to be determined.
Given: Vehicle speed $v = 30$ km/h, Braking distance $s = 13.5$ m
Determined: Mean deceleration $a = 2.5$ m/s², Retardation $z = 0.25$, Braking time $t = 3.3$ s.

¹) If final speed v_2 does not equal 0 then braking distance $s = v_1 \cdot t - at^2/2$ at v_1 in m/s.
²) Deceleration rate relative to 1 g.

Maxima for acceleration and braking (retardation)

When the motive or braking forces exerted at the vehicle's wheels reach such a magnitude that the tires are just still within their limit of adhesion (maximum adhesion is still present), the relationships between the gradient angle α, coefficient of static friction μ_r[1]) and maximum acceleration or deceleration are defined as follows. The real-world figures are always somewhat lower, as all the vehicle's tires do not simultaneously exploit their maximum adhesion during each acceleration (deceleration). Electronic traction and antilock braking systems (ASR, ABS)[2]) maintain the traction level in the vicinity of the coefficient of static friction.

k = Ratio between the load on driven or braked wheels and the total weight. All wheels driven or braked: $k = 1$. At 50 % weight distribution $k = 0.5$.
Example: $k = 0.5$; $g = 10\ \text{m/s}^2$, $\mu_r = 0.6$; $p = 15\ \%$
$a_{max} = 0.5 \cdot 10 \cdot (0.6 \pm 0.15)$
Braking on upgrade (+):
$a_{max} = 3.75\ \text{m/s}^2$
Braking on downgrade (−):
$a_{max} = 2.25\ \text{m/s}^2$

Work and power

The power required to maintain a consistent rate of acceleration (deceleration) varies according to vehicle speed.
Power available for acceleration:

$$P_a = P \cdot \eta - P_w$$

where P = engine output, η = efficiency, and P_w = motive power.

Acceleration and braking (deceleration)

	Level road surface	Inclined road surface $\alpha°$; $p = 100 \cdot \tan\alpha\%$	
Limit acceleration/ deceleration a_{max} in m/s²	$a_{max} \leqq k \cdot g \cdot \mu_r$	$a_{max} \leqq k \cdot g\ (\mu_r \cos\alpha \pm \sin\alpha)$ approximation[3]): $a_{max} \leqq k \cdot g\ (\mu_r \pm 0.01 \cdot p)$	+ Upgrade braking or downgrade acceleration − Upgrade acceleration or downgrade braking

Achievable acceleration a_e (P_a in kW, v in km/h, m in kg)

Level road surface	Inclined road surface	
$a_e = \dfrac{3600 \cdot P_a}{k_m \cdot m \cdot v}$	$a_e = \dfrac{3600 \cdot P_a}{k_m \cdot m \cdot v} \pm g \cdot \sin\alpha$	+ Downgrade acceleration − Upgrade acceleration approximation[3]) for $g \cdot \sin\alpha$: $g \cdot p/100$

Work and power

	Level road surface	Inclined road surface $\alpha°$; $p = 100 \cdot \tan\alpha\%$	
Acceleration or braking work W in J[4])	$W = k_m \cdot m \cdot a \cdot s$	$W = m \cdot s\ (k_m \cdot a \pm g \cdot \sin\alpha)$ approximation[3]) $W = m \cdot s\ (k_m \cdot a \pm g \cdot p/100)$	+ for downgrade braking or upgrade acceleration − for downgrade acceleration or upgrade braking v in m/s. Use $v/3.6$ for v in km/h.
Acceleration or braking power at velocity v in W	$P_a = k_m \cdot m \cdot a \cdot v$	$P_a = m \cdot v\ (k_m \cdot a \pm g \cdot \sin\alpha)$ approximation[3]) $P_a = m \cdot v\ (k_m \cdot a \pm g \cdot p/100)$	

[1]) See p. 329 for numerical values.
[2]) ABS = Antilock braking system; p. 610, 638. ASR = Traction control; p. 555.
[3]) Valid to approx. $p = 20\%$ (under 2 % error)
[4]) J = N · m = W · s. Conversions, p. 14.

Stopping distance

This is the distance covered between the moment when a hazard is recognized and the time when the vehicle comes to a complete stop. It is the sum of the distances traveled during the reaction time t_r, the brake initial response time t_a (at constant vehicle speed v), and the active braking time t_w. Maximum retardation a is obtained in the pressure-build-up period t_s. Alternately, half of the pressure-buildup period may be considered to be fully decelerated.

The periods in which no braking occurs are combined to form the so-called lost time t_{vz}:

$$t_{vz} = t_r + t_a + t_s/2$$

The upper limits on retardation are determined by the static coefficient of friction between tires and road surface (p. 329), while the lower extremes are defined by the legally required minima (p. 600).

The difference between the stopping time/distance and the braking time/distance is defined by t_{vz}, or $v \cdot t_{vz}$. The brake actuation time given on page 597 includes the periods $t_a + t_s/2$.

Reaction time

The reaction time is the period which elapses between recognition of the object, the decision to brake and the time it takes for the foot to hit the brake pedal. The reaction time is not a fixed value; it ranges from 0.3 to 1.7 s, depending upon the driver and on external factors (p. 333).

Special tests are necessary to determine individual reaction patterns (such as those performed by the Medical and Psychological Institute for Traffic Safety of the German Inspection, Testing, and Certification Authorities, Stuttgart [TÜV Stuttgart, e. V.]).

Deceleration and stopping distances

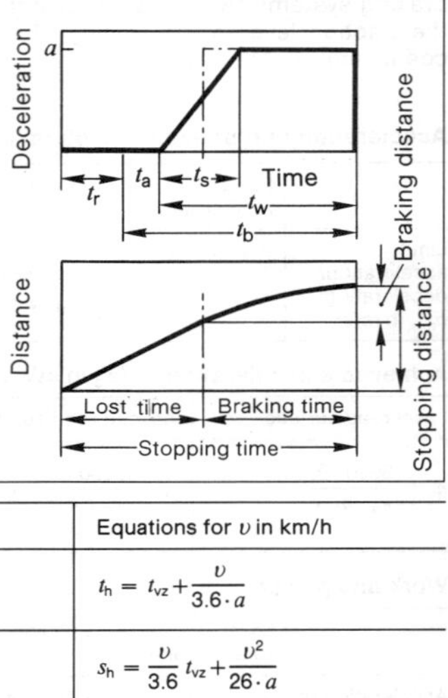

	Equations for v in m/s	Equations for v in km/h
Stopping time t_h in s	$t_h = t_{vz} + \frac{v}{a}$	$t_h = t_{vz} + \frac{v}{3.6 \cdot a}$
Stopping distance s_h in m	$s_h = v \cdot t_{vz} + \frac{v^2}{2 \cdot a}$	$s_h = \frac{v}{3.6} t_{vz} + \frac{v^2}{26 \cdot a}$

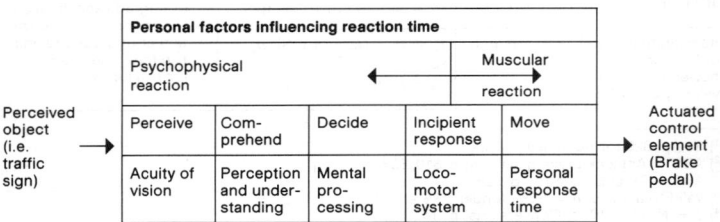

Personal factors influencing reaction time

Perceived object (i.e. traffic sign) →

Psychophysical reaction			Muscular reaction	
Perceive	Com-prehend	Decide	Incipient response	Move
Acuity of vision	Perception and under-standing	Mental pro-cessing	Loco-motor system	Personal response time

→ Actuated control element (Brake pedal)

Effect of personal and extraneous factors on reaction time

	Reduction down to 0.3 s ←	**Extension** up to 1.7 s →
A) Personal factors	Trained, reflexive response	Inexperienced, uncoordinated response
	Good frame of mind; optimal performance potential	Poor frame of mind, e.g.. fatigue
	Highly skilled driver	Lower level of driving skill
	Youth	Advanced age
	Anticipation	Inattentiveness, distraction
	Physical and mental health	Health disorders in response groups
		Panic, alcohol
B) Extraneous factors Traffic situation	Uncomplicated, easily comprehended, predictable, familiar	Complicated, difficult to comprehend, unpredictable, rarely encountered
Type of external stimulus	Explicit, conspicuous	Equivocal, inconspicuous
Location of stimulus	Within the field of vision	At edge of visual field
Type of control device	Logical control layout	Poor control layout

Brake response and pressure build-up times

The brake response and pressure build-up times t_a and t_s are determined by both the actuation and force-transmission mechanism and linkage, as well as by the condition of the brakes at the moment they are applied (for instance, wet brake disks). Consult ECE R 13 for legal regulations concerning t_a and t_s on tightly adjusted brakes. The applicable regulation[1]) for testing braking-system effectiveness uses figures of 0.36 s (vehicle class M_1) and 0.54 s (vehicle classes M_2, M_3, N_1 ... N_3) in the braking-distance equation $t_a + t_s/2$. The response and pressure build-up times are longer if the brake system is in poor condition. A response delay of 1 s results in a stopping distance of (see table):

[1]) EC Directive EEC/71/320.

Deceleration a in m/s²	Vehicle speed prior to braking in km/h 10	30	50	60	70	80	90	100	120	140	160	180	200
	Distance during delay of 1 sec (no braking) in m												
	2.8	8.3	14	17	19	22	25	28	33	39	44	50	56
	Stopping distance in m												
4.4	3.7	16	36	48	62	78	96	115	160	210	270	335	405
5	3.5	15	33	44	57	71	87	105	145	190	240	300	365
5.8	3.4	14	30	40	52	65	79	94	130	170	215	265	320
7	3.3	13	28	36	46	57	70	83	110	145	185	230	275
8	3.3	13	26	34	43	53	64	76	105	135	170	205	250
9	3.2	12	25	32	40	50	60	71	95	125	155	190	225

Passing (overtaking)

Symbol		Unit
a	Acceleration	m/s^2
l_1, l_2	Vehicle length	m
s_1, s_2	Safety margin	m
s_H	Relative distance travelled by passing vehicle	m
s_L	Distance travelled by vehicle being passed	m
s_u	Passing distance	m
t_u	Passing time	s
v_L	Speed of slower vehicle	km/h
v_H	Speed of faster vehicle	km/h

The complete passing maneuver involves pulling out of the lane, overtaking the other vehicle, and returning to the original lane. Being as passing can take place under a wide variety of highly differing circumstances and conditions, precise calculations are difficult. For this reason, the following calculations, graphs, and illustrations will confine themselves to an examination of two extreme conditions: Passing at a constant velocity and passing at a constant rate of acceleration.

We can simplify graphic representation by treating the passing distance s_u as the sum of two (straight-ahead) components, s_H and s_L, while disregarding the extra travel involved in pulling out of the lane and back in again.

Passing distance

$$s_u = s_H + s_L$$

The distance s_H which the more rapid vehicle most cover compared to the slower vehicle (considered as being stationary) is the sum of the vehicle lengths l_1 and l_2 and the safety margins s_1 and s_2.

$$s_H = s_1 + s_2 + l_1 + l_2$$

During the passing time t_u, the slower vehicle covers the distance s_L; this is the distance that the overtaking vehicle must also travel in order to maintain the safety margin.

$$s_L = t_u \cdot v_L / 3.6$$

Passing distance

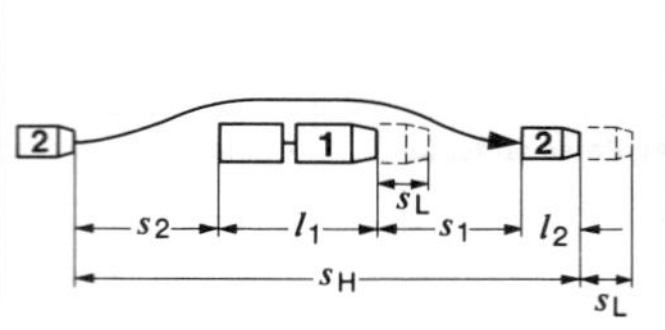

Safety margin

The minimum safety margin corresponds to the distance covered during the lost time t_{vz} (p. 332). The figure for a lost time of $t_{vz} = 1.08$ s (velocity in km/h) is $(0.3 \cdot v)$ meters. However, a minimum of $0.5 \cdot v$ is advisable outside built-up areas.

Passing at constant speed

On highways with more than two lanes, the overtaking vehicle will frequently already be traveling at a speed adequate for passing before the actual process begins. The passing time (from initial lane change until return to the original lane has been completed) is then:

$$t_u = \frac{3.6 \cdot s_H}{v_H - v_L}$$

The passing distance is

t in s, s in m, v in km/h

$$s_u = \frac{t_u \cdot v_H}{3.6} = \frac{s_H \cdot v_H}{v_H - v_L}$$

Passing with constant acceleration

On narrow roads, the vehicle will usually have to slow down to the speed of the preceding car or truck before again accelerating to pass. The attainable acceleration figures (p. 331) depend upon engine output, vehicle weight, speed and running resistance (p. 324). These generally lie within the range of 0.4 ... 0.8 m/s^2, with up to 1.4 m/s^2 available in lower gears for further reductions in passing time. The distance required to complete the passing maneuver should never exceed half the visible stretch of road.

Operating on the assumption that a constant rate of acceleration can be maintained for the duration of the passing maneuver, the passing time will be:

$t_u = \sqrt{2 \cdot s_H/a}$

The distance which the slower vehicle covers within this period is defined as $s_L = t_u \cdot v_L/3.6$. This gives a passing distance of:

$$s_u = s_H + t_u \cdot v_L/3.6 \qquad t \text{ in s, } s \text{ in m, } v \text{ in km/h}$$

The left side of the graph below shows the relative distances s_H for speed differentials $v_H - v_L$ or acceleration rates a, while the right side contains the distances which the vehicle being passed covers at various speeds v_L. The passing distance s_u is the sum of s_H and s_L.

The graph is applied as follows. First, determine the distance s_H to be traveled by the passing vehicle. Enter this distance on the left side of the graph between the Y-axis and the applicable line for $(v_H - v_L)$ or acceleration. Then extrapolate the line to the right, over to the speed line v_L.

Example (represented by broken lines in the graph):
$v_L = v_H = 50$ km/h
$a = 0.4$ m/s^2
$l_1 = 10$ m, $l_2 = 5$ m,
$s_1 = s_2 = 0.3 \cdot v_L = 0.3 \cdot v_H = 15$ m

Solution: Enter intersection of $a = 0.4$ m/s^2 and $s_H = 15 + 15 + 10 + 5 = 45$ m in the left side of the graph.
Indication: $t_u = 15$ s, $s_L = 210$ m.
Thus: $s_u = s_H + s_L = 255$ m.

Visibility

For safe passing on narrow roads, the visibility must be at least the sum of the passing distance plus the distance which would be traveled by an oncoming vehicle while the passing maneuver is in progress. This distance is approximately 400 m if the vehicles approaching each other are travelling at speeds of 90 km/h, and the vehicle being overtaken at 60 km/h.

Graph for determining passing distances

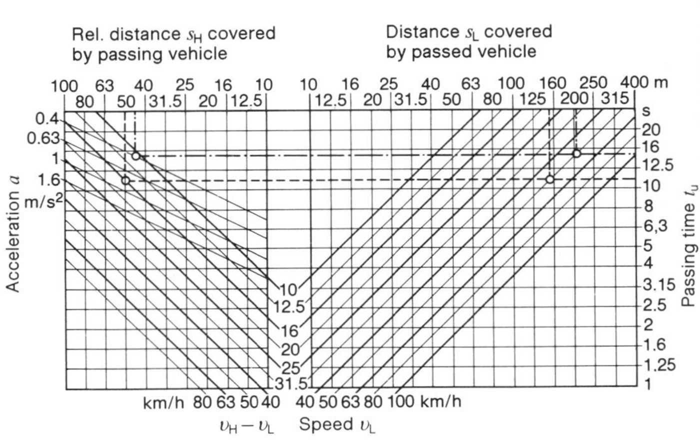

Dynamics of lateral motion

Response to crosswinds

Strong crosswinds will deflect a vehicle from its lane, particularly at high speeds. Sudden sidewinds, of the kind encountered when embankments give way to open, unsheltered roads, can evoke yaw-angle changes as well as causing the vehicle to drift off course. On vehicles which are sensitive to crosswind, these effects are substantial and can occur before the driver has had time to react and take preventive action (for reaction time see page 332). It is thus essential that the relevant factors be considered in the vehicle-design stage.

When wind impacts upon the vehicle from an oblique angle, aerodynamic drag is supplemented by a lateral component of the aerodynamic force. This force, which is distributed across the entire body, can be considered as a single force – the crosswind force – directed toward what is known as the pressure point. The actual location of the pressure point is determined by body shape and angle of impact.

The pressure point will usually be found on the front half of the vehicle, whereby it is closer to the center on conventional notchback ("three-box") bodies than on vehicles with a sloping tail section ("fastbacks" and aerodynamic designs). With the latter, the pressure point may even lie forward of the front axle in extreme cases.

The pressure point on notchback bodies generally remains in a specific location; on streamlined vehicles it tends to vary according to the angle of impact. All else being equal, the greater lateral forces will occur with the notchback.

As the above implies, the pressure point will hardly provide a suitable reference point for use in illustrating the effects of crosswinds, because it has no fixed location on the vehicle. At the same time, the center of gravity varies with vehicle load. It is thus useful to select a central location on the forward section of the body as a reference point, a practice which also ensures that the data remain unaffected by the variations in the relative positions of bodywork and suspension.

When the crosswind force is specified for a reference point other than the pressure point, it must be supplemented by the crosswind moment at the pressure point in question. The standard practice in aerodynamics is to replace the forces and moments with dimensionless coefficients which remain independent of air-flow velocity. The graph shows the curves for crosswind force and the yaw coefficients for both a notchback vehicle and a fastback body style. Due to the multiplicity of possible body designs, the present investigation can only provide general reference data; wind-tunnel measure-

Vehicle exposed to crosswind

$F_s + M_z$ impacting at O corresponds to F_s acting at D

v_s *Crosswind velocity*

v_w *Headwind velocity*

v_r *Air-flow velocity*

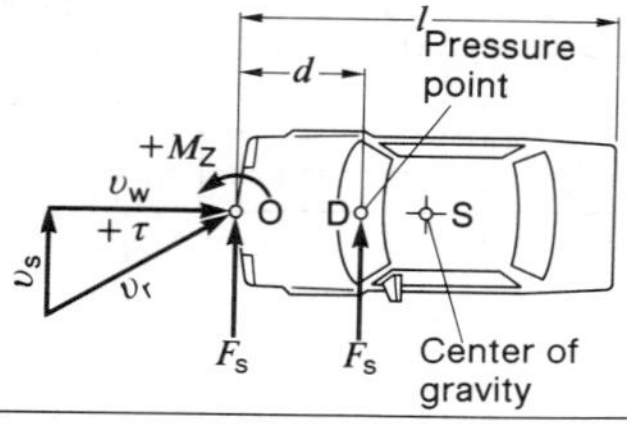

Coefficients of crosswind force c_s and yaw moment c_{MZ} relative to air-flow angle

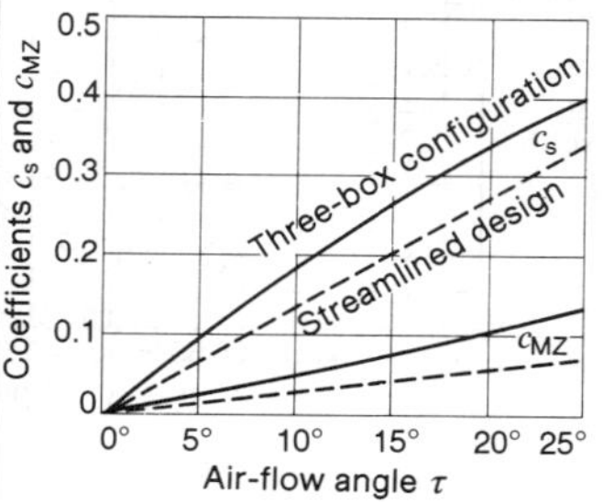

Cornering force as a function of wheel slip angle

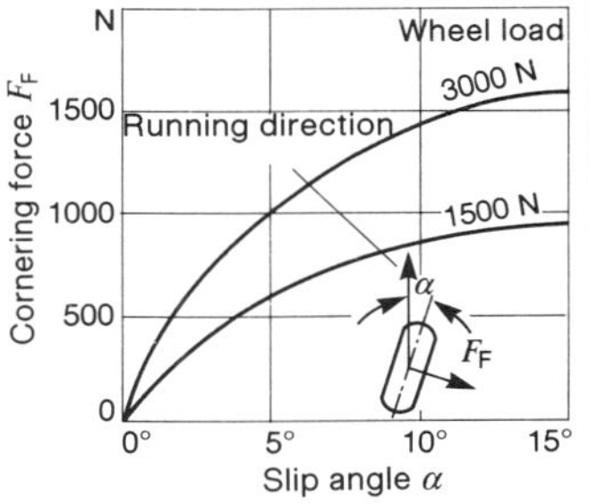

Crosswind impacting against center of gravity. Vehicle veers in or veers out

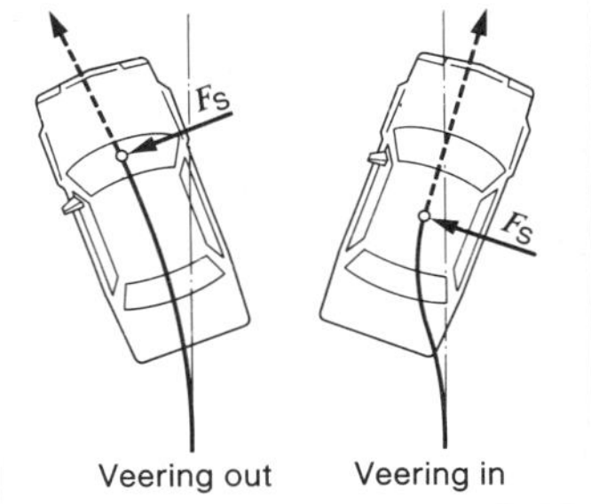

ments are essential for obtaining precise information on specific body shapes.

The following equations are applied to derive forces and moments from the coefficients:

Crosswind force: $F_s = c_s \cdot \varrho(v_r^2/2) \cdot A_s$

Yaw moment: $M_Z = c_{MZ} \cdot \varrho(v_r^2/2) \cdot A_s \cdot l$

ϱ Atmospheric density, v_r Resulting air-impact velocity, A_s Projected lateral surface of vehicle, l Total length of vehicle (in coherent units), c_s Coefficient of crosswind force, c_{MZ} Coefficient for crosswind-induced yaw.

The distance between the pressure point and the leading edge of the vehicle is calculated using

$$d = M_Z/F_s = l \cdot c_{MZ}/c_s$$

The crosswind force is resisted by the lateral cornering forces at the wheels. The degree of lateral cornering force which a pneumatic tire can provide depends upon numerous factors, such as wheel slip angle, wheel load, tire design and dimensions, tire pressure and the amount of traction afforded by the road surface.

The pneumatic tire's specific response characteristics mean that, at a constant slip angle, higher wheel loads will not evoke proportional increases in cornering forces. In the example (diagram), doubling the wheel load increases the cornering force by a factor of only 1.5 ... 1.7. The slip angle must also be increased if the cornering force is to be doubled. This explains why the axle supporting the greater load assumes a larger slip angle than its less heavily loaded counterpart, assuming that identical ratios of lateral (side) force to tire contact force act on both axles.

When the crosswind force impacts against the center of gravity, the distribution ratio for the required cornering forces between front and rear axles is a function of the wheel-load factors, i.e., the ratio of contact force to lateral force is the same at both axles. When the center of gravity is in the forward section of the vehicle, the crosswind force causes the vehicle to "veer-out" due to the front axle's necessarily greater wheel slip angle; when the center of gravity is at the rear, the vehicle "veers-in". In both cases, the vehicle's center of gravity is deflected downwind from the original path of travel. When the crosswind ceases, the "veering-out" vehicle will continue to deviate from its original path, while the "veering-in" vehicle will return to and indeed go beyond the original line.

The crosswind's impact point, however, will rarely coincide with the center of gravity; the distance forward from the center of the vehicle depends upon the individual body shape. Thus a vehicle which responds to impact at the center of gravity by veering inwards, will veer out when exposed to actual crosswinds.

Due to the forward displacement of the pressure point, vehicles with a sloping rear section display a greater tendency to veer-out; they are thus more difficult to control than notchback vehicles.

Rear-mounted vertical stabilizer fins can be installed to move the pressure point rearward, toward the center of gravity. However, except in competition vehicles and other special applications, this option has to date rarely been applied.

Placing the pressure point in the immediate vicinity of the vehicle's center of gravity results in improved directional stability. Oversteer vehicles have a minimum tendency to deviate from their path of travel when the pressure point is forward of the center of gravity. On understeer vehicles, the best pressure-point location is just to the rear of the center of gravity.

Crosswind force is generally minimal relative to contact force, and the influence of nonlinearity in the ratio of contact force to lateral force is limited when small lateral forces are applied – a vehicle's response to crosswinds is therefore not governed by tire properties alone. Among the other important factors are compliance in suspension and steering. Thus the suspension designer can also exercise a major influence on the vehicle's crosswind response characteristics.

Oversteer and understeer

Cornering forces can only be generated between a rubber tire and the road surface when the tire rolls at an angle to its longitudinal plane; that is, a certain wheel slip angle is required.

A vehicle is said to understeer when, as lateral acceleration increases, the slip angle at the front axle increases more than it does at the rear axle. The opposite applies for a vehicle which oversteers.

Avehicle will not necessarily display the same self-steering effect at all possible rates of lateral acceleration. Some vehicles always understeer or oversteer, and some display a transition from understeer to oversteer as lateral acceleration increases, while other vehicles respond in precisely the opposite manner.

References:

Barth, R.: "Windkanalmessungen an Fahrzeugmodellen und rechteckigen Körpern mit verschiedenem Seitenverhältnis bei unsymmetrischer Anströmung" (Wind Tunnel Measurements on Vehicle Models and Rectangular Bodies with Different Side Ratios under Unsymmetrical Flow). Dissertation, Stuttgart Technical College, 1958.

Barth, R.: "Luftkräfte am Kraftfahrzeug" (Aerodynamic Forces Acting on Motor Vehicles).

Deutsche Kraftfahrtforschung und Straßenverkehrstechnik (German Motor Vehicle Research and Traffic Engineering), Vol. 184, Düsseldorf.

VDI-Verlag (published by the Association of German Engineers), 1966.

Mitschke, M.: "Dynamik der Kraftfahrzeuge" (Dynamics of Motor Vehicles). Springer-Verlag, 1972.

Cornering behaviour

Centrifugal force in curves

$$F_{cf} = \frac{m \cdot v^2}{r_K}$$ (see also p. 45)

or, with v specified in km/h and r_K as the radius of the curve in m:

$$F_{cf} = \frac{m \cdot v^2}{12.96 \cdot r_K}$$

Centrifugal force when cornering
b Track width in m
h_S Height of center of gravity in m.

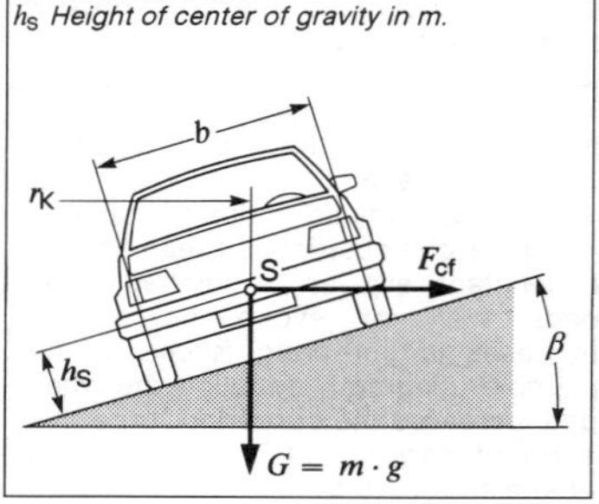

Critical speeds

The concrete example provided in the table below would apply to a vehicle with a track b = 1.5 m, height of center of gravity h_S = 0.6 m; max. adhesion coefficient μ_r = 0.8, curve radius r_K = 90 m, curve banking β = 20°.

	Flat curve	Banked curve
Speed at which the vehicle exceeds the adhesion limit (skid)	$v \leq 11.28\sqrt{\mu_r \cdot r_K}$ km/h	$v \leq 11.28\sqrt{\frac{(\mu_r + \tan\beta)\, r_K}{1 - \mu_r \cdot \tan\beta}}$ km/h
Example:	≤ 96 km/h	≤ 137 km/h
Speed at which the vehicle tips	$v \geq 11.28\sqrt{\frac{b \cdot r_K}{2 \cdot h_S}}$ km/h	$v \geq 11.28\sqrt{\frac{\left(\frac{b}{2 \cdot h_s} + \tan\beta\right) \cdot r_K}{1 - \frac{b}{2 \cdot h_s} \cdot \tan\beta}}$ km/h
Example:	≥ 120 km/h ($\mu_r \geq 1.25$)	≥ 184 km/h ($\mu_r \geq 1.25$)

Body roll in curves

Roll axis

When cornering, the centrifugal force which concentrates around the center of gravity causes the vehicle to tilt away from the path of travel. The magnitude of this rolling motion depends upon the rates of the springs and their response to alternating compression, and upon the lever arm of the centrifugal force (distance between the roll axis and the center of gravity). The roll axis is the body's instantaneous axis of rotation relative to the road surface. Like all rigid bodies, the vehicle body consistently executes a screwing or rotating motion; this motion is supplemented by a lateral displacement along the instantaneous axis.

The higher the roll axis, i.e., the closer it is to a parallel axis through the center of gravity, the greater will be the transverse stability and the less the roll during cornering. However, this generally implies a corresponding upward displacement of the wheels, resulting in a change in track width (with negative effects on operating safety). For this reason, designs are sought which combine a high instantaneous roll center with minimal track change. The goal therefore is to place the instantaneous axes of the wheels as high as possible relative to the body, while simultaneously keeping them as far from the body as possible.

Determining the roll axis

A frequently-applied means for finding the approximate roll axis is based on determining the centers of rotation of an equivalent body motion. This body motion takes place in those two planes through the front and rear axles which are vertical relative to the road. The centers of rotation are those (hypothetical) points in the body which remain stationary during the rotation. The roll axis, in turn, is the line which connects these centers (instantaneous centers). Graphic portrayals of the instantaneous centers are based on a rule according to which the instantaneous centers of rotation of three systems in a state of relative motion lie on a common pole line.

The complexity of the operations required for a more precise definition of the spatial relationships involved in wheel motion makes it advisable to employ computers capable of carrying out calculations in matrix notation (vector algebra, linear geometry, etc.).

References:

E. v. d. Osten-Sacken: "Berechnung allgemein räumlicher, vielgliedriger Gelenkgetriebe". Dissertation, Aachen Technical College, 1970. G. Prigge: "Grundsätzliches der Ermittlung der Rollachse von Kraftfahrzeugen mit räumlichen Radführungen". Dissertation, Braunschweig Technical University, 1972.

ISO procedures for evaluating operating behavior

The science devoted to studying the dynamics of operating behavior generally defines its subject as the overall behavior of the entire system represented by "driver + vehicle + environment". As the first link in the chain, the driver makes judgements on operating behavior based on the sum of various subjective impressions. Meanwhile, data on operating behavior, based on specific driving maneuvers executed without driver input ("open-loop operation") provide an objective description of the vehicle's operating response. Being as the driver still cannot be precisely defined regarding his behavior, this type of testing replaces him with a specific, objectively quantifiable interference factor. The resulting vehicular response can then be analyzed and discussed.

Standardized versions of the driving maneuvers in the list (performed on a dry road surface) below have either already been defined by the ISO or are under consideration; they serve as recognized standard procedures for vehicular evaluation [1], [2]:

- Steady-state skidpad [3],
- Transient response [4], [5], [6],
- Braking during cornering [7],

"Driver-vehicle-environment" synergism represented as a closed-loop control system

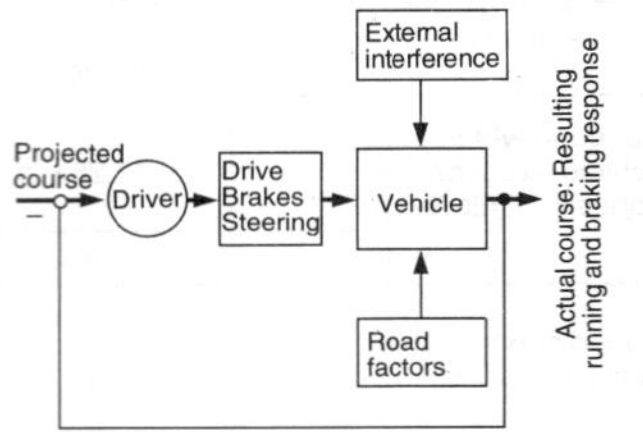

- Crosswind sensitivity,
- Straight-running stability, and
- Reaction to throttle change on skidpad.

To date, it has still not been possible to arrive at comprehensive objective definitions for the dynamic characteristics associated with closed-loop operation, as adequate data on the precise control characteristics of the human element are still unavailable.

Test quantities

The main criteria employed in evaluating vehicle dynamics are:

- Steering-wheel angle,
- Lateral acceleration,

Criteria for evaluating operating dynamics

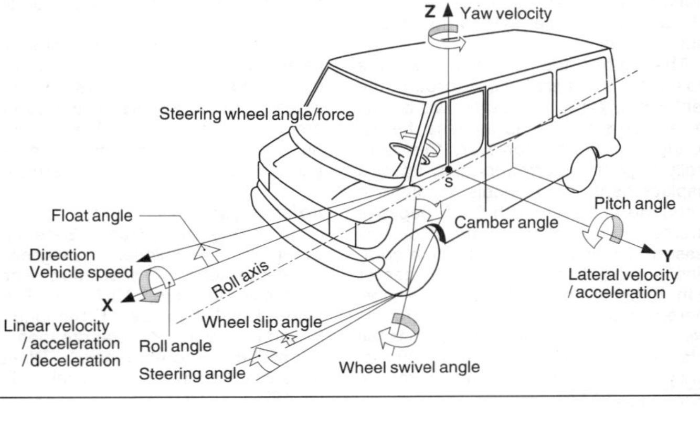

Definitions of attitude in steady-state cornering (according to Mitschke [10])
i_L Steering ratio, l Wheelbase, R (= const.) Cornering radius, i_L (l/R) Ackermann effect.

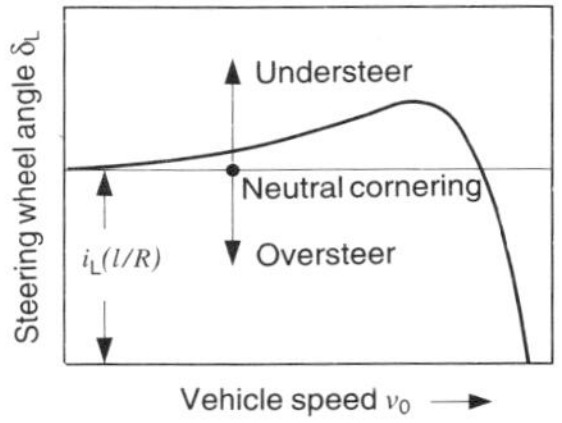

– Longitudinal acceleration and deceleration,
– Yaw speed,
– Float and roll angles.

Additional data are employed to verify and confirm the previously derived information on specific points of vehicle performance:
– Linear and lateral velocity,
– Steering angles at front and rear wheels,
– Slip angles at all wheels,
– Camber and pitch angles,
– Steering-wheel force.

Steady-state skidpad

The most important data to be derived from steady-state skidpad testing are the maximum lateral acceleration itself, and the manner in which individual dynamic parameters respond to the variations in lateral acceleration which occur up to the limit; this information is employed in evaluating the vehicle's self-steering response [2], [3]. Compliance in both the steering system and in the suspension is represented in the current standard definition of steering response, which employs the terms "oversteer, understeer and neutral steering." Several dynamic factors and their derivatives are considered in conjunction with lateral acceleration in describing vehicle response, examples being steering-wheel angle, roll angle and float angle. Other significant vehicle parameters are steering angle and slip angle.

In the following, a light utility van and a heavy truck are used to provide examples of the results gathered on a dry surface.

Steady-state skidpad *(42 m radius)*
a) Steering-wheel angle, b) Roll angle, c) Float angle, d) Rear-axle steering angle (roll steer), e) Front-wheel slip angle, f) Rear-wheel slip angle.

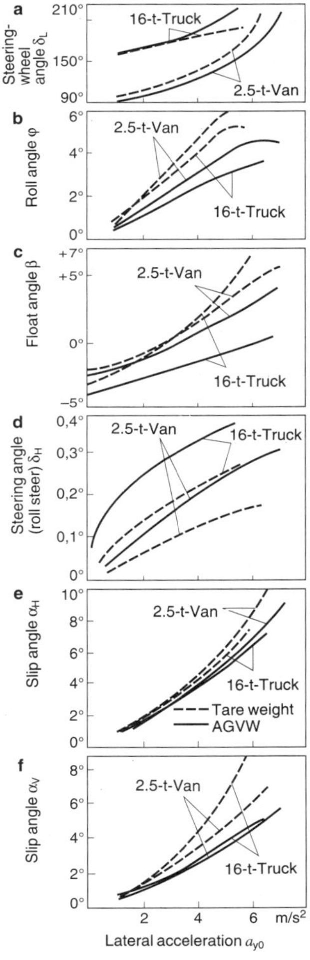

Steering-wheel angle
As small utility vehicles employ tires similar to those used in passenger cars, and are also equipped with relatively high-power engines, they achieve high rates of lateral acceleration. Both vehicle types understeer.

Roll angle
The degree of self-steering which prevails at the axles is largely determined by the roll angle. Higher loads result in more pronounced roll angles due to the greater vehicle mass and the attendant increase in effective centrifugal force.

Float angle
The float angle encountered at high rates of lateral acceleration is regarded as an index of the vehicle's response to driver input. High absolute figures or fluctuations in float angle are regarded as particularly undesirable [8].

At low rates of lateral acceleration, the float angle is determined with reference to the radius of the driven circle and the vehicle's center of gravity, which varies along with changes in vehicle load.

Rear-axle roll steer
The relationship between the steering angle at the rear axle (roll-steer angle) and lateral acceleration illustrates how the roll-steer angle at the rear axle decreases in response to higher vehicle loads.

Slip angle
The wheel slip angles at the individual wheels provide information on the vehicle's self-steering characteristics. The wheel slip angles increase in response to higher vehicle loads, a consequence of the tires requiring greater slip angles as their loading increases. [2], [9].

Transient response
In addition to self-steering in steady-state testing, yet another significant factor is the vehicle's response during directional changes (e.g., for rapid evasive maneuvers) [2]. Two test methods, have become accepted internationally. These are defined according to the type of input stimulus, and illustrate both the time and frequency ranges of the vehicle's response:
– Step-input (sharp change in steering angle),

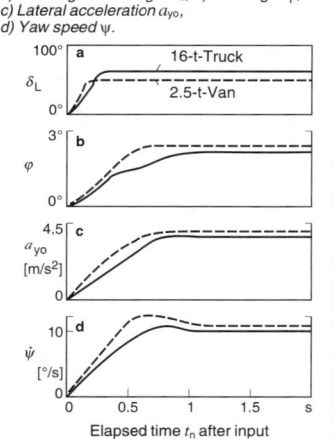

Sudden steering-angle change
(unloaded, v_0 = 20 m/s).
a) Steering-wheel angle δ_L, b) Roll angle φ,
c) Lateral acceleration a_{yo},
d) Yaw speed ψ.

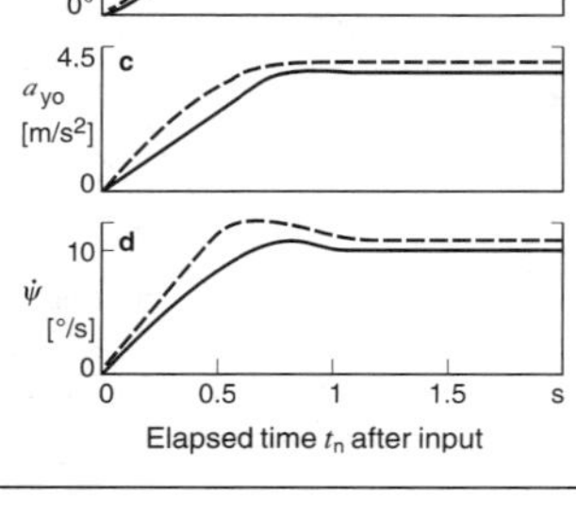

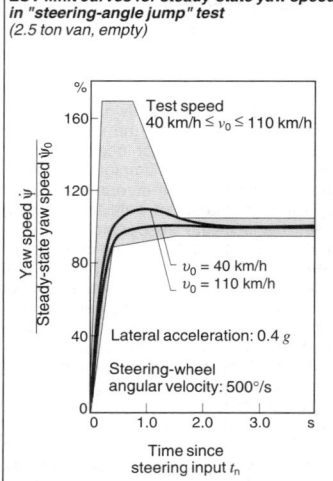

ESV limit curves for steady-state yaw speed in "steering-angle jump" test
(2.5 ton van, empty)

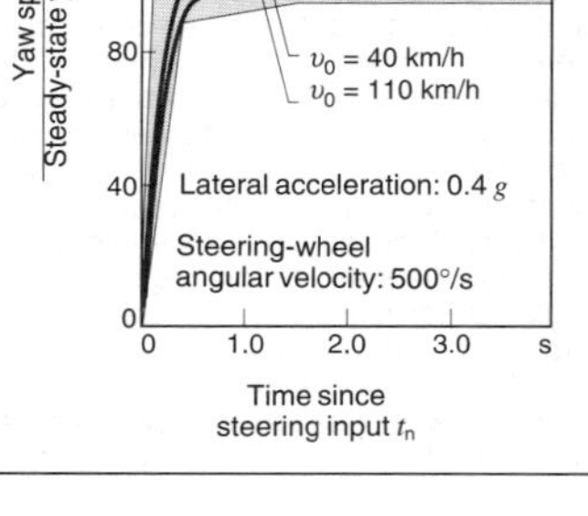

– Sinusoidal input (sinusoidal steering-angle input).

Step input (time response)
Starting with the vehicle traveling in a straight line, the steering wheel is abruptly "pulled" to a specified angle; the vehicle's response serves as the basis for evaluation. The most important quantities to be measured are [5]:
- Steering-wheel angle,
- Yaw speed,
- Vehicle speed, and
- Lateral acceleration.

The light utility van responds to the step input with a more rapid change in lateral acceleration - and thus in yaw - than the heavy truck.

US authorities have defined a steady-state yaw requirement for Experimental Safety Vehicles (ESV) [11]. Light utility vehicles may exhibit relatively pronounced overswing in the initial input phase (whereby this effect must cease after a certain period).

Sinusoidal steering-angle input
(frequency curve)
Permanent sinusoidal steering inputs at the steering wheel are also used to measure frequency-response characteristics. This provides yet another basis for evaluating a vehicle's transitional response, the intensity and phase of which varies according to the steering frequency. The most important factors for this evaluation are [6]:
- Steering-wheel angle,
- Lateral acceleration,
- Yaw speed, and
- Roll angle.

Braking in a curve
Of all the maneuvers encountered in everyday driving situations, one of the most critical – and thus one of the most important in vehicle design – is braking during cornering. The vehicle's concept must be optimized so that its reaction to this maneuver is characterized by the best possible compromise between steerability, stability and retardation [2], [7]. Testing starts from a specified initial rate of lateral acceleration, and focuses upon float angle and yaw speed relative to lateral deceleration as the significant factors.

Sinusoidal steering input
(16-ton truck, υ_0 = 60 km/h, L = 60°)
Relative to steering-wheel angle:
a) Lateral acceleration a_{y0}/δ_L,
b) Yaw speed $\dot\psi/\delta_L$ und
c) Roll angle φ/δ_L; with phase angle φ_S.

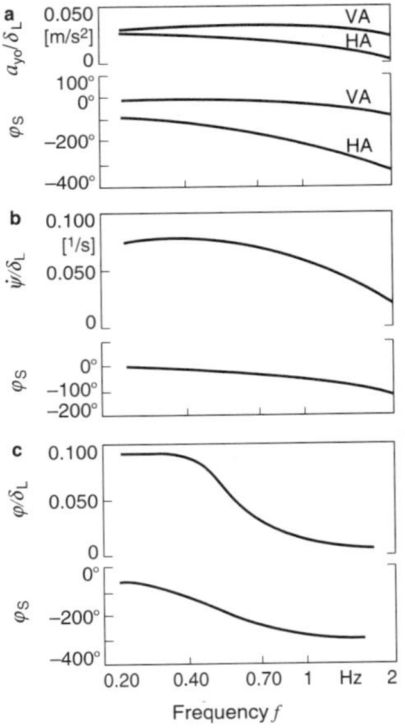

Time curve for braking in a corner
(7.5 ton truck, loaded)
1 Steady-state skidpad, 2 Initial braking,
3 Evaluation point. $\dot\psi$ Yaw speed, a_{y0} Lateral acceleration, β Float angle.

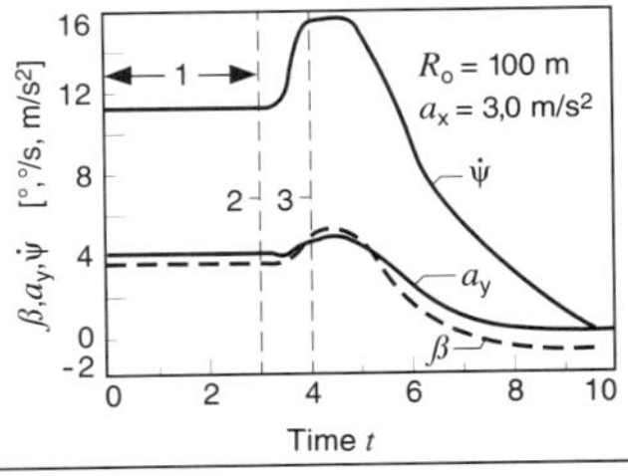

The vehicle, initially in steady-state circulation at a stipulated lateral acceleration, is braked with the rate of deceleration being increased incrementally. In every test, the time function "1 s after initial braking" is determined for vehicles with hydraulic brakes (a delay of 1.5...2 s after initial braking is applied for heavy-duty commercial vehicles with compressed-air brake systems).

Float angle
Due to the weight transfer away from the rear axle and the tires' response to this phenomenon, higher rates of retardation result in greater float angles. At high rates of deceleration, in the vicinity of the traction limit, the distribution of brake force is the decisive factor for the float angle. Meanwhile, the sequence in which the wheels lock exercises a decisive influence on the vehicle's stability.

Yaw speed
The yaw speed serves as a reference in determining whether braking performance is stable or instable. In the illustration, both vehicles' yaw-speed curves move toward zero as the vehicles progress through phases of increasing deceleration up to full lockup at both axles. This indicates acceptable braking response: The vehicle remains stable.

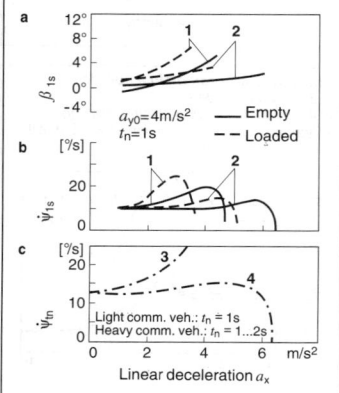

Typical yaw response to braking in a corner
a) Float angle β_{1s} *and b) Yaw speed* ψ_{1s} *1 s after initial braking* (t_n),
c) Yaw speed ψ *at moment* t_n.
1: 16-ton truck, 2: 2.5-ton van, 3: Vehicle starts to skid, 4: Vehicle remains stable.

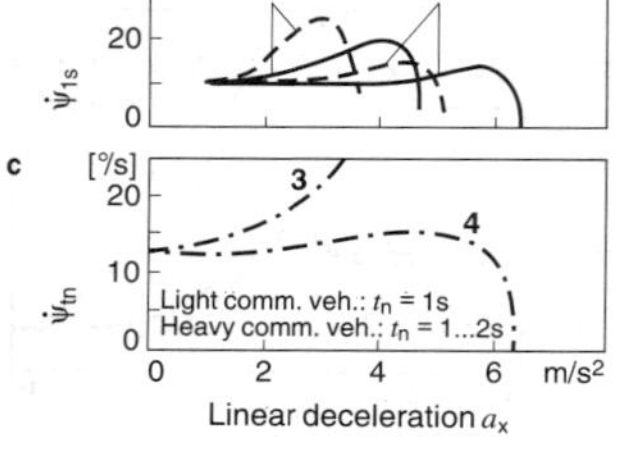

References:

[1] Rönitz R.; Braess H.H.; Zomotor A. Verfahren und Kriterien des Fahrverhaltens von Personenwagen. (Testing procedure and evalution of passenger-car driveability). AI 322, 1972, Volume 1.
[2] von Glasner E.C. Einbeziehung der Prüfstandsergebnissen in die Simulation des Fahrverhaltens von Nutzfahrzeugen. (Including test-stand results in the driveability simulation for heavy-duty commercial vehicles). Habilitation, University Stuttgart, 1987.
[3] ISO. Road Vehicles – Steady-State Circular Test Procedure. ISO, 1982, No. 4138.
[4] ISO. Road Vehicles – Double Lane Change. ISO, 1975, TR 3888.
[5] ISO. Draft Proposal for an International Standard, Road Vehicles – Transient Response Test Procedure (Step/Ramp Input). ISO/TC22/SC9/N 185.
[6] ISO. Draft Proposal for an International Standard, Road Vehicles – Transient Response Test Procedure (Sinusoidal Input). ISO/TC 22/SC9/N219.
[7] ISO. Road Vehicles – Braking in a Turn. Open-Loop Test Procedure. ISO/DIS 7975.
[8 Zomotor A.; Braess H.H.; Rönitz R. Doppelter Fahrspurwechsel eine Möglichkeit zur Beurteilung des Fahrverhaltens von Kfz? (Double Lane Change, a Method for Evaluating a Vehicle's Driveability?), ATZ 76, 1974, Volume 8.
[9] Mitschke M. Dynamik der Kraftfahrzeuge. (Dynamics of the Motor Vehicle), Springer Verlag, 1st Edition 1972, 2nd Edition 1982 and 1984, and subsequent Editions.
[10] Mitschke M. Fahrtrichtungshaltung - Analyse der Theorien. (Maintaining Direction of Travel – Analysis of the Theories). ATZ 70, 1968, Volume 5.
[11] Mischke A.; Göhring E.; Wolsdorf P.; von Glasner E.C. Contribution to the Development of a Concept of Driving Mechanics for Commercial Vehicles. SAE 83 0643.

Special operating dynamics for commercial vehicles

Symbols and units

G_V	N	Front-axle load
G_H	N	Rear-axle load
G_G	N	Total weight
G_F	N	Sprung weight
U_V	N	Unsprung weight, front
U_H	N	Unsprung weight, rear
C_{DSt}	N·m/wheel	Torsional spring rate for all stabilizers
$C_{FV,H}$	N/m	Spring rates for axle springs
$C_{RV,H}$	N/m	Spring rates for tires
$S_{FV,H}$	m	Spring track
$S_{RV,H}$	m	Tire track
$m_{V,H}$	m	Instantaneous center height
h_F	m	Height of center of gravity, sprung weight
h_G	m	Height of center of gravity, total vehicle
$C_{QV,H}$	N/m	Lateral stiffness rate of tires
r	m	Radius of curve

Self-steering properties

In the development phase in which the parameters affecting a vehicle's self-steering properties are determined, empirical and test-stand measurements and computer simulations are employed in a single process of incremental optimization. The major determinants are the geometry and compliance rates of the steering, the frame and the suspension.

The objects of analysis are those interference factors influencing straight-running stability and cornering behavior which can be traced to the interaction between steering and suspension, and which do not stem from driver inputs. The self-steering effect is examined at both the front and rear axles, in steady-state cornering, during braking and under unilateral spring compression.

When the springs are compressed on one side, a solid axle supported on leaf springs will tend to rotate about the vehicle's vertical axis. The degree of spring tilt exercises a major effect on this type of roll-steer effect. Neutral behavior or mild understeer, desirable from the safety point of view, are enhanced by tilting the front spring upward at the front and downward toward the rear, while the rear spring is mounted in the opposite manner, with the lowest end at the forward extremity.

Self-steering angle of a 16-ton truck cornering at 3 m/s² lateral acceleration

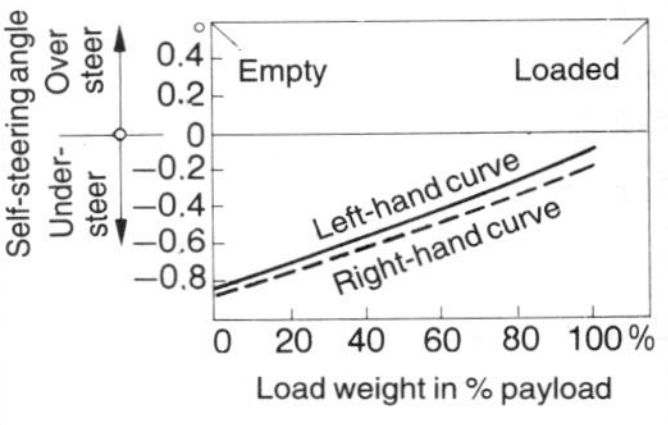

Finite element model of a 2-axle truck employed to determine self-steering property

Includes kinematic patterns of steering and suspension as well as torsional stiffness of frame.

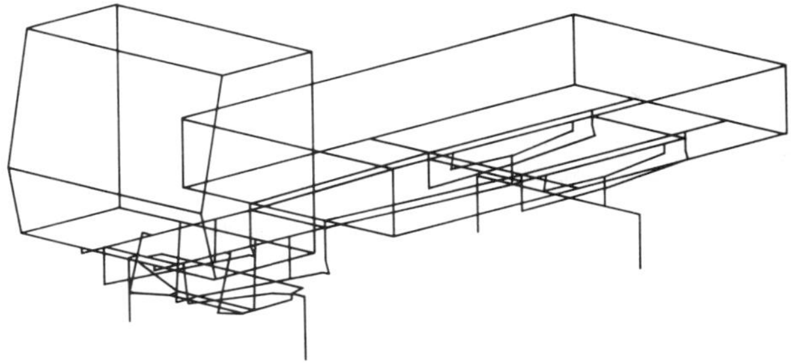

The wheel loads at the truck's rear axle vary dramatically, depending upon whether it is empty or loaded; for this reason the vehicle responds to reductions in load with more pronounced understeer.

On three-axle 6 x 4 vehicles, the non-steered tandem axle unit represents a constraining force around the vehicle's vertical axis, thus enhancing straight-line stability. The additional cornering force required at the front and rear axles during operation at low speeds is determined as follows:

Cornering forces resulting from constraint

$F_{S1} = F_{S2} - F_{S3}$ with

$F_{S2} = c_{p2} \cdot n_2 \cdot \alpha_2$

$F_{S3} = c_{p3} \cdot n_3 \cdot \alpha_3$

Slip angle

$$\alpha_2 = \frac{1}{r} \cdot \frac{c_{p3} \cdot n_3 \cdot b \cdot (a+b)}{c_{p3} \cdot n_3 \cdot (a+b) + c_{p2} \cdot n_2 \cdot a}$$

$\alpha_3 = (b/r) - \alpha_2$

c_p Coefficient of cornering stability from tire performance curve

n Number of tires per axle, other designations as in illustration

Tipping resistance

As the total height of the vehicle increases, so does its tendency to tip over to the side before starting to slide in a curve. Simulations of the tipping process for precise determination of the tip limit take into account both the elasticities and displacements of the center of gravity.

Cornering forces F_s and slip angle α on a 3-axle vehicle with non-steered tandem axle

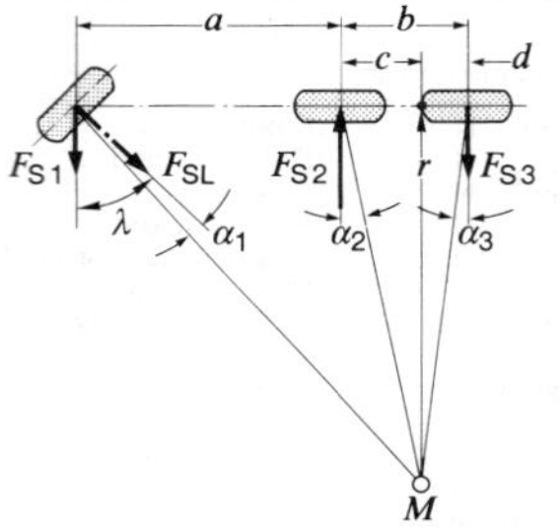

Achievable rates of lateral acceleration at the tip limit:

Van	$b = 6\ m/s^2$
Truck	$b = 5\ m/s^2$
Doubledecker bus	$b = 3\ m/s^2$

Width requirement

The width requirement of motor vehicles and truck-trailer combinations is greater during cornering than when the vehicle moves in a straight line; the precise increase depends upon the type of steering and the type of trailer connection. With respect to selected driving maneuvers, it is necessary to determine the radius described by the vehicle's outer extremities during cornering, both in order to ascertain its suitability for certain applications (e.g.,

Tipping resistance

Approximation formula for critical velocities υ_{tip} on a 2-axle truck (in km/h).

$$\upsilon_{tip} = 7.98 \cdot \sqrt{\frac{r \cdot (G_V \cdot S_{RV} + G_H \cdot S_{RH})}{G_G \cdot h_G + \frac{G_V^2}{C_{QV}} + \frac{G_H^2}{C_{QH}} + \frac{G_F^2 \cdot h_m^2}{C_D - G_F \cdot h_m}}}$$

with $C_D = \frac{C_{DF} \cdot C_{DR} \cdot i^2}{C_{DF} + C_{DR} \cdot i^2}$; $i = \frac{h_m}{h_m + m}$;

$$h_m = h_F - m; \quad m = \frac{(G_V - U_V) \cdot m_V + (G_H - U_H)\, m_H}{G_F}$$

$$C_{DF} = 1/2 \cdot (C_{FV} \cdot S_{FV}^2 + C_{FH} \cdot S_{FH}^2) + C_{DSt}$$

$$C_{DR} = 1/2 \cdot (C_{RV} \cdot S_{RV}^2 + C_{RH} \cdot S_{RH}^2)$$

narrow transit routes through constricted areas) and to confirm compliance with legal regulations.

Evaluation is conducted with reference to the tractrix principle using electronic programs.

Operating behavior

Objective analyses of operating behavior are based on various maneuvers such as steady-state circulation on the skidpad, steering impulse, wag frequency response, and braking in a curve.

The dynamic lateral response of truck-trailer combinations generally differs from that of rigid vehicles. Particularly significant are the distribution of loads between truck and trailer, and the design and geometry of the mechanical coupling device within a given combination.

Rotary oscillation, with the vehicle's masses turning against the tires (as compliance element) around a vertical axis, impairs straight-running stability. This phenomenon is induced by

– rapid steering corrections associated with evasive maneuvers,
– crosswinds, and
– pronounced slope to the side of the road, obstacles on one side, lane grooves.

Oscillation amplitudes associated with this pendulum motion must subside rapidly if vehicle stability is to be maintained.

Below is a graphic depiction of the yaw-speed progressions for various vehicle-combination types. The worst case is represented by a combination, in which the towing vehicle is empty, while the center axle trailer is loaded; the curve indicates an excessive increase in resonance ratio. This type of combination demands a high degree of driver skill and circumspection.

Tractor-semitrailer combination in the circular area as stipulated by the German Road Traffic Regulations (StVZO)

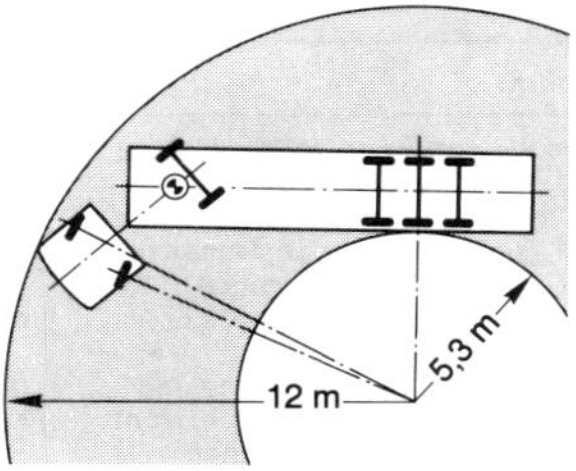

On tractor-semitrailer combinations, braking maneuvers undertaken under extreme conditions can induce jackknifing.

This process is initiated when, on a slippery road surface, loss of lateral-force is induced by excess braking force being applied at the tractor's rear axle, or due to excess yaw moment under μ-split conditions. Installation of an antilock braking system (ABS) represents the most effective means of preventing jackknifing.

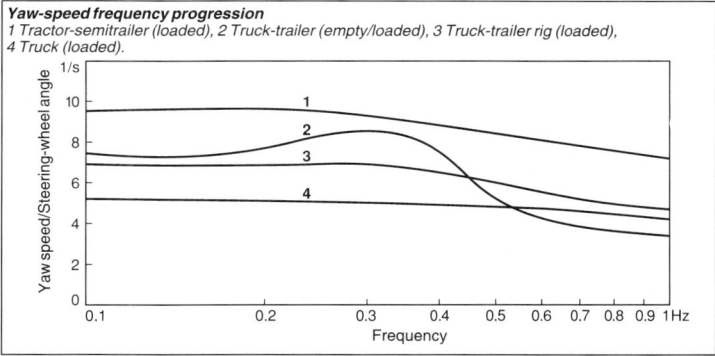

Yaw-speed frequency progression

1 Tractor-semitrailer (loaded), 2 Truck-trailer (empty/loaded), 3 Truck-trailer rig (loaded), 4 Truck (loaded).

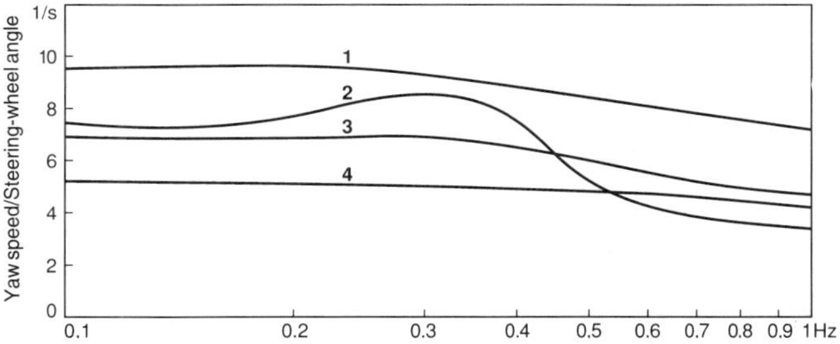

Requirements for agricultural tractors

Symbols and units

Symbol		Unit
F	Weight (wheel load) of wheel	N
F_R	Rolling resistance	N
F_{Rh}	Rolling resistance, rear axle	N
F_{Rv}	Rolling resistance, front axle	N
F_{St}	Hill-climbing resistance	N
F_T	Traction (motive) force of a wheel	N
F_{Th}	Traction (motive) force, rear	N
F_{Tv}	Traction (motive) force, front	N
F_w	Soil (ground) resistance	N
F_Z	Drawbar pull of tractor	N
F_{Zerf}	Draft requirement of implement	N
P_e	Net engine power	kW
P_{Getr}	Transmission power losses	kW
P_N	Rated engine power	kW
P_R	Auto-motive power requirement	kW
P_S	Slip power losses	kW
P_{St}	Hill-climbing power requirement	kW
P_Z	Drawbar power	kW
v	Vehicle speed	km/h
v_o	Wheel circumferential velocity	km/h
$\eta_{Getr.}$	Gear transmission efficiency	–
η_L	Tractive efficiency at tractor wheels	–
η_T	Tractive efficiency of a single wheel	–
η_Z	Tractive efficiency of a tractor including transmission	–
λ	Engine utilization ratio	–
$\varkappa$	Coefficient of traction force	–
ϱ	Coefficient of rolling resistance	–
σ	Wheel slip	%

Applications

Agricultural tractors are employed for field and for general transport duties. Depending upon the type of unit, power from the engine can be transmitted through an auxiliary PTO shaft or hydraulic lines, as well as via the drive wheels. The engine outputs for farm tractors manufactured and used in Germany range up to approximately 250 kW, with weights of over 120 kN.

Higher engine outputs exaggerate the problems associated with supporting the weight at the ground on large-volume tires of adequate capacity, as well as the difficulties encountered in transforming the engine's power into tractive power at appropriate tractor speeds.

Essential requirements of a tractor

– High drawbar pull, high tractive efficiency.

– Engine must combine high torque increase and low specific fuel consumption.

– Depending upon application and towing distances, vehicle speeds (rated speed) up to 25, 32, 40, 50 km/h, with >60 km/h for special-purpose tractors; multiple conversion ratios with appropriate gear spacing (especially important up to 12 km/h), suitable for shifting under load if possible.

– Power take-off (PTO) shaft and hydraulic connections for powering auxiliary equipment. Option of installing and/or powering equipment at the front of the tractor.

– Facilities for monitoring and operating auxiliary equipment from the driver's seat, e.g., with hydraulic control levers (p. 734).

– Clear and logical layout of control levers in ergonomically correct arrangement.

– Provision for adjusting track to suit crop-row spacing on field tractors.

– Driver protection against vibration, dust, noise, climatic influences and accident.

– Universal applicability.

Drawbar pull and drawbar power of a tractor in field work

The effective drawbar pull is essentially determined by the tractor's weight, the number of driven wheels (rear-wheel or 4-wheel drive) and the operating characteristics of its tires. The operation response of the tractor's drive tires is determined by such factors as ground conditions (moisture and porosity), tire dimensions, carcass and tread design, and tire pressure. Due to these particular operating characteristics, the farm tractor in field work develops its maximum drawbar pull only when tire slip is high, whereas the maximum drawbar power is achieved at relatively low levels of slip and drawbar pull. With the engine developing 90 % of its maximum output, the drawbar pull will not exceed 60 % of the rated engine power, even under extremely favorable conditions.

The effective engine output is:

$$P_e = P_Z + P_R + P_S + P_{Getr.}$$
$$(+P_{St} \text{ on uphill grades})$$

The drawbar power is calculated as:

$$P_Z = F_Z \cdot v$$

With rear-wheel drive, the power required to propel the tractor itself is:

$$P_R = F_{Rv} \cdot v + F_{Rh} \cdot v_o$$

The slip power losses are defined as:

$$P_S = F_T \cdot (v_o - v) = F_T \cdot \sigma \cdot v_o$$

The power losses in the transmission unit are determined with the equation:

$$P_{Getr.} = P_e \cdot (1 - \eta_{Getr.})$$

Efficiency levels:
For single wheel:

$$\eta_T = \frac{F_T}{F_T + F_R} \cdot (1 - \sigma) = \frac{\varkappa}{\varkappa + \varrho}\,(1 - \sigma)$$

For the tractor:
With rear-wheel drive:

$$\eta_L = \frac{F_{Th} - F_{Rv}}{F_{Th} + F_{Rh}} \cdot (1 - \sigma)$$

With all-wheel drive:

$$\eta_L = \frac{F_{Th} + F_{Tv}}{F_{Th} + F_{Tv} + F_{Rh} + F_{Rv}} \cdot (1 - \sigma)$$

Including transmission power losses:

$$\eta_Z = \eta_{Getr.} \cdot \eta_L = P_Z / P_e$$

The coefficients are calculated as follows:

$$\varkappa = F_T / F$$
$$\varrho = F_R / F$$
$$\lambda = P_e / P_N$$
$$\sigma = (v_o - v) / v_o$$

Draft requirements for auxiliary equipment and trailers

At a constant speed on a flat surface, the draft requirement depends either on the rolling resistance F_R (e.g., field trailers) or on soil resistance (e.g., the force needed to move a tool through the soil) or on both at the same time (e.g., beet lifter). Rolling resistance is calculated using the coefficient of rolling resistance and the sum of the weights supported at the wheels, giving:

$$F_R = \varrho \cdot \Sigma F$$

For pneumatic tires on asphalt: $\varrho \leq 0.03$
For pneumatic tires on field:

$$\varrho = 0.04 \ldots 0.35.$$

Soil resistance is determined by the type and condition of the soil, number and type of implements, working depth and vehicle speed. General reference figures for plowing would be a specific ground resistance of 400 ... 600 N/dm^2 on moderate soils, with 600 ... 1000 N/dm^2 on hard (clay) soils. On moderate ground at speeds of between 6 and 9 km/h, the soil resistance per meter of working width of a cultivator is 5500 ... 7800 N for a working depth of 13 ... 15 cm, and 11 000 ... 12 500 N for a depth of 22 ... 25 cm.

Operating characteristics of a tractor drive wheel
Tire: 16.9/14—30 AS; Wheel load: 1582 daN; Tire pressure: 1.1 bar; Ground: loamy clay, wheat stubble; treated with disk harrow, moisture: 17.3 ... 20.8 %.

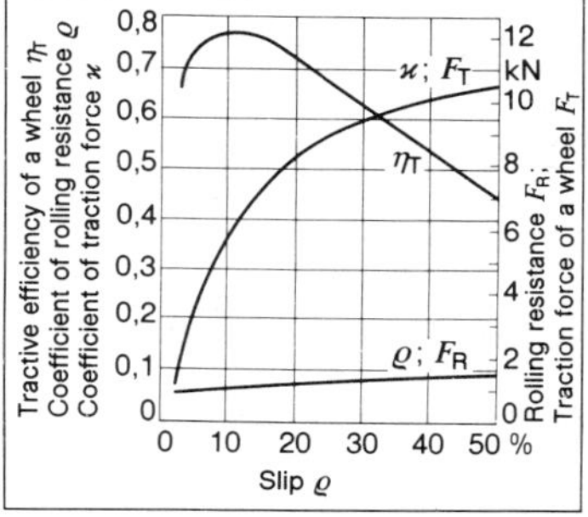

Examples of the power required by PTO-driven agricultural equipment working a 1 meter swath on moderate ground.

Implement	Required engine power kW	Working depth cm	Vehicle speed km/h
Tiller on loose soil	10.5 ... 25	8	3 ... 7
Vibrating harrow	8 ... 22	8	3.5 ... 6.5
Circular harrow	0 ... 15	8	3.5 ... 6.5

Environmental stresses on automotive equipment

Climatic factors

Climatic stress factors acting upon automotive components encompass the effects of the natural environment, i.e., the macroclimate, and influences stemming from the vehicle itself (such as fuel vapor) and the microclimate within a component (such as the heat generated in electrical devices). The following describes the individual environmental factors.

Temperature and temperature variations
The range extends from extremely low temperatures (storage, transport) all the way to the high temperatures associated with operation of the internal-combustion engine.

Atmospheric humidity and variations
This range embraces everything from arid desert climates to tropical environments, and can even extend beyond these under certain conditions (as occur for instance when water is sprayed against a hot engine block). Humid heat (high temperatures combined with high atmospheric humidity) is especially demanding. Alternating humidity results in surface condensation, which causes atmospheric corrosion.

Corrosive atmospheres
Salt spray encountered when the vehicle is operated on salt-treated roads and in coastal areas promotes electrochemical and atmospheric corrosion.
Industrial atmospheres in concentrated manufacturing regions lead to acid corrosion on metallic surfaces.

When they are present in sufficient concentrations, today's increasing amounts of atmospheric pollutants (SO_2, H_2S, Cl_2 and NO_x) promote the formation of contaminant layers on contact surfaces.

Water
Stresses of varying intensities result from rain, spray, splash, and hose water as encountered when driving in rain, during car and engine washes, and – in exceptional cases – during submersion.

Chemical fluids
The product in question must be able to resist the chemical fluids encountered in the course of normal operation and maintenance at its particular operating location. Within the engine compartment, such chemicals include fuel (and fuel vapor), engine oil and engine detergents. Certain components are confronted by additional substances, for example, brake-system components and the brake fluid used to operate them.

Sand and dust
Malfunctions result from the friction due to sand and dust on adjacent moving surfaces. In addition, under the influence of moisture, certain types of dust layers can cause current tracking in electrical circuits.

Solar radiation
The sun's rays cause aging in plastics and elastomers, and must therefore also be considered in the design of external, exposed components.

Atmospheric pressure
Fluctuations in atmospheric pressure affect the operation and reliability of differential-pressure components, such as diaphragms, etc.

Simulating stress in the laboratory

Climatic and environmental conditions are simulated both according to standardized test procedures (DIN IEC 68 – Environmental testing procedures for electronic components and equipment) and in special field-testing programs designed specifically for individual cases. The goal is to achieve the greatest possible approximation of the stresses encountered in actual practice ("test tailoring").

Simulating temperature, temperature variation and atmospheric humidity
Simulation is carried out in temperature and climate chambers as well as in climate-controlled rooms which afford access to test personnel.

The dry heat test allows evaluation of a component's suitability for storage and operation at high temperatures. Testing is not restricted to ascertaining the effects of heat upon operation; it also monitors influences on materials characteristics. Depending upon the particular application (component to be mounted on body, engine, or exhaust system), the degree of heat can embrace an extremely wide range. The stress time can be up to several hundred hours.

Testing the product's operation under cold conditions devotes particular attention to starting behavior and changes in materials characteristics at low temperatures. The testing range extends down to – 40 °C for operation, and to – 55 °C for storage. At below 100 hours, the actual testing times are shorter than those employed for dry heat.

A further test simulates the temperature fluctuation between the values to be encountered in actual operation; the temperature gradient and the dwell time also contribute to determining the degree of stress. The dwell time must be at least long enough to ensure that the sample achieves thermal equilibrium. The different levels of thermal expansion mean that the temperature variations induce both material aging and mechnical stresses within the component. The selection of appropriate test parameters makes it possible to achieve substantial time-compression factors.

Atmospheric humidity testing under steady-state damp heat (e.g., +40 °C / 93 % humidity) is employed in the evaluation of a product's suitability for operation and storage at relatively high humidity levels (tropical climates).

Simulation of corrosive atmospheres

Salt fog is produced by diffusing a 5% NaCl solution at a room temperature of 35 °C. Depending upon the intended installation location, the test times can extend to several hundred hours.

The industrial-climate test comprises up to 6 cyclical alternations between an 8-hour dwell period at 40 °C / 100 % relative humidity at 0.67 % SO_2 and 16 hours at room temperature.

The pollutant test with SO_2, H_2S, NOx and CL_2 is performed either for single gases or as a multi-substance test. Testing is carried out at 25 °C / 75 % relative humidity with concentrations in the ppm and ppb ranges, and lasts up to 21 days.

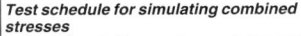

Test schedule for simulating combined stresses

t_v Dwell time, t_n Temperature-variation cycle, T Test cycle.

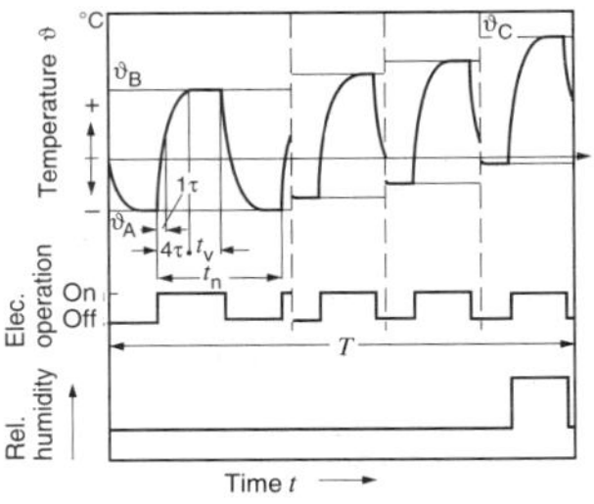

Simulation of stresses from water

A pivoting sprayer is used to simulate water spray. Water pressure, spray angle and the pivot angle can all be adjusted for different stress levels. The water-spray test employs high-pressure jets and standard steam-cleaners of the type used for cleaning engines.

Chemical fluids

For this simulation, the sample is sprayed with the respective fluid for a defined period. This is followed by 24-hour storage at elevated temperature. This test can be repeated numerous times, according to the particular application.

Simulation of stress caused by dust and sand

Dust simulation is carried out with the assistance of a device which maintains a dust density of 5 g per m^3 in moving air. A mixture of lime and fly ash is one of the substances employed.

Combined tests

Combined temperature, temperature variation and humidity test on an operating electrical product ensures a high degree of convergence with the aging effects to be anticipated under extreme operating conditions. The advantage of this test is its high level of conformity with actual practice. The disadvantage is the test duration, which is generally well in excess of that required for the corresponding individual investigations.

Internal-combustion engines

Principle of operation and classification

The internal-combustion (IC) engine is the most frequent type of drive used in motor vehicles. Internal-combustion engines generate power by converting chemical energy bound in the fuel into heat, and the heat thus produced into mechanical work.

The conversion of chemical energy into heat is accomplished by combustion, and the conversion of heat energy into mechanical work is performed by allowing the heat energy to act on a medium causing its pressure to increase, performing work as the medium expands.

Liquids which can absorb an increase in working pressure via a change of phase (vaporization), or gases whose working pressure can be increased through compression, are used as working media.

Fuels, most of which consist of hydrocarbons, require oxygen in order to burn; the required oxygen is usually supplied as a constituent of the intake air.

If fuel combustion occurs in the cylinder itself, this process is called internal combustion. In this case, the combustion gas itself is used as the working medium.

If combustion takes place outside the cylinder, the process is called external combustion.

Continous mechanical work is possible only in a cyclic process (piston engine) or a continous process (gas turbine) of heat absorption, expansion (production of work) and return of the working medium to its initial condition (combustion cycle).

If the working medium is altered as it absorbs heat, e.g., by conversion of a portion of its constituents as an oxidant, it can be returned to its initial condition only through replacement.

This cycle is called an open cycle, and is characterized by cyclic gas exchange (removal of the combustion gases and supply of the fresh charge). Internal combustion therefore always requires an open cycle.

Table 1. Classification of the internal-combustion engine

Type of process	**Open process**				**Closed process**	
	Internal combustion				External combustion	
	Combustion gas ≙ working medium				Combustion gas ≠ working medium	
					Phase change in working medium No	Yes
Type of combustion	Cyclic combustion			Continous combustion		
Type of ignition	Autoign.	External ignition				
Type of machine: Engine ≙ machine enclosing a working chamber	Diesel	Hybrid	Otto-cycle	Rohs	Stirling	Steam
Type of machine: Turbine ≙ gas turbine	–	–	–	Gas	Hot steam	Steam
Type of mixture	Heterogenous (in the combustion chamber)		Homogenous (in the combustion chamber)	Heterogenous (in a continuous flame)		

In the case of external combustion, the actual working medium remains chemically unchanged, and can therefore be returned to its initial condition by suitable measures (cooling, condensation). This enables the use of a closed process.

In addition to the main process characteristics (open/closed) and the type of combustion (cyclic/continuous), the various combustion processes of internal-combustion engines can also be differentiated according to the mixture formation and ignition.

In external mixture formation, the mixture is formed outside the combustion chamber. Because in this type of mixture formation a largely homogenous air-fuel mixture is present at the time combustion is initiated, it is also referred to as homogenous mixture formation.

In internal mixture formation the fuel is introduced directly into the combustion chamber. The later internal combustion occurs, the more heterogenous the air-fuel mixture is at the time combustion is initiated. Internal mixture formation is therefore also called heterogeneous mixture formation. External ignition involves the initiation of combustion by an electric spark or by a glow plug.

In autoignition, the mixture is ignited when the ignition temperature is achieved or exceeded during the compression of the mixture.

Cycles

The p-V-diagram

The heat energy can only be continuously converted into mechanical energy if the condition of the working medium changes; it is also desirable that as much of the working medium as possible be returned to its initial condition.

For technical work we need only be concerned with changes in pressure and the corresponding changes in volume which can be plotted on a pressure vs. volume work diagram, or p-V-diagram for short.

As the figure shows, the addition of heat and the change in condition of the working medium must occur such that as the process progresses from 1→2, the work performed is greater than the work performed in the opposite direction from 2→1, consequently leading to an area which corresponds to the amount of work which can be obtained

$L = \oint V \mathrm{d}p.$

The T-S-diagram

In order to illustrate in a similar manner the heat energies to be added and dissipated, the temperature entropy diagram, or T-S-diagram, is used.

A thermodynamic cycle illustrated using the p-V-diagram

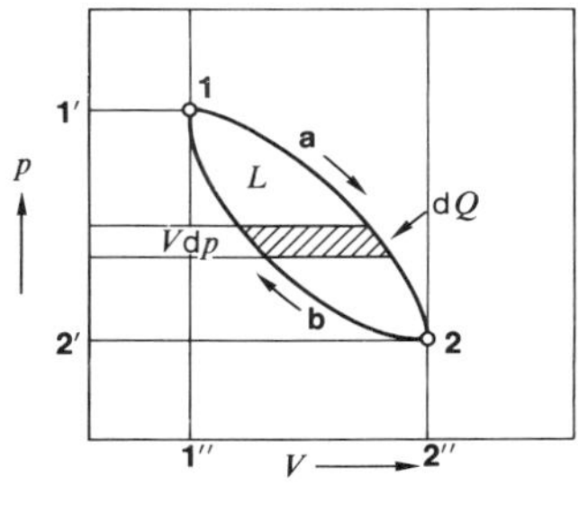

A thermodynamic cycle illustrated using the T-S- or H-S-diagram

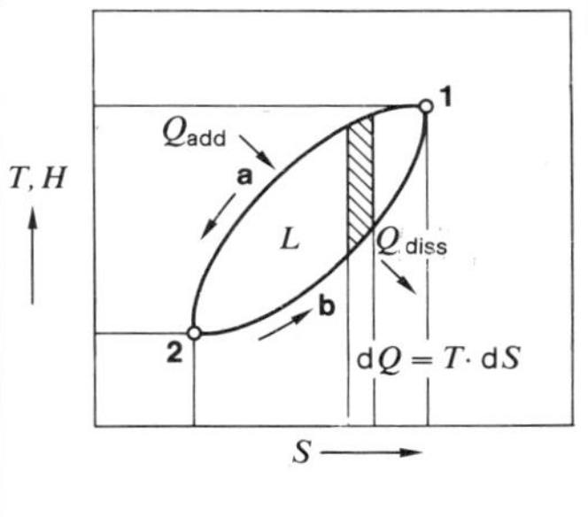

In the T-S-diagram heat quantities can be represented as areas in the same manner as work is represented as an area in the p-V-diagram. With known specific working-medium heats, the T-S-diagram can be transformed into the H-S-diagram known as the enthalpy-entropy diagram in accordance with the equation $dH = c_p \cdot dT$.

The cycle illustrated in the p-V-diagram on page 353 shows the amount of heat added along "a"

$$Q_{add} = \int_2^1 T_a \, dS$$

and the amount of heat dissipated along "b"

$$Q_{diss} = \int_2^1 T_b \, dS, \text{ where}$$

$$Q_{add} - Q_{diss} = L = \oint V dp$$

(Difference between the amount of heat added and the amount of heat dissipated) which corresponds to the obtainable amount of mechanical work. The diagram also shows that a thermal efficiency $\eta_{th} = (Q_{add} - Q_{diss})/Q_{add}$ can be defined based on the equality of mechanical work and the difference between the heat quantities, and that a cycle must theoretically exist between two given temperatures for the working medium which makes possible a maximum amount of technical work.

The Carnot cycle

This cycle, described in 1824 by Carnot, consists of two isothermal[1]) and two isentropic[2]) changes in condition which yield the maximum area between T_{max} and T_{min} in the T-S-diagram. The efficiency of the Carnot cycle is not achieved by any other cycle performing between the same two temperature limits, and would thus be the best possible way to convert heat into work:

$$\eta_{th\ Carnot} = (T_{max} - T_{min})/T_{max}$$

Internal-combustion engines operate according to other cycles, however, because isothermal compression, i.e., a pressure increase in the working medium without an increase in temperature, as well as isothermal expansion are not technically feasible.

Theoretical treatment today involves the following ideal combustion cycles: the constant-volume cycle for all piston engines with periodic combustion and generation of work, and the constant-pressure cycle for all turbine engines with continuous combustion and generation of work.

Both cycles will be dealt with in more detail in the discussion of the corresponding machines.

[1]) Isothermal change in condition: temperature does not change.
[2]) Isentropic change in condition: adiabatic (heat is neither added nor dissipated) and frictionless (reversible).
[3]) Isochoric change in condition: volume does not change; see p. 355.

The Carnot cycle in the p-V- and T-S-diagrams

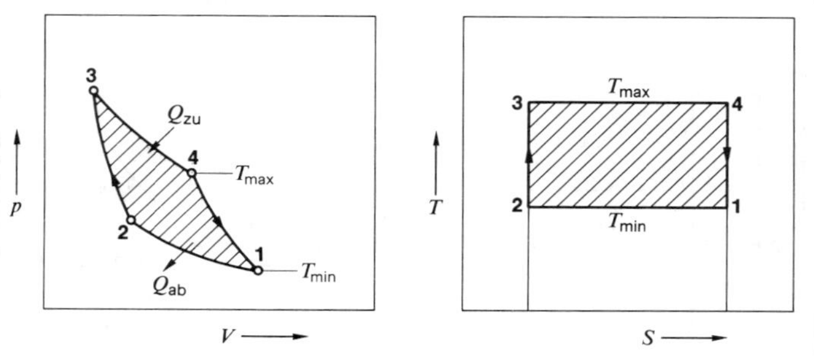

Reciprocating-piston engines with internal combustion

Operation

In all reciprocating-piston engines air or an air-fuel mixture is compressed in the working cylinder, the mixture is ignited or fuel is injected into the hot compressed air, and combustion of the fuel is initiated. The useful work so generated is converted by means of a crank mechanism into torque which is available at the end of the crankshaft.

The p-V-diagram generated along the piston path describes the actual process by which work is generated in the engine, and yields the mean effective pressure p_{mi} in the cylinder during a complete working cycle. Nowadays, in addition to the p-V-diagram, the more easily generated pressure vs. time (p–t-) diagram is used, or the pressure vs. crank angle (p–α-) diagram which is referred to the position of the crankshaft. The surfaces of these two diagrams, although they do not directly indicate the amount of work generated, nevertheless indicate important data such as firing point or peak pressure during combustion. The product of the mean effective pressure in the cylinder and the piston displacement yields the piston work, and the number of working cycles per unit time indicates the piston power or the internal ("indicated") power of an engine. The power generated by a reciprocating-piston internal-combustion engine thus increases with engine speed.

Ideal combustion cycle for piston engines with internal combustion

For reciprocating-piston engines with internal combustion, the thermodynamic ideal combustion process is the so-called "constant-volume process" consisting of isentropic compression, isochoric[3]) addition of heat as well as isentropic expansion and isochoric return of the ideal working gas to its initial condition at the beginning of the cycle. The cycle is only possible if the following conditions are met:

– no heat or gas losses, no residual gas;

– ideal gas with constant specific heats c_p, c_v and
  $\varkappa = c_p/c_v = 1.4$;

– infinitely rapid heat addition and dissipation;

– no flow losses.

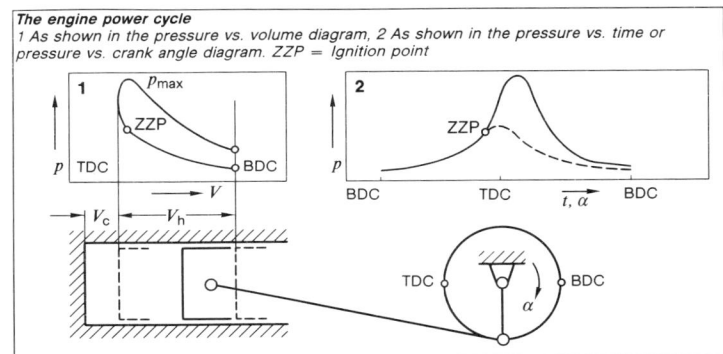

The engine power cycle

1 As shown in the pressure vs. volume diagram, 2 As shown in the pressure vs. time or pressure vs. crank angle diagram. ZZP = Ignition point

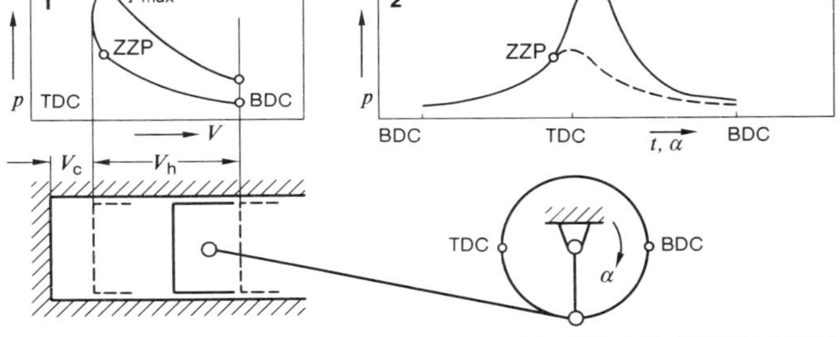

The area 4 – 5 – 1 in the diagrams below is not directly usable due to the finite expansion caused by the crank mechanism. If an exhaust gas turbine is connected downstream, section 4 – 5′ – 1 which lies above the atmospheric pressure line can be utilized.

The efficiency of the constant-volume ideal combustion cycle is calculated in the same manner as all thermal efficiencies:

$$\eta_{th} = \eta_v = (Q_{add} - Q_{diss})/Q_{add}$$

where $Q_{add} = Q_{23} = m \cdot c_v \cdot (T_3 - T_2)$ and

$$Q_{diss} = Q_{41} = m \cdot c_v \cdot (T_4 - T_1)$$

Using the same $\varkappa$ for compression and expansion:

$$\eta_{th} = 1 - Q_{diss}/Q_{add} =$$

$$1 - \frac{T_4 - T_1}{T_3 - T_2} = 1 - T_1/T_2$$

if $T_2/T_1 = \varepsilon^{\varkappa - 1}$, then $\eta_{th} = 1 - \varepsilon^{1-\varkappa}$

where the compression ratio is defined as $\varepsilon = (V_c + V_h)/V_c$ with a displacement of V_h and a compression volume of V_c.

Internal-combustion engines do not operate according to ideal cycles, however, but rather with real gas, and are therefore characterised by flow losses, thermodynamic losses and mechanical losses.

Efficiency chain (DIN 1940)

The overall efficiency η_e takes into account the sum of all losses, and can thus be defined as the ratio of the effective mechanical work to the mechanical work equivalent of the supplied fuel:

$\eta_e = W_e/W_B$ where

W_e is the effective available work at the clutch, and

W_B is the work equivalent of the supplied fuel.

In order to better distinguish among the different losses, a further differentiation can be made:

the fuel conversion factor η_B indicates the quality of combustion:

$\eta_B = (W_B - W_{Bo})/W_B$, where

W_B is the work equivalent of the supplied fuel, and

W_{Bo} is the work equivalent of the unburned fuel.

There are no operating conditions in which complete combustion takes place.

A portion of the supplied fuel does not burn (hydrocarbon constituents in the exhaust gas), or only burns incompletely (exhaust gas contains CO). Under certain operating conditions it is even desirable to inhibit complete combustion by reducing the amount of air (air-fuel ratio $\lambda < 1$, for example to increase the available full-load power), or through incomplete vaporization of the fuel during warm-up.

η_B is very often given as 1 for small diesel engines at operating temperature and for comparative studies.

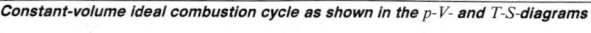

Constant-volume ideal combustion cycle as shown in the p-V- and T-S-diagrams

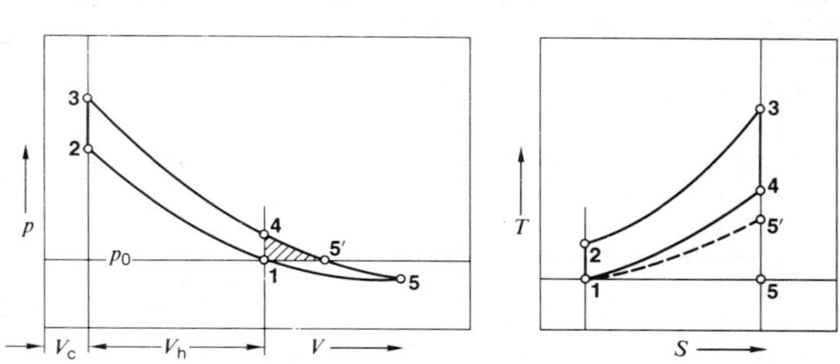

Table 2. Graphic representations and definitions of the individual and overall efficiences of the reciprocating-piston engine.

Pressure vs. volume diagram	Designation	Conditions	Definition	Efficiencies		
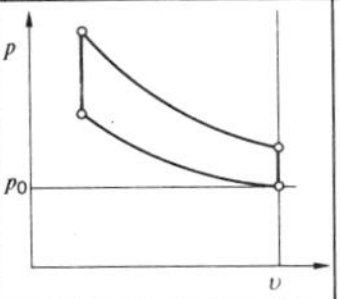	Theoretical comparative constant-volume cycle	Ideal gas, constant specific heats, infinitely rapid heat addition and dissipation, etc.	$\eta_{th} = 1 - \varepsilon^{1-\varkappa}$ Theoretical or thermal efficiency	η_{th}		
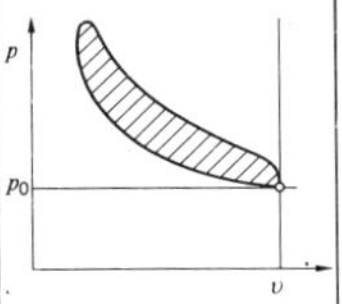	Real high-pressure working cycle	Wall heat losses, real gas, finitely rapid heat addition and dissipation, variable specific heats	η_{gHP} Efficiency factor of the high-pressure cycle		η_i	η_e
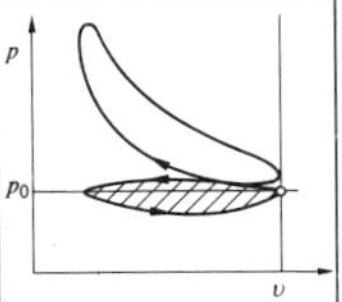	Real charge exchange (4-stroke)	Flow losses, heating of the mixture or air, etc.	η_{gLW} Charge exchange efficiency	η_g		
Mechanical losses	Losses due to friction, cooling, auxiliary units	Real engine	η_m	η_m	η_m	

The indicated efficiency η_i is the ratio of indicated work of the high-pressure section to the heat equivalent of the supplied fuel $\eta_i = W_i/W_B$.

The efficiency of cycle factor η_g comprises all internal losses of the high-pressure cycle and the low-pressure cycle such as real working gas, residual gas, wall heat losses, gas losses and pumping losses. For this reason, η_g is today more appropriately broken down into η_{gHD} for the high-pressure portion and η_{gLW} for the charge exchange portion. The efficiency of cycle factor therefore indicates the degree of compliance with the theoretical ideal combustion cycle:

$$\eta_g = \eta_{gHD} \cdot \eta_{gLW} = W_i/W_{th} \text{ where}$$

W_i is the indicated work and
W_{th} is the work generated in the ideal combustion cycle.

The mechanical efficiency η_m expresses the mechanical losses, in particular the frictional losses of the power plant and gas exchange control devices, the oil and water pumps, fuel pump, alternator, etc. in terms of the indicated work:

$$\eta_m = W_e/W_i \text{ where}$$

W_e is the effective work available at the clutch and
W_i is the indicated work.
The efficiency chain therefore appears as follows:

$$\eta_e = \eta_B \cdot \eta_{th} \cdot \eta_{gHD} \cdot \eta_{gLW} \cdot \eta_m$$

(see Table 2).

The spark-ignition (Otto) engine

The spark-ignition engine (or SI engine) is a piston engine with homogenous external or internal mixture formation and spark ignition. In a spark-ignition engine, the homogenous air-fuel mixture is compressed to approx. 20 ... 40 bar (ε = 8 ... 11) during the compression stroke. The final compression temperature of 400 ... 600 °C thus generated lies below the autoignition threshold of the mixture, so that it must be ignited by an ignition spark shortly before TDC. Subsequent combustion, and thus economy and power, are influenced primarily by the achievable flame velocity and thus the duration of combustion.

Mixture formation

The function of the mixture formation system in the spark-ignition engine is to produce a combustible, homogenous air-fuel mixture. However, homogeneity can only be achieved by gas or gas/vapor mixtures, i.e., all of the fuel must be vaporized before ignition is initiated. If some factor (such as low temperature during a cold start) inhibits complete vaporization of the fuel, then sufficient additional fuel must be provided to ensure an adequately rich — and thus combustible — air-fuel mixture (cold-start enrichment).

In addition to the formation of an homogenous mixture, the mixture formation system must also provide engine load control. Because homogenous air-fuel mixtures only burn "clean" within a narrow λ range (0.8 ... 1.2), load control must be accomplished by controlling the amount of mixture which enters the cylinder (quantity control); this is achieved by throttling the amount of air-fuel mixture entering the working cylinders under part-load operating conditions (throttle control). The air-fuel mixture must also be formed in a way which minimizes deviations in the air-fuel ratio from cylinder to cylinder and from working cycle to working cycle.

The degree to which this requirement is fulfilled varies between carburetor and fuel-injected engines, and on the engine map the curves for these two types of induction system are mutually opposed. In the case of a single-point carburetor or single-point fuel-injection system (see p. 436), the position of the throttle flap causes uneven air distribution in the lower load range and as a result uneven cylinder filling. On the other hand, intake-manifold pressure, which drops as the load decreases, causes the amount of fuel vapor to increase and thus — as shown in the figure — has a positive effect on the uniformity of mixture distribution among the engine cylinders.

As load increases, i.e., as intake manifold pressure increases, the distribution of the air-fuel mixture becomes less and less uniform.

In the case of multi-point intake-manifold fuel injection, or direct injection, the relative mixture distribution among the engine cylinders is least uniform in the lower load range. At the same time, because the distribution of air to the individual cylinders is also non-uniform in the lower range of the engine map, it is here that the difference in the amounts of air-fuel mixture distributed to the individual cylinders is more pronounced. As load increases and improves the air distribution, the λ scatter decreases.

In all mixture-formation systems, changes in the air-fuel vapor ratio (real λ) must be corrected by means of enrichment during cold starting and during the warm-up phase.

Ignition

The ignition system must be able to ignite the compressed mixture at a predetermined time, even under dynamic operating conditions which cause pronounced fluctuations in mixture movement and in the air-fuel ratio. Combustion reliability, especially in the lean range and under extreme part-load operating conditions, can be improved by positioning the spark plug in an area which provides good accessibility to the mixture and which ensures orderly mixture movement. Similar improvement can also be achieved by positioning the spark plug in small auxiliary chambers, called ignition chambers.

Mixture formation

Differences in the air-fuel ratio λ in the individual cylinders plotted as a function of load and engine speed.

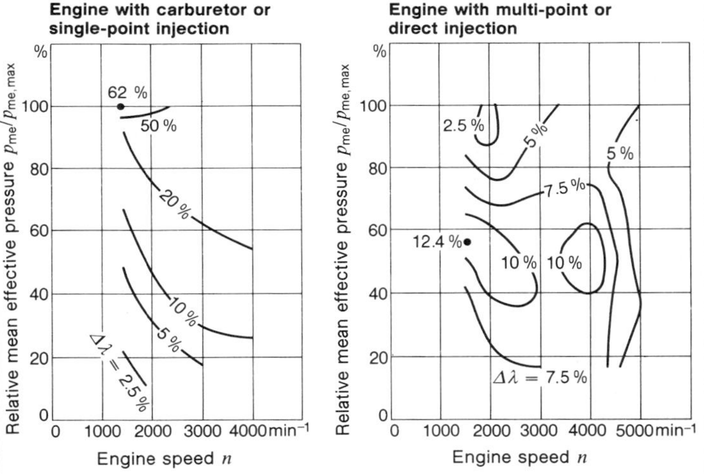

The amount of ignition energy required is a function of the air-fuel mixture. An ignition energy of 0.2 mJ is required for gasoline/air mixtures in the stoichiometric range. Rich and lean mixtures, on the other hand, require up to 3 mJ per ignition.

Combustion process

The initial thermal reaction which occurs between the addition of the ignition energy by the ignition spark and the exothermal reaction of the air-fuel mixture is called the flame development phase. This phase is roughly constant over time, and depends solely upon the mixture composition. This means that referred to piston movement an ignition lag occurs which increases as engine speed increases, and which varies as the air-fuel ratio λ changes.

The course of heat release depends primarily upon the shape of the combustion chamber and the place at which ignition occurs, and combustion time is primarily a function of the speed with which the flame propagates (combustion speed). The combustion speed is greatest at approx. 10 % excess air, i.e., $\lambda \approx 0.9$, and is 20 ... 40 m/s. Combustion speed is determined by diffusion processes in the flame front as well as by the degree of turbulence and the temperature conditions in that portion of the mixture which has not yet combusted (end gas).

The degree of turbulence in the combustion chamber and in the flame front can be influenced by a number of factors, including the design of the mixture inlet devices, the shape of the combustion chamber (e.g., incorporating edges which generate turbulence) and the use of piston movement to generate so-called squish. However, turbulence in the combustion chamber may occur spontaneously as a result of flame propagation and the attendant increase in pressure, and is in all cases a function of the engine parameters compression, intake-air temperature and engine speed.

Pressure build-up during combustion has a decisive effect on the end-gas temperature, while the significance of thermal dissipation and radiation can be ignored.

Low fuel consumption and high efficiency are promoted on the one hand by short combustion times, i.e., high combustion speeds, and on the other hand by heat release at the proper location with respect to the piston movement. The greatest heat release should occur shortly (approx. 5 ... 10° crankshaft) after top dead center. If most of the heat is released too early, wall heat losses and mechanical losses (high peak pressure) are increased. If heat release occurs too late, the heat is used inefficiently (efficiency of cycle factor) and the exhaust gas temperature increases.

The correct position for heat release must be ensured by properly selecting the ignition point while taking the following factors into consideration:

– the air-fuel mixture ratio (λ),

– the fact that turbulence depends upon the engine parameters, and

– flame development, which is constant over time, i.e., ignition lags of varying duration.

Problems and limits of combustion

In practice, reliable flame initiation and propagation in engines with external mixture formation and spark ignition prohibit use of a mixture which is leaner than $\lambda > 1.3$, although this would be desirable in order to improve the theoretical efficiency (polytropic exponent) and the gas-exchange efficiency (low throttle losses), and to reduce wall heat losses and dissociation losses (reduction of the combustion temperature). Experiments in this area are being made using stratified-charge engines.

Although higher compression ratios provide enhanced part-load efficiency, they are accompanied by increased risk of combustion knock (preignition) under full load. Combustion knock occurs when the flame propagates near the speed of sound. This can occur above all toward the end of the com-

Combustion knock in comparison with normal combustion and motored engine in the p–α-diagram.

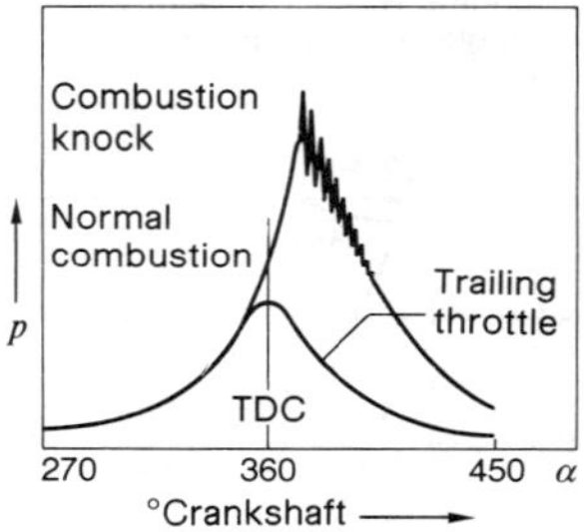

bustion process when the end gas is already highly compressed and at high temperature. In comparison to normal combustion, high pressure peaks occur during combustion knock; these pressure peaks propagate at the speed of sound in the combustion chamber and damage pistons, cylinder head, and cylinder-head gasket. The danger of combustion knock can be reduced by fuel additives or by using richer mixtures (additional internal cooling). The customary practice today of retarding the ignition point in order to eliminate combustion knock is not entirely without problems, particularly in the case of high-compression engines, because the ignition curve (mean effective pressure vs. ignition point) becomes steeper as compression increases, resulting in high exhaust-gas temperatures in addition to a lowered mean effective pressure. At compression ratios $\varepsilon = 12 \ldots 13$, it is therefore necessary to reliably detect and avoid combustion knock.

The limited degree to which the air-fuel ratio in the spark-ignition engine can be leaned out makes it necessary to perform load control by regulating the intake air mass flow over wide map ranges. This is accomplished either by throttling the air flow and thus regulating the air density, or by prematurely closing the inlet valve, thereby shortening the time during which air is drawn

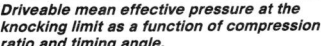

Driveable mean effective pressure at the knocking limit as a function of compression ratio and timing angle.

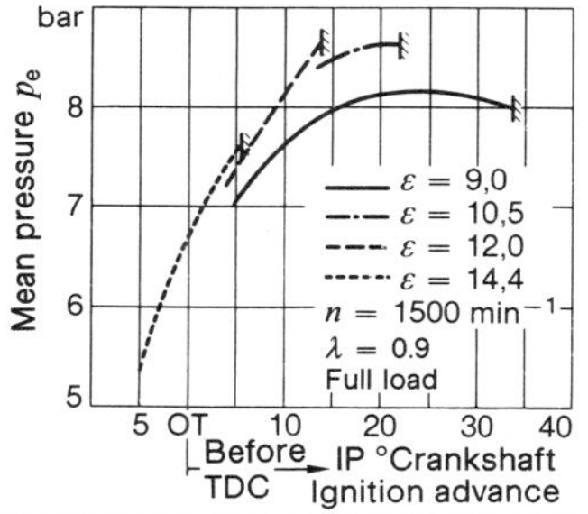

into the engine. Of the available options, throttled induction utilizes the most basic technology, but is the least efficient solution.

Power output, efficiency

The indicated efficiency of an engine with external mixture formation and spark ignition falls primarily in the lower portion of the map (see figure). This is the result of the combustion efficiency (turbulence too low, charge density too low) as well as the unfavorable gas exchange efficiency. The effective efficiency is further reduced by the unfavorable mechanical efficiency in this region of the map.

All measures which can be utilized to avoid these lower map areas thus improve the overall efficiency of the engine.

Fuel cut-off to individual cylinders allows better use to be made of those cylinders which remain in operation, thereby improving combustion efficiency and gas exchange efficiency. Valve deactivation provides further reductions in the amount of power loss by allowing the intake and exhaust valves for the deactivated cylinders to remain closed. When cylinders are switched off, the mechanical power transmission components for those cylinders are also not used. This allows the mechanical efficiency to be improved in addition.

Indicated efficiency curves of a spark-ignition engine with throttle control via load and engine speed.

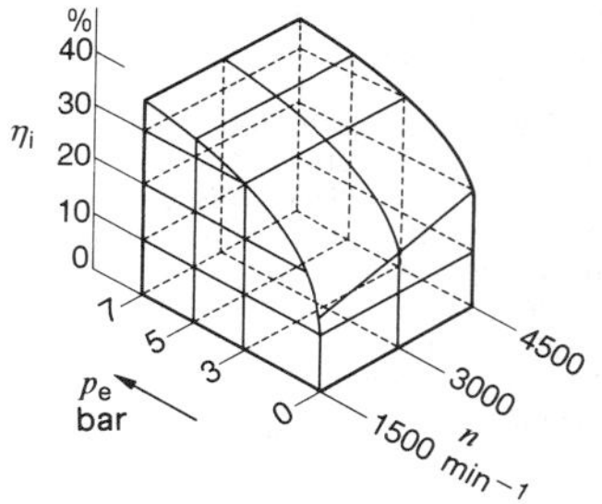

Although these measures are not yet ready for series production, engine speed reduction also improves the efficiency factor and gas exchange efficiency. In addition, the frictional mean pressure is reduced, thus improving mechanical efficiency.

Relationship between engine speed and mean pressure of friction loss

5-liter gasoline engine, P_e = 130 kW = const. at increasing engine load, p_e Mean pressure.

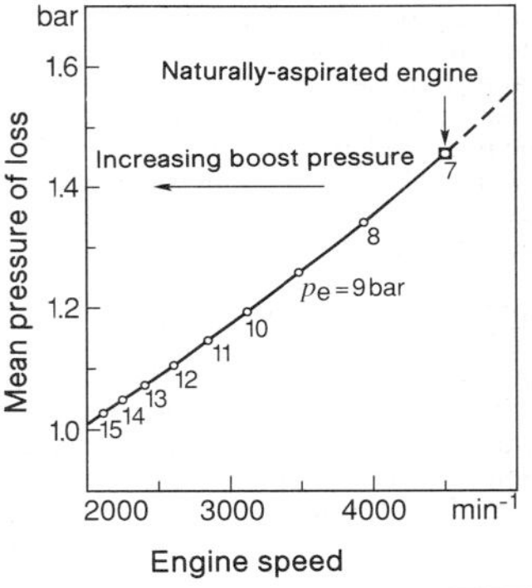

The diesel engine

A diesel engine is a reciprocating-piston engine with internal (and thus heterogeneous) mixture formation and autoignition. During the compression stroke, intake air is compressed to 30 ... 55 bar, and its temperature thereby increases to 700 ... 900 °C. This temperature is sufficient to cause autoignition of the fuel which is injected into the cylinders shortly before the end of the compression stroke and very near piston top dead center. Subsequent combustion and utilisation of the inducted combustion air, and thus the attainable mean effective pressure, depend to a great extent upon mixture formation in heterogeneous processes.

Mixture formation
In heterogeneous mixtures, the air-fuel ratio λ covers the area between pure air ($\lambda = \infty$) at the spray periphery and pure fuel ($\lambda = 0$) in the spray core.

The figure below shows schematically the λ distribution and the associated flame zone for a single drop at rest. Because this zone occurs in principle for every drop of injected mixture, load control can be performed via the amount of fuel introduced in the case of heterogeneous mixture formation. This is termed mixture quality control.

As in the case of homogenous mixtures, combustion takes place in the relatively narrow range of $0.3 < \lambda < 1.5$. The mass transport necessary for generating these combustible mixtures takes place via diffusion and turbulence, and is brought about by the mixture formation energy sources described below, and also by the combustion process itself.

Kinetic energy of the fuel spray
The kinetic energy of the fuel spray is a function of the pressure drop at the nozzle orifice, and together with the spray cone determined by the nozzle geometry and the resulting fuel velocity determines the air-fuel interaction area and the droplet size range within this space.

The spray energy is influenced by the delivery rate of the fuel-injection pump and the flow cross sections of the injection nozzle.

Heat energy
The heat energy generated by the combustion-chamber walls and the compressed air promotes the vaporization of the injected fuel in the form of film vaporization and in the form of drop vaporization.

Combustion-chamber shape
The combustion-chamber shape together with the piston movement can be used to generate turbulence (squish).

Orderly air movement (swirling action)
A movement imposed on the combustion air inside the combustion chamber, usually in the form of solid-body rotating flow, promotes the flow of air toward the fuel stream, and removes the combusted gases from the stream, if the direction of fuel flow is roughly perpendicular to the direction of the swirling air, and if the drops of fuel are in the process of being vaporized.

In the case of wall film vaporization, the swirling motion of the air removes the vaporized layer from the wall and induces thermal separation of combustion gas and fresh gas. The microturbulence superimposed on the solid-body rotating flow causes rapid mixing of the fuel and air. The orderly "solid-body

Curve of the air-fuel ratio λ in an individual drop at rest

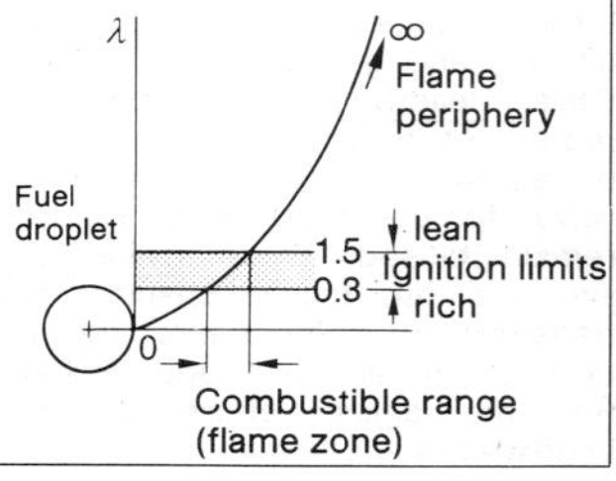

rotating flow'' of the air is generated either by the special shape of the inlet port or by transferring a portion of the cylinder charge to a swirl chamber (through a tangentially-located tract).

Partial combustion in a swirl chamber
The partial combustion of fuel in a swirl chamber increases the pressure in this chamber over that of the main combustion chamber, thereby forcing partially oxidized combustion gases and vaporized fuel through one or more connection tracts into the main combustion chamber where they are thoroughly mixed with the remaining combustion air.

The diesel combustion process makes use of at least one (but usually an appropriate combination) of these mixture formation methods.

Direct injection (DI)
This term refers to all processes in which the combustion chamber is not divided.

Quiescent injection process
The quiescent injection process uses a wide combustion-chamber recess in the piston. A 6 to 8-hole nozzle is positioned centrally with respect to the recess. This process primarily makes use of the energy of the injected fuel, and does not impart a swirling action to the air. It is applied most often in slow-running, large-size diesel engines which are operated with a large quantity of excess air.

Multiple-hole nozzle combustion process
This process incorporates a significantly narrower combustion-chamber recess in the piston. Here, a 3 to 4-hole nozzle is positioned centrally with respect to the recess. This type of process is used today in most truck engines, whereby air utilization is improved and mixture formation speed is increased through the use of swirling action in the intake passage in addition to the energy generated by injection. The intensity of the swirling action is chosen such that by virtue of the swirling air, which acts perpendicularly to the direction of injection, the A/F mixture forming around the fuel spray injected through each nozzle hole fills the combustion-chamber segment between it and the A/F mixture from the adjacent nozzle hole.

If the A/F mixture fails to completely fill the particular combustion-chamber segment, neither the air nor the power output is fully utilized. On the other hand, if there is an overlap and the A/F mixture covers more than the space between the individual sprays, this causes excessive local fuel concentration which in turn leads to air deficiency and the formation of soot. Both the quiescent injection process and the multiple-hole nozzle process are designated as combustion systems with air-distributed fuel.

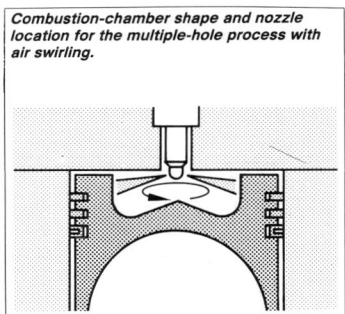

Combustion-chamber shape and nozzle location for the quiescent injection process without air swirling.

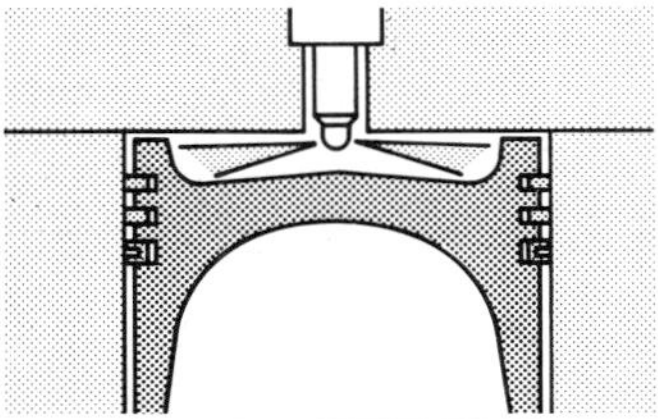

Combustion-chamber shape and nozzle location for the multiple-hole process with air swirling.

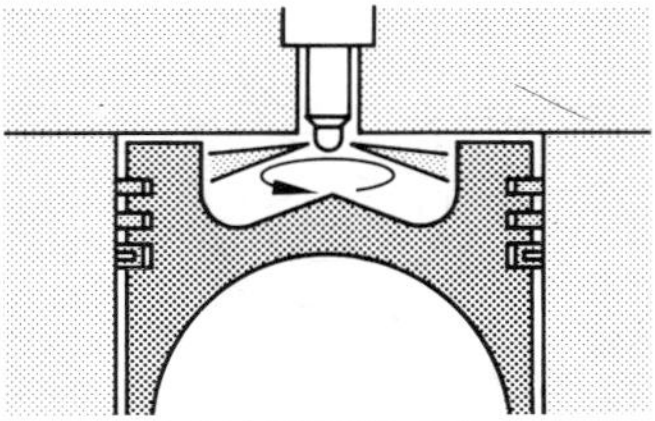

M System
The MAN wall-distribution combustion system (M system), in which the fuel is applied to the wall of the combustion chamber, makes use of the heat generated at the combustion-chamber wall and the swirling action of the air in addition to the injection energy for mixture formation. The single-hole nozzle projecting eccentrically into the narrow recess in the piston, sprays the fuel against the combustion-chamber wall and into the turbulence. The fuel forms a film which vaporizes and forms a very intense mixture with the swirling combustion-chamber air as it passes. This process makes good use of the air and is characterised by low exhaust smoke numbers.

Divided-chamber combustion systems
Divided-chamber combustion systems are well suited to small, high-speed diesel engines, usually installed in passenger cars. Here, very stringent requirements are placed on mixture formation speed and air utilization (acceptable λ). On the other hand, expensive injection equipment which generates high injection energy is to be avoided for reasons of cost. In addition, swirl-type intake passages cannot be used here without problems, for reasons of good volumetric efficiency.

The dual-chamber method combines rich mixtures in the prechamber and relatively lean charges in the main combustion chamber to achieve extremely low NO_x and HC emissions.

Combustion-chamber shape and nozzle location in the MAN M system

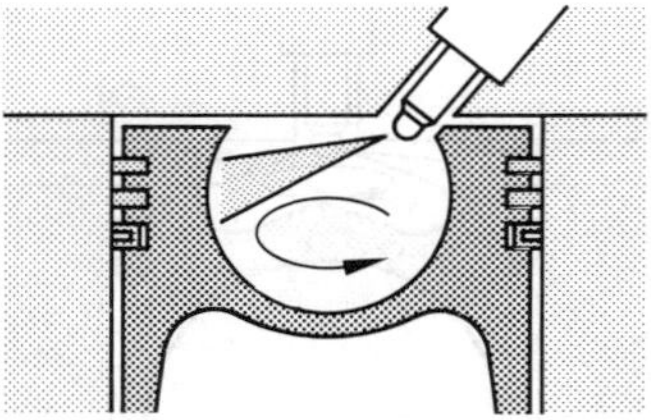

Swirl-chamber system
This process is characterised by a nearly spherical auxiliary chamber which makes up approx. 50 % of the total compression volume, and which is located at the edge of the main combustion chamber. The auxiliary chamber communicates with the main combustion chamber by means of a throat area which opens tangentially into the chamber and is directed toward the center of the piston. The nozzle and the glow plug (starting aid) are located in the auxiliary chamber. A strong air vortex is generated during the compression stroke, causing the fuel to be sprayed against the chamber wall eccentrically and in the direction of the swirling air in a manner similar to the M system. The positions of the injector nozzles and glow plugs, and the design of the swirl chamber itself (which can incorporate such features as auxiliary mixture-evaporation surfaces at the point where the injector spray hits the chamber wall) are all vital in determining the quality of the combustion process. With the correct design, this process combines high engine speeds – in excess of 5000 min^{-1} – with good air utilization and extremely limited particulate emissions.

Prechamber system
The prechamber system is characterised by an auxiliary chamber which is centrally located with respect to the main combustion chamber, with 25 ...

Combustion-chamber shape and nozzle location for the swirl chamber system

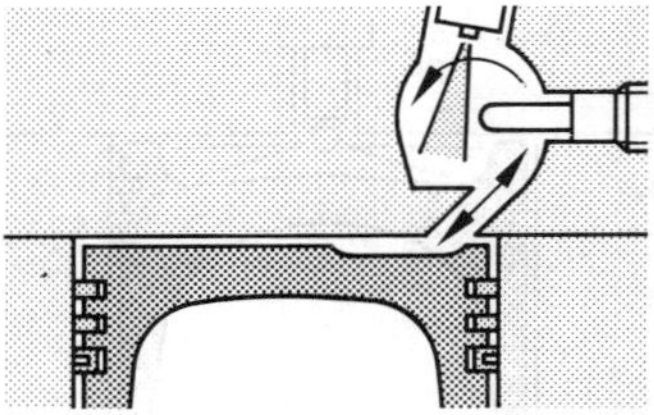

35 % of the compression volume. Here too, the injection nozzle and glow plug (starting aid) are located in the prechamber. It communicates with the main combustion chamber through several holes to allow the combustion gases to communicate as completely as possible with the main combustion air. One optimized prechamber concept utilizes the deflection surface below the injector nozzle to simultaneously induce rapid mixture formation and a controlled turbulence pattern (on some designs) in the prechamber. The turbulent flow meets the injection spray, which is also aimed into the swirl at an angle. The entire system, including the downstream glow plug, provides combustion with very low emissions and a major reduction in particulates. The process is distiguished by a high air-utilization factor, and is also suitable for high engine speeds.

Combustion process

The start of injection (and thus the start of mixture formation) and the start of the exothermal reaction (start of ignition) are separated by a certain period of time, called ignition lag. The amount of time depends upon the ignition quality of the fuel (cetane number), the compression ratio – and thus the final compression temperature – the type of fuel management selected, and the load condition of the engine (component temperature).

The combustion process, which

Combustion-chamber shape and nozzle location for the prechamber system

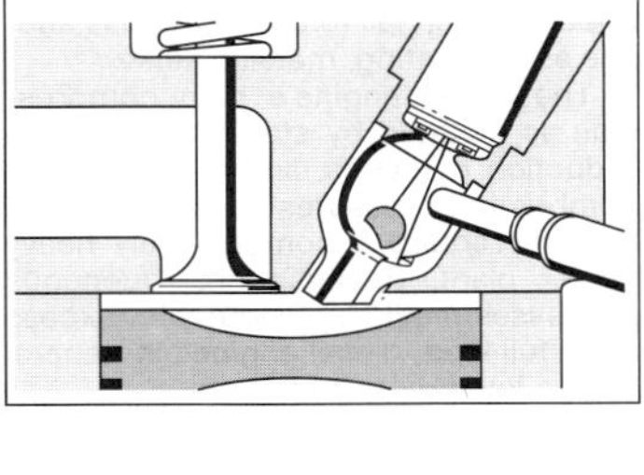

Heat release curves

1 Air-distributed direct fuel injection, 2 Wall-wetting direct injection, 3a and 3b In the auxiliary chamber and the main combustion chamber of the divided chamber system, respectively.

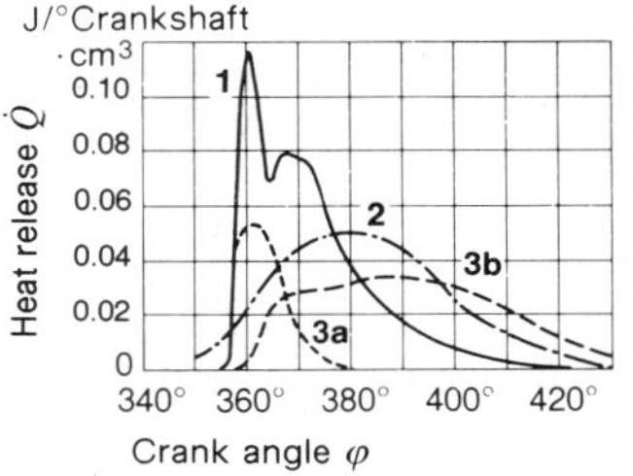

begins with the start of ignition, can be subdivided into two phases. In the "premixed flame" phase, the fuel injected prior to the start of ignition and mixed with air combusts. The fuel which is injected after the start of ignition combusts in a "diffusion flame".

That portion of the combusted fuel which burns as a very rapid premixed flame is primarily responsible for the pressure increase, and thus is the primary cause of combustion noise and the generation of oxides of nitrogen. The slower-burning diffusion flame is the primary cause of soot and unburned hydrocarbons.

The release of heat in a diesel combustion process is thus a direct function of the type of mixture formation, and can be varied over a wide range by changing the above-mentioned parameters.

The two-stage combustion cycle which is characteristic of the auxiliary-chamber process allows the combustion process to be additionally controlled via the selection of appropriate cross sections in the connection throats between the auxiliary chamber and the main combustion chamber.

The diagram shows the heat release curves with air-distributed direct fuel injection, wall-wetting direct injection and a divided-chamber system. These processes differ from one another primarily with regard to the initial combustion phase. The high conversion peak of the air-distributed direct fuel injection process at the start of combustion can be reduced by applying the fuel to the wall of the combustion chamber, and even more greatly reduced via two-stage combustion in the divided-chamber process; combustion efficiency, however, is reduced.

Combustion problems and limits

Because the fuel injected into diesel engines ignites spontaneously, the ignition quality of the fuel must be high (the fuel must have a cetane number CN ≈ 45 ... 50). In spite of a high compression ratio, ignition problems can occur during starting – particularly when starting a cold engine – because at the low cranking speed of the engine, compression does not begin until significantly after BDC, when the intake valves close. The effective compression ratio, and thus the compression temperature, are therefore greatly reduced. In addition, cold engine components promote the flow of heat out of the compressed air (polytropic exponent: $1.1 < n < 1.2$). The relationship $T_1 = T_0 \cdot \varepsilon^{n-1}$ shows that a reduction in the effective compression or the polytropic exponent causes a reduction in the final compression temperature. In addition, mixture formation is unsatisfactory at low engine speeds (large fuel droplets) and air movement is inadequate. A longer vaporization time (injection begins sooner) and an increased fuel quantity which is significantly greater than the full-load quantity (supply of a greater quantity of low-boiling fuel) can only partially solve the starting problem, because the higher-boiling fuel constituents leave the engine in the form of white or blue smoke. Starting aids which increase the temperature, such as glow plugs or flame starting systems, are therefore necessary, primarily in the case of small engines.

Because a significant portion of the mixture formation process occurs during combustion in heterogeneous processes, local concentrations of over-rich mixture occur in the diffusion flame, thereby leading to an increase in the emission of black smoke, to a certain extent even with moderate excess air. The air-fuel ratio which leads to smoke emissions which border on the legal limit is a measure of how well the air is utilized. Divided-chamber engines which emit smoke at the legal limit have excess air of 10 ... 25 %, whereas this value is 40 ... 50 % in direct-injection diesel engines. It should be noted that large-volume diesel engines must be run with a significant amount of excess air for reasons of thermal component load as well.

It is not possible to design a soot-free diesel engine, because heterogeneous combustion always produces soot. Research is therefore concentrating on the development of a regenerative particulate filter to retain and burn soot, and on catalytic oxidation processes for CO, HC and soot particles.

Due to the abrupt combustion of the vaporized fuel mixed with the air, the autoignition process is characterized by "hard" combustion which is often very loud. Noise emission can be reduced by decreasing the ignition lag (heating of the intake air, supercharging or increasing compression) and/or by reducing the amount of fuel supplied to the engine during the ignition lag (throttling pintle nozzle).

A characteristic of diesel engines, so-called "diesel knock" must not be confused with the noise generated by noisy combustion. Diesel knock is generated in the middle and lower regions of the diesel engine map, and is caused by problems in the mixture-formation system, such as fouled injection nozzles or nozzles which fail to chatter, and is audible as a pulsating, metallic noise.

The diesel engine's high compression as dictated by starting and noise-reduction demands, and the high peak combustion pressures caused by autoignition require a comparatively heavy power plant. Because heterogeneous processes must also occur with excess air at full load, diesel engines in general have a low power density.

Hybrid processes

Hybrid engines incorporate characteristics of both diesel and spark-ignition engines.

Charge stratification
In stratified-charge engines, whereas the mixture is made richer in the vicinity of the spark plug such that mixture ignition is guaranteed, the average A/F mixture involved in the combustion is highly leaned-out. The purpose of such a stratified charge is to achieve the part-load fuel consumption characteristic of a diesel engine while at the same time keeping NO_x and CO emissions at a minimum.

In open-chamber combustion systems, most of whose characteristics are similar to those of the diesel system (mixture quality control, high-pressure injection, etc.), attempts are made through internal mixture formation (Texaco TCCS, Ford PROCO, Ricardo, MAN-FM, KHD-AD) to generate an ignitable mixture at the spark plug while reducing the fuel content of the mixture down to pure air in the remainder of the combustion chamber.

Processes which use internal mixture formation have an air utilization factor comparable to that of diesel engines.

In prechamber combustion systems, whose characteristics are more like those of spark-ignition engines (throttle control, mixture induction, etc.), the spark plug is located in a small auxiliary combustion chamber which accounts for roughly 5 ... 25 % of the total compression volume, and which communicates with the main combustion chamber via one or more holes (throat areas).

In this configuration, the auxiliary combustion chamber features an additional injector which injects a portion of the overall injected fuel quantity (VW, Porsche-SKS), or it can feature an additional valve through which a portion of the A/F mixture is aspirated (Honda-CVCC).

A disadvantage of these processes is their more complex design and higher HC emissions due to the lower exhaust-gas temperatures which cause a reduction in afterburning reactions in the exhaust system, or which completely prevent such reactions.

Multifuel engines
In multifuel engines, the ignition quality or knock resistance of the fuel makes little or no difference, and fuels of differing quality can be used without causing engine damage. Due to the fact that the fuel used with multifuel engines may have a very low knock-resistance rating, external mixture formation is accompanied by the danger of combustion knock or pre-ignition. For this reason, multifuel engines always use internal mixture formation and retarded start of injection (similar to the diesel engine). The injection pump for multifuel operation has an annular lubrication channel for the pump element to lubricate the plungers with engine oil from the forced-feed lubrication system. This annular lubrication channel also prevents fuel from entering the camshaft area of the pump. Because the low ignition quality of the fuels makes autoignition difficult or even impossible, multifuel engines operate with extremely high compression (Mercedes-Benz, MTU: $\varepsilon = 25:1$), or are equipped with spark plugs or glow plugs (MAN-FM). The compression ratio of these engines with external ignition lies between that of spark-ignition and diesel engines at $\varepsilon = 14 \dots 15$.

A special type of ignition initiation is the ignition spray process which is used in alcohol and gas engines (KHD, MWM), in which an additional spray of diesel fuel is sprayed directly into the combustion chamber. This additional spray comprises 5 ... 10 % of the full-load diesel fuel quantity, thereby ensuring that the mixture will ignite. In this process, the main source of energy can be supplied via external or internal mixture formation.

None of the above-mentioned processes is in widespread use today, with the exception of military applications.

Gas exchange

In internal-combustion engines in which the open-chamber process is used, the exchange of the gas or charge (exhaust and refill cycle), must fulfill two decisive functions:

1. The working gas is returned to the initial condition of the cycle through exchange,
2. The oxygen required to burn the fuel is provided in the form of fresh air.

The parameters laid down in DIN 1940 can be used to evaluate the gas exchange. Whereas in the case of the mass of air supplied to a cylinder (mass of air corresponding to cylinder volume, $\lambda_a = m_g/m_{th}$) the entire charge m_g used during one working cycle is referred to the theoretical possible charge given by the displacement, the volumetric efficiency $\lambda_{a1} = m_z/m_{th}$ involves only the actual fresh charge m_z present or remaining in the cylinder. The fresh charge differs from the total charge used, m_g, by that portion which is directly exhausted during the overlap period, which thus does not participate in the combustion process. The catching efficiency

$\lambda_z = m_z/m_g$

is a measure of the charge remaining in the cylinder. The scavenge efficiency

$\lambda_S = m_z/(m_z + m_r)$

indicates how high the portion of the fresh charge m_z is in comparison to the existing total charge which comprises the fresh charge and the residual gas amount m_r. Here, the parameter m_r indicates the amount of residual gas from earlier working cycles which remains in the cylinder at the end of the exhaust portion of the cycle.

In a two-stroke cycle, the gas is exchanged with every rotation of the crankshaft at the end of the expansion in the area of bottom dead center. In a four-stroke cycle, a separate gas-exchange stroke comprising exhaust and intake occurs before every combustion stroke.

Four-stroke process
Valve timing — and thus gas exchange — are regulated by the camshaft, which rotates with half the frequency of the crankshaft by which it is driven. The camshaft opens the gas-exchange valves against the force of the valve springs in order to push out the exhaust gas and to draw in the fresh gas (exhaust and intake valves respectively). Shortly before bottom dead center (BDC), the exhaust valve opens and approx. 50 % of the combustion gases leave the combustion chamber under conditions of a supercritical pressure ratio during this pre-exhaust phase. As it moves upward during the exhaust stroke, the piston removes nearly all of the combustion gases from the combustion chamber.

Shortly ahead of piston top dead center (TDC), the intake valve opens with the exhaust valve still in its open position. This crankshaft top dead center position is called the gas-exchange TDC or overlap TDC (because the intake and exhaust processes overlap at this point) in order to differentiate it from the ignition TDC. Shortly after gas-exchange TDC, the exhaust valve closes and, with the intake valve still open, the piston can induct fresh air as it moves downward. This second stroke of the gas-exchange process, the intake stroke, continues until shortly after BDC.

Representation of the four-stroke gas exchange process in the p-V-diagram

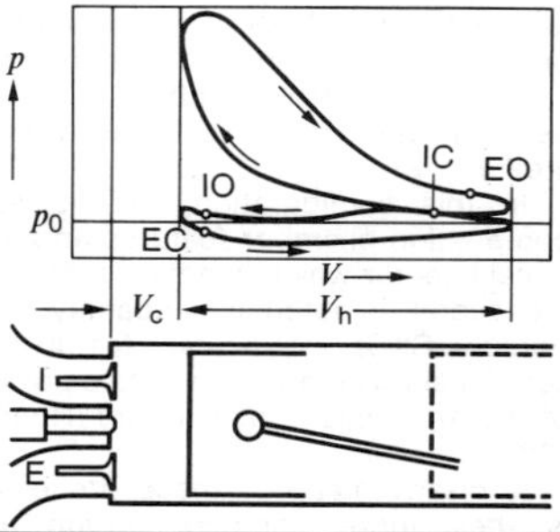

The remaining two strokes of the four-stroke process — compression and combustion (expansion) — then occur place.

During the overlap phase, in the throttle-controlled spark-ignition engine (particularly under part-load operating conditions), as a result of high manifold pressure exhaust gases flow directly from the combustion chamber into the intake passage, or from the exhaust passage directly into the combustion chamber, and from there into the intake passage.

This "internal" exhaust-gas return has an unfavorable effect, particularly at idle. It cannot be completely avoided, however, because a compromise must be found between satisfactory idle behavior on the one hand and adequate high-rpm valve overlap on the other. Early exhaust valve opening allows a high degree of pre-exhaust, and thus guarantees low residual gas compression by the piston during its upward stroke. The indicated work of the combustion gases is reduced, however. The "intake valve closes" (IC) control time has a significant effect on the charging efficiency curve as plotted against engine speed.

Four-stroke gas exchange process

E	*Exhaust*	*TDC*	*Top dead center*
EO	*Exhaust opens*	*OTDC*	*Overlap TDC*
EC	*Exhaust closes*	*ITDC*	*Ignition TDC*
I	*Intake*	*BDC*	*Bottom dead center*
IO	*Intake opens*		
IC	*Intake closes*	*IP*	*Ignition point*

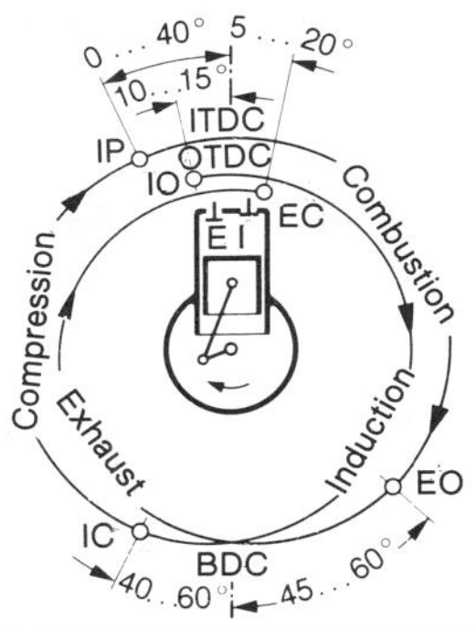

When the intake valve closes early (IC), the maximum charge efficiency occurs at low engine speeds, while delayed closing displaces the efficiency peak toward the upper end of the rpm spectrum.

Obviously, fixed valve timing will always represent a compromise between two different design objectives: Maximum brake mean effective pressure — and thus torque — at the most desirable points on the curve, and the highest possible peak output. The higher the rpm at which maximum power occurs, and the wider the range of engine operating speeds, the less satisfactory will be the ultimate compromise. Large variations in the valves' effective flow opening relative to stroke (i.e., in designs featuring more than two valves) will intensify this tendency.

At the same time, the demands for minimal exhaust emissions and maximum fuel economy mean that low idle speeds and high low-end torque (along with high specific outputs for light-weight power units) are becoming increasingly important. These imperatives have led to the application of variable valve timing (especially for intake valves), whereby the most significant concepts (with attention focused on high-speed gasoline engines in series production) have been the following:

Variable camshaft angle: A hydraulic control mechanism rotates the intake camshaft to vary the valve timing for "intake opens" (IO) and "intake closes" (IC) according to engine speed (Alfa-Romeo, Mercedes-Benz).

The camshaft is set to delayed closing of the intake valve (IC) at idle and at high engine speeds. This results in a certain amount of valve overlap at overlap top dead center (OTDC) for stability at idle and enhanced output at high rpm. The camshaft is rotated to close the intake valve early (IC) under full load in midrange operation, furnishing higher volumetric efficiency with correspondingly high levels of torque.

Selective camshaft-lobe actuation: The timing of the intake and exhaust valves is varied by alternating between separate lobes featuring two different profiles (Honda).

The first lobe features a profile tailored for optimum intake and exhaust timing and valve lift in the lower and middle engine-speed ranges. At high rpm, a rocker arm that pivots freely at low speeds is coupled to the standard rocker arm; this rocker arm rides on a second cam lobe to provide greater lift and extended opening times.

Infinitely-variable valve lift and timing: Continuous modification of valve timing as function of engine speed (Fiat).

Whereas this is the optimum concept it is the most difficult to implement. It employs a cam lobe with a curved 3-dimensional profile and lateral camshaft adjustment to achieve substantial increases in torque throughout the engine's complete rpm range.

The intake and exhaust tracts can be evaluated using stationary flow testing with flow number or passage efficiency level. It is useful to evaluate the exhaust valves in the lower lift range with reference to supercritical pressures of the kind occurring in the blowdown phase. Usual efficiency factors for the intake and exhaust passages indicate that intake-tract designs which induce combustion-charge turbulence lead to a dramatic reduction of tract efficiency and cylinder volumetric efficiency.

Advantages of the four-stroke process:
Very good volumetric efficiency over entire engine-speed range, low sensitivity to pressure losses in exhaust system, as well as relatively good controllability of the charging-efficiency curve by selection of valve timing and matching of the intake system.

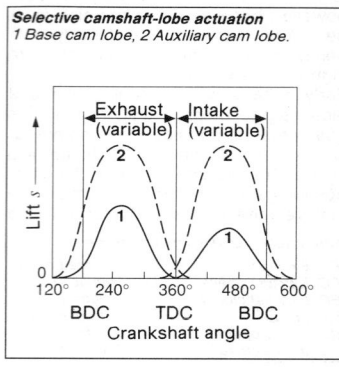

Selective camshaft-lobe actuation
1 Base cam lobe, 2 Auxiliary cam lobe.

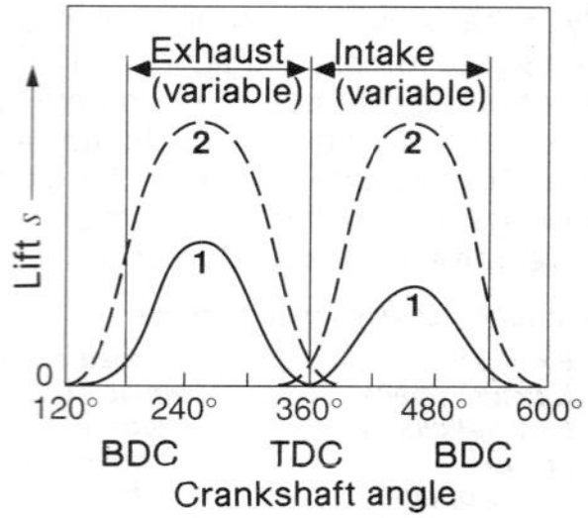

Adjustment angle for intake camshaft
1 Retard, 2 Standard, 3 Advance.

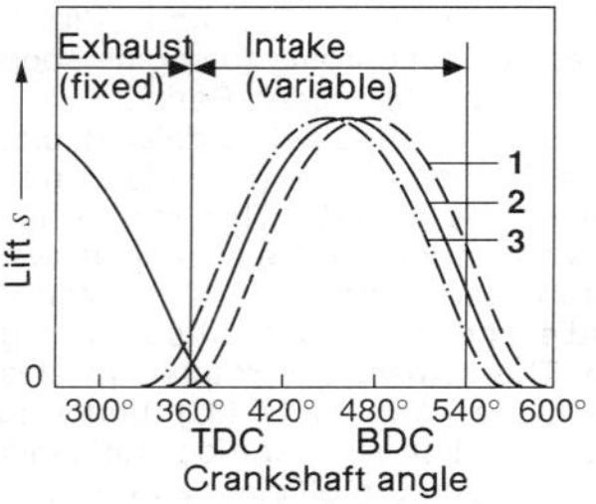

Infinitely-variable valve lift and timing
a) Minimum lift, b) Maximum lift.

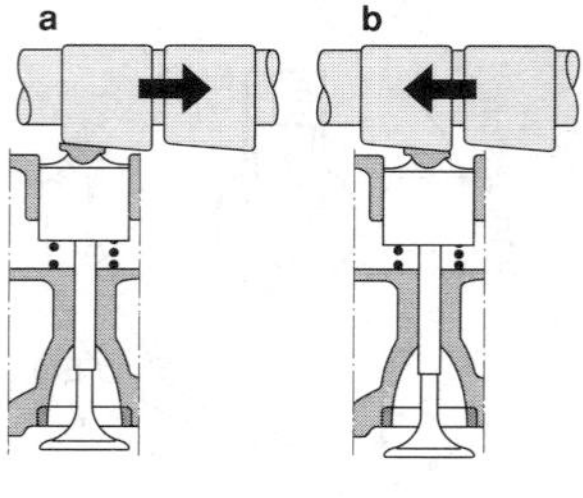

Disadvantages of the four-stroke process:
Valve control is highly complex. The power density is reduced because only every second shaft rotation is used to generate work.

Two-stroke process
To bring about gas exchange without an additional crankshaft rotation, the gases are exchanged in the two-stroke process at the end of expansion and at the beginning of the compression stroke. The times at which intake and exhaust processes occur are usually controlled by the piston which moves past intake and exhaust ports in the cylinder housing near BDC. This configuration, however, requires symmetrical control times and involves the problem of short-circuit scavenging. In addition, 15 ... 25 % of the piston stroke cannot produce work because only filling volume V_f and not displacement volume V_h can be used to produce work.

Because the two-stroke process lacks separate intake and exhaust strokes, the cylinder must be filled and scavenged using gauge pressure. Scavenging pumps are required for this purpose. In an especially simple and very frequently-used design, the bottom surface of the piston in conjunction with a crankcase with a minimized dead volume is used as the scavenging pump. The figures below show the two-

Graphical representation of the two-stroke gas exchange process in the p-V-diagram

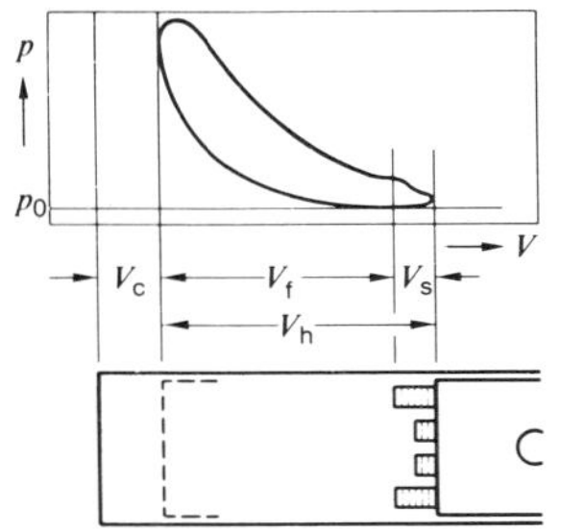

Scavenging processes
1 Cross scavenging, 2 Loop scavenging.

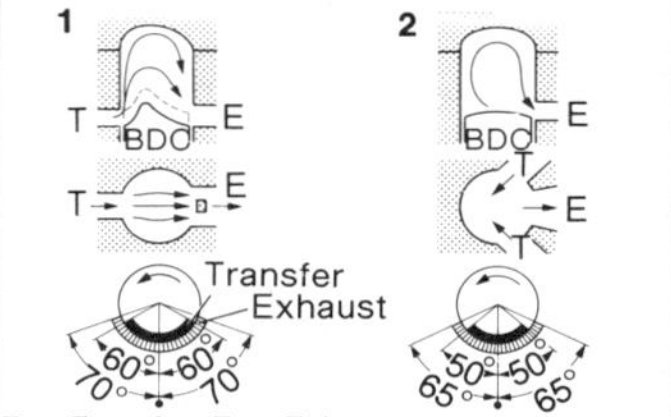

T = Transfer, E = Exhaust

3 and 4 Uniflow scavenging

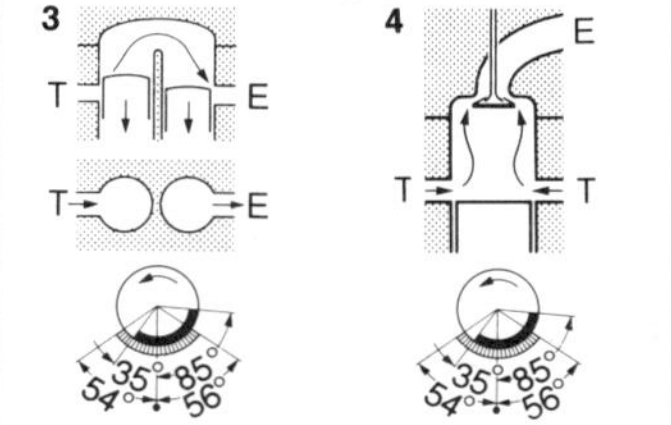

Two-stroke gas exchange process with crankcase compression

E	*Exhaust*	*T*	*Transfer passage*
EO	*Exhaust opens*	*TO*	*Transfer passage opens*
EC	*Exhaust closes*		
I	*Intake*	*TC*	*Transfer passage closes*
IO	*Intake opens*		
IC	*Intake closes*	*TDC*	*Top dead center*
IP	*Ignition point*	*BDC*	*Bottom dead center*

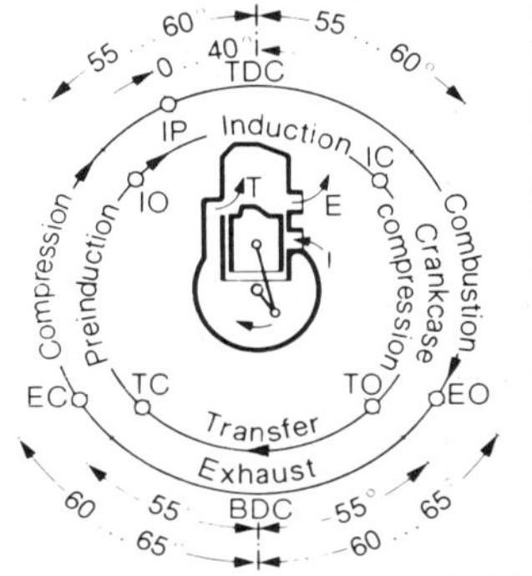

stroke engine with crankcase scavenging or crankcase compression, as well as the associated control processes. The processes which take place on the scavenging pump side are shown in the inner circle, and those which take place on the cylinder side are shown in the outer circle. Satisfactory cylinder scavenging can be accomplished by means of cross scavenging, loop scavenging or uniflow scavenging.

Advantages of the two-stroke process: Simple engine design, low weight, low manufacturing costs, more favorable torsional force diagram.

Disadvantages of the two-stroke process:
Higher fuel consumption and higher HC emissions (cylinder scavenging is problematic), lower mean effective pressures (poorer volumetric efficiency), higher thermal load (no gas exchange stroke), poor idle behavior (higher percentage of residual gas).

Supercharging processes

The power of an engine is proportional to the air throughput m_z. Because air throughput, in turn, is proportional to air density, the power of an engine, given a specific displacement and engine speed, can be increased by precompression of the air before it enters the cylinders, i.e., by supercharging. The supercharging ratio indicates the increase in density as compared to a naturally-aspirated engine. It depends upon the system used (the pressure ratio obtained), and is the greatest given a specific increase in pressure when the temperature of the compressed air (charging air) is not increased or is returned to its initial value by intercooling. In the spark-ignition engine, the supercharging ratio is limited by knocking combustion, and in the diesel engine by the maximum permissible peak pressures. In order to avoid these problems, supercharged engines usually have a lower compression ratio than naturally-aspirated engines.

Ram-pipe supercharging
Configuration and energy balance. Induction work A of the piston ≙ compression work B.

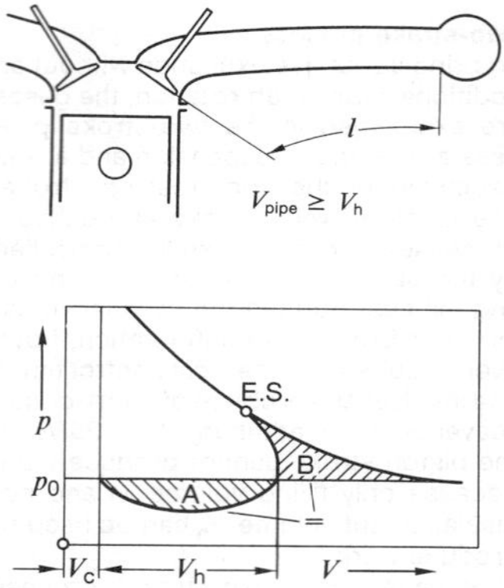

Tuned-intake tube charging
Configuration and charging efficiency curve.

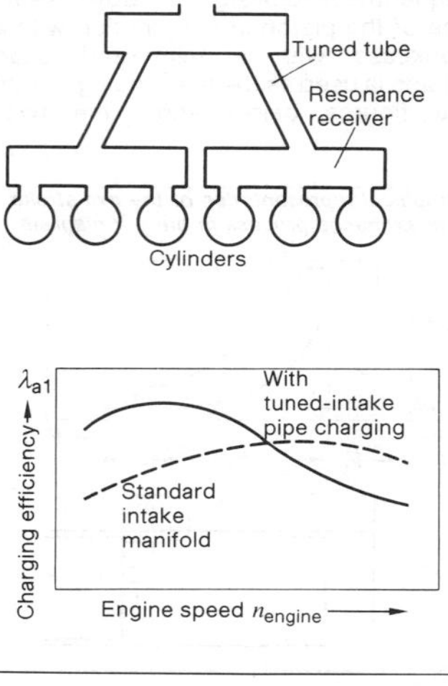

Dynamic supercharging
The simplest type of supercharging utilizes the dynamic behavior of the aspirated air.

Ram-pipe supercharging
Each cylinder has a special intake manifold of a specific length, usually connected to a common receiver. The energy balance is characterized by the fact that the intake work of the piston is converted into kinetic energy of the column of gas upstream of the intake valve, and this kinetic energy, in turn, is converted into fresh charge compression work.

Tuned-intake tube charging
In tuned-intake tube charging, groups of cylinders with the same ignition intervals are connected to resonance receivers via short tubes. These resonance receivers communicate with the atmosphere or a common receiver via tuned tubes, and act as Helmholtz resonators.

Variable-configuration intake manifold
a) Two-stage operation,
b) Three-stage operation.
A, B Cylinder groups;
1, 2 Flaps, rpm-regulated

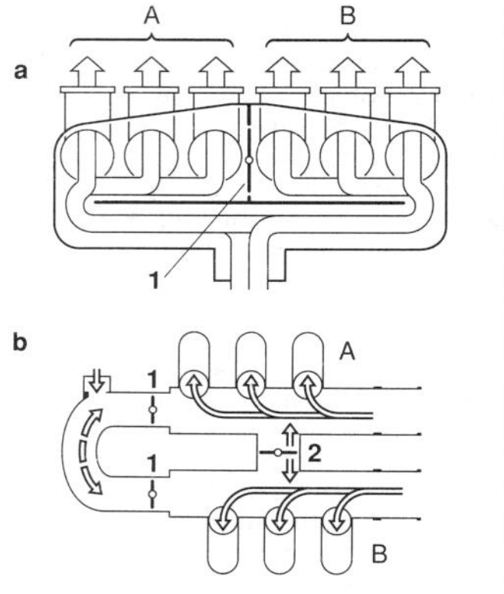

Variable-configuration intake manifold
Several manufacturers (BMW, Citroën, Opel, Ford) have already introduced systems employing the principles of dynamic boost (including combination designs). These systems enhance charge efficiency, above all in the lower engine-speed range.

The combined variable-intake system employs flaps or similar devices to alternately connect and isolate the intake passages leading to the different cylinders in response to variations in engine speed.

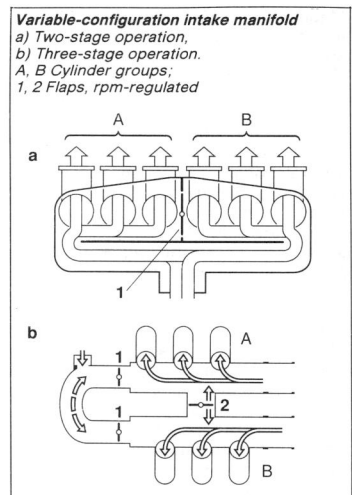

At low rpm the variable-length intake runners operate in conjunction with an initial resonance chamber. The length of the intake runners is adjusted continually as engine speed increases, the entire process culminating with the opening of a second resonance chamber.

Variable-length intake runners
1 Resonance chamber 1,
2 Adjuster,
3 Resonance chamber 2.

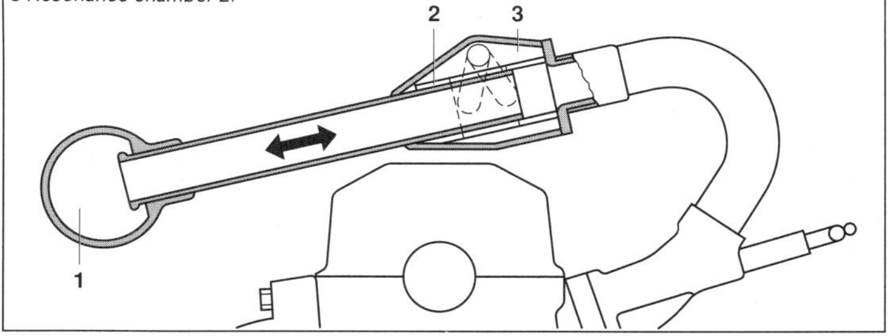

Mechanical supercharging

In mechanical supercharging, the supercharger is directly engine driven. Usually, the engine drives the supercharger at a fixed transmission ratio. Mechanical or electromagnetic clutches are often used for switching the supercharger on and off. The interrelationship between the engine and the supercharger is shown most simply using the pressure vs. volumetric flow rate map in which the pressure ratio π_c of the supercharger is plotted against volumetric flow rate $\dot{V}$.

With unthrottled four-stroke engines (diesel), the diagram is particularly descriptive because it contains sloped straight lines – so-called engine mass-flow characteristics – which represent increasing engine air-throughput values as the pressure ratio $\pi_c \triangleq p_2/p_1$ increases at constant engine speed. Those pressure ratios are indicated in this map which result at corresponding constant supercharger speeds for a positive-displacement supercharger and a turbocharger.

Only superchargers whose delivery rates vary linearly with their rotational speeds are suitable for vehicle engines. These are positive-displacement superchargers of piston or rotating-vane design or Roots blowers (see p. 418). Turbochargers are not suitable.

Advantages of mechanical supercharging:

Relatively simple superchargers on cold side of engine. Engine exhaust gas is not involved. Supercharger responds immediately to load changes.

Disadvantages of mechanical supercharging:

The supercharger must be engine-powered, causing increased fuel consumption.

Exhaust-gas turbocharging

In exhaust-gas turbocharging, the energy for the turbocharger is taken from the engine exhaust gas. On the one hand, energy is used which in naturally-aspirated engines cannot be used due to expansion conditions imposed by the crank mechanism. On the other hand, the pressure of exhaust gas is increased upon leaving the engine in order to achieve the necessary compression power. In today's turbocharged engines, exhaust gas energy is converted into mechanical energy by an exhaust-driven turbine, which permits using turbochargers for pre-compressing the fresh gas. The combination of an exhaust-driven turbine and a turbocharger is an exhaust-gas turbocharger (see p. 420).

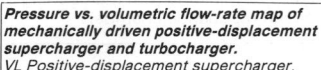

Pressure vs. volumetric flow-rate map of mechanically driven positive-displacement supercharger and turbocharger.
VL Positive-displacement supercharger, SL Turbocharger.

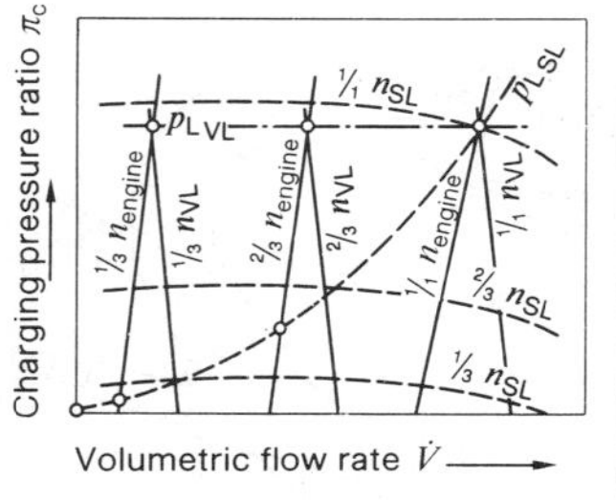

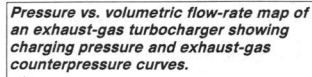

Pressure vs. volumetric flow-rate map of an exhaust-gas turbocharger showing charging pressure and exhaust-gas counterpressure curves.

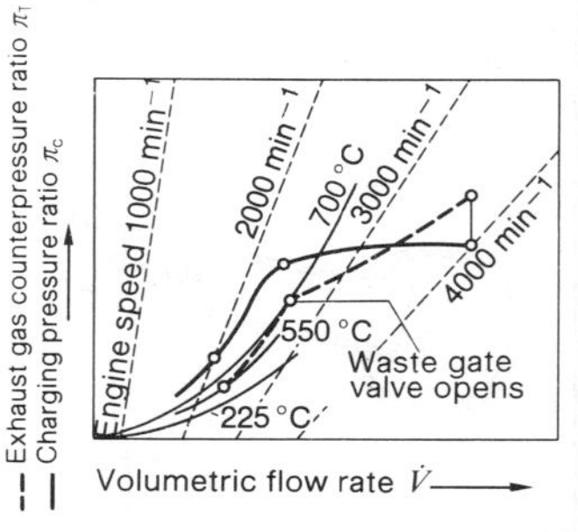

Advantages of exhaust-gas turbocharging:
Considerable increase in design power and power per unit displacement; improved torque curve over useful speed range; significant improvement in fuel consumption compared to naturally-aspirated engines of equal power; improvement in exhaust-gas emissions.

Disadvantages of exhaust-gas turbocharging:
Installation of the turbocharger in the hot exhaust-gas line requiring materials resistant to high temperatures; space must be provided for the installation of turbocharger and intercooler; low basic torque at low engine speed; throttle response is extremely sensitive to design of unit and ancillaries.

Pressure-wave supercharging
The pressure-wave supercharger achieves direct energy exchange between exhaust gas and the intake air for the purpose of increasing the density of the latter. This is accomplished by utilizing the differing speeds of the gas particles and pressure waves, and the reflection properties of these pressure waves (see p. 422). The pressure-wave supercharger consists of a cell rotor with an air or exhaust-gas housing on either rotor face; these housings incorporate specific timing edges and gas pocket configurations.

Constant and transient torque curves for turbocharged engine compared with a naturally-aspirated engine.

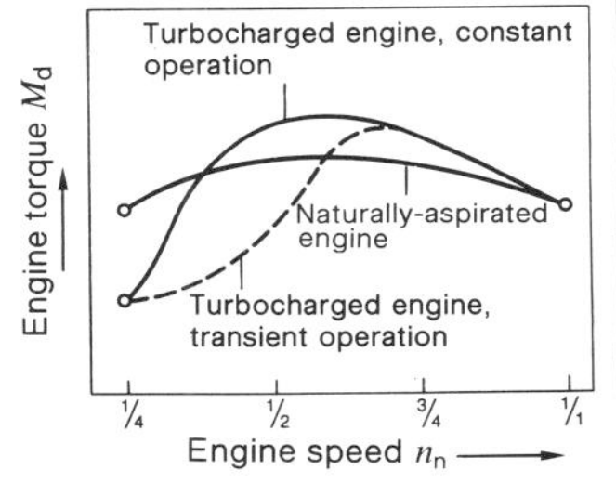

Advantages of pressure-wave supercharging:
Rapid response because energy exchange between exhaust gas and charge air occurs at the speed of sound; high compression at low engine speeds.

Disadvantages of pressure-wave supercharging:
Limited flexibility with regard to installation caused by the belt drive and gas lines; increased exhaust gas and scavenging air quantities; noisy operation; extremely sensitive to increased resistance on the low-pressure side.

Truck diesel engine with exhaust-gas turbocharging, tuned-intake tube supercharging and intercooling. *1 Tuned tubes, 2 Resonance receiver for cylinders 4–5–6, 3 Turbocharger, 4 Compensation receiver, 5 Resonance receiver for cylinders 1–2–3, 6 Radiator, 7 Intercooler, 8 Fan.*

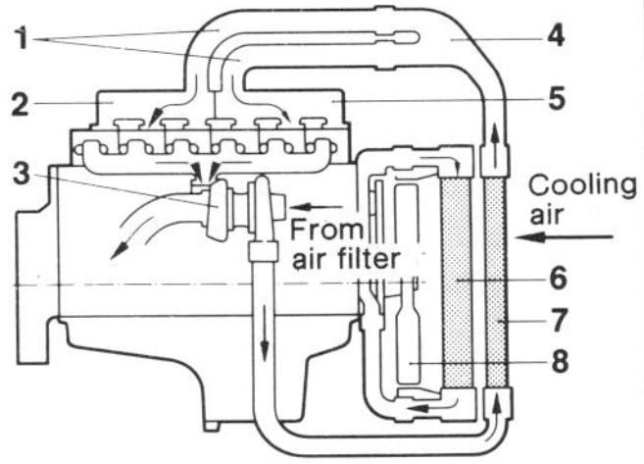

Part-load fuel consumption curves for naturally-aspirated and turbocharged engines of the same power.

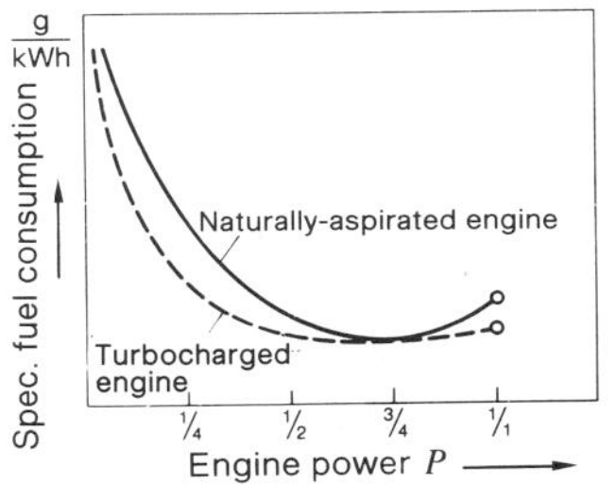

Power transmission in reciprocating-piston engines

Engine types

Mono-piston power unit
The working chamber is formed by the cylinder head, cylinder sleeve and piston.

In-line engine (1)
The cylinders are arranged in a line.

Vee engine (2)
The cylinders are arranged in two planes in a "V" configuration.

Radial engine (3)
The cylinders are arranged radially in one or more planes.

Opposed-cylinder engine (4)
The cylinders are horizontally opposed.

Multi-piston power unit
More than one (usually two) working pistons share a common combustion chamber.

U-engine (5)
The pistons move in the same direction.

Opposed-piston engine (6)
The pistons move in mutual opposition.

Reciprocating-piston engine types

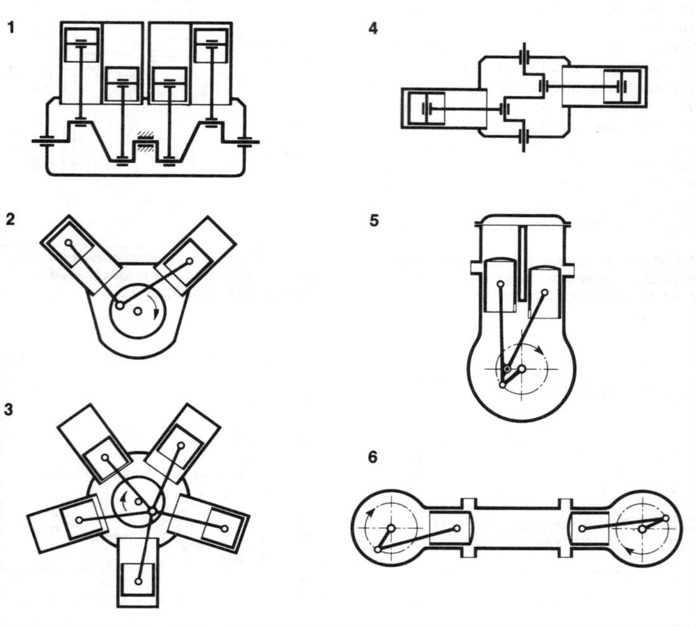

Direction of rotation

(DIN 73 021)[1]

Clockwise (cw) rotation: as viewed looking at the end of the engine opposite the power-output end.

Counterclockwise (ccw) rotation:
as viewed looking at the end of the engine opposite the power-output end.

Numbering the cylinders

(DIN 73 021)[1]

The cylinders are numbered consecutively 1, 2, 3, etc. in the order in which they would be intersected by an imaginary reference plane which, as viewed looking at the end opposite the power-output end, is located horizontally to the left when numbering begins, and which is then moved clockwise about the longitudinal axis of the engine (see figures below). If there is more than one cylinder in a reference plane, the cylinder nearest the observer is assigned the number 1 with subsequent numbers being assigned to the following cylinders. Cylinder 1 is to be identified by the number 1.

Firing order

The firing order is the sequence in which the cylinders fire. It is determined by the engine design, equal ignition intervals, easy-to-manufacture crankshaft design, favorable crankshaft loading etc.

Design	Number of cylinders	Normal firing order (examples)
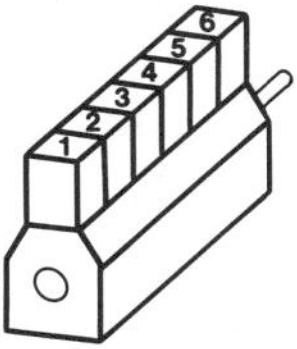	4 5 6 8	1 3 4 2 or 1 2 4 3 1 2 4 5 3 1 5 3 6 2 4 or 1 2 4 6 5 3 or 1 4 2 6 3 5 or 1 4 5 6 3 2 1 6 2 5 8 3 7 4 or 1 3 6 8 4 2 7 5 or 1 4 7 3 8 5 2 6 or 1 3 2 5 8 6 7 4
	4 6 8	1 3 2 4 1 2 5 6 4 3 or 1 4 5 6 2 3 1 6 3 5 4 7 2 8 or 1 5 4 8 6 3 7 2 or 1 8 3 6 4 5 2 7
	4	1 4 3 2

[1]) Applies to motor-vehicle engines only. In the case of internal-combustion engines for general and marine use, the reverse direction (as viewed looking at the power-output end) is standardized (ISO 1204 and 1205, DIN 6265).

Function and dynamics of power-transmission components

The purpose of the piston, connecting rod and crankshaft assembly of the reciprocating-piston engine is to convert the gas forces which are generated during combustion in the working cylinder into reciprocating piston movement and, by means of a crank mechanism, to convert this motion into useful torque available at the power-output end of the engine. The cyclic principle of operation leads to unequal gas forces, and the acceleration and deceleration of the reciprocating power-transmission components generates inertia forces. It is usual to distinguish between internal and external effects of the gas-pressure and inertia forces.

The external effects, consisting of free forces or moments, impart movement to the engine which is transmitted to the engine supports in the form of vibrations. In this context, the smooth running of an engine means freedom from low-frequency vibrations, and quiet running means freedom from high-frequency, audible vibrations.

The internal forces cause periodically changing loads on housing, piston, connecting rod and crankshaft assembly and force-transmission components. This fact must be taken into consideration when determining their dimensions and fatigue strength.

Crank mechanism and gas force

The crank mechanism of a single-cylinder power plant comprises the piston, connecting rod and crankshaft. These components are acted upon by the gas force, thereby causing them to generate inertia forces.

The gas force F_G which acts on the piston can be subdivided into the side forces F_N applied by the piston to the cylinder wall and suppported by it, and the connecting-rod force F_S. The connecting-rod force, in turn, causes the tangential force F_T to be applied at the throw of the crank mechanism. This force together with the crank radius generates the shaft torque and the radial force F_R.

These forces can be calculated as a function of the gas force using the crank angle α, the pivoting angle of the connecting rod β and the connecting-rod ratio λ:

Connecting-rod force: $F_S = F_G/\cos\beta$

Side force: $F_N = F_G \cdot \tan\beta$

Radial force: $F_R = F_G \cdot \cos(\alpha+\beta)/\cos\beta$

Tangential force: $F_T = F_G \cdot \sin(\alpha+\beta)/\cos\beta$

where $\lambda = r/l$; $\sin\beta = \lambda \cdot \sin\alpha$;

$\cos\beta = \sqrt{1-\lambda^2 \cdot \sin^2\alpha}$

All of these relationships can be represented in the form of Fourier series, a favorable method for the representation of vibration calculations.

Piston, con rod and crankshaft assembly of the reciprocating-piston engine
1 Valve train assembly, 2 Piston, 3 Con rod, 4 Crankshaft

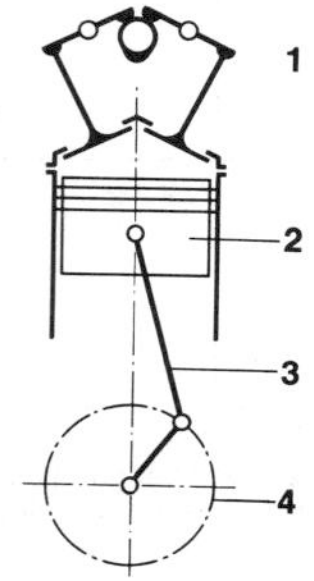

Breakdown of gas force as shown using a single crank mechanism

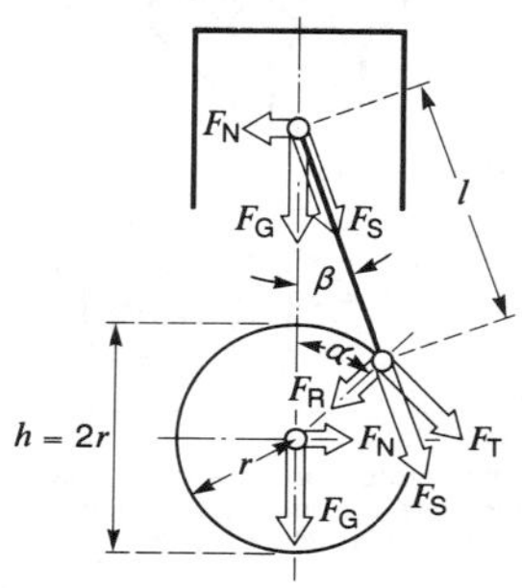

Inertia forces and moments of inertia
The inertial effects of the piston, con rod and crankshaft assembly are composed of the forces of the rotating masses of the crankshaft around their axis (x-axis) and the reciprocating masses in the cylinder direction (z-axis for in-line engines). With multiple-cylinder machines, free moments of inertia occur due to different points of application of gas and inertia forces. The mass effects of a single-cylinder engine can be determined using the piston mass m_K (purely oscillating mass), the crankshaft mass m_W (purely rotating mass) and the corresponding con-rod mass components (usually assumed to consist of oscillating and rotating con-rod masses amounting to one third and two thirds of the total mass respectively):

Oscillating mass
$$m_o = m_{Pl}/3 + m_K$$
Rotating mass
$$m_r = 2\, m_{Pl}/3 + m_W$$
The rotating inertia force acting on the crank is as follows:
$$F_r = m_r \cdot r \cdot \omega^2$$
Oscillating inertia force:
$$F_o = m_o \cdot r \cdot \omega^2 \cdot (\underbrace{\cos\alpha}_{\text{1st Order}} + \underbrace{\lambda \cdot \cos 2\alpha}_{\text{2nd Order}} + \ldots)$$

The following also applies:
$$F_y = r \cdot \omega^2 \cdot m_r \cdot \sin\alpha$$
$$F_z = -r \cdot \omega^2 \cdot [m_r \cdot \cos\alpha + m_o \cdot (A_1 \cdot \cos\alpha + A_2 \cdot \cos 2\alpha + \ldots)]$$

Reference coordinates and inertia forces *(single-cylinder engine).*

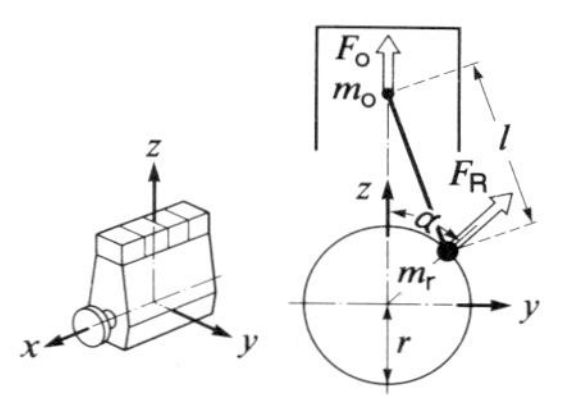

where
$\lambda = r/l$; $A_1 = 1$;
$A_2 = \lambda + 1/4 \cdot \lambda^3 + 15/128 \cdot \lambda^5 \ldots$

The inertia force components are designated as inertia forces of the 1st, 2nd or 4th order, depending upon their rotational frequencies with respect to engine speed.

In general, only the 1st and 2nd order components are significant; higher orders can be disregarded.

In the case of multiple-cylinder engines, free moments of inertia are present if all inertia forces of the entire crank mechanism yield a couple at the crankshaft. Determination of free moments of inertia therefore requires a three-dimensional observation of the crank configuration, whereas the inertia forces can be determined using a two-dimensional system.

Moments of inertia of a crankshaft with three throws (example)

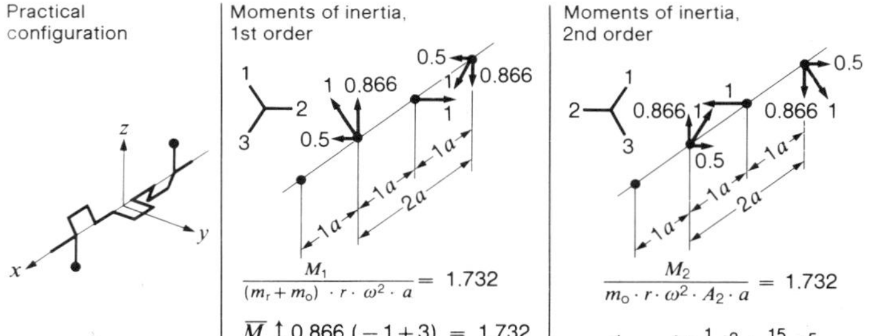

$$\frac{M_1}{(m_r + m_o) \cdot r \cdot \omega^2 \cdot a} = 1.732$$
$$\overline{M} \updownarrow 0.866\,(-1+3) = 1.732$$
$$\overleftrightarrow{M} = 0.5 \cdot 1 - 1 \cdot 2 + 0.5 \cdot 3 = 0$$

$$\frac{M_2}{m_o \cdot r \cdot \omega^2 \cdot A_2 \cdot a} = 1.732$$
$$A_2 = \lambda + \frac{1}{4} \cdot \lambda^3 + \frac{15}{128} \cdot \lambda^5$$

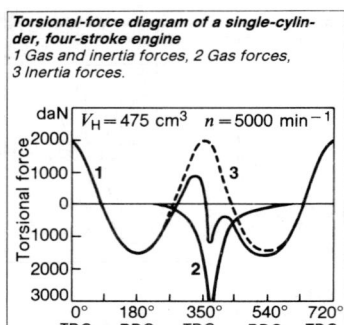

Torsional-force diagram of a single-cylinder, four-stroke engine
1 Gas and inertia forces, 2 Gas forces, 3 Inertia forces.

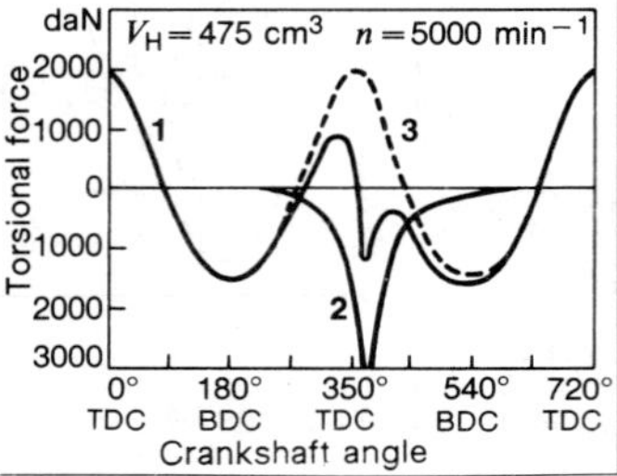

The torsional-force diagram of the reciprocating-piston engine

If the periodically changing gas force acting on the piston and the periodic effects of mass acting on the piston, connecting rod and crankshaft assembly are grouped together, they generate a sum of tangential force components at the crankpin which, when multiplied by the crank radius, yield a periodically changing torque value. If this torque value is referred to the piston surface and the crank radius, the result is a value — tangential pressure — which is independent of engine size. The indicator diagram shows the curve of this pressure value as a function of crank position. It is one of the most important characteristic curves used for assessing dynamic engine behavior.

With multiple-cylinder engines, the tangential pressure curves of the cylinders are superimposed on one another with a phase shift resulting from the number of cylinders, cylinder arrangement, crank arrangement and firing order. The resulting composite curve is characteristic for the engine design, and covers a full working cycle (i.e., 2 crankshaft rotations for 4-stroke engines). It is also called a torsional-force diagram.

By means of a harmonic analysis, the torsional-force diagram can be replaced by a series of sinusoidal oscillations with whole multiples of the basic frequencies which yield the "torsional harmonics". When referred to engine speed, these multiples are also called orders. In the case of the four-stroke engine, half orders are also produced, e.g., the 0.5th order.

In any case, the changing torsional force of reciprocating-piston engines over the course of a working cycle generates a non-uniform rotational speed at the crankshaft end, the so-called coefficient of nonuniformity

$\delta_s = (\omega_{max} - \omega_{min}) / \omega_{min}$,

which can be evened out to an acceptable degree through the use of an energy storage device (flywheel).

Complete 1st and 2nd order balancing of masses in a single-stroke system

Counterweights

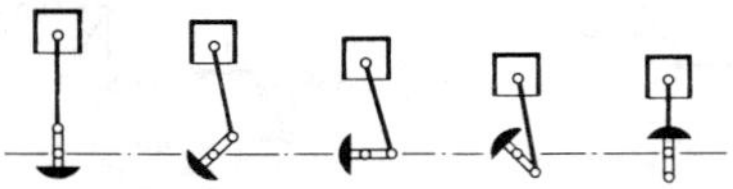

Unbalanced systems rotating in opposite directions

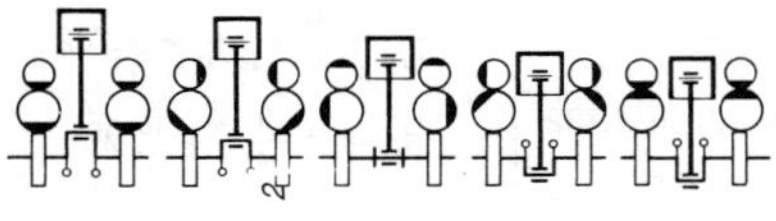

Vector diagrams of the 1st and 2nd order inertia forces.

1st Order

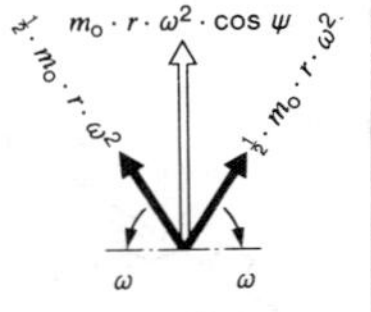

2nd Order

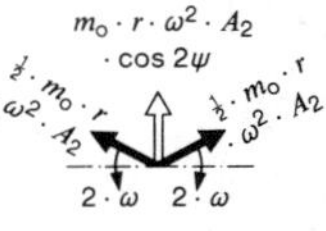

Balancing of masses in the reciprocating-piston engine

The balancing of masses refers to all measures used to partially or completely balance the inertia forces and moments of inertia of crank mechanisms. If no free inertia forces and moments of inertia occur outside the entire engine, all masses are externally balanced. However, forces and moments may still occur internally which subject the engine mounts and housing to loads, and which cause deformation and vibrations. The basic loads imposed by gas and inertia forces are shown in Table 3.

Balancing of inertia forces in the single-stroke system

Rotating masses are the easiest to balance by means of counterweights which oppose the centrifugal force. Oscillating masses generate forces which vary periodically, and which rotate in the 1st order at crankshaft

Table 3. Forces and moments applied to the piston, connecting rod and crankshaft assembly

Forces and moments at the engine	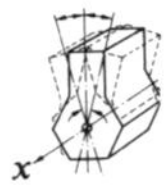	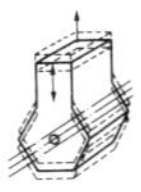	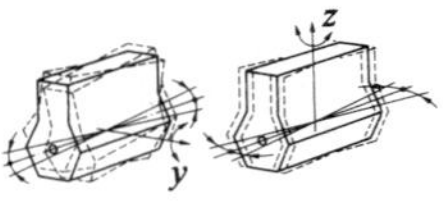	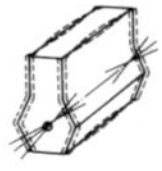
Designation	Oscillating torque, transfer tilting moment, reaction torque	Free inertia force	Free inertia moment, longitudinal tilting moment about the y-axis (transverse axis) ("pitching" moment) about the z-axis (vertical axis) ("rolling" moment)	Internal bending moment
Cause	Tangential gas forces as well as tangential inertia forces for ordinal numbers 1, 2, 3 and 4	Unbalanced oscillating inertia forces 1st order for 1 and 2 cylinders; 2nd order for 1, 2 and 4 cylinders	Unbalanced oscillating inertia forces as a couple of 1st and 2nd order	Rotating and oscillating inertia forces
Actuating variables	Number of cylinders, ignition intervals, displacement, p_i, ε, p_z, m_o, r, ω, λ	Number of cylinders, crank arrangement m_o, r, ω, λ	Number of cylinders, crank arrangement, cylinder interval, counterweight size influences inertia torque components about the y- and z-axis m_o, r, ω, λ, a	Number of throws, crank arrangement, engine length, housing stiffness
Remedy	Can be counteracted only in exceptional cases	Free mass effects can be eliminated by rotating balancing systems, however this process is complex and therefore rare; crank sequences are favored which exhibit no or very few free mass effects		Counterweights, stiff engine housing
	Shielding of the environment through flexible engine mounts (in particular for orders ≥ 2)			

Table 4. Residual inertia forces of the 1st order with differing balancing rate.

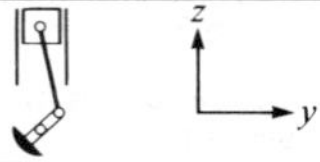		Balancing rate		
		0 %	50 %	100 %
Size of counterweight	$m_G \triangleq$	m_r	$m_r + 0.5\, m_0$	$m_r + m_0$
Residual inertia force (z) of the 1st order	$F_{1z} =$	$m_0 \cdot r \cdot \omega^2$	$0.5 \cdot m_0 \cdot r \cdot \omega^2$	0
Residual inertia force (y) of the 1st order	$F_{1y} =$	0	$0.5 \cdot m_0 \cdot r \cdot \omega^2$	$m_0 \cdot r \cdot \omega^2$

speed, and at double the crankshaft speed in the 2nd order. Balancing can be achieved by using unbalanced systems rotating in opposite directions at crankshaft speed and double the crankshaft speed. The forces thus generated must have the magnitude of the rotating inertia-force vectors, and must act in the opposite direction.

Balancing rate
The counterweights necessary to balance the rotating masses can be increased by a certain percentage of the oscillating mass such that the oscillating force acting in the direction of movement of the cylinders (z) is counteracted. The percentage of this inertia force which is counteracted then appears in the y-axis. The ratio of the

Table 5. Crank arrangements of the 1st and 2nd order for three- to six-cylinder, in-line engines.

	3-cylinder	4-cylinder	5-cylinder	6-cylinder
Crank sequence	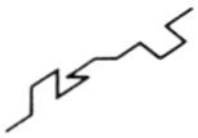		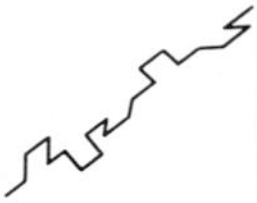	
1st order crank arrangement	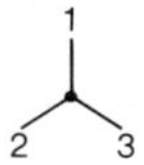			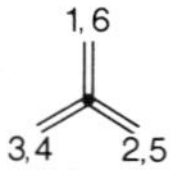
2nd order crank arrangement	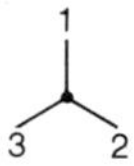			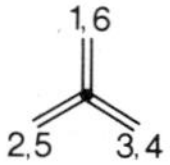

inertia force component which is counteracted in the z-axis to the initial value of the 1st order inertia force is termed the balancing rate (Table 4).

Balancing of inertia forces in the multi-cylinder engine
In the case of multi-cylinder engines, the selection of the crank arrangement (throw sequence), and thus engine design, is largely influenced by the mutual balancing of the inertia forces of the crank mechanism. The inertia forces are balanced if the common center of gravity of all of the moving piston, connecting-rod and crankshaft-assembly components lies in the center of the crankshaft, i.e., if the crankshaft is symmetrical as viewed from the front. The symmetry of the crankshaft is checked using the so-called 1st and 2nd-order crank arrangements. In the four-cylinder, in-line engine there is no symmetry in the 2nd-order crank arrangement. Thus large free inertia forces exist for this order. These forces can be balanced through the use of two countershafts rotating in opposite directions at twice the crankshaft speed (Lanchester balancing system).

Balancing inertia forces and gas forces
The tangential gas forces supply an additional periodic torque which can be detected as the reaction torque of the engine housing. In a four-cylinder in-line engine, overall free 2nd-order forces and oscillating torque values result from the 2nd-order tangential inertia forces and gas forces. 2nd-order balancing of masses and a reduction of the 2nd-order torque values can be achieved in this case via 2 offset countershafts.

Balancing inertia force and oscillating torque of the 2nd order in a four-cylinder, in-line engine via two offset countershafts.
1 Inertia torque only; 2 Gas torque only or complete balancing of inertia torque, $z_I - z_{II} = -2B_2/A_2 \cdot r$; 3 Gas and inertia torque without torque balancing; 4 Gas and inertia torque with half of the inertia torque balanced, $z_I - z_{II} \approx 0.5 \cdot l$.

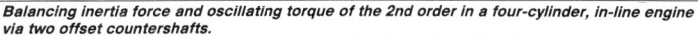

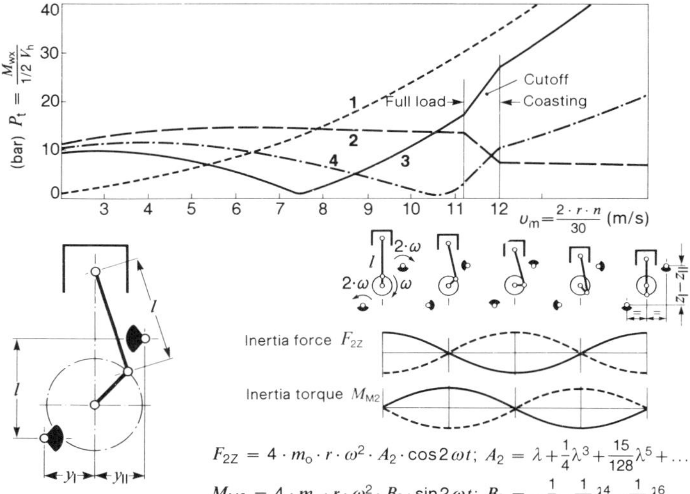

$$F_{2Z} = 4 \cdot m_o \cdot r \cdot \omega^2 \cdot A_2 \cdot \cos 2\omega t;\ A_2 = \lambda + \frac{1}{4}\lambda^3 + \frac{15}{128}\lambda^5 + \dots$$

$$M_{M2} = 4 \cdot m_o \cdot r \cdot \omega^2 \cdot B_2 \cdot \sin 2\omega t;\ B_2 = -\frac{1}{2} - \frac{1}{32}\lambda^4 - \frac{1}{32}\lambda^6$$

Table 6. Free forces and moments of the 1st and 2nd order, and ignition intervals of the most common engine designs.

$F_r = m_r \cdot r \cdot \omega^2$ $\qquad F_1 = m_0 \cdot r \cdot \omega^2 \cdot \cos\alpha$ $\qquad F_2 = m_0 \cdot r \cdot \omega^2 \cdot \lambda \cdot \cos 2\alpha$

Cylinder arrangement	Free forces of the 1st order[1])	Free forces of the 2nd order	Free moments of the 1st order[1])	Free moments of the 2nd order	Ignition intervals
3-cylinder					
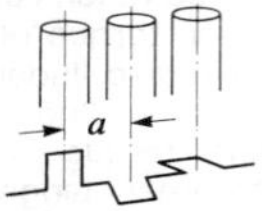 In-line, 3 throws	0	0	$\sqrt{3} \cdot F_1 \cdot a$	$\sqrt{3} \cdot F_2 \cdot a$	240°/240°
4-cylinder					
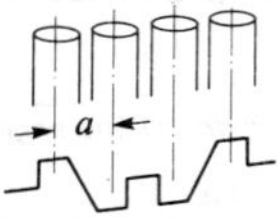 In-line, 4 throws	0	$4 \cdot F_2$	0	0	180°/180°
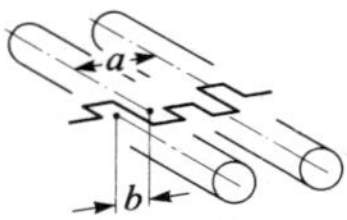 Opposed-cylinder 4 throws	0	0	0	$2 \cdot F_2 \cdot b$	180°/180°
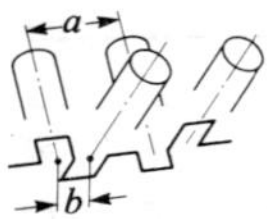 V 60°, 4 throws	0	$2\sqrt{3} \cdot F_2$	$F_1 \cdot a$	$3\,F_2 \cdot b/2$	180°/180°
5-cylinder					
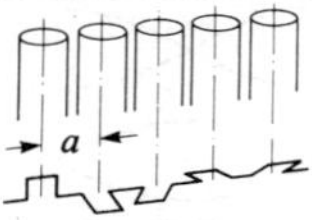 In-line, 5 throws	0	0	$0.449 \cdot F_1 \cdot a$	$4.98 \cdot F_2 \cdot a$	144°/144°

[1]) Without counterweights.

Cylinder arrangement	Free forces of the 1st order[1]	Free forces of the 2nd order	Free moments of the 1st order[1]	Free moments of the 2nd order	Ignition intervals
6-cylinder					
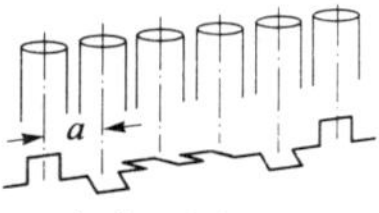 In-line, 6 throws	0	0	0	0	120°/120°
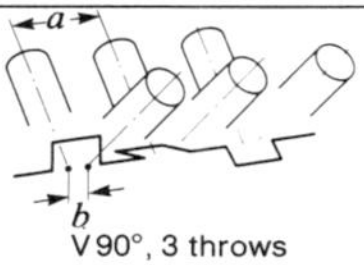 V 90°, 3 throws	0	0	$\sqrt{3} \cdot F_1 \cdot a$ [2]	$\sqrt{6} \cdot F_2 \cdot a$	150°/90° 150°/90°
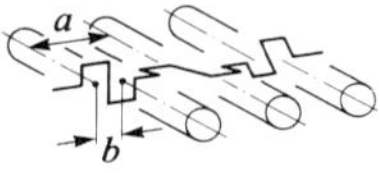 Opposed-cylinder, 6 throws	0	0	0	0	120°/120°
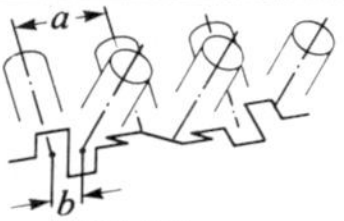 V 60°, 6 throws	0	0	$3\,F_1 \cdot a/2$	$3\,F_2 \cdot a/2$	120°/120°
8-cylinder					
 V 90°, 4 throws in two planes	0	0	$\sqrt{10} \cdot F_1 \cdot a$ [2]	0	90°/90°
12-cylinder					
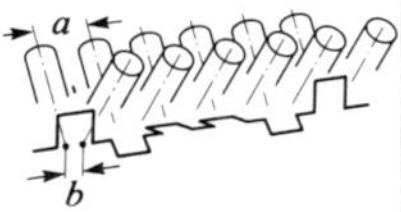 V 60°, 6 throws	0	0	0	0	60°/60°

[1]) Without counterweights. [2]) Can be completely balanced by using counterweights.

Main components of the reciprocating-piston engine

The piston

The piston in today's motor-vehicle engine must perform several functions:

— It must transfer the combustion gas forces to the connecting rod.

— As a crosshead, it must guide the connecting rod in the cylinder.

— It must support the normal force against the cylinder wall which is generated as cylinder pressure is converted into connecting-rod force.

— It must seal the combustion chamber from the crankcase through the use of sealing elements.

— It must dissipate its heat energy to the coolant.

In addition, the piston shape and the manner in which combustion gas forces are transferred via the piston pin to the connecting rod are determined largely by combustion-chamber shape and thus the piston-crown shape, as well as by the type of combustion process used and its maximum combustion pressures. The piston, the piston pin and the piston-pin bearings must be very carefully designed due to the combustion forces, the requirement that piston weight be as low as possible and the temperatures which occur at the piston. These factors together impose a load which can approach the piston-material strength limit.

Piston shapes in various engine designs

1 Strip inserts for expansion control.

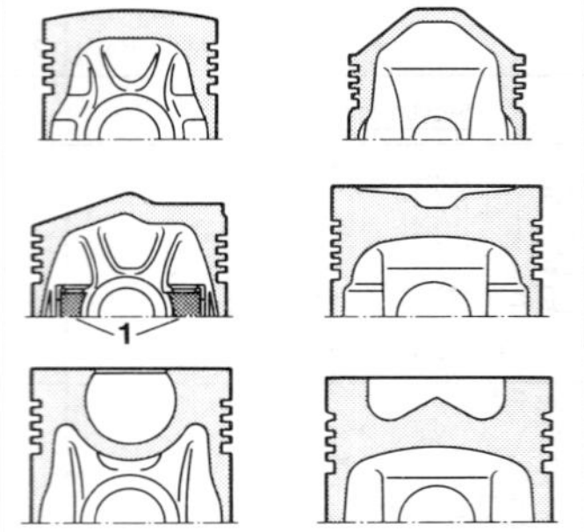

The most often used materials for cylinder liners and pistons are gray cast iron and aluminum. Piston and cylinder liner have different coefficients of expansion. Piston play in the cylinder, though, must be kept to a minimum in order to reduce noise (piston slap) and improve sealing. To this end, steel strips or the like are sometimes cast into the piston to limit its expansion. Piston rings are used to seal the combustion chamber from the engine crankcase. The two top rings are gas seals. At least one additional ring (usually a special shape) serves as oil control ring, and maintains proper oil conditions at the piston and its other rings.

Operating temperatures at the pistons of motor-vehicle engines at full load (schematic)

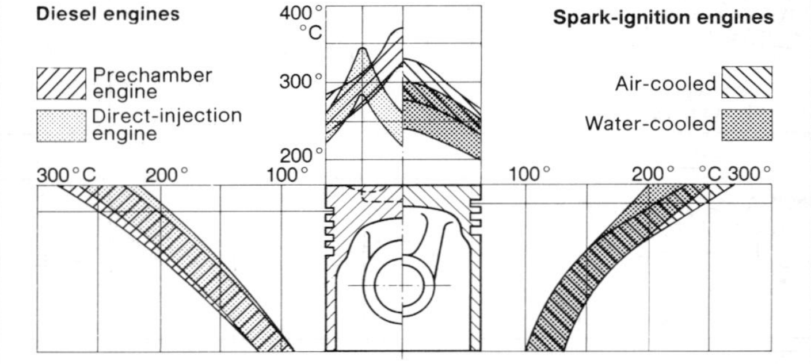

Piston-ring shapes and arrangement

Diesel engine: *1 T-ring, barrel-faced keystone ring, 2 M-ring, taper-faced compression ring with inside bevel, 3 M-ring, taper-faced napier compression ring, 4 Spring-loaded D-ring.*

Spark-ignition engine: *5 R-ring, barrel-faced plain compression ring, 6 M-ring, taper-faced compression ring with inside bevel, 7 Napier ring, 8 D-ring, narrow-land drain-oil control ring, 9 Multi-piece steel oil ring.*

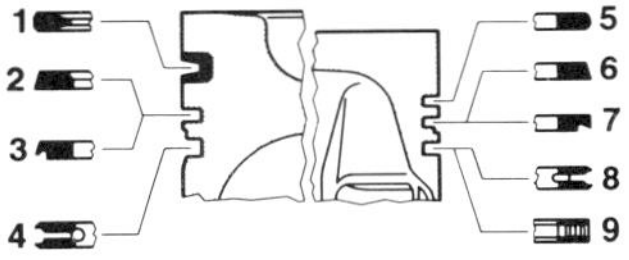

Connecting rod of a passenger-car engine

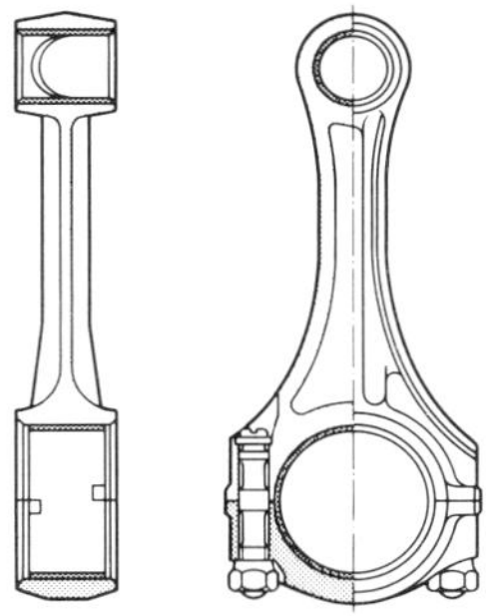

Due to their in some cases very high pretensioning forces, piston rings are a major source of friction in the reciprocating-piston engine.

Connecting rod

The connecting rod connects the piston to the crankshaft. It is subjected to very high tensile, compression and bending stresses and carries the bearings for the piston pin and the crank pin. The length of the connecting rod is determined by the piston stroke and the counterweight radius if the height of the engine is an important factor (usually the case in vehicle engines).

Crankshaft throw

Primary stresses and deformations due to gas pressure and inertia forces.

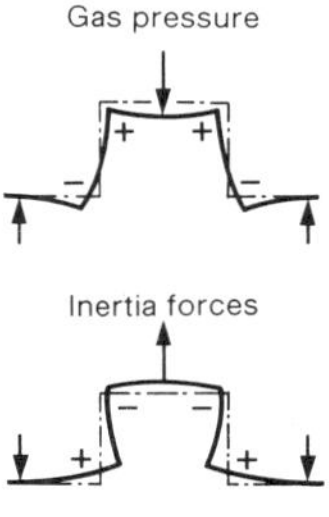

Crankshaft

By means of crankshaft throws, piston reciprocating movements are transferred by the connecting rods to the crankshaft where they are available as usable torque at the crankshaft end.

As a result of forces, torques and bending moments which are highly variable in time and location, as well as the resulting vibrations, the crankshaft is subjected to very high and complex loading. Its design must therefore incorporate careful and precise calculations and dimensions with regard to strength and vibrational characteristics. Design is even more difficult because the system is statically indeterminate due to the multiple bearing points which exist in almost every case.

The number of crankshaft bearings is primarily determined by overall load factor and maximum engine speed. All diesel engine crankshafts have a bearing after each throw due to the high working pressures, as do the crankshafts of highly-loaded, high-speed spark-ignition engines.

The crankshafts of some smaller SI-engines which are not so highly loaded have a bearing only after every second crankshaft throw for cost reasons. The number of counterweights also depends upon the above-mentioned criteria. Materials and manufacturing processes used are also determined by the engine loading.

Highly-stressed crankshafts are usually drop-forged. In smaller engines and in engines subject to lower loads, cast crankshafts are being used more and more for cost and weight reasons.

Cast crankshaft

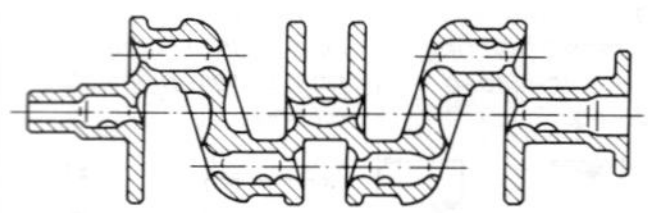

Crankshaft vibrations

Bending vibrations are significant only on engines with a small number of cylinders, because the crankshaft and the necessary large flywheel form an oscillatory system with a low natural frequency. Beginning with 3-cylinder engines, bending vibrations are uncritical. By logical extension, this also applies to the crankshaft longitudinal vibrations induced by bending vibrations. But, with increasing numbers of cylinders, the torsional vibrations of the resonant system formed by crankshaft, connecting rod and piston are dangerous. This system, in which connecting rod and piston exhibit varying mass moments of inertia depending upon crank angle, can be calculated by reducing it to a smooth, flexible shaft free of inertia with equivalent masses mounted on it. Having reduced the resonant system to the model described, its natural frequencies and vibrational impacts can now be determined.

Vibrational schematic of a 6-cylinder crankshaft (K) with flywheel (S) and transmission (G)
a Relative amplitudes, *n* engine speed.

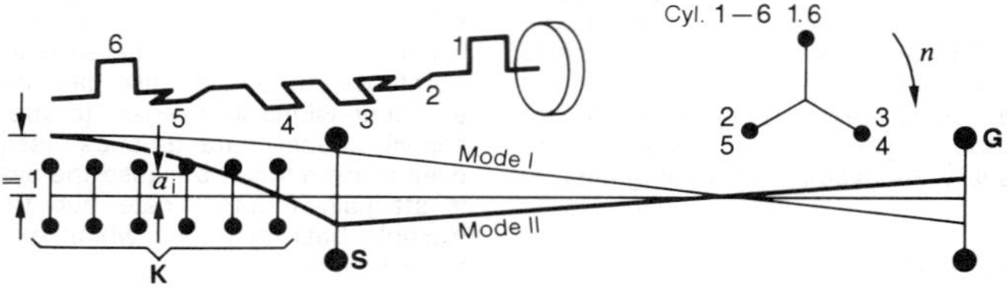

Order analysis of the crankshaft vibrations of a 6-cylinder engine, with differing firing orders, *a* Relative amplitudes

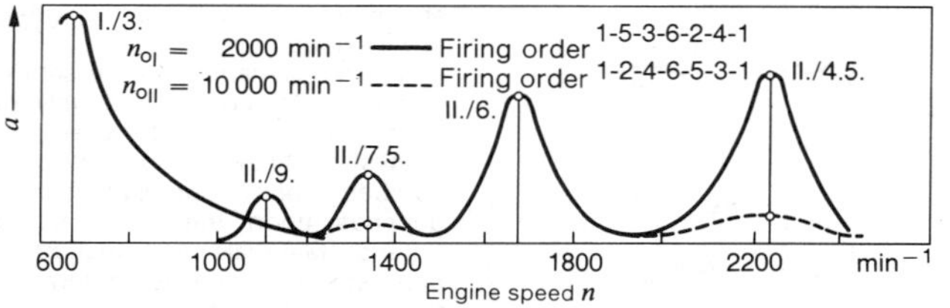

Vibrations are induced by the tangential forces at the crank pin which are composed of gas forces and oscillating inertia forces. The torsional vibrations of the crankshaft must be reduced to uncritical values through the use of vibration dampers (e.g., bonded rubber vibration dampers or viscous vibration dampers).

Crankcase
The function of the crankcase is to transfer forces between the cylinder head and the piston, connecting rod and crankshaft assembly, to support this assembly and the moving pistons, and to make an oil- and water-tight seal between the piston, connecting rod and crankshaft assembly and the coolant areas. In addition, most of the non-integral engine components are mounted on the crankcase.

On all motor-vehicle engines, the cast crankcase is standard equipment. In it, the gas forces are induced via cylinder-head bolts, which further transmit these forces to the main bearings via load-bearing transverse walls in a flow of force which is as rectilinear and free of bending moments as possible. For reasons of strength, the crankcase often extends underneath the center of the crankshaft. In spark-ignition engines, the pistons run in integrally-cast cylinder liners. In diesel engines, separate dry or wet liners made of special wear-free materials are usually used.

Whereas crankcases for truck engines are almost exclusively made of gray cast iron, crankcases for passenger-car engines are increasingly being made of aluminum in order to decrease engine weight.

Cylinder head
The cylinder head closes off the crankcase and the cylinder at the top, as well as housing the gas-exchange devices, spark plugs and/or injectors. Together with the piston, it also forms the desired combustion-chamber shape. In the vast majority of passenger-car engines, the entire valve timing gear is also mounted in the cylinder head.

Cylinder-head designation with respect to intake and exhaust passages
1 Crossflow design, 2 Counterflow design

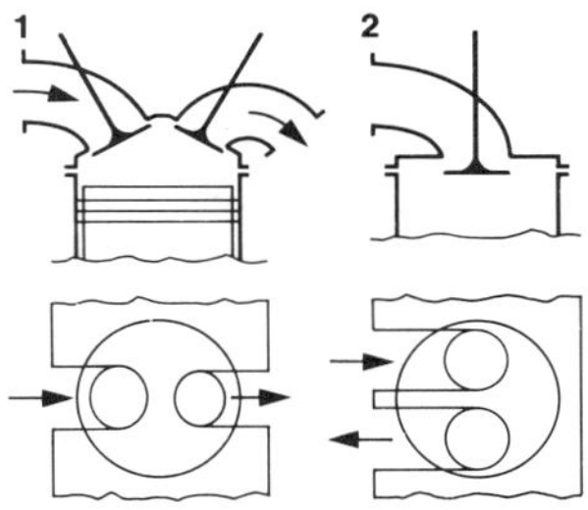

There are two basic designs, depending upon the way in which the gases are exchanged:

– Counterflow cylinder head: Intake and exhaust passages open on the same side of the cylinder head. This limits the available space for fresh-air and exhaust-gas lines, but greatly eases supercharging because its gas passages are very short. It also provides advantages in terms of line routing in transversely-mounted vehicle engines.

– Crossflow cylinder head: Intake and exhaust-gas lines are located on opposite sides of the engine, resulting in a diagonal flow of fresh air and exhaust gas. This provides more freedom for routing the lines, and facilitates sealing.

In truck and large industrial engines, individual cylinder heads are often used for each cylinder for reasons of sealing-force distribution, maintenance and repair. In air-cooled engines, individual cylinder heads are additionally used in order to promote cooling.

In passenger-car and small-scale engines, one cylinder head is usually used for all cylinders. The cylinder heads of water-cooled diesel truck engines are usually made of gray cast iron. Air-cooled cylinder heads, as well as the cylinder heads of nearly all passenger car spark-ignition and diesel engines, are made of aluminum for reasons of thermal conductivity and weight.

Valve timing-gear designs *(Source: Hütten: "Motoren").*
1 Push-rod assembly, 2 Finger follower or single rocker-arm assembly actuated by overhead cam, 3 Twin rocker-arm assembly actuated by overhead cam, 4 Overhead bucket tappet assembly. OHV = Overhead Valves, OHC = Overhead Camshaft, DOHC = Double Overhead Camshaft.

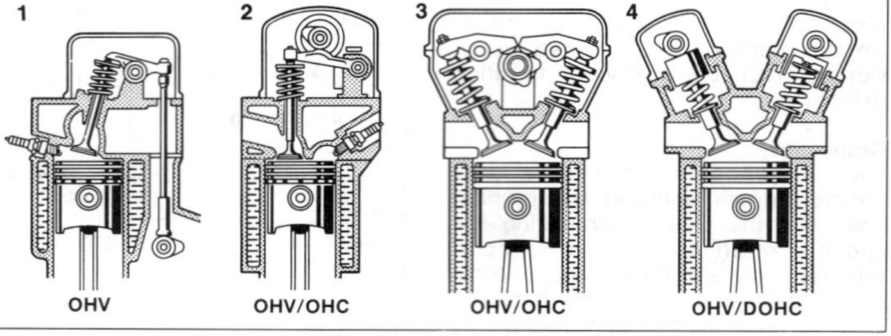

Valve-train assembly
The function of the valve-train assembly in a 4-stroke engine is to enable and to control the exchange of gases in the IC engine (see p. 368). The valve-train assembly includes the intake and exhaust valves, the springs which close them, the cam driving assembly and the force-transmission components.

Valve timing-gear designs
In the following widely-used designs the camshaft is located in the cylinder head:
– Overhead bucket tappet assembly, in which the "bucket", which moves back and forth in the cylinder head, absorbs the lateral force of the cam, and transfers the cam force to the valve.
– Finger follower or single rocker-arm assembly actuated by an overhead cam, in which cam force and lateral cam force are absorbed and transformed by a lever in the cylinder head which oscillates between the valve and the cam. The intervening rocker arm can also be designed to act as a cam lift multiplier in order to absorb lateral forces and to transmit cam force.
– Twin rocker-arm assembly actuated by overhead cam, in which the rocker arm moves about an axis located between the camshaft and the valve. Here too, the rocker arm is usually designed as a cam lift multiplier, thereby producing the desired valve lift.

With a crankcase-mounted camshaft, the rocker arm is not actuated directly by the cam but by an intervening push rod and a tappet (push-rod assembly).

Valve arrangement
The type of valve timing-gear assembly is determined mainly by the combustion-chamber shape. Today, nearly all valve timing-gear assemblies are of the overhead type mounted in the cylinder head. In diesel engines and spark-ignition engines subject to lower loads, the valves are parallel to the cylinder axis, and are usually actuated by twin rocker arms, bucket tappets or single rocker arms. In today's spark-ignition engine designs in which power is a primary consideration, valves are increasingly being tilted toward one another. This configuration, with a given cylinder diameter, enables larger valve diameters and more favorable routing of intake and exhaust passages. Twin rocker-arm assemblies actuated by overhead cams are used most often here. High-performance and racing engines are increasingly using four valves per cylinder and overhead-bucket-tappet valve assemblies.

The valve-timing diagram of an engine shows the opening and closing times of the valves, the valve lift curve and the maximum valve lift, as well as valve velocity and valve acceleration.

Valve timing diagram showing valve lift (s), valve velocity (s′) and valve acceleration (s″)

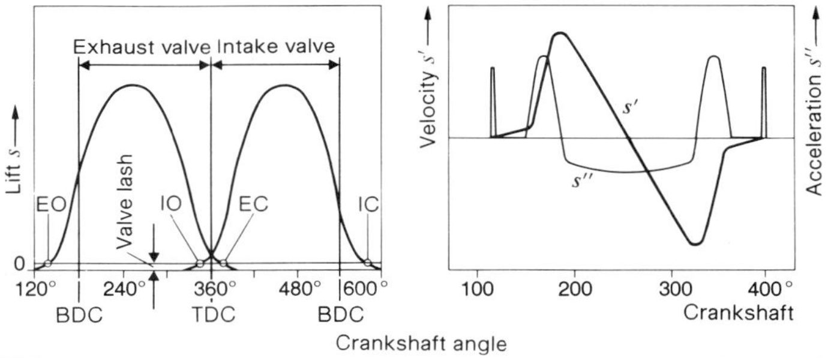

Customary valve acceleration values for passenger-car valve-train assemblies with overhead camshafts are as follows:
$s'' = 60 \dots 65$ mm $(b/\omega^2) \triangleq 6400$ m/s^2 at 6000 min^{-1} for single and twin rocker-arm assemblies,
$s'' = 70 \dots 80$ mm $(b/\omega^2) \triangleq 7900$ m/s^2 at 6000 min^{-1} for overhead-bucket tappet assemblies. For commercial-vehicle engines with bottom-mounted camshafts:
$s'' = 100 \dots 120$ $(b/\omega^2) \triangleq 2000$ m/s^2 at 2400 min^{-1}.

Valve, valve guide and valve seat
Valves are made of materials which are heat-resistant and resistant to scale. In many cases the valve seat area is hard-faced. In the case of the exhaust valve, thermal conductivity has been improved by filling the hollow stem with sodium. To improve the stability and sealing characteristics of valves, valve rotating systems (roto caps) are often used in modern valve-train assemblies. These mechanisms impart an additional rotary motion to the valves.

The valve guides of high-performance engines must have high thermal conductivity and good anti-friction properties. Valve guides are usually pressed into the cylinder head and often have valve stem seals on their cold ends in order to reduce oil consumption. Valve seat wear is generally reduced by making the valve seats out of cast or sintered materials and shrink-fitting them in the cylinder head.

Cam design and control dynamics
The function of the cam is to open and close the valves as far as possible, as fast as possible and as smoothly as possible. The closing force for the valves is applied by the valve springs which are also responsible for maintaining contact between the cam and the valves. Dynamic forces impose limits on cam and valve lift.

The entire valve-train assembly can be viewed as a spring/mass system in which the conversion from stored to free energy causes forced vibration. Valve-train assemblies with overhead camshafts can be represented with sufficient accuracy by a 1-mass system (consisting of the moving mass, the valve-train assembly stiffness and corresponding damping).

For systems with bottom-mounted camshafts and push rods, a 2-mass system is being increasingly used.

The maximum permissible contact stress, usually regarded as the parameter which limits cam-lobe radius and the rate of opening on the flank, currently lies between 600 and 750 N/mm^2 depending upon the material pairings used.

Cooling

In order to avoid thermal overload, combustion of the lubricating oil on the piston sliding surface and uncontrolled combustion due to excessive component temperatures, the components surrounding the hot combustion chamber (cylinder liner, cylinder head, valves and in some cases the pistons themselves) must be intensively cooled.

Direct cooling

Direct air cooling, removes heat directly from the components by means of intensive air flow through the usually finned surface. Although used primarily in motorcycle and aircraft engines, this form of cooling is also employed for some passenger-car and commercial-vehicle diesel and spark-ignition engines. Its main advantage is its high reliability and freedom from maintenance. The design measures required to ensure efficient heat dissipation to the cooling air increases the cost of the components however.

Indirect cooling

Because water has a high specific heat capacity and exhibits good thermal transition to the material, most vehicle engines today are water-cooled. The air/water recirculation cooling system is the most prevalent system. It comprises a closed circuit which allows the use of anti-corrosion and anti-freeze additives. The coolant is pumped through the engine and through an air/water radiator. The cooling air flows naturally through the radiator as the vehicle is driven, or is forced through it by a fan. The coolant temperature is regulated by a thermostatic valve which bypasses the radiator when necessary.

Lubrication

The internal-combustion engine uses oil in order to lubricate and cool all of the power-transmission components. The lube oil is also used to remove dirt and neutralize chemically-active combustion products, as well as to transmit forces and damp vibrations. The oil can only comply with all these requirements if it is transported in adequate quantities to the engine's critical points, and if its properties are adapted to the specific requirements by appropriate measures taken during manufacture (for instance the inclusion of additives).

In total-loss lubrication (fresh-oil lubrication), a metering system provides oil to the points to be lubricated, where the oil is then consumed. A special case of this type of lubrication is mixture lubrication in which oil is either added to the fuel in a ratio of from 1:20 to 1:100, or metered to the engine (this process is used primarily in small two-stroke engines).

In most motor-vehicle engines, force-feed lubrication systems are used in combination with splash and oil mist lubrication. In this system, oil is pumped under pressure (usually by a gear pump) to all bearing points, whereas sliding parts are lubricated by splash lubrication systems and oil mist.

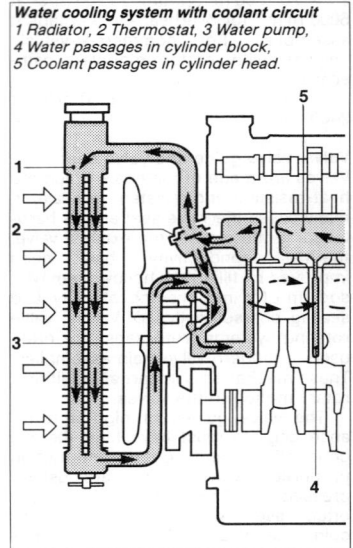

Water cooling system with coolant circuit
1 Radiator, 2 Thermostat, 3 Water pump, 4 Water passages in cylinder block, 5 Coolant passages in cylinder head.

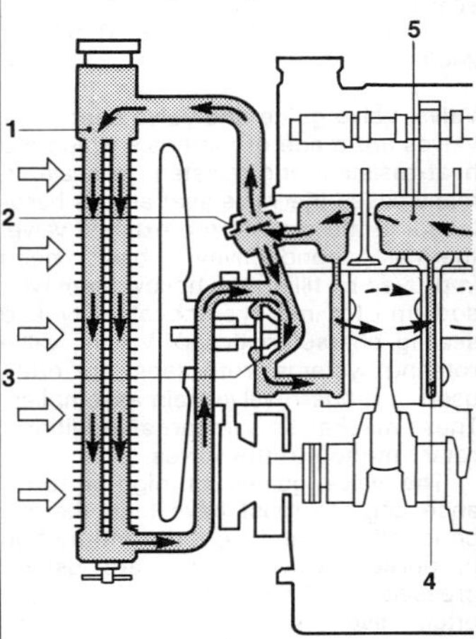

After flowing through the bearing points and sliding parts, the oil collects below the piston, connecting rod and crankshaft assembly in the oil sump. This serves to cool the oil, and to remove the foam by settling, while at the same time acting as a reservoir. Engines subject to high loads are also fitted with an oil cooler. Engine service life is significantly prolonged by keeping the engine lube oil clean.

Oil filters

Oil filters remove solid particles from the engine oil (combustion residue, metal particles and dust) and maintain the lubricating capability of the oil during maintenance intervals. Oil-filter dimensions are governed by the degree to which impurities are generated in the motor and the maintenance interval prescribed by the engine manufacturer. Filter maintenance and oil changes should be performed at the same time.

Full-flow filters protect the entire oil circuit because particles which cause wear are trapped during their first pass through the circuit. Paper fine filters have proven suitable as filter elements in the full-flow circuit. Their degree of filtration is significantly finer than strainers or disk filters. Full-flow filters must be fitted with a bypass valve in order to ensure that the engine continues to be supplied with oil if the filter gets clogged. These should always be installed in the oil circuit downstream of the pressure regulating valve. Full-flow filters usually incorporate replaceable elements.

Bypass filters remove only about 5... 10 % of the oil from the engine's lubricating system, and return this to the sump after filtering. Most bypass filters are of the fiber-filling type. It is recommended that such filters are used only in conjunction with full-flow filters. The finest particles (primarily soot) which have not been removed by the full-flow filter, are filtered out by the bypass filter, thus leading to a reduction in the concentration of very fine pollutants in the oil.

Force-feed lubrication system

1 Pressure relief valve 2 Oil filter, 3 Gear pump, 4 From main bearing to connecting-rod bearing, 5 Suction strainer, 6 Main oil-pressure line to crankshaft bearings, 7 Return flow from timing-gear case to crankcase, 8 To camshaft bearings.

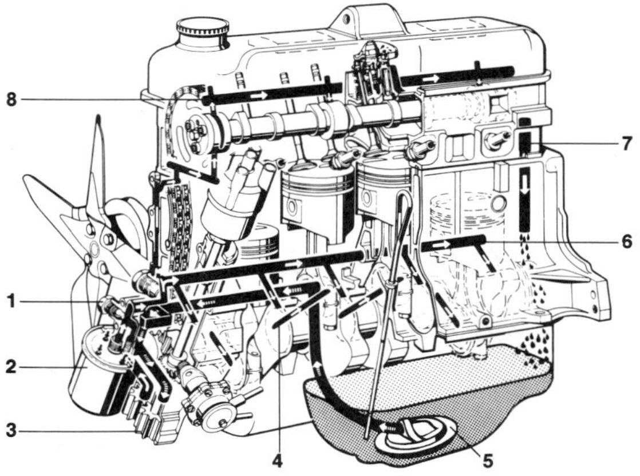

Empirical values and data for calculation

Comparisons

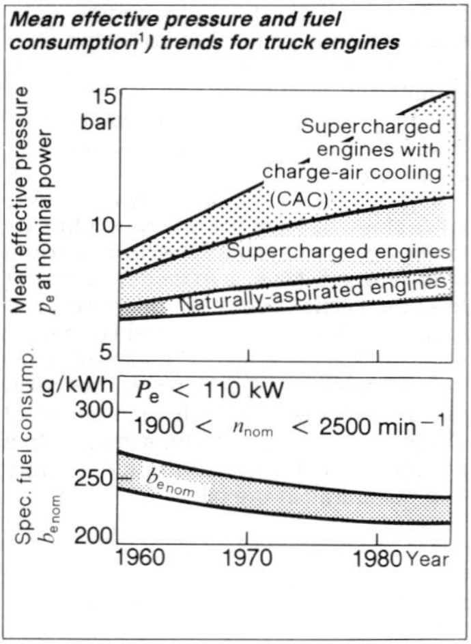

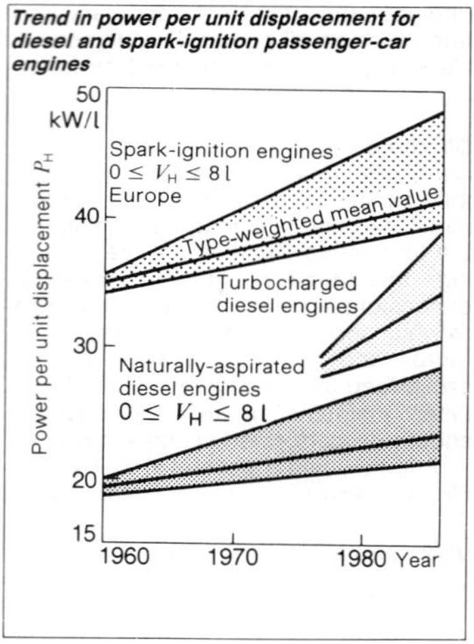

[1]) See page 323 for on-the-vehicle measures influencing fuel consumption

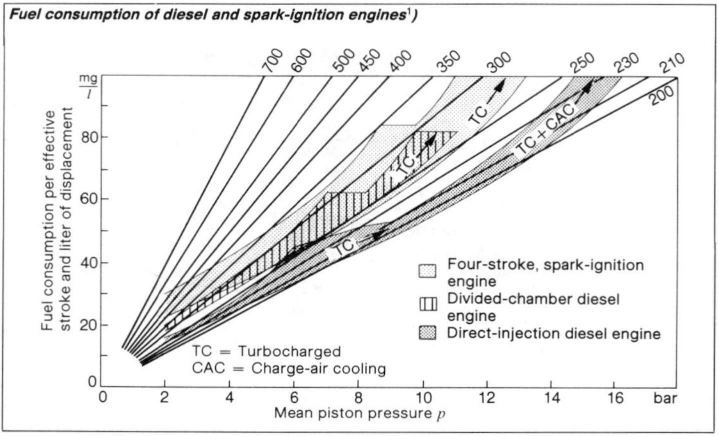

Comparative data

Type of engine		Engine speed min⁻¹	Compression ratio	Mean effective pressure bar	Power per unit displacement kW/l	Weight to power ratio kg/kW	Fuel consumption g/kWh	Torque increase %
SI engine for motorcycles and mopeds	2-stroke	4500 ... 8000	7 ... 9	4 ... 6	30 ... 50	5 ... 2.5	600 ... 400	5 ... 10
	4-stroke	5000 ... 9000	8 ... 11	7 ... 10	30 ... 70	4 ... 1	350 ... 270	5 ... 25
Passenger cars	Naturally-asp. engine	4500 ... 7500	8 ... 12	8 ... 11	35 ... 65	3 ... 1	350 ... 250	15 ... 25
	Turbo/superch. eng.	5000 ... 7000	7 ... 9	11 ... 15	50 ... 100	3 ... 1	380 ... 280	10 ... 30
Trucks		2500 ... 5000	7 ... 9	8 ... 10	20 ... 30	6 ... 3	380 ... 270	15 ... 25
Diesel engine for Pass. car	Naturally-aspirated	3500 ... 5000	20 ... 24	6 ... 8	20 ... 30	5 ... 3	320 ... 240	10 ... 15
	Turbo/supercharged	3500 ... 4500	20 ... 24	9 ... 12	30 ... 40	4 ... 2	290 ... 240	15 ... 25
Trucks	Naturally-aspirated	2000 ... 4000	16 ... 18	7 ... 10	10 ... 15	9 ... 4	240 ... 210	10 ... 15
	Turbo/supercharged	2000 ... 3200	15 ... 17	10 ... 13	15 ... 20	8 ... 3	230 ... 205	15 ... 30
	With CAC[1])	1800 ... 2600	14 ... 16	13 ... 18	20 ... 25	5 ... 3	225 ... 195	30 ... 60
Special designs	Rotary engine	6000 ... 8000	7 ... 9	8 ... 11	35 ... 45	1.5 ... 1	380 ... 300	5 ... 15
	Stirling engine	2000 ... 4500	4 ... 6	–	–	10 ... 7	300 ... 240	20 ... 40
	Gas turbine	8000...70 000	4 ... 6	–	–	3 ... 1	1000 ... 300	50...100

[1]) CAC: charge-air cooling.

Power and torque curves

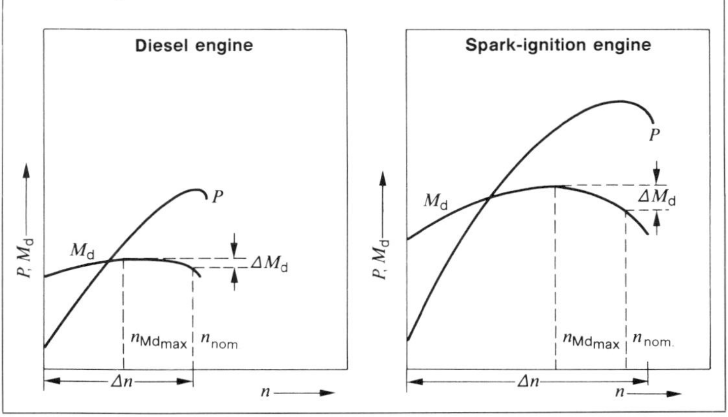

Performance curves *(part-load behavior)*
for a specific control-rack travel or specific accelerator position.

Characteristics of a diesel engine with constant control-rack position.
M_d remains roughly constant with n.

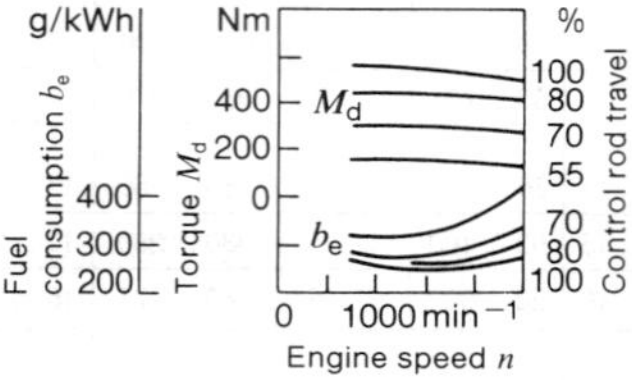

Characteristics of a carburetor spark-ignition engine (four-stroke) with constant throttle-valve position.
M_d drops rapidly as n increases;
P_{eff} remains roughly constant.

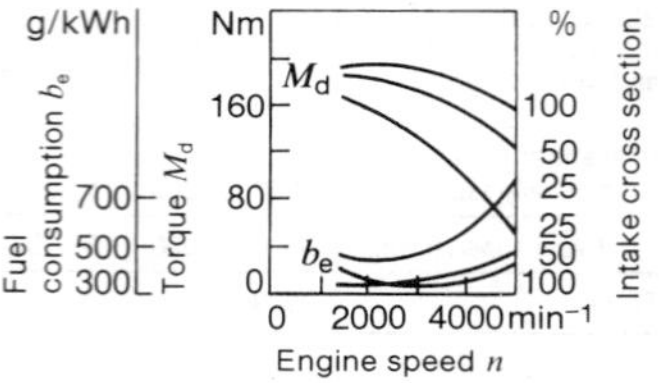

Maximum torque position
The position on the total engine-speed curve (relative to rpm for max. output) at which maximum torque is developed, specified in % ($n_{Md\,max}/n_{nominal} \cdot 100$).

Useful speed range
(minimum full-load speed/nominal speed)

Type of engine	Useful speed range Δn_N	Max. torque position %
Diesel engine for passenger cars	3.5 ... 5	15 ... 40
for trucks	1.8 ... 3.2	10 ... 60
Spark-ignition engine	4 ... 7	25 ... 35

Torque increase

Type of engine	Torque increase M_d in %
Diesel engine for passenger cars	
Nat. aspirated engine	15 ... 20
Turbo/supercharged eng.	20 ... 30
Diesel engine for trucks	
Nat. aspirated engine	10 ... 15
Turbo/supercharged eng.	15 ... 30
With CAC[1])	25 ... 60
Spark-ignition engine	
Nat. aspirated engine	25 ... 30
Turbo/supercharged eng.	30 ... 35

[1]) CAC: charge-air cooling.

Engine output, atmospheric conditions
The torque and thus the power output of an internal-combustion engine are essentially determined by the calorific content of the cylinder charge. The amount of air (or, more precisely, of oxygen) in the cylinder charge provides a direct index of calorific content. The change which the engine will display at full power can be calculated as a function of variations in the condition of the ambient air (temperature, barometric pressure, humidity), provided that engine speed, A/F ratio, volumetric efficiency, combustion efficiency and total engine power loss remain constant. The A/F mixture responds to lower atmospheric density by becoming richer. The volumetric efficiency (pressure in cylinder at BDC relative to pressure in ambient atmosphere) only remains constant for all atmospheric conditions when the throttling mechanism is opened fully (full-throttle). Combustion efficiency drops in cold, thin air as vaporization and turbulence, and combustion speed all fall. Engine power loss (friction + gas exchange + boost drain) reduces the indicated power.

Effect of atmospheric conditions
The quantity of air which an engine ingests depends upon the ambient density; thus colder, heavier, denser air increases engine output. Rule of thumb: Engine power drops by approximately 1% for each 100 m increase in

altitude. Depending upon engine design, the cold intake air is more or less heated in the intake passages, thereby reducing its density and thus ultimate output. As humid air contains less oxygen than dry air, it also results in a power-output reduction. These losses are generally small to the point of insignificance.

The warm humidity of tropical air can result in a considerable power loss.

Definitions of power

The net power is the engine's power as measured at the crankshaft or ancillary mechanism (such as the transmission) at the specified rpm. When measurements are made downstream of the transmission, then the transmission unit's losses must be taken into account. Nominal power is the maximum net power of the engine under full throttle.

Conversion formulae are used to convert the results of dynamometer testing to reflect standard conditions, thereby negating the influences of such factors as time of day and year while simultaneously allowing different manufacturers to provide mutually comparable data. The procedure converts atmospheric density — and thus the effective volume of air in the engine — to defined "standard conditions" for air mass.

The comparison data in the following table show the most important standards used in power correction.

Power correction standards (Comparison)

Standard (Date of publication)	EWG 80/1269 (4/81)	ISO 1585 (5/82)	JIS D 1001 (10/82)	SAE J 1349 (5/85)	DIN 70 020 (11/76)
Barometric pressure during testing (* subtract vapor pressure!)					
Dry p_{PT}* kPa	99	99	99	99	—
Absolute p_{PF} kPa	—	—	—	—	101.3
Temperature during testing					
Absolute T_P K	298	298	298	298	293
Engines with spark ignition, naturally-aspirated and turbo/supercharged					
Correction factor α_a	$\alpha_a = A^{1.2} \cdot B^{0.6}$ $A = 99/p_{PT}$ $B = T_P/298$				$\alpha_a = A \cdot B^{0.5}$ $A = 101.3/p_{PF}$ $B = T_P/293$
Corrected power: $P_0 = \alpha_a \cdot P$ (kW) (P measured power)					
Diesel engines, naturally-aspirated and turbo/supercharged					
Atmospheric correction factor f_a	$f_a = A \cdot B^{0.7}$ ($A = 99/p_{PT}$; $B = T_P/293$) (naturally-aspirated and mechanically-supercharged)				as α_a on SI gasoline engine
	$f_a = A^{0.7} \cdot B^{1.5}$ ($A = 99/p_{PT}$; $B = T_P/293$) (turbocharged engines with/without charge-air cooling)				
Engine correction factor f_m	$40 \le q/r \le 65$: $f_m = 0.036 \cdot (q/r) - 1.14$ $q/r < 40$: $f_m = 0.3$ $q/r > 65$: $f_m = 1.2$				$f_m = 1$
$r = p_L/p_E$ Boost pressure response, with absolute boost pressure $= p_L$, p_E Absolute pressure before compressor, q spec. fuel consumption (SAE J 1349) 4-stroke engines: $q = 120{,}000\ F/DN$, 2-stroke engines: $q = 60{,}000\ F/DN$ with F = Fuel flow (mg/s); D = Effective stroke volume (l); N = Engine speed (min^{-1})					
Corrected power: $P_0 = P \cdot f_a^{fm}$ (kW) (P measured power)					
Prescribed accessories					
Fan	Yes, with electric/viscous-drive fan at max. slip				Not defined
Emissions-control system	Yes				Not defined
Alternator	Yes, loaded with engine-current draw				Yes
Servo pumps	No				No
Air conditioner	No				No

Calculation

Quantity		Unit
a_k	Piston acceleration	m/s^2
B	Fuel consumption	kg/h; dm^3/h
b_e	Spec. fuel consumption	g/kWh
D	Cylinder diameter $2 \cdot r$	mm
d_v	Valve diameter	mm
F	Force	N
F_G	Gas force in the cylinder	N
F_N	Piston side thrust	N
F_o	Oscillating inertia force	N
F_r	Rotating inertia force	N
F_s	Rod force	N
F_T	Tangential force	N
M	Torque	N·m
M_o	Oscillating moments	N·m
M_r	Rotating moments	N·m
M_d	Engine torque	N·m
m_p	Weight-to-power ratio	kg/kW
n	Engine speed	min^{-1}
n_p	Injection pump speed	min^{-1}
P	Power	kW
P_{eff}	Net horsepower[1]	kW
P_H	Power per unit displacement	kW/dm^3
p	Pressure	bar
p_c	Final compression pressure	bar
p_e	Mean working pressure	bar
p_L	Charging pressure	bar
p_{max}	Peak pressure in the cylinder	bar
r	Crank radius	mm
s_d	Injection cross section of the nozzle	mm^2
S, s	Stroke, general	mm
s	Piston stroke	mm
s_F	Suction stroke, 2-stroke engine	mm
S_K	Piston clearance from TDC	mm
S_s	Slot height, 2-stroke engine	mm
T	Temperature	°C, K
T_c	Final compression temperature	K
T_L	Charge-air temperature	K
T_{max}	Peak temperature in combustion chamber	K
t	Time	s
V	Volume	m^3
V_c	Compression space of a cylinder	dm^3

[1]) Net horsepower P_{eff} is the usable horsepower delivered by the internal-combustion engine, whereby the auxiliary equipment necessary for operation (e.g., ignition equipment, fuel-injection pump, scavenging air and cooling air fan, water pump, fan and supercharger) are driven by the internal-combustion engine (DIN 1940). This horsepower is called net engine power in DIN 70 020 (see p. 397).

Quantity		Unit
V_E	Injected quantity per pump stroke	mm^3
V_f	Charge volume of a cylinder (2-stroke)	dm^3
V_F	Charge volume of a 2-stroke engine	dm^3
V_h	Displacement of a cylinder	dm^3
V_H	Displacement of the engine	dm^3
v	Velocity	m/s
v_d	Mean velocity of the injected spray	m/s
v_g	Gas velocity	m/s
v_m	Mean piston velocity	m/s
v_{max}	Max. piston velocity	m/s
z	Number of cylinders	–
α_d	Injection period (in ° crankshaft at the fuel-injection pump)	°
β	Pivot angle of the connecting rod	°
ε	Compression ratio	–
η	Efficiency	–
η_e	Effective efficiency	–
η_{th}	Thermal efficiency	–
ν, n	Polytropic exponent of real gases	–
ϱ	Density	kg/m^3
φ, α	Crank angle (φ_o = top dead center)	°
ω	Angular velocity	rad/s
λ	$= r/l$ connecting-rod ratio,	–
λ	Air-fuel ratio	–
$\varkappa$	$= c_p/c_v$ Adiabatic exponent of ideal gases	–

Superscripts and subscripts

0, 1, 2, 3, 4, 5	Cycle values/main values
o	Oscillating
r	Rotating
1st, 2nd	1st, 2nd Order
A	Constant
′, ″	Subdivision of main values, derivations

Conversion of units
(see also pp. 17 ... 38)

1 g/hp · h	= 1.36 g/kW · h
1 g/kW · h	= 0.735 g/hp
1 kp · m	= 9.81 N · m ≈ 10 N · m
1 N · m	= 0.102 kp · m ≈ 0.1 kp · m
1 hp (DIN)	= 0.735 kW
1 kW	= 1.36 hp (DIN)
1 at	= 0.981 bar ≈ 1 bar
1 bar	= 1.02 at ≈ 1 at

Calculation equations

Mathematical relationships between quantities	Numerical relationships between quantities

Swept volume

Swept volume of a cylinder

$$V_h = \frac{\pi \cdot d^2 \cdot s}{4}; \quad V_f = \frac{\pi \cdot d^2 \cdot s_f}{4} \text{ (2-stroke)}$$

$V_h = 0.785 \cdot 10^{-6}\, d^2 \cdot s$

V_h in dm³, d in mm, s in mm

Swept volume of the engine

$V_H = V_h \cdot z; \quad V_F = V_f \cdot z$ (2-stroke)

$V_H = 0.785 \cdot 10^{-6}\, d^2 \cdot s \cdot z$

V_H in dm³, d in mm, s in mm

Compression

Compression ratio

$$\varepsilon = \frac{V_h + V_c}{V_c}$$ (see p. 402 for diagram)

Final compression pressure

$p_c = p_o \cdot \varepsilon^{\nu}$

Final compression temperature

$T_c = T_o \cdot \varepsilon^{\nu - 1}$

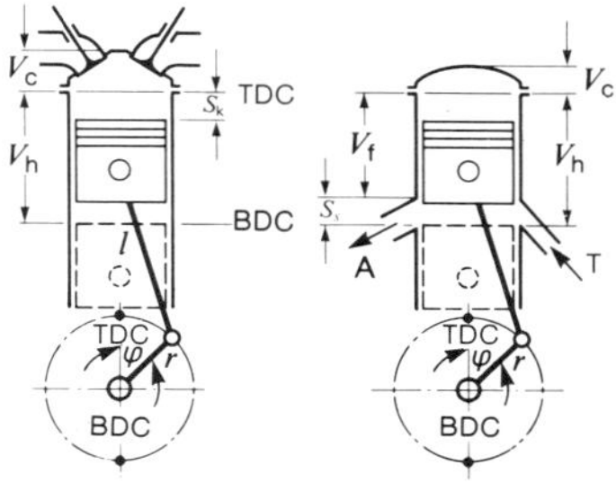

4-stroke engine ***2-stroke engine***

Piston movement

(See p. 403 for diagram)

Piston clearance from top dead center

$$S_k = r\left[1 + \frac{l}{r} - \cos\varphi - \sqrt{\left(\frac{l}{r}\right)^2 - \sin^2\varphi}\right]$$

Crank angle

$\varphi = 2 \cdot \pi \cdot n \cdot t$ (φ in rad)

$\varphi = 6 \cdot n \cdot t$

φ in °, n in min⁻¹, t in s

Piston velocity (approximation)

$$v \approx 2 \cdot \pi \cdot n \cdot r\left(\sin\varphi + \frac{r}{2l}\sin 2\varphi\right)$$

$$v \approx \frac{n \cdot s}{19{,}100}\left(\sin\varphi + \frac{r}{2l}\sin 2\varphi\right)$$

v in m/s, n in min⁻¹, l, r and s in mm

Mean piston velocity

$v_m = 2 \cdot n \cdot s$

$$v_m = \frac{n \cdot s}{30{,}000}$$ (See p. 404 for diagram)

v_m in m/s, n in min⁻¹, s in mm

Maximum piston velocity (approximate, if connecting rod is on a tangent with the big-end trajectory; $a_k = 0$)

l/r	3.5	4	4.5
v_{max}	$1.63 \cdot v_m$	$1.62 \cdot v_m$	$1.61 \cdot v_m$

(See p. 404 for diagram)

Piston acceleration (approximation)

$$a_k \approx 2 \cdot \pi^2 \cdot n^2 \cdot s\left(\cos\varphi + \frac{r}{l}\cos 2\varphi\right)$$

$$a_k \approx \frac{n^2 \cdot s}{182{,}400}\left(\cos\varphi + \frac{r}{l}\cos 2\varphi\right)$$

a_k in m/s², n in min⁻¹, l, r and s in mm

---

[1]) See p. 44 for definitions of "mathematic relationships between quantities" and "numerical relationships between quantities".

Calculation equations (continued)

Mathematical relationships between quantities	Numerical relationships between quantities
Gas velocity Mean gas velocity in the valve section $v_g = \frac{d^2}{d_v^2} \cdot v_m$	$v_g = \frac{d^2}{d_v^2} \cdot \frac{n \cdot s}{30{,}000}$ v_g in m/s, d, d_v and s in mm, n in min^{-1}

The highest volumetric efficiency values are achieved at mean gas velocities of 90 ... 110 m/s (empirical values).

Fuel supply Injected quantity per injection-pump stroke $V_E = \frac{P_{eff} \cdot b_e}{\varrho \cdot n_p \cdot z}$	$V_E = \frac{1000 \cdot P_{eff} \cdot b_e}{60 \cdot \varrho \cdot n_p \cdot z}$ V_E in mm^3, P_{eff} in kW, b_e in g/kW·h (or also P_{eff} in hp (DIN), b_e in g/hp (DIN)·h), n_p in min^{-1}, ϱ in kg/dm^3 (for fuels, $\varrho \approx 0.85\ \text{kg/dm}^3$)
Mean velocity of injected spray $v_d = \frac{2 \cdot \pi \cdot n_p \cdot V_E}{S_d \cdot \alpha_d}$ (α_d in rad)	$v_d = \frac{6\, n_p \cdot V_E}{1000 \cdot S_d \cdot \alpha_d}$ v_d in m/s, n_p in min^{-1}, V_E in mm^3, S_d in mm^2, α_d in °
Engine power $P = M \cdot \omega = 2 \cdot \pi \cdot M \cdot n$	$P = M \cdot n/9549$ P in kW, M in N·m (= W·s), n in min^{-1}
$P_{eff} = V_H \cdot p_e \cdot n/K$ $K = 1$ for two-stroke engine $K = 2$ for four-stroke engine	$P_{eff} = \frac{V_H \cdot p_e \cdot n}{K \cdot 600} = \frac{M_d \cdot n}{9549}$ P_{eff} in kW, p_e in bar, n in min^{-1}, M_d in N·m
Power per unit displacement (power per liter) $P_H = \frac{P_{eff}}{V_H}$	$P = M \cdot n/716.2$
Power-to-weight ratio $m_P = \frac{m}{P_{eff}}$	P in hp (DIN), M in kp·m, n in min^{-1}

Calculation equations (continued)

Mathematical relationships between quantities		Numerical relationships between quantities	
Mean piston pressure (mean pressure, mean working pressure)			
Four-stroke engine	Two-stroke engine	Four-stroke engine	Two-stroke engine
$p = \frac{2 \cdot P}{V_H \cdot n}$	$p = \frac{P}{V_H \cdot n}$	$p = 1200 \frac{P}{V_H \cdot n}$	$p = 600 \frac{P}{V_H \cdot n}$
		p in bar, P in kW, V_H in dm^3, n in min^{-1} or also:	
		$p = 883 \frac{P}{V_H \cdot n}$	$p = 441 \frac{P}{V_H \cdot n}$
		p in bar, P in hp (DIN), V_H in dm^3, n in min^{-1}	
$p = \frac{4 \cdot \pi \cdot M}{V_H}$	$p = \frac{2 \cdot \pi \cdot M}{V_H}$	$p = 0.1257 \frac{M}{V_H}$	$p = 0.0628 \frac{M}{V_H}$
		p in bar, M in N·m, V_H in dm^3	
Engine torque		$M_d = \frac{V_H \cdot p_e}{0.12566}$	$M_d = \frac{V_H \cdot p_e}{0.06284}$
$M_d = \frac{V_H \cdot p_e}{4\pi}$	$M_d = \frac{V_H \cdot p_e}{2\pi}$	M_d in N·m, V_H in dm^3, p_e in bar $M_d = 9549 \cdot P_{eff}/n$ M_d in N·m, P_{eff} in kW, n in min^{-1}	
Fuel consumption[1] $B =$ Measured values in kg/h $b_e = B/P_{eff}$ $b_e = 1/(H_u \cdot \eta_e)$		B in dm^3/h or kg/h V_B = Measured volume on the test dynamometer t_B = Elapsed time for measured volume consumption $b_e = \frac{V_B \cdot \varrho_B \cdot 3600}{t_B \cdot P_{eff}}$ ϱ_B = Fuel density in g/cm^3, t_B in s, V_B in cm^3, P_{eff} in kW.	
Efficiency $\eta_{th} = 1 - \varepsilon^{1-\nu}$ $\eta_e = P_{eff}/(B \cdot H_u)$		$\eta_e = 86/b_e$ where H_u = specific calorific value 42 000 kJ/kg b_e in g/(kW·h)	

[1]) See p. 323 for the effect of on-the-vehicle measures on fuel consumption.

Displacement and compression space

See p. 399 for diagram and equation.

The diagram below applies to the displacement V_h and compression space V_c of the individual cylinder, and to the total displacement V_H and total compression space V_C.

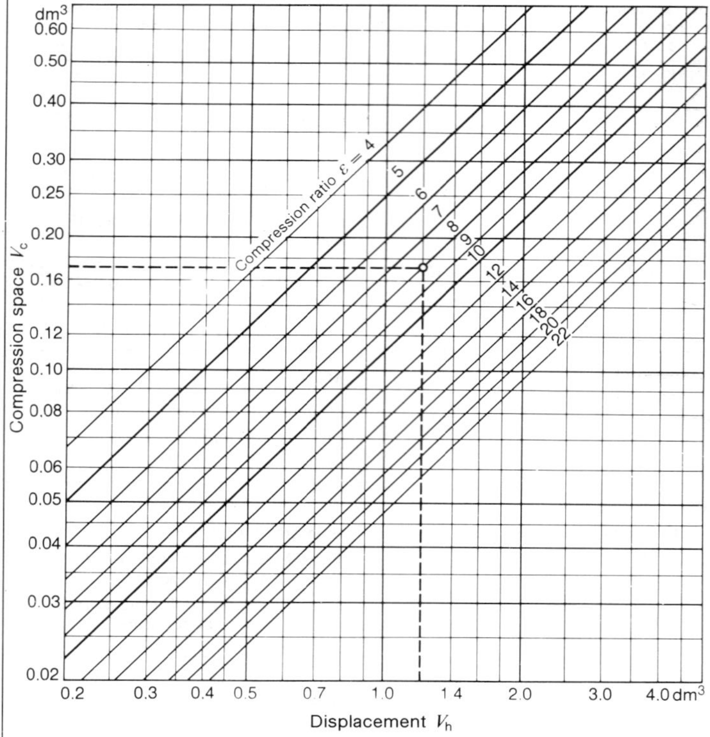

Example:
an engine with a displacement of 1.2 dm³ and a compression ratio $\varepsilon = 8$ has a compression space of 0.17 dm³.

Piston clearance from top dead center *See p. 399 for equation.*

Conversion of degrees of crank angle to mm of piston travel.

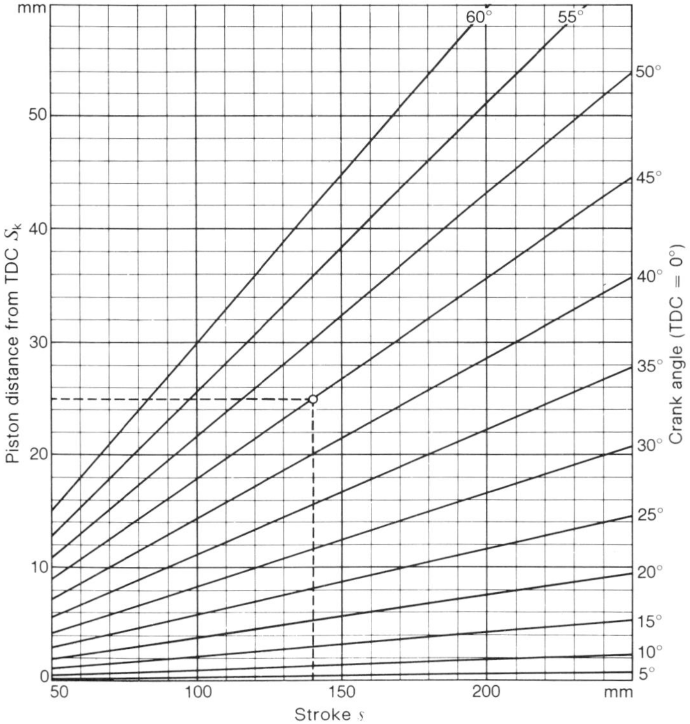

Example:
the piston clearance from top dead center is 25 mm for a stroke of 140 mm at 45° crankshaft.
The diagram is based on a crank ratio $l/r = 4$ (l connecting-rod length; r one half of the stroke length). However, it also applies with very good approximation (error less than 2%) for all l/r ratios between 3.5 and 4.5.

Piston velocity

See p. 399 for equation.

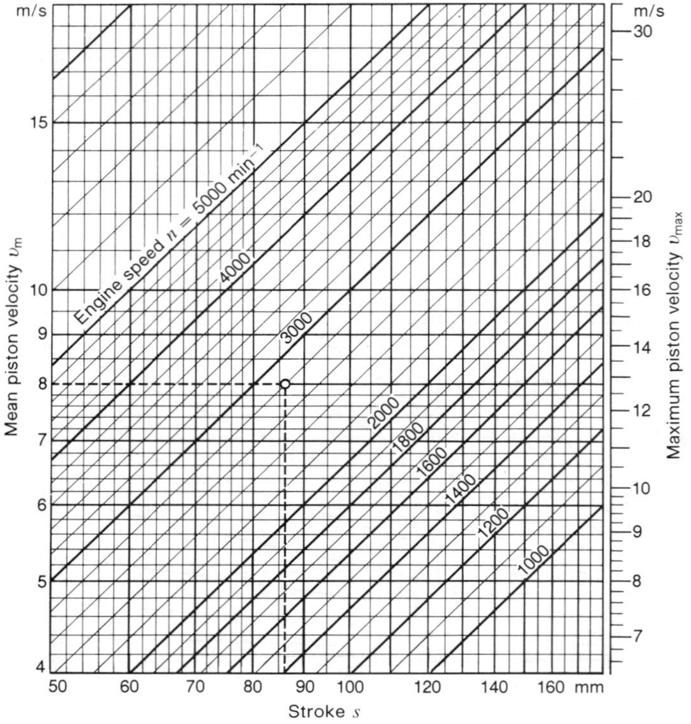

Example:
The mean piston velocity v_m = 8 m/s and the maximum piston velocity v_{max} = 13 m/s for a stroke s = 86 mm and an engine speed of n = 2800 min^{-1}.
The diagram is based on v_{max} = 1.62 v_m (see p. 399).

Increase in the density of the combustion air in the cylinder on turbo/supercharging

Increase in density on supercharging as a function of the pressure ratio in the compressor, the compression efficiency and the intercooling rate for charge-air cooling (CAC).

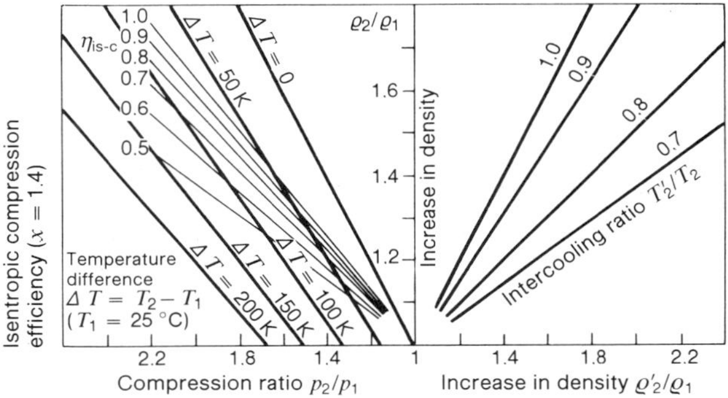

$p_2/p_1 = \pi_c =$ Pressure ratio during crankcase compression
$\varrho_2/\varrho_1 =$ Increase in density, $\varrho_1 =$ Density upstream of compressor, $\varrho_2 =$ Density downstream of compressor in kg/m³
$T_2'/T_2 =$ Intercooling rate, $T_2 =$ Temperature before CAC, $T_2' =$ Temperature after CAC in K
$\eta_{is-c} =$ Isentropic compressor efficiency

Final compression pressure and temperature

Final compression temperature as a function of the compression ratio and the intake temperature.

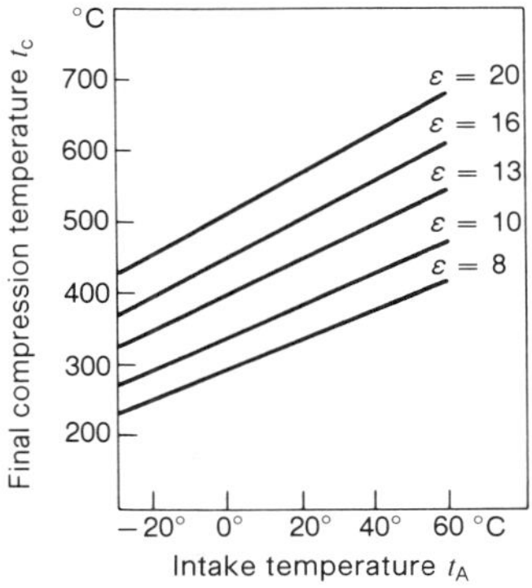

$t_c = T_c - 273.15$ K; $T_c = T_A \cdot \varepsilon^{n-1}$; $n = 1.35$

Final compression pressure as a function of the compression ratio and boost pressure.

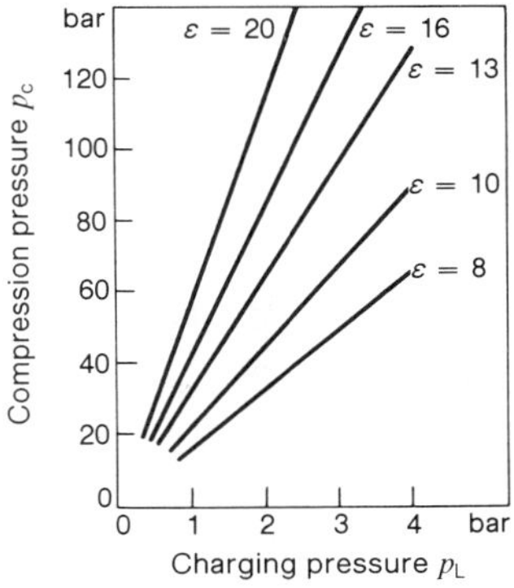

$p_c = p_L \cdot \varepsilon^n$; $n = 1.35$

Reciprocating-piston engine with external combustion (Stirling engine)

Method of operation and efficiency

Cycle sequence: In phase I, the power piston is at its lowest position and the displacer (top piston) is in its highest position; all of the working gas is expanded between the power piston and displacer in the cold space. During the transition from phase I to phase II, the power piston compresses the working fluid in the cold space. The displacer remains in its uppermost position. During the transition from phase II to phase III, the compressed working fluid is pushed by the downward motion of the displacer via the cooler into the regenerator (where it absorbs the stored heat) and from there into the heater (where it is heated to maximum working temperature). Because the power piston remains in its lowermost position, the volume does not change.

After passing through the heater, the heated gas enters the hot space above the displacer. During the transition from phase III to phase IV, the hot gas expands; the power piston and displacer are pushed into their lowermost positions, thereby performing work. The cycle is completed during the transition from phase IV back to phase I, where the gas is again pushed by the upward movement of the displacer through the heater and into the regenerator, thus giving off a large portion of its heat. The residual heat is given off in the cooler before the gas reenters the cold space.

The theoretical cycle thus comprises quasi-isothermal compression (the working gas is cooled back down to its initial temperature in the cooler after adiabatic compression), isochoric heat addition via the regenerator and heater, quasi-isothermal expansion (the working gas is reheated to its initial condition in the heater after adiabatic expansion) and isochoric heat dissipation via the regenerator and cooler.

The ideal cycle shown in the p-V and T-S diagrams could only be achieved if – as described – the movement of the power and displacer systems were discontinuous.

If both pistons are connected to a shaft, i.e., via a rhombic drive, they carry out phase-shifted sinusoidal movements which lead to a rounded work diagram with the same cycle efficiency – similar to the efficiency of the Carnot cycle – but with reduced power and total efficiency.

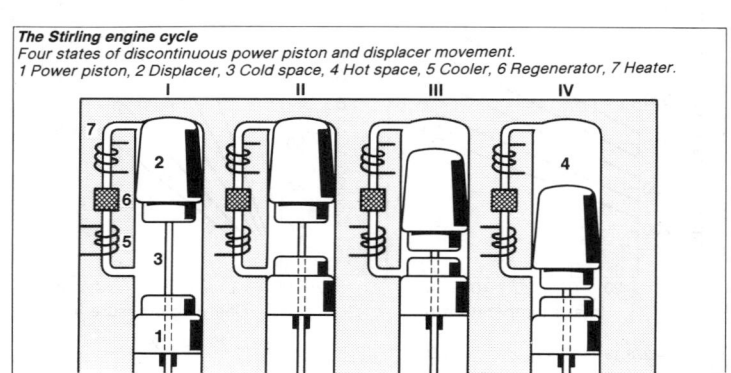

The Stirling engine cycle

Four states of discontinuous power piston and displacer movement.

1 Power piston, 2 Displacer, 3 Cold space, 4 Hot space, 5 Cooler, 6 Regenerator, 7 Heater.

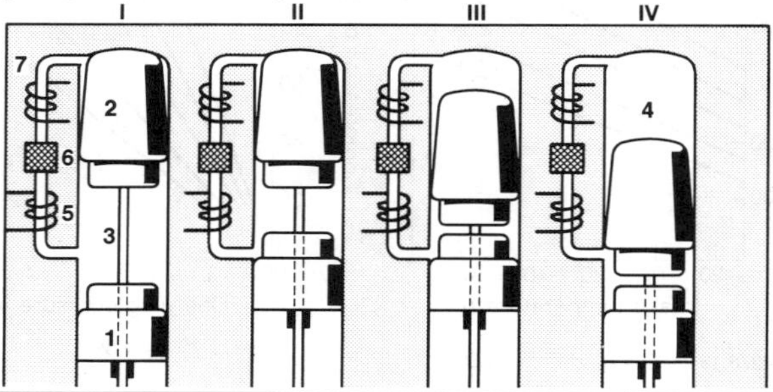

Theoretical Stirling engine cycle as shown in the p–V and T–S diagrams

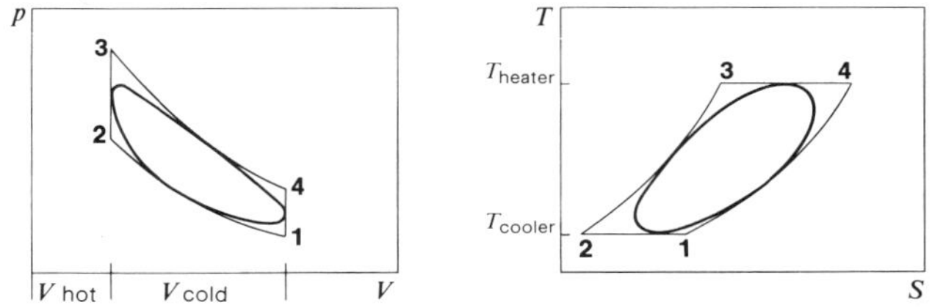

Design and operating behavior

Modern Stirling engines act as double-acting engines with 4 cylinders, for example, operating with appropriate phase shift. Each cylinder has only one piston whose top surface acts as a power piston, and whose bottom surface acts as a displacer for the following cylinder. The cooler, regenerator and heater are located between the cylinders.

In order to keep power output per unit displacement from becoming too low, the engine is run at a high pressure of from 50 to 200 bar which is variable for purposes of load control. Gases with low flow losses and high specific heats (usually hydrogen) must be used as the working fluid. Because all of the heat to be withdrawn from the cycle must be dissipated to the ambient air via the cooler, Stirling engines require considerably larger heat exchangers than IC-engines.

Advantages of the Stirling engine: very low concentrations of those pollutants which are limited by legislation (HC, CO and NO_x); quiet running without combustion noise; usable with a wide variety of different fuels (multifuel capability); fuel consumption (in the map) roughly corresponds to that of direct-injection diesel engines at equivalent speeds.

Disadvantages: high manufacturing costs due to complicated design; very high working pressures with only moderate power output per unit volume and per unit weight; expensive load control system required; large cooling surface and in some cases high fan power required.

Double-acting Stirling engine
1 Heater, 2 Regenerator, 3 Cooler.

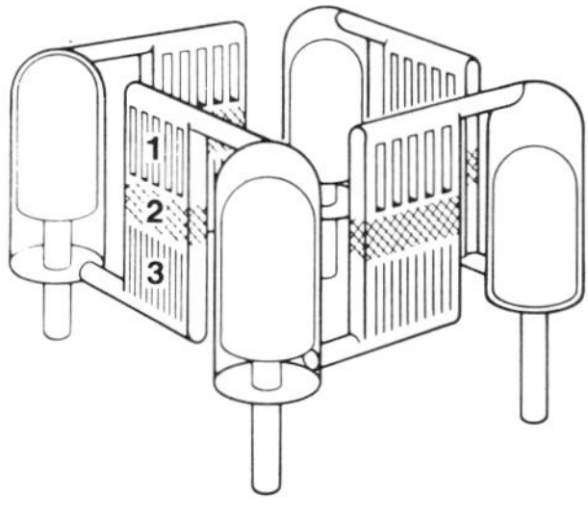

Heat balance in the Stirling engine

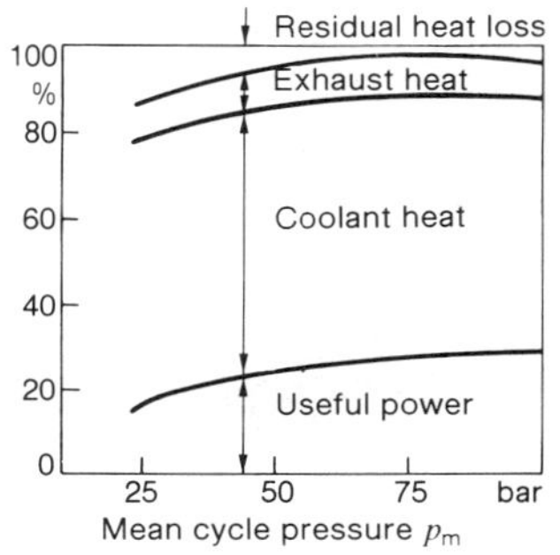

The Wankel (rotary) engine

The rotary engine is a special type of reciprocating-piston engine in which the crank mechanism is replaced by an eccentric drive and a rotor which forms the combustion chamber as it follows a trochoid path.

The cross section of the rotor is a triangle with convex sides. It moves in a water-cooled housing whose chamber is an oval curve whose cross section is slightly reduced in the center (epitrochoid). The three corners of the rotor follow the wall of the housing as the rotor rotates, thus generating three cells (A, B and C) 120° apart and sealed from one another. These cells periodically become smaller and then larger as the rotor rotates. During each rotation of the rotor, a four-stroke spark-ignition combustion process occurs in each of the cells, i.e., after one full rotation of the triangular rotor, the engine has completed the four-stroke process three times, and the eccentric shaft has rotated the same number of times.

The rotor is fitted both with face seals and apex seals. It incorporates a concentric internal ring gear and the bearings for the engine shaft's eccentric. The inside revolution of the internal ring gear is controlled by yet another gear; this block-mounted gear is in a concentric position relative to the eccentric shaft. This gear set transmits no force. Instead, it serves to maintain the rotary piston in the trochoidal orbit pattern required to synchronize piston and eccentric shaft.

The ratio of the teeth of the two gears is 3:2. The rotor rotates at two thirds of the angular velocity of the shaft and in the opposite direction with respect to the shaft such that the relative speed of the rotor with respect to the housing is only one third the angular velocity of the shaft.

Design and principle of operation of the Wankel (rotary) engine
1 Rotor, 2 Internal gear in the rotor, 3 Spark plug, 4 Stationary pinion, 5 Bearing surface of the eccentric.
a: Cell A takes in air-fuel mixture, cell B compresses the mixture, and the combustion gases are exhausted from cell C. (Depressions in the rotor flanks allow gas to pass by the trochoidal restriction.)
b: Cell A is filled with fresh gas, the combustion gases expand in cell B, thereby turning the eccentric shaft via the rotor; combustion gases continue to be exhausted from cell B. The next phase of combustion is again that shown in figure a, whereby cell C has taken the place of cell A. Thus the rotor, by turning through 120° of one rotation, has carried out the complete four-stroke process at its three flanks. During this process, the eccentric shaft has made one complete rotation.

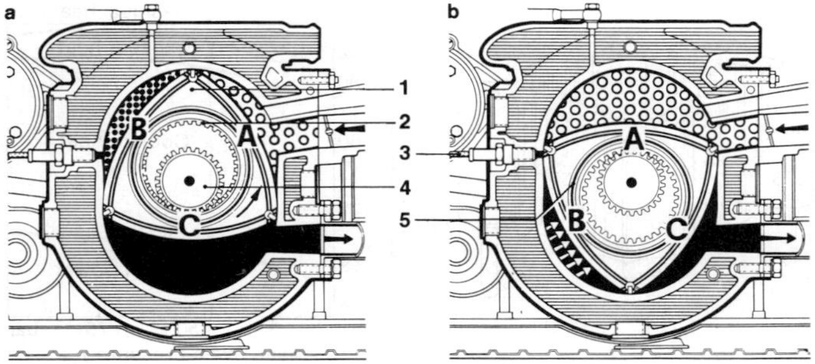

The gas exchange is regulated by the piston as it moves past slots in the housing. An alternative to this arrangement in which the peripheral intake ports are located at the outside of the trichoid path, is represented by intake ports in the side of the block (side ports).

Considerably higher gas velocities and engine speeds are made possible by the lack of narrow gas cross sections and reciprocating masses. Every rotary engine can be completely balanced mechanically. The only irregularity which remains is the degree of nonuniformity which occurs in all internal-combustion engines. However the torsional force curve of a single-rotor engine is considerably smoother than that of a conventional single-cylinder engine due to the fact that the power strokes occur over 270° of the eccentric-shaft rotation.

This degree of nonuniformity, and thus the smooth running behavior of the engine, can be additionally improved by placing several rotors on one shaft. In this context, a three-rotor engine corresponds to an eight-cylinder, reciprocating-piston engine. The torque curve can be made to assume the characteristics of a throttled engine or a racing engine depending upon port timing and intake cross section.

Advantages of the rotary engine: complete balancing of masses; favorable torsional force curve; compact design; no valve-train assembly necessary; excellent running behavior.

Disadvantages: unfavorable combustion chamber shape with long flame paths; high HC emissions; high fuel and oil consumption; higher manufacturing costs; diesel operation not possible; high location of power transmission shaft unfavorable.

Design of a twin-rotor rotary engine
1 Rotor, 2 Hydraulic torque convertor, 3 Automatic clutch.

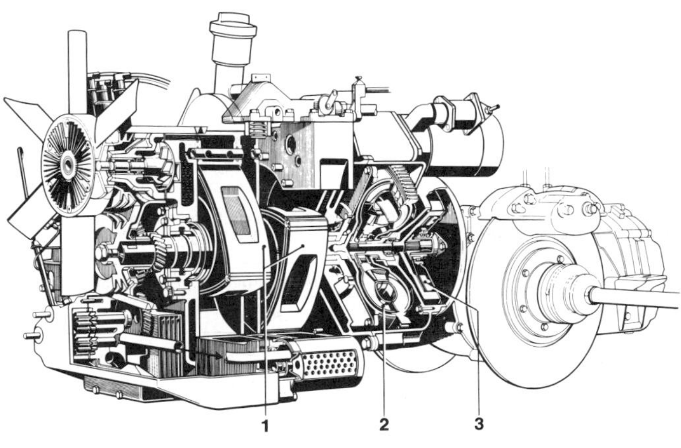

Gas turbine

In the gas turbine, the individual changes of state during the cycle take place in spatially separate components (compressors, burners and turbines), which communicate with one another via flow-conducting components (diffusers, spirals and the like). These changes of state therefore occur continuously.

Method of operation, comparative cycle and efficiency

In automotive gas turbines, the air which is continuously aspirated through filters and silencers is generally compressed in a radial-flow compressor, after which it is further heated in a heat exchanger. In today's automotive gas turbines, the heat exchanger is usually designed as a rotating regenerator.

The compressed and preheated air then flows into the burner where it is directly heated through the injection and combustion of gaseous, liquid or emulsified fuels. Energy from the compressed and heated gases is then transmitted to one, two or three turbine stages on one to three shaft groups. The radial- or axial-flow turbines initially drive compressors and auxiliary equipment. The remaining power is delivered to the cardan shaft via a power turbine, reduction gear and transmission.

In order to reduce part-load and idle consumption, as well as to improve acceleration behavior, the power turbine is generally fitted with adjustable guide vanes. In single-shaft machines, adjustable gears are also required.

The gases in the turbine, which have cooled somewhat due to expansion, flow through the gas side of the heat exchanger where most of their residual heat is dissipated into the air. These gases are then expelled through the exhaust port, where the heat which they still contain can be used by the vehicle heating system.

The thermal efficiency, and thus the fuel consumption of the gas turbine depends to a great extent on the maximum permissible operating temperature (burner exit temperature). The temperatures which can be achieved through the use of highly temperature-resistant cobalt- or nickel-based alloys do not enable fuel consumption to be brought down to the values of today's piston engines. Comparable or improved fuel consumption can only be achieved through the use of ceramic materials.

The thermodynamic comparative cycle for the gas turbine is the constant-pressure cycle or Joule cycle. It consists of isentropic compression (process 1→2), isobaric heat addition (process 2→3), isentropic expansion (process 3→4) and isobaric heat dissipation (process 4→1). Good thermal efficiency is only achievable if the addition of heat with a temperature increase of T_2 to $T_{2'}$ via a heat exchanger is coupled with heat dissipation (4→4').

Characteristic operating temperatures (orders of magnitude) at various positions in metallic and ceramic automotive gas turbines at full load:

Measuring point	Metal turbine	Ceramic turbine
Compressor exit	230 °C	250 °C
Heat exchanger exit (air side)	700 °C	950 °C
Burner exit	1000 °C ... 1100 °C	1250 °C ... 1350 °C
Heat exchanger inlet (gas side)	750 °C	1000 °C
Heat exchanger exit	270 °C	300 °C

Thermodynamic comparative cycle as shown in the p–V and T–S diagrams

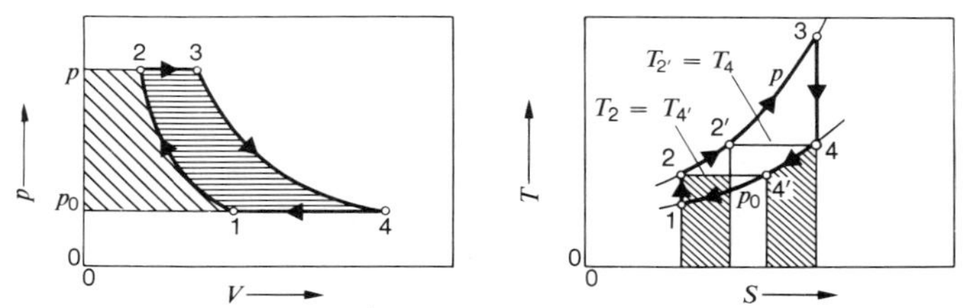

If heat is completely exchanged, the quantity of heat to be added per unit of gas is then reduced to

$$q_{in} = c_p \cdot (T_3 - T_{2'}) = c_p \cdot (T_3 - T_4)$$

and the quantity of heat to be dissipated is

$$q_{out} = c_p \cdot (T_{4'} - T_1) = c_p \cdot (T_2 - T_1)$$

The maximum thermal efficiency for the gas turbine with heat exchanger is:

$$\eta_{th} = 1 - Q_{out}/Q_{in} = 1 - (T_2 + T_1)/(T_3 - T_4)$$

Where $p_2/p_1 = (T_2/T_1)^{\frac{\varkappa}{\varkappa-1}} = (T_3/T_4)^{\frac{\varkappa}{\varkappa-1}}$
and $T_4 = T_3 \cdot (T_1/T_2)$ thus
$\eta_{th} = 1 - (T_2/T_3)$

Today's gas-turbine power units reach thermal efficiencies of up to 35 %.

Advantages of the gas turbine: low emissions without the need for additional equipment; extremely smooth running; multifuel capability; favorable stationary torque curve; long maintenance intervals.

Disadvantages: manufacturing costs still high; unfavorable throttle take-up; higher fuel consumption; less suitable for low-power applications.

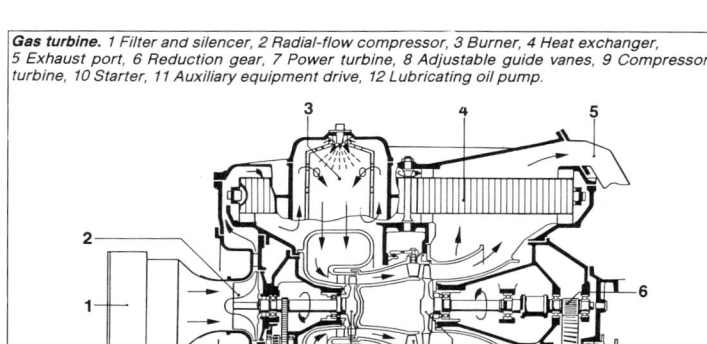

Gas turbine. *1 Filter and silencer, 2 Radial-flow compressor, 3 Burner, 4 Heat exchanger, 5 Exhaust port, 6 Reduction gear, 7 Power turbine, 8 Adjustable guide vanes, 9 Compressor turbine, 10 Starter, 11 Auxiliary equipment drive, 12 Lubricating oil pump.*

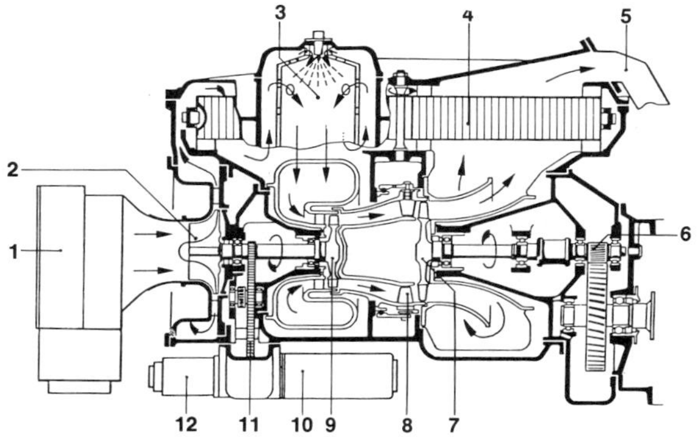

Engine cooling

Air cooling

In the case of air-cooled engines, air pressure and/or a fan produces an air stream around the finned outer walls of the cylinder casing. The amount of air can be adjusted according to load or temperature using, for instance, speed regulation or throttling arrangements. The power consumption is 3 ... 4 % of total engine output. Suitable soundproofing measures can be employed to obtain both engine-temperature consistency and noise levels comparable to those achieved with fluid-cooled engines. The heat absorbed by the engine oil is dispersed by an air-cooled oil cooler which can be mounted at a suitable position in the air stream.

Water cooling

Water cooling has practically become the standard in both passenger vehicles and heavy-duty vehicles.

Pure water is no longer employed as coolant; today's coolants are composed of a mixture of water (of drinking quality), antifreeze (generally ethylene glycol), and corrosion inhibitors appropriate to the specific application. An antifreeze concentration of 30 ... 50 % raises the coolant mixture's boiling point, and in passenger cars allows operating temperatures of up to 120 °C at a pressure of 1.4 bar. (Illustration of cooling system, p. 392).

Radiator designs and materials

The cores of the coolant radiators in modern passenger cars are almost always made of aluminum, which is also being used in an increasing number of heavy-vehicle radiators. There are two basic assembly variations: Brazing and mechanical joining.

For cooling high-output engines, or when space is limited, the best solution is a brazed, high-performance flat-tube and corrugated-fin layout with minimal aerodynamic resistance on the intake side.

The less expensive, mechanically-assembled finned-tube system is generally employed for applications with less powerful engines or when more space is available.

When the radiator is assembled mechanically, the cooling grid is formed by mounting stamped fins around oval or round tubes. The fins are corrugated and/or slotted at right angles to the direction of air flow.

In both types of radiator, turbulators are applied to enhance the thermal transfer on the coolant side (in the pipes) provided the attendant pressure losses remain within acceptable limits. On the cooling-air side,

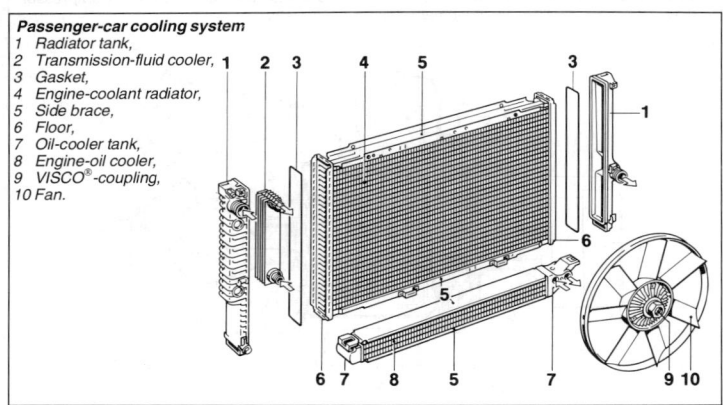

Passenger-car cooling system
1 Radiator tank,
2 Transmission-fluid cooler,
3 Gasket,
4 Engine-coolant radiator,
5 Side brace,
6 Floor,
7 Oil-cooler tank,
8 Engine-oil cooler,
9 VISCO®-coupling,
10 Fan.

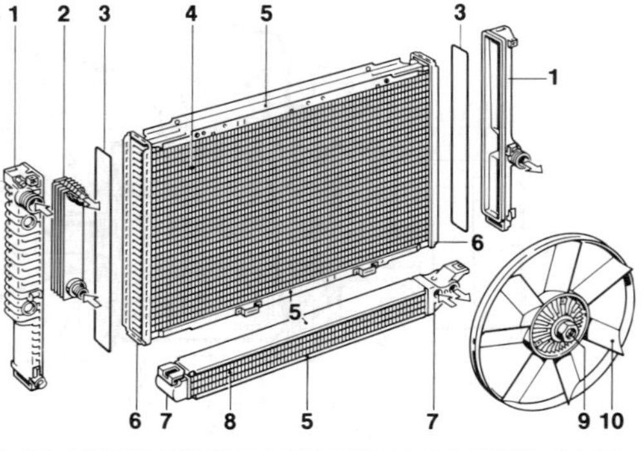

corrugations and gills provide improved thermal transfer in the fins.

The radiator tank ensures that the coolant is distributed throughout the block. Such tanks are made of fiberglass-reinforced polyamides, and are cast as an injection-molding, incorporating all connections and mountings in a single unit; they are flange-mounted on the radiator core.

Radiator design

Regardless of operating and environmental conditions, the radiator must always be capable of reliably transferring to its surroundings the heat produced in the engine. Different methods can be applied to determine radiator capacity. The cooling capacity required for a specific radiator can be determined empirically, using comparisons with reference units of the same design, or calculations employing correlation equations for thermal transfer and flow-pressure loss can be employed.

In addition to reliable cooling, other priorities in radiator design include minimal power requirements for fan operation and low vehicle aerodynamic resistance. The mass of the cooling air stream is a decisive factor, as there is an inverse relationship between fan and radiator capacities: A more powerful fan with higher energy consumption allows a smaller radiator, and vice versa. In addition, the temperature differential between the surrounding air and the coolant should be as great as possible, an objective that can only be achieved by maximizing coolant temperature, which in turn entails a corresponding increase in system pressure.

Regulation of coolant temperature

A motor vehicle's engine operates in a very wide range of climatic conditions and with major fluctuations in engine load. The temperature of the coolant – and with it that of the engine – must be regulated if they are to remain constant within a narrow range. It is recommended that a temperature-sensitive thermostat incorporating an expansion element be installed to regulate temperature independent of pressure variations in the cooling system. Responding to a drop in coolant temperature, the thermostat operates a valve which increases the amount of coolant which bypasses the radiator. This method provides consistent operating temperatures, good vehicle-heater performance, and favorable emissions, while also reducing engine wear.

Coolant expansion tank

The coolant expansion tank is a reliable means of allowing gases to escape, thus preventing cavitation of the kind that generally tends to occur on the suction side of the water pump. The air volume contained within the expansion tank must be sufficient to respond to the coolant's thermal expansion with a rapid pressure buildup, thus preventing the coolant from boiling over.

Expansion tanks are injected-molded in plastic (generally polypropylene), although simple designs can also be inflated to shape. The expansion tank can form a single unit with the radiator tank, or the two can be joined in a flange or plug connection. It is also possible to install the expansion tank remotely.

The position or shape of the filler opening can be used to limit capacity, thus preventing overfilling. A sight glass or an electronic level sensor can be employed to monitor the level of the coolant, or the expansion tank can be manufactured in colorless, transparent plastic. However, colorless polypropylene is sensitive to ultraviolet rays; it is thus important that the expansion tank not be exposed to direct sunlight.

Fan

Motor vehicles require substantial cooling capacity, even at low speeds. Thus the radiator must be provided with forced-air ventilation. Single-piece injected plastic fans are generally employed in passenger cars, while trucks and buses usually have either fans with riveted metal blades or solid plastic units which require up to 15 kW to drive them. Fans with more modest power requirements are generally operated electrically. Although blade design and arrangement can be selected to provide relatively quiet operation, the noise levels of such fans remain substantial due to their constant high rotating speed. The outlay involved for the electric-drive units for mid-size cars and larger vehicles would be excessive. For such vehicles, the fan is powered directly by the engine, via a drive belt, or, in the case of heavy trucks, the fan is fastened directly to the crankshaft, thus dispensing with an intermediate drive. The fan-control arrangement requires particular attention. Depending upon vehicle and operating conditions, the unassisted air stream can provide sufficient cooling up to 95% of the time. It is thus possible to economize on the fuel which would otherwise have to provide the energy to drive the fan. Electric fans use a two-step control system to achieve this end: An electric temperature switch activates the fan once a specific coolant temperature has been exceeded. The fluid-friction or viscous-drive fan (VISCO®-Coupling) is a mechanical-drive arrangement of proven effectiveness for application in both passenger cars and heavy vehicles. It basically consists of three sections: The engine-powered primary (or input) disk, the internally-activated secondary (or output) section, and the control. An intermediate disk divides the secondary section into a supply chamber and a working chamber through which the fluid circulates. There is no mechanical connection between the working chamber and the primary disk, which rotates freely within it. Torque is transmitted through the internal friction of the highly-viscous fluid and its adhesion to the inner surfaces. There is a degree of slippage between input and output. A wiper rotates with the secondary section, maintaining a supply of fluid medium to the supply chamber. Centrifugal force then forces the fluid through a valve and back to the working chamber. The control's bimetallic spring responds to drops in the temperature around it by closing the valve, causing the fluid medium to collect in the supply chamber while the working chamber empties. Aside from an insignificant residual torque, the coupling is disengaged. The system thus provides infinitely-variable speed regulation according to the temperature of the air stream surrounding the bimetallic element.

Charge-air cooling

Cooling the charge air reduces both the thermal loads placed on the engine and the fuel consumption, while limiting exhaust-gas temperatures, with the attendant benefits in NO_x emissions. In addition, it also improves resistance to knock in spark-ignition engines. Either the engine coolant or the ambient air can be employed to cool the charge air. When the engine coolant is used, the charge-air cooler (or intercooler) can be installed in virtually any location, a benefit associated with the water-cooled unit's modest dimensions. However, this type of system

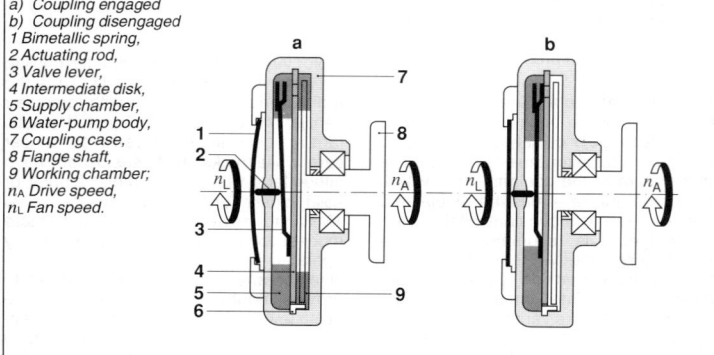

Visco®-coupling
a) Coupling engaged
b) Coupling disengaged
1 Bimetallic spring,
2 Actuating rod,
3 Valve lever,
4 Intermediate disk,
5 Supply chamber,
6 Water-pump body,
7 Coupling case,
8 Flange shaft,
9 Working chamber;
n_A Drive speed,
n_L Fan speed.

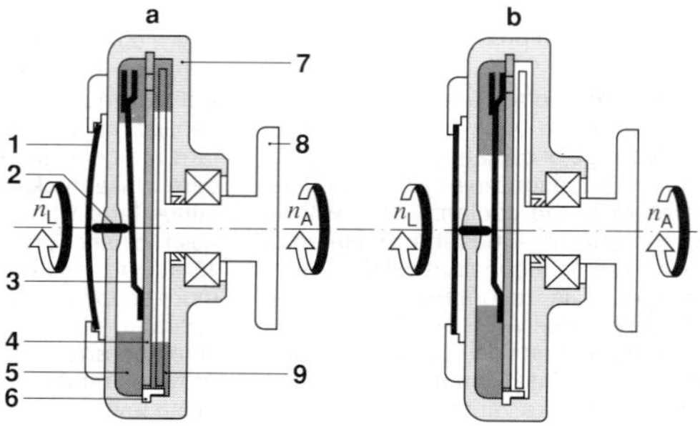

cannot cool the charge air to below the temperature range of the engine coolant unless an auxiliary cooling circuit is used.

This has resulted in the air-cooled design becoming the standard version in both passenger cars and heavy vehicles. These intercoolers can be mounted in front of, beside or above the engine radiator, or at a completely separate location. A separately-mounted intercooler can utilize either the unassisted vehicle air stream or its own fan. Extra effort is required to ensure adequate air supply when the intercooler is to be located to the front of the engine radiator. The advantage of this location lies in the fact that the fan ensures sufficient air flow across the intercooler at low vehicle speeds. A disadvantage is that the cooling air is itself heated in the process: The capacity of the engine radiator must therefore be increased accordingly.

The system of corrugated aluminum fins and tubes employed for the core is similar to that used in the radiator for the engine coolant. Wide tubes with internal fins provide superior performance and structural integrity in actual practice. Due to the high level of thermal-transfer resistance on the charge-air side it is possible to hold the fin density on the cooling-air side to a minimum. The diffusion rate is a particularly important factor on the charge-air intercooler, and defines the relationship between the cooling of the charge air and the charge-air/cooling-air temperature differential:

$$\Phi = (t_{1E} - t_{1A}) / (t_{1E} - t_{2E})$$

The equation's elements are:

Φ Diffusion rate
t_{1E} Charge-air intake temperature
t_{1A} Charge-air exit temperature
t_{2E} Cooling-air intake temperature
For passenger cars: $\Phi = 0.4 \dots 0.7$
For trucks: $\Phi = 0.65 \dots 0.85$

Whenever possible, the plenum chamber is injection-molded in fiberglass-reinforced polyamide as a single casting incorporating all connections and mounts. It is flange-mounted on the core. Plenum chambers which feature undercut shapes or are intended for high-temperature applications are die-cast in aluminum, and welded to the core.

Oil coolers

A portion of the engine's thermal loss is absorbed by its lube oil, the cooling needs of which are frequently satisfied by the surface area of the oil pan. High-performance vehicles, however, require a cooling device if the lubricant is to remain within the specified temperature range under full-load operation.

Lube-oil coolers are generally in the form of aluminum oil/air radiators, which are either installed adjacent to the engine-coolant radiator or separately. Separately mounted units depend upon either the unassisted air stream or an extra fan for operation. The oil cooler consists of a high-density system of flat tubes and corrugated fins, or of round tubes in conjunction with flat fins. The high internal pressures make it necessary to equip flat tubes with turbulence inserts.

Stainless-steel disk radiators and aluminum forked-pipe radiators are used to cool lubricating oil and engine coolant in passenger cars. Disk radiators have their own housing and are mounted between the oil filter and the block, while forked-pipe radiators have no casing, facilitating installation in oil-filter housings and in the oil pan.

When the cooling requirements are more modest, as is the case, for instance, with the cooling of automatic-transmission fluid, copper/brass double-pipe heat exchangers or aluminum flat-tube radiators are used. Both types of unit are installed in the return-side coolant tank of the engine radiator.

An oil/air radiator is used to cool transmission fluid in more powerful heavy vehicles. The unit is mounted in front of the engine radiator in order to provide good ventilation.

Engine oil in heavy vehicles is generally cooled with stainless-steel disk stacks installed in an extension of the cooling circuit; if conditions are favorable, this installation requires neither a casing nor additional lines.

Air supply

Air filters

The air filter serves to inhibit internal wear by preventing air-borne dust from being drawn into the engine.

The dust content of the air on paved roads amounts to an average of 1 mg/m^3, however, on unpaved roads and in construction areas the dust content can be high as 40 mg/m^3. This means that – depending on roads and operating conditions – a medium-sized engine can draw in up to 50 g of dust over 1000 km.

Air filters for passenger cars
In addition to filtering the air, air filters for passenger cars preheat the intake air and regulate its temperature, as well as damping the air-intake noise. Intake air temperature regulation is important for the operation of the vehicle and for the composition of the exhaust gases. The temperature of the intake air may differ under part-load and full-load operating conditions.

The required amount of hot air is drawn in in the vicinity of the exhaust and added to the cold intake air at the filter inlet by means of a flap valve mechanism. The regulating mechanism is usually an automatic arrangement employing either a pneumatic vacuum unit connected to the intake manifold or an expansion element. The constant regulated intake air temperature improves engine performance and fuel consumption, and decreases the percentage of pollutants in the exhaust gases through better fuel management and distribution of the air-fuel mixture. Preheating the intake air also shortens the warm-up phase of the engine after it is started, particularly in cold weather. It also prevents ice from forming in the carburetor.

Passenger-car air filters employ paper cartridges and can be mounted either centrally or at the side of the engine compartment. This type of filter is characterized by a high retention factor which remains insensitive to fluctuations in load. Cartridge replacement is a simple operation to be performed at the intervals specified by the vehicle's manufacturer. Passenger-car air

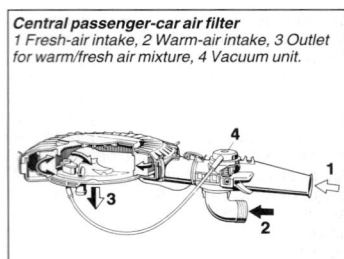

Central passenger-car air filter
1 Fresh-air intake, 2 Warm-air intake, 3 Outlet for warm/fresh air mixture, 4 Vacuum unit.

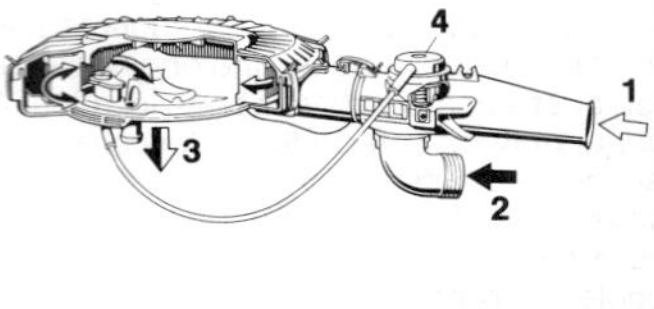

Side-mounted passenger-car air filter
1 Fresh-air intake, 2 Warm-air intake, 3 Outlet for warm/fresh air mixture.

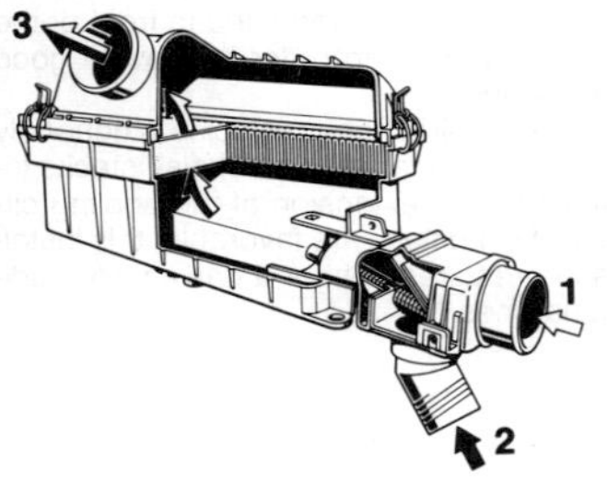

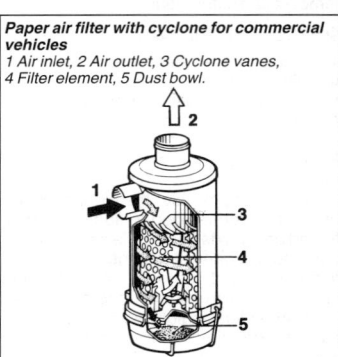

Paper air filter with cyclone for commercial vehicles
1 Air inlet, 2 Air outlet, 3 Cyclone vanes, 4 Filter element, 5 Dust bowl.

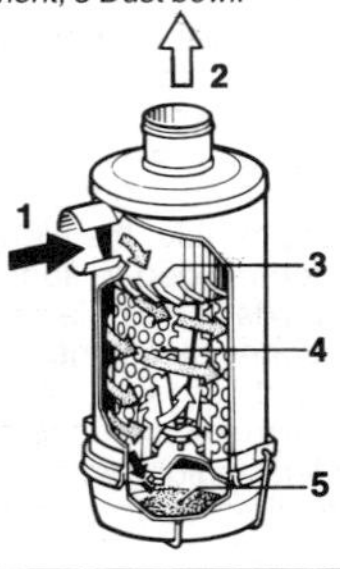

filters must be specially matched to each engine type in order to optimize power, fuel consumption, intake air temperature and noise damping.

Air filters for commercial vehicles

Most of the air filters used in heavy vehicles are of the paper-element type, although oil-bath filters are employed in some applications. Paper filters exhibit high filtering efficiency in all load ranges and increased flow resistance as the amount of dust retained by the filter increases. The paper air filter incorporates a cyclone prefilter to save space. This cyclone/paper air filter combination is the most common type in use today. The filter is serviced by either replacing the filter element or emptying the dust cup.

Paper air filters often incorporate maintenance indicators to show when the filter needs servicing.

The servicing information provided by the manufacturer of the vehicle or filter must be followed. Servicing can be simplified, according to the intensity of engine air pulsation, by using specially matched automatic dust-unloading valves.

Cyclones increase filter service life and extend the maintenance intervals. The cyclone vanes rotate the air, causing the majority of dust particles to be separated from the air before reaching the downstream air filter. Cyclones can be installed upstream of both paper air filters and oil-bath air filters. They cannot be used alone as engine air filters because their filtering efficiency is inadequate. Pertinent standard: DIN 71 459.

Intake-noise damping

The intake noise of passenger-car and commercial-vehicle air filters must be damped in order to comply with legal regulations pertaining to the overall vehicle noise level. Noise damping is achieved almost exclusively by designing the air filter to act as a reflection sound absorber having the specialized shape of a Helmholtz resonator; see p. 427.

Assuming that the air filter is of sufficient size (a good empirical value for 4-stroke engines is 15 to 20 times the displacement of one cylinder), intake noise can generally be damped by 10 to 20 dB (A). In special cases in which the noise at particular frequencies is excessive, supplemental dampers must be used.

The resonance frequency of an intake damper is

$$f_0 = \frac{c}{2\pi} \cdot \sqrt{\frac{A_m}{l \cdot V}}$$

Where
c Speed of sound in air
l Length of the intake manifold
A_m Mean cross section of the intake manifold
V Filter volume

Intake-noise damping

Damping curves of an intake-noise damper
Damper resonance f_0 = 66 Hz.
1 Theoretical damping curve without taking into account pipe resonances.
2 Curve of measured damping response with low sound energy density and without parallel flow (loudspeaker measurement).
3 Measured damping response with high sound energy density and with parallel flow (measurement at the engine).

Air filter with intake pipe
l length of the intake pipe, A_m Mean intake-manifold cross section, V Filter volume.

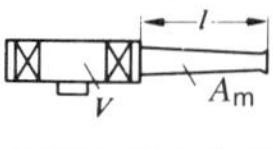

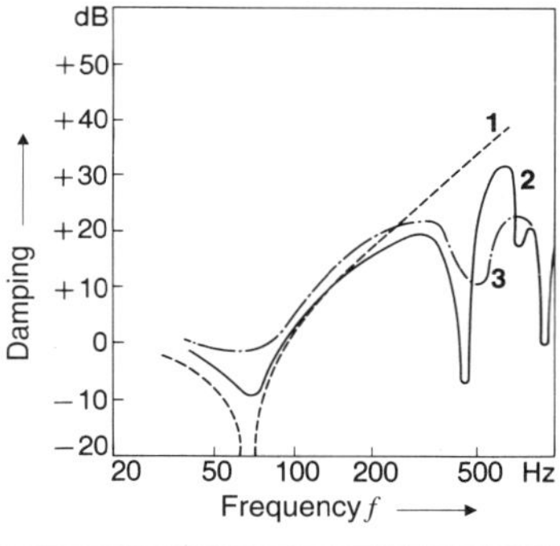

Turbochargers and superchargers for internal-combustion engines

(self-charging)

By compressing the air inducted for combustion in the internal-combustion (IC) engine, and thereby increasing its mass, charging systems also increase the output obtained for a given displacement at a given engine speed. The "compressors" generally used for IC engines are of three basic types; the mechanically-driven supercharger, the exhaust-gas turbocharger and the pressure-wave supercharger.

Mechanical superchargers compress the air using power supplied by the engine crankshaft (mechanical coupling between engine and supercharger), while the turbocharger is powered by the engine's exhaust gases (fluid coupling between engine and turbocharger).

Although the pressure-wave supercharger also derives its compression force from the exhaust gases, it requires a supplementary mechanical drive (combination of mechanical and fluid coupling).

Superchargers (mechanically driven)

These fall into two categories: mechanically-driven centrifugal superchargers (MKL) and mechanically-driven positive-displacement superchargers (MVL).

The turbo-type supercharger for the MKL corresponds to the exhaust-gas turbocharger in its essential configuration. This type of device is very efficient, providing the best ratio between unit dimensions and flow volume. However, the extreme peripheral velocities required to generate the pressure mean that drive speeds must be very high. As the secondary drive pulley (2:1 conversion ratio relative to primary drive) does not rotate fast enough to drive a centrifugal supercharger, a single-stage planetary gear with a 15:1 speed-increasing ratio is employed to achieve the required peripheral speeds. In addition, a transmission unit must be included to vary the rotational speeds if the pressure is to be maintained at a

Mechanical centrifugal supercharger *(schematic)*
1 Variable-speed primary pulley, 2 Variable-speed secondary pulley, 3 Solenoid dutch, 4 Step-up planetary-gear set, 5 Compressor, 6 Air intake, 7 Air outlet.

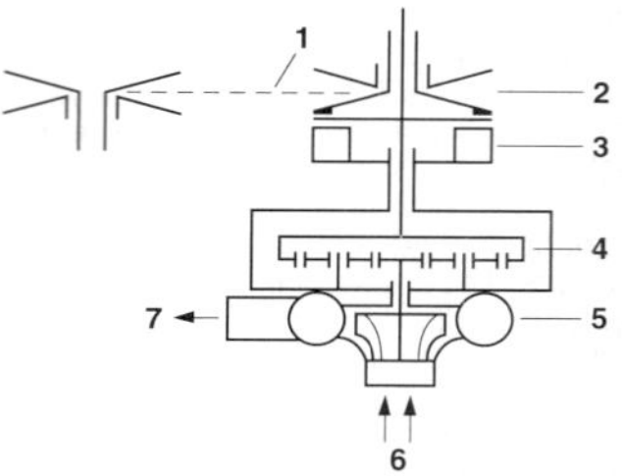

reasonably constant level over a wide range of flow volumes (~ engine speed). The necessity of using extreme rotational speeds, and the technical limits imposed on the transmission of drive power, mean that the centrifugal supercharger's range of potential applications is limited to medium and large-displacement diesel and gasoline engines in passenger cars. This design has not been extensively employed for mechanical superchargers.

Positive-displacement superchargers operate both with and without internal compression. Internal-compression superchargers include the reciprocating-piston, the screw-type, the rotary-piston and the sliding-vane compressor. The Roots supercharger is an example of a unit without internal compression. All of these positive-displacement superchargers share certain characteristics as shown in the graphic illustration for a Roots supercharger.

– The curves for the constant rotational speed n_{LAD} in the graph of p_2/p_1 against $\dot{V}$ are extremely steep, indicating that increases in the p_2/p_1 pressure ratio are accompanied by only slight reductions in the mass-flow volume $\dot{V}$. The precise extent of the drop in flow volume is basically determined by the efficiency of the gap seal (backflow

losses). It is a function of the p_2/p_1 pressure ratio and of time, and is not influenced by rotational speed.
– The p_2/p_1 pressure ratio does not depend upon the rotational speed. In other words, high pressure ratios can also be generated at low mass-flow volumes.
– The mass-flow volume $\dot{V}$ remains independent of the pressure ratio, and is, roughly formulated, directly proportional to rotational speed.
– The unit retains stability throughout its operating range. The positive-displacement compressor operates at all points of the p_2/p_1-$\dot{V}$ graph as determined by supercharger dimensions.

The two symmetrical rotary pistons of the **Roots-type supercharger** operate without directly contacting each other or the housing, with the size of the peripheral gap being a function of design, materials and manufacturing tolerances. An external gear set synchronizes the motion of the two rotary pistons.

In the **sliding-vane supercharger,** an eccentrically-mounted rotor drives the three centrally mounted sliding vanes; the eccentric motion provides the internal compression. The compression pressure for any given degree of eccentricity can be modified by changing the position of the outlet edge A in the housing.

The **spiral-type supercharger** employs an eccentrically-mounted displacement element which is designed to respond to rotation of the input shaft by turning in a double-eccentric oscillating pattern. In sequence, the working chambers open for charging, close for transport and open once again for discharge at the hub. The spirals can be extended beyond the length shown in the illustration to provide internal compression.

The displacement element is driven by a belt-driven, grease-lubricated auxiliary shaft, while the input shaft is lubricated by the engine's oil circuit. Radial sealing is via gaps, while lateral sealing strips provide the axial seal.

Characteristic map for a Roots-type compressor

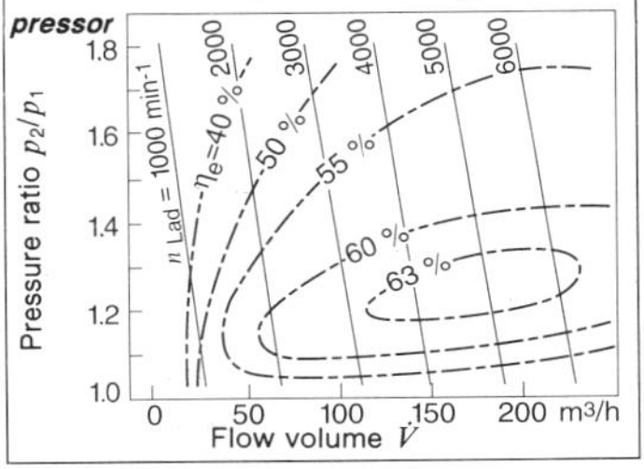

Cross section of a Roots-types compressor
1 Housing
2 Rotary piston

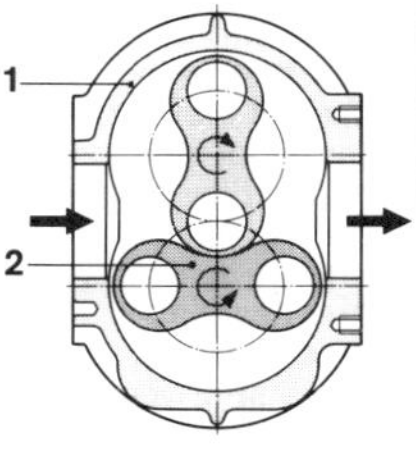

Cross section of a sliding-vane compressor
1 Housing, 2 Rotor, 3 Vanes, 4 Shaft, 5 Outlet edge A.

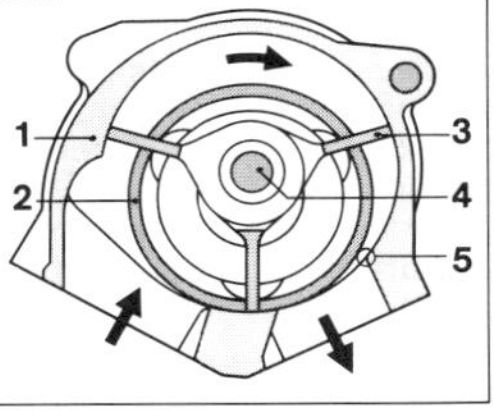

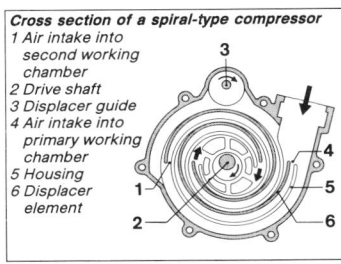

Cross section of a spiral-type compressor
1 Air intake into second working chamber
2 Drive shaft
3 Displacer guide
4 Air intake into primary working chamber
5 Housing
6 Displacer element

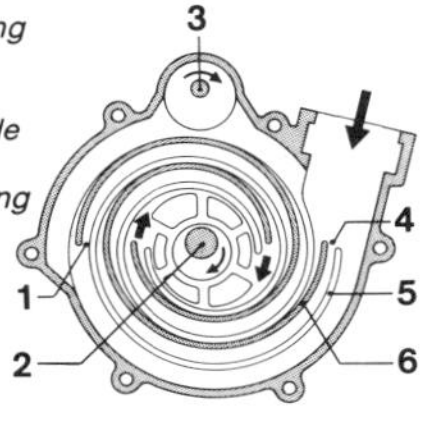

The **rotary-piston supercharger** incorporates a rotary piston moving about an internal axis. The driven inner rotor (rotary piston) turns through an eccentric pattern in the cylindrical outer rotor. The rotor ratios for rotary-piston superchargers are either 2:3 or 3:4. The rotors turn around fixed axes without contacting each other or the housing. The eccentric motion makes it possible for the unit to ingest the maximum possible volume (chamber I) for compression and discharge (chamber III). The internal compression is determined by the position of the outlet edge A.

A ring and pinion gear with sealed-grease lubrication synchronizes the motion of the inner and outer rotors. Permanent lubrication is also employed for the roller bearings. Inner and outer rotors employ gap seals, and usually have some form of coating. Piston rings provide the seal between working chamber and gear case.

Superchargers on IC engines are usually belt-driven (toothed or V-belt). The coupling is either direct (continuous engagement) or via clutch (e.g., solenoid-operated dutch, demand actuation). The step-up ratio may be constant, or it may vary according to engine speed.

Mechanical positive-displacement superchargers (MVL) must be substantially larger than their centrifugal counterparts (MKL) in order to produce a given mass flow. The mechanical positive-displacement supercharger is generally applied to small and medium-displacement engines, where the ratio between charge volume and space requirements is acceptable.

Exhaust-gas turbochargers

The exhaust-gas turbocharger (ATL) consists of two turbo elements, a turbine and a compressor, which are installed on a single shaft. The turbine uses the energy of the exhaust-gas to drive the compressor. The compressor, in turn, draws in fresh air which it supplies to the cylinders in compressed form. The air and the mass flow of the exhaust gases represent the only coupling between the engine and the compressor. Turbocharger speed does not depend upon engine speed, but is rather a function of the balance of drive energy between the turbine and the compressor.

Exhaust-gas turbochargers are used on engines in passenger cars, trucks and heavy-duty engines (marine and locomotive power plants, stationary generators).

The typical engine-performance curves for this type of application are illustrated in a compression graph (p. 421), valid for all displacements, in which the surge line separates the stable operating range on its right from the instable range. It is obvious that the instable range presents no difficulties provided that the correct turbocharger is selected, as all of the points representing potential operating conditions lie

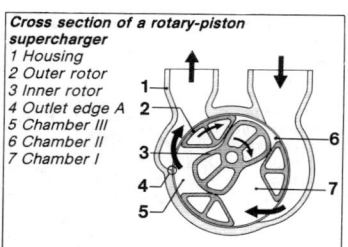

Cross section of a rotary-piston supercharger
1 Housing
2 Outer rotor
3 Inner rotor
4 Outlet edge A
5 Chamber III
6 Chamber II
7 Chamber I

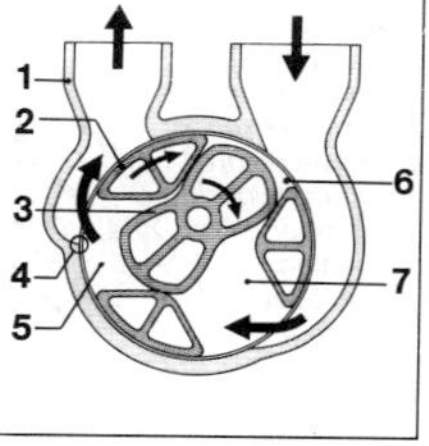

Boost-pressure regulation via exhaust-side boost-pressure control valve (wastegate)
1 Engine, 2 Exhaust-gas turbocharger, 3 Wastegate.

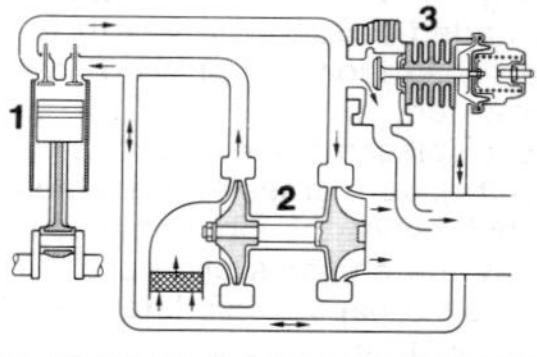

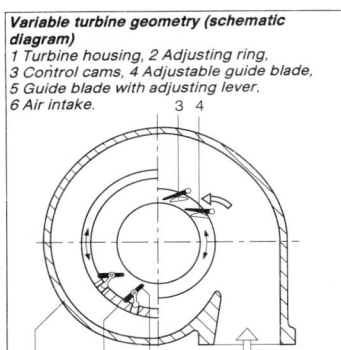

Variable turbine geometry (schematic diagram)
1 Turbine housing, 2 Adjusting ring, 3 Control cams, 4 Adjustable guide blade, 5 Guide blade with adjusting lever, 6 Air intake.

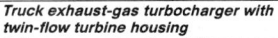

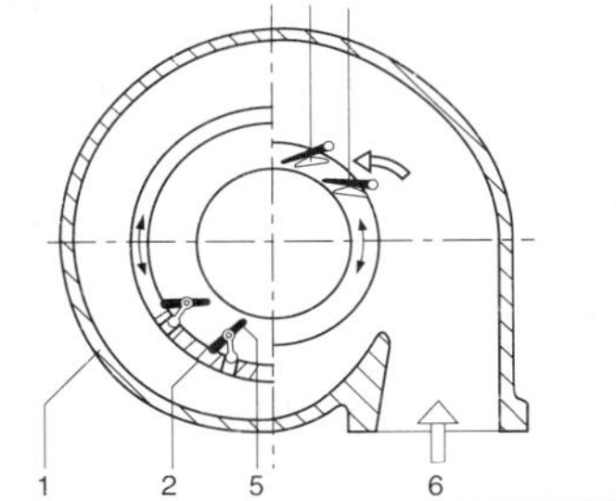

Truck exhaust-gas turbocharger with twin-flow turbine housing
1 Compressor housing, 2 Compressor wheel, 3 Turbine housing, 4 Rotor, 5 Bearing housing, 6 Incoming exhaust-gas, 7 Exhaust-gas discharge, 8 Atmospheric air, 9 Compressed fresh air, 10 Oil supply, 11 Oil return.

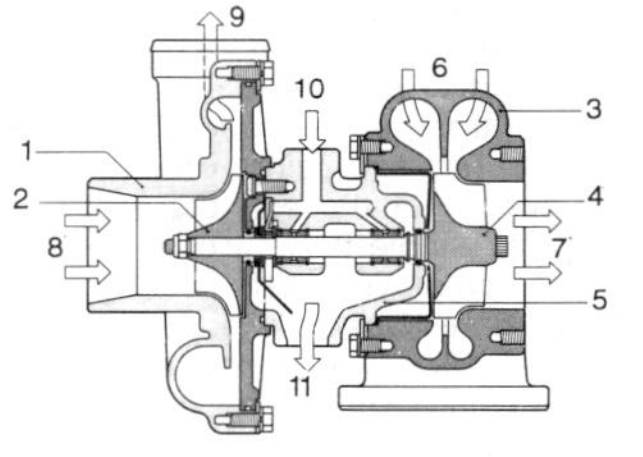

either on the engine operating curves (full load) or below them (part-load operation).

Different applications require various configurations. However, all exhaust-gas turbochargers have practically the same major components: the turbocharger rotor and shaft assembly, which combine with the bearing housing to form the so-called core assembly, and the compressor housing. Other components such as turbine housing and control elements vary according to the specific application.

Piston rings are installed on both the exhaust and intake sides to seal off the bearing housing's oil chamber. In some special applications sealing is enhanced by trapped air or a compressor-side carbon axial face seal. Friction bearings are generally used, installed radially as either floating double plain bushings or stationary plain-bearing bushings, while multiple-wedge surface bushings provide axial support. The turbocharger is connected to the engine's lube-oil circuit for lubrication, with oil supply and return lines located between the compressor and turbine housings. No additional cooling arrangements are provided for the bearing housing on standard units. The temperatures can be maintained below critical levels using devices such as a heat shield, and by

Compression graph with typical engine operation curves valid for all displacements

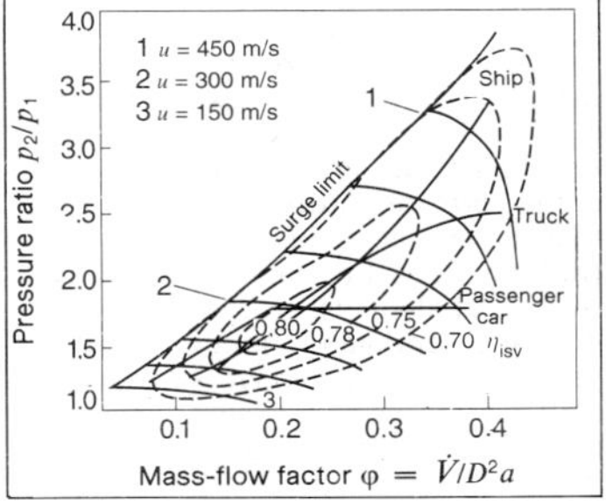

thermally isolating the bearing housing from the hot turbine housing, supplemented by incorporating suitable design elements in the bearing housing itself. Water-cooled bearing housings are employed for exhaust-gas temperatures in excess of 850 °C. The rear wall of the compressor seals the compressor side of the bearing housing.

The housing of the radial compressor is generally made of cast aluminum. An air bypass valve can be integrated in the housing for special applications.

Turbine housings differ substantially according to intended use. Casting materials for turbine housings range from GGG 40 to NiResist D5 (depending upon exhaust-gas temperature). Exhaust-gas turbochargers for trucks incorporate a twin-flow turbine housing in which the two streams join just before reaching the impeller. This housing configuration is employed to achieve pulse turbocharging, in which the pressure of the exhaust-gas is supplemented by its kinetic energy.

In contrast, in the case of constant-pressure turbocharging, only the pressure energy of the exhaust-gas is utilized, and single-flow turbine housings can be employed. This configuration has become especially popular for use in conjunction with water-cooled turbine housings on marine engines. The exhaust-gas turbochargers on heavy-duty engines often incorporate a nozzle ring upstream from the turbine. The nozzle ring provides a particularly smooth and consistent stream to the impeller while allowing fine adjustment of the flow through the turbine.

Exhaust-gas turbochargers for passenger cars generally use single-flow turbine housings. However, the car engine's wide rpm range means that some form of turbocharger governing mechanism is required if the boost pressure is to be maintained at a relatively constant level throughout the engine's operating range. Standard practice presently favors regulating flow on the exhaust side, whereby a portion of the engine's exhaust gases is routed past the turbine (bypass) using a governing mechanism (wastegate) which can be in the form of a valve or a flap.

The wastegate is actuated pneumatically. The necessary control pressure is tapped-off from the pressurized side of the turbocharger, making it possible to combine turbocharger and wastegate in a single unit.

The available energy is exploited more efficiently by governing systems incorporating turbines with variable blade geometry. With this system, the turbine's flow resistance is modified continuously to achieve maximum utilization of the exhaust energy under all operating conditions.

Of all the potential designs, adjustable guide blades have achieved general acceptance, as they combine a wide control range with high efficiency levels.

An adjusting ring is rotated to provide simple adjustment of the blade angle. The blades, in turn, are swiveled to the desired angles using adjusting cams, or directly via adjusting levers attached to the individual blades. The pneumatic actuator can operate with either vacuum or positive pressure. Microelectronic control systems can exploit the advantages of variable turbine-blade geometry by providing optimal boost pressure throughout the engine's operating range.

Pressure-wave superchargers

The pressure-wave supercharger exploits the dynamic properties of gases, using pressure waves to convey energy from the exhaust-gas to the intake air. The energy exchange takes place within the cells of the rotor (cell-type wheel), which also depends upon an engine-driven belt for synchronization and maintenance of the pressure-wave exchange process.

Pressure-wave compressor
1 Engine, 2 Cell-type compressor wheel, 3 Belt drive, 4 High-pressure exhaust-gas, 5 Pressurized air, 6 Low-pressure air intake, 7 Low-pressure exhaust outlet.

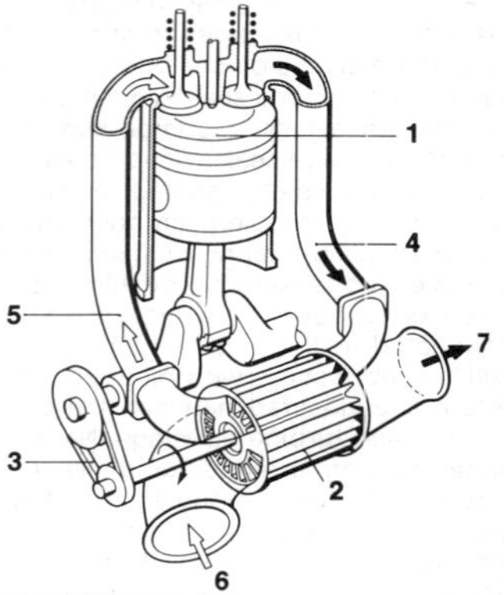

Inside the rotor, the actual energy-exchange process proceeds at the speed of sound. This depends upon exhaust-gas temperature, meaning that it is essentially a function of engine torque, and not engine speed. Thus the pressure-wave process is optimally tailored to only a single operating point if a constant step-up ratio is employed between engine and supercharger. To get around this disadvantage, appropriately-designed "pockets" can be incorporated in the forward part of the housings. These achieve high efficiency levels extending through a relatively large range of engine operating conditions and provide a good overall boost curve.

The exchange of energy occurring within the rotor at the speed of sound ensures that the pressure-wave supercharger responds rapidly to changes in engine demand, with the actual reaction times being determined by the charging processes in the air and exhaust tracts.

The pressure-wave supercharger's rotor is driven by the engine's crankshaft via a belt assembly. The rotor's cell walls are irregularly spaced in order to reduce noise. The rotor turns within a cylindrical housing, with the fresh air and exhaust-gas tracts feeding into the housing's respective ends. On one side are low-pressure air intake and pressurized air, while the high-pressure exhaust and low-pressure exhaust-gas outlet are located on the other side.

The accompanying gas-flow and state diagrams illustrate the pressure-wave process in a basic "Comprex" at full load and moderate engine speed. Developing (or unrolling) rotor and housing converts the rotation to a translation. The state diagram contains the boundary curves for the four housing openings in accordance with local conditions. The diagrams for the ideal no-loss process have been drawn-up with the assistance of the intrinsic characteristic process.

The pressure-wave supercharger's rotor is over-mounted and is provided with permanent grease lubrication, with the bearing located on the unit's air side. The air housing is of aluminum, the gas housing of NiResist materials. The rotor with its axial blades and chambers is cast using the lost-wax method. A integral governing mechanism regulates boost pressure according to demand.

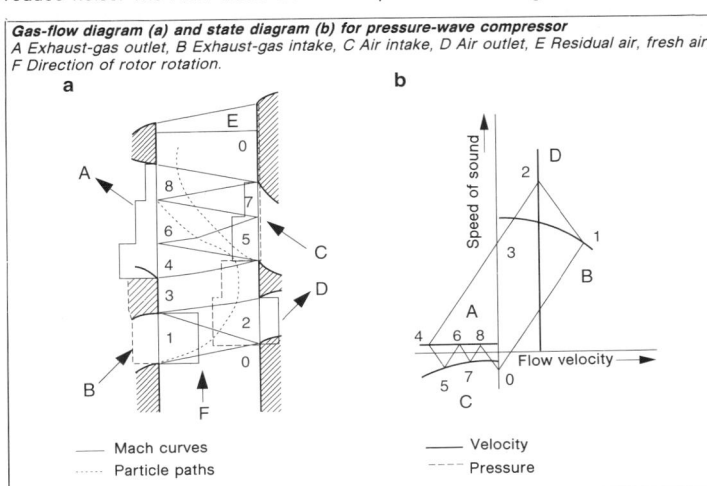

Gas-flow diagram (a) and state diagram (b) for pressure-wave compressor
A Exhaust-gas outlet, B Exhaust-gas intake, C Air intake, D Air outlet, E Residual air, fresh air, F Direction of rotor rotation.

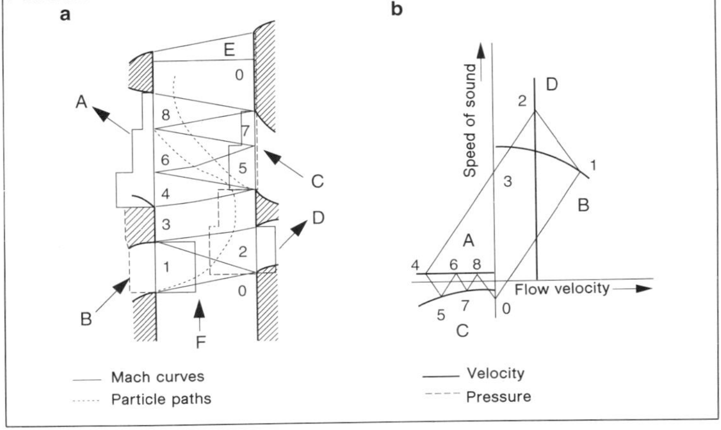

Exhaust systems

Exhaust-system purpose

The exhaust system reduces the pollutant constituents of the exhaust gas generated by combustion in the engine. The remaining exhaust gas is then discharged as quietly as possible at a convenient point on the vehicle. The engine power should be reduced as little as possible during the process.

Exhaust-system design

A passenger-car exhaust system serves here as our example. It consists basically of three main components (although some of these are also found in commercial-vehicle exhaust systems):

The catalytic converter serves as an exhaust-gas cleaning device for spark-ignition (SI) engines (as does nowadays the oxidation catalytic converter in diesel engines). It is mounted as close as possible to the engine so that it can quickly reach its operating temperature and therefore be effective in urban driving. It is fitted as supplementary equipment in place of the front muffler, whose acoustical functions it also takes over in addition to its exhaust-gas cleaning function. The acoustical changes in the vehicle must meet legal requirements.

Depending on the size of the vehicle and the engine, one or several mufflers are used. In V-engines the left and right cylinder banks are frequently run separately, each being fitted with its own catalytic converter or muffler, and only brought together at the end of the vehicle in one large muffler.

The exhaust pipes are the third and last component in the exhaust system. They combine the exhaust-gas outlets in the cylinder head into one or more pipes (manifolds), and also connect the catalytic converter(s) and the mufflers to each other. The length and cross-section of the pipes, as well as the type of junction used, influence the vehicle's performance characteristics and acoustic behavior. Exhaust systems for vehicles with larger swept volumes are therefore often fitted with twin pipes. The pipes, the catalytic converter and muffler are connected to the main body of the system by means of insert connections and flanges. Many original-equipment (OE) systems are welded into one complete element for faster mounting.

The entire exhaust system is connected with the underbody of the vehicle via flexible suspension elements. The fixing points must be carefully selected, as otherwise vibration can be transmitted to the bodywork and thus generate noise in the passenger compartment. The exhaust-system noise at the exhaust-emission point (tailpipe) can also cause bodywork resonances.

Exhaust systems
a) Without, b) With catalytic-converter system.
1 Front muffler, 2 Catalytic-converter system, 3 Center muffler, 4 Rear muffler.

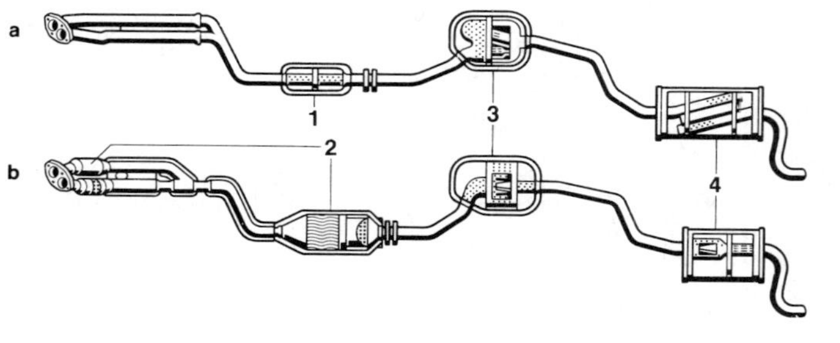

The total volume of the passenger-car muffler system is approximately three to eight times the engine's swept volume. Depending on swept volume and type of muffler, the exhaust system weighs between 8 and 40 kg.

Catalytic converter

The catalytic-converter housing is of heat-resistant, high-quality steel. It contains actively-coated ceramic monoliths. In order to compensate for the differing coefficients of thermal expansion of steel and ceramics, and to protect the sensitive monolith against bumps and vibrations, a flexible mounting is used. Two different types of mounting have been developed:

The wire-knit mounting, of highly heat-resistant stainless steel, is non-sensitive to extreme exhaust-gas temperatures and to pronounced gas pulsations in the high-speed range. Because of its poor heat-insulation qualities, the pipes and the body of the catalytic converter must often also be insulated.

The swelling-mat mounting is made of ceramic fiber felt, composed of aluminum silicate fibers and expanding mica particles. The two substances are combined using acrylic latex. Under the influence of temperature the matting expands and presses the monolith into an immovable position. As the swell matting is a good insulator, there is no need for additional insulation. However, if the exhaust gases cause excessive heating, the pressure on the monoliths can reach such a level that there is the danger of fracture. If the exhaust-gas temperatures are not high enough, the pressing force exerted on the monolith is insufficient, allowing the monolith to move and possibly be destroyed. Exhaust-gas pulsation may lead to erosion in the swell matting.

In order to restrict linear expansion and to achieve better mixing of the exhaust gases, several monoliths are frequently used in one catalytic converter. The shape of the inflow funnel into the catalytic converter must be designed carefully, so that the exhaust gases flow through the monolith evenly. The external shape of the ceramic body depends on the space available underneath the vehicle, and may be triangular, oval or round.

An alternative to the ceramic monolith is the metal catalytic converter. It is made of finely corrugated, 0.05 mm thick metal foil, wound and hard-soldered in a high-temperature process. As in the case of the ceramic catalytic converter, the surface is coated with catalytically effective material. As a result of its thin walls, more channels can be accommodated in the same area. That means less resistance to the exhaust gas, which is beneficial with regard to performance optimization in high-performance vehicles.

Dual-bed three-way catalytic converter
1 Lambda sensor for lambda closed-loop control, 2 Monolith, 3 Wire-knit mounting, 4 Heat-insulated double shell.

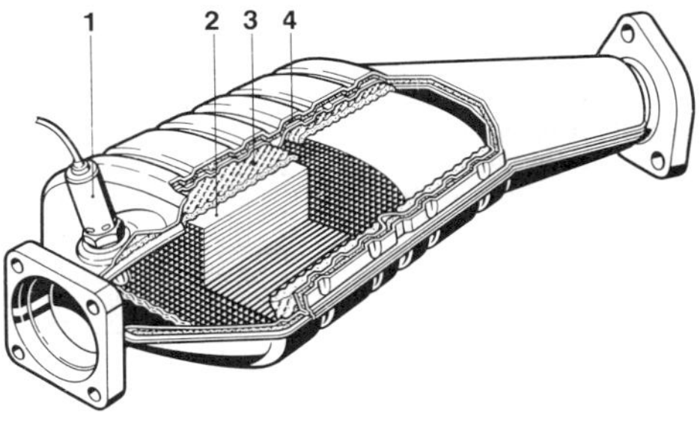

Catalytic converters also have an acoustic effect. As a result of the narrow ceramic pipes in the monolith, numerous small sound sources are formed.

The sound waves are thereby partially extinguished by interference or are damped by friction.

In the design of the exhaust system the catalytic converter must be carefully tuned, as its high level of flow resistance has a considerable influence on the system's vibration characteristics as well as on the performance of the engine (see also "Catalytic Afterburning", page 481).

Mufflers

Mufflers are intended to smooth the exhaust-gas pulsations and make them as inaudible as possible. Basically, two physical principles are concerned, reflection and absorption, and mufflers are divided into two types according to these two principles. However, they mostly comprise a combination of reflection and absorption. As mufflers together with the pipes of the exhaust system form an oscillator with natural resonance, the position of the mufflers is highly significant for the quality of sound-damping. The objective is to tune the exhaust systems as low as possible, so that their natural frequencies do not excite bodywork resonances. To avoid structure-borne noise and to provide heat insulation against the underbody of the vehicle, mufflers often have double walls and an insulating layer. Depending on the space available underneath the vehicle, mufflers are produced either as "winding cups" or from half-shells.

Reflection mufflers consist of chambers of varying lengths which are connected together by pipes. The differences in the cross-sections of the pipes and the chambers, the diversion of the exhaust gases, and the resonators formed by the connecting pipes with the chambers, produce muffling which is particularly effective at low frequencies. The more chambers used, the more efficient is the muffler.

Reflection mufflers cause a higher exhaust-gas backpressure, as a rule have greater power loss, and are heavier.

Absorption mufflers are constructed with one chamber, through which a perforated pipe is passed. The chamber is filled with sound-deadening material. The sound enters the absorption material through the perforated pipe and is converted into heat by friction. The absorption material usually consists of long-fiber mineral wool (basalt or rock wool) with a bulk density of 120 ... 150 g/l. The level of muffling depends on the bulk density, the sound-absorption grade of the material, and on the length and coating-thickness of the chamber. Damping takes place across a very broad band, but only begins at higher frequencies. The shape of the perforations, and the fact that the pipe passes through the wool ensures that the material is not blown out by the pulsation of the exhaust gas. Sometimes the mineral wool

Noise-damping principles
a) Absorption muffler
b) Reflection muffler
c) Combination of a) and b).

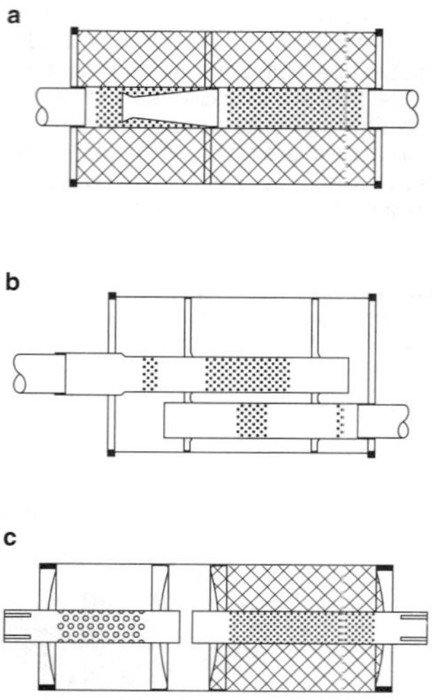

is protected by a layer of stainless-steel wool around the perforated pipe.

Absorption mufflers are principally used as rear mufflers.

Acoustic tuning devices

A number of different components can be used to remove disturbing frequency areas of the noise emitted from the tailpipe.

The Helmholtz resonator damps sound in its natural frequency range and functions as a suction resonator. It is a through-flow resonator and amplifies at its natural frequency, but thereafter it has a broad damping range.

Pipes perforated with holes work in a similar way to a watering-can rose. The one large sound source, the pipe, is converted into many small sound points, formed by the perforations (the holes in the watering-can rose). A broad-band filter effect occurs as a result of interference and swirling of the exhaust gas.

Venturi nozzles damp low-frequency sound. They must be designed so that the flow speed in the nozzle throat is always below the speed of sound. The funnel must be set at a specific angle, as otherwise hissing noises occur.

Soot filters

In order to remove solid particles from diesel-engine exhaust gas, soot filters are in development. Various kinds of filter system are used, e.g., steel-wool filters, ceramic-monolith filters, ceramic-coil filters etc.

The ceramic-monolith filter currently represents the best compromise with regard to the requirements made of the filter. In contrast to the flow-through catalytic-converter monoliths, the channels for the soot filter are alternatingly open and closed, so that the particle-laden exhaust gas is forced to flow through the uncoated, porous walls of the honeycomb structure. The particles are deposited in the pores. Depending on the porosity of the ceramic body, the effectiveness of these filters ranges from 70 to 90 %.

In order to guarantee full functioning of the filters they must be regenerated at certain intervals. Two cleaning processes are possible; in both cases the soot particles are burnt away:

In the chemical process, additives in the fuel reduce the flammability of the soot particles to the usual exhaust-gas temperature. The secondary emissions arising as a result of the additives may have a disadvantageous effect.

In the thermal process, a high-power heating element is connected, which raises the exhaust-gas temperature to approx. 700 °C. The regeneration is most simply carried out with the engine switched off. The filter regeneration point is ascertained either via a time control or an aneroid box. If it is necessary to regenerate the filter while the vehicle is running, two filters can be fitted which are alternatingly filtering or being regenerated. This is, however, very cost-intensive. A further possibility is to divert the exhaust gases via a sound muffler during regeneration, whereby the exhaust gases are emitted unfiltered for approx. 5 % of the journey. Heating elements are also being developed which permit simultaneous regeneration and filtering of engine exhaust gases (full-flow regeneration).

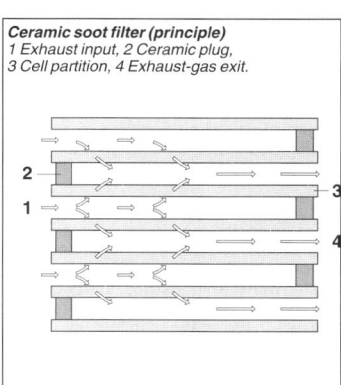

Ceramic soot filter (principle)
1 Exhaust input, 2 Ceramic plug, 3 Cell partition, 4 Exhaust-gas exit.

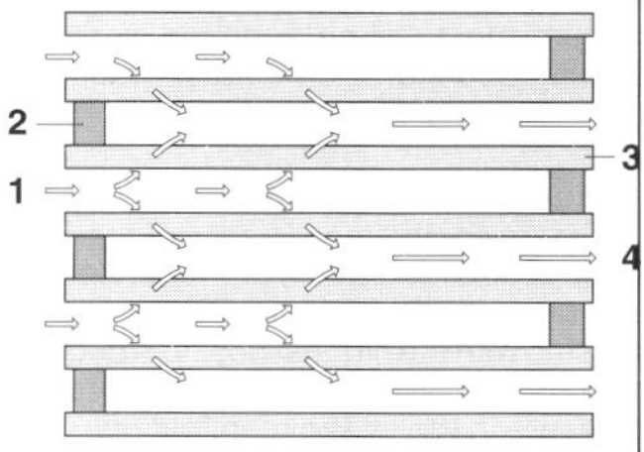

Engine management for spark-ignition (SI) engines

Control parameters and operation

Air-fuel ratio (A/F ratio)

Approximately 14.5 kg air are required for complete combustion of 1 kg gasoline. The excess-air factor which describes this so-called stoichiometric A/F ratio is

$$\lambda = \frac{\text{quantity of intake air}}{\text{theoretical air requirement}} = 1$$

A lean mixture ($\lambda > 1$) contains more air; a rich mixture ($\lambda < 1$) less air.

The A/F ratio decisively affects the engine's operating characteristics. Maximum torque and smoothest operation are obtained in the rich range at $\lambda \approx 0.9$. However, this ratio is also characterized by high CO and HC emissions as well as excessive specific fuel consumption. The rich-mixture limit for engine operation is $\lambda \approx 0.5$, with the lean limit being reached at $\lambda \approx 1.3$. It is for these reasons that engines were formerly set up to run lean under part-load operation (fuel consumption), with enrichment at full-throttle (performance), and approximately $\lambda = 1$ (smooth running) at idle. Today, almost all engines are operated at the stoichiometric A/F ratio $\lambda = 1$. This allows the 3-way catalytic converter to treat raw emissions with maximum effectiveness, thereby facilitating compliance with legal emission limits (p. 482). However, under certain operating conditions, such as starting, warm-up and acceleration, the mixture must still be enriched in order to obtain good starts, smooth operation and brisk engine response.

Air-fuel mixture quality

Optimum combustion in spark-ignition engines is obtained with a homogeneous air-fuel mixture. This requires good fuel processing with the highest possible degree of atomization. When there is high vacuum pressure in the intake manifold (idle, part-throttle, low rpm), the carburetor discharges a fine mist of fuel into it; however, large fuel droplets form in the upper load

Influence of air factor λ and ignition timing α_z on fuel consumption and torque

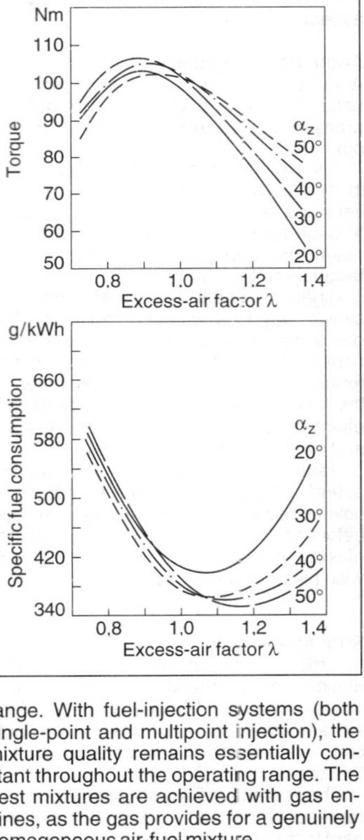

range. With fuel-injection systems (both single-point and multipoint injection), the mixture quality remains essentially constant throughout the operating range. The best mixtures are achieved with gas engines, as the gas provides for a genuinely homogeneous air-fuel mixture.

Fuel-metering

On systems with central fuel-metering devices (carburetors and single-point fuel-injection systems), the long distances and the varying lengths of the mixture-intake passages complicate distribution of the fuel to the individual cylinders. Designing carburetor systems is especially difficult, as various combinations of jets and passages are employed to discharge the fuel into the intake tract in accordance with the operating conditions. With single-point fuel injection (also known as throttle-body injection – TBI), it is possible to achieve uniform distribution through careful design of throttle-valve layout and the location of the injector. Multipoint fuel injection distributes extremely consistent quantities of fuel to the individual cylinders; the deviation between cylinders generally remains within a range of approx. 0.5 ... 3%. Sequential injection can also be applied with multipoint-injection systems to obtain further improvements in combustion along with even greater consistency between cylinders: Here, injection of the fuel into the individual cylinders is not simultaneous, but rather consecutive, being delivered at the same crankshaft angle on each cycle.

Ignition energy

The ignition system provides the high-voltage spark which initiates combustion. An ignition-spark energy of approx. 0.2 J is adequate to ignite a stoichiometric air-fuel mixture, while richer or leaner mixtures require substantially higher levels of spark energy. Excess energy, i.e., where an ignition system provides a spark of high energy and extended duration (transistorized or electronic ignition) stabilizes flame propagation, thus reducing fluctuations between cycles. The reduction in cyclic deviation results in smoother running and lower HC emissions from the engine. Increased spark penetration and thin spark-plug electrodes also have a positive effect on engine smoothness and HC emissions.

Ignition timing

Fuel consumption and exhaust emissions respond oppositely to changes in ignition timing: While more spark advance increases power and reduces fuel consumption, it also results in higher emissions of HC and, in particular, of NO_x. Excessive spark advance can cause engine knock which may lead to engine damage. Retarded ignition results in higher exhaust-gas temperatures, which can also harm the engine. An electronic system incorporating programmed ignition curves, with the ability to control ignition timing with reference to variables such as rpm, load, temperature, etc., can be employed to achieve the optimum compromise between these conflicting objectives.

Influence of air factor λ and ignition timing α_z on exhaust emissions

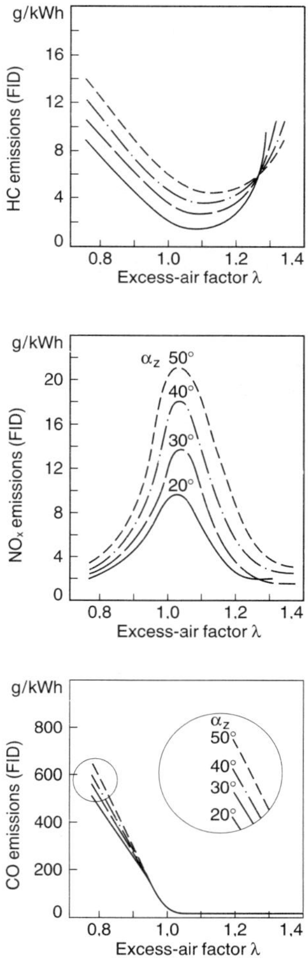

Fuel management

Fuel management for the spark-ignition engine comprises:
- Metering the air-fuel mixture according to quantity and ratio,
- Formation of the air-fuel mixture,
- Transporting the air-fuel mixture,
- Distributing the air-fuel mixture.

The driver-operated throttle valve meters the mixture quantity, while the mixture-formation device controls the A/F ratio by metering the appropriate amount of fuel to the air being drawn into the engine.

Mixture formation is significantly influenced by the type of fuel-injection device used. The fuel generally enters the intake manifold in droplet form. Some of the droplets evaporate to form fuel vapor on their way to the intake valves (desirable), while others form a film on the manifold walls (undesirable). Most of the improvement in mixture quality associated with single-point mixture formation is caused by the atomization at the throttle valve and evaporation on the warm walls of the intake manifold, and on the special heating elements. On multipoint fuel-injection systems, the excellent mixture formation at the injector is supplemented by evaporation on the hot intake valve.

With single-point mixture formation, mixture transport and mixture distribution both take place within the intake manifold. In consequence, the manifold's design has a major influence on both processes, and uniform mixture distribution under all operating conditions is very difficult to achieve.

With decentralized mixture formation, i.e., multipoint injection systems, pure air flows through most of the length of the intake tract. The fuel is generally injected directly before the intake valve, thus providing optimum conditions for uniform mixture distribution.

Mixture-preparation
a) Single-point fuel injection, b) Multipoint fuel injection.
1 Fuel, 2 Air, 3 Throttle valve, 4 Intake manifold, 5 Injector(s), 6 Engine.

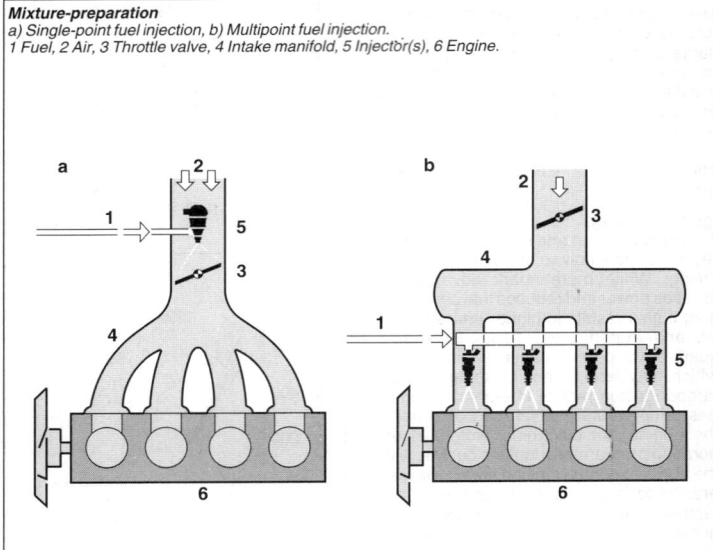

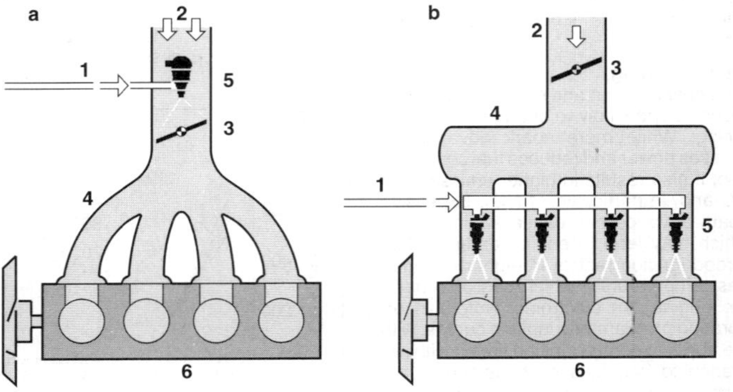

Schematic of a carburetor system
1 Fuel tank, 2 Fuel pump, 3 Fuel filter, 4 Carburetor, 5 Intake manifold.

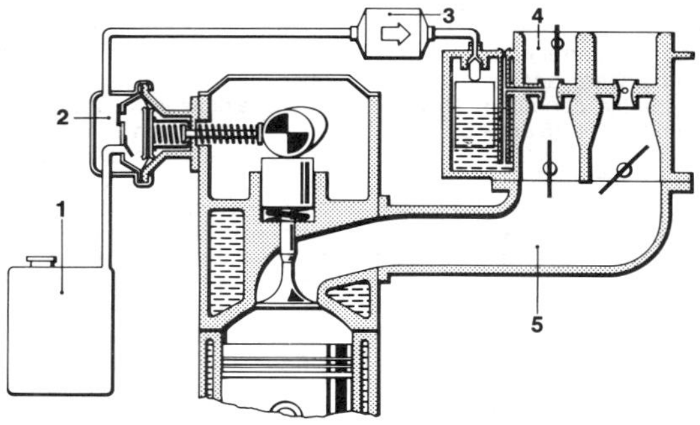

Carburetors

Carburetor system

The fuel is transported from the fuel tank to the carburetor by a fuel pump (generally a diaphragm pump); its driving force comes from the camshaft or the distributor shaft. The system is designed to limit the maximum supply pressure. A fine-mesh fuel filter can be installed upstream or downstream from the pump.

Carburetor types

Downdraft carburetors

Downdraft carburetors are the most common type of carburetor in use today. Layouts which use float chambers and metering jets to best advantage make it possible to produce effective constructions. These designs work in conjunction with the corresponding intake-manifold designs to achieve optimum mixture formation and distribution.

Sidedraft carburetors

Sidedraft carburetors (familiar as fixed-venturi and constant-depression carburetors) are advantageous in cases where the lowest possible engine height is required. Sidedraft carburetors with fixed venturi are generally employed in engines designed for high specific output.

Constant-depression carburetors feature venturi cross sections which vary in size during operation, maintaining essentially constant vacuum at the fuel outlet. The variation in the cross section of the air intake is provided by a pneumatically-actuated plunger; attached to the plunger is a needle which regulates the fuel quantity.

Carburetors for 4-cylinder engines

The single-venturi carburetor with one mixing chamber is the least expensive design, and is therefore generally used with small engines.

The two-stage carburetor featuring two mixing chambers has come to be the standard arrangement. The first barrel controls part-throttle operation. When maximum engine output is required, a mechanical or pneumatic unit activates the second stage by opening the second throttle valve. Two-stage carburetors are employed on low and medium-displacement engines of 1.3 litres and above, where their potential for more precise calibration of mixture formation provides greater latitude for meeting specific engine requirements, with attendant benefits in fuel consumption and exhaust emissions.

Carburetors for 6-cylinder engines
The double-barrel carburetor features two carburetor sections which share a single float chamber and operate in parallel. The two throttle valves open simultaneously. The two-stage four-barrel carburetor has four mixing chambers and is easier to tune for part-throttle operation. This design is also suitable for V8 engines.

Special-purpose carburetors
Carburetors for off-road vehicles use special float chambers to maintain an optimum mixture when the vehicle is tilted at extreme angles.

Design and operating principles

The driver uses the accelerator pedal to actuate the throttle valve, which determines the amount of air which is drawn into the engine. The carburetor discharges fuel in quantities proportional to the amount of air. Thus output is a function of throttle opening. The float and the flat needle valve operate together to regulate the flow of fuel to the carburetor while maintaining a constant fuel level in the float chamber. The linkage's intrinsic lever action enhances the closing force exerted upon the float needle.

The airflow is measured by means of an air funnel which is designed to induce a venturi effect. The reduction in its diameter increases the velocity of the air, producing a corresponding vacuum at the narrowest point. The resulting pressure differential relative to the float chamber – which can be further augmented with a boost venturi – is exploited to withdraw fuel from the float chamber. In fixed-venturi carburetors, adapting the amount of fuel to the air quantity is basically performed by the main jets and several auxiliary metering systems. The high flow velocities through the venturi and the throttle aperture permit extremely good mixture formation.

Schematic of a two-stage carburetor
1 Idle cut-off valve, 2 Acceleration pump, 3 Idle system, 4 Choke valve, 5 Booster, 6 Main metering circuit, 7 Full-load enrichment, 8 Float, 9 Fuel supply, 10 Float needle valve, 11 Bypass plug, 12 Idle-mixture adjustment screw, 13 Throttle valves, 14 Venturi, 15 Part-load control valve.

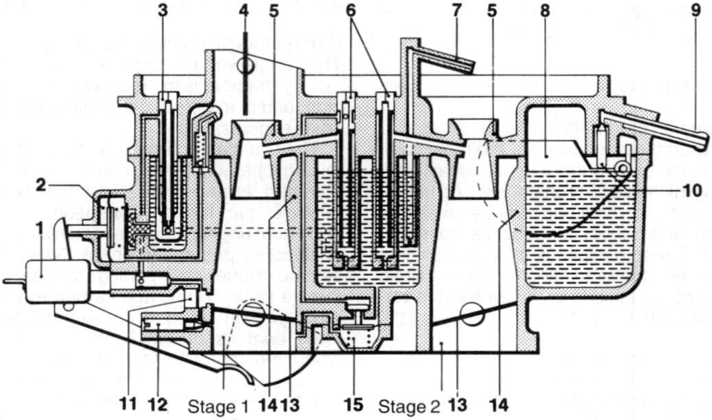

Fuel-metering systems

Main system
The fuel is metered by the main jet. An air-correction tube with lateral orifices (emulsion tube) adds air to the fuel in order to obtain the desired A/F ratio for all engine operating conditions.

Idle and progression system
At idle, the vacuum which the air stream produces at the fuel outlet is not sufficient to withdraw fuel from the main system. For this reason, there is a separate idle system with an outlet located downstream from the throttle valve at the point of maximum vacuum. The emulsion required for idling emerges from the idle circuit after initial processing by the idle fuel and air-correction jets.

The "progression system" provides for the transition to the main system. Here the throttle valve controls a series of orifices, or a slit, which receive their fuel supply from the idle system.

Correction systems for stationary engine operation
At specific points on the engine's performance curve, the part-throttle control system can provide additional fuel to the main system. An adjustable needle, regulating either the fuel jet or the air-correction jet in the main system, provides another option for controlling part-throttle operation.

The settings for full-throttle operation are essentially determined by the design of the engine (in particular valve timing, intake-manifold layout, air-filter design, etc.). A full-throttle enrichment device can be employed for compensation in cases where the mixture leans out with increasing rpm. This consists of a calibrated tube which conducts fuel from the float chamber to the carburetor inlet.

Special measures for dynamic engine operation
The fuel travels to the cylinders more slowly than the air. When the throttle valve is opened suddenly, the accelerator pump provides for smooth transition by discharging fuel from a special circuit into the mixing chamber.

Jerking and high HC emissions can occur during overrun (trailing-throttle) operation. Potential corrective measures include a time delay for throttle-plate closure, application of a pneumatically-controlled deceleration system, or an overrun fuel cutoff device.

Special measures for cold engines
The engine requires a relatively rich mixture and increased air flow for cold starting. The necessary enrichment is provided by a choke flap located above the venturi and the mixture outlets.

The throttle plate is held partially open to augment the amount of mixture available for cold idling, while the choke flap controls the mixture enrichment. The bypass plug can be heated to prevent icing.

Idle-speed reduction
Reductions in idle speed are intended to reduce the fuel consumption at idle. This can be achieved through minor adjustments to the engine, ignition and carburetor, as the carburetor continues to provide good mixture preparation, even at low airflow rates.

Lambda control
A solenoid valve can be employed to control the air correction for the main system. Adjustments on both the fuel side and the air-correction side are commonly applied to the idle system.

Overrun fuel cutoff
Further reductions in fuel consumption can be achieved by shutting off the fuel flow during overrun. On carburetors with a single idle system, the throttle plate closes to a point below the outlet for the idle mixture, thus interrupting the mixture supply. Other designs employ an idle cutoff valve.

Electronically-controlled carburetor system (ECOTRONIC)

Basic carburetor

The basic carburetor is restricted to the throttle, float system, idle and progression system, main system and choke. An idle-air control system with a choke-activated needle jet is also provided.

Additional components and actuators

The throttle-plate actuator is an electro-pneumatic servo device for controlling the cylinder charge. The actuator's plunger moves the throttle plate via a lever attached to the carburetor's throttle shaft.

Two solenoid valves regulate the operating pressure at the diaphragm by switching to atmospheric or intake-manifold pressure.

The choke serves as the actuator for adapting the A/F ratio to the particular engine operating conditons. When the choke flap is closed, the increased pressure differential in the main system and the additional effect on the idle jet produce a richer mixture. The choke functions as a torque motor: Counterforce is exerted by air pressure acting against the eccentrically-mounted choke flap and by a return spring.

Sensors

The throttle potentiometer determines the position and motion of the throttle plate, while a temperature sensor measures the coolant temperature. A second sensor may be installed for intake-manifold temperature.

An idle switch can be used to detect overrun. However, this component can be omitted by using appropriate software strategies.

Electronic control unit (ECU)

The ECU's input circuit converts the received analog signals into digital form. The processor performs further operations with the input data in order to calculate output values with reference to the programmed data map. The output signals control the servo elements which operate the choke flap and the throttle plate, as well as other outputs.

Basic functions

The basic carburetor determines the primary functions of the system. The idle, progression and full-load systems all contribute to matching performance to the programmed curves. The base calibrations can be intentionally "lean," as the choke-valve control is able to provide a corrective enrichment. In case of electrical

Schematic of an electronically-controlled carburetor (ECOTRONIC)
1 ECU, 2 Temperature sensor, 3 Carburetor, 4 Throttle actuator, 5 Choke actuator, 6 Choke valve, 7 Idle switch, 8 Throttle valve, 9 Throttle potentiometer.

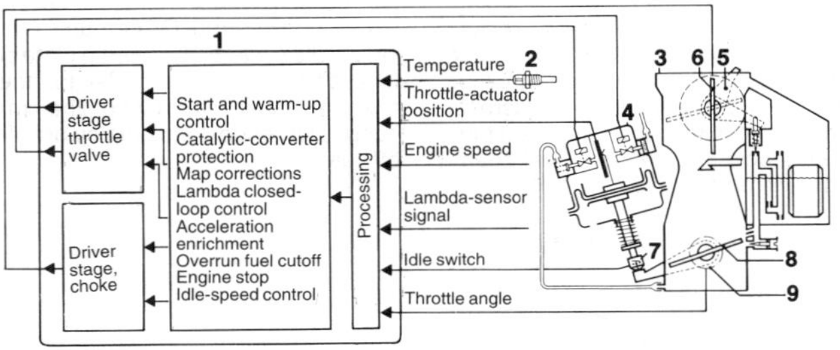

or electronic failure, the system reverts to "limp-home" settings corresponding to the carburetor's basic settings.

Electronic functions
Start and warm-up: During starting, the throttle plate is regulated according to temperature and rpm to ensure availability of the mixture quantity required for trouble-free run-up after starting. The requisite enrichment is provided by the choke control. In the subsequent warm-up phase, the throttle actuator regulates the idle speed according to coolant temperature. Here, as well, the required enrichment is obtained by adjusting the choke flap and/or the needle jet in the idle air-correction system.

Corrections to programmed data map: Precise control of the choke flap can be employed to provide any corrections in stationary operation which may be required to bring the carburetor's basic settings into conformity with the programmed performance curves (map).

Lambda control: ECOTRONIC operates with Lambda control, with the Lambda probe acting as the exhaust-gas sensor (p. 482). Adjustments are performed by the choke-valve actuator.

Acceleration: The acceleration enrichment required for dynamic operation is also provided by briefly closing the choke. This makes it possible to achieve precise enrichment for transient operation, with exact metering of fuel quantity for the respective phase: cold or full engine operating temperature.

Overrun fuel cutoff, engine-stop: As no power is required during overrun, it is possible to economize on the fuel that would normally be used in this phase. During overrun, the throttle actuator pivots the first-stage throttle plate to the overrun position. This means that the outlets for idle mixture are now above the throttle-plate metering edges, thus interrupting the fuel flow. The overrun cutoff comes into effect at engine speeds down to just above idle. A controlled overrun-transition feature ensures a smooth progression from power-off back to active engine operation.

When the engine is switched off, the throttle plate closes, thus interrupting the fuel flow and preventing the engine from running on. The throttle moves to the starting position again once the engine has stopped completely.

Idle-speed control: This system maintains the idle speed at a constant level, allowing substantial idle-speed reductions due to the fact that reserves for dealing with interference factors are no longer necessary.

If the engine speed deviates from the setpoint, the ECU transmits a correction for the throttle setting. The control system enables a mean engine-speed variance of $\pm$ 10 min^{-1}. The idle-speed setpoints are programmed with reference to temperature, thus they are increased slightly at colder temperatures.

Catalytic-converter protection: Excessive engine speed can cause damage to catalytic converters which are mounted in the direct vicinity of the engine. This can be prevented by a wafer-shaped valve capable of interrupting the flow of fuel from the float chamber. The valve is closed when the choke flap, which is connected to the valve via a linkage, receives a command to perform a counter-rotation.

Ignition control: In addition to controlling the fuel formation, the ECU can also regulate the ignition according to the programmed maps and operating conditions.

Additional functions: The ECU can refer to the fuel-consumption program and the operating conditions to calculate the fuel consumption per unit of time.

The ECU can be programmed to monitor both the incoming signals from the sensors and the signals which are transmitted to the actuators. Other options include the ability to record malfunctions; a fault-memory readout can then be performed using either a flash code or diagnosis equipment.

Further functions such as manifold-heater control, canister-purge control, EGR, etc. can also be performed by the ECU.

Single-point fuel-injection systems

Single-point fuel injection has advanced beyond the compact fuel-injection system stage to become a comprehensive engine-management system, e.g., the Mono Motronic (p. 472).

The various single-point injection systems differ in the design of the central-injection unit. All systems feature an injector located above the throttle plate; they differ from multipoint injection units in that they frequently operate at low pressure (0.7 ... 1 bar above atmospheric). This means that an inexpensive, hydrodynamic electric fuel pump can be used, which is generally installed in the fuel tank. The injector is flushed continuously by the fuel which surrounds it in order to inhibit the formation of air bubbles. This arrangement is an absolute necessity for a low-pressure system. The designation "Single-Point Injection (SPI)" corresponds to the terms Central Fuel Injection (CFI), Throttle Body Injection (TBI) and Mono-Jetronic (Bosch).

Mono-Jetronic

Mono-Jetronic is an electronically controlled, low-pressure single-point injection system for 4-cylinder engines featuring a centrally located electromagnetic fuel injector. At the heart of the system is the central injection unit, which uses the throttle plate to meter the intake air while injecting the fuel intermittently above the throttle valve. The intake manifold then distributes the fuel to the individual cylinders. Various sensors monitor all important engine operating data; these are used to calculate the control signals for the injector and the other system actuators.

Central injection unit

The injector is located above the throttle, in the intake-air path, in order to ensure homogeneous mixture and good cylinder-to-cylinder distribution. The spray pattern is directed into the sickle-shaped orifice

Schematic of a Mono-Jetronic system

1 Fuel tank, 2 Electric fuel pump, 3 Fuel filter, 4 Pressure regulator, 5 Injector, 6 Air-temperature sensor, 7 ECU, 8 Throttle actuator, 9 Throttle potentiometer, 10 EGR valve, 11 Carbon canister, 12 Lambda sensor, 13 Coolant-temperature sensor, 14 Ignition distributor, 15 Battery, 16 Ignition switch, 17 Relay, 18 Diagnostic connector, 19 Central injection unit.

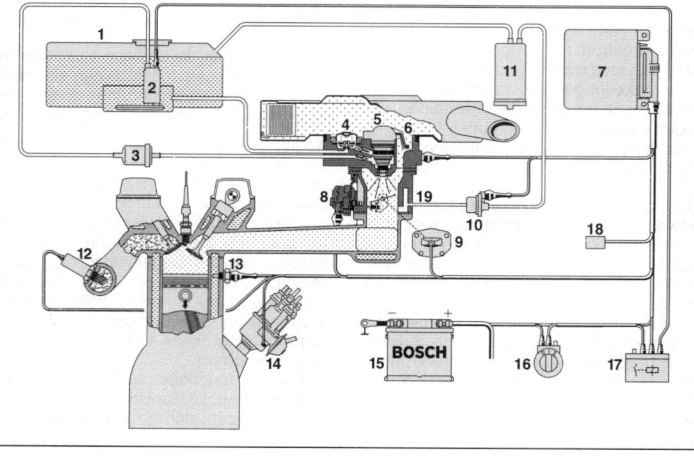

between the housing and throttle plate, where the high pressure differential produces optimum mixture preparation. This means that wall wetting is avoided to a large extent.

The injector operates at a system pressure of 1 bar (above atmospheric pressure). Its good fuel atomization ensures consistently good mixture distribution, even in the critical full-load range. Injector firing is synchronized with the ignition pulses.

System control

In addition to the engine speed n, the main actuating variables for the injection system can include the air volume/air mass flow, the absolute manifold pressure, and the throttle position α. The α/n system, which is applied with Mono-Jetronic, can meet even the most stringent emission requirements when used in conjunction with Lambda closed-loop control and 3-way catalytic converter. A self-adaptive system employs the Lambda-sensor signal as a reference to compensate for component tolerances and changes in engine condition, thus achieving precise operation throughout the lifetime of the system.

Adaptation functions

The injection time is extended to provide additional fuel for cold starts and during the post-start and warm-up phase. When the engine is cold, the throttle actuator adjusts the throttle position to supply more air to the engine, thus maintaining idle speed and exhaust emissions at a constant level. The throttle potentiometer recognizes the change in throttle position and initiates an increase in the fuel quantity via the ECU. The system regulates the enrichment for acceleration and full-load (WOT) operation in the same manner. The overrun fuel cutoff provides reductions in fuel consumption and in exhaust emissions during overrun. The adaptive idle-speed control lowers and stabilizes the idle speed, and the ECU directs the actuator to adjust the throttle position with reference to engine speed and temperature.

Mono-Jetronic central injection unit
1 Pressure regulator, 2 Air-temperature sensor, 3 Injector, 4 Upper part (hydraulics), 5 Fuel supply, 6 Fuel return, 7 Insulator plate, 8 Throttle valve, 9 Lower part.

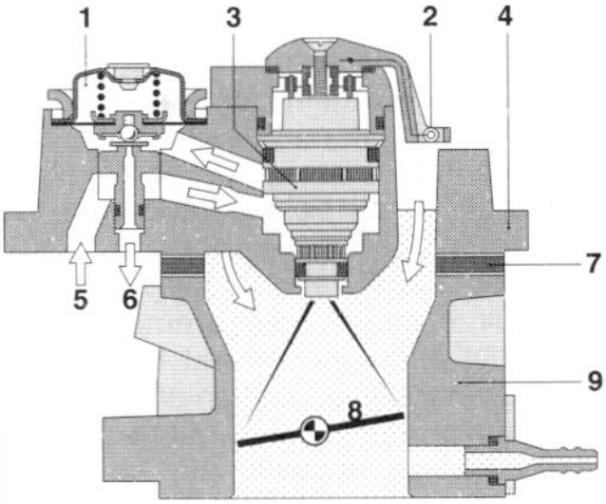

Multec central injection unit (Opel)
1 Pressure regulator, 2 Injector, 3 Fuel return, 4 Stepper motor for idle-speed control, 5 To intake manifold, 6 Throttle valve, 7 Fuel inlet.

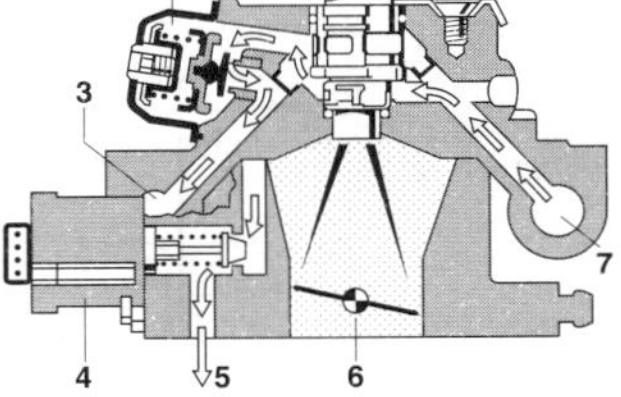

Multipoint fuel-injection systems

K-Jetronic

Operating principle
- Continuous injection
- Direct airflow measurement

The K-Jetronic is a mechanical system which does not require an engine-driven injection pump. It meters a continuous supply of fuel directly proportional to the quantity of air being drawn into the engine.

Because the K-Jetronic system incorporates direct airflow measurement, it can also detect changes caused by the engine, allowing the application of emission-control equipment which requires precise measurement of the intake air.

Operation
The intake air flows through the air filter, the airflow sensor, and the throttle before entering the intake manifold and continuing to the individual cylinders.

The fuel is pumped from the fuel tank by an electric (roller-cell) fuel pump and flows through the fuel accumulator and fuel filter to the fuel distributor. A pressure regulator in the fuel distributor maintains constant system pressure. The fuel flows from the fuel distributor to the injectors. Excess fuel not required by the engine is returned to the tank.

Mixture-control unit
The mixture-control unit consists of the airflow sensor and the fuel distributor.

Airflow sensor
The airflow sensor consists of an air funnel and a pivoting airflow sensor plate. A

Schematic of a K-Jetronic system
1 Fuel tank, 2 Electric fuel pump, 3 Fuel accumulator, 4 Fuel filter, 5 Warm-up regulator, 6 Injector, 7 Plenum, 8 Electric start valve, 9 Fuel distributor, 10 Airflow sensor, 11 Electro-hydraulic pressure actuator, 12 Lambda sensor, 13 Thermo-time switch, 14 Ignition distributor, 15 Auxiliary-air valve, 16 Throttle switch, 17 ECU, 18 Ignition switch, 19 Battery.

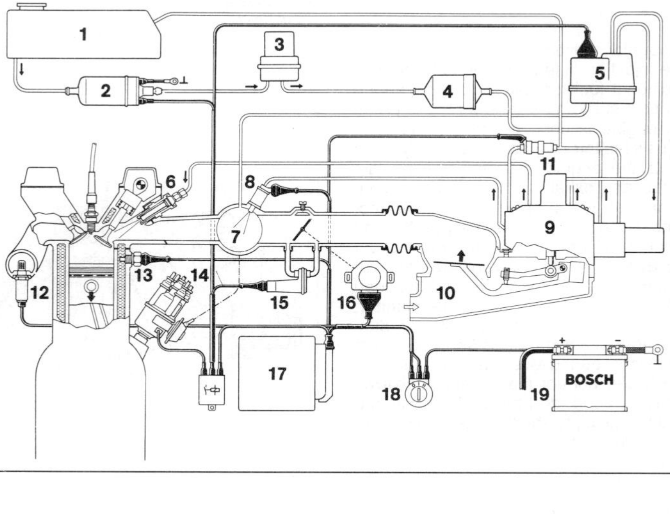

counterweight compensates for the weight of the sensor plate and pivot assembly. The sensor plate is displaced by the airflow, while the control plunger in the fuel distributor exerts hydraulic counter-pressure to maintain the system in a balanced state. The position of the airflow sensor plate is a measure for the intake airflow, and is transmitted to the fuel distributor's control plunger by means of a lever.

Fuel distributor
The amount of fuel to be supplied to the individual cylinders is determined by varying the aperture of the metering slits in the fuel-distributor barrel. The number of rectangular-shaped metering slits in the barrel corresponds to the number of engine cylinders.

The specific size of the metering-slit aperture depends on the control-plunger position. In order to ensure constant pressure drop at the slits for various flow rates, a differential pressure regulator is located downstream of each metering slit.

Injector
1 Hexagon fitting, 2 Fine-mesh strainer, 3 Valve body, 4 Valve needle, 5 Rubber molding.

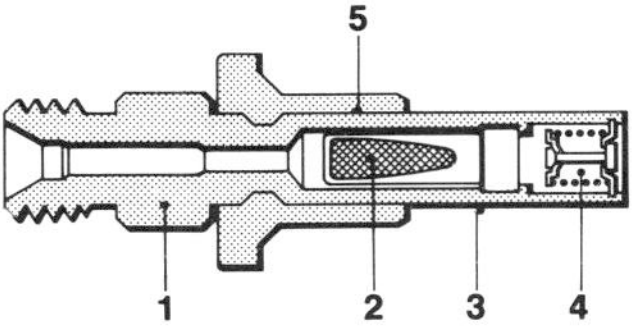

Fuel distributor in mixture-control unit
1 Diaphragm, 2 To injector, 3 Control plunger, 4 Metering slot, 5 Differential-pressure regulator.

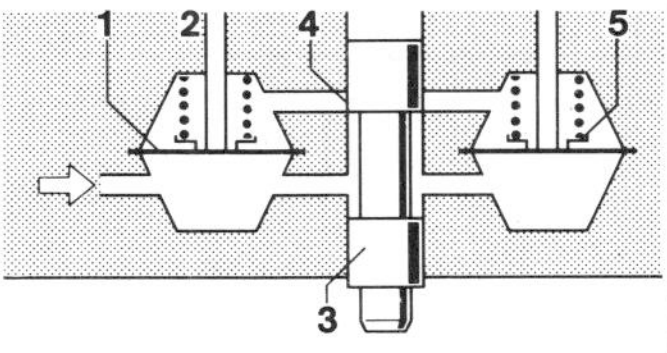

Injector
The injector opens automatically at a pressure of approximately 3.8 bar, and has no metering function. It provides good fuel induction by opening and closing at a frequency of approx. 1500 Hz ("chatter").

It is held in place by a molded rubber collar, and it is pressed, not screwed, into position. The hexagon fitting is used to retain the unit when attaching the fuel-supply line.

Warm-up regulator
The warm-up regulator is controlled by an electrically-heated bimetallic element; it enriches the mixture in the warm-up phase by reducing the counterpressure exerted against the control plunger. A reduction in the control pressure means that the stroke of the airflow sensor plate for a given airflow increases (corresponding to a larger metering-slit aperture). The result is a richer mixture during warm-up.

Where desired, the warm-up regulator can be expanded to incorporate the following functions:
- Full-load enrichment,
- Acceleration enrichment,
- Altitude compensation.

Auxiliary-air valve
The auxiliary-air valve, controlled by either a bimetallic spring or an expansion element, supplies the engine with additional air (which is monitored by the airflow sensor, but bypasses the throttle valve) during the warm-up phase of operation. This supplementary air compensates for the cold engine's higher friction losses; it either maintains the normal idle speed or increases it in order to heat the engine and exhaust more quickly.

Electric start valve,
Thermo-time switch
The thermo-time switch activates the electric start valve according to engine temperature and elapsed time. During low-temperature starts, the start valve injects supplementary fuel into the intake manifold (cold-start enrichment).

Lambda control

Open-loop control measures to regulate the A/F ratio are not sufficiently precise for achieving conformity with extremely low emission limits.

When the Lambda closed-loop control (required for operation of the 3-way catalytic converter) is installed, the K-Jetronic system must be provided with an electronic control unit which uses the Lambda-sensor signal as its main input variable.

An electromagnetic frequency valve is employed to regulate the A/F ratio by controlling the pressure differential at the metering slits. However, this principle cannot be applied to meet the more stringent emissions requirements scheduled for the future.

KE-Jetronic

KE-Jetronic represents a further development of the K-Jetronic system which has been expanded by the addition of an ECU. This allows increased flexibility and makes it possible to include extra functions. The additional components include:

- A sensor for the intake airflow,
- A pressure actuator for A/F ratio adjustment, and
- A pressure regulator, which maintains system pressure at a constant level, as well as providing a fuel-cutoff function when the engine is switched off.

Operation

An electric fuel pump generates the system pressure. The fuel flows through the fuel distributor, while a diaphragm regulator maintains the system pressure at a constant level. With K-Jetronic, the control

Schematic of a KE-Jetronic system

1 Fuel tank, 2 Electric fuel pump, 3 Fuel accumulator, 4 Fuel filter, 5 Fuel-pressure regulator, 6 Injector, 7 Plenum, 8 Electric start valve, 9 Fuel distributor, 10 Airflow sensor, 11 Electrohydraulic pressure actuator, 12 Lambda sensor, 13 Thermo-time switch, 14 Coolant-temperature sensor, 15 Ignition distributor, 16 Auxiliary-air valve, 17 Throttle switch, 18 ECU, 19 Ignition switch, 20 Battery.

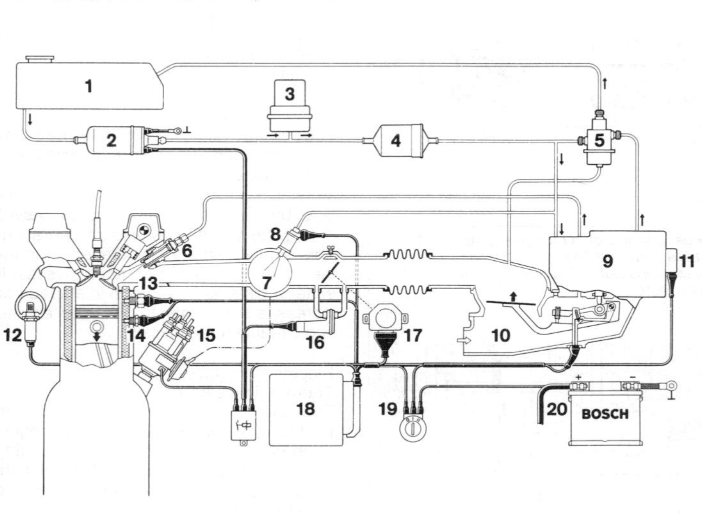

circuit performs mixture corrections via the warm-up regulator. In contrast, with the KE-Jetronic the primary pressure and the pressure exerted upon the control plunger are equal. The A/F ratio is corrected by adjusting the pressure differential in all the fuel distributor's chambers simultaneously.

The system pressure is present upstream from the metering slits, and applies a counterpressure to the control plunger. As with the K-Jetronic, the control plunger is displaced by an airflow sensor flap. A damper unit prevents the oscillations that could otherwise occur due to the forces generated by the sensor flap. From the control plunger, the fuel flows through the pressure actuator, the lower chambers of the differential-pressure valve, a fixed flow restrictor, and the pressure regulator before returning to the fuel tank. Together with the flow restrictor, the actuator forms a pressure divider, in which the pressure can be adjusted electrodynamically. This pressure is present in the lower chambers of the differential-pressure valves.

A pressure drop corresponding to the actuator current occurs between its two connections. This causes variations in the pressure differential at the metering slits, and alters the amount of fuel to be injected.

The current can also be reversed to shut down the fuel supply completely. This feature can be employed for such functions as overrun fuel cutoff and engine-speed limitation.

Electrohydraulic pressure actuator
1 Nozzle, 2 Valve plate, 3 Coil, 4 Magnetic pole, 5 Fuel inlet, 6 Adjustment screw.

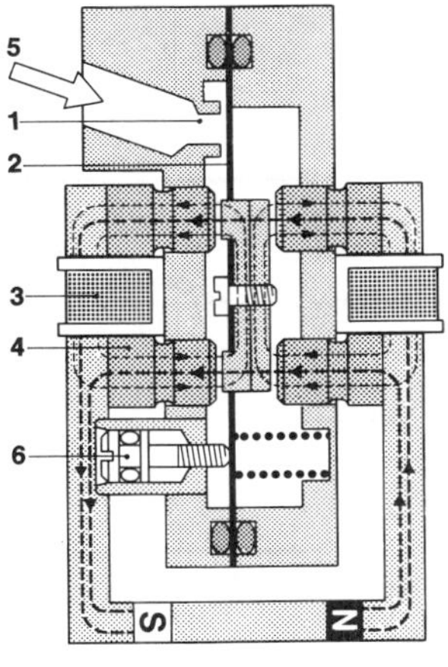

Electrohydraulic pressure actuator

This electrohydraulic actuator is mounted on a fuel-distributor flange. It is an electrically-controlled pressure regulator which operates according to the nozzle/flapper-plate system. There is a linear relationship between the current flow and the mixture-enrichment factor.

Electronic control unit (ECU)

The ECU processes signals from the ignition (engine speed), temperature sensor (coolant temperature), throttle potentiometer (intake airflow), throttle switch (idle and overrun, WOT), starter switch, Lambda sensor, pressure sensor and other sensors. Its most important functions are the control of:

- Starting and post-start enrichment
- Warm-up enrichment
- Acceleration enrichment
- Full-load enrichment
- Overrun fuel cutoff
- Engine-speed limitation
- Idle-speed control
- Altitude compensation
- Closed-loop Lambda control.

A coding switch makes it possible to select between operation with Lambda control (with catalytic converter) or without it. This permits a choice between leaded and unleaded gasoline.

Lambda closed-loop control

The signal from the Lambda sensor is processed in the KE-Jetronic's ECU. The pressure actuator carries out the necessary adjustments.

L-Jetronic

Operating principles

- Airflow measurement
- Main actuating variables: Airflow and engine speed
- Intermittent injection

The L-Jetronic combines the advantages of direct airflow measurement with the unique possibilities afforded by electronics. It is similar to the K-Jetronic in that it recognizes all changes in engine condition (due to wear, combustion-chamber deposits, changes in valve adjustment) to ensure consistently good exhaust-gas composition.

Operation

The fuel is injected through the engine's solenoid-operated injectors. A solenoid valve is assigned to each cylinder, and triggered once per crankshaft revolution. All of the injectors are wired in parallel to reduce the complexity of the electrical circuit. The differential between the fuel and manifold pressures is maintained at a constant level of 2.5 or 3.0 bar, thus the amount of discharged fuel is determined exclusively by the pulse width provided by the ECU. The pulse width (duration) depends on intake airflow, engine speed, and other parameters which are acquired by various sensors and processed by the ECU.

Fuel supply

An electric fuel pump supplies the fuel and generates the injection pressure. The fuel is pumped from the fuel tank, through a paper filter, and into a supply line at the other end of which there is a pressure regulator (spring-loaded diaphragm). The pressure regulator maintains a constant pressure at the metering orifice, regardless of the amount of fuel being injected.

Schematic of an L-Jetronic system

1 Fuel tank, 2 Electric fuel pump, 3 Fuel filter, 4 ECU, 5 Injector, 6 Fuel-pressure regulator, 7 Plenum, 8 Electric start valve, 9 Throttle switch, 10 Airflow sensor, 11 Lambda sensor, 12 Thermo-time switch, 13 Coolant-temperature sensor, 14 Ignition distributor, 15 Auxiliary-air valve, 16 Battery, 17 Ignition switch.

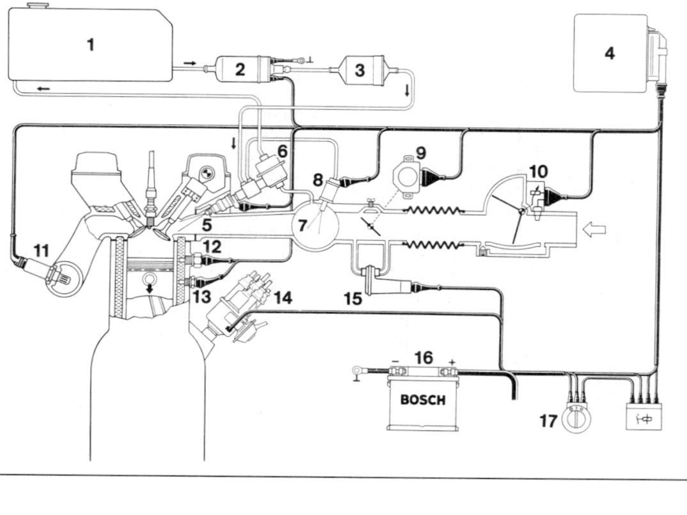

Air-flow sensor
1 Idle-mixture adjustment screw, 2 Airflow sensor flap, 3 Stop, 4 Compensation flap, 5 Damping chamber, 6 Air-temperature sensor.

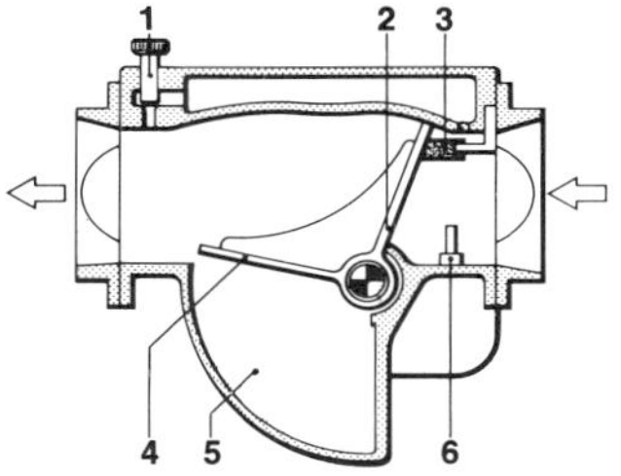

Injector
1 Pintle, 2 Needle, 3 Armature, 4 Spring, 5 Solenoid winding, 6 Electrical terminals, 7 Fuel strainer.

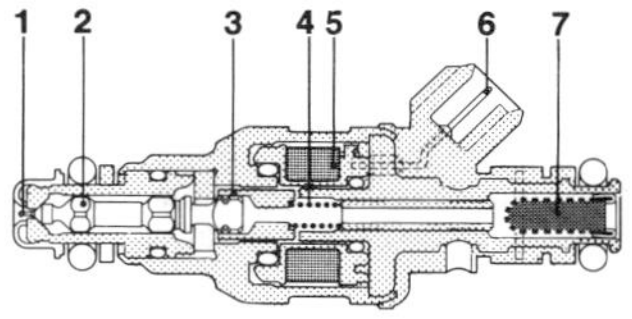

Airflow sensor
The intake air deflects the sensor flap against the constant counterforce of a spring. A potentiometer converts the deflection angles into a voltage ratio which determines the pulse length of a timing element in the ECU. A temperature sensor in the airflow sensor detects the change in air density caused by temperature changes.

Injectors
The injectors meter and atomize the fuel. When the solenoid coil is energized, the injector needle is lifted a mere 0.05 mm from its seat.

Throttle switch
This transmits a control signal to the ECU when the throttle valve is either completely closed (idle) or fully opened (full-load).

Coolant-temperature sensor
The coolant-temperature sensor is designed as a temperature-sensitive resistor (thermistor) and controls the warm-up enrichment.

Auxiliary-air valve, start-valve, thermo-time switch
Design and function are similar to those of the corresponding K-Jetronic components.

Electronic control unit (ECU)
This ECU converts the engine variables into electrical pulses. These are triggered at a point which corresponds to the ignition point, while their duration is basically a function of speed and intake airflow. Since all injectors are activated simultaneously, only a single driver stage is required. The temperature sensors cause increases in injection duration for decreasing engine and air temperatures. The throttle-switch signals enable the mixture to be adapted for idle and for full-throttle operation.

Lambda closed-loop control
The ECU compares the Lambda-sensor signal with a setpoint value before activating a two-stage controller. The control adjustment is then performed, as are all corrections, by modifying the injection time.

L 3-Jetronic
The L 3-Jetronic incorporates functions extending beyond those provided by the L-Jetronic's analog technology. In contrast to the L-Jetronic, the ECU employs digital technology to adjust the A/F ratio to a load/engine-speed map. In order to save space, the ECU is installed in the engine compartment, directly on the airflow sensor, where the two components form a single measuring and control unit.

LH-Jetronic

The LH-Jetronic is closely related to the L-Jetronic, the main difference being the method of intake airflow measurement with the LH-Jetronic using a mass airflow sensor to measure the *mass* of the intake air. Thus, the results no longer depend on the air density, which is a function of temperature and pressure.

The other LH-Jetronic components and the system operating principle are comparable to those of the L-Jetronic.

Operating-data processing in the ECU
The LH-Jetronic is equipped with a digital ECU. In contrast to the L-Jetronic, the A/F ratio is adjusted by means of a load/engine-speed map, with priority being placed on low fuel consumption and exhaust emissions. The ECU processes the sensor signals when calculating the injection duration, which is a measure for the injected fuel quantity. The ECU includes a microprocessor, program and data memories, and an A/D converter. The microprocessor is provided with a suitable voltage supply and with a stable clock rate for data processing. The clock rate is provided by a quartz oscillator.

Hot-wire mass airflow sensor
The stream of intake air to the engine is conducted past a heated wire (hot wire) which forms part of an electrical bridge circuit. The flow of current through the wire serves to maintain it at a constant temperature above that of the intake air. This principle makes it possible to employ the current requirement as an index of the air mass being drawn into the engine. A resistor converts the heating current into a voltage signal which the ECU processes along with engine speed as a main input variable. A temperature sensor is mounted in the hot-wire mass airflow sensor to ensure that its output signal is not

Schematic of an LH-Jetronic system
1 Fuel tank, 2 Electric fuel pump, 3 Fuel filter, 4 ECU, 5 Injector, 6 Fuel distributor, 7 Fuel-pressure regulator, 8 Plenum, 9 Throttle switch, 10 Hot-wire mass airflow sensor, 11 Lambda sensor, 12 Coolant-temperature sensor, 13 Ignition distributor, 14 Idle-speed actuator, 15 Battery, 16 Ignition switch.

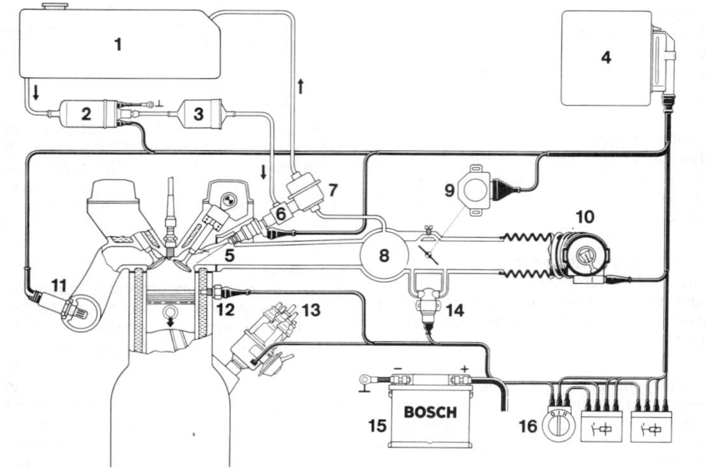

influenced by the temperature of the intake air. The A/F-ratio at idle can be adjusted with a potentiometer. As contamination on the surface of the hot wire could affect the output signal, each time the engine is shut down the wire is electrically heated for one second to burn-off any contamination. The hot-wire mass airflow sensor has no moving parts, and its aerodynamic resistance in the intake tract is negligible.

New hot-film mass airflow sensor

The operating principle of the hot-film mass airflow sensor is the same as that of the hot-wire sensor. However, in the interests of simplified design, a substantial portion of the electrical bridge circuit is installed on a ceramic substrate, in the form of thin-film resistors. In addition, there is no need to burn contaminants off the film. The contamination problem is solved by placing the areas on the sensor element which are decisive for thermal transmission at a downstream location. This prevents them from being affected by deposits on the sensor element's front edge.

New Kármán vortex volumetric flow meter

Yet another option for measuring intake air is provided by a meter which uses the Kármán vortex principle to measure the volumetric flow rate. In this type of meter, vortices are generated as the intake air flows past vortex generators. The frequency of these vortices is a measure of the volumetric flow rate. This frequency is measured by the emission of ultrasonic waves perpendicular to the direction of the intake-air flow. The propagation velocity of these waves, which is affected by the vortices, is detected by an ultrasonic receiver and the resulting signals are evaluated in the ECU.

Hot-film mass airflow sensor

a Housing, b Hot-film sensor (installed in center of housing).
1 Heat sink, 2 Spacer, 3 Driver stage, 4 Hybrid, 5 Sensor element (metallic film).

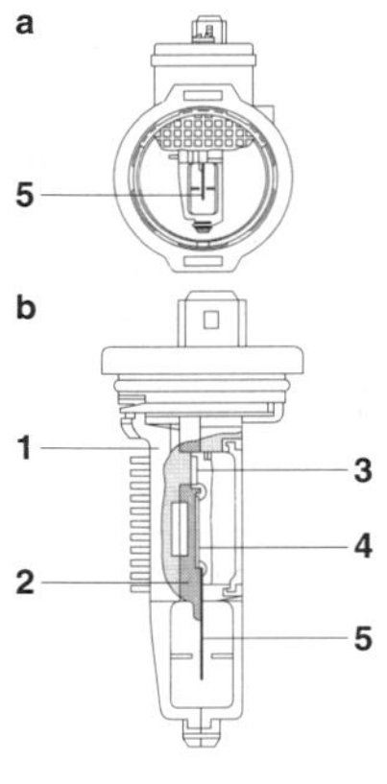

Kármán vortex flow meter

1 Oscillator, 2 Vortex generator, 3 Transmitter, 4 Ultrasonic waves, 5 Eddy currents, 6 Receiver, 7 Amplifier, 8 Filter, 9 Pulse shaper.

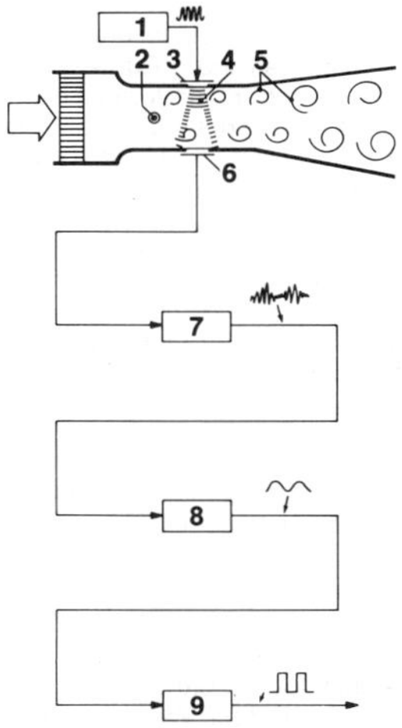

Ignition

It is the job of the ignition system to initiate combustion of the flammable air-fuel mixture by igniting it at precisely the right moment. In the spark-ignition (Otto) engine, this is achieved with an electrical spark, i.e., an arc discharged between the electrodes of the spark plug.

If the catalytic converter is to function properly, then it is essential that the ignition system operates reliably under all conditions. Misfiring can result in catalytic-converter damage or destruction caused by post-combustion of unburned mixture.

Mixture ignition

When the composition of the mixture is stoichiometric, an energy of approximately 0.2 mJ is required for each individual ignition of the air-fuel mixture via electric spark. Over 3 mJ are required for a rich or lean mixture. This energy represents only a fraction of the total energy in the ignition spark, the actual ignition energy. If sufficient ignition energy is not available, there will be no ignition, the mixture cannot ignite, and misfiring will result. For this reason, a high-enough level of ignition energy must be provided to ensure that the air-fuel mixture will always ignite, even under unfavorable conditions. It suffices for a small flammable mixture cloud to flow past the spark. The mixture cloud ignites, the flame is propagated to the remaining mixture in the cylinder, and the fuel starts to combust. Ignitability is enhanced by good fuel atomization and good access of the mixture to the electrodes, as well as through extended spark duration and spark length (large electrode gap). The spark plug determines the location and length of the spark; its duration depends upon the type and design of the ignition system, as well as on the momentary conditions for ignition.

Spark generation

The voltage must be high enough before it is possible for a spark to arc from one electrode to another. When the spark plug fires, the voltage across the electrodes abruptly jumps from zero up to the arc-over voltage (ignition voltage). As soon as the spark is discharged, the voltage at the spark plug falls to the spark voltage. The air-fuel mixture has the chance to ignite while the spark is present (spark duration). After the spark breaks down, the voltage drops to zero.

Spark-plug voltage characteristic with stationary or semi-stationary air-fuel mixture

1 Ignition voltage, 2 Spark voltage, t Spark duration.

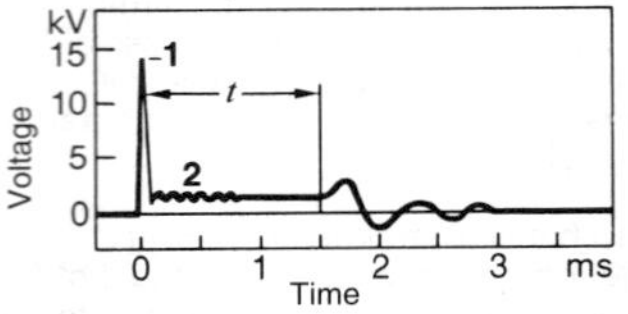

Although heavy mixture turbulence is desirable, it can extinguish the spark, thus leading to incomplete combustion. The energy stored in the ignition coil should therefore suffice for one or more consecutive sparks, according to the specific requirement.

High-voltage generation and energy storage

With battery-ignition systems, an ignition coil is generally used to provide the high voltage to the spark plug which is required for generating the spark. The ignition coil functions as an autotransformer. In coil-ignition systems it also assumes the other important function of storing the ignition energy. When the contact breaker closes, energy from the vehicle's electrical system flows into the coil's primary winding. The energy is then stored in a magnetic field until the firing point, when the secondary winding discharges it to one of the engine's spark plugs. The ignition coil is designed such that the available high voltage is sufficiently above the maximum possible ignition-voltage requirements of the spark plug. The available voltage is 25 ... 30 kV when the energy stored in the coil is 60 ... 120 mJ.

The operational reserves of high voltage and ignition energy are sufficient to compensate for all electrical losses. Improper maintenance causes a reduction in the high-voltage reserves, and results in misfiring. The engine loses power and fuel consumption increases. In addition, this phenomenon can result in damage to or destruction of the catalytic converter, should one be installed. In extreme cases, the engine either fails to start – especially when cold – or stalls.

Ignition systems are also available with capacitive energy storage (CDI) for use on high-performance and racing engines. The ignition energy is stored in the electrical field of a capacitor before a special transformer transmits it to the spark plug in the form of a high-voltage ignition pulse.

Ignition timing and adjustment

Approximately two milliseconds elapse between the mixture's initial ignition and its complete combustion. The ignition spark must therefore arc early enough to ensure optimum combustion pressure under all engine operating conditions. The firing point must be selected so that the following objectives can be met:

- Maximum engine performance
- Low fuel consumption
- No engine knock
- Low emissions.

It is impossible to fulfill all of these requirements simultaneously however, and compromises must be found on a case-to-case basis. The optimum ignition point depends on a variety of parameters, the most important being engine speed, engine load, engine design, fuel, and operating conditions such as starting, idle and overrun. Spark-advance mechanisms which respond to engine speed and to intake-manifold pressure are employed to regulate the ignition point according to the engine's current operating conditions. These two types of adjustment can come into effect either individually or simultaneously. The extent to which the ignition point is advanced or retarded is determined by the ignition-advance curves, which vary according to engine type.

Example of cumulative ignition timing consisting of centrifugal and vacuum advance
1 Part-load road operation, 2 Full load.

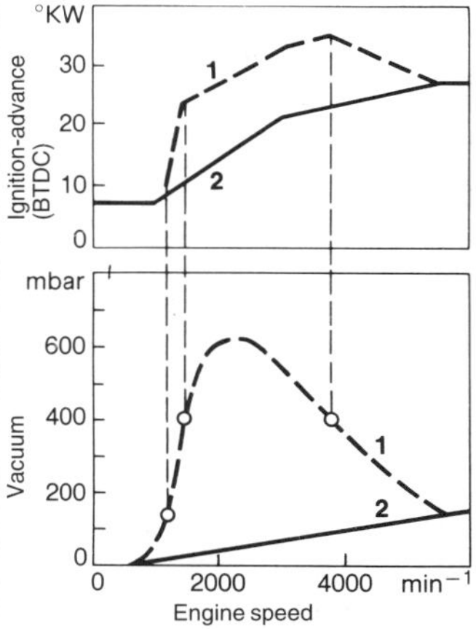

Under full load, the accelerator pedal is depressed fully and the throttle is wide open (WOT). As engine speed rises, the ignition point advances along with it in order to maintain the combustion pressure at a level which provides for optimum engine performance. The throttle is only partially opened during part-load operation, the air-fuel mixture is lean and therefore less combustible. This means that more time is required for ignition, so the ignition point must occur sooner, in other words it must be shifted further in the "advance" direction. The manifold pressure which is employed to determine the necessary degree of advance is monitored downstream from the throttle.

Initially, the vacuum increases as the throttle is opened wider; it begins to fall in the proximity of the full-throttle (WOT) position. The performance curve (part-load road operation) requires an increase in throttle opening along with rising engine speed; the result is the vacuum curve as a function of part-load engine speed on the road as shown in the diagram above.

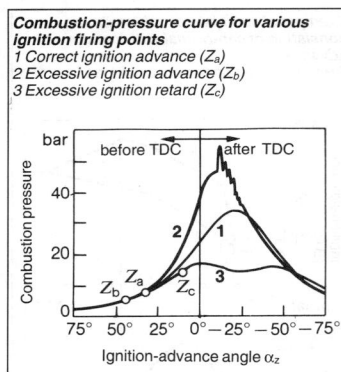

Combustion-pressure curve for various ignition firing points
1 Correct ignition advance (Z_a)
2 Excessive ignition advance (Z_b)
3 Excessive ignition retard (Z_c)

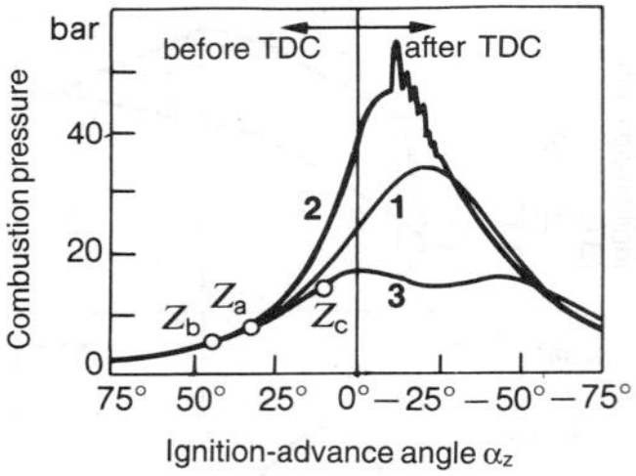

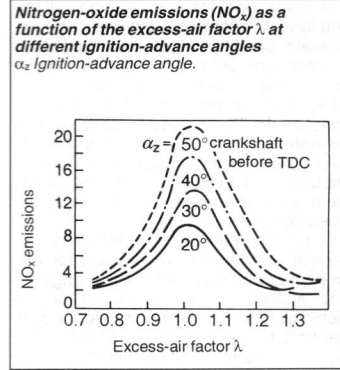

Nitrogen-oxide emissions (NO_x) as a function of the excess-air factor λ at different ignition-advance angles
α_z Ignition-advance angle.

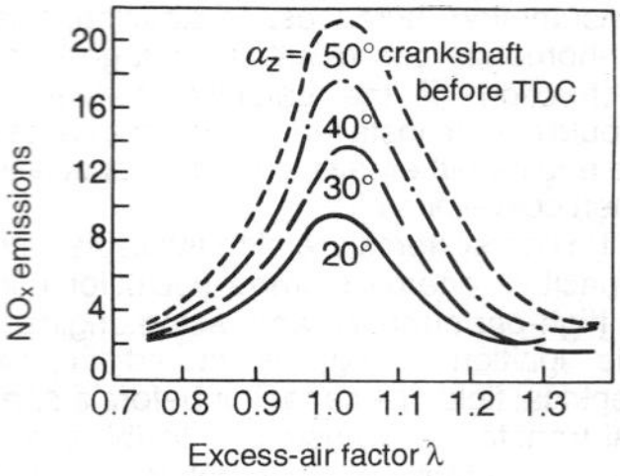

The left-hand diagram at the top of this page shows the curves associated with correct and with incorrect ignition timing for the combustion-chamber pressure of a 4-stroke engine. Even when the ignition timing is initially correct, incorrect maintenance can result in the ignition point shifting away over time. When the ignition point shifts toward a later firing point ("retard"), this leads to increased fuel consumption. When it advances, excessive advance can cause pre-ignition, with damage to the spark plugs or, in extreme cases, to the engine. The level of exhaust emissions also increases.

Ignition and emissions

Due to the fact that it has a direct influence on the various exhaust-gas components, the ignition has a significant effect upon exhaust emissions. The ig- nition angles for minimum exhaust emissions can only be partially achieved due to the fact that the optimization crite-

Overview of various ignition systems				
Function	Ignition System			
	CI	TCI	ESA	DLI
Designation	Coil ignition system	Transistor-ized coil ignition system	Electronic ignition	Distributor-less ignition system
Ignition triggering	Mechani-cal	Electronic	Electronic	Electronic
Ignition point determined from engine speed and load	Mechani-cal	Mechani-cal	Electronic	Electronic
High-voltage generation	Inductive	Inductive	Inductive	Inductive
Spark distribution to appropriate cylinder	Mechani-cal	Mechani-cal.	Mechani-cal	Electronic

ria for exhaust gas, fuel consumption, driveability, etc., do not always converge (Exhaust emissions, p. 478).

Ignition coil

The ignition coil functions as an energy-storage device and as a transformer. It is supplied with DC voltage from the vehicle electrical system, and provides the ignition pulses for the spark plugs at the required high voltage and discharge energy. Both the ignition driver stage, with its set switching current, and the primary winding, with its specific resistance and inductance characteristics, determine the amount of energy stored in the ignition coil's magnetic field. The secondary winding can be designed to provide peak voltage, spark current and discharge duration in accordance with the respective requirements.

The contact-breaker points used with coil ignition can only handle interrupt currents of up to approx. 5 A. TI, SI and BSI ignition systems can cope with almost any current. The ballast resistors which are generally employed with coil ignition (they can be bypassed to increase energy during cold starts) are redundant on electronic ignition, where the electronic circuitry triggers the ignition coil according to battery voltage and engine speed to provide full energy at the ignition point.

The ignition coil is designed to comply with the requirements of the particular application. It must charge quickly in order to achieve the voltages and ignition energies required at high engine speeds. This demands low primary inductance and, in some cases, high primary interrupt currents (so that sufficient energy can be stored).

Ignition coils (schematic)
Rotating distribution: a) Single-spark coil. Distributorless ignition: b) Single-spark coil, c) Dual-spark coil.

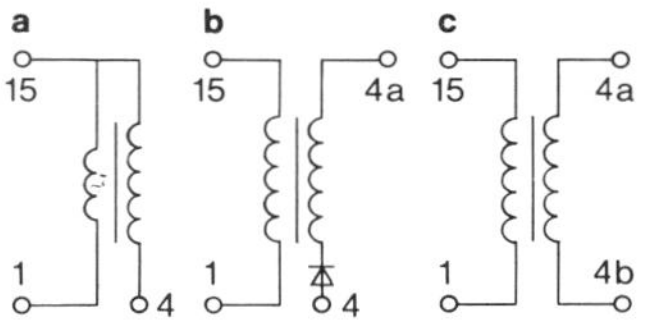

Single-spark coil
1 External low-voltage terminal, 2 Laminated iron core, 3 Secondary winding, 4 Primary winding, 5 Internal high-voltage connection via spring contact, 6 Spark plug.

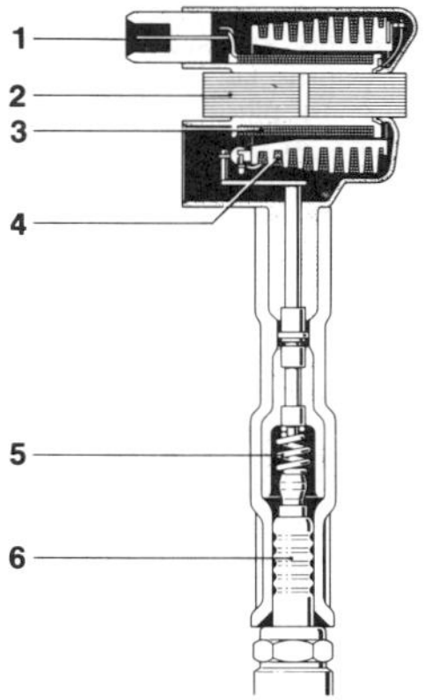

Design and operation

The traditional ignition coils with asphalt or oil insulation in metal casings are being increasingly replaced by coils which use an epoxy-resin filler. These not only allow more latitude in the selection of geometry, type and number of electrical connections, but are also characterized by more compact dimensions, better vibration resistance and lower weight. The ignition coil is generally attached to the engine or vehicle body. The primary winding, as the chief source of heat, is usually placed as close as possible to the iron core for improved thermal conductivity and to save copper.

The synthetic materials which are used provide good adhesion between all of the provide good adhesion between all of the high-voltage components and the molded epoxy resin, which penetrates into all the capillary spaces. Iron cores are sometimes also embedded on the inside of the synthetic molding.

The secondary winding is often designed as a disk or sandwich winding, with the windings distributed among a series of segments. The even distribution of stresses among the insulating elements in all chambers and the high dielectric strength permit compact dimensions, and it is possible to dispense with insulating foil and paper between wire layers. The winding's self-capacitance is also reduced.

Due to the lower beakdown voltage required for the negative (relative to engine ground) ignition spark, the positive side of the primary winding, and the positive connection of the secondary winding, are generally combined on those ignition coils which are used with rotating distribution.

Single and dual-spark ignition coils are an alternative for use in ignition systems with distributorless ignition. When one single-spark coil per spark plug is used, the primary current is switched so that the individual spark plug is provided with an ignition pulse at precisely the right moment in time. Auxiliary spark gaps or high-voltage diodes are used to prevent the positive 1 ... 2 kV high-voltage pulse from causing the spark plug to fire prematurely. On the dual-spark coil, the secondary winding is galvanically insulated from the primary winding. Each of the two high-voltage outputs is connected to a spark plug, with sparks occurring at both of these when the primary current is switched off. Generally speaking, as with rotating high-voltage distribution, this system does not require any special precautions to prevent discharge during switching.

Connection and installation are easier when several ignition coils are combined in a common casing to form a single assembly. However, the individual coils continue to operate as independent units.

The combination of ignition coils and driver stages means that a short primary lead can be used (lower voltage drop). This arrangement also prevents the ECU from heating up due to power loss in the driver stages.

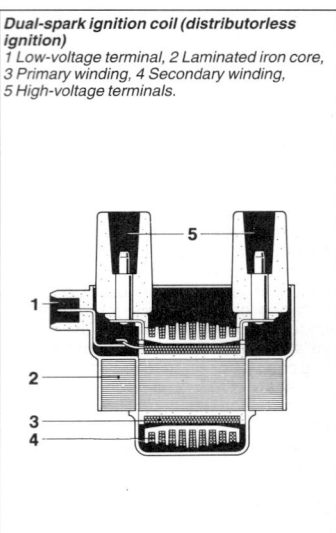

Dual-spark ignition coil (distributorless ignition)
1 Low-voltage terminal, 2 Laminated iron core, 3 Primary winding, 4 Secondary winding, 5 High-voltage terminals.

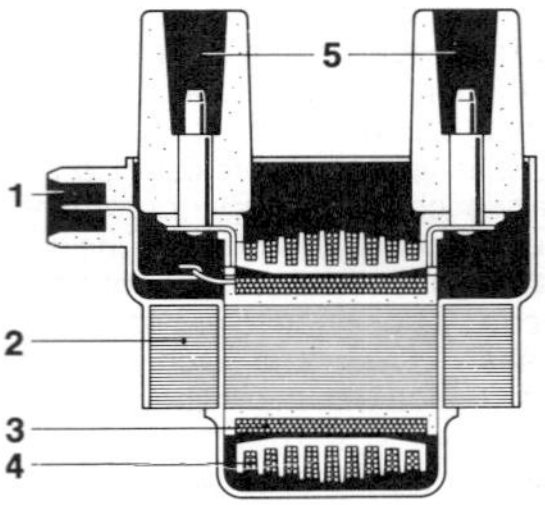

Spark plug

The purpose of the spark plug is to introduce the ignition energy into the combustion chamber. It receives this energy from the ignition coil of a rotating distribution system or from the ignition transformer in a distributorless system. The spark is required to initiate combustion of the air-fuel mixture, and depending upon engine parameters and the spark plug's electrode gap, voltage requirements can sometimes extend beyond 30 kV.

Inside the combustion chamber, the spark plug is exposed to substantial stresses; these are not only electrical, but also thermal and mechanical in nature. In a 4-stroke engine (assuming compression ratio $\varepsilon = 9$, and engine speed $n = 4500\ \text{min}^{-1}$), the following gas temperatures and pressures are present in the vicinity of the spark plug during each full-load cycle (30 ms) at normal outside temperatures:

End of intake stroke	60 °C, 0.9 bar
Ignition point	350 °C, 9 bar
Maxima	3000 °C, 40 bar
End of cycle	1100 °C, 4 bar

In the process, the spark plug stabilizes at a mean temperature which can be approx. 750 ... 950 °C at full load. Uncontrolled ignition processes (knocking) are accompanied by very high pressure peaks substantially in excess of 40 bar.

Design
An electrically-conductive, cast-glass element forms the connection between a center electrode and terminal nut in a special high-grade ceramic insulator (high Al_2O_3 content with slight quantities of flux agents for optimum sintering characteristics). The glass element acts as a mechanical support for the components while providing a gas seal against the high-pressure combustion gases. It can also incorporate resistor elements for interference suppression and burn-off.

The connection end of the insulator is glazed for improved protection against contamination. To ensure a gas-tight seal, it is shrunk (small area of the shell is heated to approx. 900 °C) and attached to the nickel-plated steel shell by shrinkage and reversal of the rim. The ground electrode, like the center electrode, is primarily manufactured using nickel-based alloys to cope with the high thermal stresses. It is welded to the shell. The thermal conduction properties of both the center and the ground electrodes are improved by using a nickel-alloy jacket material and a copper core. Silver and platinum, or platinum alloys, are employed as electrode material for special applications. The spark plugs have either an M4 or a standard SAE thread, depending upon the type of high-voltage connection. Spark plugs with metal shields are available for watertight systems and for providing maximum interference suppression.

Heat range
The spark plug's heat range is an index of its capacity to withstand thermal loads. The code number is based on compara-

Spark plug
1 High-voltage connector (terminal nut), 2 AL_2O_3 Ceramic insulator, 3 Shell, 4 Heat-shrinkage zone, 5 Conductive glass, 6 Captive gasket, 7 Composite center electrode Ni/Cu, 8 Ground electrode, 9 Pt electrode.

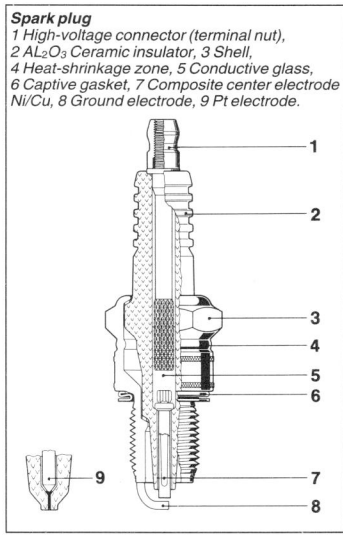

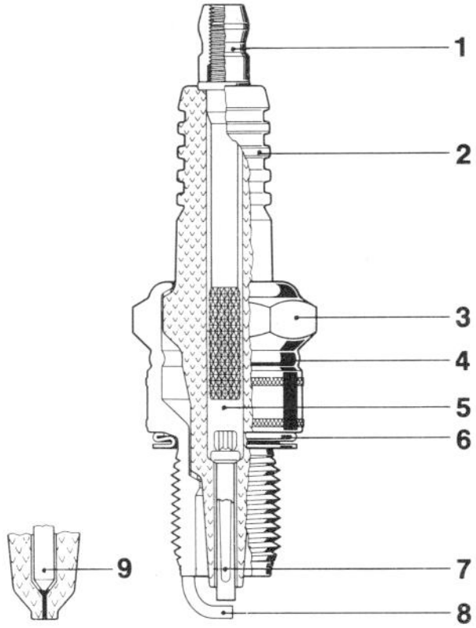

Spark-plug temperature response
1 high, 2 medium, and 3 low heat range.

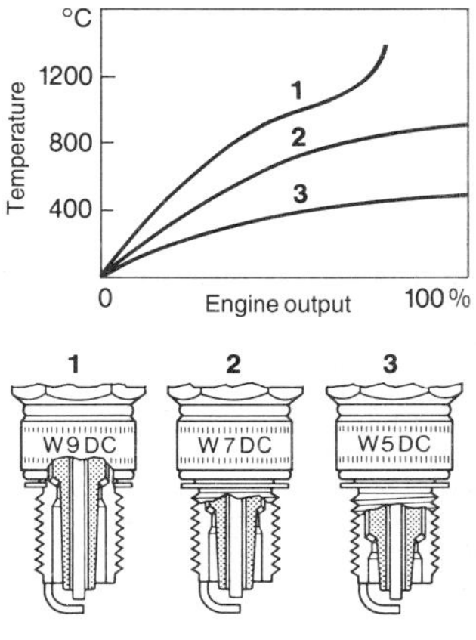

tive measurements conducted against a standard reference. The correct heat range for a specific engine depends upon the amount of heat which is to be produced and then dissipated during the combustion cycle. With modern engines, the temperature at the spark plug is no longer the sole criterium. Another important consideration is the ignition probability factor, which is determined by measuring the ionic current.

The ionic-current measurement procedure developed for ascertaining the optimum heat range can distinguish between pre-ignition and post-ignition in the combustion process. It uses the firing point as reference. The appropriate heat range is ascertained by determining the distance between the firing point and the point of pre-ignition, with the engine operating under just those conditions in which the preignition tendency is most pronounced. Incomplete combustion is particularly frequent when the engine has not yet reached its full operating temperature, at extremely low outside temperatures, and after restart. The temperatures at the center electrode and the insulator tip seldom rise beyond 150 °C, so deposits of unburned hydrocarbons and oil traces on the colder sections of the spark plug are likely. Due to the danger of cold plug fouling (risk of misfiring), the objective is to bring the spark plug to temperatures above 400 °C as quickly as possible, as the soot burns off from the insulator tip once this heat range is reached. A spark plug's "operating range" is determined with reference to these two extreme conditions:

– The plug must rapidly achieve the self-cleaning temperature of > 400 °C,
– It must maintain sufficient heat-range reserves to prevent damage to spark plugs and engine,
– In the interests of service life, a maximum temperature of 850 °C is to be observed (hot-gas corrosion).

The use of center-electrode materials with high thermal conductivity (silver or nickel-alloys with copper core), makes it possible to lengthen the insulator tip substantially without changing the plug's heat range, thus extending the plug's operating range downward in the direction of lower thermal loads. In other words, it is less liable to foul. These advantages are offered by all Bosch Super (thermoelastic) spark plugs. Reducing the probability of combustion miss and ignition miss, with their attendant massive increases in hydrocarbon emissions, provides benefits in exhaust emissions and fuel consumption during part-load operation.

Example: Recommended spark plug W 7 DC

Fitted spark plug	W 8 DC	W 6 DC
Heat range index	8	6
Insulator-tip length	longer	shorter
Tendency to preignite	greater	less
Plug-fouling tendency	less	greater

Influence of design of the spark plug's combustion-chamber end on the engine's misfire limit

The engine's misfire limit and the exhaust-gas composition can both be influenced by the design of the spark plug's combustion-chamber end: Electrodes featuring good mixture access to the spark and low thermal conductivity can be used to ignite even lean mixtures (excess air, Lambda number > 1). Larger electrode gaps serve the same objectives (to extend the engine's misfire limit into the high-Lambda range). However, such options are considerably limited by the ignition system (secondary available voltage) and the demands which are placed on insulating materials and design. In most cases, electrodes which penetrate further into the combustion chamber (extended spark location), with corresponding insulator protrusion, not only improve the engine's operating characteristics, they also feature increased resistance to deposits. The thermal loadability of such spark plugs is less critical due to their greater thermal dissipation. Where necessary, composite materials can be used to compensate for excessive electrode temperatures. Because influences fluctuate from engine to engine, extreme care must be taken during application engineering to select the optimum spark-plug design.

Electrode gap and ignition voltage

On the one hand, the electrode gap should be as wide as possible, so that the spark reaches as large an air-fuel volume as possible and the mixture is rapidly and reliably ignited so that the engine runs smoothly. On the other hand, the electrode gap must be narrow enough to guarantee that, given sufficient energy, the ignition voltage forms a reliable spark, even at the end of the spark plug's service life and under unfavorable circumstances. It is frequently impossible to achieve smooth idle when the electrode gap is too narrow. The voltage requirement is influenced by a multiplicity of factors. These include not only the electrode gap, shape, temperature and the type of material, but also factors specific to the combustion chamber such as mixture ratio (Lambda), flow velocity, turbulence and the pressure of the gas to be ignited. High ignition-voltages are required in the following cases:

– High compression ratio or turbocharging,
– Inhomogeneous mixture, especially during acceleration from idle and with lean mixtures,
– Cold electrodes and cold mixture,
– Wide electrode gap (electrode wear).

On today's high-compression, high-turbulence engines, the electrode gap must be carefully determined in order to guarantee reliable ignition and misfire-free operation throughout the required service life.

Spark-plug evaluation

Lambda closed-loop control systems are vital for meeting the stringent emissions requirements which are placed upon modern vehicles. The Lambda sensor and the catalytic converter required for such systems can only operate when unleaded gasoline is used. This means that the wear characteristics or the "face" of spark plugs which operate under such conditions differ from those of plugs used with leaded gasoline. The once-frequent spark-plug failures due to the fuel's high lead content (lead deposits on the insulator tip) are a thing of the past. This means that without appropriate equipment, it is impossible to refer to the spark plug's face when determining the plug's service life limit. The vehicle and spark-plug manufacturers conduct extensive tests to mutually determine a spark plug's service life. The recommended replacement intervals are contained in the service guidelines of the respective automobile manufacturers. Neither inspection nor adjustment is required in the periods between service. Thus it is only in extreme cases that the spark plug's face can serve as a source of information, such as when major oil or ash deposits are present, or in cases of mechanical damage or thermal overload.

HC emissions as a function of electrode gap (1) and spark penetration (2)

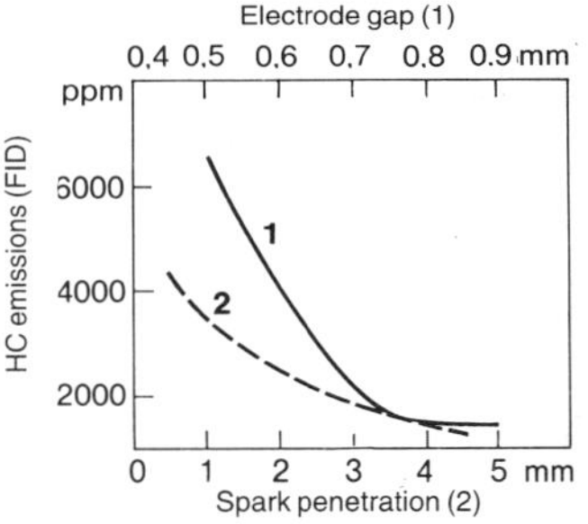

Electrode gaps

Application	Gap in mm
Standard engines with battery ignition and mixture adaptation ($\lambda = 1$)	0.7 ... 0.9
Engine designed for extremely lean operation	1.0 ... 1.2
Small engines with magneto ignition	0.5
High-compression engines (e.g., racing engines, gas engines)	0.3 ... 0.5

Selection and installation of spark plugs

The spark-plug code contains all the vital information on the spark plug, whereby no specifications are provided for electrode gaps in the range ≤ 1.1 mm. The specified tightening torque is to be selected with reference to the spark plug's design (international ISO standard). Compliance with this standard means that both loose spark plugs and damage to the cylinder-head threads are avoided. The tightening torques given in the table for installation with torque wrench apply to unlubricated spark plugs. (When installing without a torque wrench, begin by screwing the spark plug into the head until it contacts the seat. Then turn new flat-seat plugs about another 90°. Spark plugs with conical seats and used spark plugs are to be turned about another 15°.)

Type designation code for Bosch spark plugs

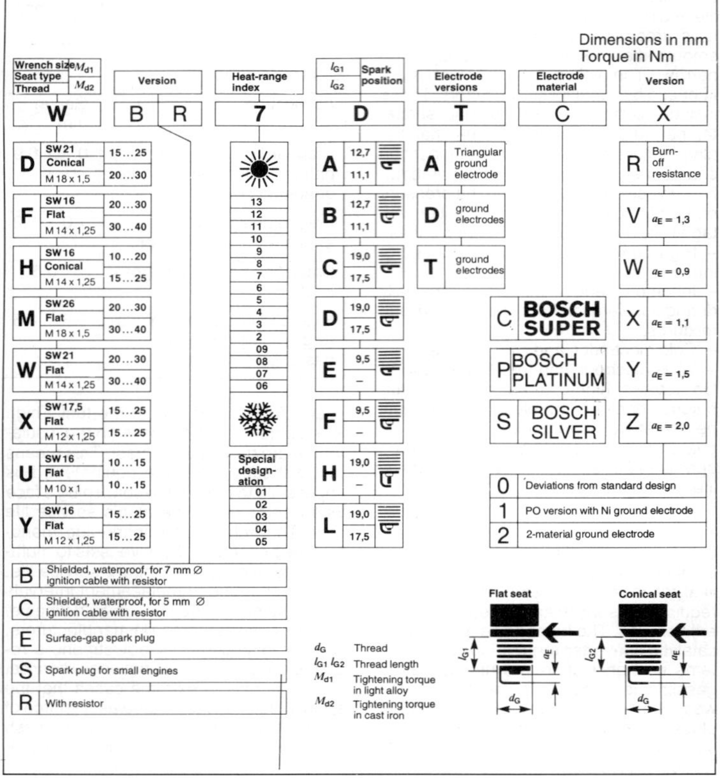

Conventional coil ignition (CI)

Many vehicles are still equipped with conventional coil ignition. When the contact breaker closes with the ignition switched on, current from the battery (alternator) flows through the ignition-coil primary winding, generating the powerful magnetic field in which the energy is stored. At the ignition point, the contact breaker interrupts the current, the magnetic field collapses, and the high voltage necessary for ignition is induced in the secondary winding. This voltage is fed from terminal 4 to the ignition distributor via the high-voltage cable, and from there to the particular spark plug.

In general, the following describes the relationship between the speed of a four-stroke SI engine and the sparking rate per minute:

$$f = z \cdot n/2$$

f Sparking rate, z Number of cylinders,
n Engine speed.

At low engine speeds, the contact breaker remains closed long enough to store the maximum possible amount of ignition energy. At higher engine speeds, this so-called dwell period is shorter, which means that the primary current is interrupted before it has had time to rise to a high enough value. The reduced storage rates result in there being less secondary voltage available from the ignition coil. However, the ignition coil is designed to provide a secondary voltage well in excess of that required by the spark plugs, even at maximum engine speeds. A layer of contamination on the insulating components acts as a capacitive and ohmic shunt, increasing the ignition loads placed upon the system, with combustion and ignition misfiring as the ultimate consequences.

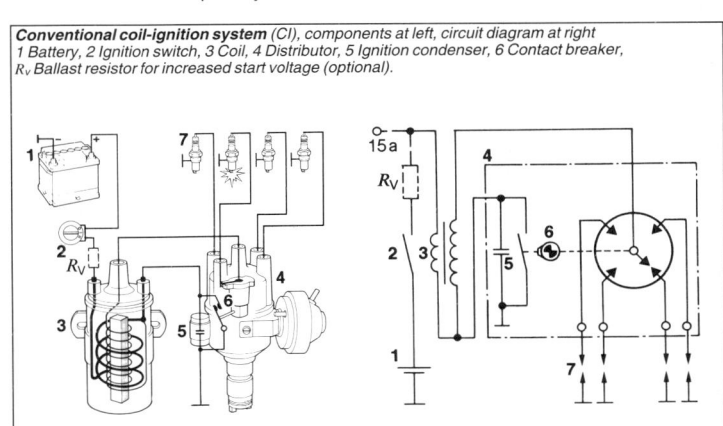

Secondary voltage as a function of sparking rate
a without ohmic shunts (R > 10 MΩ)
b 1 MΩ shunt resistor
c 0.5 MΩ shunt resistor
d Ignition voltage requirement

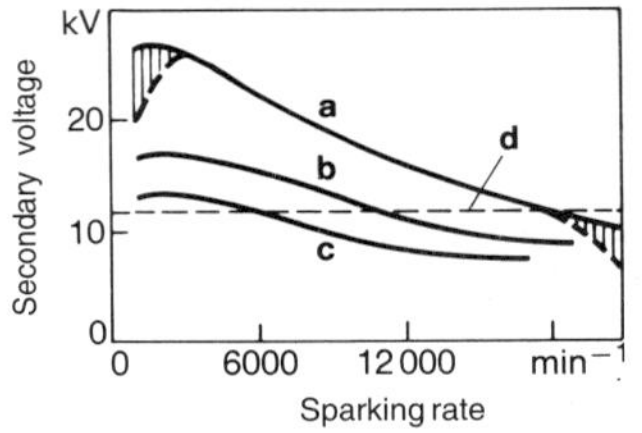

Conventional coil-ignition system *(CI), components at left, circuit diagram at right*
1 Battery, 2 Ignition switch, 3 Coil, 4 Distributor, 5 Ignition condenser, 6 Contact breaker, R_V Ballast resistor for increased start voltage (optional).

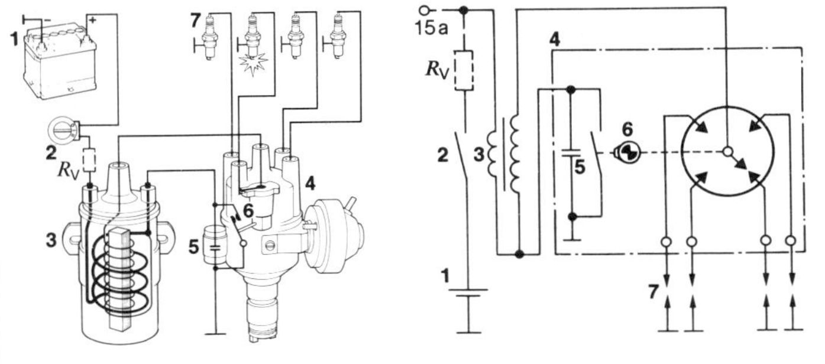

Ignition coil

Description: Page 449.

Ignition distributor

The distributor is a separate, self-contained component within the ignition system. It has the following functions:

– It distributes the ignition pulses to the engine spark plugs in a specific sequence (CI, TCI, ESA).

– It triggers the ignition pulse, either when the contact breaker interrupts the primary current, or, with breakerless systems (CI, TCI, ESA in some cases), by means of a pulse generator

– It adjusts the ignition point (timing) by means of the spark-advance mechanism on conventional ignition systems (CI, TCI).

In modern electronic ignition systems, operating either alone or in combination with the fuel-injection system (Motronic), the distributor generally comprises only a rotor arm connected to the camshaft and the distributor cap with high-voltage leads.

The contact breaker and the spark-advance mechanism perform functions which are quite different from those of the distributor proper. They are combined with it in a single unit simply because they need to be driven synchronously.

A center connection, and a carbon brush or discharge gap, are used to conduct the ignition pulse to the distributor's rotor arm. By means of sparks, this then distributes the ignition pulses to the fixed electrodes pressed into the cap around its periphery, from where they are conducted through the ignition cables to the spark plugs. A dust cover is sometimes installed to separate the high-voltage components from the rest of the housing.

Contact breaker

The contact breaker uses a cam-actuated contact to interrupt the primary current in the coil at the firing point. The number of cam lobes corresponds to the number of engine cylinders. The angle defined by that proportion of the distributor shaft's rotation during which the contact breaker is closed is termed the dwell angle β.

Contact breaker
1 Moving breaker-plate assembly, 2 Breaker lever, 3 Distributor shaft, 4 Distributor cam.

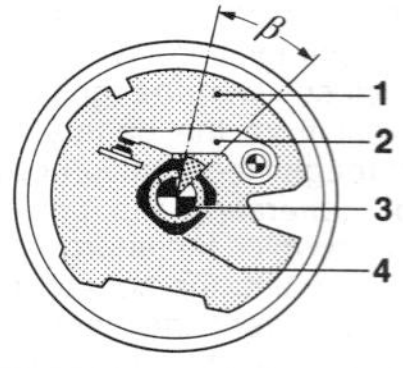

Centrifugal advance mechanism, at rest (above), in operation (below)
1 Support plate, 2 Distributor cam, 3 Contact face, 4 Advance flyweight, 5 Distributor shaft, 6 Driver.

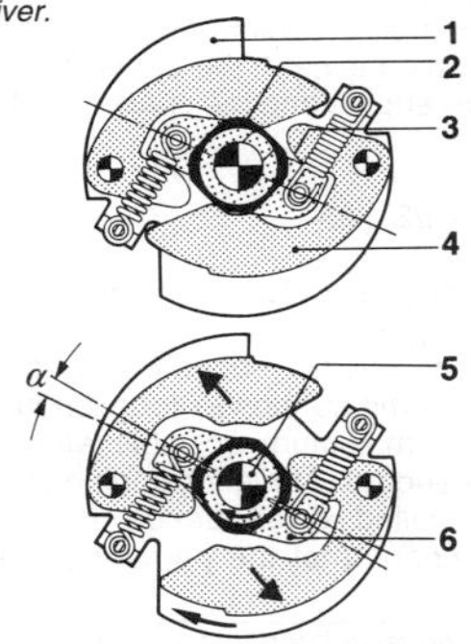

The contact-breaker contacts (points) are subject to three types of wear:

- Contact wear
- Cam-follower (rubbing-block) wear
- Physical deformation and local compressions in the contact metal.

Contact wear is caused by the breaking sparks (sparks at contact break) which result from the voltage induced when the primary current is interrupted. Although the ignition condenser has spark-quenching characteristics, it cannot fully suppress the breaking sparks. Although contact wear and rubbing-block wear are mutually counteractive, the effects of the latter are generally more pronounced, resulting in a tendency for the ignition to drift in the "retard" direction, toward a later ignition point.

Spark-advance mechanism
Ignition distributors are generally equipped with two spark-advance mechanisms: A speed-dependent, centrifugal advance mechanism and a load-dependent vacuum advance mechanism.

Centrifugal advance mechanism
The centrifugal advance mechanism adjusts the ignition point as a function of the engine speed. The support plate upon which the advance weights are mounted rotates with the distributor shaft, and the flyweights move outward as engine speed increases. By means of the contact path, they rotate the driver with respect to the distributor shaft in the direction of rotation. This causes the distributor cam to also turn through the advance angle α relative to the distributor shaft. The ignition point is advanced by this angle.

Vacuum advance mechanism
The vacuum advance mechanism adjusts the ignition point as a function of engine output/engine load. The vacuum in the intake manifold in the vicinity of the throttle valve is the reference for this ignition adjustment. The vacuum acts upon two aneroid capsules.

Operation of the advance mechanism
The lower the load, the slower the combustion of the air-fuel mixture. This means that it must be ignited earlier. Meanwhile, the proportion of those residual gases which have been burned but not discharged from the combustion chamber increases, and the mixture leans out. The vacuum for the advance mechanism is taken off immediately downstream from the open throttle valve. As the engine load decreases, the vacuum in the advance unit rises, causing the diaphragm and its actuating rod to move to the right. The rod rotates the breaker plate in the direction opposite to the distributor shaft's direction of travel, moving the ignition point further forward, that is, in the "advance" direction.

Operation of the retard mechanism
Here, the vacuum in the intake manifold is taken off downstream from the closed throttle. The "vacuum retard unit" moves the firing point back ("retard") under certain operating conditions (e.g., idle, overrun) in order to reduce exhaust emissions. The ring diaphragm and its actuating rod move to the left when vacuum is applied. The actuating rod rotates the breaker-plate assembly together with the contact breaker in the direction of rotation of the distributor shaft. This spark-retard system operates independently of the advance mechanism, whereby the advance mechanism has priority: Simultaneous vacuum in both units results in the requisite part-load adjustment in the "advance" direction.

Vacuum advance mechanism with ignition advance and retard units
a Advance adjustment up to stop, b Retard adjustment up to stop
1 Ignition distributor, 2 Breaker-plate assembly, 3 Diaphragm, 4 Vacuum retard unit,
5 Vacuum advance unit, 6 Vacuum unit, 7 Throttle valve, 8 Intake manifold.

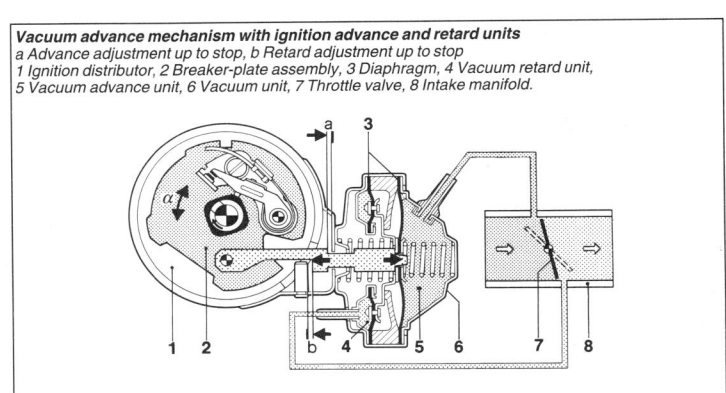

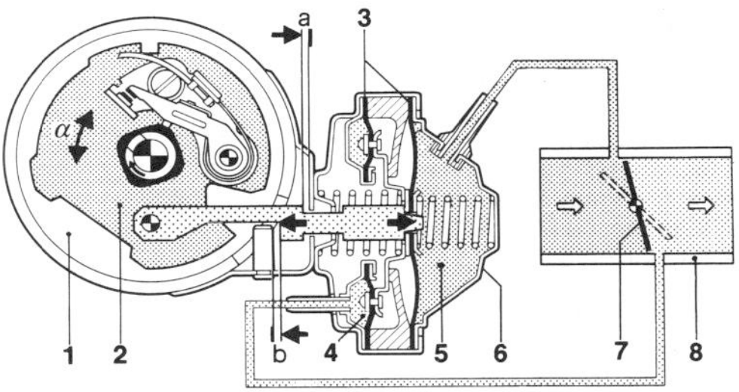

Transistorized ignition (TCI)

With conventional coil-ignition systems, ignition energy and maximum voltage are restricted by the electrical and mechanical factors which limit the switching capacity of the contact breaker. The demands placed upon battery-ignition systems are often more than the contact breaker can meet in its role as a power switch. In electronic ignition systems, semiconductor elements assume some of the contact-breaker load, or they are replaced entirely by non-wearing control devices. Transistorized (coil) ignition is available in both breaker-triggered and breakerless versions.

Breaker-triggered transistorized coil ignition is especially well-suited for retrofitting in place of conventional coil-ignition systems (CI). Breaker-triggered transistorized coil ignition systems are no longer installed as original equipment.

Breakerless transistorized ignition
On breakerless transistorized ignition systems, the cam-actuated contact breaker is replaced by a magnetic "pulse generator". This generates current and voltage pulses magnetically (without contacts) and uses these to trigger the high-voltage ignition pulse via the system electronics. The pulse generator is installed in the ignition distributor.

These types of generators operate according to various principles.

Induction-type pulse generators
The induction-type pulse generator is a permanently-excited AC generator consisting of stator and rotor (trigger wheel). The number of teeth or arms corresponds to the number of cylinders in the engine. The frequency and amplitude of the alternating current generated by the unit is determined by the engine speed. The ECU (trigger box) processes this AC voltage and uses it for ignition control.

Hall-type pulse generators
This type of ignition-pulse generator utilises the Hall effect. A speed-dependent magnetic field produces voltage pulses in a semiconductor layer which is under current; these pulses switch the ECU primary current on and off.

Pulse generators have clear advantages relative to mechanical contact breakers: They are not subject to wear, and are thus maintenance-free. They

Breakerless transistorized coil-ignition system
1 Battery, 2 Ignition switch, 3 Coil, 4 Electronic trigger box, 5 Ignition distributor with centrifugal and vacuum advance mechanism, 6a Induction-type pulse generator, 6b Hall-type pulse generator (alternative), 7 Spark plugs.

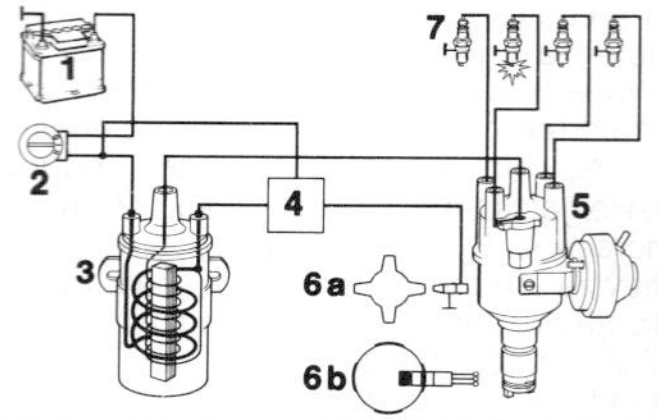

Ignition distributor with induction-type pulse generator
1 Permanent magnet, 2 Induction winding with core, 3 Variable air gap, 4 Trigger wheel.

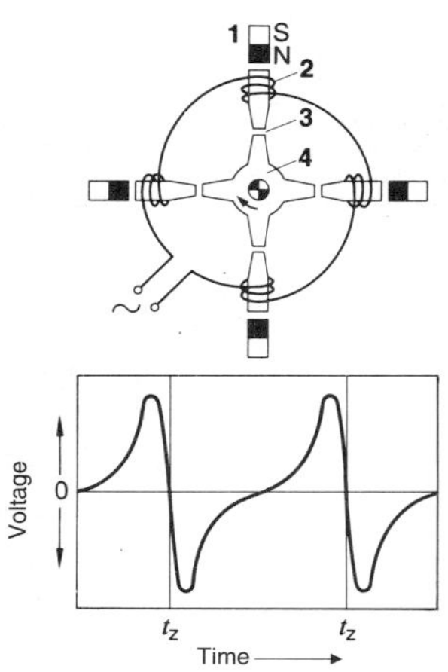

allow precise control of the ignition point, with attendant benefits for the engine's operation.

Electronic control units

Virtually all of the electronic control units (trigger boxes) in use today are equipped with primary-current regulators and closed-loop dwell-angle control.

The primary-current regulator limits the current in order to protect the ignition coil and the driver stage. When used in conjunction with a coil featuring low primary resistance, it provides high starting current at low battery voltages. This makes it possible to dispense with the ballast resistors upstream of the coil as well as with the bridging function for starting.

The closed-loop dwell-angle control ensures that the current control circuit operates for as short a time as possible in its control range. This reduces the power losses in the ECU. At the same time, it compensates for fluctuations in battery age and the effects of ignition-coil temperature.

Ignition distributor with Hall sensor
1 Vane with width b, 2 Soft-magnetic conductive elements, 3 Hall IC, 4 Air gap, U_G Hall sensor voltage (transformed Hall voltage).

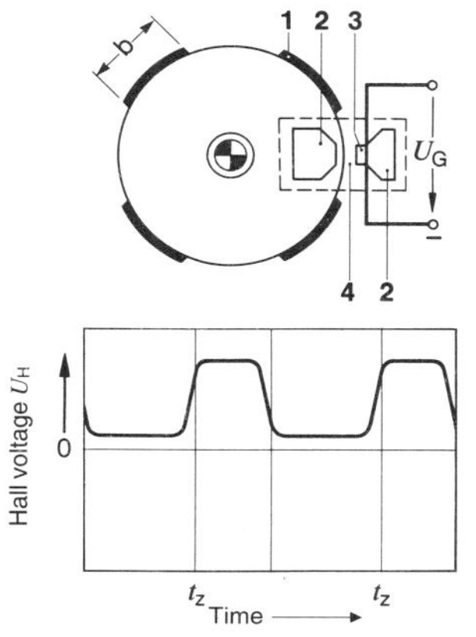

The closed-loop dwell-angle control operates up to medium engine speeds, with the exact limit depending upon the design of the respective system. At high engine speeds, the dwell angle is determined by the break time required for duration of the spark discharge. The residual energy remaining in the coil after the break time, facilitates complete charging of the coil in the case of short dwell-angles.

The sparkless closed-circuit current switch-off switches off the primary current with the ignition on and the engine off to ensure that no sparks occur at the spark plug. However, there are also TC-i systems (with induction-type pulse-generator), which feature an intrinsic closed-circuit current switch-off characteristic.

Transistorized ignition is sometimes employed together with auxiliary devices to adjust the spark advance. An example would be the idle-speed control which is installed between the Hall generator and the ECU; below idle speed it reacts to further decreases in engine rpm by advancing the ignition, thus increasing torque and preventing engine speed dropping any further. The electronic retard device reduces the amount of ignition-angle advance at high engine speeds to prevent knocking. It is connected in parallel with the ECU. Today, both of these functions are integrated in electronically adjusting ignition systems.

Hybrid units have become the ECU standard for transistorized ignition systems due to their ability to combine high packaging density with low weight and excellent reliability. The hybrid technology replaces the printed-circuit board with an Al_2O_3 substrate to which the conductor paths and resistors have been applied in a silk-screening process. Semiconductor devices and capacitors in chip form complete the circuit. As the Darlington power-transistor chip is mounted insulated on the metallic base plate, the cooling is excellent, permitting operation at high temperatures.

Ignition coils (Description on p. 449)

The performance specifications of the ignition coils for transistorized ignition differ from those of conventional coil ignitions. Care is to be taken that they are not confused with each other.

Capacitor-discharge ignition system (CDI)

The operating principle of CDI, or "thyristor ignition," as it is also called, differs from that of the ignition systems described above. It was developed for application with the high-speed, high-output multiple-cylinder reciprocating IC engines used in high-performance and racing vehicles, and for rotary-engine vehicles.

The salient characteristic of the CDI system lies in it storing the ignition energy in the electrical field of a capacitor. Capacitance and charge voltage of the capacitor determine the amount of energy which is stored. The ignition transformer converts the primary voltage discharged from the capacitor to the required high voltage. Capacitor-discharge ignition is available in both breaker-triggered and breakerless versions.

The major advantage of the CDI is that it generally remains impervious to electrical shunts in the high-voltage ignition circuit, especially those due to spark-plug contamination. For many applications, the spark duration of 0.1 ... 0.3 ms is too brief to ensure that the air-fuel mixture will ignite reliably. Thus CDI is only designed for specific types of engine, and today its use is restricted to a few applications only, as transistorized ignition systems have virtually the same performance. CDI is not suited for aftermarket installations.

CDI can also be employed for distributorless ignition with the installation of one ignition coil per cylinder, with energy distribution taking place at the medium-voltage level.

High-voltage capacitor-discharge ignition with induction-type pulse generator, schematic

1 ECU, 2 Charging device, 3 Pulse-shaping circuit, 4 Control stage, 5 Ignition transformer, 6 To induction-type pulse generator, 7 To ignition distributor.

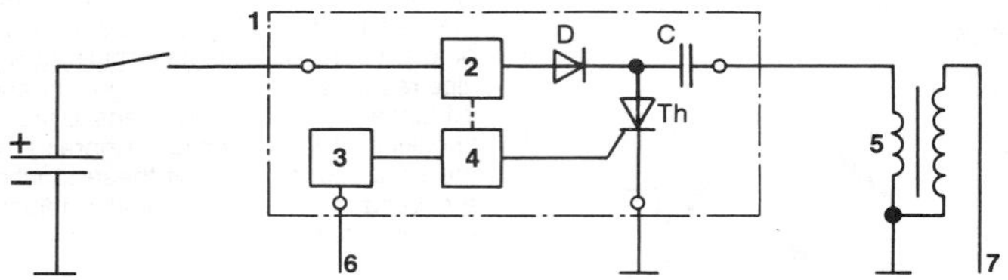

Caution

All electronic ignition systems are inherently dangerous. Before working on these systems, always switch off the ignition or disconnect the voltage supply. Such work includes:

– Replacing components such as spark plugs, ignition coil or transformer, distributor, high-tension cables, etc.

– Connecting engine test equipment such as stroboscopic timing light, dwell-angle/engine-speed tester, ignition oscilloscope, etc.

Dangerous voltages are present when the ignition is switched on. Such testing should therefore be performed by qualified personnel only.

Electronic ignition (ESA and DLI)

Electronic ignition derives its name from the fact that it calculates the ignition point electronically. The characteristic curves provided by the conventional distributor's centrifugal and vacuum-advance units are replaced by an optimized electronic ignition map. Mechanical high-tension distribution is retained with the ESA version of electronic ignition. The fully-electronic (distributorless) electronic ignition (DLI) uses stationary electronically-controlled components to replace the mechanical, rotating high-tension distributor.

Electronic ignition systems operate more precisely than mechanical systems. This is especially due to the fact that the ignition process can be triggered from the crankshaft instead of from a distributor (which means distributor drive tolerances are no longer a factor). The limitations which mechanical adjustment mechanisms place upon the performance curve (summation of curves for load and for engine speed in a single progression) are also no longer a factor. In principle, the number of input variables is also unlimited, which in general also results in the ignition angle's adjustment range being extended. The restrictions imposed on the fixed-drive ignition distributor regarding the engine's ignition-voltage requirements and ignition-angle adjustment range are such that it has difficulty coping with larger numbers of cylinders; efficient spark distribution cannot always be guaranteed. Corrective measures include dividing the ignition into two circuits (e.g., for 8 and 12-cylinder engines) and static voltage distribution.

Electronic ignition can be combined with electronic fuel-injection (Motronic), knock control, ASR, etc., making it possible to employ sensors and/or signals from other units in more than one system. The use of a serial bus (CAN, p. 776) further reduces the number of inputs and processing circuits on the ECU input-side.

Schematic of an electronic ignition system (ESA)
1 Ignition coil with ignition driver stage, 2 High-voltage distributor, 3 Spark plug, 4 ECU, 5 Coolant-temperature sensor, 6 Knock sensor, 7 Engine-speed and reference-mark sensor, 8 Sensor wheel, 9 Throttle switch, 10 Battery, 11 Ignition switch.

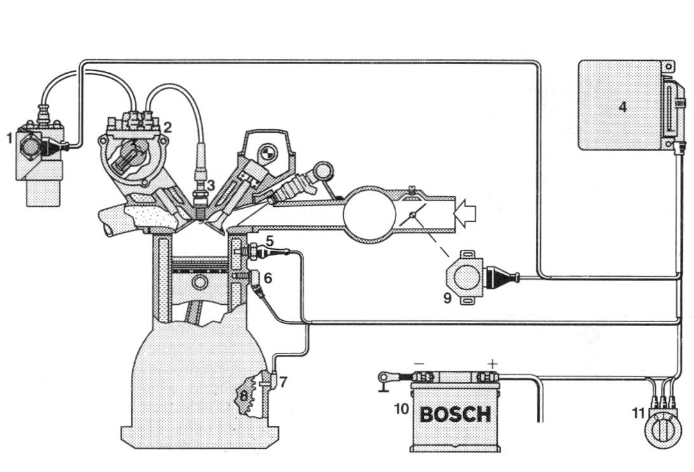

Electronic ignition. Signal processing
1 Engine speed, 2 Switch signals, 3 CAN (serial bus), 4 Intake-manifold pressure, 5 Engine temperature, 6 Intake-air temperature, 7 Battery voltage, 8 Microprocessor, 9 Analog/digital converter, 10 Driver stage.

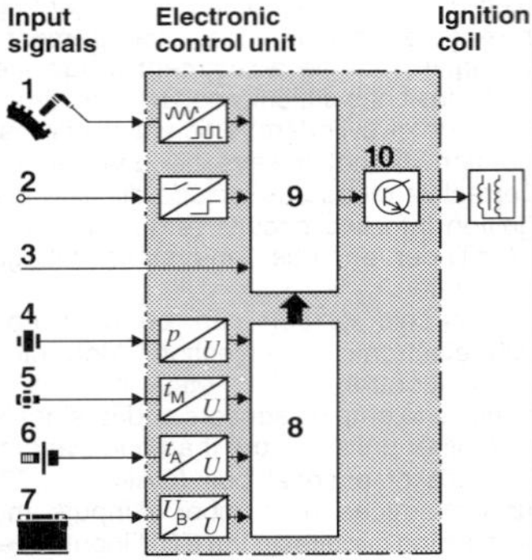

Ignition maps
Above: electronically optimized
Below: mechanical advance system.

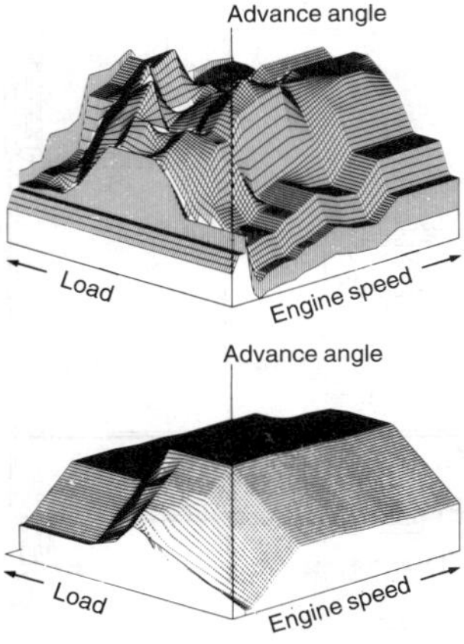

Operation

The engine speed and the crankshaft position are monitored directly at the ring gear, using either a separate wheel or a specific pin sequence employing an inductive, rod-type sensor, with two sensors being employed on older units. Triggering is either incremental or segmentary, according to whether the information is taken from teeth which are distributed evenly around the crankshaft or whether a crankshaft segment per cylinder pair is used (Beginning of segment = Maximum spark advance angle, End of segment = Starting angle).

In the incremental system illustrated here, the reference mark (represented as a tooth gap) indicates a defined crankshaft position. As from this point, electrical detection of the crankshaft angle is possible using the ring-gear teeth. A distributor without advance mechanism can also be employed for triggering; here the control signal is provided by a Hall generator. An absolute-pressure sensor in the intake manifold is the best way to monitor load, providing a better gauge of cylinder-charge than the spark-advance or retard bores on the throttle valve. It is also possible to incorporate load switches, throttle potentiometers and electronic load signals from the fuel-management system. The microcomputer in the ECU conditions the engine-speed and load signals, using them to calculate the precise ignition angle within the ignition map. The computer can also process other signals, such as engine temperature, or information on overrun or full-load operation from the throttle switch, to provide correction values or to process any other functions that may be required for an individual vehicle. The computer also specifies the dwell angle during which the coil is charged. The battery can be monitored to provide a voltage-correction factor. When the battery's voltage deviates from the specified value, the coil-charge time is lengthened or shortened accordingly. This ensures that the greatest-possible voltage remains available, while at the same time keeping the build-up of heat in ECU and coil to a minimum. The computer interrupts the current flow through the coil at engine speeds below the cranking speed in order to avoid overheating. The driver stage can be integrated within the ECU, or it can be installed externally, e.g., on the ignition coil.

Signal processing in the ECU
After initial processing, the digital signals go directly to the processor. Analog signals are first converted into digital form. There are also ECU's which can output additional digital or analog signals (e.g., for overrun fuel cutoff and exhaust-gas recirculation). There are a large number of ESA ignition-system versions of varying complexity. A comparison of the ignition map with the response curve of a distributor shows that it is possible to program each point in the ignition map independently from every other point. Thus the optimum ignition timing (e.g., according to fuel consumption) can be selected for every operating condition, according to the limits imposed by factors such as exhaust emissions, pre-ignition limit and driveability. The entire unit is completely maintenance-free, and does not require any adjustments during the engine's service life.

Rotating voltage distribution
A high-voltage distributor distributes the ignition pulses to the spark plugs of the individual cylinders (as described on p. 456). If the distributor's adjustment range is insufficient for handling a larger number of cylinders, then two ignition circuits are employed, i.e, two 4-cylinder distributors can be used for one 8-cylinder engine. Synchronization through the crankshaft can be used for "two times 4 cylinders", whereas "two times 3 cylinders" with constant ignition-angle spacing (not employed up to now) must be controlled by the camshaft.

Distributorless (stationary) voltage distribution

Systems with single-spark ignition coil
Each cylinder has its own ignition coil with driver output stage, installed either directly above the spark plug or separately. Either synchronization with the camshaft sensor or a method for detecting the compressed cylinder is required. On engines with an

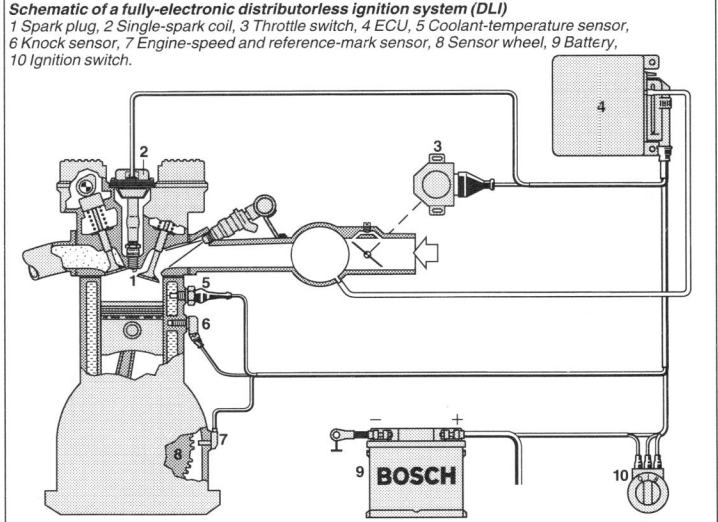

Schematic of a fully-electronic distributorless ignition system (DLI)
1 Spark plug, 2 Single-spark coil, 3 Throttle switch, 4 ECU, 5 Coolant-temperature sensor, 6 Knock sensor, 7 Engine-speed and reference-mark sensor, 8 Sensor wheel, 9 Battery, 10 Ignition switch.

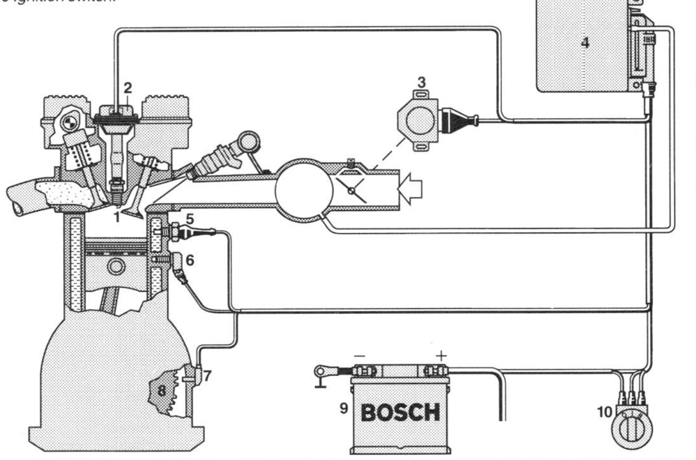

even number of cylinders, the system reverts to crankshaft triggering in the event of camshaft-sensor failure, although two coils are then always activated simultaneously (one of the sparks is discharged during an exhaust stroke). This system, suitable for engines with any number of cylinders, provides the greatest latitude for adjustment, as there is only one spark per cycle.

Systems with dual-spark ignition coil
One ignition coil is required for every two cylinders. The crankshaft can be used for synchronization. The high-voltage end of each ignition coil is connected to two spark plugs which belong to two cylinders whose operating cycles are 360° out of phase with each other.

As there is an additional spark during the exhaust stroke, care must be taken to ensure that residual mixture or fresh mixture is not ignited. Furthermore, the dual-spark system is only suited for use with even numbers of cylinders. Due to its cost advantage relative to the single-spark unit, the dual-spark ignition system is the most common distributorless ignition in use today.

Knock control

Function
Internal-combustion engines are damaged by combustion knock (see p. 360). Higher combustion ratios intended to improve fuel economy, and fluctuations in fuel quality, increase the engine's tendency to knock.

Knock control serves to prevent knocking under all operating conditions. With high compression ratios, the knock limit is often within the ignition-timing range for minimum fuel consumption. Knock control makes it possible to design the engine for operation in this range without having to provide safety reserves.

Operation
From a suitable installation location on the engine block, the knock sensor monitors structure-borne noise, which it transforms into an electrical signal suitable for transmission to the ECU. An evaluation circuit in the ECU adjusts the amplitude of the noise signal, adapting it for processing at both low or high engine speeds, and on quiet or loud engines. A "measuring window," synchronized to the crankshaft, and

Schematic of knock-control system

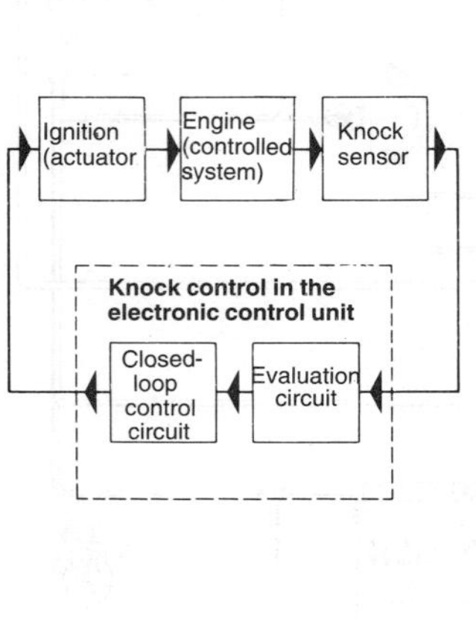

Knock control
Control algorithm for ignition adjustments with a 4-cylinder engine.
$K_{1...3}$ knock in cylinders 1 ... 3.
Cylinder 4: No knock.
a Delay prior to ignition retard
b Retardation, c Delay before return to original ignition point, d Spark advance.

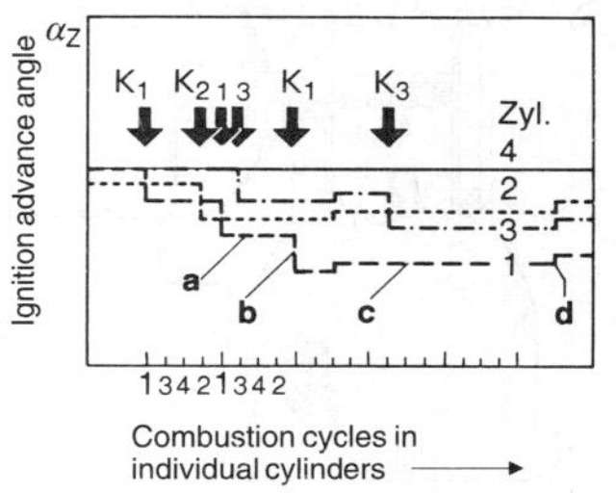

a band pass are used to filter out the data which characterize knocking. This information is then compared with signals from combustion processes in which no knock is occurring in order to determine whether knocking is present. The (closed-loop) control circuit adjusts the engine by means of an actuator and eliminates the knock. Ignition timing is an especially effective manipulated variable, as it permits the most rapid corrections.

When knock occurs, the ignition timing is retarded for a certain number of cycles, after which it again gradually moves back toward its original setting. The ability to retard the timing for each cylinder individually is of major importance. The objective is to limit the timing adjustment to the cylinders where knock is actually occurring, while allowing the others to continue operating at their respective optima.

Knock control in turbocharged engines

With turbocharged engines, ignition-timing adjustments are joined by a second option: The boost/intake pressure can be employed as a manipulated variable. In the illustration, the knock sensor is installed between cylinders 2 and 3 on the intake side. The ECU adapts the ignition while at the same time activating the duty-cycle solenoid, thus opening the exhaust-side wastegate to bypass the turbine. This reduces the boost pressure and, as a consequence, the tendency to knock. A sensor in the intake manifold provides information on load, and together with the possibility of monitoring the throttle position, this system provides for boost-pressure control. This prevents excessive boost pressures, and during steady-state operation reduces exhaust back-pressure so that fuel economy is improved (see "Boost-pressure control" p. 420 and 467).

Knock control as an additional function

It is quite easy to combine knock control with electronic ignition; this arrangement is frequently employed in Motronic systems (p. 474).

Knock sensor
1 Seismic mass, 2 Potting compound, 3 Piezoceramic element, 4 Contacts, 5 Terminals.

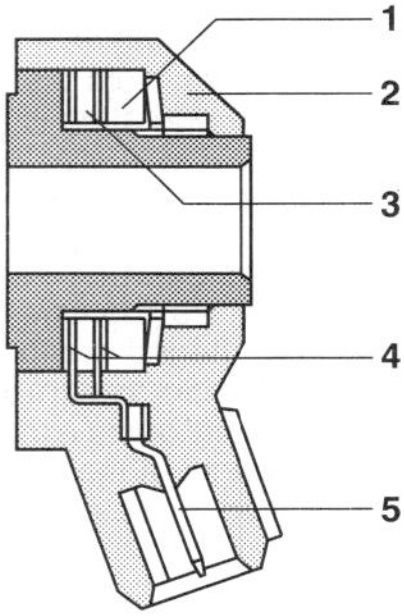

Knock sensor

The knock sensor is installed in a location which is selected for its optimum knock-detection properties. The structure-borne noise from the engine block is transmitted to an annular piezoceramic disk and induces alternating electrical voltages on its surface which are sent to the ECU through a shielded wire. When higher numbers of cylinders are concerned, two knock sensors can be used. These are then synchronized with the camshaft, allowing the system to monitor the correct knock sensor for the particular cylinder.

Monitoring functions

The driver must be informed of any failure in the knock-control system. The ECU therefore continually monitors all sensors for correct operation and performs a self-check for correct response. In case of malfunction, it protects the engine by permanently retarding the ignition. A dashboard display provides notice in case of malfunction, or if the closed-loop controller reaches the limits of its control range.

Additional engine-control functions

The "fuel preparation" and "ignition" operations described above represent the main functions of the engine's electronic engine-management system. As all important data on engine operation is available in such a system, it is a logical step to integrate additional engine-management or control functions in the same system. The result is that systems that were initially independent, such as fuel-injection and ignition, become integral components in an engine-management system the scope of which is continually being expanded.

The most important of these integrated functions are described below.

Idle-speed control

The intake-air flow, the excess-air factor λ and the ignition timing determine the SI engine's idle speed. This can be regulated by changing the air quantity (charge adjustment) and/or the ignition timing (ignition adjustment). The control of idle speed by means of the cylinder charge (idle-speed control) is a standard idle-adjustment method. Idle is one of the most frequently encountered operating conditions in city driving, and adjusting for the lowest possible idle speed is therefore an especially logical way of reducing fuel consumption and lowering exhaust emissions. An idle-speed control system is used which provides for a consistent, stable idle throughout the service life of the vehicle (maintenance-free).

Idle-speed control
1 Idle actuator, 2 Electronic idle controller, 3 Throttle valve, U_B Supply-voltage, n Engine speed, T_M Engine temperature, α_{DK} Throttle position, D/AC Signal from automatic transmission/air conditioner.

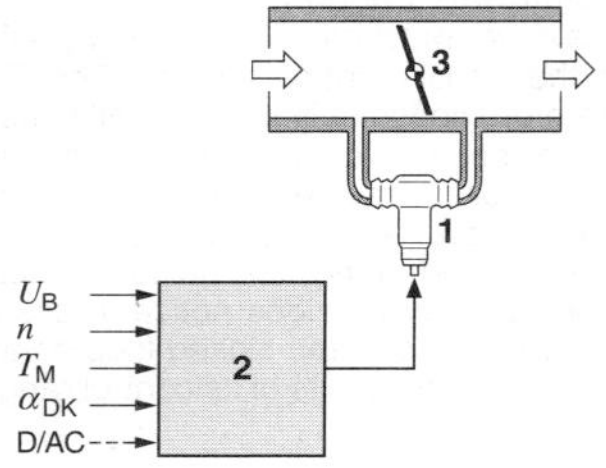

Operation
Sensors monitor engine speed, engine temperature and throttle position; additional load factors such as automatic transmission, air conditioning and other interference factors can also be monitored. The electronic controller compares the actual engine speed with the desired (setpoint) speed. The controller transmits a signal to the idle actuator, which adjusts to the desired idle speed by increasing the air flow when the idle speed is too low, and decreasing it when idle is too high. Both fast-acting and slow-acting closed-loop control concepts are applied. Fast-acting control enables a low idle speed to be used which is conducive to low fuel consumption and emissions. This is because the system can compensate, with virtually no loss of engine speed, for variations in load condition caused by the switching in of energy-consuming devices. At the same time, the response of the closed-loop control must not be so rapid as to impair stability. As slow-acting control compensates for gradual deviations (tolerance and drift), it does not allow such low idle speeds. It is thus at a certain disadvantage as a fuel-saving measure.

In addition to the charge-control systems, which employ an actuator in the throttle bypass, there are also systems available which act on the throttle plate itself.

Idle-speed actuator
The idle-speed actuator is located in the throttle bypass. The rotary valve on the armature shaft opens the air-bypass passage until the required idle speed is reached, regardless of engine load. Voltage is applied alternately to the rotary actuator's two windings (two-winding operation) and generates opposing forces on the pivoting armature. The rotary valve assumes the opening angle which corre-

sponds to the pulse-duty factor of the applied voltage. This means that the bypass opening can be adjusted by varying the pulse-duty factor. Other types of actuator, with only a single winding (single-winding operation), generally act against the force of a counterspring, while the movement of the armature can be either rotary or lateral. Under zero current conditions, some actuators revert to a "limp-home aperture" which is just sufficient to allow the SI engine to continue running at minimum idle speed. A special case is the step motor which moves by one unit (step) per control pulse. A gear-drive converts the rotation into linear motion.

Electronic engine-power control (EMS)
EMS (or "E-Gas") departs from the conventional mechanical systems which use a bowden cable or linkage to vary the position of the throttle plate. Instead, it uses an ECU and electric motor. The system is thus capable of controlling the throttle plate with reference to various operating parameters, performing tasks such as torque reduction for electronic traction control (ASR).

A travel sensor monitors the position of the accelerator pedal and transmits this information to the ECU. Taking into account the input signals from other systems (e.g., ASR and Motronic), the ECU uses this travel-sensor signal to calculate the control signal for the throttle actuator. A position control loop is applied for precise adjustment of the throttle angle, the ECU using the signal from a potentiometer inside the actuator for this purpose.

The ECU constantly monitors all components to ensure that the system is operating correctly. The sensors and the processor in the ECU are all present in pairs, making it possible to compare the respective signal pairs to obtain reliable monitoring.

In addition to those systems which employ an electrical connection between the accelerator pedal and the actuator, there are also systems on the market which incorporate a mechanical connection element (such as a bowden cable). This permits "limp-home" should a malfunction cause the the system to switch off the actuator.

Electronic engine-power control (EMS)
1 Accelerator pedal, 2 Pedal-position sensor, 3 ECU with 3b data bus and 3a microprocessor, 4 Throttle actuator.

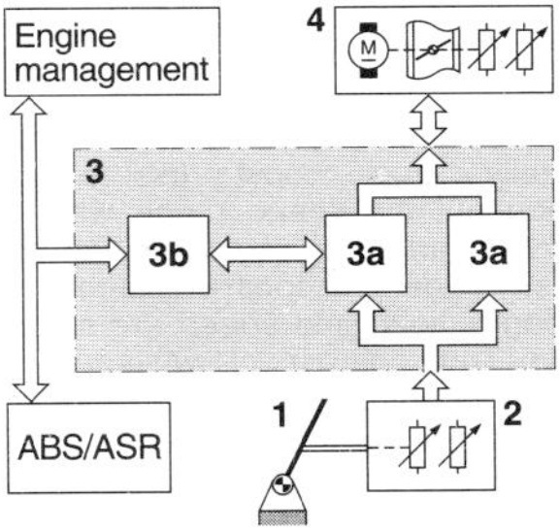

Because it regulates the throttle plate electronically, the electronic engine-power control (EMS) can perform various functions to enhance driving safety, convenience and engine management. The safety measures include both ASR and engine drag-torque control. The latter employs programmed throttle openings to reduce to a non-critical level the braking force that engine drag-torque can apply to the driven wheels.

Measures for driving convenience and comfort include the cruise control ("Tempomat") and the advantage of applying EMS to reduce load-change reactions under transient conditions.

The idle-speed control system, incorporating a separate actuator for the throttle bypass on systems without EMS, is an example of an engine-management function. Development is being carried out to adapt EMC to effect other engine-related improvements (e.g., for improved fuel consumption).

Electronic boost-pressure control
As well as being designed to generate boost at low speeds, turbocharged engines must also develop their specified power outputs. The objectives are early increase in boost pressure, a well-

balanced pressure curve, which results in smooth torque progression at all engine speeds and pedal positions, and the maximum achievable specific output. The ability of mechanically governed exhaust turbochargers to comply with these objectives is limited.

On the other hand, together with the appropriate exhaust turbocharger, electronic boost-pressure control combines a virtually ideal boost-pressure curve throughout the speed range with good control characteristics during load transitions. The data for boost pressure relative to engine load and speed are stored in maps. Turbocharger and wastegate valve are designed to ensure that a sufficiently long control stroke is available. A solenoid valve operates at a specific duty cycle and defines the optimum position for the wastegate-control valve under all operating conditions by adjusting to the programmed boost pressure. Potential sources of load information include the intake-manifold pressure, the intake-air quantity and the air mass flow.

Boost-pressure control systems are always used together with knock control in order to obtain high specific engine outputs. There is no engine damage from combustion knock, although the ignition timing is advanced as far as possible (refer to Knock Control, p. 464).

As soon as combustion knock is detected (due to low-octane fuel for instance), ignition advance is reduced as a preventive measure.

To prevent the exhaust turbocharger from being exposed to excessive exhaust-gas temperatures, excessive retardation of the ignition point is first of all countered by a richer air-fuel mixture. If this does not suffice, boost pressure is reduced.

Combined knock and boost control

1 Intake air, 2 Compressor, 3 Turbine, 4 To exhaust system, 5 Waste-gate control valve, 6 Throttle-valve, 7 Throttle potentiometer, 8 Temperature sensor, 9 Knock sensor, 10 Control valve, 11 ECU, p_1 Pressure before compressor, p_2 Boost pressure, p_2' Intake-manifold pressure, p_3 Exhaust back pressure, S_K Knock-sensor signal, S_R Engine-speed signal, T_L Boost-air temperature, V_A Exhaust-gas flow, V_T Flow through turbine, V_W Flow through wastegate, α_D Throttle angle, α_Z Ignition advance angle.

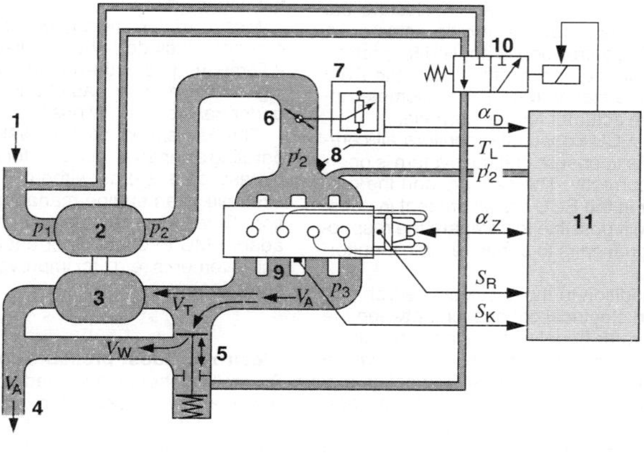

Variable-length intake manifold

Engine design objectives include both maximum low-speed torque and high rated output at maximum engine speed. The torque curve for a given engine is proportional to the mass of the inducted air over speed.

The geometrical configuration of the intake manifold represents one means of influencing torque. Intake manifolds for carburetor and single-point injection systems (Mono-Jetronic) require short and, as far as possible, equal-length manifold runners to ensure good cylinder-to-cylinder mixture distribution.

The intake runners used with multipoint fuel-injection systems conduct only air; the fuel is discharged directly before the intake valves. This configuration offers greater latitude in intake-manifold design.

Standard intake manifolds for multipoint fuel-injection consist of single induction runners and a plenum with throttle plate. The factors which influence design are as follows:

- Short induction runners are used to achieve high output, but at the cost of sacrifices in low-end torque, while long induction runners have the opposite effect.
- Large plenum volumes can provide resonance effects leading to improved cylinder charge in certain engine-speed ranges. However, the dynamics can be adversely affected (mixture fluctuations during rapid load changes).

A suitable variable-length intake-manifold design can be used to provide a virtually ideal torque curve. The possible measures, based on engine load, engine speed and throttle-valve position for instance, include the following:

- Infinitely variable adjustment of intake-runner length,
- Ability to switch between different intake-runner lengths,
- Ability to switch between different intake-runner diameters,
- Ability to deactivate a single passage per cylinder on multiple-passage intake runners,
- Ability to select from different plenum volumes.

These options mean that the variable-length intake-manifold principle can be used to either improve the operating dynamics or to maintain the initial dynamics while reducing fuel consumption (dependent upon conversion ratio).

Continuously adjustable variable-length intake manifold
1 Side wall (drum bearing), 2 Fixed housing, 3 Rotatable drum (air distributor), 4 Drum air inlet, 5 Air inlet for intake runners, 6 Seal (e.g., leaf spring), 7 Intake runners, 8 Intake valve, 9 Intake air.

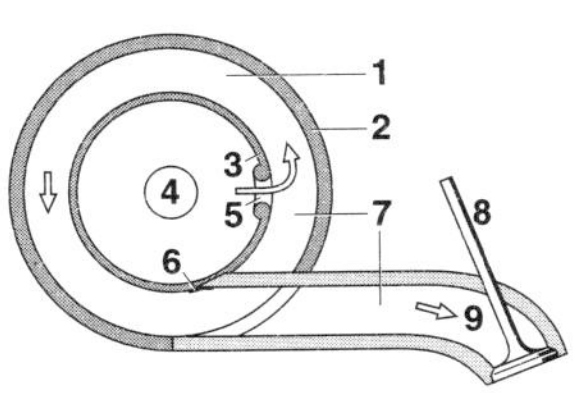

Mean effective pressure as a function of engine speed for a continuously adjustable variable-length intake manifold at 3 different lengths
L_1 Effective intake-runner length, D_1 Intake-runner diameter.

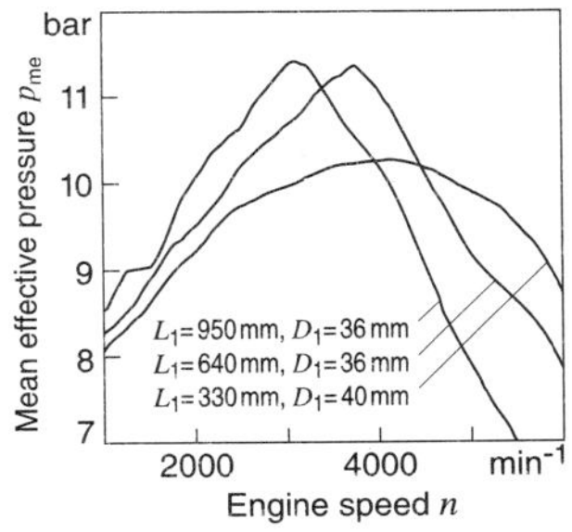

Evaporative emission control system

As fuel evaporates in the fuel tank, hydrocarbons are discharged into the atmosphere. This effect increases along with fuel-temperature increase. The legal requirements regarding evaporative emissions can be satisfied with the application of carbon canisters which store the hydrocarbons from the fuel tank ("Testing exhaust and evaporative emissions from spark-ignition vehicles," p. 483). The fuel tank is then ventilated exclusively via this carbon canister. Due to its limited storage volume, however, the carbon must be continually regenerated. With the engine running, air is drawn through the carbon canister and into the engine for combustion. If 1% of the intake air is composed of fuel vapor from the carbon canister, the A/F ratio at the engine changes by approximately 20%. This means that the entry of such vapors into the engine must be controlled, both to maintain exhaust emissions within the desired limits as well as to ensure good driveability. To this end, the engine-management system activates a regeneration valve (the so-called canister-purge valve). A programmed adaptation curve, based on the load and engine-speed parameters, makes it possible to achieve essentially progressive control of the flow quantity within the canister-purge valve's operating range.

Under certain operating conditions, the canister-purge valve is either switched off (idle) or it remains ineffective (full-load: insufficient vacuum). In addition, the Lambda control monitors whether the specified limits are maintained when the canister-purge valve is activated. If the valve's influence is excessive, the flow quantity is reduced in order to maintain driving characteristics and exhaust emissions at optimum levels.

Exhaust-gas recirculation

Exhaust-gas recirculation (EGR) provides an effective means of reducing nitrous-oxide emissions (NO_x). Exhaust gases which have already been combusted are added to the air-fuel mixture in order to reduce peak combustion temperatures. This

Evaporative emission-control system
1 Intake air, 2 Throttle valve, 3 Intake manifold (to engine), 4 Canister-purge valve, 5 From engine-management ECU, 6 Carbon canister, 7 Ambient air, 8 Fuel vapors in tank.

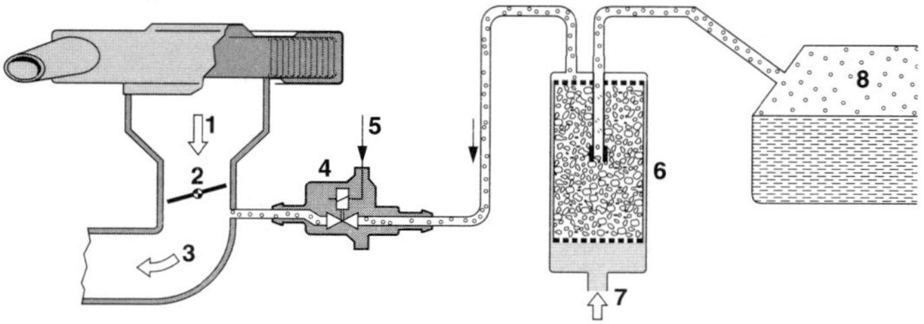

measure reduces the emissions of temperature-dependent nitrous oxides.

A certain degree of "internal" exhaust-gas recirculation is an inherent design feature in all IC engines due to the overlap between the intake and exhaust valves. A certain amount of residual exhaust gas – depending upon the degree of valve overlap – is re-inducted along with the fresh air-fuel mixture. On engines with variable valve timing, it would theoretically be possible to influence NOx emissions by using variable internal exhaust-gas recirculation.

Virtually all of the exhaust-gas recirculation systems in use today operate according to the principle of "external" exhaust-gas recirculation. A defined portion of the engine's exhaust emissions are extracted and returned to the fresh air-fuel mixture via a solenoid valve. The exhaust-gas recirculation is generally controlled by a pneumatic or mechanical system which meters the recirculated exhaust gas with reference to factors such as engine speed, intake-manifold pressure and engine temperature. In some systems, the ECU uses an electropneumatic transducer to activate the EGR valve.

By means of EGR, NOx emissions can be reduced by up to 60%. Increases in HC emissions and in fuel consumption combine with rougher engine operation to impose an upper limit upon the recirculation rate. Thus the EGR is switched off during idling, when no significant NOx emissions are produced in any case. Exhaust-gas recirculation is generally applied during part-throttle operation, as it is here that its potential is greatest. The unfavorable pressure conditions impose limitations on EGR at and in the vicinity of the upper load range.

One disadvantage common to all EGR systems is that the valves and plumbing are susceptible to clogging due to exhaust-gas deposits; and during the life of the engine this causes an ongoing reduction in the amount of gas which is recirculated.

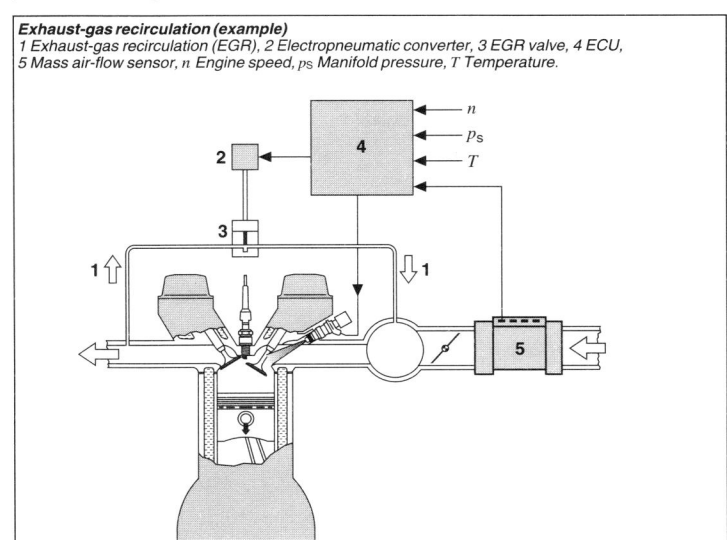

Exhaust-gas recirculation (example)
1 Exhaust-gas recirculation (EGR), 2 Electropneumatic converter, 3 EGR valve, 4 ECU, 5 Mass air-flow sensor, n Engine speed, p_S Manifold pressure, T Temperature.

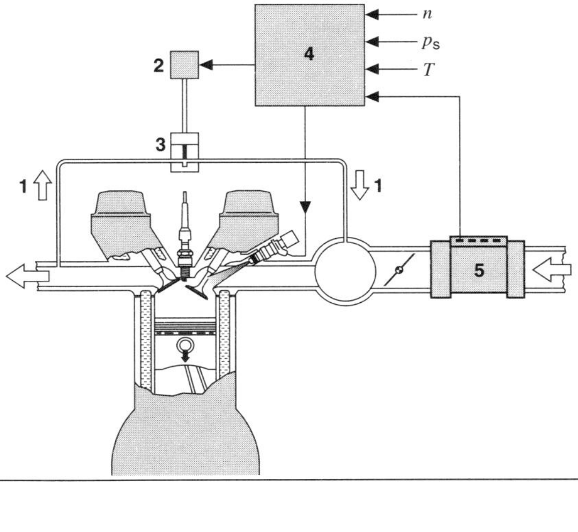

Combined ignition and fuel-injection system (Motronic)

The Motronic engine-management system has undergone substantial development since its introduction in 1979, whereby the basic constituents of this integrated system remain the fuel-injection and the fully-electronic ignition systems. The following Motronic versions are available:

– KE-Motronic, based on the KE continuously-operating fuel-injection system (p. 440).
– Mono-Motronic, based on the intermittently-operating single-point Mono-Jetronic fuel-injection system (p. 436).
– Motronic based on the intermittently-operating multipoint fuel-injection, which is described in the following.

Detection and processing of measured variables

As the section on "Control parameters and operation" (p. 428) has shown, A/F ratio, mixture preparation, ignition timing (defined as ignition-advance angle α_z) and the ignition energy, all decisively influence the combustion process in the cylinder, with attendant consequences for the engine's exhaust emissions. All the the parameters required for optimum combustion are transmitted by sensors to the ECU in the form of measured variables.

Sensors

Engine speed and engine load represent the main control variables. An inductive sensor uses the modulation of a ring-gear-induced magnetic field to measure the engine speed and crankshaft angle; the load factor is determined by measuring either the intake-air mass flow or the intake-manifold pressure. These pressure values are used in the map to determine the optimum parameters for injection and ignition timing. Only integrated systems are able to ensure the necessary simultaneous processing of both values.

Motronic control maps *(samples)*

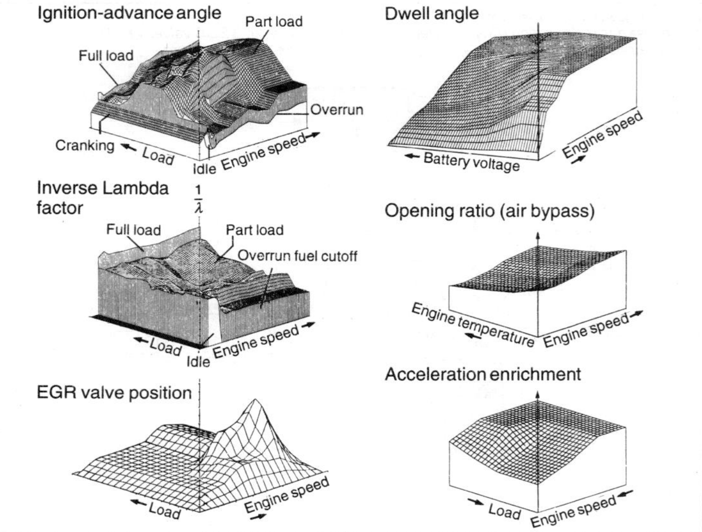

This arrangement makes it possible to prevent statistical errors, such as those that can result from load-sensor tolerances. Whereas inaccuracy in the value assignment at part load will usually only have a detrimental effect on fuel economy or exhaust emissions, it means increased risk of knocking during full-load operation in those ranges which have a more pronounced knocking tendency. Motronic systems provide unambiguous assignment of ignition angle and injection timing, even under dynamic conditions.

Electronic control unit

The ECU employs sensors to monitor the momentary engine condition at extremely short intervals (milliseconds). Input circuits suppress signal interference and convert the signals to a single unified voltage scale.

An analog/digital converter transforms the filtered signals into the digital format in which the microprocessor processes all information as far as the output signals. The driver stages convert the signal data from their low power level at the microprocessor outputs, adapting them to the levels required by the various actuators.

A semiconductor memory chip stores all programs and performance maps, which makes it possible to maintain complete consistency by remaining impervious to fluctuations caused by signal-level and component tolerances.

The digital accuracy is a function of word length, as well as of the consistency of the quarz's basic clock frequency, and the types of algorithms used for the calculations. The consistency and precision of the reference voltages and the components installed in the input circuits influence the analog accuracy.

The program design must take into account the engine's extreme real-time demands: On a 6-cylinder engine at maximum speed, only approx. 3 ms are available between each ignition spark. All essential calculations must be completed within this period. In addition to these crankshaft-synchronous processes, there are also time-synchronous operations. Both types can be suspended by interrupts.

Actuators

The individual constituent systems also supply the actuators. Modern Motronic systems are generally provided with single-spark ignition coils.

The Motronic system

Motronic consists of a number of subsystems. By operating together as the two basic elements within a single system, ignition and fuel-injection acquire a flexibility and operational scope exceeding that provided by the corresponding systems on their own. Motronic is characterized by numerous three-dimensional performance maps; there are no intrinsic programming restrictions, and the maps can be applied for a multiplicity of functions. Motronic's basic specification includes additional subfunctions for meeting emissions requirements and achieving optimum fuel economy.

Adaptive input control is now a standard feature of the Lambda control system; it is

Motronic system

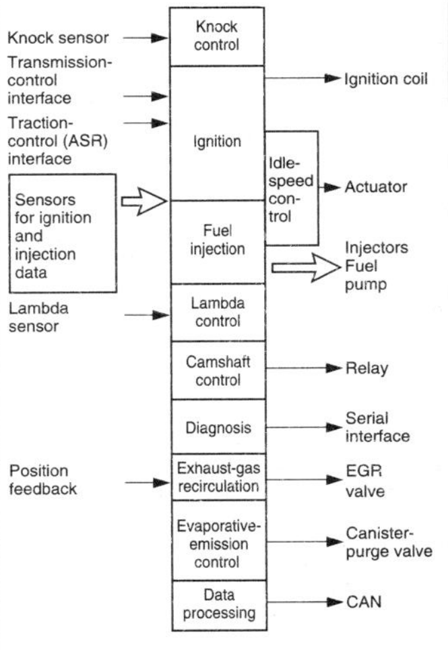

particularly important for maintaining stable exhaust emissions throughout the service life.

Improved fuel economy and increased output are the main reasons why knock control has become a standard feature. The idle-speed control, which is dependent on data from the ignition and fuel-injection systems, was a natural candidate for integration, as were the evaporative-emissions control system ("canister-purge valve") and variable-camshaft control.

Increasing microprocessor capacity has made it possible for one computer element to assume control of all of these functions.

Adaptation strategies

Closed-loop control circuits are being inreasingly supplemented by adaptive strategies, as the closed-loop circuit's dead time places a limit on its operating speed, making precise pilot-control measures necessary. The closed-loop circuit's manipulated variables serve as measured variables for the adaptive process.

Adaptation variables (Lambda map, base air at idle and throttle angle) reduce adjustment requirements both in production and during vehicle servicing.

Adaptive procedures focusing on the ignition-timing map and the fuel component from the carbon canister provide optimum engine operation regardless of the type of fuel being used.

In order to achieve additional emissions improvements and better dynamic response during transitions, some Motronic systems incorporate sequential injection. This system meters the fuel to the cylinder once per combustion cycle, at a predetermined time. Depending on operating conditions, the fuel is injected before the intake valve opens in order to improve the fuel atomization.

Integrated diagnosis

Self-diagnosis is standard with all microprocessor-controlled systems. It includes the detection of implausible signals and the provision of appropriate countermeasures. In specific cases, this ability can even be used for limp-home operation. Some versions inform the driver of malfunctions, while the ECU stores errors

Sequential fuel injection

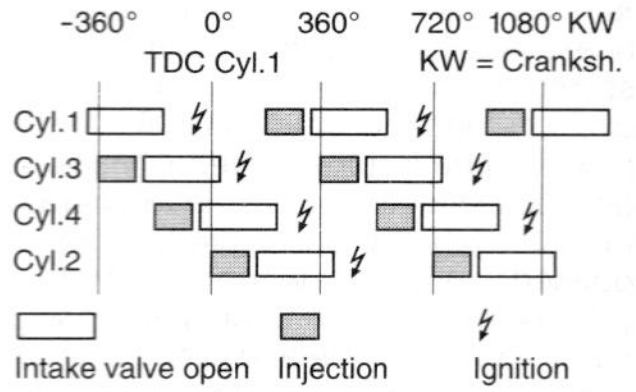

in order to simplify trouble-shooting during service.

The fault information is obtained either by a flash code or via a serial interface and a highly sophisticated tester. Supplementary information on the operating conditions present at the time the malfunction occurred (such as engine speed and temperature) are also recorded by the tester. Legal requirements (in particular those of the "California Air Resources Board" CARB) are having a continuously increasing effect upon diagnosis-system design.

System networks

The functions described thus far represent the Motronic's basic functions. The increasing use of electronics in vehicular applications, for functions such as transmission control, electronic throttle control (E-Gas), electronic traction control ASR), on-board computer, etc., makes it imperative to network these systems. Above all, the exchange of information between the systems themselves permits a reduction in the number of sensors while improving utilization of the individual systems. "Simpler" systems employ duty cycles for data exchange. More complex systems must use serial data transmission in conjunction with special CAN arrangements (CAN = Controller Area Network, p. 776) integrated within the ECU.

The numerous Motronic subsystems, the network combinations with the systems described, and the exhaust-emissions legislation in specific countries, all result in a wide variety of calibration data being needed for ECU production. To enhance the vehicle manufacturer's production flexibility and to minimize costs for inventory and servicing, some Motronic ECU's are delivered with an "end-of-line" programming feature, i.e., with a preliminary program. The specific data for a particular version are then entered either just before the vehicle is assembled, or, in case of repair, at a central service facility.

System configuration

The schematic of a typical Motronic system shows that the fuel system and the method for measuring load and temperature are similar to those of the LH-Jetronic (p. 444).

The ignition system comprises single or dual-spark coils (1 coil for each cylinder or for 2 cylinders). Conventional distribution of the ignition voltage with a camshaft-driven distributor can also be used with this system. It is essential that engine speed and reference-mark position are monitored at the crankshaft.

Racing applications

Motronic's application in motor sport is distinguished by two special characteristics:
– Engine speeds are substantially higher than those encountered in normal series-production engines.
– No loss of power is to result from the load monitoring arrangements.

Thus, throttle position is the main control parameter on naturally aspirated engines, with turbocharged engines employing the manifold pressure for this purpose. Both versions use a closed-loop Lambda system in order to maintain the A/F mixture within the $\lambda = 0.7 ... 1.3$ range. This is a major difference compared to the Motronic ECU's used for series production. To satisfy real-time requirements, only multi-processor systems are used. Results gathered from competition experience include very low specific fuel consumption and important know-how suitable for application in production vehicles.

Schematic of a Motronic system (Motronic M3)
1 Fuel tank, 2 Electric fuel pump, 3 Fuel filter, 4 Pressure regulator, 5 Carbon canister, 6 ECU, 7 Phase sensor, 8 Distributorless ignition, 9 Spark plug, 10 Injector, 11 Canister-purge valve, 12 Air-temperature sensor, 13 Hot-wire mass airflow meter, 14 Lambda sensor, 15 Coolant-temperature sensor, 16 Knock sensor, 17 Throttle actuator, 18 Idle-speed actuator, 19 CAN, 20 Diagnosis, 21 Engine speed and reference sensor, 22 Battery, 23 Ignition switch, 24 A/C switch.

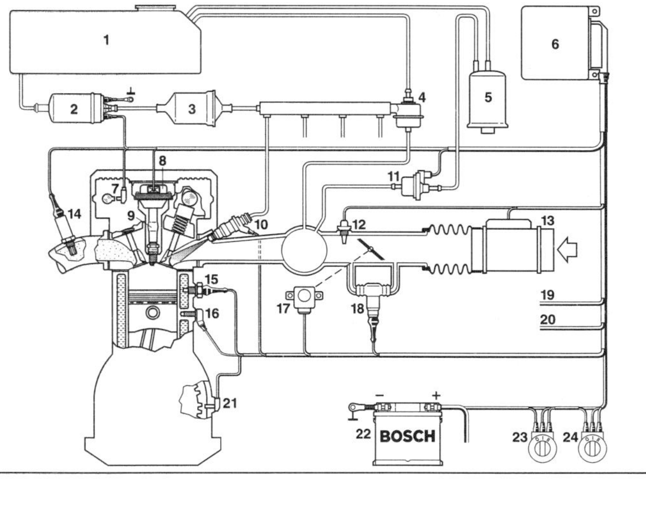

Engine-test technology

The service and maintenance requirements of modern vehicles continue to decrease; electronic systems are largely maintenance-free. But malfunctions can still occur. Factors such as wear, contamination and corrosion can impair the operation of engine and electronic systems, and settings can change over time. Rapid and reliable diagnosis of malfunctions is the most important function of any service facility, whereby it is necessary to distinguish between testing and diagnosis. Testing entails the determination of certain measured values for comparison with the prescribed specifications. In diagnosis (e.g., of the engine), correlations are sought between deviations from the specified values on the one hand, and system functions, malfunction patterns and experience on the other, in order to determine the type of malfunction or the defective component.

Engine diagnosis

Engine, ignition and fuel-metering systems are becoming more complex and less accessible. Universal automated procedures, free from the effects of subjective influences, are thus essential elements of a computer-controlled testing program in the automotive service facility. Such a program includes:

- Comparison of power output from individual cylinders through selective short-circuiting of the ignition or via analysis of smooth running referred to the momentary engine speed,
- Comparison of compression values based upon starter current draw,
- Determination of A/F mixture distribution using selective measurement of the exhaust-gas HC content,
- Analysis of the primary and secondary ignition voltages.

Electronic-system testing

Testing of engine-related electronic systems is carried out using test equipment specifically designed to utilize the on-board engine monitoring technology.

The test connection is established by inserting a universal test adapter between the plug and socket at the junction linking the peripheral device with the ECU. If only the peripheral device (sensor, actuator, wiring and power supply) is to be tested, then it is sufficient to connect the tester to the peripheral's plug, while the ECU is also connected for functional testing of dynamic operation. The individual electronic system requires only a single interchangeable, system-specific adapter cable. The program switches on the universal test adapter are then used to establish a logical test sequence specifically tailored to the requirements of the system in question.

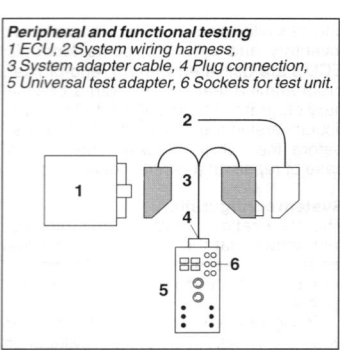

Peripheral and functional testing
1 ECU, 2 System wiring harness, 3 System adapter cable, 4 Plug connection, 5 Universal test adapter, 6 Sockets for test unit.

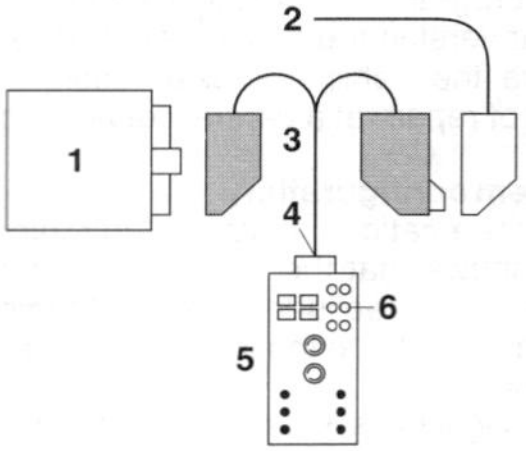

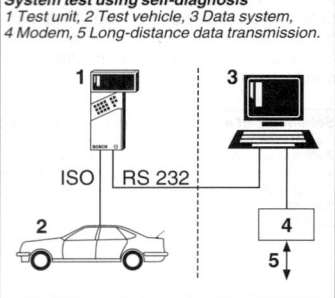

System test using self-diagnosis
1 Test unit, 2 Test vehicle, 3 Data system, 4 Modem, 5 Long-distance data transmission.

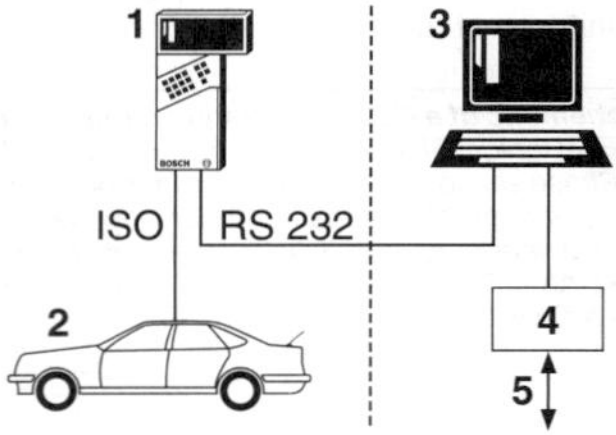

Once connected, the test unit provides a display of both measured values and of signals such as ignition and fuel-injection pulses.

When the ECU remains connected for operational testing, keys can be used to enter simulations of various operating conditions, the effects of which are then evaluated by the test unit.

Self-diagnosis

The dominant role being assumed by electronic systems in the vehicle makes it necessary to devote increased attention to the problems asociated with service. In addition, because essential vehicle functions are becoming increasingly dependent upon electronics, stringent requirements must be complied with, both in the area of reliability and in the back-up systems which must come into operation in case of malfunctions.

The solution is to incorporate self-diagnosis in the electronic system. In other words the ability of the electronic "intelligence" which in any case is already available in the vehicle's electronic equipment, to continuously monitor itself, detect faults, store them and diagnose them.

For instance, the ECU carries out its own self-check as follows: Programmed memory chips are provided with test patterns which can be retrieved and used for comparisons. In the case of program memories, a comparison with test sums is employed to ensure that data and programs are correctly stored. The data and address buses are included in the test program.

Sensors are tested for plausibility within specified limits, while open and short circuits are also recognized. Final-control elements can be tested during activation using current-draw limits.

The "off-board test devices" used for the evaluation of such "on-board diagnosis" systems, require an interface of the type stipulated in ISO 9141. The serial port can maintain communications at baud rates ranging from 10 baud to 10 kbaud. It is designed as a single or two-wire port, allowing connection of several control units to a central diagnosis plug.

A stimulation address is transmitted to all of the connected devices, whereupon each system recognizes its address and responds by transmitting back a baud-rate recognition word.

The test unit monitors the period between pulse flanks to determine the sender's baud rate, which it then adopts automatically. The key bytes that follow (assigned by the DIN Motor-Vehicle Committee) specify the protocol for subsequent data communications.

The programmable test unit converts the data which are then converted into diagnosis sequences and plain-text information designed specifically for the respective system.

The self-diagnosis is used to provide the following:
- Identification of system and ECU,
- Recognition, storage and readout of static and sporadic malfunctions together with the error path, type of malfunction and associated parameters,
- Readout of current actual values, switching conditions, specifications,
- Stimulation of system functions,
- Programming of system variations.

Individual programs for the test unit are stored in plug-in modules, while updates and communication with data systems can take place using the communications port.

Self-diagnosis in electronic systems

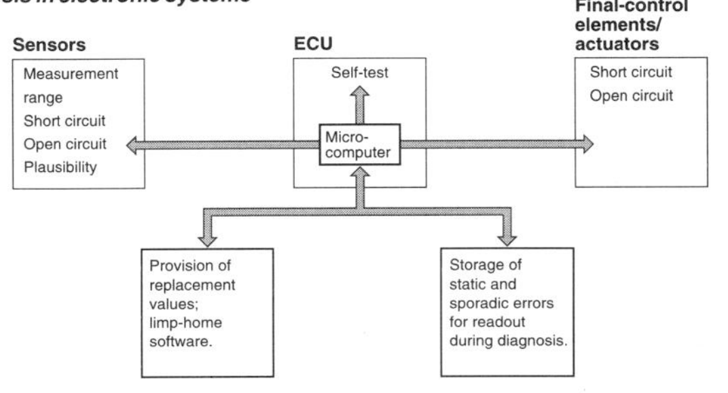

Exhaust emissions from spark-ignition engines

Combustion products

Complete combustion
The by-products of complete combustion are carbon dioxide and water.

Incomplete combustion
Unburned hydrocarbons:
C_nH_m (paraffins, olefins, aromatic hydrocarbons)
Partially-burned hydrocarbons:
C_nH_m CHO (aldehydes),
C_nH_m CO (ketones),
C_nH_m COOH (carboxylic acids),
CO (carbon monoxide).
Thermal crack products and derivatives:
C_2H_2, C_2H_4, H_2 (acetylene, ethylene, hydrogen, etc.), C (soot), polycyclic hydrocarbons.

Combustion by-products
From atmospheric nitrogen: NO, NO_2 (nitrous oxides); from fuel additives: lead oxides, lead halogenides; from fuel impurities: sulfrous oxides.

Oxidants
The following oxidants are produced when exhaust gas is exposed to sunlight: organic peroxides, ozone, peroxy-acetylnitrates.

Properties of exhaust-gas components

Major components
The major proportion of the exhaust gas is composed of the three components nitrogen, carbon dioxide and water vapor. These are non-toxic. However, emissions of CO_2 – essentially a factor of fuel consumption – are being subjected to increasing scrutiny due to their contribution to the "greenhouse effect."

The exhaust gas also contains the following toxic, dangerous, or unpleasant components:

Carbon monoxide CO: A colorless, odorless and tasteless gas. Inhalation of air with a volumetric concentration of 0.3 % carbon monoxide can result in death within 30 minutes. The CO-content of the exhaust gas from spark-ignition engines is especially high at idle. It is therefore imperative that the engine never be allowed to run in a closed garage!

Nitrogen monoxide NO: A colorless, tasteless and odorless gas; in air it is gradually transformed into NO_2. Pure NO_2 is a poisonous, reddish-brown gas with a penetrating odor. The concentrations found in exhaust gases and in extremely polluted air can induce irritation in mucous membranes. NO and NO_2 are generally referred to collectively as oxides of nitrogen NO_x.

Hydrocarbons are present in exhaust gases in a variety of forms. When exposed to sunlight and nitrous oxides they react to form oxidants, which can be a source of irritation to mucous membranes. Some hydrocarbons are considered to be carcinogenic.

Particulates (particulate matter) In accordance with American regulatory practice, particulates are defined as all substances (aside from unbound water) which under normal circumstances are present in exhaust gases in a solid (ash, carbon) or liquid state.

Air-fuel mixture formation

The fuel used in spark-ignition engines is more volatile than diesel fuel, while the air-fuel mixing process preceding combuation also extends over a longer period than in a diesel engine. The result is that spark-ignition engines operate on a more homogenous mixture than their diesel counterparts.

Spark-ignition engines run on a stoichiometric mixture or in its immediate vicinity. Diesel engines on the other hand always operate with excess air ($\lambda > 1$), i.e., they are lean-running. If the excess-air level is not high enough, this results in increased emissions of soot, CO and HC.

Combustion process

Combustion temperature, and thus the NO_x content, are determined largely by the point at which combustion begins relative to TDC. In the spark-ignition engine, the ignition timing determines the point at which the combustion process begins, while the start of the injection process initiates combustion in a diesel engine.

Emissions control

The methods used to alter the composition of the exhaust gases from spark-ignition engines are divided into two basic categories: engine-design measures and exhaust-gas treatment. The selection of procedures to be employed in any given country is determined by its specific legal requirements. The major industrial nations, with their important markets, have been moving toward implementation of the stringent American exhaust emissions regulations (or have already done so). Compliance with this legislation is achieved using emission control systems which incorporate the 3-way catalytic converter, a principle which has already proven itself in the United States.

Engine-design measures

Fuel metering:

The mixture being delivered to the engine, as defined by the excess-air factor λ, exercises a decisive influence on the composition of the exhaust gas. The engine produces its maximum torque at approximately $\lambda = 0.9$; thus this ratio is generally programmed for full-load operation. Optimum fuel economy is achieved with mixtures in the range of $\lambda = 1.1$. This coincides with the setting for low CO and HC emissions; oxides of nitrogen (NO_x) however, are at a maximum at this ratio. Excess-air factors of $\lambda = 0.9$ ... 1.05 are selected for idle. An excessively lean mixture results in the engine's lean misfire limit (LML) being reached or exceeded, and as the mixture is progressively leaned out, misfiring causes a rapid increase in HC emissions. For overrun (trailing-throttle) operation, it is frequently necessary to select an extremely rich mixture ($\lambda < 0.9$) in order to maintain an ignitable mixture, while at the same time air is added to avoid excessive vacuum.

Yet another option for overrun operation is to completely interrupt the fuel supply to the engine at speeds above idle (overrun fuel cutoff). Fuel-injection systems are employed for precise mixture control (p. 436).

The excess-air factor λ determines:
Exhaust-gas composition (CO, CO_2, O_2, NO_x, HC), torque (M) and specific fuel consumption (b). The figures are representative for a spark-ignition engine under constant part-throttle operation at moderate rpm and cylinder charge (λ factors encountered in vehicle engines range from approx. 0.85 ... 1.15, depending upon specific operating conditions).

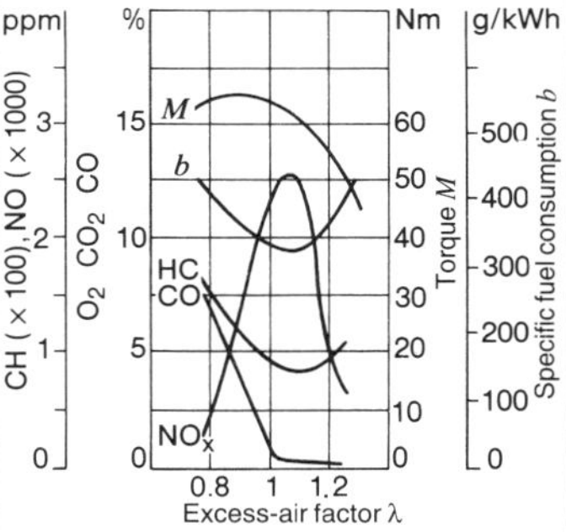

Mixture formation:

Mixture formation embraces both the air-fuel ratio and the quality of the air-fuel mixture entering the combustion chamber. The fuel's homogeneity, its stratification patterns and its temperature at ignition are all factors in determining combustibility and combustion sequence, with consequent effects upon exhaust-gas composition. Homogenous mixtures and controlled stratification (rich mixture at the spark plug, lean mixture in the vicinity of the combustion-chamber walls) represent two different development options. On engines with central mixture formation (single-point injection or TBI), preheated intake air and heated intake-manifold runners are employed to inhibit formation of a fuel film on the manifold walls.

Uniform distribution:
Maximum engine efficiency can only be achieved if every cylinder is operated with the same excess-air factor. This necessitates a system which ensures that both air and fuel are distributed evenly among the individual cylinders.

Exhaust-gas recirculation (EGR):
Exhaust gas can be conducted back to the combustion chamber to reduce peak combustion temperatures. Higher combustion temperatures induce an overproportional increase in the formation of NO_x, and because exhaust-gas recirculation reduces combustion temperatures, it represents a particularly effective means of controlling NO_x emissions. EGR can be implemented in either of two ways:

- Internal exhaust-gas recirculation is achieved with appropriate valve timing (overlap),
- External exhaust-gas recirculation employing controlled EGR valves.

Valve timing:
Internal exhaust-gas recirculation can be implemented using large valve overlaps, but at the cost of rough idling and increased hydrocarbon emissions. Thus variable valve timing is desirable as a means of reducing emissions (see section "Camshaft and valve timing", p. 369, 370).

Compression ratio:
It has long been recognized that the enhanced thermal efficiency associated with high compression ratios represents an effective means of improving fuel economy. However, the increase in peak combustion temperature also results in higher NO_x emissions.

Combustion-chamber design:
Low HC emissions are best achieved with a compact combustion chamber featuring a minimal surface area and no recesses. A centrally-located spark plug with short flame travel produces rapid and relatively complete combustion of the mixture, resulting in low HC emissions and reduced fuel consumption. Induced combustion-chamber turbulence also provides rapid combustion while making it possible to employ leaner mixtures.

External measures (such as controlled vortex in the intake tract) complement a thoroughly optimized combustion chamber design in the lean-burn engine, which is capable of running on mixtures in the range of $\lambda = 1.4$. Although the lean-burn engine features low exhaust emissions and excellent fuel economy, it does need catalytic exhaust-gas treatment in order to meet the most stringent emissions limits for CO and HC. Up to now the application potential of the lean-burn engine, with its attractive fuel economy, has been limited due to its inability to meet the stringent US emissions limits.

Ignition system:
The design of the spark plug, its position within the combustion chamber, together with the spark energy and spark duration all exercise a major influence on the ignition and combustion sequence of the mixture, with attendant effects on emissions levels. The significance of these factors increases in direct proportion to the leanness ($\lambda > 1.1$) of the mixture. Ignition timing exerts a decisive effect on both exhaust emissions and fuel economy. Using the firing point for optimum fuel economy as a baseline, the timing is retarded to a point at which the exhaust valve opens before the combustion process is completed, inducing a thermal reaction in the exhaust system. Although this method achieves reductions in NO_x and unburned hydrocarbons, this is at the price of increased fuel consumption. At the same time, fuel consumption, nitrous oxides and hydrocarbons all increase when the ignition timing is advanced beyond the optimum.

Crankcase ventilation (blowby):
The concentration of hydrocarbons in the crankcase can be many times that found in the engine's exhaust gases. Control systems conduct these gases to a suitable point in the engine's intake tract, from where they are drawn into the combustion chamber for burning. Originally, these gases were allowed to escape untreated directly into the atmosphere; today, crankcase emission-control systems are a standard legal requirement.

Exhaust-gas aftertreatment

Thermal afterburning:
Before today's catalytic treatment of exhaust emissions became standard, initial attempts to reduce emissions utilized thermal afterburning. This method employs a specific residence time at high temperatures for burning the exhaust-gas components which failed to combust during normal combustion in the engine cylinders. In the rich range (λ = 0.9 ... 1.0), the process must be supported with supplementary air injection. In the lean range (λ = 1.1 ... 1.2), the residual oxygen in the exhaust gas is sufficient for afterburning.

Today, thermal afterburning is considered to have extremely limited potential, as it is of no value in meeting low NO_x limits. However, it can be employed to reduce emissions of HC and CO in the warm-up phase, before the catalytic converter reaches operating temperature. Thus thermal aftertreatment with air injection can be used to achieve compliance with tomorrow's more stringent limits by reducing the emissions produced by the engine in the warm-up phase.

Catalytic afterburning:
The catalytic converter is composed of a carrier substrate, which serves as a base for the catalytic material, mounted within a housing using vibration-proof, heat-insulated supports. Granulate and ceramic or metallic monolith structures are employed as substrate materials. The monolith structure's suitability for automotive applications has been demonstrated in the course of an extended development period; it provides the following advantages: maximum utilization of catalytic surface, durability combined with physical strength, low thermal retention and limited exhaust back-pressure. The active catalytic layer consists of small quantities of noble metals (Pt, Rh, Pd), and is sensitive to lead. For this reason, it is essential that engines with catalytic converters be run on unleaded fuel exclusively, as lead destroys the effectiveness of the active layer. The unit's conversion rate is largely a function of operating temperature; no meaningful treatment of pollutants takes place until the converter has reached an operating temperature of approx. 250 °C. Operating temperatures of approx. 400 ... 800 °C provide ideal conditions for maximum efficiency and extended service life.

Installing the catalytic converter directly adjacent to the engine provides benefits in the form of high exhaust-gas temperature, resulting in optimum efficiency, but with the disadvantage of high thermal stresses. As the maximum permissible operating temperature is reached just slightly above 1000 °C, the units are generally installed at a less critical location under the floor of the vehicle. Engine malfunctions, such as ignition miss, can cause the temperature in the catalytic converter to increase to the point where the substrate melts, resulting in destruction of the unit. Reliable, maintenance-free ignition systems must be used to prevent this from happening. Oxidation catalytic converters oxidize CO and HC either by utilizing the excess air supplied by lean engine mixtures or by relying on secondary air injection. Reduction catalytic converters operate with an air deficiency, and thus without air injection, to reduce NO_x levels.

The reduction and oxidation converters can also be combined in series to produce a dual-bed catalytic converter, a device whose capabilities extend beyond the control of NO_x emissions – when supported with secondary air injection, it also limits HC and CO levels. The disadvantages include design complication (two converters, air injection) and the necessity of operating the engine in the high-consumption range (λ = 0.9).

The three-way or selective catalytic converter with lambda closed-loop control has proven to be an effective concept for exhaust-gas aftertreatment. It is capable of providing the required reduction of all three pollutants provided the engine is operated with a stoichiometric mixture. The "window" for treatment of the three components is narrow; this means that a conventional open-loop fuel-metering system is not sufficiently precise for application with this concept.

Lambda closed-loop control

A closed-loop control system represents the only means of controlling air-fuel mixture composition with the necessary precision. In such a system, the exhaust gases are constantly monitored to provide the information required for instantaneous adjustments to the fuel-metering system. The composition of the exhaust gases is monitored with an exhaust-gas oxygen sensor (EGOS), the so-called Lambda sensor. This reflects a stoichiometric mixture ($\lambda = 1$) by generating a voltage peak, thus indicating whether the mixture is richer or leaner than $\lambda = 1$.

Lambda oxygen sensor

One part of the sensor's ceramic surface is positioned in the exhaust stream, while the other part remains in contact with the surrounding air. The ceramic surfaces (zirconium dioxide) are coated with a thin, gas-permeable layer of platinum.

Above about 300 °C, the sensor's ceramic material conducts oxygen ions. Due to the ceramic material's special characteristics, the sensor responds to variations in the oxygen concentration between the two surfaces by generating a voltage. This voltage provides an index for the difference in oxygen content at the two surfaces of the sensor. The exhaust gas from the IC engine always contains residual oxygen, even when the engine is run on excess fuel (at $\lambda = 0.95$ this is typically 0.2 ... 0.3 vol.%). The proportion of residual oxygen is essentially a function of the composition of the air-fuel mixture drawn in by the engine for combustion. This relationship makes it possible to use the oxygen content of the exhaust gas as an index for the excess-air factor (λ). The use of an internal heating element to heat the sensor substantially improves operation at low exhaust temperatures; it also maintains emissions stable at a low level while contributing to increased service life. It is for these reasons that heated Lambda sensors (HEGOS) are generally used today.

Catalytic-converter efficiency as a function of excess-air factor λ. *1 Exhaust emissions before treatment in 3-way catalytic converter, 2 Exhaust emissions after treatment in 3-way catalytic converter, 3 Electric signal from Lambda oxygen sensor,* U_λ *Sensor voltage.*

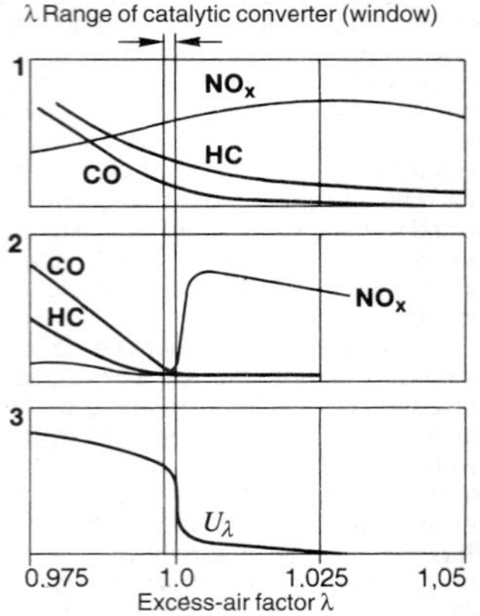

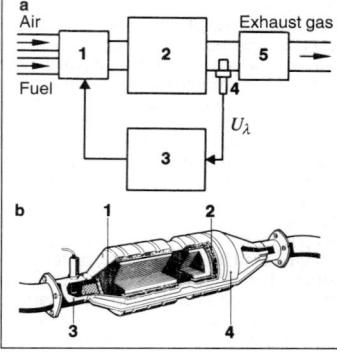

Emissions treatment with 3-way catalytic converter and lambda oxygen sensor
a) Schematic illustration. 1 Fuel-metering device, 2 Engine, 3 ECU, 4 Lambda sensor, 5 3-way catalytic converter, U_λ *Sensor voltage.*
b) 3-way catalytic converter. 1 Ceramic monolith, 2 Wire screen, 3 Lamba sensor, 4 Housing.

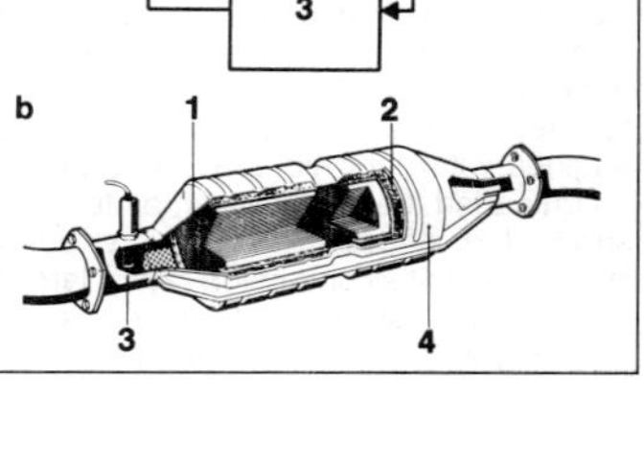

Testing exhaust and evaporative emissions

Test program

If a passenger vehicle's emission levels are to be determined precisely, then the vehicle must be tested in the emissions test cell under standardized conditions which provide an accurate reflection of actual driving conditions. This is the only means of ensuring that individual emissions tests remain mutually comparable.

The vehicle to be tested is parked with the drive wheels on special rollers with which rotating resistance can be adjusted to simulate friction losses and aerodynamic resistance, while inertial mass can be added to simulate the vehicle's weight. The required cooling is provided by a fan mounted a short distance from the vehicle. The measurement of emissions levels is based on a simulated driving pattern which progresses through a precise driving cycle incorporating various vehicle speeds. The exhaust gases produced in the course of this procedure are collected for subsequent analysis of pollutant mass. The manner in which exhaust gases are collected and the procedures for determining emissions have largely been standardized in the various countries, but the driving cycles have not. In some countries, regulations on exhaust emissions are supplemented by limits on evaporative-emissions losses from the fuel system.

Chassis dynamometer

Fluid-friction dynamometers, eddy-current brakes and DC motors simulate the inertial forces which rolling and aerodynamic resistance exert upon the vehicle by providing a corresponding, velocity-dependent braking force (resistance of the rollers to turning). Rapid couplings in various sizes are used to connect inertial masses to the rollers, thus simulating vehicle weight. The progression curve for braking loads must correspond to that for vehicle speed, and the required inertial masses must be maintained precisely (deviations result in measuring errors). Ambient conditions such as atmospheric humidity, temperature and barometric pressure also influence test results.

Driving cycles

Testing is based on a standardized driving cycle in which gearshifts, braking, idle phases and standstill periods have all been selected to provide a high level of correspondence with the velocities and acceleration that characterize typical driving in normal traffic. Five different test cycles are employed internationally. Usually, a driver sits in the vehicle to maintain the speed at the levels indicated on a display screen.

Test samples and dilution procedures (CVS Method)

The European adoption of the constant-volume sampling method (CVS) in 1982 means that there is now basically a single internationally-valid procedure for collecting exhaust gases.

Test samples and emissions analysis

The exhaust gases emanating from the test vehicle are diluted with fresh air at a ratio of 1 : 10 and extracted using a special system of pumps which is arranged to maintain the respective flow volumes of exhaust gas and fresh air at a fixed ratio, i.e., the air feed is regulated according to the vehicle's momentary exhaust volume. Throughout the test a constant proportion of the diluted exhaust gas is extracted for collection in one or several sample bags. The pollutant concentration in the sample bags at the end of the test corresponds precisely to the mean concentration in the total quantity of fresh-air/exhaust mixture which has been extracted. As the total volume of the fresh-air/exhaust mixture can be monitored, it is possible to use the pollutant concentration as the basis for calculating the masses of the substances emitted in the course of the test. Advantages of this procedure: Condensation of the water vapor contained in the exhaust gas is avoided, which provides for a substantial reduction of the NO_X losses in the bag. In addition, dilution greatly inhibits the tendency of the exhaust components (especially hydrocarbons) to react with one another. However, dilution does mean that the concentration of the pollutants decreases proportionally to the mean dilution ratio, necessitating the use of more sensitive analyzers.

Analyzers and dilution equipment

One of two different but equally acceptable pump arrangements is generally employed to maintain a constant flow volume for the test. In the first, a normal blower extracts the fresh-air/exhaust mixture through a venturi tube; the second layout employs a special vane pump (Roots blower). Either method is capable of metering the flow volume with an acceptable degree of accuracy.

Determining evaporative emissions from the fuel system

Apart from the emissions stemming from the engine's combustion process, motor vehicles also emit hydrocarbons (HC) in the form of evaporative emissions resulting from fuel vaporization in the tank and supply lines. Some countries (e.g., USA) already have laws limiting the allowable evaporative losses (planned for EC).

SHED Test

The SHED (Sealed Housing for Evaporative Determination) test is the most common procedure for determining evaporative emissions. It comprises two test phases – with varying conditioning procedures – which are conducted in a gas-tight chamber. The first part of the test is carried out with the fuel tank approx. 40% full. The test fuel is warmed from its initial temperature of 10 ... 14.5 °C, with actual testing of the HC concentration in the chamber starting once it reaches 15.5 °C. After one hour the temperature of the fuel has risen by 14 °C; at this point testing is concluded with a final sampling of the HC concentration. Evaporative emissions are determined by comparing the initial and the final measurements. The vehicle's windows and trunk lid must remain open during the test. For the second portion of the test, the vehicle is first warmed up by being run through the FTP 75 test cycle. It is then parked in the chamber. The increase in the HC concentration as

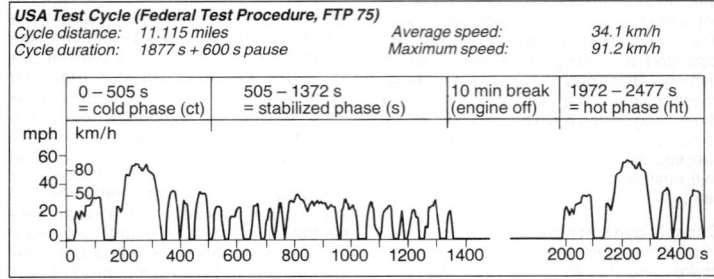

USA Test Cycle (Federal Test Procedure, FTP 75)

Cycle distance:	*11.115 miles*	*Average speed:*	*34.1 km/h*
Cycle duration:	*1877 s + 600 s pause*	*Maximum speed:*	*91.2 km/h*

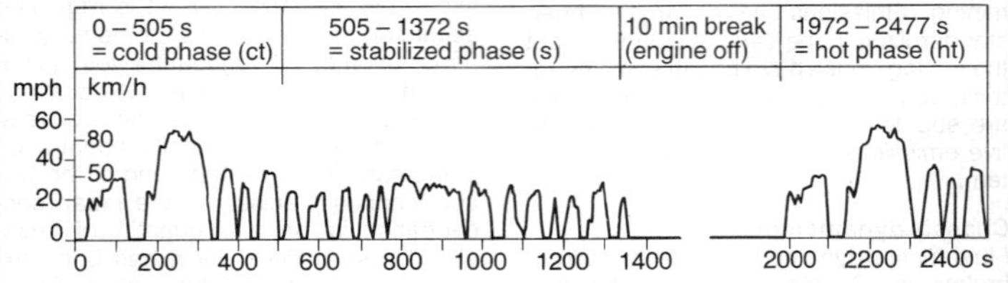

Test layout for USA Federal Test (venturi system shown here)
1 Chassis dynamometer, 2 Inertial mass, 3 Exhaust gas, 4 Air filter, 5 Fresh (dilution) air, 6 Sampling venturi, 7 Gas temperature, 8 Pressure, 9 Venturi, 10 Blower, 11 Sample bags, 12 System outlet.

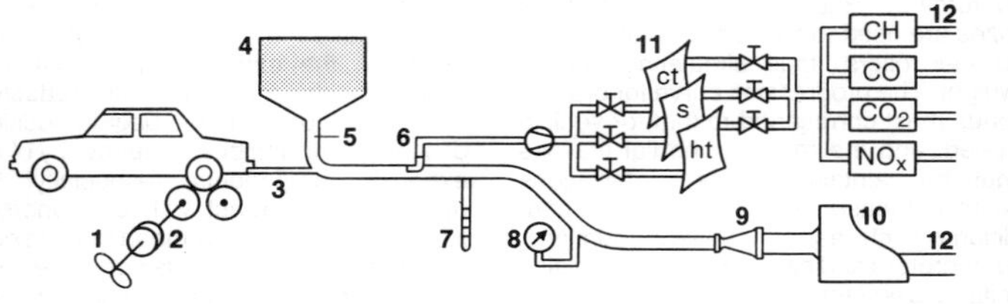

the vehicle cools during the hour it remains parked is then measured. The sum of the results from both tests must be less than the present limit value of 2 g hydrocarbon vapor. Meanwhile, a more stringent SHED test is to be implemented in the USA.

USA FTP 75 test cycle

The FTP 75 test cycle consists of three test sections. These, in turn, represent speeds measured in America on the streets of Los Angeles in morning commuter traffic:

Test section		Elapsed time (s)
Transition phase	ct	0 ... 505
Stabilized phase	s	506 ... 1372
Hot test	ht	1972 ... 2477

The vehicle to be tested is first conditioned by being left parked for 12 hours at a room temperature of 20 ... 30 °C. It is then started and driven through the prescribed driving curve:

Phase ct: Diluted exhaust gas is collected in bag 1 during the cold transition phase.

Phase s: Exhaust samples are diverted to bag 2 at the beginning of the stabilized phase (after 505 s) without any interruption in the program sequence. The engine is switched off for a 10-minute pause immediately following the end of the stabilized phase (after 1372 s).

Phase ht: The engine is restarted for the hot test (505 s in duration). The speed sequence of this phase directly corresponds to that of the cold transition phase. Exhaust gases are collected in a third

Table 1. Emissions limits under USA-FED (49-states) and California FTP 75 Test cycle

Model year	Region	CO g/mile	HC g/mile	NO_x g/mile	Evaporation g/test
since 1982	FED CAL	3.41[1]) 7.0	0.41 0.41	1.0[1]) 0.4[1])	2.0 2.0
1993	CAL	3.4	0.25	0.4	2.0
1994	FED	3.4	0.25	0.4	2.0

[1]) Waivers may be granted under certain conditions.

Table 2. Emissions limits in Australia, Austria, Brazil, Canada, Finland, Mexico, Norway, South Korea, Sweden, Switzerland. FTP 75 Test cycle

Country	Implementation	CO g/km	HC g/km	NO_x g/km	Evaporation g/test
Switzerland	10.87	2.1	0.25	0.62	2.0
Austria	87/88	2.1	0.25	0.62	2.0
Sweden	model year 89	2.1	0.25	0.62	2.0
Norway	1989	2.1	0.25	0.62	2.0
Finland	1990	2.1	0.25	0.62	2.0
Mexico Brazil	1991 1.90 1.92 1.97	7.0 24.0 12.0 2.0	0.7 2.1 1.2 0.3	1.4 2.0 1.4 0.6	2.0 – – –
Australia	1.86	9.3	0.9	1.9	2.0
		CO g/mile	HC g/mile	NO_x g/mile	Evaporation g/Test
Canada	9.87	3.4	0.41	1.0	2.0
South Korea	model year 88	3.4	0.41	1.0	2.0

sample bag. The bag samples from the previous phases are analyzed, as the probes should not remain in the bags for longer than 20 minutes.

The exhaust-gas sample in the third sample bag is analyzed once the driving sequence has been completed. The weighted sum of the pollutant emissions (HC, CO and NO_X) from all three bags are evaluated with reference to the distance covered and then expressed as emissions per mile. The limits on pollutant emissions vary among individual countries. This test procedure is used in the USA (incl. California – Table 1) and in several other countries (Table 2). Each new vehicle is required to comply with the limits for a distance of 50,000 miles, independent of vehicle weight and displacement. Under certain conditions, the US authorities grant waivers for specific model years. In addition, higher emissions limits apply when vehicles are certified for a distance of 100,000 miles. Among the various environmental-protection measures included in the Clean Air Act of 1990 is a tightening of vehicle-emissions limits, to enter effect in 1994 (Table 1). California is introducing the new, more stringent limits in 1993, and is also planning further, more drastic measures.

The cold-start enrichment process which is necessary when a vehicle is started at low temperatures, produces particularly high emissions; these are not measured in present emissions testing, which is conducted at ambient temperatures of 20 ... 30 °C. The Clean Air Act seeks to reduce these emissions by prescribing an emissions test at – 6.7 °C. However, a limit is only prescribed for carbon monoxide.

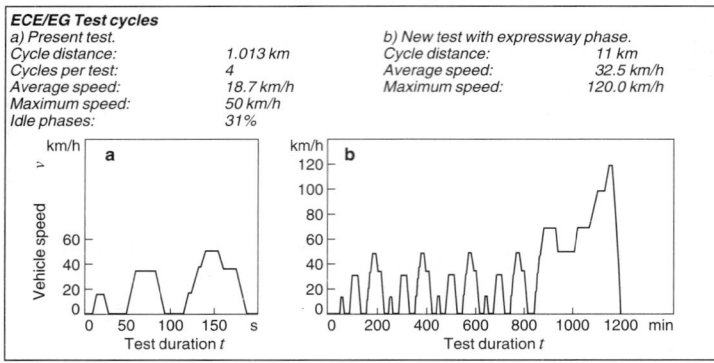

ECE/EG Test cycles

a) Present test.

Cycle distance:	*1.013 km*
Cycles per test:	*4*
Average speed:	*18.7 km/h*
Maximum speed:	*50 km/h*
Idle phases:	*31%*

b) New test with expressway phase.

Cycle distance:	*11 km*
Average speed:	*32.5 km/h*
Maximum speed:	*120.0 km/h*

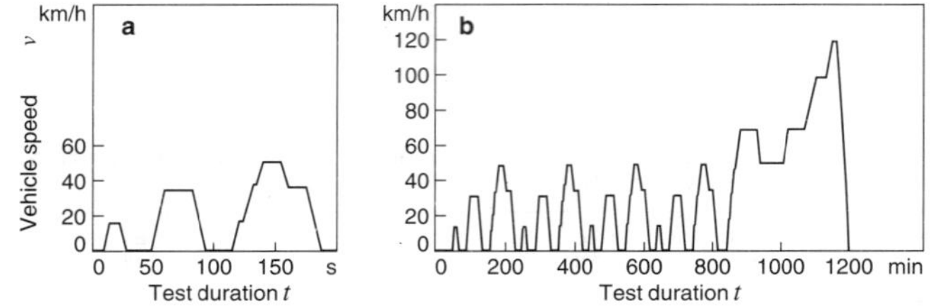

Test layout for European test (rotary-piston blower shown)

1 Chassis dynamometer, 2 Inertial mass, 3 Exhaust gas, 4 Air filter, 5 Fresh (dilution) air, 6 Cooler, 7 Gas temperature, 8 Pressure, 9 Rotary-piston blower, 10 Sample bags (≈ 100 l), 11 System outlet.

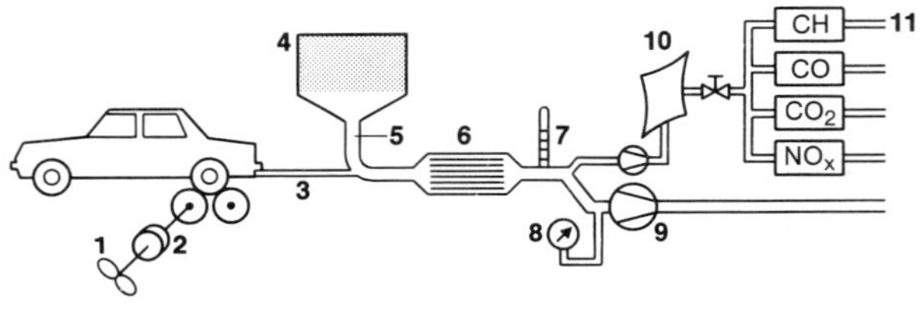

ECE/EC test cycle and limits

The ECE/EC test cycle uses a hypothetical driving curve which is calculated to provide a reasonable approximation of driver behaviour in urban traffic. The ECE test cycle is presently binding in the following countries: Belgium, Denmark, France, Germany, Great Britain, Greece, Ireland, Italy, Luxembourg, Netherlands, Portugal, and Spain.

Test cycle: After conditioning (vehicle parked at a room temperature of 20 ... 30 °C), the actual test cycle commences with a cold start and 40-second warm-up. The cycle is run four times in succession with no pauses between runs. During the test, the CVS method is used to collect exhaust in a sample bag. The pollutant levels obtained from analysis of the bag's contents are not converted to reflect a particular distance, but are provided in the form of g/test. In addition, hydrocarbons and oxides of nitrogen are combined in a composite limit ($HC+NO_x$). More rigorous limits with differing classifications according to engine displacement were introduced in 1988. This regulation is designated EWG 88/76; and is included as such in Table 4. This regulation already applies to vehicles with engine displacements below 1.4 liters or above 2.0 liters. Vehicles with a displacement between 1.4 and 2.0 litres are covered by the earlier regulation ECE R15-04, in which the limits are scaled according to vehicle weight (Table 3). In 1989 a second emissions-reduction stage was decided upon for vehicles with displacements below 1.4 litres. This regulation, scheduled for implementation in 1992, is designated EWG 89/458 (Table 4).

Uniform conditions do not apply throughout Europe. Those member states in the European Community favoring implementation of more stringent limits succeeded in securing passage of an amendment (Appendix III A) guaranteeing recognition of the FTP 75 Cycle as a basis for vehicle approval. This step also facilitates the introduction of tax incentives for such vehicles in Belgium, Denmark, the Netherlands and Germany. Since October, 1990, Denmark has permitted new-vehicle registrations only for vehicles for which compliance with US limits has been confirmed using the FTP 75 Cycle.

A new "European Driving Cycle" EWG 91/441 has been passed by the European

Table 3. ECE/EC Emissions limits relative to reference weight of vehicle (ECE R15-04). ECE/EC Test cycle

Vehicle reference weight (kg) min.	max.	CO g/test	$HC + NO_x$ g/test
	1020	58	19.0
1020	1250	67	20.5
1250	1470	76	22.0
1470	1700	84	23.5
1700	1930	93	25.0
1930	2150	101	26.5
2150		110	28.0

Table 4. Emissions limits in the EC. ECE/EC Test cycle

Engine displacement (l) min.	max.	Tentative implementation date New models	Initial registrations	Regulation	CO g/test	$HC + NO_x$ g/test	NO_x g/test
2.0		1.10.88	1,10.89	88/76/EWG	25	6.5	3.5
1.4	2.0	1.10.91	1.10.93	88/76/EWG	30	8	–
	1.4	1.10.90	1.10.91	88/76/EWG	45	15	6
		1.7.92	1.1.93	89/458/EWG	19	5	–
All engine-displacement categories		1.7.92 New European test cycle	31.12.92	91/441/EWG	2.72 g/km	0.97 g/km	–

Council of Ministers. This regulation includes a single set of stricter limits for all weights and displacements (Table 4), as well as limits on evaporative emissions of the kind applied in the USA. The test comprises both the present urban cycle and a supplementary expressway phase including speeds of up to 120 km/h, an addition intended to reflect the large amount of higher-speed, extra-urban traffic.

Japanese test cycle

Two test cycles with differing hypothetical driving curves are combined to provide the complete test. Following a cold start, the 11-mode cycle is covered four times, with all four cycles being evaluated. The 10-mode test is run through six times with the vehicle fully warmed-up; the first of the six cycles is not included in the evaluation. Preconditioning for the hot start, which includes the legally-required idle-emissions test, proceeds according to the following sequence: First, the vehicle is driven for 15 minutes in a warm-up phase. Then, the concentrations of HC, CO and CO_2 are measured in the exhaust pipe at 40 km/h. The 10-mode hot test starts after an additional warm-up period consisting of 5 minutes at 40 km/h. Both the 11-mode and the 10-mode test use a CVS unit for exhaust-gas analysis. The diluted exhaust gas for each phase is collected in a sample bag. The emissions limits for the cold test are specified in g/test, while the limits for the hot test are expressed according to distance, being converted to grammes per kilometer (Table 5). The Japanese regulations include limits on evaporative emissions as determined according to the SHED method. Japan is also planning to tighten its emissions limits (for NO_x in particular), while the 10-mode test is to be expanded to include an expressway phase.

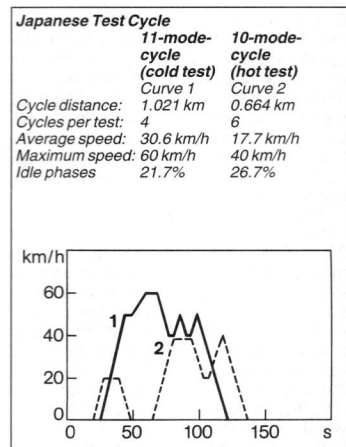

Japanese Test Cycle

	11-mode-cycle (cold test)	***10-mode-cycle (hot test)***
	Curve 1	*Curve 2*
Cycle distance:	*1.021 km*	*0.664 km*
Cycles per test:	*4*	*6*
Average speed:	*30.6 km/h*	*17.7 km/h*
Maximum speed:	*60 km/h*	*40 km/h*
Idle phases	*21.7%*	*26.7%*

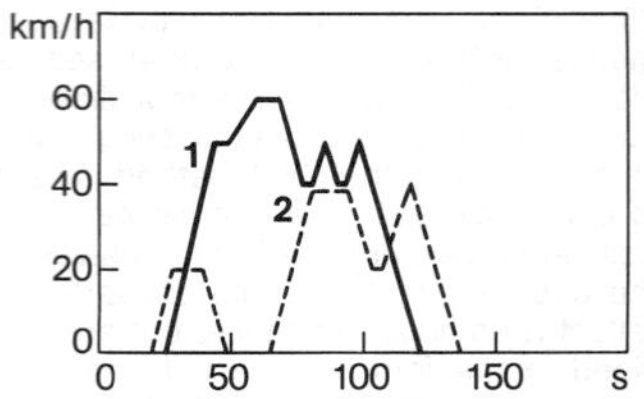

Comparison of test procedures and limits

Both the present ECE/EC test cycle and its Japanese counterparts are essentially designed to simulate traffic moving in an urban center at the speeds which are typical for this kind of driving. The FTP 75 test cycle, on the other hand, also includes higher speeds. A direct comparison of the different emissions limits is made difficult by the variations in driving programs with their attendant disparities in engine load. However, it can be maintained that the most stringent emissions regulations are presently those in effect in the USA (requiring use of a closed-loop-controlled 3-way catalytic converter).

Table 5. Emissions limits in Japan. Japanese Test Cycle

Test procedure	CO	HC	NO_x	Evaporation
10-mode (g/km)	2.1	0.25	0.25	–
11-mode (g/test)	60.0	7.0	4.4	–
SHED (g/test)	–	–	–	2.0

Exhaust-gas analyzers

Legislation reflects government efforts to reduce the quantity of toxic substances in exhaust gases by requiring that testing be carried out on vehicles which are already on the road.

In addition, exhaust-gas analyzers are also indispensible service tools, necessary both for optimal mixture adjustment and for effective engine-fault diagnosis.

Test procedure

Required is the ability to carry out precise measurements of the individual exhaust components. This has led to automotive service operations adopting the infrared method as the only suitable means for testing exhaust gases.

This method bases on the fact that individual exhaust-gas components absorb infrared light at various specific rates, according to their characteristic wave lengths. The various designs include both single-component analyzers (e.g., for CO) and multi-component devices (for CO/HC, CO/CO_2, $CO/HC/CO_2$ etc.).

Test chamber

Infrared radiation is transmitted from an emitter which has been heated to approx. 700 °C. The beam passes through a measuring cell before entering the receiver chamber. When the CO-content is to be measured, the sealed receiver chamber contains gas with a defined CO content, which absorbs a portion of the CO-specific radiation. This absorption is accompanied by an increase in the temperature of the gas, producing a gas current which flows from the current sensor with volume V_1 into the compensation area with volume V_2. A rotating chopper disk induces a rhythmic interruption in the beam, producing an alternating flow pattern between the two volumes V_1 and V_2. The flow sensor converts this motion into an alternating electrical signal. When a test gas with a variable CO content flows through the measuring cell, it absorbs radiant energy in a quantity proportional to its CO content; the energy is then no longer available in the receiver chamber. The result is a reduction of the base flow in the receiver chamber. The deviation from the alternating base signal provides an index of the CO content in the test gas.

Measuring chamber using infrared method
(schematic illustration)
1 Receiving chamber with compensation volumes V_1 and V_2, 2 Flow sensor, 3 Measuring cell, 4 Rotating chopper disk with motor, 5 Infrared emitter.

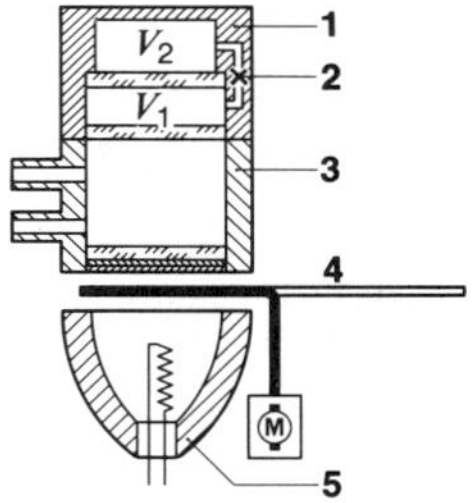

Testing of the catalytic converter

A representative component can be used to obtain an indirect measurement of converter operation on vehicles with closed-loop-controlled catalytic devices. The best-suited is CO, which is not to exceed 0.3 % volume downstream from the converter, whereby it is essential that lambda be exactly $\lambda = 1.00$ ($\pm$ 0.01). Lambda, in turn, can be determined using the composition of the exhaust gas at the catalytic converter's outlet. The exhaust-gas analyzer calculates the value for Lambda using the content of CO, HC, CO_2 and O_2 in the exhaust gas, with constants being employed for NO and fuel composition HC_V. The O_2 content is measured with an electrochemical probe.

LPG systems

Liquified petroleum gas

Liquified petroleum gas (LPG) is a mixture of propane and butane. The name is explained by the fact that the gas assumes a liquid state at pressures of 2 ... 20 bar; the actual pressure depends upon the propane/butane ratio and the temperature. (See chapter on "Fuels," p. 226).

At the start of the '90s, internal-combustion (IC) engines were consuming approximately 8.2 million metric tons of LPG annually (with 2.5 million tons being consumed in Europe). Should efforts to utilize the gas contained in petroleum succeed, then these figures could increase exponentially. Tax rates exercise a decisive effect on the cost- effectiveness of LPG.

Operation on LPG

Any vehicle equipped with an IC engine can be converted for operation on LPG. For the most part, spark-ignition (SI) engines are re-equipped for dual-fuel operation (system can be switched between gasoline and LPG). LPG-powered taxis and buses are generally set up for single-fuel operation, while regulations require this configuration on gas-powered industrial trucks intended for indoor use. When fuel-injected engines are converted, it should be remembered that these function as induction (or naturally-aspirated) powerplants while running on LPG (consumption in liters increases by approx. 20 ... 25 % over gasoline, while the figure for carburetor units is 15 ... 20 %).

Advantages
– In Europe, reasonably priced and available in adequate quatities.
– Presuming that the same level of technology (electronic control systems, etc.) is employed for both types of engine, emissions from an LPG engine, including CO_2, are substantially lower than those achieved with a gasoline engine - even one equipped with fuel injection (EFI) and a closed-loop-controlled 3-way catalytic converter. Liquified petroleum gas contains no lead or sulfur compounds; mixture formation, charge distribution and combustion properties are all excellent.

Disadvantages
– Lower performance and increased fuel consumption compared to gasoline.
– Supplementary safety regulations must be considered, as the LPG is under pressure.
– Pressurized gas cylinders require a lot of space, as the actual capacity is only 80 % of cylinder volume (the remainder serving as expansion room for the gas).

LPG system

In Germany, professional installation of the LPG system in a specialist workshop is followed by a trip to the TÜV or TÜA (German inspection authorities) to secure operating approval. In Germany this in-

Toxic emissions in gasoline and LPG operation (comparison)
Fuel-injected engine with 3-way catalytic converter and closed-loop control, US 83 test procedure.

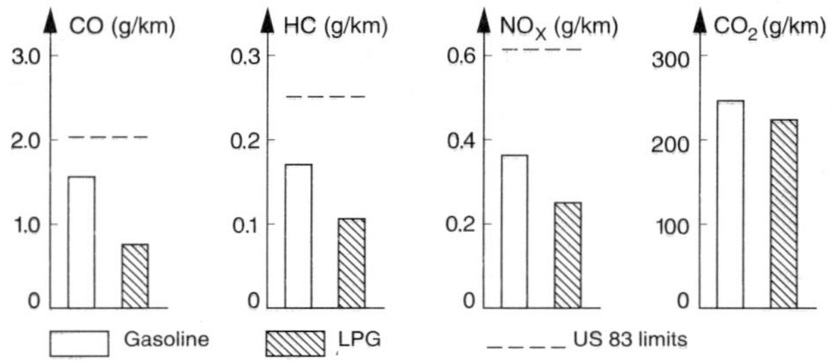

Schematic diagram of an LPG system

1 Vent line for tank fittings, 2 LPG tank, 3 Housing with tank fittings, 4 External filler valve with 80% cutoff, 5 Flow-interrupt valve, 6 Evaporator-pressure regulator with cooling system, 7 Servomotor for gas control, 8 ECU, 9 Liquified gas/gasoline switch, 10 Venturi mixing unit, 11 Lambda oxygen sensor, 12 Vacuum sensor, 13 Battery, 14 Ignition/start switch, 15 Relay.

Equipment for operation on conventional gasoline fuel

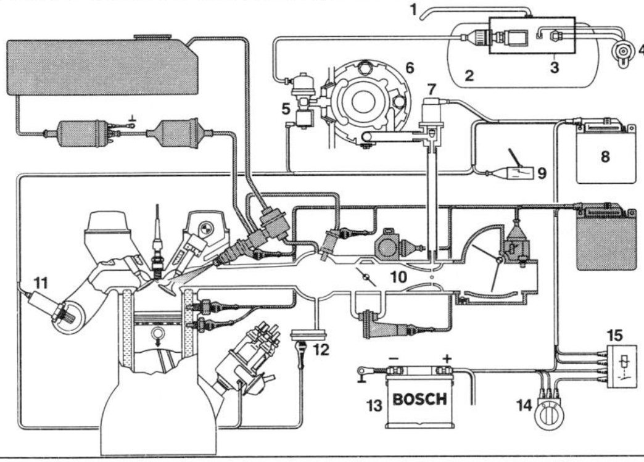

spection is based on the "Guidelines for inspecting vehicles with engines powered by liquified gases" as issued by the Federal Minister of Transportation.

A modern LPG system will incorporate the following components:

- LPG tank with external filler valve,
- Flow-interrupt valve,
- Evaporative-pressure regulator with cooling system,
- Venturi mixing unit,
- Electronic control unit (ECU),
- Servomotor for controlling gas flow,
- Switch for alternating between LPG and gasoline operation.

After emerging from its tank, the LPG flows to the evaporative-pressure regulator, where it is vaporized and its pressure reduced. The ECU processes the signals from the oxygen (Lambda) and vacuum sensors, which serve as references for controlling the servomotor used to regulate the flow of liquified gas to the venturi mixing unit.

The flow-interrupt valve shuts immediately when the ignition is switched off. A gasoline/LPG switch installed in the instrument panel allows the operator to select between the two fuels.

LPG tanks

As LPG tanks are used to store pressurized gas, they are subject to the "TRG 380" technical regulations which govern such gases. At the factory, they receive official technical approval, where each tank is also provided with an approval certificate.

The tanks are equipped with an external filler valve (with a device to limit the charge to 80%) and a solenoid-actuated extraction valve. Tank capacities range from 40 ... 128 l.

Natural gas as engine fuel

Reserves of natural gas are extensive. Together with it being used nowhere near as much as crude oil, this fact makes natural gas a very interesting alternative fuel for automotive applications. Both equipment configurations and emissions would be similar to those employed with the combination of propane and butane known as LPG. Natural gas can be transported either as a high-pressure gas (160 ... 200 bar) or in liquified form (at – 160 °C) in an insulated tank; the disadvantage of the former mode lies in its limited operating range.

Operation on alcohol (spark-ignition engines)

The finite availability of fossil fuels provides an impetus for devoting increased effort to development work on engines and injection systems capable of using alcohols, such as ethanol and methanol, as an alternative ("Alternative fuels," p. 231). Virtually the only place where ethanol is used is Brazil, a phenomenon explained by it being available locally. In the USA (and in California in particular), increasing attention is being focused on methanol, which also has benefits regarding exhaust emissions. Reduced emissions of NO_x and CO_2 along with lower levels of ozone and smog formation.

As universal availability of methanol fuels cannot be assumed, engines and engine-control systems must be designed for flexible dual-fuel operation (ranging from pure gasoline to max. 85% methanol). Alcohol fuels place special, highly critical demands upon both the engine and the fuel system. This is due to the moisture, acids and gums contained in the fuel posing a hazard to metals, synthetic materials and rubber. Because methanol has a high level of resistance to pre-ignition, engines designed to operate on methanol exclusively can feature a substantially higher compression ratio than gasoline engines, making them more efficient. On the other hand, methanol's low calorific value means that fuel consumption is almost doubled, necessitating increases in both the fuel-supply rate and the volume of the fuel tank, as well as recalibration of the injectors.

Suitable Lambda oxygen sensors can be employed for optimal emissions control together with a catalytic converter. Special lubricants are able to maintain long-term stability in the face of agression from methanol and its combustion products.

Pilot control of the fuel mixture is facilitated by a fuel sensor; the signal which this sensor transmits to the ECU reflects the proportion of methanol in the fuel. Specially-tailored programs adapt mixture and ignition timing to suit the engine's current operating conditions.

Hydrogen-powered passenger car with spark-ignition engine *(BMW 735i)*
LH_2 Liquid hydrogen, GH_2 Gaseous hydrogen. 1 Valve block for LH_2 refuelling and GH_2 supply (vacuum-insulated), 2 Hydrogen lines, vacuum-insulated, 3 LH_2 Evaporator, 4 Metering valve for regulating power with electronic control, 5 Hydrogen injectors, 6 Overcurrent and safety valves, 7 Liquid-hydrogen tank with vacuum super-insulation, 8 Hydrogen sensors for automatic leak monitoring, 10 Variable-speed centrifugal supercharger.

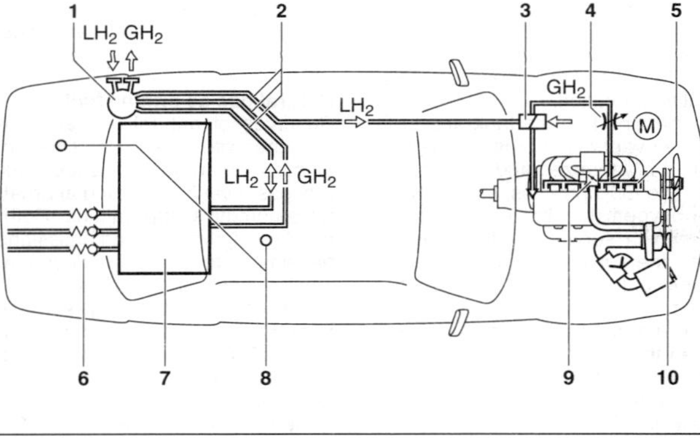

Hydrogen operation (spark-ignition engines)

The finite availability of fossil energy and concern regarding CO_2 levels have also combined to provoke increasing interest in hydrogen's potential as an automotive fuel. Although the production of hydrogen, the required infrastructure and refuelling all pose difficult problems, technically feasible solutions are on the horizon. Production of hydrogen through electrolysis assumes the availability of adequate amounts of electrical energy from atomic or solar sources.

Storing hydrogen in the vehicle

Gaseous storage in pressurized tanks
High pressures (300 bar) are required for storage in gaseous form. This results in high weight along with safety risks.

Liquid storage (cryogenic tank)
Liquid storage represents the best alternative with regard to both weight and energy density (present operating range approx. 300 km). The extremely low temperature required (– 253 °C) places substantial demands on thermal insulation. Residual heat causes hydrogen to be emitted from the safety valve, resulting in losses of about 2 % per day when the vehicle is parked. An electric evaporator maintains the specified tank pressure during operation.

Metal-hydride tanks
Hydrides are produced as hydrogen is absorbed by a metallic powder. This is an exothermic process, i.e., heat must be conducted away during fuelling. There are no storage losses. The disadvantages associated with the low energy density (range: 120 km) and high materials costs are to a degree offset by uncomplicated safety technology.

Methylcyclohexanol storage
This type of storage employs a catalyst to dehydrate the hydrogenous methylcyclohexane at 500 °C. The byproducts are hydrogen and recyclable toluene.

Mixture preparation

Regardless of storage mode, all current systems inject gaseous hydrogen into the intake manifold. Although a number of advantages could be had by injecting low-temperature hydrogen directly into the combustion chamber (improved charge dispersion for higher output, cool mixture for low NO_x emissions, no danger of backfiring into the induction tract), the short injector service life means that this type of system is not likely to come on the market in the near future.

Current external mixture-formation designs are based on a continuous-injection system in which a central electric metering valve and a hydrogen distributor conduct the vaporized hydrogen to the individual intake pipes.

Backfiring into the intake tract is prevented by lean mixtures or supplementary water injection. A supercharging device can be used to compensate for a portion of the power loss associated with lean operation.

One alternative, comprising intermittent sequential injection of hydrogen into the intake manifold, is presently in the development stage. This system's unlimited range of options for injection timing allow it to inhibit backfiring, even with rich mixtures. Injector and electronic-control system must operate with extreme precision while maintaining short valve-opening times; the technical requirements are thus substantial.

Emissions

During combustion, pure hydrogen (H_2) will oxidize into water (H_2O). No CO_2 is produced in the combustion process. H_2 is thus the only fuel which can be used to avoid all CO_2 emissions (the operative assumption being that no fossil fuels be employed as primary energy sources in the hydrogen-production process). Electric drive is the only alternative which can make a similar claim. Meanwhile, lean mixtures or a system for catalytic control of emissions (still to be developed) will meet future standards governing NO_X.

Diesel-engine management

Fuel metering

Requirements

The fuel-injection pump must supply fuel at a pressure of between 350 and 1200 bar – according to the specific diesel combustion configuration - with maximum precision in the individual injection cycles if good mixture quality is to be achieved. The start of the injection cycle must be precisely timed to within approx. 1° crankshaft in order to achieve the optimum compromise between fuel consumption, emissions and noise (combustion smoothness).

A timing device controls the start of injection, and compensates for the pressure-wave propagation times in the injection lines, by responding to increasing engine speed and advancing the pump's port-closing (actual start of pump delivery) accordingly. Load-sensitive control mechanisms are employed in some special applications.

The fuel quantity alone is used for the diesel engine's load and speed control; its intake air is not throttled. This means that presuming adequate injected fuel quantity, an unloaded diesel engine can speed-up out of control until it destroys itself. For this reason a governor is required which limits the engine's maximum speed.

Fuel-injection process

Considering the high pressures and short delivery times involved, the fuel can no longer be regarded as incompressible. Thus the processes attendant upon injection are not static (i.e., they do not conform with geometric laws of displacement), but are instead dynamic (essentially according to acoustic principles).

An engine-driven camshaft drives the injection-pump's plunger in the supply direction, generating pressure in the high-pressure gallery. The delivery valve responds to the increased pressure by opening, and a pressure wave proceeds toward the injection nozzle at the speed of sound (approx. 1400 m s^{-1}). When the injection nozzle's opening pressure is reached, the needle valve overcomes the force of the injection-nozzle spring and lifts from its seat so that fuel can be injected from the spray orifices into the engine's combustion chamber. The injection process ends with the opening of the spill port in the plunger-and-barrel assembly. Initially, the pressure in the pump chamber collapses. The delivery valve then closes, and due to the action of its relief collar, reduces the pressure in the injection line. The pressure drop to the so-called "standby pressure" is calculated to ensure that

– the injection nozzle closes quickly to provide a clean break in fuel discharge and to prevent fuel dribble,

– residual pressure waves in the lines are effectively dampened in order to prevent the nozzles from reopening and to ensure that the low-pressure undulations do not result in cavitation damage.

In-line fuel-injection pump with mechanical (flyweight) governor

1 Fuel tank, 2 Governor, 3 Fuel-supply pump, 4 Injection pump, 5 Timing device, 6 Drive from engine, 7 Fuel filter, 8 Vent, 9 Nozzle-and-holder assembly, 10 Fuel return line, 11 Overflow line.

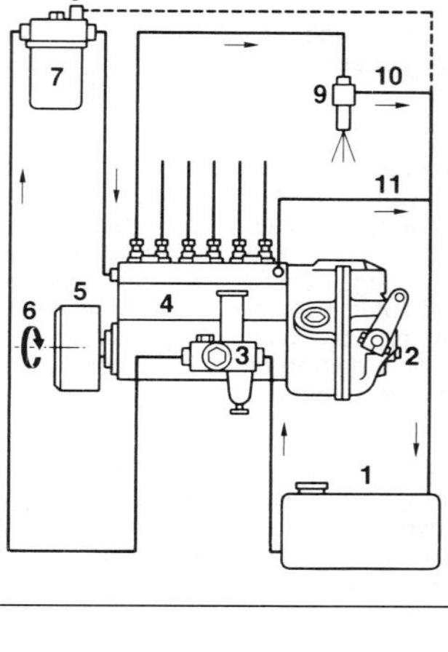

Fuel-injection system

The fuel-injection system is responsible for complying with the diesel engine's fuel-metering requirements. The components on the low-pressure side of the injection system comprise fuel tank, fuel filter, fuel-supply pump, overflow valve and fuel-supply lines. The fuel pressure required for injection is generated on the high-pressure side of the system, where the fuel is pumped through the delivery valve, high-pressure injection lines and nozzle-holder assembly on its way to the injection nozzle.

Fuel-injection pump

Current technology generally prescribes the application of one of the following high-pressure injection systems for automotive diesels:

– In-line injection pumps, with mechanical governors or electronic actuator (electronic diesel control – EDC), and timing devices as dictated by the specific application. On the in-line injection pump (particularly widespread on heavy-vehicle engines), a camshaft actuates one plunger-and-barrel assembly per engine cylinder.

Yet another design is represented by the in-line control-sleeve injection pump, with which the port closing (start of pump delivery) as well as the injected fuel quantity can be regulated.

– The distributor-type injection pump features a mechanical governor or electronic actuator (EDC) and an integral timing device. In the distributor-type pump (especially popular in high-speed diesel engines for passenger cars and light trucks), a central, cam-plate-driven plunger generates pressure and distributes the fuel to the individual cylinders, while a control collar controls the injected fuel quantity.

The components in both types of system are manufactured to precise tolerances in order to ensure long service life and consistent, exact control of port closing and injected fuel quantity, as well as minimum scatter between the individual cylinders.

In addition to the in-line and distributor-type pumps, there is also an injection pump which is actuated directly by the engine's camshaft, this is generally of the

Size P in-line fuel-injection pump
1 Delivery-valve holder, 2 Spring seat, 3 Delivery valve, 4 Pump barrel, 5 Pump plunger, 6 Lever arm with ball head, 7 Control rack, 8 Control sleeve, 9 Plunger control arm, 10 Plunger return spring, 11 Spring seat, 12 Roller tappet, 13 Camshaft.

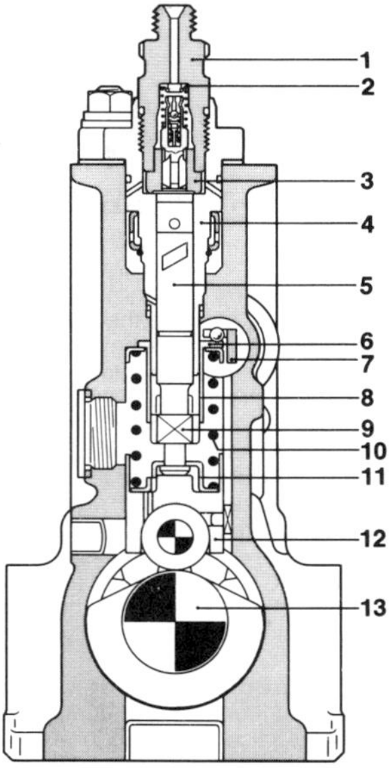

Applications for various types of in-line injection pump

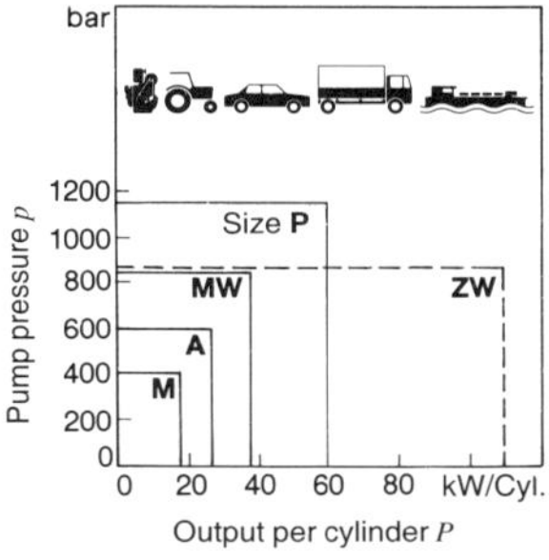

single-cylinder type (usually used with large marine engines, construction machinery and in low-displacement engines).

Another injection method is represented by the unit-injector system, in which the pump and the injection nozzle form a single unit. One unit injector is installed in the cylinder head for each cylinder. The unit is driven by the engine's camshaft, either directly via pushrod or indirectly via rocker-arm assembly.

In-line fuel-injection pump (PE)

Fuel-supply pump

A piston pump delivers the fuel to the injection pump's fuel gallery at a pressure of 1 ... 1.5 bar. The cam-driven supply-pump plunger travels to TDC on every stroke. It is not rigidly connected to the drive element; instead, a spring supplies the return pressure. It is this return stroke where the actual pumping occurs. The plunger spring responds to increases in line pressure by reducing the plunger's return travel to a portion of the full stroke. The greater the pressure in the supply line, the lower the supply quantity.

High-pressure pump

Every in-line fuel-injection pump has a plunger-and-barrel assembly for each engine cylinder. An engine-driven camshaft moves the plunger in the supply direction, and a spring presses it back to its initial position. Although there is no sealing element, the plunger is fitted to the assembly with such precision (clearance: 3 ... 5 m) that operation is virtually leak-free, even at high pressures and low engine speeds.

The plunger's actual stroke is constant. The supply quantity is moderated by turning the plunger – into which inclined helices have been machined – to vary its effective stroke. Active pumping starts when the upper edge of the plunger closes the intake port. A slot provides a connection between the plunger (pressure) chamber above the plunger and the area below the helix. Delivery ceases when the helix uncovers the intake port.

Various helix designs are employed in the plunger. On plunger-and-barrel assemblies with a lower helix only, pumping always begins at the same stroke travel, the plunger being rotated to advance or retard the end of delivery. An upper helix can be employed to vary the start of delivery. There are also plunger-and-barrel assemblies on the market which combine upper and lower helices in a single unit.

In order of their suitability for use with high injection pressures, the major types of delivery valve currently in use are:

- Constant-volume relief valve,
- Constant-volume relief valve with return-flow restriction
- Constant-pressure valve

Fuel-delivery control in the in-line fuel-injection pump
1 From pump gallery, 2 To nozzle, 3 Barrel, 4 Plunger, 5 Lower control helix, 6 Vertical groove.

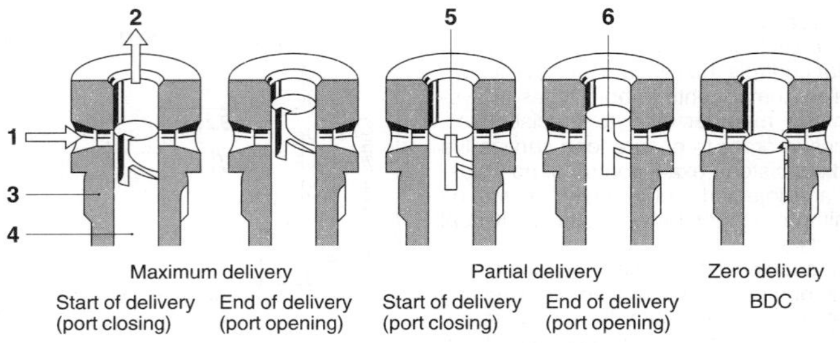

The delivery valve and pressure-relief characteristics must be specially designed for the specific application. Units incorporating a return-flow restriction or constant-pressure valve employ an additional throttle element to damp the pressure waves reflected back from the injection nozzle, thus preventing it from opening again. The constant-pressure valve is employed to maintain stable hydraulic characteristics in high-pressure fuel-injection systems and on small, high-speed direct-injection engines.

In fuel-injection pumps generating moderate pressures of up to 600 bar (e.g., Sizes M, A), the plunger-and-barrel assembly is installed in the pump housing in a fixed position, where it is retained by the delivery valve and the delivery-valve holder.

In pumps generating injection pressures in excess of 600 bar, the plunger-and-barrel assembly, delivery valve and delivery-valve holder are screwed together to form a single unit, redirecting the high sealing forces away from the pump housing (e.g., Sizes MW, P).

The in-line fuel-injection pump and the attached governor are connected to the engine's lube-oil system.

Speed governing

The main function of the governor is to limit the maximum engine speed. In other words, it must ensure that the diesel engine does not exceed the maximum rpm specified by its manufacturer. Depending upon type, the governor's functions may include maintaining specific, constant engine speeds, such as idle, or other speeds in the range between idle and maximum speed. The governor can also adjust full-load delivery in accordance with engine speed (adaptation), boost or atmospheric pressure, and it can be used to meter the extra fuel required for starting. The governor adapts the delivery quantity to these conditions by making corresponding adjustments in the position of the control rack.

Mechanical (flyweight) governors

The mechanical governor (also known as a flyweight or centrifugal governor) is driven by the engine's camshaft, and provides the performance curves described below. The flyweights, which act against the force of the governor springs, are connected to the control rack by a system of levers. During static operation, centrifugal and spring forces are in a state of equilibrium, with the control rack positioned for the delivery quantity corresponding to the engine's output at the respective point on its performance curve. A drop in engine speed - for instance, due to increased load – results in a corresponding reduction in centrifugal force, and the governor springs move the flyweights, and with them the control rack, in the direction for increased delivery quantity until equilibrium is restored. Various functions are combined to produce the following types of governor:

Variable-speed governors

The variable-speed governor maintains a virtually constant engine speed in accordance with the position of the control lever. Applications: Preferably for commercial vehicles with auxiliary power take-off, for construction machinery, agricultural tractors, in ships and in stationary installations.

Delivery-valve holder with delivery valve
a) With constant-volume valve and return-flow restriction,
b) With constant-pressure valve.
1 Delivery-valve holder, 2 Return-flow restriction, 3 Dead volume, 4 Retraction piston, 5 Valve ball, 6 Valve holder, 7 Supply valve, 8 Calibrated restriction, 9 Pressure-holding valve.

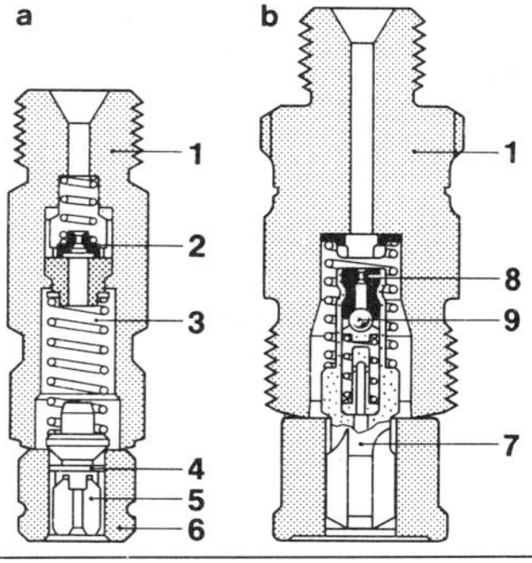

Governor characteristic curves
a Positive torque control in upper speed range, b Unregulated range, c Negative torque-control; 1 Idle-speed setpoint, 2 Full-load curve, 3 Full-load curve, turbocharged engine, 4 Full-load curve, naturally-aspirated engine, 5 Full-load curve, naturally-aspirated engine with altitude compensation, 6 Intermediate engine-speed control, 7 Temperature-sensitive starting quantity.

Variable-speed governor

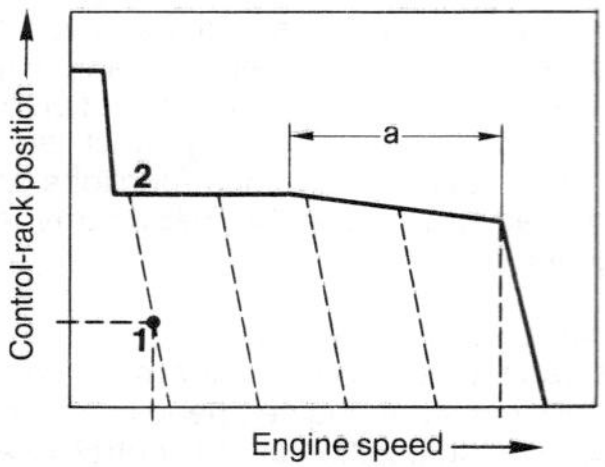

Minimum-maximum-speed governor

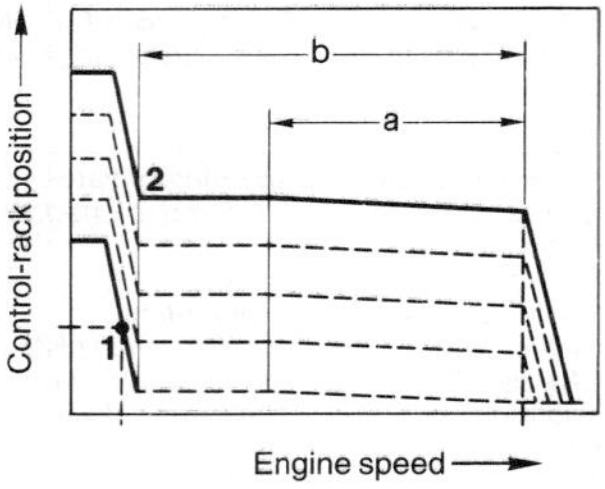

Complex governor with additional control functions

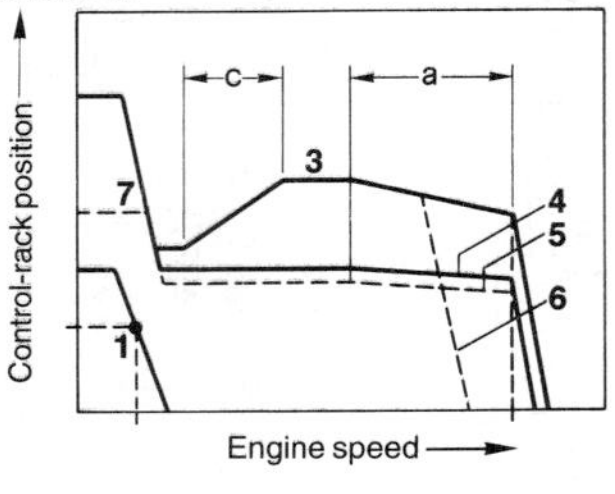

Minimum-maximum-speed governors
From the characteristic curve for the minimum-maximum-speed governor it can be seen that this type of governor is effective only at idle and when the engine reaches maximum rpm. The torque in the range between these two extremes is determined exclusively by the position of the accelerator pedal. Application: For road vehicles.

Combination governors
Combination governors are a synthesis of the two governor types described above. Depending upon the specific application, active control can be in the upper or lower engine-speed range.

Governor types
In the RQ and RQV governor, the flyweights act directly on the governor springs; control-lever movements vary the transfer ratio at the fulcrum lever.

In the RSV, RS and RSF governors, the governor spring is outside the flyweights; the transfer ratio at the fulcrum lever remains essentially constant.

Speed droop
The governor's performance characteristics are essentially a function of the

RQ Minimum-maximum-speed governor
1 Pump plunger, 2 Control rack, 3 Full-load stop, 4 Control lever, 5 Injection-pump camshaft, 6 Flyweight, 7 Governor spring, 8 Sliding bolt.

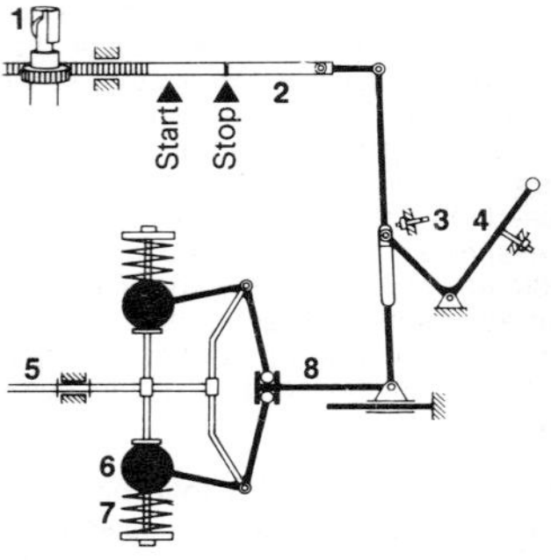

slope of the control curve, defined as speed droop δ:

$$\delta = \frac{n_{LO} - n_{VO}}{n_{VO}} \cdot 100\%$$

The smaller the differential between the upper no-load speed (n_{LO}) and the upper full-load speed (n_{VO}), the lower the speed droop, in other words, the greater is the precision with which the governor maintains a specific engine speed. Variable-speed governors on small high-speed engines generally achieve a top-end breakaway consistency of 6 ... 10%.

Mechanical add-on equipment

Torque control

An auxiliary spring (torque-control spring) is installed at a suitable position in the governor mechanism. The spring precisely adapts the governor's output curve to the diesel engine's full-load fuel requirements by lowering it slightly. When a given engine speed is reached, the spring compresses and causes the control rack to move in the direction for reduced fuel-delivery quantity (positive torque control). Negative torque control, which responds to increased engine speed by augmenting the fuel-delivery quantity (see diagram on p. 498) is also possible, albeit at the price of a substantially greater number of components and more complicated adjustment procedures.

RSV Variable-speed governor
1 Pump plunger, 2 Control rack, 3 Maximum-speed stop, 4 Control lever, 5 Start spring, 6 Stop or idle stop, 7 Governor spring, 8 Auxiliary idle spring, 9 Injection-pump camshaft, 10 Flyweight, 11 Sliding bolt, 12 Torque-control spring, 13 Full-load stop.

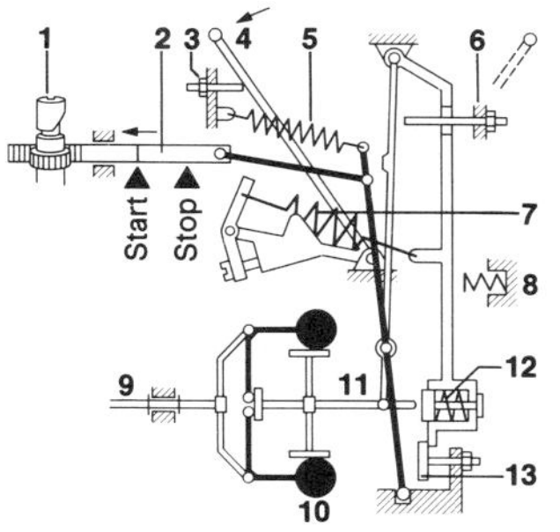

Manifold-pressure compensator (LDA)

Turbocharged engines are capable of converting greater amounts of fuel into torque as the boost pressure increases; a spring-loaded diaphragm is employed to furnish a corresponding correction in full-load fuel-delivery quantity. The diaphragm responds to increasing boost pressure on its working side by shifting the control rack (to which it is connected) to provide a commensurate increase in fuel-delivery quantity.

Manifold-pressure compensator (LDA)
1 Boost-pressure connection, 2 Diaphragm.

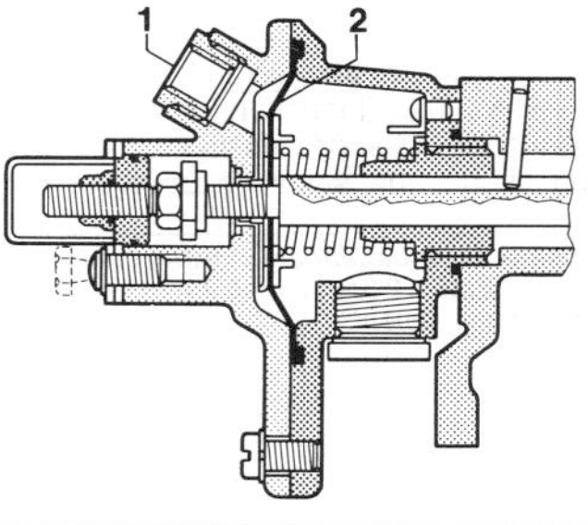

Altitude-pressure compensator (ADA)
1 Pressure capsule, 2 Atmospheric-pressure connection.

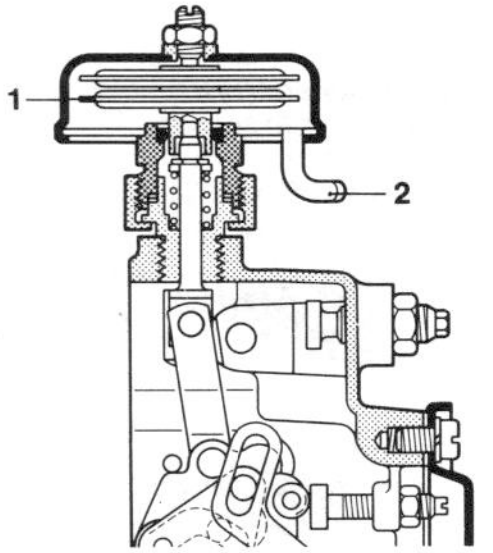

Altitude-pressure compensator (ADA)
The altitude-pressure compensator is similar to the LDA. It reduces full-load fuel-delivery in response to the low atmospheric pressure (and low air density) encountered at high altitudes. The unit includes a barometric capsule which displaces the control rack in the direction for lower fuel-delivery quantity once atmospheric pressure drops by a specific increment.

Temperature-sensitive starting device (TAS)
A cold engine requires a certain amount of enrichment for starting, in other words more fuel. This enrichment is not necessary on a warm engine, and would lead to the emission of smoke. The solution is a control-rack stop employing an expansion element to prevent the enrichment during warm starts.

Rack-travel sensor (RWG)
The RWG uses induction for rack-position monitoring. After processing in an evaluation circuit, the signal is used for such tasks as control of mechanical and hydraulic transmissions, for the provision of fuel-consumption figures, for exhaust-gas recirculation and for diagnosis.

Port-closing sensor (FBG)
The FBG is an inductive unit for monitoring on the running engine the point at which pump delivery starts (port closing); it can also check the timing device. In addition, injection pumps equipped with this device can be supplied with the camshaft locked in the port-closing position, facilitating simple and precise pump installation on the engine.

Timing devices
Centrifugally-controlled timing devices are positioned in the drive train between the engine and the injection pump. The flyweights respond to increasing engine speed by turning the injection pump's camshaft, with respect to the drive shaft, in the "delivery advance" direction. Versions: Front-mounted, clutch-driven units and gear-driven devices with an adjustment range of 3°...10° on the pump shaft.

Temperature-dependent starting device
1 Control rack, 2 Start-quantity stop with expansion element.

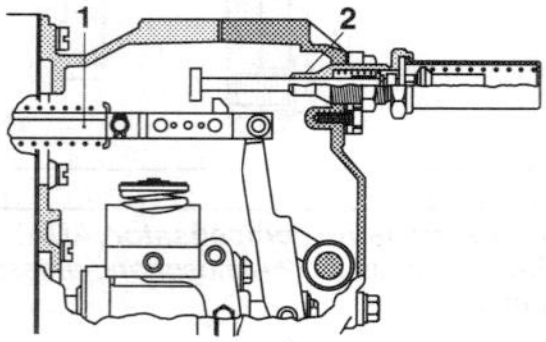

Rack-travel sensor (RWG)
1 Laminated iron core, 2 Reference coil, 3 Fixed short-circuiting ring, 4 Control rack, 5 Measuring coil, 6 Moving short-circuiting ring.

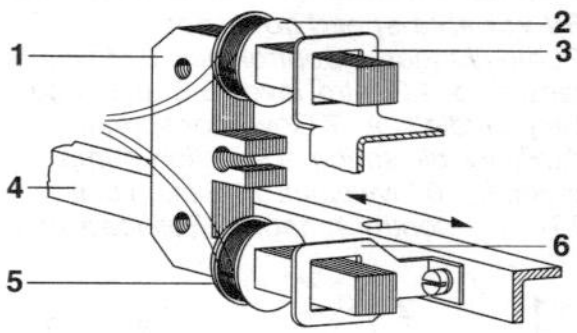

Port-closing sensor (FBG)
a) Measurement with sensor, b) Blocking position; 1 Pump camshaft, 2 Sensor, 3 Blocking pin.

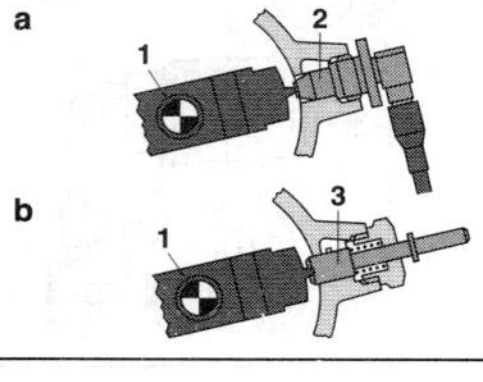

Timing device
Off position.

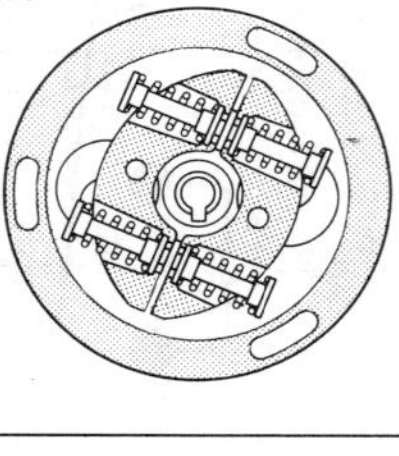

Pump shutoff

A mechanical (stop lever), electric or pneumatic shutoff device is employed to shut down the diesel engine by interrupting the fuel supply.

Electronic governor (EDC)

Instead of flyweights, the electronic governor for the in-line fuel-injection pump uses a solenoid actuator with a non-contacting inductive position sensor to position the control rack.

The solenoid actuator is triggered by an ECU, in which a microprocessor compares accelerator position, rpm and a number of additional correction factors, with the performance curves stored in its memory in order to determine the correct injection quantity (expressed as a function of control-rack position). An electronic controller compares the monitored control-rack position with the specified setpoint in order to determine the required excitation-current input to the solenoid, which operates against a return spring. When deviations are detected, the excitation current is regulated to shift the control rack to precisely the specified position.

An inductive speed sensor monitors a camshaft-mounted pulse wheel; the ECU uses the pulse intervals to calculate engine speed.

Because it can monitor a number of engine and vehicle parameters and combine them to calculate the injection quantity, an electronic governor offers a number of advantages over a mechanical unit:
– Engine can be switched on and off with key,
– Complete freedom in determining full-load response,
– Maximum injected fuel quantity can be precisely coordinated with the boost pressure in order to remain inside the smoke limit,
– Corrections for air and fuel temperatures,
– Temperature-dependent start enrichment,
– Engine-speed control for auxiliary drives,
– Cruise-control facility,
– Regulation of maximum speed,

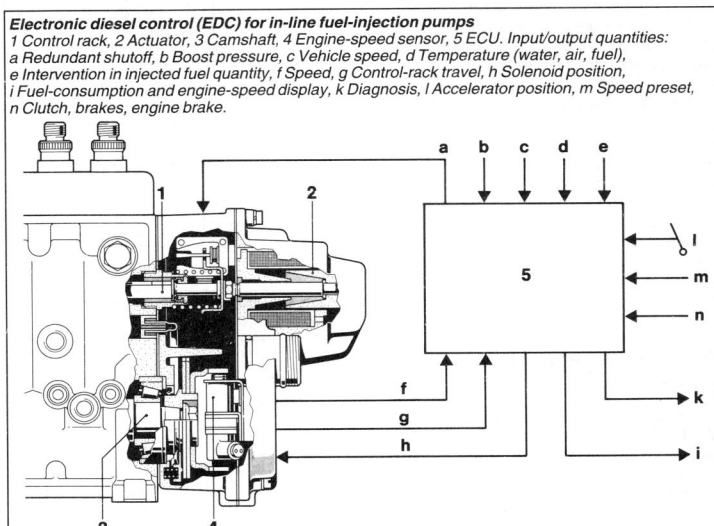

Electronic diesel control (EDC) for in-line fuel-injection pumps
1 Control rack, 2 Actuator, 3 Camshaft, 4 Engine-speed sensor, 5 ECU. Input/output quantities: a Redundant shutoff, b Boost pressure, c Vehicle speed, d Temperature (water, air, fuel), e Intervention in injected fuel quantity, f Speed, g Control-rack travel, h Solenoid position, i Fuel-consumption and engine-speed display, k Diagnosis, l Accelerator position, m Speed preset, n Clutch, brakes, engine brake.

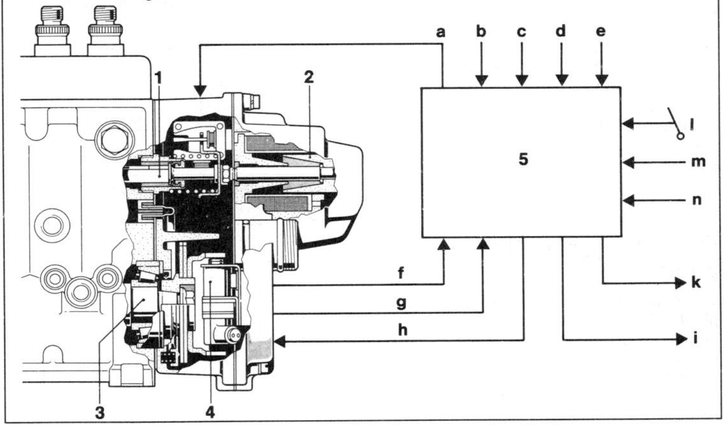

- Consistent, low idle speed,
- Active surge control,
- Option for intervention in traction control (ASR)/automatic transmission,
- Signal transmission for tachometer,
- Service support through integral fault diagnosis.

In-line control-sleeve injection pump

The in-line control-sleeve injection pump makes it possible to provide electronically-controlled adjustment of port closing (start of pump delivery). The conventional spill port is incorporated in the slide valve which is a component in each plunger-and-barrel assembly. A control shaft with actuating levers is employed to adjust the positions of all sliders at once, which it does by displacing the slider up or down to advance or retard the start of delivery relative to camshaft position. An electromagnetic positioning mechanism similar to that used in the electronically controlled in-line injection pump turns the control shaft, albeit without position feedback.

A needle-travel sensor monitors the start of injection directly at the injection nozzle. It transmits a corresponding signal to the ECU, which compares it to the programmed value as a function of rpm, injection quantity, etc., in order to adjust the solenoid-excitation current to achieve congruence between the feedback and setpoint values for start of injection.

In systems using the control-sleeve injection pump, the engine-speed sensor obtains precise information on the start of injection relative to TDC by monitoring the pulses from the reference marks on the engine's flywheel.

Distributor-type injection pump (VE)

The distributor-type injection pump is applied in 3, 4, 5 and 6-cylinder diesel engines as installed in passenger cars, tractors and light and medium-heavy trucks generating power of up to 20 kW per cylinder, according to engine speed and combustion principle. Distributor-type injection pumps for direct-injection (DI) engines achieve a maximum of 700 bar in the pump's high-pressure chamber at speeds of up to 2400 min^{-1}.

Fuel-supply pump

This integral vane-type pump draws in the fuel from the tank (should no primary pump be installed) and, together with a pressure-control valve, generates an internal pump pressure which increases in direct proportion to engine speed.

In-line control-sleeve pump
1 Pump plunger, 2 Control sleeve, 3 Control-sleeve adjustment shaft, 4 Control rack.

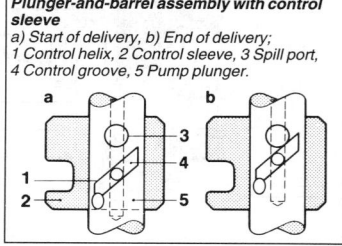

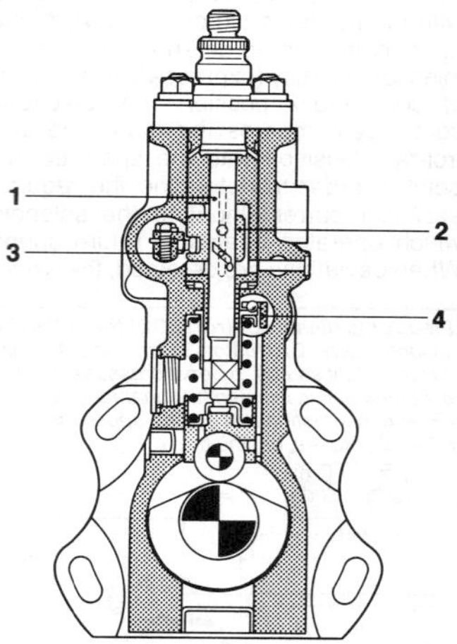

Plunger-and-barrel assembly with control sleeve
a) Start of delivery, b) End of delivery; 1 Control helix, 2 Control sleeve, 3 Spill port, 4 Control groove, 5 Pump plunger.

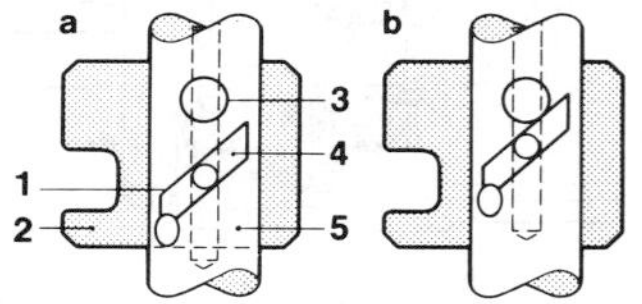

High-pressure pump

The VE pump employs only one plunger-and-barrel assembly for all cylinders. The plunger displaces the fuel during its stroke while at the same time rotating to distribute it to the individual outlets. During each rotation of the driveshaft, the plunger completes a number of strokes equal to the number of engine cylinders to be supplied. The VE pump's driveshaft turns the cam plate and the plunger to which it is connected via a cross coupling. The lobes on the bottom of the cam plate turn against the rollers of the roller ring, causing cam plate and plunger to supplement their rotating motion by executing a stroke (distribution and delivery). The pump continues to deliver fuel during its working stroke for as long as the spill port remains closed, and ceases to do so as soon as the spill port emerges from the control collar, whose position thus determines the effective stroke and injected fuel quantity. The governor determines the position of the control collar, which slides on the plunger.

Mechanical governor

A ball pin provides the connection between the control collar and the governor levers, which, in turn, respond to the centrifugal force exerted on the flyweights and the governor spring. The speed is set by adjusting the spring tension by means of the speed-control lever. The full-load adjustment screw is used to shift the entire governor-lever assembly so as to obtain maximum effective stroke. Additional springs can be installed in the governing mechanism to adapt idle and transitional behavior to the specific requirements of the engine.

Speed droop, governor types

The description of speed droop and governor types (variable-speed governors, minimum-maximum-speed governors) for in-line pumps also applies to governors used with distributor pumps.

Load signal

On distributor fuel-injection pumps equipped with minimum-maximum speed

VE Distributor-type fuel-injection pump (basic version)
1 Vane-type supply pump, 2 Governor drive, 3 Timing device, 4 Cam plate, 5 Control collar, 6 Distributor plunger, 7 Delivery valve, 8 Solenoid-actuated shutoff, 9 Governor lever mechanism, 10 Overflow throttle, 11 Mechanical shutoff device, 12 Governor spring, 13 Speed-control lever, 14 Control sleeve, 15 Flyweight, 16 Pressure-control valve.

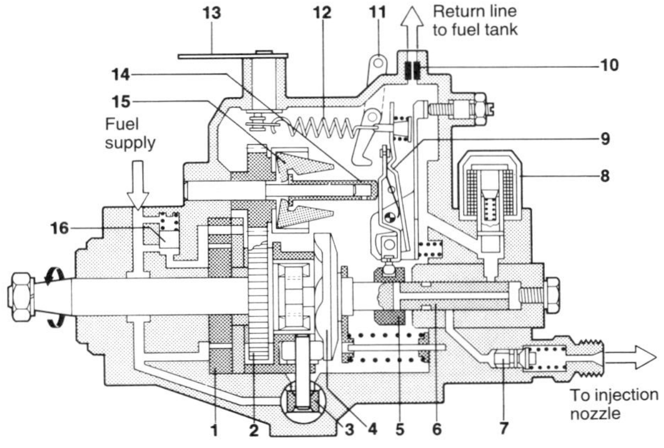

governors, the position of the outer control lever can be monitored via microswitch or potentiometer to provide information on load.

Mechanical add-on devices

A number of ancillary monitoring devices are available for the processing of additional operating parameters, in order to provide information for regulating the injection quantity (such as manifold-pressure compensator (LDA), start quantity, hydraulic and mechanical full-load adaptation) and for adjusting port closing (start of delivery) – (e.g., cold-start accelerator, load-dependent start of delivery).

Hydromechanically controlled timing device

Installed downstream from the supply pump is a pressure-control valve which allows the pump's internal pressure to rise linearly as a function of engine speed (1.5 ... 8 bar). This speed-dependent pressure is applied through a throttle bore to the front end of the spring-loaded timing-device plunger. The plunger, in turn, rotates the pump's roller ring in the opposite direction to the pump's direction of rotation, thus advancing the injection timing (port closing or start of delivery) independently of engine speed.

A mechanical (stop lever) or electric (solenoid valve) shutoff device shuts down the diesel engine by interrupting fuel delivery. The electric variant is particularly widespread in passenger cars.

Electronic governor (EDC)

An eccentrically-mounted ball pin provides the connection between the VE pump's control collar and a solenoid rotary actuator. The actuator's angular setting determines the position of the control collar, and with it the effective stroke of the pump. Connected to the actuator is a position sensor (potentiometer or inductive sensor). The ECU's microcomputer receives various signals from the sensors: accelerator-pedal position, engine speed, air, coolant and fuel temperatures, boost pressure, atmospheric pressure, etc. It uses these inputs to determine the correct injection quantity, which is converted to a specific control-rack position with the aid of performance maps electronically stored in the unit's memory. The ECU varies the excitation current to the rotary actuator

Electronic diesel control (EDC) for distributor-type fuel-injection pumps
1 Supply pump, 2 Solenoid valve, 3 Timing device, 4 Control collar, 5 Rotary actuator with sensor, 6 ECU. Inputs/Outputs: a Speed, b Start of injection, c Temperature, d Boost pressure, e Accelerator position, f Fuel return, g To injection nozzle.

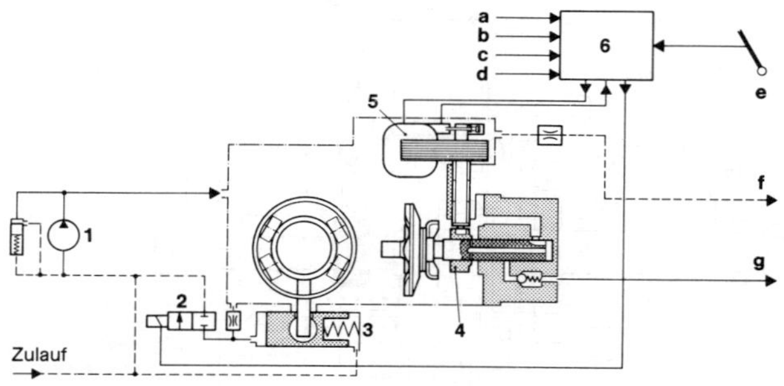

until it receives a signal indicating congruence between the setpoint and actual values for control-rack position.

Electronically-controlled timing device
The injection timing (start of injection) can also be regulated by comparing actual and setpoint values. In this process, the signal from a sensor monitoring the point at which the injection nozzle opens is compared with a programmed setpoint. A clocked solenoid valve, connected to the working chamber of the timing-device plunger, varies the pressure exerted against the plunger, and with it the setting of the timing device. A signal from a sensor in the nozzle holder indicating the start of injection, is compared with the electronically stored specification. The clock rate used to trigger the solenoid is modified until the actual and setpoint values converge.

Compared to a mechanical governor, the electronic unit has the following advantages:
– Improved control of injected fuel quantity (fuel consumption, engine power, emissions),
– Improved control of engine speed (low idle speed, adjustment for air conditioner, etc.)
– Enhanced comfort (anti-surge control, smooth operation),
– More precise start of injection (fuel consumption, emissions),
– Improved service (diagnosis).

The application options extend to embrace features such as open-loop and closed-loop control of exhaust-gas recirculation, boost-pressure control, glow-plug control, and interconnection with other on-board electrical systems.

Fuel-injection system with distributor-type pump
1 Fuel tank, 2 Fuel line, 3 Fuel filter, 4 Distributor-type fuel-injection pump, 5 Pressure line, 6 Injection nozzle, 7 Fuel-return line.

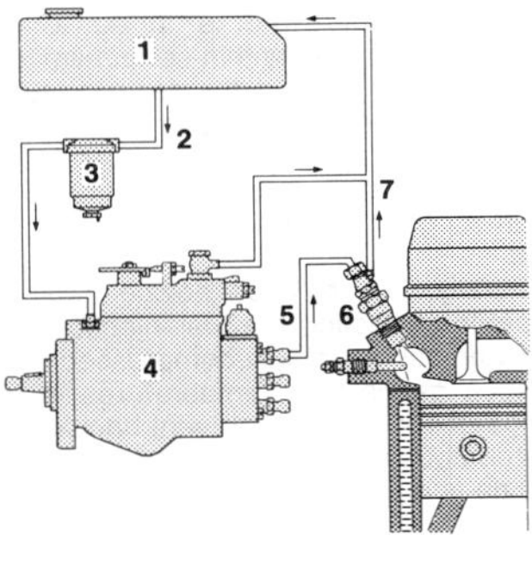

Unit injectors (PDE)

The unit injector, or pump-nozzle unit, can be directly installed in the cylinder head, and functions as a single-cylinder injection pump with integral injector. Drive is provided by the engine's camshaft. Each pump-nozzle unit includes a rapid-action solenoid valve for controlling start of injection and injected fuel quantity. When the solenoid valve opens, the unit's injector supplies fuel to the overflow line's orifice. The nozzle injects fuel into the cylinder when the solenoid retracts. The solenoid's closing point determines the start of injection, and its duration the injected fuel quantity. As the ECU controls the solenoid valve with reference to a program map, injection timing and duration can be programmed as desired, independent of the engine's crankshaft angle. These diesel-engine solenoid valves must cope with 300 to 500 times more pressure and cycle 10 to 20 times quicker than their gasoline-engine counterparts.

In conventional fuel-injection systems, maximum injection pressure is limited by the physical characteristics of the pressure lines between the injection pump and the injection nozzle. As the unit injector makes it possible to dispense with these lines, injection pressures of up to 1500 bar can be achieved. This order of injection pressure is combined with electronic programs for start of injection and duration of injection to obtain substantial reductions in diesel emissions.

Electronic closed-loop control concepts can include additional functions such as temperature-controlled start of injection, and can be used to control engine surge and to ensure smooth operation. In the future, such concepts will be used with pilot injection to further reduce noise. Finally, the unit injector can be used to switch off individual cylinders during part-load operation.

Fuel filters

The quality of the fuel filter and compliance with maintenance intervals exercise a decisive effect on the service life of a diesel injection system. The fuel filter's most important component, the filter cartridge, consists of a special hydrophobic paper element (felt is seldom used) woven in a helical pattern to form pockets. This arrangement provides the maximum filtering surface for a given area, allowing the filter to achieve maximum contamination retention for long service intervals. The degree of filtering is essentially a function of the paper's porosity, its weight and the type of fibers used. Due to the differences in requirements, systems with distributor-type injection pumps use filters with a mean pore size of 4 ... 5 µm, while pore sizes of 8 ... 10 µm are used with all other types of injection pump. Filters for diesel injection systems are either in-line (VE pumps only) or cartridge-type (consisting of filter cover and screwed-on replacement cartridge). Filter covers are available in various designs, including some with a hand-pump to assist restarting after running out of fuel or after filter maintenance. The complete in-line or cartridge filter is replaced when the specified maintenance interval has elapsed (> 30,000 km).

Filters for VE pumps incorporate a special chamber for collecting moisture. The water contained in the fuel collects on the contaminant side of the filter paper and then coalesces to form large droplets on the clean side. A sensor can be used to signal when the maximum permissible water level has been reached. A drain plug is used to discharge the water.

An electric heater can be installed in the filter to prevent obstruction due to paraffin separation in cold weather.

Nozzles and nozzle holders

Functions

Within the diesel engine's fuel-injection system, the injection nozzles and their holders serve as the connecting element between the injection pump and the engine. Their functions are:

- Assist in metering the fuel,
- Process the fuel ,
- Define the injection characteristics,
- Seal off the combustion chamber.

Diesel fuel is injected at peak pressures of up to 1000 bar, a figure which will become even higher in the future. Under these conditions the diesel fuel ceases to behave as a solid, incompressible fluid, and becomes compressible. During the brief delivery time (in the order of 1 ms), the injection system is "inflated," and a quantity of fuel – the nozzle's cross-section is one of the factors determining how much – is discharged into the engine's combustion chamber.

Through the length and diameter of the orifice, its spray direction and (to a more limited extent) its shape, the injection nozzle exercises a decisive effect on fuel processing, with corresponding consequences upon the engine's output, fuel consumption and exhaust emissions.

The rate-of-discharge curve must be calibrated to meet the specific requirements of the combustion process. This relationship has an important effect on both output and combustion noise. The correct injection duration is achieved when the pump's delivery rate is tuned to the nozzle's diameter. Within certain limits, it is possible to achieve the desired rate of discharge through optimal control of the injection nozzle's aperture (depending upon the nozzle needle's stroke) and by controlling the nozzle needle's motion pattern.

Finally, the injection nozzle must be capable of sealing the fuel-injection system against hot, highly-compressed combustion gases with temperatures in the range of 1000 °C. To prevent backflow of the combustion gases when the injection nozzle is open, the pressure in the injection nozzle's pressure chamber must always be higher than the combustion pressure. This requirement becomes particularly relevant toward the end of the injection sequence (when a stark reduction in injection pressure is accompanied by massive increases in combustion pressure), where it can only be ensured by carefully matching the injection pump, the injection nozzle and the nozzle needle for mutually satisfactory operation.

Basic design

Standard nozzle holders

The illustration shows the basic design of the combined nozzle-and-holder assembly. The injection nozzle consists of two sections: the body and the needle. The nozzle needle moves freely within the body's guide bore while at the same time providing a positive seal against high injection pressures. At the bottom of the needle is a conical seal, which the nozzle spring presses against the body's correspondingly shaped sealing surface when the nozzle is closed. These two opposed conical surfaces exhibit a slight mutual variation in aperture angle, providing linear contact with high dynamic compression and a positive seal.

The diameter of the needle guide is greater than that of the seat. The hydraulic pressure from the injection pump acts against the differential surface between the needle diameter and the surface covered by the seat. The injection nozzle opens when the product of sealing surface and pressure exceeds the force of the nozzle spring in the holder. As nozzle opening results in a sudden jump in the area around the seat which is exposed to pressure, a sufficiently high delivery rate will result in the injection nozzle snapping open very rapidly. It does not close again until the system has dropped from its opening pressure to below the relatively lower closing pressure. This hysteresis effect is of particular significance in designing hydraulic stability into fuel-injection systems. The opening pressure for nozzle-holder combinations intended for application at between 100 and 300 bar is set by installing washers beneath the nozzle spring. The closing pressure is then determined by the injection nozzle's geometry (ratio of needle diameter to seat diameter).

Nozzle-holder assemblies
a) With throttling-pintle nozzle, b) With hole-type nozzle; 1 Supply, 2 Holder body, 3 Nozzle retaining nut, 4 Spacer, 5 Injection nozzle, 6 Union nut with high-pressure tubing, 7 Edge filter, 8 Leak-off connection, 9 Pressure-adjustment shims, 10 Pressure channel, 11 Spring, 12 Pressure spindle, 13 Locating pins.

a

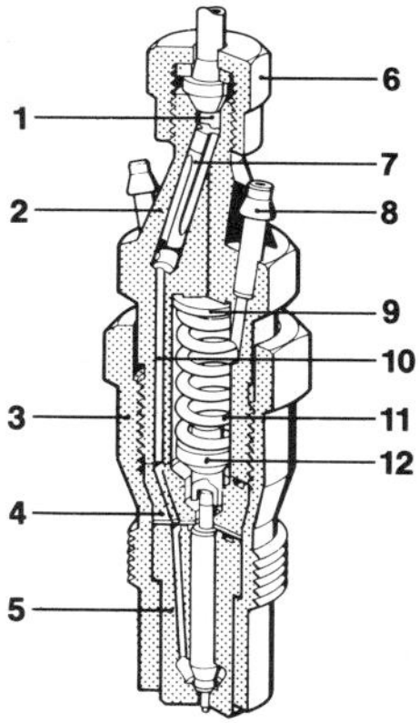

b

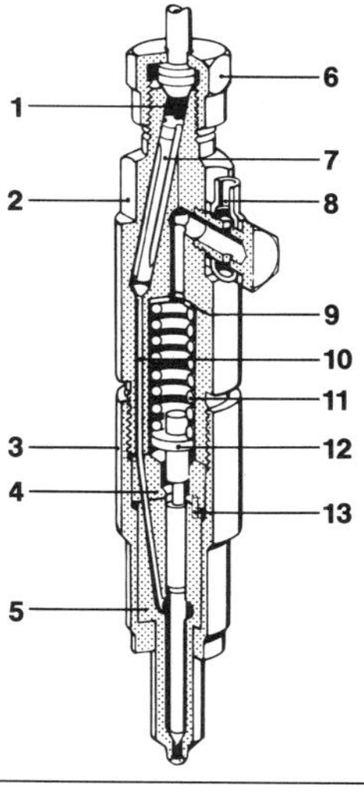

Dual-spring nozzle holders (2FH)

On dual-spring holders, the four parameters opening pressure 1, opening pressure 2, prestroke and total stroke, are set and adjusted to provide a specific rate-of-discharge curve. This type of holder can be employed to reduce the noise associated with direct-injection engines. Opening pressure 1 is set and tested as with the single-spring holder. Opening pressure 2 is the sum of the pretension figures for spring 1 and auxiliary spring 2. Spring 2 is supported by a stop sleeve which has been machined to the dimensions of the prestroke.

During injection, the opening of the nozzle needle is initially restricted to the prestroke range. Common prestroke figures are 0.03 ... 0.06 mm. As the pressure in the nozzle holder increases, the stop sleeve is raised, allowing the nozzle needle to open completely.

Dual-spring holders include special nozzles, in which the nozzle needle has no pintle, and the shoulder of the needle is level with the nozzle body.

There are also dual-spring holders available on the market for prechamber and turbulence-chamber engines. The injection figures are tailored to the respective injection system, with low opening pressures (e.g., 130/180 bar) and prestrokes of approximately 0.1 mm.

Nozzle types

Diesel engines with two-section combustion chambers require nozzle designs differing from those used in single-section chambers.

Throttling-pintle nozzles feature a coaxial spray pattern and are generally equipped with needles which retract to open; they are suitable for use in prechamber and turbulence-chamber engines.

Direct-injection engines with single-section combustion chambers generally require multi-hole nozzles.

Throttling-pintle nozzles

DN..SD.. injection nozzles and KCA nozzle holders represent the standard combination for use with prechamber and turbulence-chamber engines. The standard nozzle holder features M 24 x 2 threads and uses a 27-mm wrench fitting. DN 0 SD.. injection nozzles are generally used with a needle diameter of 6 mm and a spray aperture angle of 0°, nozzles with a defined conical spray angle are also available (for example, 12° in the DN 12 SD..). Smaller holders are used when only limited space is available (e.g., KCE holders).

Throttling-pintle nozzles vary the discharge aperture – and thus the flow rate – as a function of needle stroke. The hole-type nozzle displays an immediate, sharp

KBEL...P... Dual-spring holder

H_1 Prestroke, H_2 Main stroke, $H_{total} = H_1 + H_2$ Total stroke;
1 Holder, 2 Stop sleeve, 3 Spring seat, 4 Spring, 5 Shim, 6 Guide disk, 7 Pressure spindle, 8 Spring, 9 Shim, 10 Intermediate spacer, 11 Nozzle retaining nut, 12 Pressure pin.

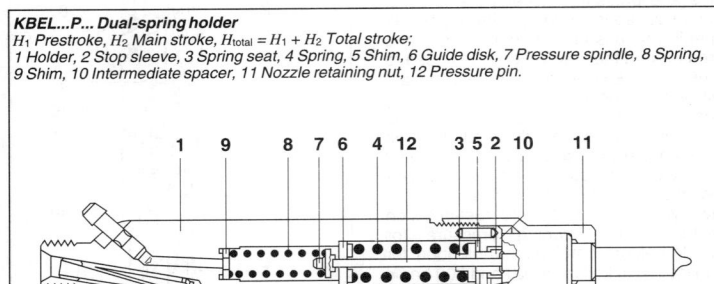

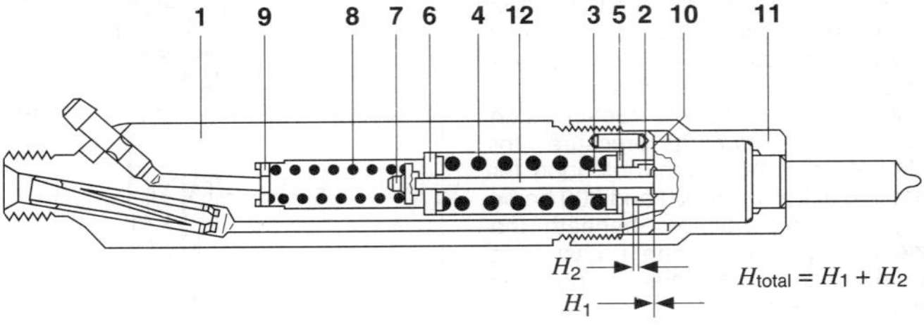

rise in aperture when the needle opens; in contrast, the throttling-pintle nozzle is characterized by an extremely flat aperture progression at moderate needle strokes. Within this stroke range, the pintle (an extension at the end of the needle) remains in the spray orifice. The flow opening consists only of the small annular gap between the larger spray orifice and the throttling pintle. As the stroke increases, the pintle emerges from the spray orifice, with an attendant substantial increase in the size of the aperture. This stroke-dependent aperture regulation can be employed to exert a certain amount of control on the rate of discharge (quantity of fuel injected into the engine within a specific period). At the start of injection, only a limited amount of fuel emerges from the injection nozzle, while a substantial quantity is discharged at the end of the cycle. This injection sequence has a particularly positive effect on combustion noise.

It must be remembered that excessively small apertures in combination with short needle strokes result in the injection pump accelerating the needle toward "open" with increased force, causing the needle to quickly emerge from the throttling stroke area. The injected fuel quantity per unit of time increases dramatically, and combustion noise rises accordingly. Similarly, negative effects result from excessively small openings at the end of the injection cycle: the volume displaced by the closing nozzle needle is restricted by the narrow aperture. The result is an undesirable extension of the injection duration. In summary, the shape of the aperture must be precisely matched to the injection-pump's delivery rate and the requirements of the combustion process (specified geometric dimensions with narrow tolerances).

During engine operation, carbon deposits form in the throttle gap. These are rather substantial and, unfortunately, extremely irregular as well. The level of deposit formation is determined by the quality of the fuel and the engine's operating conditions. In most cases only 30% of the initial throttle gap remains unobstructed. Fewer and more even deposits are found on flat pintle nozzles, in which the annular opening between the nozzle body and the throttle pintle is almost zero. The throttle pintle uses a machined surface to open the flow aperture. This type of flow passage features reduced surface

Types of injection nozzles
a) Throttling-pintle nozzle, b) Hole-type nozzle, δ Spray-orifice cone angles;
1 Pressure pin, 2 Nozzle body, 3 Nozzle needle, 4 Feed bore, 5 Pressure chamber, 6 Spray orifice, 7 Pintle, 8 Blind hole.

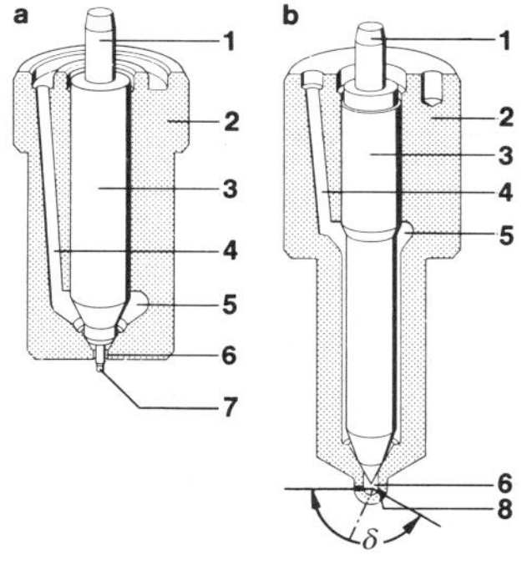

Nozzle designs
Hole-type nozzle with conical blind hole, 2 Hole-type nozzle with cylindrical blind hole, 3 Seat-hole nozzle, 4 Throttling-pintle nozzle, 5 Flat pintle nozzle with inclined surface.

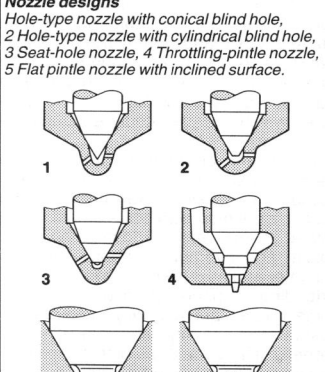

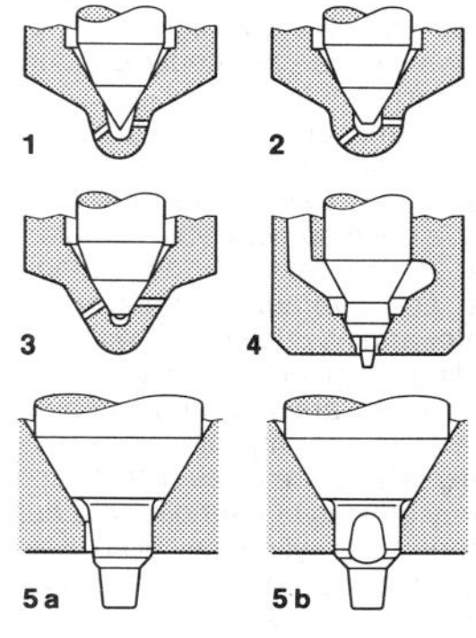

area relative to the flow opening, resulting in an enhanced self-cleaning effect. The machined surface is frequently parallel to the axis of the nozzle needle. Additional inclination can be employed to produce a more pronounced rise in the flat part of the flow curve, allowing a smoother transition to full nozzle opening. This expedient displays a positive effect on part-load noise emissions and on operating characteristics.

As deposit formation is also promoted by high temperatures at the injection nozzles, thermal shields are available to transfer the heat from the combustion chamber back to the cylinder head.

Hole-type nozzles

There are a wide variety of nozzle-and-holder assemblies (DHK) for hole-type nozzles. In contrast to throttling-pintle nozzles, multi-hole nozzles must generally be installed in a prescribed position in order to ensure the correct alignment between the variously-angled orifices and the engine's combustion chamber. For this reason, lug fittings or banjo bolts are usually employed to attach the nozzle-and-holder assemblies to the cylinder head, while an additional screw retainer provides the desired orientation. Multi-hole nozzles are available with needle diameters of 6 and 5 mm (Size S) and 4 mm (Size P). The nozzle springs must be suitable for use with the particular needle diameters and with the high opening pressures which are commonly encountered (> 180 bar).

At the end of the injection sequence there is a pronounced danger of the combustion gases being blown back into the nozzle, a development which would, in the course of time, result in destruction of the nozzle and hydraulic instability. Needle diameter and nozzle spring (with attention extending to spring oscillation patterns in some cases) are carefully calibrated to ensure that the injection nozzle seals properly. There are three different options for spray orifices in the hole-type nozzle's end cone: the cylindrical blind hole, the conical blind hole and the seat hole. Depending upon spray-orifice type, at the end of the injection cycle there remains a given volume of fuel in the nozzle which is then free to evaporate into the combustion chamber. The 3 different spray-orifice types above are listed in the order of descending retained fuel volume at the end of the injection cycle. In other words, because it retains the least fuel in the nozzle, the seat-hole nozzle contributes to a reduction in the engine's hydrocarbon emissions, because less fuel can vaporize into the combustion chamber.

The length of the spray orifice is limited by the nozzle cone's mechanical integrity. At present, the spray-orifice length is 0.6 ... 0.8 mm for cylindrical and conical blind holes, and 1 mm for seat-hole nozzles. The tendency is toward shorter holes, as these generally allow better control of smoke emissions.

Special heat-treating and drilling techniques must be employed to provide seat-hole nozzles (Size P with 4-mm needle diameter) with the required mechanical strength. Drilling can be used to achieve flow tolerances of ± 3.5 % in hole-type nozzles. Additional procedures can be applied to achieve tolerances of ± 2 % for particularly demanding applications.

The thermal resistance of the materials limits peak temperatures for hole-type nozzles to approx. 270 °C. Thermal-protection sleeves are available for operation in especially difficult conditions, and there are even cooled injection nozzles for large-displacement engines.

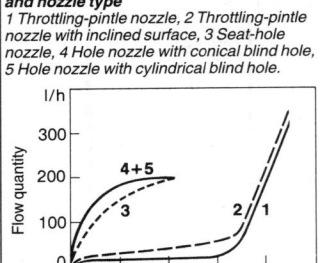

Flow quantity as function of needle stroke and nozzle type

1 Throttling-pintle nozzle, 2 Throttling-pintle nozzle with inclined surface, 3 Seat-hole nozzle, 4 Hole nozzle with conical blind hole, 5 Hole nozzle with cylindrical blind hole.

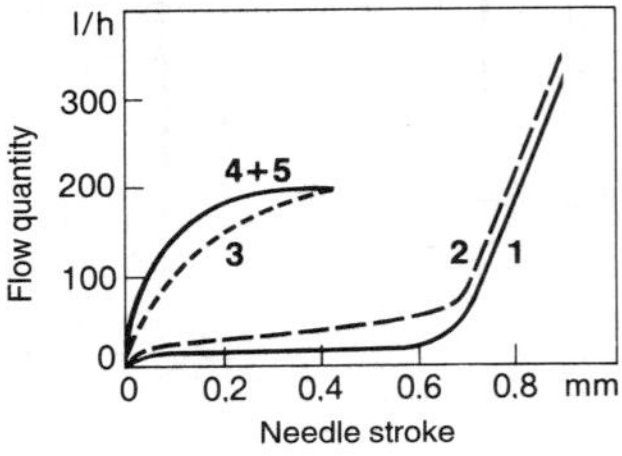

Fuel-injection pump test benches

Thorough testing and precise adjustment are indispensible if injection pumps and governors are to assist the diesel engine in achieving its optimal consumption and output while at the same time allowing it to maintain compliance with today's increasingly stringent emissions requirements. This is where the injection-pump test bench is essential. The basic specifications for test procedure and test bench are stipulated in ISO standards, which place especially stringent demands on the rigidity and drive consistency of the drive unit.

The injection pump to be tested is clamped to the test bench and its drive side is connected to the test bench's coupling. The drive unit is powered by an electric motor (with hydraulic or mechanical gear drive to flywheel and coupling, or with direct frequency control). Supply and return lines connect the injection pump to the test-bench calibration-oil supply, while pressure lines lead to the fuel-delivery measuring device which consists of test nozzles with precisely set opening pressures, and which uses spray dampers to discharge the calibrating oil into the measuring system. The pressure and temperature of the test fluid can be adjusted to comply with the test specifications.

The continuous-flow measurement method entails the use of one precision gear pump per cylinder. The gear pump's speed is regulated so that the quantity of calibrating oil which it pumps corresponds with the amount of calibrating oil being discharged. The pump's speed thus provides an index for the flow quantity per unit of time. A microprocessor analyzes the measurement results and converts them to bar-graph form for display on a monitor. This test method is characterized by a high degree of accuracy and consistently reproducible test results.

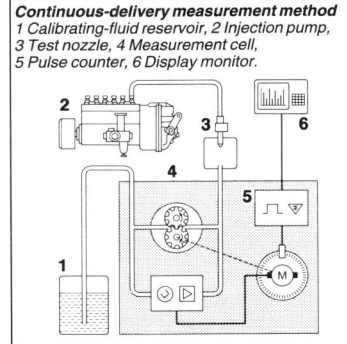

Continuous-delivery measurement method
1 Calibrating-fluid reservoir, 2 Injection pump, 3 Test nozzle, 4 Measurement cell, 5 Pulse counter, 6 Display monitor.

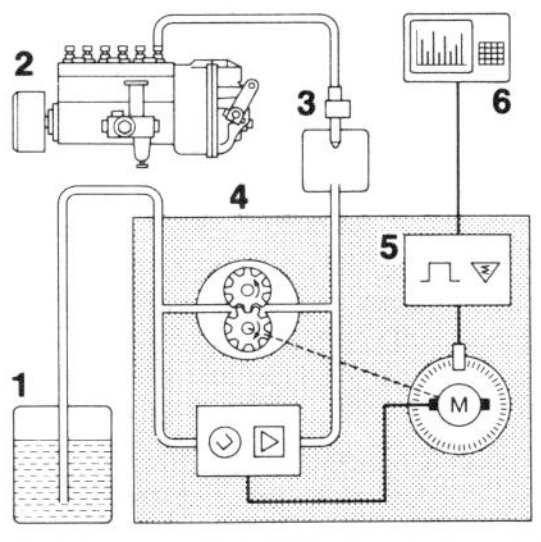

Quantity measurement with measuring glasses (graduates) starts with the calibrating oil from the test nozzles being routed past the graduates and back to the calibrating-oil reservoir. The control unit waits until the prescribed number of strokes has been entered at the stroke counter before starting the actual test by switching the calibrating-oil flow to the graduates. The flow is interrupted again once the prescribed number of strokes has been completed. The quantity of calibrating oil which has been discharged by the test nozzles can be read from the graduates.

"Motortesters" for diesel engines

The diesel-pump tester is used to calibrate the pump precisely to the engine's requirements. It monitors the pulses from the reference marks on the engine's flywheel. The unit monitors port closing (start of delivery) and timing adjustment at specific engine speeds without any need to open the high-pressure lines. An inductive clamp sensor is attached to the injection line for cylinder no. 1. In conjunction with a stroboscope or TDC sensor for monitoring crankshaft position, the diesel-pump tester determines the port closing and the degree of timing adjustment.

Another test method involves monitoring the port closing by screwing an inductive sensor into the governor housing. The sensor receives pulses from a pin located on the governor's flyweight housing. The pulses trail the signals from the TDC sensor at a specific interval; it is this interval that the unit employs to calculate the port closing.

Exhaust emissions from diesel engines

The constituents of the exhaust gases produced by diesel engines are listed together with the emissions from spark-ignition (SI) engines on pp. 478 ff. Table 1 provides information on the composition and temperature of the exhaust gases.

Mixture formation

The diesel engine operates on fuel with a higher boiling point than that burned by its gasoline-powered counterpart. The diesel also has less time to form the air-fuel mixture, which is less homogeneous as a result. Diesel engines always run on excess air ($\lambda > 1$); an insufficient quantity of excess air results in increased emissions of soot, CO and HC.

Combustion

Combustion is initiated when the injector starts to discharge fuel. The point at which combustion actually starts, as defined relative to TDC, exercises a decisive influence on combustion temperature, with attendant consequences on nitrous-oxide (NO_X) formation.

Emissions control

Engine measures

Combustion chamber

Exhaust emissions are affected by the design of the combustion chamber.

Engines featuring a divided combustion chamber (prechamber, swirl chamber) produce fewer nitrous oxides than engines with direct injection. On the other hand, direct-injection engines provide better fuel economy. The swirl pattern of the air in the combustion chamber and the fuel-discharge pattern can be matched for maximum mutual compatibility and effectiveness, resulting in a more homogeneous air-fuel mixture and more complete combustion. The combustion temperature must be high enough to ensure reliable ignition.

Fuel injection

The injection timing and sequence, and the fuel's atomization all have an effect on pollutant emissions. The point at which combustion starts is essentially a function of injection timing. Delayed injection reduces NO_X emissions; excessive delay results in higher levels of hydrocarbons in the exhaust. A deviation of 1° (crankshaft) in the start of injection can increase NO_X emissions by as much as 5%, while HC emissions climb by up to 15%. This high degree of sensitivity means that precise injection timing is essential. Electronic control systems are capable of maintaining optimum injection timing with a high degree of precision. With such an electronic diesel-control system (EDC), a crankshaft reference point provides the basis for regulating the timing device setting (port-closing control or control of start of delivery). Extremely high precision can be achieved by monitoring the start of injection directly at the injection nozzle by employing a needle-motion sensor to monitor the needle-valve's movement (control of start of injection).

Any fuel emerging into the chamber after combustion has been completed could be discharged directly into the exhaust system in unburned form, thus raising levels of hydrocarbon emissions.

To prevent this happening, the fuel volume between the injection nozzle's seat and the end of its discharge orifice is held to a minimum. It is also essential that dribble and post-injection be avoided.

A fine fuel mist promotes thorough mixture of the air and fuel, thereby contributing to reductions in emissions of soot (particulates) and hydrocarbons. This kind of fine mist is achieved with high injection pressures and optimum discharge-orifice geometry.

The maximum fuel flow for a given quantity of intake air must be limited in order to prevent the engine from producing soot emissions. Here, an excess-air factor of at least 10 ... 20 % ($\lambda =$ 1.1 ... 1.2) is required.

Intake-air temperature

Higher intake-air temperatures are accompanied by higher combustion tempera-

Table 1. Composition and temperature of exhaust gases

Exhaust-gas components		at idle	at maximum output
Nitrous oxides (NO_x)	ppm	50 ... 250	600 ... 2500
Hydrocarbons	ppm C_1	50 ... 500	150 .
Carbon monoxide	ppm	100 ... 450	350 ... 2000
Carbon dioxide	Vol%	... 3.5	12 ... 16
Water vapor	Vol%	2 ... 4	... 11
Oxygen	Vol%	18	2 ... 12
Nitrogen, etc.	Vol%	residual	residual
Soot	mg/m³	≈ 20 (SZ[2] ≈ 0.7)	≈ 200 (SZ[2] ≈ 3.5)
Exhaust-gas temperature[1]	°C	100 ... 200	550 ... 750

[1]) Downstream of exhaust valve.
[2]) SZ = Bosch sooting figure.

tures, with a commensurate increase in NO_x emissions.

On turbocharged engines, cooling the compressed intake air (intercooling) represents an effective means of inhibiting the formation of NO_x.

Exhaust-gas recirculation (EGR)
Exhaust gases can be rerouted into the intake air in order to reduce the amount of oxygen in the fresh intake charge while increasing its specific heat. Both factors engender lower combustion temperatures (thus limiting NO_x production) and reduce exhaust emissions. Excessive recirculation of exhaust gases results in higher emissions of soot, carbon monoxide and hydrocarbons, all due to insufficient air. The quantity of the recirculated exhaust gases must therefore be limited to ensure that the combustion chamber receives sufficient oxygen to support combustion of the injected fuel.

Exhaust-gas treatment
Hydrocarbon emissions are reduced with noble-metal catalytic converters in the exhaust system. In these, a portion of the gaseous hydrocarbons, including those attached to the particulates (carbon), is burned using the oxygen contained in the exhaust gas.

The catalytic converters employed to reduce NO_x emissions in gasoline engines operate with either an oxygen deficiency or a stoichiometric mixture. Diesel engines, however, can only be run on excess air (fuel economy, particulate and hydrocarbon emissions). Thus a conventional catalytic converter is not suitable for limiting NO_x emissions from diesel engines. Meanwhile, filters for installation in the exhaust system are presently being tested as a means for reducing particulate emissions (soot).

Emissions testing

Increasingly stringent regulations define the legal limits on the quantities of pollutant emissions which may be emitted by diesel engines. Such emissions are tested under defined operating conditions.

Test layout
As a general rule, exhaust emissions from car engines are tested on a chassis dynamometer, and those from truck engines on an engine test stand.

Many of the emissions limits and test procedures now in common use were first introduced in the USA, where the CVS (Constant Volume Sampling) method is prescribed as an efficient procedure for monitoring particulate emissions in dynamic test cycles. In this process, the exhaust gases produced by the vehicle are diluted with filtered ambient air and extracted with a blower during a standardized test cycle. The volume of gas extracted by the blower remains constant. Dilution inhibits condensation from forming during sample collection while also holding the temperature at the level required for particulate measurements (52 °C).

The blower provides constant extraction of the samples from the diluted exhaust gases. The sample is conducted through special filter elements, where the level of particulate emissions is determined by measuring the increase in mass.
A second, heated sample line leads to the FID (Flame Ionization Detector), which

continuously monitors the concentration of hydrocarbons (HC). A third sample is conducted into the exhaust-gas collection bags. Once the cycle has been completed, the bags' contents are fed into exhaust-gas analyzers, where the concentrations of CO, NO_X and CO_2 are measured. Calculations to determine emissions levels for the various exhaust-gas components are based on the volume of mixed gas and the concentrations of the individual components.

In the USA, the same procedures and analyzers are employed in testing emissions from passenger-car and truck engines. The exhaust gases are usually diluted twice, to make it possible to process large volumes of gases with reasonably-sized dilution tunnels while simultaneously maintaining the legally stipulated conditions. In the European stationary test cycle, partial-flow dilution is also approved for particulate measurements.

Testing for particulate levels is usually followed by an additional examination of exhaust-gas opacity in both stationary and dynamic full-throttle operation.

Driving cycles for emissions testing of diesel-powered passenger vehicles
a) USA, b) Europe, c) Japan.

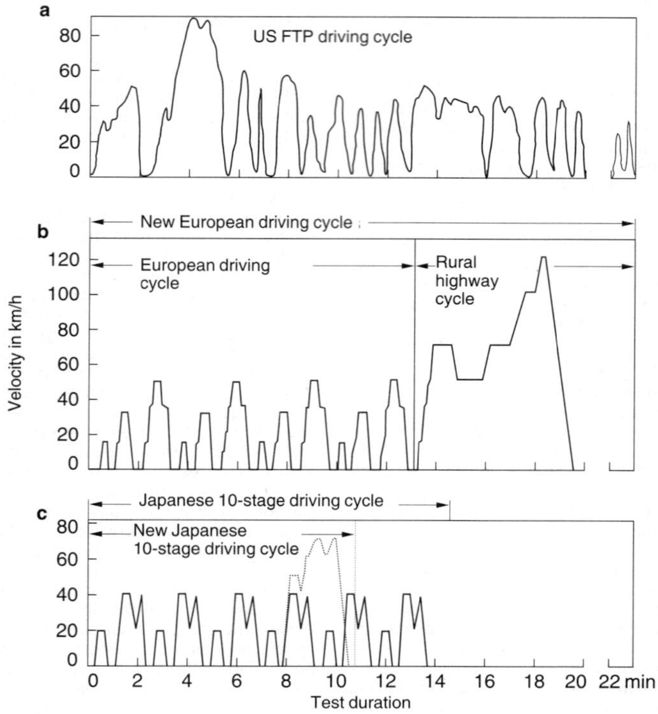

Test cycles and exhaust-emission limits in Europe

Passenger cars

The emissions regulations applied in the nations of the European Community are based on ECE Directive R15 and its appendices.

ECE Directive R15/04 for motor vehicles weighing less than 3.5 metric tons, featuring emissions limits graduated according to vehicle weight, is still partially valid. A new and more stringent series of limits classifying vehicles according to displacement is presently being introduced in several stages (Table 2). Aside from these, a particulate limit for all vehicles regardless of displacement has been in effect since 1989.

In the future, the ECE R15 driving cycle will be expanded to include a rural highway section (≤ 120 km/h), while implementation of a unified and stricter set of limits is envisaged for passenger cars (Table 2). In addition, a new driving cycle for light utility vehicles, the introduction of a limit for particulate emissions, and further reductions in permissible levels of gaseous emissions

European emissions limits

Table 2. Diesel-powered vehicles < 3.5 metric tons
European driving cycle (from ECE R15).

Reference mass	CO	$HC + NO_x$ 1)	$HC + NO_x$ 2)
kg		g/test	
≤ 1020	58	19.0	23.7
≤ 1250	67	20.5	25.6
≤ 1470	76	22.0	27.5
≤ 1700	84	23.5	29.3
≤ 1930	93	25.0	31.2
≤ 2150	101	26.5	33.1
> 2150	110	28.0	35.0

1) For passenger vehicles with transport capacity ≤ 6 persons;
2) For passenger vehicles with transport capacity > 6 persons and commercial vehicles < 3.5 tons.

Passenger vehicles with transport capacity ≤ 6 persons and < 2.5 tons approved gross vehicle weight, European driving cycle.

Displacement	Date 1)	CO	$HC + NO_x$	Particulates 2)
l			g/test	
> 2.0	1.10.88	30	8	1.1
1.4 ... 2.0	1.10.91	30	8	1.1
< 1.4	1.10.90	45	15 3)	1.1
< 1.4	1.10.92	19	5	1.1

1) Separate regulation for direct-injection engines; 2) Universal particulate limits from 1.10.89; Separate regulation for direct-injection engines; 3) NO_x limit of 6 g/test also applicable.

Planned emissions limits for passenger vehicles ≤ 6 persons and AGVW < 2.5 tons, as prescribed in the directive issued by the European Council of Ministers: European driving cycle including rural highway component.

No classification as per engine displacement	Date	CO	$HC + NO_x$	Particulates
			g/km	
	1.7.92 1)	2.72	0.97	0.14

1) 1.7.94 for displacements < 1.4 l.

are all planned. The limit on exhaust-gas opacity prescribed in ECE R24 will be maintained.

The "Stockholm Group" of nations (Sweden, Switzerland, Austria) base their emissions standards on US regulations. Drving cycle and emissions limits correspond to those contained in the US 1987 regulations (Table 3).

Commercial vehicles

In Europe, vehicles of > 3.5 tons approved gross vehicle weight which are equipped with more than 9 seats are subjected to the 13-stage test prescribed by ECE R49. The test sequence is a series of 13 different stationary operating modes. The emissions measurements from the different stages provide the basis for the calculations used to determine mean emissions levels.

The original limits for gaseous emissions have been lowered, and the regulation has been extended to include a limit on particulate emissions. Meanwhile, the stipulations governing exhaust-gas opacity as contained in ECE R24 and similar regulations have been retained (Table 4).

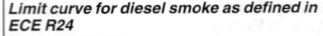

Limit curve for diesel smoke as defined in ECE R24

Lowest test rpm:
$0.45 \cdot n_{nom}$ or at least 1000 min^{-1}.

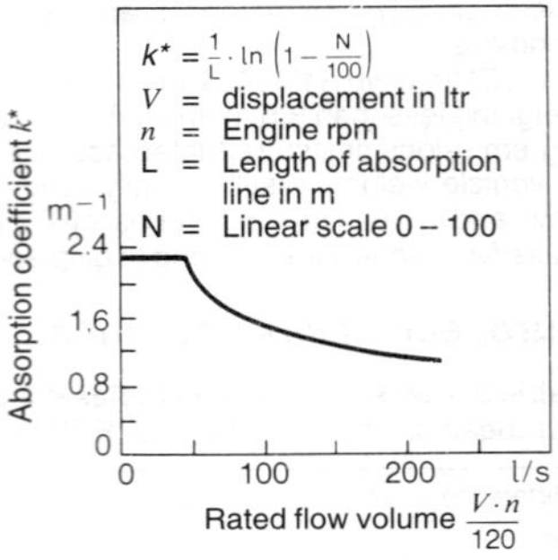

Table 3. Passenger vehicles in Sweden, Switzerland, Austria

FTP 75 Driving cycle	CO	HC	NOx	Particulates
	g/km			
Limits	2.1	0.25	0.62	0.124[1])
Sweden 10.92 (10.94)	2.1	0.25 (0.19)	0.25	0.05

[1]) Present Austrian limit = 0.373 g/km (≙ US '83). Austria and Switzerland also have limits on smoke emissions similar to those of ECE R24; in Sweden HSU 45/3.5 BSU.

Table 4. Heavy trucks (> 3.5 tons AGVW)

Test sequence: 13-stage European test (from ECE R 49) with partial or full-flow CVS unit added for measuring particulates

		ECE R49	EG	Switzerland		Austria		Sweden		EC-proposals		
Date		1983	10.90	10.87	10.91	01.88	10.91 (10.93)	1994	1993[1])	07.92		10.96
HC	g/kWh	3.5	2.4	2.1	1.23	2.8	1.2	1.2	0.6	1.1		1.1
CO		14.0	11.2	8.4	4.9	11.2	4.9	4.9	2.0	4.5		4.0
NOx		18.0	14.4	14.4	9.0	14.4	9.0	7.0	7.0	8.0		7.0
Part.		–	–	–	0.7	-	0.7 (0.4)	0.4	0.15	0.36	> 85 kW	0.15
										0.63	≤ 85kW	0.3

Smoke emissions also limited as in ECE R24 or similar.
[1]) For urban-use vehicles.

Test cycles and exhaust-emission limits in Japan

Passenger cars
A 10-stage driving cycle is used to determine the concentrations of gaseous pollutants in the exhaust gas produced by diesels. From 1993 onward, the driving cycle is to be extended to include a high-speed section (similar to Europe). The emissions limits and the more stringent requirements envisaged for the future are shown in Table 5.

Commercial vehicles
The concentrations of gaseous pollutants in diesel-engine exhaust emissions are determined during stationary testing in a 6-stage driving cycle. The results include both the maximum values and a weighted average.

A 13-stage test procedure (similar to Europe) is also planned. The exhaust-emission limits are listed in Table 6.

There is also a limit on full-throttle (WOT) exhaust-gas opacity.

Japanese emissions limits

Table 5. Diesel-powered passenger vehicles (≤ 10 persons)

Driving cycle: 10-stage test / New 10-stage test (approx. 1992)									3-stage-test
	Vehicle weight	HC		CO		NO_x		Part.	Smoke[1])
	kg	g/km							
present limits[2])	max. ≤ 1200 > 1250	max. 0.62 0.62	avg. 0.4 0.4	max. 2.7 2.7	avg. 2.1 2.1	max. 0.98 1.26	avg. 0.7 0.9	 – –	50 % or 5 BSZ[3])
approx. 1992...94	≤ 1250 > 1250	–		–		0.72 0.84	0.5 0.6	0.2 0.2	40 % 40 %
planned within next decade	–	–		–			0.4	0.08	25 %

[1]) Limit for smoke emissions under full load/acceleration. [2]) Introduction dates for domestically produced and for imported vehicles vary. [3]) BSZ = Bosch sooting figure.

Table 6. Diesel-powered commercial vehicles > 2.5 tons AGVW

Driving cycle: 6-stage test / New 13-stage test									3-stage-test
		HC		CO		NO_x		Part.	Smoke[1])
6-stage-test		ppm							
Present limits	DI[2]) IDI[3])	max. 670 670	avg. 510 510	max. 980 980	avg. 790 790	max. 520 350	avg. 400 260	 – –	50% or 5 BSZ[4])
13-stage-test		g/kWh							
approx. 1994	DI[2]) IDI[3])	–		–		6.0 5.0	6.0 5.0	0.7 0.7	40% 40%
planned within next decade	–	–		–		4.5	4.5	0.25	25%

[1]) Limit for smoke emissions under full load/acceleration.
[2]) Direct injection. [3]) Indirect injection.
[4]) BSZ = Bosch sooting figure.

US test cycles and exhaust-emission limits

The FTP (Federal Test Procedure) 75 driving cycle applies to passenger cars and light commercial vehicles with an approved gross vehicle weight of less than 8500 lbs (see diagram). The speed curve corresponds to an urban operation cycle in the USA. Testing is performed on a chassis dynamometer, and the results are measured using the CVS method. The limits are provided in Table 7.

The present US emissions regulations embrace a multiplicity of variegated options, including various long-term performance requirements, recall conditions, etc.; this work can therefore provide only a brief synopsis of this enormously complex regulatory framework. Since 1987, heavy-truck engines have been tested on an engine dynamometer in a non-stationary driving cycle (transient cycle), with emissions being measured according to the CVS method. The test cycle is based on highway operation under real-world conditions. The opacity of the exhaust gas is monitored in a separate test (Federal Smoke Cycle).
See Table 8 for limits.

Exhaust-emissions testing equipment

Emissions testing on diesel engines, whether performed as an adjunct to servicing procedures or during regular inspections of road vehicles, concentrates on determining the levels of particulate emissions.

Two standard procedures are used:
– For the filter method a specified quantity of exhaust gas is drawn through a filter element. The filter's level of discoloration then provides an index for the amount of soot contained in the exhaust gas.
– The absorption method (opacity or darkening test) bases on the attenuation in the strength of a light beam which is transmitted through the exhaust gas.

Measurements of diesel smoke emissions must be performed under load, as this is the only operating condition under which any significant quantities of particulates are produced. Here, as well, two different test procedures are in common use:
– Testing under full load, performed on a chassis dynamometer or on a measured test course against the vehicle's brakes.

US Emissions limits

Table 7. Diesel-powered passenger vehicles

Driving cycle: US FTP 75; Fed. 49 states, California						
Model year	HC	NMHC1)	NO_x	CO	Part.	Durability
	g/Mile					Miles
1887 Fed.	0.41	–	1.0	3.4	0.20	50 000
1989 Cal.	0.46	–	1.0	8.3	0.08²)	100 000
1993 Cal.³)	–	0.31	1.0	4.2	0.08²)	100 000
1994 Fed.⁴)	–	0.25	1.0	3.4	0.08	50 000
1994 Fed.⁴)	–	0.31	1.25	4.2	0.10	100 000

1) Methane-free HC; 2) for particulates: Long-term performance requirement 50,000 miles;
3) 40% of planned production must conform to new limits from 1993 model year onward;
1994: 80%; 1995: 100% of planned production; 4) 40% of planned production must conform to new limits from 1994 model year onward; 1995: 80%; 1996: 100% of planned production.

Table 8. Diesel-powered heavy commercial vehicles (> 8500 lbs AGVW)

Model year	HC	NO_x	CO	Part.	Smoke
	g/bhp · h				% Opacity
1990	1.3	6.0	15.5	0.6	A: Acceleration: 20%
1991...93	1.3	5.0	15.5	0.25¹)	B: Deceleration from
1994...97	1.3	5.0	15.5	0.1	full load: 15%
1998	1.3	4.0	15.5	0.1	C: Peak smoke: 50%

1) Urban buses 0.1 g/bhp · h.

– Testing under free acceleration with a brief application of a specified pressure to the accelerator pedal; load is provided by the reciprocating and centrifugal masses represented by the accelerating engine.

As the results of testing for diesel smoke emissions vary according to both test procedure and type of load, they are not generally suitable for direct mutual comparisons.

Smoke tester (opacity measurement)

During testing, a pump diverts a portion of the exhaust gas to a test chamber after extracting it through a sampling tube and hose. This procedure's particular virtue lies in its preventing the exhaust-gas pressure and its fluctuations from distorting the test results.

Within the test chamber, a light beam is transmitted through the diesel exhaust gases. Photoelectric equipment monitors the reduction in the beam's intensity, which is then indicated as % opacity N or as absorption coefficient K. The length of the test chamber must be precisely defined and the test chamber's window must be equipped with thermal protection against soot deposits in order to ensure consistent and precise results.

Measurement and display assume the form of a continuous process during testing under load. For free acceleration, the entire test curve is recorded in digital form. The tester automatically determines the maximum value and calculates the mean from several gas pulses.

Smoke tester (filter method)

This test device extracts a specified quantity of diesel exhaust gas through a paper filter strip. Consistent, mutually comparable test results are achieved by recording the volume of gas processed in each test step; the device converts the results to a standardized form. The system also monitors and compensates for other factors such as pressure, temperature and the dead volume between sampling tube and paper filter.

A reflective photometer is used for optoelectronic evaluation of the darkened filter paper. The result is indicated as the Bosch sooting figure (BSZ) or as mass concentration (mg/m^3).

Smoke tester (opacity measurement)
a) Schematic diagram,
b) Gas-surge measurement
1 Collection probe, 2 Switchover valve for scavenge air, 3 Measurement chamber, 4 Measurement section, 5 Lamp, 6 Receiver, 7 Pump.

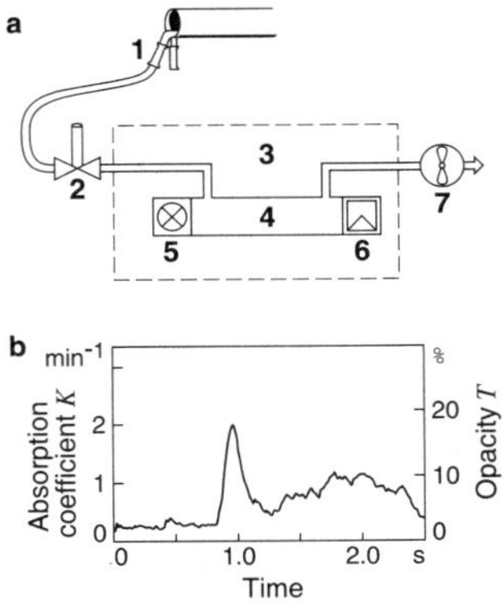

Smoke tester (filter method)
1 Paper filter, 2 Gas passage, 3 Photometer, 4 Paper transport, 5 Volume measurement, 6 Switchover valve for scavenge air, 7 Pump.

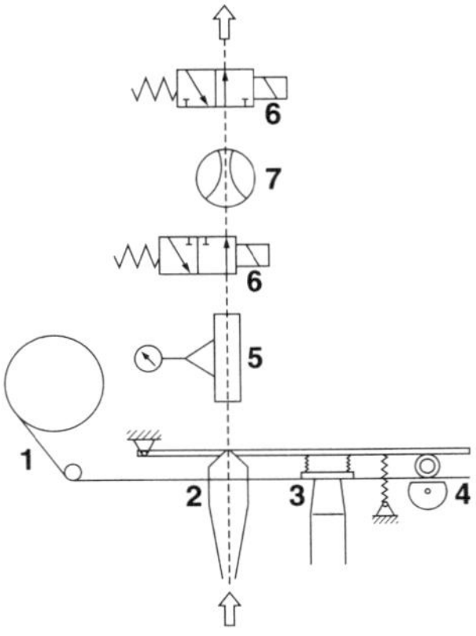

Auxiliary starting devices

Cold diesel engines are reluctant to start. Blowby and thermal losses reduce the maximum compression pressure and associated peak temperatures to such a degree as to render starting impossible without the assistance of auxiliary devices. The individual temperature threshold depends upon the specific engine design. Direct-injection (DI) engines, with their single-section combustion chambers and relatively low thermal losses, start more readily than prechamber or induced-turbulence engines (two-section combustion chamber).

On large-displacement DI engines (such as those used in heavy vehicles), a flame plug, heater plug or heater flange is employed to preheat the air in the intake tract.

Sheathed-element glow plugs

On engines featuring a divided combustion chamber and on small-displacement DI engines, starting (especially in the cold) is improved by installing an auxiliary starting device in the form of a sheathed-element glow plug adjacent to the injector.

On prechamber and induced-turbulence engines, the glow element extends into the subchamber, and on DI engines into the main combustion chamber. When heated, the sheathed-element glow plug forms a hot spot within the turbulence chamber. It is here that a portion of the fuel vaporizes before it ignites the mixture.

Modern glow-plug systems continue to operate briefly after the engine has started, improving initial operation while reducing blue-smoke emissions and combustion noise. It must be noted, however, that the high temperatures associated with this practice do subject the glow plug to additional stresses.

The electrical energy for operating the sheathed-element glow plug is provided by the vehicle's electrical system via the preglow-control unit.

Design and characteristics

The main component in the sheathed-element glow plug is the tubular heating element. Firm, gas-tight installation in the glow-plug shell ensures that it can resist both corrosion and hot gases. The ele-

Sheathed-element glow plug
1 Terminal, 2 Round nut, 3 Insulation washer, 4 Seal, 5 Sheath, 6 Threads, 7 Control coil, 8 Annular gap, 9 Conical seat, 10 Insulating powder, 11 Heater coil, 12 Glow tube.

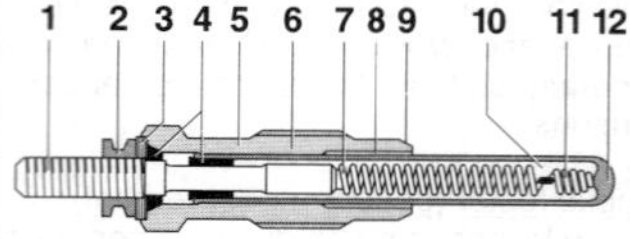

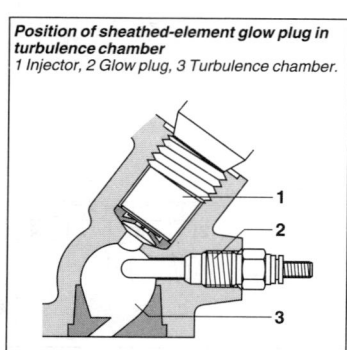

Position of sheathed-element glow plug in turbulence chamber
1 Injector, 2 Glow plug, 3 Turbulence chamber.

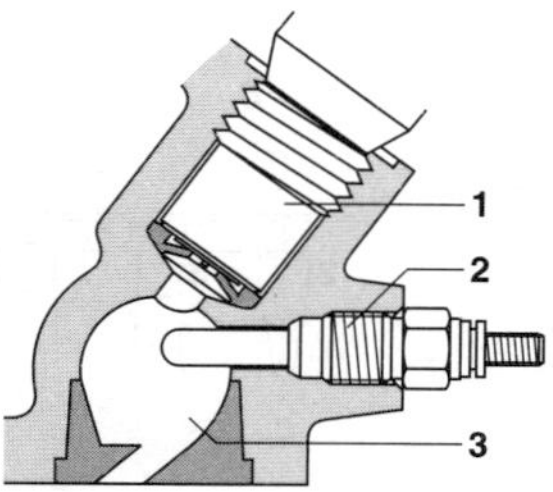

Temperature of sheathed-element glow plug as function of time
1 S-RSK, 2 GSK2.

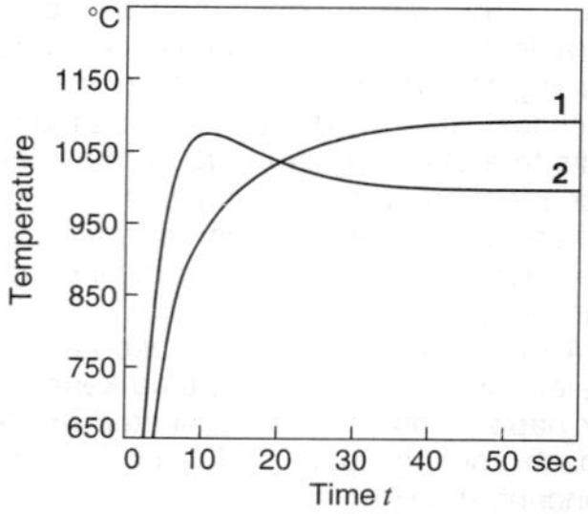

Flame plug
1 Fuel metering unit, 2 Fuel input, 3 Filter, 4 Socket threads, 5 Seal, 6 Shell, 7 Vaporizing tube with filter, 8 Glow element, 9 Flame sleeve.

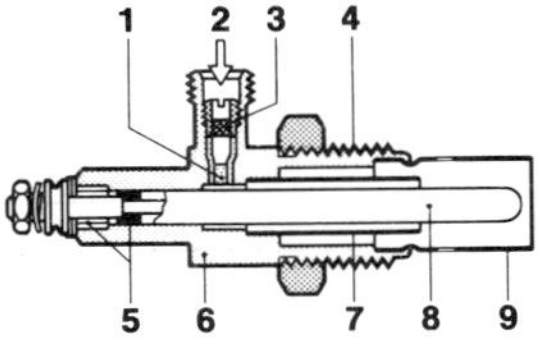

ment contains a spiral filament embedded in magnesium-oxide powder. The spiral filament comprises a heater coil installed in the tip of the glow tube and connected in series with the control coil. The heater coil's resistance is virtually insensitive to temperature.

Circuit continuity is provided by welding the ground side of the heater coil to the inner tip of the glow tube, and by connecting the control coil to the terminal screw. The terminal screw, in turn, connects the glow plug to the vehicle's electrical system.

The control coil has a PTC characteristic (resistance increases along with temperature) which means that substantially more current flows through a cold plug than through a warm one, and then decreases along with increasing temperature.

Design and materials are specially selected to provide specific heating characteristics. Conventional S-RSK sheathed-element glow plugs employ a nickel control coil, while second-generation plugs (GSK2) use a special alloy. The diagrams illustrate specific resistance relative to temperature for both types of glow plug.

Specific resistance of control coil as function of temperature
1 S-RSK, 2 GSK2.

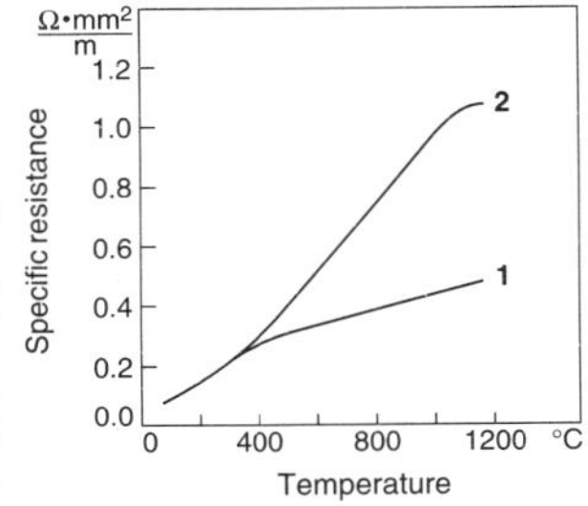

Compared to the earlier S-RSK models, the GSK2 is faster in reaching the temperature required for ignition. At the same time, its continuous-operation temperature is lower, meaning that the GSK2 can remain switched on for up to 3 minutes after starting in order to reduce exhaust emissions and noise.

Flame plug

The flame plug heats the intake air by burning fuel. The standard layout uses the injection system's supply pump to provide the flame plug with fuel via a solenoid valve. The flame plug's fuel-input fitting includes both a filter and the metering unit responsible for providing the correct amount of fuel for the specific engine. The fuel vaporizes in the vaporizing tube encompassing the flame plug before mixing with the intake air. The mixture ignites at the tip of the flame plug which reaches temperatures of over 1000 °C.

Heater plug and heater flange

Both of these devices employ electrically-heated glow elements or coils to warm the intake air. Their use is particularly widespread on small engines, where they are installed between the air filter and the cylinder head.

Glow-control unit

The complete glow-control unit includes both the glow or flame plug and a device for controlling the glow process. While today's flame plugs still generally employ a bimetallic switch to indicate when the engine is ready to start, systems with sheathed-element glow plugs incorporate electronic glow-control units. In addition to controlling the glow times and the ready-to-start indicator, these units also incorporate protective and monitoring functions.

Design

The glow-control unit essentially consists of a power relay to regulate the glow-plug current, electronic circuitry to control glow times and ready-to-start indicator, and the elements for the protective functions. The unit is generally installed in the engine compartment, where it is enclosed in a plastic housing for protection against dust and water. The glow-control unit is equipped with the following inputs

- Terminal 30 – Battery positive,
- Terminal 31 – Ground
- Terminal 15 – Glow-plug and starter switch,
- Terminal 50 – Starter control,
- NTC temperature sensor (in some applications),
- LS load switch (in some applications)

and the outputs

- Start-indicator lamp La,
- Glow-plug connections G1... G6.

Basic unit

The glow duration is controlled by a temperature sensor installed in the glow-control unit. It provides the optimal glow-plug temperature for good starting in accordance with the engine/glow plug combination. At the end of the glow period, the start-indicator lamp goes out to signal that the engine can be started. The glow process continues for as long as the starter remains in operation, or until the safety override – installed to limit loads on battery and glow plugs – is activated. A strip fuse provides protection against short circuits.

Typical glow sequence

1 Glow-start switch, 2 Starter, 3 Start-indicator lamp, 4 Load switch, 5 Glow plugs. t_V Glow time, t_S Ready to start, t_N Post-start operation.

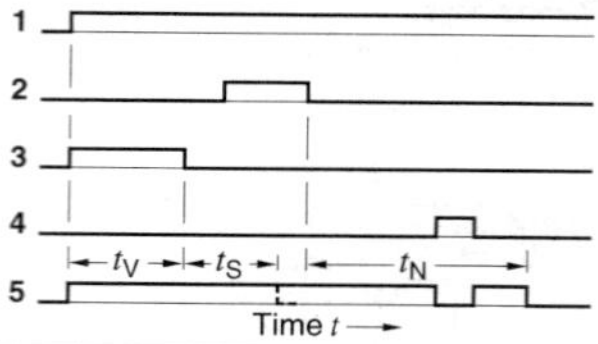

Expanded-function units

An engine-mounted sensor (NTC in coolant) provides an input to support precision control of glow times, which are also adjusted by the glow-control unit to compensate for fluctuations in battery voltage. Current continues to flow to the glow plugs once the engine has started. An engine-load monitor is used to interrupt or switch off the glow process, and an electronic override circuit provides protection against overvoltage and short circuit. A monitoring circuit detects glow-plug failure and relay errors, which are displayed through the start-indicator lamp.

Units with central glow control

This type of unit receives information on when glow-plug operation is required, and when not, directly from the engine's central ECU which is also the address to which the glow-control unit reports errors which it has detected via a diagnosis line.

Glow-plug and starting system for diesel engines

1 Battery, 2 Starter, 3 Glow-plug and starter switch, 4 Glow-control unit, 5 Coolant temperature sensor, 6 Internal temperature sensor (alternative to 5), 7 Sheathed-element glow plugs, 8 Start-indicator switch, 9 Load switch.

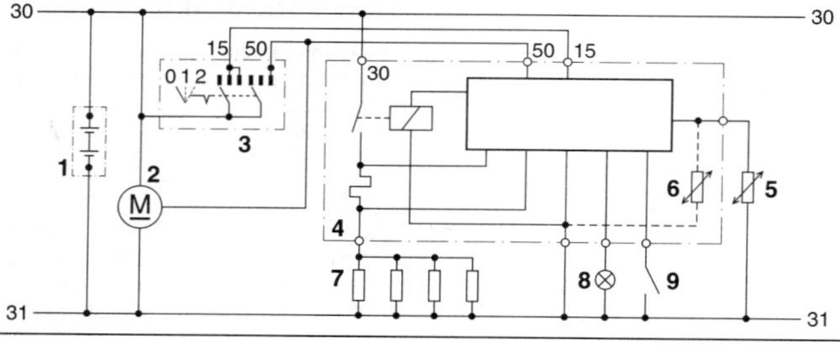

Starting systems

Most starting systems for IC engines comprise a battery-driven DC motor (starter motor), switchgear, control units and the associated wiring. The rotational speed required to start the engine (SI engines: approx. 60 ... 100 min^{-1}; diesel engines: approx 80 ... 200 min^{-1}) are far lower than the starter speed. The starter cranks the engine via a gear pair (starter pinion and engine ring gear) with a suitable step-down ratio (between approx. 10 : 1 and 20 : 1, see "Starter tooth design", p. 296).

Influencing variables

The crankshaft torque and the minimum rotational speed required to start the engine depend among other things upon engine type, engine swept volume, number of cylinders, compression, bearing friction, additional loads driven by the engine, the fuel-management system, engine oil and temperature.

The torque and rotational speed required for starting both increase with declining temperatures, with the result being a higher demand for starter output.

The battery internal resistance increases as its temperature and its state of charge drop. The battery no-load voltage decreases as temperature drops. The higher the battery output curent and the lower the temperature, the lower is the battery terminal voltage. In addition, the battery capacity decreases as temperature decreases and the battery discharge current increases. Therefore the lower the temperature, the less power the battery can supply. In addition to the engine design characteristics, the minimum temperature at which the engine will start is a central factor in determining starting system power.

Permanent field starter with intermediate transmission

1 Engaging shift lever, 2 Engagement solenoid and solenoid switch, 3 Overrunning clutch with pinion, 4 Intermediate transmission (planetary gear), 5 Armature, 6 Permanent magnets.

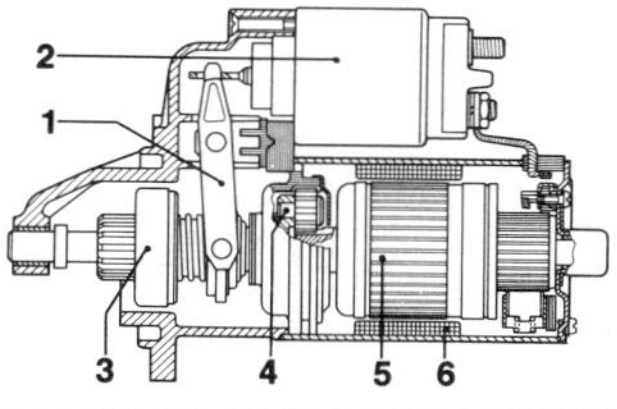

Starters

A starter comprises the following major components:

- Electric motor
- Pinion-engaging drive
- Overrunning clutch.

The functions these components must perform can be seen in the following description of the starting procedure.

The pinion must initially engage the ring gear. When the engine starts and runs up to speed, it spins the pinion faster than the starter does and would eventually destroy the starter due to centrifugal force. To prevent this, an overrunning clutch is installed between pinion and armature shaft which breaks connection between them as soon as the engine "overtakes" the starter.

Electric motor

In most cases, a DC series-wound motor is used, whose initial torque is high enough to begin cranking the IC engine, and which is characterized by a high no-load speed which supports engine run-up. In starters whose starting power is higher, an additional shunt winding promotes smoother starter operation as the starter engages the ring gear, and limits starter no-load speed during the starting process.

Progress made to date in ferrite technology permits the use of demagnetization-resistant starter motors with permanent-magnet excitation.

Starters with armatures which rotate at a higher speed but deliver lower torque can be made lighter and smaller.For such a starter to become a practical proposition, the crankshaft/starter-armature gear ratio must be increased. The ring-gear diameter cannot be increased, so the increased gear ratio is achieved through the use of an additional transmission stage which is in an integral part of the starter (reduction-gear starters).

Pinion-engaging drives
(Engaging systems)

Inertia-drive starters
The inertia drive (as employed, e.g., in lawn mowers) is the simplest form of pinion-engaging drive. A helical spline in the shaft slides the overrunning clutch forward when the armature rotates. When the starter is switched on, the unloaded armature begins to rotate freely. The pinion and overrunning clutch do not yet rotate due to their inertia, and are pushed forward by the spline. As soon as the pinion makes contact with the ring gear, it is kept from rotating and pushed further forward until contact with the stop ring is made. At this point, the overrunning clutch begins to transmit the armature torque to the ring gear via the pinion, and the engine is cranked.

As soon as the engine begins to rotate the pinion at a speed above armature speed, the overrunning clutch interrupts the transmission of force and the friction of the overrunning clutch attempts to accelerate it above armature speed. This causes the overrunning clutch and pinion to slide backward in the helical spline. This disengagement process is augmented by the return spring, which keeps the pinion disengaged when the starter is not running.

Pre-engaged-drive starters
In pre-engaged-drive starters, an engagement solenoid which incorporates the switching contacts for the starter current, engages the pinion with the ring gear. When the starting switch is closed, the hold-in winding H is energized, and current flows through the series circuit comprising pull-in winding E and electric motor. The engagement solenoid picks up and moves overrunning clutch and pinion forward via an engaging shift lever and meshing spring.

If the pinion and ring gear happen to find themselves in mutually optimal positions, then the pinion will immediately mesh with a gap in the ring gear's teeth. In this case the pinion teeth's engagement depth in the ring gear increases until the travel limit is reached and the contact bridge in the solenoid switch hits the relay contacts; at this point the full voltage is applied to the starter motor.

If the pinion teeth do not immediately mesh with the ring-gear gaps, the ring gear prevents the pinion from advancing any further. The engaging lever then compresses the meshing spring, and the main contact closes wihtout the pinion having engaged. The electric motor then turns the pinion which is in contact with the face of the ring gear until a pinion tooth finds a ring-gear gap and the meshing spring pushes the pinion and overrunning clutch forward.

When the solenoid winding is de-energized, the return spring pushes the solenoid plunger and pinion with overrunning clutch into the rest position. This disengagement procedure is augmented by the helical spline during overrunning.

Inertia-drive starter *(diagram)*
1 Starting switch, 2 Starting relay, 3 Excitation winding, 4 Ring gear, 5 Pinion with overrunning clutch, 6 Helical spline, 7 Armature, 8 Battery.

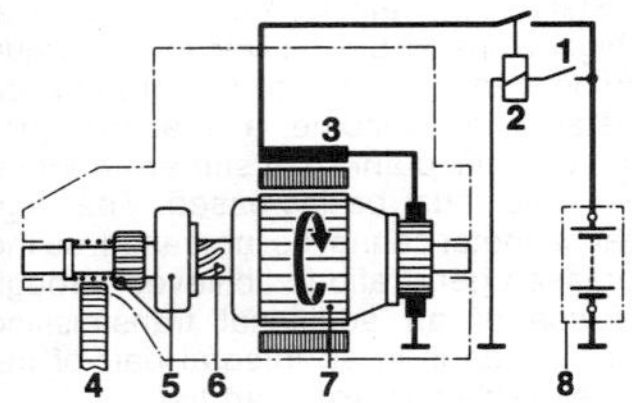

Pre-engaged-drive starter *(diagram)*
1 Starting switch, 2 Solenoid switch, 3 Excitation winding, 4 Engaging shift lever, 5 Ring gear, 6 Pinion with overrunning clutch, 7 Helical spline, 8 Armature, 9 Battery.

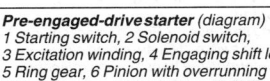

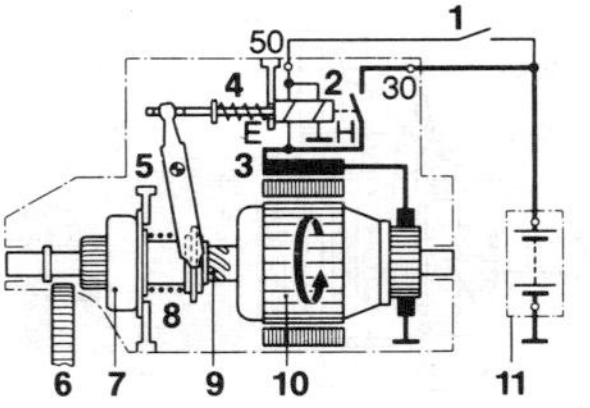

Sliding-gear starters
The sliding-gear drive switches the starter on in two stages.

When the starting switch is closed, battery voltage is applied in parallel to the hold-in winding H of the engagement solenoid and in parallel to the control relay. The control relay picks up, but is held in contact position 1 (first stage) by a tripping lever and notch. Battery voltage is applied to the pull-in winding E of the engagement solenoid and the shunt winding of the motor which are connected in parallel with one another and in series with the armature. The starter begins to rotate, however, it can only generate low torque due to the high winding resistances in series with the armature winding. The engagement solenoid simultaneously pushes the pinion in the direction of the ring gear, and allows it to engage at low torque. Shortly before the end of meshing travel is reached, the engagement solenoid releases the latched control relay which immediately moves into contact position 2 (second stage). The starting current now flows through the series winding and the armature. The changeover contact on the engagement solenoid connects shunt winding parallel to the armature and the series winding. The starter develops full torque.

Sliding-gear starter *(circuit diagram)*
1 Starting switch, 2 Control relay, 3 Tripping lever, 4 Pinion, 5 Ring gear, 6 Changeover contact, 7 Engagement solenoid, 8 Series winding, 9 Shunt winding, 10 Battery.

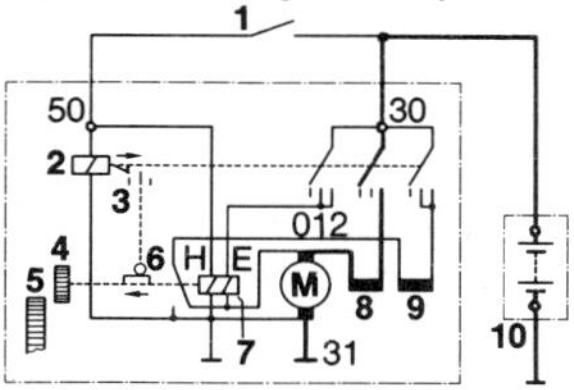

Roller-type overrunning clutch
1 Pinion, 2 Clutch shell, 3 Roller race, 4 Roller, 5 Pinion shaft, 6 Spring, a Direction of rotation.

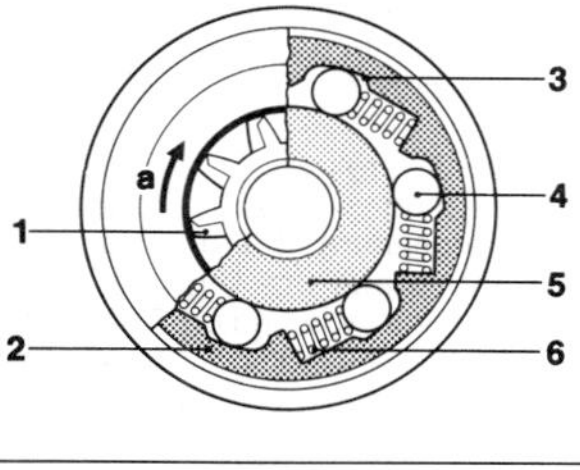

Overrunning clutch types
Overrunning clutches protect the starter armature from excessive speed when "overtaken" by the engine.

Roller-type overrunning clutch
Small and medium-sized starters generally have an overrunning clutch in which rollers are pushed by springs into wedge-shaped recesses between the clutch shell and the pinion shaft. When torque is applied by the starter, the rollers are wedged tight and torque is transmitted from the shell to the pinion shaft.

When torque is applied in the opposite direction, the rollers are forced loose and the pinion is decoupled from the starter.

Multiplate overrunning clutch
The multiplate overrunning clutch is used in large starters in commercial vehicles. The driver with the outer plates and the starter armature, and on the other side the driving shaft and the pinion are positively connected to one another. The inner plates fit in an inner clutch race which rides axially in a helical spline in the driver shaft. Under no-load conditions the plate stack is lightly compressed by the compression spring, and can only transmit low torque. As load increases, the inner clutch race is moved by the helical spline in the direction of the compression spring, which is thus more strongly compressed and presses the plates more tightly together. The multiplate overrunning clutch is therefore able to transmit increasing torque as the starter load increases.

Radial-tooth overrunning clutch
The radial-tooth overrunning clutch is also used in large commercial vehicle starters.

The entire clutch system is coupled to the armature shaft, on which it slide axially (meshing), by means of spur toothing in the dirt sleeve. The outer surface of the dirt sleeve has a helical spline, and transmits the torque to a clutch nut which further transmits the torque to the pinion by means of the steep flanks of the sawtooth-shaped radial teeth. During overrun, the pinion pushes the clutch nut backwards by means of the shallow flanks of the radial teeth, and interrupts the transmission of force. The disengaging ring is also moved backward, and held in the disengaging position by the flyweights. The centrifugal force developed by the flyweights at low pinion speeds no longer suffices to keep the overrunning clutch in its disengaged position, and the spring again pushes the clutch nut into the pinion.

Multiplate overrunning clutch
1 Drive shaft (connected to pinion), 2 Compression spring, 3 Driver with outer plates, 4 Inner clutch race with inner plates, 5 Helical spline, 6 Drive end (connected to armature).

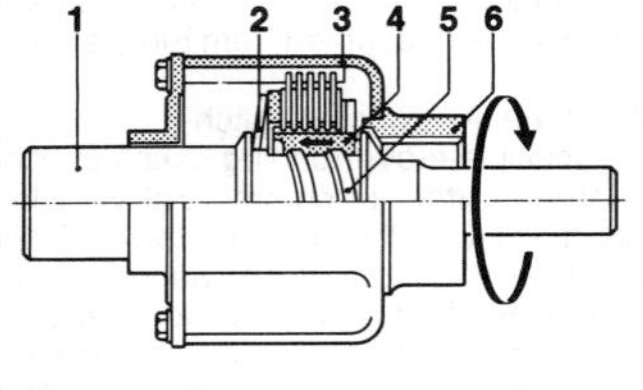

Radial-tooth overrunning clutch
1 Pinion, 2 Flyweight, 3 Radial teeth, 4 Disengaging ring, 5 Clutch nut, 6 Spring, 7 Helical spline, 8 Rubber buffer, 9 Dirt sleeve, 10 Spur toothing.

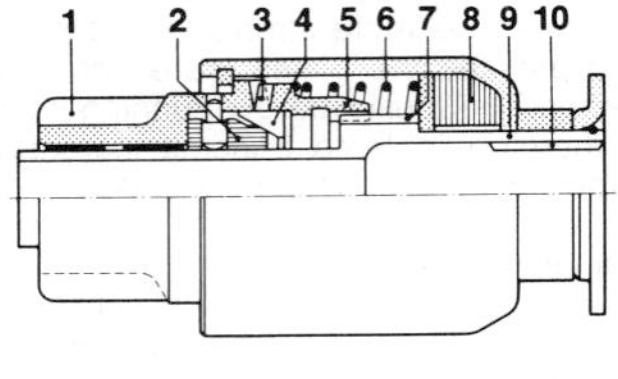

Starter protection

Starter power is also a function of the size of the vehicle battery. Thermal loads in the current-carrying parts and mechanical loads in the torque transmission parts increase as battery size increases. It is for this reason that a maximum permissible battery size is usually specified for each starter type. Although the starter is designed to operate for only short periods of time, its design must allow for longer cranking times and thus increased thermal load at low temperatures.

Small starters are designed such that they can be operated at low temperatures using a battery of maximum permissible size until the battery charge is completely exhausted. In the case of larger starters, excessively long operating times are prevented by built-in thermo-switches (e.g., in the carbon brushes). In remote control starting system (e.g., rear-engine buses, emergency power generator sets, diesel railroad cars, etc.) on the other hand, the starting procedure cannot always be monitored by the driver.

Operating errors can damage the starter or ring gear.

Start-locking relays

Start-locking relays keep the starter from engaging an already running engine and running for too long after the engine has started. The start-locking relay uses the alternator voltage, which increases as the engine runs, as an indicator of engine operation. As the engine slows down after the ignition switch is turned off, the alternator no longer produces a usable voltage "signal"; in this case a timer in the start-locking relay blocks any repeated attempt to use the starting system for a few seconds.

Start-repeating relays

Start-repeating relays interrupt the starting procedure if the pinion is still unable to engage the ring gear, but the starter remains switched on. These relays prevent the windings from being energized for too long without the starter operating.

Electric drives

Electric drives represent an alternative power source for all vehicles from which quiet, emissions-free operation is required in applications where relatively modest operating ranges and performance levels are sufficient.

Vehicles with electric drive units emit no exhaust gases, and, at speeds of up to approx. 50 km/h, they are virtually silent as well. Electric vehicles (EV's) can be classified as either road-going or internal-transport vehicles (industrial trucks), depending upon the intended application. Internal-transport vehicles are employed in industry for transport duties on company premises, and are generally not registered for operation on public roads. Their top speed is below 50 km/h. More than half of all internal-transport vehicles rely on electric drive units, while the number of similarly-equipped road vehicles is still quite limited.

Electricity supply

The infrastructure for providing a large number of electric vehicles with power is already available. Two million electric highway vehicles would require less than 1 % of the electricity production in Germany; the energy supply for the road-going electric vehicles expected up to the year 2000 is thus ensured.

An electric-drive vehicle for road use can be recharged from any normal household socket. The socket's power limitation (short-term charging 3.6 kVA, long-term charging 2.2 kVA) provides the maximum output levels for the battery-charging unit installed in the vehicle. Based on the battery charge curve, this gives a charging time in the order of 8 hours for a 10 kWh lead-acid battery. Three-phase current supplies make it possible to employ battery chargers with substantially higher output levels than those normally found in internal-transport vehicles. This permits substantial reductions in charging time.

Batteries

At the present time, due to economic considerations, lead-acid batteries represent the only realistic alternative for widespread application in electric vehicles. However, a number of other battery systems are on the threshold of series production.

Lead-acid battery

Although the essential design of the lead-acid battery remains the same as that of the starter battery (s. "Starter battery," p. 763), the combinations of materials and the cell design are specially adapted to the particular requirements of traction oper-

Electric-vehicle drive (block diagram)

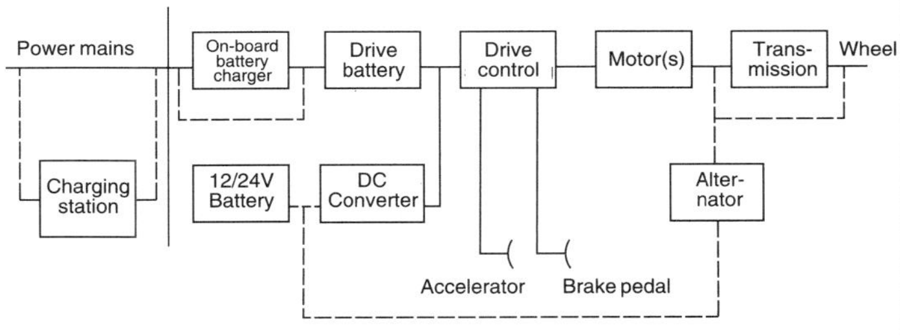

ation. The batteries commonly used in industrial transport are generally combinations of individual cells; while due to the high energy density which then becomes available, electric cars and transporters have largely adopted a modular design based on 3 or 6 cells. Industrial-transport vehicles generally employ lead-acid batteries with a liquid electrolyte, which must be topped-up with water on a regular basis. As a battery-charging station is generally already available, the maintenance requirements are viewed as acceptable. Because they do not require maintenance, solid-electrolyte lead-acid batteries offer substantial advantages in road-going vehicles.

Under real-world conditions, vehicles equipped with lead-acid batteries have a range of approx. 50 km between charges in city driving. It is not possible to achieve any substantial increase in this range in larger transporters and buses. With the appropriate recharging technology, the daily driving range amounts to many times 50 km.

The amount of energy available from a lead-acid battery decreases along with falling temperature. This means that a battery-heating arrangement is required in some climates if a reduction in driving range during winter is to be avoided.

Due to the substantial thermal capacity, the battery heating produced during charging with electrical energy is sufficient.

Because their electrolyte participates in the chemical reaction, the capacity of lead batteries depends upon the time over which discharge occurs. For instance, if the discharge time is shortened from two hours to one hour, the result is a reduction in available capacity of about 20 %.

Fleet testing with electric cars has indicated a life expectancy of approx. 4 years, corresponding to 700 cycles. A service life

Battery systems (discharge time 2h / charging time 10h)

Battery system	Cell voltage	Energy density	Energy efficiency without heating	Service life in cycles	Maintenance free	Operating temperature
Pb/PbO	2.0 V	25 Wh/kg	75 %	700	(gel) yes	0...55°C
Ni/Cd	1.2 V	50 Wh/kg	60 %	projected 1500...2000	no	– 20...55°C
Ni/Fe	1.2 V	50 Wh/kg	50 %	projected 1500...2000	no	– 20...55°C
Na/S	2.0 V	90 Wh/kg	88 %	projected 1000...1500	yes	300...380°C

Examples of electric vehicles (EV's)

Vehicle	Battery type	Acceleration 0...50 km/h	Top speed	Typical range per charge	Tare Weight	Payload	Typical consumption from power mains
Passenger car	Lead-gel	12 s	100 km/h	50 km	1420 kg	270 kg	30 kWh/100 km
Small transporter	Lead-gel	18 s	65 km/h	50 km	1240 kg	400 kg	30 kWh/100 km
Transporter	Lead-acid	12 s	70 km/h	60 km	2200 kg	800 kg	50 kWh/100 km
Urban bus	Lead-acid	23 s	70 km/h	70 km	15700 kg	7600 kg	260 kWh/100 km

of 7 ... 8 years with 1200 ... 1500 cycles can be achieved in industrial-transport vehicles. The shorter life expectancy in electric-powered road vehicles is essentially due to the substantially higher specific loads to which the battery is subjected. The mean discharge time for electric road vehicles is two hours or less, while industrial transporters generally run for 7 ... 8 hours. The situation is aggravated by the higher specific current loads to which the batteries in street vehicles are subjected.

Alkaline batteries
In addition to the nickel-iron system, this category also includes the nickel-cadmium system frequently employed in batteries for appliances. While appliance batteries employ closed systems, the open nickel-cadmium cell is dominant in electromotive applications (such as driverless transport systems).

Nickel-iron and nickel-cadmium batteries – the electrolyte is potassium hydrate in both cases – have a cell voltage of 1.2 V, contrasting with a cell voltage of 2 V in lead-acid batteries. Thus a six-volt module requires 5 cells instead of 3. The indications are that a battery life of up to 10 years/2000 cycles may be anticipated, although this has yet to be confirmed in actual vehicle testing. The considerably higher costs associated with the use of relatively expensive materials and complicated production could be amortized by a service life which is substantially longer than that of the lead-acid battery. A disadvantage associated with electric-powered road vehicles lies in the maintenance which is still required for both nickel-cadmium and nickel-iron cells. Nickel-iron systems, in particular, have an extremely high water consumption. Due to their higher losses, alkaline batteries for road-going electric vehicles must be cooled; auxiliary heating is only required at temperatures below – 20 °C. The available capacity is a function of discharge time.

The alkaline battery's higher energy density can be exploited both to increase the payload and to extend the vehicle's radius of action. Electric-powered cars typically achieve driving ranges of approx. 80 km with alkaline batteries, a figure exceeded by some transporters. Nickel-iron and nickel-cadmium systems for installation in electric vehicles for road use are already in limited production.

Sodium-sulfide batteries
The sodium-sulfide battery's electrolyte consists of an ionically-conductive, ceramic aluminum element. In order for a chemical reaction to occur, the sodium and sulfur which form the electron material must be maintained in a fluid state; the operating temperature thus lies between 300 and 380 °C. Super-insulation is required to maintain the battery system's thermal losses within acceptable limits. The battery consists of numerous individual cells, which contrast with those used in other battery types by being connected both in series and in parallel. Each individual cell is shaped like a cup. The sulfur is incorporated in a graphite matrix on the wall of the cup in order to enhance conductivity. The ceramic electrolyte element, also in cup form, is located between the sulfur and the sodium. The battery is completely sealed and maintenance-free. The electrical charge efficiency level of this battery is 1, resulting in an energy efficiency of more than 88 %. A portion of the energy required to maintain the operating temperature is derived from the losses attendant upon battery operation itself, while the remaining energy must be supplied by the power mains. An actual battery with an energy-storage capacity of 10 kWh displays a heat-radiation level of 80 W.

Using sodium-sulfide batteries, electric vehicles with an operating range in excess of 100 km can be produced, making them suitable for use in virtually all short-distance applications. Development on this type of battery has meanwhile progressed to the point where series production can be anticipated in the near future.

Drivetrains

The drivetrain of the electric vehicle generally includes the control element, the motor and the transmission. The control element relays the current-voltage demands from the pedal to the motor.

***F-v* diagram with limit curves for E-vehicle (EV) with 2-speed transmission**
F_W Moving resistance, I_{Bmax}/I_{Smax} Maximum battery/controller current, P_{Blimit} Maximum battery output, P_S Installed controller output.

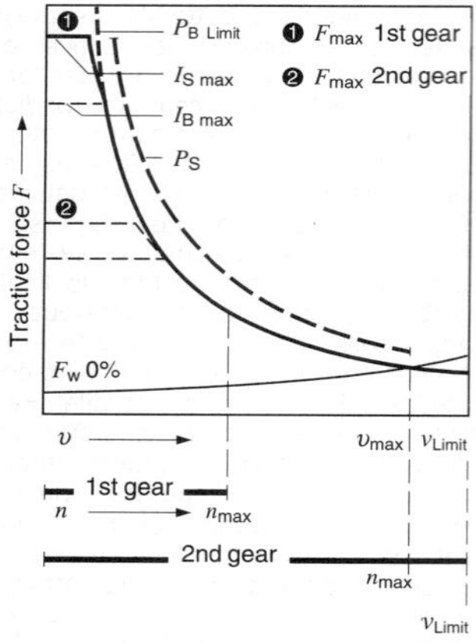

Driving with series-wound motor
B Battery, T_h Drive controller, M Electric motor (drive mode), D_F Free-wheeling diode, E-F Series field.

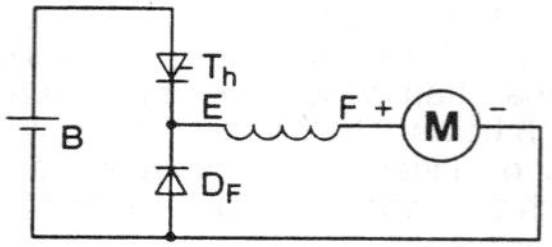

Braking with series-wound motor
B Battery, T_h Drive controller, G Electric motor (generator mode), D_F Free-wheeling diode, D_R Feedback diode, F-B Relay for switching between driving and braking modes

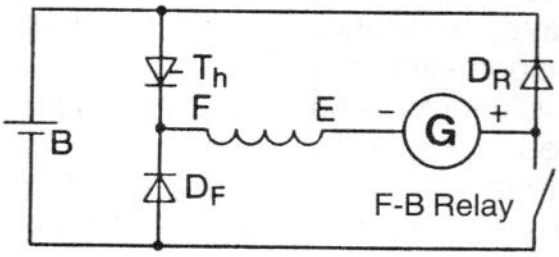

The motor's complication and expense are largely a function of the required torque rather than its output; thus financial considerations dictate that the flywheel speed be stepped-down to a maximum before reaching the drive wheels. Either one or several conversion ratios may be selected, depending upon the potential rotational-speed range of the motor being used. The limit curves for a particular battery and drive arrangement can be illustrated in the vehicle's tractive-force/speed diagram (*F-v* diagram). As the power limits of the electric motor are generally well in excess of the control element's limits, it is these which define the drive force. The rating for the controller to be installed in a particular application is calculated as the product of maximum motor current and maximum voltage from the battery or intermediate circuit. It is possible to design the controller to provide a maximum control current which is substantially higher than the maximum battery current. Optimal efficiency is achieved when the maximum controller output and the maximum battery output coincide. In contrast to the IC-engine, with electric drive units it is necessary to differentiate between short-time, or maximum output (1 ... 3 min) and continuous operation over a period of hours. This distinction also applies to most battery systems. Depending upon the type of drive being used, short-time and continuous output ratings vary by a factor of 1.5...3. The drive output is to be throttled in accordance with the thermal limits of the control element, motor and battery.

Direct-current series-wound drive

This type of drive unit employs the most basic control-element design. A power switch (thyristor or transistor(s)) directs the battery current to the motor at a variable pulse-duty frequency and/or clock frequency, adjusting the voltage at the motor to provide the desired current (step-down chopper). For the recovery of braking energy, the controller must operate as a step-up chopper, which means that additional components are needed. As the motor's field and armature are in series, exceeding the rated motor speed results in a decrease in output proportional to the square of the motor's rpm. This means that a transmission with several conversion ratios is almost always required. The entire output must be switched-in for setpoints which lie below the motor's nominal curve; this results in lower efficiency levels than those achieved, for instance, with separately-excited direct-current drive units. In electric vehicles for road use, the efficiency ratings for series-wound motors are about 5 ... 10 % lower than those derived from separately-excited drive units.

Due to its simplicity of design and its low costs, thyristor technology is still employed in virtually all industrial transporters with this type of drive unit. The low top speeds of these vehicles make it possible to employ a transmission unit with only a single conversion ratio.

Separately-excited direct-current drive

In this type of drive unit, the motor's magnetic excitation is provided by its own controller (field rheostat). Depending upon the size of the motor, the field is weakened by ratios between 1 : 3 to 1 : 5. The increase in the rotational speed relative to the nominal speed is directly proportional to the field-weakening ratio. The nominal speed

Limit curves

a) DC series operation, b) Separately-excited DC drive, c) Asynchronous operation, d) Synchronous operation with permanent excitation. I_{Bmax}/I_{Smax} Maximum battery/controller current, $P_{B\ limit}$ Max. battery output, P_S Installed controller output.

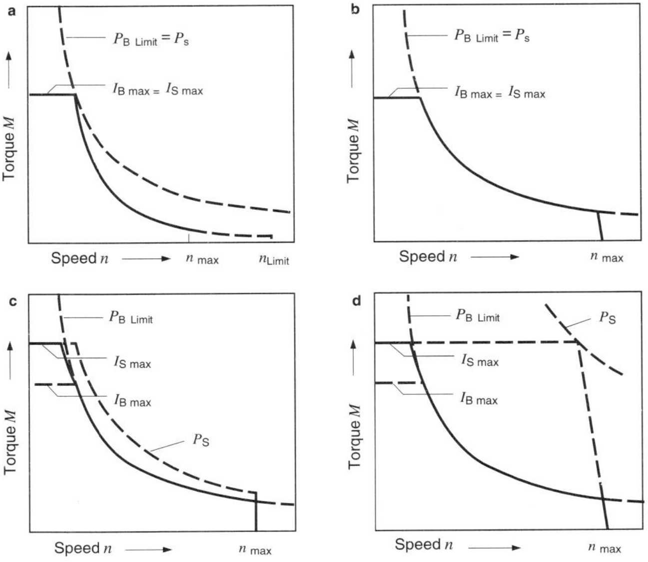

Constant-efficiency curves for DC motor with separate excitation

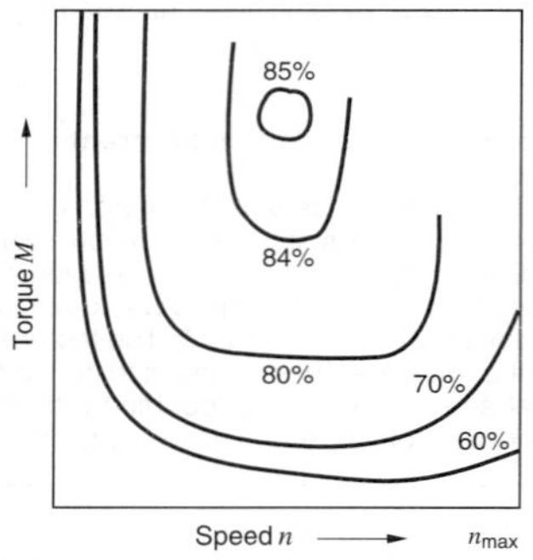

is obtained with full motor voltage at the armature and maximum field current. Within the weakened-field range, a constant drive current provides constant output from the drive unit.

As a commutation pole is required, this design is somewhat more complicated than a series-wound motor. For operation below the nominal speed and for starting, either an electronic armature positioner or a starting resistor must be employed. When a starting resistor is used, the resulting idle speed is equal to the nominal speed. The resulting operating characteristics are similar to those of an internal-combustion engine.

The transmission must be in neutral when the vehicle is not moving.

The mechanical commutator limits the maximum rotational speed to approx. 7000 min^{-1}. A transmission incorporating several conversion ratios is generally required.

Being as only the field power is used for normal driving (2 ... 5% of total power), high efficiency levels result. Increasing the field current represents a simple and efficient expedient for returning braking energy to the battery.

Asynchronous drive

Asynchronous units are characterized by having the simplest, least expensive motor design, although the use of a three-phase drive unit means that the control mechanism is more complicated than that employed for DC drives. As with the separately-excited DC motor, weakened-field operation is possible, but full power must be used. As there is no mechanical commutator, speeds of up to 20,000 min^{-1} can be achieved with appropriate motor designs, meaning that single-ratio transmission units can be used, even for road-going vehicles. Braking energy can be recovered with a high degree of efficiency. Weakened-field operation provides extremely good utilization of the installed controller output throughout the entire tractive-force/speed range.

Permanently-excited synchronous drive

Extremely small motors can be used with this type of drive unit. As permanent magnets are employed to generate the magnetic field, no losses are generated in the rotor. The result is extremely high efficiency levels. However, the rare-earth magnets required to achieve the very small size concerned make the motor expensive. Because genuine weakened-field operation is not possible with this type of motor, the controller power must either be several times maximum battery output, or a multi-stage transmission must be used. If a DC drive unit allows a field-control range of 1 : 3, then the rated output of the three-phase AC chopper must be increased by a factor of 3 in a drive unit with a permanently-excited synchronous motor. Recent developments in drive units have concentrated on achieving semi-weakened field operation in order to reduce the controller dimensions. However, this is not sufficient to obtain a speed range comparable to that of the asynchronous unit. Thus a transmission incorporating at least two drive ratios is required for economically feasible application.

Hybrid drives

In the broadest sense, the term "hybrid drives" is used to denote vehicle drives with more than one drive source. Hybrid drives can incorporate several similar or different types of energy storage devices and/or power converters. The goal of hybrid-drive developments is to combine two different drive components, such that the advantages of each are utilized under varying operating conditions in such a manner that the overall advantages of the hybrid-drive developments outweigh the increased expenditure for its configuration.

Classification of hybrid drives

In terms of available performance and range, the IC engine as a drive source is superior to all other drive systems. Its disadvantages – a drop in efficiency at part load, and the production of toxic emissions – have led to the development of hybrid drives which incorporate the IC engine. IC engines in hybrid drives are designed for average-power operation, whereby the differences between generated power and the power required at any given time are compensated by the additional mechanical or electrical energy-storage device.

A hybrid drive incorporating an IC engine and flywheel, as shown on page 534, can be operated in a number of ways by engaging and disengaging the three couplings K1, K2 and K3. The IC engine can be directly coupled to the power-shift transmission or the flywheel. In addition, the diesel engine can start the two kinetic energy storage devices (flywheel and vehicle mass) from standstill via the continuously variable transmission. This configuration also permits parallel operation of the two drive sources, diesel engine and flywheel. Here, only the power developed by the flywheel is transmitted to the power-shift transmission via the less efficient continuously variable transmission using hydrostatic converters, whereas the engine power is fed directly to the transmission input.

Hybrid drives which use only electrical drive components and do not incorporate IC engines have been developed. This was an attempt to apply the hybrid configuration in order to avoid the disadvantages of the purely battery-based electric drive.

Classification of hybrid drives

▽ *Proposals under study*
○ *Prototype vehicles*
● *Experimental operation under practical driving conditions*

Drive sources	*Internal-combustion engine only*		*Electric drive only*				*Internal-combustion engine and electric drive*		
Mechanical energy storage									
Flywheel	○			▽		○			▽
Hydraulic storage	○								
Electrical energy sources									
Battery			○	▽	▽		●		▽
Fuel cell					▽				
External supply			○			○		●	

Hybrid drive incorporating internal-combustion engine with flywheel
VM Internal-combustion engine, SR Flywheel, SRG Flywheel reduction gear, NA Auxiliary drive, F Freewheel, K Coupling, P Planetary gear set, H1, 2 Continuously-variable hydrostatic transmission, LSG Power shift transmission (automatic planetary transmission), HA Drive axle.

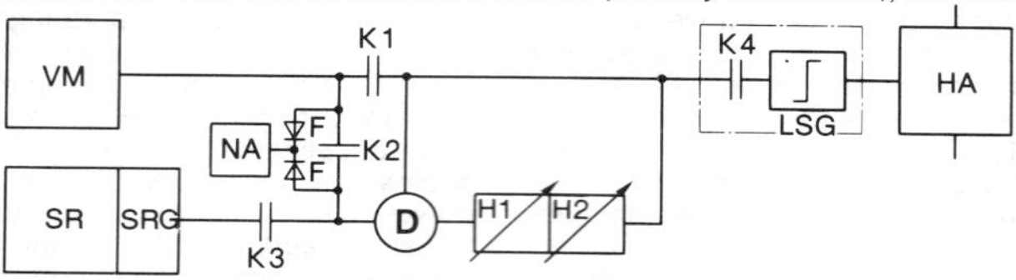

The useful energy stored in the battery allows only a limited driving range, and is further reduced as power demand increases. Combining a mechanical energy store with the battery prevents it being affected by power peaks, thus contributing to more efficient utilization of the battery energy. A hybrid system which uses a combination of two different electrochemical energy sources (battery and fuel cell) separates the energy sources such that one source has a high power, and the other has good energy-storage capability. In the case of hybrid electric drives with an external supply of energy (trolley systems), the vehicle's own energy store is used as a short-time storage medium for short distances of autonomous travel. This type of configuration reduces the high costs associated with overhead contact wires and relieves some of the restrictions associated with the trolley system.

Hybrid drive designs

Hybrid drives which combine an internal-combustion (IC) engine and an electric drive are the only hybrid drives which have warranted serious attention to date. The electric drive component of such drives is powered either by an on-board battery or via an overhead contact wire and current collector system. The diagram at the right shows the various basic drive configurations. The battery indicated in each configuration can be replaced by the external power supply arrangement. The main difference between the various configurations is the series or parallel arrangement of the power sources. In the series arrangement (1), the individual drive components are connected in series, whereas in the parallel arrangement (2 and 3) the driving power of both drive sources is mechanically added. The letters M and G indicate whether the operation of the electric machines is motor or generator-based. As the diesel engine in the series arrangement is mechanically decoupled from the vehicle drive, it is possible to

Hybrid drive configurations
1 Series arrangement, 2, 3 Parallel arrangement, VM Internal-combustion engine, EL Electric drive (motor or generator-based operation), BA Battery or external power supply, LSG Power shift transmission.

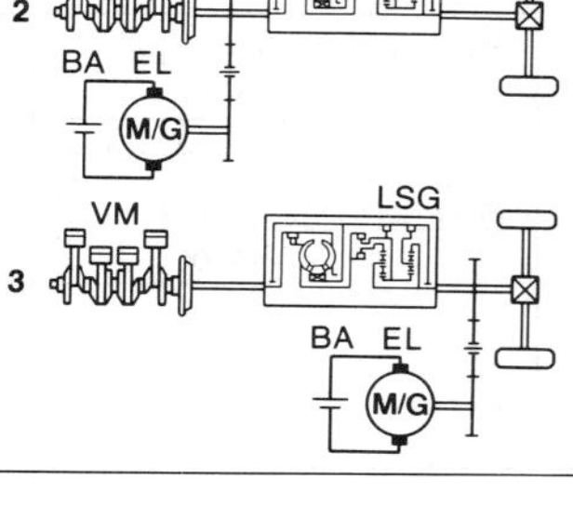

operate the diesel engine at a constant speed only in the vicinity of its optimum operating point in terms of efficiency and emissions. Regardless of the advantages of the series arrangement, this configuration has disadvantages in that energy must be converted several times. Including battery storage efficiency, the mechanical efficiency between the diesel engine and the drive axle is hardly greater than 55 %.

Parallel hybrid arrangements 2 and 3 have the advantage that operation incorporating an IC engine is just as efficient as the operation of a conventional vehicle. In arrangement 2, the mechanical starting devices and the gearing which are required by the diesel-engine drive are included in the electric drive branch, and – as illustrated – can be integrated as a conventional power-shift transmission. In this drive variant it is therefore sufficient to vary the electric-machine speed only within a specific range above a basic speed, similar to the way in which the diesel engine is operated. Here, a separately-excited motor can be used which can only be controlled in the field-weakening range. Due to the configuration of the electric motor, arrangement 3 has better transmission efficiency than arrangement 2, however, arrangement 3 must incorporate a drive control which can control the electric machine throughout its complete speed range between standstill and maximum speed. In addition, the electric motor in arrangement 3 must provide an increased torque roughly proportional to the ratio of the mechanical transmission. This leads to an equivalent increase in motor mass which is roughly proportional to motor torque.

The drive configuration of a hybrid electric bus is the same as variation 1. Depending upon the particular application, the electric drive is designed so that driving performance under electric battery power is approximately the same as that of a standard diesel-powered bus.

Because the weight of the batteries amounts to only 16 % of the gross vehicle weight, the batteries are subjected to high specific loads. The increased internal battery losses caused by these loads make necessary the use of additional auxiliary equipment (water cooling, central degassing) for the battery, as shown in the illustration below.

Hybrid electric bus
1 Electric drive motor, 2 Compressor and power-steering pump, 3 Cooling fan for drive motor, 4 Diesel engine with alternator, 5 Fan for battery ventilation, 6 Electronic control, 7 Traction batteries, 8 Equipment for battery cooling, 9 Braking resistor.

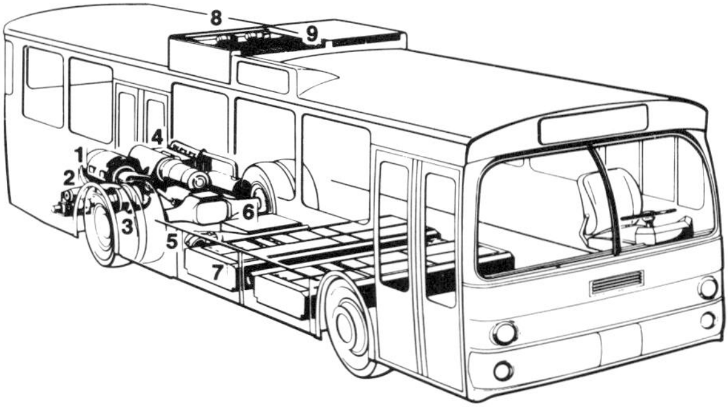

Drivetrain

Quantities and units

Quantity		Unit
a	Acceleration	m/s^2
c_w	Aerodynamic drag	–
e	Rotational inertia coefficient	–
f	Coefficient of rolling resistance	–
g	Gravitational acceleration	m/s^2
i	Conversion ratio	–
m	Vehicle mass	kg
n	Rotational speed	1/min
r	Dynamic tire radius	m
υ	Vehicle velocity	m/s
A	Face area	m^2
J	Mass moment of inertia	$kg \cdot m^2$
M	Torque	N·m
P	Power	kW
α	Ascent angle	°
φ	Overdrive factor	–
η	Efficiency	–
λ	Power number	–
μ	Conversion	–
ρ	Density	kg/m^3
ω	Angular velocity	rad/s
ν	Rotational speed ratio	–

Subscripts:

rms	root mean square	m	engine
tot	total	o	pertaining to max. power
hydr	hydraulic	A	drivetrain
max	maximum	G	transmission
min	minimum	P	pump
h	final drive	R	wheel
		T	turbine

Function

The automotive drivetrain is charged with providing the thrust and tractive forces required to overcome running resistance and induce motion. Energy in chemical (fuels) or electrical form (batteries, solar cells) is converted into mechanical energy in the power unit, with spark-ignition and diesel internal-combustion engines representing the powerplants of choice. Every power unit operates within a specific revolution range as defined by two extremities:
the idle speed and the maximum rpm. Torque and power are not delivered at uniform rates throughout the operating range; the respective maxima are available only within specific bands. The drivetrain's conversion ratios adapt the available torque to the momentary requirement for tractive force.

Drivetrain configurations

The layout of the automotive drivetrain varies according to the position of the engine and the drive axle:

Drive layout	Engine position	Driven axle
Standard	front	rear
Front-wheel drive	front, longitudinal or transverse	front
All-wheel drive	front, center (rear in isolated applications)	front and rear permanent or driver-selected (between single and two-axle drive), gradual transition also possible
Rear drive	rear	rear

Equilibrium relation between drive forces and tractive resistance

The equation defining the equilibrium between drive forces and resistance factors is applied to determine various quantities, such as acceleration, top speed, climbing ability, etc.

Available power = Tractive resistance at drive wheels (power requirement)

$$M_m \cdot \frac{i_{tot}}{r} \cdot \eta_{tot} = m \cdot g \cdot f \cdot \cos\alpha + m \cdot g \cdot \sin\alpha + e \cdot m \cdot a + c_w \cdot A \cdot \frac{\rho}{2} \cdot \upsilon^2$$

Drive force at tire contact patches | Rolling resistance | Ascent resistance | Acceleration resistance | Aerodynamic resistance

With rational inertia coeffic. $e = 1 + \frac{J}{m \cdot r^2}$ and mass moment of inertia $J = J_R + i_h^2 \cdot J_A + i_h^2 \cdot i_G^2 \cdot J_m$

Drivetrain elements

The drivetrain components must satisfy the basic requirements associated with vehicle operation in all ranges, from the stationary state, through all desired operating points, up to top speed. This entails fulfilment of the following:

- achieving the transition from a stationary to a mobile state,
- converting torque and rotational speed,
- moving both forward and backward,
- compensating for wheel-speed variations in curves,
- ensuring that the power unit remains within a range on the operating curve commensurate with minimum fuel consumption and exhaust emissions.

Stationary idle, transition to motion and interruption of the power flow are all made possible by the clutch. The clutch slips to compensate for the difference in the rotational speeds of engine and drive train when the vehicle is being set in motion. When a change in operating conditions makes it necessary to change gears, the clutch disengages the engine from the drive train for the duration of the procedure. In automatic transmissions hydrodynamic clutches or torque converters assume responsibility for the starting-off process.

The transmission modifies the engine's torque and rpm to adapt them to the vehicle's momentary tractive requirements, maintaining the power $P = M \cdot \omega$ at a relatively constant level.

The total conversion ratio is generally a composite of the ratios provided by a transmission (gearbox), with several selectable ratios (less commonly with infinitely-variable arrangements), and a constant-ratio final-drive unit. Positive-transfer gear transmissions are more common than non-positive units due to their superior performance-to-weight ratio.

Gear transmissions generally fall into one of two categories: the manually-shifted spur-gear transmission in an arrangement with main and countershaft (layshaft, idler shaft), and the planetary-gear unit featuring power-demand shifting (in automatic transmissions). The transmission also allows the selection of different rotational directions for forward and reverse operation.

The differential allows laterally opposed axles and wheels to rotate at varying rates during cornering while providing uniform distribution of the driving forces. Limited-slip final drives respond to slippage at one of the wheels by limiting the differential effect, transmitting additional force to the wheel at which traction is available.

In the control system, final-control elements (actuators) and switches supervise execution of the required ratio conversions. The control-elements are actuated

Tractive force/speed diagram

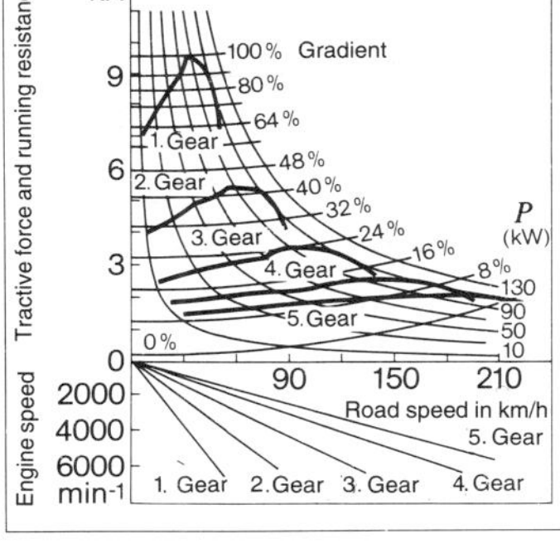

Multiple-ratio transmission in drivetrain
1 Engine, 2 Clutch, 3 Manual transmission, 4 Final-drive unit, 5 Front splitter unit, or, alternatively, 6 Rear range group, 7 Planetary-gear set.

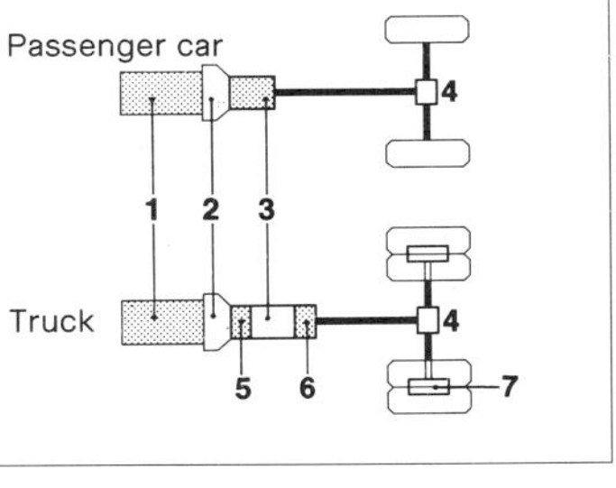

either directly, by the driver, or automatically, as sensor signals are processed in an electronic or hydraulic control unit in accordance with a specific program.

Torsion dampers, mass compliance systems and hydraulic transmission elements are all available to attenuate high-frequency vibrations. These protect the power unit from excessive loads and enhance comfort by reducing vibration.

Clutches and couplings

Friction clutch

The friction clutch found in vehicles equipped with a manually-shifted transmission consists of a massive pressure plate, a clutch disk – featuring bonded or riveted friction surfaces – and the second friction surface represented by the engine-mounted flywheel. The flywheel and pressure plate provide the thermal absorption required for friction operation of the clutch; flywheel and pressure plate are connected directly to the engine, while the clutch disk is mounted on the transmission's input shaft.

A spring arrangement, frequently in the form of a central spring plate, applies the force which joins the flywheel, pressure plate and clutch disk for common rotation; in this state, the clutch is engaged for positive torque transfer. To disengage the clutch (e.g., for shifting), a mechanically or hydraulically actuated throwout bearing applies force to the center of the pressure plate, thereby releasing the pressure at the periphery. The clutch is activated either with a clutch pedal or with an electrohy-

Clutch with dual-mass flywheel
1 Dual-mass flywheel, 2 Flexible element, 3 Pressure plate, 4 Diaphragm spring, 5 Clutch disk, 6 Throwout bearing.

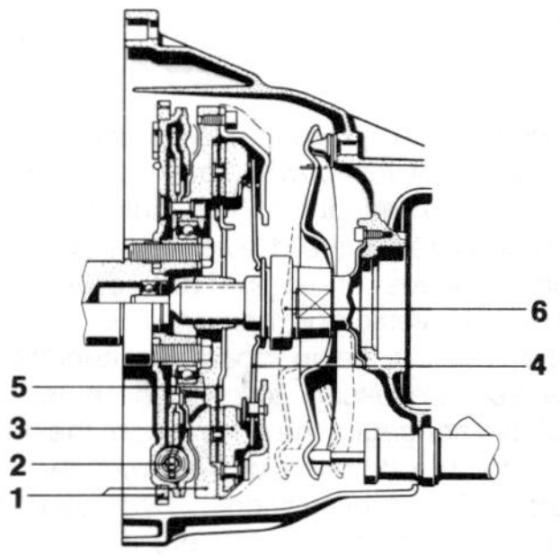

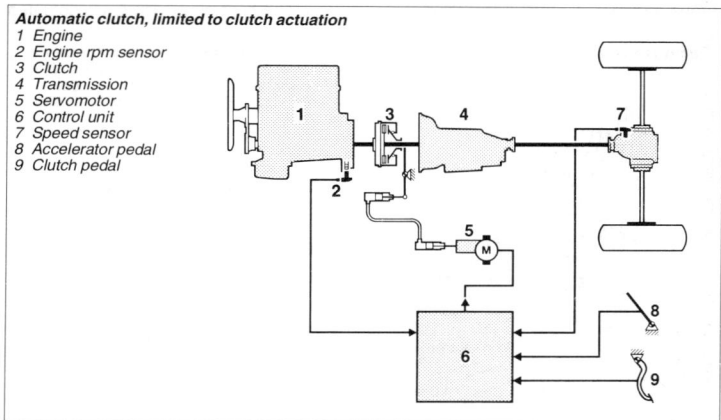

Automatic clutch, limited to clutch actuation
1 Engine
2 Engine rpm sensor
3 Clutch
4 Transmission
5 Servomotor
6 Control unit
7 Speed sensor
8 Accelerator pedal
9 Clutch pedal

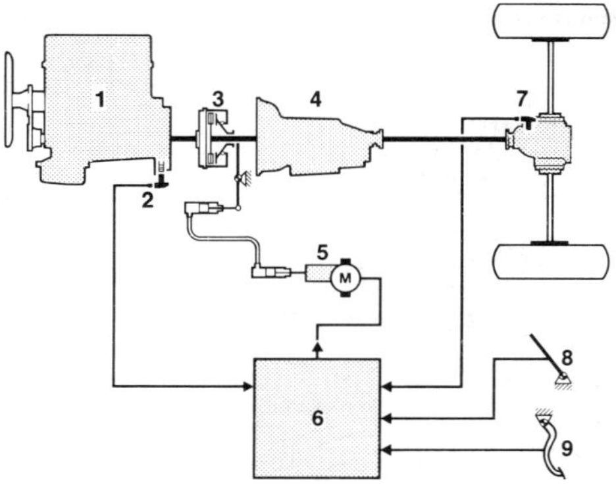

draulic or electromechanical final-control element.

When used together with an electronic control unit, the automatic clutch can provide either gradual engagement for starting off, or it can be applied in conjunction with a servo-operated shifting mechanism to form a fully-automatic transmission unit. Among such a device's other potential functions are traction control under acceleration and interruption of power transfer during braking. A system consisting of a two-section flywheel (dual-mass flywheel) with an intermediate elastic element can be installed at the front of the clutch assembly for vibration insulation.

Because the intrinsic resonating frequency of this spring-mass system is below the excitation (ignition) frequency of the engine at idle, it lies outside the normal rpm range. It thus insulates the engine from the other drive-train components ("low-pass filter").

Hydrodynamic couplings and converters

Hydrodynamic couplings and torque converters employ the force represented by a moving fluid to transmit engine torque. Because these devices compensate for differences in the rotating speeds of engine and drivetrain, they are ideal for effecting the transition from stationary to mobile operation. The torque converter also multiplies torque. First, an impeller converts the mechanical energy emanating from the power unit into fluid energy (hydraulic fluid – ATF – is the preferred medium); a second transformation, back into mechanical energy, occurs at the blades within the turbine.

The impeller's input torque M_P and the input power P_P are calculated as follows:

$$M_P = \lambda \cdot \rho \cdot D^5 \cdot \omega_P^2$$
$$P_P = \lambda \cdot \rho \cdot D^5 \cdot \omega_P^3$$

λ Power number
ρ Density of medium (≈ 870 kg/m^3 for hydraulic fluid)
D Circuit diameter in m
ω_P Angular velocity of impeller in rad/s

The mutual relationship between input torque M_P and input power P_P on the one side, and D^5 on the other, is characteristic for all hydropneumatic drive systems.

The ratio of turbine torque M_T to impeller force M_P determines the torque-conversion factor $\mu = -M_T/M_P$.

The ν factor is defined as the ratio of turbine speed to impeller speed; it exercises a determining influence on both the power number λ and the conversion factor μ. The relevant equation is: $\nu = \omega_T/\omega_P$.

The slip factor $s = 1 - \nu$ and the force conversion together determine the hydraulic efficiency:

$$\eta_{hydr} = \mu\,(1 - s) = \mu \cdot \nu.$$

Among the benefits offered by hydrodynamic couplings and torque converters are the following attributes: infinitely-variable, stepless variations in torque and rpm, vibration insulation, absorption of torque peaks and virtually wear-free power transfer. These devices offer economical operation when used together with mechanical variable-ratio transmissions; operation with non-positive engagement (slip) is limited in the interests of efficiency. It is also possible to divert torque flow from the hydrodynamic element to a friction clutch to achieve further reductions in undesirable slip, with

Hydrodynamic coupling
1 Turbine, 2 Impeller.

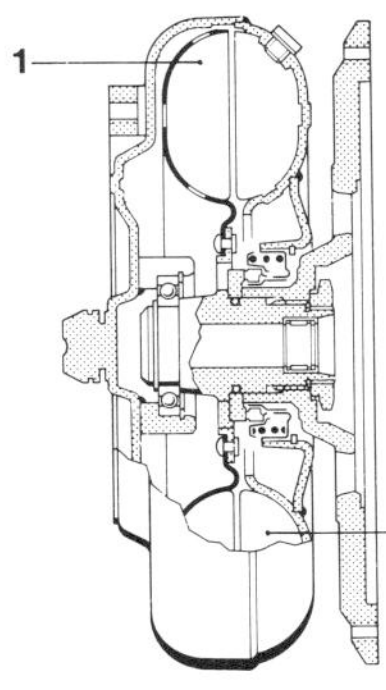

commensurate improvements in the efficiency factor.

Hydrodynamic couplings

In its standard configuration, the hydrodynamic (or Föttinger) coupling is composed of an impeller and a turbine with (normally) radial blades. The impeller is often expanded to include a housing enclosing the turbine. The absence of a stator means that there is no flow diversion between turbine and impeller; thus the torque at the turbine is equal to that at the impeller $M_T = -M_P$. This means that $\mu = 1$ (force ratio) and $\eta_{hydr} = \nu$. The factor ν is determined by blade geometry, although the coupling's volumetric efficiency may also exercise some influence. The normal automotive operating range is around $\nu \approx 0.95$, with up to $\nu \approx 0.98$ possible in highway applications.

Hydrodynamic torque converters

The hydrodynamic torque converter – also known as the Föttinger speed transformer or converter – consists of an impeller, a turbine and a stator. The converter is capable of operation in two distinct ranges, providing torque multiplication in the first stage, and functioning as a simple hydrodynamic coupling with no torque gain in the second. Operation is similar to that of the basic hydrodynamic coupling; the vehicle's power unit drives the impeller to produce fluid energy in the hydraulic medium, while the turbine connected to the transmission input shaft transforms this hydraulic energy back into mechanical force. A stator located between impeller and turbine diverts the hydraulic medium back to the input side of the impeller.

This raises the torque beyond the initial engine output as exerted at the impeller. The degree of torque multiplication $\mu = M_T/M_P$ increases as a function of the difference in the respective rotating speeds (expressed as slip) of impeller and turbine. Maximum torque multiplication is achieved at $\nu = 0$, i.e., with the turbine at stall speed. Further increases in turbine speed are accompanied by a virtually linear drop in multiplication until a torque ratio of 1:1 is reached at the coupling point. Above this point the stator, which is housing-mounted with a one-way clutch, freewheels in the flow.

A Föttinger torque converter featuring a centripetal turbine – the Trilok converter – has become the standard for automotive applications. The geometrical configuration of this unit's blades is selected to pro-

Hydrodynamic converter with lockup clutch
1 Lockup clutch, 2 Turbine, 3 Impeller, 4 Stator, 5 One-way clutch.

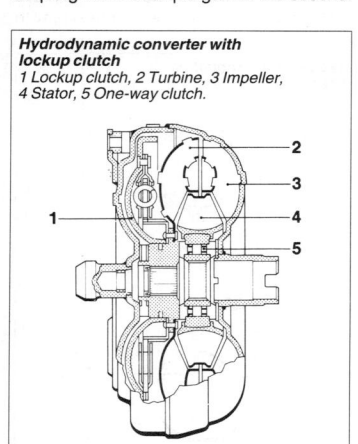

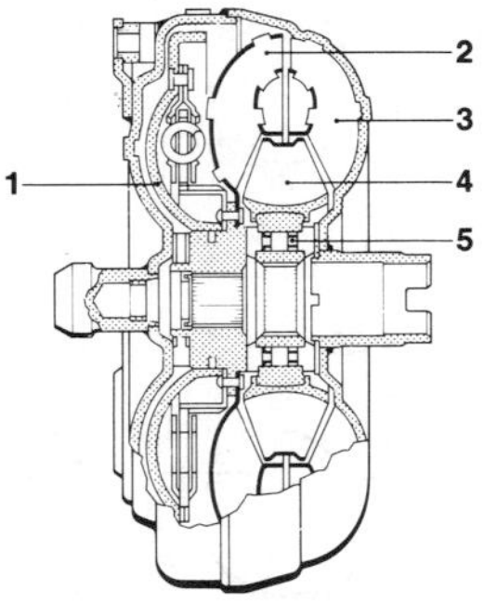

Trilok converter
(typical passenger-car performance curve).

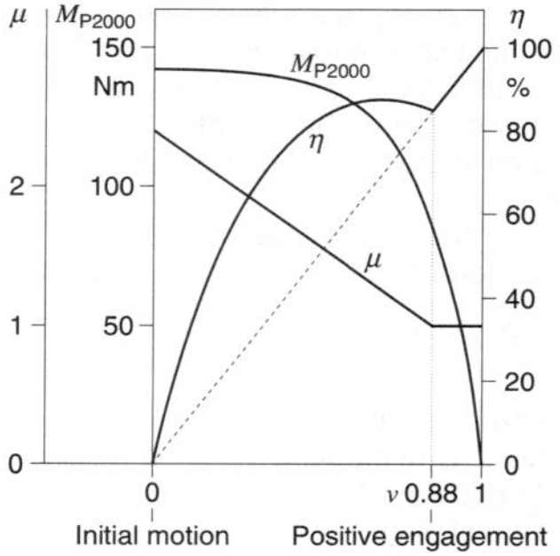

vide torque multiplication in the range of 1.9 ... 2.5 at stall speed ($\nu = 0$). The curve defining the hydraulic efficiency factor $\eta_{hydr} = \nu \cdot \mu$ in the conversion range is roughly parabolic. Above the coupling point, at which the slip rates lie in a range of 10 ... 15%, the efficiency level is equal to the rpm ratio ν, reaching levels around 97% at high rpm. Fluid couplings form the initial input element of automatic transmissions (where they operate together with planetary-gear sets, clutches, brake bands and one-way clutches). They are also used in converter-clutch units for semi-automatic transmissions.

Converter lockup clutch

The converter lockup clutch provides a friction coupling between impeller and turbine to avoid the efficiency losses associated with slip under those conditions in which torque multiplication and damping are not required. The converter lockup clutch consists of a plunger with friction surface; this is connected to the turbine hub via a torsion damper. As far as basic principles are concerned, both the layout and the operation of the torsion damper correspond to those of the dry friction clutch. The transmission's valve body regulates the direction in which the fluid flows through the converter to regulate locking of the coupling.

Transmission (gearboxes)

The required total conversion range I is approximately:

$$I \approx \frac{\tan \alpha_m \cdot \upsilon_0}{(P/G)_{eff} \cdot \varphi}$$

$\tan \alpha_m$ is maximum hill-climbing ability, $\upsilon 0$ is the power-specific top speed, $(P/G)_{eff}$ is the effective specific output, φ is the overdrive factor, with

$$\varphi = \frac{(i/r)_{min}}{\omega_0 / \upsilon_0}$$

r dynamic tire radius, $(i/r)_{min}$ = minimum conversion, ω_0 is the engine's rated angular velocity.

Calculations of effective specific output are always to be based on the power P which is actually available for tractive application (net power, minus driven ancillaries, power losses, altitude loss). Special conditions, such as automobile trailer towing, must be factored into the weight G. $\varphi = 1$ when the curve for cumulative running resistance in top gear directly intersects the point of maximum output. For passenger cars, the

Engine performance curve with curves for running resistance
(Example). Car engine with P_0 = 100 kW at ω_0 = 500 rad/s and T_{max} = 230 N · m at ω = 250 rad/s.

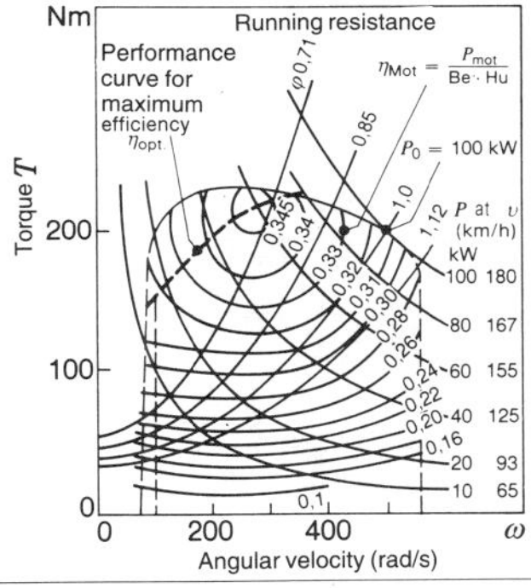

Operating diagram for truck with multiple gear ratios
Specific output 8.5 kW/t. P_0 Nominal output

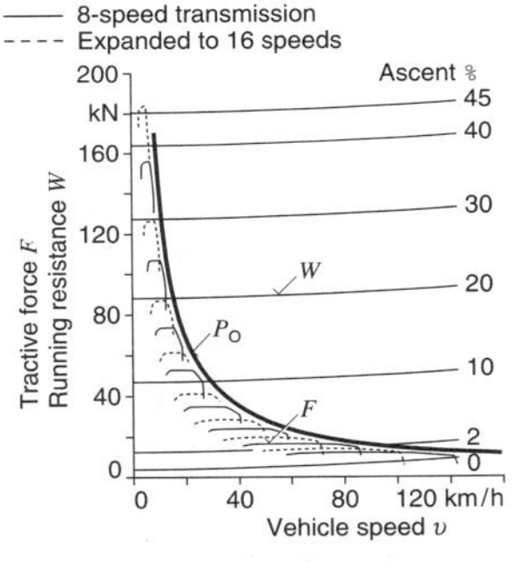

required conversion range I is 3 ... 4 at $\varphi = 1$; for a truck with a minimum specific output of 4.5 kW/t the figure is 8 ... 10. Because the φ factor determines the relative positions of the curves for running-resistance and engine output during top-gear operation, it also defines the efficiency level at which the engine operates.

$\varphi > 1$ displaces operation into an inefficient engine-performance range, but also enhances acceleration reserves and hill-climbing ability in top-gear. On the other hand, selecting $\varphi < 1$ will result in reduced fuel consumption, albeit accompanied by substantially slower acceleration and lower climbing reserves. Minimum fuel consumption is achieved on the operating curve η_{opt}. $\varphi > 1$ reduces, $\varphi < 1$ increases the conversion range I.

Multiple-ratio transmissions

Gear transmissions featuring several fixed ratios can maintain a correspondence between the respective performance curves for engine and vehicle at extremely high efficiency levels of up to $\eta = 0.99$. The correspondence with the hyperbola for maximum engine output will be acceptable or indeed quite good, depending upon a multiplicity of factors including the number of available gears, the spacing of the in-

Manually-shifted transmission
a) Single-band synchromesh
b) Dual-band synchromesh

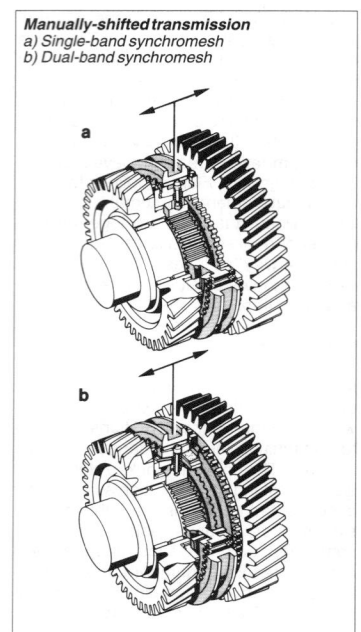

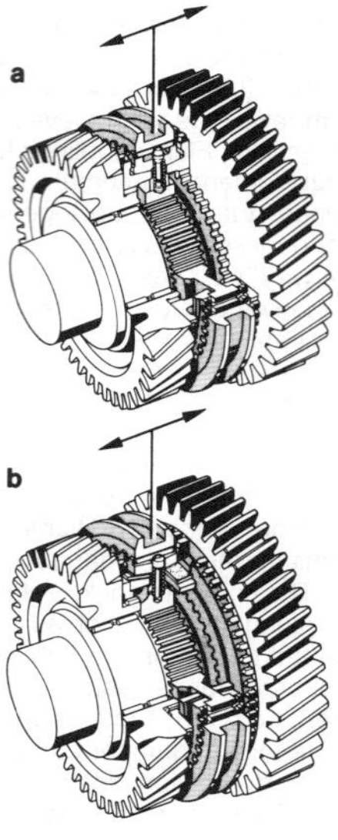

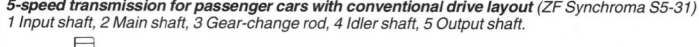

5-speed transmission for passenger cars with conventional drive layout *(ZF Synchroma S5-31)*
1 Input shaft, 2 Main shaft, 3 Gear-change rod, 4 Idler shaft, 5 Output shaft.

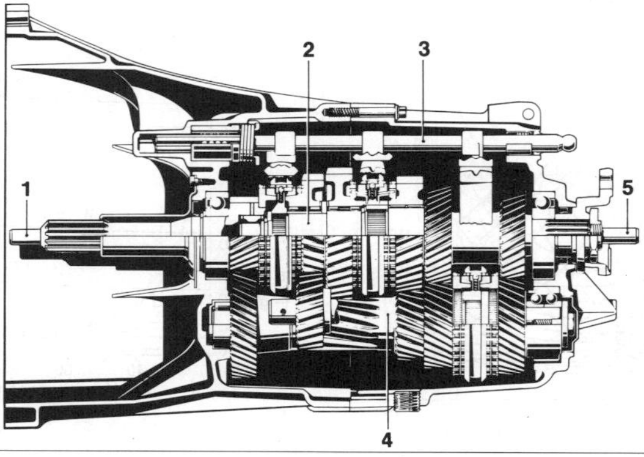

dividual ratios within the required conversion range, and the engine's full-load torque curve.

Gear selection on the multiple-ratio unit is either manual or automatic. The manually-shifted transmissions installed in passenger cars and in most heavy vehicles are two-axis units with main and countershaft (layshaft, idler gears). Transmissions in heavy commercial vehicles sometimes incorporate two or even three countershafts to reduce the load on the individual gears. Such layouts must incorporate special arrangements to achieve uniform power distribution.

A Simpson planetary gear set (3 forward gears and one reverse) is frequently used in fully-automatic transmissions; this type of unit can be coupled to additional planetary sets to obtain more ratios. Ravigneaux and other types of planetary-gear arrangements are also employed.

Manually-shifted transmissions

The basic elements of the manually-shifted transmission are:

– Single or multiplate dry clutch for interrupting the power flow and for starting off; actuation may be power-assisted to deal with high operating forces,

– Variable-ratio gear transmission unit featuring permanent-mesh gears in one or several individual assemblies,

– Shift mechanism with shift lever.

The force required for gear selection is transmitted via shift linkage rods or cable, while dog clutches or synchronizer assemblies lock the active gears to the shafts. Before a shift can take place, it is necessary to synchronize the rotating speeds of the transmission elements being joined. When the transmission incorporates dog clutches (of the type still sometimes used in transmissions for heavy commercial vehicles), the driver performs this task by double-clutching on both upshifts and downshifts, with the latter being accompanied by the application of throttle.

Virtually all transmissions in passenger cars, and the majority of those in commercial vehicles, employ locking synchronizer assemblies. These include a friction coupling for initial equalization of rotating speed and a lockout mechanism to prevent positive gear engagement prior to completion of the synchronization process; these are generally single-band designs. Multiplate and double-band synchronizers are sometimes employed in extremely demanding applications and/or to reduce shifting effort.

5-speed transmission for transverse-engine passenger car with 4wd *(Audi quattro)*
1 Input shaft, 2 Front-axle output, 3 Center differential, 4 Center differential lock, 5 Rear-axle output.

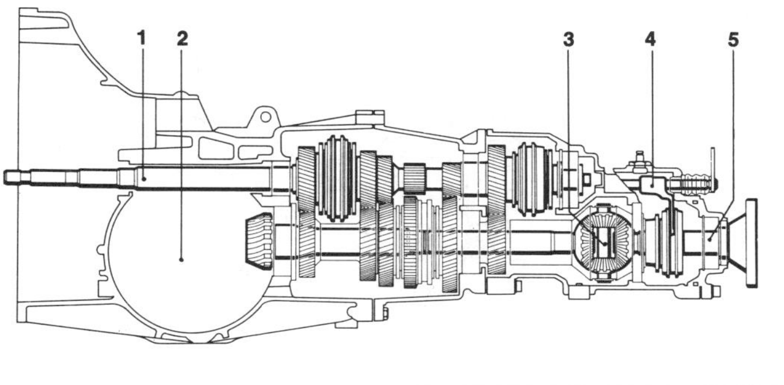

16-speed split-range truck transmission with integral retarder *(ZF-16 S 220 Ecosplit)*
1 Input shaft, 2 Gearchange connection, 3 Main shaft, 4 Gear-change rod with shift fork, 5 Planetary-gear set, 6 Output shaft, 7 Layshaft, 8 Integral hydrodynamic retarder.
A Splitter group, B Main group, C Range group.

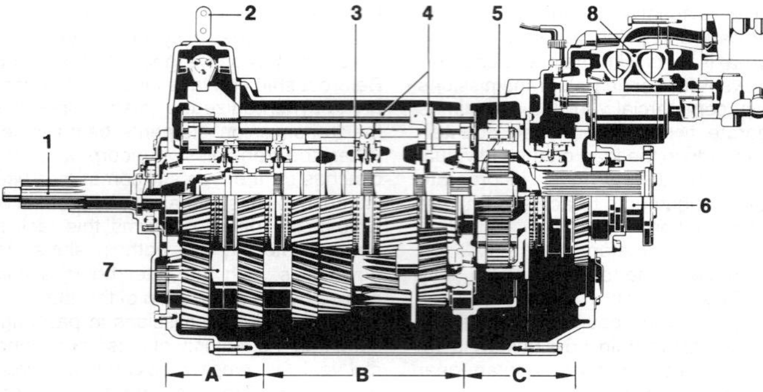

Input torque max. N · m	Individual conversion ratios (optional)								LO = low; HI = high									
	1st gear		2nd gear		3rd gear		4th gear		5th gear		6th gear		7th gear		8th gear		Reverse	
	LO	HI	LO	HI	LO	HI	LO	HI	LO	HI	LO	HI	LO	HI	LO	HI	LO	HI
2200	16.47	13.79	11.32	9.48	7.79	6.52	5.48	4.58	3.59	3.01	2.47	2.07	1.70	1.42	1.20	1.00	13.32	11.15
2300	13.80	11.55	9.59	8.02	6.81	5.70	4.58	3.84	3.01	2.52	2.09	1.75	1.49	1.24	1.00	0.84	12.23	10.24

Converter-clutch unit *(ZF Transmatic WSK 400)*
1 Hydrodynamic torque converter with lockup clutch
2 Fluid pump
3 Mechanical disconnect clutch
4 Servo-assist for operation of dry clutch

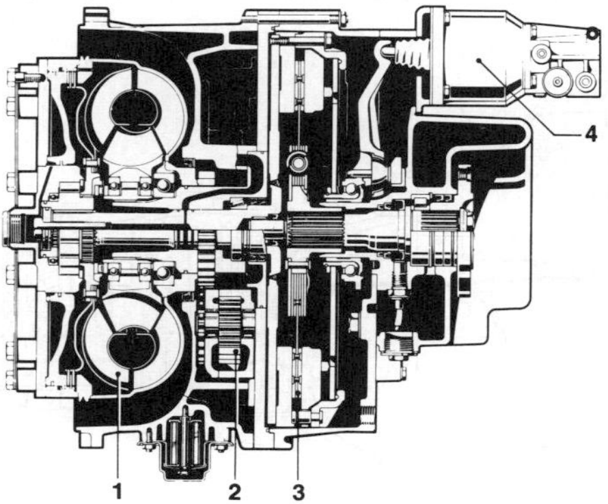

Transmissions in passenger cars include 4 or 5, occasionally even 6 forward ratios. The conversion range lies between approx. 3.8 and 5.5, depending upon the number and respective ratios of the gears. Individual transmission designs vary according to vehicle layout (conventional layout, front-wheel drive with transverse or longitudinal engine, four-wheel drive). Thus the input and output shafts may share a single axis, or they may be mutually offset; the final-drive and differential assembly may also be included in the unit. Transmissions in heavy commercial vehicles can have between 4 and 16 gears, depending upon the type of vehicle and the specific application. Transmissions with up to 6 gear ratios feature a single-assembly design; the conversion range lies between 4 and 9. Two assemblies (including a pneumatically-actuated range group) are combined to obtain transmissions with up to 9 speeds. The conversion range extends to 13.

For still higher numbers of ratios – up to 16 – three transmission elements are employed: the main transmission, a splitter group and the range group, with pneumatic actuation for the latter two units. The conversion range is as high as 16.

Automatic shift mechanism for synchromesh transmission
1 Gear indicator, 2 Selector buttons, 3 ECU, 4 to vehicle electrical system, 5 Central connection for converter-clutch control, 6 Inductive rpm sensor before and after shift clutch, 7 to E-Gas final-control element, 8 Accelerator pedal with load sensor and kickdown device, 9 Non-return overflow valve, 10 Compressed-air tank, 11 Compressed-air filter, 12 Converter clutch, 13 Reverse-gear display, 14 Reverse-gear shift cylinder, 15 Sensor for gear-shifted display, 16 Sensor for neutral display, 17 Main shift valve, 18 Central valve body, 19 Sensor for splitter-group display, 20 Shift cylinder for gears 3/4 (7/8), 21 Shift cylinder for gears 1/2 (5/6), 22 Sensor for range-group display, 23 Electronic speedometer, 24 Shift valve for range group, 25 Shift valve for splitter group.

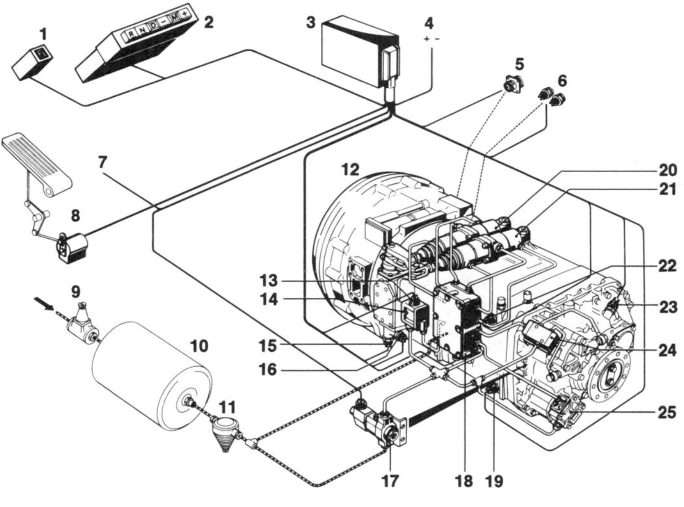

Power take-offs (auxiliary drives)
Numerous options are available for connecting auxiliary equipment to the transmissions in heavy vehicles. A basic distinction is made between clutch and engine-driven PTO's. The individual selection depends upon the specific application.

Retarders
Hydrodynamic and electrodynamic retarder assemblies (p. 630) are installed between the transmission output shaft and the drive axle to reduce the thermal load on the brakes during extended braking. Hydrodynamic retarders can be integrated within the transmission on either the input or output side. Advantages: compact dimensions, low weight, fluid shared with the transmission in a single circuit.

Transmissions with converter-clutch unit
The manually-shifted transmission can be combined with a converter-clutch unit to facilitate starting off in heavy vehicles. This unit consists of a hydrodynamic torque converter with a lockup coupling and a mechanical clutch which can be disengaged for gear shifting. A fluid pump maintains pressure in the converter circuit. During trailing-throttle operation a free-wheeling arrangement provides the diversion around the converter. Servo assistance is provided for the disengagement clutch.

Semiautomatic transmissions
Semiautomatic transmissions featuring manual gear selection combine simplified transmission operation with improved economy (especially in heavy commercial vehicles). The disadvantage of these transmissions relative to fully-automatic demand-response units lies in the fact that each shift entails an interruption of the power flow. However, there are also important advantages:
– narrower spacing of ratios, with up to 16 gears,
– enhanced-efficiency power transfer,
– reduced costs,
– same basic transmission unit for manual and automatic layouts.

Operation
A central valve block on the transmission converts electrical signals into the pneumatic or hydraulic pressure for activating the shift cylinder for the gear-changing process. Depending on which system is used, the electrical control signals can come directly from a driver-activated shift lever or from an electronic control.

Design variations
On the most basic systems, the remote control simply takes the place of the mechanical shift linkage; the shift lever (slap stick or conventional shift lever moving in H pattern) only supplies electrical signals. The vehicle is started from rest, and the clutch is used as with a standard manually-shifted transmission. More complex versions combine these systems with a recommended shift point.
Advantages are:
– reduced shifting effort,
– simplified installation (no shift linkage),
– engine overspeed protection.

On fully-automatic systems both the transmission and the drive-engagement mechanism are automated. The driver's control device consists of either a lever or push buttons, with an override provision in the shape of a driver-selected manual mode or +/– buttons. Complex shift programs are required to control a multi-ratio transmission. A system which engages the gears according to a fixed pattern will not be adequate. Current running resistance (as determined by load and road conditions) must be factored in to achieve the optimal balance between drivability and fuel economy. This task is assumed by a microcomputer control system.

The electronic engine-management system adjusts the throttle opening (up or down, depending upon direction of shift) to facilitate effective synchronization. The advantages are:
– Optimum operating economy through automatic, computer-controlled shifting,
– Reduced driver workload,
– Improved security for both driver and vehicle.

Automatic transmissions

Load-sensitive automatic transmissions perform the operations associated with starting off, ratio selection and shifting with no additional driver input required. The drive take-up element for starting off is always a hydrodynamic torque converter. The power losses in the automatic transmission are inherently larger than those in its manual counterpart. However, this fact is more than balanced by shift programs designed to maintain the engine in the maximum economy range. The components are:

5-speed automatic transmission *(ZF 5 HP 18).*
The main assemblies are:
A Hydrodynamic torque converter with lockup clutch
B 5-speed planetary-gear set
C Electronic-hydraulic transmission control.

1	*Input shaft*
2	*Lockup clutch*
3	*Hydrodynamic torque converter*
4	*Brake bands*
5...11	*Multi-plate clutches and brakes*
12...14	*One-way clutches*
15 & 16	*Planetary-gear set*
17	*Output shaft*

Torque-flow diagram

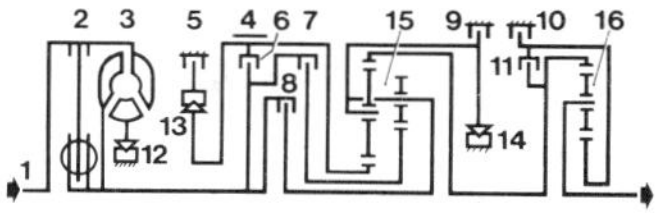

Shift diagram

Gear	Shift element									Mech. con-version
	2	4	5	6	7	8	9	10	11	
1	○				●		○	●		3.67
2	○	●	●		●			●		2.00
3	○	●	●		●				●	1.41
4	○		●		●	●			●	1.00
5	○	●	●			●			●	0.74
R	○			●			●	●		4.10

● Closed ○ May be closed

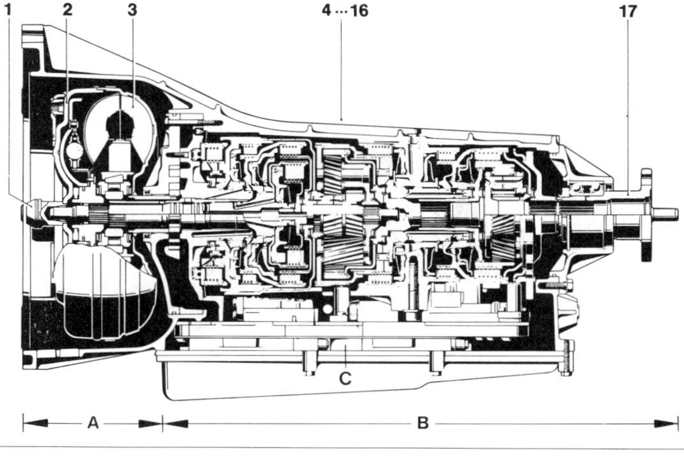

– Hydrodynamic torque converter (always employed with passenger-car transmissions, while heavy commercial vehicles generally use the Trilok design); for starting off, for torque multiplication and for absorption of harmonic vibrations. On passenger-car transmissions generally, and on heavy commercial vehicles virtually always supplemented by a lockup clutch.
– Several planetary-gear sets downstream from the hydrodynamic torque converter. Number and arrangement according to number of gears and ratios.
– Hydraulically-actuated multiplate clutches, plate or band brakes. Assigned to the individual elements within the planetary-gear sets to execute shifts without interrupting the flow of power.
– One-way clutches together with shift elements for optimal activation under load.
– A transmission-control system to define gear selections and shift points and to regulate demand-response shifting, as dictated by the driver-selected shift program (selector lever), accelerator pedal, engine operating conditions and vehicle speed. The control mechanism can be either hydraulic-only, or a combined electronic-hydraulic system.
– An engine-driven hydraulic-fluid pump (occasionally supplemented by a second fluid pump at the output end) provides hydraulic pressure for valve body and shift elements as well as supplying fluid to the hydrodynamic torque converter. It also supports lubrication and cooling in the transmission.

Design variations
The automatic transmissions installed in passenger cars most commonly incorporate 4 forward ratios, while 5-speed boxes have recently been gaining ground. The mechanical conversion range lies between 3.0 (3-speed transmission) and 5.0 (5-speed unit). Figures for initial multiplication range from 2.0 to 2.5.

Automatic transmissions in heavy commercial vehicles can have between 3 and 6 forward gears. The mechanical conversion range extends from 2 to 8. These transmissions frequently incorporate integral hydrodynamic retarders, as the requisite peripheral systems (fluid pump, large fluid pan, fluid cooler) are already in place.

Electronic transmission control
Systems which rely on hydraulics alone are being superseded by increased numbers of combined electronic-hydraulic units for the control of automatic transmissions. Hydraulic actuation is retained for the clutches, while the electronics assume responsibility for gear selection and for modulating the pressure in accordance with the torque flow. The advantages are:

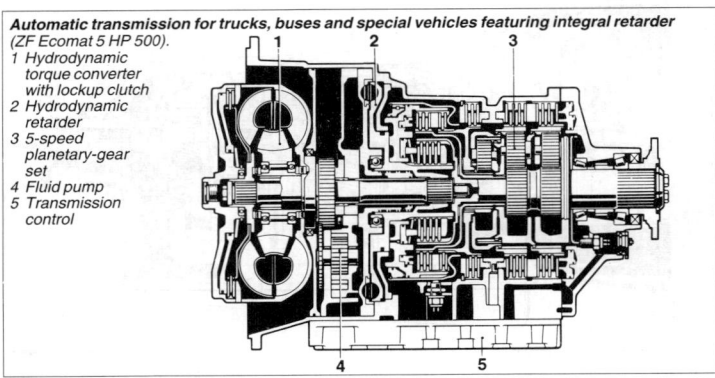

Automatic transmission for trucks, buses and special vehicles featuring integral retarder
(ZF Ecomat 5 HP 500).
1 Hydrodynamic torque converter with lockup clutch
2 Hydrodynamic retarder
3 5-speed planetary-gear set
4 Fluid pump
5 Transmission control

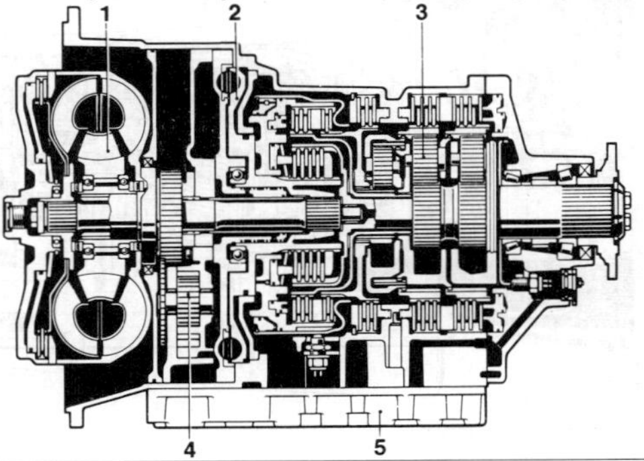

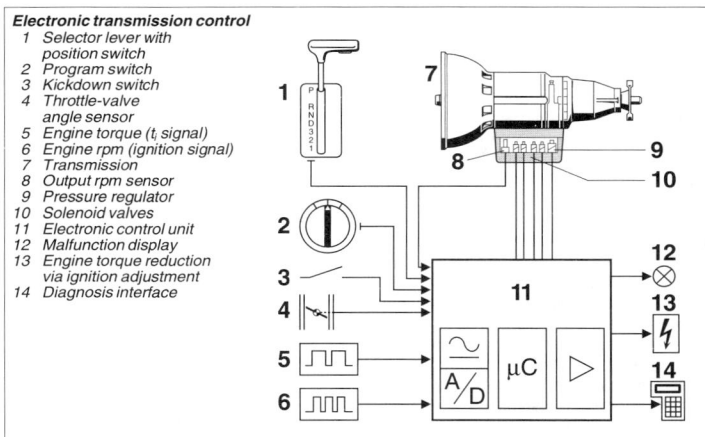

Electronic transmission control
1 Selector lever with position switch
2 Program switch
3 Kickdown switch
4 Throttle-valve angle sensor
5 Engine torque (t_i signal)
6 Engine rpm (ignition signal)
7 Transmission
8 Output rpm sensor
9 Pressure regulator
10 Solenoid valves
11 Electronic control unit
12 Malfunction display
13 Engine torque reduction via ignition adjustment
14 Diagnosis interface

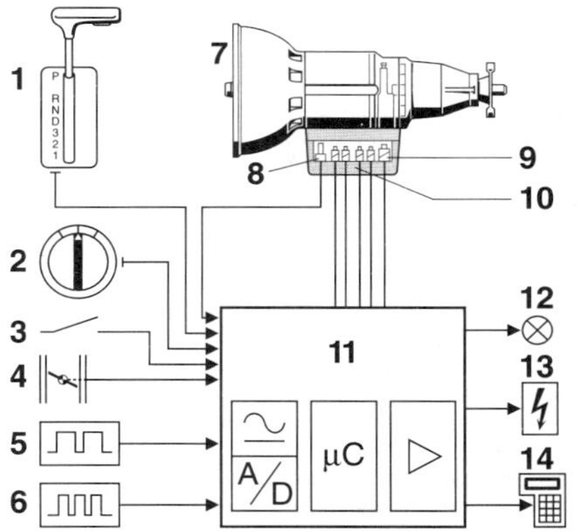

several different shift programs, smoother shifts, flexibility for adaptation to various vehicle types, simplified hydraulic control circuits and the ability to dispense with one-way clutches.

The system's sensors monitor load, selector-lever position, program and kickdown switch positions, and rpm at both the engine and the transmission's output shaft. The control unit processes this data according to a specific program to produce the control signals for the transmission. Electrohydraulic converters form the link between the electronic and hydraulic circuits, while standard solenoid valves activate and disengage the clutches. Analog or digital pressure regulators ensure precise control of pressures at the friction surfaces. A typical system includes:

Shift-point control
In selecting the gear to be engaged, the system refers to the rotating speeds of the transmission output shaft and of the engine before triggering the appropriate solenoid valves. The driver may select from among different shift programs (e.g., for maximum fuel economy or for maximum performance). Shifting can also be influenced manually with the selector lever.

"Intelligent" shift programs improve drivability by supplementing the standard transmission-control data with additional parameters such as forward and lateral acceleration, and the speed of accelerator and brake pedal actuation. A complex control program selects the appropriate gear for the current operating conditions and driving style using such expedients as suppressing trailing-throttle upshifts on the approach to and during corners, or automatically responding to low throttle openings by activating a shift program for low-rpm upshifts. Example: The Porsche Tiptronic[1]) features a ZF 4 HP 22 transmission operating with an intelligent shift program. This system combines enhanced driving convenience in the automatic mode with the option of active individual control. In addition to the standard positions, the selector lever may be moved to a second parallel gate in which a simple nudge suffices to trigger an immediate gear change (provided that excessive engine speed would not result).

[1]) Registered trademark.

Converter lockup

A mechanical lockup clutch can be employed to improve the efficiency of the transmission unit by eliminating torque-converter slip. The variables employed to determine when conditions are suitable for activation of the converter lockup mechanism are engine load and transmission output-shaft rpm.

Control of shift quality

The accuracy with which the pressure at the friction elements is adjusted to the level of torque being transmitted (determined with reference to engine load and rpm) has a decisive influence on shift quality; this pressure is regulated by a pressure regulator. Shifting comfort can be further enhanced by briefly reducing engine output for the duration of the shift (e.g., by retarding the ignition timing). This practice also reduces friction loss at the clutches and extends component service life.

Safety circuits

Special monitoring circuits prevent transmission damage stemming from operator error, while the system responds to malfunctions in the electrical system by reverting to a backup mode.

Final-control elements

Electrohydraulic converter elements such as solenoid valves and pressure regulators form the link between the electronic and hydraulic circuits.

Infinitely-variable-ratio transmission

(Ford CTX 811)

1 Input, 2 Transfer set with drive elements, 3/5 Primary/secondary shaft, each with moving taper disks, 4 Fluid pump, 6 Steel-link belt, 7 Intermediate shaft, 8 Final drive with differential.

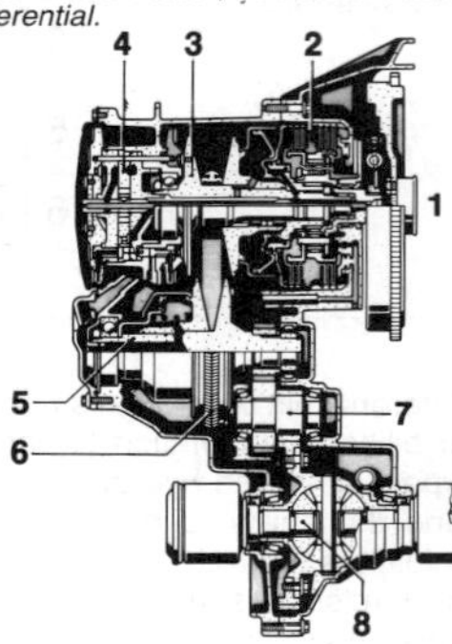

Tiptronic shifting strategies (process diagram)

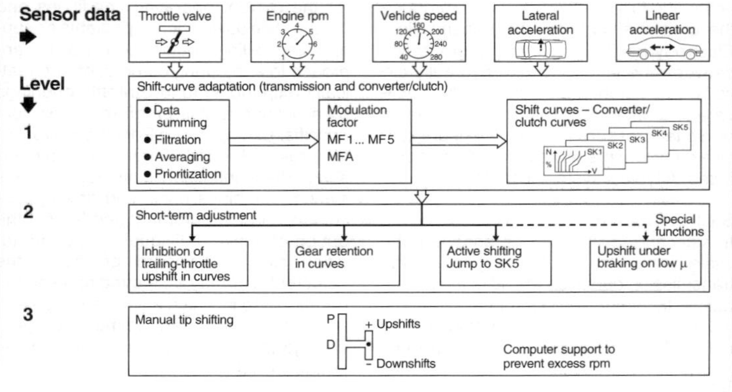

Continuously-variable transmissions

The continuously-variable transmission can convert every point on the engine's operating curve to an operating curve of its own, and every engine operating curve into an operating range within the field of potential driving conditions. Its advantage over conventional fixed-ratio transmissions lies in the potential for enhancing performance and fuel economy while reducing exhaust emissions (by maintaining the engine in the performance range for maximum fuel economy). However, full exploitation of this theoretical capability would entail an overdrive factor of $\varphi = 0.5$, or double the conversion at $\varphi = 1.0$.

The continuously-variable transmission (CVT) can operate mechanically (belt or friction-roller), hydraulically or electrically. The highest level of development has been achieved with mechanical continuously variable units employing steel belts (as installed in low-output series-production cars), where the unit's offset axes make it ideal for installation in front-wheel drive cars with transverse-mounted engines. The conversion range is 5.5 ... 6. The major elements in the continuously variable mechanical transmissions for passenger cars are:

- engagement mechanism for start off (wet multiplate clutch, magnetic-particle coupling or hydrodynamic torque converter),
- primary and secondary disks with axially adjustable taper-disk sections and power transfer via steel bands,
- electronic-hydraulic transmission control,
- reversing mode, and
- final drive unit with differential.

The continuously-variable transmission's remaining design principles have not been adopted up to now, as they still exhibit substantial disadvantages (size, weight, conversion range, manufacturing expense, transmission efficiency, restrictions on potential installation layouts) relative to fixed-ratio units.

Final-drive units

The total conversion ratio between engine and drive wheels is produced by several elements operating in conjunction: a transmission with several fixed ratios (automatic or manual), an intermediate transmission in some applications (transfer case with 4wd), and the final-drive unit.

Longer distances between transmission and final drive are bridged by the driveshaft (in one piece or in several sec-

Truck pinion axle with hub-mounted spur-gear drive
1 Twin wheel
2 Wheel bearing
3 Wheel hub
4 Spur-gear drive

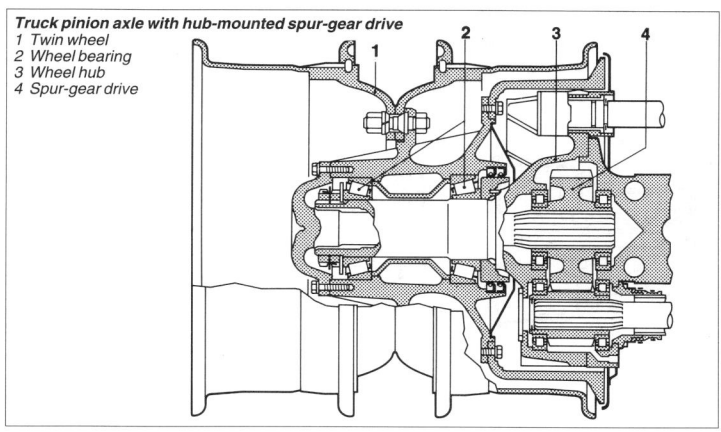

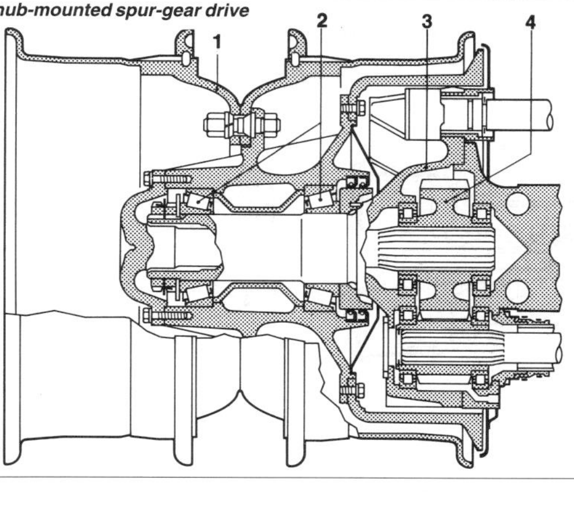

tions with intermediate bearings). Universal joints, constant-velocity joints or flexible-disk couplings compensate for angular variations between adjacent sections. When the drive line consists of a transmission with several ratios i_G and a final drive unit with conversion i_h, then the relationship between the rpm of the power unit n_m and that of the wheels n_R (with tire radius r) is defined as:

$$n_R = n_m / (i_G \cdot i_h)$$

Vehicle speed is then:

$$\upsilon = \frac{2 \cdot \pi \cdot n_m \cdot r}{i_G \cdot i_h}$$

In most automotive applications the final-drive unit consists of a ring-and-pinion unit with hypoid-bevel gears (longitudinal engine) or a spur-gear set (transverse engine). The tooth ratio determines the conversion factor, which generally lies within a range of between 2.2:1 and 5.0:1 for production vehicles.

On heavy commercial vehicles, it will seldom be possible to achieve the required conversion range with a single ring-and-pinion set; more complicated arrangements are usually employed:

- Single-ratio axles (for up to $i_h = 7$),
- Dual-shaft axle with front or top-mounted pinion drive,
- Two-speed axle (overall conversion $i_h = 9$),
- Pinion drive (spur-gear assembly in hub unit),
- Hub-mounted planetary-gear set (variable-ratio in special applications).

Large-diameter sun gears reduce ground clearance beneath the differential. The use of supplementary pinion-gear sets and outside planetary-gear axles to divide final conversion into two stages makes it possible to reduce the dimensions of both differential unit and axle shafts, allowing adequate ground clearance to be maintained in high-performance configurations.

Planetary-gear sets

Major areas of application for planetary-gear sets include final-drive units, front and rear range divider (splitter) units, and automatic transmissions. The basic planetary-gear set consists of the sungear, internal ring gear and the planet gears with carrier. Each element can act as input or output gear, or may be held stationary. The coaxial layout of the three elements makes this type of unit ideal for use with friction clutches and brake bands, which are employed for

Hub planetary-gear axle for trucks
1 Planetary-gear set, 2 Differential lock, 3 Differential, 4 Final drive.

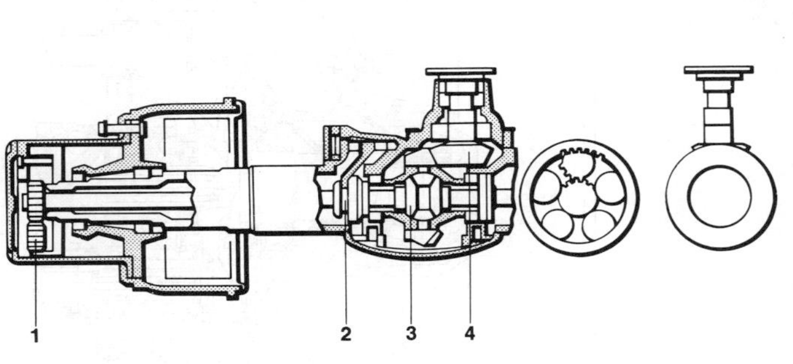

selective engagement and retention of individual elements. The engagement pattern can be changed – and a different conversion ratio selected – without interrupting torque flow; this capability is of particular significance in automatic transmissions.

Because the forces are distributed among several gears in simultaneous, parallel engagement, dimensions remain compact. The gear unit exhibits no free bearing forces, is suitable for high torques, and can be used for torque division and/or addition. Efficiency is high.

Differential

The differential unit compensates for discrepancies in the respective rotation rates

Planetary-gear set for various conversion ratios
A Sun gear, B Internal ring gear, C Planet gears with carrier.

Basic equation for planetary-gear sets: $n_A + (Z_B / Z_A) \cdot n_B - [1 + Z_B / Z_A] \cdot n_C = 0$

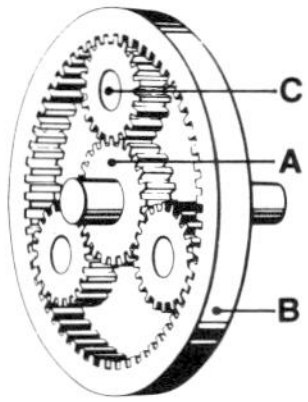

Input	Output	Locked	Ratio	Remarks
A	C	B	$i = 1 + Z_B / Z_A$	$2.5 \leq i \leq 5$
B	C	A	$i = 1 + Z_A / Z_B$	$1.25 \leq i \leq 1.67$
C	A	B	$i = \frac{1}{1 + Z_B / Z_A}$	$0.2 \leq i \leq 0.4$ Upward conversion
C	B	A	$i = \frac{1}{1 + Z_A / Z_B}$	$0.6 \leq i \leq 0.8$ Upward conversion
A	B	C	$i = - Z_B / Z_A$	Stationary transmission with direction reversal $-4 \leq i \leq -1.5$
B	A	C	$i = - Z_A / Z_B$	Stationary transmission with direction reversal $-0.25 \leq i \leq -0.67$

Final-drive unit with electronic-hydraulic limited-slip differential
1 Input side, 2 Drive pinion, 3 Ring gear, 4 Differential gears, 5 Plate set, 6 Hydraulic plunger, 7 Hydraulic connection, 8 Output side.

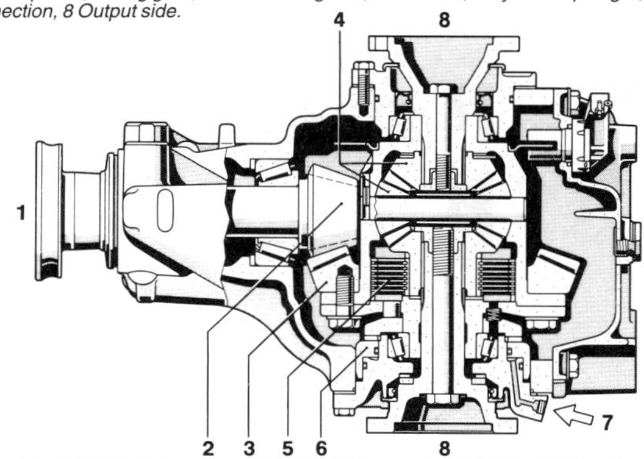

of the drive wheels: between inside and outside wheels during cornering, and between different drive axles on 4wd vehicles.

With rare exceptions for special applications, the differential is a bevel-gear drive unit. When the output bevel gears on the left and right sides (most common arrangement) are of equal dimensions, the differential gears act as a balance arm to equalize the distribution of torque to the left and right wheels.

When unilateral variations in road surface result in different coefficients of friction at the respective wheels, this balance effect limits the effective drive torque to a level defined as twice the tractive force available at the wheel (tire) with the lower coefficient of friction. This wheel then responds to the application of excessive torque by spinning.

The limited-slip differential combats this undesirable tendency by employing friction plates, friction cones, self-locking gears, or multiplate units in high-viscosity fluid media to limit the differential effect. The locking factor defines the effectiveness of the limited-slip differential:

$$S = \frac{|M_{\text{left wheel}} - M_{\text{right wheel}}|}{M_{\text{left wheel}} + M_{\text{right wheel}}} \cdot 100\ \%$$

Typical locking factors for passenger vehicles lie between 25 and 40%. The locking effect increases in response to variations in input torque (normal multiplate limited-slip unit), to differences in torque

4wd layout
1 Engine, 2 Transmission, 3 Transfer case, 4 Driveshaft to rear differential, 5 Differential, 6 Driveshaft to front differential.

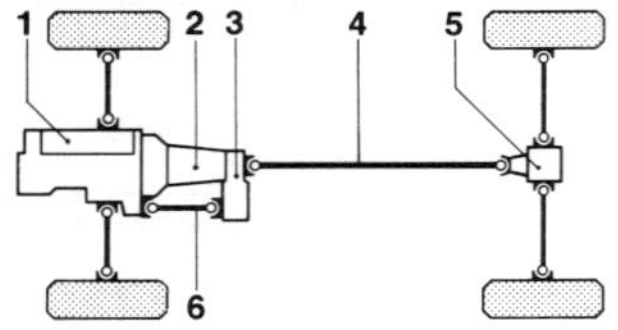

Locking-torque curve for viscous-coupling transfer case

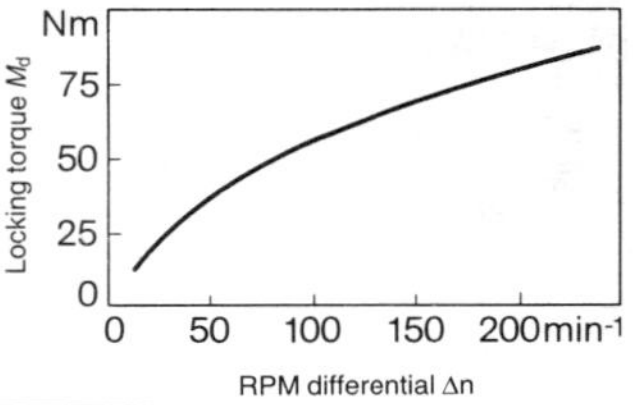

Transfer case for 4wd with viscous coupling
1 Input shaft
2 Planetary-gear set
3 Viscous coupling
4 To rear axle
5 Chain drive
6 To front axle

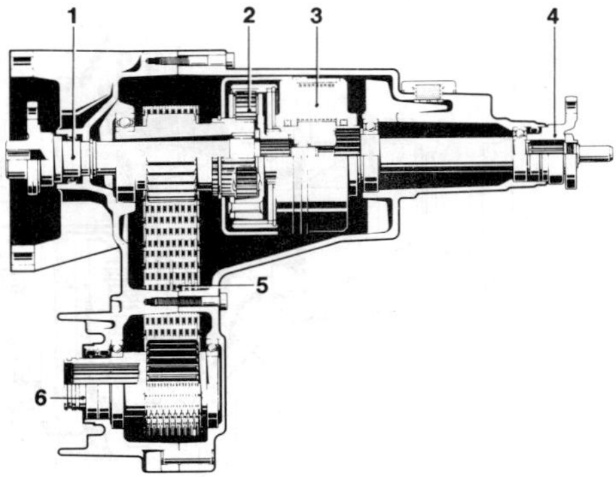

(self-locking gear sets) or rotating speed (viscous limited slip).

Limited-slip differentials can also employ electronic control to adapt to a widely variegated range of operating conditions: A high locking factor for starting off can be succeeded by a lower factor as speed increases or as the traction limit is reached. Driver-activated positive-action differential locks are available for use under special conditions (e.g., off-road).

Adhesion/slip curves
1 Wet asphalt $\mu_{A,B}$, 2 Packed snow $\mu_{A,B}$, 3 Cement $\mu_{A,B}$, 4 Wet asphalt μ_S. Adhesion coefficient $\mu_{A,B}$ Acceleration/Braking, μ_S Lateral force coefficient, $\lambda_{A,B}$ Slip under acceleration/braking.

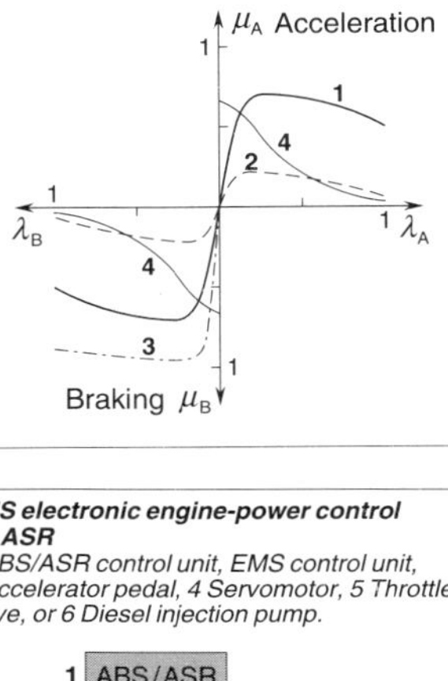

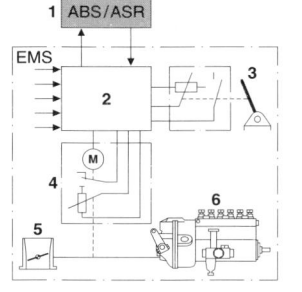

EMS electronic engine-power control for ASR
1 ABS/ASR control unit, EMS control unit, 3 Accelerator pedal, 4 Servomotor, 5 Throttle valve, or 6 Diesel injection pump.

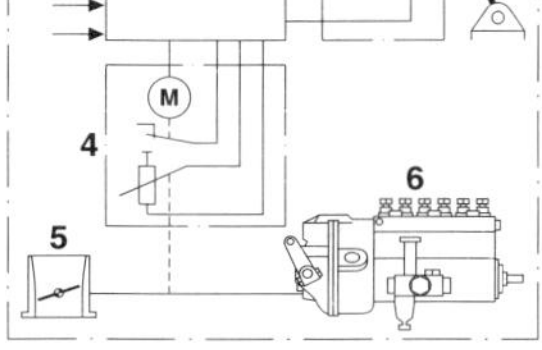

All-wheel drive, transfer case

All-wheel drive must meet especially stringent requirements for traction while simultaneously reducing the effects which this traction exerts on active vehicle response. Various types of systems are employed:

– Permanent 4-wheel drive, with 50:50 distribution using a bevel-gear differential or asymmetrical distribution via planetary-gear unit. The theoretical torque distribution is modified by the effect of automatic or controlled limited-slip differentials.

– Driver-selected 4-wheel drive (solid couplings at front/rear, viscous coupling or transfer case), with driver-actuated differential locks in transfer case and final drive. Transfer cases for off-road vehicles incorporate an additional driver-controlled conversion range for steep gradients, low speeds and high torque transfer.

The viscous coupling, an encapsulated multiplate unit with a high-viscosity silicone fluid, represents yet another means of activating the 4-wheel drive. When the traction limit at the permanently-engaged axle is exceeded, the unit responds to variations in slip by transferring torque to the secondary drive axle in accordance with the viscous-drive response curve. A unidirectional coupling interrupts the power flow to the secondary axle in the trailing-throttle mode, making the system suitable for use with ABS.

ASR traction control

A number of conditions contribute to wheelspin: the road surface may provide only limited adhesion on one or both sides, ice can make it difficult to accelerate away from parking lots or from the road shoulder. Loss of traction can also occur under acceleration, during cornering or when starting off on an uphill grade. Spinning or locked wheels afford only limited lateral adhesion (instable response). They also contribute to high rates of wear in both tires and drive-line components (such as the differential), particularly when a freely-spinning wheel suddenly finds traction. ASR ensures optimal application of tractive forces by preventing wheelspin. ASR represents an extension of ABS, with which it shares numerous components. The amount of force which can be transferred when starting off or during acceleration is (as for braking) a function of the amount of slip between tire and road surface. The adhesion/slip curves for acceleration and for braking display the same basic pattern (see illustration). The vast majority of acceleration and braking manoeuvres entail only limited amounts of slip, allowing response to remain within the stable range in the diagram; any rise in slip will be accompanied by a corresponding increase in available adhesion. Further increases in slip take the curves through the maxima and into the instable range, in which any additional growth in slip will generally result in a reduction in adhesion. A wheel will lock in a few tenths of a second under braking, while the build-up of excess torque during acceleration leads to a rapid increase in the rotational speed of one or both drive wheels. ABS prevents the wheels from locking. ASR prevents them from spinning by maintaining slip within acceptable limits during acceleration. The system actually performs two functions by enhancing traction while maintaining vehicle stability (true tracking).

Closed-loop traction-control devices for passenger cars

ABS/ASR 2I (Bosch)

To provide optimal closed-loop control of torque at the drive wheels, the mechanical connection between accelerator pedal and throttle valve (or pedal and injection-pump control lever on diesel engines) is replaced by the electronic engine-power control (EMS) (featuring the drive-by-wire accelerator pedal). A sensor converts the position of the accelerator pedal into an electrical signal, which the control unit then uses to generate a control voltage. A servomotor responds to this signal by repositioning the throttle valve (or injection-pump control lever on diesels); it then transmits a position report back to the control unit. Brief, simultaneous activation of the service brakes is employed to supplement the EMS (improved tractive performance via limited-slip effect). The standard ABS hydraulic modulator is expanded to include an ASR section, both to provide additional energy for brake-force application and for switching to ASR operation. The ABS solenoid valves have three positions – "accumulate pressure", "maintain pressure" and "bleed pressure" – to obtain the pressure modulation required for rapid and precise control of braking force.

ABS/ASR 2I System for passenger cars
1 Wheel-speed sensor, 2 ABS/ASR hydraulic modulator, 3 ABS/ASR control unit, 4 EMS control unit, 5 Throttle valve.

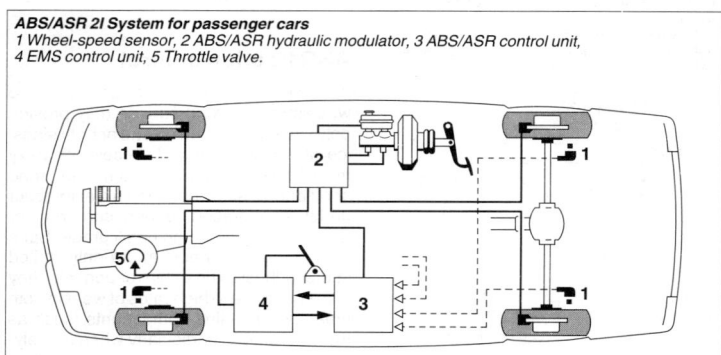

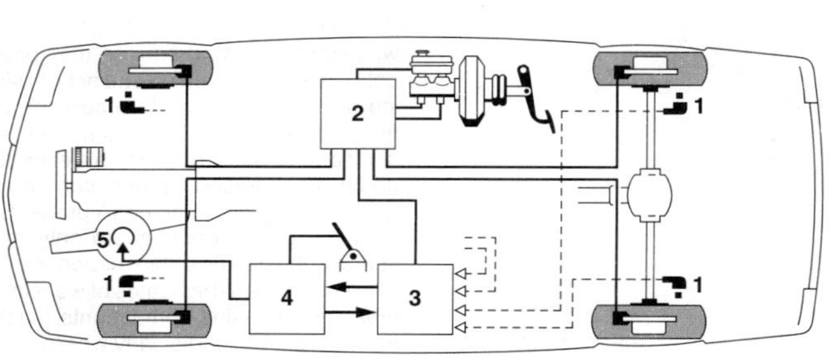

An interface connects the ABS/ASR CPU with the EMS control unit which varies the throttle-valve position in order to control engine torque.

ABS/ASR 2P (Bosch)
This system also employs EMS and brake-force modulation at the drive wheels; a salient difference being the two "plungers" to apply braking force. A hydraulically-controlled 2/2 valve is installed between solenoid valve and plunger to restrict the flow once a specific minimum pressure level is exceeded. This layout enhances braking smoothness by combining rapid initial brake-fluid delivery with subsequent moderate pressure build-up at the brake.

The ignition timing is also retarded briefly to provide supplementary support for the relatively slow reaction times achieved when the engine torque is controlled via throttle valve alone.

ABS/ASR 2E (Bosch)
This system furnishes the basic ASR benefits in stability and driver control in a simplified package. On road surfaces affording relatively constant adhesion, control of the throttle valve and the ignition timing, aided by the blanking-out of ignition pulses, can provide adequate control of engine torque for optimum vehicle stability.

A servomotor is employed for direct reduction of throttle-valve aperture, while a potentiometer monitors the valve's pos-

ABS/ASR control for passenger cars
1 ABS/ASR control unit, 2 Motronic control unit, 3 EMS control unit, 4 Engine, clutch, transmission, 5 Differential, 6 ASR pressure source, 7 ABS Hydraulic modulator, 8 Brake master cylinder, 9 Wheel brakes, 10 Wheel 1, 11 Wheel 2, 12 Wheel-speed sensor, 13 Road surface, Wheel 1, 14 Road surface, Wheel 2, 15 Vehicle mass m_P, p Brake pressure, v Wheel speed, v_F Vehicle speed, λ Slip, θ_R Wheel inertia, M_A Drive force, M_B Braking force, M_R Total forces acting on drive wheel, M_S Surface forces. Indices 1, 2: Wheel 1, 2.

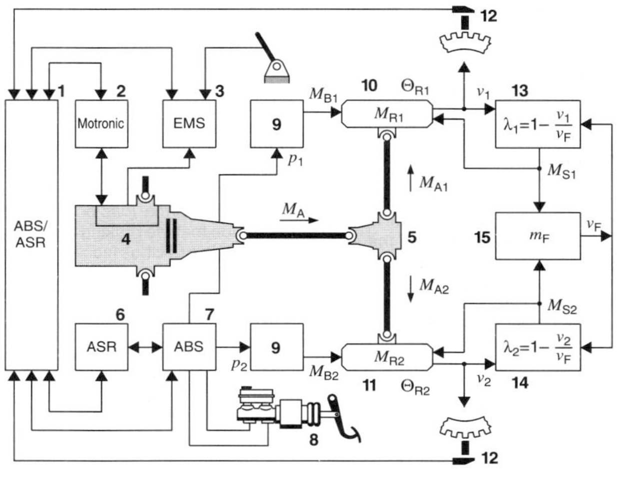

ition in an arrangement designed to allow the system to operate independently of the EMS facility which is needed for other engine-management functions. The "slow-response" engine-torque control is supplemented by "rapid-response" timing adjustment and blanking-out of ignition pulses. Under normal circumstances, application of supplementary braking force will only be required to provide additional traction when starting off on " split" surfaces (i.e., with differing left/right traction coefficients).

The standard ABS hydraulic unit receives a supplementary switchover solenoid (for mutual insulation of the circuits for braking and ASR), individual hydraulically-actuated pressure-relief valves and on/off valves. A self-priming return pump and a pressure-relief valve maintain the brake-fluid pressure at the correct level. Individual ABS solenoid valves modulate brake pressure at the drive wheels.

MSR Engine drag-torque control

The ASR unit installed in passenger cars can be expanded to include the MSR engine drag-torque control system. On slick road surfaces, a downshift or a sudden throttle closure can provoke excessive engine braking at the drive wheels. The MSR responds to these conditions by gently adjusting the throttle-valve for increased engine torque in order to reduce the braking forces at the wheel to the level corresponding to maximum operating stability.

ASR traction control for heavy commercial vehicles

This type of traction control comprises two circuits: one for braking and one for engine control. ASR is integrated within the ABS control unit for shared use of ABS components such as wheel-speed sensors and pressure-control valves. A supplementary two-way valve for each drive wheel and an ASR valve are required for control of the ASR brake-circuit, while a servo device for reducing engine torque must be incorporated in the engine-control circuit.

Brake-control circuit

When the vehicle moves off on a low-adhesion or μ-split surface, the wheelspin which accompanies excessive throttle will frequently be limited to a single drive wheel. Due to the low coefficient of friction at this wheel, only minimal tractive forces will be available to move the vehicle. The braking controller responds by applying braking pressure to the spinning wheel; this force is conveyed through the differential and acts as drive torque at the stationary wheel. The braking-force control circuit thus serves as a limited-slip device between the two wheels, increasing the available tractive force. First, the control unit switches the ASR valve to the open position for initial braking at the spinning wheel. The control circuit then uses the ABS pressure-relief valve to modulate the pressure at the wheel cylinder. Pressure can be increased, maintained, or discharged, according to the momentary condition of the wheel.

The braking-force control circuit's locking effect can be compared to that achieved with a mechanical limited-slip differential. A difference lies in the fact that the sum of the drive torques at the two wheels determines the force distribution pattern in a mechanical limited-slip differential. In contrast, in the active braking-force control circuit torque distribution is a function of the sum of the drive forces plus the applied braking force.

The benefits of the brake controller are generally felt when starting off, under acceleration or in alpine conditions on μ-split surfaces. High braking forces are required from the control circuit when a fully-loaded vehicle operates on μ-split on mountain roads. The thermal load on the brakes can be so high that the braking efficiency is impaired. The ASR thus incorporates two default modes:

a) The braking controller remains inactive at speeds in excess of 30 km/h (under most conditions),

b) The system monitors controller activity and wheel speed in order to estimate the thermal load at the brakes; the controller switches off when the limit is exceeded (occurs only under extreme conditions).

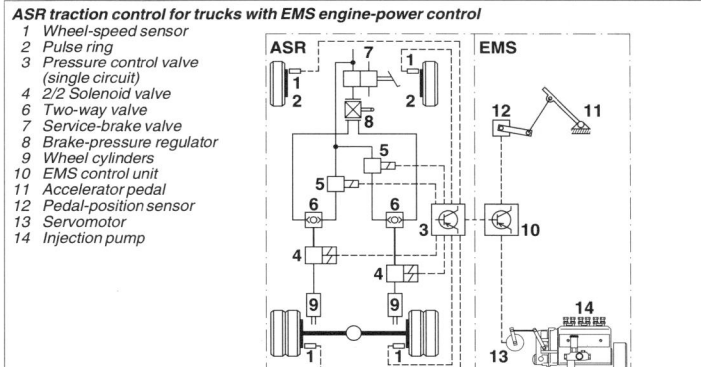

ASR traction control for trucks with EMS engine-power control

1 *Wheel-speed sensor*
2 *Pulse ring*
3 *Pressure control valve (single circuit)*
4 *2/2 Solenoid valve*
6 *Two-way valve*
7 *Service-brake valve*
8 *Brake-pressure regulator*
9 *Wheel cylinders*
10 *EMS control unit*
11 *Accelerator pedal*
12 *Pedal-position sensor*
13 *Servomotor*
14 *Injection pump*

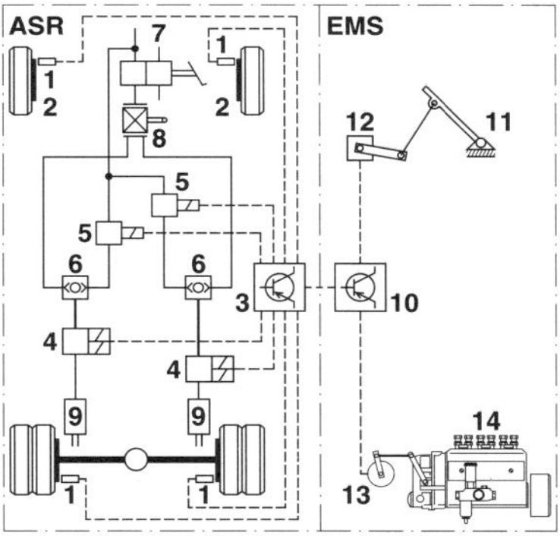

Engine-control circuit
The drive wheels respond to excess throttle by spinning.

The tractive force available to the vehicle corresponds to the diminishing adhesion coefficients found on the instable section of the adhesion/slip curve. Attempts to accelerate a stationary or crawling vehicle on ice or snow "polish" the surface, resulting in a further, substantial reduction of traction. Vehicle instability is the result. The engine control circuit responds to these conditions by reducing the drive slip to an acceptable level, thereby enhancing traction and vehicular stability.

This particular control system for reducing engine torque employs electric servo elements or pneumatic elements in one of two versions: a) interface connected to electronic engine-control devices, b) direct control of an electric ASR servomotor.

Interface: The ABS/ASR control unit receives the signals reflecting driver commands from the engine-management CPU (e.g., accelerator-pedal position or desired fuel-injection quantity). The ABS/ASR control unit consults both this signal and various other data such as wheel slip in calculating the torque reduction requirement to be implemented by the engine-management control unit. Examples of such control units are the EMS (electronic engine-power control) and EDC (electronic diesel control). These incorporate all engine-management functions (e.g., cruise control, rpm limiter, idle control) and are capable of immediate and precise implementation of the torque-reduction commands which they receive from the ASR.

ASR servomotor: The ASR servomotor receives its commands directly from the ABS/ASR control unit. The servomotor is a DC device with an integral position feedback for precise position control; control thus remains independent of variables such as positioning forces at the injection pump and friction-loss in the throttle linkage. ASR's capabilities are restricted to reductions in linkage travel, obviating the possibility of inadvertent application of additional throttle. The vehicle-speed limiter (FGB) limits the maximum speed to either the legal maximum (e.g., 80 km/h) or to a level selected by the driver (specified range: 40 km/h < vehicle velocity < maximum). With the supplementary engine rpm limiter, the driver must depress the accelerator beyond the position which would otherwise correspond to the desired speed or engine rpm limit. The ABS/ASR control unit compensates for the excess.

Suspension

Types of oscillation

Suspension springing and damping operate chiefly on the vertical oscillations of the vehicle. Driving comfort (loads on passengers and cargo) and operating safety (distribution of forces against the road surface as wheel-load factors fluctuate) are determined by the suspension. Several spring-damper systems will serve to illustrate the synergetic operation of the vehicle components.

Dual-mass model as quarter-vehicle model
h Excitation amplitude, z Oscillation amplitude, c Spring resistance, k Damping constants, m Mass. Indices: 1 Tires and axle, 2 Body.

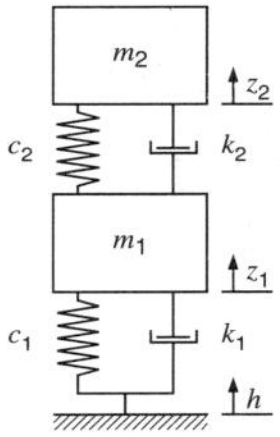

Table 1
Effects of design parameters on vertical oscillations of the vehicle

Design parameter	Effects of characteristic body frequency	Effects of characteristic axle frequency
Body data Spring constants	Major on driving comfort	Minor on driving safety
less compliance	Frequency and amplitude increase, less comfort	Increased frequency, mild reduction in amplitude
more compliance	Decreased frequency and max. amplitude, increased comfort	Mild increase in amplitude at low excitation frequencies
Shock-absorber constants	Major on driving comfort	Major on dynamic wheel-load fluctuation
	Must be tailored to application	
more damping (stiffer shock absorber)	Minor on acceleration	Major on acceleration, minor on dynamic wheel-load fluctuation
less damping (softer shock absorber)	Increased acceleration	Decreased amplitude, increased dynamic wheel-load fluctuation
Mass	Minor on amplification ratio for wheel-load fluctuation; amplification ratio for acceleration decreases with increasing load (empty vehicle is less comfortable than a loaded vehicle, and is not as safe)	
Tire and wheel data Springing (with increasing tire compliance)	Characteristic frequency and amplitude remain virtually constant	Decrease in characteristic frequency and amplitude of body acceleration and wheel-load fluctuation roughly proportional to reduction in vertical tire rigidity
Damping	Frequency and amplitude not affected by changes in tire damping	Stiffer damping results in minor reduction in amplitude during body acceleration and wheel-load fluctuation
	Due to heating, tire damping should be held to a minimum, to allow major compliance with soft tire	
Wheel mass	Reduced wheel mass has virtually no effect on comfort	Minimal wheel mass enhances safety

Driving comfort is largely determined by the degree of body oscillation. Root mean square of vertical body acceleration:

$$\overrightarrow{\ddot{z}_2} / \overrightarrow{h}$$

Axle oscillations (and thus, indirectly, fluctuations in wheel load) are the salient factor in determining driving safety. Root mean square of vertical axle oscillations:

$$\overrightarrow{\ddot{z}_1} / \overrightarrow{h}$$

Both types of motion are characterized by specific frequency relationships which assume the form of amplitude ratios.

Table 1 enumerates the relative effects of parameter variations in a dual-mass model (also applicable to actual vehicles).

In addition to determining the vertical-oscillation pattern, springing and shock absorbers also affect the vehicle's tendency to roll and pitch.

Pitch: Gyration around the vehicle's transverse axis, such as that encountered under acceleration from rest (front-suspension expansion and rear-suspension compression). The kinematic properties of the suspension (suspension-arm design) are selected so as to minimize pitching during drive-off and braking.

Roll: Gyration around a longitudinal axis which generally runs from the lower front to the upper rear of the vehicle; roll motion occurs in response to steering inputs (suspension compresses at the outside and expands on the inside of the curve). Stabilizers (anti-roll bars) at front and rear axles reduce this effect.

Types of spring

(See Table 2)

Controlled suspension systems

Load-levelling system

Partially loaded systems

The use of soft springs (comfort) results in long spring travel, such as that encountered with the vehicle loaded. In order to maintain vehicle-body height at an acceptable level, auxiliary air springs or hydropneumatic springs are employed.

The springing element is provided by the volume of the gas, while vehicle level is monitored mechanically directly at the suspension. Valves are used to control the input or output of the air or hydraulic fluid to/from the

Effect of frequency on kinematic amplitudes

$\ddot{z}_1$ Amplitude of axle acceleration, $\ddot{z}_2$ Amplitude of body acceleration, h Excitation amplitude. 1 Characteristic frequency of body, 2 Characteristic axle frequency.

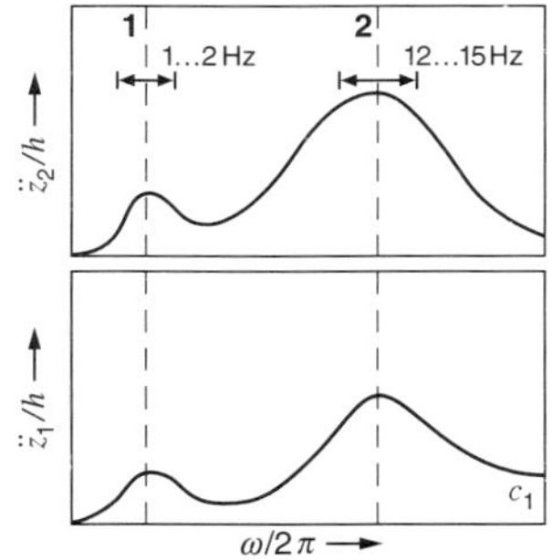

Air-suspension load-levelling system (partially loaded system)

1 Air connection, 2 Steel spring, 3 Auxiliary air-spring element, 4 Gas volume, 5 Shock absorber.

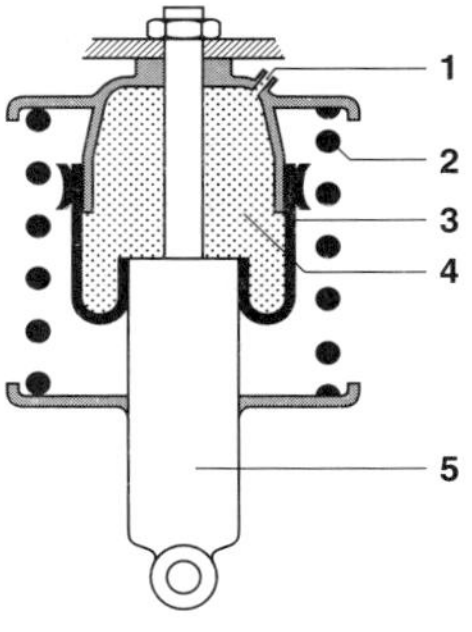

suspension element; the system can also incorporate intermediate electronic load-levelling control units acting upon solenoid valves.

Advantages of the electronic system:

– Reduced energy consumption achieved by avoiding transitional cycles during braking, acceleration and in curves,
– System reacts to increased vehicle speed by reducing ride height, resulting in fuel savings,
– Increase in vehicle height on poor road surfaces,
– Enhanced stability in curves achieved through lateral blocking of the suspension elements on a single axle.

Additional advantages for heavy vehicles:

– Automatic limitation of suspension travel for accomodating interchangeable bodies and piggyback containers,
– Vehicle height can be adjusted as desired, e.g., to align cargo surface with loading ramps,
– Control of lift axles (ride height raised automatically when lift axle is elevated), lowers automatically when approved drive-axle weight is exceeded, lift axle raised briefly (2 ... 3 minutes) to increase weight on drive axle (to increase drive traction).

Hydropneumatic load-levelling system (partially loaded system)
1 Fluid supply, 2 Steel spring, 3 Accumulator, 4 Gas volume, 5 Rubber diaphragm, 6 Fluid, 7 Hose, 8 Shock absorber.

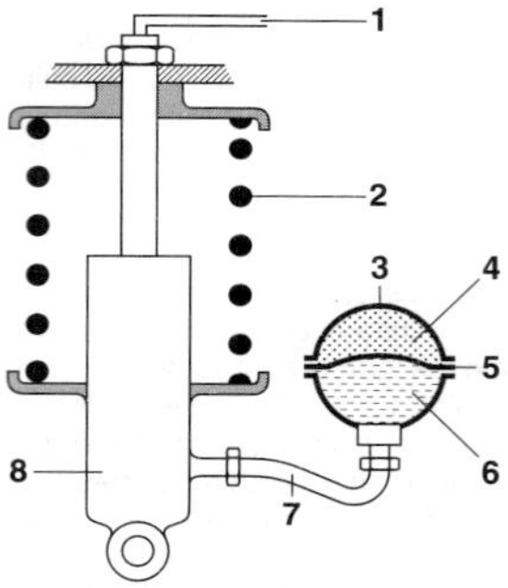

Fully loaded suspension systems

The cushioning effect is provided by the gas suspension element alone in a system in which coil springs are dispensed with. Either a single axle (generally the rear

Load-levelling (fully loaded systems)
a) Open system b) Closed system. 1 Filter, 2 Compressor, 3 Dryer, 4 Directional-control valve, 5 Bellows, 6 Non-return valve, 7 Pressure tank, 8 Pressure switch.

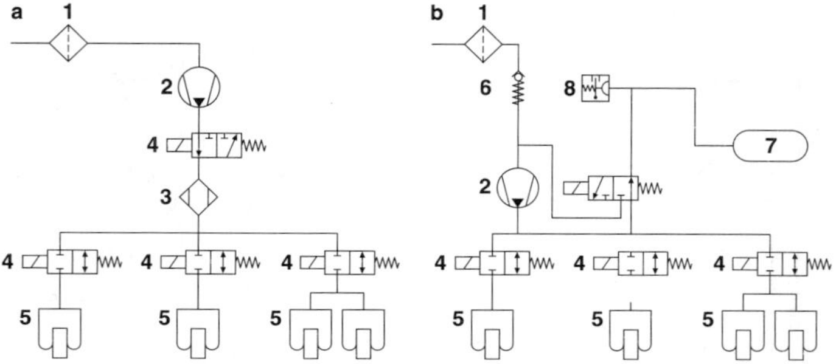

axle) or both axles of the vehicle can be controlled. If all axles are to be controlled, then the system must include an electronic control unit with a specific control strategy. The control strategy responds to factors such as fluctuations in axle load (to prevent the vehicle from tilting) while monitoring control times and recognizing system errors.

Open system:
Advantages: Relatively simple design and control.

Disadvantages: High compressor output required for brief periods of active control, air dryer required, noise during suction and exhaust.

Closed system:
Advantages: Low compressor output (minimal pressure differential between accumulator and suspension element), no problems with moisture.

Disadvantages: Relatively complicated design (accumulator, pressure switch, nonreturn valve).

Air-filled suspension elements weigh less than their hydropneumatic counterparts.

Active suspension

Active suspension controls both the "springing" and the "damping" functions. Various types of design concepts have been realized.

Designs incorporating hydraulic cylinder
An external source generates energy for rapid adjustments within a hydraulic cylinder, while sensors provide the link between cylinder and vehicle body. Sensors for wheel load, travel and acceleration transmit signals to an electronic control unit (ECU) featuring a control cycle of just a few milliseconds.

The control system achieves virtually constant wheel-load factors while maintaining a constant mean vehicle height. Steel springs or hydropneumatic suspension elements are employed to support the static wheel load.

Active suspension
a) Hydraulic cylinder, b) Hydropneumatic suspension, c) Air suspension.
1 Vehicle body, 2 Wheel-load sensor, 3 Travel sensor, 4 Accumulator, 5 Pumping circuit, 6 Servo valve, 7 Actuating cylinder, 8 Acceleration sensor, 9 Damper, 10 Valve, 11 Tank, 12 Compressor, 13 Solenoid valve.

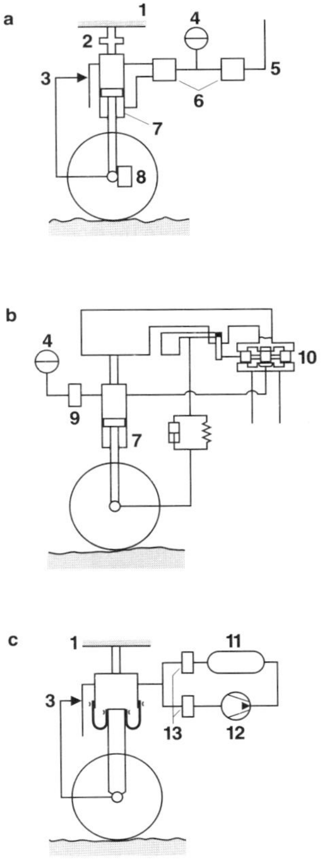

Designs incorporating hydro-pneumatic suspension (fluid control)

Structural oscillations are regulated by controlling the hydraulic fluid in the hydro-pneumatic suspension circuit, while it is being directed to the hydropneumatic element or discharged from the spring strut. In order to reduce energy requirements, the system's action is restricted to smoothing low-frequency irregularities; a gas accumulator installed adjacent to the spring strut is responsible for higher-frequency undulations.

The damping element can be set to concentrate on wheel movements.

Air-suspension designs

Body motion is controlled by regulating the air supply to the air-spring bellows. The closed bellows system is limited to controlling low-frequency oscillations and steering roll.

Because the system equalizes transverse forces, it is also suitable for application with spring struts.

Shock absorbers

Telescopic shock absorbers convert oscillations in body and suspension into heat. They are attached to body and axle with elastic mounting elements to provide noise insulation.

Single-tube shock absorbers

A sliding separating-piston and gas cushion form the gas-pressure damper in the single-tube shock absorber.

Advantages: Easy to tailor to specific applications, as the large piston diameter allows low working pressures. Sufficient room for valves and passages. Heat is dissipated directly via the outer tube. The shock absorber can be installed in any position.

Disadvantages: Length. The outer tube, which acts as guide cylinder for the piston, is susceptible to damage from stone throw etc. Suspension layout must provide sufficient room for the tube which, with its very close tolerances, is not to be mechanically impeded in any way. This is a disadvantage when lines must be routed around the shock absorber in restricted bodywork areas. The piston-rod seal is subjected to the damping pressure.

Single-tube shock absorber
1 Atmospheric pressure, 2 Valve, soft spring, 3 Valve, hard spring, 4 Non-return valve.

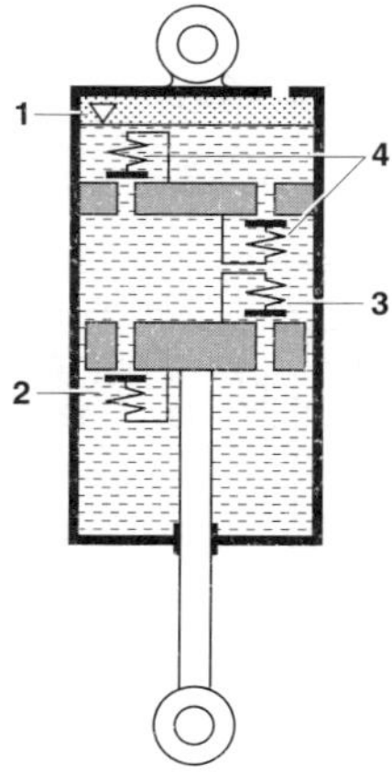

Twin-tube shock absorber
1 Atmospheric pressure, 2 Reserve chamber, 3 Base valve.

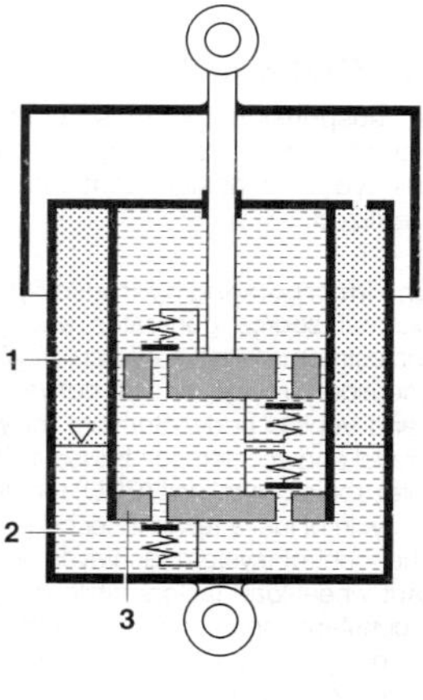

Twin-tube shock absorber

This type of damper is available as the atmospheric or low-pressure twin-tube type.

Advantages: Insensitive to external damage. Here, in contrast to the single-tube shock absorber, mechanical measures can be taken at the outer tube to permit routing of lines in restricted bodywork areas. This shock-absorber type is short, as the balance chamber is next to the working cylinder.

Disadvantages: Shock absorber is sensitive to overloading (damping ceases). Only certain specific installation positions are possible.

Damping characteristics

The damping characteristics are the result of the cumulative function of orifice damping and of the spring-loaded valve which closes the passage; the spring responds to pressure by increasing the free aperture of the outlet orifice. Piston bore and spring can be specifically tailored to provide linear to mildly degressive damping curves. An internal adjustment mechanism can be used to obtain several performance curves from a single shock absorber. The compression-stage values are frequently only 30 ... 50% of those for the rebound mode.

Electronically-controlled adjustable shock absorbers (active adaptation to operating conditions) can be used to enhance driving comfort and safety. Fixed damping parameters, on the other hand, result in defined relationships between comfort and safety.

The control law is frequently a semi-active "skyhook" type, in which the shock absorber adjusts with reference to body speed.

Vibration absorbers

The vibration absorber is a supplementary mass providing both springing and damping for the vehicle to which it is attached. The vibration absorber assimilates the oscillations of the main system, i.e., the main system ceases to oscillate - the motion is restricted to the vibration damper (see "Oscillations" p.39).

Vibration absorbers act upon body motion; their effect upon the suspension is extremely limited.

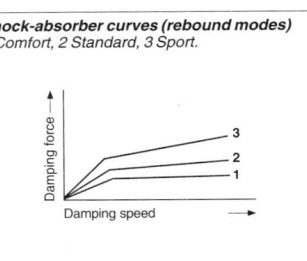

Shock-absorber curves (rebound modes)
1 Comfort, 2 Standard, 3 Sport.

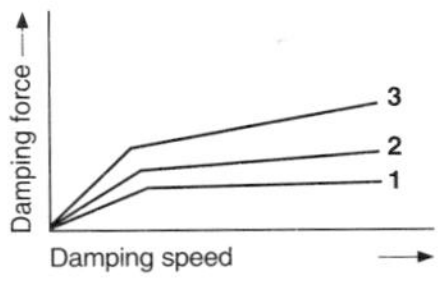

Amplification function of axle acceleration
1 With absorber, 2 Without absorber.
a_l Amplitude of z_l, h Excitation amplitude.

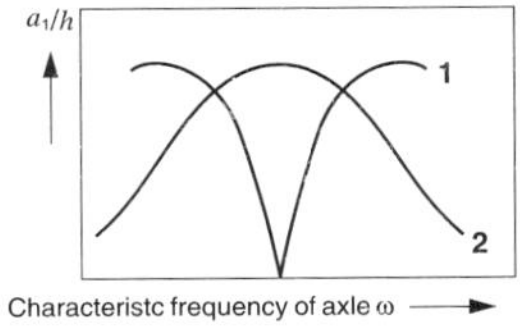

Vibration absorption
a) Installation on vehicle, b) Mechanical equivalent system.
1 Absorption spring and damper, 2 Absorption mass, 3 Wheel mass, 4 Tire spring

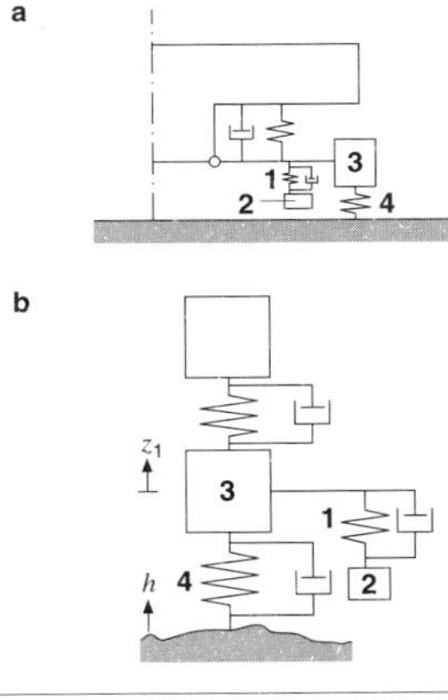

Suspension design elements (Table 2)

Spring elements	Illustration	Effects of load factor on natural frequency of body	Characteristics
Steel springs Leaf spring	Leaf springs on car  Leaf springs and auxiliary spring on truck 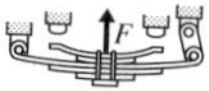	$\frac{\nu_{loaded}}{\nu_{empty}} = \sqrt{\frac{m_{empty}}{m_{loaded}}}$ Natural frequency decreases along with increasing load. Generally speaking, characteristics are linear.	Single or multi-layer. Is also used to determine wheel travel in some applications. Interleaf friction in some types, can be reduced with plastic inserts (noise possible). Generally without inserts in trucks, maintenance required. Good transfer of forces to frame.
Coil spring	Cylindrical spring 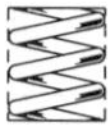 Barrel spring 		Variable compliance rates or conical-wire design provides a progressive characteristic. Shock absorber can be mounted within spring. No self-damping, self-induced spring oscillation possible. Advantages: Limited space requirement, low weight, maintenance-free. Disadvantages: Additional components required to control wheel travel.
Torsion bar	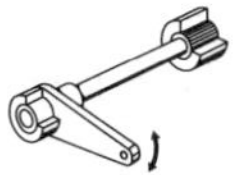		Made of round bar stock or flat steel (lower weight with round bar). Vehicle height adjustment possible, depending on design. Wear and maintenance-free. Flat-steel bundle employed for additional flexural loads.
Air springs Roll bellows Toroid bellows	Element with constant gas volume. 1 Vehicle frame, 2 Roll bellows, 3 Piston, 4 Air supply, 5 Clamping plate. Roll bellows 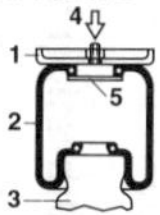 Toroid bellows 	$\frac{\nu_{loaded}}{\nu_{empty}} = 1$ Natural frequency remains contant under load. Performance curves determined by gas properties, piston form, cord angle in bellows.	As spring strut or single-spring element, especially in trucks and buses. Increasingly widespread use in cars for load-levelling control at rear axle and for suspension on all wheels. Achieves high vertical compliance (increased comfort). Wheel travel must be defined by separate suspension components. Low pressure (10 bar) means that large volumes are required. Geometric design of toroid bellows not suitable for achieving low vertical spring rates.

Hydropneumatic suspension Hydraulic diaphragm accumulator Piston accumulator	Spring element with constant gas mass. 1 Gas, 2 Fluid, 3 Diaphragm, 4 Steel spring. Hydraulic diaphragm accumulator  Piston accumulator 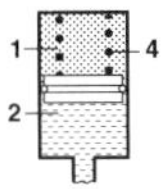	$\frac{v_{loaded}}{v_{empty}} = \sqrt{\frac{m_{loaded}}{m_{empty}}}$ Natural frequency increases under load. Curves are progressive and are a function of initial accumulator pressure.	Response characteristics determined by gas volume in accumulator (separated from fluid by piston). The fluid compresses the gas according to wheel load. Damping valves are integrated in the shock absorber and in the connection between spring strut and accumulator. The rubber diaphragm requires maintenance due to gas diffusion.
Rubber suspension	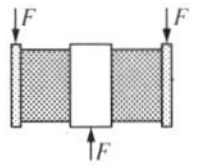 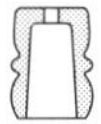	Natural frequency affected by load due to non-linear compliance rates.	Vulcanized rubber thrust elements between metal parts, increasingly with integrated hydraulic damping. Used for mounting assemblies (engine, transmission) and steering components, and as auxiliary compliance elements.
Stabilizer (Anti-roll bar)	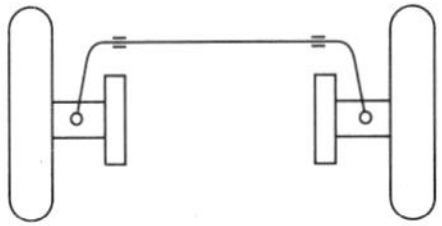	No effect with equal deflection on both sides of the wheel. Half the total anti-roll stiffness acts against unilateral deflection, while entire torsional resistance responds to mutually opposed wheel travel.	Reduces body roll while influencing cornering characteristics (over and understeer). Generally made of U-shaped bar or tube stock, sides frequently flattened to cope with flexural loads. Attachment points must be at extreme outside of axle to allow minimal stabilizer diameter. Relative positions of stabilizer and control rod radii must be selected to ensure that stabilizer is subjected to torsional stress with no bending.

Suspension linkage

The suspension layout employed to connect the individual wheels to the vehicle structure defines the suspension-linkage design. The linkage enables the wheel for the most part to move vertically in order to compensate for irregularities in the road surface. In addition, the front wheels are steered (although the future will see an increasing trend toward rear-wheel steering), and the front and rear suspension-linkage systems differ due to the special demands imposed by the steering mechanism. Appropriate design measures are taken for the suspension geometry and springing so as to limit vertical body travel while also reducing pitch and roll.

Kinematics

The front wheels pivot around an inclined axis whose position is determined by the joints and the suspension components.

The following kinematic data are of essential importance for the wheel's response to steering input and the transfer of forces between tire and road surface:

Toe-in δ_{VS}

Toe-in is the angle between the vehicle's longitudinal axis and a plane through the center of the (steered-wheel) tire. It can also be defined as the difference in the distance between this plane and the front and rear rims of the steered wheel. Toe-in compensates for elastokinematic forces which lateral forces exert on the tire. Toe-in is 2 ... 3 mm with rear-wheel drive, whereas a toe-out of up to – 2 mm is employed with front-wheel drive (to compensate for drive forces).

Deflection-force lever arm r_{st}

The deflection-force lever arm is the shortest distance between the wheel center and the inclination angle of the steering axis. Its length provides an index of the effect of drive forces on the steering.

Caster n

Positive caster is the distance between the wheel's contact point and the point at which the steering axis intersects the road as viewed from the side. Caster determines the degree of self-centering action in the steering as well as influencing straight-line stability and steering force in curves.

Toe-in

δ_{VS} *Toe-in angle, Distance between wheels: a Front, b Rear, $b–a$ Toe-in (in mm), s Track.*

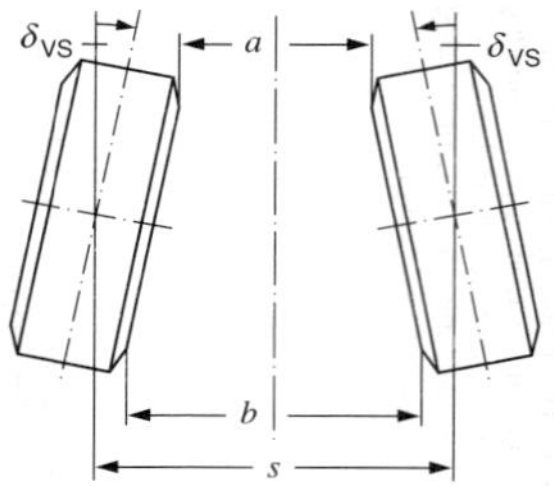

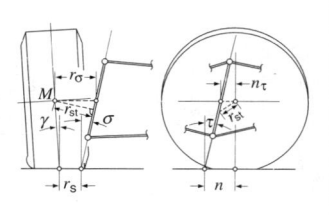

Wheel position

M Wheel center, r_{st} Deflection-force lever arm, n_τ Caster offset, n Positive caster, τ Caster angle, r_σ Kingpin inclination offset, r_s Kingpin offset, γ Camber angle, σ Kingpin angle.

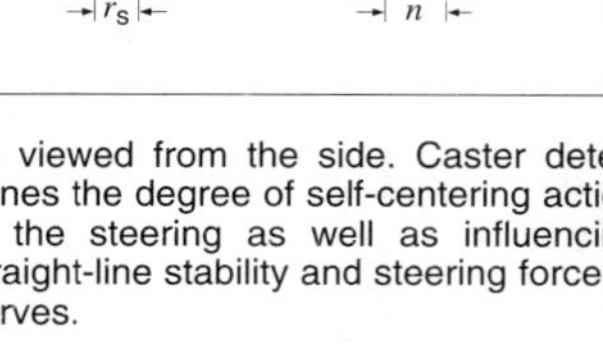

Caster offset n_τ

Caster offset is the displacement of the wheel center relative to the steering axis, as measured at the wheel center. It influences the degree of positive caster independently of the positive-caster angle.

Caster angle τ

The caster angle is defined as the angle between the steering axis and the vertical plane as viewed from the side. It influences the self-centering effect of the steering without large amounts of caster offset.

Kingpin inclination offset r_σ
The kingpin inclination offset is the horizontal distance between the wheel center and the kingpin axis.

Kingpin offset r_s
The kingpin offset, or steering offset, is the distance between the wheel center and the point at which the steering axis intersects the road surface. It is negative when the point of intersection is between the center and the outside of the wheel. Kingpin offset combines with the effects of longitudinal forces to generate steering motions and self-centering action at the steered wheel (driver information). Negative kingpin offset results in self-stabilizing steering angles.

Camber angle γ
Camber angle is the inclination of the wheel toward the vehicle's longitudinal plane as measured in the vehicle's transverse plane. The camber angle is negative when the top of the wheel is inclined toward the center of the vehicle. It influences lateral control (today's vehicles generally employ moderate cambers of $< 5 \ldots 3°$ out of consideration for the tires).

Kingpin angle σ
The kingpin angle is the angle between the steering axis and the vehicle's longitudinal plane, as measured in the vehicle's transverse plane. It influences steering force (steering feel) along with caster and the steering roll radius.

Basic types (table, p. 570ff.)

Elastokinematics

The wheel's travel pattern is dictated by the suspension geometry – as determined by the components (toe-in, track and camber) – and by the variations in kinematic properties attendant upon spring compression. The forces acting upon the suspension (acceleration, deceleration, vertical and lateral forces) also have an effect upon the wheel's dynamic position due to compliance in mountings and in the components themselves (kinematic response due to elastic deformation: elastokinematics). The usual objective is to avoid such changes in wheel orientation as might derive from either kinematic or elastokinematic effects. To this end, kinematic and elastokinematic properties are designed into the axle which are calculated to provide a self-compensating response to force and spring action. Specially-aligned component mountings result in cardanic angles during springing. According to the design of the rubber mount they define the options for the compensation of elasto kinematic effects.

Some modern rear suspensions employ elastokinematics to reduce reaction to changes in dynamic load. Differing longitudinal and vertical forces at the wheels allow the flexibly-mounted axle carrier or individual locating member to pivot, providing the wheels at the outside of the curve with more toe-in (stabilizing steering effect at the rear wheels).

Elastic wheel positioning through lateral force F_x
F_1,F_2 Forces at locating-member mount, a Distance between wheel axes and locating-member, b Distance between locating-member mounts, δ_{vs} Toe-in.

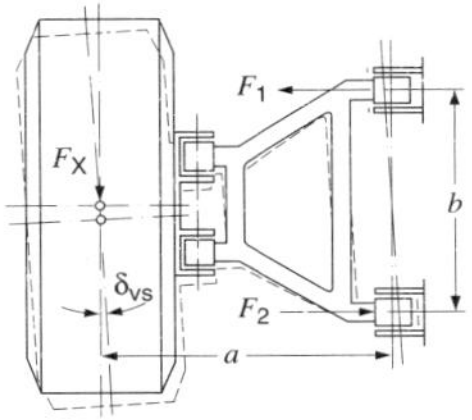

Positioning locating-member mounts to compensate for elastic deflection
S_F Center of gravity; c_{ax}, c_{rad} Compliance constants, axial/radial, α Positioning angle.

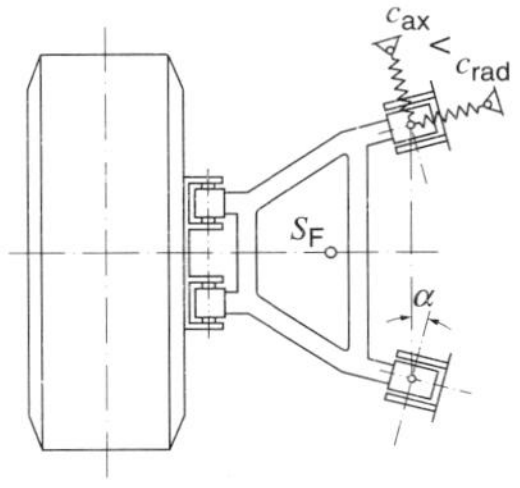

Basic suspension types and their characteristics

<table>
<tr><th colspan="5">Rigid axles</th></tr>
<tr>
<td>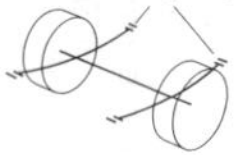</td>
<td>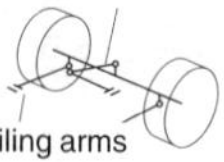</td>
<td>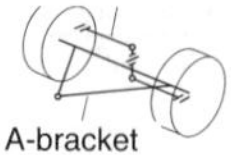</td>
<td>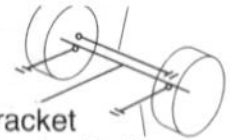</td>
<td></td>
</tr>
<tr><td colspan="5">Used for rear axle with conventional (rear-wheel) drive; for front and rear axle on heavy and off-road vehicles</td></tr>
<tr><td colspan="5">Track, toe-in, camber remain constant relative to road surface, even with body roll, good tracking</td></tr>
<tr><td rowspan="2">Low manufacturing costs, axle tramp, high unsprung weight, poor compliance characteristics under lateral force and torque</td><td colspan="4">No lateral body motion during springing, no undesirable wheel positions due to lateral or longitudinal forces, large amount of space required</td></tr>
<tr><td>Pitch axis as desired
High weight and expense</td><td></td><td>Panhard rod incites lateral body motion under compression</td><td>Pitch axis as desired</td></tr>
<tr><th colspan="5">Semi-rigid axles</th></tr>
<tr>
<td>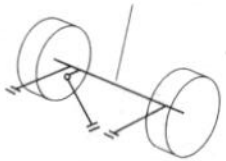</td>
<td></td>
<td></td>
<td rowspan="4"></td><td rowspan="4"></td>
</tr>
<tr><td colspan="3">Employed for rear axle in conjunction with front-wheel drive</td></tr>
<tr><td colspan="3">Large distance between mounts minimizes structural stresses, favorable force transfer at rigid longitudinal members, simple manufacture, two attachment points, simple assembly, extremely robust, limited kinematic possibilitiest</td></tr>
<tr><td>Roll center above wheel center according to position of Panhard rod</td><td>Roll center below center of wheel (according to attachment point)</td><td>Roll center at road surface (all roll centers in centre of vehicle)</td></tr>
</table>

Independent suspension

Trailing arms	Semi-trailing arms	Semi-trailing arms	Swing axle	Swing axle
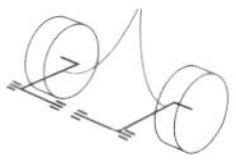		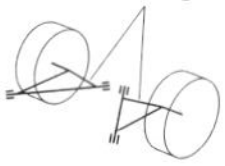	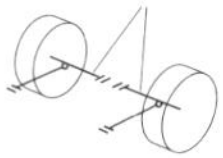	
Rear axle designs for front or rear-wheel drive				
Modest space requirement, low cost, limited range of kinematic options: Camber change, substantial caster change, position of roll center, high stresses	Ease of manufacture, positive kinematic possibilities, poor elasto-kinematic properties, lateral and peripheral forces oversteer, high steering forces	Modest expense, limited kinematic possibilities, lateral forces force body upward in curves, support effect with positive camber		
McPherson strut		Upper and lower A-arms	Lateral and transverse links	
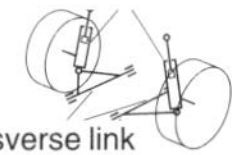		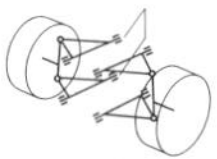	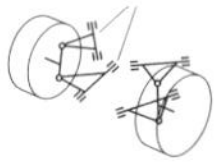	
Used at front and rear axle with front and rear-wheel drive;			At front axle with front and rear-wheel drive	
Modest space requirement (vehicle width), large support base results in minimal stress to structure, few joints, easy to install, low weight, insensitive to tolerances, limited kinematic possibilities in the areas of camber change, track angle, position of roll-and-pitch center, space required for springs, tire width, installation height		Maximum kinematic possibilities, expense associated with large number of joints, narrow structure tolerances (without subframe), due to relatively small distance between attachment points, stiff mounts are required to avoid major changes in wheel attitude (reduced comfort)		
			Forces from upper link are fed into rigid firewall	

Wheels

Modern vehicle wheels generally comprise a rim and nave or wheel disc. The rim is that part of the wheel on which the tire is mounted. The nave joins the rim to the wheel hub. Wheel size is primarily determined by the load-bearing capacity of the tire. The most important terms are: rim width, rim diameter, center hole, hole circle diameter, number of mounting holes, countersunk and stud design, and rim offset.

Rim designs
Rims differ from one another (depending upon the type of tire) in terms of number of parts and cross-sectional rim shape. The most important rim details are: rim flange, rim bead seat and rim base. Rims have one of the following cross-sectional shapes:
- Drop center,
- Flat base,
- 5° tapered bead seat and
- 15° tapered bead seat.

Wheel mounting
Mounting the wheel to the wheel hub fulfills two requirements: centering the wheel in order to ensure that it runs true, and transmission of the wheel forces to the wheel hub. Correct wheel mounting affects the service life of the wheel system as a whole.

Passenger-car wheels

Mass-produced wheels are made of sheet steel, with forged or cast aluminum and (less commonly) magnesium being used primarily for special wheels and aftermarket wheels. Sheet aluminum, although used in some cases, has not become popular for reasons of cost. The use of plastic as a material for wheels is still in the developmental stage due in particular to insufficient high-temperature strength and difficult wheel mounting and manufacture.

The disc and rim are welded together on sheet-steel wheels; in the case of forged and cast light-alloy wheels, these two components are usually manufactured in one piece. Multiple-piece designs, even those which are made of different materials (e.g.,

Disc wheel (e.g., 6J × 14 H2)
1 Rim flange (e.g., J flange), 2 5° tapered-bead seat, 3 Hump (e.g., double hump H2), 4 Rim, 5 Drop center, 6 Ventilation hole, 7 Wheel nave, D Rim diameter (e.g., 14″) L Hole circle diameter, M Rim width (e.g., 6″), N Center hole, ET Rim offset.

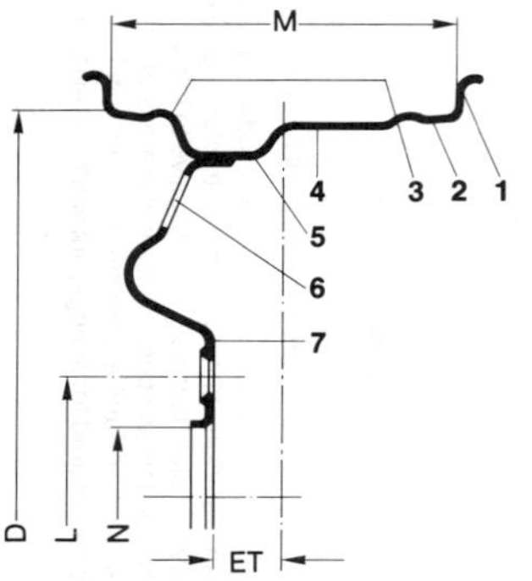

Rim designs
1 Flange, 2 5° tapered-bead seat, 3 Hump, 4 Drop center, 5 15° tapered-bead seat.
M Rim width, D Diameter.

Passenger-car hump rim as per DIN 7817

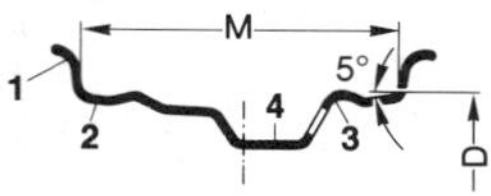

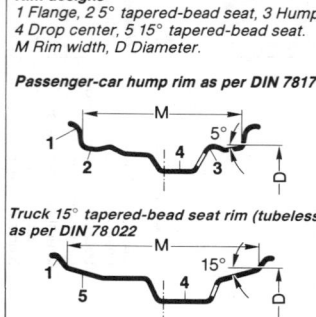

Truck 15° tapered-bead seat rim (tubeless) as per DIN 78 022

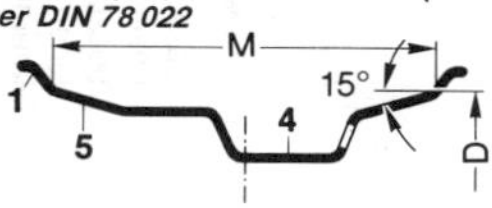

Truck 5° tapered-bead seat rim as per DIN 7820

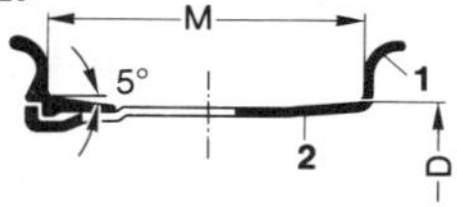

magnesium disc and aluminum rim), are available only in special cases and for racing vehicles. Passenger-car rims are almost exclusively designed as drop-center rims with double hump H2 (less commonly with flat hump FH), 5° tapered-bead seat and J flange. The lower flange shape B is frequently found on smaller vehicles; the higher flange shapes JK and K are only rarely seen, and only on higher-weight vehicles.

More recent rim developments which have been put into series manufacture on a limited basis are the TR rim (with metric dimensions) developed by Michelin for use with matching TRX tires, which permit more room for the brakes, as well as the Dunlop rim with "Denloc" groove, which also requires a matched tire. The Dunlop rim and tire combination provides improved safety in case of loss of air. The TD system (TRX-Denloc) brings together both wheel/tire systems. As opposed to previous designs, combinations incorporating other rim and tire designs are either not possible at all, or are possible only to a very limited extent.

In a completely new development, the tire grips the outside of the rim (CONTINENTAL). This design changes the way some tire/rim properties react with one another, and allows the driver to drive at reduced speed for several hundred kilometers with a flat tire or tires. This design could eliminate the need for a spare tire.

Based on American efforts to reduce the amount of space taken up by the spare tire as well as – to a very limited extent – to reduce overall vehicle weight, European vehicles are increasingly being fitted with a space-saving spare wheel which has a matching, lower-performance tire. Opinions on the usefulness of this substandard combination vary.

Design criteria for passenger-car wheels include high component strength, efficient brake cooling, reliable wheel mounting, high concentricity, small space requirements, good corrosion protection, low weight, low cost, easy tire mounting, a good tire seat, good balance-weight attachment and aesthetically pleasing design (particularly in the case of light-alloy wheels). Recent attention has also been given to wheel designs which reduce the vehicle drag coefficient.

Wheels are usually mounted to the vehicle by means of three to five wheel lugs or lug nuts whose collars have a special shape which conforms to the wheel. A central wheel mount designed as a Rudge hub or incorporating driving pins is only used with racing wheels.

Wheel covers are fastened to the wheels by means of clips, or less commonly by means of a threaded joint, for reasons of aesthetic design, reduction of the drag coefficient c_w, and improvement of wheel and/or brake cooling. Traditional materials for wheel covers are steel and aluminum. Plastics have recently been used much more frequently in order to reduce weight and cost.

Commercial-vehicle wheels

The primary requirements to be met by commercial-vehicle wheels are:
– high fatigue strength and long service life in order to maximize traffic safety,
– lowest possible wheel weight because the wheel, as an unsprung, rotating mass, influences the oscillation system "vehicle",
– high load capacity via appropriate wheel shape and use of optimum materials,
– reduction in wheel-disc unevenness,
– reduction of radial and lateral run-out and wheel imbalance,
– easy assembly of tire to rim during manufacture and in practical use.

15° Tapered-bead seat rims

A modern design for tubeless commercial-vehicle tires is the one-piece 15° tapered-bead seat rim.

Advantages:
– The one-piece wheel allows a reduction in wheel weight of up to 10% as compared to the two-piece rim, and exhibits improved true-running and less lateral run-out,

— increased rim diameter,
— sufficient free space,
— unified valve in a precise position and at a sufficient distance from the brake drum,
— unified balance-weight shapes,
— introduction of central centering and
— use of fully- or semi-automatic tire-fitting equipment.

Radial and lateral run-out, imbalance
Radial run-out of the wheel is one of the main causes of vehicle vibrations. The reduction of the permissible radial run-out of 15° tapered-bead seat rims in use today to 1.25 mm (peak-to-peak value) has resulted in great improvement as compared to flat-base rims. As opposed to radial run-out, lateral run-out is a less critical problem. Wheel imbalance is also not nearly as much of a problem as tire imbalance, which is of a greater magnitude. Maximum permissible static imbalance is limited to 2000 cmg.

Wheel centering
Lug centering via spherical washers or solely via ball-seat nuts has been replaced by central centering in order to reduce excessive radial run-out; this arrangement also permits different maximum and minimum play depending upon wheel size (especially with 22.5″ wheels). This requires tolerances which are as close as possible.

Flatness of the contact surface
Any unevenness of the wheel contact surface (waviness, inclination, shielding, etc.) is transmitted to the brake drum when the wheel nuts are tightened, causing fluctuations in braking force as the wheel rotates. These fluctuations, in turn, cause vibrations in the steering system. Driving tests have led to the establishment of a maximum value for waviness of 0.15 mm and 0.2 mm for inclination from the center of the wheel outward.

Trilex wheel system
The Trilex wheel system with cast steel "spoked wheels" comprises a rim and spider. The removable rims are connected to the spider by means of clips and screws. In order to simplify mounting and dismounting of tube tires, the rim consists of three parts with transverse pitch. The same spider can be used in conjunction with the so-called Tublex rim for mounting tubeless tires.

A new development is the one-piece cast MONOLEX 15° tapered-bead seat rim which weighs the same as a comparable steel wheel of optimal design.

Light-alloy rims
One reason for using light-alloy rims is to reduce the weight of 15° tapered-bead seat wheels. Light-alloy rims are available as cast or forged rims. In spite of weight reduction and sufficient strength characteristics, light-alloy rims are used on commercial vehicles only in special cases for reasons of cost.

Commercial-vehicle wheel loading

Prestress
Prestress occurs through the combination of stresses caused by assembling the wheel with those which result from inflating the tire.

Static nominal wheel stress
If the wheel is allowed to roll slowly on a perfectly flat road surface under static nominal wheel load, the stress in the wheel section in question varies periodically as the wheel rotates.

Additional dynamic stresses
These similar additional stresses are caused by dynamic wheel forces which result as the vehicle is driven straight ahead over an uneven road surface. As a result, quasi-static wheel forces are generated due to vehicle maneuvers such as cornering, turning the steering wheel of a stationary vehicle, braking and accelerating.

The resulting group of stresses caused by the above-mentioned types of wheel loading is used today as the basis for wheel dimensioning and testing.

Significant weak points

Highly stressed wheel sections which are thus susceptible to cracking are the nave flange or flat, the ventilation holes, the nave/rim weld and the rim drop-center radius. The flange joint is particularly susceptible.

Centrally aligned (or centered) wheels usually crack tangentially above the hole circle. In the case of lug centering, cracks usually occur radially outward from the lug holes.

Monolex wheel with rim offset (left) and without rim offset (right)

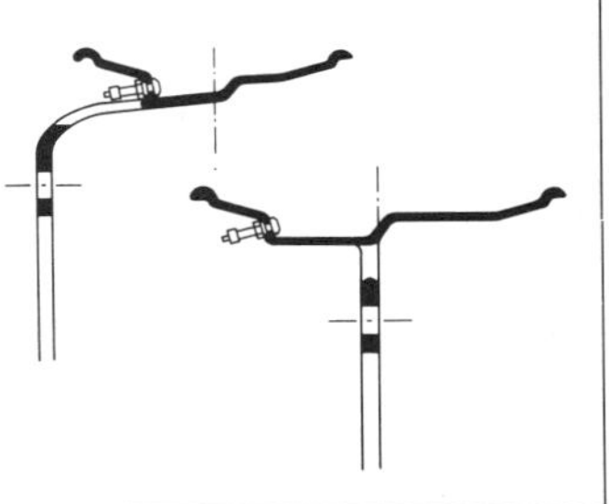

Types of wheel loading and stress distributions

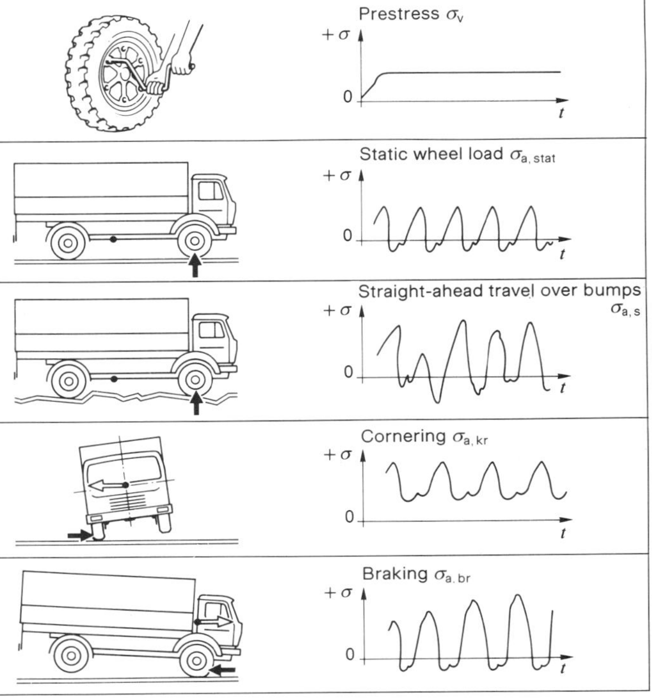

Tires

Tire groups

Tires are classified with reference to the respective requirements of various vehicle types and sizes, and operating conditions. The essential data – tire dimensions, load ratings, specified inflation pressures and authorized speeds – are standardized in the interests of interchangeability in the 7 tire groups or categories listed in Table 1. In addition to pneumatic tires, solid tires are also in use which are approved for speeds of up to 25 km/h (up to 16 km/h for unsprung drive wheels).

The classifications in tire groups 2 through 4 are based upon road conditions:
- "Standard" highway (summer) tires,
- "Special" high-traction (M+S and off-road) tires. That is, tires for combined highway and off-road use, as well as tires restricted to off-road use only.

The same basic set of operating requirements applies for all tires (Table 2), although it should be noted that the emphasis shifts toward the final three criteria (esp. Nr. 6) on heavier vehicles.

Tire structure

The older cross or bias-ply design has been largely replaced by the increasingly popular radial-ply concept (for instance in tire groups 2 through 4).

The once-dominant bias-ply tire received its name from the diagonal or bias to the center of the tread running cords of the casing (cross-ply). However, the more complex radial tire, with its radial design comprising two main sections, represents the only means of satisfying the increasingly variegated range of operating capabilities demanded of the tires used on today's passenger cars and heavy commercial vehicles. The cords in the radial tire's casing layers run in the shortest and most direct path – radially – from bead to bead. A belt surrounds the relatively thin, elastic casing in order to provide sufficient

[1]) The corresponding European standards can be found in the "Data Book of Tires and Rims" of the ETRTO (European Tyre and Rim Technical Organization, Brussels).

[2]) Guideline of the Economic Association of the German Rubber Industry, Frankfurt.

Table 1. Tire categories and applicable standards

No.	Tire application	German Standards (selection)[1]) DIN	WdK[2])
1	**Motor-driven, two-wheeled vehicles** Motorcycles, motor scooters, motorcycles of less than 50 cm^3 engine displacement, mopeds	7801, 7802, 7810	119
2	**Passenger cars** Including station wagons and special spare tires	7803	128, 203
3	**Light duty commercial vehicles** Including delivery trucks	7804	132, 133
4	**Commercial vehicles** Including multi-purpose vehicles	7805, 7793	134, 135, 142 143, 144, 153
5	**Earth-moving machines** Transport vehicles, loaders, graders	7798, 7799	145, 146
6	**Industrial trucks** Including solid rubber tires	7811, 7845	171
7	**Agricultural vehicles and machinery** Tractors, machines, implements, trailers	7807, 7808, 7813	156, 161

Examples of radial-tire construction (tubeless version)
1 Hump, 2 Bead seat, 3 Flange, 4 Casing, 5 Airtight inner liner, 6 Belt, 7 Tread, 8 Sidewall, 9 Bead, 10 Bead core, 11 Valve, 12 Cover ring, 13 Balance weight, 14 Rim shoulder.

Radial tire for passenger cars
***Casing:** Two radial rayon-cord plies.*
***Belts:** Two crossed steel-cord plies and two circumferential nylon-cord layers.*

CT tires

Radial tire for heavy commercial vehicles
***Casing:** Single radial steel-cord ply (monoply).*
***Belts:** Four crossed steel-cord plies.*

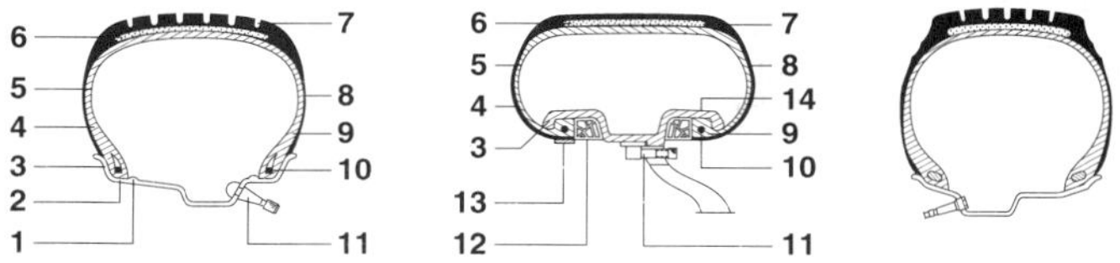

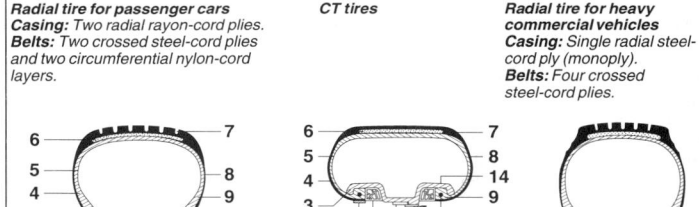

stability. The "bias-belted" design, more widespread in the US than elsewhere, incorporates an additional belt outside the diagonal casing. The performance of this type of tire is nowhere near as good as that of the radials.

CT tires feature run-flat properties. The tire reacts to deflation by supporting itself against the well of the wheel rim, and can be used for several hundred kilometers in this condition. In the TR/Denloc System, a specially-designed protrusion in the bead fits into a corresponding groove in the wheel rim. This arrangement locks the bead in position to prevent it from slipping into the center of the wheel, and thus provides limited run-flat properties.

Tubeless tires, already popular on passenger cars, are being used with increasing frequency on heavy commercial vehicles. The essential requirement is a single-piece, air-tight wheel rim, or a multipiece rim capable of accepting the required flexible rim-seal rings. On tubeless tires, the tube is replaced by a vulcanized, airtight inner liner. The bead of the tubeless tire must press more tightly against the wheel rim in order to provide the necessary seal. Special, supplementary bead seals in the form of elastomer rings are sometimes used. Dispensing with the inner tube reduces weight and simplifies mounting procedures.

Table 2. Service requirements

No.	Main criteria	Sub-criteria
1	Ride comfort	Soft suspension, low noise, smooth running (low out-of-roundness)
2	Steering behavior	Steering-force, steering precision[3])
3	Driving stability	Straight-ahead stability[3]), cornering stability[3])
4	Driving safety	Tire seat on rim, tire/road adhesion[3])
5	Durability	Structural stability, high-speed performance, bursting pressure, puncture resistance
6	Economy	Expected service life (mileage), wear pattern, sidewall wear, rolling resistance, retreadability

[3]) Main criteria for driving on roads in winter.

Diameter and design of the wheel rim
In tire groups 3 and 4, the single-piece 15° tapered drop-center rim (for tubeless tires) has been gaining ground against its multi-piece 5° counterpart. This type of rim is identified by the diameter code (1 unit = 25.4 mm) ending in .5, as in 17.5, 19.5, 22.5. The figures 16 and 20 are common codes for 5° tapered drop-center wheels. Both the standard drop-center wheel rims, with their whole-number diameter codes (10, 12, 13, etc.), and special designs with diameter specified in mm are available for passenger-car tires.

Aspect ratio (height-to-width ratio)

Aspect ratio = (H/W) x 100
H Cross-section height
W Cross-section width

The aspect ratio (H/W = Height relative to Width) on today's standard passenger-car tires ranges between 80 and 50; the figure ranges down to 30 for sports-car tires, and is between 60 and 100 for the tires on heavy commercial vehicles.

Passenger-car tires with low aspect ratios provide high levels of cornering stability. The different aspect ratios are all based on a single outside diameter in order to facilitate interchangeability. At a constant internal diameter for tire and wheel rim, a tire with a low aspect ratio will be wider, with a larger contact surface, and it will be distinguished by a more impressive appearance. A low aspect ratio makes it possible to maintain the width of the footprint while increasing the internal diameter of the wheel rim; thus providing more space for the brakes. The introduction of the 15° tapered drop-center rim for heavy commercial vehicles was only made possible by the development of a suitable tubeless tire with a low aspect ratio. This was because a reduction of the rim-base diameter was impossible due to the brake-drum diameter having to remain unchanged. Wider tires with low aspect ratios also represent the only feasible option for applications where minimum tire diameters (in other words, maximum usable height) are stipulated, e.g., for container transport.

Tire designation symbols

The tire's designation is stamped on the sidewall (see Table 4), and reflects standards mandatory in a number of European countries. These include ECE Directive Nr. 30 for passenger car tires (excepting VR and ZR tires which are homologated for speeds over 210 km/h (VR) and over 240 km/h (ZR)); Nr. 54 for tires for heavy commercial vehicles (speeds of 80 km/h and above); and ECE Directive Nr. 75 concerning tires for motorized two-wheeled vehicles (vehicles with engine displacement exceeding 50 cm^3 or attaining speeds in excess of 40 km/h). Excepted are V, VB, VR, ZB and ZR tires for over 210 and/or over 240 km/h.

Tires tested for compliance with ECE regulations are identified by the code molded into the sidewall adjacent to the bead. The code consists of a circle containing a large E followed by the code number of the responsible agency, which is in turn followed by an approval number.

Example: (E4) 020 427.

The tire's width, its construction (R = Radial; "–" = Cross-ply; B = Bias-belted), and its rim diameter represent the minimum information requirement for tire designation. The diameter of the tire is also usually included on tires for industrial trucks. On tires for two-wheeled vehicles, passenger cars and heavy commercial vehicles, this information is frequently supplemented by the aspect ratio in % which is appended directly behind the width information from which it is separated by a slash. ECE regulations require this information for all new tires. Although it is not stipulated by the ECE directives, tires for passenger cars and two-wheeled vehicles may also feature a speed-rating code letter behind the aspect ratio or tire width. On cross-ply tires the code letter replaces the horizontal line.

On VR, VB, ZR and ZB tires, it is mandatory that the code letter forms an integral part of the tire-size designation.

The PR (ply rating) follows the tire size, and is now employed as a code to distinguish the load ratings for various versions of the same size. This element was formerly used to indicate the number of plies in the casing.

The service description is an additional suffix combining the load index (LI) and the speed-rating symbol (GSY). ECE regulations prescribe it as a replacement for the PR number or the speed-rating letters in the tire size (exceptions: VB, VR, ZB and ZR tires). Specific values are assigned to the codes in the service description (Table 3).

For passenger-car tires:
Rated speed = Top speed. Vehicles whose design only allows top speeds of 60 km/h and below may exploit supplementary load-carrying capabilities.

Reductions in tire load can be traded for higher top speeds on most tires for motor-scooters and heavy commercial vehicles. Conversely, both types of tire may be used to carry higher loads throughout virtually the entire speed range when operated below their rated (reference) speed, provided that the vehicle be specifically designed to operate at the lower maximum speed. Again, increased maximum load ratings are approved for tires on passenger-car trailers for speeds up to 100 km/h, and on certain commercial vehicles used for short-distance haulage and transportation.

The correct inflation pressure for a particular tire size and PR rating or service description are specified in the standards and/or the manuals provided by the tire's manufacturer (Table 1). The suffix containing the speed-rating symbol always indicates the actual rated speed. When the speed code letters appear alone within the tire-size designation, the following supplementary designations indicate a reduction in speed rating:

"MS": – 20 km/h } Total:
"reinforced": – 10 km/h } – 30 km/h

Special stipulations apply to passenger-car tires mounted on rims smaller than 13 inches or larger than 16 inches. Special spare tires (low-weight and "space-saver" designs) are identified on the sidewall as intended for temporary use at limited speeds.

Correspondence between the speed rating for M+S tires on passenger cars, heavy commercial vehicles and motorcycles, and the respective maxima of the vehicles upon which they are mounted is not mandatory. However, a sticker indicating the lower speed for which the tires are approved must be affixed to the inside of the vehicle within the driver's field of vision. The following categories of tires may feature additional data prescribed by US highway safety legislation. These data, molded into the sidewall adjacent to the bead, are valid for Canada, and are also used in Israel:

- FMVSS 109 for passenger-car tires,
- FMVSS 119 for two-wheeled and heavy commercial vehicles.

These data are stamped adjacent to the letters "DOT", following which come the tire identification code and the date of manufacture, as well as further data on maximum load rating, maximum inflation pressure, and the cord plies which make up the casing and belts.

Australian Safety Regulation ADR 23, which applies to tires for passenger cars, employs the identification codes from FMVSS 109 and ECE-R 30.

Table 3. Service description codes (examples)

Load index

Li	50	51	88	89	112	113	145	149	157
kg	190	195	560	580	1120	1150	2900	3250	4125

Speed symbol

GSY	F	G	K	L	M	N	P	Q	R	S	T	H	V	W
km/h	80	90	100	120	130	140	150	160	170	180	190	210	240	270

Table 4. Tire identification examples

Tire group	Vehicle	Identification example: Tire size[1][2]	PR[3] number	Serv. description [4] Li	[5] GSY	Example contains specifications for: Tire dia. Ø *A*	Tire width *B*	Aspect ratio *H/B* %	Rim dia. Ø *d*
MC	Mopeds	$2^{1}/_{4}$ – 16 Mopeds	–	–	–	–	inches	–	inches
	Motorcycles less than 50 cm^3 swept volume	3 – 17 reinforced	–	51	J	–	inches	–	inches
	Motorcycles	3 – 17 reinforced	–	50	P	–	inches	–	inches
		110/80 R 18	–	58	H	–	mm	80	inches
		120/90 H 18	–	65	H	–	mm	90	inches
	Motor scooters	3.50 – 10	–	51	J	–	inches	–	inches
Passenger cars		165 R 14 M+S	–	84	Q	–	mm	–	inches
		165 R 14 reinforced	–	88	R	–	mm	–	inches
		200/60 R 365	–	88	H	–	mm	60	mm
		205/60 ZR 15	–	–	–	–	mm	%	inches
		CT 235/40 ZR 475	–	–	–	–	mm	%	mm
CV	Delivery trucks	185 R 14 C	8 PR	102/100	M	–	mm	–	inches
	Light-duty trucks	8 R 17.5 C	–	113/112	M	–	inches	–	inches
	Trucks	11/70 R 22.5	–	146/143	K	–	inches	70	inches
	Trailers	14/80 R 20	–	157	K	–	inches	80	inches
	Buses	295/80 R 22.5	–	149/145	K	–	inches	80	inches
MPV	Multi-purpose vehicles	10.5 R 20 MPT	14 PR	134	G	–	inches	–	inches
EM	Transport vehicles	18.00 – 25 EM	32 PR	–	–	–	inches	–	inches
	Loaders	29.5 – 29 EM	28 PR	–	–	–	inches	–	inches
IT	Industrial trucks	6.50 – 10[6]	10 PR	–	–	–	inches	–	inches
	Carts	21 x 4[6]	4 PR	–	–	inches	inches	–	–
	Industrial trucks	28 x 9 – 15[7]	14 PR	–	–	inches	inches	–	inches
		300 x 15[7]	18 PR	–	–	–	mm	–	inches
AG	Tractors	20.8 R 38	–	153	A 8	–	inches	–	inches
		7.50 – 16 AS Front	6 PR	–	–	–	inches	–	inches
	Implements	11.0/65 – 12 Impl.	6 PR	–	–	–	inches	65	inches

[1] C = light-duty truck (delivery-truck) tires (also for high-load-capacity motor-scooter tires).
[2] reinforced = additional designation for reinforced tires for two-wheeled motor vehicles and passenger cars.
[3] PR = load-range class.
[4] Load-range code for single/dual tires.
[5] Speed code for vehicle nominal (reference) speed.
[6] Pneumatic tires.
[7] Solid rubber tires.

Tire applications

Tire selection based upon the recommendations of the tire manufacturer is essential for obtaining satisfactory performance. Optimal operating characteristics can only be obtained when tires of one single design are mounted on all wheels (for instance, radial tires). During seasonal storage of the tires, inner tubes and bead bands tend to age and become brittle more rapidly when exposed to direct sunlight. Moving air promotes this process.

Intact packaging is particularly important for ensuring that the tube remains in good condition. The storage area should thus be cool, dry and dark, while contact with oil or grease is to be avoided.

Particular care is required when mounting tires. They must never be mounted on anything other than undistorted, undamaged, rust-free wheel rims which show no signs of more than minimal wear. When a loose flange is used, that side should receive especially critical attention.

New valves, and, where applicable, new tubes and bead bands are always to be installed with new tires. Caution is also advised when used inner tubes are refitted following repairs: Inner tubes expand during use, a condition which can result in dangerous folds forming when the tube is reinstalled. If there are any doubts at all, new tubes should be used.

Tire tread (see examples)
It is illegal to regroove the tread on tires for two-wheeled vehicles and passenger cars; manufacturer's approval is required for other tire groups.

Tire rotation is recommended to deal with variations in tread wear between axles. Low tread depth is accompanied by a commensurate reduction in the size of the protective layer covering belts and casing. This aspect should be considered when planning operation under demanding operating conditions extending over a long period of time. In addition, reduced tread depth results in a more than proportional increase in braking distances; the attendant loss of traction encountered on wet roads is of particular significance on passenger cars and high-speed commercial vehicles. The following provides figures for a passenger vehicle being braked from 100 km/h:

Tread depth in mm		8	4	3	2	1
Stopping distance	in mm	70	82	87	97	118
	in %	100	117	124	139	169
Increased stopping distance permm of wear	in %	4	7	15	30	

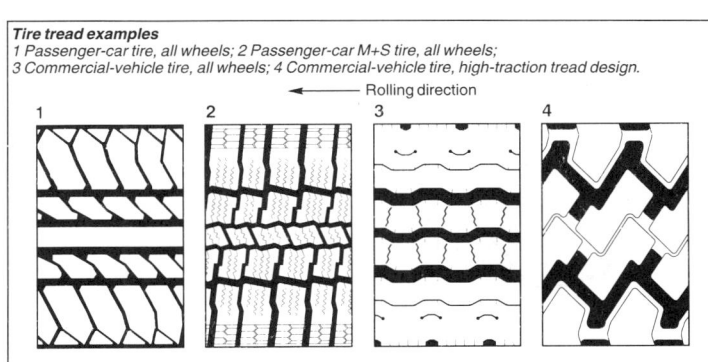

Tire tread examples
1 Passenger-car tire, all wheels; 2 Passenger-car M+S tire, all wheels;
3 Commercial-vehicle tire, all wheels; 4 Commercial-vehicle tire, high-traction tread design.

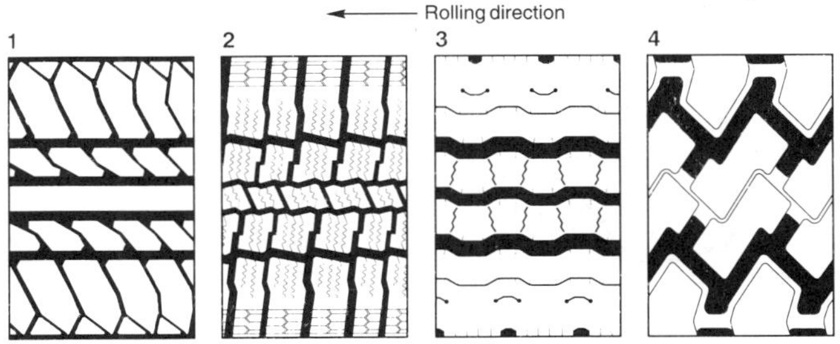

Tire traction

Units and symbols

Symbol		Unit
f	Frequency	Hz
F_B	Braking force	kN
F_R	Wheel load	kN
F_S	Side force	kN
M_R	Aligning torque	N m
n_S	Caster	mm
p_i	Tire pressure	bar
v_0	Test velocity	km/h
α	Slip angle	°
γ	Camber angle	°
λ	Slip	–

It is essential that accurate tire-performance maps are available for the engineering and optimization of the vehicle's handling, driveability, and comfort, and for the reduction of it's drivetrain vibration.

Representative tire-performance maps for passenger-cars and light commercial vehicles are already familiar and are available in various publications [1, 3, 4]. For this reason, the following will concentrate on tires for heavy-duty commercial vehicles in the dimensions 11 R 22.5. These tires are in widespread use [2].

All data in the performance maps refer to the Michelin XZA 11 R 22.5 tire.

Gough tire-performance map (B)

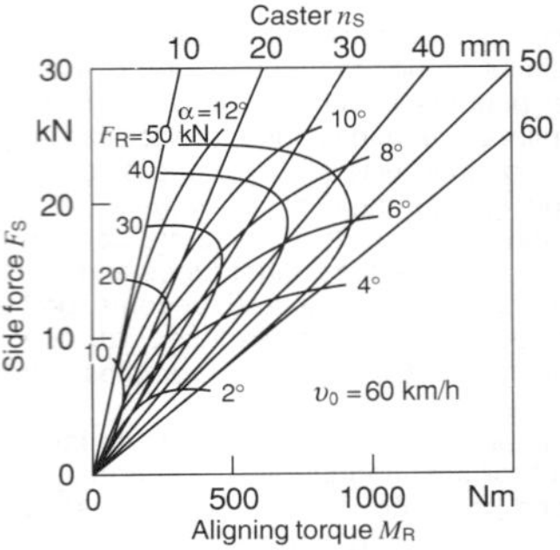

Tire performance with wheel rotating freely at a given slip angle

When the tire rotates at a slip angle, side

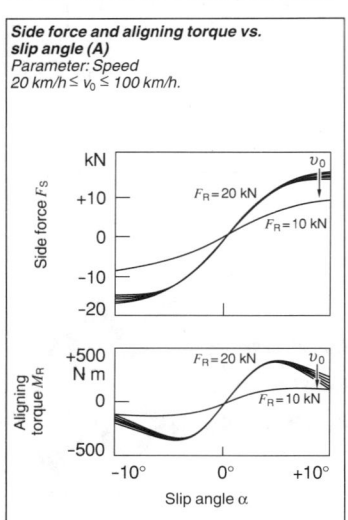

Side force and aligning torque vs. slip angle (A)
Parameter: Speed
20 km/h ≤ v_0 ≤ 100 km/h.

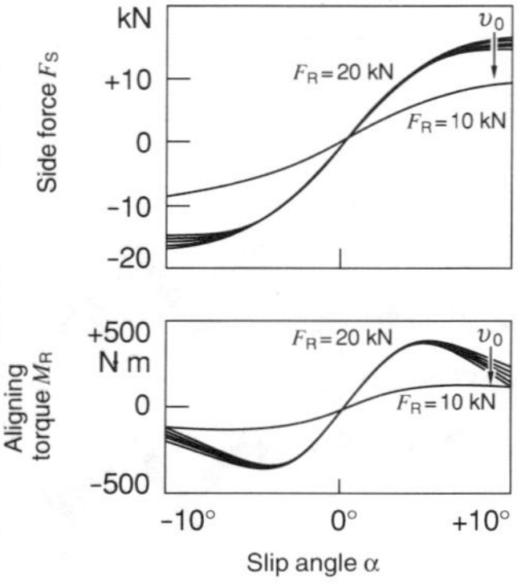

Side force vs. slip angle (C)
Parameters: Wheel load and camber angle.

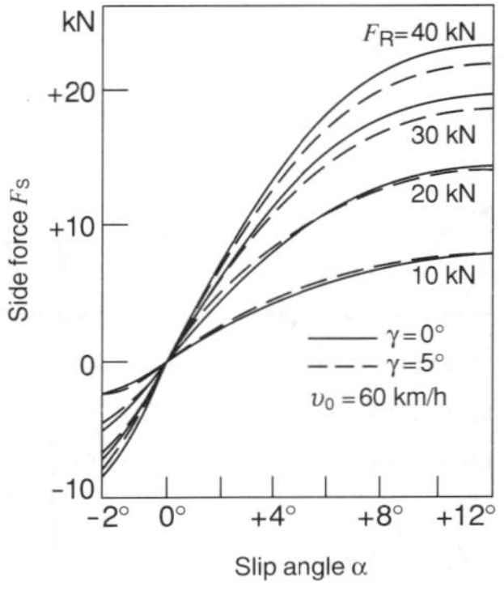

forces are generated. These side forces are accompanied by an aligning torque (Diagram B). The Gough diagram [3] is frequently employed to illustrate this phenomenon. The side force is dependent on the slip angle and displays a degressive increase as higher loads are applied to the wheel (Diagram C). The maximum side force is inversely proportional to speed, while the influence of speed increases as a function of wheel load (Diagram A).

When dealing with tires for passenger-cars and light commercial vehicles, the situation is thus: If a wheel rotating at a given slip angle is subjected to camber, the camber and side forces cause a parallel displacement of the side-force/slip-angle curves. Tires on heavy-duty commercial vehicles also display additional displacements of the side-force/slip-angle curves due to the side forces accompanying the camber; this phenomenon only occurs at larger slip angles. The result is that practically all curves intersect the coordinate origin (Diagram C).

On dry roads, reduced tread depth results in steeper side-force/slip-angle curves, with an accompanying increase in the maximum side forces which can be transferred (Diagram D).

Tire performance under acceleration and braking with wheel rolling straight ahead

The tire's response to "slip" is similar to its reaction to slip angles (Diagram E). The maximum circumferential force will generally lie within the range of 10 % to 20 % slip on a dry road surface. The coefficient of adhesion responds to higher wheel loads with a less striking, more degressive increase in the circumferential than in the lateral direction.

On larger tires, the influence which speed exerts on the level of the lateral coefficient of adhesion is less pronounced in the normal speed range for heavy-duty commercial vehicles than with tires similar to those used on passenger cars (Diagram E).

Tire pressure has only a minimal effect on maximum circumferential forces at low wheel loads. At higher wheel loads, reduced tire pressures result in a substantially more pronounced rate of increase in

Side force vs. slip angle (D)
Parameter: Tread condition.

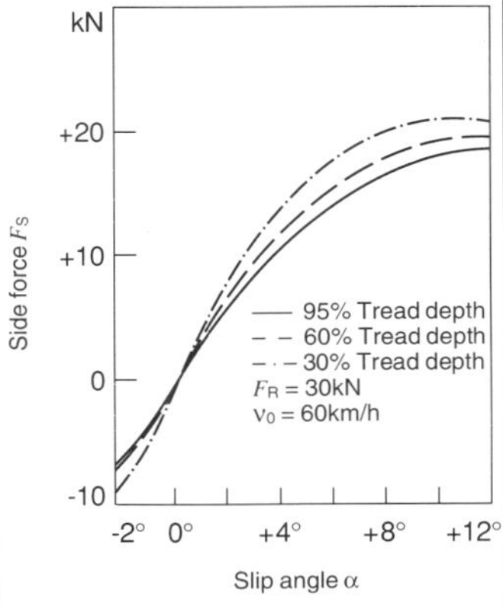

Braking force vs. slip (E)
Parameters: Wheel load and speed.

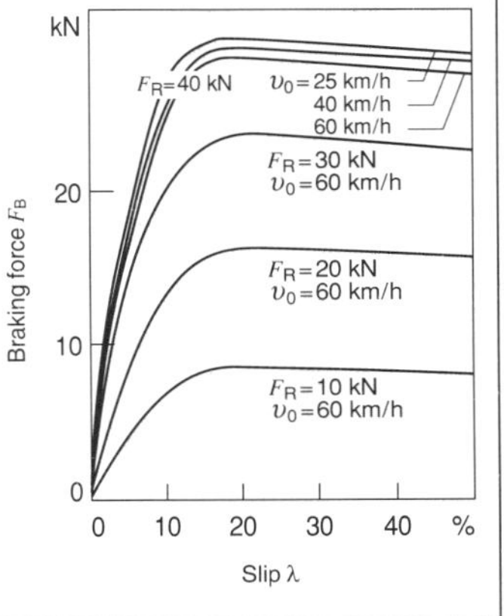

the maximum circumferential force (Diagram G).

Side and circumferential forces respond to high tire loads by displaying mutually opposed reactions to variations in tire pressure (Diagram F, G).

Tire performance at slip angles and slip

If a tire operating under circumferential forces or slip is subjected to an additional slip angle, at all slip rates the usable circumferential forces will decrease with increasing slip angle. The higher the slip angle, the more the curve for maximum circumferential force is displaced toward higher slip rates (Diagram I).

The elliptical curves for side force vs. circumferential force (braking force) vary according to wheel load (Diagram H). For critical wheel-load factors, this curve represents the adhesion limit for vehicles equipped with ABS.

The performance curves resulting from measurements actually taken, indicate the propagation of side force as a function of braking force within the slip-angle range of 0 ... 10°. The parameters for wheel load, speed and tire pressure remain constant (Diagram K).

Dynamic tire-performance curves

The illustrated tire-performance curves are based on parameters which are only subject to gradual change during the course of the measurements, i.e. quasi-static conditions. Actual operation, on the other hand, is characterized by dynamic processes. Increases in the speed at which the influencing parameters vary will induce certain maneuver-specific changes in tire response, the magnitude of which makes it imperative that they be considered.

The most significant influencing parameters are dynamic changes in:

- Slip angle
- Trackwidth,
- Camber,
- Slip,
- Wheel load.

Generally, the tire's response to these rapidly changing parameters is graphically portrayed as a function of frequency.

Side force vs. slip angle on heavy-duty commercial-vehicle tires (F)

Parameters: Tire pressure and wheel load.

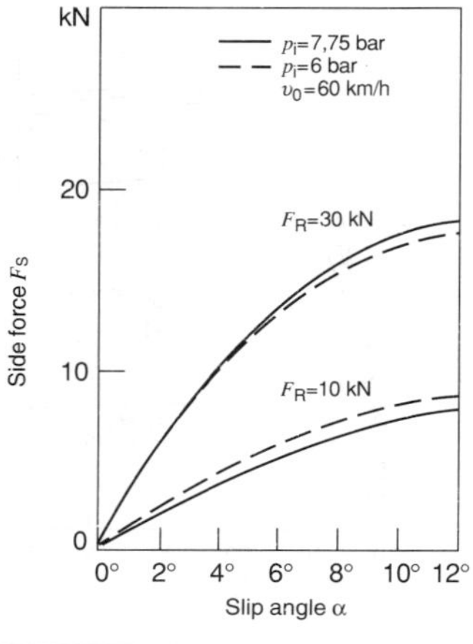

Braking force vs. slip on heavy-duty commercial-vehicle tires (G)

Parameters: Tire pressure and wheel load.

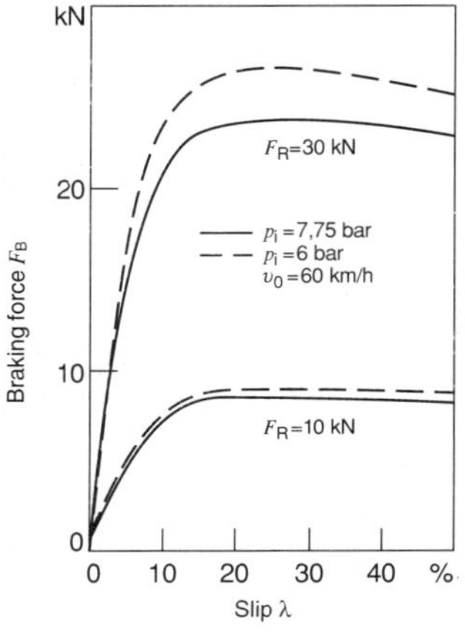

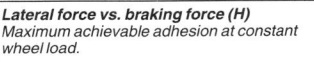

Lateral force vs. braking force (H)
Maximum achievable adhesion at constant wheel load.

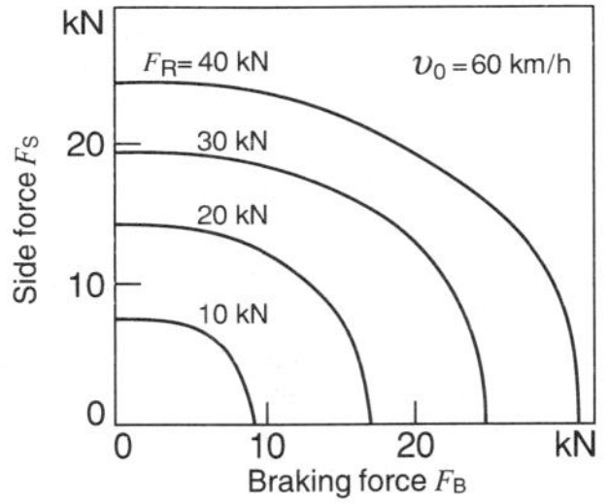

Measured tire-performance curves at a wheel load of 30 kN (K)
Side force as function of braking force. Parameter: Slip angle.

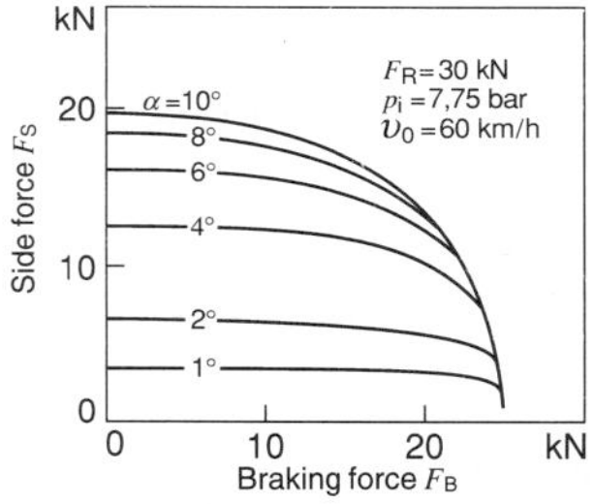

That is, amplitudes and phase angles of the tire forces and moments are illustrated relative to frequency, as a function of the forces acting on the tire, under inclusion of the frequency-dependent progression of mean values for tire forces [5, 6].

Braking force vs. slip (I)
Parameter: Slip angle.

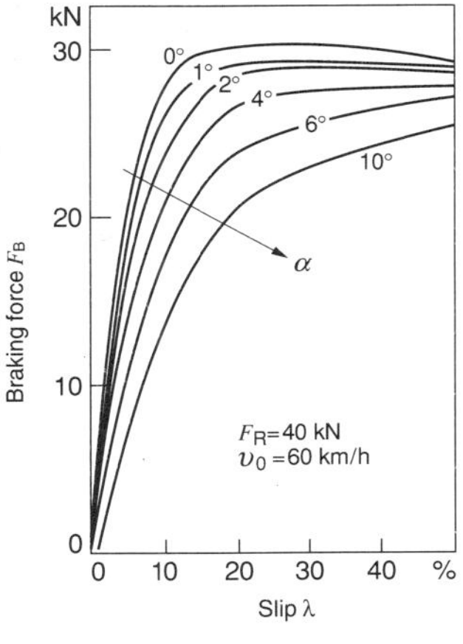

Literature

[1] Gengenbach, W.: Experimentelle Untersuchung von Reifen auf nasser Fahrbahn (Experimental investigation of tires on wet road surface). ATZ, 1968, Hefte 3, 8, and 9,

[2] von Glasner, E.C.: Einbeziehung von Prüfstandsergebnissen in die Simulation des Fahrverhaltens von Nutzfahrzeugen (Including test-bench results in the simulation of commercial-vehicle handling). Habilitation, Universität Stuttgart, 1987.

[3] Gough, V. E.: Cornering Characteristics of Tires. Automobile Engineer, 1954, Heft 44.

[4] Weber R.: Beitrag zum Übertragungsverhalten zwischen Schlupf- und Reifenführungskräften (Contribution concerning the transmission behavior between slip and circumferential/side forces). AI, 1981, Vol. 44.

[5] Fritz, G. Seitenkräfte und Rückstellmomente von Personenwagenreifen bei periodischer Änderung der Spurweite, des Sturz- und Schräglaufwinkels (Side forces and aligning torques of passenger-car tires under the influence of periodic change of track width, camber, and slip angle). Dissertation, Universität Karlsruhe, 1978.

[6] Weber, R.: Reifenführungskräfte bei schnellen Änderungen von Schräglauf und Schlupf (Circumferential/side forces as a function of rapid changes in slip angle and slip). Habilitation, Universität Karlsruhe, 1981.

Steering

The steering converts the steering-wheel rotary motion into a turn motion of the vehicle's steered wheels.

Requirements on steering systems

In accordance with § 38 StVZO German Road Licensing Regulations (FMVSS/CUR) the steering system must guarantee easy and safe steering of the vehicle: it must be possible to turn the front wheels into the position corresponding to a turning circle with a radius of 12 m within a maximum of 6 seconds. If the actuating force at the steering wheel exceeds 250 N, power assistance is necessary. If such power assistance fails, 600 N must not be exceeded. The actuating force must be harmonious from the center as far as the end stop and must not decrease. It must be possible to drive the vehicle accurately, i.e., without any unusual steering corrections. Play in the mechanical parts is impermissible.

Steering assembly *(diagram)*
1 Steering arm, 2 Drag link, 3 Idler arm, 4 Tie rod, 5 Steering wheel, 6 Steering shaft, 7 Steering box, 8 Pitman arm.

Basic principle

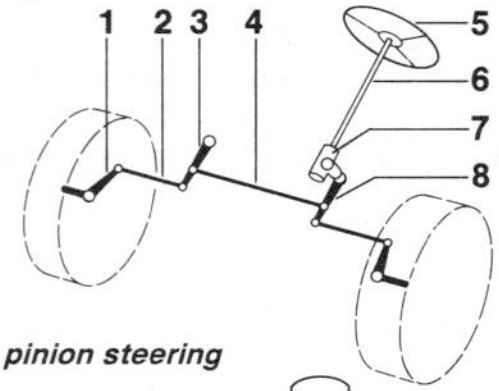

Rack and pinion steering

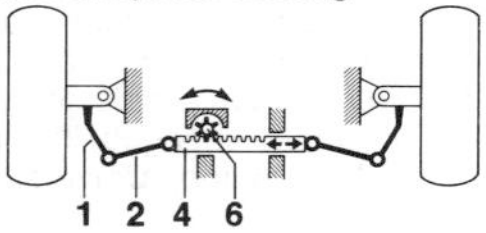

The entirety of the mechanical transmission devices must be able to cope with all loads and stresses occurring in operation. Unusual driving manœuvers, such as driving over obstacles, accident-like occurrences etc, must not lead to any cracks or breakages.

Steering behavior

The requirements in terms of steering behavior can be summarized as follows:

1. Jolts from irregularities in the road surface must be damped as much as possible in being transmitted to the steering wheel. However, such damping must not cause the driver to lose contact with the road.
2. The basic design of the steering kinematics must satisfy the Ackermann conditions: the extensions of the wheel axes of the left and right front wheels, when at an angle, intersect on an extension of the rear axle.
3. By means of suitable stiffness of the steering system (particularly if rubber-elastic connections are used) the vehicle must react to minute steering corrections.
4. When the steering wheel is released, the wheels must return automatically to the straight-ahead position and must remain stable in this position.
5. The steering should have as low a ratio as possible (number of steering-wheel turns from lock to lock) in order to obtain ease of handling. The thereby occurring steering forces are determined not only by the steering ratio, but also by the front-axle loading, the size of the turning circle, the wheel suspension (caster, steering-axis inclination, steering roll radius) and the tire tread.

Handling characteristics

Verdicts on vehicle handling often make use of the terms "oversteer" and "understeer". When a vehicle oversteers, it covers a smaller curve radius than that corresponding to the steering-wheel angle; when a vehicle understeers, it covers a larger curve radius. This inherent steering behavior is a consequence of different requirements on the slip angles of the wheels which arise when, with increasing centrifugal force, the ratio of lateral force to wheel load develops differently at the front and rear axles. Normally, neutral cornering behavior is required.

Although this allows the optimum utilization of the lateral forces (i.e., maximum cornering speeds), it reduces the subjective impression of the stability limit of the vehicle. In addition, the break-away of the vehicle is incalculable, since it may break away both at the front and at the rear. For this reason, the goal of most vehicle manufacturers is to achieve a light understeer, since, in this case, breaking away of the vehicle leads to a calculable straight-ahead course.

Rack and pinion steering
1 Pinion, 2 Rack.

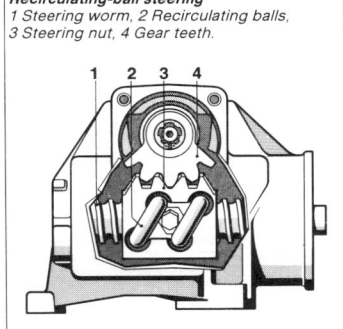

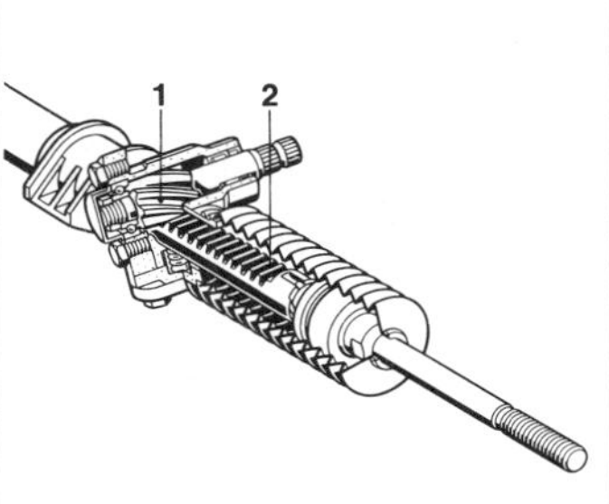

Types of steering box

A steering box must have the following qualities:
- no play in the straight-ahead position,
- low friction, resulting in high efficiency,
- high rigidity,
- readjustability.

For these reasons, only two types have become established to date:

Rack and pinion steering
Basically, rack and pinion steering consists of a rack and a pinion. The steering ratio is defined by the ratio of pinion revolutions (= steering-wheel revolutions) to rack travel. Suitable toothing of the rack allows the ratio to be made variable over the travel. This lowers the actuating force or reduces the travel for steering corrections.

Recirculating-ball steering
The forces generated between steering worm and steering nut are transmitted via a low-friction recirculating row of balls. The steering nut acts on the steering shaft via gear teeth. A variable ratio is possible with this steering box.

Recirculating-ball steering
1 Steering worm, 2 Recirculating balls, 3 Steering nut, 4 Gear teeth.

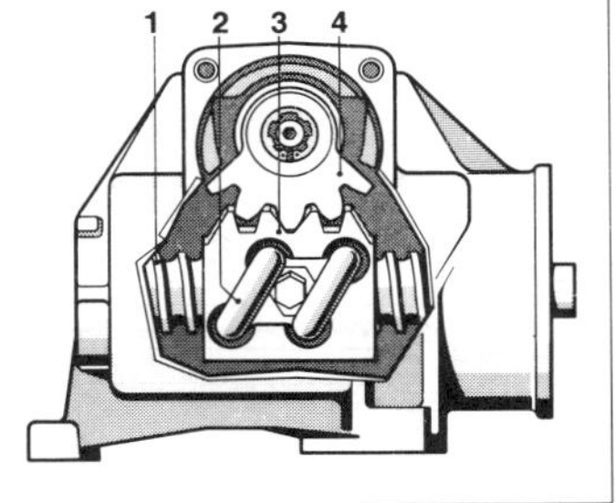

Steering kinematics

Steering kinematics and axle design must be such that, although the driver receives feedback on the adhesion between wheels and road surface, the steering wheel is not subjected to any forces from the spring motion of the wheels or from driving forces (front-wheel drive) (see p. 568).

The steering-axis inclination causes the front section of the vehicle to lift when the wheels are at an angle. This leads to a steering-angle-dependent caster return torque.

The toe-in (toe-out) is a slip angle present even during straight-ahead driving which tensions the linkages and causes a rapid build-up of transverse forces when the wheels are at an angle.

The caster produces a lever arm for lateral forces: i.e., a speed-dependent return torque.

The steering roll radius determines the extent to which the steering system is affected by disturbance forces (brakes pulling unevenly, driving forces under traction/overrun conditions with front-wheel drive). Today, the goal is to achieve a steering roll radius which is "zero" to "slightly negative".

Classification of steering systems

§ 38 StVZO German Road Licensing Regulations (FMVSS/CUR) distinguishes three types of steering systems:

– muscular-energy steering systems in which the steering force is produced exclusively by the driver (see mechanical steering boxes on p. 587)

– power steering systems in which the steering force is produced exclusively by an energy source in the vehicle. Not suitable for high-speed vehicles.

– power-assisted steering systems in which the steering force is produced by the muscular energy of the driver and by an energy source. Used for high-speed vehicles.

Power-assisted steering

Energy source

The energy source consists of a pump (usually driven by the engine), an oil reservoir and corresponding hoses and pipes.

The pump – usually a vane-type pump with internal bypass – must be dimensioned such that, even with the engine idling, it delivers a flow of oil

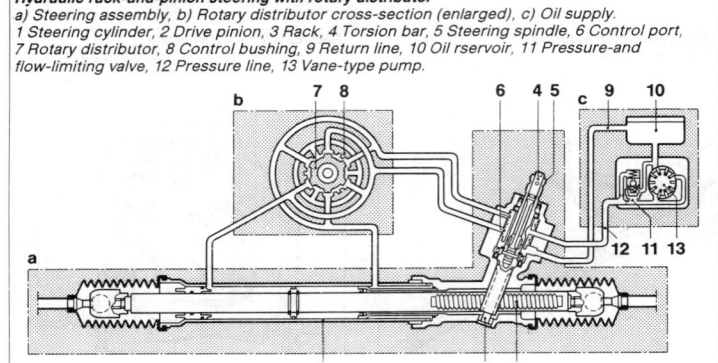

Hydraulic rack-and-pinion steering with rotary distributor

a) Steering assembly, b) Rotary distributor cross-section (enlarged), c) Oil supply.
1 Steering cylinder, 2 Drive pinion, 3 Rack, 4 Torsion bar, 5 Steering spindle, 6 Control port, 7 Rotary distributor, 8 Control bushing, 9 Return line, 10 Oil rservoir, 11 Pressure-and flow-limiting valve, 12 Pressure line, 13 Vane-type pump.

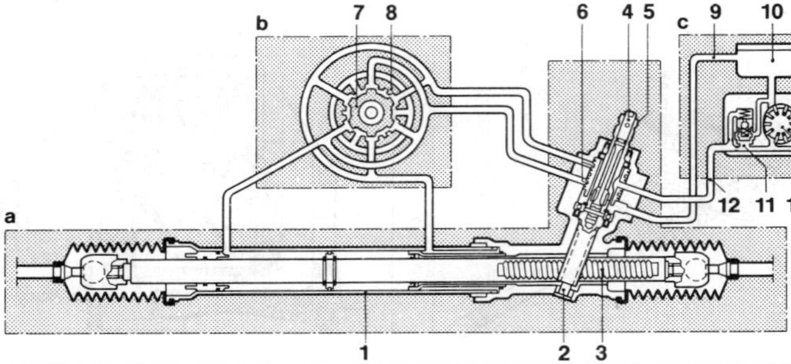

with which it is possible to achieve a steering-angle velocity of at least 1.5 s^{-1} at the steering wheel.

At higher engine speeds a further rise in the pressure of the oil flow is prevented by a flow-limiting valve integrated in the pump. Likewise usually integrated in the pump is the pressure-limiting valve which is required for the operation of a hydraulic system.

The pump must be designed such that the operating temperature of the hydraulic fluid does not rise to an excessive level (max. 100 °C) and such that no noise is generated and the oil does not foam.

Control valve

The control valve provides the steering cylinder with an oil pressure which corresponds to the rotary motion of the steering wheel. A flexible torque-measuring element (e.g., torsion bar, spiral spring, leaf spring) converts the torque precisely and with zero play into as small a control travel as possible. The control edges, which are in the form of chamfers or bevels, move as a result of the control travel and thus form the corresponding opening cross section for the oil flow.

Control valves are usually built according to the "open center" principle, i.e., when the control valve is not actuated, the oil delivered by the pump flows back to the oil reservoir at zero pressure.

Steering cylinder

The double-acting steering cylinder converts the applied oil pressure into an assisting force which acts on the rack and which intensifies the steering force exerted by the driver. The steering cylinder is normally integrated in the steering box. The steering cylinder must be particularly low in friction: this is why there are particularly high demands on piston and rod sealing.

Parameterizable power-assisted steering

Increasing demands regarding vehicle operating comfort and safety have led to the introduction of power-assisted steering systems with modulation capability. The electronically controlled power-assisted rack-and-pinion steering system is an example. It operates dependent on speed, i.e., the vehicle speed as measured by the electronic speedometer controls the actuating force of the steering system. A control unit evaluates the speed signals and determines the level of hydraulic reaction, and therefore the actuating force on the steering wheel. This level of hydraulic reaction is transmitted to the steering-system control valve via an electrohydraulic converter, in the course of which the hydraulic reaction changes in relation to the vehicle speed. The special design of the steering characteristic means that when parking, and when moving the steering wheel while standing still, only minimal forces need be applied to the steering wheel, whilst the level of assistance is reduced as speed increases. Thus precise and accurate steering is made possible at high speeds. With this system, it is important that oil pressure and volume flow are at no time reduced, so that they can be called on immediately in emergency situations. These qualities permit outstanding steering precision and safety, while at the same time providing optimum steering comfort.

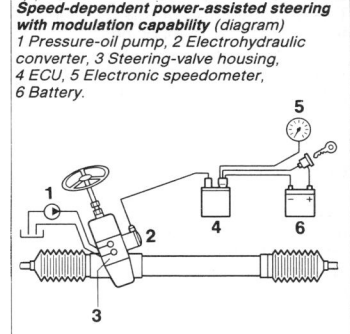

Speed-dependent power-assisted steering with modulation capability *(diagram)*
1 Pressure-oil pump, 2 Electrohydraulic converter, 3 Steering-valve housing, 4 ECU, 5 Electronic speedometer, 6 Battery.

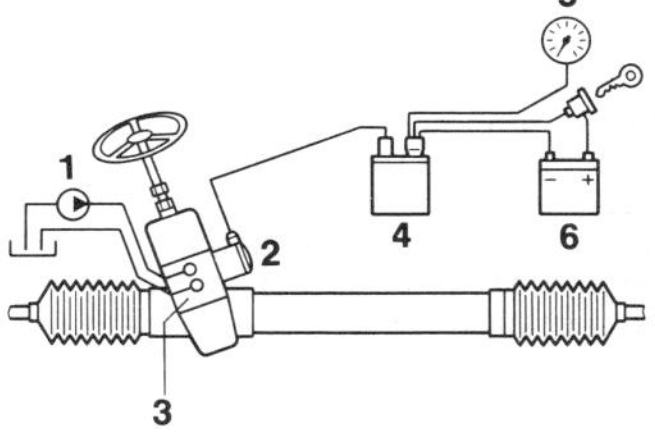

Parameterizable power-assisted steering *(characteristic curves)*
The characteristic curve form can be adjusted to the vehicle data.

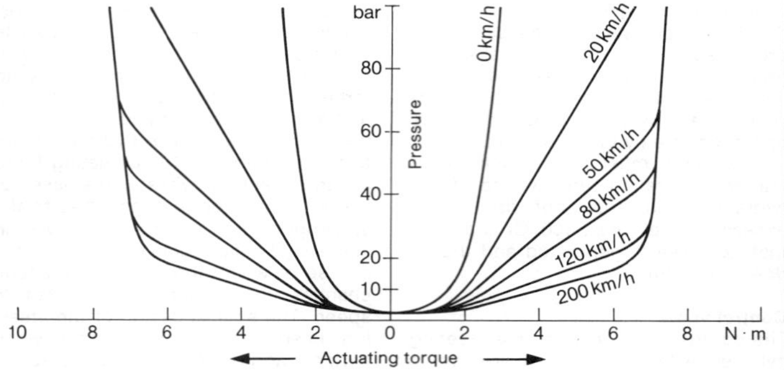

Power-assisted steering with all-hydraulic transmission

With "hydrostatic steering" there is no mechanical connection between steering wheel and road wheels. The steering force is hydraulically boosted and is transmitted exclusively by hydraulic means. Located in the control unit is a metering pump which supplies the steering cylinder with an oil pressure corresponding to the movement of the steering wheel. Owing to unavoidable leakage losses in the metering pump, the straight-ahead position of the steering wheel is no longer defined. This is why the use of this steering system is confined to machines.

The maximum permissible speed is 25 km/h in many European countries; in Germany it is 50 km/h and, with dual-circuit design, could be increased to 62 km/h.

Dual-circuit power-assisted steering system for heavy commercial vehicles

Dual-circuit steering systems are necessary where the actuating forces on the steering wheel exceed 600 N in the case of failure of the power assistance.

These steering systems are characterized by hydraulic redundancy.

Power-assisted steering with all-hydraulic transmission
1 Oil reservoir, 2 Steering pump, 3 Control unit with metering pump, 4 Steering cylinder.
Connections: R Oil flow for right-hand steering angle, L Oil flow for left-hand steering angle.

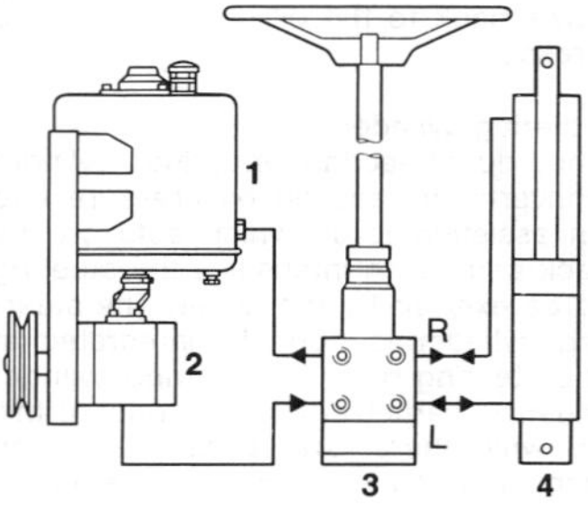

Both steering circuits of such a system are functionally tested by means of flow indicators.

The steering-circuit supply pumps must be driven in differing ways (e.g., engine-dependent, vehicle-speed-dependent or electrically).

In accordance with legislation, if the engine or one of the steering circuits fails, the vehicle can be steered with the still functioning circuit.

Single-circuit power-assisted steering system for commercial vehicles

Commercial vehicles are usually fitted with recirculating-ball power steering. In modern systems the control valve is integrated into the steering worm, which leads to compact design and optimum weight.

Only minor modification of the control valve components is necessary, to permit the actuating force in modern recirculating-ball power-steering systems to be adjusted with the aid of control electronics to vehicle speed and to other parameters such as lateral acceleration or load condition.

Dual-circuit power-assisted steering system

1 Oil reservoir, 2 Engine-driven pump, 3 Wheel-driven pump, 4 Flow indicator, 5 Dual-circuit power steering, 6 Steering cylinder.

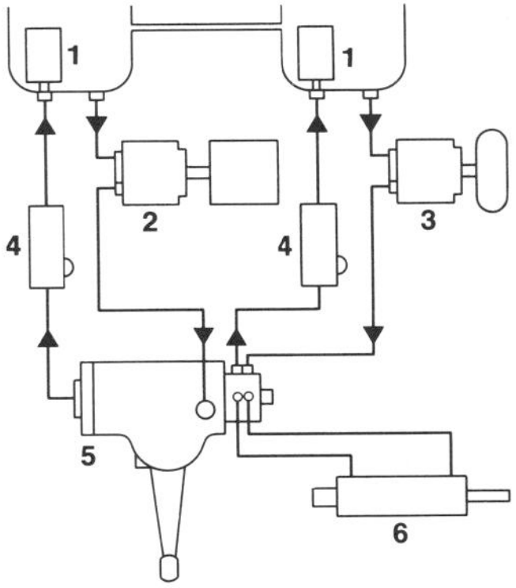

Recirculating-ball power-steering system

a) Steering assembly, b) Rotary distributor cross-section (enlarged), c) Oil supply. 1 Housing, 2 Piston, 3 Torsion bar, 4 Rotary distributor/steering spindle, 5 Control bushing/worm, 6 Sector shaft, 7 Pressure-limiting valve, 8 Replenishing valve, 9 Inlet slot, 10 Return slot, 11 Axial groove, 12 Return groove, 13 Vane-type pump, 14 Flow-limiting valve, 15 Oil reservoir.

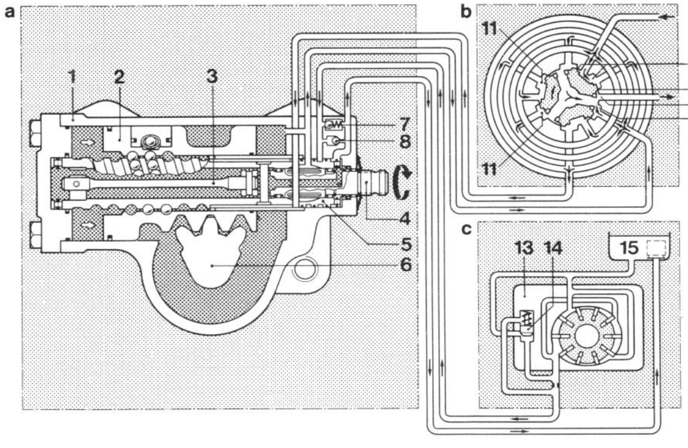

Rear-wheel steering for passenger cars

Rear-wheel steering systems serve to improve the stationary and dynamic steering characteristics.

Principles
At medium and high-speeds, turning the rear wheels in the same direction as the front wheels for a controlled, brief period of time, coordinates the vehicle's veer-in and lateral movement characteristics. This leads to an increase in stability. At low speeds, turning them in the opposite direction improves manœuverability (reduction of the turning circle by approx. 10 %).

Function
The input variables of the system are the steering-wheel angle and the driving speed. For system safety reasons, these are recorded redundantly. From these figures the control unit determines the optimum angle (desired value) of the rear wheels, compares this value with the actual value and generates the appropriate output signal for the servo actuator. The servo actuator quickly and precisely adjusts the rear-wheel steering angle to the prescribed desired value. The required dynamic control of the cylinder position is by means of a digital position controller. This enables even the most disturbing effects caused by extremely bumpy road conditions, potholes for instance, to be compensated for quickly and within the permissible tolerances.

With the aid of additional input variables, running characteristics can be improved still further.

Components

Sensors
A non-contact, inductive sensor ascertains the front-wheel steering angle indirectly via the steering-wheel angle. It supplies a coarse signal across the entire steering wheel angle range, as well as two fine signals offset by 90°. The steering-wheel angle sensor is located at the steering-box input. The driving speed is ascertained by means of the ABS wheel-speed sensors and via the speedometer signal.

Control unit
The control unit is a two-channel design and works with diversified computer hardware and software. The incoming sensor signals are redundantly processed for two different computers. The first computer applies a rapid algorithm to control the rear-wheel angle, and intervenes in the steering process. The second computer operates in parallel as a check, and in doing so uses a complex model

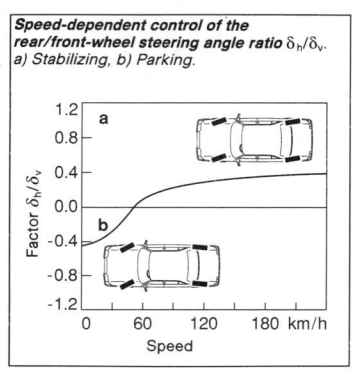

Speed-dependent control of the rear/front-wheel steering angle ratio δ_h/δ_v.
a) Stabilizing, b) Parking.

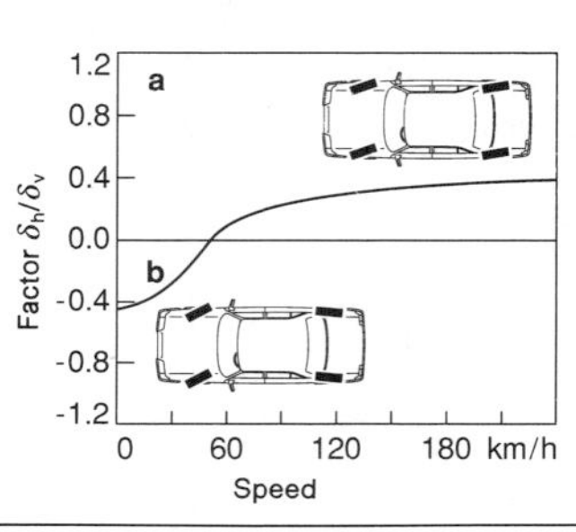

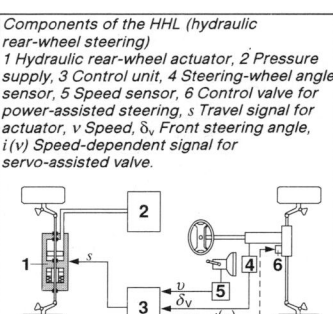

Components of the HHL (hydraulic rear-wheel steering)
1 Hydraulic rear-wheel actuator, 2 Pressure supply, 3 Control unit, 4 Steering-wheel angle sensor, 5 Speed sensor, 6 Control valve for power-assisted steering, s Travel signal for actuator, v Speed, δ_v *Front steering angle, i(v) Speed-dependent signal for servo-assisted valve.*

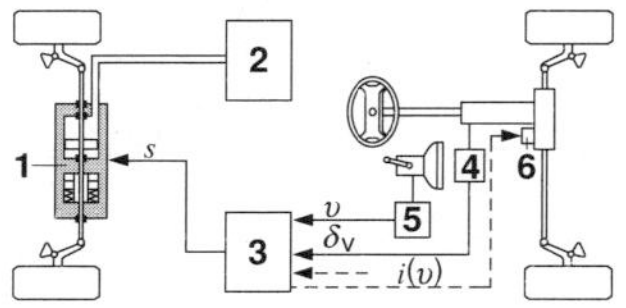

which recreates the control process (analytical redundancy). The output of the control signal for the rear-wheel actuator is effected via a switched-mode power stage.

The two computers compare their results with each other. In case of discrepancies, in accordance with the fault strategy the servo controlling element is either locked in its current position, or first brought to a center position and then locked. In such cases, conventional front-wheel steering is retained.

Actuator

The actuator can be either electrical, mechanical or hydraulic, and sets the desired rear-axle steering angle. In current applications, in view of the demands made in terms of forces and adjustment speed, a hydraulic actuator is used (HHL = Hydraulic rear-wheel steering). This is fitted parallel to the rear axle and actuates the rear wheels via steering tie rods fitted on both sides. It includes electrically controllable hydraulic valves, a servo cylinder as well as sensors for the rear-wheel angle. The servo-actuator pressure supply circuit consists of a pressure accumulator, an accumulator charge valve, a pressure sensor and the radial piston pump driven by the IC engine.

If a system fault occurs, or if the hydraulic or electrical power supply fails, the servo cylinder is held in position by means of two independent locking devices. Should even an extremely serious fault occur, this means that only very small servo-actuator movements are possible.

Running

The HHL is tested on road surfaces with high and low coefficients of static friction. In the test, various algorithms and performance data are optimized for the manœuvers: Steering-angle jump, lane-changing, slalom, steering towards a target and circling on the spot.

For example, with the aid of the active hydraulic HHL, during a simple lane change made close to maximum speed, the maximum yaw speed can be reduced by up to 50 % compared to conventional steering. The lack of overshoot when the steering is returned to straight-ahead clearly demonstrates the level of assistance provided to the driver, as well as the safety gain.

System interlinking

With HHL, handling when cornering and during fast obstacle-avoidance manœuvers is improved. Yaw-moment compensation (interlinking of ABS + HHL) also permits a significant increase in directional stability during μ-split braking (where there are considerable differences in the road-surface adhesion between the wheels on the left and right side of the vehicle). Future systems, employing vehicle dynamics sensors, offer a transition to closed-loop-controlled design concepts. In a further step, HHL will be incorporated into an overall vehicle-dynamics control concept (ABS, ASR, FWR, HHL), whereby handling during braking is also improved.

Simple lane change (v 125 km/h, coefficient of static friction 0.9)

a) Without hydraulic RWS, b) With RWS, $\dot{\Psi}$ Yaw speed, δ_n Front steering angle, δ_h Rear steering angle, 1 Phase angle, 2 Steering corrections, 3 Break-away.

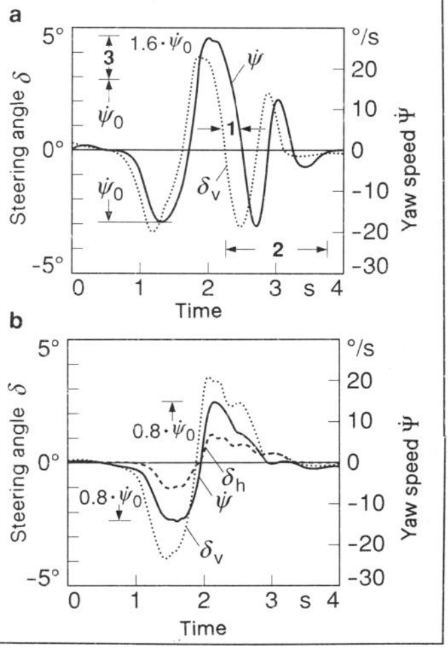

Braking systems

Definitions, Principles

(ISO 611)

Braking equipment
All the braking systems fitted to a vehicle and whose function is to reduce the speed of a moving vehicle stationary if it is already halted.

Braking sytems

Service braking system
All the elements allowing the driver to reduce of halt, directly or indirectly, the speed of a vehicle during normal driving. Its action is gradual.

Secondary braking system
All the elements allowing the driver to reduce or halt, directly of indirectly, the speed, or change in speed, of a vehicle in case of failure of the service braking system. Its action is gradual.

Parking braking system
All the elements allowing the vehicle to be held stationary mechanically even on an inclined surface, and particularly in the absence of the driver.

Additional retarding braking system
All the elements allowing the driver directly or indirectly to stabilize or to reduce the speed of the vehicle, particularly on a long incline.

Automatic braking system
All the elements which automatically brake the towed vehicle as a result of intended or accidental separation from the towing vehicle.

Anti-lock braking system (ABS)
Aggregate of all devices within the service-brake system which provide automatic slip-rate regulation for one or several wheels under braking conditions.
The braking force at wheels featuring direct regulation is controlled using data provided by the wheel's own wheel-speed sensor, while indirectly-regulated wheels rely on data provided by the wheel-speed sensor(s) at one or more of the other wheels.

Constituent elements

Energy supplying device
Parts of a braking system which supply, regulate and, if necessary, condition the energy required for braking. It terminates at the point where the transmission device starts, i.e. where the various circuits of the braking systems, including the circuits of accessories if fitted, are protected either towards the energy-supplying device or from each other. It is equally applicable in the case of a towed vehicle.

The energy source is the part of the energy-supplying device which generates the energy. It may be located away from the vehicle (for example in the case of a compressed-air braking system for atrailer) and can also be the muscular strength of an individual.

Control device
Parts of a braking system which initiate the operation and control the effect of this braking system. The control signal can be conveyed within the control device by, for example, mechanical, pneumatic, hydraulic or electrical means, including the use of auxiliary or non-muscular energy.

The control device is defined as starting at that component to which the control force is directly applied, and can be operated:
– by direct action of an individual, either by hand or foot;
– by indirect action of the driver of without any action (only in the case of towed vehicles);
– by variation of the pressure in a connecting pipe, or of the electric current in a cable, between the towing and the towed vehicle at the time of operation of one of the braking systems of the towing vehicle, or in the case of a failure;
– by the inertia of the vehicle or by its weight or that of one of its main constituent elements.

The mechanism is defined as ending at the point at which the braking energy is distributed, or where a portion of the energy is diverted to control braking energy.

Transmission device
Parts of a braking system which transmit the energy distributed by the control device. It starts either at the point where the control device terminates or at the point where the energy-supplying device terminates.

It terminates at those parts of the braking system in which are created the forces opposing the movement or the tendency towards movement of the vehicle. It can, for example, be of the mechanical, hydraulic, pneumatic (pressure above or below atmospheric), electric, or combined (for example hydro-mechanical, hydro-pneumatic) type.

Brake
Parts of a braking system in which the forces opposing the movement of the vehicle are produced, such as friction brakes (disk or drum) or retarders (hydrodynamic or electrodynamic retarders, engine brakes).

Supplementary device of the towing vehicle for the towed vehicle
Parts of a braking system on a towing vehicle which are intended for the supply of energy to, and control of, the braking systems on the towed vehicle. It comprises the components between the energy-supplying device of the towing vehicle and the supply-line coupling head (inclusive), and between the transmission d evice(s) of the towing vehicle and the control-line coupling head (inclusive).

Definitions relating to the energy supplying device:

Muscular energy braking system
Braking system in which the energy necessary to produce the braking force is supplied solely by the physical effort of the driver.

Energy assisted braking system
Braking system in which the energy necessary to produce the braking force is supplied by the physical effort of the driver and one or more energy-supplying devices.

Non-muscular energy braking system
Braking system in which the energy necessary to produce the braking force is supplied by one or more energy-supplying devices excluding the physical effort of the driver.

Note: However, a braking device in which the driver can increase the braking force, in the total failed energy condition, by muscular effort acting on this device, is not included in the above definition.

Inertia braking system
Braking system in which the energy necessary to produce the braking force arises from the approach of the trailer to its towing vehicle.

Gravity braking system
Braking system in which the energy necessary to produce the braking force is supplied by the lowering of a constituent element of the trailer (e.g. trailer drawbar), due to gravity.

Definitions relating to the design of the transmission device

Single-circuit braking system
Braking system having a transmission device embodying a single circuit. The transmission device comprises a single circuit if, in the venet of a failure in the transmission device, no energy for the production of the application force can be transmitted by this transmission device.

Multi-circuit braking system
Braking system having a transmission device embodying several circuits. The transmission device comprises several circuits if, in the vent of a failure in the transmission device, energy for the production of the application force can still be transmitted, wholly or partly, by this transmission device.

Definitions relating to vehicle combinations

Single-line braking system
Assembly in which the braking systems of the individual vehicles act in such a way that the single line is used both for the energy supply to, and for the control of, the braking system of the towed vehicle.

Two- or mult-line braking systems
Assembly in which the braking systems of the individual vehicles act in such a way that several lines are used separately and simultaneously for the nergy supply to, and for the control of, the braking system of the towed vehicle.

Continuous braking system
Combination of braking systems for vehicles forming a vehicle combination offering the following characteristics:
– the driver, from his driving seat, can operate gradually by a single operation a directly operated control device on the towing vehicle and an indirectly operated control device on the towed vehicle:
– the energy used fot the braking of each of the vehicles forming the combination is supplied by the same energy source (which can be the muscular effort of the driver);
– simultaneous or suitable phased braking of each of the vehicles forming the combination.

Semi-continous braking system
Combination of braking systems for vehicles forming a vehicle combination offering the following characteristics:
– the driver, from his driving seat, can operate gradually by a single operation a directly operated control device on the towing vehicle and an indirectly operated control device on the towed vehicle;
– the energy used for the braking of each of the vehicle forming the combination is supplied by at least two different energy sources (one of which can be the muscular effort of the driver);
– simultaneous or suitable phased braking of each of the vehicles forming the combination.

Non-continous braking system
Combinations of the braking systems of the vehicles forming a combination which is neither continuous nor semi-continous.

Braking-system control lines

Wiring & conductors
These are employed to conduct electrical energy.

Tubular lines
Rigid, semirigid or flexible tubes used to transfer hydraulic or pneumatic energy.

Lines connecting the braking equipment of vehicles in a vehicle combination

Supply line
A supply line is a special feed line transmittting energy from the towing vehcile to the energy reservoir of the towed vehicle.

Control line
A control line is a special pilot line by which the energy essential for control is transmitted from the towing vehicle to the towed vehicle.

Common supply and control line
Line serving equally as supply line and as control line (single-line braking system).

Secondary line
Special actuating line transmitting from the towing vehicle to the towed vehicle the energy essential for the secondary braking of the towed vehicle.

Braking mechanics

Mechanical phenomena occurring between the initiation of actuation of the control device and the end of the braking action.

Gradual braking
Braking which, within the normal range of operation of the control device, permits the driver, at any moment, to increase or reduce, to a sufficiently fine degree, the braking force by operation of the control device.

When an increase in braking force is obtained by action of the control device, an inverse action shall lead to a reduction of that force.

Braking system hysteresis
Difference in control forces between application and release for the same braking torque.

Brake hysteresis
Difference in application force between application and release for the same braking torque.

Forces and torques

Control force F_c
Force exerted on the control device.

Application force F_s
In friction brakes, the total force, applied to the lining, which causes the braking force by friction effect.

Braking torque
Product of the frictional forces resulting from the application force and the distance between the points of application of these forces and the axis of rotation.

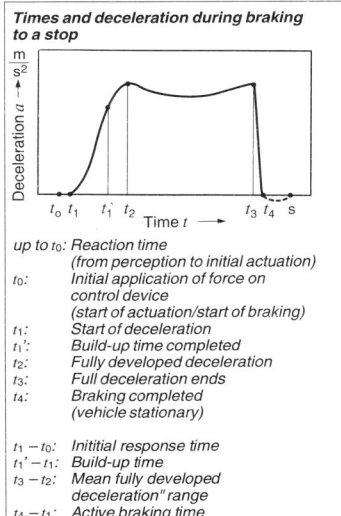

Times and deceleration during braking to a stop

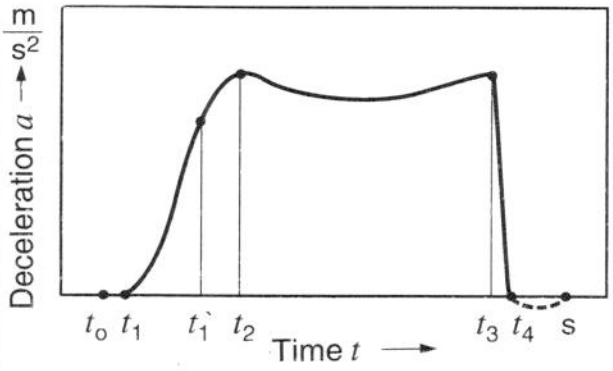

up to t_0: *Reaction time (from perception to initial actuation)*
t_0: *Initial application of force on control device (start of actuation/start of braking)*
t_1: *Start of deceleration*
t_1': *Build-up time completed*
t_2: *Fully developed deceleration*
t_3: *Full deceleration ends*
t_4: *Braking completed (vehicle stationary)*

$t_1 - t_0$: *Inititial response time*
$t_1' - t_1$: *Build-up time*
$t_3 - t_2$: *Mean fully developed deceleration" range*
$t_4 - t_1$: *Active braking time*
$t_4 - t_0$: *Total braking time*

Total braking force F_t
Sum of the braking forces at the interfaces between all the wheels and the ground, produced by the effect of the braking system, which oppose the movement or the tendecy to movement of the vehicle.

Braking-force distribution
Specification of braking force according to axle, given as % of the total braking force F_t. Example: Front axle 60 %, rear axle 40 %.

Brake coefficient C^*
Defines the relationship between the total circumferential force at the effective radius of the brake and the brake's application force.

$$C^* = F_u / F_s$$

F_u Total circumferential force
F_s Application force

The mean is employed when there are variations in the application forces at the individual brake shoes

$$F_s = \sum F_{si} / i$$

i Number of brake shoes

Times

Reaction time
The time which elapses between perception of the state or object which induces the response, and the point at which the brakes are applied (t_0).

Actuating time
Elapsed time between the moment when the component of the control device on which the control force acts starts to move, and the moment when it reaches its final position corresponding to the applied control force (or its travel). (This is equally true for application and release).

Initial response time $t_1 - t_0$
Elapsed time between the moment when the component of the control device on which the control force acts starts to move and the moment when the braking force takes effect.

Build-up time $t_1' - t_1$
Elapsed time between the moment when the braking force takes effect and the moment when this force reaches a certain value. (75 % of asymptotic value of the pressure in the wheel-brake cylinder (Defined in EC 71/320, ECE Appendix

III/2.4 as 75% of the asymptotic value for wheel-cylinder pressure).

Response time
The sum of the initial response and build-up times is used to access how the brake system behaves in time until the moment at which the full braking effect is reached.

Active braking time $t_4 - t_1$
Elapsed time between the moment when braking force takes effect and the moment at which it ceases. If the vehicle stops before braking force ceases, the time of the end of movement constitutes the end of the active braking time.

Release time
Elapsed time between the moment when the actuating time for release starts and the moment when the braking force ceases.

Total braking time $t_4 - t_0$
Elapsed time between the moment when the control device component on which the control force acts starts to move, and the moment when the braking force ceases. If the vehicle stops before the braking force ceases, the time of the end of movement constitutes the end of the total braking time.
See the graph on p. 597.

Braking distance s
Distance travelled by the vehicle during the total braking time. If the time of the end of movement constitutes the end of the total braking time, this distance is called the "stopping distance".

Braking work W
Integral of the product of the instantaneous total braking force, F_f, and the elementary movement, ds, over the braking distance, s:

$$W = \int_0^s F_f \cdot ds$$

Instantaneous braking power P
Product of the instantaneous total braking force, F_f, and of the vehicle speed, υ.

$$P = F_f \cdot \upsilon$$

Braking deceleration
Reduction of speed obtained by the braking system in the considered time, t. The following can be identified:

Instantaneous deceleration a

$$a = d\upsilon/dt$$

Main deceleration a_{ms}
The mean deceleration value over the stopping distance:

$$a_{ms} = \upsilon_0^2/(2 \cdot s_0)$$

in which υ_0 and s_0 refer to the point t_0 (see diagram, p. 597).

Mean deceleration a_{mt} within a section of time
Deceleration between two points in time t_i and t_j.

$$a_{mt} = (\upsilon_i - \upsilon_j)/(t_j - t_i)$$

This formula is used for the evaluation of the braking efficiency of retarders.

Main fully developed deceleration a_{mf}
The mean deceleration value over the period of the fully developed deceleration $t_3 - t_2$.

$$a_{mf} = \frac{1}{t_3 - t_2} \cdot \int_{t_2}^{t_3} a \cdot dt$$

Braking factor z
Ratio between the total braking force, F_f, and the static weight, G_s, on the axle or the axles of the vehicle:

$$z = F_f/G_s$$

Legal regulations

The testing of braking equipment pursuant to the issuance of the type approval for a vehicle in Germany may take place in accordance with one of the following three groups of regulations as chosen by the vehicle manufacturer:

– In Germany, national regulations as set forth in § 41 StVZO (Federal Motor Safety Standards) and pertinent guidelines for brake testing.
– Council Directive of the European Communities: Directive 71/320/EEC and the Amending Directives and Annexes or
– ECE Regulation 13 and 78 of the UN Economic Commission in Geneva.

The requirements governing ABS (antilock braking systems) contained in Paragraph 41b of the StVZO German Motor Vehicle Licensing Regulations (FMVSS/CUR) are more stringent than the corresponding EC directives. The stipulations of Paragraph 41, EC Directive ECE 71/320 and ECE Directive 13 are basically the same in all other points.

Braking equipment as prescribed in Paragraph 41 of the StVZO German Motor Vehicle Licensing Regulations (FMVSS/CUR), EC Directives and ECE Directives 13 and 78
(see p. 647 for vehicle classifications)

Category L vehicles (less than 4 wheels)
Motorized two- and three-wheeled vehicles must be equipped with 2 mutually independent braking systems. In the case of heavy category L5 vehicles, the two braking systems must both act on two wheels, and these vehicles must additionally be equipped with a parking braking system.

Category M and N vehicles
These vehicles must meet the requirements which üertain to the service braking system, secondary braking system and parking braking system. These 3 braking systems may have common components. Such vehicles must have at least 2 mutually independent control devices. The apportioning of braking force among the individual axles is prescribed. Certain vehicles as from M_2 and N_2 may be equipped with antilock braking systems (ABS). Additional retarding braking systems can be used in vehicles of category M_3 and N_3 in order to fulfil braking requirements on long inclines. Category M_3 buses with a weight of more than 10 metric tons must fulfil the downgrade-braking requirements exclusively through operation of an additional retarding braking system.

Category O trailers
Category O_1 trailers are not required to have a braking system, however, there are requirements governing the safety connection to the towing vehicle. Beginning with category O_2, trailers must be fitted with a service braking service and a parking braking system which may have common components. The parking-braking system must be able to be operated by a person standing next to the vehicle. The apportioning of the braking force among the individual axles is prescribed. An antilock braking system (ABS) is prescribed for some trailers in Class O_3 and above.

Inertia braking systems are permissible for trailers up to category O_2.

The trailer must brake automatically if it becomes decoupled from the tractor vehicle while moving, or it must be equipped with a safety connection to the towing vehicle.

Vehicles equipped with antilock braking systems (ABS)
When an antilock braking system is prescribed for vehicles in Classes M_2, M_3 and N_2, N_3, then the system must conform to the Category 1 stipulations contained in EC Directive ECE/71/320, Appendix X. The major requirements are:
– No directly-controlled wheel is to lock-up at speeds in excess of 15 km/h, regardless of road surface,
– Operating stability and steering control are to be maintained.
– Optimal utilization of tire adhesion, whether the road surface affords equal or different frictional coefficients on the different sides of the vehicle.

Minimum standards are in force for trailer ABS. The ABS on tractor and trailer should be mutually compatible in order to ensure safety and prevent tire damage.

Tractor vehicles and trailers with compressed air braking systems
The compressed-air connections must be of the two- or multi-line design. When the service- or secondary braking system of the tractor vehicle is operated, the service braking system of the trailer must be operated gradually.

The braking effect as a function of the pressure at the coupling head of the control line is prescribed.

Note: The following tables represent a summary of all major legal requirements.

Requirements according to StVZO*, EC Directive 71/320 & ECE Directive 13

Vehicle class	Passenger cars & motor coaches			Commercial vehicles			Trailers			
(Classifications, see p. 647)	M_1	M2	M_3	N_1	N_2	N_3	O_1	O_2	O_3	O_4
Service braking system	Acting on all wheels Prescribed force distribution to the axles						No brakes or as O_2	Inertia brakes or as O_3		
ABS as per StVZO ($\upsilon_{max} \geq 60$ km/h)	–	+	+	–	+	+	–	–	+	+
ABS as per EC ($\upsilon_{max} \geq 25$ km/h)	–	–	+ ≥12t[1]	–	–	+ ≥16t[2]	–	–	–	+
Type O test. eng. disengaged										
Test speed km/h	80	60	60	80	60	60	–		60	60
Braking distance ≤ m	50.7	36.7	36.7	61.2	36.7	36.7			$z \geq 0.50$	
Formula for braking distance	$0.1\upsilon + \frac{\upsilon^2}{150}$	$0.15\,\upsilon + \frac{\upsilon^2}{130}$							Semi trailer $z \geq 0.45$	
Mean fully developed deceleration ≥ m/s²	5.8	5.0								
Control force ≤ N	500	700							at ≤ 6.5 bar	
Type O Test (eng. engaged)	Vehicle response when braking from 30% – 80% υ_{max} and braking effectiveness									
Test speed $\upsilon = 80\%\ \upsilon_{max}$, but ≤ km/h	160	100	90	120	100	90	–	–	–	–
Braking distance ≤ m	212.9	111.6	91.8	157.1	111.6	91.8				
Formula for braking distance	$0.1\upsilon + \frac{\upsilon^2}{130}$	$0.15\,\upsilon + \frac{\upsilon^2}{103.5}$								
Mean fully developed deceleration ≥ m/s²	5.0	4.0								
Control force ≤ N	500	700								
Type I Test	Repeated braking at 3 m/s² Loaded, eng. engaged							Continuous braking, loaded		
$\upsilon_1 = 80\%\ \upsilon_{max}$, but ≤ km/h $\upsilon_2 = 1/2\ \upsilon_1$	120	100	60	120	60	60	–	40 km/h 7% incline 1.7 km		
Nr. of braking cycles n	15	15	20	15	20	20				
Braking cycle duration s	45	55	60	55	60	60				
Effectiveness of hot brakes following Typ I Test	≥ 80% for Type O Test (eng. disengaged) specified braking effectiveness and ≥ 60% of braking effectivenes (eng. disengaged) achieved in Type O Test							$z \geq 0.36$ and $z \geq 60\%$ or figure measured in Typ O Test at 40 km/h		
Type II Test on long inclines	Energy corresponding to 30 km/h, 6% incline and 6 km, loaded, engine engaged, retarder engaged.									
Effectiveness of hot brakes following Typ II Test	Measurement as in Type O Test (eng. disengaged)							at 40 km/h		
Formula for braking distance	M_3: $0.15\,\upsilon + \frac{1.33\,\upsilon^2}{130}$			N_3: $0.15\,\upsilon + \frac{1.33\,\upsilon^2}{115}$			–			
Braking distance ≤ m			45.8			50.6				
Mean fully developed deceleration ≥ m/s²	–	–	3.75	–	–	3.3		$z \geq 0.33$		

[1]) Buses & motor coaches for intercity and long-distance routes.
[2]) Approved for towing Class O_4 trailers.
* StVZO = German equivalent of FMVSS/CUR

Vehicle class (Classifications, see p. 647)	Passenger cars & motor coaches M_1	$M2$	M_3	Commercial vehicles N_1	N_2	N_3	Trailers O_1	O_2	O_3	O_4
Type IIa Test For additional retarding braking system	Energy corresponding to 30 km/h, 7 % incline, 6 km, loaded, only additional retarding braking system engaged. Only at $M_3 > 10$ t (excl. city buses)						–	–		
Residual braking effect Upon failure in transmission device/circuit failure, eng. disengaged			Full or partial graduated operation of trailer brakes is stipulated.							
Test speed km/h	80	60	60	70	50	40	–			
Braking dist., loaded ≤ m	150.2	101.3	101.3	152.5	80.0	52.4	–			
Braking dist., empty ≤ m	178.7	119.8	101.3	180.9	94.5	52.4	–			
Mean fully developed deceleration loaded ≥ m/s²	1.7	1.5	1.5	1.3	1.3	1.3	–			
empty ≥ m/s²	1.5	1.3	1.5	1.1	1.1	1.3	–			
Control force ≤ N		700			700					
Secondary braking system (Performed as Type O Test, eng. disengaged)			Full or partial graduated operation of trailer brakes is stipulated.							
Test speed km/h	80	60	60	70	50	40	–			
Braking distance ≤ m	93.3	64.4	64.4	95.7	54.0	38.3	–			
Formula for braking distance	$0.1\upsilon + \frac{2\upsilon^2}{150}$	$0.15\,\upsilon + \frac{2\upsilon^2}{130}$		$0.15\,\upsilon + \frac{2\upsilon^2}{115}$			–			
Mean fully developed deceleration ≥ m/s²	2.9	2.5		2.2			–			
Control force Manual ≤ N	400	600		600			–			
Pedal ≤ N	500	700		700						
Parking braking system (Loaded test) Holding stationary on incline (downgrade or upgrade) ≥ %	18			18			–	18		
Together with unbraked Class O vehicle ≥ %	12			12			–	–		
Control force Manual ≤ N	400	600		600			–	600		
Pedal ≤ N	500	700		700			–	–		
Type O Test*) (eng. disengaged, loaded) Test speed km/h	80	60	60	70	50	40	–			
Mean fully developed deceleration & deceleration before stop ≥ m/s²	1.5			1.5			–			
Automatic braking system Trailer braking with compressed-air systems with pressure loss in supply line										
Test speed km/h							–	40		
Braking factor ≥ %							–	13.5		

*) With parking braking system or via auxiliary control device for service braking system.

Requirements according to ECE Directive 78 for Class L vehicles

Vehicle class		2 and 3-wheeled motor vehicles				
(Classifications, see p. 647)		L_1	L_2	L_3	L_4	L_5
Service braking systems						
Test speed	km/h	40	40	60	60	60
or $0.9 \cdot \upsilon_{max}$, if υ_{max}	≤ km/h	45	45	67	67	67
Manual control force	≤ N	200	200	200	200	200
Pedal control force	≤ N	350	350	350	350	500
Type O Test loaded as per manufacturer's specs.						
Front brakes						
Braking distance	≤ m	21.8	26.9	37.3	43.9	54.0
Mean fully developed deceleration	≥ m/s^2	3.4	2.7	4.4	3.6	2.9
Rear brakes						
Braking distance	≤ m	26.9	26.9	54.0	43.9	54.0
Mean fully developed deceleration	≥ m/s^2	2.7	2.7	2.9	3.6	2.9
Both brakes simultaneously (when individual brakes fail to achieve figures)						
Mean fully developed deceleration	≥ m/s^2	–	4.4	5.8	–	5.0
Type O Test, not loaded (driver only) Front & rear brakes, each						
Braking distance	≤ m	28.6	28.6	61.4	61.4	61.4
Mean fully developed deceleration	≥ m/s^2	2.5	2.5	2.5	2.5	2.5
Combination brake system*, loaded & unloaded						
Braking distance	≤ m	17.9	17.9	33.3	31.7	33.7
Mean fully developed deceleration	≥ m/s^2	4.4	4.4	5.1	5.4	5.0
Secondary braking system On vehicles with combination brakes						
Braking distance	≤ m	28.6	28.6	61.4	61.4	61.4
Mean fully developed deceleration	≥ m/s^2	2.5	2.5	2.5	2.5	2.5
Parking brake, loaded		None, or as L_5				
Holding stationary on incline						
(downgrade and upgrade	≥ %	–				18
Manual control	≤ N	–				400
Pedal control	≤ N	–				500

Type I Test (Classes L_3 through L_5 only)
Loaded, eng. engaged, 10 applications from υ_1 to υ_2 at mean deceleration rate of 3 m/s^2 or max. deceleration if $a_{max} < 3 m/s^2$ when braked the first time. Control force from 1st braking is retained.
Distance from braking start to braking start: 1000 m.
Test speed υ_1 (always lower figure)

Front brakes	υ_1 = 70% of υ_{max} or ≤ 100 km/h
Rear brakes	υ_1 = 70% of υ_{max} or ≤ 80 km/h
Interconnected brake system	υ_1 = 70% of υ_{max} or ≤ 100 km/h

Test speed $\upsilon_2 = 1/2 \cdot \upsilon_1$

Effectiveness of hot brakes following Type I Test
Eng. disengaged, > 60% of deceleration achieved in Type O Test or corresponding braking distance.

Effectiveness of wet brakes (measured as in Type O Test, eng. disengaged)
Wet distance ≥ 500 m
Brake effectiveness after 0.5 to 1.0 sec. operation:
Mean deceleration ≥ 60% of mean fully developed deceleration achieved with dry brakes in Typ O Test, and ≤ 120% of mean fully developed deceleration.

* Also integral or interconnected brake system:
Braking force at all wheels is controlled from a single control device.
Secondary braking system acting upon at least one wheel is also required.

Design and components of a braking system

Basic components of a braking system:

The braking system consists of:
- An energy-supplying device,
- A control device,
- A transmission device for controlling braking force, and for activating the engine brake, retarder, parking brake,
- Additional equipment in the towing vehicle for braking the trailer.
- Wheel brakes.

Each of these components exercises an influence on the forces which determine the effectiveness of vehicle braking. Different ranges of applications for different vehicle types result in highly variegated demands being placed on braking systems. The inescapable result is a multiplicity of highly diversified braking systems, differing from one another in both design and application.

Braking-system applications

Legal regulations stipulate that the braking system on a heavy commercial vehicle will consist of:
- service brakes,
- secondary brakes,
- parking brake, and (in some cases)
- additional retarding braking systems, and
- automatic braking system.

The service and parking brakes are equipped with separate individual control and transmission devices. The service brakes are generally applied with the foot, while the parking brake can be actuated with either hand or foot. The secondary braking system frequently shares components with the service or parking brakes. For instance when one circuit in a dual-circuit service-braking system also functions as secondary brake. The additional retarding braking system, which acts as a supplementary, wear-free unit, is especially useful for relieving the service brakes on long downgrades (see "Additional retarding braking system, p. 628). Automatic braking systems apply to trailers only.

***Brake system layout** (truck tractor)*

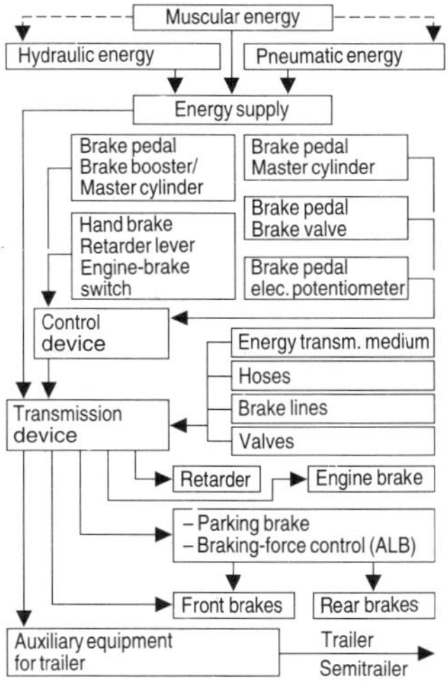

Type of energy and transmission media

Depending upon the type of energy applied to control the braking system, a distinction is drawn between:
- muscular-energy braking systems,
- energy-assisted braking systems,
- non-muscular-energy braking systems,
- inertia braking systems.

The various systems can also be installed in combination. In contrast to the non-muscular-energy braking system, for instance, the energy-assisted system also depends to some degree on the force exerted at the pedal.

Energy-assisted and non-muscular-energy systems are distinguished not only by energy type, but also by media used to transmit the energy. Pneumatic (vacuum, compressed air) and hydraulic energy are the most common, electrical energy is sometimes also employed.

Electronic/compressed-air braking system for two-axle tractor
1 3-D Force sensor, 2 Brake-pad wear sensor, 3 Control valve, 4 Front-wheel brake cylinder, 5 Rear-wheel brake cylinder, 6 Control unit ECU, 7 Brake pedal, 8 Compressed-air reservoir, 9 Compressed-air supply to trailer, 10 Trailer pilot line, 11 Coupling-force sensor.

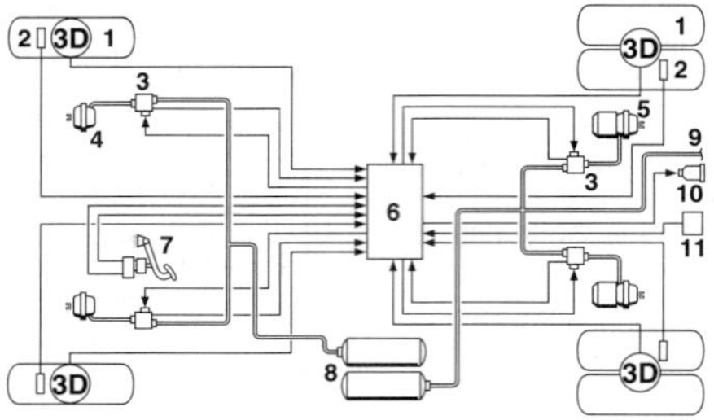

Type of transmission device
The means employed to transmit energy within the braking system may be mechanical, hydraulic, pneumatic or electric/electronic. Combinations may also be used in transmitting the force to the wheel brakes. Electric/electronic transmission mechanisms will play an important role in the electronic-pneumatic and electronic-hydraulic braking systems for the next generation of vehicles.

Braking-system design

The braking system is designed with reference to both the requirements of the vehicle and the intrinsic imperatives of the system itself.

In the case of the vehicle-oriented design, the vehicle's center of gravity and the specified distribution of braking force to the front and rear axles, determine the amount of braking force which can be applied before the wheels lock at any specific level of adhesion between tire and road surface. The braking-force-distribution diagram is used to illustrate this relationship. The coordinate axes show the braking force at front and rear axles relative to weight. The intersection of the straight lines representing equal adhesion coefficients at front and rear axles form the parabola describing "ideal" braking-force distribution. Lines representing constant braking complete the diagram.

If no braking-force proportioning device is provided, then the distribution of the braking force as installed in the unit also forms a straight line. The slope is the ratio of the braking forces at front and rear axles as determined by the dimensions of the brakes. The wheels will always lock on the front as long as axle first the line for as-installed distribution remains below the ideal distribution (stable distribution of

Distribution of braking force without braking-force proportioning device
Ideal distribution of braking force at 1 Approved gross vehicle weight, 2 Curb weight, with driver, 3 Braking-force distribution as installed, 4 Front brakes locked.
F_{Bh} Rear braking force, F_{Bv} Front braking force, G Weight, a Braking. Adhesion coefficients: rear μ_H, front μ_V.

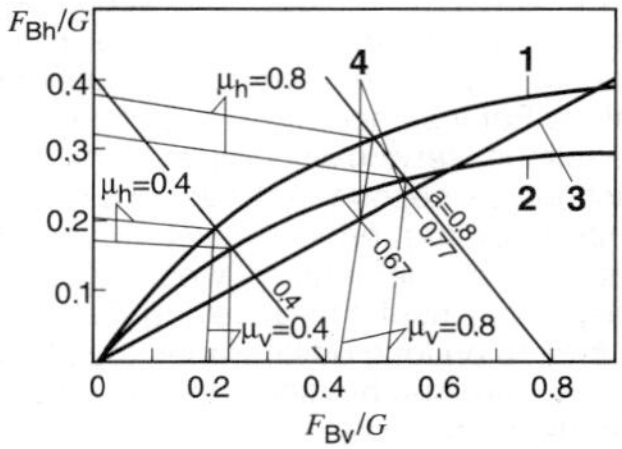

braking forces). The point at which the front wheels lock is found at the intersection of "as-installed distribution" and the lines representing the respective coefficient of adhesion.

The essential design criteria are:
– regulations governing minimum braking force required before the onset of lock, and locking sequence,
– distribution of load weight,
– influence of fading,
– engine braking,
– failure of a brake circuit,
– braking-force proportioning device (if fitted),
– failure of booster (if fitted),
– retarder (if fitted).

System-oriented design concentrates on the dimensions for the wheel brakes and on the control devices.
Design criteria for the wheel brakes:
– brake type (disk or drum),
– endurance (resistance to wear and severe use),
– space available for installation,
– acceptable pressure levels,
– rigidity (on hydraulic brakes: volume of brake fluid required for actuation).
Design criteria for the control device:
– pedal travel and pedal force during normal braking, in panic stops, with failure of a brake circuit, with brake-booster failure,
– comfort requirements,
– installation space,
– combination with brake-pressure regulators.

Brake-circuit configurations

Legal regulations stipulate a dual-circuit tranmission system as mandatory.

Of the five available options (DIN 74000, see below), versions TT and K have become standard. As the brake lines, hoses, connections, and static and dynamic seals remain at a low level of complication, the probability of failure due to leaks is comparable to that achieved with a single-circuit system. The potential response to failure of a circuit due to overheating at one wheel points up a serious weakness in the HT, LL and HH distribu-

Designation of braking-force apportioning (DIN 74 000)

Symbol	Type of apportioning ← Direction of travel	Remarks
TT	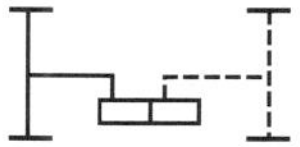	**Front-axle/rear-axle split** One axle is braked in each circuit
K		**Diagonal split** One front wheel and the diagonally opposite rear wheel are braked in each circuit.
HT	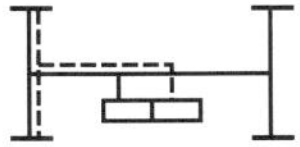	**Front-axle and rear-axle/front-axle split** One circuit brakes the front and rear axles, and one-circuit brakes only the front axle.
LL	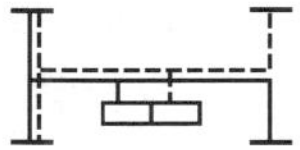	**Front-axle and rear-wheel/front-axle and rear-wheel split** Each circuit brakes the front axle and one rear wheel.
HH	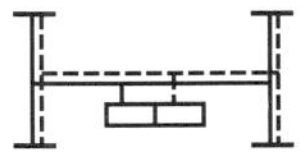	**Front-axle and rear-axle/front-axle and rear-axle split** Each circuit brakes the front axle and the rear axle.

tion patterns, where loss of both brakes on a wheel could lead to total brake-system failure.

Vehicles with a forward weight bias use distribution pattern K to fulfill the regulatory requirements. A minimal or negative roll radius or brake-force-induced, elastokinematic toe-in enhancement (p. 569) counteracts the pronounced yaw tendency associated with one of the front-wheel brakes having a tendency to pull.

Version TT is particularly well-suited for use on rear-heavy vehicles, and mid-range and heavy commercial vehicles.

Vacuum-operated brake booster
Effect of design parameter
1 Master-cylinder surface area, 2 Pedal leverage, 3 Boost factor, pedal leverage, 4 Diaphragm surface area, vacuum level, 5 Effect of pedal force, 6 Effect of servo assist, 7 Output point.

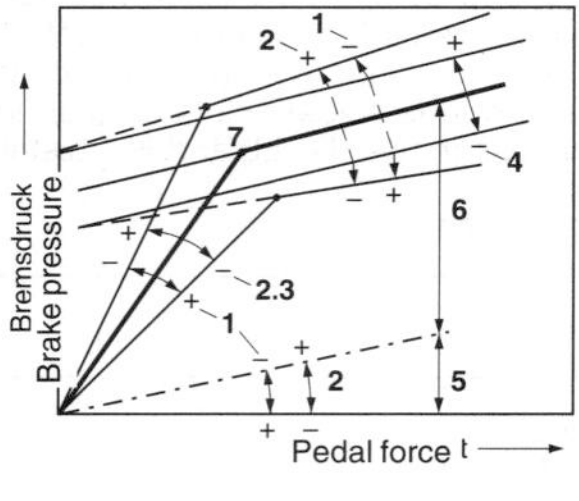

Braking systems for passenger cars and light utility vehicles

Control devices

The control device consists of:
- brake pedal,
- vacuum brake booster,
- master cylinder,
- brake-fluid reservoir,
- device to warn of brake-circuit failure and
- low brake-fluid level.

Vacuum-operated brake booster
1 Push rod, 2 Vacuum chamber with vacuum connection, 3 Diaphragm, 4 Piston, 5 Bell valve, 6 Air filter, 7 Piston rod, 8 Rear chamber, 9 Backing plate.

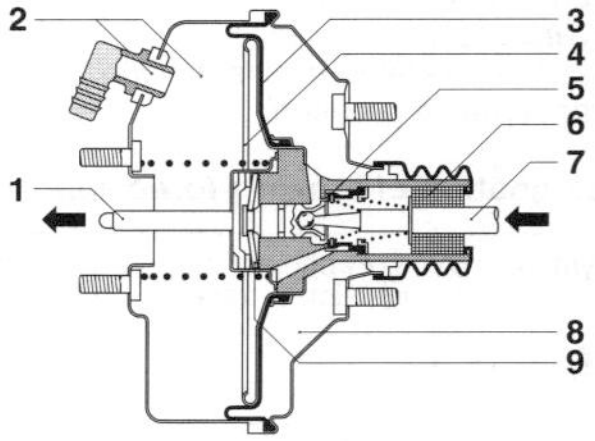

Tandem master cylinder with central valve in secondary circuit
1 Cylinder housing
2 Pressure chamber
3 Pressure supply
4 Reservoir connection
5 Push-rod piston
6 Intermediate piston
7 Central valve
8 Central valve stop
9 Primary sleeve
10 Intermediate sleeve
11 Snifter hole

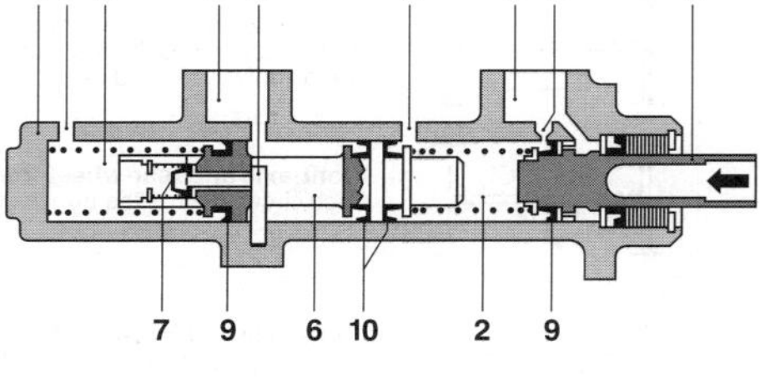

In addition to the basic equipment listed above, hydraulic boosters or hydraulic non-muscular-energy braking systems may be used in certain applications. In non-muscular-energy systems, the brake booster and master cylinder are replaced by a brake valve. The force at the pedal is modulated to achieve the desired brake pressure. High-pressure pumps and accumulators are included to generate and to store the requisite energy.

A vacuum brake booster is generally used due to its inexpensive and uncomplicated design. On this type of booster, the force applied at the pedal regulates the amount of outside air which is applied to a diaphragm, while vacuum remains present on the diaphragm's other side.

The pressure differential at the diaphragm generates force to supplement that applied at the pedal. The simplified diagram provides a schematic illustration of the main factors which influence the braking pressure; working losses and efficiency levels are not considered:

Pedal conversion, boost factor, diaphragm surface area, vacuum pressure, surface area of master cylinder.

The brake pressure is the result of a combination of the force at the pedal and an auxiliary assist. The proportion represented by the assist increases steadily up to full boost; the designed-in boost factor determines the precise rate. At full boost, the maximum pressure difference between outside air and vacuum has been reached. Additional augmentation of the output force is only possible via a substantial increase in the force applied at the pedal. Thus it is important that the booster be designed to ensure that high rates of deceleration can be achieved without exceeding full boost to any appreciable degree.

The major determinant of output force is the surface area of the diaphragm. Two diaphragms in tandem are employed to satisfy higher pressure requirements. Technical considerations limit the maximum feasible diaphragm diameter to approx. 250 mm. The maximum vacuum, as obtained at the intake manifold of a spark-ignition engine with the throttle closed, is approx. 0.8 bar. A vacuum pump is required on diesel engines.

As the demand for boost pressure in heavy vehicles is characteristically greater, the logical choice is a hydraulic booster, which can be designed to function on the same principles.

The energy is frequently provided by the power-steering pump, with an intermediate hydraulic accumulator being incorporated in the circuit to reduce the tendency of brakes and steering to influence each other.

A push rod carries the output force directly to the piston in the tandem master cylinder. The hydraulic pressure thus generated is transmitted to the "floating" intermediate piston, resulting in roughly equal pressures in the two chambers which supply the respective circuits.

Failure in one of the brake circuits can have one of two results: Either the push rod comes up against the intermediate piston, or hydraulic force presses the intermediate piston back against the wall of the master cylinder. This condition will be felt at the pedal, which will continue moving with virtually no resistance.

A master cylinder which responds in several stages has proven a useful expedient on vehicles with the TT distribution pattern. The intermediate piston, which has a smaller diameter than the push-rod piston, applies pressure to the rear-axle circuit. The system responds to failure in the front-axle circuit by increasing the pressure which is transmitted to the rear circuit at a constant pedal pressure. The degree of augmentation bases on the ratio of the piston areas of the push-rod and intermediate pistons.

A brake-fluid reservoir is connected to the master cylinder to compensate for the effects of brake-lining wear and even leakage. Releasing the brakes allows either a valve located in the main piston to open or, alternatively, a piston sealing sleeve covering a supply orifice (snifter hole) to open. This arrangement ensures that the brake system is not under pressure when released, while also providing compensation for fluid losses. The chief disadvantage of this simple layout lies in the fact that vapor bubbles in the brake fluid due to overheating cause the fluid to drain from the affected brake circuit when the brakes are released. This could make it impossible to build up pressure when the brakes are applied again.

In order to prevent complete drainage in the event of a major leak, the brake-fluid reservoir is designed – at least as from a given brake-fluid level – with two chambers. One or two float-actuated switches trigger an optical display once the fluid falls below a certain level. The float-actuated switches can be replaced by differential pressure switches on the master cylinder, these then indicate failure of a brake circuit.

Wheel brakes

The wheel brakes must meet the following requirements:

– uniform effectiveness,
– smooth, graduated response,
– resistance to contamination and corrosion,
– extreme reliability,
– durability,
– resistance to wear,
– ease of maintenance.

Whereas on small passenger cars and commercial vehicles, various types of drum brakes fulfill these demands satisfactorily; disk brakes represent the only means of achieving even response and good control on heavier and faster passenger cars.

Gray cast-iron brake disks with bilaterally acting calipers have proven to be the most satisfactory layout. The brake disk is usually located within the well of the wheel rim, an arrangement which makes it necessary to provide for adequate heat dissipation through radiation, convection and thermal conductance. Additional expedients such as internally-ventilated brake disks, air ducts and optimal-flow wheel designs are employed to reduce disk temperatures, particularly on high-performance vehicles.

Brake calipers fall into one of two categories: Floating calipers and fixed calipers.

In the case of the fixed caliper, the housing is rigid and "grips" the brake disk from both sides (see above). Two pistons in the caliper housing, one on each side of the brake disk, force the brake pads up against the brake disk.

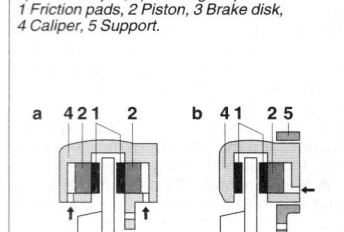

Disk brakes
a) Fixed caliper, b) Floating caliper.
1 Friction pads, 2 Piston, 3 Brake disk, 4 Caliper, 5 Support.

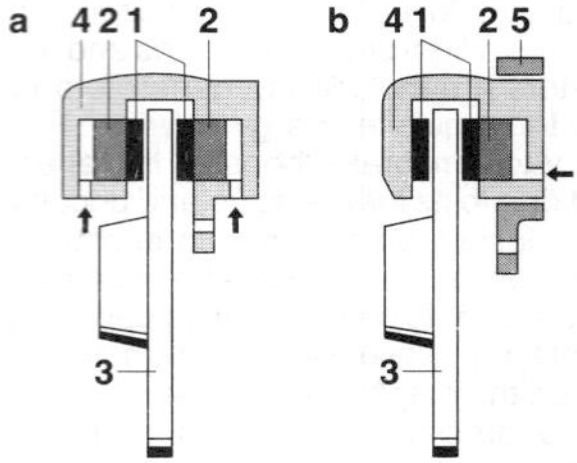

Two basic subcategories of floating caliper have established themselves: the floating-caliper (or sliding caliper) type and the so-called Mark II caliper. On both types, one or more pistons exert direct pressure on the inside friction pad. The sliding- caliper frame or the caliper then pulls the outer pad against the disk.

Compared to fixed calipers, the floating units offer the following advantages:

– Modest space requirement between brake disk and wheel dish (convenient where suspension employs small or negative steering-roll radius),
– Reduced thermal stress on the fluid, as no fluid lines are located in the critical area directly above the brake disk.

Constructive measures effectively alleviate inherent disadvantages (tendency to rattle and squeak, uneven wear of friction pads, corrosion in transmission elements).

Braking-force proportioning valve

The braking-force proportioning device is not a closed-loop control element, like the brake-pressure regulating valve as used for ABS, but rather an open-loop control element. The individual valves differ according to their function as braking-force limiters or reducers, or their control parameters, such as brake pressure, axle load or rate of deceleration.

The valve adjusts the apportionment of the braking force between front and rear axles as determined by the brakes' particular dimensions in order to achieve a closer approximation to the ideal distribution, i.e., the parabolic curve. The ideal braking-force distribution is determined solely by the vehicle's center of gravity and the nature of the particular braking maneuver. These relationships can be shown in a dimensionless braking-force-distribution diagram. The weight-related braking forces at the front and rear axles are entered on the coordinate axes. The lines for identical braking appear as straight lines with a negative slope (–1). The ideal braking-force-distribution curves for the vehicle conditions "curb weight" and "approved gross vehicle weight" are in the form of parabolas. Diagram "a" is for a braking-force limiter and diagram "b" a braking-force reducer.

Pressure-sensitive proportioning valves achieve good approximation of ideal distribution with the vehicle in the "curb weight" state. On the other hand, under "approved gross vehicle weight" conditions (upper parabola), they deviate from the ideal once the limiter or reducer becomes operative (bend in the curve), i.e., the proportion of the total braking force directed toward the rear axle decreases as the rear-axle load increases.

The load-sensitive apportioning valve responds to increased loads by displacing the triggering point upward, allowing a reasonable approximation of ideal braking-force distribution under all load conditions.

The deceleration-sensitive apportioning valve is triggered by a specific rate of deceleration, and is thus basically insensitive to load.

The proportioning valve must be designed to ensure that the distribution of braking force remains on or below the ideal curve. The potential effects of fluctuations of the pad friction coefficient, as well as of engine torque and tolerances of the valve itself, must all be considered in

Braking-force-distribution diagram.
a) Braking-force limiter, b) Braking-force reducer. F_{Bh} Rear braking force, F_{Bv} Front braking force, G Weight. 1 Loaded, 2 Empty, 3 Loaded, according to load, 4 Empty, according to pressure; empty, according to deceleration; and loaded, empty according to load, 5 Loaded, according to pressure.

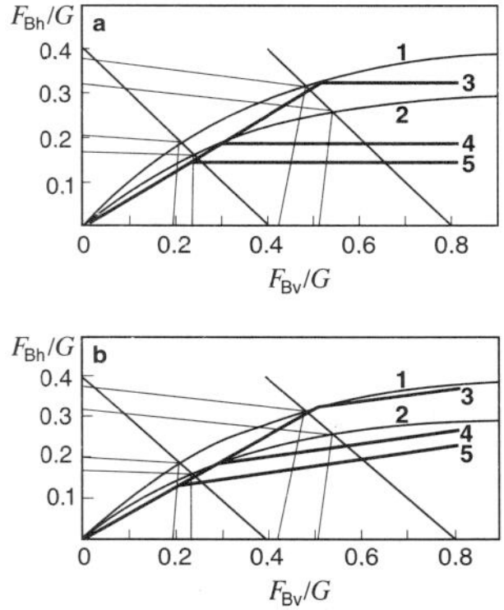

preventing over-brake of the rear axle. In practice, this means that actual installed distribution (with bend in curve) must remain well below the ideal.

The criteria according to which the proportioning valve is designed include the following:

– ABS compatibility,
– Additional outlay involved with separate brake circuits at rear axle (e.g., K distribution pattern),
– Bypass function for dealing with brake-circuit failure, esp. with braking-force limiters,
– Facility for testing of setting and operation.

Vehicles with balanced load conditions are not necessarily equipped with a proportioning valve, as the disadvantages of an undetected defect in the valve outweigh its minimal advantages.

ABS antilock braking systems for passenger cars

ABS antilock braking systems are closed-loop control devices within the braking system which prevent wheel lock-up during braking.

Closed-loop control process

On iltial braking, the brake pressure is raised; the brake slip λ increases and at the maximum point on the adhesion/slip curve, it reaches the limit between the stable and unstable ranges. From this point on, any futher increase in brake pressure or braking torque does not cause any further increase in the braking force F_B. In the stable range, the brake slip is largely deformation slip, it becoming increasingly skidding in the unstable range.

Brake slip $\lambda = (v_F - v_R)/v_F \cdot 100\%$
Wheel speed $v_R = r \cdot \omega$
Braking force $F_B = \mu_B \cdot G$
Lateral force $F_S = \mu_S \cdot G$
μ_B Braking-force coefficient,
μ_S Lateral-force coefficient.

There is a more or less sharp drop in the braking-force coefficient μ_B, depending upon the shape of the slip curve. The rsulting excess torque causes the wheel to be braked to a stop in an extremely short period of time (when braking without ABS); this is expressed as a sharp increase in wheel deceleration.

The wheel-speed sensor monitors the motion of the wheel. If one wheel shows signs of locking, there is a sharp rise in peripheral wheel deceleration and in wheel slip. If these exceed defined critical values, the controller sends commands to the solenoid-valve unit to stop or reduce the buildup of wheel-brake pressure until the danger of lock-up has passed. The brake pressure must then be built up again in order to ensure that the wheel is not underbraked. During automatic brake control, it is constantly necessary for the stability or instability of the wheel motion to be detected, and the wheel must be kept in the slip range with maximum braking force by a succession of pressure-buildup, pressure-reduction and pressure-holding phases.

Forces at the braked wheel
G Force due to weight, F_B Braking force, F_S Lateral force, v_F Vehicle speed, α Slip angle, ω Angular velocity.

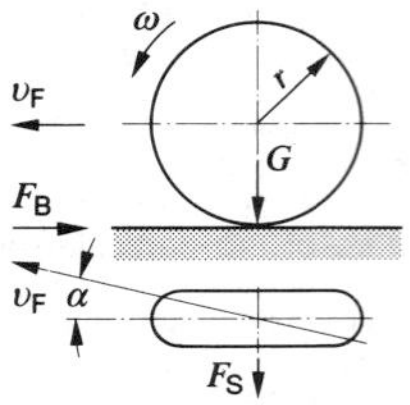

Adhesion/slip curve
The curve shape differs greatly as a function of road surface and tire condition.

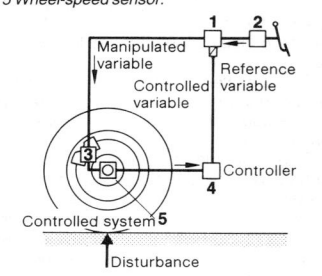

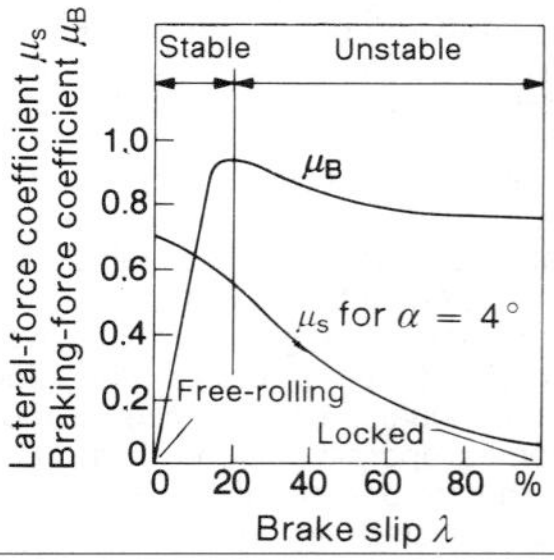

ABS closed control slip
1 Solenoid-valve unit, " master cylinder, 3 Brake cylinder, 4 Electronic controller, 5 Wheel-speed sensor.

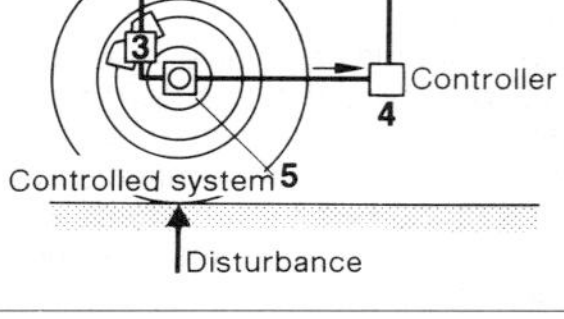

Disturbances in the closed control loop
The ABS system must take the following disturbances into account:
– Variations in the adhesion between tire and road caused by changes in the road surface and int the wheel loads, e.g. during cornering.
– Irregularities in the road surface causing the wheels and axles to vibrate.
– Out-of-roundness, brake hysteresis.

Criteria of control quality
The following criteria for control quality must be fulfilled by efficient antilock braking systems:
– Maintenance of driving stability through provision of sufficient lateral guiding forces at the rear wheels.
– Maintenance of steerability through provision of adequate lateral guiding forces at the front wheels.
– Reduction in stopping distance as opposed to braking with locked-up wheels through optimum utilization of the adhesion between tires and road.
– Rapid matching of the braking force to different adhesion coefficients.
– Guaranteeing of low braking-torque control amplitudes to prevent vibrations in the running gear.

ABS system variants
The diagram below shows six system variants, which are described in the following according to the number of channels and sensors.

4-channel system with individual control of all wheels (variant 1)
When braking on split-coefficient road surfaces, the yaw moment (torque about the vertical axis) is so great that driving stability is not adequately ensured. This system allows the rear-wheel brake control to be switched to select-low mode and vice versa.

4-channel system with diagonally split brake circuits (variant 2)
In this case, the front wheels are controlled individually, but the rear wheels are controlled jointly by the select-low method (the rear wheel with the lower adhesion coefficient determines the brake pressure applied jointly to both rear wheels). Owing to the diagonally split brake circuits, two valve units are required at the rear wheels. In this system as well as in the following

3-channel system (variant 3)
the yaw moment when braking on split-coefficient road surfaces is reduced to such an extent that passenger cars with a long wheelbase, and a high moment of mass inertia about the vertical axis, are

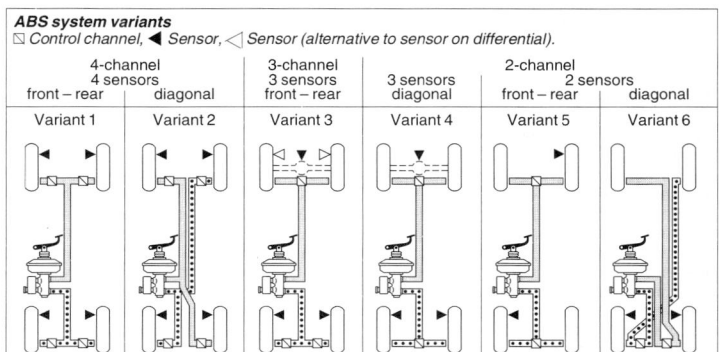

ABS system variants
Control channel, ◀ Sensor, ◁ Sensor (alternative to sensor on differential).

4-channel, 4 sensors, front – rear	4-channel, 4 sensors, diagonal	3-channel, 3 sensors, front – rear	2-channel, 3 sensors, diagonal	2-channel, 2 sensors, front – rear	2-channel, 2 sensors, diagonal
Variant 1	Variant 2	Variant 3	Variant 4	Variant 5	Variant 6

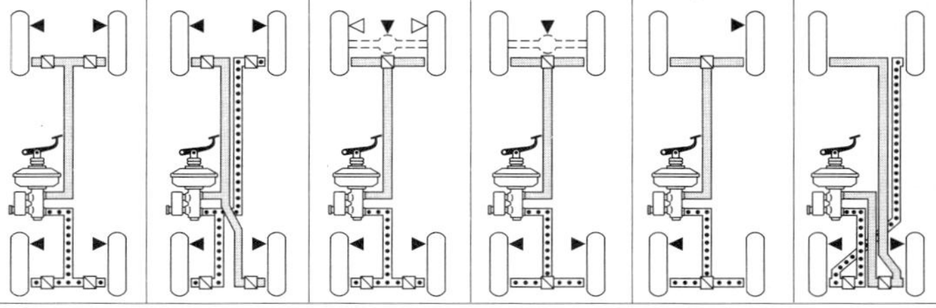

well able to control this braking situation, too. Passenger cars with a short wheelbase and a low moment of mass inertia, however, require electronic delaying of the yaw-moment buildup. When braking on split-coefficient road surfaces, this causes a delayed buildup of the braking torque at the front wheel with the high adhesion coefficient. This provides the driver with sufficient time to correct the yaw moment by a suitable movement of the steering wheel.

2-channel systems (variants 4, 5, 6)
With variants 4 and 5 in select-high mode (the front wheel with the higher adhesion coefficient determines the brake pressure applied jointly to both front wheels), steerability and driving stability on split-coefficient road surfaces are adversely affected. If the front wheels are braked on a split-coefficien road surface and the front wheels then come onto a homogeneous road surface with a high adhesion coefficient, builds up suddenly at the wheel which was previously locked. This results suddenly in a high yaw moment.

Variant 6 can be used only with diagonally split brake circuits. In this version, the brake pressures at the front wheels are controlled individually, while the brake pressures at the rear wheels are jointly controlled. Because the front-to-rear distribution of braking force bears the responsibility for ensuring that the rear wheels do not lock, this system provides somewhat lower deceleration rates than a 3 or 4-channel system.

ABS versions

ABS 2S-3-channel/-4-channel systems (Bosch)
In this system, the ABS and the brake booster are separate units.

The 3-channel hydraulic modulator for front-rear-split brake circuits comprises three solenoid valves, which permit three positions, and a return pump with electric drive motor. In the first, de-energized position, there is an unhindered passage from the master cylinder to the wheel-brake cylinder, with the result that the wheel-brake pressure rises during initial braking and during automatic brake control. In the second, semi-energized position, the passage from the master cylinder to the wheel-brake cylinder is interrupted, with the result that the wheel-brake pressure is kept constant. In the third, fully energized position, the wheel-brake pressure drops. The pressure-bleed phase lasts for about 20 ms, while the pressure buildup requires approx. 200 ms.

The 4-channel hydraulic-modulator valve for diagoanlly split brake circuits calls for four solenoid valves, because the rear-wheel brakes belong to different brake circuits. However, both the rear-wheel valves are jointly energized, so that there is the same pressure in the rear-wheel-brakes. The depicted control cycle shows automatic brake control in the case of a high adhesion coefficient. The change in wheel speed (deceleration) is calculated in the electronic controller. After th evalue falls below the ($-a$) threshold, the hydraulic modulator valve unit is switched to the pressure-holding mode. If

ABS control cycle for high adhesion coefficients

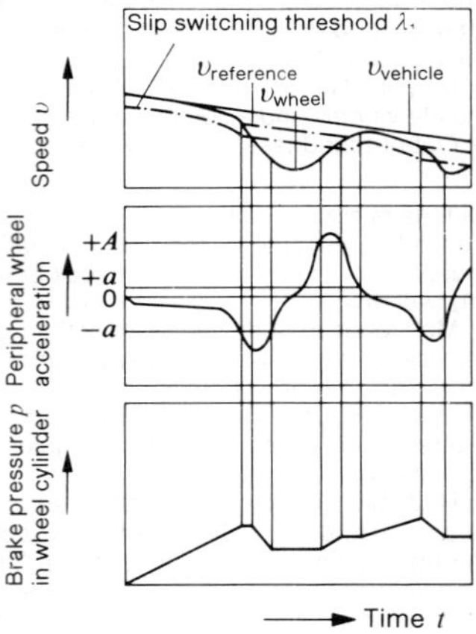

the wheel speed then also drops below the slip-switching threshold λ_1, the valve unit is switched to pressure reduction; this is done as long as the ($-a$) signal is present. During the subsequent pressure-holding phase, the peripherical wheel acceleration increases until the ($+a$) threshold is exceeded; thereupon, the brake pressure continues to be kept constant. After the relatively high ($+A$) threshold has been exceeded, the brake pressure is increased, so that the wheel is not accelerating excessively as it enters the stable range of the adhesion/slip curve. After the ($+a$) signal has dropped out, the brake pressure is slowly raised until, when the wheel acceleration again falls below the ($-a$) threshold, the second control cycle is initiated, this time with an immediate pressure reduction. In the first control cycle, a short pressure-holding phase was necessary initially for the filtering of disturbances. In the case of high wheel moments of inertia, low braking-force coefficient and slow pressuree rise in the wheel-brake cylinder (cautious initial braking, e.g., on black ice), the wheel might lock up without the deceleration switching threshold having responded. In this case, therefore, the wheel slip, too, is used in automatic brake control.

Under certain road-surafce conditions, passenger cars with all-wheel drive and with differential locks engaged pose problems when the ABS system is in operation; this calls for special measures to support the reference speed, lower the wheel-deceleration thresholds, and reduce the engine drag torque.

Brake control with yaw-moment build-up delay

When the brakes are applied on an asymmetrical road surface (left wheels on dry asphalt, right wheels on ice), the result is vastly different braking forces at the front wheels. This difference induces a turning motion (yaw moment) around the vertical axis of the vehicle.

When a heavy passenger car with ABS is braked, the resulting yaw sets in slowly and the driver has time for corrective steering maneuvers. On smaller cars, the ABS must be supplemented by an additional yaw-moment buildup-delay device

Buildup of yaw moment induced by large differences in coefficients of braking-force
M_{yaw} Yaw moment, F_B Braking-force, μ_B Coefficient of braking forcre.
1 "High" wheel, 2 "Low" wheel.

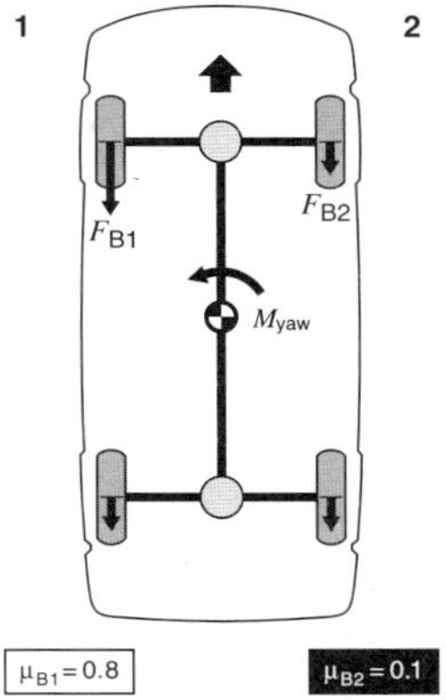

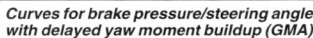

Curves for brake pressure/steering angle with delayed yaw moment buildup (GMA)
1 Master-cylinder pressure p_{HZ},
2 Brake pressure p_{high} without GMA,
3 p_{high} with GMA 1,
4 p_{high} with GMA 2, 5 p_{low} am "Low"-Rad,
6 Steering angle α without GMA, 7 Steering angle α with GMA.

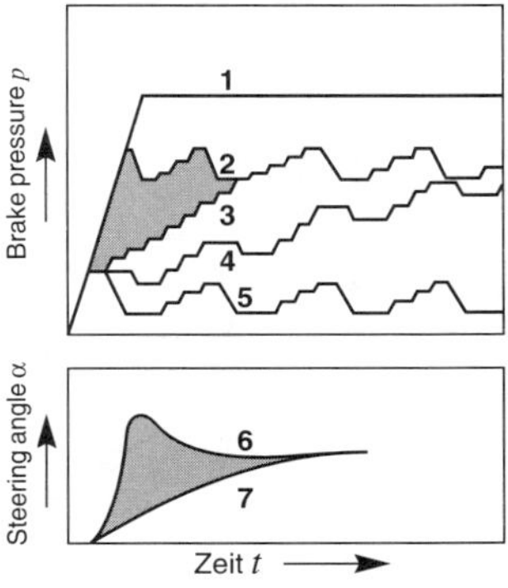

(GMA) to ensure that control is maintained during panic stops on asymmetrical surfaces.

GMA delays the pressure buildup in the wheel cylinder of the front wheel with the higher coefficient of braking force at the surface ("high" wheel).

The GMA concept is demonstrated in the diagram: Curve 1 represents the master cylinder pressure p_{HZ}. Without GMA, the wheel on asphalt soon arrives at the pressure p_{high} (Curve 2), while the wheel which is running on ice goes to p_{low} (Curve 5); each wheel achieves the maximum retardation available under the given circumstances (individual control).

The GMA 1 System (Curve 3) is suited for use with vehicles with a less critical response pattern, while GMA 2 is designed for cars which display an especially marked tendency toward yaw-induced instability (Curve 4).

ABS 2E (Bosch)

This is an inexpensive "full-function" ABS system offering the range of functions and extensive safety provided by ABS 2S with only minor sacrifices in brake-pedal feel and noise of operation.

Under normal braking, without active ABS, brake fluid flows to the right rear wheel through the rear-axle solenoid valve, while the central valve supplies the left rear wheel. When the ABS is activated, each of the left-side solenoid valves controls a front brake, while the rear-axle solenoid assumes control of the

ABS 2E hydraulic system for diagonal brake circuits

1 Brake booster
2 Solenoid valves
3 Accumulators
4 Rear-axle solenoid valve
5 Dual return pump
6 Central valve
7 Floating piston
V Front
H Rear
R Right
L Left

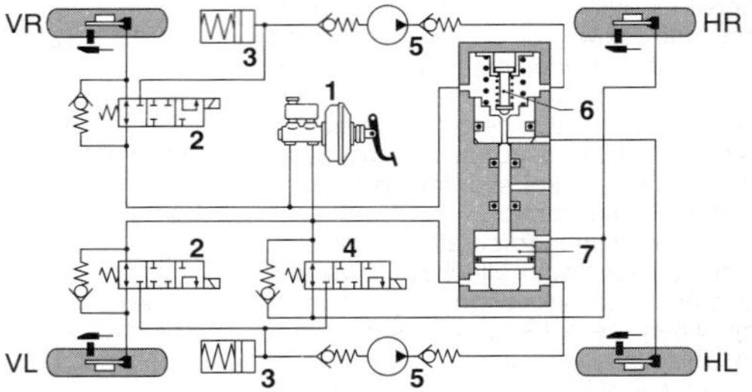

Passenger car with ABS 3

1 Wheel-speed sensor
2 Wheel-brake cylinder
3 Hydraulic pressure modulator unit with master cylinder
4 ECU
5 Warning lamp

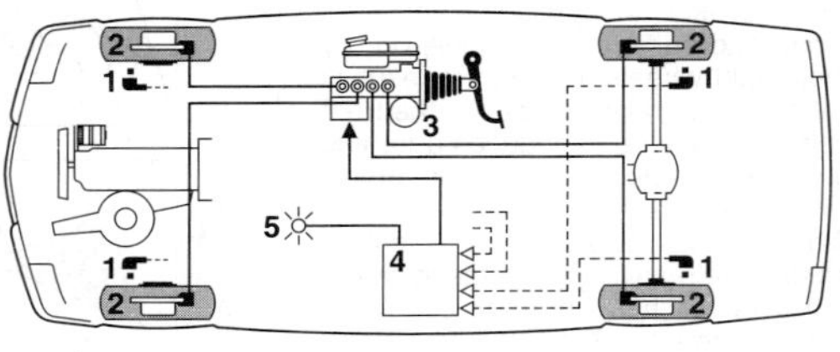

right rear. The rear-axle solenoid valve switches to the "hold-pressure" position upon receiving the corresponding command from the control unit.

When the pressure in the lower plunger chamber – which is directly joined to the master cylinder – increases relative to that in the upper chamber – which is connected to the rear-axle solenoid valve – the resulting imbalance pushes the plunger upward, closing the central valve. As braking pressure drops in the right rear brake, the plunger continues to move upward until the braking pressures at the rear wheels are roughly equal.

ABS 3 (Bosch)

The hydraulic brake booster and the ABS valve block form a single, compact integrated unit in the engine compartment. Because there is no direct connection between the brake pedal and the main piston in the master cylinder, the booster's response curve can be tailored to individual requirements: Should the supply pressure fail, a given amount of force at the pedal will result in greater braking pressures than are provided by conventional brake boosters, while the pedal also maintains stable travel resistance in the event of a brake circuit failing. This prevents the brake pedal from losing all feel and traveling right to the floor.

ABS with ASR (Bosch)

See chapter "ASR traction control," p. 556.

ALB (Honda)

The ALB (Anti-lock Brake) for front-wheel-drive passenger cars is based on the plunger priciple. Brake booster and ABS are separate units.

Whe braking without ALB, chamber A is connected to the ALB reservoir via the open outlet valve (see p. 616). The inlet valve blocks the line from the pressure accumulator, so that there is atmospheric pressure in chamber A. When, during braking, pressure is produced in the brake master cylinder, hydraulic fluid flows from chamber D into chamber B: the piston moves to the left and increases the pressure in chamber C.

If braking torque becomes too great and one of the wheels threatens to lock, the outlet valve closes first of all. Consequently, pressure in chamber A rises and prevents a futher movement of the piston to the left. If risk of lock-up remains, the inlet valve opens and allows hydraulic fluid to flow under high pressure from the pressure accumulator into chamber A. This pressure moves the piston to the right, increases the volume of chamber C and thus reduces the wheel-brake cylinder pressure. When there is no futher risk of lock-up, the inlet valve closes and keeps the brake pressure in the wheel-brake cylinder constant. If wheel acceleration increases again, the outlet valve opens: the brake pressure in the wheel-brake cylinder rises again.

The control operation of the ALB is noticeable by brake pedal pulsation.

The Honda ALB is a simplified anti-lock braking system with two control channles. The front wheel with the higher adhesion coefficient determines the joint pressure level at both front-wheel brakes, with the result that, in general, one of the front wheels locks during panic braking. Steerability is thus reduced by half, because the locked-up front wheel is not able to transmit any lateral guiding forces. In addition, the locking of the wheel can lead to heavy tire wear. The rear wheel with the lower adhesion coefficient determines the joint pressure at the rear-wheel brakes.

MK II (Teves)

The hydraulic components – brake booster and ABS – form a compact integrated unit for installation on the firewall. Under normal braking, the booster piston impels brake fluid directly to the rear brakes while pushing the master cylinder piston to the left, supplying brake fluid to the front brakes.

When the ABS is activated, the main valve opens, connecting the booster chamber with the primary side of the master cylinder piston while closing off the connection between the primary side and the reservoir. Brake fluid flows from the booster chamber to the front brakes via the connecting line and seal of the master cylinder piston.

During braking with operational ABS, booster pressure is exerted against the left side of the positioning sleeve, maintaining master cylinder and booster piston in a middle position. This ensures that sufficient piston travel remains available for front-wheel braking in the event of ABS failure.

The supply and discharge valves provide optimal regulation of the pressures in the wheel cylinders during ABS-controlled braking maneuvres, with the brake fluid which is ejected from the wheel cylinder flowing back to the reservoir.

The front brakes are controlled individually. The rear brakes are regulated together, with the wheel with the lower coefficient of traction determining the level of pressure (select low).

MK 4 with ASR (Teves)
This version is used with a conventional vacuum booster to provide "separate ABS". The system can also be extended to include ASR.

When the start of active ABS control makes it necessary to reduce the brake pressure at one of the wheels, the discharge valve is opened while the supply valve remains closed, allowing brake fluid to flow back to the reservoir from the brake. When the supply valve opens to increase the pressure, brake fluid flows from the master cylinder chamber, and the pedal gives way somewhat. The hydraulic unit must supply new energy, as repeated cycles would otherwise cause the pedal to drop too far.

The ABS hydraulic energy-supply unit employs an electrically-driven, dual piston pump which is actuated when the system recognizes incipient wheel lock. The pump extracts brake fluid from the reservoir and pumps it through the supply-valve orifice and to the brake at a suitably increased pressure.

The excess flow quantity from the pump flows into the chambers of the master cylinder, where it presses back the master-cylinder piston and the brake

Schematic diagram of ALB *(Honda)*
1 Wheel brake, 2 Modulator, 3 Chamber A, 4 Chamber B, 5 Chamber C, 6 Inlet valve, 7 Outlet valve, 8 Pressure accumulator, 9 Brake master cylinder, 10 Chamber D, 11 Fluid reservoir, 12 Piston, 13 Pump, 14 ALB reservoir.

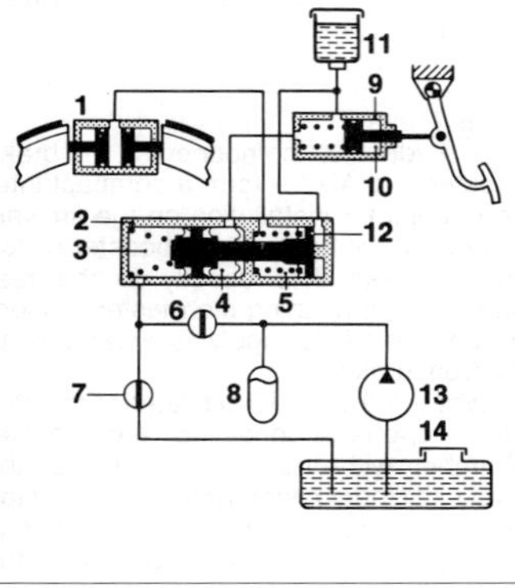

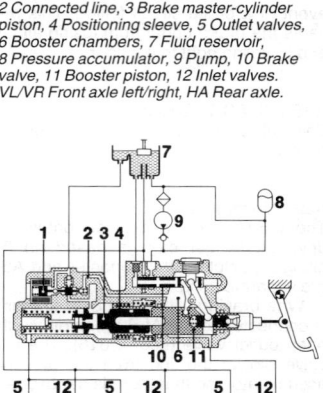

Schematic diagram: ABS MK 2 *(Teves)*
Brakes not actuated. 1 Main valve, 2 Connected line, 3 Brake master-cylinder piston, 4 Positioning sleeve, 5 Outlet valves, 6 Booster chambers, 7 Fluid reservoir, 8 Pressure accumulator, 9 Pump, 10 Brake valve, 11 Booster piston, 12 Inlet valves. VL/VR Front axle left/right, HA Rear axle.

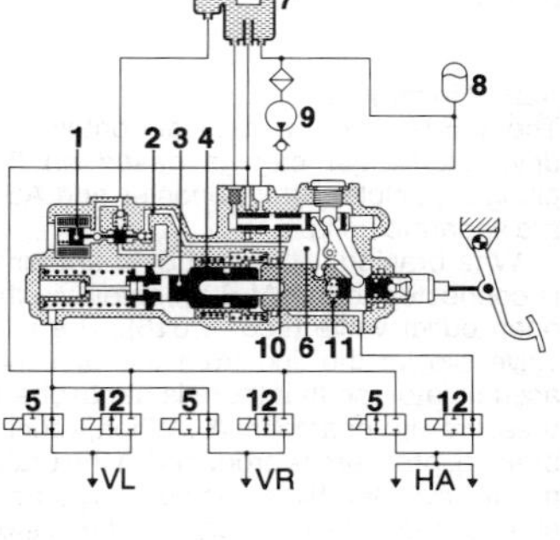

pedal. The position sensor triggers and switches off the pump so as to ensure that the intermittant flow which it produces results in adequate feel and travel at the pedal.

The hydraulics can be expanded for traction control by adding 2 ASR solenoid valves, which serve to isolate the master cylinder from the ASR, and 2 pressure-relief valves, responsible for regulating pressure in the ASR system.

The rotation sensor is a security device for monitoring the operation of the pump motor.

SCS (Lucas Girling)

The SCS (Stop Control System) for front-wheel-drive passenger cars is a purely mechanical antilock system featuring only two control channels. A pair of pressure modulators provides individual control for the front wheels, while a pressure-reduction valve adjusts hydraulic pressure to the diagonally-connected rear wheels. The pressure-reduction valves are designed to prevent the rear wheels from locking in straight-line braking on homogeneous road surfaces at constant adhesion levels (provided that the front brakes do not fade).

The front axle powers a belt-driven shaft. Coupling and ball-ramp guide are adjusted in such a way that shaft and flywheel maintain synchronous rotation under normal braking. Delay at a wheel, indicative of incipient lock, triggers the control cycle. Substantial deceleration at the wheel will cause the speed of the shaft to drop well below that of the flywheel. The flywheel responds by sliding axially along the ball-ramp guide, activating the plunger to trigger a reduction in brake pressure. When shaft and flywheel return to a state of mutually synchronized rotation, the flywheel returns to its original position. The plunger can then allow pressure to be built up once again.

Addonix ABS (Bendix)

Addonix (add on) ABS functions according to a return-flow concept. Energy is provided by an electrically-powered dual

***Schematic diagram: ABS/ASR MK 4** (Teves)*
1 Energy supply, 2 Wheel-speed sensor, 3 Master-cylinder piston, 4 Position sensor, 5 Pressure-relief valve, 6 ASR Solenoid valves, 7 Supply valve, 8 Discharge valve. V Front, H Rear, R Right, L Left.

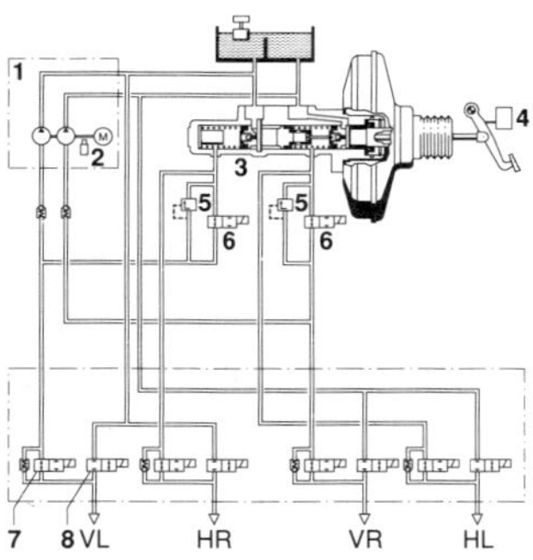

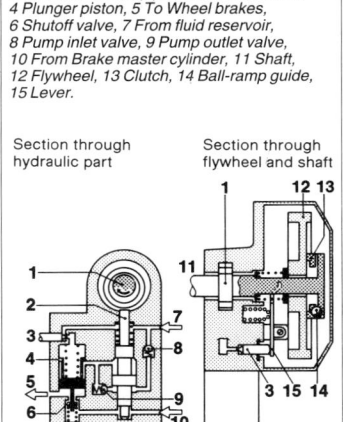

Diagram of SCS pressure modulator unit
(Lucas Girling)
1 Eccentric, 2 Pump piston, 3 Outlet valve, 4 Plunger piston, 5 To Wheel brakes, 6 Shutoff valve, 7 From fluid reservoir, 8 Pump inlet valve, 9 Pump outlet valve, 10 From Brake master cylinder, 11 Shaft, 12 Flywheel, 13 Clutch, 14 Ball-ramp guide, 15 Lever.

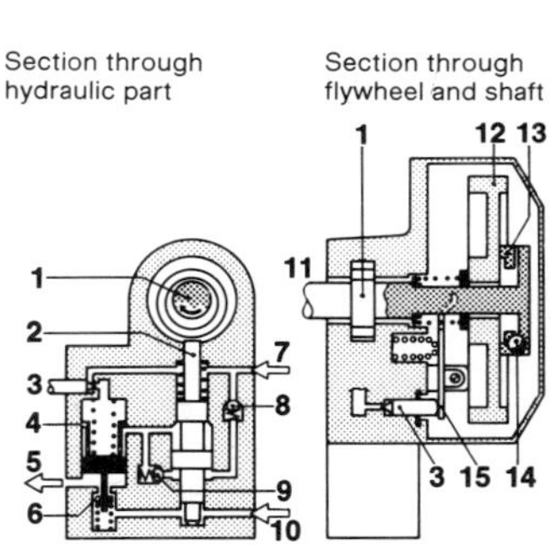

piston pump which responds to pressure reductions by pumping brake fluid from the wheel brakes back to the master cylinder.

The supply valve functions together with the flow restrictor to provide a rapid pressure buildup at the brake under moderate braking (with supply valve closed) and a gradual increase in brake pressure during ABS operation. The discharge valve can bleed off pressure from the brake by allowing brake fluid to flow through the accumulator chamber and to the return-flow pump.

This combination of supply valve, discharge valve and flow-restrictor cannot provide steady-state braking pressures at intermediate levels; brake pressure assumes a sawtooth pattern with alternating buildup and bleed phases.

The reversing valves assume full responsibility for governing the pressure at the rear brakes; the system is unable to vary the pressure-modulation rate on initial braking or for ABS.

ABS components (Bosch)

Wheel-speed sensor
The inductive wheel-speed sensor provides the control unit (ECU) with information on wheel speed.

ECU unit with vehicle-specific LSI circuits
The ECU for a 4-channel system illustrated in the block diagram receives, filters and amplifies the signals from the wheel-speed sensor before employing them to determine brake slip and wheel acceleration at the individual wheels.

Input circuit: The input circuit consists of a low-pass filter and input amplifier; the circuit suppresses interference and amplifies the signals from all rotation-speed sensors (Channels 1 ... 4).

Digital controller: The digital controller consists of two identical, mutually independent digital LSI circuits. These vehicle-specific circuits work in parallel, with each circuit processing the information from

Schematic diagram: Addonix ABS *(Bendix)*
1 Energy supply, 2 Master cylinder, 3 Supply valve, 4 Throttle, 5 Discharge valve, 6 Accumulator, 7 Reversing valve. V Front, H Rear, R Right, L Left.

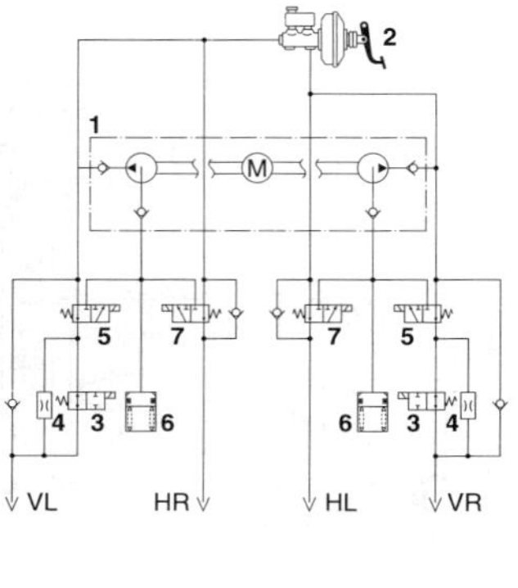

Control unit *(4-channel layout)*
1 Wheel-speed sensors, 2 Battery, 3 Input circuit, 4 Digital controller, 5 LSI circuit 1, 6 LSI circuit 2, 7 Voltage stabilizer/fault memory, 8 Output circuit 1, 9 Output circuit 2, 10 Output stage, 11 Solenoid valves, 12 safety relay, 13 Stabilized battery voltage, 14 Warning lamp.

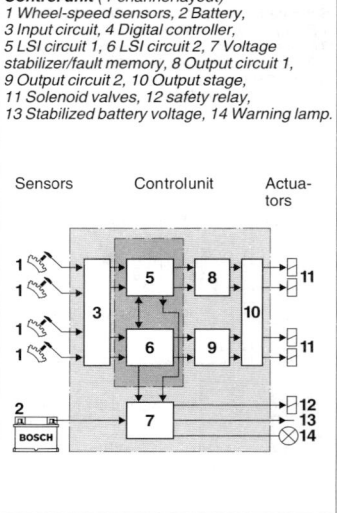

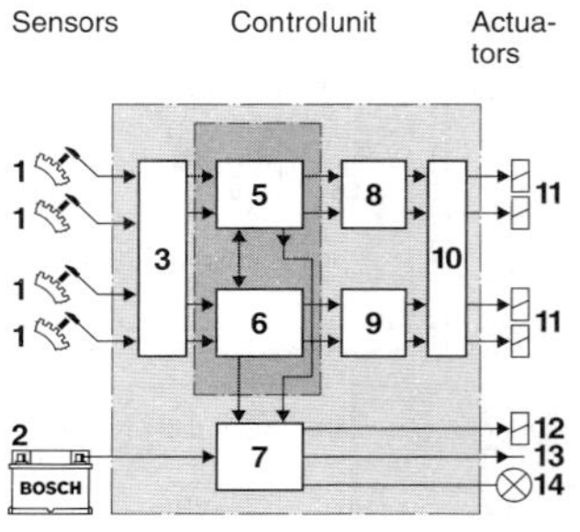

two wheels (Channels 1+2 and 3+4) and carrying out the logical computations. Once processed, the wheel frequency data continues in the circuit to a serial arithmetic-logic unit. This logic unit, in turn, uses the data to calculate the values for "wheel slip" and "circumferential deceleration" or "circumferential acceleration" required for closed-loop control. A self-adapting, complex controller logic converts the control signals into position commands for the solenoid valves. A serial interface, connected to the input stage, arithmetic-logic unit and controller logic via data link, maintains data communications between the two digital LSI circuits.

Yet another function block contains the monitoring circuit for error recognition and analysis. Should the ECU malfunction, a warning lamp informs the vehicle operator that the ABS is no longer operational. However, the braking system retains full normal operating capability when the ABS is deactivated.

Output circuits: Two output circuits function as current regulators for Channels 1 + 2 and 3 + 4 while receiving the position commands employed for solenoid regulation from the LSI circuits.

Output stage: The output stage employs the input from the current regulators in the output circuits in providing the activation current for the solenoid valves.

Voltage stabilizer, fault memory:
This function block stabilizes the supply voltage and monitors it to ensure that it remains within the tolerances required for reliable operation. The block also incorporates undervoltage recognition, which reacts to insufficient on-board voltage by shutting down the unit, as well as relays and the warning-lamp control circuit.

Control unit with microprocessors
In this ECU, the vehicle-specific LSI circuitry is replaced by two microprocessors which assume such duties as signal processing, "running" the controller program and the ABS self-monitoring function. The unit also carries out diagnosis in accordance with ISO standards, making it possible to track down defective ABS components with the aid of either the warning lamp or an "intelligent" tester.

Diagram of hydraulic modulator
D Damper, HZ Mastercylibder, M Electric motor, MV Solenoid valve, P Pump, R Control Channel, RZ Wheel cylinder, S Accumulator.

Three-channel hydraulic modulator

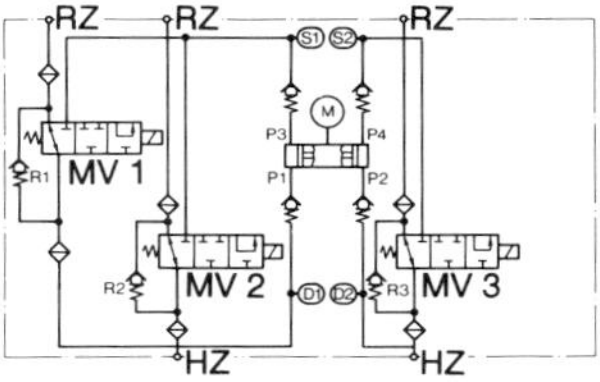

Four-channel hydraulic modulator

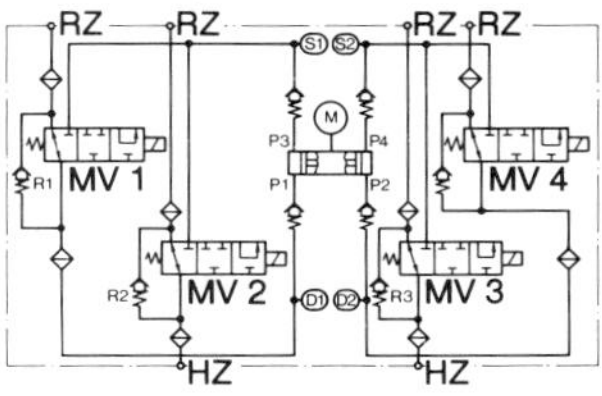

Hydraulic modulator (for ABS 2S)
The hydraulic modulator consists of return pump, solenoid valves, and an accumulator chamber for each brake circuit.

Return pump: The return pump takes the brake fluid emerging from the wheel cylinder and returns it to the master cylinder via the appropriate accumulator.

Accumulators: The accumulators provide temporary storage of brake fluid to dampen the surge which accompanies pressure bleed-off.

3/3 solenoid valves: Each wheel (4-channel unit) or each front wheel and the two rear wheels together (3-channel layout) is equipped with a 3/3 solenoid valve. The valve serves to modulate the pressure in the wheel cylinders during active ABS control.

Braking systems for commercial vehicles above 7.5 t laden weight

System and configuration

Power-braking systems of medium and heavy-duty commercial vehicles mostly operate with:

– Compressed air (normal pressure level) as a medium for energy supply and as a transmission device.

– Pneumatic-hydraulic power transmission in the service-braking system and pneumatic power transmission in the parking-brake system, or

– With pneumatic high pressure level (Figs. B & C, page 622).

Service-braking system for towing (tractor) vehicles

For practical operations, in medium and heavy commercial vehicles, the force exerted by the driver's foot alone is not sufficient to generate adequate braking deceleration. For this reason, compressed-air power-brake systems are principally used; these systems use compressed air as a stored form of energy to control or actuate the service-braking system. Diaphragm or piston actuators create the brake application forces on the wheel brakes. "Air-over-hydraulic" brake systems are becoming less and less common, as the air pressure required to control the wheel brakes must be converted into hydraulic pressure by means of brake servo-unit cylinders, compact brake assemblies or actuating cylinders.

A modern dual-circuit compressed-air brake system with trailer-brake connection, spring-type brake actuator, secondary and parking-brake system consists of the following main components:

– Energy supply,
– Compressed-air reservoir,
– Brake valves,
– Braking-force controller,
– Wheel brakes, and
– Control and air supply for the trailer braking system (diagram D, page 623).

The energy supply comprises a compressor and pressure regulator (operating pressure approx. 8 bar). Where necessary, antifreeze pumps, automatic water drainage, air filters, air driers and intermediate reservoir are added, providing clean and well-drained air.

As there may be a number of air-consuming installations apart from the braking system in the tractor-trailer combinations used in modern-day commercial-vehicle operations, it is advisable to install considerably more powerful compressors than those, for instance, required by EC/ECE brake regulations.

The four-circuit protection valve is located at the interface point between the energy supply and the compressed air reservoir. In the event of a fault, this protection valve ensures the security and continuing supply of the individual brake circuits and of priority secondary consumers.

The service-braking system's control device begins at the brake pedal and ends at the mechanically actuated components of the dual-circuit brake valve.

Sometimes, in commercial vehicles, the limited space available makes it necessary to fit the brake valve on the frame behind the cab instead of in the (tipping) cab itself. The problem of left-hand and right-hand drive trucks with the brake valve in the same position on the frame is solved by means of a dual-circuit hydraulic transmission device for the braking-circuit control. In this process an electrical warning system monitors the level of fluid in the compensating reservoirs of both circuits.

Additional installations in towing vehicles for pulling trailers/semitrailers with compressed-air brake systems (see "Basic components of a braking system") help to supply air to the trailer/semitrailer braking system, and provide a controlling function with regard to the braking effect (trailer control valve, coupling heads etc.).

Braking system for trailers

Towing-vehicle braking systems can be differentiated according to the number of connecting lines leading to the trailer/semitrailer. In other words, into single-line, two-line or multiple-line braking systems. In the case of older-type single-line braking systems (diagram E, page 623), one and the same line is used for filling the energy reservoir as well as for actuating the trailer wheel brakes via a trailer brake valve. The line is pressurized while the vehicle is being driven, and this pressure is released for braking. In the same way, if the trailer is accidentally separated from the towing vehicle, this causes pressure to be released from the control line and automatic braking of the trailer is guaranteed. If leaks occur during prolonged braking on a downgrade, the pressure in the reservoir drops, thus reducing the braking force; in other words, the braking system can become "exhausted". The single-line braking system is no longer allowed in new vehicles, in accordance with EC/ECE guidelines.

In the case of the two-line braking system, which is the standard European design version, one line (supply line) connects the energy reservoirs in the towing vehicle with those in the trailer/semitrailer; and this line is permanently under pressure. The second line (brake line) leads from the trailer control valve in the towing vehicle to the trailer brake valve in the trailer/semitrailer (diagram F, page 623). Braking occurs as a result of pressure increase. Automatic braking when the trailer/semitrailer accidentally comes loose from the towing vehicle is ensured in this system by the supply line. If the supply line comes loose or breaks, air flows out of it and the brake valve in the trailer/semitrailer activates the brakes. With the aid of a dual-circuit trailer control valve and the four-circuit protection valve, it is possible to continue the supply of air to the trailer/semitrailer and to control braking, even if one circuit of the dual-circuit braking system in the towing vehicle fails. The standardized coupling heads for "supply" and "brake" are fitted with an automatic shutoff element, which opens during the coupling process.

In the case of the three-line braking systems which are also used in France and Great Britain, the third line transmits the brake pressure for the secondary braking system in the trailer/semitrailer.

Automatic load-sensitive device for braking-force metering

The automatic device for correcting braking forces as a function of load (ALB) is a vital element of the braking-system transmission device. With the vehicle partially-loaded or empty, braking-force metering valves permit the braking forces to be adjusted to the reduced axle loading (e.g., by sensing of the axle ride clearances) and thus permit a correction of braking-force metering to the vehicle's axles ("kinked load-sensitive braking-force metering"), or they permit a set level of braking (important for vehicles in road train or tractor-trailer operation). There are three kinds of load-sensitive braking-force metering valves.

1. Braking-force limiters

Above a given "switchover point", the braking-force limiter restricts the increase

Load-sensitive braking-force metering device *(diagram A)*

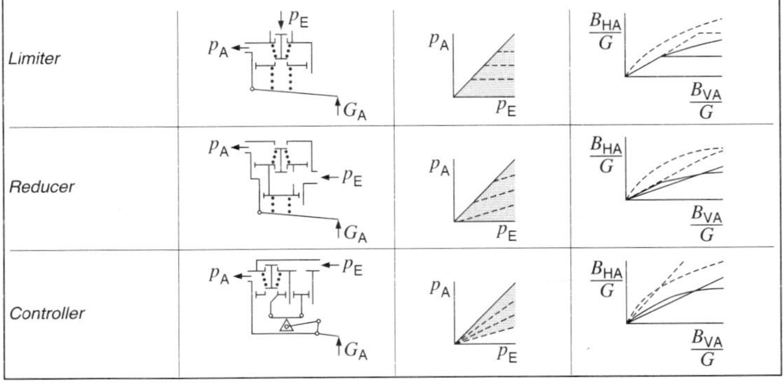

Compressed-air braking systems for trucks

1 Compressor
2 Pressure regulator
3 Antifreeze pump
4 Four-circuit protection valve
5 Air reservoir
6 Coupling head with automatic closing element
7 Water-drain valve
8 Non-return valve
9 Verification valve
10 Parking-brake valve
11 Trailer-control valve
12 Coupling head without closing element
13 Spring-brake actuator
14 Front axle
15 Automatic load-sensitive braking-force metering (ALB)
16 Rear axle
17 Service brake valve
18 Brake cylinder

Dual-circuit two-line power-brake system with pneumatic transmission device *(Fig. B)*

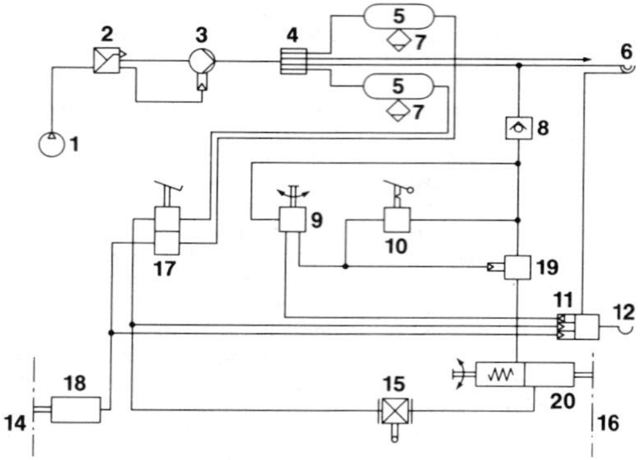

Dual-circuit two-line power-brake system ("Air-over-hydraulic" braking system) with hydraulic transmission device *(Fig. C)*

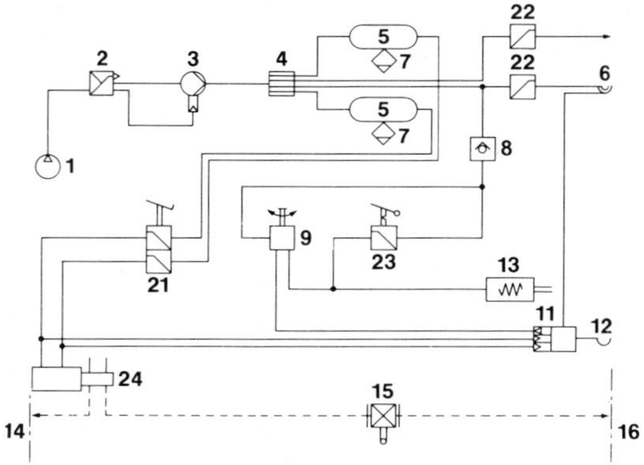

19 Relay valve
20 Combination brake cylinder
21 Service-brake valve with pressure limiting
22 Pressure-limiting valve
23 Parking-brake valve with pressure limiting
24 Actuating cylinder, dual-circuit
25 Double pressure gauge
26 Dual-circuit protection valve
27 Parking-brake mechanism
28 Trailer-brake valve
29 Load/empty valve
30 Secondary consumers (e.g., exhaust brake)

Main components of a modern compressed-air power-brake system *(Fig. D)*
a) Energy supply device, b) Reservoir, c) Brake valves,
d) Trailer control and supply device, e) Braking-force control, f) Wheel brakes.

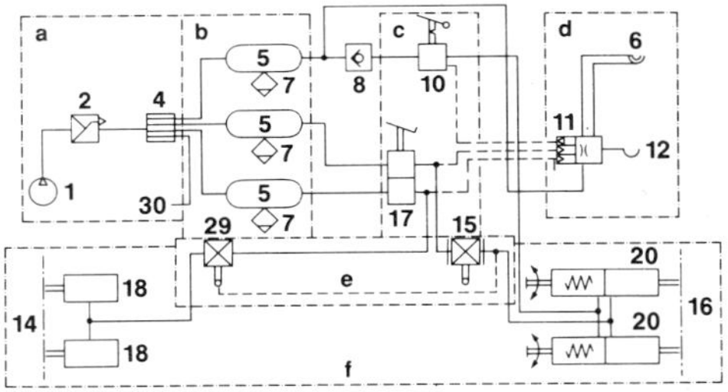

Dual-circuit single-line power-brake system *(Fig. E)*

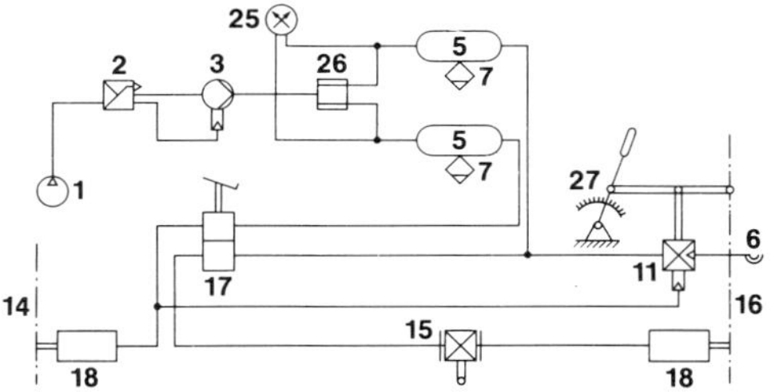

Two-line braking system for trailer/semitrailer *(Fig. F)*

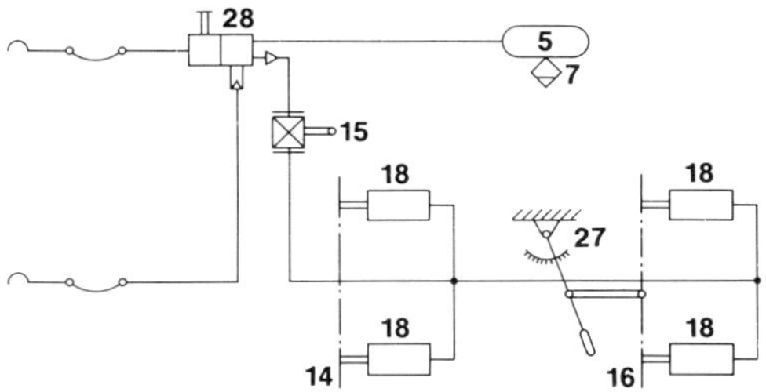

of braking force (e.g., on the rear axle), that is to say there is a "kink" in the braking-force metering characteristic.

2. Braking-force reducers
Even under most unfavorable load conditions, load-sensitive braking-force reducers permit a braking-force metering which approaches the parabola of the dynamic (ideal) braking-force metering characteristic (see "Design of a braking system"). In the area above the switchover point the braking forces on the particular axle are reduced with respect to the original braking-force metering level. Here, the installed braking-force metering is dependent on the transmission ratio and on the switchover pressure (which in turn is dependent on axle load) of the braking-force metering valve.

3. Braking-force controllers
Braking-force controllers, that is to say axle-load-sensitive braking-force reducers with their switchover point at the origin coordinates of the braking-force graph, are elaborate devices which are only used in special cases. They ensure optimum braking-force metering even under unfavorable load conditions.

ALB function diagram for four-wheel vehicles *(Fig. G)*
1 Service-brake valve, 2 From pressure supply, 3 Load/empty valve (VA), 4 ALB valve (HA), 5 From parking brake, 6 Diaphragm actuator (VA), 7 Combination brake cylinder (HA).

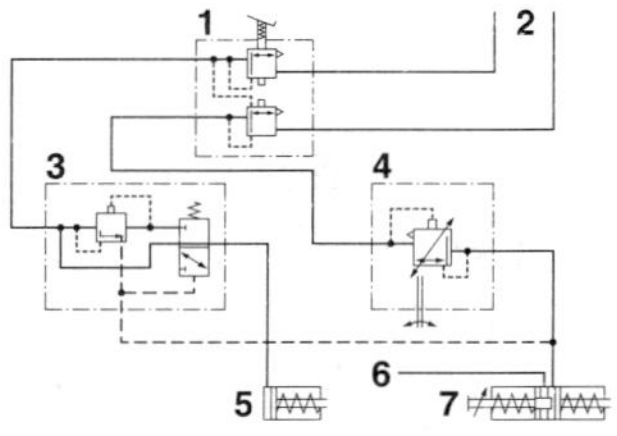

Basic comments on "kinked" braking-force metering
Load-sensitive braking-force metering devices adjust the installed braking-force metering to the dynamic (ideal) metering level and prevent the wheels of a given axle locking prematurely. However, at low adhesion coefficients and low rear-axle load, it is possible for the wheels to lock. This is because the metering device's switchover point can enter the unstable range of braking-force metering if high engine braking torque (retarder braking torque), tolerance fluctuations in the metering device and/or high fluctuations at the wheel brakes occur.

A braking system which works precisely under all braking conditions is only possible if braking-force metering is optimized. Commercial vehicles with extreme differences between empty and fully laden conditions require braking systems with automatically load-sensitive braking-force control (ALB) on the rear axle together with empty/load valves (in order to increase the working range of the ALB, Fig. G, page 624).

Wheel brakes
In future, instead of the currently prevalent drum brakes, disk brakes will be fitted more and more on medium to heavy-duty commercial vehicles (at least on the towing-vehicle's front axles).

The brake factor C^* as an assessment criterion for brake performance, indicates the ratio of braking force to actuating force. This value takes into account the influence of the internal transmission ratio of the brake as well as the friction coefficient, which in turn is mainly dependent on the parameters speed, brake pressure and temperature (Fig. H).

Drum brakes
The actual construction of the drum brake depends upon the requirements imposed by brake-shoe actuation, anchorage, and adjustment.

Simplex drum brakes (Fig. I): These differ in particular according to their type of application (floating, fixed) and type of support or anchorage (rotating shoes, sliding shoes). Wheel brakes with floating-brake application and rotating-shoe support are common. In the case of hydraulic braking-force actuation, for instance, the brakes are applied by means of floating pressure pistons whose travel is not fixed, and which develop actuating forces which are equal in both directions. One of the shoes is the leading shoe and the other the trailing shoe. In the former, the frictional forces between the brake lining and the brake drum support the actuating force, whereas in the latter the frictional forces oppose it.

In the case of the Simplex drum brake, C* is the sum of the values for the individual shoes, and is ≈ 2.0 (referred to a coefficient of friction of $\mu = 0.38$; it appears in the following C^* observations always as the basis value). A disadvantage of this design is the considerable difference in the braking effect between the two brake shoes, and the resulting greatly increased wear on the leading shoe as compared to the trailing shoe. For this reason, the trailing shoe often has a much thinner lining than the leading shoe.

Brake factor C^* as a function of the coefficient of friction and initial road speed *(Fig. H)*
1 Duo-servo drum brake, 2 Duo-duplex drum brake, 3 Simplex drum brake, 4 Disc brake.

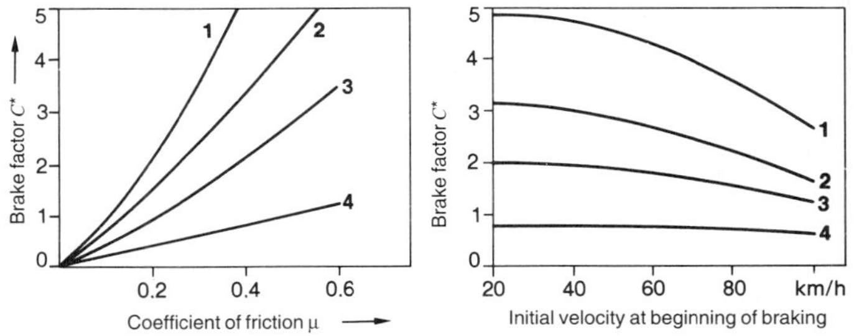

Simplex drum brakes (Fig. I)

Design	Rotating shoe	Wedge	S-cam
Operating principle	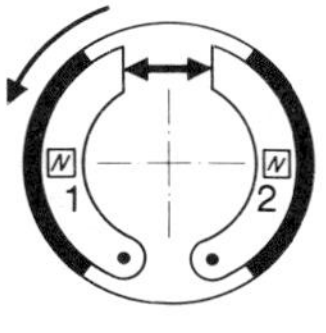	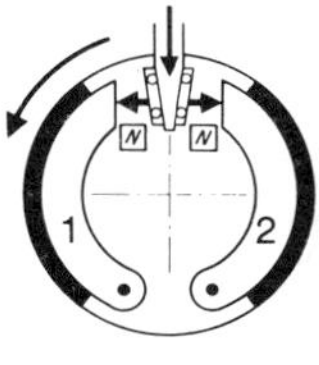	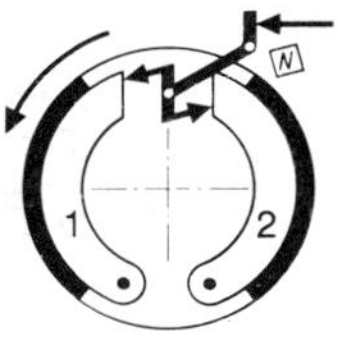
Brake factor	$C^* = C_1 + C_2$		$C^* = 4/(1/C_1 + 1/C_2)$
Brake shoes	1 Leading shoe, 2 Trailing shoe		

The simplex drum brake can also be actuated by means of a wedge unit (with integrated adjusting mechanism). This has become more and more prevalent, particularly in light and medium commercial vehicles with compressed-air braking systems (Figs. I, L, page 627).

The type of wheel brake used most often in heavy-duty commercial vehicles is the pneumatic S-cam simplex drum brake with fixed application (diagram K, page 626). Its advantages are:
- Uniform lining wear on leading and trailing shoes as a result of fixed application,
- Long lining life,
- An application mechanism which is simple, reliable and insensitive to temperature. It comprises diaphragm cylinder, automatic slack adjuster, brake shaft and S-cams,
- Little change in brake factor C^*,
- Simple operation of the parking-brake system via spring-brake actuators,
- Precise adjustment by means of automatic slack adjusters.

Its disadvantages are:
- High internal forces and thus relatively heavy brake construction, as unequal cam forces occur and lead to high free bearing forces,
- Relatively low brake factor C^*, which means considerable application work when braking,
- Due to the roughly equal application travel of leading and trailing shoes, compared to individual shoes, the application forces behave in the opposite manner.
- For the same coefficient of friction, the brake factor C^* is somewhat lower than that of simplex brakes with hydraulic or pneumatic application.

Simplex drum brake with S-cam *(Fig. K)*
1 Diaphragm actuator, 2 S-cam, 3 Brake shoes, 4 Return spring, 5 Brake drum.

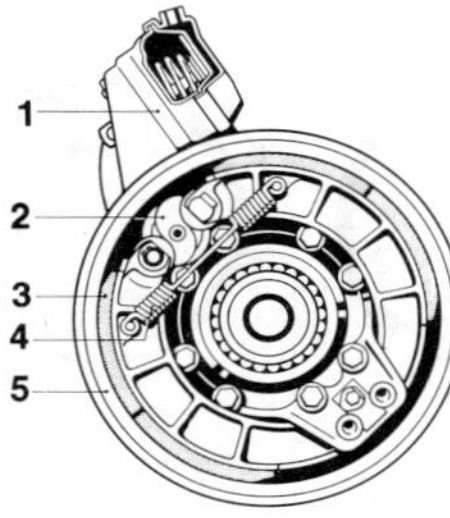

Duo-duplex drum brakes: The Duo-duplex brake with two leading shoes (for instance with wedge-unit control) (Fig. L, page 627) is rarely used nowadays.

This brake features floating application and the resulting sliding shoe anchorage. An advantage of the brake type is the practically equal brake-lining wear on both shoes and the significantly higher internal transmission ratio in comparison to simplex drum brakes. With two leading shoes, brake factors of $C^* \approx 3.0$ are achieved, although these figures cannot be held constant throughout a long period of braking due to this type of brake's susceptibility to fading.

Duo-servo drum brakes: In the past, these were widely used in light commercial vehicles (particularly on the rear axle). This brake's primary characteristic is the fact that both when driving forwards and when reversing, the support force of the primary shoe is used as the actuation force for the secondary shoe. The brake factor is $C^* \approx 5.0$.

The popularity of the duo-servo brake lies in the fact that the high brake factors achieved permit even relatively heavy vans and light-duty trucks up to a weight of approx. 7.5 t to be equipped with vacuum-assisted braking systems. At the same time, the manually operated parking brake incorporated in such systems generates a braking torque of considerable magnitude. However, under conditions of high thermal stress, significant brake-factor fluctuations occur. This fact limits the range of application of this type of brake and necessitates a braking-force metering system which is precisely adapted to the vehicle in question. In future wheel-braking systems, duo-servo drum brakes will for the most part no longer be used for the service-braking system.

Disc brakes

Apart from their use in express coaches, disc brakes are currently primarily fitted to the front axles of medium and heavy commercial vehicles.

The advantages of disc brakes in comparison to drum brakes are:

– Brakes can be applied with far more sensitivity,
– Equal wear of the inboard and outboard brake pads if the appropriate degree of heat dissipation is provided,
– Less tendency to brake noise,
– Relatively constant brake factor with less susceptibility to fading.

The disadvantages of disc brakes are:

– Shorter brake-lining life,
– Usually higher acquisition and operating costs (in comparison to drum brakes).

The high degree of adaptive braking required at high highway speeds is handled better by disc brakes. The brake discs are less susceptible to cracking than the drums of the drum brakes, apart from which disc brakes are less subject to fading. The brake factor of the disc brake is $C^* \approx 0.76$, referred to the basis value of $\mu = 0.38$.

Floating-caliper disc brakes are increasingly replacing the fixed-caliper brakes used in the past. This development is the result of efforts to design lighter and cheaper brake assemblies which are more temperature-resistant. The caliper itself is not subject to braking torque, and this fact promotes the sensitivity of application and the braking-effect consistency.

Automatic adjustment of wheel brakes

Brake-lining wear increases the clearance between brake lining and brake drum, and thus increases the braking distance. If the clearance is not adjusted correctly, in extreme cases the piston stroke in the brake cylinder may increase to such an extent that there is no braking effect. Automatic adjustment to the correct clearance is effected when the wheel brake is released. When the vehicle is braked, the piston stroke in the brake cylinder necessary to bridge the total clearance can be divided into three sections:

– Pre-set constructive clearance between brake lining and brake drum/disc,
– Clearance resulting from lining wear,
– Clearance dependent on the elasticity of the brake drum/disc and of the brake linings, as well as on the transmission of force between brake cylinder and wheel brake ("elasticity clearance").

A slack adjuster automatically ensures the correct adjustment (Fig. M, page 628).

Duo-drum brakes and disc brake (Fig. L)

Design	**Duo-Duplex** Wedge	**Duo-Servo** Positive-action adjustment	**Disc brake**
Operating principle	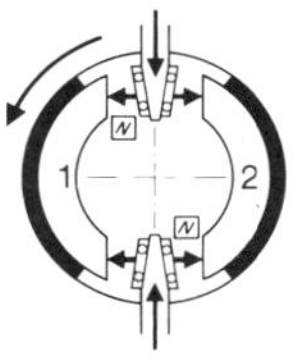	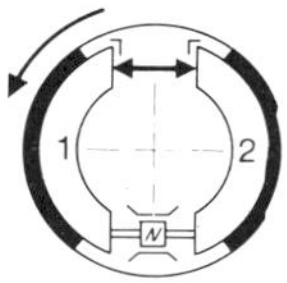	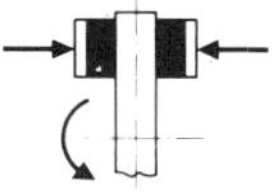
Brake factor	$C^* = C_1 + C_2$	$C^* = C_1 + C_2\,(k_1 + k_2 \cdot C_1)$	$C^* = 2 \cdot \mu$
Brake shoes	1 Leading shoe, 2 Trailing shoe		–

Parking-brake system

The braking systems with spring-type brake actuators which are usual in commercial vehicles above 7.5 t are a convenient form of parking-brake and service-braking system. In these, in a purely compressed-air braking system, spring-type brake cylinders from the parking-brake system and diaphragm brake cylinders from the service-braking system are combined.

In the disengage position the four-circuit protection valve and the handbrake valve connect the reservoirs of the service-braking system with the spring compression chamber, and maintain the spring under tension. In vehicles with a connection for the trailer/semitrailer braking system a buffer reservoir is also located in this line. When the handbrake valve is actuated, the pressure in the compression chamber is reduced. Consequently partial braking occurs at first and, with the handbrake valve still actuated, a pressure reduction down to the "surrounding conditions" takes place, and thus full braking of the spring-brake actuator (secondary braking), occurs. Further actuation defines a "Parking setting". With the aid of a further lever setting, in tractor-trailer vehicles only the powered towing vehicle is braked, and not the entire tractor-trailer rig. As well as this test setting for mechanical parking-brake effects when a trailer is being towed, EC/ECE legislation for instance stipulates a safeguard emergency-air supply, as well as a nine-fold actuation and release using the energy reserve, a warning device indicating that the spring-brake is beginning to function, and an auxiliary release device.

Retarder braking systems (additional retarding braking systems)

The wheel brakes used in passenger cars and commercial vehicles are not designed for continued retarding operation. In a prolonged period of braking (e.g., when driving downhill) the brakes can be thermally over-stressed, causing the braking effect to be reduced ("fading"). In extreme cases (particularly if the service-braking system has been badly maintained) this may even lead to complete braking-system failure. Therefore, in order to deal with the excessive thermal stresses which result from continuous braking during downhill operation, particularly vehicles with a high laden weight are frequently fitted with a wear-free supplementary retarding braking system in addition to their normal wheel brakes. This system is independent of the wheel brakes, and is also used for braking the vehicle so as to comply with speed limits. This

Brake clearances *(Fig. M).*
a Due to elasticity, b Due to wear, c Constructive. 1 Brake shoe, 2 Diaphragm cylinder, 3 Automatic slack adjuster.

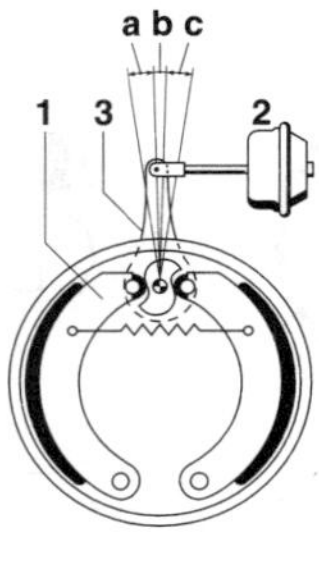

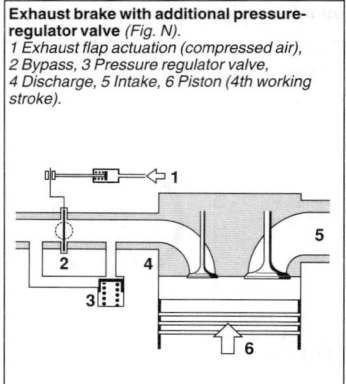

Exhaust brake with additional pressure-regulator valve *(Fig. N).*
1 Exhaust flap actuation (compressed air), 2 Bypass, 3 Pressure regulator valve, 4 Discharge, 5 Intake, 6 Piston (4th working stroke).

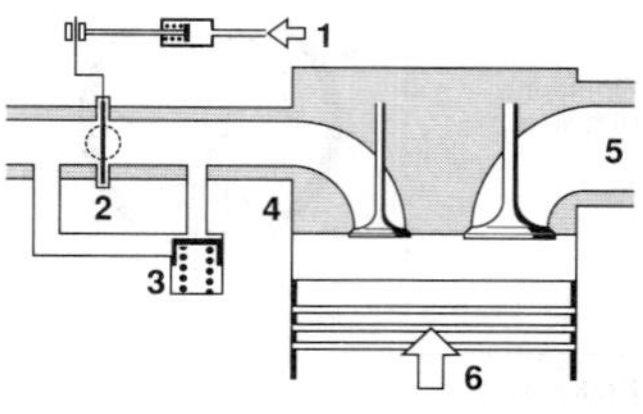

reduces brake wear as well as increasing braking comfort for the driver. In commercial vehicles two basic types of additional retarding braking system are used:

1. Exhaust (engine) braking system
The exhaust braking power is comprised of the drag power together with the braking power (effected by the throttling of exhaust gas flow in the exhaust stroke). The maximum drag power of standard engines is 5 ... 7 kW/l depending upon engine swept volume. In contrast, standard engines with conventional exhaust brakes ("exhaust-flap brakes") achieve braking powers of 14 ... 20 kW/l. A further increase in exhaust braking power is only possible by means of additional design modification. Decompression exhaust brakes (e.g., "C-brake", "Jake brake", "Dynatard" or "Powertard") as well as the constant-throttle exhaust brake can significantly improve braking power (Fig. R, page 630).

Exhaust brake with exhaust flap: The exhaust-flap brake is still the most common system in use today. In this system the driver is able to close a butterfly valve in the exhaust tract by means of compressed air (relatively little constructional outlay is involved). As a result, a counterpressure is generated in the exhaust-gas system which must be overcome by each piston during its exhaust stroke (Fig. N).

Through the use of a pressure-regulator valve in the bypass, in conjunction with an exhaust flap, the braking power can be increased in the engine's lower and medium speed ranges. At higher revs, the pressure-regulator valve prevents pressure increases beyond the limits which could lead to valve or valve-gear damage.

Exhaust brake with constant throttle: The conventional exhaust brake with exhaust flap utilises only the energy available in the engine's gas-exchange process, i.e. during the 4th (exhaust) and 1st (intake) working strokes. Specific decompression during the 2nd and 3rd working strokes releases part of the compression energy. The pressure-volume diagrams below show the pressure curves in a cylinder for the "exhaust flap" and "constant throttle" exhaust braking systems as well as for the combination of both systems (Fig. O). The braking power when using the constant throttle system, as opposed to the flap system, is obtained principally in the engine's high-pressure cycle.

The installation of a small restriction valve in the bypass to the exhaust valve

Operating principle of exhaust-braking systems in pressure-volume p-v diagram form (n_m = 1700 min^{-1}) *(Fig. O)*
a) Exhaust-brake flap closed, b) Constant throttle actuated, c) Exhaust-brake flap closed and constant throttle actuated.

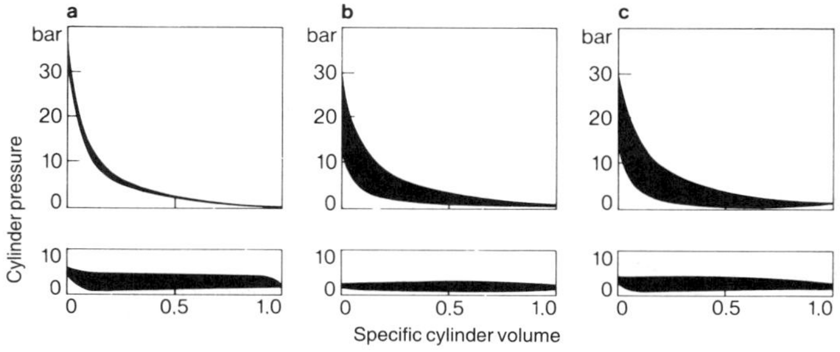

permits an increase in braking power. This valve is actuated by compressed air, in the same way as in the servo cylinder of the exhaust-brake flap. During exhaust-brake operation the valve can be continually opened, thus providing a constant throttle cross-section (Fig. P below).

2. Retarders

Retarders are increasingly being used as wear-free additional retarding braking systems in trucks and buses. In this way the demands of legislation are met, the active safety of the vehicles is increased due to the reduction of the stress placed on the service-braking system, and the economy of the vehicles is increased as a result of higher average speeds and the reduction of brake-lining wear.

Retarders can be fitted between the engine and the transmission (primary retarders) or between the transmission and the driven axle(s) (secondary retarders). The disadvantage of primary retarders lies in the unavoidable interruption of power transmission, and thus braking effect, which occurs during gear changing with manual transmissions. Primary retarders can be employed in conjunction with power-shift transmissions. However, the performance differences between primary and secondary retarders underline the need for ongoing development in the future (Fig. S, page 631).

Currently, two basic design concepts represent the latest technology:

Exhaust brake with exhaust flap and constant throttle *(Mercedes-Benz) (Fig. P)*
1 Compressed air, 2 Exhaust flap, 3 Exhaust, 4 Constant throttle, 5 Intake, 6 Piston (2nd working stroke).

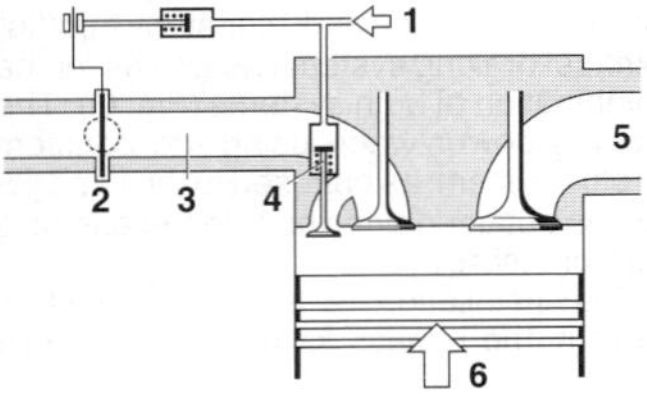

Braking-power curves *(V8 engine) (Fig. R)*
1 Exhaust flap and constant throttle, 2 Constant throttle, 3 Exhaust flap

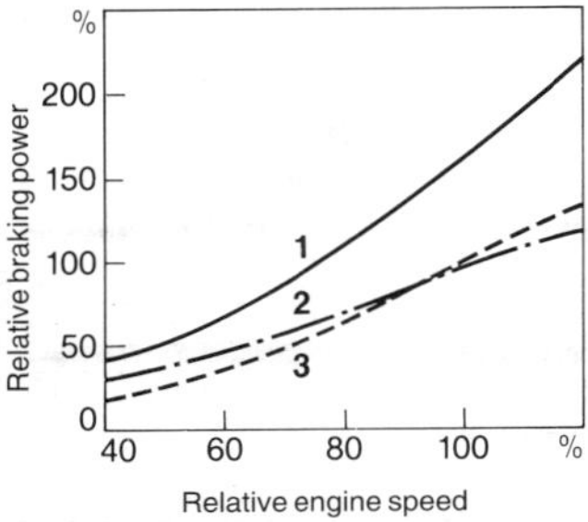

Hydrodynamic retarders: This retarder works in the same way as the Foettinger clutch (Fig. T, page 631). The rotor converts the mechanical energy supplied by the drive shaft into kinetic energy of a fluid. This kinetic energy is in turn converted into heat at the stator, which means that the fluid used must be cooled.

A hand lever or the brake pedal (in the case of an integrated retarder) transmits the driver's braking-power requirements. In conjunction with an electronic control circuitry, a defined control air pressure is set. This control air pressure then forces a quantity of oil, by means of a corresponding quantity of air, into the retarder's working area between rotor and stator. The flow energy absorbed by the oil as a result of the vehicle speed and the associated rotor motion is braked by the stator's fixed blades. This in turn effects braking of the rotor and thus of the entire vehicle. Characteristics are:

- Adequate cooling-circuit dimensioning is necessary in order to dissipate to the engine cooling circuit the heat generated by braking. An oil/water heat exchanger is used,
- Relatively complex design,
- Low weight of the hydrodynamic retarder which is integrated directly into the transmission,
- High specific braking powers,

– Very sensitive control of applied braking torque
– Fan losses occurring when the retarder is not running must also be taken into consideration in retarder design.

In the hydrodynamic secondary retarder, an almost constant braking torque is available over a broad propshaft-speed range (Fig. U below). Below approx. 1000 min^{-1} the braking torque drops steeply. As a result of this characteristic, conventionally designed hydrodynamic retarders are particularly suited to high-speed transport vehicles (overland transport).

Modern retarder designs rectify the unfavorable braking torque characteristic of the secondary retarder design described above by providing high braking torques even at still low propshaft speeds. A spur-

Braking torques of hydrodynamic retarders
1 Secondary retarder, 2 Cooling power limit, 3 Primary retarder. (Fig. S)

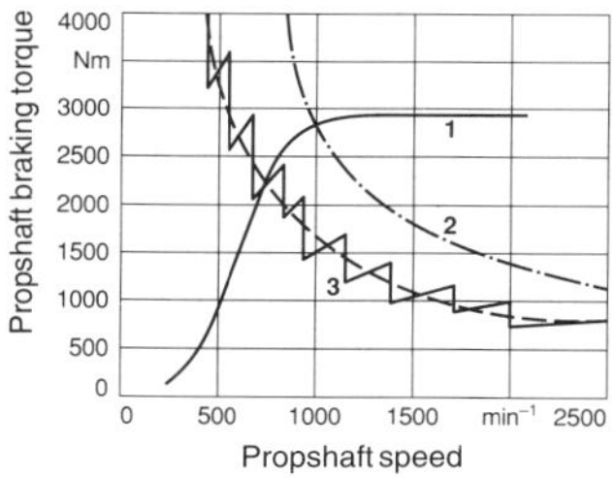

Hydrodynamic retarder performance characteristics *(Fig. U)*
1 Boost retarder, 2 Conventional retarder, max./min. braking torque, 3 Cooling power limit at continuous load (300 kW).

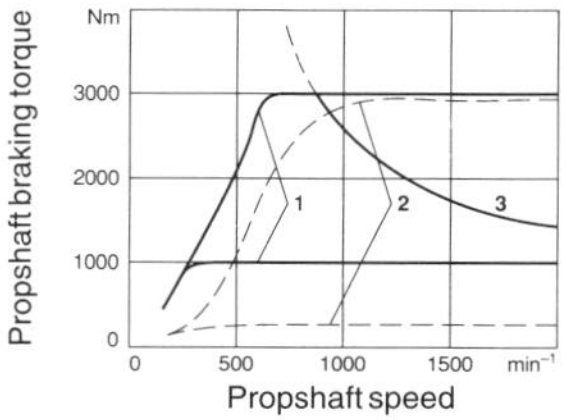

Hydrodynamic retarder *(Fig. T)*
1 Braking stator, 2 Drive shaft, 3 Mounting flange, 4 Braking rotor, 5 Heat exchanger (oil/water).

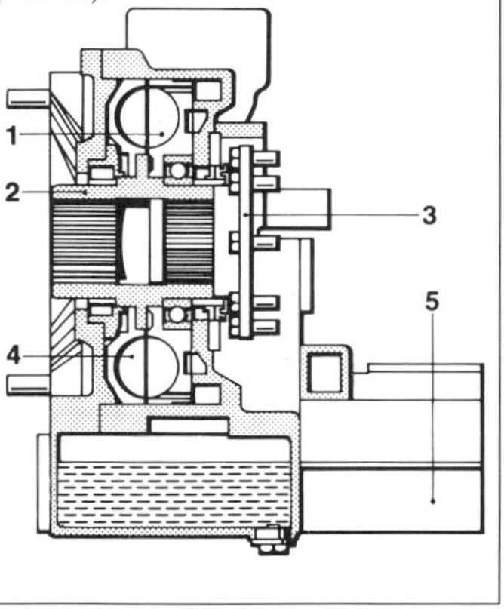

Electrodynamic retarder *(Fig. V)*
1 Rotor on transmission side, 2 Rotor on rear axle-side, 3 Stator with coils, 4 Star-shaped bracket, 5 Transmission cover, 6 Intermediate flange, 7 Transmission output shaft, 8 Air gap, 9 Shim rings (air-gap setting).

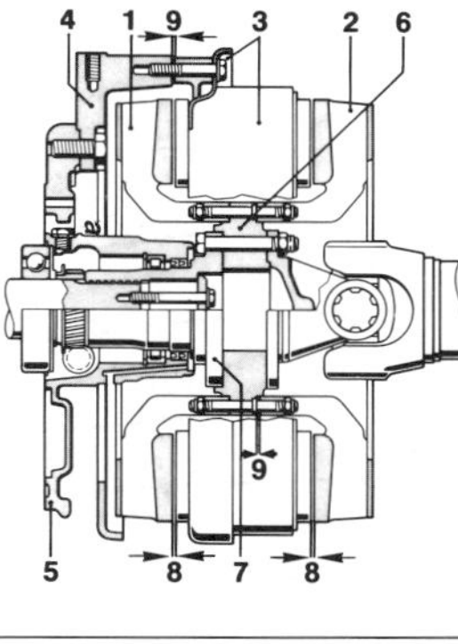

gear stage with a transmission ratio of approx. 1 : 2 drives such "boost retarders", which are fitted to the side of the transmission.

A microprocessor control ensures acceptable braking-torque levels even in the propshaft lower speed range via a proportional valve.

Hydrodynamic retarders can only be used as additional retarding braking systems in certain situations for limited periods. The maximum cooling power of modern diesel engines is approx. 300 kW. Thus, as a result of the coupling of the engine and retarder cooling circuits, there exists a risk for both engine and retarder if additional safety measures are not undertaken. For this reason, thermo switches are used to restrict the retarder's braking power so that thermal equilibrium is ensured.

Electrodynamic retarders: Currently common electrodynamic retarders have a mounting in the form of a stator, on which field coils are mounted (Fig. V, page 631). The rotors mounted on both sides of the drive shaft are ribbed for better heat dissipation. In order to brake the vehicle, voltage is applied to the field coils (from the battery or alternator) which thus generate a magnetic field which induces eddy currents in the rotors as they pass through the field. This generates a braking-torque level which is dependent on the stator excitation and on the air gap between rotor and stator.

Characteristics:

- Dissipation to the atmosphere of the heat produced,
- Relatively simple design,
- Relatively heavy construction,
- Uninterrupted continuous operation only with sufficient current supply,
- Heating of the retarder leads to a reduction in braking torque,
- High braking powers even at low vehicle speeds,
- Braking power influenced by rotor blading, air-flow conditions around the eddy-current brake, and by ambient temperature.

In contrast to the conventional hydrodynamic secondary retarders, electrodynamic retarders provide relatively high braking torques at low drive-shaft speeds (Fig. W, page 632).

The significant reduction in braking torques of the electrodynamic retarder as the rotor temperature increases result from the thermal safeguard (Fig. Z, page 632). Vehicle deceleration is reduced as thermal stress on the electrodynamic retarder increases.

In order to prevent temperature-related destruction of the retarder when the vehicle is braking, a bimetal switch restricts the current supply to half of the eight coils when the stator temperature reaches approx. 250 °C (Fig. Z,page 632).

Braking-torque characteristic of an electrodynamic retarder *(Fig. W)*

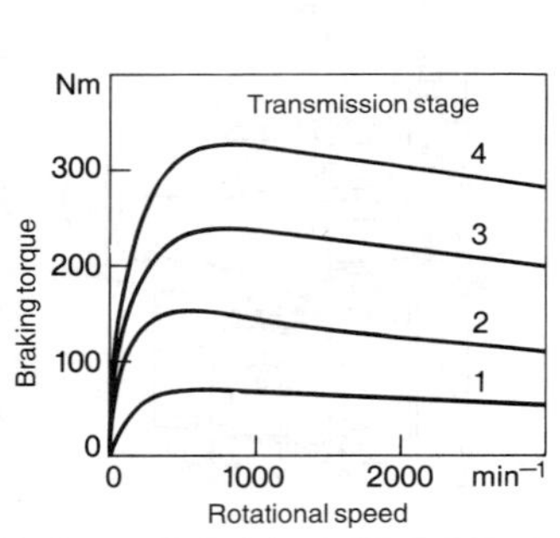

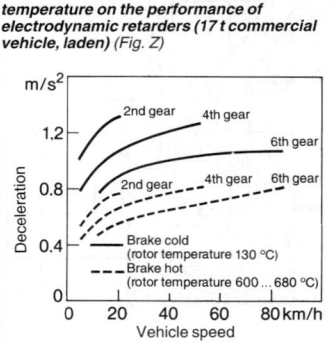

Influence of transmission ratio and rotor temperature on the performance of electrodynamic retarders (17 t commercial vehicle, laden) *(Fig. Z)*

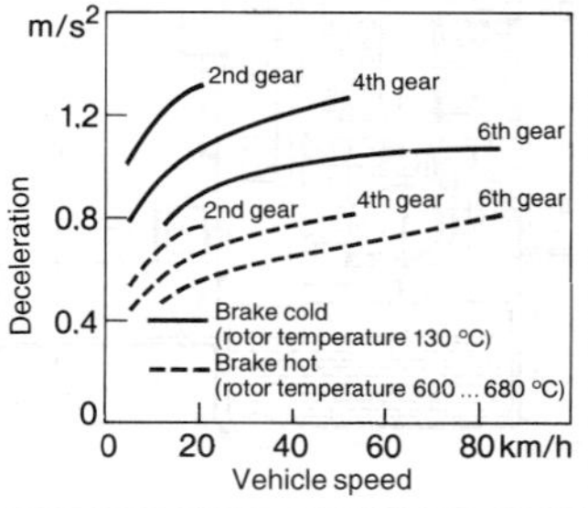

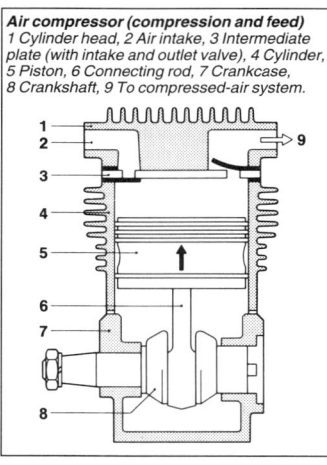

Air compressor (compression and feed)
1 Cylinder head, 2 Air intake, 3 Intermediate plate (with intake and outlet valve), 4 Cylinder, 5 Piston, 6 Connecting rod, 7 Crankcase, 8 Crankshaft, 9 To compressed-air system.

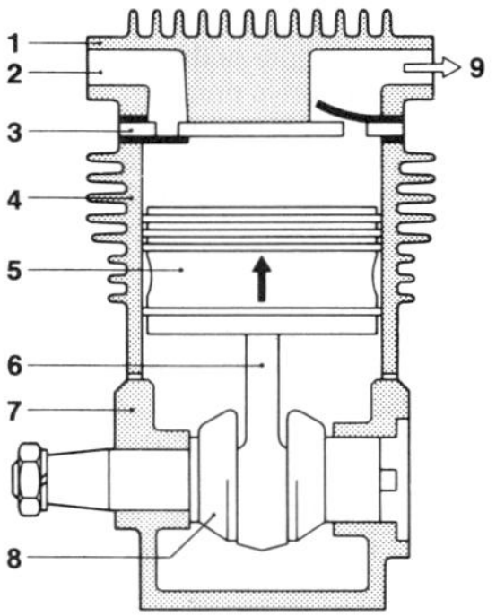

Pressure regulator
1 From air compressor, 2 To air reservoirs, 3 Blow-off.

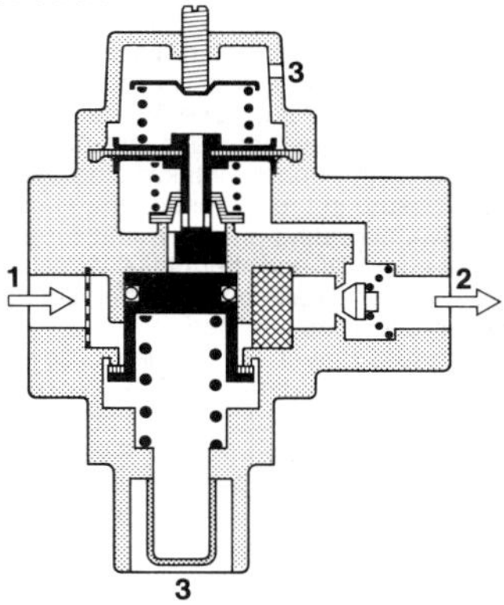

Components for compressed-air brakes

Energy supplying device
The energy supplying device comprises the following:
- Energy source
- Pressure regulator
- Air conditioning.

Energy source: The energy source is a continuously running air compressor which is driven by the engine via V-belts or toothed gears. It consists of:
– Crankcase with crankshaft (driver for power-steering pump at the free end of the shaft), bearing assembly and connections for circulating engine lubrication;
– Cylinder with piston and connecting rod;
– Intermediate plate with intake and outlet valves;
– Cylinder cover with suction and pressure connections for air and, if appropriate, the fittings required for liquid-cooled versions.

The air compressor is usually mounted on the vehicle engine by means of base or flange attachment. In some cases, it is already integrated into the crankshaft housing.

During its downward stroke, the piston draws in air in a downward direction after the intake valve has automatically opened as a result of the vacuum. The intake valve closes at the beginning of the return movement of the piston. The air is now compressed and, after reaching a set pressure, it is conveyed via the outlet valve, which also opens automatically, into the downstream compressed-air system.

In terms of delivery rate, the aim is a volumetric efficiency of 70% and in terms of oil consumption a maximum of 0.5 g/h is desirable.

Pressure regulation: The pressure regulator ensures that the desired pressure level is maintained. Two principal types of regulation are used:
1. Regulation in which the pressure regulator has no influence on the energy source (in compressors with maximum speeds > 2500 min^{-1}).

The pressure regulator (see Fig. above) switches off when the desired maximum operating pressure is reached, and returns the air supplied by the compressor to atmosphere during the subsequent no-load period. If the pressure in the air reservoirs reaches the lower operating-pressure limit the pressure regulator switches on again and supplies the air delivered by the compressor to the air reservoirs.

2. Regulation in which the pressure influences the energy source (in compressors with maximum speeds < 2500 min^{-1}).

When the desired maximum operating pressure is reached, the regulator applies pressure to a plunger in the compressor and opens its intake valve. Without being supplied to the air reservoirs, the intake air is expelled through the intake fitting. When the pressure in the air reservoirs reaches the lower operating-pressure limit, the regulator switches and the intake valve can again automatically open and close, and the air reservoirs are filled.

Pressure level: In today's towing vehicles, values between 7 and 10 bar (low pressure) and between 14 and 20 bar (high pressure) are used. In the two-line braking system, the pressure in the lines connecting towing vehicle and trailer is between 6 and 8 bar.

Compressed-air conditioning: The air must be conditioned in order to ensure proper operation of the downstream braking-system components. Impurities in the air can cause leaks in the control valves, and water in the compressed air leads to corrosion or icing-up during frost. Air cleaners, antifreeze pumps, water-drain valves and air driers are used to combat these problems.

Control device

Normally, the control device comprises the brake pedal and all devices up to the point where influence is exerted on the control equipment.

Transmission device

The transmission device comprises the following:

- Circuit isolation (e.g., multiple-circuit protection valve
- Energy storage (e.g., air reservoirs)
- Control equipment (e.g., brake valves
- Load-sensitive braking-force metering (e.g., automatic load-sensitive braking-force control)
- Brake cylinders or servo cylinders

These components work together as shown in the block diagram on the right of a power-braking system with dual-circuit service-braking system (see also the braking-system diagram on p. 622)

Functions and design of components:

Circuit isolation

Separation of the circuits with respect to one another in the event of damage in one circuit, as well as preservation of the operational integrity of the intact circuits.

Circuit isolation is primarily achieved by a combination of overflow valves grouped together as a unit; the operation of these valves is ensured at both low and high delivery rates.

Energy storage

Provision of the required volume of energy for all circuits in the braking system, including provision of energy in the event of failure of the energy source.

Commercially available welded sheet-steel air reservoirs are used for this purpose; these have corresponding safety allowances for excess pressure and rust.

Control equipment

This equipment is used to provide the desired degree of pressure metering in the corresponding part of the system.

Mechanically, hydraulically or pneumatically actuated or controlled reaction

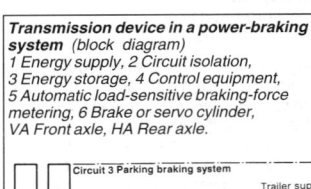

Transmission device in a power-braking system *(block diagram)*
1 Energy supply, 2 Circuit isolation, 3 Energy storage, 4 Control equipment, 5 Automatic load-sensitive braking-force metering, 6 Brake or servo cylinder, VA Front axle, HA Rear axle.

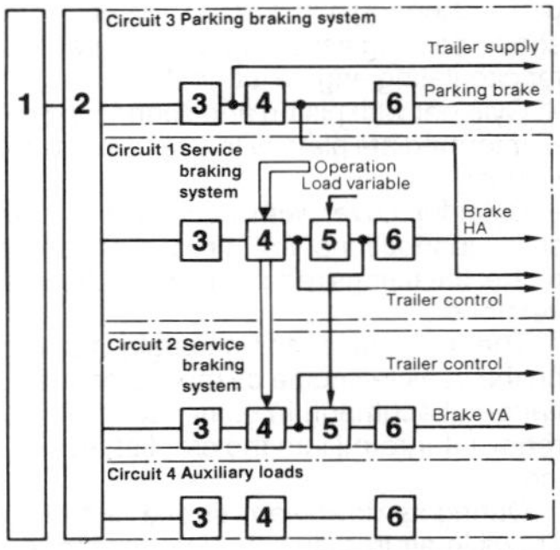

valves are used to control the pressure at the output of each valve as a function of the input variable. Due to the wide range of applications, a correspondingly large number of different components are in use. Dual-circuit control valves are also required for dual-circuit service-braking systems. Proper braking-system operation requires good control behavior, good pressure-metering capability, fast reaction times and low braking-system hysteresis.

Automatic load-sensitive braking force metering (ALB)
Automatic pressure control as a function of vehicle load.

Load is often determined by spring compression (in the case of steel suspension springs) and bellows pressure (in the case of pneumatic suspension). A control valve with a variable reaction-surface area reduces the output pressure in the valve in relation to the input pressure as a function of spring compression or bellows pressure.

Brake cylinders or servo cylinders
Used to convert the applied system pressure into braking force.

Single-box air drier
1 Dessicant box, 2 From pressure regulator, 3 From air compressor, 4 Heating element, 5 Bleeder valve, 6 Exhaust, 7 To regeneration-air reservoir, 8 To supply-air reservoir.

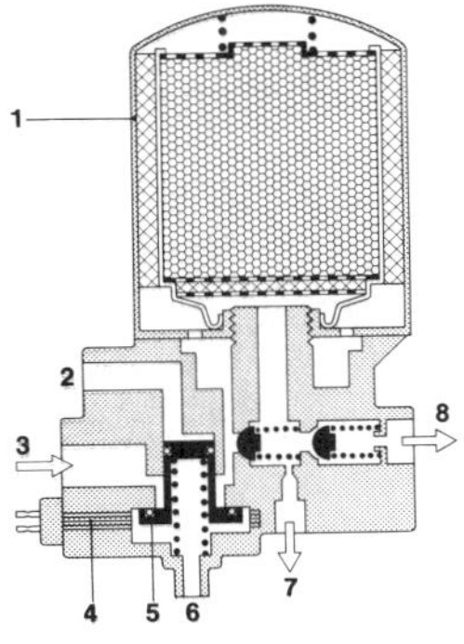

Both plunger- and diaphragm-type cylinders are used. Diaphragm-type cylinders are primarily used for the service-braking system, while spring-brake actuators are used for the parking system. In the case of axles which are acted upon by both the service-braking system and the parking-brake system, use is made – in braking systems with hydraulic force transmission – of combined single-chamber spring-brake actuators (so-called combination cylinders).

Single-box air drier
Basically, an air drier consists of a dessicant box and a housing, in which, as well as the air duct, a bleeder valve and a connection to the regeneration air reservoir with integral regenerating throttle are located.

When the bleeder valve is closed, the compressed air supplied from the air compressor flows through the dessicant box and from there to the supply-air reservoirs. At the same time a regeneration-air reservoir with a volume of approx. 4 ... 6 liters is filled with dry compressed air. When flowing through the dessicant box, water is removed from the moist compressed air by means of condensation and adsorption.

The granulate in the dessicant box has a limited water absorption capacity and must therefore be regenerated at regular intervals. In the reverse regeneration process, dry compressed air from the regeneration air reservoir is reduced to atmospheric pressure via the regenerating throttle, flows back through the moist granulate, drawing off the moisture from it, and flows as moist air via the opened bleeder valve into the atmosphere. In air driers with integrated pressure regulator the control element is installed at connection 4 of the air-drier valve housing.

Wheel brakes (see p. 624)

Service-brake valve
Two tandem-arranged control valves are actuated by a common device (brake pedal with transmission). The synchronized opening of both circuits is ensured by identical spring and valve sealing forces as well as by the mechanical overcoming of the opening forces in both con-

trol valves. In the braking position, the rocking piston between the control circuits is subjected on its two sides to the currently applied braking pressure and thus guarantees that the circuits are synchronized. The preloaded travel spring provides small response travels of the service-brake valve. The interaction of the force of the reaction piston with the travel spring enables the system to execute the necessary control travels independently. Dual-circuit sealing of the rocking piston ensures the required safety.

Parking-brake valve

Today's compact design of the parking-brake valve is a direct result of the lack of installation space at the instrument panel (where is used to be fitted). The parking-brake valve always actuates the brake cylinders via relay valves.

A rotary hand lever (actuating lever) adjusts an internal valve seat by means of an eccentric and a linking strap. In doing so, it controls a double-seat valve in which compressed air from above and the force of compression springs from below act on a valve piston.

In the brake position the actuating lever latches into position automatically, and the space above the valve piston is purged of air. As many intermediate settings between the drive and brake settings as desired are possible.

If the actuating lever is moved beyond the brake position, the auxiliary (test) valve is actuated and compressed air flows from the supply-air reservoir into the connecting line to the trailer-control valve. This leads to the towing-vehicle braking effect being retained, although it is cancelled for the trailer.

Automatic load-sensitive braking-force regulator

This device is connected between the service-brake valve and the brake cylinders. Depending on the vehicle load, it regulates the applied braking pressure.

The device has a reaction diaphragm of variable active area. The diaphragn rests on two radially arranged and interlocking rakes. Depending on the position of the control-valve seat in the vertical direction, there is a large reaction area (valve position at bottom) or a small reaction area (valve position at top). Consequently, the brake cylinders are supplied via an integrated relay valve with a pressure which is lower than (unladen), or which is the same

Service-brake valve

1 Actuation, 2 Reaction piston, 3 Brake circuit 1, 4 Rocking piston, 5 Brake circuit, 6 Exhaust, 7 Travel spring, 8 Supply circuit 1, 9 Control valves, 10 Supply circuit 2.

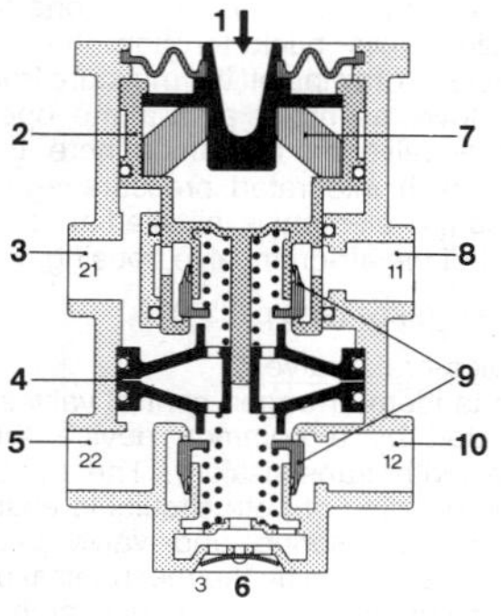

Automatic load-sensitive braking force regulaor

1 Exhaust, 2 Rake, 3 Reaction diaphragm, 4 From air reservoir, 5 Exhaust, 6 From service-brake valve, 7 Control valve, 8 Relay piston, 9 To brake cylinders, 10 Rotary cam.

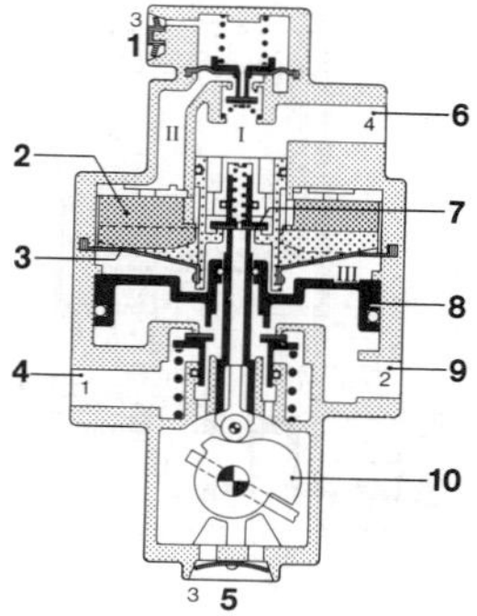

as (fully laden), that coming from the service-brake valve. The device is mounted on the vehicle frame and senses the compression position of the axle by a rotary lever via linkages. The rotary cam moves the valve pipe accordingly in the vertical direction and thus determines the valve position. The pressure limiter which is integrated into the device at the top allows a small partial pressure to flow in on the top side of the diaphragm. Thus, up to this pressure there is no reduction in the brake-cylinder pressure. This results in the synchronous application of the brakes on all vehicle axles. If the rotary lever breaks, the applied pressure flows to the brake cylinders at a ratio of 2 : 1.

Combination brake cylinder for wedge brakes

The combination brake cylinder consists of a single-chamber diaphragm cylinder for the service brakes and a spring-brake actuator for the parking brakes. The cylinder and spring-brake actuator are in tandem and act on a common pressure rod. They can be actuated independently of each other. Simultaneous actuation results in the addition of their forces.

The central release screw (see Fig. below left) permits tensioning the spring of the spring-brake actuator without compressed air having to be applied. This is the mounting position when installed. After installation, the release screw is screwed into the actuator, and the spring acts via the piston rod on the wedge-spreading mechanism. Inflow of compressed air in front of the actuator piston (parking-brake release) moves the piston against the force of the spring, therby tensioning the spring and releasing the brake (as shown in Fig. below left). When the service brake is actuated, compressed air flows behind the diaphragm and acts via piston plate and pressure rod on the wedge-spreading mechanism. Pressure reduction leads again to brake release.

Trailer-control valve

In two-line braking systems, the trailer-control valve which is installed in the towing vehicle controls the service brakes of the trailer. This multi-circuit relay valve is energized by both service-brake circuits and by the parking-brake system.

In the driving position, the supply chamber as well as the chamber of the parking-

Combination brake cylinder for wedge brakes
1 Single-chamber cylinder control line,
2 Spring-brake actuator control line,
3 Pressure rod, 4 Piston rod, 5 Release screw.

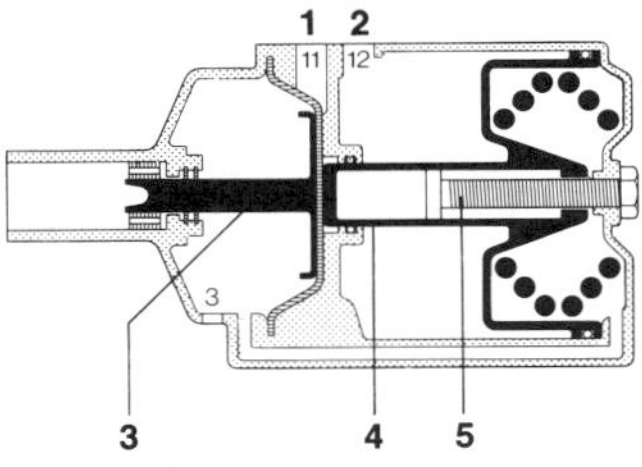

Trailer-control valve
1 Service-brake circuit 1, 2 Parking-brake circuit, 3 Service-brake circuit 2, 4 Pilot spring, 5 Control piston 1, 6 Control line to trailer, 7 Control-piston unit, 8 Supply line to trailer, 9 Control piston 2, 10 Exhaust.

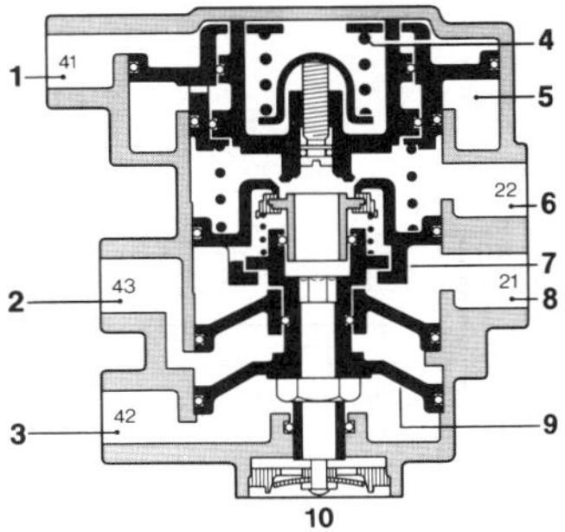

brake circuit are each subjected to equal pressure, and the trailer-control line is exhausted through the central exhaust port. A rise in pressure upstream of the control piston of brake circuit 1 (top) and/or of brake circuit 2 (bottom) leads to a corresponding rise in pressure in the trailer-control line. Brake circuit 1 is equipped with a larger control piston than brake circuit 2, which means that it has priority over the control piston of circuit 2. This priority ends when the pilot pressure is reached, at which the pressure on the control piston exceeds the force of the pilot spring. A reduction in pressure in the service-brake circuits leads to the same reduction in the trailer-control line.

The exhausting of the parking-brake circuit (braking) increases the pressure in the chamber to the trailer-control line. The application of air to the parking-brake circuit (releasing) again exhausts the trailer-control line.

Mufflers

Current and future legislation stipulates the reduction of compressed-air valve exhaust noise. Absorption-principle mufflers are used whose size depends on the exhaust-air quantity, air pressure, exhaust duration, and required noise level.

The muffler is a cylinder with radial and axial slits, and is filled with insulating material. Noise damping is due to inflow geometry, the insulation cartridge, and the exhaust slits with spherical exhaust flow. Mufflers are attached to the valves via threaded, snap-action or pipe connections. Some versions fulfill the "Low-Noise Vehicle" conditions [72 dB(A)].

Examples of ABS systems for commercial vehicles

a) Two-wheel systems (semitrailers),
b) Four-wheel systems,
c) Six-wheel systems (articulated buses)
1 Wheel-speed sensors
2 ECU
3 Pressure-modulation valve
4 Service-brake valve
5 Brake cylinder
6 Pulse ring

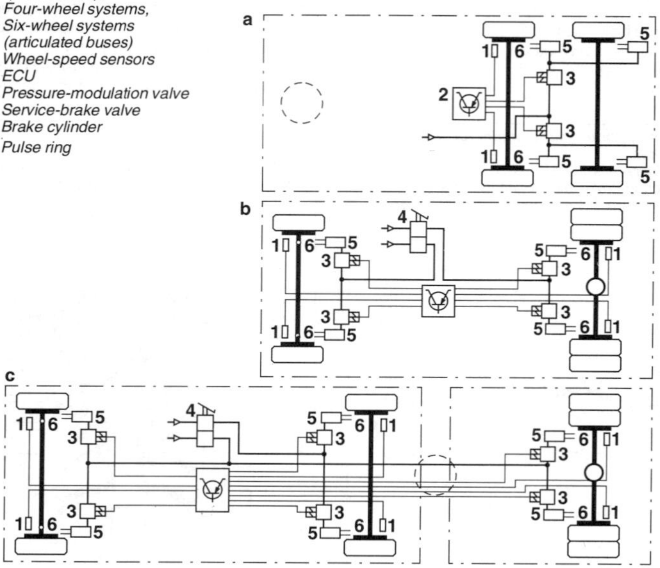

Antilock braking systems (ABS) for commercial vehicles

The ABS prevents the wheels from locking when the vehicle is overbraked. The vehicle therefore retains its directional stability and steerability even under emergency braking on a slippery road surface. The stopping distance is often shorter as opposed to braking with locked wheels. ABS prevents the danger of jackknifing in the case of vehicle combinations.

In contrast to passenger cars, commercial vehicles have pneumatic braking systems. Nevertheless, the functional description of the ABS control circuits for passenger cars (see p. 610) applies also to commercial vehicles.

The antilock braking system as used in commercial vehicles consists of wheel-speed sensors, an electronic controller (ECU) and pressure-modulation valves. The ABS regulates the brake pressure in each brake cylinder by increasing the pressure, holding it constant or reducing it by exhausting to atmosphere.

Individual control (IR)

This process, which sets and controls the optimum brake pressure individually for each wheel, produces the shortest braking distances. Under μ-split conditions (different friction coefficients between right-hand and left-hand wheels, e.g., black ice at edge of road surface, good grip at center of road surface) braking produces a high yawing moment about the vertical axis of the vehicle, thus making short-wheelbase vehicles difficult to control. In addition, this is coupled with a high steering moment as a result of the positive steering roll radii in commercial vehicles.

Select-low control (SL)

This process can reduce the yawing and steering moments to zero. The brake-pressure level is the same in both wheels of a given axle. The pressure level is based on the wheel which is running at the lower friction coefficient (select low). Under μ-split conditions this results in longer braking distances.

ABS control processes

Example: Braking on μ-split, a) IR individual control (rear axle), b) IRM individual control modified (steering axle). HV/AV = Holding valve/Outlet valve.
Subscripts: FZ vehicle, R/L wheel right/left, 0,1,2 thresholds.

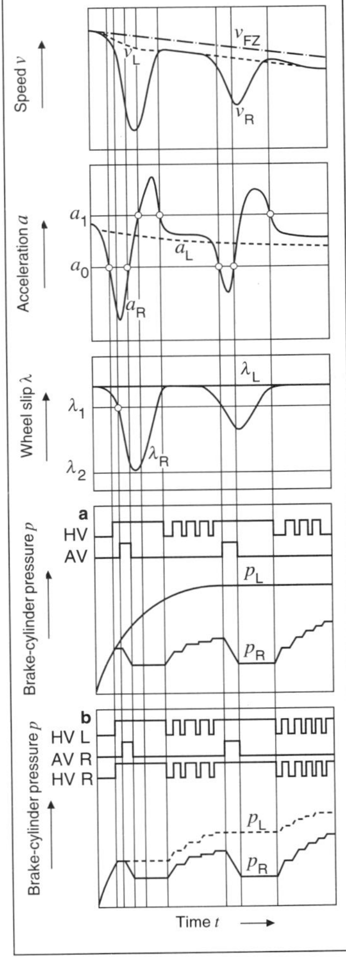

Individual control modified (IRM)
This process reduces yawing and steering moments only as far as necessary, and limits brake-pressure difference between left and right sides to a permissible level. This leads to the wheel which is running at the high friction coefficient being braked less strongly. This compromise results in a braking distance which is only a little longer than that for individual control, but it does ensure the safe control of vehicles which tend to handle critically.

Commercial-vehicle ABS versions
Depending on the number of controlled axles, two-wheel, four-wheel and six-wheel ABS systems are available. Two-wheel systems, mainly suitable for semi-trailers, control the wheels of one axle individually. The same brake pressure as for the controlled axles is applied to the trailer's remaining axles. Four-wheel systems are used in four-wheel buses, trucks and trailers. Axles located close together can be controlled jointly on each side as in two-wheel systems, so that six-wheel vehicles can be fitted with a four-wheel system. Six-wheel systems are primarily designed for longer wheelbase vehicles (e.g., articulated buses). For four-wheel and six-wheel systems, either the IRM or the SL process is applied on the steering axle if it is only equipped with one pressure-modulation valve. In commercial vehicles the rear axle is always IR-controlled.

The range of available ECU's permits further control combinations (not described here). An example: If both axles of a four-wheel semitrailer have wheel-speed sensors and each side of the vehicle has a pressure-modulation valve, the wheels of one side of the vehicle are SL-controlled. In this case, one axle may be a lifting axle, which is automatically excluded from the control process when lifted.

When the vehicle is running on a low friction coefficient, the operation of an additional retarding brake can lead to excessive slip at the driven wheels. This would severely impair vehicle stability. ABS therefore monitors the brake slip and controls it to permissible levels by switching the additional retarding brake on and off.

All ABS systems can be equipped with single-channel pressure-modulation valves, although special trailer-ABS systems can also be fitted with ABS relay valves with solenoid-valve pilot control.

In commercial vehicles with pneumatic/hydraulic converters, ABS intervenes in the pneumatic brake circuit and in doing so defines the hydraulic brake pressure.

In vehicle combinations (tractor-trailer rigs, road trains), the ideal situation is one in which both the towing vehicle and the trailer are equipped with ABS. However, even a partial ABS facility (ABS only in the towing vehicle or in the trailer) suffices to make the vehicle combination easier to control.

Towing vehicles and trailers with ABS systems of different manufacturers may be combined as desired if an ABS plug and socket connection in accordance with DIN ISO 7638 is used betwen the two vehicles.

ABS/ASR control unit
1 Wheel-speed sensors, 2 Interface ASR engine control, 3 Self-diagnosis, 4 Vehicle electrical-system voltage, 5 Input stages, 6 Microcomputers 1.1 ... 2.2, 7 Power supply, protective unit, 8 Final stages, 9 Pressure-modulation valve, 10 ASR solenoid valve, 11 Warning lamp, 12 ASR information lamp, 13 Retarder relay, 14 Valve relay.

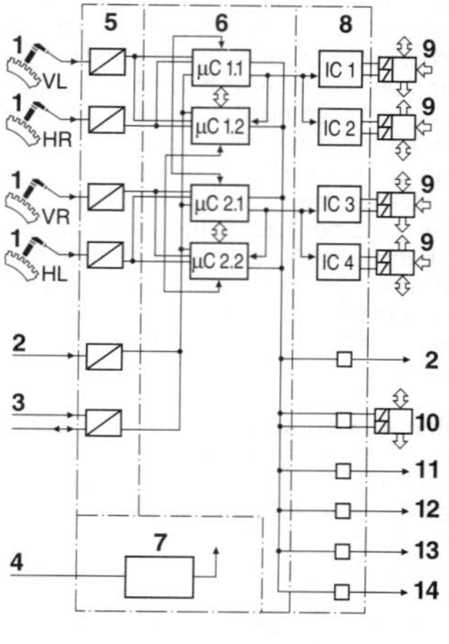

ABS components

Wheel-speed sensors

A pulse ring mounted on the hub produces an AC voltage in the wheel-speed sensor when the wheels are spinning. Its frequency is proportional to the wheel speed (description of function page 106).

The wheel-speed sensor is held in its mounting hole by a spring sleeve. When first installed in the vehicle it is positioned up against the pulse ring. The wheel-bearing play and the elastic deformations of the axle result in the pulse ring automaticaly positioning itself at the correct distance to the sensor. Depending upon pulse-ring diameter, this air gap can be up to a few millimeters. If the air gap is excessive, the ECU switches off the control at the wheel in question.

Electronic control unit (ECU)

The ECU's input stages (which use digital-circuitry techniques) are convert the incoming sinusoidal signals from the wheel-speed sensors into square-wave signals. The wheel speed and the wheel acceleration are calculated from the frequency of the square-wave signals by (redundant) microcomputers. Using the speeds from two diagonally opposite wheels, the microcomputers then generate a vehicle reference speed. With this reference speed and the individual wheel speeds it is possible to calculate the brake slip for each wheel. If a wheel has a tendency to lock, this is determined from the wheel-acceleration and slip signals. In such a case, the microcomputer energizes (via the ECU output stages) the solenoids of the pressure-modulation valves which control the brake pressure in the individual brake cylinders.

The ECU contains a comprehensive program for the detection of faults throughout the entire anti-lock system (wheel-speed sensors, ECU, pressure-modulation valves, wiring harness). If a fault is detected, it switches off the defective part of the system and stores a code detailing the faulty signal path. The service braking system remains fully functional. The ECU self-diagnosis facility incorporates two methods for fault-code read-out in the workshop: Display by a flashing diagnosis lamp at the press of a button, or interrogation by means of an "intelligent" tester via a serial interface, in accordance with ISO proposals.

The ECU's of some European ABS manufacturers include not only the ABS function but also functions for ASR traction control and in some cases for cruise control (see also page 559). The most important factor is that depending upon the model, the ECU automatically configures itself to the required function. In other words, if the vehicle concerned is only ABS-equipped, the ECU only carries out the ABS function; if the vehicle has ASR components the control unit also controls wheel slip.

ECU for trailer recognition

If the ABS is used in vehicle combinations, each of the two vehicles has its own ABS. The towing vehicle is additionally equipped with the ECU for trailer recognition which, by means of a warning lamp, informs the driver of the equipment on the trailer:

– Lighting-up of information lamp only means "trailer without ABS".

– Lighting-up of warning lamp and information lamp means "malfunctions in trailer ABS".

Pressure-modulation valve

Single-channel pressure-modulation valves are available with and without relay action. The relay-action valves are suitable for semitrailers and drawbar trailers. The standard trailer-braking system often includes relay valves which can then be replaced by ABS relay-action valves. Non-relay-action ABS valves are used in all other vehicles, i.e. in buses, trucks and tractor-trailer rigs, as well as in trailers and special vehicles.

Both types of valve have 3/2 pilot valves. The non-relay-action valves thereby control 2/2 diaphragm valves, which have a sufficiently large cross-section for almost all applications. In the relay-action valves, the 3/2 pilot valves influence the pressure in the control chamber of a relay valve. The ECU actuates the pilot valves in the appropriate combinations to achieve the "maintain pressure" or "reduce pressure" functions as required. If no pilot-valve actuation takes place, "pressure build-up" is the result.

When braking normally (that is, without ABS response = no locking tendency of a wheel), the air flows through the pressure-modulation valves unhindered in both directions when pressure is applied to or removed from the brake cylinders. This ensures fault-free functioning of the service-braking system.

Electronically controlled braking system (ELB) for commercial vehicles

The development of an electronically controlled braking system (ELB) is intended to optimize the braking process for pneumatically braked vehicles (particularly road trains and tractor-trailer rigs). There are systems available today which are almost at the standard equipment stage. An ELB system includes at least the following function blocks:

– Electronically controlled service-braking system (EPB),
– Antilock braking system (ABS),
– Traction control (ASR) in towing vehicles.

The description of a system equipped with ELB, together with the circuit diagram, is given below (for ABS and ASR see pages 639 and 558 respectively). The compressed-air supply, conditioning and storage equipment, as well as the wheel-brake cylinders, which are components of existing braking systems, are employed here too.

Pressure-modulation valve (schematic)
1 Holding valve, 2 Outlet valve, 3 Solenoid valve for "Maintain pressure", 4 Solenoid valve for "Reduce pressure", 5 Control piston, 6 Valve plate, 7 Compression spring, 8 Brake cylinder, 9 Service-brake valve, 10 Supply air, 11 Exhaust.

Single-channel pressure-modulation valve

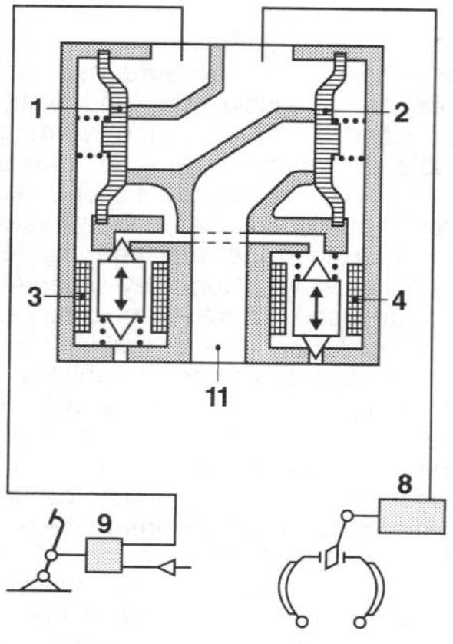

Pressure-modulation valve with relay action

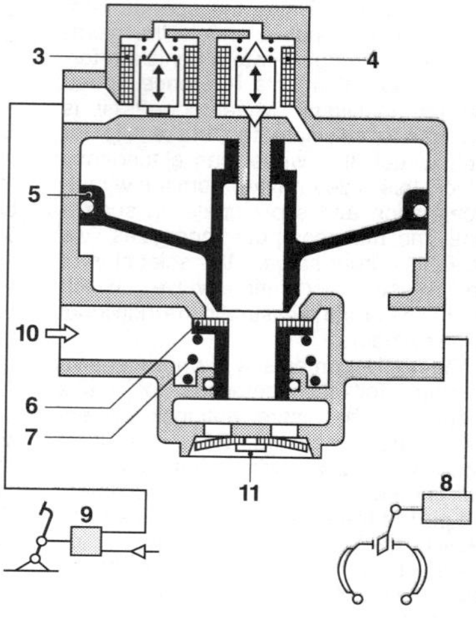

The pressure level to be set during braking (setpoint level) is calculated from the measured brake-pedal position. One pressure buildup valve per axle provides uniformity of pressure buildup in the right and left-side brake cylinders. The simultaneous rapid release of the brakes at all axles is effected by releasing air via the ABS valves.

On vehicles which are controlled with such systems, the synchronous braking effect extending from the towing-vehicle steering axle to the final axle of the trailer has a beneficial effect. For instance, a similar level of braking comfort and sophistication can be achieved in a 38 t road train as in a passenger car. Reaction times for brake-application and release are minimized.

At the basic current-free setting (non-braking position or fault in the electrical system) the pneumatic backup circuit has continuity from the service brake valve through to the wheel-brake cylinders.

The pneumatic triggering of the trailer brakes is effected from the service brake valve and from the brake pressure on the rear axle of the towing vehicle. The rear-axle brake pressure is blocked by an on-off valve when ASR is in use.

Additional factors can be taken into account for setting the brake pressures: load condition in order to optimize adhesion stress on the wheels, coupling force between towing vehicle and trailer in order to minimize coupling forces when braking; measurement of lining wear etc.

Electronically controlled braking system ELB
1 Air reservoir, 2 Service-brake valve, 3 Pressure-buildup valve, 4 Relay valve, 5 ABS pressure-modulation valve, 6 Brake cylinder, 7 Pressure sensor, 8 Wheel-speed sensor, 9 Load sensor, 10 Trailer-control valve, 11 ASR lock valve, 12 Shuttle valve, 13 Muffler, 14 ECU.

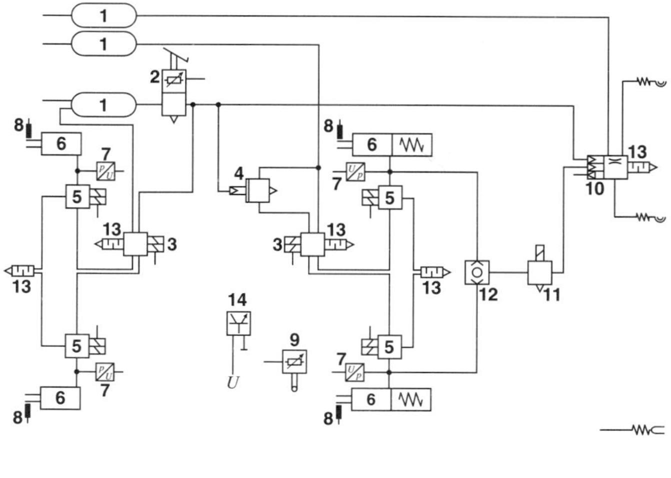

Brake test stands

The brakes are of decisive importance in maintaining high technical standards of vehicle safety; it is therefore imperative that the brake system be inspected on a regular basis. The German motor vehicle inspection prescribed by Paragraph 29 of the StVZO Road Licensing Regulations (FMVSS/CUR) normally employs brake test stands (roller dynamometers) for this purpose, as do automotive service centers for inspections and repairs. The braking forces monitored at the wheel's circumference provide the basis for evaluating the operation and effectiveness of the brake system. Brake stands employed for the inspections stipulated in Paragraph 29 must conform to the "Regulations governing use, design and testing of brake test stands" as administered by the Federal Transport Minister.

Layout

The brake test stand's main components are two mutually independent roller sets, for the left and right sides of the vehicle respectively. The vehicle is driven onto the test stand so that the wheels of the axle being tested rest upon the rollers.

A stable frame supports the roller sets, which assume the form of a drive roller and a secondary roller in a parallel layout, while a drive chain provides the positive dynamic connection between the two rollers. An AC motor powers the drive roller through a gear set with an upward conversion ratio, while the drive unit itself is suspended on an extension of the drive roller's shaft. Pressure exerted against a torque lever flanged onto the gear-drive unit is transferred through the load sensor, with the frame providing positive support for the entire assembly. The braking force F_{Br} is actually measured by monitoring the reaction torque M_R. The electric motors set the rollers in motion and then maintain a constant rotational speed against the considerable opposing forces that occur when the vehicle's brakes are applied. The suspended drive unit with torque lever transmits the braking forces to the load-sensing device. This load device can assume the form of an aneroid unit, incorporated within the hydraulic system, which acts directly upon a gauge. The gauge, whose scale is calibrated in newtons, provides an analog display of braking force.

Electrical load-sensing systems can employ flexural sensors with a wire strain gauge, or they may be designed to use an inductive short-circuit-ring sensor working in combination with a linear-motion spring strut.

The system's computer employs digital technology in the subsequent evaluation of the various data derived from braking-force testing, such as fluctuations or differences in braking force. Once processed, the information is presented in either analog or digital form, depending upon the specific system, while a printer can be connected to provide a hardcopy test protocol.

Operation

The drive motors for the roller sets may be activated in one of two ways, either by remote control or with an integral automatic on/off switch. An automatic-activation test stand is distinguished by the pressure-sensitive rollers located between the main test rollers on each roller set. When the vehicle is driven onto the test stand, it pushes down the pressure-sensitive rollers and activates the stand. When the vehicle leaves the stand the pressure-sensitive rollers are released and the unit is switched off. Should the applied braking force start to exceed the available traction between tires and test rollers, the wheel will respond by starting to slip and will then lock. Tire slip, however, makes it impossible to perform useful measurements of braking force. Under these conditions, it is the slip resistance between tire and roller (as a function of wheel load) that is measured and this is of no use. Here assistance is provided by an automatic override device which recognizes this kind of slip by monitoring the test-roller speed, and which responds to it by switching off the test unit when a given maximum figure is exceeded. This avoids both false measurements and possible tire damage. The display, meanwhile, continues to show the maximum braking force achieved before the override device was activated. On analog displays, the reading is maintained by an indicator lock, while an electronic memory circuit stores the data for readout on units with digital displays. Both arrangements ensure that the final display remains in place long enough to be recorded by the operator.

In addition, the vehicle and/or axle weight can also be measured at the test stand or entered remotely; the test unit can then use this information to calculate the effective retardation.

The brake test stand employs specific test sequences to provide extremely rationalized examination procedures, allowing the operator to carry out complete testing of both front and rear brakes without leaving the vehicle.

Vehicles with permanent 4-wheel drive and variable torque distribution are tested on special stands which are constructed to prevent the forces generated at the test axle from being transferred to that axle which is at rest.

Brake test stand measurement sensor

1 Adjustment plate, 2 Alignment pin, 3 Flexural sensor with wire strain gauge, 4 Thrust block, 5 Torque lever.

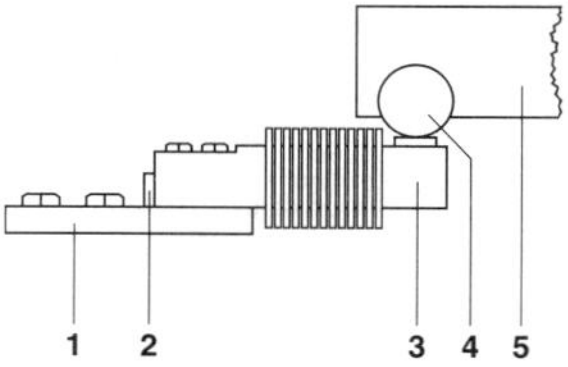

Determining braking force F_{Br} via measurement of reaction torque M_R

1 Vehicle tire
2 Roller set with spacing a
3 Motor with gear set
4 Torque lever with length l
5 Measurement sensor
6 Display

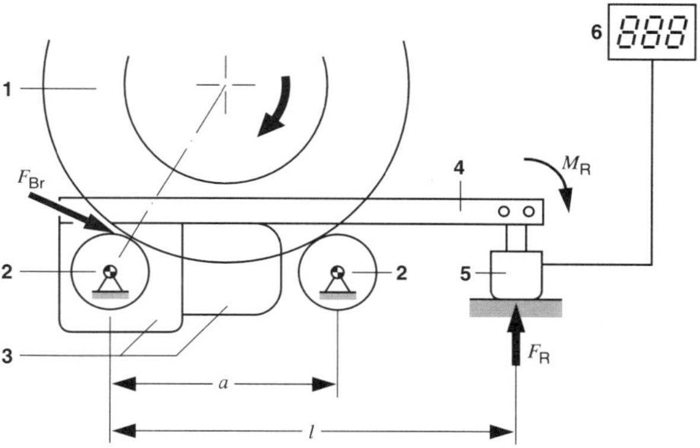

Road-vehicle systematics

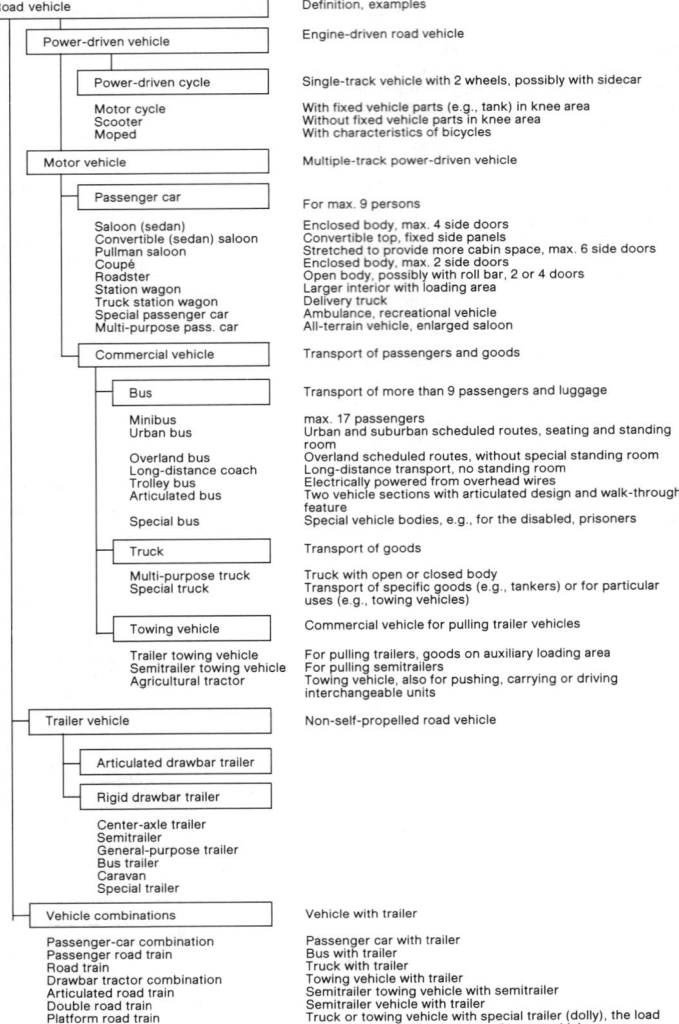

Road vehicle	Definition, examples
Power-driven vehicle	Engine-driven road vehicle
Power-driven cycle	Single-track vehicle with 2 wheels, possibly with sidecar
Motor cycle	With fixed vehicle parts (e.g., tank) in knee area
Scooter	Without fixed vehicle parts in knee area
Moped	With characteristics of bicycles
Motor vehicle	Multiple-track power-driven vehicle
Passenger car	For max. 9 persons
Saloon (sedan)	Enclosed body, max. 4 side doors
Convertible (sedan) saloon	Convertible top, fixed side panels
Pullman saloon	Stretched to provide more cabin space, max. 6 side doors
Coupé	Enclosed body, max. 2 side doors
Roadster	Open body, possibly with roll bar, 2 or 4 doors
Station wagon	Larger interior with loading area
Truck station wagon	Delivery truck
Special passenger car	Ambulance, recreational vehicle
Multi-purpose pass. car	All-terrain vehicle, enlarged saloon
Commercial vehicle	Transport of passengers and goods
Bus	Transport of more than 9 passengers and luggage
Minibus	max. 17 passengers
Urban bus	Urban and suburban scheduled routes, seating and standing room
Overland bus	Overland scheduled routes, without special standing room
Long-distance coach	Long-distance transport, no standing room
Trolley bus	Electrically powered from overhead wires
Articulated bus	Two vehicle sections with articulated design and walk-through feature
Special bus	Special vehicle bodies, e.g., for the disabled, prisoners
Truck	Transport of goods
Multi-purpose truck	Truck with open or closed body
Special truck	Transport of specific goods (e.g., tankers) or for particular uses (e.g., towing vehicles)
Towing vehicle	Commercial vehicle for pulling trailer vehicles
Trailer towing vehicle	For pulling trailers, goods on auxiliary loading area
Semitrailer towing vehicle	For pulling semitrailers
Agricultural tractor	Towing vehicle, also for pushing, carrying or driving interchangeable units
Trailer vehicle	Non-self-propelled road vehicle
Articulated drawbar trailer	
Rigid drawbar trailer	
Center-axle trailer	
Semitrailer	
General-purpose trailer	
Bus trailer	
Caravan	
Special trailer	
Vehicle combinations	Vehicle with trailer
Passenger-car combination	Passenger car with trailer
Passenger road train	Bus with trailer
Road train	Truck with trailer
Drawbar tractor combination	Towing vehicle with trailer
Articulated road train	Semitrailer towing vehicle with semitrailer
Double road train	Semitrailer vehicle with trailer
Platform road train	Truck or towing vehicle with special trailer (dolly), the load forms the connection between the two vehicles

Classification[1])

Category L

Motor vehicles with fewer than 4 wheels, motorized two-wheeled and three-wheeled vehicles.

Category	Design	Displacement	Maximum speed
L_1	two-wheeled	$\leq/50\ cm^3$	$\leq/50$ km/h
L_2	three-wheeled	$\leq/50\ cm^3$	$\leq/50$ km/h
L_3	two-wheeled	$>50\ cm^3$	>50 km/h
L_4	three-wheeled asymmetrical to longitudinal vehicle axis	$>50\ cm^3$	>50 km/h
L_5	three-wheeled symmetrical to longitudinal vehicle axis	$>50\ cm^3$ $\leq/1$ t laden weight	>50 km/h

Category M

Passenger vehicles with at least 4 wheels or with 3 wheels and an overall weight >1 t.

Category	Driver's seat + passenger seats	Laden weight
M_1	$1 \leq 9$	
M_2	>9	<5 t
M_3	>9	>5 t

Class N

Goods transport vehicles with at least 4 wheels or with 3 wheels and a laden weight >1 t.

Category	Laden weight
N_1	≤ 3.5 t
N_2	>3.5 t ≤ 12 t
N_3	>12 t

Category O

Trailers and semitrailers

Category	Laden weight
O_1 only single-axle trailers	≤ 0.75 t
O_2	>0.75 t ≤ 3.5 t
O_3	>3.5 t ≤ 10 t
O_4	>10 t

[1]) Vehicle classification in accordance with the Directives of the European Community (71/320/EEC) and ECE Regulation No. 13 with regard to brake equipment.

Vehicle bodies, passenger cars

Main dimensions

Interior-dimensions

Dimensional layout depends upon body shape, type of drive, scope of aggregate equipment, desired interior size, luggage compartment volume and other considerations such as driving comfort, driving safety and operating safety. Seats are designed in accordance with ergonomic findings and with the aid of templates (DIN or SEA): body template as per DIN 33 408 for men (5th, 50th, and 95th percentile) and women (1st, 5th and 95th percentile). For example, the 5th percentile template represents "small" body size, i.e., only 5 % of the population have smaller bodies, and 95 % have larger body dimensions.

SAE H-point template in accordance with SEA J826 b: 10th, 50th and 95th percentile thigh segments and lower leg segments. For legal reasons motor vehicle manufacturers in several countries must use the SAE H-point template for determining the seating reference point. The body template in accordance with DIN 33 408 is particularly well suited to dimensional design of seats and passenger areas.

The hip point (H-point) is the pivot center of torso and thigh, and roughly corresponds to the hip joint location. The seating reference point (in accordance with ISO 6549 and US legislation) or R-point (ISO 6549 and EEC Guidelines/ECE Regulations) indicates the position of the design H-point in the rearmost normal driver seating position in the case of adjustable seats. In determining the design H-point position, many vehicle manufacturers use the 95th percentile adult-male position or, if this position is not reached, the rearmost seat position. In order to check the position of the measured H-point relative to the vehicle, a three-dimensional, adjustable H-point machine weighing 75 kg is used. The seating reference point, accelerator heel point, vertical and horizontal distance between these two points, as well as body angles specified by the vehicle manufacturer form the basis for determining the dimensions of the driver's seating position.
The seating reference point is used
— to define the positions of the eyellipse (SAE J941) and the eye points (RREG 77/649) as a basis for determining the driver's direct field of view;
— to define hand reach envelopes in order to correctly position controls and actuators;
— to determine the accelerator heel point (AHP) as a reference point for positioning the pedals.
The space required by the rear axle as well as location and shape of the fuel tank primarily determine the rear seating arrangement (height of the seating reference point, rear seating room, headroom) and thus the shape of the roof rear portion. There are different body angles of the SAE template and different distances between the seating reference point of the driver's seat and the rear seats, depending upon the type of vehicle being developed, the projected main dimensions and the required passenger sizes.

The longitudinal dimensions are greatly affected by the height of the seats. Lower seats require a more stretched passenger seating position, and thus greater interior length.

The width of the interior is dependent upon the projected exterior width, the shape of the sides (curvature), the door mechanisms and the space required by various assemblies (propeller-shaft tunnel, location of the exhaust system, etc.).

Luggage-compartment dimensions

The size and shape of the luggage compartment depend upon the design of the rear of the vehicle, the position of the fuel tank, the tank volume, the position of the spare tire and the location and size of the main muffler.

Luggage compartment capacity is determined in accordance with DIN-ISO 3832 or, more commonly, in accordance with the VDA* method using the VDA unit module (a right parallelepiped with dimensions of 200 × 100 × 50 mm — corresponds to a volume of 1 dm³).

* VDA (Verband der Automobilindustrie) = German Automotive Industry Association

Typical internal and external dimensions *(in accordance with VDA Guideline 239-01)*

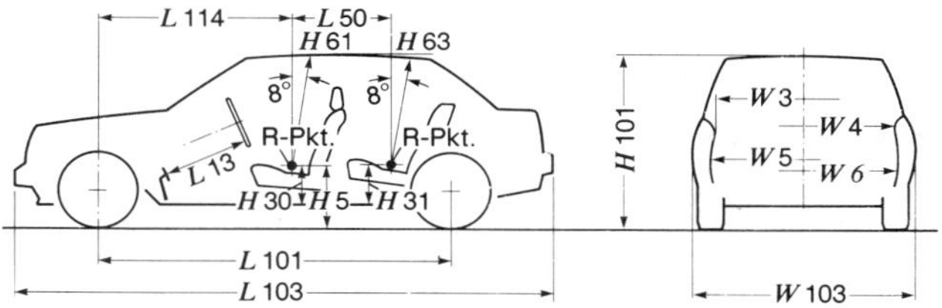

Dimension			Subcompact car mm		Long car mm
H	5	R-point to ground, front	460	to	510
H	30	R-point to accelerator heel point, front	240		300
H	31	R-point to accelerator heel point, rear	300		310
H	61	Effective headroom, front	940		980
H	63	Effective headroom, rear	920		950
H	101	Vehicle height	1360		1400
L	13	Steering wheel to brake pedal	480		630
L	50	R-point distance (front to rear seat)	710		830
L	101	Wheelbase	2430		2880
L	103	Vehicle length overall	3840		4930
L	114	Center of front wheel to R-point, front	1250		1590
W	3	Shoulder room, front	1310		1430
W	4	Shoulder room, rear	1290		1420
W	5	Hip room, front	1260		1430
W	6	Hip room, rear	1240		1470
W	103	Vehicle width overall	1620		1820

Exterior dimensions

The following factors must be taken into consideration:

- Seating arrangement and luggage compartment.
- Engine, transmission, radiator.
- Auxiliary and special equipment.
- Space required by sprung and turned wheels (allowance for snow chains).
- Type and size of drive axle.
- Position and volume of fuel tank.
- Front and rear bumpers.
- Aerodynamic considerations.
- Ground clearance (approx. 100 to 180 mm).
- Effect of body structure width on windshield wiper system (ADR 16, FMVSS 104).

Parameters which determine passenger-car driver's seat location

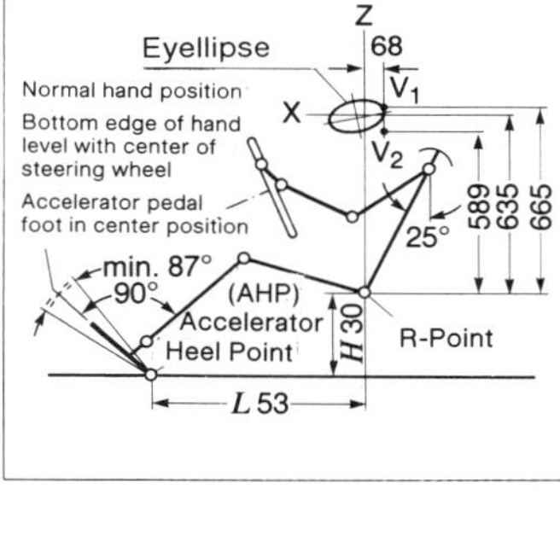

Vision

A compromise must be found between optimum vision and the functional layout of components which tend to obstruct the field of vision. The following influencing factors must be taken into consideration:

— Obscuration by pillars, the roof, the hood and the luggage-compartment lid. The eye ellipse in accordance with SAE J941 and the "eye points" in accordance with RREG 77/649[1]) are the basis for assessing the field of vision,
— Location, size and shape of the rear-view mirror in accordance with RREG 79/795.
— Windshield wiper pattern in accordance with FMVSS 104[2]) and RREG 78/318,
— Windshield curvature,
— View of instruments (obstruction of vision by steering wheel, ADR 18A[3])).

Body design

The following technical requirements must be met in interior and exterior body design:

— Mechanical functions (lowering of side windows, opening of the hood, luggage-compartment lid and sunroof, positions of lamps),
— Manufacturability and ease of repair (gap widths, bodywork assembly, window shape, protective molding rails, paint feature lines),
— Safety (position and shape of bumpers, no sharp edges or points),
— Aerodynamics (air resistance, dirt on the vehicle body, wind noises, ventilation openings, windshield-wiper operation),
— Optics (distortion caused by window type and slope, glare due to reflection),
— Legal requirements (position and size of lamps, rear-view mirror, license plates),
— Design and layout of controls (positions, shapes and surface contours),
— Ease of parking.

1) Guidelines published by the Council of the European Community.
2) Federal Motor Vehicle Safety Standard (USA).
3) Australian Design Rule.

Aerodynamic effects on vehicle functions

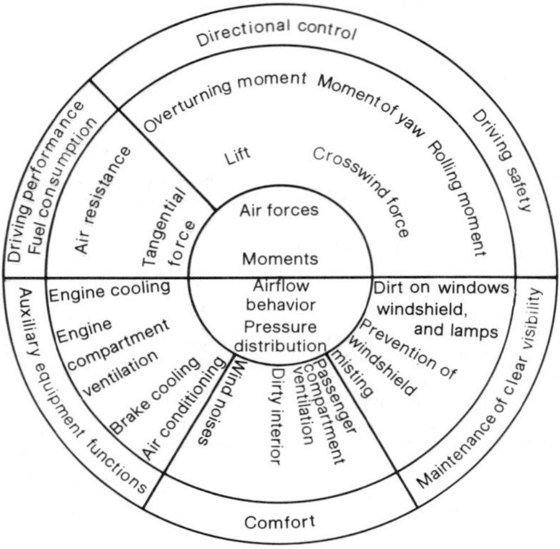

Aerodynamics

Aerodynamics deals with all processes which are observed as air flows through and around a vehicle.
Air resistance $W = c_w A \cdot v^2 \cdot \varrho/2$
where c_w = drag coefficient, A = cross-sectional area, v = driving speed, ϱ = air density (see also p. 325 f).

Factors which can be influenced by the vehicle manufacturer are:
- Drag coefficient c_w as a measure of the aerodynamic quality of the vehicle shape,
- Projected vehicle cross-sectional area A.

Vehicle (Examples)	c_w —	A m_2
Audi 100	0.30	2.05
Porsche 944	0.35	1.82
Mercedes 190 E/2.3-16	0.32	1.92

Attemps to reduce the c_w value by adding spoilers, underbody panels, etc. are not practical, since their effect depends upon the aerodynamic characteristics of the basic vehicle body (see table for effect of individual modifications on drag coefficient). These types of modifications in optimized form are standard features of modern vehicle design.

The c_w value can be influenced by individual aerodynamic or design measures. Airflow through the vehicle as well as roof-mounted fixtures will always increase the c_w value. Examples (− = better, + = worse):

Effect of	Δc_w %
Lowering vehicle height by 30 mm	approx. −5
Smooth wheel covers	−1 ... −3
Wide tires	+2 ... +4
Windows flush with exterior	approx. −1
Sealing body gaps	−2 ... −5
Underbody panels	−1 ... −7
Concealed headlamps	+3 ... +10
Outside rear-view mirrors	+2 ... +5
Airflow through radiator and engine compartment	+4 ... +14
Brake cooling devices	+2 ... +5
Interior ventilation	approx. +1
Open windows	approx. +5
Open sunroof	approx. +2
Roof-mounted surfboard rack	approx. +40

Effect of $c_w \cdot A$ on fuel consumption (mid-sized vehicle)

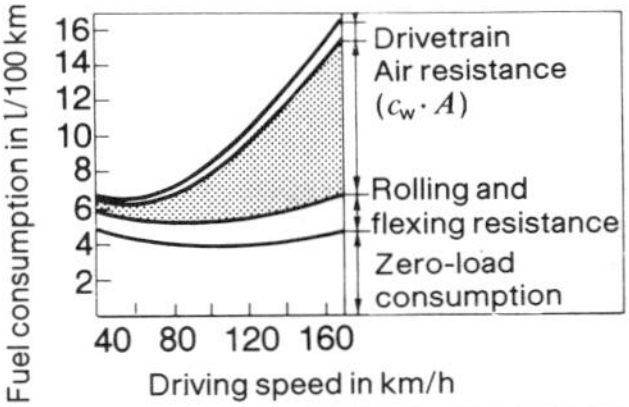

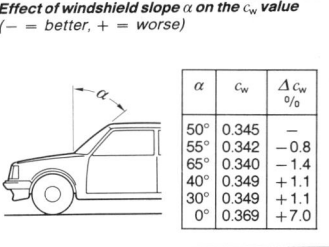

Effect of windshield slope α on the c_w value
(− = better, + = worse)

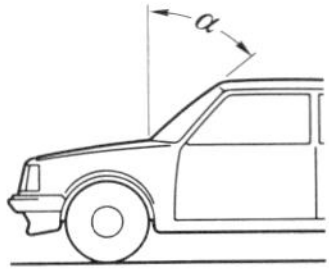

α	c_w	Δc_w %
50°	0.345	–
55°	0.342	−0.8
65°	0.340	−1.4
40°	0.349	+1.1
30°	0.349	+1.1
0°	0.369	+7.0

Measures for optimising the c_w value and axle lift and their effects
using the Mercedes 190 E/2.3-16 as an example.
(− = better, + = worse).
W = Air resistance; A_V = Lift, front;
A_H = Lift, rear.
1 Front apron, 2 Side trim panel,
3 Rear apron, 4 Rear spoiler.

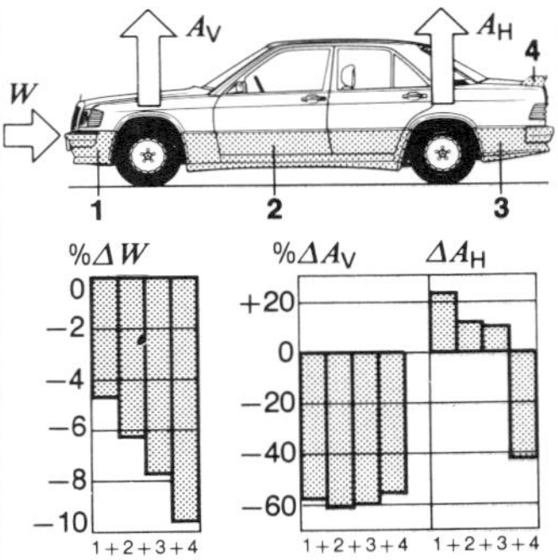

Body structure

Unitized all-steel body

(Standard design)

A self-supporting body comprises hollow sheet-steel components onto which body panels are welded by welding robots or in multi-spot welding units. Depending upon vehicle type, roughly 5000 spot welds must be made along a flange length of 120 ... 200 m. The flange widths are 10 ... 18 mm. Other parts (front fenders, doors, hood and luggage-compartment lid) are bolted to the supporting structure of the body. Other types of body construction include frame and sandwich designs.

General requirements:

Rigidity

Torsional and bending rigidity should be as great as possible in order to minimize elastic deformation of the apertures for the doors, hood and luggage-compartment lid. The effect of body rigidity on the vibrational characteristics of the vehicle must be taken into consideration.

Vibrational characteristics

Body vibrations as well as vibrations of individual structural components as a result of excitation by the wheels, suspension system, engine and drive train can severely impair driving comfort if resonance occurs.

The natural frequency of the body, and its components which may vibrate, must be detuned by means of creasing and changing the wall thicknesses and cross sections, such that resonance and its consequences are minimized.

Operational integrity

Alternating stresses which can affect the body as the vehicle is driven can lead to incipient structural cracks or weld failure. Areas which are particularly susceptible are the bearing points of the running gear, the steering system and engine units.

Body stresses due to accidents

In the event of a collision, the body must be capable of transforming as much kinetic energy as possible into deformation work while minimizing deformation of the vehicle interior (see page 656, Safety).

Ease of repair

Those components which are most susceptible to damage as a result of minor accidents ("fender-benders") must be easily replaceable or repairable (access to exterior body panels from inside, access to bolts, favorable location of joints, feature lines for the repainting of individual components).

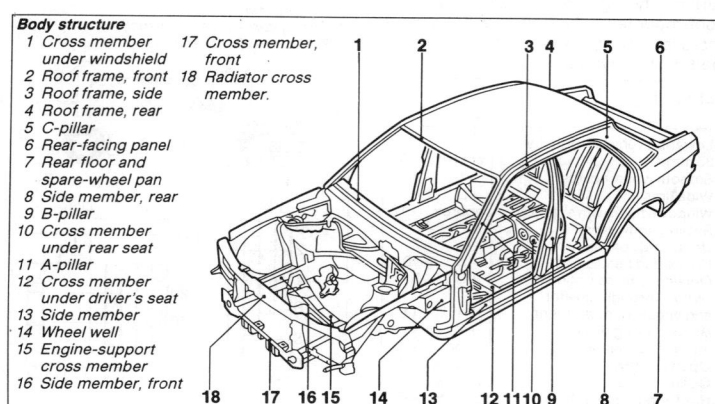

Body structure

1 Cross member under windshield
2 Roof frame, front
3 Roof frame, side
4 Roof frame, rear
5 C-pillar
6 Rear-facing panel
7 Rear floor and spare-wheel pan
8 Side member, rear
9 B-pillar
10 Cross member under rear seat
11 A-pillar
12 Cross member under driver's seat
13 Side member
14 Wheel well
15 Engine-support cross member
16 Side member, front
17 Cross member, front
18 Radiator cross member.

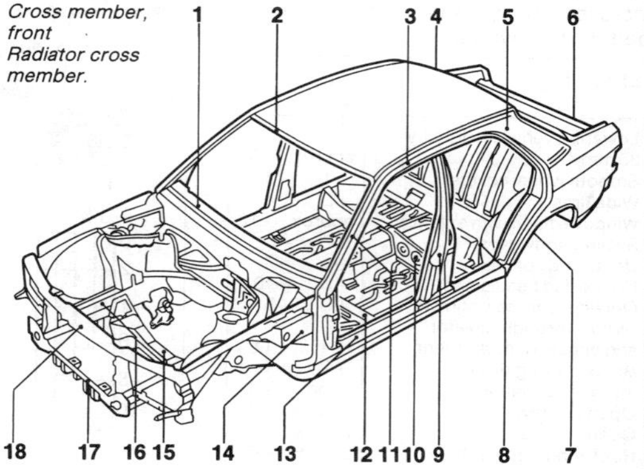

Body materials

Sheet steel

Sheet steel of various grades (see table on p. 189) is customarily used for the vehicle body structure.

Sheet thickness ranges from 0.6 to 3 mm, with most pieces being between 0.8 and 1.0 mm thick. Due to the mechanical properties of steel with regard to stiffness, strength, economy and ductility, alternative materials for the vehicle body structure are not yet available.

High-strength, low-alloy (HSLA) sheet steel is used for highly-stressed structural components. The increased strength of these components allows their thickness to be reduced.

Aluminum

Aluminum can be used for separate body components such as the hood, luggage-compartment lid, etc. for the purpose of weight reduction. Aluminum costs significantly more than sheet steel however, which limits its use in mass-produced vehicles.

Due to its lower modules of elasticity, aluminum is less suitable for the load-bearing members of the body structure, because the cross-sectional dimensions and/or sheet thicknesses must be increased over those of a steel body structure. In addition, different material characteristics must be taken into consideration when spot-welding aluminum: The thermal and electrical conductivity of aluminum are three times greater than for steel, and an aluminum spot-weld is only half as strong.

Plastics

Plastics as materials for separate body components can be used in a limited number of cases in place of steel (see Table below).

Examples of application	Material	Abbreviation	Processing method
Load-bearing components, e.g., bumper beams	Glass-fiber-reinforced, unsaturated polyester resins	GF-UP	Pressing of resin compounds e.g., SMC (Sheet Molding Compound)
Moldings/covers, e.g.,front apron, spoiler, front section, radiator grille, wheel-well liners, wheel covers	Glass-fiber-reinforced, unsaturated polyester resins	GF-UP	
	Polyurethane	PUR	RIM (Reaction Injection Molding) RRIM (Reinforced Reaction Injection Molding)
Separate vehicle-body components, e.g., hood, fender, luggage-compartment lid, sunroof	Polyamide Polypropylene Polyethylene Acrylonitrile-butadiene-styrene copolymeres Polycarbonate (with polybutadiene theraphthalate mod.)	PA PP PE ABS PC-PBTP	Injection molding, glass-fiber constituent determines elasticity
Protective molding rails	Polyvinyl chloride Ethylene-propylene Terpolymers Elastomer-modified polypropylene	PVC EPDM PP-EPDM	Injection molding/ extrusion
Energy-absorbing foam	Polyurethane	PUR	Liquid reaction foaming

Body surface

Corrosion protection

Allowance must be made for corrosion protection as early as during the body design phase ("Anti-Corrosion Code", Canada). Corrosion protection measures:
– Minimize flanged joints, sharp edges and corners,
– Avoid areas where dirt and humidity can accumulate,
– Provide holes for pretreatment and electrophoretic enameling,
– Provide good accessibility for the application of corrosion inhibitor,
– Allow for ventilation of hollow spaces,
– Prevent the penetration of dirt and water to the greatest extent possible; provide water drain openings,
– Minimize the area of the body exposed to stone chips,
– Prevent contact corrosion.

Precoated sheet steel (inorganic zinc, electrolytically galvanized, hot-dip galvanized) is often used for those components which are particularly endangered, such as doors and load-bearing members at the front of the vehicle. Flanges which are exposed to particularly high corrosive stress receive a coating of spot-welding paste (PVC or epoxy cement; approx. 10 ... 15 m total seam length per vehicle) before assembly.

Painting

Measures subsequent to electrophoretic enameling:
– Covering the spot-welded seams (up to 115 m), folds and joints with PCV sealing compound,
– Coating the underbody with a layer of PVC (0.3 ... 0.8 mm thick, 10 ... 18 kg per vehicle) to protect it from damage due to stone chips,
– Preservation of hollow components using penetrating, non-ageing wax,
– Use of corrosion-resistant, separate plastic components in highly susceptible areas such as the front wheel wells (PVC coating is not suitable here).
– Preservation of underbody and engine compartment after final assembly.

Coating system, overall thickness	140 ... 160 μm
Zinc-phosphate coating	≈ 2 μm
Electrophoretic enameling (cathodic)	13 ... 18 μm
Stone-chip protection coating	≈ 30 μm
Primer coat[1])	30 ... 35 μm
Foundation-paint coat[1])	25 ... 30 μm
Top-paint coat	35 ... 45 μm
Varnish coat (only for metallic paint)	40 ... 45 μm

[1]) The primer and foundation paint coat are frequently combined as a filler.

Body finishing components

Bumpers

The front and rear of the vehicle should be protected in such a manner that low-speed collisions will only damage the vehicle slightly, or not at all. Prescribed bumber evaluation tests (US Part 581, Canada CMVSS 215, and ECE-R 42, currently not obligatory) specify minimum requirements in terms of energy absorption and installed bumper height (4 km/h barrier collision, 4 km/h pendulum tests). Bumper evaluation tests in accordance with US Part 581 must be passed by a bumper system whose energy absorber is of the no-damage absorber type. The requirements of the ECE standard are satisfied by plastically deformable retaining elements located between the bumper and the vehicle body structure. In addition to sheet steel, many bumpers are manufactured using fiber-reinforced plastics and aluminum sections.

Exterior trim, impact strips

Plastics have become the preferred materials for exterior impact strips,

Bumpers
1 Shock-absorber system,
2 Energy-absorbing PUR-foam system.

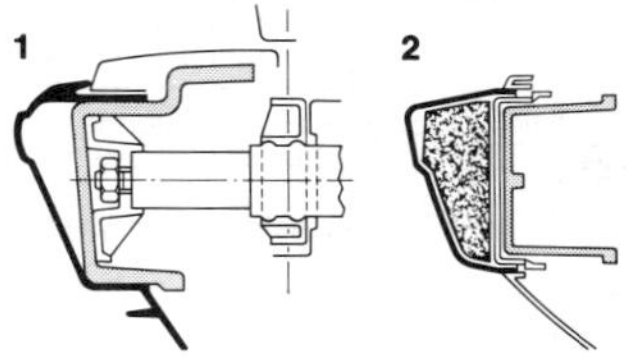

trim, skirts and spoilers, and particularly for those components whose purpose is to improve the aerodynamic characteristics of the vehicle. Criteria used in the selection of the proper material are flexibility, high-temperature shape retention, coefficient of linear expansion, notched-bar toughness, resistance to scratches, resistance to chemicals, surface quality and paintability (see p. 653 for examples).

Glazing
The windshield and rear window are usually held in rubber strips and sealed or bonded in place.

The total weight of the windows in a vehicle ranges from 25 to 35 kg. Plastics (PC, PMMA) have not been used as substitutes for glass for the purpose of weight reduction due to several disadvantages. Recently, due to its heat-insulation and noise-damping properties, 2-layer insulating glass has come into use for door windows (see p. 698 for glazing).

Door latches
Door latches are of great importance with regard to passive accident safety (pertinent regulations: ECE-R 11 and FMVSS 206, among others):
– Fully latched and secondary latched positions,
– Complete integrity under a longitudinal load of up to 12 kN and a transverse load of up to 10 kN (fully latched position),
– Complete integrity under a longitudinal or transverse inertia load of up to $30 \cdot g$.

Individual manufacturers have varying solutions with regard to ease of operation, anti-theft protection and child-proof operation.

Seats
The strength requirements which must be met by the seats in a collision pertain to the seat cushion and backrest, the head restraints, the seat adjustment mechanism and the seat anchors (pertinent regulations: FMVSS 207, 202; ECE-R 17, 25; RREG 74/408, 78/932 and others). One component of active safety is seating comfort. Seats must be designed such that vehicle occupants with different body dimensions do not suffer from driving fatique. Parameters:
– Support of individual body areas (distribution of pressure),
– Lateral support when cornering,
– Seating ambience,
– Freedom of movement so that an occupant may change his sitting position without readjusting the seat,
– Vibrational and damping characteristics (matching of the natural frequency with the excitation frequency band),
– Adjustability of seat cushion, backrest and head restraint.

The above parameters are affected by the following:
– Dimensions and shapes of the upholstery in the seat cushion and backrest,
– Distribution of the spring rates of individual cushioned zones,
– Overall spring rate and damping capacity, of the seat cushions in particular,
– Thermal conductivity and moisture absorption capacity of the covers and upholstery,
– Operation and range of the seat adjustment mechanisms.

Interior trim
A section of trim consists of a dimensionally stable core (sheet steel, sheet aluminum or plastic) with mounting hardware, and energy-absorbing cushion made of foam material (e.g., PUR) and a flexible surface layer (e.g., of PVC or ABS film). One-piece plastic trim sections made of injection-molded thermoplastic material are also used.

The headliner is made either as a stretched liner or finished liner. The materials used must be flame-retardant and must burn slowly (FMVSS 302).

Section through an A-pillar with trim
(Principle)
1 Core, 2 Foam, 3 Film, 4 Windshield, 5 Side window, 6 Door frame.

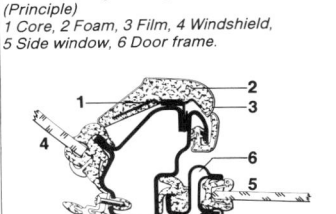

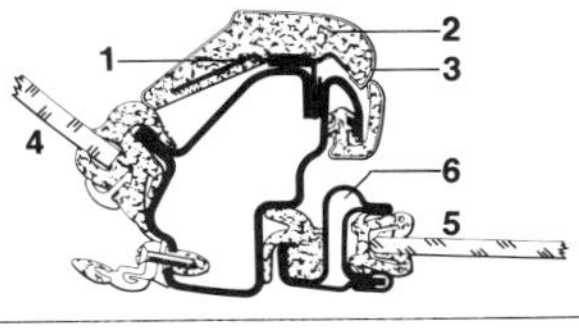

Safety

Active safety:
Prevention of accidents
Passive safety:
Reduction of accident consequences

Active safety
Drive safety is the result of a harmonious suspension design in terms of wheel suspension, springing, steering and braking, and is reflected in optimum dynamic vehicle behavior.

Conditional safety results from keeping the physiological stress that the vehicle occupants are subjected to by vibration, noise, and climatic conditions down to as low a level as possible. It is a significant factor in reducing the possibility of incorrect manœuvers in traffic.

Vibrations within a frequency range of 1 to 25 Hz (stuttering, shaking, etc.) induced by wheels and drive components reach the occupants of the vehicle via the body, seats and steering wheel. The effect of these vibrations is more or less pronounced, depending upon their direction, amplitude and duration.

Noises as acoustical disturbances in and around the vehicle can come from internal sources (engine, transmission, propshafts, axles) or external sources (tire/road noises, wind noises), and are transmitted through the air or the vehicle body. Sound intensity is measured in dB (A) (see also p. 62 f.).

Noise reduction measures are concerned on the one hand with the development of quiet-running components and the insulation of noise sources (e.g., engine encapsulation), and on the other hand with noise damping by means of insulating material or anti-noise materials. Climatic conditions inside the vehicle are primarily influenced by air temperature, air humidity, rate of air flow through the passenger compartment and air pressure (see p. 350 for additional information).

Perceptibility safety
Measures which increase perceptibility safety are concentrated on
– lighting equipment (see p. 668),
– acoustic warning devices (see p. 691),
– direct and indirect view (see p. 650) (Driver's view: The angle of obscuration caused by the A-pillars for both of the driver's eyes – binocular – must not be more than 6 degrees.).

Operating safety
Low driver stress, and thus a high degree of driving safety, requires optimum design of the driver's surroundings with regard to ease of operation of the vehicle controls.

Safety in traffic. *Terms and influencing factors*

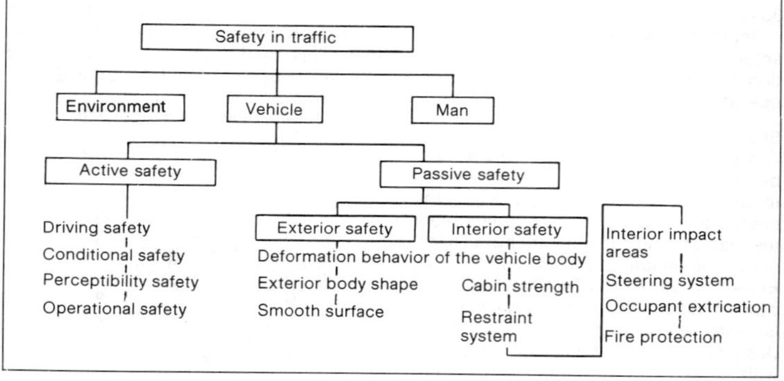

Passive safety

Exterior safety

The term "exterior safety" covers all vehicle-related measures which are designed to minimize the severity of injury to pedestrians and bicycle and motorcycle riders struck by the vehicle in an accident. Those factors which determine exterior safety are:

– Vehicle-body deformation behavior,
– Exterior vehicle-body shape.

The primary objective is to design the vehicle such that its exterior minimizes the consequences of a primary collision (a collision involving persons outside the vehicle and the vehicle itself).

The most severe injuries are sustained by passengers who are hit by the front of the vehicle, whereby the course of the accident greatly depends upon body size. The consequences of collisions involving two-wheeled vehicles and passenger cars can only be slightly ameliorated by passenger-car design due to the often considerable inherent energy component, the two-wheeled vehicle's high seat position and the wide dispersion of contact points. Those design features which can be incorporated into the passenger car are, for example:

– Movable front lamps,
– Recessed windshields wipers,
– Recessed drip rails,
– Recessed door handles.

See also ECE-R 26, RREG 74/483.

Interior safety

The term "interior safety" covers vehicle measures whose purpose is to minimize the accelerations and forces acting on the vehicle occupants in the event of an accident, to provide sufficient survival space and to ensure the operability of those vehicle components critical to the removal of passengers from the vehicle after the accident has occurred. The determining factors for passenger safety are:

– Deformation behavior (vehicle body),
– Passenger-compartment strength, size of the survival space during and after impact,
– Restraint system,
– Impact areas (vehicle interior),
– Steering system,
– Occupant extrication,
– Fire protection.

Laws which regulate interior safety (frontal impact) are:

– Steering system movable toward rear (FMVSS 204, ECE-R 12, RREG 74/297),
– Protection of vehicle occupants in the event of an accident, in particular restraint systems (FMVSS 208, injury criteria),
– Windshield mounting (FMVSS 212),
– Penetration of the windshield by vehicle body components (FMVSS 219),
– Storage-compartment lids (FMVSS 201).

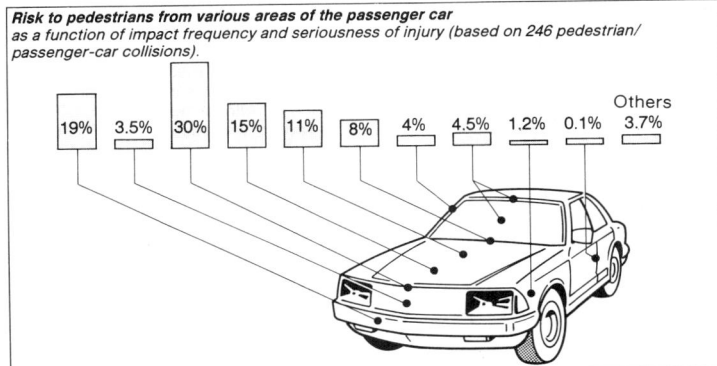

Risk to pedestrians from various areas of the passenger car
as a function of impact frequency and seriousness of injury (based on 246 pedestrian/passenger-car collisions).

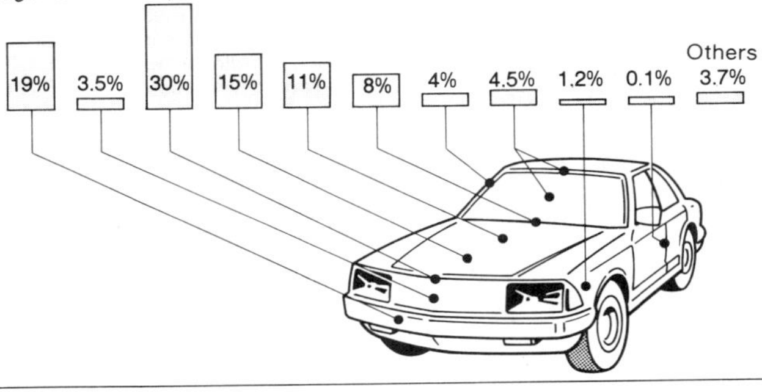

Deformation behavior of vehicle body

Due to the frequency of frontal collisions, an important role is played by the legally stipulated frontal impact test in which a vehicle is driven at a speed of 48.3 km/h (30 mph) into a rigid barrier which is either perpendicular or inclined at an angle of up to 30° relative to the longitudinal axis of the car.

Because 50 % of all frontal collisions in right-hand traffic primarily involve the left-hand half of the front of the vehicle, some manufacturers conduct left asymmetrical front impact tests covering 30 ... 50 % of the vehicle width.

In a frontal collision, kinetic energy is absorbed through deformation of the bumper, the front of the vehicle, and in severe cases the forward section of the passenger compartment (dash area). Axles, wheels (rims) and the engine limit the deformable length. Adequate deformation lengths and displaceable vehicle aggregates are necessary, however, in order to minimize passenger-compartment acceleration. Depending upon vehicle design (body shape, type of drive and engine position), vehicle mass and size, a frontal impact with a barrier at approx. 50 km/h results in permanent deformation in the forward area of 0.4 ... 0.7 m. Damage to the passenger compartment should be minimized. This concerns primarily

– dash area (displacement of steering system, instrument panel, pedals, toe-panel intrusion),

Distribution of accidents by type of collision
Symbolized by test methods yielding equal results

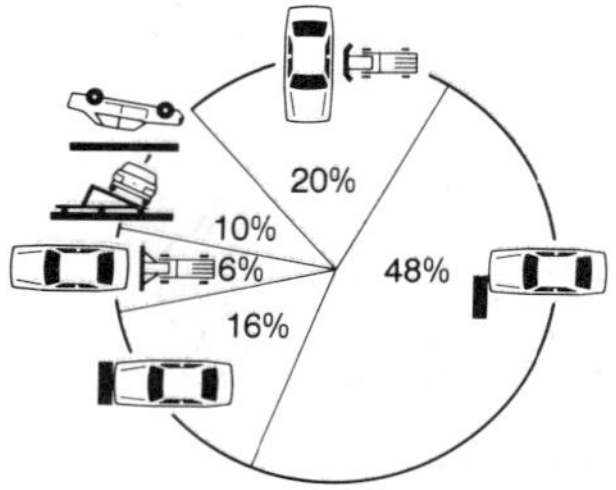

– underbody (lowering or tilting of seats),

– the side structure (ability to open the doors after an accident).

Acceleration measurements and evaluations of high-speed films permit deformation behavior to be precisely analyzed. Dummies of various sizes are used to simulate vehicle occupants, and measure head and chest acceleration as well as forces acting on the thighs. Head acceleration values have been used to determine the head injury criterion (HIC). The comparison of measured values supplied by the dummies with the permissible limit values as per FMVSS 208 (HIC: 1000, chest acceleration: 60 g/3 ms, upper leg force: 10 kN) only provides limited data.

The side impact, as the next most frequent type of accident, places a high risk of injury on the vehicle occupants due to the limited energy absorbing capability of trim and structural components, and the resulting high degree of vehicle interior deformation. The risk of injury is largely influenced by the structural strength of the side of the vehicle (pillar/door joints, top/bottom pillar points), load-carrying capacity of floor cross-members and seats, as well as the design of inside door panels.

In the rear impact test, deformation of the vehicle interior must be minor at most. It should still be possible to open the doors, the edge of the trunk lid should not penetrate the rear window and enter the vehicle interior, and fuel-system integrity must be preserved.

Roof structures are investigated by means of rollover tests and quasi-static car-roof crush tests (FMVSS 216). In addition, at least one manufacturer subjects his vehicles to the inverted vehicle drop test in order to test the dimensional stability of the roof structure (survival space) under extreme conditions (the vehicle falls from a height of 0.5 m onto the left front corner of its roof).

Steering system

Legal requirements (FMVSS 203 and 204) regulate the maximum displace-

Acceleration, speed and distance travelled, of a passenger compartment when impacting a barrier at 50 km/h

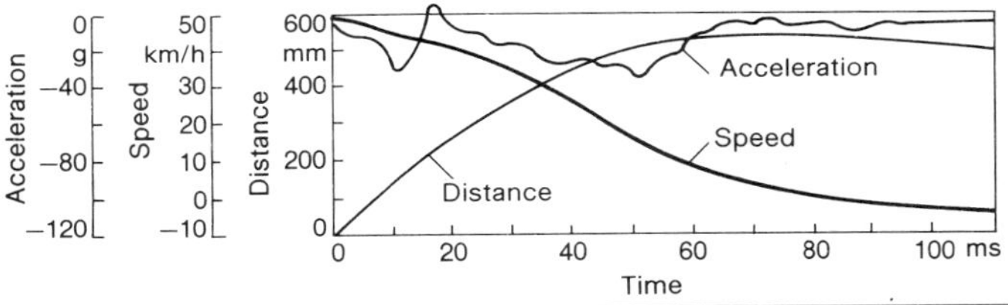

ment of the top end of the steering column toward the driver (max. 127 mm, frontal impact at 48.3 km/h) and the limit of the impact on the steering system (max. 1111 daN at an impact speed of 24.1 km/h). Slotted tubes, corrugated tubes and breakaway universal joints (among others) are used in the design of the lower section of the steering column spindle so that it can be deformed both longitudinally and transversely.

Passenger restraint systems (P. 717)
Automatic seat belt (manual systems)
The most frequently installed three-point seat belt with retractor mechanism ("automatic seat belt") represents a good compromise between effective safety, ease of buckling, comfort and cost. When a specific vehicle-deceleration value is reached, a built-in, quick-response interlock inhibits the seat-belt roller.

Seat-belt tightener systems
Seat-belt tightener systems represent a further development and improvement of three-point automatic seat-belt systems. By reducing seat-belt slack, they eliminate excessive forward passenger movement in serious accidents. This in turn reduces the differential speed between the vehicle and passengers, and thus also reduces the corresponding forces acting on the passengers.

Air bag (automatic systems)
The purpose of the air-bag systems is to eliminate or reduce the impact of the driver against interior vehicle components, in particular the steering wheel.

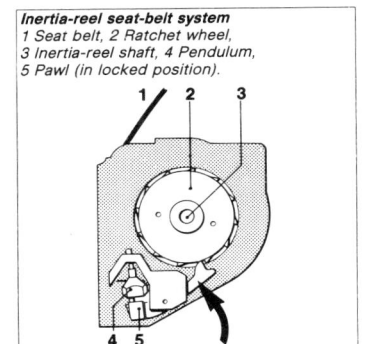

Inertia-reel seat-belt system
1 Seat belt, 2 Ratchet wheel, 3 Inertia-reel shaft, 4 Pendulum, 5 Pawl (in locked position).

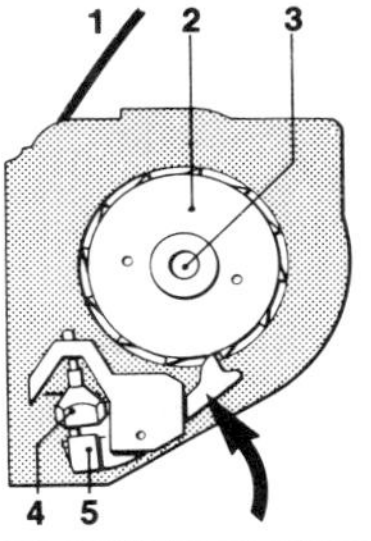

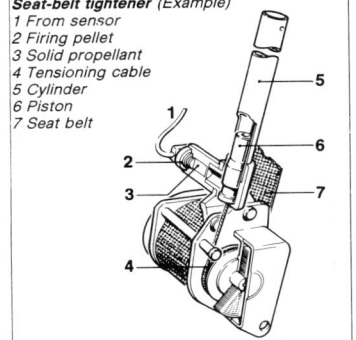

***Seat-belt tightener** (Example)*
1 From sensor
2 Firing pellet
3 Solid propellant
4 Tensioning cable
5 Cylinder
6 Piston
7 Seat belt

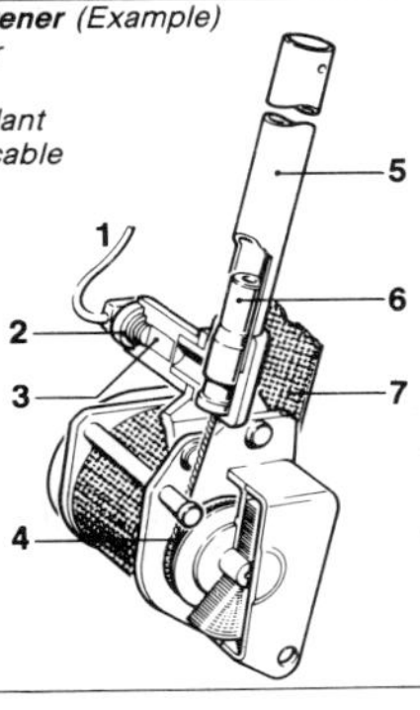

Calculation

Finite-Element Method
The Finite-Element Method (FEM) can be used to calculate static, dynamic and acoustic characteristics of components and complete bodies. In finite-element analysis, a support structure of any degree of complexity is broken down into simple structural elements (beams, shells and solid elements etc.), of which the elastic behavior is known and can be easily defined. These elements are then assembled to form the overall structure, taking into account compatibility conditions. This enables a mathematical model to be constructed in such a manner that it sufficiently corresponds to the actual body in terms of its elastic characteristics. A number of systems are available for practical FE calculation, such as PERMAS, NASTRAN, ABAQUS and DYNA3D.

Advantages of FEM: Characteristics of structures of any level of complexity can be calculated; anisotropic and non-linear material properties can be taken into account; variations can be rapidly examined; tried and tested program systems are available; easy to incorporate into the CAD/CAM chain.

Limits of FEM: Accuracy is dependent on element type and precision of element distribution within the structure; changes in sheet-metal thicknesses and material characteristic values resulting from the deep-drawing process are not taken into account; welding joints cannot be precisely replicated in the model.

Complete body calculation
For the calculation, the bodywork structure is broken down into elements with the required level of precision depending on the problem to be solved (as at 1990: up to approx. 65,000 elements with over 300,000 unknowns). Results under static load are supplied in the form of deformations, stresses and deformation work.

Strength analysis
For individual parts and body areas which are subject to specific stresses caused by factors such as restraint systems or trailer loads, detailed examinations are carried out with the aim of providing proof of sufficient strength or of reducing unacceptable stresses by modifying the design.

Analysis of dynamic behavior
Dynamic analyses are carried out both for the complete body and for the individual components. In these analyses, the natural vibration (frequencies, forms of vibration) and the system's response to periodic or generally time-dependent excitation is determined. In this way, critical resonances can be

Calculation of a vehicle body structure

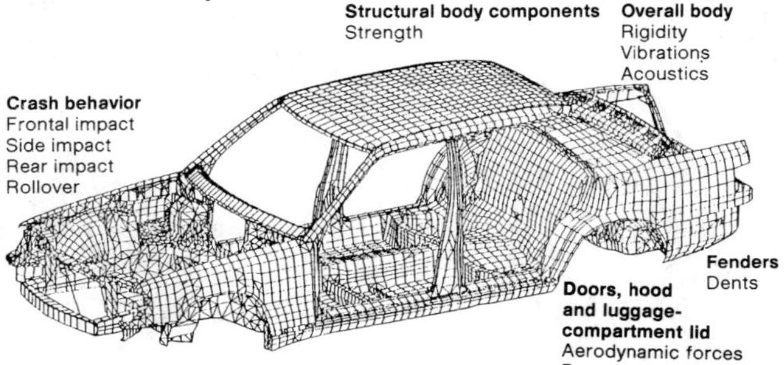

The structural analysis process using the finite-element method

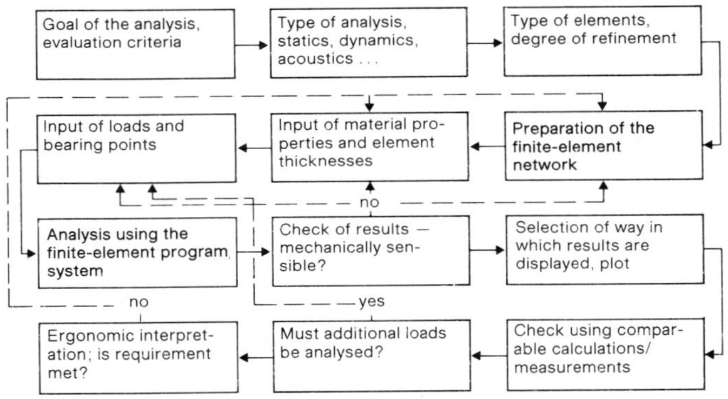

identified and the loads which determine operational integrity can be defined.

For the examination of ride comfort and acoustical behavior in the vehicle interior, FE models of the chassis, engine, doors etc, as well as a model of the interior, are added to the body model.

Analysis of crash behavior
Accident tests carried out by automobile manufacturers (frontal, rear and side impacts, rollover and drop tests) as well as traffic accidents, are dynamic, to a large degree non-linear processes which cannot be described using the current FE programs. Special FE program systems (e.g., DYNA3D, PAM-CRASH) have been developed for numerical simulation of these processes, and are providing increasingly successful results in the field. These systems include analysis of severe plastic deformations as well as recording of the contact areas arising between various vehicle parts during crash processes.

Recycling, environmental protection
Significant progress has been made by the automobile manufacturers in maintaining clean water and air, preventing noise pollution and recycling raw materials:
– The recycling quota for metallic materials is 95 %.
– The recycling quota for plastics is approximately 5...10 %. In cooperation with the chemical industry, intensive efforts are being made to improve this figure, and prospects for solving the problem are highly promising.
– Exhaust-gas purification and recovery of high-value catalyst materials (rhodium, platinum).
– Recycling of battery materials such as lead.
– Chlorofluorocarbons (CFC's) are no longer used as expanding agents in the manufacture of plastics, and CFC-free refrigerant is about to be introduced.
– Solvents for body degreasing are almost entirely free of chlorinated hydrocarbons; water-based paint is used in dip-priming.
– Water-based paints for top coating are in development.
– Reprocessing of manufacturing agents, e.g., oil, coolant, antifreeze.
– Recycling of some 60 % of so-called residual materials (e.g., scrap metal, waste paper, leather, textile and wood waste).

Vehicle bodies, commercial vehicles

Commercial vehicles

Commercial vehicles are used for the safe and economical transportation of persons and goods, whereby the economic efficiency is determined by the ratio of usable space to overall vehicle volume, and of useful load to laden vehicle weight. Dimensions and weights are limited by legal regulations.

From the design concept viewpoint, a distinction must be made between cab-over-engine (COE) and cab-behind-engine (CBE) vehicles.

A wide variety of vehicle types meet the demands of local and long-distance transportation, as well as on those encountered on building sites and in special applications.

Delivery trucks and vans

These are light-duty trucks (2 ... 7 t) used in the transportation of persons and in local goods distribution. In fulfilling this function stringent demands are made on the vehicle in terms of mobility, maneuverability, performance and operating comfort. The design concepts are based on front-mounted engine, front or rear-wheel drive, independent suspension or rigid axle

Commercial vehicles	
All-terrain vehicle	
Delivery truck/van	
Truck	
Road train	
High-capacity road train	
Tractor-trailer rig	
Bus	
Agricultural vehicle	
Off road, construction dump truck	

Delivery trucks and vans	
Van	
Double-cab low-bed truck	
High-bed flatbed truck	
Chassis	

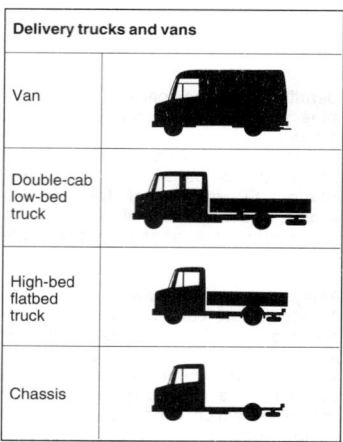

Delivery-truck load-bearing unit

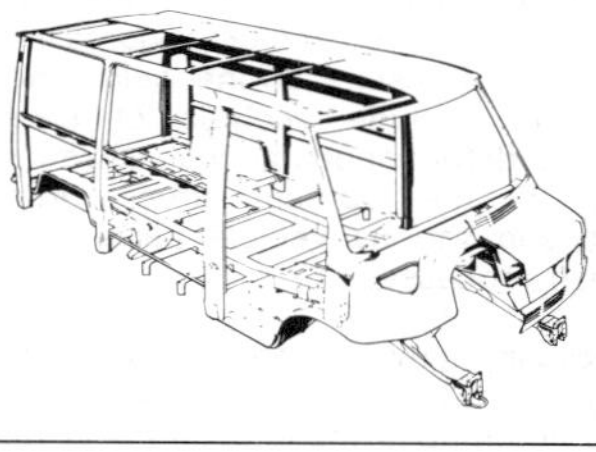

and, from 3.5 t laden weight, twin tires on the rear axle.

The product range includes enclosed-body multi-purpose vehicles and vans, as well as low-bed and high-bed platform-body vehicles with special superstructures and double cabs.

In small delivery trucks and vans, the bodies form an integral load-bearing unit together with the chassis.

The body and chassis frameworks consist of sheet-metal pressed elements and flanged profiles. Platform-body vehicles have a ladder-type frame with open or closed side members and cross members as the primary load-bearing structure.

Medium and heavy-duty trucks and tractor vehicles

In this sector the division between load-bearing chassis and partially load-sharing bodies has become prevalent. In most cases the engine is at the front. It is seldom fitted as an underfloor engine between the axles. Drive is via the twin-tire rear axle. For building-site (off-road) use with high traction requirements, all-wheel drive with longitudinal and cross-lock technology is applied.

Type of truck undercarriage (see Figure below):
N x Z/L
N = Number of wheels
Z = Number of driven wheels
L = Number of steered wheels

Normal chassis have leaf- or pneumatically-sprung rigid front and rear axles. Pneumatic suspension facilitates the simple mounting and removal of interchangeable bodies and unhitching of semi-trailers. Three-axle vehicles (6 x 2) are fitted with either a leading or a trailing axle (in front of or behind the driven axle) to increase the useful load. High-traction 6 x 4 vehicles for use on building sites have a dual-axle configuration with axle-load compensation and center bearing point.

Chassis frames

The chassis frame is the commercial vehicle's actual load-bearing element. It is designed as a ladder-type frame, consisting of side and cross members. The choice of profiles decides the level of torsional stiffness. Torsionally flexible frames are preferred in medium and heavy-duty trucks because they enable the suspension to comply better with uneven terrain. Torsionally stiff frames are more suitable for smaller delivery vehicles and vans.

Apart from the force introduction points, critical points in the chassis-frame design are the side-member and cross-member junctions. Special gusset plates or pressed cross-member sections form a broad connection basis. The junctions are riveted, bolted and welded. "Fish belly" frames with higher side members between the axles provide greater bending stiffness. Additional reinforcement at specific points is provided by [-shaped or L-shaped inserts.

Driver's cab

There are a variety of cab designs available depending on the vehicle concept. In delivery vehicles and vans, low, convenient entrances are an advantage, whereas in long-distance transport space and comfort are more important. Modular design concepts allow for short, medium

Types of truck undercarriage (examples)

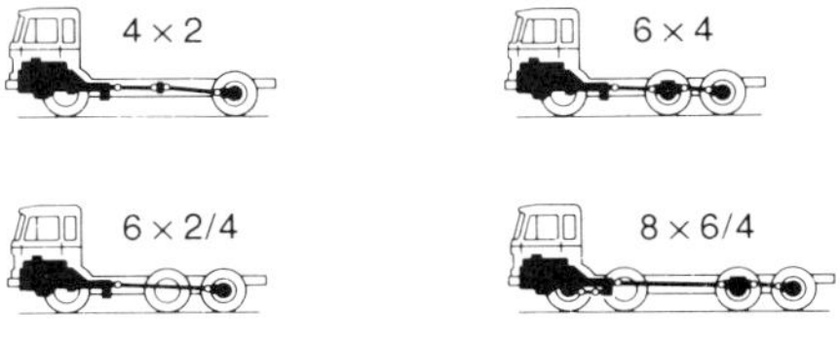

and long cab versions while retaining the same front, rear and doors.

In the case of cab-over-engine (COE) vehicles, the steering system is positioned right at the front of the vehicle. The engine is located under the cab or underneath a hood in the vehicle interior between the driver and the co-driver. The entrance is positioned (somewhat uncomfortably) in front of or above the front axle. A mechanical (pretensioned torsion bar) or hydraulic cab-tipping mechanism ensures good access to the engine.

In the conventional cab-behind-engine (CBE) truck, the engine/transmission assembly is mounted ahead of the actual cab interior beneath a steel or plastic hood (which is usually tiltable for reasons of accessibility). The driver enters the cab behind the front axle.

Bodies

Specific body structures such as flatbeds, standard vans, box vans, dump-truck deep-beds, tankers, concrete mixers etc. permit the economical and efficient transportation of a wide variety of goods and materials. Connection between body and load-bearing chassis frame is effected in part by means of auxiliary frames with non-positive or positive attachments.

Road trains and tractor-trailer rigs are used in long-distance transport. As the size of the transportation unit increases, the costs relative to the freight volume decrease.

Load volume is increased by reducing the empty spaces between cab, cargo area and trailer (high-capacity road train). Advantages of tractor-trailer operation are the greater uninterrupted loading length of the cargo area and the shorter inoperative times of the tractor units.

Measures to improve aerodynamics, such as front and side trim on the vehicle and specially adapted air deflectors from the cab to the body, are applied to minimise fuel consumption.

Buses

Buses are used for passenger transportation. The main design aspects are: design layout dependent on area of use; safety; environmental tolerability; good ride and springing comfort, and high maintenance of value.

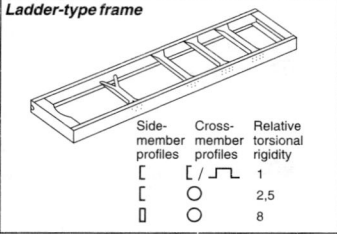

Truck assemblies
1 Body, 2 Axle, 3 Chassis frame, 4 Transmission, 5 Engine, 6 Cab.

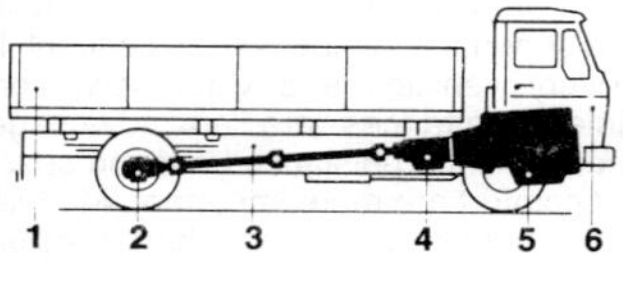

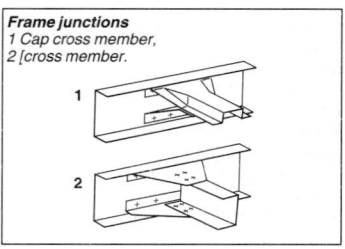

Frame junctions
1 Cap cross member, 2 [cross member.

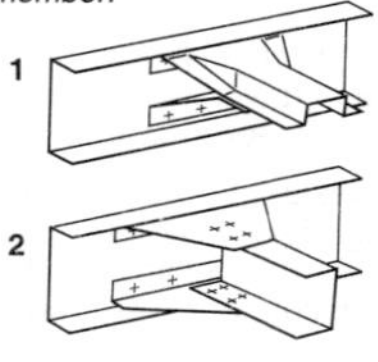

Ladder-type frame

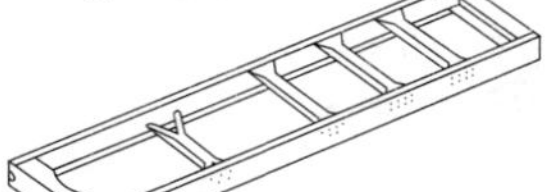

Side-member profiles	Cross-member profiles	Relative torsional rigidity
[	[/ ⊓	1
[	O	2,5
▯	O	8

Cab
1 Cab over engine (COE), 2 Cab-behind-engine (CBE)

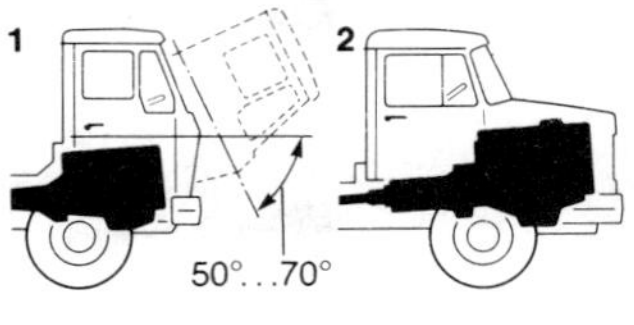

Microbuses

Microbuses carry up to 25 passengers. The vehicles are assembled on ladder-type chassis or are developed from delivery trucks or vans. Soft main suspension and elastic supports between the body and the chassis provide a high degree of ride comfort.

City buses

These are equipped with seating and standing room for scheduled routes. The short intervals between stops in local traffic necessitate rapid passenger turnover, which means wide doors and a low vehicle floor (300....700 mm).

Main data for the standard public bus:

Vehicle length approx. 11.8 m
Laden weight approx. 17.5 t
Number of seats 38 to 44
Total passenger capacity approx. 108 persons.

Doubledecker buses (approx. 130 persons) and articulated (approx. 185 persons) buses provide increased transport capacity.

Bus types	
Micro-bus	
Standard public bus	
Double-decker public bus	
Articulated bus	
Overland bus	
Tour bus (long-distance coach)	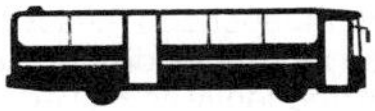

Integral bus body

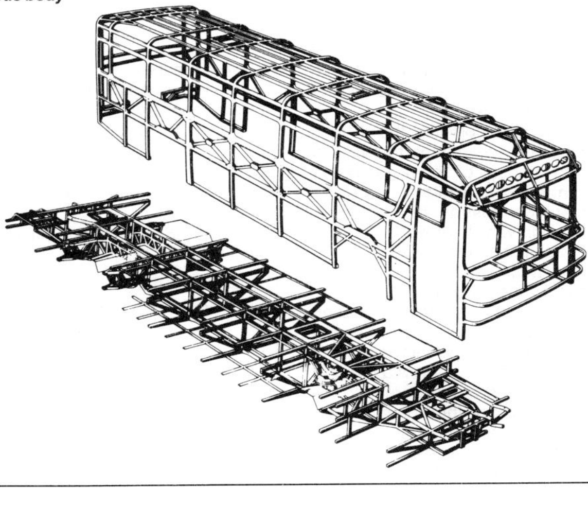

Overland buses
With standing room in the aisle and small compartments for luggage, they represent a compromise between the city bus and the tour bus.

Tour buses (long-distance coaches)
Tour buses are designed to provide a comfortable ride over medium and long distances. They range from the low, two-axle standard bus to the doubledecker luxury coach with a separate cabin for the driver.

Body structure
Light design based on an integral body. The body and base frames, which are firmly welded together, consist of pressed grid-type support elements and rectangular tubes.

Undercarriage
The horizontal or vertical rear-mounted engine drives the rear axle. Pneumatic suspension at all axles permits ride-level stabilization and a high degree of ride comfort. Independent suspension at the front axle as well as disc brakes and retarders are frequently employed.

Passive safety in commercial vehicles

Passive safety is intended to limit the consequences of accidents and to protect other road users. Systematic recording of accidents as well as accident tests with complete commercial vehicles assist in devising safety measures.

In the event of a collision, the driver's cab and the passenger compartment must maintain the amount of room necessary for occupant survival, while at the same time deceleration must not be excessive. Depending upon vehicle design, there are a variety of solutions to this problem.

In delivery trucks and vans, front-section design is energy-absorbing as in passenger cars. Despite short deformation routes and the high level of released energy, physiologically permissible limits are not exceeded in the event of a 50 km/h frontal impact against a rigid barrier.

In the case of trucks, the side members extend up to the front bumper and can absorb high longitudinal forces. Such passive-safety measures are based on accident analyses and are intended to improve the structural design of the cab. Static and dynamic stress and impact tests on the front and rear surfaces of the cab, as well as on its roof, simulate the stresses involved in a frontal impact and in accidents in which the vehicle overturns or rolls over, as well as in which the load shifts.

Statistical analyses have proved that the bus is one of the safest means of passenger transportation. Static roof-load tests and dynamic overturning tests provide evidence of body strength. The use of flame-retardant and self-extinguishing materials for the interior of the vehicle minimises the risk of fire.

Because road traffic involves many different kinds of vehicles, collisions between light and heavy vehicles are unavoidable. As a result of the differences in vehicle mass, and incompatibility in terms of vehicle geometry and structural stiffness, the risk of injury in the lighter vehicle is greater.

The formulas below define the change in speed during a normal (non-oblique) plastic impact for frontal or rear collisions between two vehicles:

Vehicle 1 $\Delta c_1 = \dfrac{\mu \cdot \Delta v}{1+\mu}$

Vehicle 2 $\Delta c_2 = \dfrac{\Delta v}{1+\mu}$

where $\mu = m_2/m_1$

m_1, m_2 = masses of the vehicles involved,
v = relative speed prior to impact.

Side, front and rear underride guards assist in reducing the dangerous situations in which the lighter vehicle drives under the heavier vehicle when a collision occurs, and thus help to protect other road users.

Rear underride guard for commercial vehicles

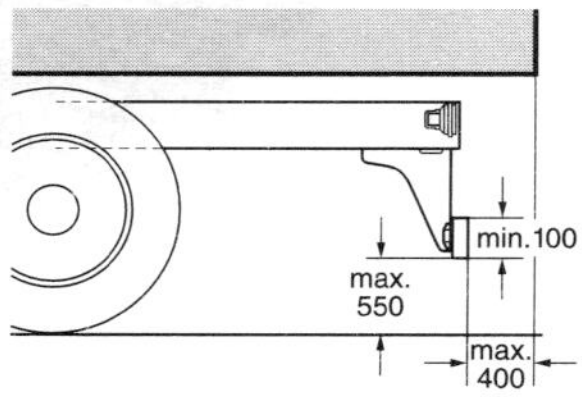

Noise reduction in commercial vehicles

Measures taken in the vehicle to lower the level of noise serve to reduce traffic noise in general and improve ride comfort. By means of noise-source analysis, the contribution of the individual sound sources to the overall noise is examined, and the effectiveness of noise-emission-reduction measures is determined.

The starting points for noise reduction at source are low engine revs, intervention in the combustion process, low-noise gear teeth in transmissions and axles, and resonance-free interaction of all engine components, as well as of the exhaust gas and induction systems.

Appropriate connection elements between the noise sources on the one hand and the frame, body and cab on the other, can restrict the propagation of structure-borne noise. Such measures are supported by flexible suspension using composite rubber and metal parts which effectively damp structure-borne noise from the engine, transmission, drive shafts, axle assemblies, cab mounts etc. Covering and encapsulation of the noise sources are effective secondary measures.

Engine-attached encapsulation has not become an established method of noise reduction. In trucks, delivery trucks and vans, a staged partial chassis-attached encapsulation of the engine/transmission assembly is common, as is full body-attached encapsulation in rear-engine buses.

With purely vehicle-attached measures the sound pressure level is reduced by 10 dB(A) in acceleration drive-by tests, which means that the definition limit for low-noise commercial vehicles of 80 dB(A) is attained (Regulations: see "Acoustics", page 62). At a speed of over approx. 50 km/h on the flat, tire noise is the dominant factor. The random combinations which occur between road surface and tire, cover a range of over 7 dB(A) for drive-by noise. Current developments are aiming at the production of "whispering" asphalt and low-noise tires.

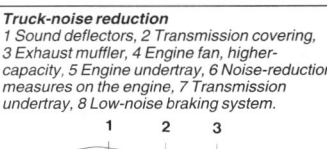

Truck noise-source analysis
1 Total noise, 2 Engine, 3 Exhaust system, 4 Fan, 5 Air intake, 6 Rest.

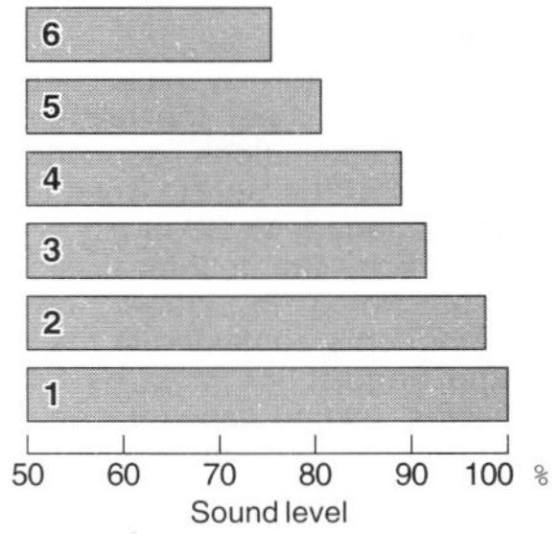

Truck-noise reduction
1 Sound deflectors, 2 Transmission covering, 3 Exhaust muffler, 4 Engine fan, higher-capacity, 5 Engine undertray, 6 Noise-reduction measures on the engine, 7 Transmission undertray, 8 Low-noise braking system.

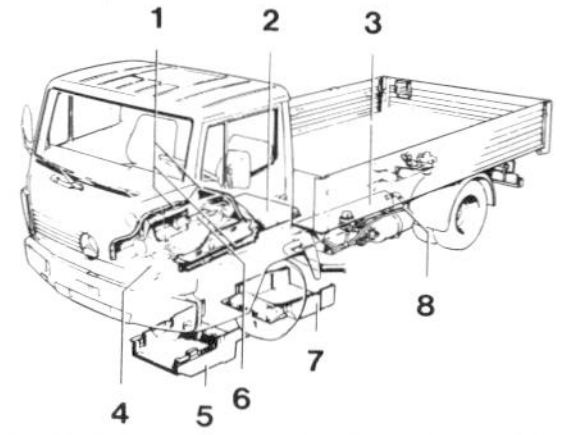

Commercial-vehicle drive-by noise
1 Road/tire scatter range.

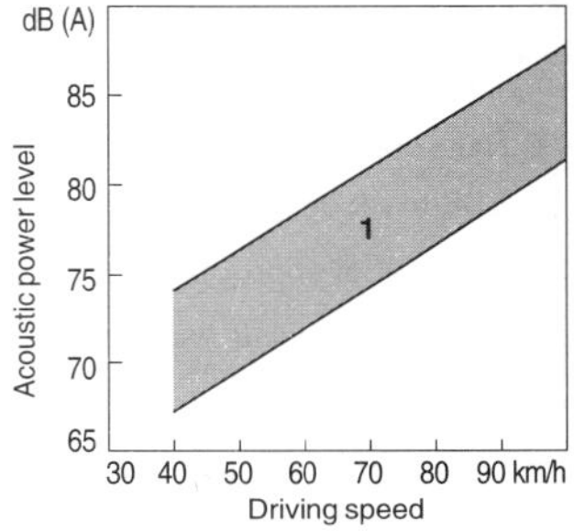

Lighting

Legal regulations

Germany
In Germany, motor-vehicle lighting equipment must meet the design and operating specifications contained in §§ 49a to 54 of the StVZO Road Licensing Regulations (FMVSS/CUR).

An addition, the technical requirements pertaining to lighting devices and components contained in the Road Licensing Regulations must be fulfilled during type testing (acceptance testing) in accordance with § 22a. Other European countries have similar national specifications.

Europe
In Europe, all vehicular illumination and signalling devices are to be installed in accordance with the regulations contained in ECE-R448 (Jurisdiction: ECE Geneva) and/or 76/756/EC (EC Brussels).

USA
Standard FVMSS 108 (Federal Motor Vehicle Safety Standard) applies in the USA. Its contents correspond to the European regulations. The acceptance requirements for the individual devices are laid down in the SAE specifications for photometric and technological tests.

Marks of approval
A different mark of approval has been specified for each lighting function; these marks must appear on the lens of the lighting device.
Examples:

~K National mark of approval

(E1) ECE mark of approval

e 1 EC mark of approval.

The number 1 following each letter indicates that approval was granted in Germany.

Photometric terms and definitions
(See p. 131 for further terms and definitions).

Range of a headlamp
That distance at which the luminous intensity of the headlamp beam has a specified value, e.g. "1 lux range".

Geometric range of a headlamp
This is the distance to the horizontal portion of the light-dark cutoff on the road surface. A low-beam inclination of 1 %, or 10 cm per 10 m, results in a geometric range equalling 100 × headlamp mounting height (as measured between road surface and the center of the reflector).

Visual range
Distance at which an object within the luminous distribution of the field of vision remains visible. Visual range is influenced by the following factors: shape, size and reflectance of objects, type of road surface, headlamp design and cleanliness, and the physiological condition of the eyes. Therefore, numerical values cannot be specified for visual range. The visual range, for example, can drop to below 20 m under extremely unfavorable conditions (with RH traffic, object on left side of a wet road), and can exceed 100 m under very favorable conditions (object on right side of road).

Signal identification distance
Maximum distance at which optical signals (e.g. fog warning lamp) can be identified under misty or foggy conditions.

Glare, physiological
Physiological glare results in a measurable reduction in the driver's ability to see caused by sources of glare, i.e. a reduced visual range as two vehicles approach one another.

Glare, psychological (Discomfort glare)
Psychological glare occurs when a source of glare causes "discomfort" without reducing the driver's ability to see. Pyschological glare is assessed according to a scale which ranges from comfortable to uncomfortable.

Reflector focal length
Reflectors for headlamps and other lamps usually have a parabolic shape. The focal length f (distance between

the vertex of the parabola and the focal point) lies between 15 and 40 mm.

Reflector illuminated area
The parallel projection of the entire reflector opening onto a transverse plane. This plane is usually perpendicular to the direction of travel.

Effective luminous flux
That portion of the luminous flux of the filament which can act via the reflective or refractive components of a lighting device (e.g., via the headlamp reflector to the road surface). A short reflector focal length makes efficient use of the incandescent filament because the reflector broadly encompasses the bulb, and can therefore convert a greater part of the luminous flux into a beam of light.

Parabolic reflector
F Focal point, S Vertex, f Focal length

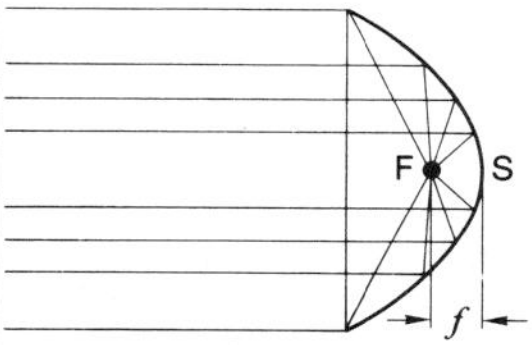

Angles of geometric visibility
Those angles, measured with respect to the device axis, at which the entire lighted lens area of the device must be visible.

Table 1. Angles of geometric visibility and luminous-intensity values for lighting devices on the motor vehicle

Direction from which vehicle is seen	Angle of geometric visibility to the device axis				Luminous intensity in the reference axis (cd)	
	Outside	Inside	Above	Below	min.	max.
From the front						
Low-beam headlamp	45°	10°	15°	10°	–	–
High-beam headlamp	5°	5°	5°	5°	–	–
Fog lamp	45°	10°	5°	5°	–	–
Side-marker lamp	80°	45°	15°	15°4)	4	60
Front turn-signal lamp	80°	45°	15°	15°4)	1751) (250 or 400)	700
Daylight running lamp (S, SF only)	80°	45°	15°	15°	300	800
From the rear						
Rear turn-signal lamp	80°	45°	15°	15°4)	50	200
Auxiliary side turn-signal lamp, visible from rear	5 ... 60°	–	15°	15°4)	0.62)	2002)
Tail lamp	80°	45°	15°	15°4)	4	12
Clearance lamp	80°	–	5°	20°	4 4	60 to front 12 to rear
Stop lamp	45°	45°	15°	15°4)	40	100
Supplemental high-mounted stop lamp	–	–	–	–	40	100
Fog warning lamp	25°	25°	5°	5°	150	300
Backup lamp 1	45°	45°	15°	5°	80	600 (300)3)
Backup lamp 2	45°	30°	15°	5°	80	600 (300)3)
From the front and rear						
Parking lamp	45°	–	15°	15°4)	2 2	60 to front 30 to rear

1) Applies to a distance of > 40 mm between the edges of the light emission areas of turn-signal indicator and headlamp, or turn-signal indicator and fog lamp. A luminous intensity of 250 cd is required when distance 20 ≤ 40 mm, and 400 cd at < 20 mm.
2) Throughout the entire range of geometric visibility.
3) Max. 300 cd above a horizontal line passing through the reference axis, max. 600 cd below the line.
4) Only 5° at installation height < 750 mm.

Terms and definitions relating to device design[1])

Grouped design
Common housing, but with individual lenses and bulbs. Example: multiple-compartment lamp at the rear of the vehicle which fulfills various lighting functions.

Combined design
Common housing and bulb, but with individual lenses. Example: combined tail lamp and license-plate lamp.

Nested design
Common housing and lens, but with individual bulbs. Example: headlamp with built-in side-marker lamp.

Main headlamps, European system

Low beam

The density of today's traffic has greatly reduced the use of high-beam headlamps. The low beam is therefore most often used for driving. The past several years have seen significant improvements in low-beam headlamps:

– Introduction of asymmetrical low-beam headlamps with an extended visual range at the front-seat passenger's side of the road

– Approval of various types of halogen lamps with an increase of the luminous intensity at the road surface of 50 ... 80 %.

The "Litronic" gaseous-discharge headlamp (with arc) supplies more than twice as much light as a comparable halogen unit.

All headlamp units employed up to 1990 used a low-beam light source which was mounted forward of the parabolic reflector's focal point, endowing the light with a post-reflection inclination toward the reflector's axis.

A cap keeps the lower portion of the beam of light from hitting the lower area of the reflector and being reflected in an upward plane. The edge of the cap appears as a light/dark cutoff on the road surface. A "dark above/light below" pattern produces a distribution of light which yields long-range visibility in all traffic situations. Glare in

Low-beam *(pattern of reflection)*
1 Low-beam filament, 2 Cap

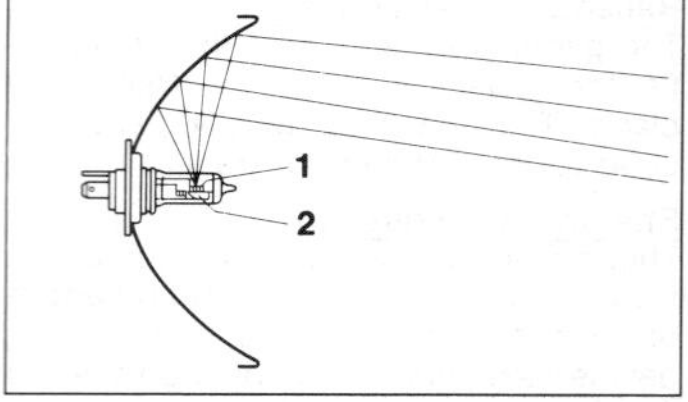

Low-beam light/dark cutoff
The cap within the bulb limits the upper portion of the light beam.

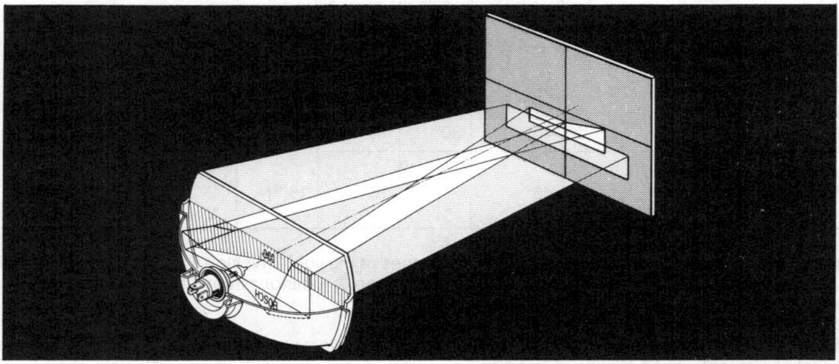

[1]) All illustrations and diagrams refer to right-hand traffic.

the direction of oncoming traffic can be kept within limits while at the same time achieving a high luminous intensity below the light/dark cutoff.

There are also reflectors on the market which use the lower section of the reflector. On these, the light source lies to the rear of the focal point (relative to the lower section). The cap consists only of fins on each side of the light source; some special applications dispense with the cap entirely.

The light/dark cutoff contrast, on the other hand, must not exceed an average value for practical driving reasons. For example, during pitching motions of the vehicle, an extremely sharp light/dark cutoff produces unfavorable dynamic contrast on the road surface.

In addition to achieving a maximum visual range and minimum glare, the distribution of light close to the vehicle must also meet certain requirements. It must be possible to navigate curves safely, i.e. the distribution of light must extend over the right-hand and left-hand edges of the road surface. It is not possible to achieve constant luminance on the road surface throughout the entire area between the vehicle and the geometric headlamp range. It is possible, however, to greatly reduce contrasts in luminance within the illuminated portion of the road surface. In addition to the use of asymmetrical projection patterns, and halogen and gaseous-discharge lamps, changes in reflector size and shape can greatly help to improve visual range and low-beam balance.

Reflector size
Increasing the reflector size improves the low-beam efficiency. Geometric range is increased by mounting the headlamp as high as possible. On the other hand, the front of the vehicle must be kept low for aerodynamic reasons.

Under these conditions, larger reflectors (low-beam efficiency) can only be achieved at the cost of wider headlamps. For photometric reasons it is of advantage that the horizontal diameter of the reflector is the determining factor for the achievable luminous intensity in the form of flat radiation. If the width of the reflector is doubled from 130 to 260 mm, the luminous intensity at the right-hand edge of the road surface at a distance of 50 m from the vehicle is roughly doubled, thereby greatly improving the visual range.

Luminous intensity at the front-seat passenger's side of the road *as a function of the horizontal reflector diameter*

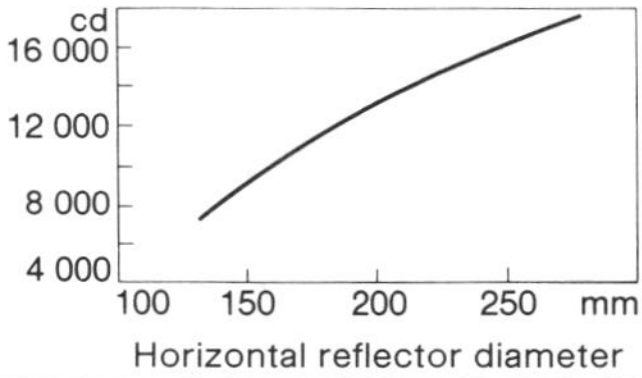

Reflectors of the same size also perform differently depending upon their focal lengths. Shorter focal lengths produce broader beams with better near-field and lateral illumination. This is particularly advantageous on cornering. When mounted on the vehicle, however, these deeper reflectors take up more room.

Stepped reflectors
Stepped reflectors consist of paraboloid sections of different focal lengths,

Light distribution on the road surface produced by headlamps of different sizes and shapes *(as seen from above)*
The advantage of wider headlamps is clearly evident.

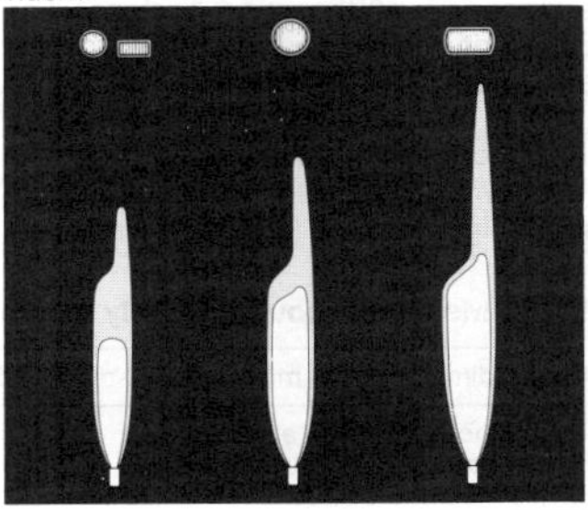

Homofocal reflector
1 Basic reflector, 2 Supplementary reflector

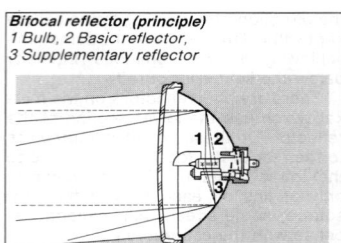

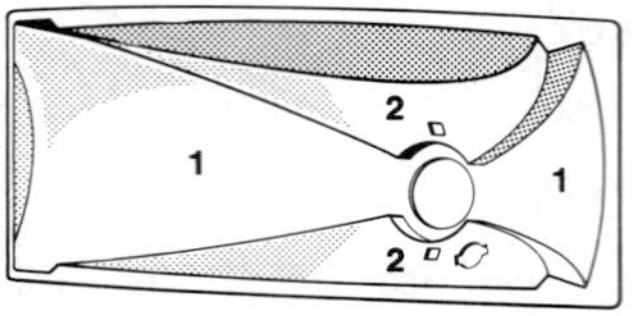

Bifocal reflector (principle)
1 Bulb, 2 Basic reflector,
3 Supplementary reflector

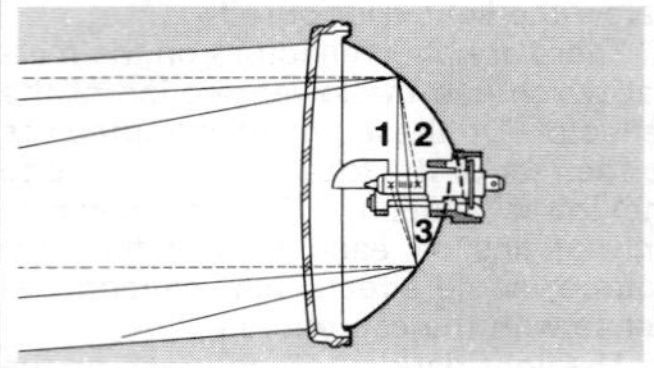

and exhibit the advantages of deep reflectors in spite of their reduced depth.

Homofocal reflectors
The supplemental sectors of the homofocal reflector with a common focal point have a shorter focal length than the basic reflector, and thus measurably increase the effective luminous flux. The light from the supplemental reflectors only improves near-field and lateral illumination, and does not increase the range of the headlamp. The unit's lamp incorporates two light sources (low and high beam). The reflector is made of plastic due to the large steps between the individual reflector sections.

Bifocal reflectors
The bifocal reflector (reflector sections with different focal points) additionally takes advantage of the lower reflector area which normally receives no light. Here, a parabolic sector is positioned such that the light which impinges on this area is also reflected downward in the direction of the road surface. The focal point should be located in front of the filament. The additional light gained by using this reflector principle is also only effective in the near field.

The bifocal reflector's lamp employs a single light source (low beam); its use is thus restricted to application in four-headlamp systems.

Variable-focus (stepless) reflectors
CAD programs make it possible to design variable-focus reflectors (VFR) employing non-parabolic sections to achieve a smooth-transition geometry. The shape of the reflector is optimized to correspond to a specified light-distribution pattern as projected onto a screen. The focal point of the various reflector zones can change its position relative to the light source. Application of this principle makes it possible to employ the entire reflector surface to achieve virtually any desired light-distribution pattern.

PES headlamps
The PES (Poly-Ellipsoid System) headlamp system with imaging optics provides lighting improvements in comparison with conventional headlamps. A light-opening area of only 28 cm^2 permits light distributions of the kind achieved with previous large-area headlamps. This is achieved with a CAD-calculated elliptic reflector and projection optics. An imaging screen projects precisely defined cutoffs, either with a high degree of sharpness, or with intentional lack of sharpness, or with any desired characteristics.

Table 2. Mean luminous intensity at the point of maximum high-beam intensity

Reflector dimensions in mm	130 dia	165 dia	180 dia	200 × 140	220 × 140	240 × 130
Mean luminous intensity at point of max. intensity at the high-beam 25 m distance	60 lx	75 lx	80 lx	90 lx	100 lx	110 lx

PES headlamps with an overall height of approx. 80 mm can form a lighting-strip unit together with conventional high beam, side-marker lamps and PES fog lamps.

The PES-PLUS concept is intended for use in taller units (approx. 130 mm). PES-PLUS makes use of the light which is projected against the screen and is thus wasted on the 80 mm PES unit. This additional light is projected over a section of the reflector below the screen, improving illumination directly forward of the vehicle.

Litronic

The Litronic (Light-Electronic) headlamp system incorporates a xenon-filled, "D-1" gaseous-discharge lamp as its central element. The unit combines a high degree of illumination with minimal space requirements, allowing aerodynamic styling of the vehicle's front end.

The 35-W "D 1" lamp's arc emits a luminous flux which is twice as intense as that produced by the H 1 lamp. The color temperature (4500 K) is higher, and it contains — similar to sunlight — relatively large components of green and blue. Full illumination, corresponding to approx. 90 lm/W, is produced once the quarz element reaches its operating temperature of almost 1000 K. A current of up to 2.6 A (continuous operation: approx. 0.4 A) can be applied to obtain immediate light. The service life of 1500 h corresponds to the average total operating time to be expected during the vehicle's life. The fact that failure is not sudden, as in filament units, facilitates early diagnosis and replacement.

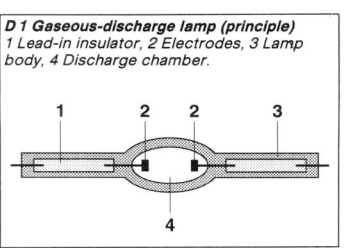

D 1 Gaseous-discharge lamp (principle)
1 Lead-in insulator, 2 Electrodes, 3 Lamp body, 4 Discharge chamber.

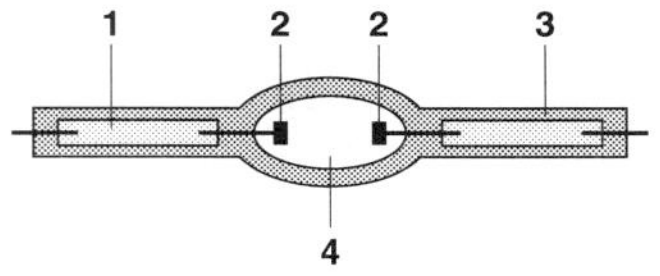

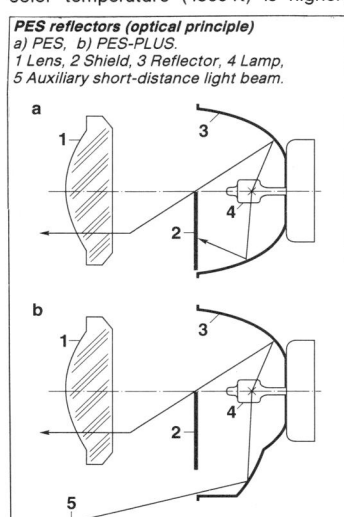

PES reflectors (optical principle)
a) PES, b) PES-PLUS.
1 Lens, 2 Shield, 3 Reflector, 4 Lamp,
5 Auxiliary short-distance light beam.

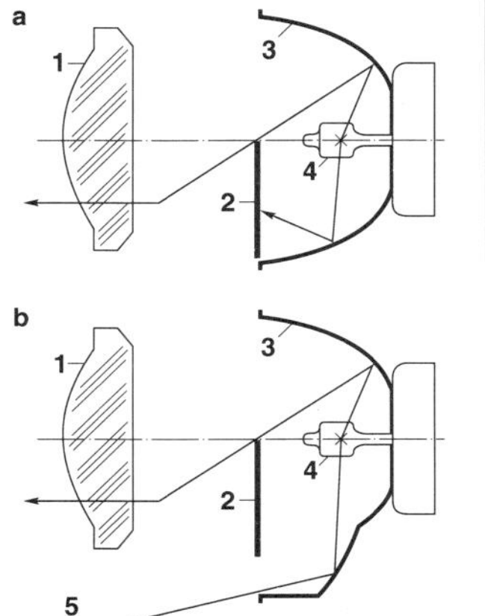

Light distribution (at road-surface level)
a) PES H 1 lamp, b) Litronic PES D 1 lamp.

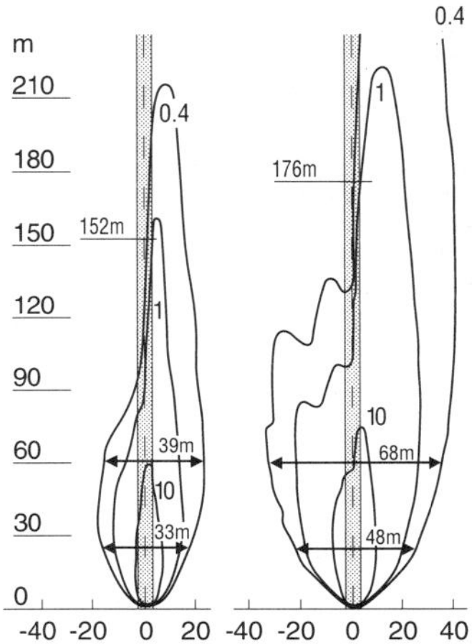

Electronic ballast unit

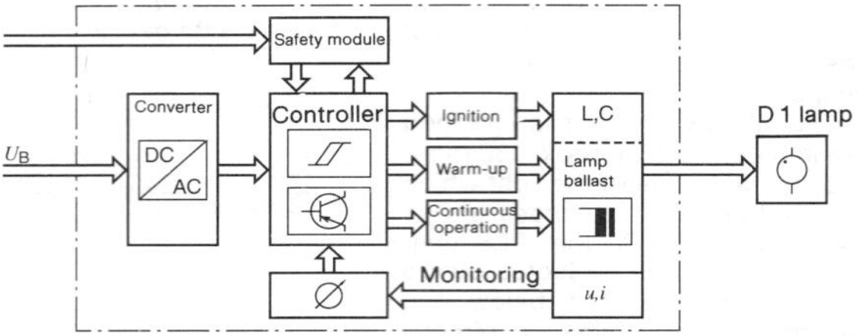

An integral part of the headlamp is the electronic ballast unit (EVG) responsible for lamp control and monitoring. Its chief functions are:

— ignition of the gaseous discharge (6 ... 12 kV),

— regulation of current supply in the warmup phase, and

— demand-oriented supply in static operation (AC voltage, $f < 10$ kHz).

Should the lamp go out (for instance, due to a momentary lapse in the voltage supply from the vehicle system), reignition is spontaneous and automatic. The headlamp switches off in response to damage in the front-glass area or when a lamp connection is exposed, thus ensuring protection against inadvertent contact and UV exposure.

Litronic is being introduced as the low-beam unit in four-headlamp systems. Reflective and PES designs are an open option. Dispensing in part with "miniaturization" results in substantial enhancements in road illumination, providing the peripheries of curves and the edges of wide roads with the kind of illumination that halogen units have hitherto afforded on straight stretches of road. Concentrated-beam halogen high-beam units are incorporated in the circuits for simultaneous operation.

High beam

The high beam always emanates from a light source situated at the reflector's focal point, causing the light to be reflected so as to exit in the direction of the reflector's axis.

The luminous intensity which can be achieved axially by the high beam depends upon the illuminated area of the reflector. Table 2 gives general figures for attainable luminous intensity. In the case of larger reflectors, the luminous intensity has been intentionally limited by the optical design of the lens in order to comply with legal requirements.

Designs

In accordance with regulations which are in force worldwide, every dual-tracked road vehicle must have 2 low-beam headlamps and at least 2 high-beam headlamps (4 high-beam headlamps are also permissible).

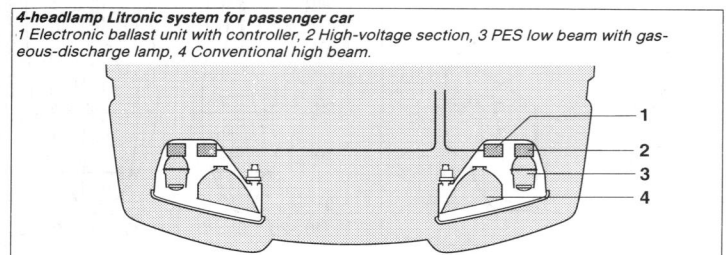

4-headlamp Litronic system for passenger car
1 Electronic ballast unit with controller, 2 High-voltage section, 3 PES low beam with gaseous-discharge lamp, 4 Conventional high beam.

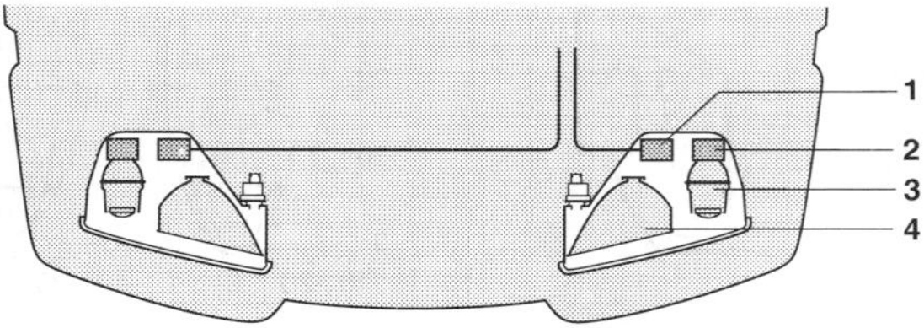

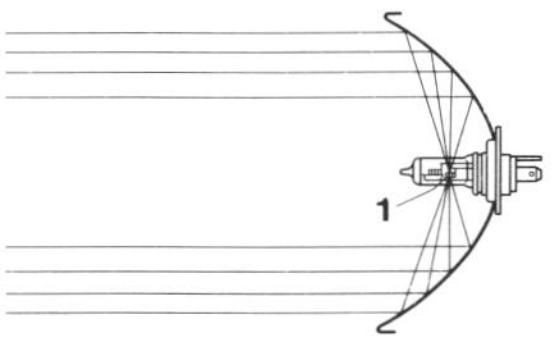

High beam (pattern of reflection)
1 High-beam light source located at focal point.

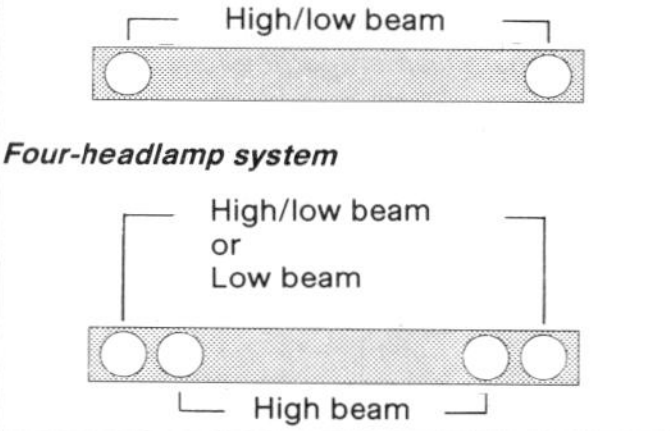

Two-headlamp system
This system uses bulbs which have two filaments (Bilux, Duplo), and employs the same reflectors for both the high and low beams.

Four-headlamp system
In this system, one pair of headlamps produces both the high and low beams, or only the low beam. The second pair of headlamps provides the high beam. The following designs are in use today:

Lens movable in vehicle body
The lens and reflector are mounted to one another forming a headlamp unit. The headlamp is aimed by moving the entire unit. In unfavorable circumstances, the lens may assume a slightly tilted position in the vehicle body. Headlamp units usually have seal bonnets and special ventilation systems in the area of the bulb.

Lens attached to vehicle body
The lens is attached to the vehicle body, and is not connected to the reflector. The headlamp is aimed by moving only the reflector (non-unitized construction). Because the lens is fixed, it can be fully integrated into the vehicle body design. The entire headlamp is either sealed or ventilated.

Components

Reflectors
Reflectors are made of sheet steel or plastic. Steel reflectors are made as follows: The steel is first deep-drawn and given a parabolic shape. It is then galvanized or powder-coated to protect it from corrosion, after which its surface is smoothed by coating, and the reflective aluminum layer is applied by evaporation. A protective layer is then evaporated onto the aluminum. This process hermetically seals the sheet steel, making the reflective surface extremely smooth with a residual roughness of max. 1/10,000 mm.

Plastic reflectors are produced by injection or compression molding; no special anti-corrosion treatment is required.

Lenses
Lenses are made of high-purity glass (free from bubbles and streaks). During the lens molding process, particular attention is paid to high surface quality in order to prevent light from being deflected upward, causing glare for oncoming traffic. The type and configuration of the lens prisms depend upon reflector size and focal length, as well as the desired light distribution pattern. When a VFR reflector is used, only a minimal prismatic effect is required from the lens, as light distribution is essentially determined by the reflector. In order to reduce the weight of the lens, plastics will most likely be used as lens materials in the future.

Aerodynamic front-end design frequently entails designing the lens to conform to the specific contours of the vehicle.

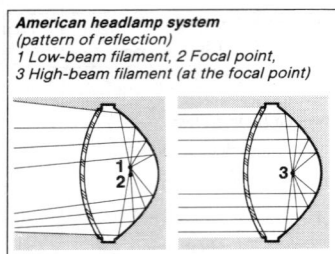

American headlamp system
(pattern of reflection)
1 Low-beam filament, 2 Focal point,
3 High-beam filament (at the focal point)

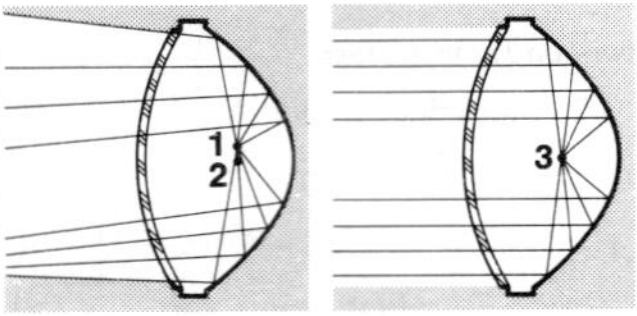

European headlamp system
(low beam)

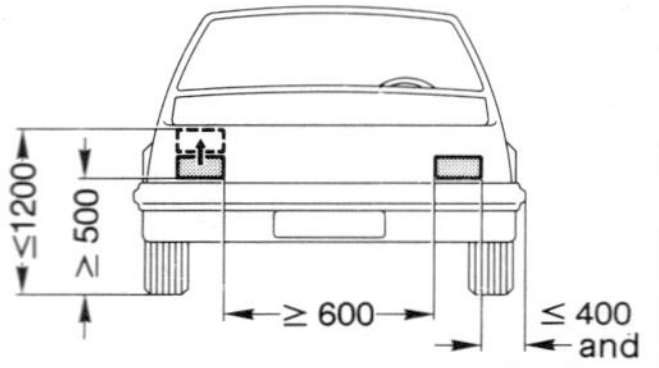

Main headlamps, American system

Low beam

As viewed in the direction of travel, the low-beam filament is located above and slightly to the left of the reflector focal point. This causes almost all the effective luminous flux to be reflected downward toward the road surface, with a certain percentage of the luminous flux being directed toward the right. The result is an asymmetrical beam. There is no protective cap under the filament, so the entire reflector area can be utilized. The lack of a clearly defined light/dark cutoff, however, means that the visual range is only average on the side exposed to oncoming traffic (the LH side in countries with RH traffic), and glare is more pronounced than with the European system.

High beam

As in the European system, the filament is located at the focal point of the parabolic reflector.

Designs

Sealed-beam

The glass reflector with an evaporated aluminum reflective layer must make a gas-tight seal with the lens, because the filaments are not encapsulated. This molded unit, the sealed-beam headlamp unit, is filled with inert gas. If a filament fails, the entire unit must be replaced. Halogen lamp units are also in use in which the halogen bulbs with their own glass envelope are molded into the sealed-beam unit. It is therefore no longer absolutely necessary that the unit be hermetically sealed. The limited range of available sealed-beam headlamps severely restricts the latitude for front-end styling variations.

Replaceable-bulb headlamp (RBH)

This headlamp uses a replaceable bulb. The headlamp's size and shape can be adapted to suit individual styling requirements. The trend is toward increasing use of plastic for the reflector and the lens.

European regulations

Regulations and guidelines for main headlamps

76/761/EEC and ECE Regulations 1 and 2: Headlamps and Bulbs for High and Low Beams.
ECE Regulation 5: Sealed-Beam Headlamps for European Asymmetrical Low Beam.
ECE Regulation 8: Headlamps with H 1, H 2 and H 3 Bulbs.
ECE Regulation 20: Headlamps with H 4 Bulbs.
ECE Regulation 31: Sealed-Beam Headlamps with Halogen Bulbs.
In Germany, StVZO § 50 Road Licensing Regulations (FMVSS/CUR): Headlamps for High and Low Beams.
76/756/EEC and ECE Regulation 48 for installation and application.

Low-beam headlamps, mounting

Regulations require 2 white low-beam headlamps for multiple-tracked vehicles (yellow headlamps are required in France).

Grouped and nested designs which include high beams and all other lamps at the front of the vehicle are permissible. Combinations incorporating other devices are not permissible.

Low beam, illumination engineering
Within Germany, the technical stipulations of the StVZO Road Licensing Regulations (FMVSS/CUR) apply to symmetrical low beams. In the case of asymmetrical low beams, only international regulations and guidelines are in force. These contain precise regulations covering the photometric measurement of the particular type of low beam concerned (with normal or conventional halogen lamp).

A headlamp is type-tested using test bulbs which have closer tolerances than commercially available series-manufactured bulbs.

The glare effect of a headlamp is governed by § 50 (6) of the StVZO, according to which the problem of glare is considered resolved if the luminous intensity is a maximum of 1 lx at a distance of 25 m in front of the headlamp at the height of the center of the headlamp. This measurement should be made with the engine running at medium speed.

Low beam, switching
When switching from high beam to low beam, all high-beam headlamps must be switched off simultaneously. Dimming (delayed switch-off) is permissible. The dimming delay must not exceed 5 s. A response time of 2 s must be ensured so that the headlamps are not dimmed during momentary flashing. The low beam may remain on when the dimmer switch is in the high-beam position. Headlamp bulbs may generally be operated only for a brief period of time with both filaments on.

Low beam, aiming
Aiming requirements:
— Correct tire pressure
— Vehicle loaded:
for passenger cars: one person or 70 kg in the back seat; for trucks: unloaded; for single-track vehicles and single-axle tractor vehicles: one person or 70 kg in the driver's seat.
— The vehicle must be rolled a few meters so that the suspension can adapt to the added load.
— The vehicle must be parked on a flat surface.
— A test surface must be set up at a distance of 10 m from the vehicle such that the center mark is located in the direction of travel in front of each headlamp when it is aimed.
— The headlamps are to be aimed individually, during which time the remaining headlamps are to be covered.
— With vehicles having manual headlight-levelling devices, each headlamp must be set to the manufacturer's specified position.
See Table 3 for adjustment value e.
The headlamps must be re-aimed if headlamp adjustment is affected by modifications of or changes to vehicle equipment (e.g., suspension). The headlamps should also be re-aimed if the bulbs are replaced.

High-beam headlamps, mounting
The vehicle must be equipped with at least 2 but no more than 4 high-beam headlamps.

Horizontal headlamp configuration: The outside edges of the illuminated areas of the headlamps must not be further from the center of the vehicle than the outside edges of the low-beam headlamps. Mounting height is not specified.

Grouped and nested designs which include low beams and all other lamps at the front of the vehicle are permissible. Combinations which include other lamps are not permissible. A blue or yellow high-beam indicator lamp must be installed inside the vehicle.

High beam, illumination engineering
High-beam light distribution is described in the ordinances and guidelines in conjunction with the low beams. The most important specifications in this regard are: symmetrical distribution about a vertical line passing through the center of the headlamp; maximum luminous intensity at the center line of the headlamp.

Table 3: Adjustment value "*e*" for headlamp aiming.[1])

Type of vehicle	Head-lamp	Fog lamp
	Adjustment value *e*	
	cm	cm
1. Vehicles in which the headlamp-reflector upper edge is not higher than 135 cm above the road surface a) Passenger cars (see also 1 i) b) Vehicles which have self-leveling suspensions or automatic tilt-compensating lighting systems[2]) c) Multiple-axle tractor vehicles or prime movers d) Single-tracked motor vehicles e) Trucks with front loading areas	10	20
f) Trucks with rear loading areas[3]) g) Articulated road trains[3]) h) Buses[3]) i) Station wagons[3])	30	40
2. Vehicles in which the headlamp-reflector upper edge is higher than 135 cm above the road surface.	$H/3$	$H/3+7$
3. Single-axle tractor vehicles or prime movers with permanent low-beam headlamps where the degree of inclination of the light beam center is specified.	$2N$	20

Headlamp test surface

The configuration of the adjustment marks and lines applies to main headlamps mounted at the standard height. The center mark is moved to height H at the center of the headlamp. The adjustment value e = 10 cm specifies the vertical distance between the center mark and the separating line.

In the case of headlamps which have an adjustment value $e > 10$ cm, the separating line is brought to the corresponding lower position. The center mark in these cases naturally does not lie at the height of the center of the headlamp. However it is used to check the position of the high beam (if equipped).

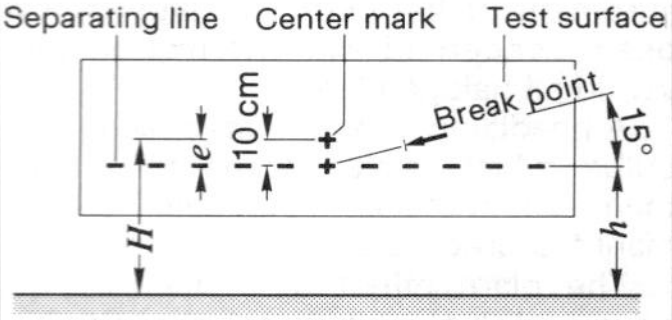

H *Height of the center of the headlamp above the road surface in cm*

h *Height of the separating line of the test surface above the road surface in cm*

$e = H-h$ *adjustment value*

N *Distance in mm by which the center of the light beam must be inclined at a distance from the vehicle of 5 m*

A *Headlamp center-to-center distance*

The left-hand (horizontal) portion of the light/dark cutoff must be set to coincide with the separating line.

Position of the test surface with respect to the longitudinal vehicle axis

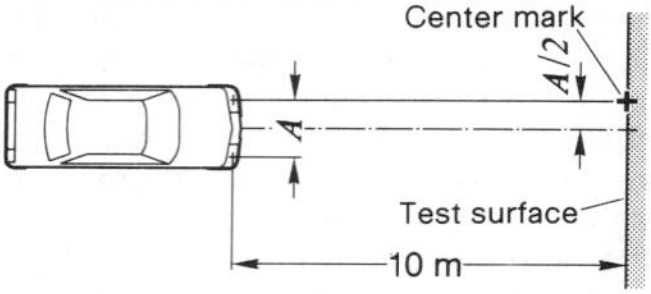

Table 4. Geometric range of the horizontal portion of the low-beam light/dark cutoff. Headlamp mounting height: 65 cm.

Inclination of the light/dark cutoff in % (1% = 10 cm/10 m)	1	1.5	2	2.5	3
Geometric range in m of the horizontal portion of the light/dark cutoff	65	43.3	32.5	26	21.7

The sum of the individual luminous intensity values of all high-beam headlamps installed on the vehicle must not exceed 225,000 cd. This value is checked by means of reference numbers which are located in the vicinity of the mark of approval on each headlamp. A value of 225,000 cd corresponds to the number 75. The luminous intensity of the high-beam headlamp is specified by a number (e.g. 20) to the right of the round ECE mark of approval (p. 668).

If a vehicle is equipped only with these headlamps (no auxiliary driving lamps), the sum of the individual luminous intensity values is roughly 40/75 of 225,000 cd, i.e. 120,000 cd.

High beam, aiming

If the high-beam headlamp also includes an asymmetrical low beam (Bilux or Duplo bulbs), the high beam is aimed by bringing the low beam into the desired position. Separate high-beam headlamps are aimed horizontally and symmetrically with reference to the center of the headlamp and the center mark.

European sealed-beam units

Sealed-beam units are approved for use in Europe in accordance to ECE Regulations 5 (for standard lighting) and 31 (for halogen lighting). As in the case of American sealed-beam units, the complete headlamp must be replaced if a bulb fails.

[1]) The results achieved using headlamp aiming devices must meet the values given in the table.

[2]) The specific characteristics of these devices must be strictly observed in accordance with the directions of the manufacturer.

[3]) Excluding motor vehicles as per 1 b.

Specifications for North America

Ordinances and guidelines

Federal Motor Vehicle Safety Standard (FMVSS) No. 108 and SAE Lighting Equipment and Photometric Tests (Standards and Recommended Practices).

The regulations which pertain to headlamp mounting and switching are comparable to European regulations.

The primary differences concern the headlamp systems. Only the following headlamp sizes were permissible in the USA up to 1983:

Two-headlamp systems:
- 178 mm dia., round
- 200 × 142 mm, rectangular

Four-headlamp systems:
- 146 mm dia., round
- 165 × 100 mm, rectangular

The use of replaceable-bulb lamps in any size and shape – RBH or Replaceable Bulb Headlamps – has been permitted since the promulgation of FMVSS Amendment Nr. 108 in 1983.

Headlamps in accordance with ECE or EEC Guidelines are not permissible for dual-tracked vehicles in the USA. They can, however, be used on motorcycles.

Aiming

Whereas in Europe headlamps are always visually aimed by observing the beam of light, the use of mechanical aiming devices has become the most common method of aiming headlamps in the USA. For mechanical aiming, headlamp units in the USA have 3 aiming pads on the lens which form the aiming planes. A headlight aiming device is placed against these pads. The headlamps are aimed with a level (water-bubble).

Headlight leveling devices

Table 4 gives the geometric ranges for various angles of headlamp inclination and a headlamp mounting height of 65 cm. The inspection tolerance extends to include inclination angles of up to 2.5 % (1.5 % below standard setting). European Community regulations specify the following headlight-range adjustment:

The basic setting according to specification *e* is (10 ... 15 cm)/10 m with the weight of a single person on the driver's seat. The specifications for the basic setting are provided by the vehicle manufacturer.

An automatic or manually-operated headlight-leveling (range adjustment) device has been mandatory for all vehicles registered in Germany from 1 January 1990 onward, except in cases in which other equipment (e.g., vehicle-level control) ensures that the inclination of the light beam will remain within tolerances. Other countries do not require this type of equipment; however, its use is allowed.

Automatic headlight-leveling devices

Automatic headlight-leveling devices must be designed such that the low beam is raised or lowered according to the vehicle load, and remains within 5 cm/10 m (0.5 %) and 25 cm/10 m (2.5 %).

Manual headlight leveling

This is regulated from the driver's seat and must incorporate a detent at the basic setting; beam adjustment is also performed in this position. Markings corresponding to those vehicle load conditions requiring adaptive adjustment are to be placed adjacent to the switch on both infinitely-variable and fixed-position units. All design variations employ an adjustment mechanism which serves to move either the headlamp reflector (housing design) or the entire headlight unit up or down. Manually-controlled units employ a driver-operated switch to control the setting, while automatic systems rely on level sensors at the vehicle's suspension. The sensors transmit a signal – proportional to suspension travel – to the final-controlling elements.

Hydromechanical systems

These systems are designed such that an amount of fluid proportional to the magnitude of the required adjustment moves through hydraulic lines which connect the manual switch (or level sensors) with the adjustment devices.

Vacuum systems

The manual switch (or level sensors) in these systems modulates the intake manifold vacuum used to move the adjustment devices.

Electrical systems

These employ electric gear motors as final-controlling elements, actuated via the driver's control switch or by suspension-travel sensors.

Automatic headlight leveling system

1 Adjustment device, 2 Addition point, 3 Level sensor.

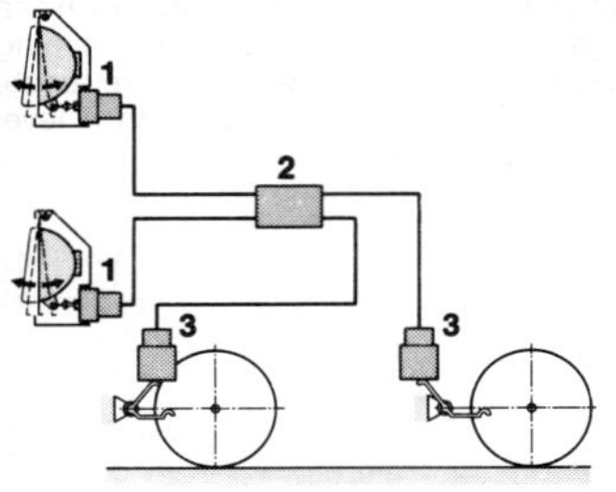

Manual headlight leveling system

1 Adjustment device, 2 Manual switch.

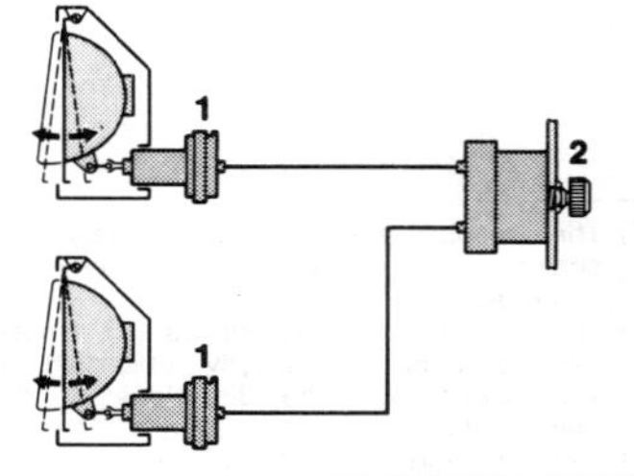

Fog lamps

The purpose of fog lamps is to improve road surface illumination in fog, snow, heavy rain or dusty conditions.

Optical principle
A parabolic reflector with a light source at the focal point reflects light which is axially parallel (like the high-beam headlamp). The lens then stretches out this beam of light to form a horizontal band. A mask blocks the upward portion of the beam. Under practical driving conditions, a light distribution which has a sharp upper light/dark cutoff is favorable in order to keep that portion of the field of vision above the boundary as dark as possible. Lateral dispersion to both sides should be approximately 50°. PES fog lamps represent a particularly effective means of fulfilling these requirements.

Designs
Fog lamps mounted on the exterior of the vehicle with an optical unit in the housing are mounted either upright on top of the bumper or suspended beneath it. For style and aerodynamic reasons, fog lamps are increasingly being integrated as units into the vehicle body, or they are designed as a component in a single lighting unit (fog lamps which are combined with the headlamps to form a single unit feature adjustable reflectors).

Most fog lamps produce white light. There are no physiologically justifiable advantages in yellow light. The effect of fog lamps depends upon the size of the illuminated area and the focal length of the reflector. For a given illuminated area and focal length, there are no major differences between round and rectangular fog lamps in terms of the light produced.

Regulations
2 white or yellow fog lamps are permissible on the vehicle in accordance with 76/756/EEC, ECE Regulation 19 and § 52 of the StVZO Road Licensing Regulations. Fog lamps may also be grouped together with other lamps at the front of the vehicle and with headlamps; other combinations are not permissible. Fog lamps may be nested with high-beam headlamps, side-marker lamps and parking lamps. Fog lamps must be switchable independently of high- and low-beam headlamps. In accordance with the Road Licensing Regulations valid within Germany, fog lamps may be mounted more than 400 mm away from the widest point on the vehicle contour if the lamp circuitry provides for fog-lamp operation only in conjunction with the lower beam. Fog lamps are levelled in the same manner as main headlamps. The adjustment values e are given in Table 3.

***Fog lamp** (parabolic reflector)*
1 Mask, 2 Lens, 3 Reflector,
4 Vertical aiming axis

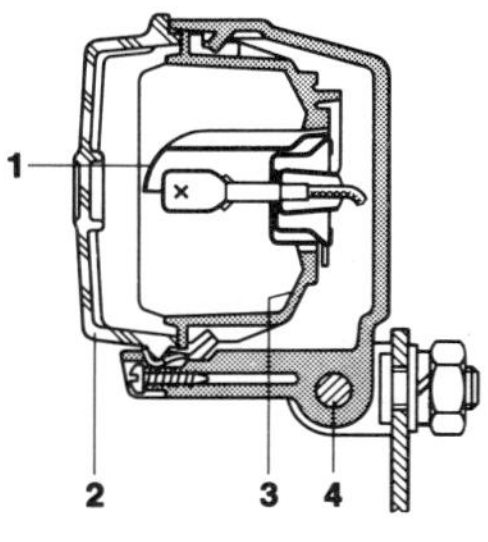

***Fog lamps** (mounting location)*

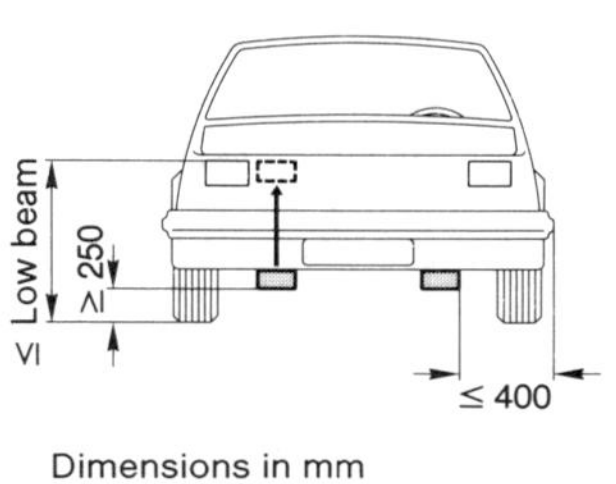

Auxiliary driving lamps

Auxiliary driving lamps enhance the high-beam visibility provided by two and four-headlamp systems. From the optical viewpoint, auxiliary driving lamps are similar to fog lamps. However the lens is designed to meet high-beam requirements. Auxiliary driving lamps and fog lamps are often of the same size and shape.

Auxiliary driving lamps are mounted and aimed in the same way as regular high-beam headlamps, and their photometric specifications are the same. Auxiliary driving lamps are subject to the same regulations with regard to maximum permissible luminous intensity on the vehicle, whereby the sum of the reference numbers must not exceed 75 (see p. 677, 679). In the case of older headlamps without a reference number in the mark of approval, the number 10 is assumed.

Signal and marker lamps

Design and mounting specifications are contained in 76/756/EEC and § 49 a of the StVZO.

The purpose of such lamps is to allow the vehicle and its actual or intended direction of travel to be recognized. In principle, there are two possible lamp designs which meet illumination requirements.

Lamps with reflectors
Light emitted by the bulb is reflected by a reflector of no specific shape (often parabolic) such that the beam is nearly parallel to the lamp axis, passing through a lens which distributes it by means of optical dispersion elements.

Lamps with fresnel optics
There is no reflector to provide intermediate reflection in this type of unit, in which the lamp transmits a beam of light directly to a fresnel lens for refraction. Fresnel optics are usually less efficient.

Illumination engineering
The luminous intensity of all lamps must fall within minimum and maximum limits in the direction of the reference axis (Table 1). This ensures that the signal will be recognized, while eliminating the effect of glare for other drivers. Referred to this reference axis value, luminous intensity to either side and above and below the reference axis may be lower. Percentage figures exist for these values (so-called unified spatial light distribution). Photometric measurement of the various luminous intensity values at the vehicle is easier than with the low beam, because only the luminous intensity value on the reference axis is measured with the engine running. Only the light emitted by the lamps may be measured (under daylight conditions).

Lamp with reflector *(principle)*
1 Housing, 2 Reflector, 3 Lens with cylindrical dispersion elements.

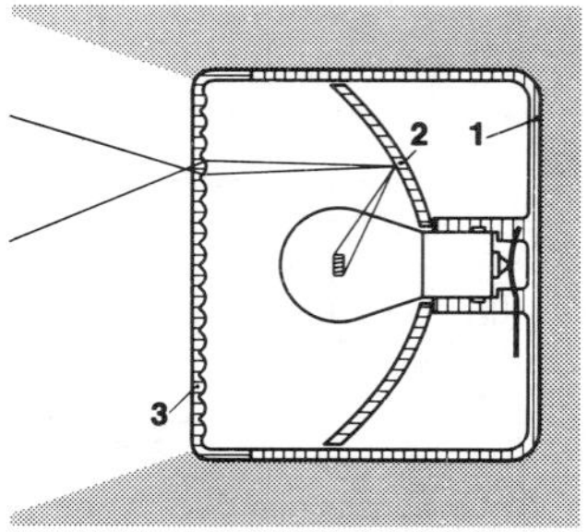

Lamp with fresnel optics *(principle)*
1 Housing, 2 Lens with fresnel optics.

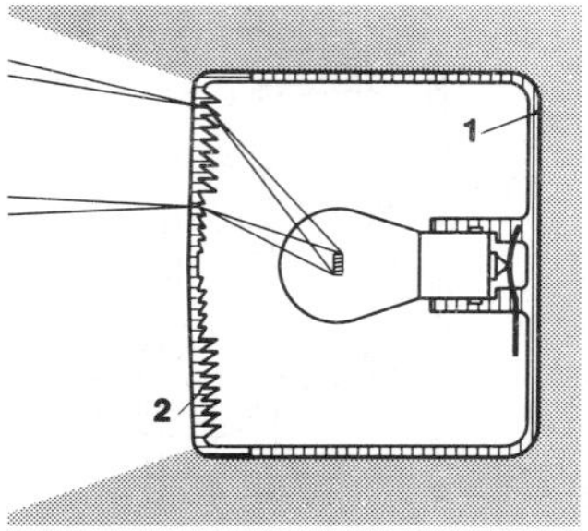

Turn-signal lamps

76/759/EEC, ECE Regulation 6, § 54 of the StVZO Road Licensing Regulations (FMVSS/CUR). For dual-tracked vehicles, Group 1 (front-mounted), Group 2 (rear-mounted) and Group 5 (side-mounted) turn-signal lamps are required.

Group 5 turn-signal lamps can be omitted if the vehicle is less than 6 m in length. Group 2 turn-signal lamps are sufficient for motor cycles and mopeds.

No particular color is specified for the turn-signal indicator lamp.

Flash frequency: 90 ± 30 cycles per minute.

Front-mounted turn-signal lamps
2 yellow turn-signal lamps are stipulated.

Turn-signal lamps may be grouped together with one or more other lamps. Combination allowed only with turn-signal lamps from other groups. Turn-signal lamps may be nested only with parking lamps. Function indicator required.

Rear-mounted turn-signal lamps
2 yellow turn-signal lamps are stipulated.

Mounting positions as for front-mounted turn-signal lamps, however additional limitation with regard to distance from tail lamp: < 300 mm.

Regulations regarding grouping, combination, nesting, as for front-mounted turn-signal lamps.

Side-mounted turn-signal lamps
2 yellow turn-signal lamps are stipulated.

Grouping and nesting as for front-mounted turn-signal lamps. Side-mounted turn-signal lamps may only be combined with turn-signal lamps of other groups.

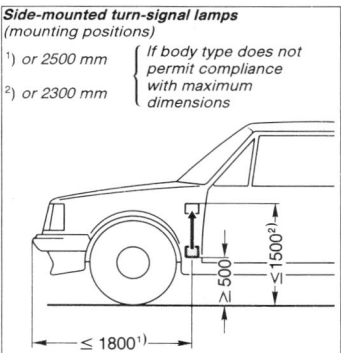

Side-mounted turn-signal lamps
(mounting positions)
[1]) or 2500 mm; [2]) or 2300 mm — If body type does not permit compliance with maximum dimensions

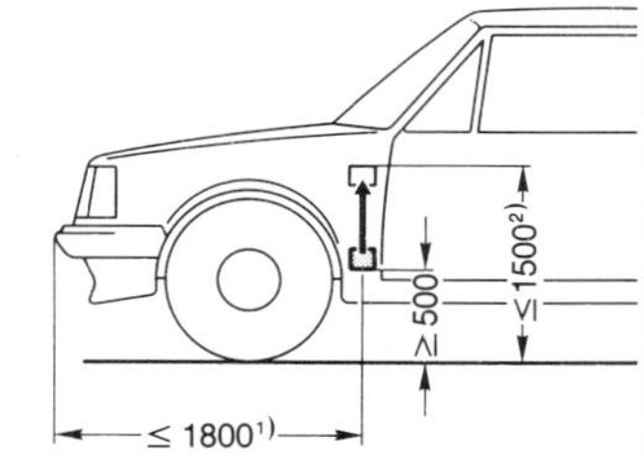

Front-mounted turn-signal lamps
(mounting positions)
[1]) ≤ 2100 mm in cases where the design of the vehicle's body prevents compliance with regulations on maximum height.

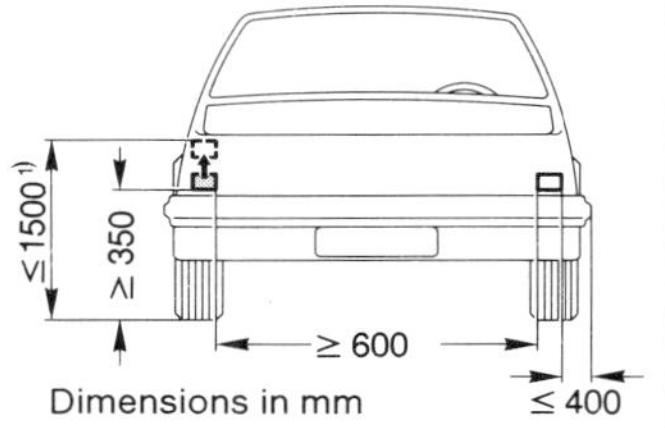

Rear-mounted turn-signal lamps
(mounting positions)
Height and width as for front-mounted turn-signal lamps; if the vertical distance between the turn-signal lamp and the tail lamp is < 300 mm, the horizontal distance must be no more than 50 mm.

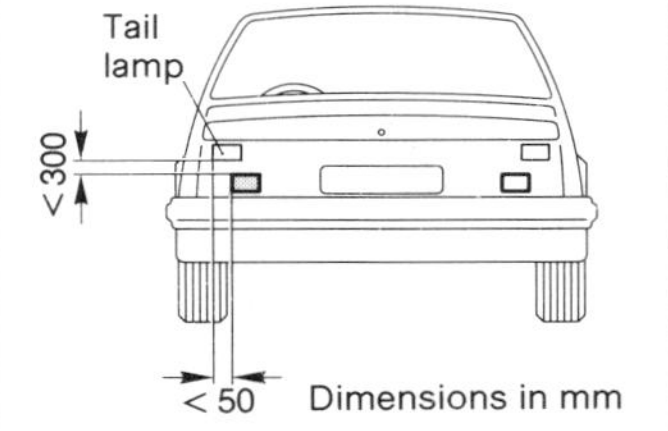

Side-marker, clearance and tail lamps

76/758/EEC, ECE Regulation 7, §§ 51 and 53 of the StVZO Road Licensing Regulations (FMVSS/CUR). Side-marker lamps (visible from the front) are required on vehicles and trailers whose width exceeds 1600 mm, while tail lamps (projecting toward the rear) are required for vehicles of all widths. If the vehicle width is greater than 2100 mm (e.g., trucks), the vehicle must also be equipped with clearance lamps visible from the front and rear.

Side-marker lamps
2 white side-marker lamps are stipulated. The color yellow is permissible if the side-marker lamps are nested with yellow headlamps (France).

For mounting positions, see "Front-mounted turn-signal lamps".

Side-marker lamps may be grouped and nested with all other front-mounted lamps (or headlamps). Side-marker lamps are very often nested with headlamps. Side-marker lamps may not be combined with other lamps (or headlamps).

Tail lamps
2 red tail lamps are stipulated.

For mounting positions, see "Rear-mounted turn-signal lamps".

Tail lamps may be grouped with all other rear lamps. They may be combined with rear license-plate lamps. They may be nested with stop lamps, parking lamps and fog warning lamps. If nested with tail lamps and stop lamps, the actual luminous intensity ratio of the individual functions must be at least 1:5. Tail lamps must operate together with side-marker lamps.

Clearance lamps
2 white lamps visible from the front, 2 red lamps visible from the rear.

Mounting positions: as far apart as possible and as high as possible on the vehicle.

Clearance lamps may be grouped together with other lamps. They may not be combined or nested with other lamps.

Stop lamps

76/758/EEC, ECE Regulation 7, § 53 of the StVZO Road Licensing Regulations (FMVSS/CUR).

In addition to the primary stop lamps, supplemental high-mounted stop lamps are permissible in Germany, Austria, Great Britain, Sweden and Norway.

Primary stop lamps
2 red stop lamps are stipulated on all vehicles.

Primary stop lamps may be grouped together with tail lamps. They may be combined only with license-plate lamps if they are simultaneously nested in tail lamps. They may be nested in tail lamps or parking lamps. If stop lamps and tail lamps are nested, the actual luminous intensity ratio of the individual functions must be at least 5:1.

Supplemental high-mounted stop lamps
In some countries, 2 red supplemental high-mounted stop lamps are permissible. These lamps may be mounted either on the exterior of the vehicle or inside the vehicle (in front of the rear window).

The luminous intensity values given in Table 1 must be met in order to keep drivers following the vehicle from being blinded. A maximum value of 60 cd is aimed for. Supplemental high-mounted stop lamps must operate together with the primary stop lamps.

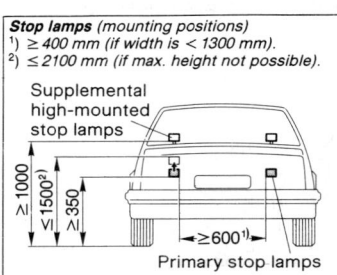

Stop lamps *(mounting positions)*
[1]) *≥ 400 mm (if width is < 1300 mm).*
[2]) *≤ 2100 mm (if max. height not possible).*

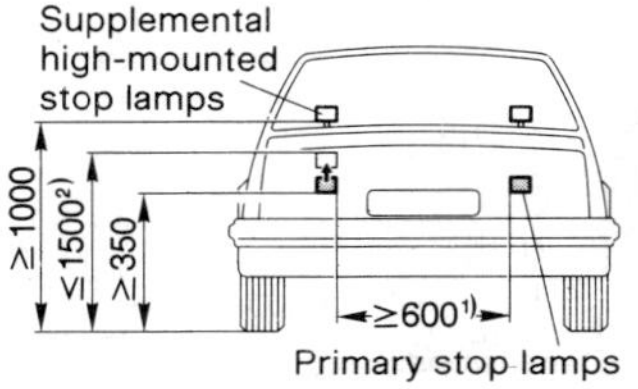

Fog warning lamps
(rear fog lamps)

77/538/EEC, ECE Regulation 38, § 53 d of the StVZO Road Licensing Regulations (FMVSS/CUR).

The countries of the European Community prescribe one or two fog warning lamps for all vehicles being registered for the first time.

Fog warning lamps may be grouped together with all other rear lamps. They may not be combined with other lamps. They may be nested with tail lamps or parking lamps.

The visible illuminated area in the direction of the reference axis must not exceed 140 cm². The fog warning lamp circuit must ensure that the lamps can only be switched on if the fog lamps or the low-beam or high-beam headlamps are operating. It must be possible to switch off fog warning lamps independently of fog lamps.

Fog warning lamps must have yellow indicator lamps (vehicles licensed before January 1981 may also have green indicator lamps).

Backup lamps

77/539/EEC, ECE Regulation 23, § 52 of the StVZO Road Licensing Regulations (FMVSS/CUR). 1 or 2 white backup lamps are permissible.

Backup lamps may be grouped together with all other rear lamps. They may not be combined or nested with other lamps.

The backup-lamp circuitry must ensure that backup lamps will operate only with the vehicle in reverse gear and the ignition system turned on.

Parking lamps

77/540/EEC, § 51 of the StVZO Road Licensing Regulations (FMVSS/CUR). Either 2 parking lamps at the front and rear or 1 parking lamp on each side are permissible. Front parking lamps must be white, and rear parking lamps must be red. Yellow rear parking lamps are permissible if grouped together with turn-signal lamps. For mounting positions, see "Turn-signal lamps". Parking lamps may be grouped together with all other lamps. They may not be combined with other lamps. They may be nested with side-marker lamps, headlamps and fog lamps, tail lamps, stop lamps and fog warning lamps, as well as with side-mounted turn-signal lamps.

Parking lamps must operate without other lamps (or headlamps) being turned on. In most cases, the tail lamps and side-marker lamps fulfill the function of parking lamps.

Backup lamps *(mounting positions)*
Number: 1 or 2 lamps

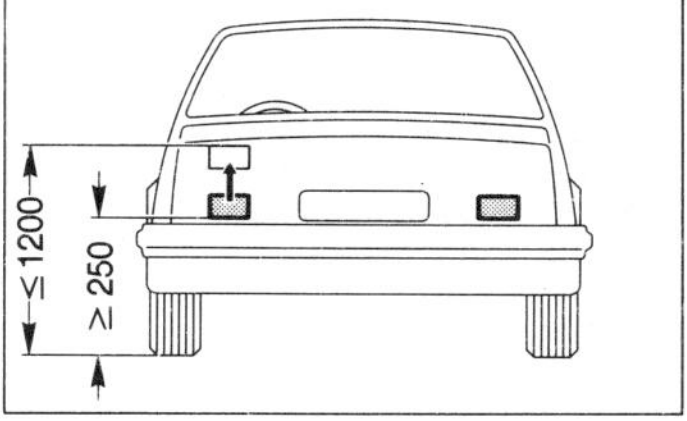

Fog warning lamps *(mounting positions)*
Layout for one lamp on LHD vehicle.

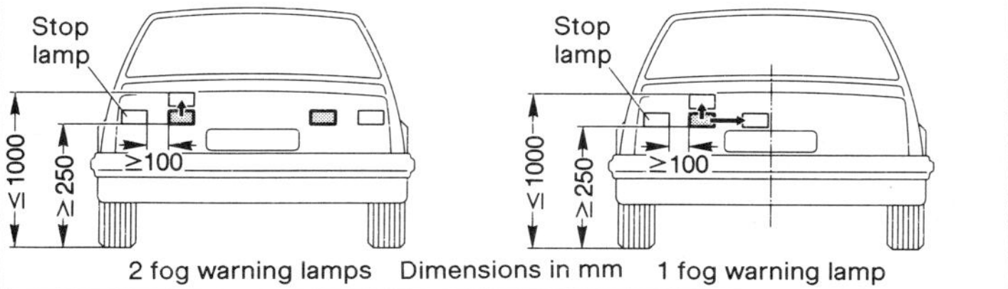

License-plate lamps

76/760/EEC, ECE Regulation 4, § 60 of the StVZO Road Licensing Regulations (FMVSS/CUR). The rear license plate must be illuminated such that it can be read at night at a distance of 25 m.

License-plate lamps may be grouped together with all rear lamps or combined with tail lamps. They may not be nested with other lamps.

The luminance at all points on the license plate surface must be at least 2.5 cd/m^2. Test points are distributed over the license plate surface between which the luminance gradient of $2 \times B_{min}$/cm must not be exceeded. B_{min} represents the lowest luminance value measured at the test points.

Daytime running lamps

2 white or yellow daytime running lamps are stipulated by law for dual and single-track vehicles in Sweden and Finland. These lamps indicate to other drivers that the vehicle in question is moving or is about to move.

Daytime running lamps may be grouped together and combined with other lamps and headlamps.

Daytime running lamps must be switched on with the ignition, and may only operate together with the tail lamps.

Low-beam headlamps or fog lamps can also be used to achieve compliance with the lighting requirement for daytime driving when their light is of the specified intensity (Table 1). It is to be anticipated that still more countries will promulgate regulations stipulating the use of daylight running lights or of the low beam for daytime driving.

Daytime running lamps *(mounting positions shown for Sweden and Finland)*

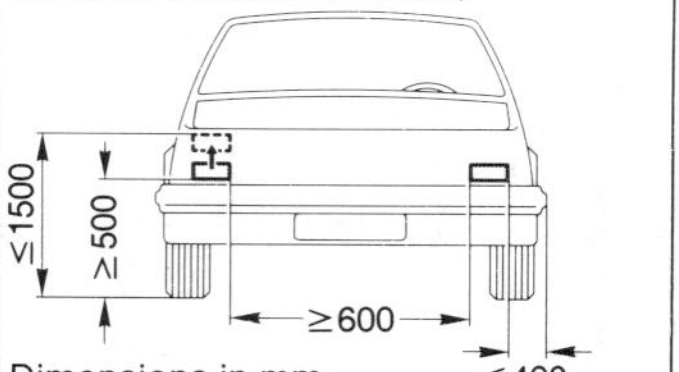

Dimensions in mm

Other lighting devices

Floodlamps

When the vehicle is moving, floodlamps may be used only if the vehicle's movement pertains to an assignment which requires illumination by means of floodlamps, e.g., in the case of agricultural tractors, forestry vehicles, self-propelled machinery, and rescue vehicles.

These floodlamps are not subject to photometric regulations. The distribution of light is such that the working area is broadly and uniformly illuminated. Such lamps are often installed on special mounts so that they can be aimed as required.

Spot lamps

Spot lamps generate a narrow beam of high luminous intensity. A small area can therefore be illuminated at a great distance.

Identification lamps

§ 52 of the StVZO Road Licensing Regulations (FMVSS/CUR). Blue identification lamps are permissible equipment on authorized vehicles. Yellow identification lamps are used as hazard warning lamps. Identification lamps must project light through a 360° arc, and must give the appearance of flashing. The flashrate f lies between 2 and 5 Hz.

Identification lamps are photometrically evaluated in terms of flashing intensity. This is the product of the mean luminous intensity over time within the light beam (max. 400 cd) and a value which is a function of the "on" time of the flashing signal (max. $0.6/f$).

Table 5. Stipulated minimum flashing intensity for identification lamps

Location of measurement	Flashing intensity Blue	Yellow
Parallel to the plane of the road surface	>20 cd	>40 cd
Within the light beam at an angle to the plane of the road surface of ±4°	>10 cd	
±8°		>30 cd

Lamp bulbs

ECE Regulation 37.

Bulbs for motor-vehicle lighting devices are available for 6, 12 and 24 volt electrical systems. In order to prevent bulbs of the wrong voltage from being used, most of the bulb types have differently shaped bases. Some bulbs which have identical bases are so different in terms of electrical power that it is impossible to use them incorrectly. The type of bulb required by each lighting device is indicated on the device.

One of the identifying characteristics of incandescent bulbs is luminous efficacy (lumens/watt). Luminous efficacy indicates the photometric efficiency referred to the applied electrical power. The luminous efficacy of non-halogen bulbs is 10 ... 18 lm/W.

The enhanced luminous efficacy provided by H 1 ... H 4 and H 7 halogen lamps (HS 1 and HS 2 for motorcycles) – in the order of 22 ... 26 lm/W – is essentially due to the higher gas pressure. The halogen process prevents deposits from clouding the bulb, ensuring that it remains clear for the life of the filament.

D 1 gaseous-discharge lamps (Litronic) provide still further improvements in low-beam illumination with a luminous efficacy of 85 lm/W.

Table 6. Motor-vehicle bulb specifications (not including bulbs for motorcycles and mopeds)

Application	Category	Nominal voltage Volt	Nominal power Watt	Specified luminous flux Lumen	Base type IEC	Illustration
High/ low beam	R 2	6 12 24	45/40[1]) 45/40 55/50	600 min/ 400 – 550[1])	P 45 t – 41	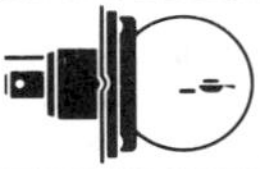
Fog lamps, supplementary high beam, low beam in 4-headlamp systems	H 1	6 12 24	55 55 70	1350[2]) 1550 1900	P 14.5 e	
High beam, low beam in France	H 2	6 12 24	55 55 70	1300[2]) 1800 2150	X 511	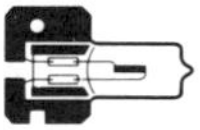
Fog lamps, supplemental high beam	H 3	6 12 24	55 55 70	1050[2]) 1450 1750	PK 22 s	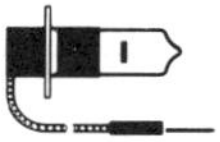
High/low beam	H 4	12 24	60/55[1]) 75/70	1650/1000[1]),[2]) 1900/1200	P 43 t – 38	
Low beam in 4-headlamp systems, fog lamp since 1992	H 7	12	55	1500[2])	PX 26 d	

1) High/low beam
2) Specified values for a test voltage of 6.3; 13.2 or 28.0 V.
3) Specified values for a test voltage of 6.75; 13.5 or 28.0 V.

Continued →

Table 6. Continued

Application	Category	Nominal voltage Volt	Nominal power Watt	Specified luminous flux Lumen	Base type IEC	Illustration
Stop lamps, signal lamps, fog warning lamps, backup lamps	P 21 W	6, 12, 24	21	460[3])	BA 15 s	
Stop/tail lamps	P 21/5 W	6 12 24	21/5[4]) 21/5 21/5	440/35[3]),[4]) 440/35 440/40	BAY 15 d	
Side-marker lamps, tail lamps	R 5 W	6, 12, 24	5	50[3])	BA 15 s	
Tail lamps	R 10 W	6, 12, 24	10	125[3])	BA 15 s	
License-plate lamps, tail lamps	C 5 W	6, 12, 24	5	45[3])	SV 8.5	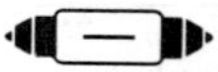
Backup lamps	C 21 W	12	21	460[3])	SV 8.5	
Side-marker lamps	T 4 W	6, 12, 24	4	35[3])	BA 9 s	
Side-marker lamps, license-plate lamps	W 5 W	6, 12, 24	5	50[3])	W 2.1 × 9.5 d	
Side-marker lamps, license-plate lamps	W 3 W	6, 12, 24	3	22[3])	W 2.1 × 9.5 d	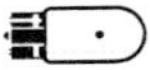
Low beam in 4-headlamp systems (as from about 1993)	D 1 Gaseous-discharge lamp[5])	85 12[6])	35 approx. 45[6])	3000	PK 32 d	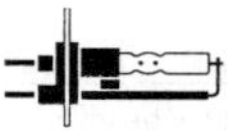

[1]) High/low beam
[2]) Specified values for a test voltage of 6.3; 13.2 or 28.0 V.
[3]) Specified values for a test voltage of 6.75; 13.5 or 28.0 V.
[4]) Main/auxiliary filament.
[5]) Standardization not yet completed.
[6]) With ballast unit.

Headlamp aiming devices

Purpose
Motor-vehicle headlamps must provide sufficient light without blinding on-coming drivers. The vertical and lateral beam angles must therefore be set in accordance with legal requirements as contained in the "Guideline for Adjustment of Motor Vehicle Headlamps" in § 50 of the German StVZO Road Licensing Regulations (FMVSS/CUR). Headlamp adjustment is primarily performed using optical aiming devices.

Design of aiming device
Headlight aiming devices are portable imaging chambers which comprise a single lens (objective) and a collecting screen located in the focal plane of the lens and rigidly connected to it. The collecting screen has markings for proper headlamp adjustment, and can be viewed by the operator using suitable devices such as windows or movable mirrors.

The prescribed headlamp adjustment, i.e. the inclination with respect to the center line of the headlamp given in cm for a distance of 10 m, is set by turning a knob which moves the collecting screen.

The aiming device is aligned with the vehicle axis by means of a sighting device, e.g., a mirror with a sighting line. It is turned and aligned such that the sighting line uniformly touches two outside vehicle reference marks. The imaging chamber can be moved vertically and clamped at the level of the vehicle headlamp.

Testing the headlamps
Once the optical system has been positioned properly in front of the lens of the headlamp under test in accordance with the above procedure, an image of the distribution of light emitted by the headlamp is produced on the collecting screen. Some testers are additionally equipped to measure luminous intensity by means of a photodiode and associated display.

In the case of headlamps with asymmetrical low beams, the cutoff boundary must touch the marked boundary lines; the point of intersection of the horizontal and vertical components must lie on the center mark of the vertical line.

After the cutoff boundary of the low beam has been adjusted properly, the center of the high beam (when the high and low beams are set together) must lie on the center mark within the boundary corners.

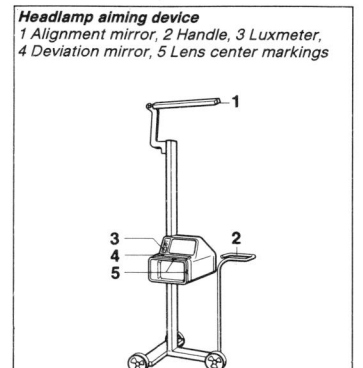

Headlamp aiming device
1 Alignment mirror, 2 Handle, 3 Luxmeter, 4 Deviation mirror, 5 Lens center markings

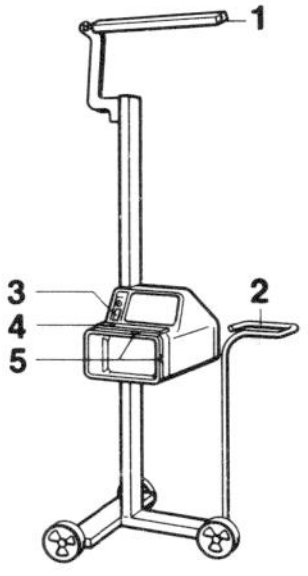

Cutoff boundary line for asymmetrical low beams

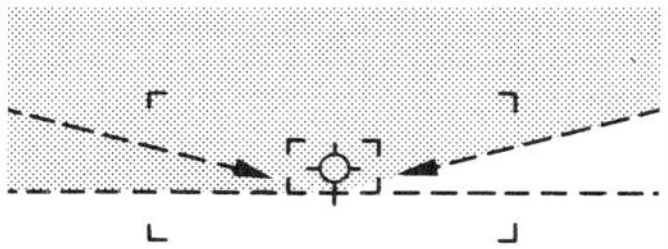

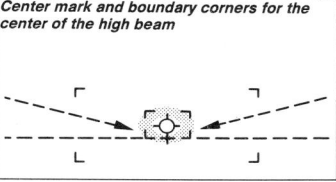

Center mark and boundary corners for the center of the high beam

Visual signaling systems

Regulations

The StVZO Road Licensing Regulations (FMVSS/CUR) and EC Directive EEC 76/756 specify that the vehicle lighting system be supplemented by visual turn signals and hazard-warning flashers on all vehicles with a top speed > 25 km/h.

Flashing signals: Signals flashing at 60 ... 120 pulses per minute, with a relative flash duration of 30 ... 80 %. Light must be emitted within < 1.5 sec. after system switch-on. Should one lamp fail, the remaining lamps must still radiate visible signals.

Turn signals: Use synchronized flashing of all turn-signal lamps on one side of the vehicle. Lamp functioning is monitored electrically, and system defects are indicated at the signal lamp or by means of considerable variation in the blinker-signal frequency.

Hazard flashers: Use synchronized flashing of all turn-signal lamps (four-way signal), and function regardless of whether the engine is running or not. A device to indicate operation is stipulated.

Turn-signal systems for vehicles without trailer

The electronic hazard-warning and turn-signal flasher incorporates an oscillator unit for triggering the relay that operates the lamps, and a current-activated control unit which modifies the flashing frequency as soon as a lamp fails. The blinker switch controls the turn signals, while the hazard-flasher switch operates the hazard flashers.

Turn-signal systems for vehicles with/without trailer

This type of hazard-warning and turn-signal flasher differs to that used on single vehicles with respect to the manner in which turn-signal operation is monitored.

Single monitoring circuit

The towing vehicle and the trailer share a common monitoring circuit which triggers two indicator lamps at the turn-signal frequency. In the event of a failure of the first or second turn signal on the towing vehicle or trailer, the first or first and second indicator lamp respectively remain off. No means is provided for localizing the malfunction at either the towing vehicle or the trailer. The flasher frequency remains unchanged.

Dual monitoring circuit

Towing vehicle and trailer are provided with separate monitoring circuits. The indicator lamps remain off selectively, allowing localization of the malfunction at the towing vehicle or the trailer. The flasher frequency remains unchanged.

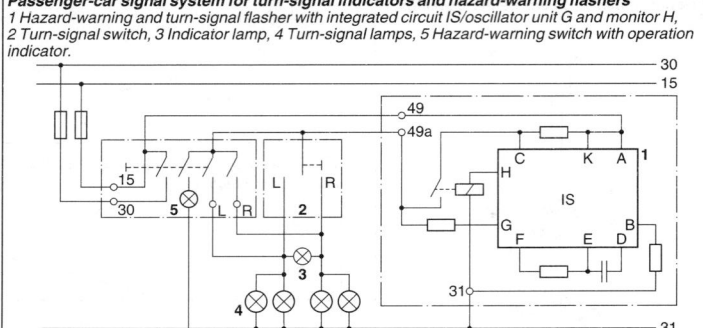

Passenger-car signal system for turn-signal indicators and hazard-warning flashers
1 Hazard-warning and turn-signal flasher with integrated circuit IS/oscillator unit G and monitor H, 2 Turn-signal switch, 3 Indicator lamp, 4 Turn-signal lamps, 5 Hazard-warning switch with operation indicator.

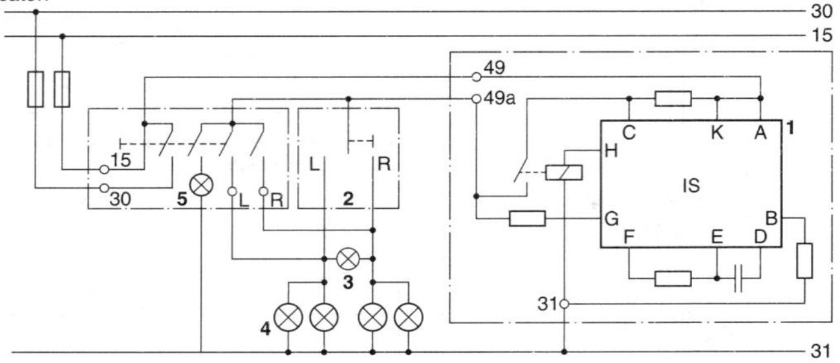

Acoustic signaling devices

Regulations
The internationally-applied ECE Regulation Nr.28 specifies that the acoustic signals produced by motor vehicles will maintain a uniform sound quality with no perceptible frequency fluctuations during operation. Sirens or bells, and the like, are forbidden, as well as the playing of melodies by means of sound generators operating in a given sequence.

Installation
Elastic couplings must be used to decouple electric horns from the vehicle's body, as the horn would otherwise induce sympathetic oscillations in the adjacent bodywork. The resulting feedback would diminish both volume and tone quality. Both electric and electropneumatic horns are sensitive to resistance in their control circuits. When horns are installed in pairs, they should be triggered by relays.

Horns

Standard horns
The mass of the armature together with the flexible diaphragm forms an oscillating system within the horn. When voltage is applied to the contacts controlling the solenoid coil, the armature impacts against the magnetic core at the horn's fundamental frequency. A fixed tone disk, directly attached to the armature, responds to these intense periodic impacts by radiating harmonic waves. Legal regulations stipulate that the maximum sound energy must lie within a band of 1.8 ... 3.55 kHz. This frequency explains the horn's relatively piercing note. This sound, which is essentially emitted along the horn's axis and out toward the front, can be heard above the background noise in traffic, even over longer distances.

The horn's size is one of the factors which determine the fundamental frequency and volume.

Supertone horns
The supertone horn employs both a larger diameter and a more powerful electric drive to produce warning signals which can still be heard even under extreme conditions (inside a truck cab with its high noise level, for instance).

Fanfare horns

The electropneumatic fanfare horn employs the same basic actuating system as its standard counterpart, the salient difference being that the armature is allowed to vibrate freely in front of the coil with no impact occurring. The oscillating diaphragm induces vibration of an air column within a tube. The resonant frequency of the diaphragm and the air column are tuned to one another, and they determine the pitch of the signal. The tube is in the shape of a funnel, with a wide opening to enhance the efficiency of sound propagation. The funnel tube is generally coiled to minimize the unit's size.

The presence of upper harmonics in the lower range of the frequency spectrum endows the fanfare horn with a rich, melodious sound. The tone is less penetrating than that of a standard horn due to the more consistent distribution of sound energy over a wide spectrum.

Selecting the correct horn
The warning produced by the impact horn is more conspicuous; it thus represents the better choice for vehicles which are frequently used on long hauls on roads with a large amount of truck traffic. Alternatively, the fanfare horn is superior for urban driving, as pedestrians often find the standard horn excessively loud and unpleasant. Both sets of requirements can be fulfilled by installing the two horn types together in a single system with a selection switch for urban or rural traffic. Standard and fanfare horns both operate at standardized frequencies. High and low tones can be combined to produce a harmonious dual-tone sound.

Theft-deterrent systems

Regulations

Theft-deterrent systems (car alarms) installed in motor vehicles must conform to the regulations defined in Paragraph 38 b of the StVZO Road Licensing Regulations (FMVSS/CUR) as well as ECE Directive R18. A primed alarm system responds to attempts at unauthorized entry by emitting warning signals.

Approved warning signals

– Intermittent acoustical signals of max. 30 s in length emitted by either the vehicle's own horn or an auxiliary unit.

– Optical flashing signals of max. 5 min in length provided by the hazard warning flashers, with supplementary activation of the interior lights (StVZO) or 30 s flashing of the low beams (ECE).

In order to signal repeated manipulation on the vehicle, the system may only produce a further acoustic alarm once the previous alarm has expired. The driver must be able to deprime the alarm immediately. It must be impossible for those alarm units which affect the vehicle's operating systems when primed to become active when the engine is running. The alarm is not to be triggered by vehicle movements (such as tremors etc.) not caused by attempted unauthorized entry.

Automotive alarm systems

The schematic diagram below is of an actual unit available on the market. The central ECU evaluates the signals at its input terminals, activates the system and switches on the warning signals (horn and visual signals) via its outputs.

The system is primed and deprimed with an infrared remote-control unit. The unit works with individual codes to secure the vehicle against unauthorized use.

The ignition must be off (i.e., engine off) before the system can be primed.

The switches for the doors and hood are connected at the input terminals T-, S-, S1. Opening one of these will trigger an imme-

Theft-deterrent system *(Car alarm)*
1 Battery, 2 Driving switch, 3 Start disable, 4 Ignition, 5 Starter, 6 Remote control (6.1 Transmitter, 6.2 Receiver), 7 Alarm relay, 8 Alarm horn, 9 Radio, 10 Passenger-compartment protection, 11 Tilt alarm, 12 Flashing display "Primed", 13 Door contact switch, 14 Contact switches for hood and trunk, 15 Status display: Primed/Deprimed, 16 Visual signal (Hazard-warning and turn-signal system). H Rear, V Front, L Left, R Right.

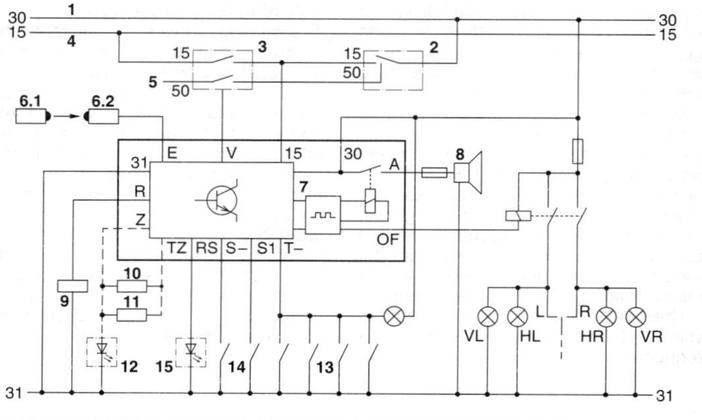

diate alarm, as will an open circuit at the radio-monitoring loop or switching on the ignition. Output Z activates the external ancillaries which trigger the alarm via input TZ. All of the mutually independent inputs are able to trigger consecutive alarms. The start-disable facility protects the engine from unauthorized starting. A lamp at output RS signals the unit's operating status (primed/deprimed) for approximately 3 seconds, and the lamp at output Z flashes when the unit is primed.

Optional extras

Electronic wheel and tow-away protection

This unit consists of a position sensor and an evaluation unit. When primed, the alarm unit stores the inclination or tilt angle at which the vehicle has been parked (on a level surface or on a hill) as the reference angle. An alarm is triggered when either the rate of variation in the angle or the angle itself exceeds the programmed limits. Normal changes in the vehicle's position (due to air loss in the tires, deliberate rocking of the vehicle, or settling in soft ground) are recognized as such by the electronics, and do not trigger an alarm.

Ultrasonic passenger-compartment protection

An ultrasonic field is generated inside the vehicle. An ultrasonic detector registers motion or pressure variations (such as those that occur when a hand reaches into the vehicle or when a window is broken) that cause the field to fluctuate, and the electronic evaluation unit responds with an immediate alarm. The alarm threshold can be adjusted to optimize the system's effectiveness.

Units which monitor the passenger compartment with the aid of ultrasonics or similar methods are only allowed to issue three alarms, an initial alarm and two follow-ups.

Electronic wheel and tow-away protection

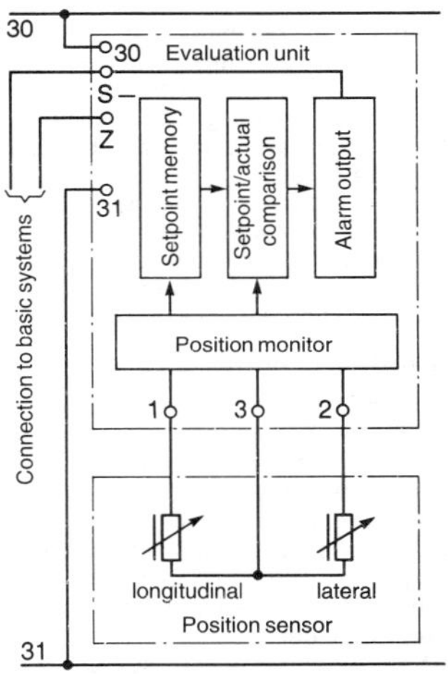

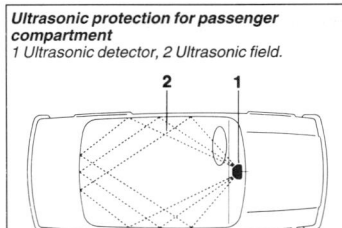

Ultrasonic protection for passenger compartment
1 Ultrasonic detector, 2 Ultrasonic field.

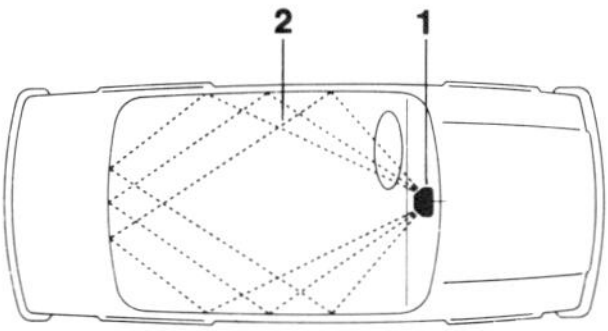

Windshield and rear-window cleaning

Systems for cleaning the vehicle's windshield, headlamps, and rear window are needed in order to comply with legal stipulations for good visibility at all times. Such systems can be subdivided as follows:

- Windshield wiper systems
- Rear-window wiper systems
- Headlamp wiper systems
- Headlamp washer systems
- Combination wiper-washer systems.

Windshield wiper systems

The following are the most important windshield-cleaning systems, using the passenger car as an example. These systems are based on the legally prescribed areas of vision (Europe, USA and Australia). The wiped areas may be changed by additional controls acting on the wiper blades (parallelogram, general four-bar mechanism).

The windshield wiper system must meet the following requirements:

- Removal of water and snow
- Removal of dirt (mineral, organic or biological),
- Operation at high temperature (+80°C) and low temperature (−30°C),
- Corrosion resistance against acids, alkalis, salts (240 h), ozone (72 h),
- Service life: passenger cars 1.5×10^6 wipe cycles, commercial vehicles 3×10^6 wipe cycles,
- Stall test.

Mechanical wiper mechanism

Series- or parallel-coupled four-bar mechanisms are used, with transversely jointed linkage or additional controlled four-bar linkages also being used for large wipe angles or difficult mechanical transmission configurations.

Optimization of the mechanism is important. Smooth operation can be achieved by matching the maximum values of angular acceleration and/or the force-transmission angles near to the wiper reversal points.

A second step towards optimization of the wiper mechanism involves the working position of the wiper-blade lip

Windshield cleaning systems

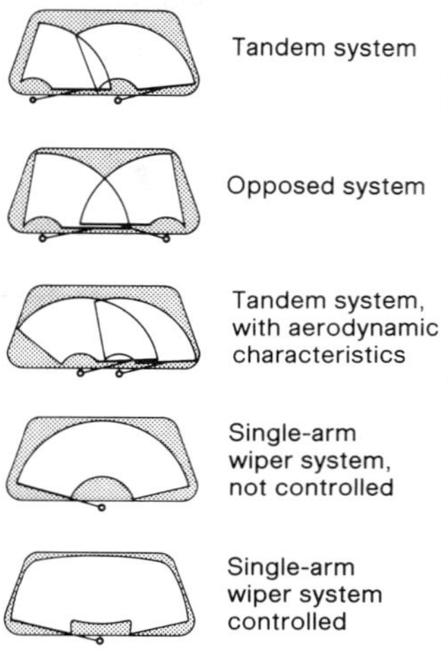

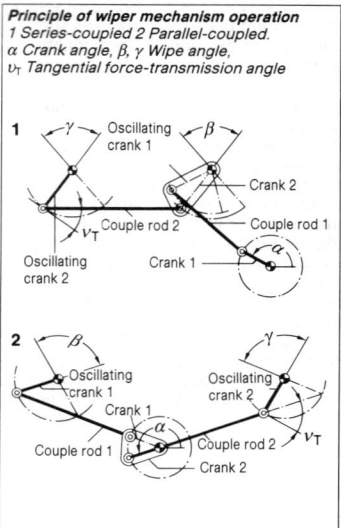

Principle of wiper mechanism operation
1 Series-coupled 2 Parallel-coupled.
α Crank angle, β, γ Wipe angle,
υ_T Tangential force-transmission angle

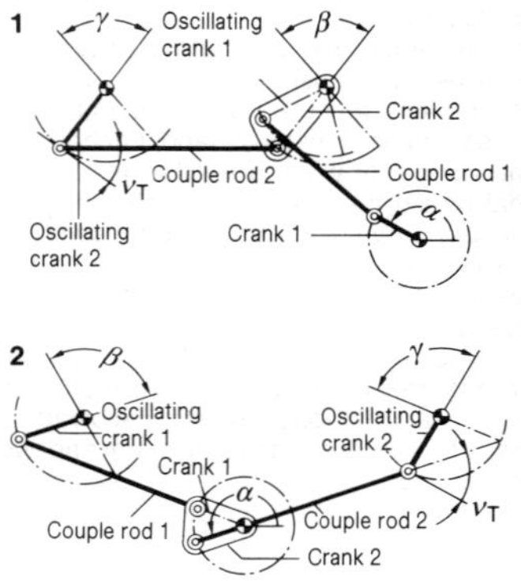

relative to the surface of the windshield or rear-window.

A second optimization step of the mechanism relates to the normal-deviation curve. By positioning the wiper bearings at the proper angle to the windshield, and by applying additional torsion to the wiper arms, the position of the wiper blades is defined so that at their reversal points they are inclined laterally towards the wiped-area bisector, thus assisting the wiper-blade elements to swivel into their new working position when reversal takes place.

Wiper blades

Wiper blades are used in lengths of 260 ... 1000 mm. Their dimensions for mounting (e.g., slide-in or hook mounting) are standardized. Minimum-wear operation is achieved by eliminating play in their mountings and joints. The tops of the center brackets are perforated to prevent blade lift-off at high speeds. In special cases aerodynamic deflectors are integrated in the wiper arms or blades to press the blades against the windshield.

Tandem wiper system, series-coupled
Right-hand part of mechanism designed as: 1 Oscillating crank, 2 Transversely jointed linkage, 3 Additional controlled four-bar linkage, 4 Controlled crank with attached coupling link.

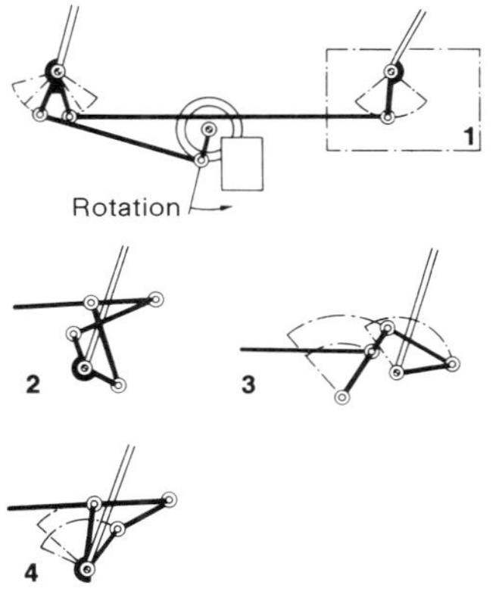

Rubber elements

The most important component of a wiper system is the rubber element. It is loaded by the claws of the bracket system, and supported by spring strips. Its double microedge is pressed against the windshield, and at its point of contact has a width of only 0.01 ... 0.015 mm. When moving across the windshield, the wiper-blade element must overcome coefficients of dry friction of 0.8 ... 2.5 (depending upon air humidity), and coefficients of wet friction of 0.6 ... 0.1 (depending upon frictional velocity). The correct combination of wiper-element profile and rubber properties must be chosen so that the wiper lip can wipe the complete wiped area of the windshield surface at an angle of approx. 45°.

Rear-window cleaning systems

These systems perform similar to windshield-cleaning systems. However, service life is limited to 0.5×10^6 wipe cycles. In right-hand traffic vehicles,

Rubber wiper element in working position
1 Claw bracket, 2 Spring strip, 3 Lip, 4 Double microedge, 5 Windshield.

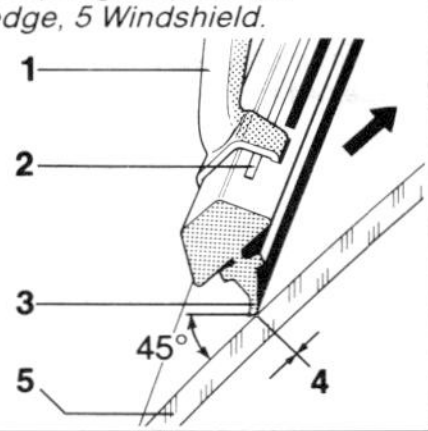

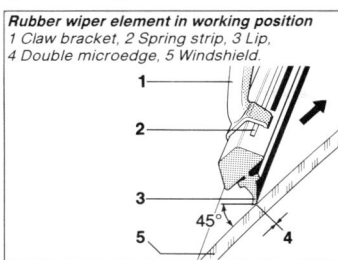

Rear-window wiped areas
The shaded areas indicate impaired visibility with regard to passing vehicles.

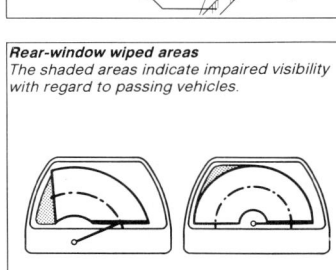

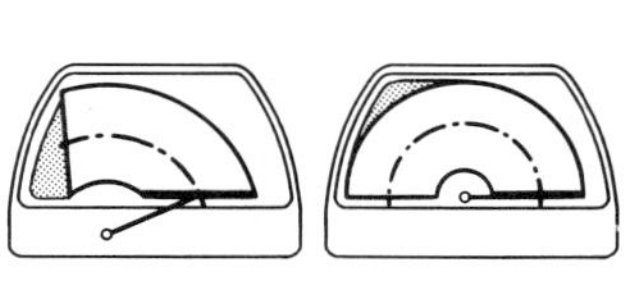

the wiped area is preferred with parking position on the right-hand side (as viewed in the direction of travel). The 180° system is used when rear-window dimensions permit.

Headlamp cleaning systems

Two systems have been adopted for cleaning headlamps: the wipe/wash system and the wash-only system. For the wipe/wash system a wiper arm is driven directly by a motor with a step-down gear unit; the water required to clean the headlamps is taken from the windshield-washer reservoir.

The advantages of the headlamp-wash system lie in its simplicity and often in its easier adaptation to the vehicle styling concept. It is important that the nozzles are positioned correctly so that water jets properly cover the headlamps at all driving speeds.

The law requires that a dirty headlamp whose luminous intensity has been reduced to only 20 % be cleaned within 8 s so that its luminous intensity again reaches 80 %. The system must be able to complete at least 50 cycles on one charge of cleaning fluid.

Location of headlamp cleaning nozzle (wipe/wash system)

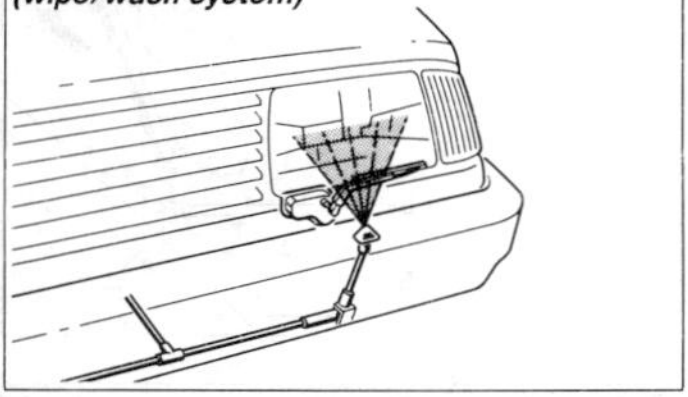

Wiper motor with worm gear
1 DC motor with permanent magnets, 2 Worm gear, 3 Shaft end.

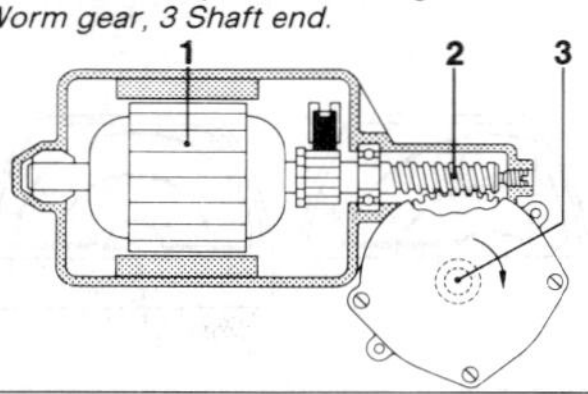

Wiper motors

DC motors with permanent magnets are used as wiper motors. For normal use in windshield-wiper systems, they incorporate a worm-gear unit, but when used in rear-window and headlamp cleaning systems, they often incorporate an additional gear unit for translating rotary motion into oscillating motion (four-bar linkage, rack-and-pinion mechanism or crank-wheel mechanism).

The output of wiper motors for windshield and window cleaning systems is rated differently from that of common electric drives. Legal regulations and application requirements usually specify that the operating speed of the first wipe frequency be $n_{B1} = 45\ \text{min}^{-1}$, and $n_{B2} = 65\ \text{min}^{-1}$ for the second wipe frequency. Taking the maximum friction between rubber element and window, this results in a torque for each wiper arm which the wiper motor must produce at a speed of at least $n_A = 5\ \text{min}^{-1}$. The starting torque M_{An} in Nm for operation of <u>one</u> wiper arm is calculated as follows:

$$M_{An} = F_{WFN} \cdot \mu_{max} \cdot f_s \cdot f_T \cdot L_A \cdot (\omega_{H\,max}/\omega_{Mot}) \cdot (1/\eta_{Gear}) \cdot (R_{Aw}/R_{Ak})$$

F_{WFN} Downward nominal load of the wiper arm in N (arm movement to the windshield or rear window, approx. 15 N per meter wiper blade),

μ_{max} Max. coefficient of dry friction of the rubber element (2.5 at $\varphi = 93\,\%$ relative humidity),

f_s Multiplier to account for wiper-arm joint friction (usually 1.15),

f_T Tolerance factor to account for wiper-arm load tolerance (usually 1.12),

L_A Wiper arm length in m,

$\omega_{H\,max}$ Max. angular velocity of the wiper arm,

ω_{Mot} Mean angular velocity of the wiper-motor crank,

$$\omega_{H\,max}/\omega_{Mot} \approx 0.15 \cdot (0.01 \cdot \omega_w)^2 + \sin(\omega_w/2)$$

ω_w Wiper-angle β or γ

η_{gear} Efficiency of the gear unit, usually assumed to be 0.8; must be measured separately when using special mechanism components (e.g., transversely

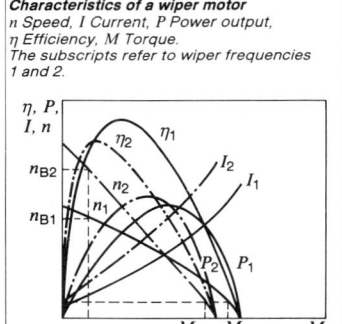

Characteristics of a wiper motor
n Speed, I Current, P Power output,
η Efficiency, M Torque.
The subscripts refer to wiper frequencies 1 and 2.

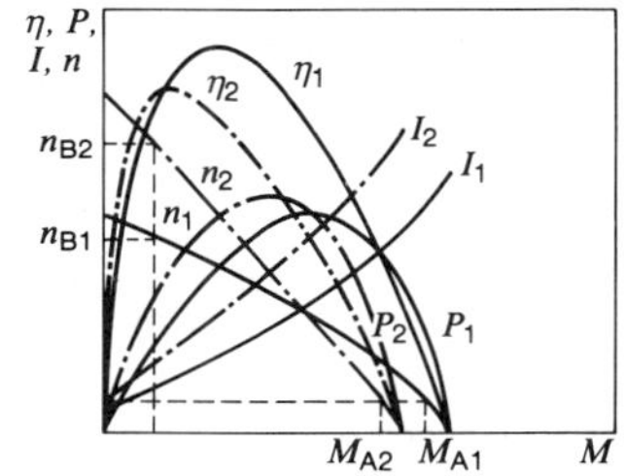

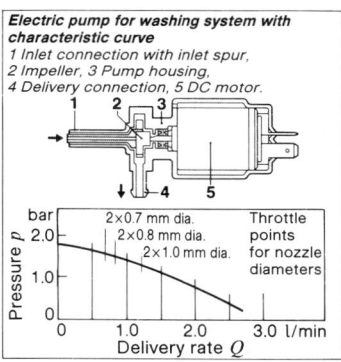

Electric pump for washing system with characteristic curve
1 Inlet connection with inlet spur,
2 Impeller, 3 Pump housing,
4 Delivery connection, 5 DC motor.

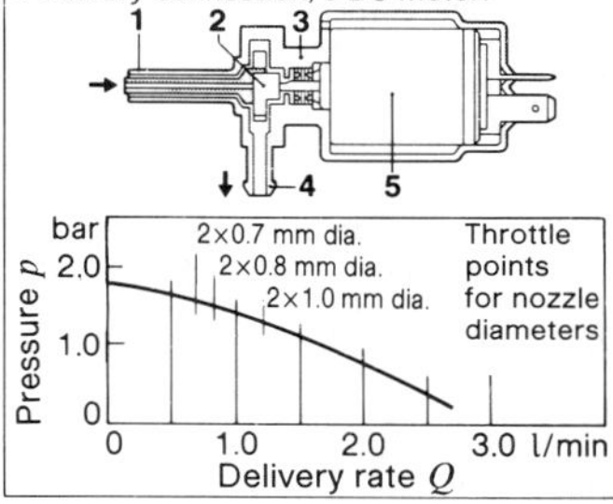

jointed linkage, additional controlled four-bar linkage, multiple O-ring seals),

R_{Aw} Electrical resistance of the rotor winding heated by nominal operation,

R_{Ak} Electrical resistance of the cold rotor winding,

(R_{Aw}/R_{Ak}) is usually 1.25.

The motor's short-circuit strength is another important factor in its design. This is defined as the length of time during which the stalled motor must withstand the full test voltage without short-circuiting its windings (usually specified as $t_K = 15$ min).

Together, the frictional load and the step-down ratio result in a running torque on wet glass which is 0 ... 20 % of the starting torque. In the case of very large windshield wiper systems operating on nearly vertical windshields (e.g., in buses), the torque of the wiper arm resulting from the effect of gravity must also be taken into consideration (separately calculated allowance).

In the case of drive motors with pendular mechanism (rear window and headlamp cleaning systems), the torque at the oscillating shaft must also be determined as follows:

$$M_H = F_{WFN} \cdot \mu_{max} \cdot f_s \cdot f_T \cdot L_A \cdot (R_{Aw}/R_{Ak})$$

Washing systems

To ensure good visibility in the wiped areas, it is imperative that wiper system is backed up by a washing system. Electrical centrifugal pumps of simple design are used (characteristic pump curve) to pump the water through 2 to 4 nozzles and onto the windshield in a narrow spray pattern. The water, to which a cleaning additive is added, is contained in a reservoir of 1.5 ... 2 *l* capacity. If the same water is used also to clean the headlamps, a larger volume of 5 ... 7 *l* is necessary. A separate reservoir is provided for the rear-window cleaning system. The washing system is often coupled to the corresponding wiper system by means of an electronic control in such a way that water is sprayed onto the window or windshield while a pushbutton is pressed, with the wiper system continuing to operate for several additional cycles after the pushbutton is released.

Automotive windshield and window glass

Silica glass is used for automotive windshields and windows.
Approximate composition:
72 % SiO_2 as vitrifier
14 % Na_2O as flux
10 % CaO } as stabilizer
4 % MgO }

Windows are made of flat glass which is poured using the float glass process. Fusion occurs at a temperature of 1550 °C; the melt then passes through a refining zone of 1500 °C to 1100 °C. The melt is then poured onto the so-called float bath (liquid tin) and is cooled to a temperature of 600 °C. It is at this stage that the two plane-parallel surfaces of exceptionally high quality are produced (tin bath surface below, fire-finished surface above). After passing through a cooling zone, the glass is then cut to pieces of 6.10 m × 3.35 m.

The glass can now be further processed in one of two ways:
– As single-pane toughened safety glass (TSG) or
– As laminated safety glass (LSG) which is primarily used for windshields.
TSG windows differ from LSG windows in that they exhibit higher mechanical and thermal strength as well as different breakage and shattering behavior. TSG panes pass through a toughening process which greatly prestresses the surface of the glass. In case of breakage, these windows break into many small dull-edged pieces.

The LSG window, on the other hand, exhibits a normal shattering pattern. When an LSG window is cracked, it is easier to see through than a TSG window.

Material properties and physical data of automotive glass (finished windshields and windows)

Property	Dimension	TSG	LSG
Density	kg/m^3	2500	2500
Surface hardness	Mohs	5 ... 6	5 ... 6
Compressive strength	MN/m^2	700 ... 900	700 ... 900
Modulus of elasticity	MN/m^2	68 000	70 000
Bending strength			
before prestressing	MN/m^2)	30[2])	30[1])
after prestressing	MN/m^2	50[2])	
Impact-ball strength (DIN 52 306) (at room temperature)	Nm	> 7 (227 g ball)	> 90[1]) (2.26 kg ball)
Arrow-drop strength (DIN 52 307) (at room temperature)			> 18[1])
Specific heat	kJ/kgK	0.75 ... 0.84	0.75 ... 0.84
Coefficient of thermal conductivity	W/mK	0.70 ... 0.87	0.70 ... 0.87
Coefficient of thermal expansion	m/mK	$9.0 \cdot 10^{-6}$	$9.0 \cdot 10^{-6}$
Dielectric constant		7 ... 8	7 ... 8
Light transmittance (DIN 52 306), clear	%	≈ 90	≈ 90[1]
Index of refraction		1.52	1.52[1]
Deviation angle of wedging	Angle minute	< 1.0 flat < 1.5 bent	≤ 1.0 flat[1]) ≤ 1.5 bent[1])
Dioptric faults (DIN 52 305)	Dptr.	< 0.03	≤ 0.03[1])
Temperature resistance	°C	200	90[1]) (max. 30′)
Resistance to temperature shocks	K	200	

[1]) Properties of the finished laminated safety glass. In calculating the permissible bending stress, the coupling effect of the PVB film may be neglected.
[2]) Calculated values; these values already contain the necessary safety margins.

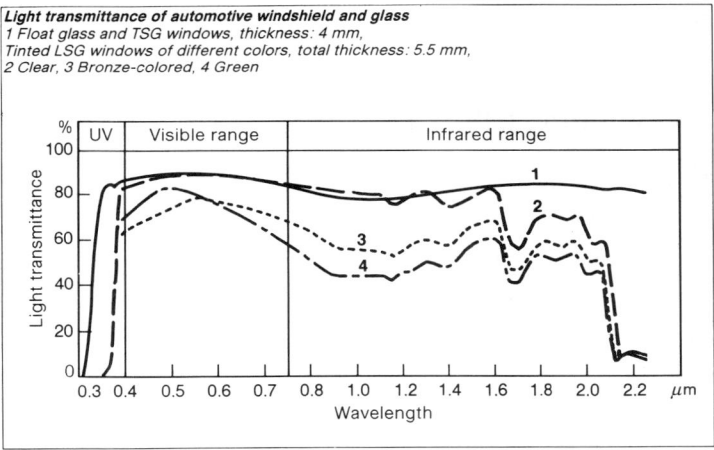

Light transmittance of automotive windshield and glass
1 Float glass and TSG windows, thickness: 4 mm,
Tinted LSG windows of different colors, total thickness: 5.5 mm,
2 Clear, 3 Bronze-colored, 4 Green

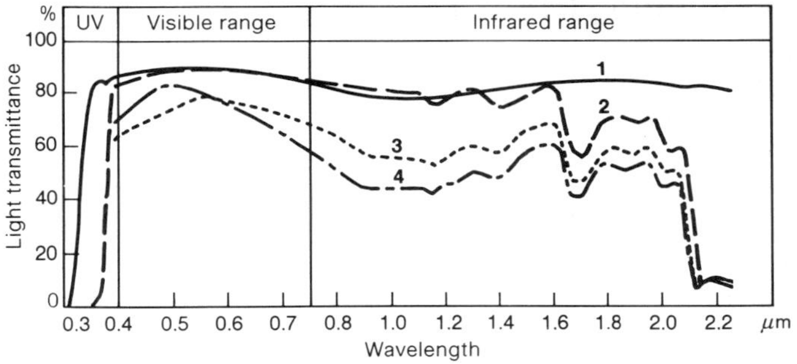

Laminated glass is made of two panes of glass bonded to each other by means of an intermediate film of plastic (polyvinylbutyral).

This type of window design helps to reduce danger of injury because the glass shatters into many small, blunt pieces which are held in place by the plastic film. In the case of the Sekuriflex window (a refinement of the LSG window), an additional plastic film with excellent optical and mechanical properties (e.g., abrasive and scratch resistance) is applied to the inside surface of the window.

Green or bronze-colored windows are used for heat absorption because they block the transmission of infrared light more strongly than light of shorter wave lengths. On the other hand, light transmission in the visual spectrum is reduced from 90 % to 80 %.

Optical properties

The optical properties of TSG and LSG windows are roughly the same, because the optical properties of the PVB film are very nearly the same as those of glass.

Heatable safety glass

In the case of heatable safety glass (TSG), heating conductors are applied to the window (not yet prestressed) using the silk screen process, and are sintered in place during the prestressing process. Subsequent galvanization increases the strength of the heating conductors, tempers them and protects them against environmental influences. Window areas treated in this way can be kept free of mist by heating, and even of ice if the heating power is high enough.

Heated window areas must never be cleaned using caustic or scouring cleansers (e.g. chlorine, ammonia, sand or acids).

In the case of LSG windows, very thin, nearly invisible heating wires are applied in wavy lines to the plastic adhesive film. They are connected in series and/or parallel in order to achieve the intended electrical resistance. The thin wires provide even better heating coverage. The heating power of passenger-car rear window heating systems is approximately 3 ... 5 W/dm^2.

Passenger-compartment heating, ventilation, and air conditioning (HVAC)

Requirements

The vehicle's climate-control system provides for the following:
- a comfortable climate for all passengers,
- an environment calculated to minimize driver stress and fatigue,
- more recent units use filters to remove particulate matter (pollen, dust) and even odors from the air,
- good visibility through all windows, and windshield.

In many countries the performance of the heater unit is governed by legal requirements, with emphasis on the defroster's ability to maintain clear windows and windshields (such as EEC Directive 78/317 within the European Community, and MVSS 103 in the USA).

Comfortable interior temperature and air flow rate as a function of outside temperature

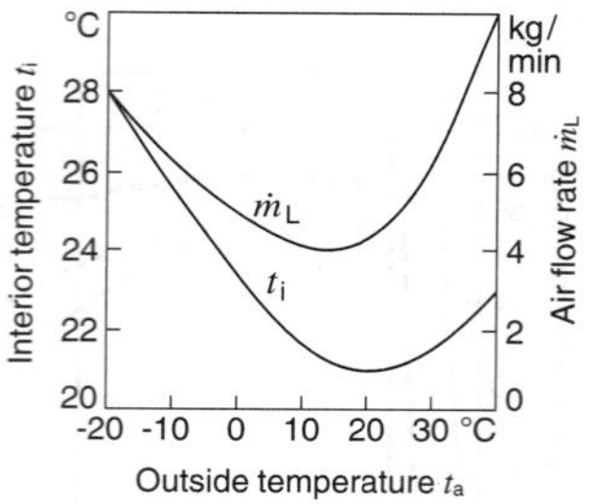

Systems deriving heat from the engine

On vehicles with liquid-cooled engines, the engine heat (by-product of the combustion process) contained in the coolant is used to warm the passenger compartment. With air-cooled engines, engine heat is taken from the exhaust or, in some cases, from the engine's lubrication circuit. The heater core consists of tubes and fins, and employs the same basic design as the engine radiator. Coolant flows through the core's tubes while air flows through its fins. Two design concepts are available for regulating the heater's thermal output.

Coolant-side heater control

With this system, the entire air flow is usually directed through the heater core, while a valve controls the heat level by regulating the flow of coolant through the unit. Extreme precision is required from the valves, which must be capable of providing consistent, stable settings for accurate control at the minimal flow rates necessary for maintaining low heat levels (important during seasonal transitions). A disadvantage lies in the fact that heater output varies according to the coolant's temperature and pressure, meaning that heater performance is affected by engine speed and load.

Air-side heater control

In this type of system the flow of coolant through the heater core is unrestricted. The heat is regulated by dividing the air flow before it reaches the core: A portion of the air flows through the core, while the rest is directed around it. The two currents are subsequently reunited in the plenum chamber. An air flap can be used to regulate the distribution of the two currents, thereby determining the amount of heat taken from the coolant. This type of control arrangement is less sensitive to fluctuations in engine load, and air-temperature adjustments take effect immediately. Water and/or air-side blocks prevent undesirable residual warmth from emerging from the hot core when the heater is not in operation.

One disadvantage of the air-side control layout lies in the larger installation volume required for housing the bypass duct and the plenum chamber.

The air-ventilation current is provided by a constant-speed or adjustable-speed electric blower, whereby aerodynamic pressure can also become a significant factor as vehicle speed increases. The minimum hourly air-flow rate is 30 m^3 per person (figure for reference purposes only). Factors such as passenger-compartment temperature, outside temperature, air flow and heat radiation (to a degree) all affect the process of achieving a comfortable climate (see illustration). Because the precise data on these variables vary substantially from one vehicle to the next, actual figures must be derived empirically.

As motor vehicles have relatively small passenger compartments, drafts and sunlight entering through windshield and windows confront the heating, ventilation, and air-conditioning (HVAC) systems with extreme challenges. In order to enhance passenger comfort, an attempt should be made to maintain the temperature in the footwell 4 ... 8 °C above that of the air around the upper body.

Electronic heater control

Variations in outside-air temperature and vehicle speed cause fluctuations in the temperature of the passenger compartment. On standard systems, constant manual readjustment of the heater controls is necessary for maintaining equilibrium. Electronic heater control dispenses with this requirement by maintaining the interior temperature at the desired level automatically.

On heater units featuring water-side regulation, sensors monitor the temperatures of the vehicle's interior and of the emerging air; the control unit processes this information and compares it with the preselected temperature. Meanwhile, a solenoid valve installed in the cooling circuit opens and closes at a given frequency in response to the signals which it receives from the control unit. The adjustments in open/close ratio in the cycle periods regulate the flow rate from the closed position up to the maximum. A servo-actuated adjustment flap is usually employed to provide infinitely-variable temperature regulation in air-side systems (pneumatic linear adjusters are also occasionally used). Sophisticated systems allowing separate adjustment for the left and right sides of the vehicle are also available.

Air conditioners

The heater unit alone is not capable of providing a comfortable environment at all times. When the outside temperature climbs beyond 20 °C, the air must be cooled to achieve the required interior temperatures. Here, compressor-driven refrigeration units with R 12 (to be phased out in favor of the more environmentally-compatible R 134a by 1995) refrigerant are used. An engine-driven pump compresses the vaporous refrigerant, generating heat in the process. The refrigerant is then pumped to the condenser, where it cools and returns to a liquid state; here, the refrigerant releases the energy which it receives in the compressor and the heat absorbed in the evaporator into the environment. An expansion valve sprays the cooled liquid into the evaporator, where the evaporation process serves to extract heat from the incoming stream of fresh air,

Air conditioner with electronic water-side control (schematic)
1 Blower, 2 Evaporator, 3 Evaporator temperature sensor, 4 Heater core, 5 Solenoid valve, 6 Air exit-temperatur sensor, 7 Setpoint control, 8 Interior sensor (ventilated), 9 Control unit, 10 Compressor; a) Fresh air, b) Recirculated air, c) Defrost, d) AC Bypass, e) Ventilation, f) Footwell, g) Condensation drain.

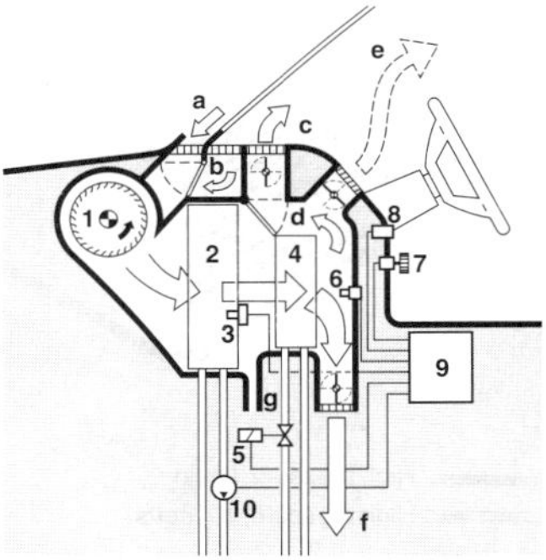

thereby cooling it. Moisture is extracted from the refrigerated air as condensation, reducing the air's humidity to the desired level. Evaporators and condensers are generally designed as tube-and-fin heat exchangers. The evaporator is located before the heater core in the fresh-air stream. Because precise regulation of the cooling process cannot be achieved by simply activating and deactivating the refrigeration circuit, the evaporator must permanently furnish undercooled air, which the heater core then warms to the desired temperature.

Automatic climate control

Automatic climate control is particularly useful for vehicles in which both air conditioner and heater are installed, because the constant monitoring and adjustment required to maintain a temperate climate presents the occupants with a complicated task. This rule applies to bus drivers in particular, as they are exposed only to the conditions at the front of the vehicle. An automatic climate control system incorporating a preselection feature can automatically maintain the correct temperature, air flow and air distribution in the passenger compartment. These parameters are mutually interdependent, and changes to one will affect the others. At the center of the system is a temperature-control circuit for interior temperature. The control unit continuously monitors both the preselected temperature and all essential variables which affect the system, using this information to calculate a setpoint t_i. The setpoint is compared with the actual temperature, and the control unit uses the difference between the two as the basis for determining the required heating, refrigeration, and air-flow rate. Another function controls the position of the air-distribution flaps with reference to the program which the occupants have

Coolant circuit of an air-conditioning system

1 Compressor, 2 Electric clutch (for compressor on/off function), 3 Condenser, 4 Auxiliary fan, 5 High-pressure switch, 6 Fluid reservoir with desiccant insert, 7 Low-pressure switch, 8 Temperature switch or on/off control (for compressor on/off function), 9 Temperature sensor, 10 Condensate drip pan, 11 Evaporator, 12 Evaporator fan, 13 Fan switch, 14 Expansion valve.

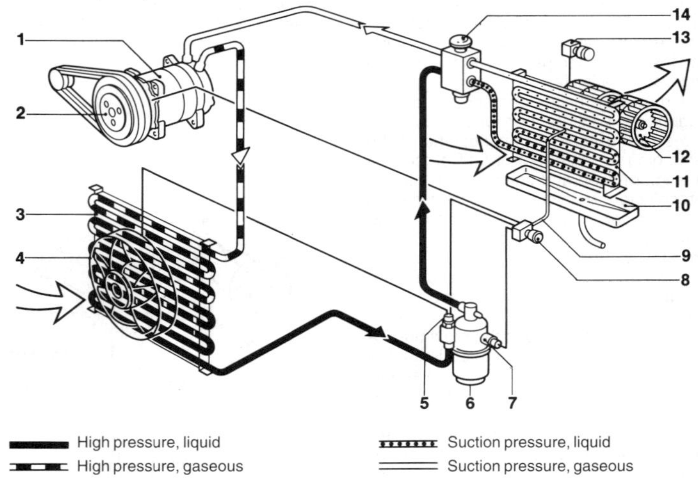

selected. Meanwhile, all control circuits continue to respond to manual inputs.

The setpoint temperature determined by the control unit is achieved by means of water or air-side adjustments (as described in "Electronic heater control).

Infinitely-variable or graduated blower control is used to adjust the air flow to the specified level. There is generally no setpoint processing involved in this operation. This type of arrangement is inadequate for dealing with the increases in flow rate caused by aerodynamic pressure at high speeds. Here, a special control function can compensate by responding to increasing vehicle speeds, initially by reducing the blower speed to zero, and then, should the flow continue to rise, by using a restriction flap to throttle the stream of incoming air.

Control of air distribution to the three levels – defroster, upper compartment and footwell – is effected manually, with preselection, or with a fully-automatic program. Especially popular are units featuring program control buttons in which each button provides a specific air-distribution pattern for the three levels.

The defroster represents a special case. In order to clear the windows as rapidly as possible, the temperature control must revert to maximum heat and maximum blower speed while directing the air flow through the upper defroster outlets. On systems with program switches and fully-automatic units, this operating mode is selected with a single button; at temperatures above 0 °C the refrigeration unit is also activated to extract humidity from the air. To prevent the still unheated air giving rise to drafts, the blower is switched off electronically after cold starts in winter, except when "DEF" and cooling are in operation.

The variations described above are used in both passenger cars and trucks. Buses require more complicated layouts. The passenger compartment can be divided into several control zones, in which the temperature is controlled by electronically regulating the speed of the zone's individual water pump.

Auxiliary heater installations

The fuel for units which produce heat without the aid of the engine is supplied either by the standard vehicle tank, or, on large vehicles, by a separate tank. An electric pump supplies the fuel to an injector, which sprays a fuel mist into the combustion chamber; the mist mixes with the air and burns. The hot exhaust gases are then directed to a heat exchanger. The heat exchanger can function in one of two ways, either warming the interior air directly, or by transferring heat to the engine's coolant circuit. In the latter case circulation is maintained by a separate electric pump, making it possible to use the standard heating unit to warm the passenger compartment. This type of auxiliary heating for the engine coolant also improves cold-start response in the winter.

Auxiliary air heater (independent of engine)
1 Air heater with blower for combustion and heating air, combustion chamber and heat exchanger, 2 Hot-air intake, 3 Air outlet to vehicle interior, 4 Combustion-air intake, 5 Fuel supply, 6 Exhaust system, 7 Electronic control unit, 8 Thermostat and timer for preselecting switch-on time.

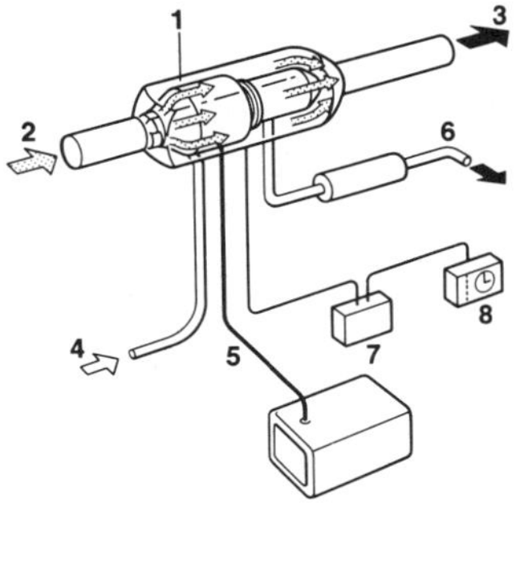

Automotive sound systems

Reception conditions

Common phenomena which reduce the quality of FM reception include path interference (mountain effect), such as briefly occurs when the signal path is interrupted by a mountain or building (producing hiss), and delayed reception of the broadcast waves that have been reflected by these obstacles (producing multipath distortion). Other sources of interference: Cross-talk from adjoining high-power transmitters, interference at one frequency emanating from intermodulation products of two other – more powerful – transmitters.

Technical terms

ARI (radio information for the driver): This traffic-information system is the product of a cooperative development project involving Blaupunkt, the ADAC (the largest German motorists' association) and the German ARD radio network. The system is in active use in Germany, Switzerland, Austria, and Luxembourg.

Those FM broadcasters participating in the traffic-information network constantly transmit a special identification signal (SK), which is recognized by all ARI-equipped radios. If the ARI button has been activated, the channel scanner will pause only at traffic-information stations.

The stations also transmit a supplementary regional identification (BK) code to identify the specific area for which traffic information is being broadcast. A code letter (A through F) appears in the display on radios which are capable of regional recognition (letters correspond to those found on the blue signs on German highways).

Yet another signal, the announcement code, is transmitted for the actual traffic announcements. This signal ensures that the driver always hears the traffic information at an appropriate volume (adjustable), quite aside from whether the radio is turned down or a cassette or CD is playing (playback mechanism pauses for the duration of the announcement).

Antenna-diversity recognition: This is a receiver system for vehicles which are equipped with several – usually two – antennas (e.g., window antennas). It's chief function is to alleviate the effects of the multipath distortion induced by reflected radio waves. As multipath interference is characterized by substantial local fluctuations in field strength (within a range of 50 ... 100 cm), at least one of the vehicle's antennas can usually be counted on to be positioned for clear reception, provided that there is sufficient distance between them. The diversity system automatically switches over to the antenna with the best reception. Different systems are characterized by varying degrees of technical complexity.

a) Conventional scanner (1-tuner diversity): Should the reception quality at antenna "A" fall below a specified level, the unit responds by tentatively switching to antenna "B". If "B" is even worse, then the unit reverts to "A". If "B" is better, the unit remains at "B".

b) Selective process (multi-tuner diversity): Each antenna feeds to its own tuner. The system can compare the reception quality at the respective antennas on a continuous, uninterrupted basis, using this information to select the antenna providing the best signal.

ADA (Auto-Directional Antenna): This is a multi-antenna reception system which uses a separate tuner with each antenna in a layout similar to that of the "selective process" described above. The salient difference lies in the fact that there is no alternation between antennas with ADA. Instead, the system processes all – up to four – antenna/tuner signals, modifying amplitudes and phase lengths as required for subsequent summation. A special control algorithm automatically processes amplitude and phase to ensure that minimal interference is reflected in the cumulative signal. The system can thus selectively deactivate reception from individual directions, electronically simulating the response of a directional antenna.

ADA has been designed for application with several window antennas and/or simple wire and foil antennas in bumpers.

ASU: Automatic interference suppression for car radios, suppresses ignition noise in the FM band.

Output power: Amplified output which the car radio or auxiliary amplifier (amplifier, booster) transmits to the speakers. DIN 45 324 draws a distinction between RMS output (max. continuous power) and music output (brief maxima); both are rated in watts. The relationship between "volume" and "output" is exponential. The increase in volume produced by doubling the output is just barely audible (3 dB). More important is the speakers' efficiency factor (volume in dB/1W/1m). Although "output variations in watts" are of limited practical value, technical justification for the installation of ultra-high-output systems may well be present in the form of reduced low-frequency distortion (→ Automotive speakers → Subwoofers).

CD (Compact Disk): 12 or 8-centimeter sound-reproduction medium featuring signals stored in digital form and playing times extending to 74 minutes. A laser beam is directed toward a reflective information layer for contactless optical scanning. Variations in this layer (pits) dampen the reflected beam received by the prism. A light diode monitors this information for binary transmission to a digital-analog converter. A new 16-bit amplitude value is processed 44,100 times per second, providing the D/A converter with the data required to reconstitute the original sound signal.

PCI (Program Comparison and Identification): This separate station-identification system is found in the Blaupunkt Berlin IQR 85/88, where it operates independently of the RDS network. Continuing updates on transmitter information by means of data cassette. The automatic frequency-diversity system uses dual-tuner technology for inaudible selection of the best reception.

RDS (Radio Data System): Digitalized data-transmission system for FM broadcasters, who transmit the RDS "data telegram" in a single standardized format throughout Europe. The data, which can be interpreted by car (or home) radios equipped with RDS decoders, include the following (status as of 1991):

– The call letters or identity of the station being received (e.g., "BAYERN 3" or "BBC 1") appear on the radio's display (PS Code).

– Also transmitted is a list of alternative frequencies on which the current broadcast can also be received (AF Code). The RDS receiver responds to reductions in the quality of reception from the station to which the radio is tuned by searching through the AF list for alternative frequencies for the same station. If the first alternative provides better reception, then the unit locks onto the new frequency. If it is worse, then RDS continues to the next substitute frequency. The process is virtually inaudible under ideal conditions (depending on individual unit design).

– Each station also has an identification number (PI Code) for backup verification. The PI code must remain constant when the system selects a substitute frequency, otherwise the system registers an unallowed station change.

– Traffic-information and announcement codes (TP and TA Codes). The RDS receiver evaluates TP and TA in a process analogous to that employed for ARI-SK and DK (→ ARI). As most European countries are still without an ARI traffic-information system, implementation with RDS was a logical step. The present ARI system will remain in place though, operating parallel to RDS, for some time to come. Stations with the RDS features listed above – usually the national networks, but including some private broadcasters – can be received in the following countries (status: 1991):

D, CH, A, F, I, E, PO, B, NL, LUX, GB, IRL, DK, S, N, SF, YU.

The RDS format incorporates further options which will be available for future requirements:

– **PTY Code (Program Type):** Classifies up to 16 different program types according to their content, i.e., news, classical music, etc.

– **"PTY 31":** Control signal for superimposition of civil defense messages for the general population (similar to TA). The PTY 31 function cannot be deactivated.

– **EON Code (Enhanced Other Networks):** Provides the driver with the option of directly selecting another broadcast from the same transmitting station. "EON" also informs the receiver when a traffic announcement is being transmitted on a parallel program, and can switch to this parallel broadcast for the announcement's duration (GB, S).
– **TMC Code (Traffic Message Channel):** For future application as a source of standardized information bits, e.g., on traffic congestion. The information bits can be triggered for reproduction - in any language, at any time - via speech synthesizer. Driver guidance systems can monitor warnings on obstructions for immediate calculation of the best route for the given conditions.
– **MS Code (Music/Speech):** Automatically adjusts volume and tone for optimal reproduction of either speech or music.
– **CT Code (Clock/Date):** Time, date.
– **DI Code (Decoder Information):** Control information for the receiver unit, for instance, whether the current broadcast is being transmitted in Dolby stereo.
– **PIN Code (Program-Item Number):** Corresponds to the VPS function used to trigger video recordings of televised broadcasts. Automatic control for recording preselected programs
– **RT Code (Radio Text):** Text transmission and corresponding display (such as music titles) for home receivers - not for mobile receivers.
– **RP Code (Radio Paging):** Call paging and message relay for individual subscribers. The available network of FM stations is utilized to provide paging service (S, N, DK, F, PO).
– **TDC Code (Transparent Data Channel):** Intended for text displays on video screens, also suitable for graphic displays and program transmissions.
– **NWS Code (National Warning System):** Intended to provide national civil defense and disaster-control services with a means of internal communication.

Auxiliary equipment

– **Amplifier, booster:** → Output power
– **Equalizer:** Equalizers are employed to improve bass and treble response through graduated amplification and/or suppression of individual frequency ranges. The specific acoustical properties of the motor vehicle's interior result in distortions of emphasis (non-linear propagation). The equalizer can compensate for these distortions, with parametric equalizers providing optimal results.
– **CD Changer:** CD player for installation in the luggage compartment. The CD changer is loaded with a disk magazine capable of holding up to 12 disks, depending upon the precise configuration. The CDs and the individual tracks are selected using either a suitably-equipped radio or a separate remote-control unit.

Automotive speakers

The acoustical properties of the vehicle's interior, the speakers' locations and the speakers themselves all influence the quality of musical reproduction. The larger the speakers, the better the bass response (e.g., four x 160 mm system). Separate subwoofers are becoming popular in sound systems at the higher end of the price range; they can be hidden below the rear tray or on the panel between passenger compartment and trunk. For optimal reproduction, subwoofer systems generally require → Amplifiers.

Antennas

The effectiveness of a vehicle's antenna is directly proportional to its distance from the vehicle's major ground masses. Good reception is ensured by the telescoping rod antenna, also available as a motor-driven "automatic antenna". An alternative is the integral window or windshield-mounted antenna which is also available as an aftermarket unit for attaching to the inner surface of windshield or windows. Although it is more sensitive to direction, which puts it at a slight disadvantage relative to the rod-type unit, its advantages are no maintenance and no wear. In contrast to the rod antenna, the window unit causes no aerodynamic drag, and it requires no retraction space. A third alternative is a short, flexible whip antenna which is technically a compromise between the other two extremes.

Vehicle monitoring system (Check-Control)

This unit monitors important operational and safety-related vehicle components. The status of the following parameters can be checked before and during vehicle operation: Engine oil level (two levels: "static" and "dynamic") – engine coolant level – windshield washer-fluid level (level sensor) – operation of low-beam headlamps, stop lamps, back-up lamps and license-plate lamps.

The system

A sensor is provided for each of the monitored functions. The system also watches the condition of the wires with transmit current to the lamps, and includes an additional check for the stop-lamp fuses. To enhance safety, failure of both stop lamps is indicated to the driver immediately, even without the brake pedal being depressed. Defects at other lamps are indicated only once an attempt is made to switch them on. Open circuits also trigger a malfunction display.

German law requires an initial test of stop-lamp condition when the vehicle is started. The system simulates a brake defect between the time the ignition is switched on and the first application of the brake pedal. The lamp indicates satisfactory operation by going out, and responds to defects by remaining on.

Operation

In the course of a 50 ms test sequence, the microprocessor registers the conditions of each sensor, of the current lines and of the stop-lamp fuses. A defect (e.g., bulb failure, blown fuse, open wire) triggers the start of the individual delay period for the fault block in question (approximate delays of 0.5 sec. for lamps, 1 sec. for fluids with engine off, and 10 sec. for fluids with engine running). Due to the delay feature, even the levels of "sloshing" fluids can be monitored accurately. If a malfunction cannot be verified before expiration of the programmed delay period for the single process check (e.g., due to the effects of extraneous interference factors), the fault memory is reset, and added up again if the malfunction continues to exist. As each function block is equipped with its own counter, all malfunctions are monitored and registered separately. Should a counter indicate that the value corresponding to a specific delay period has been exceeded, the system triggers a blinking warning lamp and the LED for the function in question, providing a visual fault display. The driver can cancel the flashing warning by pressing a button, but the LED will remain on until the malfunction has been rectified, thereby providing the driver with a constant reminder of the defect. The engine-oil fault memory is reset by adding oil to the engine with the ignition switched off.

Locations of the components in the vehicle

1 Test pushbutton, 2 Engine coolant, 3 Engine oil, 4 Windshield washer fluid, 5 Stop lamps, 6 Back-up lamp, 7 License-plate lamp, 8 Low-beam headlamps, 9 Additional equipment for specific countries; Seat-belt monitor, air bag, O_2 sensor, 10 Central information lamp.

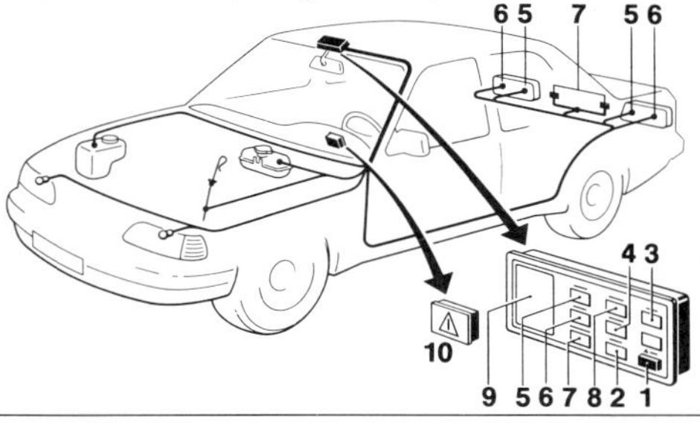

Trip computers

The trip computer provides: Time, instantaneous fuel consumption, average fuel consumption, average speed, remaining operating range, trip time (stopwatch function), outside temperature.

The unit is divided into three function blocks: Control, central-processing unit and the display section.

The control unit is a panel containing the keys used to activate the desired functions. The function keys provide sequential selection of the individual displays, while the default key calls up the time display. Instantaneous fuel consumption and outside temperature are displayed as current values, while the figure for average consumption is based on the immediately preceding 30 km. The fuel-range-warning function is triggered automatically when the data for current consumption and remaining fuel indicate a remaining range of less than 50 km.

The central processing unit consists of a microcomputer with voltage regulator and the special peripherals for processing incoming sensor signals. When the ignition is switched on, separate counters and A/D converters begin continuous monitoring of the signals relaying information on fuel supply, outside temperature, pulses for distance, fuel-injection, and flow rate. The sensors then convert the data to a format suitable for computer processing before transmitting it to the computer in the appropriate time-slot pattern. The process calculations for the individual functions are performed at one-second intervals. Each time a key is activated, the unit responds by initiating a new calculation, providing immediate display of the desired information. Meanwhile, the operating voltage is scrutinized to verify that it remains within the specified limits, and the display is updated. The wiring is coded to allow installation in various types of vehicle, providing the computer with access to the assorted data stored in the ROM (distance codes, injection system, tank sensors, etc.). A connector plug furnishes the link between the CPU and vehicle wiring on the one hand, and input panel and display on the other.

The display unit usually consists of an LCD with variable-intensity illumination. There is also an operating mode allowing display of all monitored data, vehicle version, and test results; this mode facilitates diagnosis during production and in service and maintenance.

Trip recorder (schematic diagram)

Connections: 1 Instrument illumination, 2 Tank sensor, 3 Temperature sensor, 4 Distance pulse, 5 Fuel-injection pulse, 6 Flow-rate sensor, 7 Function, Default, Reset keys, 8 Vehicle type code.

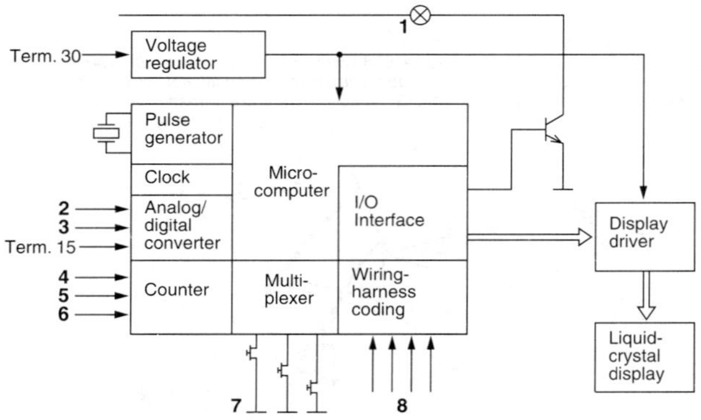

Park Pilot

Many modern automotive designs severely restrict rearward vision, frequently making it difficult or even impossible to discern obstacles behind the vehicle. A particular hazard is posed by boundary stones and vehicles with low hoods. As the driver cannot estimate the actual distance between vehicle and obstacle, it is often impossible to make full use of the available parking space. The Park Pilot with its integrated software furnishes a direct display of the distance separating the vehicle from the object(s) to the rear.

Design

The Park Pilot's individual components are the control unit, the display (options: lamps or LCD in digital format) and the sensors which incorporate the ultrasonic transmitters and receivers.

Distance monitoring

The principle is the same as that employed for echo depth soundings. All sensors are triggered for a brief period (approx. 150 µs) at regular intervals (cycles of approx. 30 ms). The unit transmits ultrasonic waves (approx. 30 kHz) both in the triggering period and in the subsequent, physically-induced resonance period at the diaphragm. The sensors then switch to the reception mode in which they monitor the ultrasonic waves which are reflected back. The distance between vehicle and object is determined with reference to the transit time (delay) for the first echo signal:

Pulse shapes
a) Transmit pulse , b) Echo pulse,
t_n Post-pulse oscillation period (approx. 1 ms),
t_e Transit time.

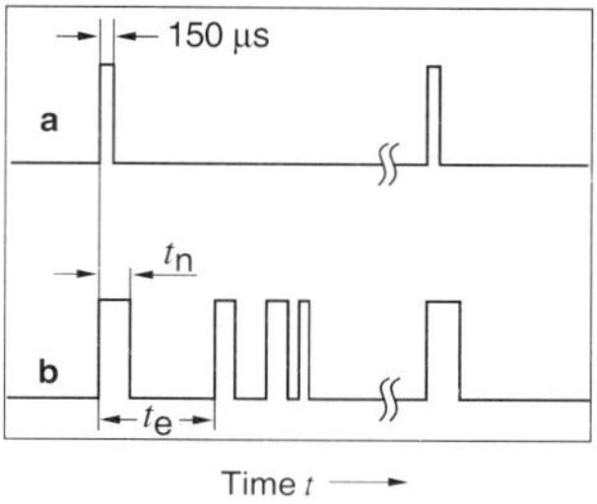

Distance $s = 0.5 \cdot t_e \cdot v_s$
with t_e Transit time
$v_s = 340$ m/s
(Speed of sound in air).

Operation

The unit is activated when reverse gear is engaged. Operation starts with an initial self-test in which all display elements and sensors are activated and checked for correct operation. Upon completion of the self-test, the unit provides one of three displays: The ready display, indicating that the device is functioning properly, the distance to an obstacle, or a recognized unit error. The unit monitors an area to the rear of the vehicle extending between 0 ... 160 cm; this distance, in turn, is divided into four warning zones (Table).

A special calibration mode makes it possible to adapt the system for use in various installation positions.

Zone	Distance to obstacle in cm	Warning mode
I	160 ... 100	Continuous optical signal
II	100 ... 50	Continuous optical signal, intermittent acoustic signal (cycle duration inversely proportional to distance from obstacle)
III	50 ... 30	Continuous optical signal, continuous acoustic signal
IV	30	Flashing optical display, continuous acoustic signal

Trip recorders

These devices record the vehicle speed, the distance covered (odometer), and the time. They also incorporate a warning lamp which is triggered when vehicles exceed a preset speed (such as the legally-permitted limit, or the maximum speed commensurate with economical operation). The following data is also recorded on the tachograph chart along with the corresponding clock time: Road-speed curve, wheel time and pauses, distance covered. The trip recorder, which is designed specifically so that it can be calibrated, is mandatory for certain vehicle categories within Germany (Paragraph 57b, StVZO). Various other countries also have specific national regulations governing the use of trip recorders.

Mode of operation

The EC tachograph is a special form of trip recorder which incorporates an auxiliary feature allowing differentiated recording of wheel time and Test periods (time-group monitor); different versions are available, for either one driver or two. The EC tachograph meets all the requirements set forth in EEC Directive 3821/85, i.e., the EC tachograph charts serve as the driver's official daily record. Within the European Community, the EC tachograph is obligatory equipment on specific types of vehicle, where it monitors compliance with the wheel time and rest periods prescribed in EEC Directive 3820/85. The supplementary features on the EC tachograph include a clock-function display and an LED which confirms to the driver that the charts are installed and that all styluses are functioning properly.

Some tachographs also display and record engine speed, while operation control and further parameters can also be recorded when the appropriate options are installed. These include the two-stage auxiliary stylus (e.g., for recording fuel consumption) and contacts which trigger

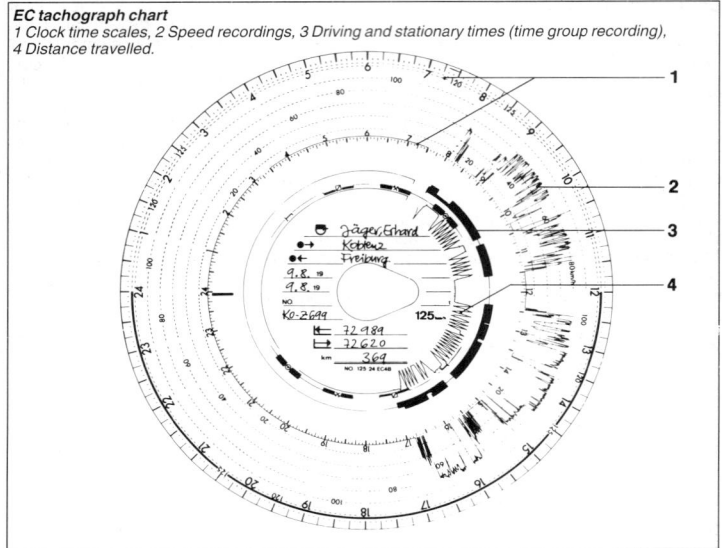

EC tachograph chart

1 Clock time scales, 2 Speed recordings, 3 Driving and stationary times (time group recording), 4 Distance travelled.

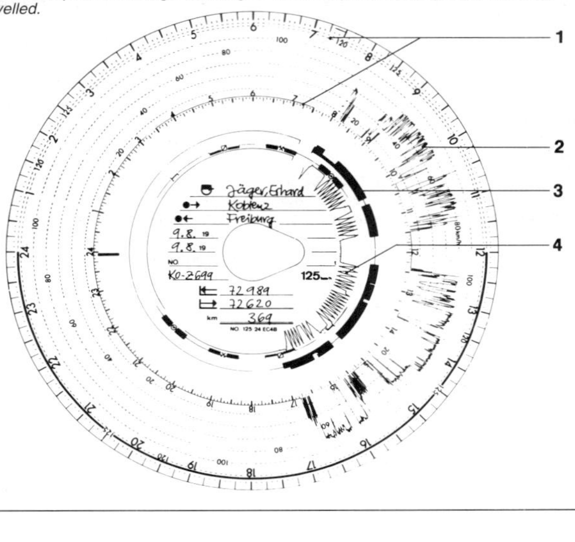

other warning and control devices in response to vehicle and engine speed.

Trip recorders and EC tachographs must maintain the strict operating tolerances defined in the German Calibration Regulations, in Paragraph 57b of the StVZO and in EEC Directive 3821/85. These regulations also extend to govern periodic inspection of tachograph and related equipment at authorized facilities.

The tachograph chart can be interpreted using any of several methods, including visual, electronic and microscopic evaluation. Visual evaluation is the simplest method, as the chart disk makes it possible to appraise and check an entire day's operation at a glance. Systematic visual evaluation embraces the following individual checks: Written entries, working time, breaks, rest periods, assessment of driving style, fuel consumption and engine speed, as well as manipulated or incorrect recordings. Microscopic examination uses a special microscope to analyze the recording down to a precision range measured in seconds and meters. The data gathered can be entered in a time/distance graph (see illustration) for precise reconstruction, e.g., of the events preceding an accident.

The tachograph charts can also serve as part of a fleet-management program, with partially or fully-automatic computerized analysis and processing.

Pulse drive is employed on tachographs featuring electronic monitoring systems. It runs on signals produced by a pulse generator, installed either within the vehicle or at the transmission's speedometer-drive gear, which converts the mechanical rotation of the speedometer pinion into electronic pulses.

The most modern electronic trip recorders and EC tachographs incorporate an integral conversion feature to adapt the unit for variations in the number of pulses per meter traveled. No extraneous devices are required. On vehicles with variable-ratio rear axles, a conversion-gear unit modifies the ratio of the tachograph's drive signal to maintain synchronization with vehicle conditions.

Accident chart with microscopically determined driving-speed curve

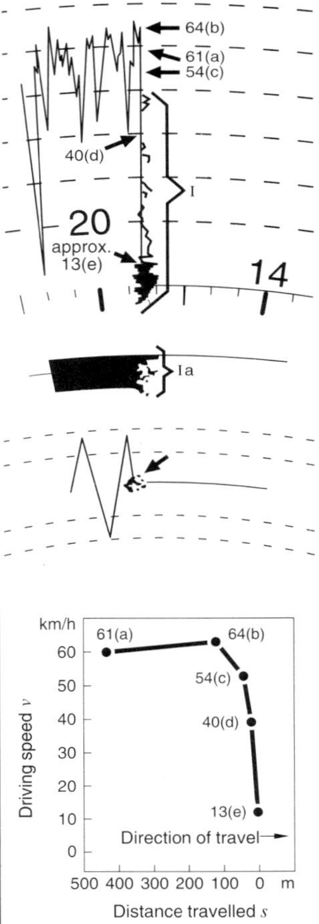

Navigation systems

The range of navigation systems extends to embrace everything from simple orientation aids to guidance systems featuring automatic route determination. All of the navigation systems include the same basic components: An orientation device with sensors for determining instantaneous vehicle position, a means of entering the destination and a readout mechanism for providing the driver with information on the best routes to the specified target point. The type and number of components depend upon the complexity of the specific system, while additional systems, such as data memories for storing digital road maps, represent a useful supplement.

Orientation

Systems based on compound navigation - or dead reckoning - are acquiring prominence as the standard for automotive applications. Such units require no external transmitter infrastructure. Vehicle motion is monitored and registered with cyclical tabulation of increment and direction (coupling). As the accumulated error tends to be on the order of 2% of the total trip distance, the composite-navigation process must be abetted by some form of supplementary aid. On simple systems this assist assumes the shape of a periodic manual position correction. In more complex systems, such as "Travel Pilot," the control computer compares the information of vehicle motion with a digitalized representation of the local street network and makes the necessary corrections automatically (map matching).

The area coverage provided by the GPS satellite positioning system is expanding at the same time that the cost for suitable receivers is coming down; thus orientation via satellite signal represents an additional source of information for the future.

Sensor core in geomagnetic sensor
1 Sensor winding (x), 2 Sensor winding (y), 3 Excitation winding, 4 Core ring.

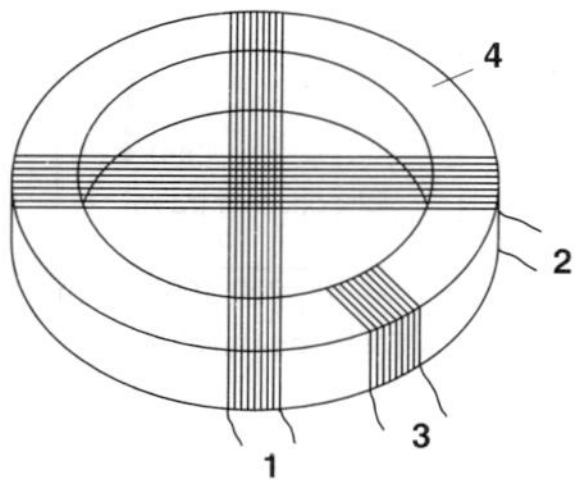

Sensors

The composite navigation process depends on two types of sensors, monitoring wheel motion and geomagnetism.

Wheel sensors

The wheel sensors record the rotation of the wheels at one axle, generating the pulses which provide the basis for periodic calculations of distance traveled and changes in direction. Changes in direction are indicated by a discrepancy in the rotational speeds on the inside and outside wheels; here the number of pulses per rotation must be high enough to ensure adequate recognition of variations in angle. In addition, the sensors must also be capable of monitoring vehicle movement at extremely low speeds in order to prevent disorientation during parking manoeuvres or in stop-and-go driving.

Geomagnetic sensors

The geomagnetic sensors frequently operate on the flux-gate principle. They contain an annular core in which an excitation winding generates a triangle-shaped alternating field, which the earth's continuous field overlaps. Saturation at the annular core induces voltage pulses at the sensor windings arranged on the core at right angles, providing an index for the horizontal component of the earth's magnetic field. When the system is installed, the magnetic fields emanating from the vehicle's ferrous masses and the current flow from major loads must be measured in an initial calibration process, providing the control unit's microcomputer with the data it needs for compensatory calculations.

Destination entry

Destinations are entered into the more basic systems in the form of coordinates. These, in turn, are derived from appropriate maps using different methods representing varying levels of convenience. Some systems feature memories with adequate storage capacity for street and name directories, allowing the driver to enter postal addresses. These systems convert the information into the required coordinates automatically.

Route and direction recommendations

The computer bases its route recommendations on the result of a comparison of actual and target positions which it performs. Less complex systems indicate the linear distance to and direction of the destination. The driver must interpret the data to determine the best route, with no supplementary information on the surrounding street network being provided.

The "Travelpilot" furnishes additional information in the guise of a map section. The unit scrolls and turns the map in response to vehicle motion and changes in direction, while the driver may select from a number of scales. The system makes it much easier to decide on the best route to a given destination.

Future versions of the "Travelpilot" will also carry out automatic route calculations and highlight the recommended path on the map in the monitor. To minimize demands on the driver, the display will be limited to the next intersection and the direction in which to continue, while the recommendation can be provided in acoustic form in order to avoid distracting the driver from the road.

Travelpilot
Map display.

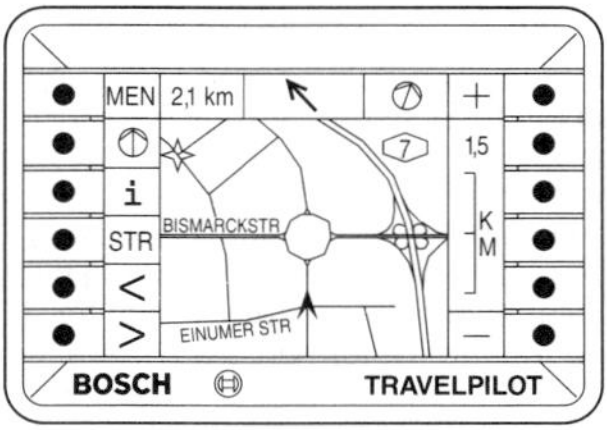

Route calculations

Those systems that already use stored road-network data as a backup for correcting dead-reckoning errors can also use this same information to automatically determine the best route, the proviso being that the control computer must possess adequate processing reserves.

When a given route recommendation is not followed, the subsequent route calculations should always be processed quickly enough to ensure that the driver receives a new recommendation before reaching the next intersection.

Depending upon the desired data quality, it may be necessary to equip the system to provide supplementary information on topics such as driving time for individual stages, bridges, one-way streets, limited-access roads.

Map memory

The map memory's storage capacity must be large enough to ensure access to all the data required for a large area. A change of storage medium should only be required under special circumstances. A CD ROM with a capacity of about 600 Mb is suitable for this type of application. A useful estimate of the capacity required to store a given area in digital form is 1 or 2 bytes per inhabitant; this figure varies according to the extent of the available details. The CD ROM drives must feature shorter access times and greater shock resistance than their counterparts in audio applications.

Mobile radio

Mobile radio systems can be divided into two categories: Public radio networks (car phones, etc.) and private mobile radio (or PMR). The public radio networks are – like their land-line counterparts – universal-access systems. In contrast, access to a PMR system is restricted to specific groups. Mobile radio networks consist of mobile transmitter/receiver units (mobile stations) and the requisite infrastructure (system administration, stationary units and base stations). Attempts to economize on the number of necessary frequencies have led to the establishment of cellular networks; these make it possible to use the same frequency repeatedly in numerous cells, provided that the distances between the cells are sufficient. The precise number of stationary transmitters employed in a single network will depend upon the size of the area being served and/or the number of subscribers. Mobile radio units fall into three categories: Vehicle units, portable radios and hand-held devices.

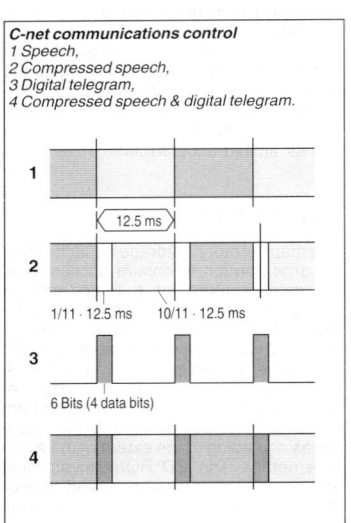

C-net communications control
1 Speech,
2 Compressed speech,
3 Digital telegram,
4 Compressed speech & digital telegram.

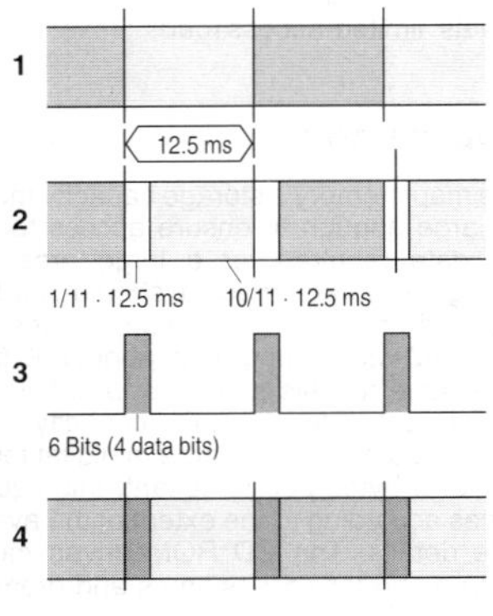

Cellular telephone networks

Communications within the mobile telephone network are always established via a stationary base station; the network is not restricted to providing communications between mobile units, and access to and from the standard land-line telephone system is also possible.

C Net

This radio-telephone network operates in the 450 MHz band within Germany, where there were approximately 350,000 C-Net subscribers in mid-1991. The network has been expanded repeatedly to cope with the considerable growth rates in the number of participants, with frequent reductions in cell size in urban areas.

The communications path between two units is established and monitored with digital telegrams relayed on special organization channels. The system administration facility continually monitors existing communications links on the oral-communications channels by slotting digital telegrams into gaps in the speech transmission. The speech transmission is subdivided into blocks of 12.5 ms. Before transmission, these blocks are compressed into time units of 10/11 x 12.5 ms. The digital telegrams are inserted into the resulting gaps of 1/11 x 12.5 ms.

Upon arrival at the receiver, the telegram is filtered from the transmission signal and the speech is re-expanded to its original value of 12.5 ms.

GSM Net

In 1987, in a step aimed at resolving compatibility problems among the various European systems and at providing a uniform system for the future, the Conference of European Postal and Telecommunications Administrations, or CEPT, decided to set up a digitalized cellular mobile telephone system for all of Europe. The system entered operation in mid-1991. The number of potential subscribers within Germany is placed at about 2.5 million, with 10 ... 15 million expected for Europe as a whole.

Private mobile radio systems

These are mobile-radio networks designed specifically to meet the individual operational requirements of various customer groups. The essential object is to provide total radio coverage within a specific, well-defined area, thus ensuring consistent access to the mobile stations. At less than 1 second, the typical times for establishing the link are substantially below those for mobile telephone networks.

The most important subscriber groups are:
- Electric utilities,
- Public transport authorities,
- Official agencies and security organizations,
- Common-frequency subscribers,
- Taxi and rental-car agencies.

Within Germany, the total number of PMR users stands at approximately 750,000. Various signaling procedures are employed to administer the communications links. Selective-call networks allow the user to call a specific individual station. The most important signaling procedures are the 5-tone sequence and the digital calling methods.

The five digits of the 5-tone sequence contain the code for the station address of the party being called, with each digit being assigned a value of 0 ... 9. Each number represents a frequency. The transmission time for each number is 70 ms.

Upon receiving and processing the 5-tone sequence, the target station transmits an acknowledge signal in the form of its own 5-tone sequence, while a call tone is also generated to alert the caller. This establishes the communications link.

Systems employing a digital calling system represent a further development of the tone sequence method. The data in the "call" and "acknowledge" telegrams are contained in binary codes. Frequencies of 1800 Hz and 1200 Hz are assigned to the bits "0" and "1" respectively. The advantage over the tone-sequence method lies in the fact that the digital telegram can relay additional information over and beyond the target address.

Trunk radio networks

In order to eliminate the increasing frequency-crowding which was plagueing the PMR networks, in 1989 the German Post Office's TELEKOM division decided to set up trunk radio networks in the 400 MHz band. The object is to increase utilization efficiency through common use and administration of several radio channels. Under the same conditions, the system accomodates more users on each channel than a conventional network. It provides good access within the trunk radio network and exclusive communications links. The possibility of dialling from the mobile station into the public land-line telephone system should be mentioned.

The link is administered through a special radio frequency within the frequency group (organization channel), as defined by Specification MPT 1327 (MPT, Ministry of Post and Telecommunications). The system administration transmits periodic status-request telegrams to the mobile stations; these signals are contained within specified time slots. When one mobile station wishes to establish communications with another, it responds to this status request with its own telegram containing the corresponding request. The system administration then transmits a channel-change telegram to both mobile stations, requesting they switch from the organization channel to the assigned communications frequencies. In addition to standard radio communications, this system can also accomodate data transmissions in the form of status telegrams (5 data bits) and report telegrams (186 bits of useful information) transmitted over the organization channel.

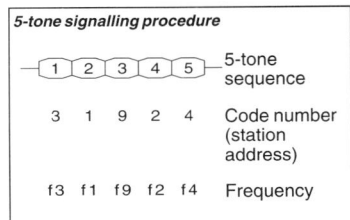

5-tone signalling procedure

1	2	3	4	5	5-tone sequence
3	1	9	2	4	Code number (station address)
f3	f1	f9	f2	f4	Frequency

Board Information Terminal (BIT)

Vehicle-related display and control elements are being joined by an increasing number of similar devices for external communications systems. The car radio is now virtually standard, and mobile telephones, navigation systems, etc., are becoming widespread. Equipping each new device with its own display and control elements – with an agglomeration of several different operating philosophies as the possible result – places additional burdens on the driver. For numerous reasons, including those related to safety, this type of arrangement will not satisfy future requirements.

One solution is to combine the display and operating elements from several subsystems within a single display and control unit. This unit – the board information terminal (BIT) – maintains communications with peripheral devices and systems via a data bus (e.g., with CAN protocol) through which the telegrams used for control and for providing information displays are transmitted and received.

The BIT can be used to provide a single "user interface" for several different applications. A substantial reduction in the number of input and output elements facilitates implementation of an ergonomically satisfactory control layout. The BIT's primary controls are arranged for convenient, "blind" operation, featuring convenient input elements; these are within the driver's immediate reach and can be identified and operated by touch. More extensive programming tasks – such as storing automatic-dialing codes for telephone numbers – can be performed by remote control; safety considerations dictate that this type of programming operates only when the vehicle is stationary. Oral input is a possible future option.

The central monitor, mounted in an ergonomically optimal location, can display information in various formats, including symbols, text, digitalized road displays. High-resolution color graphics (e.g., thin-film transistorized LCD) are suitable here. Machine-generated oral response could provide additional support.

In the face of increasing complexity, the BIT furnishes an opportunity to design clear, convenient vehicle instrumentation, an endeavor in which traffic safety is one of the chief beneficiaries.

Structure of the Board Information Terminal (BIT)

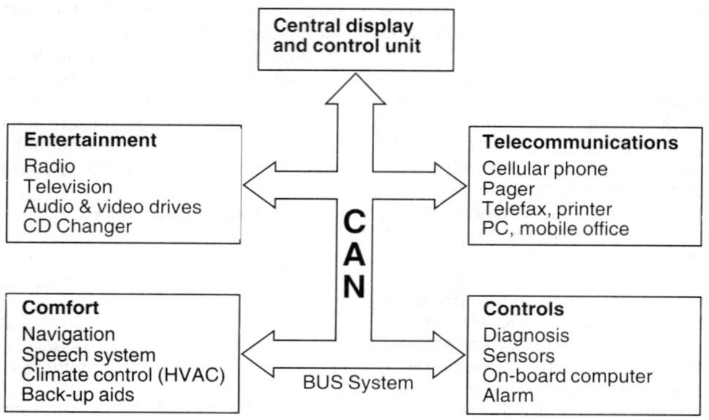

Safety systems

Occupant safety systems

Occupant safety systems provide protection automatically in the event of a collision or rollover, without any effort on the part of the vehicle occupants. For this reason seat belt and airbag systems are also known as "passive occupant restraint systems".

Seat-belt tightener system

Electronic triggering system
In the case of a frontal collision at a speed of 50 km/h the seat belts must absorb a level of energy which approximately equals the kinetic energy of a person in free fall from the 4th floor of a building.
Because of the slackening of the belt, the so-called film-reel effect and the belt stretch, normal three-point automatic belts only offer a limited amount of protection in frontal impacts with fixed obstacles (≥ 40 km/h). The seat-belt tightener system overcomes the problem of belt slack and the film-reel effect by means of retraction (that is to say tightening of the belts) and thus guarantees a significant improvement in their protective effectiveness.
A prerequisite for optimum protection is that the vehicle occupants are able to participate in the deceleration of the vehicle after being propelled forward out of their seats to as small a degree as possible. This is achieved by the triggering of the seat-belt tightener as soon as impact occurs and by the earliest possible commencement of passenger restraint. The maximum forward movement with tightened seat-belts should be approximately 1 cm, and the maximum duration of mechanical tightening should be 12 ms.

A belt-tightener trigger unit installed centrally in the passenger compartment records the acceleration in the direction of the longitudinal axis of the vehicle with a piezoelectric sensor and ignites the pyrotechnical belt tighteners as soon as the change in speed on impact, calculated from the acceleration, exceeds the trigger threshold.

In order to protect against false triggering as a result of malfunctions in the electronic trigger function, the belt-tightener unit includes an acceleration-sensitive electromechanical safety switch ("Hamlin Switch"). The trigger threshold for frontal impacts (approx. 18 km/h) ensures that

Passenger restraint systems
1 Seat-belt tightener, 2 Co-driver airbag, 3 Driver airbag, 4 Sensor and power stand-by.

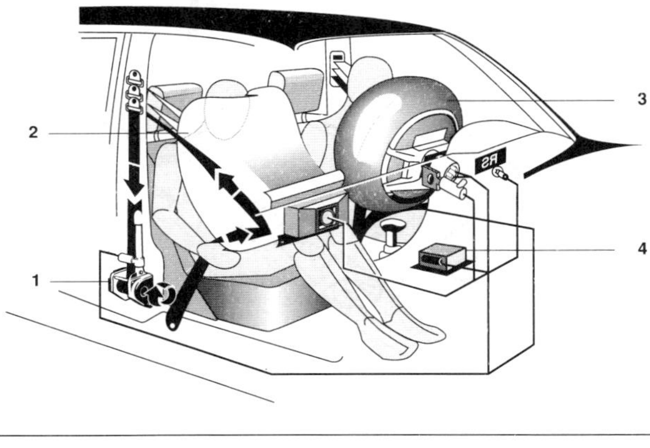

the electronic trigger unit does not activate the belt tighteners in the case of minor accidents (< 15 km/h), hammer blows or driving on rough surfaces.

Mechanical triggering systems
One of these systems uses only the energy of the frontal impact (relative displacement between engine block and body at ≥ 25 km/h) to tighten the front seat-belts via control cables, at the same time pulling the entire steering column forward away from the driver (Audi safety system procon-ten).

Other systems trigger a pretensioned spring via a mechanical sensor. This pulls the belt latch mechanism backwards and thus – as in the case of the pyrotechnic tightener – tightens the seat-belts. A disadvantage of this type of system is the relatively late response of the mechanical system.

Another simple system is the "Belt Brake". The belt is mechanically clamped at its point of emergence from the retractor. However, this eliminates the film-reel effect but not belt slack.

Airbag system
Upon vehicle collision a pyrotechnic gas generator inflates an air cushion (airbag) in such a way that when impacted by the occupants it partially deflates again, and absorbs their impact energy. An airbag each for the driver and front-seat passenger protects against head and chest injuries occuring on impact (≤ 60 km/h) against a solid obstacle. Even a belt tightener cannot exclude the possibility of the head being propelled against the steering wheel.

Airbags also protect occupants who are not wearing seat belts, and are therefore of particular benefit in countries in which the wearing of a seat belt is not obligatory. In the USA passive restraint systems (airbag or automatic seat belts) have been legally required since mid-1989 (FMVSS 208).

The gas generator fills the driver airbag installed in the steering-wheel hub with nitrogen (N_2, volume 60 ... 80 l) in 30 ... 35 ms, and fills the passenger airbag (volume approx. 150 l) installed in place of the glove compartment in approx. 50 ms, also with nitrogen (N_2). The longer inflation time for the passenger airbag is permissible because the geometric distance from the front-seat passenger to the glove compartment, and therefore the permissible forward movement, is greater than that from the driver to the steering wheel.

Mechanical belt-tightener system
(Audi, procon-ten)

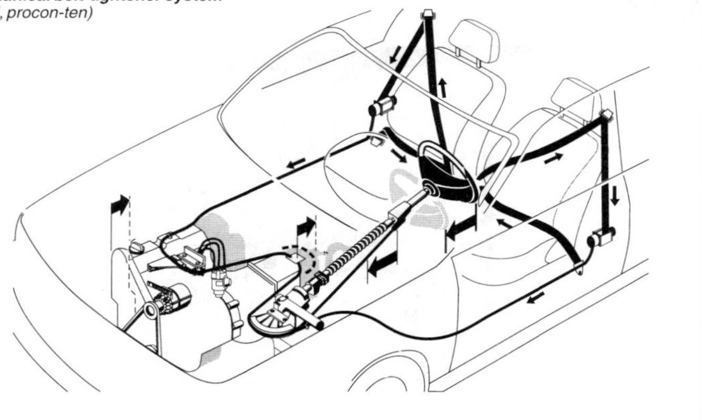

The decisive factor in determining the quality of the protection provided is the triggering of the airbag at exactly the correct moment. The occupants should make contact with the airbag while it is still fully inflated but is just beginning to deflate. The maximum permissible forward movement on the driver's side is usually 12.7 cm (the "5 inches rule") and the permissible airbag deflation time is approx. 100 ms. The entire impact and energy absorption process is therefore completed after approx. 150 ms.

Decentralized system
(electromechanical impact detection)
In this process the electromechanical "satellite sensors" located at the front of the vehicle register the accelerations occurring on impact. An electromechanical safety switch in the diagnostic unit fitted in the passenger compartment is located in series with these sensors. When at least one of the forward switches and the safety switch are activated, the firing current flows directly to the airbag trigger unit. In the case of mechanical sensors the trigger sensitivity can only be set by the appropriate selection of mechanical parameters (seismic mass, spring constant, contact travel, damping). In addition to the system monitoring, the diagnostic unit contains a voltage transformer and a power stand-by in order to guarantee extended functioning in case of loss of battery power.
A crash recorder records the function sequence on impact and stores the system state (types of fault and duration of faults when a crash occurs) in its memory. After identification of a fault the failure warning indicator lights up in the instrument panel. Stored types of fault and fault durations can be read out via a serial diagnostic interface.

Centralized system
(electronic impact detection)
In this process an electronic trigger unit installed centrally in the passenger compartment uses an electronic acceleration sensor to measure the acceleration occurring on impact. A piezoelectric sensor is suitable for this purpose.
The centralized electronic trigger unit in its entirety contains the following functions:
– Impact identification by the electronic acceleration sensor and mechanical safety switch,
– Triggering of the airbag and belt-tightener firing circuits at the right moment for the varying kinds of impact (e.g., frontal and oblique-angle impacts) by employ-

Airbag system *(block diagram)*
U_B Battery voltage, U_{st} Control voltage, ADW analog/digital converter,
1 Sensor, 2 External switches, 3 Data storage, 4 Monitoring, 5 Final stages, 6 Power stand-by (6a digital, 6b analog), 7 Warning lamp, 8 Test/diagnosis, 9 Airbag, 10 Seat belts, 11 Firing agent.

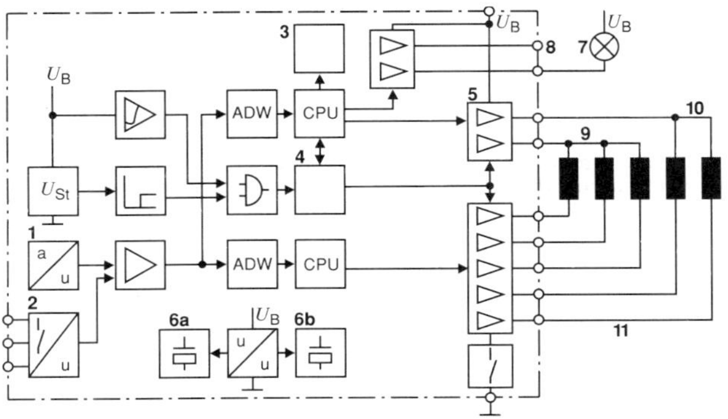

ment of the appropriate triggering algorithms (crash-identification processes),
– Voltage transformer and power standby,
– Selective triggering of the belt tightener by belt-latch interrogation,
– Setting of two trigger thresholds, dependent on whether the occupant is wearing a seat-belt or not (high or low trigger threshold),
– Adaptation to varying vehicles, with the differences in the energy-absorption behavior of their forward structures, by programming of appropriate triggering parameters,
– Diagnosis of functions inside and outside the unit and of system components,
– Non-volatile memory storage of fault types and fault durations,
– Serial diagnostic interface,
– Crash recorder,
– Warning lamp output,
– Protection against false triggering by means of mechanical safety switch – redundant with signal processing (parallel processing).

Rollover protection system
In convertibles with swing-out roll bars an electronic trigger unit (rollover sensor) effects a "lightning-fast" extension of the roll bar when the vehicle rolls over. In such cases, a strong electromagnet releases a pretensioned spring. As a rollover can occur in any direction horizontally, the rollover sensor must react in every direction.

Roll-bar triggering
The rollover sensor identifies a vehicle rollover based on:
– vehicle acceleration, or
– vehicle tilt and rear-wheel rebound.

The omnidirectional registration of acceleration is achieved by two acceleration sensors, one in the longitudinal and one in the lateral direction of the vehicle. The rollover sensor microcomputer squares and totals the sensor signals and compares the resulting acceleration with the programmed trigger threshold of approx. 5 g.

A tilt switch evaluates the vehicle tilt as a second triggering criterion. Roll-bar triggering also takes place as soon as the vehicle inclination reaches ≥ 27° and at least one of the two rear-axle switches has opened as a signal indicating rear-wheel rebound. The microcomputer and an analog hardware path redundantly evaluate the second triggering condition in order to increase functional safety.

Rollover protection system
a) Normal position, b) Rollover.

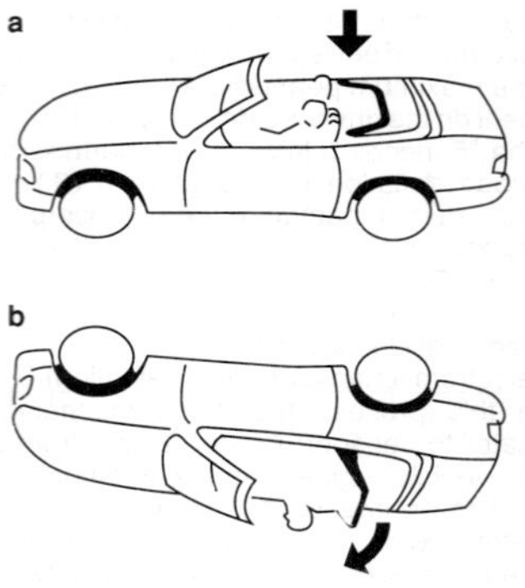

Belt locking
A simple mechanical belt-locking mechanism is not possible in a convertible fitted with belt-integral seats (seats with belt retractors built into the seat backs). In such cases, the rollover sensor also takes on the function of electrically blocking the front automatic belts. To do this it activates a locking-mechanism relay for each belt under the following conditions:
– Vehicle acceleration ≥ 0.45 g omnidirectional in the horizontal plane (evaluated analog to the 5 g threshold of the microcomputer),
or
– vehicle tilt ≥ 27°.

The microcomputer and an analog hardware path also redundantly evaluate the conditions for locking based on vehicle tilt.

Additional functions
As well as the triggering functions, the rollover sensor also carries out self-diagnosis, in which the external actuators, the rear-axle switches, the vehicle electrical system voltage and the warning lamp are diagnozed. It has a non-volatile memory, a fault clock and a serial diagnostic interface.

Tire-pressure monitoring system (RKS)

Safety and tire pressure
Tires loose pressure when they are damaged by the entry of foreign bodies or if the driver is careless when driving over obstacles. Even in intact tires the pressure loss through diffusion is as much as 30% in a year.

The tire's safety-related characteristics, such as durability at high loads and speeds, the ability to transmit high braking and cornering forces to the road surface, as well as good aquaplaning behavior, are only guaranteed if the tire is used with the prescribed air pressure.

The electronic tire-pressure monitoring system warns the driver in good time when pressure loss occurs. As well as improved safety, the system also provides for greater economic efficiency, as insufficient tire pressure increases tire wear and fuel consumption.

Design and function
The electronic tire-pressure monitoring system consists of a pressure switch, high-frequency sensor and evaluation electronics.

The pressure switch, which is bolted into the wheel rim, contains an aneroid box filled with inert gas and sealed with a stainless steel diaphragm. The tire pressure is applied to the exterior of the diaphragm, and the inert-gas reference pressure to the interior. If the tire pressure exceeds the reference pressure the diaphragm curves inwards and closes a contact. On the other hand, if the pressure drops below the reference pressure, the diaphragm curves outward and opens the same contact.

Tire-pressure monitoring system (RKS)
1 Pressure switch, 2 High-frequency sensor, 3 Evaluation electronics, 4 Wheel-speed signal, 5 Display.

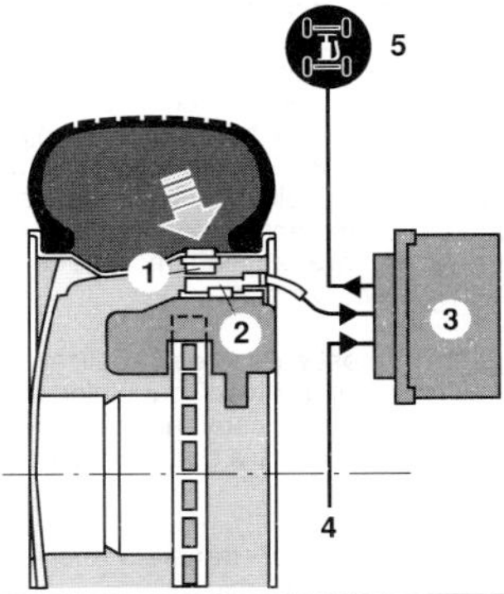

There is no display due to pressure fluctuations in the tire resulting from temperature changes, as the reference-gas temperature remains extremely close to that of the air in the tire.

The high-frequency sensor, which is fixed to the axle, identifies the contact status of the pressure switch. To do so, a series oscillating circuit in parallel with the pressure-switch contact draws off energy from the oscillator's high-frequency sensor when the pressure switch rotates past with its switch contact closed. This results in a brief interruption of oscillation which causes a pulse at the output of the HF sensor. Thus, pulses only occur at the sensor output if the tire pressure exceeds the reference pressure. If the tire pressure falls below the reference pressure these pulses disappear.

The evaluation electronics processes the signals from each wheel's HF sensor, together with the wheel-speed signals. Being as a fixed ratio exists between these two pulse frequencies, a warning is given if this condition is not fulfilled over a certain distance.

Comfort and convenience systems

Power windows

The power windows in motor vehicles are generally operated by electric drive units, with three system types accounting for approximately 90% of the market requirement. The available installation space assumes a prominent place among the criteria which are applied in determining which system to install.

System 1 (most widespread application): An electric motor-driven spur pinion transmits the force to a conventional window-winder mechanism via gear segment.

System 2: The electric motor transfers the force through a bowden cable.

System 3: A gear-driven, torsion and pressure-resistant stiff operating cable provides the connection between the motor and the window.

Power-window motors

The space available inside the door makes narrow drive-unit design imperative (flat motors). Apart from being self-locking, the worm-gear pair responsible for furnishing the reduction ratio must be designed to resist involuntary, undesired or forced opening. A flexible dog clutch provides good damping characteristics during operation.

Power-window control

Manual control is via rocker switch, while convenience can be enhanced by combining the power windows with the central locking system. When the passengers exit the vehicle, such a system responds by automatically closing the windows, either entirely or with a gap for ventilation. During closing, a force-limitation device (anti-squeeze or finger protection), must be active. The device serves to prevent human appendages from being caught by the

Window lift drives
1 Electric gear motor, 2 Guide rail, 3 Driver, 4 Lift mechanism, 5 Flexible drive cable, 6 Stiff operating cable.

System 1 with gear segment

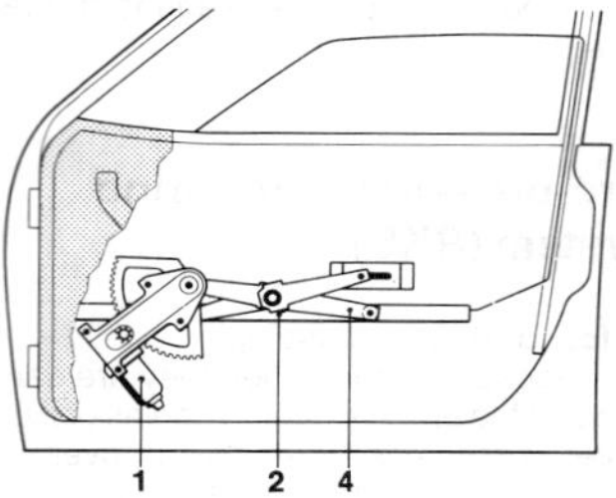

System 2 with flexible bowden cable

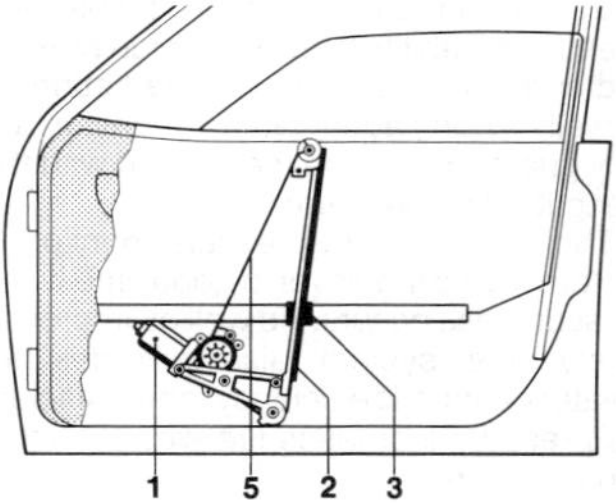

System 3 with stiff operating cable

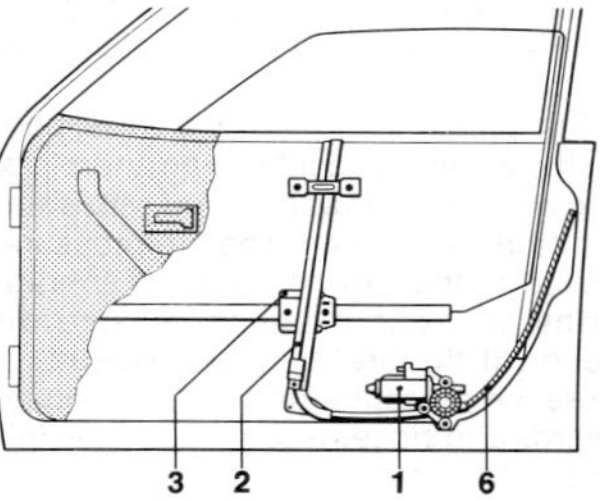

closing window. Paragraph 30 of the StVZO Road Licensing Regulations (FMVSS/CUR) stipulates that this protection mechanism remain effective while the window moves upward through the 200 ... 4 mm adjustment range (as measured from the upper edge of the window opening).

The window drive units include integral Hall sensors to monitor motor speed during operation. The system responds to a reduction in motor speed by reversing the motor, whereby the thrust forces are not to exceed 100 N, while the maximum force rate is 10 N/mm. The unit automatically overrides the anti-squeeze protection immediately before the window enters the door seal, allowing the motor to run to its end position and making it possible for the window to close completely. The window position is initialized at this point in the cycle.

Electronic control may be concentrated in a central control unit, or the control elements may be dispersed among the individual window motors in order to reduce the complexity of the wiring. Such actuators are ideally suited for use in multiplex systems.

Power sunroof

Modern power-sunroof units are combination tilting and sliding designs. The special controls required by these mechanisms can be either electronic or electromechanical. With the electromechanical control (see Fig.), mechanical interlocks on the limit switches a) and b) ensure that the roof can be either opened or tilted from the closed position, depending on the polarity at Terminals I and II. Once the sunroof has been tilted or opened, a polarity shift will initiate the corresponding lowering or closing process. An electronic control unit featuring integrated anti-squeeze protection offers certain benefits when the roof is included in a central-locking system. Supplementary functions such as

- Preset position control,
- Closing via rain sensor,
- Multiplex control

can all be included in the package at relatively modest expense.

Sunroof drive unit with electromechanical control of opening and closing as well as of lifting and closing functions

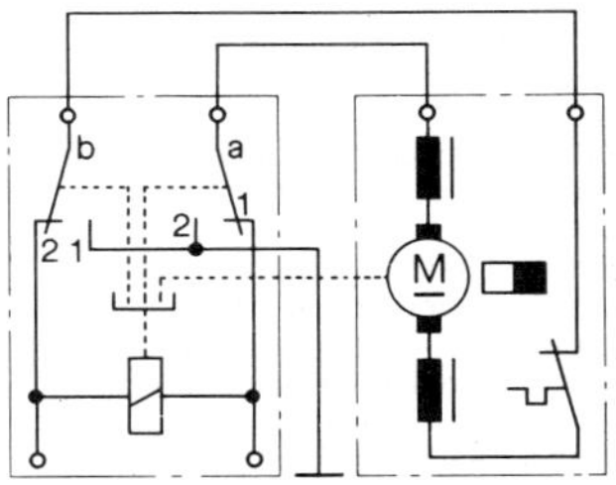

Power-window control unit featuring electronic force limitation
1 Microcomputer, 2 Relay output stage, 3 Position commands, 4 Multiplex bus, 5 Hall sensors, 6 Motor-temperature sensor.

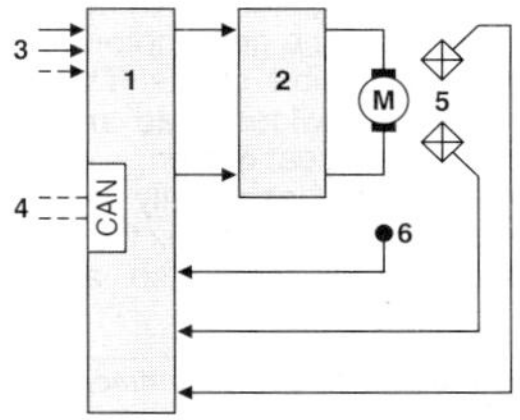

Drive for the roof is provided by a torsion and pressure-resistant operating cable. The drive motor can either be installed in the roof or at the rear of the vehicle (e.g., in the trunk). Permanently-excited worm-gear motors with power ratings of approx. 40 W are used, and thermal circuit breakers protect them against overheating.

A provision must also be made for ensuring that the roof can be closed with the on-board tools in the event of a failure in the electrical system.

Seat and steering-column adjustment

Electrically-adjustable seats are an especially useful feature in vehicles which are driven by several different persons, as they assist each new driver in finding his or her optimal driving position. Up to five motors perform the following functions at each front seat:

- Seat-cushion height adjustment, front
- Seat-cushion height adjustment, rear
- Longitudinal travel adjustment
- Backrest tilt adjustment
- Head-restraint height adjustment.

One common seat-adjustment system includes three direct-drive motors and two compact gearsets. One of the gearsets governs longitudinal adjustment, while the other is designed for combined longitudinal and height adjustment. Yet another concept features three identical gear motors with four height and two linear-adjustment gearsets. The gear motors drive the gearsets via flexible shafts. This type of system is quite widespread and can be installed on any seat design.

Modern seats (especially for sporting vehicles) do not merely affix the lap belt to the seat frame, they also attach the shoulder strap – together with its height adjuster, automatic extender and tightener – to the backrest. This type of seat design ensures optimal belt positioning for a wide range of different-sized passengers at all available seat positions, thereby making an important contribution to occupant safety. The seat frame must be reinforced for this type of design, while both the gearset components and their connections to the frame must be strengthened.

The optional programmable electric seat adjuster ("memory seat") can recall several previously set seat positions.

Electrically-adjustable steering columns are also seeing increased use as yet another means of enhancing driver comfort. The adjustment mechanism, consisting of a single electric motor and self-arresting gearset for each adjustment plane, forms an integral part of the steering column. The gearset for telescopic adjustment must be capable of absorbing any and all impact forces ("crash" forces) which might be applied to the steering column. The adjustment can be triggered in either of two ways, using either the manual position switch, or through the programmable seat adjustment.

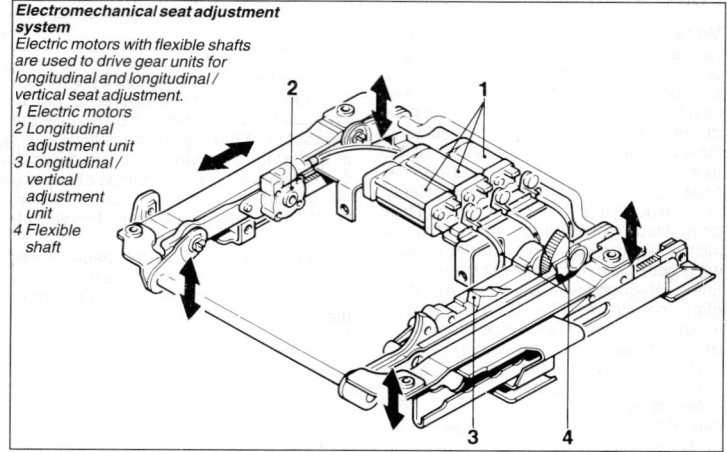

Electromechanical seat adjustment system
Electric motors with flexible shafts are used to drive gear units for longitudinal and longitudinal / vertical seat adjustment.
1 Electric motors
2 Longitudinal adjustment unit
3 Longitudinal / vertical adjustment unit
4 Flexible shaft

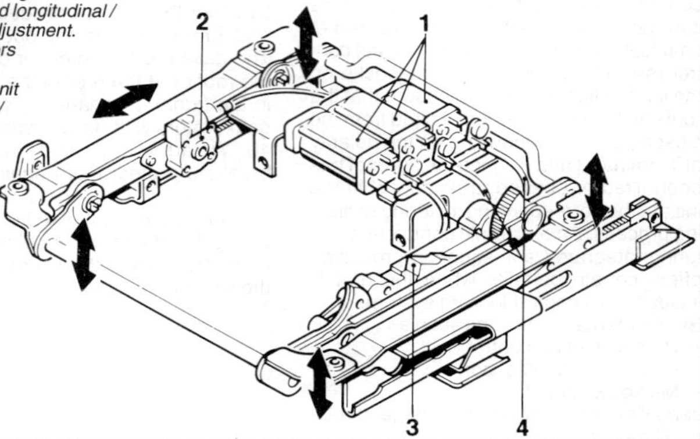

Central locking system

Either pneumatic or electric actuators can be used to power central locking systems for vehicle doors, luggage compartments and fuel-filler flaps.

In pneumatic systems, an electric motor drives the reversible dual-pressure pump which provides the required system pressure (positive or vacuum). The unit is controlled with a central position switch in the vehicle's interior or with the key at the driver's door lock, while multipoint activation (from the luggage compartment as well as the driver's and passengers' doors) is available as an option.

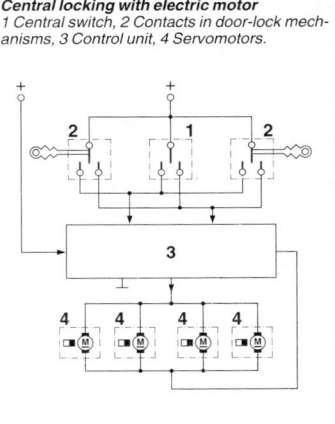

More widespread than the pneumatic systems are those which depend on electric motors for central locking. Although various technologies are used, according to the functional range and lock type, the basic principle remains constant: A small electric motor featuring a reduction-gear drive unit powers the actuating lever responsible for opening and closing the lock. Provision must be made to ensure that the door can always be unlocked with the key and the interior handle in the event of a power failure. Central locking systems incorporating special theft-deterrence features must be so designed as to preclude deactivation of the "Theft deterrent" without the vehicle key.

An ultrasonic remote control unit can provide enhanced operating convenience.

Central locking with electric motor
1 Central switch, 2 Contacts in door-lock mechanisms, 3 Control unit, 4 Servomotors.

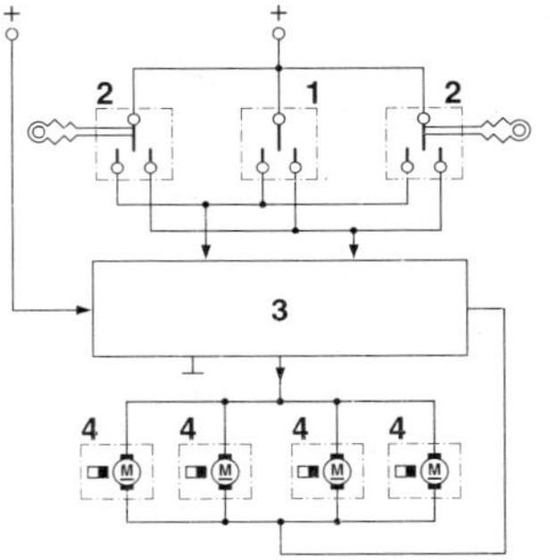

Central locking, servo unit
1 Wiring connection, 2 Flexible end-position coupling, 3 Gear unit, 4 Electric motor, 5 Actuating lever, h Travel range.

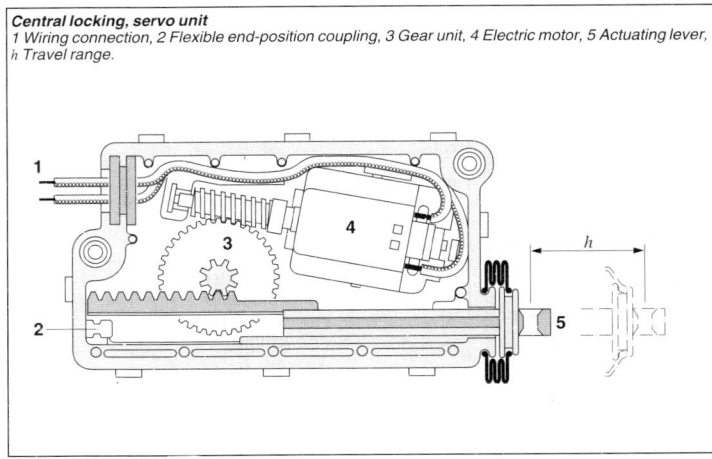

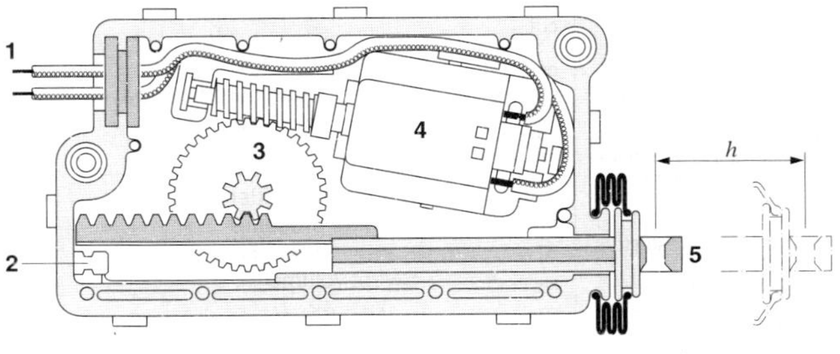

Automotive hydraulics

Symbols and units

Symbols		Units
A	Area of flow cross section	cm^2
A_D	Cross-sectional area of restriction	cm^2
A_K	Piston area	cm^2
A_R	Cross-sectional area of line	cm^2
b	Gap width	mm
d	Line diameter	mm, cm
E_{Fl}	Modulus of elasticity, liquid	$N \cdot mm^{-2}$
E_{oil}	Bulk modulus, oil	$N \cdot mm^{-2}$
e	Eccentricity offset	mm
F	Force	N
g	Acceleration due to gravity	$m \cdot s^{-2}$
H	Cylinder stroke length	cm, mm
h	Gap height	µm, mm
l	Gap length, line length	mm, m
l_o	Output length	cm
M_1	Input torque	$N \cdot m$
M_2	Output torque	$N \cdot m$
M_{th}	Theoretical input or output torque	$N \cdot m$
M_{verl}	Torque loss	$N \cdot m$
n	Rotational speed	min^{-1}
P_{an}	Input power	kW
P_{ab}	Output power	kW
p_z	Cylinder pressure	$MPa \cdot W^{-1}$
Δp	Pressure difference	$MPa \cdot W^{-1}$
Q	Delivery rate of hydraulic pump, or intake rate of hydraulic motor or hydraulic cylinder	$l \cdot min^{-1}$
Q_1	Delivery rate	$l \cdot min^{-1}$
Q_2	Intak rate	$l \cdot min^{-1}$
Q_L	Leakage rate	$l \cdot min^{-1}$
Q_{th}	Theoretical delivery or intake rate	$l \cdot min^{-1}$
Re	Reynolds number	—
r	Line radius	mm
t	Stroke time of hydraulic cylinder	s
U	Perimeter of flow cross section	cm
V_{Fl}	Fluid volume	cm^3
V_H	Displacement of hydraulic cylinder	cm^3
V_o	Output volume	cm^3
V_{th}	Theoretical delivery displacement/intake displacement	$cm^3 \cdot min^{-1}$
υ	Line flow rate	$m \cdot s^{-1}$
υ_1	Stroke rate	$m \cdot s^{-1}$
α_D	Flow coefficient of restrictors, orifices, etc.	—
η	Dynamic viscosity	$Ns \cdot m^{-2}$
η_{hm}	Hydromechanical efficiency	—
η_{vol}	Volumetric efficiency	—
λ	Coefficient of flow resistance	—
ν	Kinematic viscosity	$m^2 \cdot s^{-1}$
ρ	Density	$kg \cdot dm^{-3}$
ω	Angular velocity	s^{-1}

Calculation of coefficient of flow resistance λ

$\lambda = \frac{64}{Re}$ for laminar flow and isothermal change of state

$\lambda = \frac{75}{Re}$ for laminar flow and adiabatic change of state

for turbulent flow up to Re = 80,000 and smooth lines

$Re = \upsilon \cdot D_H/\nu$ where $D_H = 4\,A/U$

Terms and formulas

Hydraulic pump

Delivery rate

$$Q_1 = V_{th} \cdot n \cdot \eta_{vol}$$

Output power

$$P_{ab} = Q_1 \cdot \Delta p$$

Input torque

$$M_1 = \frac{V_{th} \cdot \Delta p}{10 \cdot 2\pi} \cdot \frac{1}{\eta_{hm}}$$

Input power

$$P_{an} = M_1 \cdot \omega$$

Volumetric efficiency

$$\eta_{vol} = \frac{Q_1}{Q_{th}} = \frac{Q_{th} - Q_L}{Q_{th}} = 1 - \frac{Q_L}{Q_{th}}$$

Hydromechanical efficiency

$$\eta_{hm} = \frac{M_{th}}{M_1} = \frac{M_{th}}{M_{th} + M_{verl}}$$

Hydraulic motor

Intake rate

$$Q_2 = V_{th} \cdot n/\eta_{vol}$$

Output power

$$P_{ab} = M_2 \cdot \omega$$

Output torque

$$M_2 = \frac{V_{th} \cdot \Delta p}{10 \cdot 2\pi} \cdot \eta_{hm}$$

Volumetric efficiency

$$\eta_{vol} = \frac{Q_{th}}{Q_2} = \frac{Q_{th}}{Q_{th} + Q_L}$$

Hydromechanical efficiency

$$\eta_{hm} = \frac{M_2}{M_{th}} = \frac{M_{th} - M_{verl}}{M_{th}}$$

Hydraulic cylinder

Cylinder pressure

$$p_z = F/(A_K \cdot \eta_{hm})$$

Swept volume

$$V_H = A_K \cdot H$$

Stroke time

$$t = V_H/Q_1$$

Stroke rate

$$\upsilon_1 = Q_1/A_K$$

Flow rates in lines and gaps

Required line cross section

$A_R = Q_1/\upsilon$

Pressure loss in straight lines

$$\Delta p = \lambda \cdot \frac{l}{d} \cdot \frac{\rho}{2} \cdot \upsilon^2$$

Flow through a pipe (according to Hagen-Poiseuille)

$$Q = \frac{\pi \cdot r^4}{8 \cdot \eta \cdot l} \cdot \Delta p$$

Flow (laminar) through a smooth gap

$$Q = \frac{b \cdot h^3}{12 \cdot \eta \cdot l} \cdot \Delta p$$

Flow (laminar) through an eccentric sealing gap

$$Q = \frac{d \cdot \pi \cdot \Delta r^3}{12 \cdot \eta \cdot l} \cdot \left[1 + 1.5 \cdot \left(\frac{e}{\Delta r}\right)^3\right] \cdot \Delta p$$

($2 \cdot \Delta r$ = clearance between piston and bore)

Flow through restrictors and orifices

$Q = \alpha_D \cdot A_D \cdot \sqrt{2\,\Delta p/\rho}$

(α_D at control slide valves: 0.6 to 0.8)

Compressibility of an hydraulic fluid

$\Delta V_{Fl} = A_K \cdot \Delta l = V_o \cdot \Delta p/E_{Fl}$

where the initial volume is

$V_o = A_K \cdot l_o$

and the bulk modulus for oil is

$$E_{oil} \approx 1.6 \cdot 10^9 \frac{\text{N}}{\text{mm}^2}$$

Gear pumps

Gear pumps are designed either with one external-toothed and one internal-toothed gear or with two external-toothed gears. External-toothed pumps are cheaper to manufacture and are therefore in much more common use. The displacement per revolution is constant, and is determined by the gear diameter, the center-to-center distance and the width of the teeth. The rotating (meshed) gears transport the hydraulic fluid in the spaces between the teeth from the low-pressure to the high-pressure side, and the teeth immersed in the fluid force it into the delivery line. There is almost no clearance between the housing and the tips of the teeth; thus the pump exhibits a good radial seal. The pump chamber is axially sealed by plates or bushings which are hydraulically pressed against the gears. These plates or bushings simultaneously act as bearings for the gears. This design achieves the high efficiency characteristic of high-pressure pumps. Drive speeds of up to 4000 min^{-1}, maximum permissible pressures of up to approx. 250 bar and high power densities (6 kW/kg) make gear pumps particularly well suited for use in mobile (automotive) hydraulic systems. 4 ... 5 pump sizes satisfy flow-volume requirements ranging from 0.5 ... 300 l/min.

***Gear pumps and motors** (Direction of fluid flow and gear rotation shown for pump operation)*

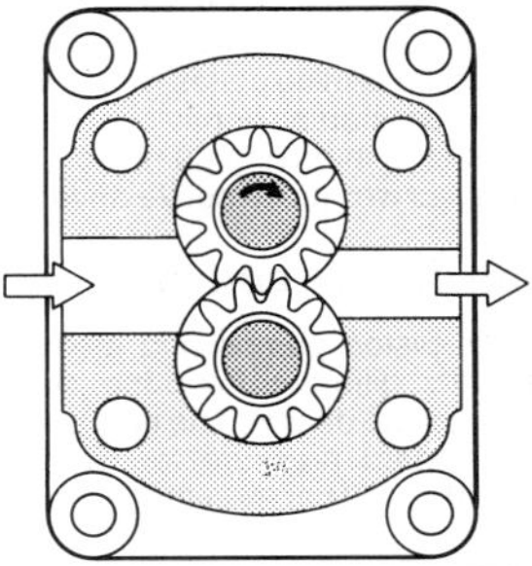

High-pressure Bosch gear pump
Volumetric efficiency η_v and overall efficiency η_t as a function of the delivery rate at Δp = 210 bar.

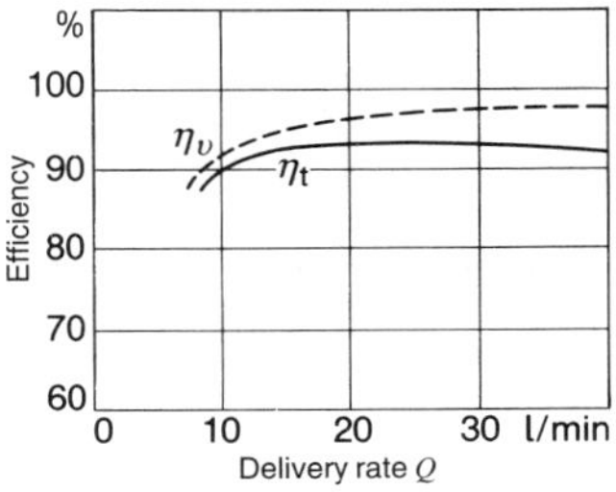

Gear motors

Like gear pumps, the simplest gear motors are designed to operate in only one direction of rotation. If oil flows from the high-pressure to the low-pressure side, the gears in the motor rotate in a direction opposite to the direction in which they rotate during pumping. Motors suitable for use as vehicle drives, i.e. motors which can be operated in both directions of rotation and which can be loaded in the reverse direction, have also been derived from gear pumps through appropriate design of the axial pressure field and the leakage fluid passages. The advantages of external-toothed pumps such as high power density, small installation-space requirements and low manufacturing costs also apply to gear motors. They are therefore chosen for road vehicles, construction equipment and agricultural machinery for driving cooling and cleaning fans, screw conveyors, sweepers, spreading plates, vibrators, etc. The excellent starting behavior of gear motors is utilized in driving pumps and compressors, as well as in motive drives.

Piston pumps and motors

Hydraulic piston pumps and motors are significantly different from the classical piston-machine design. The high pressure level (standard pressure for hydrostatic drives 350 ... 400 bar) results in high piston forces which necessitate sturdy and rigid mechanical drive systems. The drive mechanisms of modern machines are nevertheless highly compact, particularly due to the hydrostatic transmission of force between the two primary reciprocating components. The good lubricating and cooling qualities of the hydraulic fluid promote such space-saving designs. Hydraulic piston machines are thus able to achieve a maximum power density of more than 5 kW/kg.

In order to achieve a uniform volumetric flow rate, hydraulic piston machines are designed with an odd number of piston elements. A differentiation is made between radial- and axial-piston machines, depending upon the configuration of the drive mechanism. Both types are available as pumps and motors with constant or variable displacement, suitable for use in open and closed circuits. The displacement of these motors and pumps is varied by changing the length of the piston stroke. Phase control of hydraulic machines was not adopted because a rotating crankshaft is unsuitable as a means of stroke adjustment. Rotating, stroke-generating mechanisms, such as eccentric shaft or crankshaft (radial), and swashplate (axial), are therefore unsuitable for stroke adjustment and are only used in some fixed-capacity machines.

All variable-capacity and many fixed-capacity devices operate with other drives

Axial-piston machine
(swash plate unit)
1 Drive shaft, 2 Swash plate, 3 Cylinder barrel (rotates), 4 Retaining plate, 5 Slippers, 6 Piston, 7 Control plate

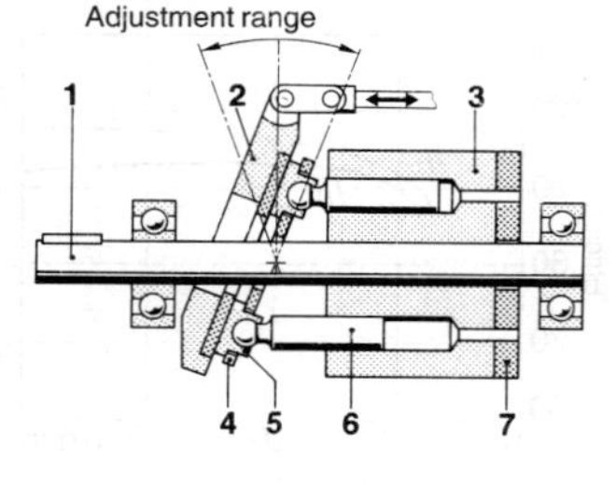

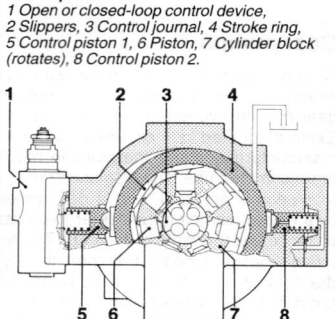

Radial-piston machine
1 Open or closed-loop control device, 2 Slippers, 3 Control journal, 4 Stroke ring, 5 Control piston 1, 6 Piston, 7 Cylinder block (rotates), 8 Control piston 2.

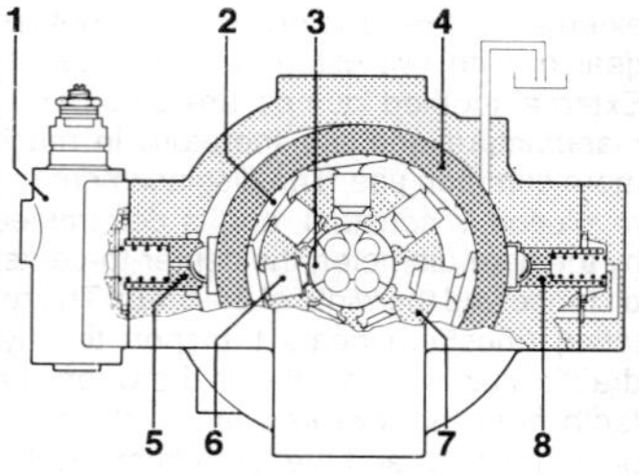

specifically designed for hydraulic applications. This type of unit incorporates a rotating cylinder assembly. Together with a stationary control plate or control journal, the cylinder assembly forms a rotary slide valve which alternately exhausts and fills the cylinders. Axial-piston machines are designed as swash-plate units.

The centrally-ported machine has been adopted as the standard radial design. The cylinder block rotates on the control journal, and the bearing forces are supported at hydrostatic pressure fields on the journals. Similar pressure fields transmit the forces between the rotating piston slippers and the stationary cam ring. The ring's variable eccentric position relative to the control journal generates the piston stroke. In the case of pumps in which the delivery direction can be reversed, the stroke ring can be moved in both directions via its adjustment piston. All control elements are located in the stator, allowing rapid and precise adjustments in flow volume using hydraulic or electronic servo elements and controllers. The adjustable piston unit can be integrated within the electronic control circuit using either proportional valves in the control circuit or servo adjusters which regulate according to flow.

Electrohydraulic pumps and small units

An electrohydraulic pump is a combination of a hydraulic pump and an electric motor. A DC motor is used in most mobile hydraulics applications, however AC and three-phase motors are also used in stationary operation.

Gear pumps are characterized by a low degree of pulsation and quiet operation. As such, these hydraulic components have proven useful for generating pressure in electrohydraulic pumps. Sizes B and F with capacities of 1 ... 22.5 cm^3 per revolution are used, and achieve operating pressures of up to approx. 280 bar. Together with size I to T electric motors which generate a maximum nominal output of 8 kW, they are used in a number of different mobile-hydraulics applications.

Electrohydraulic pumps are used to supply the hydraulic energy for the "raising" and "steering" functions in all kinds of vehicles, in particular in industrial trucks (fork lift trucks and pallet trucks), mobile lifting platforms, trucks, special construction, transport and rescue vehicles, and passenger cars.

In passenger cars, electrohydraulic pumps, including increasing numbers of miniaturized versions, are finding application in functions such as ride-level control, and power-assists for steering and parking. Safety-related braking and acceleration control represent a special area of application. At the heart of the ABS and ASR systems (see p. 610 and 556) is a hydraulic unit to generate regulation pressure.

In addition to electrohydraulic pumps, various valves or valve assemblies must be installed in motor vehicles in order to implement the wide variety of control functions. This has led to the development of small, compact units with outputs of up to 4 kW.

In these units, the electric motor and hydraulic pump are supplemented by a valve body, a hydraulic-fluid tank, and filters for both fluid and air. The design concept accommodates individual modifications for specific control functions. Sleeve and seat valves can be combined in a compact valve block or at unions in the system. Small and miniaturized units are used in those applications where high power is required despite limited space being available. Examples include municipal vehicles (street sweepers, rotary snow plows, utility tractors, industrial trucks, special-purpose vehicles, and passenger-transport vehicles with lifts and pivoting equipment for carrying handicapped persons).

Novel applications are found in passenger vehicles. The most advanced convertibles utilize hydraulic mechanisms to operate the top; these devices fold the top, stow it in a specified manner, and lock it into place.

Valves

Directional-control valves

OC valves (open-center)
When the valve unit is in the neutral position, the flow from the pump is directed through up to 10 valves (neutral circulation pattern). The fluid flow is restricted when a valve is actuated prior to the opening of the line to the servo unit.
Disadvantages:
– High pressure loss = Energy loss in neutral position
– Control precision affected by load pressure

LS Valves (load-sensing)
Used in systems with variable-capacity pumps or constant-capacity pumps and auxiliary pressure compensator. In the neutral position, the LS control line removes the pressure from the pump and pressure compensator. When the valve unit is actuated, the pump controller/pressure compensator maintains the pressure differential at the valve spool at a constant level. The result: The flow of hydraulic fluid to the servo unit is not affected by the load pressure.
Advantages:
– Minimal neutral-position loss
– Improved precision control independent of load pressure.

OC directional-control valve
1 Neutral flow.

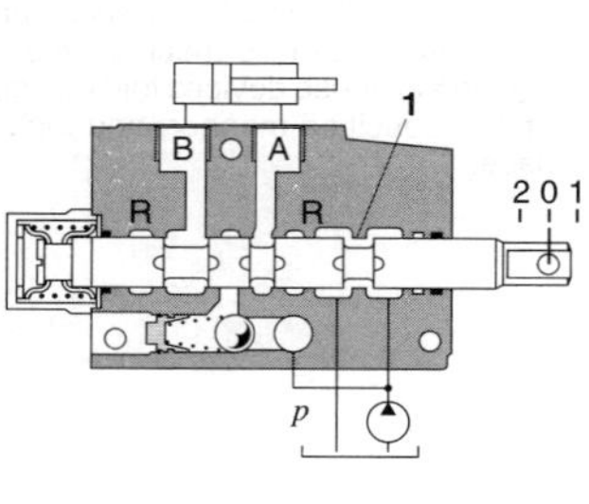

LS directional-control valve
1 Measuring diaphragm, 2 Pressure compensator, 3 Constant-displacement pump, 4 Variable pump.

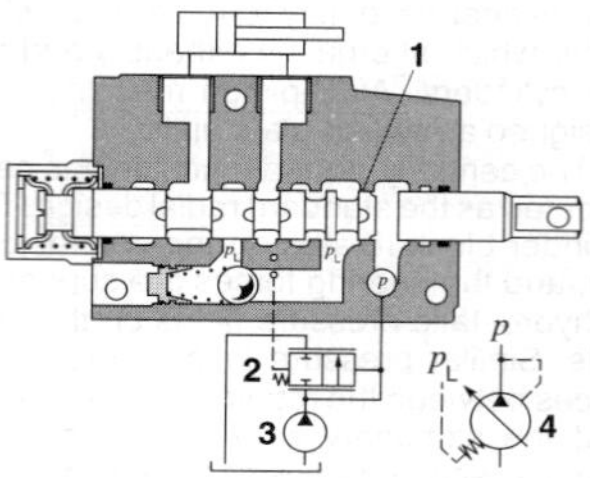

Throttle valve

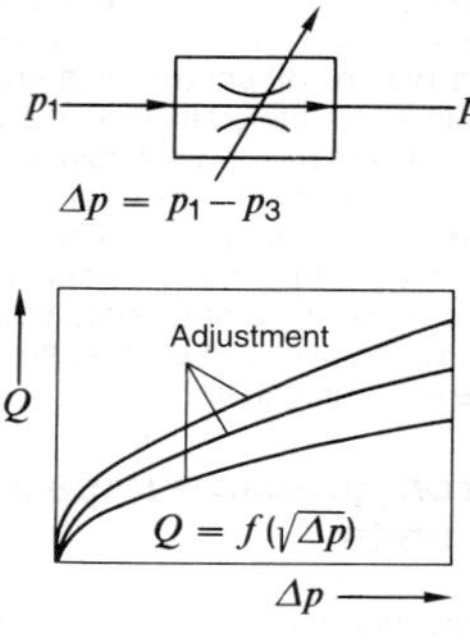

2-way flow control valve
1 Spring, 2 Measuring diaphragm,
3 Regulating throttle (pressure compensator).

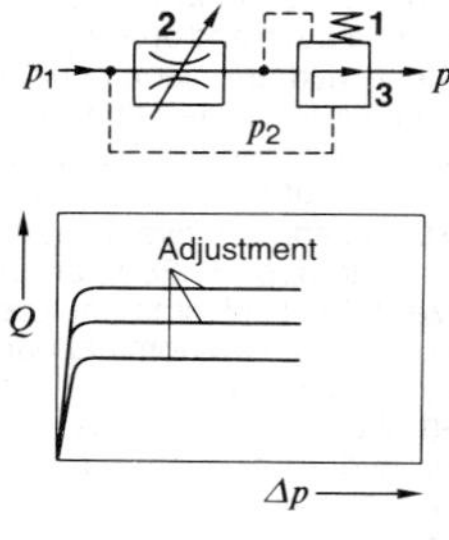

Flow-control valves

Throttle valves

Throttle valves are used to adjust the oil flow rate by changing the flow cross section. According to the law of fluid flow, this flow-limiting function is pressure-dependent; it is therefore used only for simple flow adjustment. Pressure-independent adjustment requires the use of control valves.

Flow-pressure-compensated control valves

In order to be able to set the oil flow Q independently of the load pressure p_3 at 2-way flow-control valves, the pressure difference at the metering orifice $(p_1 - p_2)$ is held constant by a variable restrictor (pressure drop). The pressure difference $p_1 - p_2$ corresponds to the spring force acting on the pressure compensator. In this type of control, the surplus oil flows via the pressure-relief valve in the system.

Losses can be reduced by using 3-way flow-control valves which have an additional drain through which the surplus oil flows back to the tank or to other loads.

3-way flow control valve
1 Pressure compensator, 2 Measuring diaphragm.

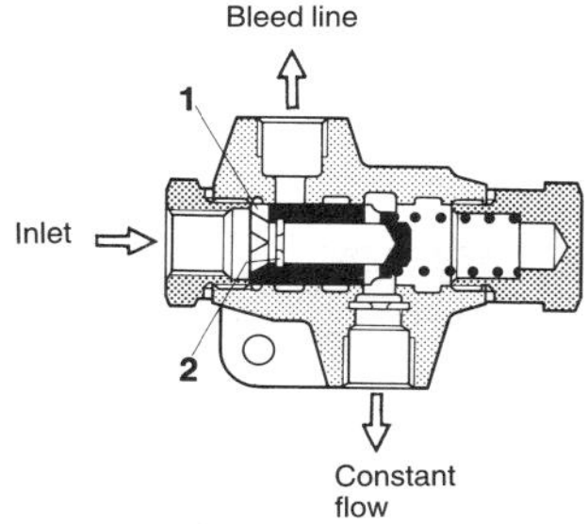

Pressure-control valves

Pressure relief valve

Hydraulic circuits incorporate a pressure-relief valve in order to protect the components as well as to ensure the operational safety of the system. If the pressure acting on the seat diameter exerts a force equal to the force exerted by the precompressed spring, the closure member lifts off its seat and the oil flows to the tank.

Pilot-operated pressure-relief valves are used for greater oil flows and to achieve valve characteristics which are independent of the flow rate. The pilot valve re-

Directly controlled pressure-relief valve
1 Valve seat, 2 Cushioning piston.

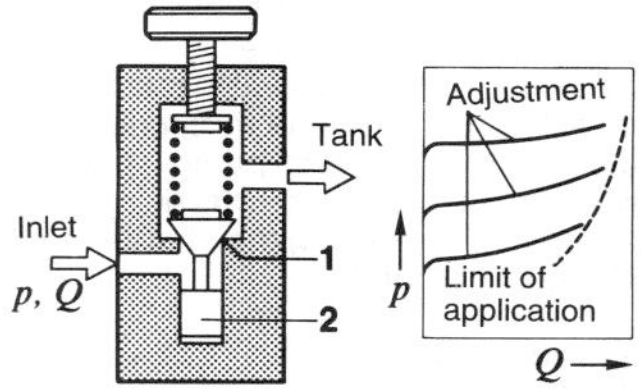

Pilot-operated pressure relief valve
1 Pilot valve, 2 Main valve

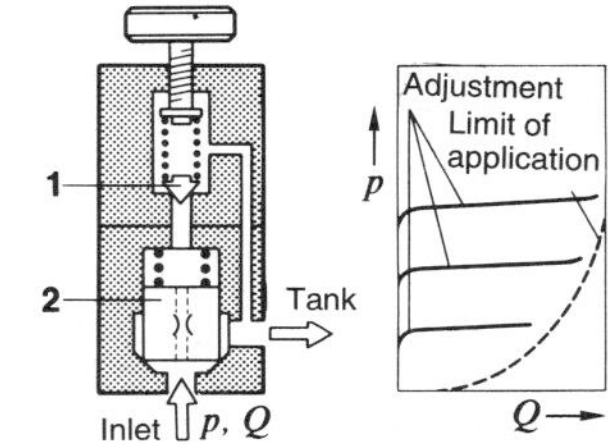

Shuttle valve

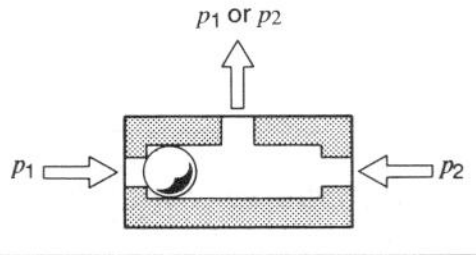

Double check valve with hydraulic pilot control
1 Seat valve, 2 Release piston.

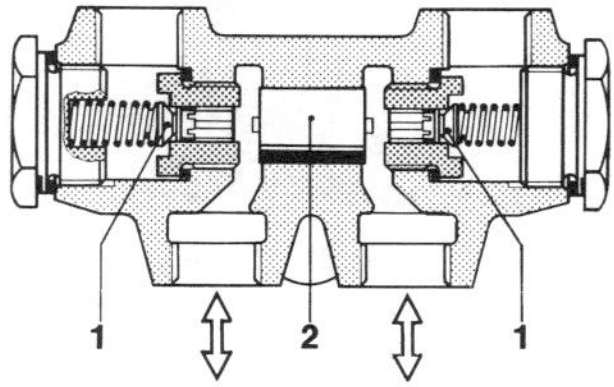

lieves the spring chamber of the main valve which controls oil flow to the tank.

Pressure-reducing valve
This valve reduces the pressure applied to a specific load in the system.

Sequence valve
This valve assigns priority to the primary circuit of a system until the set pressure is reached, whereafter the valve releases the connection to the secondary circuit. In systems which have several pumps, energy is saved by diverting oil which is not required at any given time along the shortest route to the tank via cutoff valves.

Non-return valves
This valve type maintains load pressure against the effects of external forces and mass forces. The leaklightness required is only possible with poppet valves.

Shuttle valve
A shuttle valve selects the higher of two applied pressures and supplies this pressure to the output. The closure member blocks the low-pressure output.

Check valve
A simple check valve allows flow in only one direction, while blocking the flow in the opposite direction.

With load-holding functions, the non-return valve must be opened for lowering. In pilot-controlled check valves, this is achieved by mechanically, hydraulically or electrically lifting a closure member off its seat.

Directional-control valve with direct solenoid actuation
1 Tractive electromagnet, 2 Return spring.

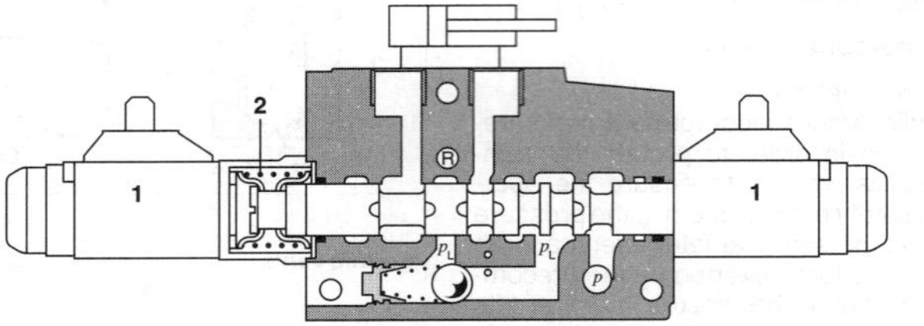

Directional-control valve with electrohydraulic actuation
1 Pilot valve, 2 Valve piston, 3 Supply and return lines for control fluid, 4 Return spring, 5 Position spring.

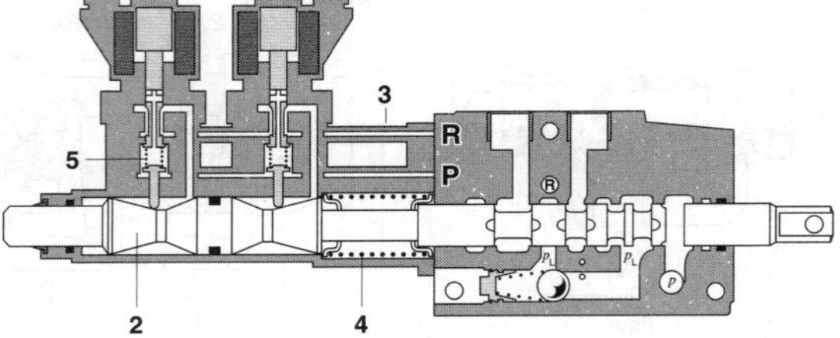

Electric proportional valves
The advantages in both installation and application has impelled automobile manufacturers to employ electric actuators despite the higher costs.

Direct solenoid actuation
A tractive electromagnet responds to the activation current by moving the proportional valve sleeve by a corresponding increment against the force of a spring. The application limit is determined by the available solenoid force, e.g., 30 l/min, 200 bar. The short stroke limits application of this principle to 3-position valves.

Electrohydraulic actuation
The "Electrohydraulic Servo Unit," or EHS, generates high actuation forces to provide high switching power. The position control for the directional-control valve sleeve compensates for interference factors. Mechanical position control using force comparison can be used to meet the requirements of automotive hydraulic systems. The valve piston is controlled via two 3/2 solenoid valves. Valve deflection is initiated by applying a specific current to the pilot valve so that the sleeve is pressed against the monitoring spring: the valve piston is activated. The tracer pin tensions the monitoring spring via the return ball. When a condition is achieved in which the spring force and the solenoid force are equal, the pilot sleeve reverts to the blocked position, terminating the motion. The compensatory effect completely negates the influence of interference factors such as flow forces. The flow of hydraulic fluid, which is proportional to the solenoid current, has a hysteresis of less than 3 %, while the positioning time for a 100 % jump in setpoint is less than 0.1 second.

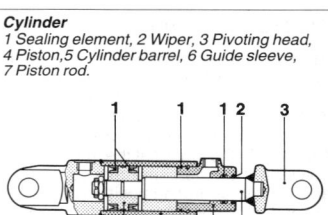

Cylinder
1 Sealing element, 2 Wiper, 3 Pivoting head, 4 Piston, 5 Cylinder barrel, 6 Guide sleeve, 7 Piston rod.

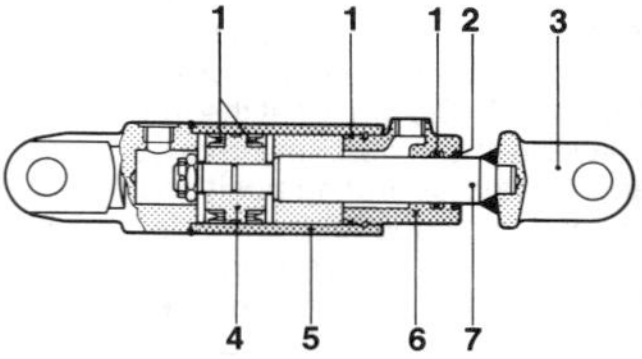

Cylinders

Cylinders convert hydraulic power (pressure, oil flow) into rectilinear motion (force, velocity). They are characterized by high power density and relatively simple design. Cylinder efficiency is determined by the seals, the operating pressure and the piston surface quality. In addition to force and velocity, buckling strength is an important design criterion which is used to determine cylinder dimensions and piston-rod extension length. Types of cylinder mounting at the head and bottom include holes, clevises, pivoting bearings and threads.

Table 1. Cylinder designs

Design	Remarks	
Single-acting	Drive possible in only one direction.	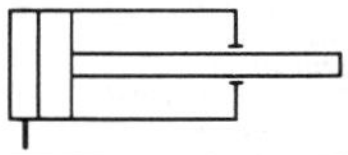
Double-acting	Two drive directions; different effective areas on the two sides of the piston.	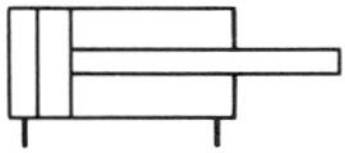
	Two drive directions; both piston surface areas equal; through-rod piston.	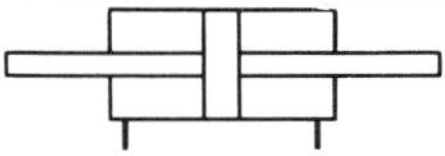

Tractor hydraulics

An oil-hydraulic system transforms the tractor into a universal and mobile vehicle for agricultural and forestry applications. With the aid of hydraulics, the wide variety of implements used can be quickly mounted to the tractor at the front, rear and between the axles, and moved into their appropriate operating positions by means of open or closed-loop controls. Quick-disconnect hydraulic couplings are used to control additional linear and rotary motors on the implement itself. Operation of the tractor is facilitated by means of hydraulic power-assisted steering (see also the section on steering systems), brake systems, clutches and gear-shifting systems. Pressure relief valves prevent the tractor from being overloaded. Trailers pulled by the tractor and matched to its brake system can be hydraulically braked. High power density and flexibility account for the wide use of hydraulics in tractors. The wide variety of applications ranging from small vineyard tractors rated at approximately 20 kW to large center-pivot steered tractors which produce roughly 300 kW of power, and including tool carriers, standard tractors, forestry tractors and construction-work tractors, represent a number of different requirements in terms of hydraulic power, hydraulic systems and system operation.

Hydraulic systems for tractors
Tractor hydraulic systems in general have at least one high-pressure circuit which operates at pressures of up to max. 250 bar and oil flow rates of up to max. 120 l/min, as well as a low-pressure system with roughly 30 bar and a flow rate of roughly 20 l/min. There are basic differences among the high-pressure systems in use today. Important criteria in the selection of a system are energy losses, complexity and cost.

Open-center system
(Q = const., $p \neq$ const.)
This system is the most common due to its favorable price/performance ratio, and

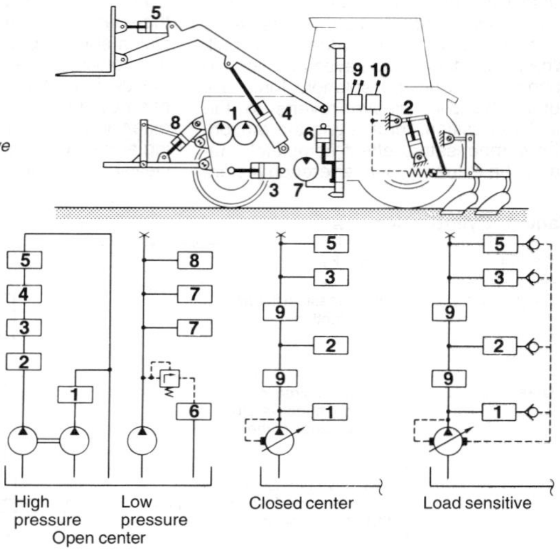

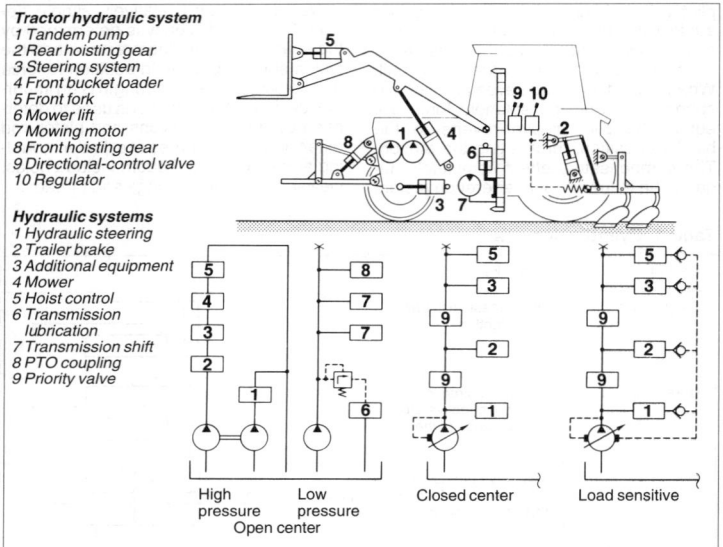

Tractor hydraulic system
1 Tandem pump
2 Rear hoisting gear
3 Steering system
4 Front bucket loader
5 Front fork
6 Mower lift
7 Mowing motor
8 Front hoisting gear
9 Directional-control valve
10 Regulator

Hydraulic systems
1 Hydraulic steering
2 Trailer brake
3 Additional equipment
4 Mower
5 Hoist control
6 Transmission lubrication
7 Transmission shift
8 PTO coupling
9 Priority valve

most often incorporates gear pumps. With all valves in their unactuated positions, the hydraulic fluid flows neutrally to the tank, and its volume flow rate varies only as a function of diesel engine speed. In order to swing one or more loads into working position, the neutral-flow channel in the valve is throttled, and hydraulic fluid is supplied to the working ports in accordance with the degree of movement. Priority circuits for safety-related functions incorporate an upstream valve(e.g., for a trailer brake), an additional pump (e.g., for the steering system) as well as flow control/priority valves. In addition, the main working circuit can be broken down into three output levels (Q_1, Q_2, $Q_1 + Q_2$) by reconfiguring the connections of two pumps.

Closed-center system:
($Q \neq$ const., $p =$ const.)
With the valves in their neutral positions, a variable-capacity piston pump works against a closed system, and at a constant maximum pressure pumps only the leakage losses. When a valve is actuated, the pump automatically increases its delivery in accordance with the increased amount of fluid demanded by the working system. Additional priority valves are used to perform safety-related functions in various systems such as the steering and trailer brake circuits.

Load-sensitive system
($Q \neq$ const., $p \neq$ const.)
As in the closed-center system, a variable-capacity pump is used in this system as well, however, the maximum load pressure used in control operations is picked off via additional control lines. The pump maintains a constant control pressure drop between the pressure at the pump outlet and the load pressure. The delivery rate of the pump thus corresponds to the instantaneous valve opening cross section. In parallel operation with differing load pressure, additional two-way flow control valves regulate the flow of fluid. This system is used in the case of high installed hydraulic power when only a partial flow is tapped off over a long period of time (e.g., relatively small rotating hydraulic motors).

Rear hoisting-gear control

The rear hoisting gear with its standardized 3-point coupling is the most frequently used type of mount for implements. The attached implements can be raised, lowered and held in position. In addition, the tractive force in the hitch linkage can be held constant, or the position of the implement with respect to the tractor can be held constant. Tractive force regulation primarily used in working the soil, e.g., plowing (a constant tractive force produces a constant working depth in homogeneous soil). High control quality, i.e. small fluctuations in tractive force, is required for full utilization of engine characteristics and small fluctuations in depth. Because the implements are guided and thus largely supported by the hoisting-gear control, the resistance associated with the implement's movement through the soil generates additional downward force at the drive wheels. This reduces wheel slip, and thus energy losses. Position control is used primarily for implements which do not penetrate the ground. In addition, a certain

Electronic hoist control mechanism (EHR – D)
1 Electronics, 2 Control panel, 3 Position sensor, 4 Force sensor pins, 5 Rear actuation, 6 Pump, 7 Control valve, 8 Cylinder, 9 External sensor, 10 Radar sensor, 11 RPM sensor.

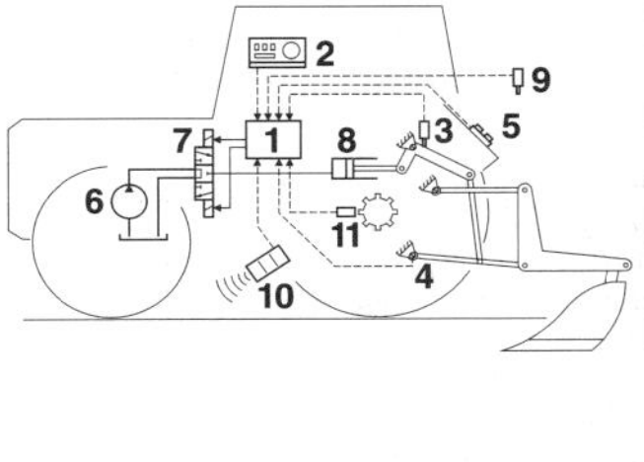

percentage of the position control can be mixed with the tractive-force control (mixed control) in order to limit depth fluctuations in the case of highly variable soil resistance.

Mechanical hoisting-gear control (MHR)
The sensor signals are monitored and processed as mechanical travel. The tractive force is monitored as spring travel at the upper or lower control arms, while the actual position can be taken at a cam plate on the hoist mechanism. A control rod relays the signals to the control valve according to the selected ratio. At the control valve, the actual values are compared with those selected by the operator. The hoisting mechanism is then raised or lowered to compensate for any control deviations.

Electronic hoisting-gear control (EHR)
The salient feature of EHR lies in the fact that the monitored and control signals are derived, transmitted and processed electronically. The tractive force is measured directly by force-sensor pins at the hitch coupling point. It is possible to supplement position and force regulation with other functions by expanding the electronic controller and the number of sensors. Rear activation eases attachment of implements. An external sensor can be installed to monitor the travel height of an attached implement (e.g., beet lifter). A speed sensor (radar) and a wheel-speed sensor make it possible to determine slip, providing the basis for a slip-control feature. Active suspension control is useful for enhancing safety and comfort when heavy attachments are being towed.

Hoisting-gear control with hydraulic signal transmission
The basis of this hydraulic signal-transmission system is a hydraulic bridge. The setpoint and actual values of the controlled variable are applied via throttles to the bridge's arms and, if the setpoint and actual values do not coincide, this causes the control valve to be shifted against the force of a spring by the diagonally tapped-off differential pressure.

Directional-control valves for tractors
Depending upon the type of hydraulic system, directional-control valves for the high-pressure circuit have either open or closed neutral positions with load sensing. Poppet valves or slide valves (see the section on directional-control valves) are used with downstream mechanically or hydraulically pilot-operated poppet valves in the cylinder port in order to hold heavy loads over a long period of time, as well as for reasons of safety. In addition to the three positions for load extension, retraction and holding, the valves often have a fourth position (free-floating position) in order to permit the implement to be guided on the soil, for example by means of supporting wheels. Detent mechanisms with hydraulic maximum-pressure release automatically reset a valve which has moved past its neutral position in the event of an overload, or if a cylinder reaches its limit position (operating convenience). Integrated flow regulators allow pressure-independent parallel connections and constant speed of linear and rotary motors. Built-in shock absorbers protect the tractor from overloads if the cylinder port is closed.

Solenoid valves are used to actuate a number of hydraulic functions on the implement, and are controlled from the tractor by means of cables (e.g., beet lifters).

Hydraulic fluid is supplied via hydraulic quick-disconnect couplings or by a separate pump driven by the tractor's power take-off shaft. Electromagnetic switching valves for gear-shifting purposes, and for actuating the various clutches in the tractor, are increasingly being incorporated in the low-pressure circuit.

For the trailer braking, a braking valve is included in the high-pressure circuit. It is actuated by the tractor brake, and supplies a correspondingly controlled brake pressure to the trailer.

Hydraulic accumulators

Objectives: Energy storage, impact and pulsation damping, operation as spring element.

The hydraulic accumulator consists of a shell, the interior of which is separated by a solid or flexible barrier. On one side of the barrier is gas, on the other fluid. There are three basic types of units: The bladder, the diaphragm and the piston accumulator.

Nitrogen is employed as gas medium. During operation, the pressure from the fluid compresses the gas. The minimum operating pressure p_1 should lie at least 10% above the initial gas pressure p_0. The pressure variation between the initial gas pressure and the maximum operating pressure p_2 should not exceed the following: 1 : 8 in diaphragm accumulators; 1 : 4 in bladder accumulators; 1 : 10 in piston accumulators. The three operating states illustrated in the diagram are governed by the laws of polytropic changes in state:

$$p_0 \cdot V_0^n = p_1 \cdot V_1^n = p_2 \cdot V_2^n$$

With nitrogen, the polytropic exponent is $n = 1$ for isothermic changes in state, and $n = 1.4$ for adiabatic changes. The available fluid volume between operating pressures is a function of the volume differential:

$$\Delta V = V_1 - V_2.$$

Auxiliary drives

Electrohydraulic devices are employed as drive units in numerous auxiliary automotive applications. The advantages associated with a positive power-to-weight ratio are accompanied by flexibility in installation. Electrohydraulic devices are used to control hoists and trailing axles, and for raising tractor axles. They are also used for controlling the steering and lifting mechanisms on industrial trucks and other vehicles. Platform lifts for loads of 500 to 5000 kg represent a major area of application for electrohydraulic devices.

The motion of the platform can be divided into two states: lowering and raising. While the stroke is controlled by a single central or two outside cylinders, the tilt function is usually governed by two cylinders. These are either single-action cylinders with return springs, or double-action cylinders. The tilt-control functions are generally governed hydraulically. In addition to the "raise" and "lower" functions, another important feature is a "floating" position for loading at fixed-position docks. Other features include the ability to position the unit at any position (tilt under full load) and to maintain the specified travel speeds during raising and lowering.

Diaphragm accumulator
1 Screw cap, 2 Gas chamber, 3 Diaphragm, 4 Fluid chamber, 5 Plug, 6 Steel case.

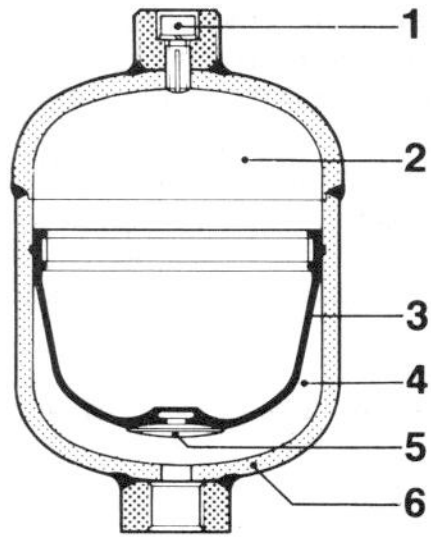

Operating states of hydraulic accumulator
p_0 Initial gas pressure, p_1 Minimum operating pressure, p_2 Maximum operating pressure, V_0 Volume at initial gas pressure, V_1 Volume at minimum operating pressure, V_2 Volume at maximum operating pressure.

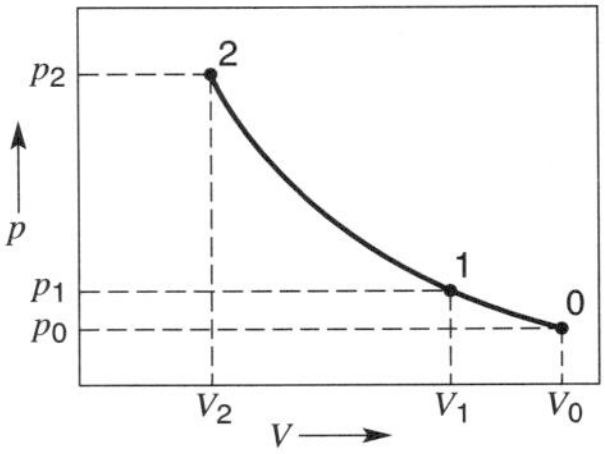

Hydrostatic fan drives

The influence of the air stream on the temperature of the engine coolant is regulated via thermostatic control of fan speed. Hydrostatic fan drives are frequently applied for high-output engines (buses, trucks, construction and agricultural machinery, stationary powerplants) in applications where scope is required in specifying the radiator's position in the vehicle (space constraints, engine encapsulation). Aside from the flexibility in positioning the radiator, these units also have the advantages of high power-to-weight ratios (low weight, compact component dimensions), uncomplicated control and regulation, reliability, and the reduced component wear which results from the hydraulic fluid's lubrication effect.

The essential components of the hydrostatic fan drive are the hydraulic pump, the motor (high-pressure gear or piston units), and the temperature-controlled valve in the bypass line to the hydraulic motor for controlling fan speed. The engine powers the hydraulic pump either directly or indirectly via drive belt (conversion ratio). The pump, in turn, powers the hydraulic motor in the fan assembly. The motor speed depends on the fan's specific response properties ($n_L \sim \sqrt{\Delta p_M}$) and the effective pressure differential (Δp_M). If losses associated with transmitting the power are discounted, the speed will be directly proportional to system pressure (p).

Both continuous-action and discontinuous-action control are employed to govern the engine-coolant temperature. With two-point control (discontinuous), the bypass valve is in the form of an electrically-triggered directional-control valve, with actuation controlled by a thermoswitch in the engine's coolant circuit. A pressure valve mounted in a parallel circuit determines the maximum fan speed – and thus cooling power – which will be obtained when the directional-control valve is closed. The precise regulating response is a function of the system pressure to which the valve is set (usually 200 bar). Continuous-control systems feature a bypass valve in the form of a pressure valve or throttle valve with a supplementary bypass-pressure valve for limiting system pressure. The unit is adjusted by a temperature-sensitive control mechanism with proportional response

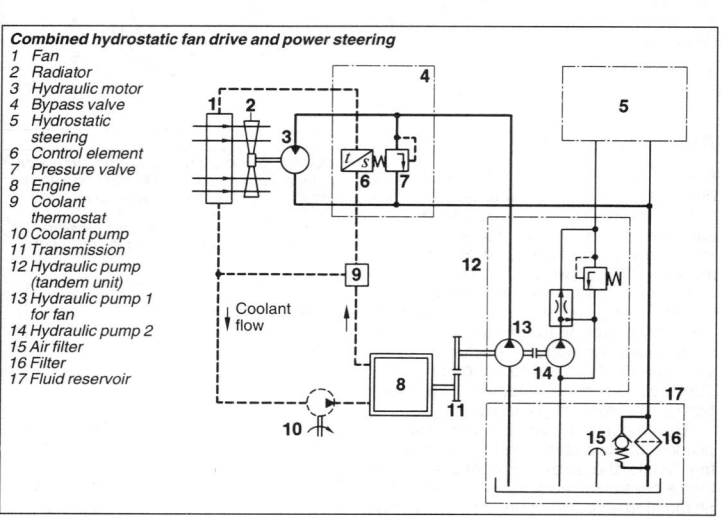

Combined hydrostatic fan drive and power steering

1 Fan
2 Radiator
3 Hydraulic motor
4 Bypass valve
5 Hydrostatic steering
6 Control element
7 Pressure valve
8 Engine
9 Coolant thermostat
10 Coolant pump
11 Transmission
12 Hydraulic pump (tandem unit)
13 Hydraulic pump 1 for fan
14 Hydraulic pump 2
15 Air filter
16 Filter
17 Fluid reservoir

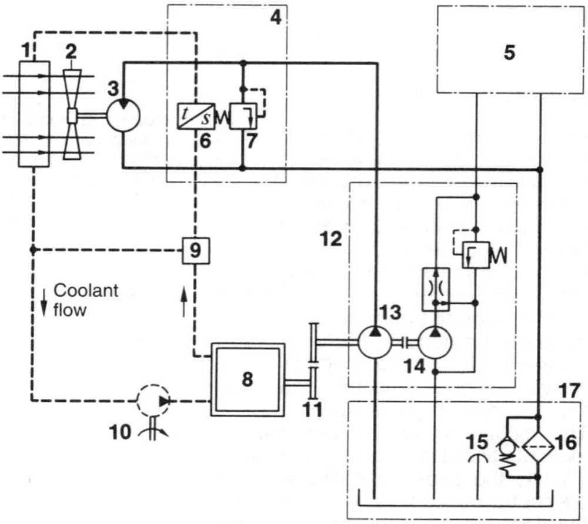

characteristics. It provides continuous, progressive control of system pressure (in the case of the throttle valve via outgoing bypass flow). The control mechanism can be a thermostatic element (expansion element with wax) located in the coolant stream.

Electrohydraulic systems in which the valve is adjusted by a solenoid (proportional solenoid or solenoid with pulse-modulated switching) are becoming increasingly important. This type of solenoid is controlled by the output signal of an electrical temperature sensor located within the coolant stream. This type of unit provides proportional control of the system pressure as a function of temperature. It continually adjusts the fan speed for the required cooling power, remaining within a control range of 5 K. The proportion of operating time during which the fan operates at maximum speed is only roughly 5 %, meaning that the fan rotates at reduced speed most of the time. Reductions in fuel consumption and noise emissions are the result. The inherent system losses with this type of slip regulation, a maximum of roughly 15 %, are commensurate with the requirements of economy. In order to ensure adequate ventilation in the engine compartment beyond the base speed – of particular importance with compartments for encapsulated engines on low-noise vehicles – there is also a limit on minimum system pressure. The control electronics can also be expanded to process additional analog (such as internal and external temperature) and digital input signals. These can serve as the basis for generating output signals to the control solenoid, allowing additional adjustment of fan speed. An example is the combined application of the fan drive to regulate coolant, boost-air and engine-compartment temperatures, and to switch the fan to maximum rpm during retarder operation. Electrohydraulic systems can be integrated within the engine-management system. Hydrostatic fan-drive installations can also be employed in conjunction with other equipment, and they can be employed to power other ancillaries such as the clutch, transmission, compressors, water pump, alternator, hydraulic power steering, rear-axle steering, hydraulic dump-bed lifts. Systems with appropriate control technology and combinations using multiple pumps can deal with operational priorities and safety requirements.

Electrohydraulic fan drive
1 Gear motor with proportional pressure valve, 2 Control unit, 3 Current regulator, 4 Voltage regulator, 5 Retarder operation.
Temperature sensors for: 6 Coolant, 7 Boost air, 8 Outside air.
U_B Battery voltage.

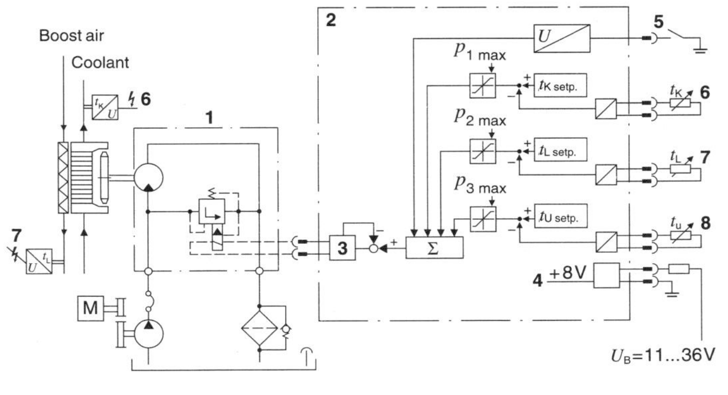

Hydrostatic drives

If the pressure outlet of an adjustable hydraulic pump is connected to a constant-speed or adjustable hydraulic motor (piston or gear motor), the result is an infinitely-variable power-transmission device. The mechanical input power (torque x rpm) emerges as mechanical output at the output. The specific conversion ratio is determined by the quotients of the preset pump flow volume and the motor's displacement volume. Parallel layouts incorporating several motors (differential effect) and series layouts (constant velocity) are also possible. However, a basic transmission within an open circuit can neither change direction nor apply braking force without the assistance of auxiliary mechanisms. This type of layout is suitable for adjustable ancillaries, such as fans, spreader plates, etc.

Main drives

Hydrostatic drive systems for automotive application must be able to cope with turning under power and with braking. For this reason, it is the closed circuit which has gained predominance. The main (reversible) pump is combined with a charge pump, which is usually flange-mounted. The flow from the charge pump into the low-pressure line compensates for leakage and losses in compression volume. Because there is always pressure on the low-pressure side, the main pump's maximum permissible speed is higher than in suction operation. At a constant conversion ratio, this type of transmission provides almost the same degree of positive drive as a mechanical unit. It is especially well-suited as a device for powering machinery. Meanwhile, "automotive" controls have been developed to provide drive characteristics similar to those of cars (for industrial trucks, etc.). In these, the ve-

Open-circuit hydrostatic drive
1 Engine, 2 Adjustable hydraulic pump, 3 Hydraulic motor, 4 Pressure relief valve, 5 Output, 6 Fluid reservoir.

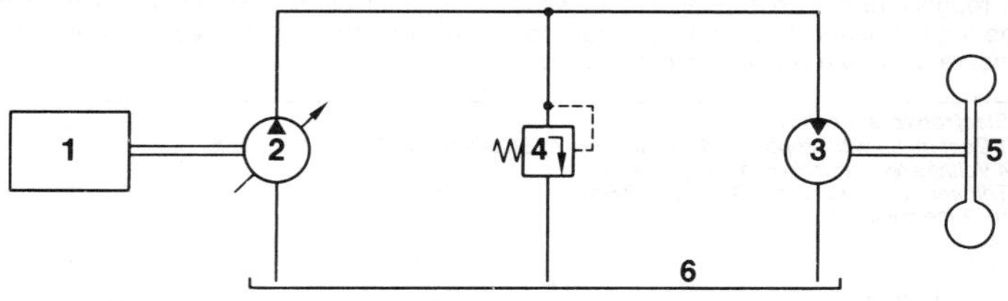

Basic closed circuit
1 Engine, 2 Adjustable hydraulic pump, 3 Charge pump, 4 Charge-pressure relief valve, 5 High-pressure relief valve, 6 Charge non-return valve, 7 Reversible hydraulic motor, 8 Output.

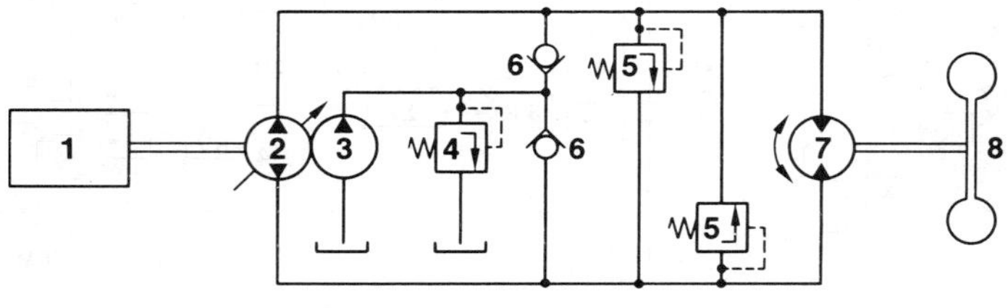

hicle's IC engine and the transmission are governed by a single pedal. Most familiar are the circuits in which the operator uses the pedal to control the engine speed only. The engine power is directed through an auxiliary pump and a throttle circuit (generally incorporating several stages) to generate the control pressure which corresponds to the specific engine speed. This pressure, in turn, determines the main pump's flow volume via a control mechanism with proportional pressure response. This control concept is uncomplicated, and prevents the engine from stalling, as the pump responds to losses in input rpm by switching down to lower flow rates requiring lower torques. However, more complicated circuits are required to satisfy more stringent demands for power control and fuel economy. Electrically-adjustable pumps and modern sensor technology provide for elegant solutions using electronics.

Auxiliary drives

Yet another application for hydrostatic drives is as auxiliary units on otherwise free-wheeling truck axles for slow operation in difficult terrain. When required, this unit acts as a hydrostatic substitute for driveshaft and transfer case. For normal road operation, some form of low-loss switch-off is required for the unit. The solution is provided by a constant-displacement pump at the engine; this pump features variable ratios, and can also be disengaged completely. Low-velocity hub motors are located on the auxiliary-drive axle. Springs retract the motor pistons for normal road operation, making it possible to design the hydraulic circuit specifically for low-speed operation. Neither rotating losses nor substantial friction losses are encountered under normal operating conditions.

Schematic diagram of "automotive" transmission

1 Pedal, 2 Engine with speed governor, 3 Hydraulic pump with adjustable pressure, 4 Charge pump, 5 Restrictor network for rpm-dependent control pressure, 6 Hydraulic motor, 7 Output.

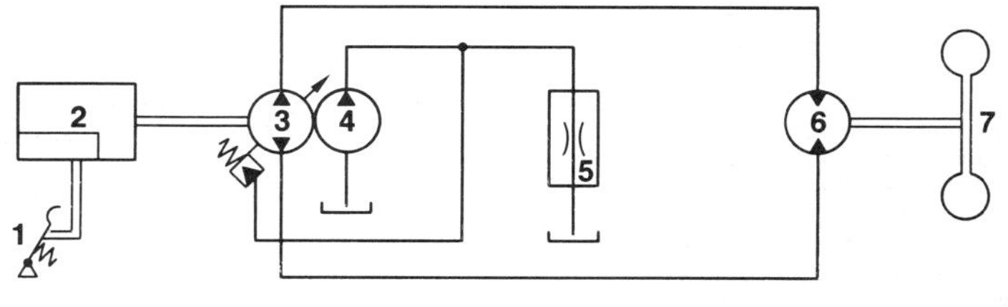

Electrostatic auxiliary drive

1 Electric control for road operation/auxiliary drive, 2 Variable-speed constant-displacement pump with disengagement feature, 3 Fluid reservoir, 4 Detachable connection hoses, 5 Hydraulic lines, 6 Hub motors.

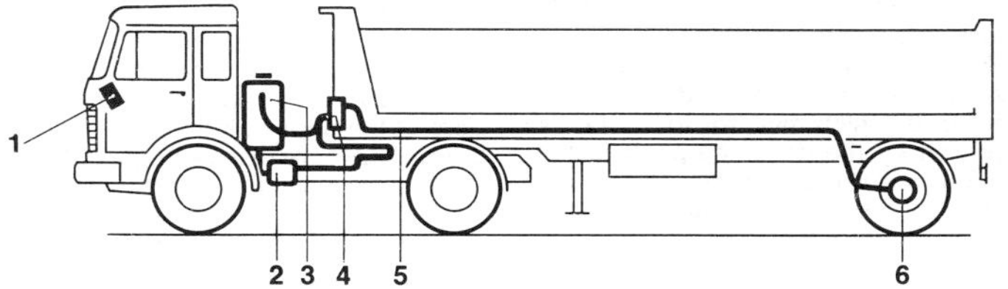

Automotive pneumatics

Pneumatic systems are used in motor vehicles as sources of energy for
- locking, operating and controlling doors, radiator louvers, etc.,
- suspension-level control (p. 561),
- pneumatic braking equipment (p. 620).

Door operation (buses)

Bus doors are operated via double-acting working cylinders. Piston motion is transmitted to the door. The two cylinder chambers are alternately pressurized and exhausted, thereby opening and closing the door. Three drive systems are in use:
- The piston cylinder rotates the door spindle via a lever. Spindle motion is transmitted to the door by means of levers mounted at the top and bottom of the door.
- The piston cylinder is axially flange-mounted to the door spindle. The reciprocating motion of the cylinder piston is converted into rotary motion in the door spindle.
- The piston cylinder is axially mounted to the door spindle. The reciprocating motion of the cylinder piston is converted into rotary motion in the door spindle.

In order to damp the movement of the door as it reaches its end position while opening or closing, a pressure- or travel-dependent cushioning device can be installed in the cylinder to reduce the speed of the door shortly before it reaches either end position. The end-position cushioning effect can be either increased or decreased by adjusting a throttle screw.

A 4/2-way solenoid valve is used to reverse the motion of the door. A current pulse, which may, for example, be triggered by the driver by pushing the pushbutton which operates the doors, causes the solenoid armature to move the rocker into the opposite position via a rod.

When this happens, the rocker closes the inlet valve and opens the outlet on one end of the cylinder, while the outlet is opened and the inlet closed on the other end. Additional valve and control functions must be designed into the system to fulfill the requirements of the vehicle manufacturers as well as the safety requirements contained in § 35 e of the StVZO Road Licensing Regulations (FMVSS/CUR), the Guidelines for power windows, doors and gates, ZH 1/494 of the Main Association of the Commercial Mutual Indemnity Association and the Guidelines of the Association of Public Transport Services (VÖV) for standard city buses.

The closing door must reverse its direction if it encounters resistance (VÖV standard city bus), or the closing force must be interrupted. The opening force must be limited to 150 N or be interrupted upon meeting a resistance. After the emergency valve has been operated, the opening or closing force of the door must be cancelled, so that the door can be operated by hand. After the emergency valve has been returned to its normal position, door movement must not begin until a separate pushbutton (located on the driver's console or in a box above the door) is pressed or sufficient safety functions have been initiated. Abrupt door movements must be prevented.

City bus systems

Door reversal in city buses is achieved through installation of pressure-sensitive devices in the rubber door lips, differential-pressure switches, light barriers or potentiometers which generate electrical switching pulses if the doors meet with resistance, thereby reversing the door valve. If the door meets with resistance while opening, these devices can be actuated while unpressurized, or pressure can be applied to both chambers of the door cylinder. In the case of buses with more than two doors, the rear third door must be automatically controlled. The driver only releases the door for operation. Door opening, open time and closing are electronically controlled on the basis of driver and passenger information.

It is often desirable that only the front half of the front door be operated while the other half remains closed. This function is achieved by a 2/2-way solenoid valve located in the closing line of the cylinder for the second door section.

Tour bus systems
Where the emergency valve is located upstream of the door valve (as in the diagram) an electromagnetic door unlocking process is used, which releases the valve plunger to reverse the door motion when the pushbutton for door operation is actuated.

When this power operation is triggered, banging of the door is prevented by the start-up throttle. In normal operation the start-up throttle is kept open by the secondary pressure.

If the emergency valve is installed downstream of the door valve in the line leading to the closing chamber of the door cylinder, the emergency-valve lock is pneumatically actuated. After medium pressure is reached, the control rod is pneumatically released and the emergency valve is reversed.

Door and flap locking
In large tour-bus doors which swing outward, it is essential that the door is locked during the journey. This is done either by lifting the door immediately after the closing process or by additional locking devices, with single-acting actuating cylinders installed in the door frame. At the conclusion of a door-closing process these are activated by the door itself, e.g., via a 3/2-way reversing valve, thus supporting the door actuator at the end of the closing process. This closing and locking device is installed in such a way that it releases the locking effect when there is a drop in pressure. The door is then held only by the door lock which can be opened manually in an emergency.

In the case of luggage-compartment flaps, on the other hand, locking is by spring force when pressure drops.

Radiator louvers
The radiator louver is actuated by a single-acting cylinder controlled by a thermostatic valve. This contains a wax filling element which, when it expands at a temperature of 80° C, reverses a 3/2-way valve.

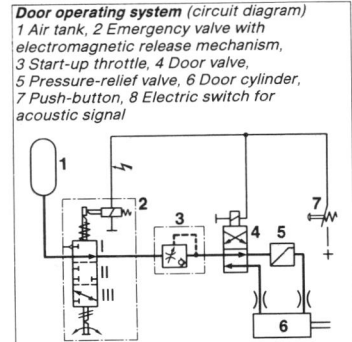

Door operating system *(circuit diagram)*
1 Air tank, 2 Emergency valve with electromagnetic release mechanism, 3 Start-up throttle, 4 Door valve, 5 Pressure-relief valve, 6 Door cylinder, 7 Push-button, 8 Electric switch for acoustic signal

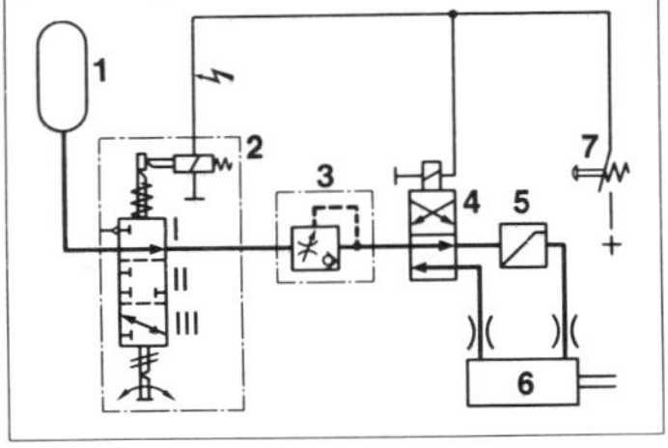

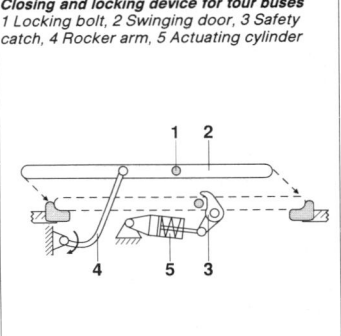

Closing and locking device for tour buses
1 Locking bolt, 2 Swinging door, 3 Safety catch, 4 Rocker arm, 5 Actuating cylinder

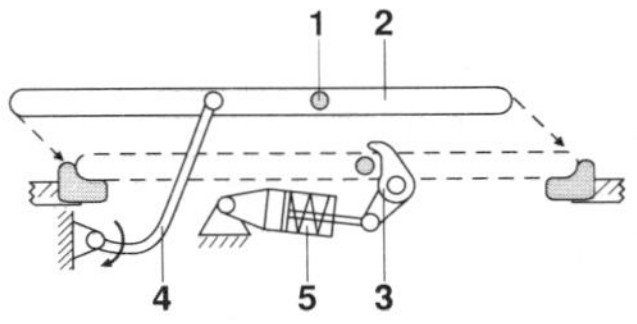

Symbols used in vehicle electrical systems

(Excerpts from DIN Standards 40900)

Connections

Electrical conductor; crossover without and with connection

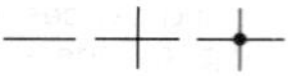

Shielded conductor, single-pole

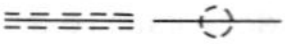

Pneumatic and hydraulic lines

Mechanical lines; crossover without and with connection

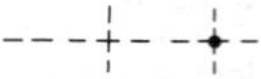

Junction point, general; separable connection (if representation necessary)

Plug connection; male contact; female contact. Three-contact plug connection

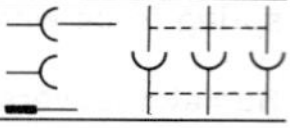

Ground (equipment ground, vehicle ground)

Mechanical functions

Switch positions (basic position: solid line)

Time delay function (shown by double line) toward the right and toward the left and right

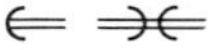

Manual actuation, actuation by follower (cam), thermal actuation (bimetallic strip)

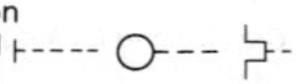

Detent, non-automatic, automatic return in direction of arrow (pushbutton)

Actuation (mech., pneum., hydraul.); general, piston actuator, actuation by rotational speed n, pressure p, flow rate Q, time t, temperature $t°$

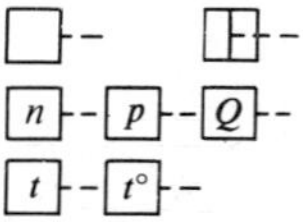

Variability and adjustability, non-inherent, externally applied, general

Variability/adjustability, inherent, internal, due to physical variable; linear, nonlinear

Switches

Switch in general, make contact, break contact

Detent switch, make contact, break contact with non-automatic return

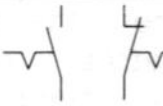

Changeover switch; break before make, make before break

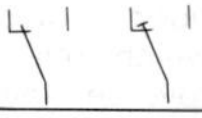

Switch with two-way make contact and center position "Off" (e.g., turn-signal switch)

Switch with ganged make and break contacts, double make contact

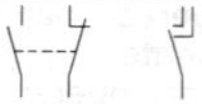

Multiple-position switch

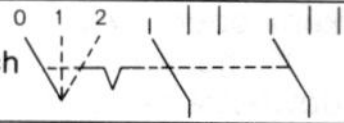

Cam-operated switch, normally closed contact, e.g., contact-breaker points

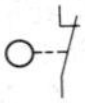

Thermostatic switch, release switch

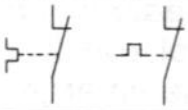

Relays

Actuator with one winding, with two opposed windings

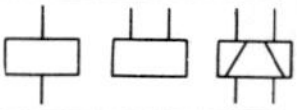

Electrothermal actuator of a thermal relay

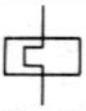

Electromagnetic actuator, solenoid; solenoid valve in closed position

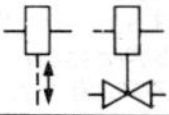

Relay (actuator and switch) Example: instantaneous break contact and delayed make contact

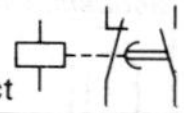

Resistors

Resistor, potentiometer (with three connections)

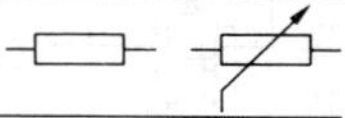

Heating resistor, sheathed-element glow plug, glow plug, window defroster

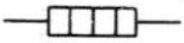

Inductors, windings

Winding, coil, inductance, choke; general	
Variable inductance, transformer (ignition coil)	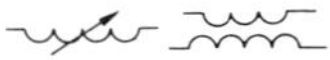

Capacitors, condensers

Capacitor or condenser, general; variable, polarized	
Feedthrough capacitor coaxial, non-coaxial	

Semiconductor devices

PNP and NPN transistor, E Emitter, B Base, C Collector	
Rectifier diode, Zener diode	
Reverse-blocking triode thyristor; anode- and cathode-side controlled	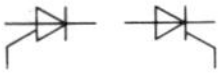

Indicators

Indicator, general; voltmeter; clock	
Rotational speed indicator, temperature indicator, linear speed indicator	

Batteries

Battery, general; multiple-cell battery	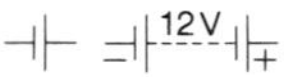

Incandescent lamps

Incandescent lamp with one filament; with two filaments	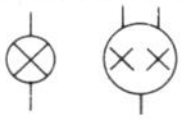

Various components

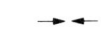

Antenna	
Fuse	
Permanent magnet	
Spark gap, spark plug	
Horn or fanfare horn, speaker, microphone	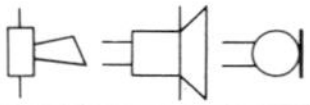
Piezoelectric module	
Hall generator	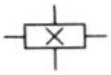

Devices with internal circuitry

Dot/dash border used to delineate circuit sections or to group parts together to form one device	
Shielded device; the dashed line is connected to ground	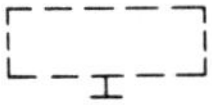

Devices without internal circuitry

Device or circuit element. Explanations may be placed inside the basic symbols; e.g., symbols, formula symbols, characteristics, device designations	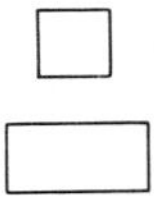
Converter, transducer, memory, general	
Regulator; controlled variable is placed within the triangle: e.g., U = voltage regulator	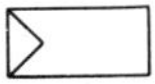

Examples of device symbols

Analog to digital converter (ADC)	
Amplifier	
Frequency converter	
Frequency multiplier	
Frequency divider	
Pulse inverter	
Pulse shaper	
Transducer (temperature/current)	
Gear unit, speed converter	

Electric rotating machines

Armature, rotor with winding, brush (only if necessary)	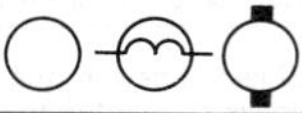
Windingless rotor (pick-up), rotor with permanent magnet	
Direct current, alternating current, three-phase current	
Star-connected winding, delta-connected winding, windings	
DC generator; DC motor; AC generator; Alternator	
Shunt, series, compound-wound machine	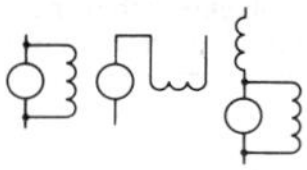
Inductive sensor	
Star-connected alternator; collector-ring rotor with excitation winding	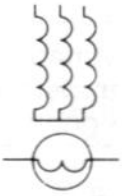

Devices in the motor vehicle

(see circuit diagrams on pages 752–754)

Battery	
Socket (female contact)	
Light, headlamp	
Horn, fanfare horn	
Rear window defroster	
Switch, general; without and with indicator light	
Pressure switch	
Relay, general	
Solenoid valve, injector, cold-start valve	
Thermotime switch	
Throttle-valve switch	
Rotary actuator	
Auxiliary air valve with electrothermal actuator	
Spark plug	

Ignition coil

Ignition distributor, general

Voltage regulator, alternator with regulator

Starter motor with engagement solenoid

Electric fuel pump, motor drive for hydraulic pump

Motor with blower, fan

Wiper motor

Car radio

Speaker

Trigger box, control unit

Voltage stabilizer

Inductive sensor

Turn-signal flasher, pulse generator, intermittent relay

Piezoelectric sensor

Lambda sensor

Air flow sensor

Air-mass meter

Flow-rate sensor, fuel-level sensor

Temperature switch, Temperature sensor

Identification of electrical devices

(Excerpts from DIN Standard 40 719/2)

Identification letter	Type of device / Examples
A	**System, subassembly, parts group**
	Car radio, combination unit, trigger box, control unit
B	**Transducer for conversion of non-electrical variables to electrical variables, or vice versa**
	Sensor, probe, pick-up, fanfare horn, horn, microphone, speaker, air flow sensor
C	**Condensers and capacitors of all types**
D	**Binary devices, memory devices**
	Digital device, integrated circuit (IC), memory, time delay device, timer
E	**Various other devices and equipment**
	All types of lighting, heater, air conditioner, spark plug, ignition distributor
F	**Protection devices**
	Polarity protection device, fuse, current protection circuit, overvoltage protection device
G	**Power supply**
	Battery, alternator (generator), rectifying device, battery charger, transformer
H	**Indicators, alarms, signaling devices**
	Acoustic alarm, indicator lamp, turn-signal indicator lamp, turn-signal lamp, stop lamp, high-beam indicator lamp, alternator indicator lamp, indicator lamp, signal lamp, warning buzzer
K	**Relays**
	Battery relay, turn-signal flasher, turn-signal relay, engagement solenoid, starting solenoid, hazard-warning-signal flasher
L	**Inductors**
	Coil, winding

Identification letter	Type of device / Examples
M	**Motors**
	Blower motor, fan motor, windshield-washer motor, windshield-wiper motor, starter motor
N	**Regulators, amplifiers**
	Regulator (electronic or electromechanical), voltage stabilizer
P	**Measurement, display, test devices**
	Ammeter, diagnostic connection, test point, measuring point, tachometer, speedometer, clock
R	**Resistors**
	Flame glow plug, glow plug, glow-plug indicator resistor, heating resistor, potentiometer, variable resistor (rheostat), dropping resistor, resistance cable, cigarette lighter
S	**Switches**
	Switches/pushbuttons of all types, pressure switch, contact breaker
T	**Transformers**
	Ignition transformer, ignition coil
U	**Converters of electrical variables into other electrical variables, modulators**
	DC transformer, converters of all types
V	**Semiconductors**
	Diode, rectifier, semiconductors of all types, transistor, thyristor, Z-diode
W	**Transmission paths, conductors, antennas**
	Car antenna, shielding component, shielded conductor, wiring harness, conductor, common ground line
X	**Terminals, plugs, plug-and-socket connections**
	Terminal stud or screw, terminal, terminal strip, socket, plug, plug-and-socket connection, distributor connector
Y	**Electrically-actuated mechanical devices**
	Permanent magnet, injector, electric fuel pump, electromagnet, solenoid, solenoid valve, door lock, centralized locking system
Z	**Electrical filters**
	Interference suppressor, filter network

Terminal designations

(Excerpts from DIN Standard 72552)

The terminal designations do not identify the conductors, because devices with different terminal designations can be connected at the two ends of each conductor. If the number of terminal designations is not sufficient (multiple-contact connections), the terminals are consecutively numbered using numbers or letters whose representations of specific functions are not standardized.

Term.	Definition
1	**Ignition coil, ignition distributor** Low voltage
	Ignition distributor with two separate electrical circuits
1 a	To ignition contact breaker I
1 b	To ignition contact breaker II
2	Short-circuit terminal (magneto ignition)
4	Ignition coil, ignition distributor, high voltage
	Ignition distributor with two separate electrical circuits
4 a	From ignition coil I, terminal 4
4 b	From ignition coil II, terminal 4
15	Switched + downstream of battery [output of ignition/driving switch]
15 a	Output at dropping resistor to ignition coil and starter
	Glow plug and starter switch
17	Start
19	Preheat
	Battery
30	Input from + battery terminal, direct
	12/24 V series-parallel battery switch
30 a	Input from + terminal of battery II
31	Return line to battery − battery terminal or ground, direct
31 b	Return line to negative battery terminal or ground, via switch or relay (switched negative)
	12/24 V series-parallel battery switch
31 a	Return line to − terminal of battery II
31 c	Return line to − terminal of battery I

Term.	Definition
	Electric motors
32	Return line [1])
33	Main terminal connection [1])
33 a	Self-parking switch-off
33 b	Shunt field
33 f	For second lower-speed range
33 g	For third lower-speed range
33 h	For fourth lower-speed range
33 L	Counterclockwise rotation
33 R	Clockwise rotation
	Starter
45	Separate starter relay, output; starter, input (main current)
	Two-starter parallel operation
	Starting relay for engagement current
45 a	Output, starter I
	Input, starters I and II
45 b	Output, starter II
48	Terminal on starter and on start-repeating relay for monitoring starting procedure
	Turn-signal flasher (pulse generator)
49	Input
49 a	Output
49 b	Output, second turn-signal circuit
49 c	Output, third turn-signal circuit
	Starter
50	Starter control (direct)
	Series-parallel battery switch
50 a	Output for starter control
	Starter control
50 b	with parallel operation of two starters with sequential control
	Starting relay for sequential control of the engagement current during parallel operation of two starters
50 c	Input at starting relay for starter I
50 d	Input at starting relay for starter II
	Start-locking relay
50 e	Input
50 f	Output
	Start-repeating relay
50 g	Input
50 h	Output

[1]) Polarity reversal possible at terminals 32—33.

Term.	Definition
	Alternator
51	DC voltage at rectifier
51 e	DC voltage at rectifier with choke coil for daytime driving
	Trailer signals
52	Signals from trailer to towing vehicle, general
53	**Wiper motor,** input (+)
53 a	Wiper (+), self-parking switch-off
53 b	Wiper (shunt winding)
53 c	Electric windshield-washer pump
53 e	Wiper (brake winding)
53 i	Wiper motor with permanent magnet and third brush (for higher speed)
	Trailer signal
54	For lamp combinations and trailer plug connections
	Stop lamp
54 g	Pneum. valve for additional retarding brake, electromagnetically actuated
55	**Fog lamp**
56	**Headlamp**
56 a	High beam, high-beam indicator lamp
56 b	Low beam
56 d	Headlamp-flasher contact
57	**Side-marker lamp:** m-cycles, mopeds. Abroad also cars, trucks, etc.
57 a	**Parking lamp**
57 L	Parking lamp, left
57 R	Parking lamp, right
58	**Side-marker lamps, tail lamps, license-plate lamps and instrument-panel lamps**
58 b	Tail-lamp changeover for single-axle tractors
58 c	Trailer plug-and-receptacle assembly for single-conductor tail-lamp cable with fuse in trailer
58 d	Variable-intensity instrument-panel lamp, tail-lamp and side-marker lamp
58 L	Left
58 R	Right, license-plate lamp
	Alternator
	(magneto generator)
59	AC voltage, output
	Rectifier, input
59 a	Charging armature, output
59 b	Tail-lamp armature, output
59 c	Stop-lamp armature, output

Term.	Definition
61	**Alternator charge-indicator lamp**
	Tone-sequence control device
71	Input
71 a	Output to horns 1 & 2, low
71 b	Output to horns 1 & 2, high
72	**Alarm switch** (rotating beacon)
75	**Radio, cigarette lighter**
76	Speaker
77	**Door-valve control**
	Switch Break-contact and changeover switches
81	Input
81 a	1st output, break side
81 b	2nd output, break side
	Make-contact switch
82	Input
82 a	1st output
82 b	2nd output
82 z	1st input
82 y	2nd input
	Multiple-position switch
83	Input
83 a	Output, position 1
83 b	Output, position 2
83 L	Output, left-hand position
83 R	Output, right-hand position
	Current relay
84	Input, actuator and relay contact
84 a	Output, actuator
84 b	Output, relay contact

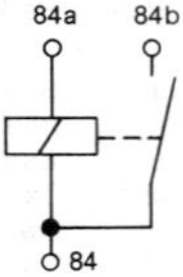

Term.	Definition
	Switching relay
85	Output, actuator (end of winding to ground or negative) Input, actuator
86	Start of winding
86 a	Start of winding or 1st winding
86 b	Winding tap or 2nd winding

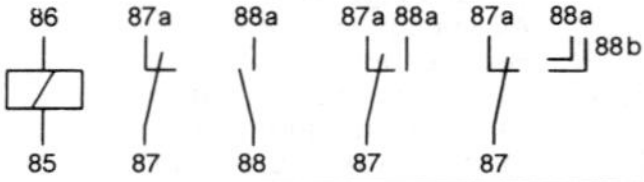

Term.	Definition
	Relay contact for break and changeover contacts
87	Input
87 a	1st output (break side)
87 b	2nd output
87 c	3rd output
87 z	1st input
87 y	2nd input
87 x	3rd input
	Relay contact for make contact
88	Input
	Relay contact for make and changeover contacts (make side)
88 a	1st output
88 b	2nd output
88 c	3rd output
	Relay contact for make contact
88 z	1st input
88 y	2nd input
88 x	3rd input

Alternator and voltage regulator

B +	Battery positive
B –	Battery negative
D +	Dynamo positive
D –	Dynamo negative
DF	Dynamo field
DF 1	Dynamo field 1
DF 2	Dynamo field 2
	Alternator
U, V, W	Alternator terminals

Directional signals (turn-signal flasher)

C	First indicator lamp
C0	Main terminal connection for separate indicator circuits actuated by the turn-signal switch
C2	Second indicator lamp
C3	Third indicator lamp (e.g., when towing two trailers)
L	Turn-signal lamps, left
R	Turn-signal lamps, right

Comparison of terminal designations: DIN 72 552 vs. other terminal designations

DIN 72 552 and Bosch	DF	D–	D+	B+	F	D+/61	61	31–
Autolite	F FLD	–	+	BAT B	Field	ARM A	I	G GND
Butec	F	–	+					
Delco Remy	F	GRD	+	BAT B	F	GEN	L	– GND
Ducellier	Exc E	–	+	BAT B	Exc	DYN D		M–
Elmot	67	31	15	30	67	51/15		31
Femsa	Exc	31	+	30 BAT	67 Exc	51 DIN		31
Fiat	67	31	15	30	67	51/15		31
Ford				BAT	Field	ARM		G
Hitachi	F	E	IG					
Iskra	DF	D–	D+	B+	DF	D+		D–
Japan, other manufacturers	F	E	IG (=15)	A, B (N = center point of stator)			L	E
Lada (Shiguli)	67	31	15	30	67	51/15		31
Lucas	F	–	+ SW=15	A, B, B+ A1[1])	F F1, F2	D	WL IND	E/–
Magneton-Pal	M	–	R	+B	M	R	D/61	–B
Marelli	67	31	15	B+ 51	F DF	D+	61	31–
Mitsubishi	F	E	IG					
Mopar	Exc	–	IGN					
Motorola, SEV-Motorola	Exc	–	+					
Nippon Denso	F	E	B					
Paris-Rhône	Exc	–	+ BOB	BAT	Exc	DYN		M–
Prestolite	Exc	–	IGN					
Seri-Ducellier	DF	D–	+					
SEV-Marchal	DF	–	+					

[1]) A1 = loads.

Circuit diagram for a passenger car with spark-ignition engine

(not showing internal circuitry of devices)

A1 Device designation in accordance with DIN 40 719 (page 747)
15 Terminal designation in accordance with DIN 72 552 (page 748)
1 Section identification in accordance with DIN 40 719

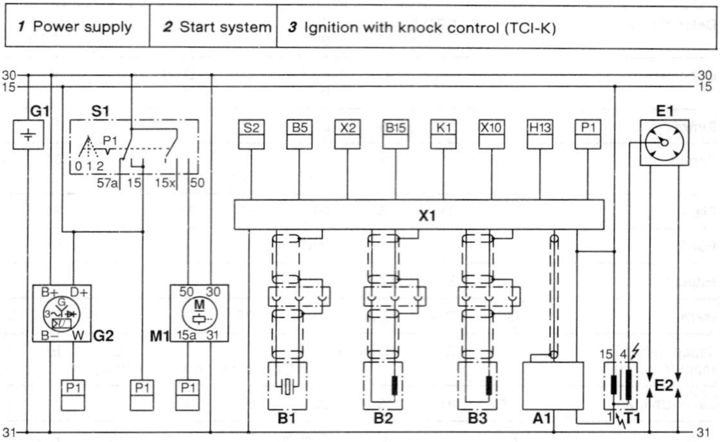

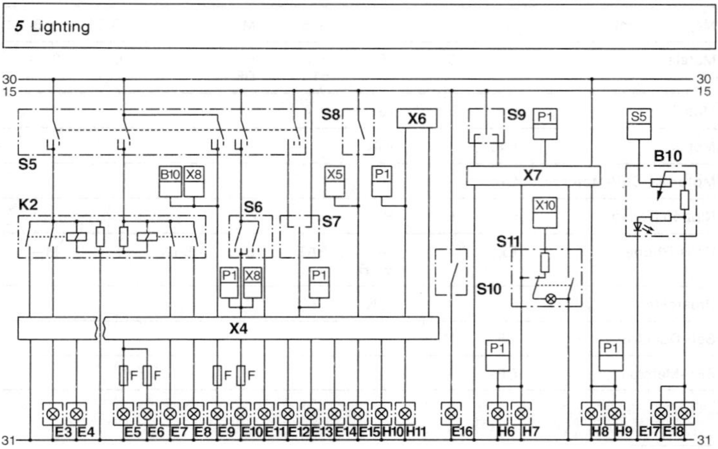

The following circuit diagrams show examples of automotive circuitry. The diagrams serve as explanatory illustrations to the text. They are not intended as the basis for design or installation.

"Assembled" and "detached" representations are used in automotive electrics.

Reference: Bosch Technical Instruction "Automotive Symbols and Circuit Diagrams".

4 Gasoline fuel-injection (KE-Jetronic)

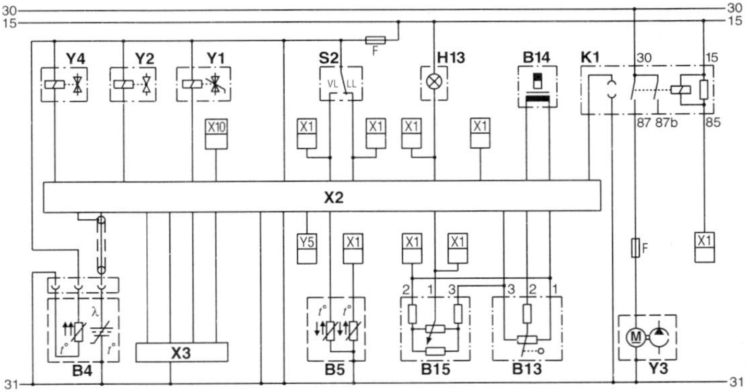

6 Wipe/ wash system	***7*** Cooling, ventilation	***8*** Signaling system	***9*** Clock, radio

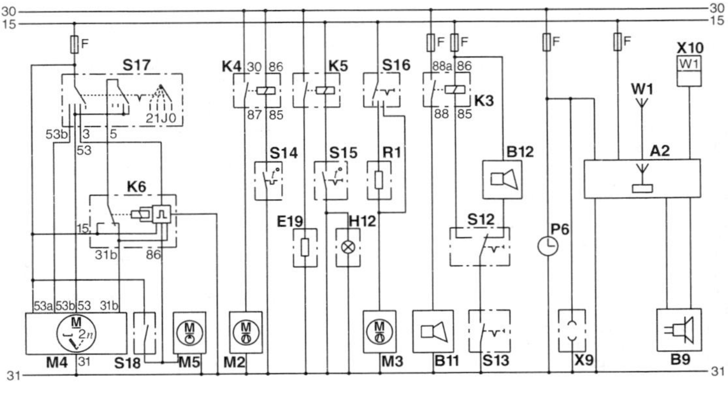

10 Indicators and displays	*11* ABS

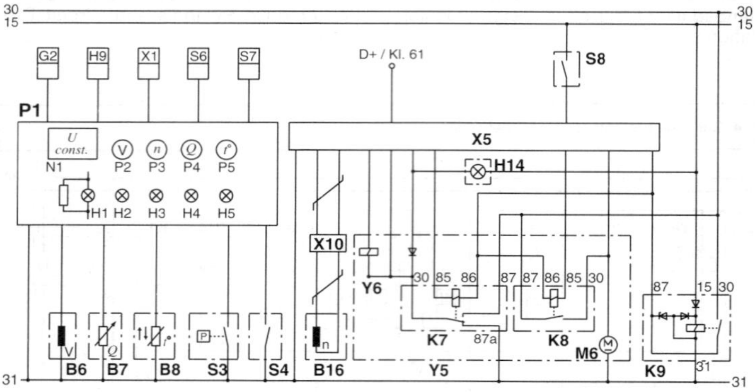

Device design.	Device	Section
A1	Trigger box (EI-K)	*3*
A2	Radio	*9*
B1	Knock sensor	*3*
B2	Rotational-speed and reference-mark sensor	*3*
B3	Cylinder identification sensor	*3*
B4	Lambda sensor	*4*
B5	Dual temperature sensor (engine)	*4*
B6	Vehicle-speed signal sensor	*10*
B7	Fuel-level sensor	*10*
B8	Coolant-temperature sensor	*10*
B9	Loudspeaker	*9*
B10	Brightness control, instrument lighting	*5*
B11	Supertone horn	*8*
B12	Horn	*8*
B13	Air flow sensor	*4*
B14	Electrodynamic pressure actuator	*4*
B15	Altitude sensor	*4*
B16	ABS wheel-speed sensor	*11*
E1	High-voltage distributor	*3*
E2	Spark plugs	*3*
E3, E4	Fog-warning lamps	*5*
E5, E6	Driving lamps	*5*
E7, E8	Fog lamps	*5*
E9, E10	Lower-beam headlamps	*5*
E11, E12	Side-marker lamps	*5*
E13	License-plate lamp	*5*
E14, E15	Tail lamps	*5*

Device design.	Device	Section
E16	Backup lamp	*5*
E17	Instrument lighting	*5*
E18	Instrument-panel lighting	*5*
E19	Rear-window defroster	*7*
F...	Fuses	
G1	Battery	*1*
G2	Alternator	*1*
H1	Alternator charge-indicator lamp	*10*
H2	Oil-pressure indicator	*10*
H3	Handbrake-indicator lamp	*10*
H4	High-beam indicator	*10*
H5	Turn-signal indicator lamp	*10*
H6...H9	Turn-signal lamps	*5*
H10, H11	Stop lamps	*5*
H12	Rear-window defroster indicator lamp	*7*
H13	Diagnosis lamp	*4*
H14	Fault indicator/warning lamp (ABS)	*11*
K1	Fuel-pump relay	*4*
K2	Side-marker lamp interrogation relay	*5*
K3	Relay, supertone horn	*8*
K4	Relay, engine fan	*7*
K5	Relay, rear-window defroster	*7*
K6	Relay, wiper interval	*6*
K7	Valve relay	*11*
K8	Engine relay	*11*
K9	Relay, overvoltage protection	*11*

Wiring diagram in detached representation

In the detached representation method, the continuous connecting lines between the individual devices are omitted. The devices are shown in the form of squares, rectangles, or symbols, and designated in accordance with DIN 40719/2. The terminal designation of the device is also given. Each outgoing conductor from a device receives a code containing the terminal designation of the destination device as well as the device designation. If necessary, the conductor color is also given.

Reference: Circuit Diagrams for Passenger Cars, published by Autodata-Verlag. Sold by: Fust, Wever & Co. GmbH, Essen.

Example: alternator

Example: Alternator
a Device designation (code letter and code number)
b Terminal designation on device
c Device to ground
d Destination (code letter and code number) (terminal designation) (conductor color)

Device representation — Destination

G 1 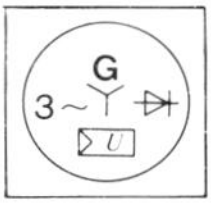

D + O— H 1/sw
B + O— G 2 :+/rt
B – ●—|

sw = black
rt = red

a b c d

Device design.	Device	Section
M1	Starter motor	2
M2	Cooling-fan motor	7
M3	Fresh-air blower motor	7
M4	Wiper motor	6
M5	Windshield-washer motor	6
M6	Return pump	11
N1	Voltage stabilizer	10
P1	Instrument cluster	10
P2	Electric speedometer	10
P3	Tachometer	10
P4	Fuel-level indicator	10
P5	Engine-temperature indicator	10
P6	Clock	9
R1	Fan resistor	7
S1	Ignition/starting switch	2
S2	Throttle-valve switch	4
S3	Oil-pressure switch	10
S4	Handbrake switch	10
S5	Light switch	5
S6	Fog-lamp switch	5
S7	Lower-beam switch	5
S8	Stop-lamp switch	5
S9	Turn-signal switch	5
S10	Switch, backup lamp	5
S11	Switch, hazard warning system	5
S12	Horn change-over switch	8
S13	Horn button	8
S14	Thermo switch	7
S15	Switch, rear-window defroster	7
S16	Fan switch	7
S17	Wiper switch	6
S18	Washer switch	6
T1	Ignition coil	3
W1	Car antenna	9
X1	Plug, EI-K control unit	3
X2	Plug, KE-Jetronic control unit	4
X3	Coding plug	4
X4	Plug, lamp-control module	5
X5	Plug, ABS control unit	11
X6	Plug, Check-Control	5
X7	Plug-in base, hazard-warning relay	5
X8	Plug, base module, central bodywork electronics	5
X9	Diagnosis socket	9
X10	Wheel-speed sensor (ABS)	11
Y1	Idle actuator	4
Y2	Injectors	4
Y3	Electric fuel pump	4
Y4	Canister-purge valve	4
Y5	Hydraulic modulator	11
Y6	Solenoid valves	11

Calculation of conductor sizes

Quantities and units

Quantity		Unit
A	Conductor cross section	mm^2
I	Current	A
l	Conductor length	m
P	Power required by load	W
R	Resistance (load)	Ω
S	Current density in conductor	A/mm^2
U_N	Nominal voltage	V
U_{vl}	Permissible voltage drop in insulated conductor	V
U_{vg}	Permissible voltage drop in entire circuit	V
ϱ	Resistivity	$\Omega \cdot mm^2/m$

Calculation

In determining the conductor cross section, allowance must be made for voltage drop and the effect of elevated temperatures.

1. Determine the current I of the load:

$$I = P/U_N = U_N/R$$

2. Calculate the conductor cross section A using the U_{vl} values given in Table 2 ($\varrho = 0.0185\ \Omega \cdot mm^2/m$ for copper):

$$A = I \cdot \varrho \cdot l / U_{vl}$$

3. Round-off the value for A to the next larger conductor cross section in accordance with Table 1.

Individual conductors which have cross sections less than 1 mm^2 are not recommended because their mechanical strength is inadequate.

4. Calculate the actual voltage drop U_{vl}:

$$U_{vl} = I \cdot \varrho \cdot l / A \text{ and}$$

5. Check the current density S in order to avoid excessive conductor temperatures (in brief operation, $S < 30\ A/mm^2$; see Table 1 for values for continuous operation).

$$S = I/A$$

Table 1. Electrical copper conductors for motor vehicles
Single-core, untinned, PVC-insulated. Permissible working temperature: 70° C.[2])

Nominal conductor cross-section mm^2	Approximate number of individual wires[1])	Maximum resistance per meter[1]) at +20° C mΩ/m	Maximum conductor diameter[1]) mm	Nominal thickness of insulation[1]) mm	Maximum cable outer diameter[1]) mm	Permissible continuous current (standard value)[2]) at ambient temperature 30+° C A	at +50° C A
1	32	18.5	1.5	0.6	2.7	19	13.5
1.5	30	12.7	1.8	0.6	3.0	24	17.0
2.5	50	7.60	2.2	0.7	3.6	32	22.7
4	56	4.71	2.8	0.8	4.4	42	29.8
6	84	3.14	3.4	0.8	5.0	54	38.3
10	80	1.82	4.5	1.0	6.5	73	51.8
16	126	1.16	6.3	1.0	8.3	98	69.6
25	196	0.743	7.8	1.3	10.4	129	91.6
35	276	0.527	9.0	1.3	11.6	158	112
50	396	0.368	10.5	1.5	13.5	198	140
70	360	0.259	12.5	1.5	15.5	245	174
95	475	0.196	14.8	1.6	18.0	292	207
120	608	0.153	16.5	1.6	19.7	344	244

[1]) As per DIN ISO 6722, part 3.
[2]) As per DIN VDE 0298, part 4.

The values given for U_{vl} in Table 2 are used to calculate the dimensions of the positive conductor. The voltage drop in the ground return is not taken into account. In the case of insulated ground cables, the total length in both directions should normally be used.

The U_{vg} values given in the table are test values and cannot be used for conductor calculations because they also include the contact resistance of switches, fuses, etc.

Notes

1 *The lengths and resistances of all three control leads should be as equal as possible.*

2 *In special cases in which a very long main starter cable is used, the U_{vl} value can be exceeded if the starting limit temperature is reduced.*

3 *If the main starter return cable is insulated, the voltage loss in the return line should not exceed that of the incoming line; voltage loss values of 4 % of the nominal voltage in each line are permissible, for a total of 8 %.*

4 *The U_{vl} values apply to solenoid-switch temperatures of from +50 to +80° C.*

5 *Make allowance for the cable to the starter switch if necessary.*

Table 2. Permissible voltage drop

Type of conductor	Permissible voltage drop in positive conductor U_{vl}		Permissible voltage drop in entire circuit U_{vg}		Notes
Nominal voltage U_N	12 V	24 V	12 V	24 V	
Lighting conductors from terminal 30 of light switch to lamps < 15 W to trailer socket from trailer socket to lamps	0.1 V	0.1 V	0.6 V	0.6 V	Current at nominal voltage and nominal power
from terminal 30 of light switch to lamps > 15 W to trailer socket	0.5 V	0.5 V	0.9 V	0.9 V	
from terminal 30 of light switch to headlamps	0.3 V	0.3 V	0.6 V	0.6 V	
Charging cable from terminal B+ of alternator to battery	0.4 V	0.8 V	–	–	Current at nominal voltage and nominal power
Control leads from alternator to regulator (terminals D+, D–, DF)	0.1 V	0.2 V	–	–	At maximum excitation current (note 1)
Main starter cable	0.5 V	1.0 V	–	–	Starter short-circuit current at +20°C (notes 2 and 3)
Starter control lead From starter switch to terminal 50 of starter Solenoid switch with single winding Solenoid switch with pull-in and hold-in windings	1.4 V 1.5 V	2.0 V 2.2 V	1.7 V 1.9 V	2.5 V 2.8 V	Maximum control current (notes 4 and 5)
Other control leads from switch to relay, horn, etc.	0.5 V	1.0 V	1.5 V	2.0 V	Current at nominal voltage

Electrical energy supply in the motor vehicle

The vehicle must be able to draw upon sufficient reserves of electrical energy to satisfy a number of requirements. The available current supply must be capable of ensuring that the vehicle can be started and operated at all times. Operation of electrical accessories for a reasonable period of time with the engine off should not make subsequent engine starts impossible. Battery, starter, alternator and the electrical system as a whole must be designed for mutually compatible operation. The criteria for designing the optimal system are low weight, compact dimensions and low fuel consumption, whereby fuel economy is generally the predominating concern. The following factors must receive special consideration:

Starting temperature
The lowest temperature at which the engine can be started depends upon a number of factors including the battery (capacity, internal resistance, state of charge, etc.) and the starter (size, with or without intermediate transmission, electrical/permanent-magnet excitation, etc.). If the engine is to be started at a temperature of −20°C, for example, the battery must have the minimum state of charge p.

Alternator output
The current output of the alternator varies as a function of engine speed. The alternator can only supply a certain percentage of its rated current at idle n_L. If the current I_V consumed by the loads is greater than the current I_G output by the alternator, e.g., at idle, the battery will discharge and the voltage in the vehicle electrical system will drop.

If on the other hand, the consumer current I_V consumed by the loads is less than the current I_G output by the alternator, some of this current difference is used for battery charging (I_B).

Driving
The speed at which the alternator turns depends upon the particular type of operation for the vehicle in question. The cumulative speed frequency distribution shows how often a certain speed is achieved or exceeded during vehicle operation.

Due to traffic congestion or stops at traffic lights, a passenger car driven in commuter traffic is run at idle a high percentage of the time. Under highway driving conditions, on the other hand, the percentage of time the vehicle is run at idle is generally lower. Additional idle time is accumulated by city buses because they must make frequent stops. The state of charge of the battery is further reduced when loads must be left on with the engine turned off (e.g., at bus terminals). Long-dis-

Possible starting temperature as a function of battery charge
p Minimum charge

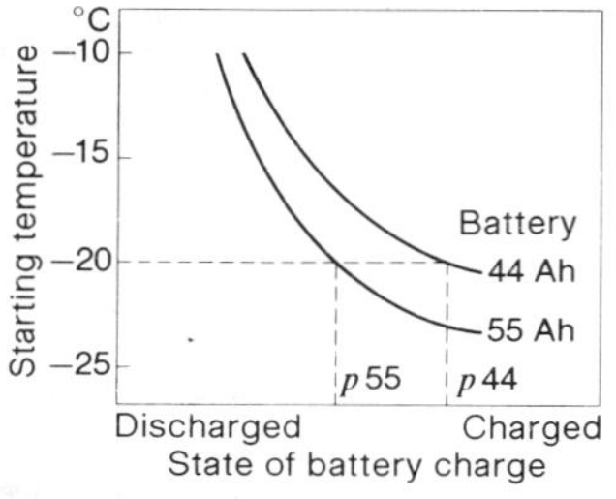

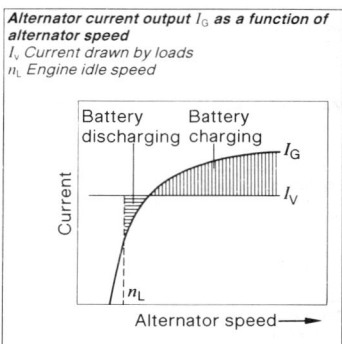

Alternator current output I_G as a function of alternator speed
I_V Current drawn by loads
n_L Engine idle speed

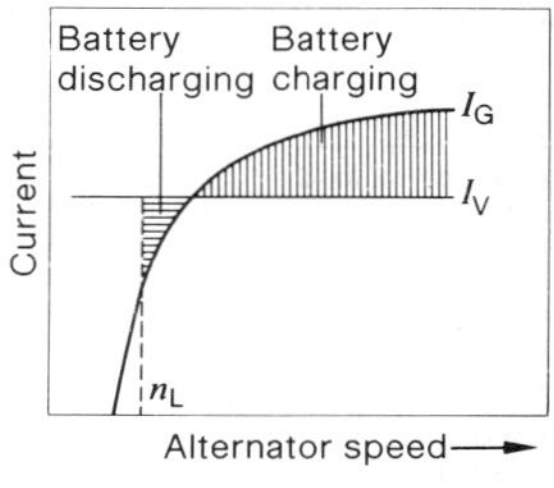

tance tour buses generally run only a small percentage of the time at idle.

Electrical loads
Electrical loads have different duty cycles. A differentiation is made between continuous loads (ignition, fuel injection, etc.), long-time loads (lighting, heated rear window, etc.) and short-time loads (turn signals, stop lamps, etc). Use of some electrical loads is seasonal (air conditioners in summer, seat heaters in winter). The on-time of electrical radiator fans depends upon temperature and driving conditions. In winter, lights are generally used when driving in commuter traffic.

Charging voltage
The battery charging voltage must be higher in cold weather and lower in warm weather in order to accommodate the chemical processes which take place inside the battery. The gassing voltage curve indicates the maximum permissible charging voltage at which the battery does not "gas".

Vehicle loads require a voltage which is as constant as possible. The voltage applied to lamp bulbs must have very close tolerances so that lamp bulb service life and light intensity remain within specified limits. The voltage regulator limits the maximum voltage. It affects the lower voltage limit when the potential alternator current I_G is larger than the system's load-current requirement I_V. The voltage regulator is usually mounted on the alternator.

In the event that significant deviations can be expected between the temperature of the voltage regulator and that of the battery electrolyte, it is advantageous to monitor the voltage-regulation temperature directly at the battery. It is possible to compensate for the voltage loss in the charge cable between the alternator and the battery by using a regulator to monitor actual voltage directly at the latter (over a supplementary wire).

Dynamic system characteristic
The interrelationships between the battery, alternator, loads, temperature, engine speed and engine/alternator speed ratio determine the system characteristic.

It is specific for each combination of parameters and each set of operating conditions, and is thus dynamic in nature. The dynamic system characteristic can be measured at the battery terminals using an X-Y recorder.

Charging balance calculation
The charging balance calculation must take into consideration the above-mentioned influencing variables. A computer program is used to determine the state of battery charge at the end of a typical driving cycle. A typical passenger-car cycle consists of vehicle operation in commuter traffic (engine

Cumulative engine speed frequency for city and highway driving

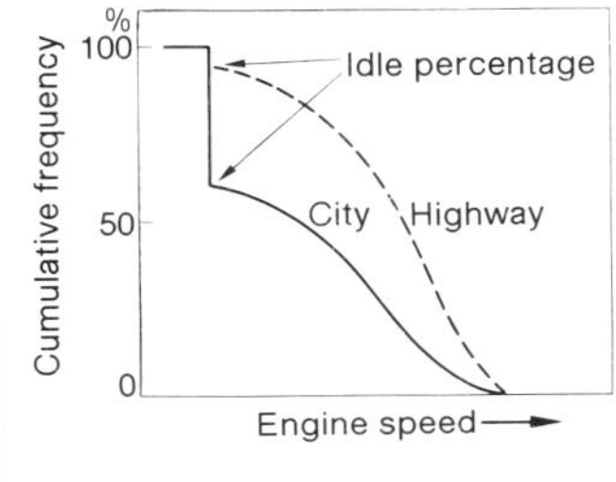

Dynamic system characteristics
(Envelopes for city driving).
1 with large alternator and small battery,
2 with small alternator and large battery.

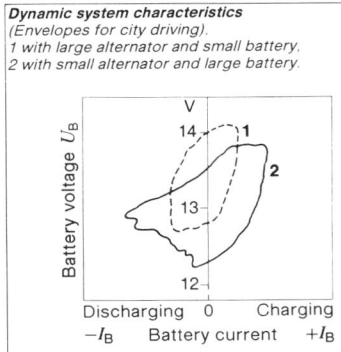

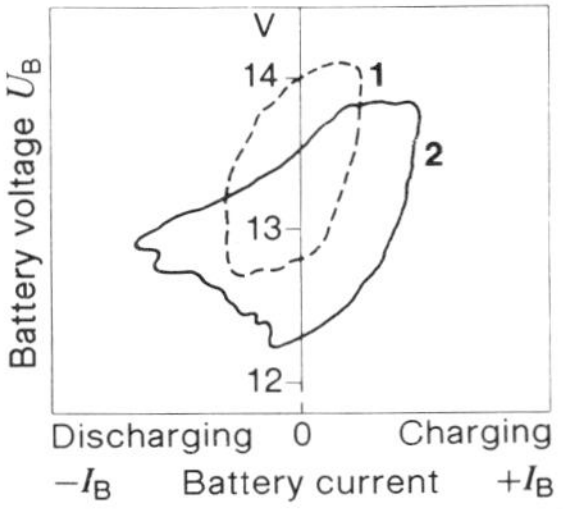

speeds are low) combined with winter operation (at which time charging current consumption by the battery is low). Summer operation may place even greater loads on the system when the vehicle is equipped with an air conditioner (high current draw). The battery's charge at the end of the cycle must – at the very least – be sufficient to allow a subsequent engine start at the temperature in question.

Lead-acid batteries

The active materials in a lead-acid battery are lead oxide (PbO_2) on the positive plates, spongy, highly porous lead (Pb) on the negative plates and the electrolyte, diluted sulfuric acid (H_2SO_4). The electrolyte is simultaneously an ion conductor for charging and discharging. The PbO_2 and Pb assume typical electrical voltages (individual potentials) with respect to the electrolyte; the algebraic sum of these individual voltages produces a cell voltage which can be externally measured. At rest, the cell voltage is approx. 2 V, increasing during charging and decreasing when the cell is subjected to a load. When the cell discharges, PbO_2 and Pb combine with H_2SO_4 to form $PbSO_4$ (lead sulfate).

This conversion causes the electrolyte to lose SO_4 (sulfate) ions, and its density decreases. When the cell charges, the active materials PbO_2 and Pb are reconstituted from the $PbSO_4$.

$$PbO_2 + 2\,H_2SO_4 + Pb \rightleftarrows PbSO_4 + 2\,H_2O + PbSO_4$$

→ Discharging, ← Charging

If the charging voltage continues to be applied after the cell has reached a state of full charge, only the electrolytic decomposition of water occurs, producing oxygen at the positive plate and hydrogen at the negative plate (oxyhydrogen gas).

Electrolyte density can be used an indication of the state of charge of the battery. The accuracy of this relationship depends upon battery design (see table below with ranges of deviation) as well as electrolyte stratification and battery wear with a certain degree of irreversible sulfating and/or a high degree of shedding of the plate material.

Behavior at low temperatures

The more the battery discharges, the more dilute the electrolyte becomes. As the density of the electrolyte decreases its freezing point increases.

A battery whose electrolyte is frozen is only capable of supplying a low current which is not sufficient for starting the vehicle.

Mixing instructions

Desired electrolyte density in kg/l	Volumetric ratio of concentrated sulfuric acid (96 %) to distilled water
1.23	1:3.8
1.26	1:3.2
1.28	1:2.8

Density and freezing point of dilute sulfuric acid

State of charge	Battery design	Electrolyte density kg/l[1]	Freezing point °C
Charged	standard	1.28	−68
	tropicalized	1.23	−40
Half charged	standard	1.16/1.20[2]	−17 ... −27
	tropicalized	1.13/1.16[2]	−13 ... −17
Discharged	standard	1.04/1.12[2]	−3 ... −11
	tropicalized	1.03/1.08[2]	−2 ... −8

[1]) At 20 °C: The electrolyte density rises and falls with temperature by approx. 0.01 kg/l per 14 °C.
[2]) Low value: high electrolyte utilization. High value: low electrolyte utilization

Mixing fresh electrolyte

To avoid splashing, always add concentrated sulfuric acid to distilled water, never the reverse. Stir with an acid-resistant rod (glass or plastic) while adding acid. The table on p. 760 shows how to mix electrolyte to produce some standard acid concentrations. The values given can be extrapolated linearly to achieve other concentrations.

Battery characteristics

Designation

In addition to mechanical parameters such as dimensions, mounting and terminal design, batteries are characterized by electrical values measured as per test standards (e.g., DIN 43539, Part. 2). Starter batteries manufactured in Germany are marketed with a 5-digit type number, nominal voltage, nominal capacity and cold-discharge test current (only for starter batteries) as per DIN 72310 and 72311. Example: 56618, 12 V 66 Ah 300 A.

Capacity

Battery capacity, rated in Ah, is the current which can be delivered by the battery under specified conditions. Capacity decreases as discharge current increases and temperature decreases.

Nominal capacity K_{20}

As defined by DIN, nominal capacity is the current which the battery can deliver within 20 h at constant discharge current down to a cutoff voltage of 1.75 V/cell. The battery nominal capacity depends upon the quantities of active material used (positive mass, negative mass, electrolyte), and is relatively unaffected by the number of plates.

Cold-discharge test current I_{KP}

This figure provides an index of the battery's current delivery capacity when cold (i.e., cold-starting capability). As per DIN Standards, the terminal voltage during discharge at I_{KP} and −18 °C must be at least 1.5 V/cell 30 s, and at least 1 V/cell 150 s after the start of discharge. The short-time behavior of the battery when discharged at I_{KP} is largely determined by the number of plates, their surface area, and the gap between plates and separator material.

Battery voltage curves as a function of discharge time for various discharge currents

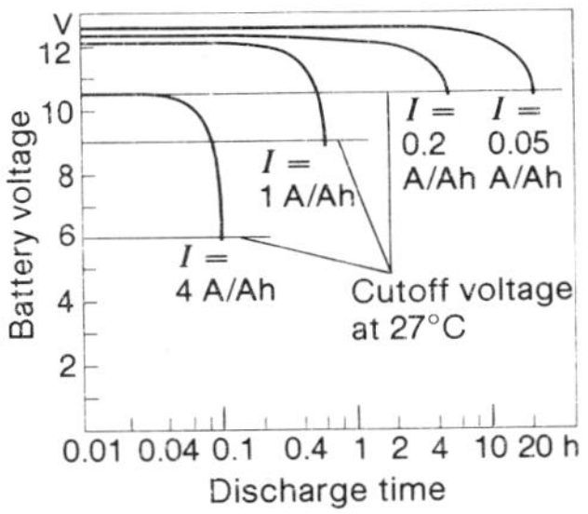

Battery capacity as a function of discharge current and temperature

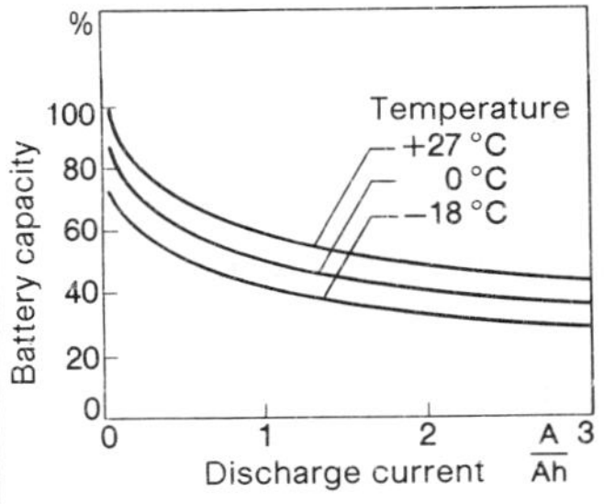

Correction factor for internal battery resistance as a function of electrolyte temperature and state of discharge

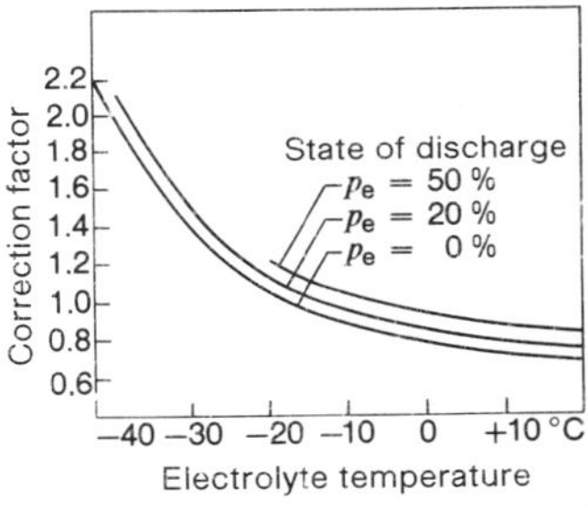

Another variable which characterizes starting behavior is internal resistance R_i. The following equation applies to a fully-charged battery (12 V) at −18 °C: $R_i = (2100...2400)/I_{KP}$ (mΩ), where I_{KP} is given in A. The battery internal resistance and other resistances in the starter circuit determine the cranking speed.

Vehicle electrical system

The voltage level in the vehicle electrical system, and thus the battery charge, are also affected by the wiring between alternator, battery and electrical loads. If all loads are connected on the battery side, the total current in the charging cable is $I_G = I_B + I_V$. The charging voltage is lower due to the high voltage drop. If all loads are connected on the alternator side, the voltage drop is less and the charging voltage is higher. This could be disadvantageous to loads (such as electronic circuitry) which are sensitive to voltage peaks or high voltage ripple. Those electrical devices which feature high current draw and relative insensitivity to overvoltage should therefore be connected at the alternator, and voltage-sensitive loads with low current draw should be connected at the battery. Voltage drops can be minimized by suitable conductor cross sections and good connections whose resistance remains low even after a long period.

Fuel consumption

A small portion of the fuel used by the vehicle is used to drive the alternator and transport the combined weight of starter, battery and alternator (approx. 5 % in a medium-sized car). Average fuel consumption per 100 km: For a weight of 10 kg, approx. 0.1 l; for 100 W of drive power: approx. 0.1 l. Alternators with a high part-load efficiency therefore contribute to fuel economy even though they are slightly heavier.

Vehicle electrical system with loads connected to alternator and battery

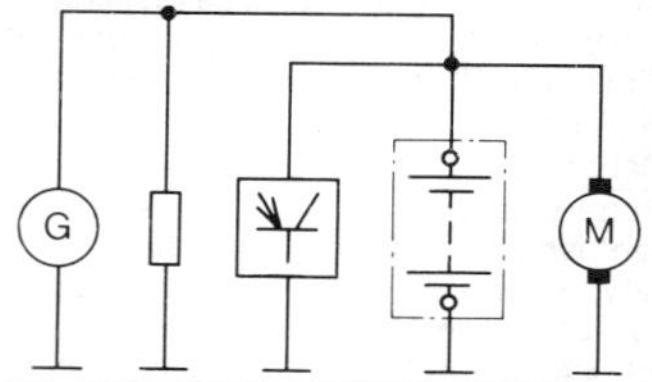

Installed loads with absolute power consumption and average power consumption as a function of duty cycle

Load	Absolute power consumption	Average power consumption
Ignition	40 W	40 W
Radio	10 W	10 W
Side-marker lamps	8 W	7 W
Low-beam headlamps	110 W	90 W
License-plate lamp, tail lamps	30 W	25 W
Indicator lamp, instrument-panel lamps	7 W	5 W
Heated rear window	80 W	34 W
Vehicle heating system	120 W	50 W
Electric radiator fan	60 W	25 W
Windshield wipers	30 W	5 W
Stop lamps	42 W	11 W
Turn-signal lamps	42 W	6 W
Fog lamps	110 W	20 W
Fog warning lamps	21 W	2 W
Total		
Installed loads	710 W	
Average power consumed by loads		330 W

Starter batteries

Requirements

Modern vehicles are placing increasingly exacting demands on their batteries: Enhanced cold-starting power (higher currents, especially at low temperatures) is needed with diesel engines, while vehicles equipped with large numbers of sophisticated electrical accessories require large amounts of electrical energy, not only when driving, but also when stationary. Maintaining a positive charging balance is especially difficult with frequent town and commuter driving because these are always accompanied by substantial current consumption.

Within the automotive electrical system, the battery assumes the role of a chemical storage unit for the electrical energy produced by the alternator. The battery must be capable of limited-duration high-current delivery for starting (especially critical at low temperatures), and it must be able to furnish some or all of the electrical energy for other important system components for limited periods with the engine at idle or off. The lead-acid storage battery represents the usual means of meeting these demands. Typical system voltages are 12 V for passenger cars, and 24 V for large utility vehicles (achieved by connecting two 12 V batteries in series).

Batteries must be specifically designed to meet individual system requirements for starting power, capacity and current consumption at temperatures ranging from approx. –30 ... +70 °C. There are also additional specifications which must be satisfied for particular applications (e.g., maintenance-free batteries, vibration-proof batteries).

Battery design

The 12-volt automotive battery contains six series-connected, individually partitioned cells in a polypropylene case. Each cell consists of a positive and negative plate set. These sets, in turn, are composed of the plates (lead grid and active mass) and the microporous material (separators) which insulates the plates of opposite polarities. The electrolyte is a solution of sulfuric acid which permeates the pores in the plates and separators and the voids in the cells. The terminals, the cell connectors, and the plate straps are made of lead; the openings in the partitions for the cellular connectors are tightly sealed.

Maintenance-free automotive battery
1 One-piece cover
2 Terminal-post cover
3 Cell connector
4 Terminal post
5 Frit
6 Plate strap
7 Case
8 Bottom mounting rail
9 Positive plates, inserted into envelope separators
10 Negative plates

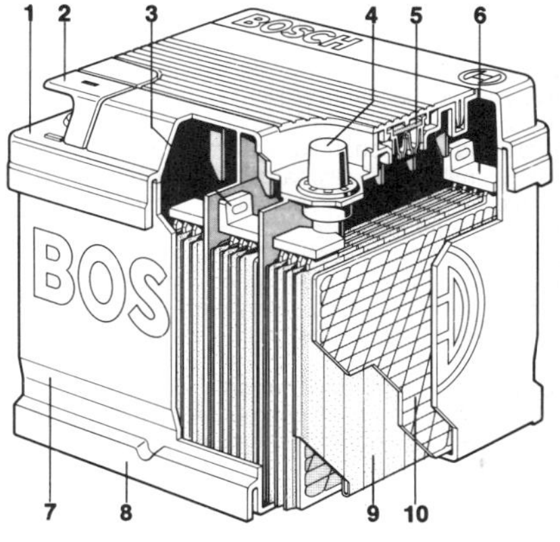

A hot-molding process is employed to permanently bond the one-piece cover to the battery case, providing the battery's upper seal.

On conventional batteries, each cell is sealed by its own vent plug, which when removed permits initial battery filling and topping-up during service. When screwed in, the vent plugs allow charge gases to escape. Maintenance-free batteries frequently appear to be completely sealed units, but they also require escape vents.

Battery designs

Maintenance-free battery

The maintenance-free battery defined in DIN standards features lead-alloy grids with a low antimony content to reduce gas generation and the attendant water losses during charging. This prolongs the electrolyte check intervals to:

– every 15 months or 25,000 km on low-maintenance batteries, and

– every 25 months or 40,000 km (DIN definition) for maintenance-free batteries.

There is never any need (and generally no means provided) to check the electrolyte level on the completely maintenance-free (lead-calcium) battery. With the exception of two extremely small vent orifices, this type of battery is completely sealed. As long as the electrical system is operating normally (U = constant), water decomposition is minimal, and the electrolyte reserves above the plates will last for the life of the battery. This type of calcium battery affords the additional advantage of extremely limited self-discharge, making it suitable for storage for periods of up to several months (provided that it carries a full charge at the outset). When a maintenance-free battery is recharged remote from the vehicle's electrical system (i.e., with battery charger), the charge voltage is never to exceed 2.3 ... 2.4 V per cell; overcharging at constant currents, or the use of chargers with a W charge curve will always lead to water consumption in the lead-acid battery.

Deep-cycle battery

Due to their particular design characteristics (plate thickness, separator materials), standard automotive batteries are poorly suited for applications in which frequent and extreme discharge occurs; normal batteries respond to these conditions with substantial wear at the positive plates (particularly through separation and sedimentation of the active material). In the deep-cycle battery, the separators include fiberglass mats to provide the positive mass with extra support to prevent premature shedding which otherwise leads to sludge formation. The service life, as measured in charge/discharge cycles, is roughly twice as long as that of a standard battery. Deep-cycle batteries featuring pocket separators and felt layers have an even longer service life.

Vibration-proof battery

In the vibration-proof battery, an anchor of cast resin and/or plastic prevents the plate stacks from moving relative to the battery case. According to DIN standards, this type of battery must survive 20 hours at 22 Hz sinusoidal vibration and a maximum acceleration of 6 g, a requirement that is approximately ten times that for standard batteries. Vibration-proof batteries are used primarily in utility vehicles, construction equipment, tractors, etc. Designation: "Rf".

Heavy-duty battery

The heavy-duty battery combines the attributes of the deep-cycle and vibration-

Battery charging: W-curve

1 Charging voltage, 2 Charging current

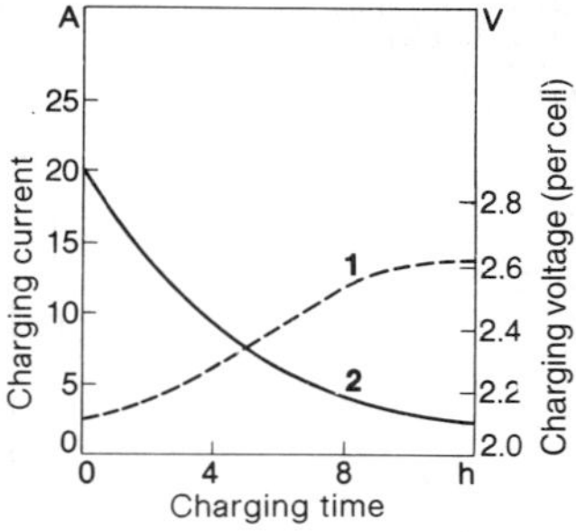

proof units. It is used in heavy vehicles to cope with both vibration and extreme cyclic discharge. Designation: "HD".

"S" battery
The Kt (or "S") battery shares the basic design of the deep-cycle device, compared to which it has thicker plates, but fewer of them. Although no cold-discharge current is specified for the Kt battery, its starting power lies well (35 ... 40 %) below that of comparably sized standard units. This battery is used in applications characterized by extreme cyclic variations, e.g., as a drive battery (p. 527, Drive batteries).

Operating states

Discharge
Soon after the start of the discharge process, the battery's voltage drops by a specific increment; it then remains relatively consistent, falling slowly under continuing load. The ultimate voltage collapse occurs only just before complete discharge, upon exhaustion of one or several active components (positive mass, negative mass, electrolyte).

Charging
Voltage limiting takes place when the battery is charged in the vehicle. This corresponds to the IU charging pattern, in which the charge current drops automatically in response to increasing battery voltage. The IU method prevents harmful overcharging and ensures a long battery service life. In contrast, many service-station and home chargers still operate with constant current or with a W-shaped charging curve. In either case, there is little or no reduction in charge current once the battery is fully charged, resulting in substantial water consumption and corrosion at the positive grid.

Battery charging: IU-curve
1 Charging voltage, 2 Charging current.

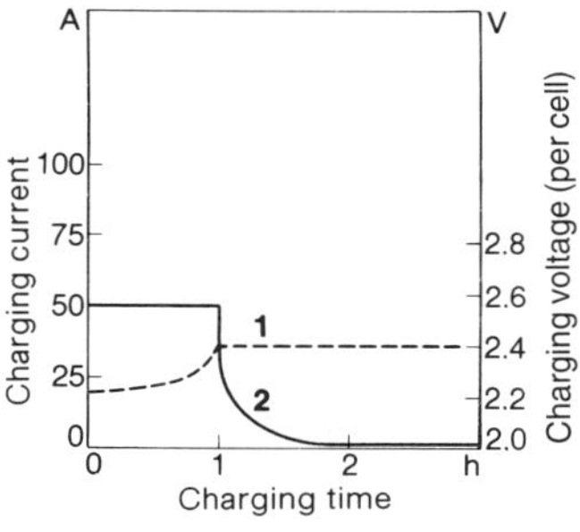

Self-discharge (see also "Battery maintenance")
Batteries discharge themselves continually, even when no loads (electrical devices) are attached. At room temperature, a modern low-antimony battery will lose about 0.1 ... 0.2 % of its total charge each day. As the battery ages, the rate can increase to as much as 1 % per day as a result of antimony transfer to the negative plate and various other sources of contamination. This phenomenon can ultimately lead to battery failure. Rule of thumb regarding the influence of temperature: The rate of self-discharge doubles with every 10 °C increase in temperature.
The self-discharge rate of the lead-calcium battery is only one fifth as high, and it remains constant throughout the life of the battery.

Battery maintenance

On low-maintenance batteries, the electrolyte level should be inspected in accordance with the manufacturer's instructions; when indicated, it should be replenished to the MAX graduation with distilled or demineralized water. To minimize self-discharge, the battery should be kept clean and dry. An additional prewinter examination of the electrolyte's specific-gravity – or, should this be impossible, of the open-circuit voltage – is also advisable. The battery should be recharged when the specific gravity is below 1.20 g/ml, or the open-circuit voltage is under 12.2 V. Terminals, terminal clamps and installation clamps should be coated with acid-protection grease.
Batteries temporarily removed from service should be stored in a cool, dry

place. The electrolyte's specific gravity and/or the open-circuit voltage should be checked every 3-4 months. The battery should be recharged whenever the figures drop below 1.20 g/ml or 12.2 V. Low-maintenance and maintenance-free batteries are best recharged with the IU method (see "Charging") at a maximum voltage of 14.4 V. This method allows adequate charging times in the order of 24 hours without any attendant risk of overcharging. If a constant-current or W-curve battery charger is used, the current should be reduced to max. $^1/_{10}$ of the rated capacity in A when gassing is seen to start. That is, for example, 6.6 A for a 66 Ah battery. The battery charger should be switched off about 1 hour afterwards. Ventilate the charging area (explosive gases, explosion danger. Avoid open flames and sparks).

Battery malfunctions

Battery failures which are traceable to internal faults (such as short circuits accompanying separator wear or loss of active mass, broken connections between cells and plates) can rarely be rectified through repair; the battery must be replaced. Internal shorts are indicated by major variations in the specific-gravity readings between cells (difference between max. and min > 0.03 g/ml). It is frequently possible to charge and discharge a battery with defective cell connectors provided that the currents remain small, but attempts to start the engine will result in total voltage collapse, even if the battery is fully charged.

If no defects can be found in a battery which consistently loses its charge (indication: low specific gravity in all cells, no starting power) or is overcharged (indication: high water loss), this suggests a malfunction in the vehicle's electrical system (alternator faulty, electrical equipment remains switched on when the engine is off due to faulty relays for instance, voltage regulator set too high or too low, or regulator completely inoperative). When a battery remains severely discharged for a longer period of time, the $PbSO_4$ crystals in the active mass become coarse, making the battery more difficult to recharge. Such a battery should be recharged by applying a minimal charge current (approx. $^1/_{40}$ of the rated capacity in A) for roughly 50 hours.

Safety precautions

The instructions manual accompanying the battery should always be studied prior to installation or removal in order to obviate the possibility of injury due to improper handling. The chief sources of danger are the battery acid and the explosive gas (combination of oxygen and hydrogen) which is generated during charging.

Tipping the battery for extended periods or carelessness during electrolyte checks can lead to burns from the sulfuric acid. Extra caution should be used during charging and when connecting and disconnecting jumper cables due to the danger of the oxyhydrogen gas exploding. The danger of gas explosions associated with sudden shorts or breaks in a circuit can be considerably reduced by avoiding sparks and open flames, but a residual risk will always remain. For the reasons listed above, battery-charging areas should always be well-ventilated, while eye protection and gloves should be worn when handling the battery.

In order to prevent sparks when the battery is connected or disconnected, all electrical equipment must be switched off, and the terminals must be connected in the proper sequence. The rules are as follows:

– When installing the battery, always connect the positive cable first, and the negative cable last. When removing the battery, first disconnect the negative, and only then the positive cable (assuming that negative is ground).

– When connecting a charger or an external battery to boost a low battery which remains installed in the vehicle, always start by connecting the positive terminal of the battery being charged to the positive terminal of the external booster. Then connect the negative cable from the external charger or booster battery to an exposed metallic surface on the vehicle, at least 0.5 m away from the battery.

– Always disconnect the cable from the

negative terminal before commencing work in the vicinity of the battery or on the vehicle's electrical system. Shorts (with tools) generate sparks, and can also cause injury.

Testing starter batteries

The specifications and test procedures for standard automotive starter batteries are defined in DIN 43 539. Whereas these tests were conceived to determine and monitor the quality of new batteries, they make no claim to cover fully all aspects of battery performance throughout the wide range of varying conditions encountered in practice.

The nominal capacity is the battery's rated ampere-hour (Ah) capacity at a specified discharge current which is dependent upon the discharge duration. The K_{20} specification stipulates that the battery must maintain a specified current output I_{20} (discharge current) for 20 hours at 27 °C without dropping below the specified terminal discharge voltage of 10.5 V. The rated discharge current I_{20} is the discharge current which corresponds to the rated capacity supplied by the battery during the specified discharge period: $I_{20} = K_{20}$ / 20 h. The cold-discharge test current is a high-discharge current assigned to each individual battery; it provides an index of low-temperature cold-start response under specific load conditions. For the cold-starting test, the specified cold-discharge test current is discharged starting at an initial battery temperature of -18 ± 1 °C, and continuing until a cut-off voltage (final discharge voltage) of 6 V.

Battery chargers

Charging curves

The most common charging pattern is defined by the W curve, which is generally provided by non-regulated chargers. Due to the charger's internal resistance, these chargers respond to increasing battery voltage by steadily lowering the charge current (charging times 12 ... 14 hours).

Because these chargers do not incorporate any means for limiting the charging voltage, they are only conditionally suitable for use on maintenance-free batteries. For these, chargers which operate according to the IU or WU pattern should be used. With the IU curve, the lead battery (2.4 V per cell) is supplied with constant charging current (to protect the charger against overload) until gassing commences. The charging voltage is then held constant and the charging current reduced sharply (to protect the battery against over-charging). Provided that the initial current is high enough, recharging times of < 5 hours can be achieved with IU chargers.

Special variations on both the IU and the W charging patterns are available (e.g., Wa, WOW, IUW). These can be applied in combination to meet individual demands for charging time, terminal voltage and low maintenance.

Charging-current and charging-voltage settings

In chargers with controlled charging patterns (e.g., IU curve), a regulator continually monitors the instantaneous actual values for charging current and voltage. It compares the monitored (actual-value) data with stored setpoints, and uses a final-control element to reduce the deviation to 0. This type of unit also compensates for fluctuations in its mains input voltage which could otherwise lead to variations in charging current. This has positive consequences for battery life and maintenance intervals.

Charging current

In normal charging the battery is supplied with current corresponding to approximately 10% of its capacity in Ah. Several hours are required to charge the battery completely. Boost charging ($I_L = 5 \cdot I_5$) can be used to bring an empty battery back up to about 80 % of its rated capacity with no damage. Once the gassing voltage is reached, the charging current must either be switched off (e.g., Wa curve) or reduced to a lower level (e.g., WOWa). These current-switching functions are controlled by an adjustable charge limiter or an automatic switch-off device.

Alternators

Current generation

The alternator must furnish the vehicle's electrical system with a sufficient supply of current under all operating conditions in order to ensure that the state of charge in the energy storage device (battery) is consistently maintained at an adequate level. The object is to achieve balanced charging, i.e., the curves for performance and speed-frequency response must be selected to ensure that the amount of current generated by the alternator under actual operating conditions is at least equal to the consumption of all electrical equipment within the same period.

The alternator actually produces alternating current. The vehicle's electrical system, on the other hand, requires direct current to recharge the battery and operate the electrical equipment; it is thus direct current that must ultimately be supplied to the electrical system.

The essential requirements are:

– Maintenance of direct-current supply to all electrical equipment in the system,

– Supplementary charging reserves for (re)charging the battery, even with a constant load from electrical devices in continuous operation,

– Maintenance of a constant alternator voltage throughout the entire ranges of engine speeds and load conditions,

– Robust design capable of withstanding externally-imposed stresses such as vibration, high ambient temperatures, pronounced temperature variations, dirt, moisture, etc.,

– Low weight, compact dimensions and long service life,

– Minimal operating noise.

Design factors

Rotational speed

The alternator's operating efficiency (its power-to-weight ratio expressed as the ratio of energy generated to component mass in kg) increases as a function of rotational speed. This factor alone would dictate as high a conversion ratio as possible between the engine's crankshaft and the alternator.

The following factors though must also be considered:

– Increasing centrifugal forces at high alternator speeds,

– Alternator noise,

– Effect of high speeds on the service lives of the wear components (bearings, collector rings, carbon brushes),

– Effect of the inertial forces exerted by the alternator on the crankshaft and the attendant stresses on the belt drive.

Typical conversion factors for automotive applications lie within a range of 1 : 2 to 1 : 3, with ratios of up to 1 : 5 being used in large utility vehicles.

Temperatures

The losses that accompany energy conversion in any machine lead to high component temperatures. The effective performance of the fan increases proportionally to operating speed, long after current generation has flattened off; the actual maximum currents tend to lie within an alternator-speed range extending to approximately 4000 min^{-1}.

High alternator temperatures are also a result of heat radiation from engine components and ancillaries (such as exhaust systems and turbochargers); the amount of heat depends upon the relative installation positions, and is greatest when the engine operates at high speeds and under high load factors. The supply of cooling air is generally drawn in from the engine compartment. As engine-compartment encapsulation is becoming increasingly widespread as a noise-reduction measure, an separate fresh-air supply for the alternator is an effective means of reducing component temperatures and enhancing alternator performance.

External influences

Installing the alternator on an IC engine means exposing it to extreme stresses. Depending upon the installation configuration and the engine's vibration patterns, accelerations of 500 ... 800 m/s^2 are possible. This subjects the alternator's mountings and components to extreme forces, necessitating the application of suitable countermeasures. Among other things, it is imperative that critical resonances be avoided.

Further detrimental influences include spray water, dirt, oil and fuel mist, and road salt in winter. These factors expose all components to the risk of corrosion. It is important that tracking between conducting parts be avoided, as electrolysis could otherwise lead to the early failure of vital operating components.

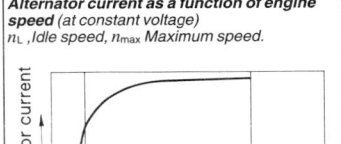

Alternator current as a function of engine speed *(at constant voltage)*
n_L, Idle speed, n_{max} Maximum speed.

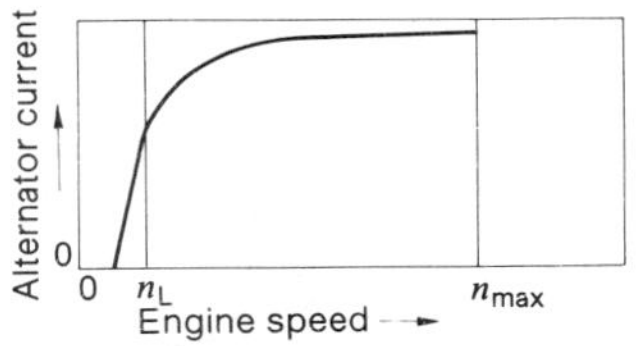

Characteristics and operation

Automotive alternators are designed to supply charge voltages of 14 V (with 28 V for heavy utility vehicles) in order to maintain an adequate charge in 12 V (or 24 V) batteries.

As direct current is required for charging the battery, a rectifier must be provided to convert the alternator's three-phase alternating current into DC. This arrangement also prevents the battery from discharging when the vehicle is stationary. A supplementary relay of the kind used with DC generators is not required.

The current-generation curve has a sharp bend, with no current production until after the so-called "0-ampere speed" is exceeded. At high speeds, the effect of the reverse magnetization field generated by the load current prevents the curve from climbing further. This characteristic prevents excessive demand from the system causing further increases in current flow, thereby protecting the alternator from the thermal damage associated with electrical overload.

Alternators are self-excited 12 or 16-pole synchronous devices. The AC winding is wound in the stator's slots, while the excitation winding is housed within the rotor. The DC exciting current required by the excitation winding is conducted to the rotating rotor through collector rings and sliding contacts (carbon brushes). The current produced in the AC winding is channeled in two directions: Most of it flows through the positive diodes of the main rectifier bridge and into the vehicle's electrical system, from where it returns through the negative diodes. A smaller portion of the current acts as excitation current, flowing through the three exciter

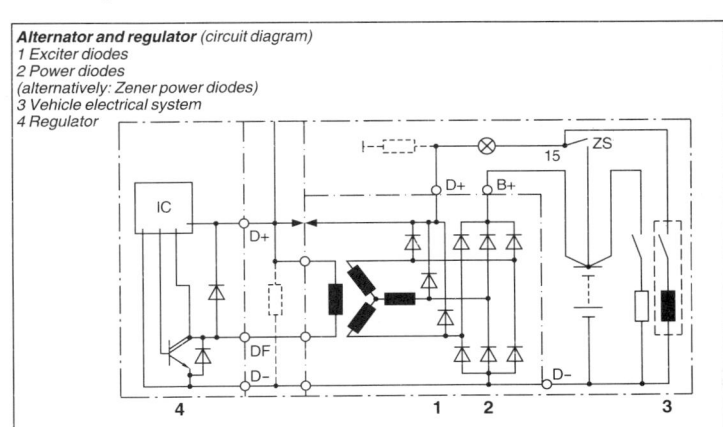

Alternator and regulator *(circuit diagram)*
1 Exciter diodes
2 Power diodes
(alternatively: Zener power diodes)
3 Vehicle electrical system
4 Regulator

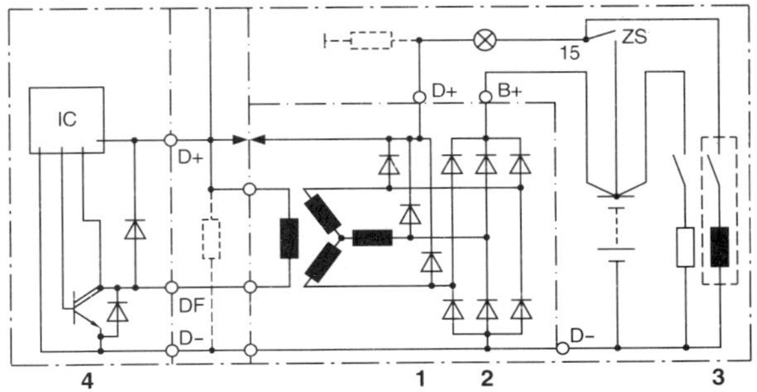

diodes to terminal D+, and through the regulator and collector rings to the rotating excitation winding. From there, it returns via the three negative diodes on the main rectifier.

The D+ terminal assumes several functions: It operates in conjunction with the battery terminal B+ and the charge indicator lamp to provide alternator pre-excitation. Once the alternator has been excited, the voltage level at terminal D+ is similar to that at B+; certain electrical devices can be supplied with voltage via relay.

To ensure that the alternator comes on line when the engine is started, the charge indicator lamp must draw the specific minimum power required for pre-excitation (a resistor in a parallel circuit is required with lamps rated at 1.2 W and less at 12 V). The pre-excitation current determines the "on-line" speed at which initial excitation occurs when the engine is started. This speed is well above the "0-ampere speed", with the precise figure being largely determined by the power of the pre-excitation circuit. A resistor (about 68 ohms) can be installed between lamp and ground (but as close to the lamp as possible) to indicate an interruption in the excitation circuit during operation. The charge indicator lamp should come on when the ignition is switched on prior to starting (monitoring function) and go out as the engine starts to run.

The loads at terminal D+ must be restricted to the regulator current, the charge indicator lamp and an additional current of 0.2 A.

Circuit showing an indication of malfunction due to an open excitation circuit
1 Alternator, 2 Charge indicator lamp, 3 Resistor, 4 Ignition and starting switch, 5 Battery.

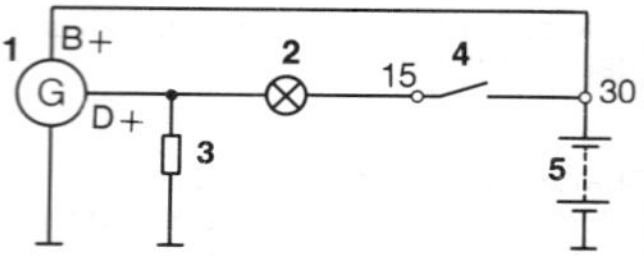

Design variations

Claw-pole alternators

The already very familiar mechanical concept embodied in this alternator type has completely replaced the earlier DC generator as the standard design in automotive applications. Based on equal outputs for both concepts, the alternator weighs 50 % less, and is also less expensive to manufacture. Large-scale application only be-

Claw-pole alternator
1 Collector-ring end shield
2 Rectifier heat sink
3 Power diode
4 Exciter diode
5 Transistor regulator
6 Stator
7 Claw-pole rotor
8 External fan
9 Fan pulley
10 Drive end shield with mounting flanges

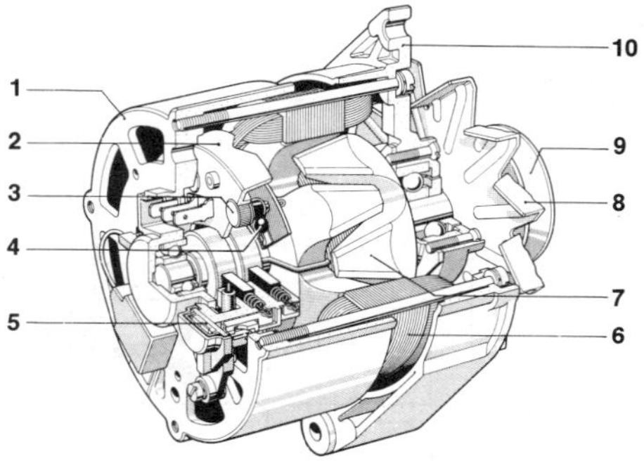

came feasible with the introduction of compact, powerful, inexpensive and reliable silicone diodes. The classic alternator design is characterized by the external fan providing single-flow axial ventilation.

The leakage flux between the claw poles limits the length – and thus the output – that can be achieved for any given diameter with this type of layout. It is possible to incorporate two systems in a common housing for special applications; the stators are then wired parallel on the AC side and operate through a common rectifier.

Compact alternators

The compact alternator is a new variant of the claw-pole concept based on dual-flow ventilation with two smaller internal fan elements. The cooling flow is extracted from the surrounding air in the axial plane, and exits the alternator radially in the vicinity of the stator winding heads, at the drive and collector-ring end shields. The major advantages of the compact alternator are:

– Higher maximum operating speeds for enhanced efficiency,
– Smaller fan diameters for reduced aerodynamic noise,
– Substantial reduction in magnetic noise.

Compact alternator
1 Casing with dual-flow ventilation, 2 Stator, 3 Claw-pole rotor, 4 External collector rings, 5 Internal fan, 6 External rectifier.

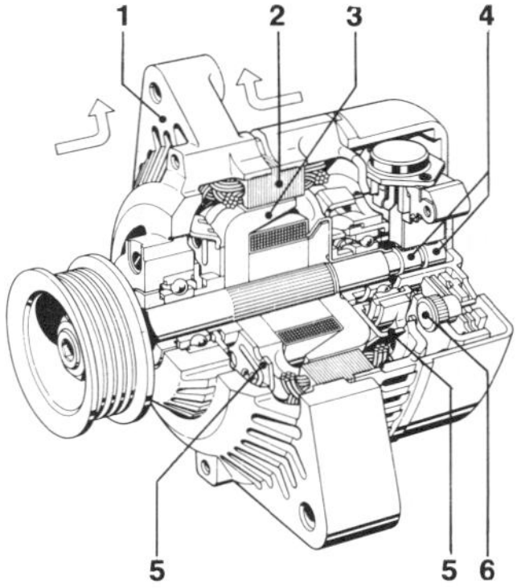

Salient-pole alternator

Alternators based on the salient-pole concept are required in those special applications which are characterized by extreme power demands (as in touring coaches).

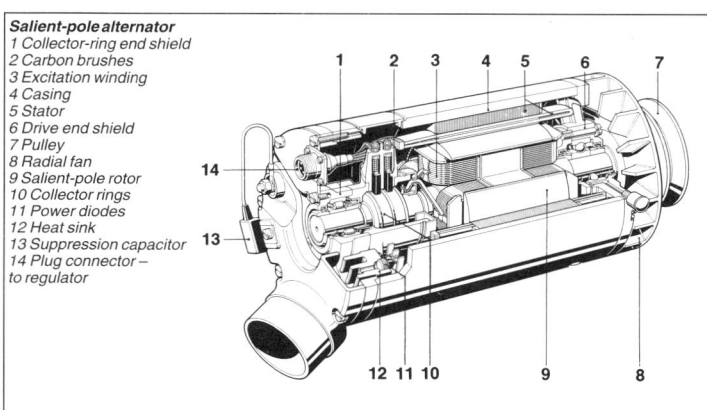

Salient-pole alternator
1 Collector-ring end shield
2 Carbon brushes
3 Excitation winding
4 Casing
5 Stator
6 Drive end shield
7 Pulley
8 Radial fan
9 Salient-pole rotor
10 Collector rings
11 Power diodes
12 Heat sink
13 Suppression capacitor
14 Plug connector – to regulator

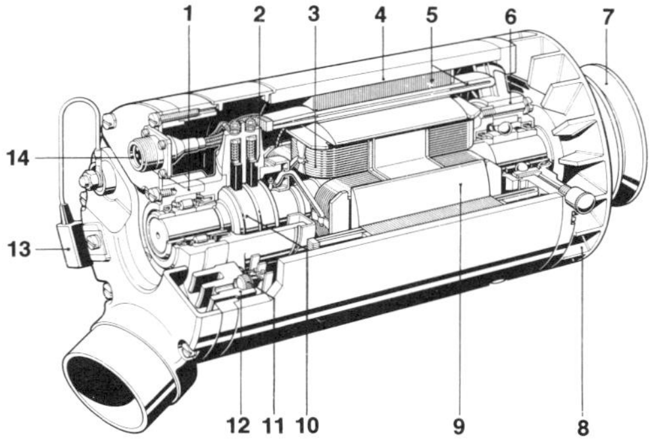

The rotor is equipped with individual magnetic poles, each of which is provided with its own field winding. This layout allows the stator to be substantially longer (relative to its diameter) than would be possible with a claw-pole alternator, meaning that output relative to diameter can be increased. The excitation currents required for the salient-pole alternator though are substantially higher than those for the claw-pole unit and develop far more heat. The electronic regulator therefore has to be installed away from the alternator in a separate housing.

Alternators with windingless rotors

The windingless-rotor alternator is a special design variation on the claw-pole unit in which only the claw poles rotate, while the excitation winding remains stationary. Instead of being connected directly to the shaft, one of the pole wheels is held in place by the opposite pole wheel via a non-magnetic ring. The magnetic flux must cross two additional air gaps beyond the normal working gap. With this design, the rectifier supplies current to the excitation winding directly through the regulator; collector rings and their sliding contacts are not required. This arrangement obviates the wear factor represented by the collector ring and carbon brush assemblies, making it possible to design alternators for a substantially longer service life (important for construction equipment and railroad generators). The units weigh somewhat more than claw-pole alternators of comparable generating capacity due to the fact that additional iron is required to conduct the magnetic flux through two additional air gaps.

Operating conditions

Ventilation

Ventilation for automotive alternators is virtually always supplied by attached or internal radial cooling fans, while fresh-air induction is becoming increasingly popular as a means of dealing with extreme temperatures in the engine compartment. The dimensions of the ventilation arrangement must be adequate for ensuring that component temperatures remain below the specified limits under all conceivable operating conditions. It may be necessary to replace the rectifier's aluminum heat sinks with copper units in some special applications.

On alternators for heavy-duty vehicles, the entire collector-ring and carbon-brush assembly is usually encapsulated in order to prevent the entry of dust, dirt and water. Fresh-air induction is almost always beneficial, especially with higher outputs.

Alternator with windingless rotor

1 Pulley
2 Fan
3 Drive end shield with stationary inner pole
4 Stator
5 Stationary excitation winding
6 Windingless rotor
7 Rear end shield
8 Regulator
9 Power diode
10 Bracket
11 Conductive element

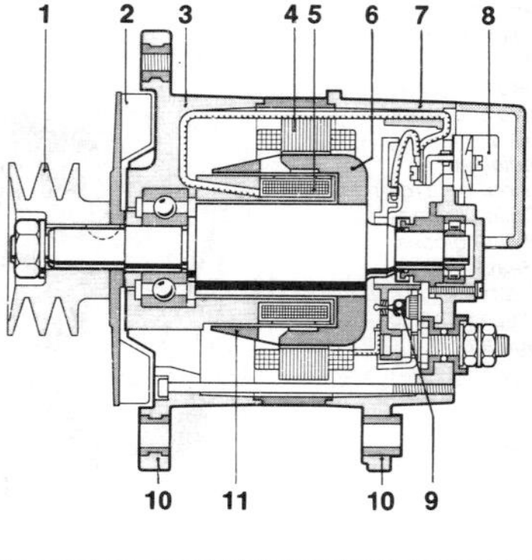

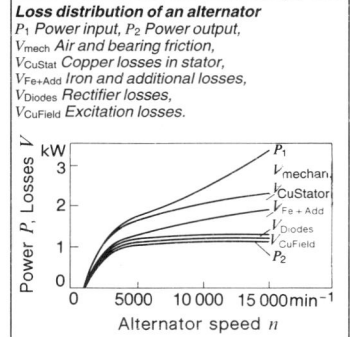

Loss distribution of an alternator
P_1 Power input, P_2 Power output,
V_{mech} Air and bearing friction,
V_{CuStat} Copper losses in stator,
V_{Fe+Add} Iron and additional losses,
V_{Diodes} Rectifier losses,
$V_{CuField}$ Excitation losses.

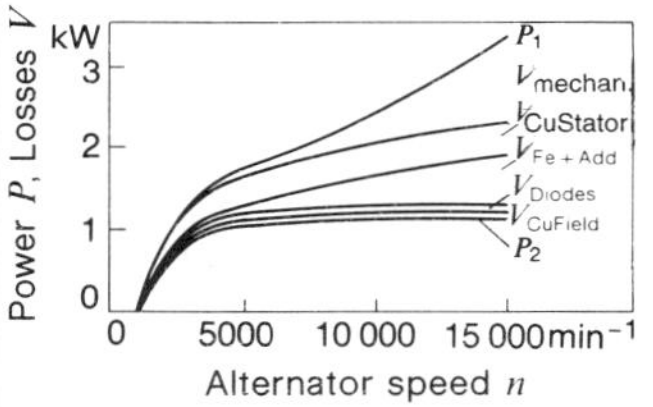

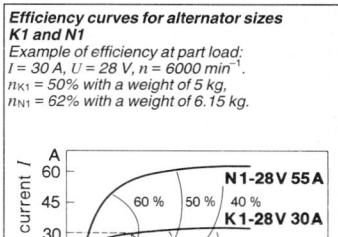

Efficiency curves for alternator sizes K1 and N1
Example of efficiency at part load:
I = 30 A, U = 28 V, n = 6000 min^{-1}.
η_{K1} = 50% with a weight of 5 kg,
η_{N1} = 62% with a weight of 6.15 kg.

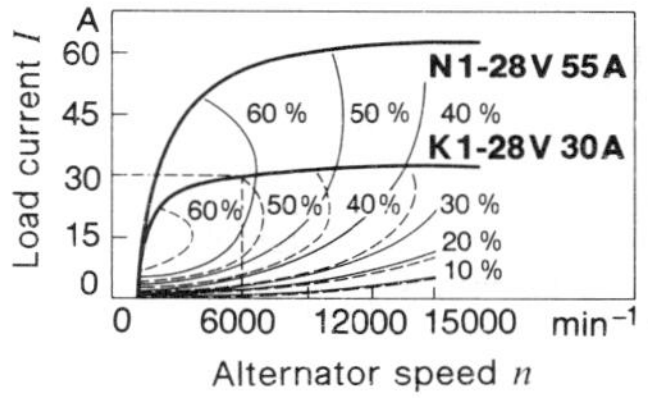

Sealed alternators with ventilation ribs on the outside for surface cooling are employed under certain conditions, while enclosed alternators with fluid cooling (e.g., oil) may be required in especially critical applications.

Installation
Virtually all those engine-powered alternators which are driven by standard V-belts are installed on bracket assemblies which allow the belt tension to be adjusted by pivoting the alternator. When ribbed V-belts are used, the alternator is generally installed in a fixed position, and belt tension is maintained by a separate mechanism. Larger alternators can be attached directly to a recess on the engine in special cases.

The load imposed by the drive belt is the decisive factor in selecting the bearing dimensions for the alternator's drive side. The belt forces are determined by both the geometry of the drive layout and the power requirements of all the other devices being driven by the belt. Yet another factor is the effective radius of the pulley; larger radii can produce a substantial lever effect between the pulley's load-bearing surface and the drive-side bearings. The stresses emanating from these static factors are supplemented by the dynamic forces associated with torque and speed fluctuations. These factors must be considered in determining ball-bearing dimensions and in alternator testing.

Drive layout
Although standard V-belts with conversion factors of up to 1 : 2.5 are usually employed to drive the alternator, ribbed V-belts are also used in automotive applications. Because this design allows shorter bend radii, smaller alternator pulleys and higher conversion ratios can be achieved. Railroad alternators are operated by helical-gear assemblies driven directly from the axle. It is imperative that special precautions be taken to dampen rotary oscillations when direct mechanical drive (without an intermediate belt, e.g., centrally at the crankshaft or via gears) is used to power the alternator.

Efficiency
Losses are an unavoidable byproduct of all processes in which mechanical or kinetic energy is converted into electrical energy. The efficiency rating is the ratio between the power which is supplied to the unit and that which emerges. The three major sources of power depletion are iron losses, copper losses and mechanical losses. Iron losses result from the hysteresis and eddy currents produced by the alternating magnetic fields in the iron in the stator and rotor. Copper losses are produced by resistance in the rotor and stator windings. Their extent is proportional to the power-to-weight ratio, i.e., the ratio of generated electrical power to the mass of the effective components. The mechanical losses include friction at

the roller bearings and at the collector ring, aerodynamic friction at the fan, and, above all, the power required to drive the fan itself, which increases dramatically at higher speeds.

In normal automotive operation, the alternator operates in the part-load range. The efficiency level at moderate engine speeds is then approximately 50 %. A larger (and heavier) alternator can be used to move the efficiency curve for identical part-load conditions into a more favorable range. The efficiency gains provided by the larger alternator more than compensate for the losses in fuel economy associated with the greater weight. However, it must also be remembered that more energy will be required to rotate this larger inertial mass. When alternators are being designed for typical operating conditions, an attempt should be made to find the optimal compromise between weight and efficiency in order to minimize fuel consumption.

Voltage regulators

The voltage regulator serves to place an upper limit on alternator voltage in the face of wide fluctuations in alternator speed and load. The level to which the alternator voltage is limited by the regulator usually depends upon the temperature. The voltage is somewhat higher in the winter to compensate for the fact that the battery is then more difficult to charge. In the summer, the voltage regulator maintains the system voltage at a lower level to prevent the battery from overcharging. Constant-voltage regulators are also found in some specialized applications. It is also possible for the voltage of the electrical system to drop below the regulation voltage when there is substantial current consumption at low rpm.

Voltage regulators were formerly constructed using discrete components, but today they incorporate hybrid or monolithic circuits. A modern transistorized regulator featuring hybrid technology combines all control and regulation functions within a single hermetically-sealed housing. The housing contains a ceramic base, with discrete resistors and capacitors, and a bonded IC (integrated circuit). The power transistor and the free-wheeling diode are soldered directly to the metal socket to ensure good heat dissipation. When monolithic technology is applied, the control and regulator IC, the power transistor and the free-wheeling diode are all located on a single chip. Voltage regulators with auxiliary functions, known as multifunction regulators, are becoming increasingly widespread.

Regulator operation

$I_{exc.}$ Exciting current, T_{ON} On time, T_{OFF} Off time, I_m Mean exciting current, n_1 Lower speed, n_2 Higher speed.

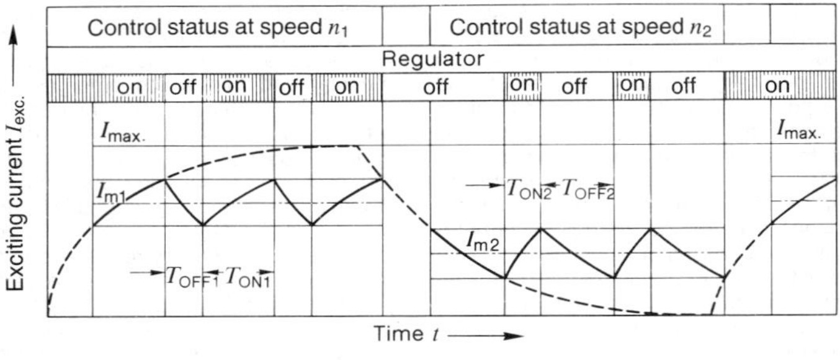

Overvoltage protection

The electric strength of alternators and voltage regulators usually suffices to ensure that their semiconductor elements will operate reliably together with the vehicle's battery. Emergency operation without the battery is characterized by extreme voltage peaks. Especially critical is the phenomenon known as "load-dump," in which the current to major consumers is suddenly interrupted. Thus additional measures are necessary to ensure complete reliability. There are three options available for protecting against overvoltage:

Zener diodes

Zener diodes can be installed in the rectifier in place of the power diodes. Zener diodes limit the high-energy voltage peaks to levels which are harmless for the alternator or the regulator. In addition, Zener diodes can be used to provide remote protection for other voltage-sensitive equipment in the vehicle's electrical system. The response voltage of a Zener-diode-equipped rectifier is 25 ... 30 V on a 14 V alternator.

Alternators and regulators with enhanced electric strength

In such alternators, the semiconductor elements have higher electric strength ratings. In addition, a capacitor is fitted between the alternator's B+ terminal and ground, where it provides short-range interference suppression. The enhanced electric strength of such alternators and regulators only protect the units themselves; these measures furnish no additional protection for other electrical equipment in the system.

Overvoltage protection devices

These semiconductor devices are connected to the alternator's D+ and D– (ground) terminals. The system responds to voltage peaks by shorting the alternator at the excitation winding. The main beneficiaries of these overvoltage protection devices are the alternator and regulator, with only secondary protection being provided for other voltage-sensitive equipment in the electrical system. Overvoltage protection devices can be combined with another unit specially designed to inhibit consequential damage; such a layout prevents the battery from boiling-off its electrolyte should the regulator malfunction and stick in the "on" position.

Circuit diagram of an automatically actuated overvoltage protection device

1 Battery
2 Overvoltage protection device
3 Ignition and starting switch
4 Regulator
5 Alternator

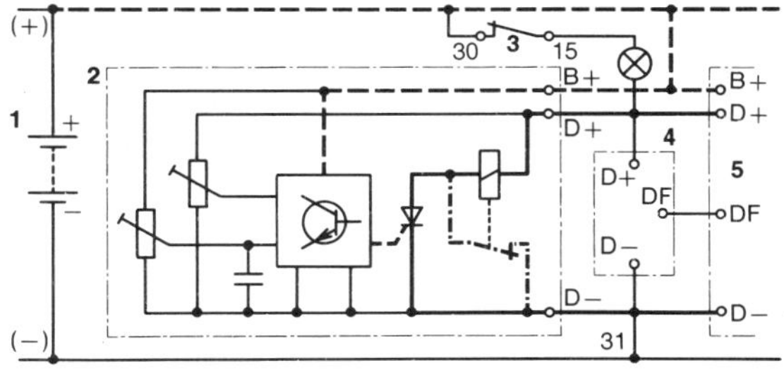

Controller Area Network (CAN)

Increasing numbers of vehicular control units (ECU's) are being integrated within synergistic networks; this trend is assuming particular significance at a time when more and more innovative functions are being incorporated in automotive electronic systems. The conventional method for organizing these interrelationships is to assign single dedicated wires to the signals. This level of circuit technology no longer suffices for mastering the requirements associated with the growth in data communications between automotive electronic components. The wiring harness for a top-of-the-range vehicle, for instance, becomes unmanageably complex and bulky, while the number of pins at the individual ECU's also becomes excessive. The CAN serial bus system has been especially developed to provide solutions to these problems in automotive applications.

Applications

CAN's applications within the vehicle can be divided into three main areas:
- Communications between ECU's,
- Bodywork, comfort and convenience electronics (multiplex), and
- Mobile communications.

Communication between ECU's

Communication between individual controls units becomes necessary when electronic systems such as Motronic, electronic transmission-shift control, electronic engine-power control (EMS or "drive-by-wire") and traction control (ASR) are interconnected. Typical data-transmission speeds range from about 125 kbit/s to 1 Mbit/s, and must be high enough to ensure that the required real-time response is maintained. Serial data transmission is superior to conventional interfaces operating with pwm, switching signals and analog signals, as it provides higher data-transfer speeds without placing additional burdens on the CPU. The number of pins at the ECU's can also be reduced.

Multiplex

Multiplex systems can be designed in a variety of different versions and subsystems. A serial interface provides the connection for electronic components such as vehicle-lighting control, seat adjustment ("memory" seat), HVAC control and the driver interface. Typical data-transmission speeds lie within a range of 10 to 100 kbit/s.

The fact that compared to a conventional wiring harness, the multiplex bus considerably reduces the number of wires, pins and couplers is a considerable advantage. This, in turn, allows more flexibility in routing the wiring.

Mobile communications

A serial bus connects mobile communications equipment, such as radio, telephone and navigation devices to a central unit which can incorporate both the driver interface and a high-resolution color display. The objective is to apply ergonomically optimized design to minimizing the degree of driver distraction associated with operation of these units. Data transfer rates of 50 ... 100 kbit/s are sufficient, provided that no digital audio or navigation data are to be transmitted through the bus system.

Bus configuration

CAN operates according to the multi-master principle, in which a linear bus structure connects several control units each of which has equal rights. The advantage of this type of structure lies in the fact that a malfunction at one node does not impair bus-system access for the remaining devices. Thus the probability of a total system failure is substantially lower than with other logical architectures (such as ring or active star struc-

Linear bus structure

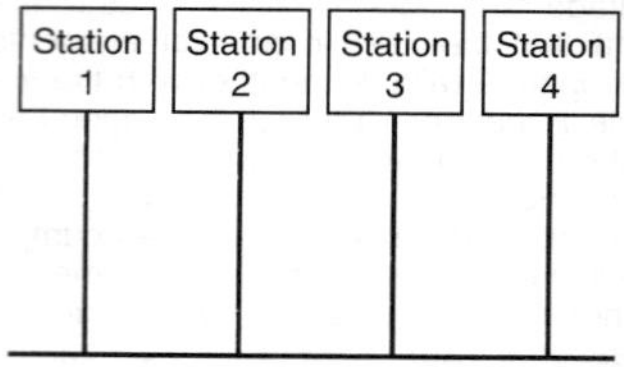

tures). When a ring or active star structure is employed, failure at a single node or at the CPU is sufficient to cause a total failure.

Content-based addressing

The addressing scheme employed with CAN assigns a label to every message, with each message receiving a unique 11-bit or 29-bit "identifier". The identifier classifies the content of the message (e.g., engine speed). Each station processes only those messages whose identifiers are stored in its acceptance list (message filtering). Thus CAN requires no station addresses for data transmission, and the nodes are not involved in administering system configuration. This facilitates adaptation to variations in equipment levels.

Logical bus states

The CAN protocol is based on two logical states: The bits are either "recessive" (logical 1) or "dominant" (logical 0). When at least one station transmits a dominant bit, then the recessive bits simultaneously sent from other stations are overwritten.

Priority assignments

The identifier labels both the data content and the priority of the message being sent. Identifiers corresponding to low binary numbers enjoy a high priority and vice versa.

Bus access

Each station can begin transmitting its most important data as soon as the bus is unoccupied. When several stations start to transmit simultaneously, the system responds by employing "Wired-AND" arbitration to sort out the resulting contentions over bus access. The message with the highest priority is assigned first access, without any bit loss or delay. Transmitters respond to failure to gain bus access by automatically switching to receive mode; they then repeat the transmission attempt as soon as the bus is free again.

Message format

A data frame with a length of less than 130/150 bits (11/29-bit identifier) is constructed for transferring data on the bus. This ensures minimal waiting time until the subsequent transmission (which could be urgent). The data frame consists of seven consecutive bit fields:

Start of frame
Start of frame indicates the beginning of a message and synchronizes all stations.

Arbitration field
The arbitration field consists of the message's identifier and an additional control bit. While this field is being transmitted, the transmitter accompanies the transmission of each bit with a check to ensure that no higher-priority message is being transmitted (which would cancel the access

Message filtering

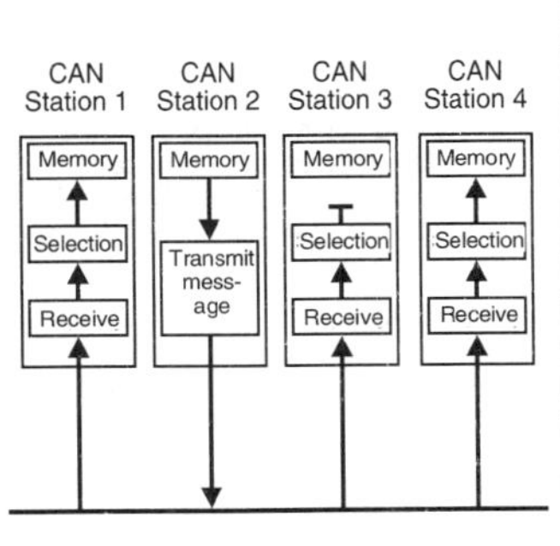

Message format

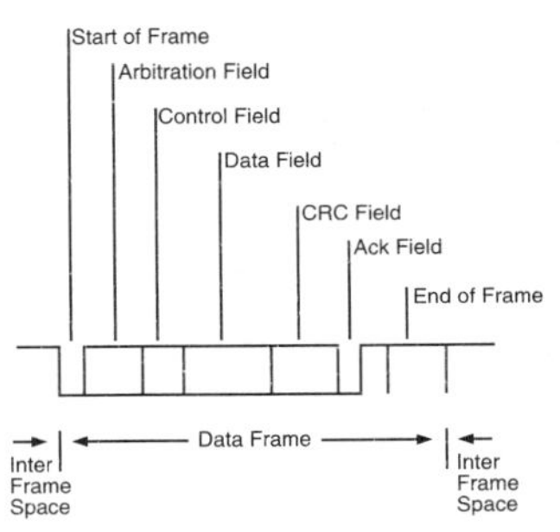

authorization). The control bit determines whether the message is classified under "data frame" or "remote frame."

Control field
The control field contains the code indicating the number of data bytes in the data field.

Data field
The data field's information content comprises between 0 and 8 bytes. A message of data length 0 can be used to synchronize distributed processes.

CRC field
The CRC (Cyclic Redundancy Check) field contains the check word for detecting possible transmission interference.

Ack field
The "Ack field" contains the acknowledgement signals with which all receivers indicate receipt of non-corrupted messages.

End of frame
End of frame marks the end of the message.

Transmitter initiative
The transmitter will usually initiate a data transfer by sending a data frame. However, the receiver can also send a remote frame to request data from the transmitter. This remote frame has the same identifier as the corresponding data frame, with the bit following the identifier serving to distinguish between the two.

Error detection
CAN incorporates a number of monitoring features for detecting errors. These include:
– 15-bit CRC: Each receiver compares the CRC sequence which it receives with the calculated sequence.
– Monitoring: Each transmitter compares transmitted and scanned bit.
– Bit stuffing: Between "start of frame" and the end of the CRC field each data frame or remote frame may contain a maximum of 5 consecutive bits of the same polarity. The transmitter follows up a sequence of 5 bits of the same polarity by inserting a bit of the opposite polarity in the bit stream; the receivers eliminate these bits as the messages arrive.
– Frame check: The CAN protocol contains several bit fields with a fixed forma for verification by all stations.

Error handling
When a CAN controller determines the presence of an error, it aborts the current transmission by sending an error flag. An error flag consists of 6 dominant bits; it functions by deliberately violating the conventions governing stuffing and/or formats.

Fault confinement with local failure
Because defective stations can severely impair the ability to process bus traffic, the CAN controllers incorporate mechanisms which can distinguish between intermittent and permanent errors and local station failures. This process is based on statistical evaluation of error conditions.

Implementations
In order to provide the proper CPU support for a wide range of different requirements, the semiconductor manufacturers have introduced implementations representing a broad range of performance levels. The various implementations differ neither in the message they produce, nor in their arrangments for responding to errors. The difference lies solely in the type of CPU support required for message administration.

As the demands placed on the ECU's processing capacity are extensive, the interface controller should be able to administer a large number of messages and expedite data communications with only minimal demands on the CPU's computational resources. Powerful CAN controllers are generally used in this type of application.

More basic and less expensive chips are preferred for multiplex systems, and present-day mobile communications, as the demands which these types of systems place on the controller are more modest.

Standardization
The ISO (International Organization for Standardization) is adopting CAN as the standard for automotive applications with data-transfer rates exceeding 125 kbit/s, with CAN being employed with two other protocols for data transmission speeds of up to 125 kbit/s.

Electromagnetic compatibility (EMC) and interference suppression

The expression "electromagnetic compatibility" (EMC) defines an electrical system's ability to remain neutral in the vicinity of other systems. In other words, it is compatible and besides not interfering with other systems, it also remains impervious to such interference as might emanate from them. In automotive applications, this means that the various electrical systems such as the ignition, the electronic fuel injection, ABS, and the radio must function in close mutual proximity without interfering with each other. It also means that the vehicle as a whole must remain neutral within the larger environment; it is not to interfere electrically with other vehicles, and it must not interfere with broadcast or communications transmissions of any kind. At the same time, the vehicle must itself remain fully operational when exposed to strong electromagnetic fields from the outside (e.g., in the vicinity of radio transmitters).

It is in view of these considerations that automotive electrical systems and complete vehicles are designed to ensure that electromagnetic compatibility is maintained.

Sources of interference

On-board electrical system, ripple

The alternator supplies the vehicle's electrical system with rectified alternating current. Although the current is smoothed by the battery, a residual ripple remains. The amplitude of the ripple depends upon system load and circuit design, while its frequency varies as a function of alternator (and thus engine) speed. The ripple's fundamental frequency lies in the kHz range. It can penetrate into the vehicle's sound system – either directly (galvanically) or through inductance – where its presence is heard as a whine in the speakers.

On-board electrical system, pulses

Interference pulses are generated when electrical equipment in the vehicle is switched on and off. These pulses are received by adjacent systems either directly via the voltage supply, or indirectly, as a result of coupling effects. If the interference source, and the system which receives the interference pulse it generates, are not appropriately matched to each other, this phenomenon can lead to malfunctions and even to destruction of adjacent systems.

The wide variety of pulses that occur in the vehicle can be classified in five basic groups. Classification according to amplitude provides the best basis for matching the interference sources and the potentially susceptible equipment to achieve maximum compatibility between them.

Influence of electrical-system design on voltage ripple

Example: I_{alt} = 130 A, n_{alt} = 18 000 min^{-1}, Battery 12 V 55 A · h.

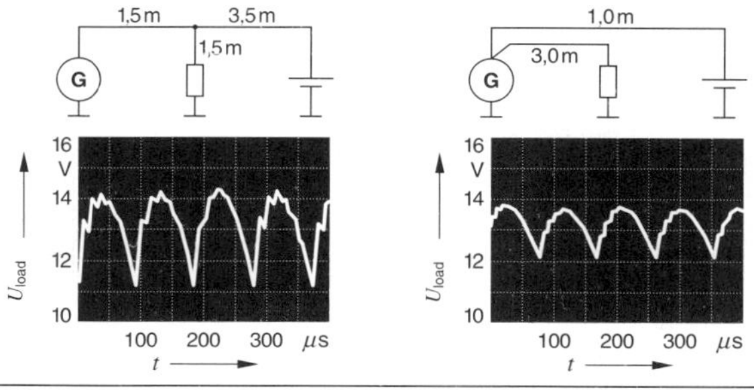

This matching procedure can, for example, entail prescribing Class II for all a vehicle's interference sources, while potentially susceptible devices (such as control units) can be designed to conform to Class III requirements, thus providing a safety margin. Reallocation to Classes I/II is advisable in cases where suppression at the source is easier than providing the corresponding protection at the susceptible devices. The principle can also be inverted; if protective measures at the potentially susceptible equipment are easier and less expensive then a move to Classes III/IV.

On-board electrical system, high-frequencies

Switching operations and current commutation induce high-frequency internal oscillations in many components. These oscillations travel through the components' circuits – especially the current-supply lines – and back into the vehicle's electrical system, where they arrive at variously attenuated intensities.

Depending upon whether the interference voltage's spectrum is continuous or a collection of individual curves, a distinction is drawn between two kinds of interference source: "broad-band" (electric motors, as used for wipers, fans, fuel pump, alternator) and "narrow-band" (electronic control units with microcomputers).

Sources of broad and narrow-band interference

a) Signal progression referred to time $y(t)$,
b) Corresponding spectrum $\tilde{y}(f)$,
c) Observation of spectrum with monitoring device of bandwidth B: with $B{\cdot}T < 1$ individual bars, indicates "narrow-band" interference; $B{\cdot}T > 1$ continuous curve, indicates "broad-band" interference.

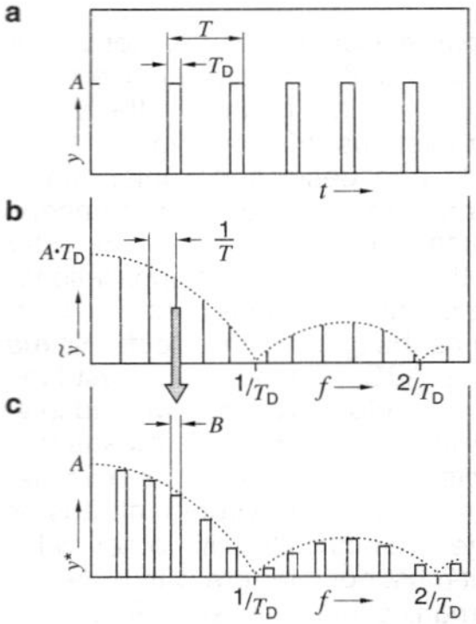

The classification depends upon the bandwidth of the test instrument being used.

High-frequency oscillations can represent a permanent source of interference for communications systems in the vehicle; they lie within the same frequency and amplitude ranges as the transmitted

Test pulses as per DIN 40 839, Part I

Test pulses				Classification of allowed pulse amplitudes			
Pulse shape	Source	Internal resistance	Pulse duration	I	II	III	IV
1	Switch-off of inductive devices, e.g., relays or valves	10 Ω	2 ms	– 25 V	– 50 V	– 75 V	– 100 V
2	Switch-off of motorized devices, e.g., fan motor, which produce positive overvoltage on run-on.	10 Ω	50 µs	+ 25 V	+ 50 V	+ 75 V	+ 100 V
3a	Overvoltages due to switching processes	50 Ω	0.1 µs	– 40 V	– 75 V	– 110 V	– 150 V
3b				+ 25 V	+ 50 V	+ 75 V	+ 100 V
4	Supply-voltage curve during starting	10 mΩ	to 20 s	12 V – 3 V	12 V – 5 V	12 V – 6 V	12 V – 7 V
5	Load dump [1])	1 Ω	to 400 ms	+ 35 V	+ 50 V	+ 80 V	+ 120 V

[1]) Load dump occurs when the alternator is feeding high current into the battery and the connection between the two is suddenly interrupted.

or received signals, and are thus ideally situated for entering the vehicle's communications system either directly at the sensor (antenna) or through the antenna cable.

At the OE (Original Equipment) stage, the process of matching the interference sources and susceptible devices for mutual compatibility can be facilitated by applying the system for classifying interference voltage in supply lines which is defined in DIN 57 879/VDE 0879.

Should the interference level initially approved for OE purposes prove excessive upon subsequent installation of a communications system, there is a limited range of remedial measures which can be taken:

– If the source of the interference derives its current directly from terminal 15 or 30 via an adequately dimensioned switch, then the interference can be combatted with suppression capacitors and filters of a type suitable for automotive application. The capacitors are generally connected directly to the source's terminal, with the ground wire being kept as short as possible. Coupling from conductors carrying interference voltage can be reduced by passing such wires through a braided metal screen which is grounded as directly as possible at both ends.

– If the interference source is controlled by an ECU, it is generally forbidden to suppress it by means of suppression components (quenching), as this would modify the control unit's switching response.

– If the (narrow-band) interference emanates from the ECU itself, an attempt must be undertaken to solve the problem by finding a suitable position for the antenna and its cable.

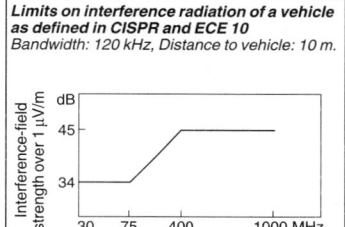

Limits on interference radiation of a vehicle as defined in CISPR and ECE 10
Bandwidth: 120 kHz, Distance to vehicle: 10 m.

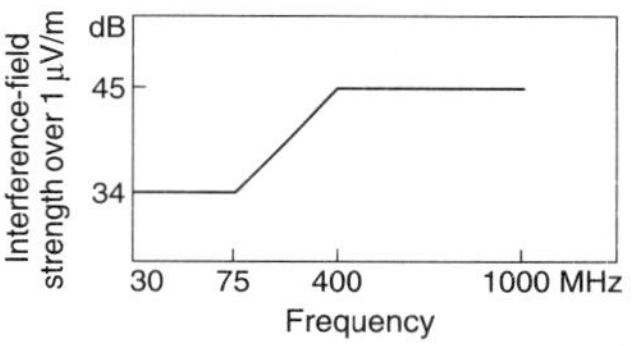

The vehicle as an interference source

The ignition systems is the major source of vehicle interference. The levels of electromagnetic radiation which may be emitted by the ignition are defined in legal stipulations (EC Directive ECE 10). These are aimed at ensuring interference-free radio and TV reception in other vehicles and in nearby buildings.

Simple adherence to ECE 10 will rarely be sufficient for vehicles which are equipped with communications systems. When a telephone or radio is installed in the vehicle, it must be equipped with special suppressors to reduce the interference radiated by the spark plugs and, in some cases, by the distributor; the precise requirement will vary from vehicle to vehicle. It may be necessary to partially or completely screen the ignition system on

Maximum radio-interference voltage levels for suppression levels in the individual frequency ranges as defined in DIN 57 879, Part 3/VDE 0879, Part 3.

	Frequency range			
Suppression level	LW 0.15 to 0.3 MHz	MW 0.5 to 1.65 MHz	KW 5.95 to 26.1 MHz	UKW 87.5 to 108 MHz
	Approved radio-interference voltage levels in dB			
5	60	50	40	24
4	70	58	46	30
3	80	66	52	36
2	90	74	58	42
1	100	82	64	48
0	Unlimited			

vehicles equipped with two-way radios. These suppression measures can be accompanied by negative effects on the ignition system's secondary available voltage. In such cases, it is necessary that an authorized workshop checks the feasibility of these measures.

Potentially susceptible devices

Electronic control units are susceptible to interference signals penetrating into the system from outside. The interference signals emanate either from neighboring systems within the vehicle itself or from sources in the immediate vicinity (such as a powerful broadcast transmitter). Malfunctions start to occur at the point where the system loses the ability to distinguish between useful or information signals and interference signals. If the relationship between the output signal y and the input signal x at operating point y_0, x_0 in the system or its subsystem is:

$$y - y_0 = a_1\,(x - x_0) + a_2\,(x - x_0)^2$$

and if the input signal is a combination of a useful and an interference signal (index N or S)

$$x - x_0 = x_N \cdot \cos\,(\omega_N \cdot t) + x_S \cdot \cos\,(\omega_S \cdot t)$$

then the output signal becomes

$$y - y_0 = a_1\,[x_N \cdot \cos\,(\omega_N t) + x_S \cdot \cos(\omega_S t)]$$
$$+ \tfrac{1}{2} \cdot a_2\,[x_N^2\,(1 + \cos\,(2\,\omega_N t))$$
$$+ 2 \cdot x_N \cdot x_S \cdot \cos\,((\omega_N - \omega_S)t)$$
$$+ 2 \cdot x_N \cdot x_S \cdot \cos\,((\omega_N + \omega_S)t)$$
$$+ x_S^2\,(1 + \cos(2\omega_S t))]$$

It therefore becomes apparent that there is the danger of interference in the case of harmonic convergency between the useful signal ω_N and ω_S or $2 \cdot \omega_S$. The same applies when $\omega_S >> \omega_N$ due to the DC component which occurs on demodulation, or, with $w_S < w_N$ with the oscillations attendant upon intermodulation, with $\omega_N \pm \omega_S$.

Interference coupling

Signals from interference sources penetrate susceptible devices in any of three ways:

– Direct (galvanic) coupling occurs when the source and the device affected by the interference share common current paths, a condition which can hardly be avoided with a common voltage source. The vehicle's wiring harness should be designed with the smallest possible dimensions. Whether a parallel, serial or multipoint structure is best for the supply lines will depend upon the current magnitude, the frequency range and the general design of the system being connected.

– Coupling occurs on connecting lines when they are laid in parallel between the source and the device being exposed to the interference.

Interference model

Electronic system: S Sensor(s), V_1 Signal amplification and conditioning, SV Signal processing, V_2 Power amplification, A Actuator(s)

An interference-signal flow is superimposed on the useful-signal flow through direct (galvanic) coupling U_1 ... U_3, coupling on connecting wires L_1 ... L_4, direct coupling in sensor or actuator D_1, D_2.

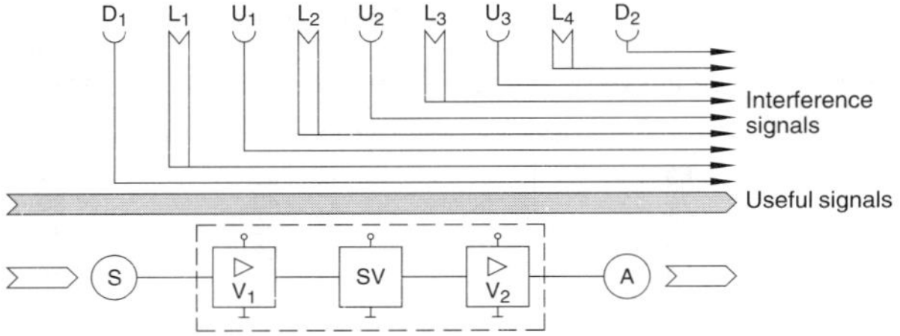

$$U_b = \frac{k \cdot R_2 \cdot \sinh(\gamma \cdot l)}{(R_1 + R_2) \cdot \cosh(\gamma \cdot l) + W\left(k_a + \frac{R_1 \cdot R_2}{W^2} \cdot k_b\right) \cdot \sinh(\gamma \cdot l)} \cdot \left(\frac{R_1}{W} \cdot U - W \cdot I\right)$$

In the model above, shown at the top of this page, the voltage U_b which is coupled into the device receiving the interference is calculated as shown with the parameters

$k = C/C_0;\ k_a = (C_a + C)/C_0;\ k_b = (C_b + C)/C_0$

$C_0 = \sqrt{C_a \cdot C_b + C \cdot (C_a + C_b)}$

$\gamma \cdot l = j(\omega/c) \cdot l$; $W = 1/(c \cdot C_0)$

c = 30 cm/ns (speed of light)

U_b consists of two parts: a "capacitive" component, which depends on the voltage U, and an "inductive" component, which is a function of the current I. If the wavelength of the interference signal is larger than the conductor length l, then the simplification is applied:

$$U_b \approx k \cdot (\gamma \cdot l) \cdot [U(R_1 \cdot R_2)/(R_1 + R_2) - W \cdot I \cdot R_2/(R_1 + R_2)]$$

This indicates that coupling can be kept to a minimum the shorter the length l and the lower the standardized coupling capacity k. k decreases as the distance between the conductors increases, and can be further reduced with a screen connected to ground at both ends.

– Direct interference is possible in cases where sensor S or actuator A (see right-hand Figure below) reacts directly to electromagnetic fields, e.g., if S is a radio antenna, a microphone or the magnetic head on a cassette player. Here the object is to increase the physical distance between interference source and exposed susceptible equipment until the interference disappears.

Measuring techniques

– The interference signals are generally registered as reference values in dB (decibels). The reference quantity for interference voltage is 1 µV; for electric field strength it is 1 µV/m, for power it is 1 mW, thus:

$u^* = 20 \cdot \lg U$

$e^* = 20 \cdot \lg E$

$p^* = 10 \cdot \lg P$

with u^*, e^*, p^* in dB; U in µV; E in µV/m; P in mW.

– Under standardized conditions, artificial networks are used to examine the pulses or high-frequency interference voltages which emanate from a device.

– Wire-borne interference waves, to be injected into the wiring harness of the electrical system under investigation, are produced either with the aid of a stripline, a TEM (transversal electromagnetic field) cell or BCI (bulk current injection). With the stripline, the wiring is inserted between a strip-shaped conductor and a base plate. When the TEM cell is used, the control unit and a section of the wiring harness are arranged at right angles to the electromagnetic waves' direction of propagation. BCI employs a current transformer to inject current into the wiring.

Model of coupling mechanism of line-conducted electromagnetic waves

a) Conductor on which the electromagnetic waves from the interference source are propagated,

b) Target wire, component in interference-susceptible system.

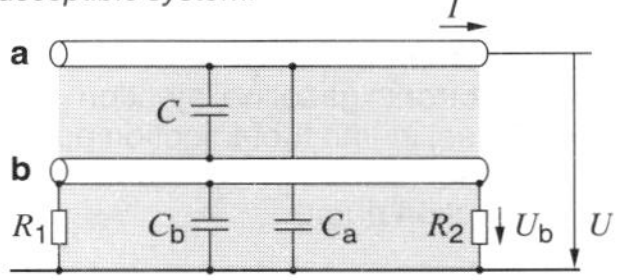

Schematic diagram of the equivalent circuit of an automotive electrical system as per DIN 57 879, Part 3/VDE 0879, Part 3

Connections: P–B Unit being tested, A–B Current, M–B Radio-interference monitor, S Switch, B Reference ground (sheet-metal plate, screen for equivalent circuit).

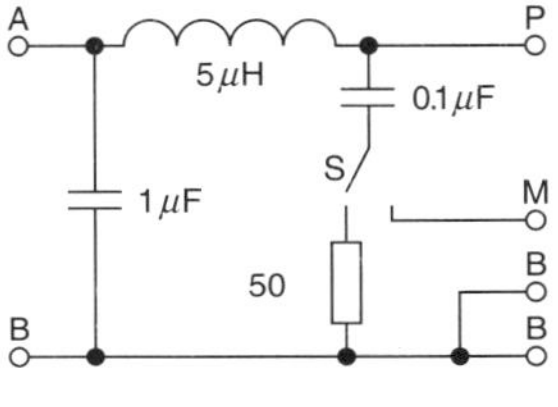

Motor vehicle specifications

The following table contains data on selected passenger cars manufactured both inside and outside Germany (Validity: First half of 1991 calendar year).
The list is intended only as a representative selection; inclusion in or exclusion from the list is not intended as the reflection of a qualitative judgement of any kind.

Abbreviations

A	Automatic transmission
ABS	Antilock braking system
AT	Exhaust-gas turbocharger
Bf	Leaf spring
Br	Opposed-cylinder engine
Bx	Braking-force regulator
Ca	Convertible
Co	Coupé
D	Axle with bilateral CV joints
Db	Damper strut
De	De Dion axle
Dl	Diagonal control arm
DPa	Diagonal swing axle
DQl	A-arm
DQu	Twin control arm
DSl	Twin semi-trailing arms
E	Axle with single CV joint
Ea	Independent suspension
El	Electronic gasoline injection
EP/R	Diesel in-line fuel-injection pump
EP/V	Diesel distributor-type fuel-injection pump
F	Spring strut
G	G-Supercharger
Gf	Rubber spring
h	Rear
Hf	Hydropneumatic suspension
K	Floor shift
Kl	Torsion-beam trailing-arm axle
Km	Rotary-piston engine (Wankel)
Ko	Station wagon
Kom	Compressor
La	Lambda closed-loop control
lä	Longitudinal installation
Le	Gearshift lever or selector lever on steering column
Lf	Longitudinal leaf spring
Li	Sedan
Ll	Trailing arm
Ls	Longitudinal radius arm
M	Selector lever in center
Ma	Multi-link axle
Mm	Mid-engine
O	Overdrive
Om	Omega axle
P	Panhard rod
Pa	Swing axle
q	Transverse installation
Qf	Transverse leaf spring
Ql	Control arm
R	In-line engine
Ra	Multi-link independent-suspension axle (5 control arms per wheel)
Ro	Roadster
Sa	Rigid axle
Sb	Disc brake
Sf	Coil spring
Sl	Semi-trailing arm
Sv	Brake booster (servo)
Ta	Torsion crank axle
Tb	Drum brake
Tfl	Longitudinal torsion bar
Tfq	Transverse torsion bar
v	Front
V	Vee-type engine
Ve	Valves per cylinder
Vla	Trailing-arm torsion-beam axle
Vtl	Four-joint trapezoidal-link axle
W	Water
Wa	Watt linkage
Ze	Single-point injection (TBI)
Zl	Supplementary link

Explanations

Line	

1 **Vehicle body**
Example: 3/5 KoLi 5 indicates a three- or five-door station wagon with five seats.

2 **Net engine horsepower**
The net engine output in kW/HP as per DIN 70 020

4 **Maximum speed**
The maximum speed (in accordance with DIN 70 020) which the vehicle can maintain over a measured distance of 1 km.

6 **Curb weight**
The weight of the vehicle when ready for use, excluding the driver.

8 **Power-to-weight ratio**
Calculated from the brake horse power and weight of the vehicle when ready for use, excluding the driver (curb weight). The smaller the power-to-weight ratio, the greater the acceleration and climbing ability.

9 **Fuel consumption**
In the case of European motor vehicles usually in accordance with DIN 70 030 (see p. 322); specified for a constant speed of 90 km/h, a constant speed of 120 km/h, city traffic; otherwise average consumption.

15 **Specific power output**
Ratio of brake horse power to swept volume (displacement).
Conversion: 1 kW/l = 1.36 HP/l.

16 **Engine type**
Specified in the following order: Engine orientation, number of cylinders, cylinder configuration.
Examples: q 4 R indicates a transverse 4-cylinder in-line engine; 2 Km indicates a 2-chamber rotary-piston engine; 4 Ve indicates 4 valves per cylinder.

20 **Drive configuration**
Letters which precede the hyphen indicate the location of the engine, and letters which follow the hyphen indicate the location of the driven wheels, e.g., v-h indicates that the engine is at the front of the vehicle and the driven wheels are at the rear; v-v+h indicates that the engine is at the front of the vehicle, and that the vehicle has all-wheel drive.

21 **Transmission ratio**
Individual transmission-conversion ratios between engine and gearbox output shaft (standard equipment).

22 **Final drive ratio**
Conversion ratio between gearbox output shaft and axle drive shaft.

23 **Gearshift**
The numeral indicates the number of forward speeds or automatic transmission speeds, and the letters indicate the type of actuation.
Examples:
4 Le indicates four forward speeds, gearshift lever on steering column, manual shift; 5 K indicates five forward gears, floor shift; 3 A – Le indicates 3-speed automatic transmission, selector lever on steering column. Information in ( ) applies to other variations whose data, such as transmission ratios, are not given here.

24 **Cooling**
W 12 indicates water cooling with a radiator capacity of 12 l.

32 **Wheel suspension**
Examples: Ql-F indicates a control arm with spring strut; Sa-Ll-Sf indicates a rigid axle with trailing arms and coil spring.

34 **Tires**
See p. 578 for explanation of tire designations.

35 **Service braking system**
Example: Sb-Tb-Br-Sv indicates front disk brakes, rear drum brakes, braking-force regulator and brake booster.

Country		Germany				
Vehicle make Model		Audi 80 1.8 S	80 quattro 16V	80 turbo D	Cabriolet	Coupé S 2
1	Body style	4 Li 5	4 Li 5	4 Li 5	2 Ca 4	3 Co 5
2	Net engine horsepower kW (HP) at engine speed min⁻¹	66 (90) 5500	101 (137) 5800	59 (80) 4500	98 (133) 5500	162 (220) 5900
3	Max. torque Nm at engine speed min⁻¹	142 3250	181 4500	152 2300–2800	186 4000	309 1950
4	Maximum speed km/h	182	208	174	198	248
5	Acceleration from 0 to 100 km/h s	12.4	9.1	14.6	10.8	6.1
6	Curb weight kg	1050	1270	1090	1350	1420
7	Gross vehicle weight kg	1510	1730	1550	1750	1880
8	Power-to-weight ratio kg/kW	15.9	12.6	18.5	13.8	8.8
9	Fuel consumption *l* / 100 km	5.4/6.9/10.6	6.8/8.6/12.6	3.8/5.3/6.9	6.8/8.5/12.3	7.6/9.3/14.3
10	Type of fuel	Regular unleaded	Premium unleaded	Diesel	Premium unleaded	Premium unleaded
11	Fuel tank capacity *l*	68	70	68	70	70
12	Engine swept volume cm³	1781	1984	1588	2309	2226
13	Bore/stroke mm	81.0/86.4	82.5/92.8	76.5/86.4	82.5/86.4	81.0/86.4
14	Compression ratio	9.0	10.8	23.0	10.0	9.3
15	Specific power output kW / *l*	37.1	50.9	37.1	46.9	72.8
16	Engine type	lä 4 R	lä 4 R, 4 Ve	lä 4 R	lä 5 R	lä 5 R, 4 Ve
17	Fuel management	Mono-Motronic	Motronic	EP/V, AT	KE-Jetronic	Motronic, AT
18	Alternator V/A	14/65	14/90	14/65	14/90	14/90
19	Battery V/Ah	12/40	12/50	12/63	12/63	12/63
20	Drive configuration	v-v	v-v+h	v-v	v-v	v-v+h
21	Transmission ratios 1st/2nd gear 3rd/4th gear 5th gear	3.545/1.857 1.156/0.838 0.683	3.545/2.105 1.300/0.943 0.769	3.545/1.857 1.156/0.838 0.683	3.545/2.105 1.429/1.029 0.838	3.500/1.842 1.222/0.903 0.714
22	Final-drive ratio	4.111	4.111	4.111	3.889	4.111
23	Gearshift	5 K (3 A)	5 K	5 K	5 K	5 K
24	Cooling	W 6.5	W 6.5	W 6.5	W 8.0	W 8.5
25	Vehicle length mm	4403	4403	4403	4366	4400
26	Vehicle width mm	1695	1695	1695	1716	1715
27	Vehicle height mm	1397	1364	1397	1379	1375
28	Wheelbase mm	2546	2537	2546	2545	2550
29	Track, front/rear mm	1411/1432	1408/1421	1411/1432	1453/1447	1455/1440
30	Turning circle diameter m	11.2	11.1	11.2	11.1	11.3
31	Ground clearance mm	127	113	127	131	120
32	Wheel suspension, front	Ea-DQl-F	Ea-DQl-F	Ea-DQl-F	Ea-DQl-F	Ea-DQl-F
33	Wheel suspension, rear	Ta-Ll-F	Ea-DQl-F	Ta-Ll-F	Ta-Ll-F	Ea-DQl-F
34	Tires	175/70 R 14 T	195/60 R 14 V	175/70 R 14 T	195/65 R 15 V	205/55 R 16 Z
35	Braking system	Sb-Tb-Sv-Br	Sb-Sb-Sv-ABS	Sb-Tb-Sv-Br	Sb-Sb-Sv-Br	Sb-Sb-Sv-ABS

See pp. 784/785 for abbreviations and explanations.

				BMW			
100	100 2.5 TDI	100 quattro 2.8 E	V 8 L	318 i	320 i	325 i	
4 Li 5	4 Li 5	4 Li 5	4 Li 5	4 Li 5	4 Li 5	4 Li 5	1
74 (101) 5500	85 (115) 4000	128 (174) 5500	206 (280) 5800	83 (113) 5500	110 (150) 5900	141 (192) 5900	2
157 2750	265 2250	250 3000	400 4000	162 4250	190 4700	245 4700	3
182	195	218	249	198	214	233	4
12.6	11.1	8.0	7.9	11.3	9.8	7.9	5
1310	1425	1500	1770	1145	1270	1295	6
1860	1975	2050	2310	1605	1730	1755	7
17.7	16.8	11.7	8.6	13.8	11.5	9.2	8
6.4/7.8/10.7	4.8/6.7/7.5	8.0/10.0/13.5	9.2/11.0/17.5	6.4/7.8/10.6	7.1/8.7/12.8	7.0/8.4/13.2	9
Regular unleaded	Diesel	Premium unleaded	Premium unleaded	Regular unleaded	Premium unleaded	Premium unleaded	10
80	80	80	80	65	65	65	11
1984	2460	2771	4172	1796	1991	2494	12
82.5/92.8	81.0/95.9	82.5/86.4	84.5/93.0	84/81	80/66	84/75	13
9.2	21.0	10.3	10.6	8.8	10.5	10.0	14
37.3	34.6	46.2	49.4	46.2	55.2	56.5	15
lä 4 R	lä 5 R	lä 6 V	lä 8 V, 4 Ve	lä 4 R	lä 6 R, 4 Ve	lä 6 R, 4 Ve	16
Mono-Motronic	EP/V, AT	Motronic	Motronic	Motronic	Motronic	Motronic	17
14/90	14/90	14/90	14/110	14/65	14/90	14/90	18
12/50	12/110	12/63	12/92	12/50	12/65	12/65	19
v-v	v-v	v-v+h	v-v+h	v-h	v-h	v-h	20
3.545/2.105 1.429/1.029 0.838	3.50/1.89 1.23/0.87 0.67	3.500/1.842 1.300/0.943 0.789	2.48/1.48 1.00/0.73	4.23/2.52 1.6/1.22 1.00	4.23/2.52 1.67/1.22 1.00	4.20/2.49 1.67/1.24 1.00	21
4.111	3.88	4.111	3.781	3.45	3.45	3.15	22
5 K (4 A)	5 K (6 K)	5 K (4 A)	4 A (6 K)	5 K	5 K (5 A)	5 K (5 A)	23
W 7.0	W 9.4	W 12.0	W 10.5	W 6.0	W 10.5	W 10.5	24
4790	4790	4790	5190	4433	4433	4433	25
1777	1777	1777	1814	1698	1698	1698	26
1429	1430	1437	1420	1393	1393	1393	27
2687	2687	2692	3018	2700	2700	2700	28
1526/1524	1526/1524	1526/1527	1514/1531	1418/1431	1418/1431	1418/1431	29
11.4	11.4	11.4	12.9	10.4	10.4	10.4	30
129	127	122	94	110	110	110	31
Ea-Ql-F	Ea-Ql-F	Ea-Ql-F	Ea-DQl-F	Ea-Ql-F	Ea-Ql-F	Ea-Ql-F	32
Ta-Ll-F	Ta-Ll-F	Ea-Vtl-F	Ea-Vtl-F	Ea-Sl-Ql-Sf	Ea-Sl-Ql-Sf	Ea-Sl-Ql-Sf	33
195/65 R 15 T	195/65 R 15 V	195/65 R 15 V	215/60 R 15 Z	185/65 R 15 87 H	205/60 R 15 91 V	205/60 ZR 15	34
Sb-Tb-Sv-Br	Sb-Sb-Sv-Br	Sb-Sb-Sv-ABS	Sb-Sb-Sv-ABS	Sb-Tb-Sv-Br	Sb-Sb-Sv-Br	Sb-Sb-Sv-ABS	35

Country			Germany				
Vehicle make Model			**BMW** (Continued) 524 td	535 i	730 i	750 i	850 i
1	Body style		4 Li 5	4 Li 5	4 Li 5	4 Li 5	2 Co 2+2
2	Net engine horsepower at engine speed	kW (HP) min^{-1}	85 (115) 4800	155 (211) 5700	138 (188) 5800	220 (300) 5200	220 (300) 5200
3	Max. torque at engine speed	Nm min^{-1}	220 2400	305 4000	260 4000	450 4100	450 4100
4	Maximum speed	km/h	192	235	222	250	250
5	Acceleration from 0 to 100 km/h	s	12.9	7.7	9.3	7.4	6.8
6	Curb weight	kg	1480	1525	1600	1800	1790
7	Gross vehicle weight	kg	1990	2035	2130	2320	2210
8	Power-to-weight ratio	kg/kW	17.4	9.8	11.6	8.2	8.1
9	Fuel consumption	*l* / 100 km	5.1/6.6/9.5	8.0/9.8/17.3	7.6/9.4/16.3	8.8/10.9/19.8	8.8/10.4/19.8
10	Type of fuel		Diesel	Regular unleaded	Regular unleaded	Regular unleaded	Regular unleaded
11	Fuel tank capacity	*l*	80	80	90	102	90
12	Engine swept volume	cm^3	2443	3430	2986	4988	4988
13	Bore/stroke	mm	80/81	92/86	89/80	84/75	84/75
14	Compression ratio		22	9.0	9.0	8.8	8.8
15	Specific power output	kW / *l*	34.8	45.2	46.2	44.1	44.1
16	Engine type		lä 6 R	lä 6 R	lä 6 R	lä 12 V	lä 12 V
17	Fuel management		EP/V, AT	Motronic	Motronic	Motronic	Motronic
18	Alternator	V/A	14/80	14/90	14/90	14/140	14/140
19	Battery	V/Ah	12/85	12/84	12/84	12/85	2 x 12/65
20	Drive configuration		v-h	v-h	v-h	v-h	v-h
21	Transmission ratios	1st/2nd gear 3rd/4th gear 5th /6th gear	4.35/2.33 1.39/1.00 0.81	3.83/2.20 1.40/1.00 0.81	3.83/2.20 1.40/1.00 0.81	2.48/1.48 1.00/0.73	4.25/2.53 1.68/1.24 1.00/0.83
22	Final-drive ratio		3.25	3.64	3.64	3.15	2.93
23	Gearshift		5 K (4 A)	5 K (4 A)	5 K (4 A)	4 A	6 K (4 A)
24	Cooling		W 12	W 12	W 12	W 12	W 12
25	Vehicle length	mm	4720	4720	4910	4910	4780
26	Vehicle width	mm	1751	1751	1845	1845	1855
27	Vehicle height	mm	1412	1412	1411	1400	1340
28	Wheelbase	mm	2761	2761	2833	2833	2684
29	Track, front/rear	mm	1466/1487	1470/1495	1530/1558	1530/1558	1554/1562
30	Turning circle diameter	m	11.0	11.0	11.6	12.0	11.5
31	Ground clearance	mm	120	120	120	120	140
32	Wheel suspension, front		Ea-Ql-F	Ea-Ql-F	Ea-Ql-F	Ea-Ql-F	Ea-Ql-F
33	Wheel suspension, rear		Ea-Sl-Zl-Sf	Ea-Sl-Zl-Sf	Ea-Sl-Zl-Sf	Ea-Sl-Zl-Sf	Ea-Ql-Ll-Sf
34	Tires		195/65 R 15 H	225/60 ZR 15	205/65 R 15 94 V	225/60 ZR 15	235/50 ZR 16
35	Braking system		Sb-Sb-Sv-Br	Sb-Sb-Sv-ABS	Sb-Sb-Sv-ABS	Sb-Sb-Sv-ABS	Sb-Sb-Sv-ABS

See pp. 784/785 for abbreviations and explanations.

Ford Fiesta 1.4 i CLX	Escort 1.6 i Ghia	Orion 1.8 D CL	Sierra 2.0 i GL	Scorpio 2.4 i Ghia	Scorpio 2.9 i GL 4x4	Probe GT	
3/5 Li 5	5 Li 5	4 Li 5	4 Li 5	4 Li 5	5 Li 5	2 Co 4	1
52 (71) 5500	77 (105) 6000	44 (60) 4800	88 (120) 5500	92 (125) 5800	143 (195) 5750	108 (147) 4300	2
103 4000	138 4500	110 2500	171 2500	182 3500	275 4500	258 3500	3
162	186	152	190	190	225	220	4
							5
13.0	10.6	18.9	10.0	11.0	8.8	8.6	
820	1015	1070	1140	1365	1385	1338	6
1250	1425	1550	1675	1850	1925	1732	7
15.8	13.2	24.3	13.0	14.8	9.7	12.4	8
5.6/7.3/8.8	5.9/7.5/9.8	4.4/6.0/6.3	6.1/7.8/9.4	7.6/9.2/14.0	8.4/10.1/15.1	6.1/8.1/11.3	9
Premium unleaded	Premium unleaded	Diesel	Premium unleaded	Premium unleaded	Premium unleaded	Premium unleaded	10
42	55	55	60	70	70	57	11
1391	1596	1753	1898	2394	2935	2184	12
77.2/74.3	79.96/79.52	82.5/82.0	86.0/86.0	84.0/72.0	93.03/71.99	86.0/94.0	13
8.5	9.75	21.5	10.3	9.5	9.7	7.8	14
37.4	48.2	25	46.4	38.4	48.7	49.4	15
q 4 R	q 4 R	q 4 R	lä 4 R	lä 6 V	lä 6 V, 4 Ve	q 4 R, 3 Ve	16
Ze	El	EP/V	El	L-Jetronic	El	El, AT	17
14/55	14/55	14/70	14/70	14/90	14/90	14/70	18
12/43	12/43	12/63	12/43	12/48	12/48	12/56	19
v-v	v-v	v-v	v-h	v-h	v-v-h	v-v	20
3.15/1.91 1.28/0.95 0.76	3.154/1.913 1.281/0.951 0.756	3.583/1.913 1.281/0.951 0.756	3.890/2.084 1.342/1.000 0.822	3.890/2.084 1.342/1.000 0.822	2.474/1.474 1.000/0.750	3.250/1.772 1.194/0.926 0.711	21
3.84	3.824	3.588	3.62	3.92	3.64	4.1	22
5 K	5 K	5 K	5 K (4 A)	5 K (4 A)	4 A	5 K	23
W 7.0	W 8.0	W 9.3	W 8.0	W 8.5	W 8.0	W 7.5	24
3743	4036	4229	4467	4744	4669	4496	25
1606	1692	1690	1698	1760	1766	1735	26
1389	1395	1395	1407	1440	1435	1321	27
2446	2525	2525	2608	2761	2765	2515	28
1392/1384	1440/1439	1440/1439	1452/1468	1477/1500	1482/1500	1455/1465	29
10.3	10.5	10.5	11.0	11.0	11.0	11.2	30
140	140	140	120	120	120	130	31
Ea-Ql-F	Ea-Ql-F	Ea-Ql-F	Ea-Ql-F	Ea-Ql-F	Ea-Ql-F	Ea-DQl-F	32
Vla-Sf	Vla-Sf	Vla-Sf	Ea-Sl-Sf	Ea-Sl-Sf	Ea-Sl-Sf	Ea-Ql-Ll-F	33
170/55 SR 13	175/70 HR 13	175/70 R 13	185/65 R 14	195/65 R 15	205/60 VR 15	205/60 VR 15	34
Sb-Tb-Sv-Br	Sb-Tb-Sv-Br	Sb-Tb-Sv-Br	Sb-Tb-Sv-Br	Sb-Sb-Sv-ABS	Sb-Sb-Sv-ABS	Sb-Sb-Sv-ABS	35

Country		Germany				
Vehicle make Model		Mercedes-Benz 190 E 1.8	190 E 2.5-16	190 D 2.5 Turbo	230 CE	250 D
1 Body style		4 Li 5	4 Li 5	4 Li 5	2 Co 5	4 Li 5
2 Net engine horsepower at engine speed	kW (HP) min⁻¹	80 (109) 5500	143 (195) 6750	93 (126) 4600	97 (132) 5100	69 (94) 4600
3 Max. torque at engine speed	Nm min⁻¹	150 3700	235 5000–5500	231 2400	198 3500	158 2800
4 Maximum speed	km/h	185	230	195	200	175
5 Acceleration from 0 to 100 km/h	s	12.7	7.7	11.5	10.6	16.2
6 Curb weight	kg	1160	1300	1300	1380	1390
7 Gross vehicle weight	kg	1660	1800	1800	1870	1910
8 Power-to-weight ratio	kg/kW	14.5	9.1	14.0	14.2	20.1
9 Fuel consumption	*l* / 100 km	7.0/8.8/11.0	7.3/9.0/13.3	5.6/7.6/9.3	6.9/8.6/12.1	5.4/7.0/8.9
10 Type of fuel		Premium unleaded	Premium unleaded	Diesel	Premium unleaded	Diesel
11 Fuel tank capacity	*l*	55	70	55	70	70
12 Engine swept volume	cm^3	1797	2488	2497	2298	2497
13 Bore/stroke	mm	89.0/72.2	95.5/87.2	87.0/84.0	95.5/80.2	87.0/84.0
14 Compression ratio		9.1	9.7	22	9.0	22.0
15 Specific power output	kW / *l*	44.5	57.2	37.2	42.2	27.6
16 Engine type		lä 4 R	lä 4 R, 4 Ve	lä 5 R	lä 4 R	lä 5 R
17 Fuel management		KE-Jetronic	KE-Jetronic	EP/R	KE-Jetronic	EP/R
18 Alternator	V/A	14/55	14/55	14/55	14/55	14/55
19 Battery	V/Ah	12/42	12/62	12/72	12/62	12/72
20 Drive configuration		v-h	v-h	v-h	v-h	v-h
21 Transmission ratios	1st/2nd gear 3rd/4th gear 5th gear	3.91/2.17 1.37/1.00	4.08/2.52 1.77/1.26 1.00	3.86/2.18 1.38/1.00 0.75	3.91/2.17 1.37/1.00 0.81	3.91/2.17 1.37/1.00 0.81
22 Final-drive ratio		3.46	3.07	3.46	3.46	3.64
23 Gearshift		4 K (5 K. 4 A)	5 K (4 A)	5 K (4 A)	5 K (4 A)	5 K (4 A)
24 Cooling		W 8.5	W 8.0	W 8.5	W 8.5	W 8.5
25 Vehicle length	mm	4448	4430	4448	4655	4740
26 Vehicle width	mm	1690	1706	1690	1740	1740
27 Vehicle height	mm	1375	1361	1375	1395	1431
28 Wheelbase	mm	2665	2665	2665	2715	2800
29 Track, front/rear	mm	1437/1418	1446/1429	1437/1418	1501/1491	1501/1491
30 Turning circle diameter	m	10.6	10.6	10.6	10.9	11.2
31 Ground clearance	mm	155	125	155	160	160
32 Wheel suspension, front		Ea-DQl-Db-Sf	Ea-DQl-Db-Sf	Ea-DQl-Db-Sf	Ea-DQl-Db-Sf	Ea-DQl-Db-Sf
33 Wheel suspension, rear		Ea-Ra-Sf	Ea-Ra-Sf	Ea-Ra-Sf	Ea-Ra-Sf	Ea-Ra-Sf
34 Tires		185/65 R 15 87 H	205/55 ZR 15	185/65 R 15 87 H	195/65 R 15 91 H	195/65 R 15 91 T
35 Braking system		Sb-Sb-Sv-Br	Sb-Sb-Sv-ABS	Sb-Sb-Sv-ABS	Sb-Sb-Sv-ABS	Sb-Sb-Sv-ABS

See pp. 784/785 for abbreviations and explanations.

260 E	300 E 4-Matic	300 SL-24	300 TD Turbo 4-Matic	400 SE	500 SL	600 SEL	
4 Li 5	4 Li 5	2 Ro 2+2	5 KoLi 5	4 Li 5	2 Ro 2+2	4 Li 5	1
118 (160) 5800	132 (180) 5700	170 (231) 6300	108 (147) 4600	210 (286) 5700	240 (326) 5500	300 (408) 5200	2
220 4600	255 4400	272 4600	273 2400	410 3900	450 4000	580 3800	3
215	217	240	188	245	250	250	4
9.0	8.5	8.1	11.8	7.9	6.2	6.3	5
1420	1560	1690	1710	1990	1770	2190	6
1940	2080	2080	2310	2510	2160	2650	7
12.0	11.8	9.9	15.8	9.5	7.4	7.3	8
8.0/10.1/14.5	9.1/11.0/13.8	8.8/10.4/16.2	7.5/9.7/10.2	10.1/12.2/16.7	10.1/12.0/16.6	11.8/13.7/20.7	9
Premium unleaded	Premium unleaded	Premium unleaded	Diesel	Premium unleaded	Premium unleaded	Premium unleaded	10
70	70	80	70	100	80	100	11
2597	2960	2960	2996	4196	4973	5987	12
82.9/80.2	88.5/80.2	88.5/80.2	87.0/84.0	92.0/78.9	96.5/85.0	89.0/80.2	13
9.2	9.2	10.0	22.0	10.0	10.0	10.0	14
45.4	44.6	57.4	36.0	50.0	48.3	50.1	15
lä 6 R	lä 6 R	lä 6 R, 4 Ve	lä 6 R	lä 8 V, 4 Ve	lä 8 V, 4 Ve	lä 12 V, 4 Ve	16
KE-Jetronic	KE-Jetronic	KE-Jetronic	EP/R, AT	LH-Jetronic	KE-Jetronic	LH-Jetronic	17
14/70	14/70	14/100	14/70	14/120	14/110	14/120	18
12/62	12/62	12/92	12/72	12/100	12/92	12/100	19
v-h	v-v+h	v-h	v-v+h	v-h	v-h	v-h	20
3.86/2.18 1.38/1.00 0.80	3.87/2.25 1.44/1.00	4.15/2.52 1.69/1.24 1.00	3.68/2.41 1.44/1.00	3.87/2.25 1.44/1.00	3.87/2.25 1.44/1.00	3.87/2.25 1.44/1.00	21
3.92	3.27	3.46	2.65	2.82	2.65	2.65	22
5 K (4 A)	4 A	5 K (4/5 A)	4 A	4 A	4 A	4 A	23
W 8.5	W 8.5	W 9.0	W 11	W 16.5	W 13	W 20	24
4740	4740	4470	4765	5115	4470	5115	25
1740	1740	1812	1740	1885	1812	1885	26
1431	1431	1293	1490	1500	1293	1500	27
2800	2800	2515	2800	3040	2515	3040	28
1501/1491	1501/1491	1535/1523	1497/1488	1600/1575	1535/1523	1600/1575	29
11.2	12.15	10.75	12.15	12.2	10.75	12.5	30
160	160	124	160	150	124	150	31
Ea-DQl-Db-Sf	Ea-DQl-Db-Sf	Ea-DQl-Db-Sf	Ea-DQl-Db-Sf	Ea-DQu-Sf	Ea-DQl-Sf	Ea-DQu-Sf	32
Ea-Ra-Sf	Ea-Ra-Sf	Ea-Ra-Sf	Ea-Ra-Sf	Ea-Ra-Sf	Ea-Ra-Sf	Ea-Ra-Sf	33
195/65 VR 15	195/65 VR 15	225/55 ZR 16	195/65 R 15 91 H	235/60 ZR 16	255/55 ZR 16	235/60 ZR 16	34
Sb-Sb-Sv-ABS	Sb-Sb-Sv-ABS	Sb-Sb-Sv-ABS	Sb-Sb-Sv-ABS	Sb-Sb-Sv-ABS	Sb-Sb-Sv-ABS	Sb-Sb-Sv-ABS	35

Country		Germany				
Vehicle make Model		Opel Corsa 1.2 i Swing	Astra 1.6 i GL	Astra 2.0 i GSi	Vectra 1.8 i GL	Vectra 2.0 i CD
1 Body style		3/5 Li 5	3/5 Li 5	3 Li 5	4 Li 5	5 Li 5
2 Net engine horsepower at engine speed	kW (HP) min^{-1}	33 (45) 5000	55 (75) 5200	85 (115) 5400	66 (90) 5400	85 (115) 5200
3 Max. torque at engine speed	Nm min^{-1}	88 2400	125 2800	170 2600	140 3000	170 2600
4 Maximum speed	km/h	143	170	200	183	198
5 Acceleration from 0 to 100 km/h	s	18.0	14.0	9.5	12.5	10.5
6 Curb weight	kg	775/800	930/950	1050	1075	1085
7 Gross vehicle weight	kg	1250/1275	1455	1545	1610	1645
8 Power-to-weight ratio	kg/kW	23.5	16.9	12.4	16.3	12.8
9 Fuel consumption	l / 100 km	5.4/7.0/7.9	5.2/6.9/8.6	6.4/8.1/11.0	5.5/7.1/10.2	5.6/7.1/10.3
10 Type of fuel		Premium unleaded	Premium unleaded	Premium unleaded	Premium unleaded	Premium unleaded
11 Fuel tank capacity	l	42	52	52	61	61
12 Engine swept volume	cm^3	1195	1598	1998	1796	1998
13 Bore/stroke	mm	72.0/73.4	79/81.5	86/86	84.8/79.5	86/86
14 Compression ratio		9.1	9.2	9.2	9.2	9.2
15 Specific power output	kW / l	27.5	34.4	42.5	36.7	42.5
16 Engine type		q 4 R	q 4 R	q 4 R	q 4 R	q 4 R
17 Fuel management		El	Ze	Motronic	Ze	Motronic
18 Alternator	V/A	14/55	14/55	14/55	14/70	14/70
19 Battery	V/Ah	12/44	12/44	12/44	12/44	12/44
20 Drive configuration		v-v	v-v	v-v	v-v	v-v
21 Transmission ratios	1st/2nd gear 3rd/4th gear 5th gear	3.55/1.96 1.30/0.89	3.55/1.96 1.30/0.89 0.71	3.55/2.16 1.48/1.13 0.89	3.55/1.95 1.28/0.89 0.71	3.55/1.95 1.28/0.89 0.71
22 Final-drive ratio		3.94	3.94	3.55	3.94	3.55
23 Gearshift		4 K	5 K (3 A)	5 K	5 K (4 A)	5 K (4 A)
24 Cooling		W 6.1	W 5.6	W 6.5	W 6.7	W 7.2
25 Vehicle length	mm	3652	4051	4086	4430	4350
26 Vehicle width	mm	1535	1688	1688	1700	1700
27 Vehicle height	mm	1365	1410	1410	1400	1400
28 Wheelbase	mm	2343	2517	2517	2600	2600
29 Track, front/rear	mm	1320/1307	1430/1429	1430/1432	1420/1423	1426/1426
30 Turning circle diameter	m	10.0	10.5	10.5	11.0	11.0
31 Ground clearance	mm	140	135	135	140	140
32 Wheel suspension, front		Ea-Qi-Ll-F	Ea-DQl-F	Ea-DQl-F	Ea-DQl-F	Ea-DQl-F
33 Wheel suspension, rear		Vla-Sf	Vla-Sf	Vla-Sf	Vla-Sf	Vla-Sf
34 Tires		145 R 13-74 S	175/70 R 13-82 T	195/60 R 14-85 H	175/70 R 14-82 T	195/60 R 14-85 V
35 Braking system		Sb-Tb-Sv-Br	Sb-Tb-Sv-Br	Sb-Sb-Sv-ABS	Sb-Tb-Sv-Br	Sb-Sb-Sv-ABS

See pp. 784/785 for abbreviations and explanations.

				Porsche			
Calibra 2.0 i 16V 4x4	Omega 2.3 TD Caravan	Omega 2.6 i CD	Senator 3.0 i 24V CD	911 turbo	928 S4	944 S2	
2 Co 4	5 Ko 5	4 Li 5	4 Li 5	2 Co 2+2	2 Co 2+2	2 Co 2+2	1
110 (150) 6000	74 (100) 4200	110 (150) 5600	150 (204) 6000	235 (320) 5750	235 (320) 6000	155 (211) 5800	2
196 4800	218 2000	220 3600	270 3600	450 4500	430 3000	280 4100	3
215	176	215	235	270	265	240	4
							5
9.5	15.0	9.8	8.8	5.0	6.3	7.1	
1280	1390	1415	1499	1470	1600	1340	6
1700	1990	1955	1995	1810	1920	1680	7
11.6	18.8	12.9	10.0	6.3	6.8	8.6	8
6.6/8.0/11.5	5.5/7.2/8.5	7.7/9.4/10.4	7.4/9.0/14.5	8.5/10.4/21.0	10.0/11.8/16.6	7.4/9.1/14.3	9
Premium unleaded	Diesel	Premium unleaded	Premium unleaded	Premium unleaded	Premium unleaded	Premium unleaded	10
63	70	75	75	77	86	80	11
1998	2260	2594	2969	3299	4957	2990	12
86/86	92/85	88.8/69.8	95.0/69.8	97.0/74.4	100.0/78.9	104.0/88.0	13
10.5	23	9.2	10.0	7.0	10.0	10.9	14
55.0	32.7	42.3	50.5	71.2	47.4	51.8	15
q 4 R	lä 4 R	lä 6 R	lä 6 R	lä 6 Bx	lä 8 V, 4 Ve	lä 4 R, 4 Ve	16
Motronic	EP/V, AT	Motronic	Motronic	KE-Jetronic.,AT	LH-Jetronic	Motronic	17
14/70	14/70	14/90	14/90	14/115	14/115	14/115	18
12/44	12/70	12/55	12/66	12/72	12/72	12/63	19
v-v+h	v-h	v-h	v-h	h-h	v-h	v-h	20
3.55/2.16 1.48/1.13 0.89	3.954/2.187 1.386/1.000 0.845	3.954/2.187 1.386/1.000 0.845	2.40/1.48 1.00/0.72	3.154/1.789 1.269/0.967 0.756	3.87/2.25 1.44/1.00	3.500/2.059 1.400/1.034 0.829	21
3.72	3.45	3.70	3.70	3.444	2.538	3.875	22
5 K	5 K	5 K (4 A)	4 A	5 K	4 A	5 K	23
W 7.2	W 10.8	W 11.5	W 9.9	Luft	W 16	W 8.0	24
4492	4768	4738	4845	4250	4520	4230	25
1688	1760	1760	1763	1775	1836	1735	26
1320	1480	1445	1450	1310	1282	1275	27
2600	2730	2730	2730	2272	2500	2400	28
1426/1446	1462/1476	1462/1478	1450/1468	1434/1493	1551/1546	1472/1451	29
11.45	11.0	11.0	10.95	11.5	11.7	10.8	30
140	140	140	140	120	120	175	31
Ea-DQl-F	Ea-DQl-F	Ea-DQl-F	Ea-DQl-F	Ea-Ql-F	Ea-DQu-Sf	Ea-Ql-F	32
Ea-Sl-Sf	Ea-Sl-Sf	Ea-Sl-Sf	Ea-Sl-Sf	Ea-Sl-F	Ea-Dl-Ll-Sf	Ea-Sl-Tfq	33
205/55 R 15- 87 V	195/65 R 15 V	195/65 R 15 V	205/65 R 15- 93 V	1)	2)	3)	34
Sb-Sb-Sv-ABS	Sb-Sb-Sv-Br	Sb-Sb-Sv-ABS	Sb-Sb-Sv-ABS	Sb-Sb-Sv-ABS	Sb-Sb-Sv-ABS	Sb-Sb-Sv-ABS	35

1) Front 205/50 ZR 17, rear 225/40 ZR 17.
2) Front 225/50 ZR 16, rear 245/45 ZR 16.
3) Front 205/55 ZR 16, rear 225/50 ZR 16.

Country			Germany				
Vehicle make Model			VW (Volkswagen) Polo GT Coupé	Polo CL Diesel	Golf CL	Golf GTI 16V	Golf syncro GT
1	Body style		3 Co 4	3 KoLi 4	3/5 Li 5	3/5 Li 5	3/5 Li 5
2	Net engine horsepower at engine speed	kW (HP) min^{-1}	40 (55) 5000	35 (48) 4500	66 (90) 5250	95 (129) 5800	72 (98) 5400
3	Max. torque at engine speed	Nm min^{-1}	95 3200–3400	85 2700-3500	142 3000	168 4250	143 3000
4	Maximum speed	km/h	154	142	175	200	180
5	Acceleration from 0 to 100 km/h	s	15.5	19.5	11.9	9.0	11.3
6	Curb weight	kg	785	805	935/960	985/1010	1090/1115
7	Gross vehicle weight	kg	1230	1250	1440	1465	1580
8	Power-to-weight ratio	kg/kW	19.6	23.0	14.2	10.4	15.1
9	Fuel consumption	l / 100 km	5.2/7.2/8.3	4.2/5.9/5.7	6.3/8.3/10.5	6.9/8.8/11.3	6.8/9.0/11.7
10	Type of fuel		Regular unleaded	Diesel	Regular unleaded	Premium unleaded[1])	Regular unleaded
11	Fuel tank capacity	l	42	42	55	55	55
12	Engine swept volume	cm^3	1272	1398	1781	1781	1781
13	Bore/stroke	mm	75.0/72.0	75.0/79.1	81.0/86.4	81.0/86.4	81.0/86.4
14	Compression ratio		9.5	22.3	9.0	10.0	10.0
15	Specific power output	kW / l	31.4	25.0	37.1	53.3	40.4
16	Engine type		q 4 R	q 4 R	q 4 R	q 4 R, 4 Ve	q 4 R
17	Fuel management		Mono-Motronic	EP/V	Mono-Jetronic	KE-Jetronic	EI
18	Alternator	V/A	14/55	14/55	14/65	14/65	14/55
19	Battery	V/Ah	12/36	12/50	12/45	12/45	12/45
20	Drive configuration		v-v	v-v	v-v	v-v	v-v+h
21	Transmission ratios	1st/2nd gear 3rd/4th gear 5th gear	3.45/1.96 1.25/0.89 0.74	3.45/1.96 1.25/0.89 0.74	3.46/1.94 1.29/0.91 0.75	3.46/2.12 1.44/1.13 0.91	3.46/1.94 1.29/0.91 0.75
22	Final-drive ratio		4.06	4.06	3.67	3.67	4.47
23	Gearshift		5 K	5 K	5 K (4 A)	5 K	5 K
24	Cooling		W 6.0	W 6.0	W 6.3	W 6.3	W 6.3
25	Vehicle length	mm	3725	3765	3985	4040	3985
26	Vehicle width	mm	1570	1570	1665	1680	1680
27	Vehicle height	mm	1350	1350	1415	1405	1415
28	Wheelbase	mm	2335	2335	2475	2475	2475
29	Track, front/rear	mm	1320/1346	1320/1346	1427/1422	1427/1422	1427/1432
30	Turning circle diameter	m	10.0	10.0	10.5	10.5	10.5
31	Ground clearance	mm	105	105	130	105	130
32	Wheel suspension, front		Ea-QI-F	Ea-QI-F	Ea-DQI-F	Ea-DQI-F	Ea-DQI-F
33	Wheel suspension, rear		KI-F	KI-F	Vla-F	Vla-F	Ea-SI-F
34	Tires		165/65 R 13 T	145 R 13 S	175/70 R 13 H	185/60 R 14 H	185/60 R 14 H
35	Braking system		Sb-Tb-Sv-Br	Sb-Tb-Sv-Br	Sb-Tb-Sv-Br	Sb-Sb-Sv-Br	Sb-Tb-Sv-ABS

See pp. 784/785 for abbreviations and explanations.

Jetta GT	Jetta GTD	Corrado G 60	Passat GL	Passat GT	Passat GL Diesel Variant	Passat GL VR6	
4 Li 5	2/4 Li 5	3 Co 5	4 Li 5	4 Li 5	5 KoLi 5	4 Li 5	1
79 (107) 5400	59 (80) 4500	118 (160) 5600	55 (75) 5000	100 (136) 5800	50 (68) 4400	128 (174) 5800	2
157 3800	155 2500–3000	225 4000	140 2500	180 4400	127 2200–2600	235 4200	3
184	167	225	171	206	155	224	4
							5
10.6	13.7	8.3	15.5	10.2	19.4	8.2	
1000	985/1010	1115	1100	1210	1205	1300	6
1495	1495	1505	1650	1760	1750	1840	7
12.7	16.7	9.4	20.0	12.1	24.1	10.2	8
6.6/8.7/10.7	4.5/6.4/6.3	6.4/8.4/12.1	5.9/7.7/10.5	6.3/8.1/12.3	4.7/6.6/7.4	7.4/9.0/12.5	9
Premium unleaded[1])	Diesel	Premium unleaded	Regular unleaded	Premium unleaded[1])	Diesel	Premium unleaded	10
55	55	55	70	70	70	70	11
1781	1588	1781	1781	1984	1896	2792	12
81.0/86.4	76.5/86.4	81.0/86.4	81.0/86.4	82.5/92.8	79.5/95.5	81.0/90.3	13
10.0	23.0	8.0	9.0	10.8	22.5	10.0	14
44.4	37.2	66.3	30.9	50.4	26.4	45.8	15
q 4 R	q 4 R	q 4 R	q 4 R	q 4 R	q 4 R	q 6 VR	16
EI	EP/V, AT	EI, G	Mono-Motronic	KE-Motronic	EP/V	Motronic	17
14/65	14/65	14/65	14/90	14/90	14/90	14/70	18
12/45	12/63	12/45	12/36	12/54	12/63	12/54	19
v-v	v-v	v-v	v-v	v-v	v-v	v-v	20
3.46/2.12 1.44/1.13 0.89	3.46/1.94 1.29/0.91 0.75	3.78/2.12 1.43/1.03 0.84	3.78/2.12 1.43/1.03 0.84	3.78/2.12 1.43/1.03 0.84	3.78/2.12 1.34/0.97 0.80	3.78/2.12 1.43/1.03 0.84	21
3.67	3.67	3.68	3.94	3.68	3.68	3.68	22
5 K	5 K	5 K (4 A)	5 K	5 K (4 A)	5 K	5 K (4 A)	23
W 6.3	W 6.3	W 6.9	W 5.0	W 5.0	W 7.0	W 12.0	24
4385	4385	4048	4575	4575	4575	4575	25
1675	1675	1674	1705	1705	1705	1705	26
1405	1415	1318	1430	1430	1460	1430	27
2475	2475	2470	2625	2625	2625	2625	28
1427/1422	1427/1422	1435/1428	1479/1422	1479/1422	1479/1422	1479/1422	29
10.5	10.5	10.5	10.7	10.7	10.7	10.7	30
130	130	110	110	110	110	110	31
Ea-DQI-F	Ea-DQI-F	Ea-DQI-F	Ea-DQI-F	Ea-DQI-F	Ea-DQI-F	Ea-DQI-F	32
Vla-F	Vla-F	Vla-F	Vla-F	Vla-F	Vla-F	Vla-F	33
185/60 R 14 H	185/60 R 14 H	195/50 R 15 V	185/65 R 14 T	195/60 R 14 V	185/65 R 14 T	205/50 R 15 V	34
Sb-Sb-Sv-Br	Sb-Tb-Sv-Br	Sb-Sb-Sv-ABS	Sb-Tb-Sv-Br	Sb-Sb-Sv-ABS	Sb-Tb-Sv-Br	Sb-Sb-Sv-ABS	35

[1]) Regular unleaded also permitted.

Country		France				
Vehicle make Model		Citroën AX 14 TGD	AX GT	ZX Aura	BX 19 TZI	BX 19 TGD Break
1 Body style		3/5 Li 5	3 Li 5	5 Li 5	5 Li 5	5 KoLi 5
2 Net engine horsepower at engine speed	kW (HP) min^{-1}	38 (52) 5000	55 (75) 6200	65 (89) 6400	80 (109) 6000	47 (64) 4600
3 Max. torque at engine speed	Nm min^{-1}	83 2500	109 4000	132 3000	158 3000	118 2000
4 Maximum speed	km/h	155	176	181	189	154
5 Acceleration from 0 to 100 km/h	s	16.5	10.4	13.5	10.7	18.4
6 Curb weight	kg	710	740	995	1010	1060
7 Gross vehicle weight	kg	1150	1160	1540	1480	1595
8 Power-to-weight ratio	kg/kW	18.7	13.5	15.3	12.6	22.5
9 Fuel consumption	*l* / 100 km	3.6/5.0/5.2	5.2/7.0/8.1	5.4/7.1/9.3	6.6/8.7/10.7	5.1/6.8/6.7
10 Type of fuel		Diesel	Premium unleaded	Premium unleaded	Premium unleaded	Diesel
11 Fuel tank capacity	*l*	43	43	56	66	52
12 Engine swept volume	cm^3	1360	1360	1580	1905	1905
13 Bore/stroke	mm	75.0/77.0	75.0/77.0	83.0/73.0	83.0/88.0	83.0/88.0
14 Compression ratio		22.0	8.8	8.95	9.2	23.5
15 Specific power output	kW / *l*	27.9	40.4	41.2	42.0	24.7
16 Engine type		q 4 R	q 4 R	q 4 R	q 4 R	q 4 R
17 Fuel management		EP/V	Mono-Jetronic	Ze	Motronic	EP/V
18 Alternator	V/A	14/55	14/55	14/55	14/50	14/50
19 Battery	V/Ah	12/50	12/29	12/35	12/33	12/50
20 Drive configuration		v-v	v-v	v-v	v-v	v-v
21 Transmission ratios	1st/2nd gear 3rd/4th gear 5th gear	3.418/1.810 1.276/0.975 0.767	3.418/1.950 1.357/1.054 0.854	3.455/1.850 1.360/1.069 0.865	3.450/1.850 1.360/1.069 0.865	3.450/1.850 1.280/0.969 0.757
22 Final-drive ratio		3.939	3.939	3.814	3.688	4.063
23 Gearshift		5 K	5 K	5 K	5 K	5 K
24 Cooling		W 4.8	W 4.8	W 7.5	W 6.5	W 6.5
25 Vehicle length	mm	3495	3495	4070	4237	4399
26 Vehicle width	mm	1555	1555	1690	1682	1682
27 Vehicle height	mm	1355	1355	1400	1360	1431
28 Wheelbase	mm	2280	2280	2540	2655	2655
29 Track, front/rear	mm	1380/1300	1392/1312	1420/1415	1430/1364	1420/1364
30 Turning circle diameter	m	10.6	10.6	10.5	11.0	11.0
31 Ground clearance	mm	97	97	110	163	163
32 Wheel suspension, front		Ea-DQI-F	Ea-DQI-F	Ea-DQI-F	Ea-DQI-F-Hf	Ea-DQI-F-Hf
33 Wheel suspension, rear		Ea-LI-Tfq	Ea-LI-Tfq	Ea-LI-Tfq	Ea-LI-Hf	Ea-LI-Hf
34 Tires		145/70 R 13	155/65 R 14	175/65 TR 14	175/65 R 14	165/70 R 14
35 Braking system		Sb-Tb-Sv-Br	Sb-Tb-Sv-Br	Sb-Tb-Sv-Br	Sb-Sb-Sv-Br	Sb-Sb-Sv-Br

See pp. 784/785 for abbreviations and explanations.

XM Injection	XM V6 · 24 Pallas	CX 25 TGI Familiale	**Peugeot** 205 XL	205 GRD	309 GR	309 GTI	
5 Li 5	5 Li 5	5 Li 8	3/5 Li 5	3/5 Li 5	5 Li 5	3 Li 5	1
89 (121) 5600	147 (200) 6000	89 (121) 5000	44 (60) 6200	47 (64) 4600	55 (75) 6200	88 (120) 6000	2
170 4000	260 3600	191 4000	87.5 3800	118 2000	109 4000	150 3000	3
201	235	190	164	162	170	202	4
11.9	8.6	12.5	13.9	14.2	11.1	8.7	5
1310	1465	1420	790	880	910	930	6
1845	1920	2165	1220	1300	1330	1350	7
14.7	10.0	16.0	17.9	18.7	16.5	10.6	8
6.8/8.8/12.8	8.2/10.2/15.9	8.6/10.3/14.7	4.8/6.3/7.1	4.4/5.6/5.9	5.6/7.4/8.1	6.5/8.3/9.9	9
Premium unleaded	Premium unleaded	Regular unleaded	Premium unleaded	Diesel	Premium unleaded	Premium unleaded	10
80	80	68	50	50	55	55	11
1998	2975	2482	1124	1905	1360	1905	12
86.0/86.0	93.0/73.0	93.0/92.0	72.0/69.0	83.0/88.0	75.0/77.0	83.0/88.0	13
8.8	9.5	8.0	9.4	23	9.3	9.2	14
44.5	49.4	35.9	39.1	24.7	40.4	46.2	15
q 4 R	q 6 V, 4 Ve	q 4 R	q 4 R	q 4 R	q 4 R	q 4 R	16
Motronic	EI	L-Jetronic	Mono-Jetronic	EP/V	Mono-Jetronic	Motronic	17
14/70	14/70	14/80	14/54	14/54	14/54	14/54	18
12/62	12/66	12/60	12/29	12/50	12/33	12/33	19
v-v	v-v	v-v	v-v	v-v	v-v	v-v	20
3.455/1.850 1.360/1.069 0.800	3.168/1.834 1.250/0.969 0.767	3.166/1.833 1.250/0.939 0.733	3.418/1.810 1.276/0.975 0.767	3.308/1.882 1.280/0.969 0.757	3.418/1.810 1.276/0.975 0.767	2.923/1.850 1.360/1.069 0.865	21
4.19	4.067	4.07	3.938	3.588	4.29	3.69	22
5 K	5 K	5 K	5 K	5 K	5 K	5 K	23
W 7.3	W 10.0	W 12.3	W 5.8	W 8.3	W 5.8	W 8.0	24
4708	4708	4960	3705	3705	4051	4051	25
1794	1794	1770	1572	1572	1628	1628	26
1393	1393	1465	1373	1373	1380	1380	27
2850	2850	3095	2420	2420	2469	2469	28
1520/1445	1520/1445	1552/1398	1350/1304	1364/1318	1410/1378	1410/1378	29
11.7	11.7	13.4	10.5	10.5	11.1	11.0	30
141	141	155	120	120	130	130	31
Ea-DQI-F-Hf	Ea-DQI-F-Hf	Ea-QI-Hf	Ea-QI-F	Ea-QI-F	Ea-QI-F	Ea-QI-F	32
Ea-LI-Hf	Ea-LI-Hf	Ea-LI-Hf	Ea-LI-Tfq	Ea-LI-Tfq	Ea-LI-Tfq	Ea-LI-Tfq	33
195/60 R 15	205/60 ZR 15	195/70 R 14 91 H	145 R 13 S	165/70 R 13 S	165/70 R 13 S	185/55 R 15 V	34
Sb-Sb-Sv-Br	Sb-Sb-Sv-ABS	Sb-Sb-Sv-Br	Sb-Tb-Sv-Br	Sb-Tb-Sv-Br	Sb-Tb-Sv-Br	Sb-Sb-Sv-Br	35

Country		France				
Vehicle make Model		Peugeot (Continued) 405 GRI	405 GRDT	405 MI 16 X 4	605 SRi	605 SV 24
1	Body style	4 Li 5	4 Li 5	4 Li 5	4 Li 5	4 Li 5
2	Net engine horsepower kW (HP) at engine speed min^{-1}	65 (89) 6400	66 (90) 4300	108 (147) 6400	89 (121) 5600	147 (200) 6000
3	Max. torque Nm at engine speed min^{-1}	128 3000	180 2100	166 5000	170 4000	260 3600
4	Maximum speed km/h	178	180	205	199	235
5	Acceleration from 0 to 100 km/h s	12.5	12.2	9.8	10.7	8.3
6	Curb weight kg	1070	1140	1240	1325	1460
7	Gross vehicle weight kg	1550	1620	1690	1825	1960
8	Power-to-weight ratio kg/kW	16.5	17.3	11.5	14.9	9.9
9	Fuel consumption *l* / 100 km	5.8/7.8/9.8	4.7/6.2/7.5	7.6/9.3/12.0	6.8/8.8/12.8	8.2/10.2/15.9
10	Type of fuel	Premium unleaded	Diesel	Premium unleaded	Premium unleaded	Premium unleaded
11	Fuel tank capacity *l*	70	70	70	80	80
12	Engine swept volume cm^3	1580	1769	1905	1998	2975
13	Bore/stroke mm	83.0/73.0	80.0/88.0	83.0/88.0	86.0/86.0	93.0/73.0
14	Compression ratio	8.95	22.5	9.7	8.8	9.4
15	Specific power output kW / *l*	41.1	37.3	56.7	44.5	49.4
16	Engine type	q 4 R	q 4 R	q 4 R	q 4 R	q 6 V, 4 Ve
17	Fuel management	Ze	EP/V, AT	Motronic	Motronic	El
18	Alternator V/A	14/54	14/54	14/55	14/80	14/80
19	Battery V/Ah	12/42	12/67	12/42	12/75	12/75
20	Drive configuration	v-v	v-v	v-v+h	v-v	v-v
21	Transmission 1st/2nd gear ratios 3rd/4th gear 5th gear	3.455/1.850 1.280/0.969 0.757	3.455/1.850 1.148/0.829 0.658	3.455/1.850 1.280/0.969 0.800	3.455/1.850 1.360/1.069 0.800	3.418/1.834 1.250/0.969 0.767
22	Final-drive ratio	4.188	4.063	4.429	4.429	4.067
23	Gearshift	5 K	5 K	5 K	5 K (4 A)	5 K
24	Cooling	W 6.6	W 6.6	W 7.2	W 7.3	W 9.5
25	Vehicle length mm	4408	4408	4408	4721	4721
26	Vehicle width mm	1716	1716	1716	1799	1799
27	Vehicle height mm	1406	1406	1406	1426	1426
28	Wheelbase mm	2669	2669	2669	2800	2800
29	Track, front/rear mm	1450/1443	1450/1443	1440/1443	1528/1525	1537/1535
30	Turning circle diameter m	11.0	11.0	11.0	12.0	12.0
31	Ground clearance mm	125	125	125	100	100
32	Wheel suspension, front	Ea-DQl-F	Ea-DQl-F	Ea-DQl-F	Ea-DQl-F	Ea-DQl-F
33	Wheel suspension, rear	Ea-Ll-Tfq	Ea-Ll-Tfq	Ea-Ll-Tfq	Ea-DQu-Sf	Ea-DQu-Sf
34	Tires	175/70 R 14 T	185/65 R 14 T	195/55 R 15 V	195/65 R 15 H	205/55 ZR 16
35	Braking system	Sb-Tb-Sv-Br	Sb-Tb-Sv-Br	Sb-Sb-Br-ABS	Sb-Sb-Sv-ABS	Sb-Sb-Sv-ABS

See pp. 784/785 for abbreviations and explanations.

Renault

Clio RT 1.2	Clio RV 1.9 D	R 19 GTR 1.4	R 19 16V	R 21 GTS	R 21 GTD Nevada	R 25 TI	
3/5 Li 5	3/5 Li 5	3/5 Li 5	3/5 Li 5	4 Li 5	5 Ko Li 5	4 Li 5	1
40 (55) 6000	47 (64) 4500	43 (58) 4750	99 (135) 6500	66 (90) 5250	53 (72) 4500	99 (134) 6000	2
83 3500	118 2250	100 3000	158 4250	135 4000	137 2250	174 4300	3
155	161	161	210	185	164	203	4
16.0	14.8	14.8	8.5	10.7	16.1	9.9	5
825/835	915/925	925/945	1060	1010	1155/1170	1288	6
1265/1275	1350/1360	1375/1395	1505	1495	1715/1780	1740	7
20.6	19.5	21.5	10.7	15.3	21.8	13.0	8
4.7/6.3/7.3	4.1/5.7/6.6	5.3/6.9/8.5	6.3/7.6/10.6	5.9/7.5/10.5	4.9/6.6/7.4	6.8/8.5/12.6	9
Regular unleaded	Diesel	Regular unleaded	Premium unleaded	Premium unleaded	Diesel	Premium unleaded	10
43	43	55	55	66	66	72	11
1171	1870	1390	1764	1721	2068	1995	12
75.8/64.9	80.0/93.0	75.8/77.0	82.0/83.5	81.0/83.5	86.0/89.0	88.0/82.0	13
9.25	23.5	9.0	10.0	9.5	21.5	9.3	14
34.2	25.1	30.9	56.1	38.3	25.6	49.6	15
q 4 R	q 4 R	q 4 R	q 4 R, 4 Ve	q 4 R	q 4 R	lä 4 R, 3 Ve	16
El	EP/V	Ze	El	El	EP/V	El	17
14/60	14/70	14/60	14/70	14/60	14/60	14/60	18
12/40	12/70	12/40	12/50	12/50	12/65	12/50	19
v-v	v-v	v-v	v-v	v-v	v-v	v-v	20
3.091/1.864 1.321/0.967 0.795	3.727/2.048 1.321/0.967 0.795	3.727/2.048 1.321/0.967 0.795	3.091/1.842 1.320/0.967 0.795	3.091/1.864 1.321/0.967 0.756	4.091/2.176 1.409/1.030 0.861	4.091/2.176 1.536/1.162 0.930	21
4.214	3.294	3.867	4.067	4.067	3.222	3.556	22
5 K	5 K	5 K	5 K	5 K (4 A)	5 K	5 K	23
W 6.7	W 7.4	W 6.7	W 7.3	W 5.6	W 7.5	W 7.3	24
3709	3709	4155	4155	4528	4693	4713	25
1625	1625	1694	1694	1726	1726	1806	26
1395	1395	1416	1416	1514	1450	1415	27
2472	2472	2545	2545	2659	2809	2723	28
1362/1336	1362/1336	1418/1417	1418/1414	1454/1408	1454/1408	1502/1474	29
10.6	10.6	11.0	11.0	11.6	11.6	12.0	30
120	120	120	120	120	120	120	31
Ea-DQl-F	Ea-DQl-F	Ea-DQl-F	Ea-DQl-F	Ea-DQl-F	Ea-DQl-F	Ea-DQl-Ql-Sf	32
Ea-Ll-Tfq	Ea-Ll-Tfq	Ea-Ll-Tfq	Ea-Ll-Tfq	Ea-Ll-Tfq	Ea-Ll-Tfq	Ea-Ll-Ql-Sf	33
155/70 R 13 S	155/70 R 13 T	165/70 R 13 T	195/50 R 15 V	175/70 R 13 T	175/70 R 13 T	195/60 R 15 V	34
Sb-Tb-Sv-Br	Sb-Tb-Sv-Br	Sb-Tb-Sv-Br	Sb-Sb-Sv-Br	Sb-Tb-Sv-Br	Sb-Tb-Sv-Br	Sb-Sb-Sv-Br	35

Country			France			Great Britain 2)	
	Vehicle make Model		Renault (Continued) R 25 TX V6	Espace GTX	Alpine A 610	Bentley Turbo R (Cat.)	Daimler 4.0 (Cat.)
1	Body style		4 Li 5	5 KoLi 5–7	2 Co 2 + 2	4 Li 5	4 Li 5
2	Net engine horsepower at engine speed	kW (HP) min^{-1}	110 (150) 5400	79 (107) 5000	184 (250) 5750	235 (320) 4300	163 (222) 5250
3	Max. torque at engine speed	Nm min^{-1}	225 2500	170 3500	350 2900	658 2250	369 3600
4	Maximum speed	km/h	208	175	265	217	222
5	Acceleration from 0 to 100 km/h	s	9.3	12.9	5.9	7.0	8.1
6	Curb weight	kg	1308	1282	1420	2410	1800
7	Gross vehicle weight	kg	1800	2070	1740	2860	2245
8	Power-to-weight ratio	kg/kW	11.9	16.2	7.7	10.3	11.0
9	Fuel consumption	*l* / 100 km	7.4/9.3/14.5	7.5/9.7/11.8	7.3/9.2/14.7	13.5/17.3/24.8	8.0/9.8/16.3
10	Type of fuel		Premium unleaded	Regular unleaded	Premium unleaded	Premium unleaded	Premium unleaded
11	Fuel tank capacity	*l*	72	77	80	108	87
12	Engine swept volume	cm^3	2849	2165	2975	6750	3980
13	Bore/stroke	mm	91.0/73.0	88.0/89.0	93.0/73.0	104.1/99.1	91.0/102.0
14	Compression ratio		9.5	9.2	7.6	8.0	9.5
15	Specific power output	kW / *l*	38.6	36.5	61.8	34.8	41.0
16	Engine type		lä 6 V	lä 4 R	lä 6 V	lä 8 V	lä 6 R, 4 Ve
17	Fuel management		El	El	El, AT	Motronic, AT	El
18	Alternator	V/A	14/90	14/60	14/90	14/108	14/90
19	Battery	V/Ah	12/50	12/50	12/50	12/68	12/68
20	Drive configuration		v-v	v-v	h-h	v-h	v-h
21	Transmission ratios	1st/2nd gear 3rd/4th gear 5th gear	3.364/2.059 1.381/0.964 0.756	4.091/2.176 1.409/1.030 0.861	3.364/2.059 1.381/0.964 0.756	2.48/1.48 1.00	3.55/2.04 1.39/1.00 0.76
22	Final-drive ratio		3.889	3.778	3.444	2.69	3.58
23	Gearshift		5 K (4 A)	5 K	5 K	3 A M	5 K (4 A)
24	Cooling		W 9.5	W 8.4	W 12	W 18	W 12.3
25	Vehicle length	mm	4713	4429	4415	5270	4990
26	Vehicle width	mm	1806	1795	1760	1885	1795
27	Vehicle height	mm	1415	1707	1190	1485	1360
28	Wheelbase	mm	2723	2580	2339	3060	2870
29	Track, front/rear	mm	1502/1474	1517/1508	1505/1470	1550/1550	1500/1500
30	Turning circle diameter	m	12.0	12.4	11.9	13.1	12.4
31	Ground clearance	mm	120	150	125	130	130
32	Wheel suspension, front		Ea-DQl-Ql-Sf	Ea-DQl-Ql-Sf	Ea-DQl-Sf	Ea-DQl-Sf	Ea-DQl-Sf
33	Wheel suspension, rear		Ea-Ll-Ql-Sf	Sa-Ll-Sf	Ea-DQl-Sf	Ea-Sl-Sf	Ea-DQl-Sf
34	Tires		195/60 R 15 V	195/65 R 14 89 T	1)	255/65 VR 15	225/65 VR 15
35	Braking system		Sb-Sb-Sv-ABS	Sb-Tb-Sv-Br	Sb-Sb-Sv-ABS	Sb-Sb-Sv-ABS	Sb-Sb-Sv-ABS

See pp. 784/785 for abbreviations and explanations.

1) Front 205/45 ZR 16, rear 245/45 ZR 16.

Jaguar XJ-S V12 Coupé (Cat.)	**Rolls Royce** Silver Spirit II (Cat.)	**Rover** Mini Cooper (Cat.)	100 1.1 S (Cat.)	214 GSi 16V (Cat.)	416 GTi 16V (Cat.)	827 Vitesse 24V (Cat.)	
2 Co 4	4 Li 5	2 Li 4	3/5 Li 5	3/5 Li 5	4 Li 5	4 Li 5	1
209 (284) 5550	162 (220) 4200	45 (61) 5500	44 (60) 5900	66 (90) 6250	90 (122) 6800	124 (169) 5900	2
415 2800	460 1500	91 3000	90 3500	122 4000	140 5700	225 4500	3
237	204	148	152	167	196	212	4
							5
8.2	10.0	12.1	14.8	12.6	9.5	8.8	
1825	2350	695	825/840	1020/1070	1100	1400	6
2175	2800	1000	1290	1580	1570	1930	7
8.7	14.5	15.4	18.8	15.5	12.2	11.3	8
11.0/13.4/19.9	13.1/16.1/24.6	5.7/7.3/7.6	4.7/6.3/7.3	5.4/6.9/9.2	6.4/8.4/10.0	7.5/8.6/12.8	9
Premium unleaded	Premium unleaded	Premium unleaded	Premium unleaded	Premium unleaded	Premium unleaded	Premium unleaded	10
91	108	34	35.5	55	55	68	11
5343	6750	1275	1113	1396	1590	2675	12
90.0/70.0	104.1/99.1	70.6/81.3	75.0/63.0	75.0/79.0	75.0/90.0	87.0/75.0	13
11.5	8.0	9.75	9.75	9.5	9.5	9.0	14
39.2	24.0	35.3	39.5	47.3	56.6	46.4	15
lä 12 V	lä 8 V	q 4 R	q 4 R	q 4 R, 4 Ve	q 4 R, 4 Ve	q 6 V, 4 Ve	16
El	Motronic	El	Carburetor	Ze	El	El	17
14/60	14/108	14/34	14/55	14/65	14/60	14/65	18
12/68	12/68	12/30	12/35	12/45	12/47	12/63	19
v-h	v-h	v-v	v-v	v-v	v-v	v-v	20
2.5/1.5 1.0	2.48/1.48 1.00	3.647/2.185 1.425/1.000	3.417/1.800 1.138/0.810	3.417/1.947 1.333/1.054 0.854	3.250/1.944 1.346/1.033 0.848	2.923/1.789 1.222/0.909 0.750	21
2.88	2.69	3.11	4.068	3.937	4.25	4.20	22
3 A M	3 A M	4 K	4 K (5 K)	5 K	5 K (4 A)	5 K (4 A)	23
W 21.3	W 18	W 3.6	W 5.0	W 5.0	W 5.4	W 8.0	24
4765	5270	3050	3520	4220	4370	4810	25
1795	1885	1410	1560	1680	1680	1730	26
1260	1485	1350	1375	1400	1400	1400	27
2590	3060	2035	2270	2550	2550	2670	28
1490/1505	1535/1535	1205/1170	1340/1295	1475/1470	1475/1470	1490/1450	29
13.7	13.1	8.6	9.8	10.2	10.2	11.1	30
140	135	150	120	150	150	145	31
Ea-DQl-Sf	Ea-DQl-Sf	Ea-Ql-Gf	Ea-DQl-Hf	Ea-Ql-F	Ea-Ql-F	Ea-Ql-Sf	32
Ea-Ll-Ql-Sf	Ea-Sl-Sf	Ea-Ll-Gf	Ea-Ll-Hf	Ea-Ls-Ql-Sf	Fa-Ls-Ql-Sf	Ea-Ql-Ll-Sf	33
235/60 VR 15	235/70 VR 15	145/70 SR 12	155/65 R 13	185/60 HR 14	185/60 HR 14	195/65 VR 15	34
Sb-Sb-Sv-Br	Sb-Sb-Sv-ABS	Sb-Tb-Sv	Sb-Tb-Sv	Sb-Sb-Sv	Sb-Sb-Sv	Sb-Sb-Sv	35

2) Ford: See Ford models for Germany.

Vauxhall: See corresponding Opel models (Germany): Nova → Corsa. Cavalier → Vectra. Carlton → Omega

Country		Italy				
Vehicle make Model		**Alfa Romeo** Alfa 33 Boxer 16V	 Alfa 75 1.8 IE	 Alfa 164 Quadrifoglio	 Spider 2.0	 Coupé SZ
1 Body style		5 Li 5	4 Li 5	4 Li 5	2 Ca 2	2 Co 2
2 Net engine horsepower at engine speed	kW (HP) min^{-1}	97 (132) 6500	88 (120) 5800	147 (200) 5800	88 (120) 5800	154 (210) 6200
3 Max. torque at engine speed	Nm min^{-1}	155 4600	152 5000	274 4400	161 4200	245 4500
4 Maximum speed	km/h	203	190	237	190	245
5 Acceleration from 0 to 100 km/h	s	8.4	11.0	7.7	9.4	7.0
6 Curb weight	kg	1000	1110	1430	1110	1260
7 Gross vehicle weight	kg	1425	1525	1855	1280	1430
8 Power-to-weight ratio	kg/kW	10.3	12.6	9.7	12.6	8.2
9 Fuel consumption	l / 100 km	5.9/7.9/10.5	6.9/9.1/10.5	7.3/9.3/13.0	6.6/8.7/10.6	7.2/9.2/13.2
10 Type of fuel		Premium unleaded	Premium unleaded	Premium unleaded	Premium unleaded	Premium unleaded
11 Fuel tank capacity	l	50	49	70	46	68
12 Engine swept volume	cm^3	1712	1779	2959	1962	2959
13 Bore/stroke	mm	87.0/72.0	78.0/82.0	93.0/72.6	84.0/88.5	93.0/72.6
14 Compression ratio		10.0	9.0	10.0	10.0	10.0
15 Specific power output	kW / l	56.7	49.5	49.7	44.9	52.0
16 Engine type		4 Bx, 4 Ve	lä 4 R	q 6 V	lä 4 R	lä 6 V
17 Fuel management		Motronic	Motronic	Motronic	Motronic	Motronic
18 Alternator	V/A	14/65	14/65	14/85	14/55	14/70
19 Battery	V/Ah	12/50	12/55	12/60	12/50	12/70
20 Drive configuration		v-v	v-h	v-v	v-h	v-h
21 Transmission ratios	1st/2nd gear 3rd/4th gear 5th gear	3.143/1.864 1.323/1.027 0.854	2.875/1.720 1.226/0.946 0.780	3.500/2.176 1.523/1.156 0.916	3.304/1.988 1.355/1.000 0.791	2.875/1.720 1.226/0.946 0.780
22 Final-drive ratio		3.89	4.3	3.411	4.1	3.909
23 Gearshift		5 K	5 K	5 K	5 K	5 K
24 Cooling		W 7.8	W 8.0	W 9.5	W 7.5	W 10.0
25 Vehicle length	mm	4075	4330	4555	4258	4060
26 Vehicle width	mm	1614	1630	1760	1630	1730
27 Vehicle height	mm	1350	1400	1400	1290	1310
28 Wheelbase	mm	2475	2510	2660	2250	2510
29 Track, front/rear	mm	1366/1365	1368/1358	1515/1488	1324/1274	1465/1425
30 Turning circle diameter	m	10.4	10.9	10.8	10.7	10.1
31 Ground clearance	mm	120	120	140	125	120
32 Wheel suspension, front		Ea-Ql-F	Ea-DQl-Ql-Tfl	Ea-DQl-F	Ea-DQl-Ql-Sf	Ea-DQl-Ql-Sf
33 Wheel suspension, rear		Sa-Wa-P-Sf	De-Sl-Wa-Sf	Ea-DQu-F	Sa-Ql-Ll-Sf	De-Sl-Wa-Sf
34 Tires		185/60 R 14 H	185/70 HR 13	195/65 VR 15	195/60 R 13	[1]
35 Braking system		Sb-Tb-Sv-Br	Sb-Sb-Sv-Br	Sb-Sb-Sv-ABS	Sb-Sb-Sv-Br	Sb-Sb-Sv-Br

See pp. 784/785 for abbreviations and explanations.

[1]) Front 205/55 ZR 16, rear 225/50 ZR 16.

Ferrari	**Fiat**						
F 40	Panda 750 L	Uno 1.0 i.e.	Uno Turbo i.e.	Tipo 1.4 i.e.	Tipo 2.0 i.e. Granturismo	Tipo T. ds	
2 Co 2	3 Li 5	3/5 Li 5	3 Li 5	5 Li 5	5 Li 5	5 Li 5	1
351 (478) 7000	25 (34) 5250	33 (45) 5250	74 (100) 6000	51 (70) 6000	83 (113) 5750	66 (90) 4100	2
577 4000	57 3000	74 3250	142 3500	106 3000	156 3300	186 2400	3
324	125	145	192	161	190	176	4
4.1	23.0	17.7	8.9	13.0	10.5	12.0	5
1235	700	755	940	990	1150	1160	6
1400	1150	1220	1360	1490	1650	1660	7
3.5	28.0	22.9	12.7	19.4	13.9	17.6	8
8.6/10.3/18.4	5.0/–/6.2	4.6/6.4/6.7	6.0/7.8/9.2	5.3/7.2/8.5	7.0/8.7/11.0	4.9/6.6/6.2	9
Premium	Premium unleaded	Premium unleaded	Premium unleaded	Premium unleaded	Premium unleaded	Diesel	10
2 x 60	40	40	40	48	48	48	11
2936	770	999	1301	1372	1995	1929	12
82.0/69.5	65.0/58.0	70.0/64.9	80.5/63.9	80.5/67.4	84.0/90.0	82.6/90.0	13
7.7	9.4	9.0	7.7	9.2	9.5	19.2	14
119.7	32.5	33.0	56.9	37.2	41.6	34.2	15
lä 8 V, 4 Ve	q 4 R	q 4 R	q 4 R	q 4 R	q 4 R	q 4 R	16
El, AT	Ecotronic	Mono-Jetronic	LU-Jetron., AT	Mono-Jetronic	El	EP/V, AT	17
14/105	14/45	14/45	14/65	14/55	14/65	14/65	18
12/60	12/30	12/32	12/45	12/40	12/45	12/65	19
Mm-h	v-v	v-v	v-v	v-v	v-v	v-v	20
2.769/1.722 1.227/0.963 0.767	3.909/2.056 1.344/0.978	3.909/2.056 1.344/0.978 0.780	3.909/2.267 1.440/1.029 0.875	3.909/2.267 1.469/1.043 0.849	3.545/2.267 1.541/1.156 0.891	3.545/2.267 1.541/1.156 0.794	21
2.727	3.727	3.733	3.562	3.765	3.563	3.052	22
5 K	4 K	5 K	5 K	5 K	5 K	5 K	23
W 17	W 5.2	W 4.6	W 7.7	W 6.5	W 9.0	W 8.8	24
4360	3408	3689	3689	3958	3958	3958	25
1970	1494	1558	1558	1700	1700	1700	26
1125	1420	1430	1430	1445	1430	1445	27
2450	2159	2362	2362	2540	2540	2540	28
1595/1605	1263/1265	1346/1300	1353/1309	1418/1415	1429/1415	1418/1415	29
11.6	10.5	10.5	10.6	11.4	11.4	11.4	30
125	130	150	150	150	150	150	31
Ea-DQl-Sf	Ea-Ql-F	Ea-Ql-F	Ea-Ql-F	Ea-DQl-F	Ea-DQl-F	Ea-DQl-F	32
Ea-Ql-Sf	Om-Ll-Sf	Ea-Vla-Sf	Ea-Vla-Sf	Ea-Ll-Sf	Ea-Ll-Sf	Ea-Ll-Sf	33
[2]	135 R 13	155/70 R 13 S	175/60 R 13 H	165/70 R 13 76 S	185/60 R 14 80 H	175/65 R 14 80 T	34
Sb-Sb	Sb-Tb-Br	Sb-Tb-Sv-Br	Sb-Sb-Sv-Br	Sb-Tb-Sv	Sb-Sb-Sv-ABS	Sb-Tb-Sv	35

[2] Front 245/40 ZR 17, rear 335/35 ZR 17.

Country		Italy				
Vehicle make		Fiat (Continued)				Lamborghini
Model		Tempra 1.6 i.e. SX	Tempra 2.0 i.e. SX	Croma 2.0 i.e. turbo	Croma 2.5 TD	Diablo
1 Body style		4 Li 5	4 Li 5	5 Li 5	5 Li 5	2 Co 2
2 Net engine horsepower at engine speed	kW (HP) min⁻¹	57 (78) 6000	83 (113) 5750	110 (150) 5500	85 (115) 3900	362 (492) 7000
3 Max. torque at engine speed	Nm min⁻¹	124 3000	156 3300	247 2750	245 2200	580 520
4 Maximum speed	km/h	170	195	210	195	325
5 Acceleration from 0 to 100 km/h	s	13.8	10.1	7.9	11.0	4.1
6 Curb weight	kg	1080	1190	1238	1303	1575
7 Gross vehicle weight	kg	1580	1690	1775	1840	1840
8 Power-to-weight ratio	kg/kW	18.9	14.3	11.6	15.3	4.4
9 Fuel consumption	l / 100 km	6.2/7.8/10.9	6.8/8.4/11.4	6.4/8.4/10.2	5.3/7.0/8.6	13.3/15.2/20.9
10 Type of fuel		Premium unleaded	Premium unleaded	Premium unleaded	Diesel	Premium unleaded
11 Fuel tank capacity	l	65	65	70	70	100
12 Engine swept volume	cm^3	1581	1995	1995	2500	5703
13 Bore/stroke	mm	86.4/67.4	84.0/90.0	84.0/90.0	93.0/92.0	87.0/80.0
14 Compression ratio		9.2	9.5	8.0	21.0	10.0
15 Specific power output	kW / l	36.0	41.6	55.1	34.0	63.5
16 Engine type		q 4 R	q 4 R	q 4 R	q 4 R	lä 12 V, 4 Ve
17 Fuel management		Mono-Jetronic	EI	LU-Jetron., AT	EP/V, AT	EI
18 Alternator	V/A	14/55	14/65	14/85	14/85	14/85
19 Battery	V/Ah	12/40	12/45	12/70	12/70	12/55
20 Drive configuration		v-v	v-v	v-v	v-v	Mm-h
21 Transmission ratios	1st/2nd gear 3rd/4th gear 5th gear	3.909/2.267 1.542/1.156 0.968	3.545/2.267 1.542/1.156 0.875	3.750/2.176 1.519/1.132 0.929	3.500/2.176 1.379/0.975 0.723	2.31/1.52 1.12/0.88 0.68
22 Final-drive ratio		3.765	3.563	2.944	3.421	3.83
23 Gearshift		5 K	5 K	5 K	5 K (4 A)	5 K
24 Cooling		W 5.5	W 6.9	W 9.6	W 9.0	W 15
25 Vehicle length	mm	4354	4354	4520	4520	4460
26 Vehicle width	mm	1695	1695	1760	1760	2040
27 Vehicle height	mm	1445	1445	1435	1435	1105
28 Wheelbase	mm	2540	2540	2660	2660	2650
29 Track, front/rear	mm	1435/1415	1435/1415	1496/1488	1490/1482	1540/1640
30 Turning circle diameter	m	11.3	11.4	11.7	11.7	12.0
31 Ground clearance	mm	150	150	140	140	140
32 Wheel suspension, front		Ea-DQl-F	Ea-DQl-F	Ea-DQl-F	Ea-DQl-F	Ea-DQl-Sf
33 Wheel suspension, rear		Ea-Ll-Sf	Ea-Ll-Sf	Ea-Ql-F	Ea-Ql-F	Ea-DQl-Sf
34 Tires		175/65 R 14 T	185/60 R 14 H	195/60 R 14 V	185/70 R 14 H	1)
35 Braking system		Sb-Tb-Sv	Sb-Sb-Sv	Sb-Sb-Sv-ABS	Sb-Sb-Sv	Sb-Sb-Sv

See pp. 784/785 for abbreviations and explanations.

1) Front 245/40 ZR 17, rear 335/35 ZR 17.

Lancia Y 10 fire 1.1 i.e.	Y 10 GT i.e.	Delta 1600 GT i.e.	Dedra 2.0 i.e.	Thema V6	Thema 8.32	Maserati 228	
3 Li 5	3 Li 5	5 Li 5	4 Li 5	4 Li 5	4 Li 5	2 Co 5	1
37 (50) 5250	53 (72) 5750	66 (90) 6250	83 (113) 5750	108 (147) 5000	151 (205) 6750	184 (250) 6000	2
84 3000	100 3200	123 4250	156 3300	225 3500	263 5000	373 3500	3
150	170	175	195	205	234	235	4
15.8	12.0	11.3	10.8	8.4	7.2	5.8	5
800	855	1025	1218	1250	1410	1240	6
1200	1255	1475	1710	1750	1890	1800	7
21.6	16.1	15.5	14.7	11.6	9.3	6.7	8
4.7/6.2/7.3	5.6/7.2/7.9	6.4/8.4/10.1	6.8/8.4/11.4	7.4/9.4/14.0	8.9/11.0/16.8	9.2/11.8/18.2	9
Premium unleaded	Premium unleaded	Premium unleaded	Premium unleaded	Premium unleaded	Premium unleaded	Premium	10
43	43	55	63	70	70	82	11
1108	1297	1585	1995	2849	2927	2790	12
70.0/72.0	76.0/71.5	84.0/71.5	84.0/90.0	91.0/73.0	81.0/71.0	94.0/67.0	13
9.6	9.5	9.5	9.5	9.5	9.5	7.7	14
33.4	40.9	41.6	41.6	37.9	51.6	66.0	15
q 4 R	q 4 R	q 4 R	q 4 R	q 6 V	q 8 V, 4 Ve	lä 6 V, 3 Ve	16
Mono-Jetronic	L-Jetronic	Ze	El	LH-Jetronic	KE-Jetronic	El. 2 AT	17
14/55	14/55	14/65	14/65	14/85	14/85	14/65	18
12/40	12/40	12/40	12/45	12/60	12/60	12/60	19
v-v	v-v	v-v	v-v	v-v	v-v	v-h	20
3.909/2.056 1.344/0.978 0.836	3.909/2.056 1.344/0.978 0.836	3.545/2.267 1.541/1.156 0.967	3.545/2.267 1.541/1.156 0.875	3.500/2.176 1.519/1.132 0.929	3.500/2.176 1.519/1.156 0.916	3.42/1.94 1.39/1.00 0.79	21
3.733	3.867	3.562	3.563	2.944	3.563	3.31	22
5 K (A)	5 K	5 K	5 K	5 K (3 A)	5 K	5 K (4 A)	23
W 4.6	W 5.6	W 7.5	W 6.9	W 6.0	W 9.8	W 12	24
3392	3392	3895	4340	4590	4590	4460	25
1507	1507	1620	1700	1758	1758	1865	26
1440	1440	1355	1417	1385	1420	1330	27
2160	2160	2475	2540	2660	2660	2600	28
1280/1280	1280/1280	1400/1400	1436/1417	1495/1490	1495/1490	1540/1550	29
10.1	10.1	11.6	11.4	11.7	12.1	11.7	30
160	160	145	150	140	140	135	31
Ea-Ql-F	Ea-Ql-F	Ea-DQl-F	Ea-Ql-F	Ea-Ql-F	Ea-Ql-F	Ea-Ql-F	32
Om-Ll-Sf	OM-Ll-Sf	Ea-DQl-Ll-F	Ea-Ll-Sf	Ea-Ql-Ll-F	Ea-Ql-Ll-F	Ea-Sl-Sf	33
135 R 13 69 S	155/70 R 13 72 S	165/65 R 14 78 T	185/60 R 14 82 H	195/60 VR 14	205/55 VR 15	[2]	34
Sb-Tb-Sv	Sb-Tb-Sv	Sb-Sb-Sv	Sb-Sb-Sv	Sb-Sb-Sv-ABS	Sb-Sb-Sv-ABS	Sb-Sb-Sv	35

[2]) Front 205/55 VR 15, rear 225/50 VR 15.

Country		Japan				
Vehicle make Model		Honda Civic 1.5 i	CRX 1.6 i–16 VT	Concerto 1.6 i	Accord 2.2 i	Prelude 2.0 i –16
1 Body style		4 Li 5	3 Li 4	5 Li 5	4 Li 5	2 Co 2+2
2 Net engine horsepower at engine speed	kW (HP) min^{-1}	66 (90) 6300	110 (150) 7600	82 (112) 6300	110 (150) 5900	103 (140) 6000
3 Max. torque at engine speed	Nm min^{-1}	112 4500	144 7100	137 5200	198 5000	175 4500
4 Maximum speed	km/h	170	222	190	212	205
5 Acceleration from 0 to 100 km/h	s	10.1	8.1	10.6	8.4	8.6
6 Curb weight	kg	945	1010	1085	1305	1155
7 Gross vehicle weight	kg	1400	1470	1530	1840	1620
8 Power-to-weight ratio	kg/kW	14.3	9.2	13.2	11.9	11.2
9 Fuel consumption	l / 100 km	5.6/7.6/8.5	5.8/7.2/8.8	7.1/9.1/9.8	6.8/8.5/11.7	7.0/8.8/11.2
10 Type of fuel		Regular unleaded	Premium unleaded	Regular unleaded	Premium unleaded	Regular unleaded
11 Fuel tank capacity	l	45	45	55	65	60
12 Engine swept volume	cm^3	1493	1595	1590	2156	1958
13 Bore/stroke	mm	75.0/79.0	81.0/77.4	75.0/90.0	85.0/95.0	81.0/95.0
14 Compression ratio		9.2	10.2	9.1	9.8	9.4
15 Specific power output	kW / l	44.2	69.0	51.6	51.0	52.6
16 Engine type		q 4 R	q 4 R, 4 Ve	q 4 R, 4 Ve	q 4 R, 4 Ve	q 4 R, 4 Ve
17 Fuel management		El	El	El	El	El
18 Alternator	V/A	14/70	14/70	14/60	14/70	14/70
19 Battery	V/Ah	12/47	12/47	12/47	12/65	12/50
20 Drive configuration		v-v	v-v	v-v	v-v	v-v
21 Transmission ratios	1st/2nd gear 3rd/4th gear 5th gear	3.250/1.894 1.259/0.937 0.771	3.250/2.052 1.416/1.103 0.870	3.250/1.894 1.259/0.937 0.771	3.307/1.809 1.230/0.933 0.757	3.166/1.857 1.259/0.935 0.794
22 Final-drive ratio		4.250	4.133	4.250	4.266	4.062
23 Gearshift		5 K (4 A)	5 K	5 K (4 A)	5 K (4 A)	5 K (4 A)
24 Cooling		W 4.7	W 4.7	W 5.5	W 7.4	W 7.1
25 Vehicle length	mm	4230	3755	4265	4685	4510
26 Vehicle width	mm	1690	1675	1690	1695	1695
27 Vehicle height	mm	1360	1270	1395	1390	1295
28 Wheelbase	mm	2500	2300	2550	2720	2565
29 Track, front/rear	mm	1450/1455	1440/1445	1475/1470	1475/1480	1480/1470
30 Turning circle diameter	m	10.4	10.4	10.3	11.8	11.4
31 Ground clearance	mm	160	160	160	160	145
32 Wheel suspension, front		Ea-DQl-Ql-Sf	Ea-DQl-Ql-Sf	Ea-DQl-Ql-Sf	Ea-DQl-Ql-Sf	Ea-Ql-Sf
33 Wheel suspension, rear		Ea-Ls-Ql-Sf	Ea-Ls-Ql-Sf	Ea-Ls-Ql-Sf	Ea-Ll-Ql-Sf	Ea-Ql-Sf
34 Tires		175/70 R 13	195/60 R 14 85 V	175/65 R 14 82 H	195/60 R 15	195/60 R 14 85 V
35 Braking system		Sb-Tb-Sv-Br	Sb-Sb-Sv-Br	Sb-Sb-Sv-ABS	Sb-Sb-Sv-ABS	Sb-Sb-Sv-ABS

See pp. 784/785 for abbreviations and explanations.

Legend	Mazda 121 LX	323 1.6 i GLX	626 2.2 l GLX 4WD	929 3.0 i GLX V6	MX-5	RX-7	
4 Li 5	4 Li 5	3 Li 5	4 Li 5	4 Li 5	2 Ro 2	2 Co 2+2	1
151 (205) 5500	39 (53) 5500	62 (84) 5200	85 (115) 5000	123 (167) 5300	85 (115) 6500	147 (200) 6500	2
293 4400	97 2800	125 2500	180 3000	242 4000	135 5500	265 3500	3
226	150	172	181	205	195	240	4
8.1	13.7	11.2	11.2	10.2	8.8	6.7	5
1545	810	945	1285	1470	955	1315	6
2150	1300	1500	1750	2040	1190	1715	7
10.2	20.8	15.2	15.1	11.9	11.2	8.9	8
8.3/10.2/13.9	5.2/7.2/7.0	5.6/7.3/8.8	7.1/9.3/11.4	8.0/10.0/14.1	6.1/7.8/9.6	8.8/10.8/16.7	9
Premium unleaded	Regular unleaded	Regular unleaded	Regular unleaded	Premium unleaded	Regular unleaded	Premium unleaded	10
68	43	50	60	75	45	72	11
3206	1324	1598	2184	2954	1598	2 x 654 [1])	12
90.0/84.0	71.0/83.6	78.0/83.6	86.0/94.0	90.0/77.4	78.0/83.6	–	13
9.6	9.4	9.3	8.6	9.2	9.4	9.1	14
47.1	29.5	38.8	38.9	41.2	53.2	56.2	15
lä 6 V, 4 Ve	q 4 R, 4 Ve	q 4 R	q 4 R, 3 Ve	lä 6 V, 3 Ve	lä 4 R, 4 Ve	2 km, AT	16
El	Ze	El	L-Jetronic	El	L-Jetronic	L-Jetronic	17
14/70	14/65	14/65	14/70	14/70	14/60	14/70	18
12/65	12/45	12/60	12/60	12/65	12/32	12/55	19
v-v	v-v	v-v	v-v+h	v-h	v-h	v-h	20
2.937/1.692 1.515/0.868 0.682	3.45/1.94 1.39/1.03 0.81	3.42/1.84 1.29/0.92 0.73	3.31/1.83 1.23/0.91 0.72	3.48/2.02 1.39/1.00 0.76	3.14/1.89 1.33/1.00 0.81	3.48/2.02 1.39/1.00 0.72	21
4.505	4.06	4.11	v 4.39. h 3.91	3.73	4.3	4.1	22
5 K (4 A)	5 K	5 K (4 A)	5 K	5 K (4 A)	5 K	5 K	23
W 8.8	W 5.0	W 5.0	W 7.5	W 9.4	W 6	W 8.7	24
4950	3810	3995	4535	4885	3975	4335	25
1810	1655	1675	1690	1725	1675	1690	26
1410	1470	1380	1410	1425	1230	1265	27
2910	2390	2450	2575	2710	2265	2430	28
1550/1540	1420/1400	1430/1435	1455/1465	1440/1450	1410/1430	1450/1440	29
11.4	10.0	10.4	11.6	11.8	9.8	10.6	30
155	150	150	150	170	115	150	31
Ea-DQl-Sf	Ea-Ql-F	Ea-DQl-F	Ea-DQl-F	Ea-Ql-F	Ea-DQl-Sf	Ea-DQl-F	32
Ea-Ql-Sf	Vla-F	Ea-Ql-Ll-F	Ea-Ql-Ll-F	Ea-Ql-Ll-F	Ea-DQl-Sf	Ea-Sl-Zl-F	33
205/65 ZR 15	165/70 R 13 74 R	175/70 R 13 82 H	185/70 HR 14	205/60 R 15 90 V	185/60 R 14 82 H	205/55 ZR 16	34
Sb-Sb-Sv-ABS	Sb-Tb-Sv-Br	Sb-Tb-Sv-Br	Sb-Sb-Sv-ABS	Sb-Sb-Sv-ABS	Sb-Sb-Sv-Br	Sb-Sb-Sv-ABS	35

[1]) Chamber volume, equivalent diisplacement 2615 cm^3.

Country			Japan				
	Vehicle make		Mitsubishi				
	Model		Colt 1500 GLX i	Lancer GLX Diesel	Space Wagon 2000 GLX i	Galant 2000 GTi–16V	Sigma V 6
1	Body style		3 Li 5	4 Li 5	5 Li 7	4 Li 5	4 Li 5
2	Net engine horsepower at engine speed	kW (HP) min^{-1}	66 (90) 6000	44 (60) 4500	74 (101) 5000	106 (144) 6500	130 (177) 5500
3	Max. torque at engine speed	Nm min^{-1}	126 3000	113 3000	157 4000	171 5000	251 3000
4	Maximum speed	km/h	170	148	170	205	220
5	Acceleration from 0 to 100 km/h	s	11.7	16.4	11.4	8.8	9.0
6	Curb weight	kg	945	1040	1155	1271	1468
7	Gross vehicle weight	kg	1465	1500	1750	1720	2070
8	Power-to-weight ratio	kg/kW	14.3	23.6	15.6	12.0	11.3
9	Fuel consumption	*l* / 100 km	5.5/7.5/8.5	4.6/6.6/6.5	6.9/9.5/11.1	6.4/8.0/11.0	7.8/9.4/13.6
10	Type of fuel		Premium unleaded	Diesel	Premium unleaded	Premium unleaded	Premium unleaded
11	Fuel tank capacity	*l*	50	50	50	60	72
12	Engine swept volume	cm^3	1468	1796	1997	1997	2972
13	Bore/stroke	mm	75.5/82.0	80.6/88.0	85.0/88.0	85.0/88.0	91.1/76.0
14	Compression ratio		9.2	22.2	9.0	9.8	10.0
15	Specific power output	kW / *l*	45.0	24.5	37.0	53.1	43.7
16	Engine type		q 4 R, 3 Ve	q 4 R	q 4 R	q 4 R	q 6 V
17	Fuel management		EI	EP/V	EI	EI	EI
18	Alternator	V/A	14/65	14/65	14/65	14/65	14/90
19	Battery	V/Ah	12/65	12/80	12/65	12/65	12/65
20	Drive configuration		v-v	v-v	v-v	v-v	v-v
21	Transmission ratios	1st/2nd gear 3rd/4th gear 5th gear	3.363/1.947 1.285/0.939 0.777	3.363/1.947 1.285/0.939 0.756	3.454/1.947 1.285/0.939 0.756	3.038/1.947 1.258/0.939 0.756	3.090/1.833 1.217/0.888 0.741
22	Final-drive ratio		4.021	3.752	4.018	4.592	4.153
23	Gearshift		5 K (4 A)	5 K (4 A)	5 K (3 A)	5 K	5 K (4 A)
24	Cooling		W 5.0	W 6.0	W 7.0	W 6.5	W 8.0
25	Vehicle length	mm	3950	4235	4295	4540	4750
26	Vehicle width	mm	1670	1670	1640	1695	1775
27	Vehicle height	mm	1380	1405	1525	1425	1435
28	Wheelbase	mm	2385	2455	2625	2600	2720
29	Track, front/rear	mm	1430/1430	1430/1430	1410/1375	1460/1450	1535/1530
30	Turning circle diameter	m	10.6	10.8	11.4	11.5	12.1
31	Ground clearance	mm	155	155	180	160	155
32	Wheel suspension, front		Ea-DQI-F	Ea-DQI-F	Ea-QI-F	Ea-DQI-F	Ea-DQI-F
33	Wheel suspension, rear		Vla-F	Vla-F	Ea-Ls-Sf	Vla-F	Ea-Ls-QI-Sf
34	Tires		175/70 R 13	175/70 R 13	185/70 R 13 82 S	!95/60 R 15	205/65 R 15
35	Braking system		Sb-Tb-Sv-Br	Sb-Tb-Sv-Br	Sb-Tb-Sv-Br	Sb-Sb-Sv-ABS	Sb-Sb-Sv-ABS

See pp. 784/785 for abbreviations and explanations.

Nissan Micra LX	Sunny SLX 1.6	Prairie Pro SLX 4x4	200 SX Turbo 16V	Primera 2.0 GT	Maxima	Subaru Legacy 2.2 GX 4WD	
3 Li 5	5 Li 5	5 KoLi 5–7	2 Co 2+2	4 Li 5	4 Li 5	4 Li 5	1
40 (54) 5200	66 (90) 6000	72 (98) 5200	124 (169) 6400	110 (150) 6400	125 (170) 5600	100 (136) 6000	2
93 3200	133 4000	150 2400	224 4000	181 4800	248 2800	189 4800	3
150	180	160	220	220	220	200	4
							5
14.5	10.7	14.0	7.5	8.4	8.7	9.0	
720	1037	1379	1220	1220	1359	1285	6
1135	1505	1920	1675	1685	1915	1870	7
18.0	15.7	19.2	9.8	11.1	10.9	12.9	8
5.3/8.0/7.0	5.4/7.2/8.6	7.3/9.6/11.1	7.2/9.2/11.0	6.2/8.1/10.6	7.2/9.0/13.3	7.5/9.4/13.1	9
Regular unleaded	Premium unleaded	Regular unleaded	Premium unleaded	Premium unleaded	Premium unleaded	Premium unleaded	10
40	50	60	60	60	70	60	11
1235	1597	1974	1809	1998	2960	2212	12
71.0/78.0	76.0/88.0	84.5/88.0	83.0/83.6	86.0/86.0	87.0/83.0	97.0/75.0	13
9.0	9.8	8.5	8.5	10.0	10.0	9.5	14
32.4	41.3	36.5	68.5	55.0	42.2	45.2	15
q 4 R	q 4 R, 4 Ve	q 4 R	lä 4 R, 4 Ve	q 4 R, 4 Ve	q 6 V	4 Bx. 4 Ve	16
Carburetor[1])	Carburetor[1])	EI	EI, AT	EI	EI	EI	17
14/50	14/50	14/70	14/80	14/80	14/90	14/70	18
12/45	12/44	12/60	12/55	12/48	12/55	12/52	19
v-v	v-v	v-v+h	v-h	v-v	v-v	v-v+h	20
3.41/1.96 1.26/0.92 0.72	3.06/1.83 1.21/0.90 0.76	3.71/2.10 1.34/0.95 0.74	3.59/2.06 1.36/1.00 0.82	3.06/1.83 1.21/0.93 0.76	3.29/1.85 1.27/0.95 0.80	3.55/2.11 1.45/1.09 0.87	21
3.81	4.17	4.47	3.92	4.18	3.65	3.90	22
5 K (3 A)	5 K	5 K	5 K (4 A)	5 K	5 K (4 A)	5 K (4 A)	23
W 4.0	W 5.0	W 9.0	W 7.0	W 7.0	W 9.0	W 7.0	24
3735	4145	4360	4535	4400	4780	4510	25
1560	1690	1690	1690	1700	1760	1390	26
1395	1395	1650	1290	1390	1405	1690	27
2300	2430	2595	2475	2550	2650	2580	28
1345/1335	1435/1420	1460/1430	1465/1465	1470/1460	1510/1490	1460/1450	29
10.8	11.1	11.5	10.8	11.7	11.8	10.1	30
140	140	165	135	140	145	175	31
Ea-DQl-F	Ea-Ql-F	Ea-DQl-F	Ea-Ql-F	Ea-DQl-Ql-F	Ea-DQl-F	Ea-DQl-F	32
Sa-Ll-Sl-F	Ea-DQu-Ll-F	Ea-DQu-Sl-F	Ea-Ma-Sf	Ea-DQu-Ll-F	Ea-DQu-Ll-F	Ea-DQu-Ll-F	33
155/70 R 13 75 S	175/65 R 14 82 H	185/70 R 14 86 S	195/60 R 15 87 V	195/60 R 14 85 V	205/65 R 15 94 V	185/70 R 14	34
Sb-Tb-Sv-Br	Sb-Tb-Sv-Br	Sb-Tb-Sv-Br	Sb-Sb-Sv-ABS	Sb-Sb-Sv-ABS	Sb-Sb-Sv-ABS	Sb-Sb-Sv-ABS	35

[1]) Electronically controlled.

Country			Japan				
Vehicle make Model			**Toyota** Starlet 1.3 XLi	Corolla 1.6 GLi Liftback	Camry 2.0 GLi	Previa	MR 2
1	Body style		3 Li 4/5	5 Li 5	4 Li 5	4 KoLi 7–8	2 Co 2
2	Net engine horsepower at engine speed	kW (HP) min⁻¹	55 (75) 6000	77 (105) 6000	89 (121) 5600	97 (132) 5000	115 (156) 6600
3	Max. torque at engine speed	Nm min⁻¹	101 4800	142 3200	176 4400	204 4000	186 4800
4	Maximum speed	km/h	170	185	192	175	220
5	Acceleration from 0 to 100 km/h	s	10.3	10.4	9.4	11.5	7.9
6	Curb weight	kg	720	1045	1205	1670	1190
7	Gross vehicle weight	kg	1225	1490	1720	2450	1515
8	Power-to-weight ratio	kg/kW	13.1	13.6	13.5	17.2	10.3
9	Fuel consumption	*l* / 100 km	5.2/6.7/7.1	5.8/7.4/8.6	6.4/8.3/9.8	8.6/11.7/12.8	6.0/7.8/10.3
10	Type of fuel		Regular unleaded	Premium unleaded	Premium unleaded	Premium unleaded	Premium unleaded
11	Fuel tank capacity	*l*	40	50	60	75	55
12	Engine swept volume	cm^3	1296	1587	1998	2438	1998
13	Bore/stroke	mm	73.0/77.4	81.0/77.0	86.0/86.0	95.0/86.0	86.0/86.0
14	Compression ratio		9.5	9.5	9.8	9.3	10.0
15	Specific power output	kW / *l*	42.4	48.5	44.5	39.8	57.6
16	Engine type		q 4 R, 3 Ve	q 4 R, 4 Ve	q 4 R, 4 Ve	lä 4 R, 4 Ve	q 4 R, 4 Ve
17	Fuel management		El	El	L-Jetronic	L-Jetronic	L-Jetronic
18	Alternator	V/A	14/55	14/60	14/70	14/80	14/70
19	Battery	V/Ah	12/50	12/40	12/60	12/65	12/60
20	Drive configuration		v-v	v-v	v-v	v-h	Mm-h
21	Transmission ratios	1st/2nd gear 3rd/4th gear 5th gear	3.545/1.904 1.310/0.969 0.815	3.166/1.904 1.310/0.969 0.815	3.285/2.041 1.322/1.028 0.820	3.704/2.020 1.368/1.000 0.854	3.285/1.960 1.322/1.028 0.820
22	Final-drive ratio		4.058	4.058	3.944	3.909	3.944
23	Gearshift		5 K	5 K (3 A)	5 K (3 A)	5 K (4 A)	5 K
24	Cooling		W 4.8	W 5.6	W 6.5	W 11.6	W 13.6
25	Vehicle length	mm	3720	4215	4520	4765	4180
26	Vehicle width	mm	1600	1655	1710	1800	1700
27	Vehicle height	mm	1385	1365	1400	1845	1240
28	Wheelbase	mm	2300	2430	2600	2860	2400
29	Track, front/rear	mm	1390/1370	1430/1410	1475/1445	1560/1550	1470/1450
30	Turning circle diameter	m	9.8	10.4	11.6	12.2	10.6
31	Ground clearance	mm	145	155	160	150	135
32	Wheel suspension, front		Ea-DQl-F	Ea-DQl-F	Ea-Ql-F	Ea-Ql-F	Ea-Ql-F
33	Wheel suspension, rear		Vla-F	Ea-DQu-F	Ea-DQu-F	Ea-DQl-Sf	Ea-Ll-Ql-F
34	Tires		145 R 13	175/70 R 13	185/70 R 14	215/65 R 15	[1])
35	Braking system		Sb-Tb-Sv	Sb-Sb-Sv	Sb-Tb-Sv	Sb-Sb-Sv-Br	Sb-Sb-Sv-ABS

See pp. 784/785 for abbreviations and explanations.

1) Front 195/60 R 14, rear 205/60 R 14.

	Sweden						
	Saab		**Volvo**				
Supra 3.0 i turbo	900 i 2.1–16	9000 CD 2.3 Turbo S	460 GLE Injection	480 Turbo	940 GL Turbodiesel	960	
3 Co 4	3/5 Li 5	4 Li 5	4 Li 5	3 Co 4	4 Li 5	4 Li 5	1
175 (239) 5600	100 (136) 6000	143 (195) 5000	75 (102) 5600	88 (120) 5400	80 (109) 4800	150 (204) 6000	2
350 3200	175 2900	323 2000	142 3900	175 3300	205 4200	267 4300	3
245	185	230	190	200	182	215	4
							5
6.3	11.0	8.0	10.5	9.0	12.1	9.5	
1620	1200	1370	1039	1022	1430	1550	6
2070	1830	1960	1580	1440	1945	2010	7
9.3	12.0	9.6	13.9	11.6	17.9	10.3	8
8.0/10.3/14.4	7.3/10.1/12.9	7.0/9.0/12.5	6.1/7.2/10.1	6.3/8.1/11.0	6.0/8.6/9.6	8.2/10.2/14.5	9
Premium unleaded	Premium unleaded[2]	Premium unleaded[2]	Premium unleaded	Premium unleaded	Diesel	Premium unleaded[2]	10
70	63	62	60	60	60	80	11
2954	2119	2290	1721	1721	2383	2922	12
83.0/91.0	93.0/78.0	90.0/90.0	81.0/83.5	81.0/83.5	76.5/86.4	83.0/90.0	13
8.4	10.1	8.5	10.0	8.1	23.0	10.7	14
59.2	47.2	62.4	43.6	51.1	33.6	51.3	15
lä 6 R, 4 Ve	lä 4 R, 4 Ve	q 4 R, 4 Ve	q 4 R	q 4 R	lä 6 R	lä 6 R, 4 Ve	16
L-Jetronic, AT	LH-Jetronic	LH-Jetronic	LH-Jetronic	LH-Jetron., AT	EP/V, AT	Motronic	17
14/80	14/70	14/80	14/70	14/70	14/55	14/120	18
12/60	12/60	12/62	12/55	12/55	12/60	12/66	19
v-h	v-v	v-v	v-v	v-v	v-h	v-h	20
3.251/1.955 1.310/1.000 0.753	3.83/2.20 1.46/1.05 0.84	3.38/1.76 1.18/0.89 0.70	3.727/2.053 1.320/1.000 0.967	3.091/1.842 1.320/0.967 0.758	4.03/2.16 1.37/1.00 0.79	2.80/1.53 1.00/0.75	21
3.727	3.89	4.05	3.733	3.733	3.54	3.73	22
5 K (4 A)	5 K (3 A)	5 K (4 A)	5 K (4 A)	5 K (4 A)	4 K+O (4 A)	4 A	23
W 8.2	W 10.0	W 10.0	W 7.0	W 7.0	W 8.5	W 10.7	24
4630	4680	4780	4405	4258	4870	4870	25
1745	1690	1806	1678	1710	1750	1750	26
1300	1420	1405	1379	1318	1410	1410	27
2595	2515	2672	2503	2503	2770	2770	28
1485/1480	1430/1440	1534/1504	1416/1426	1416/1416	1470/1460	1470/1520	29
11.6	10.3	10.9	10.1	10.1	9.9	9.9	30
140	140	150	125	125	105	105	31
Ea-DQl-F	Ea-DQu-Sf	Ea-Ql-F	Ea-DQl-F	Ea-DQl-F	Ea-Ql-F	Ea-DQl-F	32
Ea-DQl-F	Sa-Ll-P-Sf	Sa-Ll-P-Sf	Sa-Wa-P-Sf	Sa-Wa-P-Sf	Ea-Ql-Ll-Sf	Ea-Ql-Ll-Sf	33
225/50 R 16	185/65 R 15 87 H	205/50 ZR 16	185/60 HR 14	185/60 HR 14	185/65 HR 15	195/65 VR 15	34
Sb-Sb-Sv-ABS	Sb-Sb-Sv	Sb-Sb-Sv	Sb-Sb-Sv	Sb-Sb-Sv	Sb-Sb-Sv	Sb-Sb-Sv-ABS	35

2) Regular unleaded also permitted.

Country			Spain		USA		
Vehicle make Model			**Seat** Ibiza 1.2 i GLX	 Malaga 1.5 i GLX	**Buick** Park Avenue	**Cadillac** Seville Sedan	**Chevrolet** Caprice Sedan
1	Body style		3/5 Li 5	4 Li 5	4 Li 6	4 Li 5	4 Li 6
2	Net engine horsepower at engine speed	kW (HP) min^{-1}	51 (70) 6000	66 (90) 6000	127 (173) 4800	150 (204) 4100	128 (174) 4400
3	Max. torque at engine speed	Nm min^{-1}	95 4000	121 4000	298 3200	373 3000	347 2400
4	Maximum speed	km/h	157	165	ca. 195	ca. 210	
5	Acceleration from 0 to 100 km/h	s	14.5	12.8			
6	Curb weight	kg	890/910	975	1698	1578	1847
7	Gross vehicle weight	kg	1400	1450			
8	Power-to-weight ratio	kg/kW	17.4	14.8	13.4	10.6	14.4
9	Fuel consumption	l/100 km	4.8/6.4/8.6	5.5/7.2/9.1	ca. 10 ... 17	ca. 12 ... 17	ca. 10 ... 17
10	Type of fuel		Premium unleaded	Premium unleaded	Regular unleaded	Regular unleaded	Regular unleaded
11	Fuel tank capacity	l	42	42	68	71	87
12	Engine swept volume	cm^3	1193	1461	3785	4894	5002
13	Bore/stroke	mm	75.0/67.5	83.0/67.5	96.5/86.3	92.0/92.0	94.89/88.39
14	Compression ratio		10.8	10.5	8.5	9.5	9.2
15	Specific power output	kW/l	42.7	45.3	33.6	30.7	25.6
16	Engine type		q 4 R	q 4 R	q 6 V	q 8 V	lä 8 V
17	Fuel management		LU-Jetronic	LU-Jetronic	EI	EI	EI
18	Alternator	V/A	14/55	14/45	14/105	14/140	14/100
19	Battery	V/Ah	12/45	12/45	12/54	12/69	12/54
20	Drive configuration		v-v	v-v	v-v	v-v	v-h
21	Transmission ratios	1st/2nd gear 3rd/4th gear 5th gear	3.50/1.95 1.32/0.97 0.77	3.50/1.95 1.32/0.97 0.77	2.92/1.57 1.00/0.70	2.92/1.57 1.00/0.70	3.06/1.63 1.00/0.70
22	Final-drive ratio		4.294	3.737	2.84	2.97	2.56
23	Gearshift		5 K	5 K	3 A + O – Le	3 A + O	3 A + O – Le
24	Cooling		W 8.7	W 8.9	W 11.8	W 10.1	W 15.8
25	Vehicle length	mm	3683	4273	5211	4846	5439
26	Vehicle width	mm	1610	1650	1903	1828	1956
27	Vehicle height	mm	1394	1400	1405	1352	1440
28	Wheelbase	mm	2443	2443	2814	2743	2945
29	Track, front/rear	mm	1421/1387	1421/1387	1537/1529	1522/1522	1568/1542
30	Turning circle diameter	m	9.6	10.1	13.0	12.9	12.7
31	Ground clearance	mm	125	125	140	150	180
32	Wheel suspension, front		Ea-QI-F	Ea-QI-F	Ea-DQI-F	Ea-LI-QI-F	Ea-DQI-QI-Sf
33	Wheel suspension, rear		Ea-DQI-Qf-Db	Ea-DQI-Qf-Db	Ea-DQI-Db-Sf	Ea-QI-Db-Tfq	Sa-LI-SI-Sf
34	Tires		165/65 SR 14	165/65 SR 14	P 205/70 R 15	P 205/70 R 15	P 225/70 HR 15
35	Braking system		Sb-Tb-Sv	Sb-Tb-Sv	Sb-Tb-Sv-ABS	Sb-Sb-Sv-ABS	Sb-Tb-Sv-ABS

See pp. 784/785 for abbreviations and explanations.

Chrysler Voyager SE	Dodge Monaco	Ford Mustang GT	Crown Victoria S	Mercury Cougar LS	Oldsmobile Eighty-Eight	Pontiac Bonneville SSE Sedan	
4 KoLi 7	4 Li 5	2 Co 4	4 Li 6	2 Co 4	4 Li 6	4 Li 5–6	1
104 (141) 5200	112 (152) 5000	78 (106) 4600	142 (193) 4200	104 (141) 3800	127 (172) 4800	122 (166) 4800	2
228 2400	232 3600	183 2600	353 3200	292 2400	298 2000	284 2000	3
177	ca. 195	ca. 165	ca. 190	ca. 180	ca. 195	ca. 190	4
							5
1625	1355	1250	1700	1625	1580	1676	6
2210							7
15.6	12.1	16.0	12.0	15.6	12.4	13.7	8
7.7/10.2/14.2	ca. 10 ... 15	ca. 9 ... 14	ca. 10 .. 18	ca. 10 ... 16	ca. 10 ... 17	ca. 10 16	9
Premium unleaded	Regular unleaded	Regular unleaded	Regular unleaded	Regular unleaded	Regular unleaded	Regular unleaded	10
75	60.5	58	75.5	72	68	68	11
2972	2975	2301	4601	3797	3791	3785	12
91.1/76.0	93.0/73.0	96.04/79.4	90.2/90.0	96.8/86.0	96.52/86.36	96.52/86.36	13
8.9	9.3	9.5	9.0	9.0	8.5	8.5	14
35.0	37.6	33.9	30.9	27.4	33.5	32.2	15
q 6 V	lä 6 V	lä 4 R	lä 8 V	lä 6 V	q 6 V	q 6 V	16
EL	EL	El	El	El	El	El	17
14/90	14/96	14/75	14/95	14/75	14/105	14/105	18
12/66	12/66	12/48	12/58	12/58	12/54	12/54	19
v-v	v-v	v-h	v-h	v-h	v-v	v-v	20
2.84/1.57 1.00/0.69	2.58/1.41 1.00/0.74	3.97/2.34 1.46/1.00 0.79	2.40/1.47 1.00/0.67	2.40/1.47 1.00/0.67	2.92/1.57 1.00/0.70	2.92/1.57 1.00/0.70	21
3.47	3.58	3.45	3.08	3.27	2.84	2.97	22
4 A – Le	4 A – Le	5 K (4 A)	4 A – Le	4 A	3 A + O – Le	3 A + O – Le	23
W 9.5	W 8.2	W 8.2	W 13.6	W 10.2	W 12.3	W 11.8	24
4468	4900	4560	5395	5080	5090	5044	25
1522	1780	1735	1975	1850	1880	1832	26
1637	1390	1320	1440	1340	1415	1386	27
2847	2695	2555	2905	2870	2815	2815	28
1522/1578	1480/1450	1440/1450	1590/1610	1565/1530	1545/1540	1532/1518	29
12.5	11.8	11.9	13.1	12.0	12.2	13.0	30
100	125	115	130	130	140	150	31
Ea-DQl-F	Ea-DQl-F	Ea-DQl-Ql-Sf	Ea-DQl-Sf	Ea-DQl-Ql-Sf	Ea-DQl-F	Ea-DQl-F	32
Sa-Bf	Ea-Ll-Tfq	Sa-Ll-Sl-Sf	Sa-Ll-Sl-Sf	Ea-DQl-Ql-Sf	Ea-DQl-Db-Sf	Ea-DQl-Db-Sf	33
P 205/70 R 15	205/70 R 14	195/75 R 14	215/70 R 15	205/70 R 15	205/70 R 14	P 215/60 R 16	34
Sb-Tb-Sv	Sb-Tb-Sv	Sb-Tb-Sv	Sb-Sb-Sv	Sb-Tb-Sv	Sb-Tb-Sv	Sb-Tb-Sv-ABS	35

Road-traffic legislation

The regulatory framework governing highway traffic in Germany is codified in a number of legal standards.

– The Road Traffic Act or Highway Code (*Straßenverkehrsgesetz*, or StVG) contains the basic provisions governing traffic safety, liability and penalties.

– The Highway (or Road) Traffic Regulations (*Straßenverkehrsordnung*, or StVO) contains stipulations governing road-traffic behavior.

– The Road Licensing Regulations (*Straßenverkehrszulassungs-Ordnung* or StVZO) are equivalent to the FMVSS and CUR. They contain the regulations governing the granting of official approval for operation on public highways (persons and vehicles).

– The Mandatory Liability Insurance Act (*Pflichtversicherungs-Gesetz,* or PflversG) regulates liability insurance.

– The Penal Code (*Strafgesetzbuch*, or StGB) is applied in conjunction with the StVG and the Code of Criminal Procedure (*Strafprozeßordnung*, or StPO) to regulate the administration of sanctions and penalties.

– Other infringements are covered by the Regulatory Offences Act (*Ordnungswidrigkeitengesetz*, or OWiG) and the official catalogue of warnings and fines.

The following is restricted to a discussion of the significant points in the German road-traffic legislation which are of importance with regard to the vehicle.

Loads (Paragraph 22 StVO)
Loads which project more than one meter beyond the rear reflector are to be marked:

– During daylight hours by a red flag or a bright red sign. The latter is to be suspended at right angles to the direction of travel, while the specified dimensions are 30 x 30 cm. Another alternative is a bright red cylinder of at least 30 cm in height and 35 cm in diameter. All of these devices are to be positioned ≤ 1.5 m above the road surface.

– At night by a red lamp and a red reflector ≤ 1.5 m above the road surface.

If the load projects sideways more than 40 cm beyond the side-marker or tail lamps, it is to be marked by the following devices at dawn, dusk, during darkness or in conditions affording limited visibility:

– A white lamp projecting toward the front, and

– A red lamp projecting toward the rear.

These are to be installed ≤ 40 cm from the load's lateral extremities and ≤ 1.5 m above the road surface.

Homologation, issuance and validity
(Paragraph 19 StVZO)
Modifications to components will result in suspension of a vehicle's homologation approval in cases where the component is governed by official specifications or when the use of the component represents a potential hazard. The vehicle's homologation can be renewed upon acceptance by an officially authorized inspector with a corresponding entry in the vehicle's documents.

This stipulation does not apply in cases in which a General Homolgation (*Allgemeine Betriebserlaubnis*, or ABE), or General Design Certification (*Allgemeine Bauartgenehmigung*, or ABG) has been issued, as long as no special validation from an official inspector is required. This ruling also applies to registered test vehicles belonging to manufacturers.

Homologation approval is also issued when, instead of fulfilling the applicable StVZO regulation(s), the vehicle achieves conformity with a corresponding EC regulation(s).

Homologation for vehicle components
(Paragraph 22 StVZO)
Separate homologation approval can be issued for components which form a single technical assembly on the vehicle and which can be removed and installed in a prescribed manner. In the case of volume-production parts, once-only homologation approval with the approval code on each part is sufficient. Special components need only be entered in the vehicle's documents if specifically listed in the vehicle's General Homologation (ABE). EEC General Homologation for individual vehicle components are also recognized as substitutes for a national ABE.

Design approval for vehicle components (Paragraph 22a StVZO)
The following components and assemblies

must conform to the official specifications regardless of whether they are installed in vehicles which are subject to licence approval or in vehicles which are not subject to licence approval:
1. Vehicle heaters, excepting those depending on heat which is generated electrically or derived from the cooling system,
2. Anti-skid devices, excepting snow chains,
3. Safety-glass windshields and windows,
4. Overrun brakes,
5. Devices employed to connect separate vehicles,
6. Headlights (high and low beams),
7. Fog lamps and backup lamps,
8. Tail and stop lamps,
9. Turn signals
10. Side-marker lamps, track-orientation lamps, parking lamps, license-plate lamps, clearance lamps, and fog warning lamps,
11. Emergency-vehicle rotating beacons (yellow and blue),
12. Reflectors (yellow and red),
13. Warning triangles, warning lamps and parked-vehicle warning devices,
14. Emergency horns, tachographs,
15. Light bulbs,
16. Seatbelts, incl. children's belts,
17. Lamps marking projecting cargo.

Those components for which official design certification approval is issued must be provided with the prescribed approval symbol (wavy line ∿, with letter and number or (E) in accordance with ECE regulations or [e] to indicate EEC approval).

Design certification is not required for new equipment being tested on public highways provided that the operator of the vehicle is in possession of documentation

Speed limits (Paragraphs 3 and 18 StVO)

Within built-up areas, the general speed limit for all vehicle types is 50 km/h.

Vehicle class and AGVW (motorcycles with & without sidecar, trucks incl. combination tractors, cars incl. multi-purpose vehicles)	Outside built-up areas, except on Autobahn & similar limited-access highways km/h	Autobahn and similar limited-access highways (featuring a median strip or similar division between lanes for each direction) km/h
Motorcycles, passenger cars & other vehicles ≤ 2.8 t	100[1])	No speed limit[2])
Vehicles (except passenger cars) > 2.8 t & ≤ 7.5 t Passenger cars with trailer Trucks ≤ 2.8 t with trailer, buses *), also with baggage trailer	80	80*)
Vehicles > 7.5 t	60	80
Vehicles (except trucks ≤ 2.8 t & passenger cars) with trailer Buses with standing passengers, also with baggage trailer	60	60*)
*)Special cases		
Motorcycles with trailer	60	60
Motor homes with trailer	60	80
Trucks with trailer		
– ≤ 2.8 t	80	80
– > 2.8 t	60	80
Self-powered machinery with trailer	60	60
Tractors with 1 trailer	60	80
Tractors with 2 trailers	60	60
Buses without trailer with "100 km/h" sticker	80	100
Vehicles with snow chains	50	50

[1]) No speed limit on limited-access highways with median or similar division between lanes for each direction and at least two marked lanes for each direction; recommended speed limit 130 km/h.
[2]) Recommended speed limit 130 km/h.

indicating that the required official dispensation has been granted.

Vehicle owner and registered user: Registration obligation
(Paragraph 27 StVZO)
The information contained in the vehicle's certificate of title *(Kfz-Brief)* and registration certificate *(Kfz-Schein)* must correspond to the actual status at all times; changes and modifications are to be reported to the registration office without delay.

If the vehicle's registered location is to be changed to a different registration district for a period exceeding three months, application for a new license plate is to be made without delay. Notification provided to the registration authorities who issued the original plate is sufficient in cases where the change of address is expected to be only temporary.

When the vehicle is sold, the seller is to send to the registration office both the address of the buyer and the buyer's signed statement acknowledging receipt of the vehicle's official documents. The buyer must apply for a new registration certificate, with a new license plate also being required when the district has changed.

Should the buyer fail to comply with these obligations, the registration office can rescind the vehicle's approval for operation on public roads until such time as the obligations have been fulfilled.

When a vehicle is taken off the road for a period exceeding one year, the owner is to inform the registration office, presenting the vehicle's documents and the license plates (for removal of the registration stamp) to the authorities. If the vehicle has been taken off the road permanently (the official definition being more than one year), the registration office issues a new Certificate of Title in the event that the vehicle is registered again.

Periodic inspection of vehicles and trailers
(Paragraph 29 and Appendix VIII StVZO)
The vehicle is to be submitted for regular periodic general inspections at the owner's expense. The inspection tag (attached to the license plate) indicates the month in which the vehicle is again to be presented for its periodic general inspection. The inspection tag is to be affixed by the registration office or the officially-authorized inspector when the results of the inspection indicate concurrence between the vehicle's condition and the regulatory requirements. The date of the next general inspection is also entered in the vehicle's registration certificate.

The inspection tag becomes invalid two months after the month indicated for the next general inspection. The registration office can prohibit or restrict the operation on public highways of vehicles without a valid inspection tag.

Horsepower requirements
(Paragraph 35 StVZO)
The power requirement for buses, trucks, truck tractors, and for combination vehicles is ≥ 4.4 kW/metric ton, and for road tractors ≥ 2.2 kW/t of the approved gross vehicle weight. This regulation does not apply to electric vehicles and vehicles designed to operate at ≤ 25 km/h.

Seats, seat belts and occupant-restraint systems (Paragraph 35a StVZO)
Passenger cars, truck tractors, and trucks, as well as other motor vehicles featuring passenger compartments and chassis of the same general configuration, initially registered from 1.1.1992 onward with a designed top speed in excess of > 25 km/h, are to be equipped with three-point automatic seat and shoulder belts at the outside seating places, with lap belts representing the minimal requirement for all other seats. Excepted are folding occasional seats and seats whose occupants do not face the front of the vehicle. Lap belts satisfy the requirement for convertibles (all seats) and motor homes (rearward-facing seats).

The anchorage points for the seatbelts must conform to the requirements in EEC Directive 76/115.

Seatbelts are required at all seats on vehicles initially registered before 1.1.92 (and after 1 May, 1979), but only for passenger vehicles and trucks ≤ 2.8 metric tons.

Tires and tread surfaces
(Paragraph 36 StVZO)
Motor vehicles and trailers are to be equipped with pneumatic tires having a

minimum tread depth of 1.6 mm across the entire width at all points on the circumference.

Both passenger vehicles and motor vehicles with an approved gross vehicle weight of $\leq$ 2.8 metric tons designed for a top speed $>$ 40 km/h and their trailers must be equipped with either bias-ply or radial tires exclusively; this stipulation applies only to the individual vehicles in combinations. It does not apply to trailers towed by a motor vehicle at speeds $\leq$ 25 km/h.

Windshields, windows and wipers (Paragraph 40 StVZO)
All windshields and windows – except mirrors and covers on instruments and lighting devices – must be made of safety glass. Windshields and windows are to cause no dangerous injuries upon breakage. Homologation approval as defined in Paragraph 22a StVZO is required for all safety glass.

Power-operated windshield wipers are prescribed for the windshield. The windshield wipers must be so dimensioned as to provide the driver with an adequate field of vision. A wiper-washer unit, although not officially prescribed, is standard equipment.

Brakes (Paragraph 41 StVZO)
(See p. 594, Brake systems.

Weights of trailers towed by motor vehicles (Paragraph 42 StVZO)
The weight of a trailer towed by a motorcycle, passenger car or truck is to exceed neither the AGVW – or 1.5 times the AGVW on a truck and trailer combination featuring a unified brake system – of the towing vehicle nor the figure specified by the manufacturer. Single-axle car trailers with inadequate brakes or no brakes at all may only be towed by vehicles with four-wheel brakes. This stipulation does not apply to other tow vehicles.
The maximum allowed weight for this type of unbraked single-axle trailer is half the empty weight of the towing vehicle plus 75 kg, but not more than 750 kg.

Approved dimensions and weights (Paragr. 32 and 34 StVZO) excluding Saarland
Width 2.5 m (agricultural and forestry vehicles 3.0 m), height 4.0 m.
Agricultural and forestry vehicles together with their loads may exceed 4.0 m in height but must not exceed 3.0 m in width (Paragraph 22 StVO).

Vehicle class	Length m	Weight t
Single vehicles except semitrailers with $\leq$ 2 axles	12	18
Vehicles with 3 axles – general – with dual wheels and pneumatic suspension on drive axle	 12 12	 25 26
Trailers with $>$ 2 axles	12	24
Vehicles with $>$ 3 axles	12	32
Articulated buses	18	28
Vehicle combinations – Truck/trailer combinations – Articulated vehicle or in special cases – with $<$ 4 axles – with 4 axles 2-axle towing vehicle + 2-axle trailer 2-axle truck tractor + 2-axle trailer – with $>$ 4 axles – 5-6 axles for articulated-vehicles for 40-foot ISO containers	 18 15.5 16.5	 28 36 36...38 40 44
Axle weights: Single axles: 10 t; single drive axles: 11.5 t, tandem axles according to axle spacing and design: 11.5 t ($<$ 1 m), 16 t ($\geq$ 1 m & $<$ 1.3 m), 18 t ($\geq$ 1.3 m & $<$ 1.8 m) or 19 t for dual-wheel-equipped drive axles with pneumatic suspension; corresponding figures for trailers: 11 t, 16 t, 18 t and 20 t ($\geq$ 1.8 m). Triple-axle weights: 21 t ($\leq$ 1.3 m) and 24 t ($>$ 1.3 m & $\leq$ 1.4 m).		

Trailer couplings and drawbar loads (Paragraph 44 StVZO)
On a single-axle trailer, in cases where even load distribution results in a drawbar load > 50 kg, a provision must be present to allow adjustment of the trailer-coupling height. This requirement does not apply to trailers being towed by vehicles equipped with suitable jacking equipment.

A passenger car drawing a single-axle trailer must be capable of supporting at least ≥ 4 % of the trailer weight, although as prescribed by law this figure need not exceed 25 kg. Neither the maximum drawbar load for trailer coupling and towing mechanism, nor the approved drawbar load specified by the towing vehicle's manufacturer is to be exceeded. The respective approved drawbar loads are to be indicated at visible locations on both the towing vehicle and the trailer.

Fuel tanks (Paragraph 45 StVZO)
The fuel tank must resist corrosion and display no leakage at a pressure defined as double that of the normal operating pressure, but at least 0.3 bar. Suitable orifices, safety valves, etc., must be provided to allow excess pressure to escape. Neither the filler opening nor the pressure-equalization device is to permit fuel to escape as a result of road shocks, or in curves, or when the vehicle is tilted.

The fuel tank must be insulated from the engine in such a manner as to prevent the fuel from being ignited in the event of an accident. This provision does not apply to two-wheeled vehicles and tractors with exposed operating positions.

The fuel tanks in buses are to be located neither in the passenger nor in the driver compartment; they are to pose no direct threat to the exits in case of fire. The tanks are to be located at the sides or under the floor at a distance of at least 500 mm to the door openings. Should it prove impossible to maintain this distance, then a metal shield is to be installed to protect the portion of the tank in question (exception: tank bottom).

Fuel lines (Paragraph 46 StVZO)
The fuel lines must be installed so as not to be negatively affected by torsional motion, engine movement and similar phenomena. The fuel lines can be made of seamless flexible metal tubes or flame and fuel-resistant synthetic hoses. The lines are to be protected against physical damage.

All fuel-conducting components must be protected against heat which might impair operation. They are positioned so as to obviate the possibility of dripping or evaporating fuel accumulating on hot components or being ignited by electrical devices.

Fuel lines on buses are not to be in the passenger or driver compartment; gravity-feed designs are forbidden.

Emissions (Paragraph 47 StVZO)
Emissions data which is decisive for homologation approval is contained in App. XIV StVZO. Stipulations contained in the most recent version are identical with contents of ECE Regulation Nr. 15 with Amendment 04 and EEC Directive 70/220 with Amendment EEC 83/351. App. XIV has been superseded by EEC Directive 70/220 with Amendments EEC 88/76 and EEC 88/436. Amendments also specify the deadlines after which the EC norms replace all national regulations.

Emissions are measured in three individual test procedures:
Type 1: Emissions under various operating conditions (motor vehicles ≤ 3.5 tons)
1. European test as defined in Appendix III to the EC Directive, or
2. Alternate test procedure for engine swept volumes ≥ 1400 cm^3 as defined in App. IIIA, as introduced in EEC 88/76 through 70/220; (corresponds to the EPA 49-state cycle in the USA).
Test description on page 483.
Type II: Carbon-monoxide emissions at idle (presently ≤ 3.5 % vol.).
Type III: Gaseous crankcase emissions.

The crankcase ventilation system must prevent gaseous emissions from escaping into the atmosphere.

Diesel-powered vehicles are only subjected to Type I testing (Type II and Type III do not apply); however, the following additional tests apply:
– EEC 88/436 – Test Type I to include a supplementary test for diesel particulates,
– Appendix XV StVZO – Diesel smoke (identical with EEC 72/306 and ECE-R24),
– Appendix XVI StVZO for tractors used for agriculture and forestry,

– EEC 88/77 – Emissions from heavy utility and commercial vehicles.

The rates for vehicle taxes are assessed on the basis of separate tests and regulations independent of those for homologation. Alternatively, voluntary advance compliance with tighter EC Regulations is accepted as a basis for both fiscal classification and homologation approval.

Compliance with the applicable regulations leads to classification as a "low-emissions" or "qualified low emissions" vehicle; the applicable classification instruments are contained in the Vehicle Taxation Code and Appendices XXIII, XXIV and XXV StVZO, as well as the still voluntary, supplementary EEC Directives 89/458 and 89/491 to 70/220. Two-wheeled vehicles > 50 cm³ and > 50 km/h are governed by the emissions regulation ECE R40, while ECE R47 applies to motorcycles and scooters ≤ 50 cm³ and ≤ 50 km/h.

Exhaust-gas emissions test (ASU) (Paragraph 47a and Appendix XI StVZO)
In the annual exhaust-gas emissions test (*Abgassonderuntersuchung*, or ASU), an authorized service facility or officially sanctioned inspection station examines the vehicle to ensure that CO emissions at idle, idle speed, ignition timing and dwell angle conform to the manufacturer's specifications. Proper adjustment is indicated by a decal affixed to the front license plate and by a test certificate.

Diesel-powered vehicles are excepted from this requirement as are vehicles operated with a red license plate (temporary 5-day registration), vehicles with initial registration dates prior to 1 July, 1969, motor vehicles < 50 km/h, motor vehicles < 4 wheels, motor vehicles ≤ 400 kg AGVW, self-powered machinery and tractors used in forestry or agriculture. Under the presently applicable exemption clause, an ASU decal can be issued to low-emissions vehicles (App. XXIII or XXV StVZO, Code Nr. 01 or 03) and qualified low-emissions C/XXIII vehicles (Code Nr. 02) without an inspection; the decal remains valid until the next major inspection as prescribed in Paragraph 29 StVZO. The code number is on the second line of the vehicle registration certificate.

Noise emissions (Paragraph 47 StVZO)
The levels of operating noise emanating from motor vehicles and trailers are not to exceed the technically feasible minima.

The corresponding EC Directives define both the limits for operating noise and the prescribed test procedures, and are mandatory for the vehicle types listed below:
– EEC 70/157 for vehicles which transport persons or cargo,
– EEC 74/151 for tractors used in forestry and agriculture,
– EEC 78/1015 and Appendix XX StVZO for two-wheeled vehicles,
– Appendix XI StVZO for low-noise motor vehicles.

Should cause exist to believe that a vehicle's noise emissions exceed the

Motor-vehicle noise limits

Vehicle class	dB(A)
1. Passenger vehicles with ≤ 9 seats incl. driver	77¹)
2. Passenger vehicles with > 9 seats incl. driver, and cargo vehicles	
– AGVW ≤ 2 t	78¹)
– AGVW > 2 and ≤ 3.5 t	79¹)
3. Passenger vehicles with > 9 seats incl. driver with AGVW > 3.5 t:	
– Engine output < 150 kW	80
– Engine output ≥ 150 kW	83
4. Cargo vehicles with AGVW > 3.5 t:	
– Engine output < 75 kW	81
– Engine output ≥ 75 and < 150 kW	83
– Engine output ≥ 150 kW	84
Vehicle classes 1 through 4: Special limits for off-road vehicles with AGVW > 2 t:	
– Limit with engine output < 150 kW	+ 1
– Limit with engine output ≥ 150 kW	+ 2
5. Agricultural and forestry tractors and equipment:	
– Empty weight ≤ 1.5 t	85
– Empty weight > 1.5 t	89
6. Motorcycles	
– ≤ 80 cm³	77
from 1 Oct., 1993	75
– > 80 and ≤ 175 cm³	79
from 31 Dec., 1994	77
– > 175 cm³	82
from 1 Oct., 1993	80
7. Light motorcycles	75
8. Mopeds	
– Designed for top speed > 25 km/h	72
– Designed for top speed ≤ 25 km/h	70

¹) Add 1 dB(A) for direct-injection diesel engines.

specified level, the operator is obliged to respond to an official request to have the noise emissions measured, but only when the test station is not more than 6 km distant. The operator assumes responsibility for the test expenses should it be determined that the vehicle exceeds the limits.

Lighting equipment
(Paragraph 49a StVZO). See p. 668.

Acoustic warning devices
(Paragraph 55 StVZO)
Vehicles must be equipped with at least one device capable of generating a sound suitable for warning pedestrians and drivers of possible danger, without startling them or disturbing others more than is absolutely necessary. If several such devices are installed, only one device is to operate at once; sequences of several different base frequencies are forbidden. Horns are to generate a pure tone in a constant base frequency (harmonic chord). Volume is not to exceed 105 dB(A) at any point as measured 7 meters from the horn's installation location on the vehicle and 500 ... 1500 mm above the road surface.

Use of warning devices employing a series of various high-pitched sounds is restricted to official and emergency vehicles.

Interference suppression
(Paragraph 55a StVZO)
Engine ignition systems must incorporate interference suppression, as must electric vehicles. Compliance with DIN 57879, Part 1/VDE 0879, Part 1/6.79 satisfies this requirement. The official interference-suppression symbol must be present on all high-tension ignition components.

Rear-view mirrors (Paragraph 56 StVZO)
Vehicles must be equipped with mirrors which allow the driver to observe traffic to the rear. Required are:
1. For two-wheeled vehicles $\leq$ 80 km/h including mopeds: One rear-view mirror (left),
2. For two-wheeled vehicles > 80 km/h: Two rear-view mirrors (left and right).
3. General requirements for motor vehicles:
– One left-mounted outside mirror <u>and</u>
– one interior-mounted rear-view mirror <u>or</u>, should the latter not provide an adequate field of vision,
– one right-mounted outside mirror.
4. Additional requirements for heavy commercial vehicles > 7.5 tons:
– one right-mounted wide-angle mirror <u>and</u>
– one mirror for observing the front of the vehicle, right-mounted at a height $\geq$ 2 m.

Rear-view mirrors are not required on vehicles designed to operate at speeds < 25 km/h with an exposed driving position. Rear-view mirrors must conform to the regulations contained in EEC 71/127, Appendix III, Items 3, 4 and 5.

Speedometers and odometers
(Paragraph 57 StVZO)
Dual and multi-track vehicles designed for speeds > 30 km/h, and two-wheeled vehicles and mopeds, are to be equipped with a speed-monitoring device within the operator's field of vision. It may incorporate a distance-monitoring apparatus. The device must indicate vehicle speed in kilometers per hour while fulfilling the requirements defined in EEC/75/443, App. II.

Trip recorders and monitoring devices
(Paragraph 57a StVZO)
The following classes of vehicles are to be equipped with a basic trip recorder (tachograph) unit:
1. Motor vehicles with an approved gross vehicle weight $\geq$ 7.5 metric tons.
2. Tractors with engines producing $\geq$ 40 kW, unless used exclusively in agricultural and forestry applications.
3. Passenger vehicles for transporting $\geq$ 8 persons.

These stipulations do not apply to vehicles designed for top speeds $\leq$ 40 km/h, nor to vehicles of the Federal armed forces, the fire departments or civil defense, or vehicles equipped with an EC monitoring device as defined in EEC Directive Nr. 3821/85. Such a device is prescribed for vehicles used for commercial transportation of cargo where the AGVW of the vehicle alone, or of the vehicle plus trailer attached, exceeds 3.5 metric tons, as well as for buses in non-scheduled service.

Exemptions from the obligation to install an EC monitoring device or trip recorder are listed in Articles 4 and 14 of EEC Directive Nr. 3820/85 and in the Operators' Directive, Paragraph 7.

The monitoring device or trip recorder is to provide a continuous record of vehicle operation and pauses; all connections in the chain of data-transmission devices must be sealed. Trip recorders and monitoring devices must be tested and provided with an installation plate by an authorized person every two years and after each tire change.

Design and mounting of official license plates (Paragraph 60 StVZO)

Regional codes and numbers on official license plates are to be indicated with black letters and numbers on a white background. Green characters on a white background being used for tax-exempt vehicles.

License plates must not mirror light, or be obscured or dirty. Newly-issued license plates must be reflective, but older non-reflective plates may continue in use.

The rear license plate may be tilted at an angle of up to 30° toward the front of the vehicle. If the vehicle has extremely sloping bodywork, two license plates at the front and two at the rear may be substituted for the single license plates. This means there will be a front and rear license plate on each side of the vehicle.

Up to an adequate distance away from the vehicle, the plates must be legible at angles of 30° to each side of the vehicle's longitudinal axis.

On all vehicles except electric carts and their trailers, regulations stipulate the prescribed distances above the road surface as ≥ 200 mm to the lower edge of the front license plate, ≥ 300 mm to the lower edge of the rear plate, with ≥ 200 mm on motor scooters. The license plates are not to diminish the vehicle's ground clearance.

A lamp must be provided to make the rear license plate legible from 20 or 25 m (depending upon vehicle category).

In addition to the registration number, the international "D" symbol may be affixed to the plate. Mounting on the vehicle of any other object which might be mistaken for an official license plate is prohibited.

Mopeds, motor-driven cycles, motorcycles

1. Mopeds: ≤ 50 cm^3 and n ≤ 4800 rpm < 25 km/h, pedals, single-seat, headlamp with permanent 15 W low beam (must also be on in daylight operation), high-pitched ringing device, 1 left-mounted mirror, no operator's license required – moped test certificate sufficient, helmet required.
2. Light mopeds: as in 1, with exceptions ≤ 30 cm^3 and ≤ 20 km/h, bicycle characteristics, no helmet required.
3. Mokicks and motor-driven bicycles (moped): ≤ 50 cm^3, ≤ 50 km/h, one or two-seater, headlamp with low and high beam; permanent 15 W low beam allowed when electrical supply is limited, low beam required during daylight operation, 1 left-mounted mirror sufficient, horn, stop lamp and turn signals not required, but allowed. Class IV operator's license (or Class V if issued prior to 1 April, 1980).
4. Light scooters and motorcycles, as in 3, except: ≤ 80 cm^3 and ≤ 80 km/h, high and low-beam headlights, and stop lamps required, Class 1b operator's license (or Class 3 or 4 if issued prior to 1 April, 1980).

Vehicle classes 1 ... 4: General operating approval sufficient.

5. Motorcycle, as 3 and 4, except: Turn signals required, left and right-mounted mirrors, Class 1a operator's license if ≤ 20 kW and ≥ 7 kg empty weight/kW, otherwise Class 1. Registration with vehicle title and registration certificate.

Trailers towed by mopeds are classified as bicycle trailers as long as the designed top speed of the towing vehicle does not exceed 25 km/h. Homologation approval is required for trailers towed by other types of motorized two-wheeled vehicle.

License-plate dimensions

Vehicle class	Maxima Height x width mm x mm
Light motorcycles, electro carts ≤ 20 km/h, agricultural & forestry tractors ≤ 30 km/h, trailers for same	130 x 240
Other motorcycles, Light vehicles	200 x 280
Other vehicles and trailers	110 x 520 or 200 x 340
Light motorcycles ≤ 50 km/h, Mopeds, Rollchairs	
– Insurance license plate	130 x 105.5
– Official license plate (with insurance exemption)	116 x 140

Alphabets and numbers

German alphabet

Gothic type

𝔄	𝔞	a	𝔍	𝔧	j	𝔖	ſ 𝔰	s
𝔅	𝔟	b	𝔎	𝔨	k	𝔗	𝔱	t
ℭ	𝔠	c	𝔏	𝔩	l	𝔘	𝔲	u
𝔇	𝔡	d	𝔐	𝔪	m	𝔙	𝔳	v
𝔈	𝔢	e	𝔑	𝔫	n	𝔚	𝔴	w
𝔉	𝔣	f	𝔒	𝔬	o	𝔛	𝔵	x
𝔊	𝔤	g	𝔓	𝔭	p	𝔜	𝔶	y
ℌ	𝔥	h	𝔔	𝔮	q	ℨ	𝔷	z
ℑ	𝔦	i	ℜ	𝔯	r			

Phonetic alphabets

	German	International	2-way radio
A	= Anton	Amsterdam	Alpha
Ä	= Ärger	—	—
B	= Berta	Baltimore	Bravo
C	= Cäsar	Casablanca	Charlie
CH	= Charlotte	—	—
D	= Dora	Danmark	Delta
E	= Emil	Edison	Echo
F	= Friedrich	Florida	Foxtrott
G	= Gustav	Gallipoli	Golf
H	= Heinrich	Habanna	Hotel
I	= Ida	Italia	India
J	= Julius	Jerusalem	Juliett
K	= Kaufmann	Kilogramm	Kilo
L	= Ludwig	Liverpool	Lima
M	= Martha	Madagascar	Mike
N	= Nordpol	New York	November
O	= Otto	Oslo	Oscar
Ö	= Ökonom	—	—
P	= Paula	Paris	Papa
Q	= Quelle	Quebec	Quebec
R	= Richard	Roma	Romeo
S	= Samuel	Santiago	Sierra
Sch	= Schule	—	—
T	= Theodor	Tripolis	Tango
U	= Ulrich	Uppsala	Uniform
Ü	= Übermut	—	—
V	= Viktor	Valencia	Victor
W	= Wilhelm	Washington	Whiskey
X	= Xanthippe	Xanthippe	X-Ray
Y	= Ypsilon	Yokohama	Yankee
Z	= Zeppelin	Zürich	Zulu

Greek alphabet

Letter		Name	Letter		Name
Α	α	Alpha	Ν	ν	Nu
Β	β	Beta	Ξ	ξ	Xi
Γ	γ	Gamma	Ο	ο	Omicron
Δ	δ	Delta	Π	π	Pi
Ε	ε	Epsilon	Ρ	ϱ	Rho
Ζ	ζ	Zeta	Σ	σ ς	Sigma
Η	η	Eta	Τ	τ	Tau
Θ	ϑ	Theta	Υ	υ	Upsilon
Ι	ι	Iota	Φ	φ	Phi
Κ	ϰ	Kappa	Χ	χ	Chi
Λ	λ	Lambda	Ψ	ψ	Psi
Μ	μ	Mu	Ω	ω	Omega

Cyrillic alphabet

Letter		Pronunciation	Letter		Pronunciation
А	а	a	Р	р	r
Б	б	b	С	с	s
В	в	v	Т	т	t
Г	г	g	У	у	oo
Д	д	d	Ф	ф	f
Е	е	ye	Х	х	h as in "human"
Ё	ё	yaw			
Ж	ж	zh	Ц	ц	ts
З	з	s	Ч	ч	ch
И	и	ee	Ш	ш	sh
Й	й	i	Щ	щ	shch
К	к	k	Ъ	ъ	hard sign
Л	л	l	Ы	ы	i
М	м	m	Ь	ь	soft sign
Н	н	n	Э	э	e
О	о	o	Ю	ю	yoo
П	п	p	Я	я	ya

Roman numerals

I	1	XXX	30
II	2	XL	40
III	3	L	50
IV	4	LX	60
V	5	LXX	70
VI	6	LXXX	80
VII	7	XC	90
VIII	8	C	100
IX	9	CC	200
X	10	CD	400
XI	11	D	500
XX	20	DC	600
XXI	21	M	1000
XXIX	29	MCMXCII	1992

Index of headings

A

A-pillar 652
ABS see Antilock Braking
Systems 610...612, 638
ABS select-low control, comm. vehs 639
ABS, hydraulic modulator 619
ABS, individual control 611, 639
ABS, modified individual control,
commercial vehs 639
AC machines, single phase 126
AC see alternating current 75
Acceleration and braking 330
Acceleration 328
Acceleration and braking graph 330
Acceleration of free fall 11
Acceleration rest
Acceleration resistance 323
Acceleration sensors 107
Acceleration, passenger-car 786...813
Accelerator pump 432
Accuracy, manufacturing 157
Accuracy, measuring 157
Ack field (CAN) 778
Acoustic impedance 60
Acoustic quality control 65
Acoustic signaling devices 691
Acoustic tuning devices 427
Acoustic warning devices 820
Acoustics, general terms 60
Acoustics, symbols and units 60
Action limits, statistics
Active power 75
Active suspension 563
Active-gas metal-arc welding 308
Actuator, electrodynamic 119
Actuator, electromechanical 116
Actuator, fluid-mechanical 120
Actuator, hydraulic 120
Actuator, pneumatic 120
Actuators 116...122
ADA see Auto Directional
Antenna 704
Adaptation strategies, Motronic 474
Add-on equipment, mechanical
(diesel fuel-injection pumps) 499
Addendum modification coefficient 296
Addendum modification, gears 292, 293
Additional retarding braking
system 594, 628
Additives, diesel fuels 230
Additives, SI-engine fuels 228
Addonix ABS 617
Adhesion to road surface 329
Adhesion/slip curve 555, 610
Adhesive technology 309
Adiabatic change of state for gases 69
Adjustment of injection timing,
control-sleeve inj. pump 502
Adjustment screw, full-load 503
Advance mechanism, centrifugal 457
Advance mechanism, ignition 457
Advance mechanism, vacuum 457
Aerodynamic drag 325, 651
Aerodynamics, passenger cars 651
Afterburning 481
Agricultural tractor 348, 646
Air cooling 412
Air filter, central 416
Air filter, oil-bath 417
Air filters 416
Air requirement 428
Air springs 566
Air supply 416
Air-conditioning systems 701
Air-flow angle, motor vehicle 336
Air-flow sensor 438, 443
Air-flow sensor, Pitot-tube 112
Air-fuel (A/F) mixture 396, 428
Air-fuel (A/F) ratio 428
Air-mass meters 113
Air-mass sensor, hot-film 113, 445
Air-mass sensor, hot-wire 113, 444
Airbag 659, 718
Alarm systems 692
ALB (1) see Anti-Lock Brake 615
ALB (2) see Autom. load-sensing
braking-force metering 635
Alcohol operation, SI engines 492
Alcohols, fuels 231
All-wheel drive (AWD) 555
Allowances, ISO 266, 267
Alphabet, German (Gothic type) 822
Alphabet, Greek 822
Alphabet, Russian 822
Alternating current (AC) 75
Alternative drive systems 527
Alternative fuels 231
Alternator output 758
Alternator, claw-pole 770
Alternator, salient-pole 771
Alternator, windingless-rotor 772
Alternator-current characteristics 769
Alternators 768...775
Altitude-pressure compensator
(ADA) 500
Aluminum body 653
American gear standards 297

American units 17...38
Ampere 10
Ampere turns 81
Amplifier, car radio 705
Amplitude 39
Analog technology 100
Analog/Digital converter 100
Angle, air-flow 336
Angle, dwell 456
Angle, roll 342
Angle, steering-wheel 342
Angström 12
Angular frequency 13, 39
Annealing 257
Announcement identification, car radio 704
Annulus 142
Anode 74
Anodic corrosion protection 247
Anodizing 248
Antenna-diversity recognition 704
Antennas, motor vehicle 706
Anti-corrosion code 654
Anti-Lock Brake (ALB) 615
Anti-foaming agents 231
Anti-aging additives 228
Antiferromagnets 176
Antifreeze 412
Antiknock quality 227
Antilock braking system (ABS), commercial vehicles 639...642
Antilock braking system (ABS), passenger cars 610...619
Aperture, numerical 134
API classification, engine oils 223
API classification, transmission lubricants 224
Apparent power 75, 77
Application-specific IC (ASIC) 96
Approved dimensions, regulations 817
Aquaplaning 329
Arc, mathematics 138
Arc discharge, spark plug 446
Arc pressure welding 308
Arc-over voltage 446
Areas, mathematics 142
Area of circles 141, 142
Area, reflector 669
Arithmetic series 140
Articulated bus, definition 646
Articulated road train, definition 646
Artificial network, EMC 783
Ash, lubricants 218
ASR see Traction control 467, 555
Asynchronous drive, electric vehicles 532
ATF oils 224
ATF see Automatic Transmission Fluid 218, 224
Atmospheric conditions and engine output 396
Atmospheric humidity and variations, stresses 350
Audit, quality 144
Austempering 254
Austenitic structure 252
Auto-Directional Antenna (ADA) 704
Autoignition 353
Autom. load-sensitive device for braking-force metering 621
Automatic adjustment, wheel brakes 627
Automatic antenna 706
Automatic clutch system 538
Automatic FM interference suppression 705
Automatic headlight leveling 680
Automatic load-sensing braking force metering (ALB) 635
Automatic seat belt 659
Automatic transmissions 547
Automatic Transmission Fluid (ATF) 218, 224
Automotive electrical systems 758...778
Automotive speakers 706
Automotive paints, properties 216
Automotive transmission, hydraulic 740, 741
Auxiliary drives, hydraulic 737
Auxiliary driving lamps 682
Auxiliary logic 94
Auxiliary starting devices, diesel engines 520...522
Auxiliary-air valve 439, 443
Average peak-to-valley-height 265
Axial clamping forces, bolted joints 286
Axial piston machine, hydraulics 728
Axis, neutral 52
Axle oscillation 561

B

B-pillar 652
Backup lamps 685
Backup warning, Park Pilot 709
Balancing of inertia forces, single-stroke system 381
Balancing of masses 381
Balancing rate 382
Bar, unit 14

Barrel spring 566
Barrel, conversion 22
Barrier impact 659
Basic holes and shafts 263
Batteries 763...767
Battery characteristics 761
Battery chargers 767
Battery charging 765
Battery charging current 767
Battery charging voltage 759
Battery designs 527...529
Battery ignition 458
Battery internal resistance 761
Battery malfunctions 766
Battery, capacity 761
Battery, cold-discharge test current 761
Battery, deep-cycle 764
Battery, electric drive 527
Battery, heavy-duty 764
Battery, IU characteristic 765
Battery, Kt 765
Battery, lead-acid 760
Battery, nickel-cadmium 529
Battery, nickel-iron 529
Battery, nominal capacity 761
Battery, open-circuit voltage 765
Battery, self discharge 765
Battery, sodium-sulfide 529
Battery, starter 763
Battery, vibration-proof 764
Battery, W-curve 764
BDC see Bottom Dead Center, piston 368
Bearing load 268
Bearings 268...275
Bearings, ball 275
Bearings, carbon graphite 273
Bearings, dry sliding 272
Bearings, grooved sliding 269
Bearings, metal-backed composite 272
Bearings, multi-layer 269
Bearings, Polymer 272
Bearings, rolling 275
Bearings, sintered-metal 272
Bearings, sliding, hydrodynamic 268, 270
Bearings, thrust 268
Beats 39
Bell-shaped curve 151
Belt drives 302
Belt force 302
Belt tightener, pyrotechnical 717
Bending 52
Bending moment 52
Bending strength 55
Bending stress 52
Benedicks effect 85
Bevel gears 293, 554
Bifocal reflector 672
Bimorphous spring element, sensor 108
Binary system 100
Bingham bodies 218
Binomial distribution 156
Bipolar transistors 89
BIT see Board Information Terminal 716
Bit stuffing (CAN) 778
Black-body radiator 67
Black ice, static coefficient of friction 329
Black smoke emission 366
Bleeding, lubrication 218
Blind rivet 310
Blowby 480
Board Information Terminal (BIT) 716
Body design, passenger car 650
Body finishing components, passenger cars 654
Body roll 339
Body stresses due to accidents 652
Body structure, passenger cars 652
Body template 648
Boiling curve, fuels 228
Boiling range, diesel fuels 230
Bonding and joining techniques 306...311
Boost-pressure control, electronic 468
Boost retarder 631
Booster, carburetor 432
Booster, car radio 705
Bore/stroke, pass.-car engine 786...813
Boron treatment 256
Bottom clearance, gears 294
Bottom Dead Center (BDC), piston 368
Brake test stands 644
Brake cylinder 634
Brake factor 625
Brake fluids 234
Brake fluids, wet boiling point 234
Brake pressure 607
Brake pressure build-up time 333
Brake response time 333
Brake system, dual-circuit compressed-air 620
Brake, definition 595
Brake-circuit configurations 605
Braking deceleration 598
Braking distance 598
Braking equipment 594...643
Braking force 610
Braking in a curve 343
Braking resistance 323

Braking system, actuating time 597
Braking system, air-over-hydraulic 622
Braking system, application force 597
Braking system, automatic 594
Braking system,
control device 594, 606, 634
Braking system, control force 597
Braking system, electronic. controlled,
comm. vehs. 642
Braking system, electronic/
compressed-air 604
Braking system, energy source 594, 633
Braking system, energy supplying
device 594, 633
Braking system, inertia 595
Braking system, multi-circuit 595
Braking system, muscular energy 595
Braking system, non-muscular
energy 595
Braking system, parking 594, 628
Braking system, energy-assisted 595
Braking system, secondary 594
Braking system, service 594
Braking system, single-line 595
Braking system, three-line 621
Braking system, transmission
device 595, 634
Braking system, two-line 596, 621, 623
Braking system, gravity 595
Braking systems for pass. cars and
light comm. vehs. 606...619
Braking systems for commercial
vehicles 620...643
Braking systems, configurations 605
Braking systems, definitions and
principles 594...606
Braking system, hysteresis 597
Braking system, multi-line 595
Braking system, supply line, 596
Braking time, total 598
Braking times 597
Braking torque 597
Braking valve, service 636
Braking work 598
Braking-force coefficient 610
Braking-force controller 621, 624
Braking-force limiter 621, 624
Braking-force metering,
automatic load-sensing 635
Braking-force proportioning valve 609
Braking-force reducer 621, 624
Breakdown voltage, semiconductor 88
Breaking spark 456
British units 17...38
Broadband interference source 780
Browning 248
Buckling 53
Bulk Current Injection (BCI) 783
Bulk modulus, oil 726
Bumpers 654
Bus access, CAN 777
Bus circuitry, data processing 94, 163
Bus configuration, CAN 776
Bus, bodies 664
Bus, definition 646
Bus, passenger, hybrid electric 535
Butt-seam welding 307

C

C-Net 714
C-pillar 652
Cab Behind Engine (CBE) 664
Cab Over Engine (COE) 664
Caliper, disk brakes 608
Cam brake 626
Cam design 391
Camber angle 569, 582
CAN see Controller Area
Network 776...778
Candela, unit 10
Canister-purge valve 470
Cantilever spring 276
Capacitance 15, 71, 76
Capacitive reactance 76
Capacitor 72, 76
Car alarms see Theft-deterrent
systems 692
Car radio 704...706
Carbon deposits, diesel fuels 230
Carbon monoxide 478
Carbonitriding 255
Carburetors 431...435
Carburetor system, electronically
controlled 434
Carburetor, constant-depression 431
Carburetor, double-barrel 432
Carburetor, downdraft 431
Carburetor, main system 433
Carburetor, mixing chamber 431
Carburetor, sidedraft 431
Carburetor, single-venturi 431
Carburetor, two-stage 431
Carburizing 255
Carnot cycle 69, 354
Case depth 256
Case-depth steel 186
Case-hardening 255
Cast iron, properties 185
Cast-aluminum alloys 191
Caster 588

Catalyst, reduction 481
Catalytic afterburning 481
Catalytic converter 424, 481
Catalytic converter, dual-bed 481
Catalytic converter, metal 425
Catalytic converter, noble-metal, diesel engine 513
Catalytic converter, selective 481
Catalytic converter, three-way 481
Cathode 74, 91
Cathodic corrosion protection 247
Cations 74
CBE see Cab Behind Engine 664
CD see Compact Disc 705
Cells, solar 91
Cells, dry 75
Cells, Galvanic 75
Cells, Leclanché 75
Cells, Weston 75
Cellular telephone networks 714
Celsius degree, conversion 33
Celsius, unit 15
Central injection unit, Mono-Jetronic 436
Central locking system 725
Central Processing Unit (CPU) 94, 160
Centrifugal advance mechanism 457
Centrifugal force in curves 338
Ceramics 174, 200, 207
Cetane improvers 230
Cetane Number (CN) 229
Change in condition 354
Change in condition for gases 69
Characteristic axle frequency 560
Charge stratification 367
Charge-air cooling 414
Charging air 372
Charging balance calculation 759
Charging efficiency, gas exchange 368
Charging systems 418...423
Chassis dynamometer 483, 644
Chassis frame, trucks 663
Chassis, passenger bus 665
Check valve 732
Check-Control 707
Chemical deposition 249
Chemical elements 168...171
Chemicals, names 236...241
Chip 88
Choke 434
Choke flap 433
Chromizing 248
Circle, area 142
Circuit diagrams 752...754
Circuit family 94
Circuit isolation, air brakes 634
Circuit, magnetic 81
Circuit-board technology 97
Circular cask, volume 143
Circular cone, volume 143
Circular Pitch (CP), gears 297
Circumference, table 141
Cladding 249,250
Classification, road vehicles 647
Cleaning systems, headlamp 696
Cleaning systems, rear-window 695
Clearance, wheel brakes 627
Climbing power 327
Climbing resistance 327
Clinching 311
Clock generator 94
Clockwise (cw) rotation, IC engine 377
Closed control loop 164
Closed-center system, hydraulic 735
Closed-circuit current switch-off, transist. ign. 459
Closed-loop control 164...167
Cloud point, oils, definition 218
Clutches 538...541
Coal liquefaction 231
Coalescing, fuel filters 506
Coarse thread, UNC 290
Coating, powder 250
Coatings, inorganic nonmetallic 248
Coatings, metallic 249
Coatings, organic 250
COE see Cab Over Engine 664
Coefficient of adhesion 583
Coefficient of contraction 51
Coefficient of thermal expansion 173
Coefficient of flow resistance 726
Coefficient of nonuniformity 380
Coefficient of static friction 329
Coefficient of thermal expansion 173
Coefficient, addendum modification 296
Coefficient, contraction 51
Coefficients of friction 49, 285
Coefficients, drag 47
Coefficients, friction 49
Coefficient of yaw moment 336
Coercive field strength 79, 173
Coil ignition 446...448, 455
Coil spring, suspension 566
Coils 76, 745
Cold adhesives 309
Cold riveting 310
Cold starting 433
Cold-flow properties, diesel fuels 229
Collector (transistor) 89
Colloid, chemical, definition 172
Color filters 130

Combination brake cylinder
for wedge brakes 637
Combination of vehicles,
systematics 646
Combustion by-products 478
Combustion cycle, ideal 355
Combustion efficiency 396
Combustion process 479
Combustion process,
diesel engines 365
Combustion process, SI engines 359
Combustion products,
diesel engines 512
Combustion products, SI engines 478
Combustion smoothness,
diesel engines 494
Combustion speed 359
Combustion systems,
divided-chamber 364
Combustion, complete 478
Combustion, cyclic 352
Combustion, external 352
Combustion, incomplete 478
Combustion, internal 352, 355
Combustion-chamber design 480, 512
Combustion-chamber shape 362, 512
Comfort and convenience
systems 722...725
Commercial vehicles, definition 646
Commercial vehicles, noise reduction
667
Commercial vehicles, transmissions 545
Commercial vehicles, bodies 662...667
Communication and information
systems 704...706
Communication between ECU's,
CAN 776
Compact alternators 771
Compact Disk (CD) 705
Complete body calculation 660
Complex admittance 77
Composite materials 175
Compound, chemical, definition 172
Compressed-air brakes,
components 633
Compressibility, brake fluids 234
Compression pressure 405
Compression space 402
Compression spring 278
Compression strength 55
Compression, calculation 399
Compressor map 421
Comprex supercharger 423
Computing power 160
Conductance 77
Conductivity, electrical 86, 204
Conductivity, thermal 173
Conductor calculations 756
Confidence interval 153
Conformability, bearings 269
Connecting rod 387
Connecting-rod force 378
Connecting-rod ratio 378
Connections, symbols 744...755
Consistency, lubricants 218
Constant pressure cycle,
gas turbine 410
Constant throttle, exhaust brake 629
Constant Volume Sampling (CVS) 513
Constant-pressure cycle 354
Constant-pressure turbocharging 422
Constant-pressure valve 497
Constant-velocity joints, final drive 552
Constant-volume cycle 354
Constant-volume ideal
combustion cycle 356
Constant-volume valve 497
Consumption graph, engine 322
Contact breaker, ignition 455,456
Contact corrosion 242
Contact force, crosswind 338
Contact potential 83
Contact pressure, gears 299
Contact wear, contact breaker 456
Contact-point electrode, welding 306
Contamination sensor 115
Content-based addressing, CAN 777
Continous-time control 166
Continuous combustion 352
Continuous division, mathematics 140
Continuous sound level, equivalent 64
Continuous-flow measurement
method, fuel-inj. pumps 511
Continuously variable transmissions 551
Contrast, technical optics 131
Control bit, CAN 777
Control coil, glow plug 521
Control dynamics 391
Control engineering 164...167
Control field, CAN , 778
Control of lift axles 562
Control rack, in-line fuel-injection
pump 497
Controller Area Network
(CAN) 776...778
Controlling system 164
Convection 66
Conversion products, diesel fuel 229
Conversion tables 17...38
Converter and clutch unit 544, 546

Converter lockup 550
Converter, hydrodynamic 328
Convertible (sedan) saloon, definition 646
Coolant 413
Coolant circuit 392
Cooling, engine 392, 412...415
Coolant circuit, air-conditioning system 702
Copper conductors, motor vehicles 756
Copper losses, alternator 773
Copper wire, round 205
Core assembly, turbocharger 421
Core hardness 253
Core roughness 265
Cornering behavior 338
Cornering force, tires 337, 582
Cornering resistance 325
Correcting range 165
Corrosion 242...251
Corrosion inhibitors, fuels 231
Corrosion protection 229, 234, 242, 247, 654
Corrosion testing 245
Corrosive atmospheres 350
Cosine 138
Cotangent 138
Coulomb's Law 71
Counterclockwise (ccw) rotation, IC engine 377
Counterflow cylinder head 389
Coupé, definition 646
Coupling, fluid friction 414
Coupling, galvanic 782
Coupling, vibration/oscillation 40
Coupling, Visco 414
Covering layers, corrosion prot'n. 248
CPU see Central Processing Unit 94, 160
Crack products 478
Crank angle 378
Crank angle, convers. of degrees to mm piston travel 403
Crank arrangement, IC engine 382
Crank mechanism, IC engine 378
Crankcase 389
Crankcase compression 372
Crankcase scavenging 372
Crankcase ventilation 480
Crankshaft 379, 387
Crankshaft throw 387
Crankshaft vibrations 388
Crash behavior, analysis 661
CRC field, CAN 778
Creep 57
Creep behavior 57
Crevice corrosion 245
Critical speeds 339
Cross scavenging 371
Crossflow cylinder head 389
Crosswind forces, motor-vehicle dynamics 336
Crosswind sensitivity 340
Crosswinds, response to 336
Cruise control 467
Crushing strength, radial 172
Cryogenic tank 493
CT tires 577
Cumulative frequency curve 150
Curb weight, passenger cars 785..813
Curie point, definition 173
Curie temperature, ferrites 198
Current, electric 10, 72, 75...77
Current-carrying conductor with magnetic field 82
CVS method (Constant Volume Sampling) 483, 513
CW value 651
Cycle, Carnot 69, 354
Cycle, Stirling engine 406
Cycles, thermodynamic 353
Cyclic Redundancy Check (CRC) 778
Cycloidal teeth 292
Cyclone 416
Cylinder charge 396
Cylinder charge control, ECOTRONIC 434
Cylinder head 389
Cylinder liner 386
Cylinder numbering 377
Cylinder pressure, hydraulic cylinder 726
Cylinder switch-off 361
Cylinders, hydraulic 733
Cylinder, regular 143
Cylindrical gears 293
Cylindrical spring 566

D

Damage, tribological 315
Damping characteristics 565
Damping, oscillations 39
Dash area 658
Data field, CAN 778
Data processing in motor vehicles 160...163
Daytime running lamps 686
DC see Direct Current 72...75
Deceleration, braking 331
Decibel 62, 783

Decimal system 136
Decoder Information (DI Code) 706
Deep-drawing presses 313
Deep-drawing technology 312
Deformation behavior of vehicle body 658
Degree of reflection 129
Degrees of protection, electric machines 127
Delivery rate, hydraulic pump 726
Delta connection 77
Demagnetization curves 81
Demodulation, EMC 782
Denloc groove 573
Density 172, 230
Density increase of combustion air on supercharging 405
Density, magnetic flux 78
Design approval, regulations 814
Detergent additives, fuels 229, 231
Deviations of form 264
Device for correcting braking force, load-sensitive 636
Devices, semiconductor 88...91
Devices, symbols 744...747
Dezincification 245
DI-Code see Decoder Information 706
Diagnosis, motor-vehicle 474
Diamagnetic materials 78
Diamagnets 176
Diametral pitch (P), gears 297
Diaphragm accumulator, hydraulic 737
Diaphragm-type cylinder, braking syst., comm. vehs. 635
Dielectric constant 71
Dielectric displacement 71
Diesel engine 362...366, 494...522
Diesel engine, full-load speed 499
Diesel engine, M-System 364
Diesel fuel-injection pumps, see Fuel-injection pumps, Diesel 494...506
Diesel fuels 229
Diesel knock 366
Diesel-smoke emissions, measurement 518
Differential 537, 553
Differential lock 552
Diffusion flame 365
Diffusion potential 87
Diffusion process 248
Diffusion rate 415
Digital calling system 715
Digital conversion 101
Digital integrated circuit 94
Dilatant flow behavior, lubricants 220
Dimensional tolerances 263
Dimensions of passenger cars 649
Dimensions, exterior, ISO 266
Dimensions, exterior, passenger cars 649
Dimensions, internal, ISO 267
Dimensions, internal, passenger cars 648, 649
Diode thyristor 91
Diode, Light Emitting (LED) 135
Diode, photo 89
Diode, Schottky 88
Diode, switching 88
Diode, varactor 88
Diode, Zener 88
Direct cooling 392
Direct current 72...75
Direct hardening 255
Direct injection (DI) 363
Direct interference, EMC 783
Direct-current circuits 73
Direct-current machines 83, 123
Direct-current relays, materials 177, 196
Direct-current drive, electric vehicles 530
Direction of action 165
Directional-control valves, hydraulic 730
Directly controlled variable 164
Disc brakes 608, 627
Disc wheel 572
Disc-type flexible couplings, final drive 551
Discharge rate 51
Discharge time, energy-storage device 320
Discharge, gas 85
Discrete-time control 166
Dispersion, chemical, definition 172
Display elements, technical optics 135
Dissociation losses, combustion 360
Distributorless ignition, ignition energy 450
Distributorless voltage distribution, electr. ign. 463
Distribution , binomial 156
Distribution, normal 151
Distribution, Poisson 156
Distribution, Weibull 155
Distributor cap 456
Disturbance point 165
Disturbance range 165
Disturbances 165
Dog clutch 543
Dominant bit, CAN 777

Door latches, passenger cars 655
Door locking 743
Door operation, buses 742
Doped lubricants 218
Doping, semiconductors 86
Doppler effect 61
Double check valve, hydraulic 731
Double road train, definition 646
Double-action presses 313
Downgrade force 327
Drag coefficient 47
Drag, aerodynamic 325
Draw tempering, steel 254
Drawbar load, regulations 818
Drawbar tractor combination, definition 646
Drive configuration, motor-vehicle specifications 785...813
Driveability, road vehicle 320
Driven plate, clutch 538
Driver information systems 713
Driver's cab 663
Drives, hydrostatic 740
Drivetrain 536...559
Driving resistance, external 323
Dropping point, lubricants 218
Drum brakes 608, 624...626
Dry cells 75
Dry or boundary friction 315
Dual-circuit indicator systems 690
Dual-circuit steering systems 590
Dual-component adhesives 309
Dual-fuel operation 490
Dual-spark coil 450, 464
Dual-spring nozzle holders 508
Dummy (manikin) 658
Dust unloading valve 417
Dust, stresses 350
Duty types, electric machines 126
Dwell angle 456
Dynamic behavior, vehicle body 660
Dynamic loadability, bearings 275
Dynamic supercharging 373
Dynamic tire-performance curves 584
Dynamic viscosity 220
Dynamic voltage system characteristic 759
Dynamics of lateral motion 336
Dynamics of linear motion 324

E

E-Gas 467
E-Series 137
Ease of repair, body 652
EDC see Electronic diesel control
EC tachograph 710
Eccentricity, bearings 268
ECE/EG driving cycle, SI engines 486
ECOTRONIC 434
ECU see Electronic Control Unit 160
EDC, distributor injection pump 504
EDC, in-line injection pump 501
EEPROM, microcomputer 94
Effective luminous flux 669
Effective value, vibration/oscillation 40
Effects, electrical 83...85
Effects, galvanomagnetic 85
Effects, thermomagnetic 85
Efficiency chain 356
Efficiency of cycle approximation 357
Efficiency, combustion 396
Efficiency, indicated 357
Efficiency, mechanical 357
Efficiency, overall 356
Efficiency, thermal 69, 354
EFI see Fuel-injection, gasoline 436...445
EGR see Exhaust-Gas Recirculation 470, 480, 513
Elastic limit under bending 55
Elastokinematics, wheel suspension 569
Elastomer swelling 234
Elastomers 175
Electric drives, motor vehicles 527...532
Electric fuel pumps 436...444
Electric machines 123...127
Electric start valve 439, 443
Electrical conductivity 86
Electrical devices, identification 747
Electrical energy supply, automotive electrical systems 758...762
Electrical engine-power control (EMS) 467
Electrical engineering 70...85
Electrical loads, motor vehicles 759
Electrical properties, materials 204
Electrical systems, automotive 758...778
Electrochemical corrosion testing 245
Electrode gap, spark plug 453
Electrode-potential series 83
Electrodynamic retarder 632
Electrodynamic rotary actuator 119
Electrodynamic short-stroke linear motor 119
Electrohydraulic pumps 729
Electrohydraulic servo unit 733
Electrolysis 74
Electrolytes 74

Electromagnetic compatibility (EMC) 779...783
Electromagnetic fields 70
Electron-beam welding 308
Electron-hole pair 87
Electronic boost-pressure control 468
Electronic Control Unit (ECU) 160, 443
Electronic Diesel Control (EDC) 501...504
Electronic engine-power control 467, 555, 559
Electronic heating control 701
Electronic ignition 460...463
Electronic transmission control 548
Electronic-system testing 476
Electronics 86...101
Electrophoretic enameling 654
Electroplating 249
Electropneumatic fanfare horns 691
Elements, chemical 168
Ellipse, area 142
Ellipsoid 143
Elongation after fracture table 185
Embeddability, bearings 269
EMC see Electromagnetic compatibility 779...783
Emissions see Exhaust emissions
Emittance, luminous 131
Emitter, transistor 89
Empirical distribution 151
Emulsion, chemical, definition 172
Enameling 248
Energy, magnetic field 83
Energy storage, compressed-air brakes 634
Energy, heat (diesel engines) 362
Energy, ignition, 429
Energy-absorbing foam 653
Energy-storage density 320
Engaging systems, starter 524
Engine and vehicle speed 328
Engine cooling 412...415
Engine diagnosis 476
Engine drag-torque control 467, 558
Engine fuel-consumption graph 322
Engine management, diesel engines 494...511
Engine management, integrated 472
Engine management, SI engines 428...477
Engine oils 222
Engine output 396, 400
Engine power loss 396
Engine power, regulations 816
Engine ring-gear, starting systems 523
Engine torque, calculation 401
Engine type, motor-vehicle specifications 785...813
Engine, internal-combustion 352...411
Engine, ignition intervals 384
Engine, in-line 376
Engine, internal-combustion 352...411
Engine, lean-burn 480
Engine, opposed-cylinder 376
Engine, opposed-piston 376
Engine, radial 376
Engine-control circuit, comm. vehs, ASR 559
Engine management, integratedŸ
Engine-power control, electronic 467, 556
Engine-test technology 476
Engineering statistics 150...157
Engines, closed-process 352
Enhanced Other Network (EON), car radio 706
Enthalpy (heat content) 66
Enthalpy-entropy diagram 354
Entropy 69
Environmental protection and recycling 661
Environmental stresses on automotive equipment 350
EON see Enhanced Other Network 706
EP (Extreme Pressure) lubricants 218
EPROM, Microcomputer 95
Equalizer, car radio 706
Equation, Eytelwein 302
Equation, quadratic 140
Equilibrium boiling point, brake fluids 234
Equilibrium relation, drive and traction resistances 536
Equivalent, electrochemical 74
Error flag, CAN 778
Ethanol (ethyl alcohol) 182
Ethylene glycol 412
Euler's formula 138
European test, test system (SI engines) 486
Evaluation of inspection by attributes, statistical 155
Evaporative emission control 470
Evaporative-pressure regulator 491
Excess-air factor 428
Exhaust brakes 629...632
Exhaust-emissions, diesel engines 512...519
Exhaust-emissions, SI engines 478...489

Exhaust-emissions testing, diesel engines 513...519
Exhaust-emissions testing, SI engines 483...489
Exhaust-emissions testing equipment, diesel engines 518
Exhaust-emissions testing equipment, SI engines 489
Exhaust-gas analyzer, single-component 489
Exhaust pipe 424
Exhaust systems 424...427
Exhaust valves 390
Exhaust-gas aftertreatment, diesel engines 513
Exhaust-gas aftertreatment, SI engines 481
Exhaust-gas analyzers, SI engines 484, 489
Exhaust-gas collection bag 514
Exhaust-gas components 478
Exhaust-gas control, diesel engines 512
Exhaust-gas control, SI engines 479
Exhaust-gas emissions test 819
Exhaust-gas limits, diesel engines 515
Exhaust-gas limits, SI engines 485
Exhaust-Gas Recirculation (EGR), diesel engines 513
Exhaust-Gas Recirculation (EGR), SI engines 470, 480
Exhaust-gas testing, diesel engines 513
Exhaust-gas testing, infrared process 489
Exhaust-gas testing, SI engines 483
Exhaust-gas turbocharger 420
Exhaust-gas turbocharging 374
Exhaust-gas, diesel engines 512...519
Exhaust-gas, measuring chamber 489
Exhaust-gas, regulations 818
Exhaust-gas, SI engines 478...489
Exhaust-gas, test samples 483
Expansion tank, coolant 413
Extension spring 278
External filler valve 491
Extremely heavy metals 187
Eytelwein equation 302

F

Fabric-base laminate 209
Factor, power 75
Factor, stress concentration 58
Factor, tooth profile 300
Factor, velocity 300
Failure Mode and Effects Analysis (FMEA) 144, 158
Failure phases 159
Failure rate 155, 158
Fan drive, hydrostatic 738
Fan, cooling 413
Farad, unit 15
Faraday's Laws 74
Fastback, crosswind response 336
Fatigue limits 56, 142...151
Fatigue strength, bearings 269
Fatigue strength of structure 57
Fault-Tree Analysis (FTA) 158
Federal Test Procedure, SI engines 484
Ferrimagnets 176
Ferrit cores 177
Ferromagnetic materials 78
Ferromagnets 176
FET see Field Effect Transistors 89, 90
Fiber composite materials 175
FID see Flame Ionization Detector 513
Field constant, electrical 71
Field strength, coercive 79
Field strength, electrical 71
Field strength, limiting 79
Field, electric 71
Field, electromagnetic 70
Field, magnetic 78, 81
Field-Effect Transistors (FET) 89, 90
Filler metals for brazing 202
Filter method, exhaust-gas emissions 518
Filters, air 416
Filters, bypass 393
Filters, cartridge-type 506
Filters, ceramic-monolith 427
Filters, color 130
Filters, diesel fuels 506
Filters, full-flow 393
Filters, oil 393
Filters, side-mounted 416
Filters, soot 427, 513
Filtration properties, diesel fuels 229
Final controlling elements 164...167 see Actuators 116
Final drive 551
Final drive ratio, motor-vehicle specifications 785...813
Fine thread, ISO 289
Fine thread, UNF 290
Finite-Element Method (FEM) 312
Fire point/flash point 218
Firing order 377
Fischer-Tropsch synthesis 231
Fixed-caliper disk brakes 608

Flame hardening 253
Flame Ionization Detector (FID) 513
Flame plug 521
Flame, diffusion 365
Flange mounting, fasteners 282
Flapper-nozzle system 122
Flash frequency, signal lamps 683, 686
Flash point 218, 229
Flash welding 307
Flashing intensity 686
Flatness of the contact surface, wheels 574
Float angle 342, 344
Float chamber; carburetor 432
Float glass process 698
Float, carburetor 432
Floating-caliper disk brakes 608
Flow curves 220
Flow improvers, diesel fuels 229
Flow meter 111
Flow pressure, lubricants 218
Flow rate 51
Flow rates in lines 727
Flow resistance 121
Flow, change in cross section 51,
Flow-control valves 730
Flow-interrupt valve, LPG system 491
Fluid friction 315
Fluid-friction coupling 414
Fluids, brake 234
Fluids, glycol-ether 234
Fluids, hydraulic 235
Fluids, mineral-oil 235
Fluids, Newtonian 220
Fluids, silicone 235
Fluids, stresses 350
Flux, magnetic 78
Flux-gate principle 712
Fluxing agents 308
Flywheel, hybrid drives 533
FMEA see Failure Mode and Effects Analysis 144, 158
Foam, energy-absorbing 653
Focal length, reflector 668
Force of attraction, magnetic 81
Force of attraction, masses 47
Force sensors 111
Force, connecting-rod 378
Force, contact 338
Force, cornering 337
Force, crosswind 336
Force, downgrade 327
Force, equation 45
Force, friction 315
Force, gas 378
Force, Lorentz 71, 117
Force, motive 328
Force, radial 378
Force, tangential 378
Force, thermoelectromotive 84
Force, transverse 52
Force-feed lubrication 392
Form factor 41
Forward state, semiconductor 87
Föttinger coupling 540
Four-circuit protection valve 620
Four-headlamp system, Litronic 673, 674
Four-stroke process 368...371
Fourier series 39
Fracture toughness 172
Frame junction, truck 664
Free corrosion 242
Free fall 46
Free floating position 736
Free forces, engine design 384
Free moments, engine design 384
Frequency 39
Fresh charge, gas exchange 368
Fresnel optics 682
Fretting corrosion 245
Friction 49, 315
Friction clutch 538
Friction hardening 253
Friction modifier, lubricants 218
Friction welding 308
Frontal impact of two vehicles 666
Frontal impact test 658
Frustrum 143
FTA see Fault-Tree Analysis 158
Fuel consumption 322, 401, 785
Fuel cut-off 361, 433
Fuel distributor, K-Jetronic 439
Fuel filters 506
Fuel for SI engines 226...229
Fuel injection, diesel 494...511
Fuel injection, direct 363
Fuel injection, gasoline 436...445
Fuel injection, multipoint 438
Fuel injection, SI engines 436, 438
Fuel injection, single-point, Mono-Jetronic 436
Fuel lines, regulations 818
Fuel metering, diesel engines 494
Fuel metering, SI engines 428, 479
Fuel pumps 431, 436...444
Fuel pump, hydrodynamic electric 436
Fuel spray, kinetic energy 362
Fuel supply, calculation 400
Fuel tanks, regulations 818

Fuel-delivery control,
in-line fuel-injection pumps 496
Fuel-injection pump test benches 511
Fuel-injection pump,
distributor-type 495, 502
Fuel-injection pump,
high-pressure 496, 503
Fuel-injection pump, in-line 496...502
Fuel-injection pump,
in-line control-sleeve 495, 502
Fuel-injection pumps,
diesel 494...506
Fuel-injection system,
low-pressure single-point 436
Fuel-supply pump,
diesel engines 496, 502
Fuels 226
Fuels, basic requirements 321
Fuels, diesel 229
Fuels, SI engines 226
Full bodywork encapsulation 667
Full bridge, hydraulic 122
Full custom IC 96
Full-depth teeth 297
Full-load adjustment screw 503
Full-load enrichment 433, 437, 441
Fully developed deceleration 598
Fusion welding 308

G

Galvani potential 83
Galvanic coupling 782
Gas discharge 85
Gas exchange 352, 368
Gas force, reciprocating-piston
engine 378
Gas friction 315
Gas laser (CO_2) 314
Gas turbine, automotive 410
Gas turbine, IC engines 352
Gas velocity, calculation 400
Gas-shielded metal-arc
welding 308
Gaseous fuels 233
Gaseous hydrocarbons 233
Gaseous storage, hydrogen 493
Gasoline, leaded 226
Gasoline, premium 232
Gasoline, regular 226
Gasoline, unleaded 226
Gasoline/Petrol 226
Gate array 97
Gear motors, hydraulic 728
Gear pair with modified
center distance 293
Gear pair with reference
center distance 293
Gear pumps , hydraulic 727
Gear shifting 542
Gear types 293
Gears 292...301
Gears, load-bearing capacity 298
Gears, operating pitch diameter 294
Gel-type greases 218
General corrosion 244
General inspection, motor vehicles 816
Geomagnetic sensor 712
Geometric range, headlamp 668
Geometric series 140
Geometric visibility, lighting 669
German alphabet 822
Glare, physiological 668
Glass ceramics 249
Glass fibers see optical fibers 133
Glass-mat-base laminate 209
Glasses 175
Glazing 655
Glow control unit 521
Glycol-ether fluids 234
GMA see Yaw-moment build-up
delay 613
Golden section 140
Gough tire-performance map 583
Governor, combination 498
Governor, mechanical 497
Governor, minimum-maximum-
speed 498
Governor, variable-speed 497
Governors, diesel engine 497...504
Graded-index fiber 133
Graphite 218
Gravimetric measurement,
fuel consumption 322
Gravitation 47
Greases, lubricating 224
Greek alphabet 822
Greenhouse effect 478
Gross calorific value 226
Ground clearance,
passenger-car 786...813
GSM Net 714
GTO thyristor 91
Guldin's rule for plane surfaces 142
Guldin's rule for solids 143
Gyrometer, oscillation 107

H

H-point 648
Half-bridge, hydraulic 122
Half-differential sensor 105

Half-value width, vibration/oscillation 40
Hall constant 85
Hall effect 85
Hall-effect vane switch 106
Hamlin switch 717
Handling characteristics, steering 587
Hard metals 187
Hard soldering 308
Hardening 252
Hardening potential 253
Hardening temperatures 252
Hardness 258...262
Hardness tests 258
Hardness, ball impression 262
Hardness, Brinell 259
Hardness, Knoop (HK) 262
Hardness, Rockwell (HR) 258
Hardness, Shore 262
Hardness, Vickers (HV) 260
Hazard flashers 690
Headlamps 129, 132, 670...680
Headlamp aiming 678
Headlamp aiming devices 689
Headlamp cleaning systems 696
Headlamps, main 670...676
Headlamps, nested design 670
Headlamps, PES 672
Headlamps, sealed-beam 676
Headlight leveling devices 680
Heat 66
Heat capacity, specific 173
Heat content 66
Heat exchanger 410
Heat of evaporation 173, 226
Heat of fusion, specific 173
Heat range, spark plugs 451
Heat transfer 66
Heat treatment 252...257
Heatable safety glass 699
Heated Lambda sensor 482
Heater flange 521
Heater plug 521
Heating systems, engine-dependent 700
Heating systems, engine-independent 703
Heating, Ventilation, and Air-Conditioning (HVAC) 700
Heavy metals 190
Helical gear 294
Helical spring 278
Helmholtz resonator 417, 427
Hexagon, area 142
High beam 674, 676
High-lubricity oils 223
High-pressure lubricants 218
High-pressure pumps, hydraulics 727
Hip point 648
Histogram 150
Hoisting gear control 735
Hologram 134
Holography 134
Homofocal reflector 672
Homogeneuous mixture, formation 358
Homologation, regulations 814
Hooke's Law 53
Horns, fanfare 691
Horns, supertone 691
Hot adhesives 309
Hot dipping 249
HP (horsepower), conversion 30, 31
Hump rim, passenger car 572
Hybrid circuits 97
Hybrid drives 533
Hybrid electric bus 535
Hybrid engines 367
Hybrid fuels 231
Hydraulic accumulators 737
Hydraulic cylinder 726
Hydraulic diaphragm accumulator 567
Hydraulic fluids 234
Hydraulic half-bridge 122
Hydraulic motors 726
Hydraulic pumps 726
Hydraulic valves 730
Hydraulics, automotive 726...741
Hydrocarbons 478
Hydrodynamic converters 328, 539
Hydrodynamic couplings 540
Hydrodynamic retarders 630
Hydrodynamics 220
Hydromechanical efficiency 726
Hydropneumatic suspension 564, 567
Hydrostatic press 51
Hysteresis loop 78

I

I-element, control engineering 166
IC (1) see Integrated Circuit 93, 96, 97
IC (2) see Internal-Combustion Engines 352...411
IC engines, reciprocating-piston 355, 376, 386
IC engines, comparative data 395
IC engines, definition of power 397
IC engines, direction of rotation 377
IC engines, maximum torque position 396
IC engines, multifuel 367
IC engines, polytropic exponent 360, 366

IC engines, power and
torque curves 395
IC engines, torque increase 396
IC engines, values and data
for calculations 394
Icing protection, fuels for
SI engines 229
Ideal combustion cycle 355
Identifier (CAN) 777
Idle air-correction jet 433
Idle fuel-correction jet 433
Idle-speed actuator 466
Idle-speed control 459, 466
Idle-speed reduction 433
Ignition 358, 446...464
Ignition angle, determination 448
Ignition angle, effect upon
exhaust-gas 448
Ignition chamber 358
Ignition coils 449
Ignition curve 360
Ignition distributors 456
Ignition energy 429, 446
Ignition point 429, 447
Ignition quality 229
Ignition spark 446
Ignition system, influence on
exhaust-gas 480
Ignition systems 455...464
Ignition timing, adjustment 447, 466
Ignition voltage 4461
Ignition voltage and electrode gap 453
Ignition, capacitor-discharge
(CDI) 460
Ignition, distributorless semiconductor
(DSI) 463
Ignition, high-voltage 446
Ignition, mixture 446
Ignition, Motronic 473
Ignition, transistorized,
breaker-triggered 458
Ignition, transistorized, breakerless 458
Ignition-pulse generator 458
Ignition-triggering sensor 106
Illuminance 131
Imaging chamber 689
Imbalance, tire 574
Imbalance, wheel 574
Impact detection 719
Impedance 76
Incandescent lamps, symbols 745
Increment system, ignition 462
Independent suspension 571
Indicated efficiency 357
Indices of refraction 129
Individ. efficiency, reciprocating-
piston engine 357
Inductance 76, 82
Induction 78, 82
Induction period, lubricants 219
Inductive hardening 253
Inductive sensors 106
Industrial atmospheres, stresses 350
Inert-gas welding 308
Inertia forces 379
Inhibitors 219, 248
Inhibitors, vapor-phase 251
Initial sample inspection 146
Inorganic materials 174
Input power, hydraulic pump 726
Input signals 160
Input torque, hydraulic motor 726
Input torque, hydraulic pump 726
Inspection tag 816
Inspection, initial sample 146
Insulated-gate FET 89
Insulating materials,
electrical properties 206
Insulators 86
Intake runners, variable-length
intake manifold 469
Intake valves, IC engine 369, 390
Intake-air temp., effect on
exhaust-gas (diesel eng.) 512
Intake-noise damping 417
Intake-system contamination
inhibitors 228
Integral window-mounted antenna 706
Integrated Circuit (IC) 92
Integrated sensors 103
Integration level, IC 93
Integration, monolithic 92
Intercooling, diesel engines 512
Intercrystalline corrosion 245
Interface reaction, corrosion7 242
Interference coupling 782
Interference model, EMC 782
Interference radiation 781
Interference source, motor vehicle 781
Interference suppression 781, 820
Interference, vibration/oscillation 40
Interior rim 655
Intermittent duty 126
Internal-combustion engines
see IC engines 352...411
Internal-transport vehicles 527
Interval, acoustic 61
Intrinsic conduction, semiconductors 87
Intrinsically viscous flow behavior 220
Involute function 139

Involute teeth 292
Iron losses, alternator 773
Isentropic change of state
for gases 69, 354
ISO allowances 266
ISO metric screw threads 289
ISO tolerance classes 263
Isobaric change of state
for gases 69
Isochoric change of state
for gases 69, 354
Isothermal change of state
for gases 69, 354

J

Jackknifing 347
Jetronic see Fuel-injection,
gasoline 436...445
Jetronic, K- 438
Jetronic, KE- 440
Jetronic, L- 442
Jetronic, LH 444
Jetronic, L3 443
Jetronic, Mono- 436
Joining and bonding
techniques 306...311
Jointed drive shaft, final drive 551
Joule cycle, gas turbine 410
Junction FET 90

K

K-Jetronic 438
K-values, bolted joints 286
Karman vortex path 112
Karman vortex volume-flow
sensor 112, 112, 445
KE-Jetronic 440
Kelvin 10, 15, 33
Kesternich test, corrosion 246
Kickdown 548
Kilogramm 10, 12
Kinematic viscosity 220
Kinetic energy 45
Kinetic energy, fuel spray 362
Kingpin inclination offset 569
Kingpin offset 569
Kirchhoff's laws 72
Knock control, electronic ignition 464
Knock control, Motronic 473
Knock inhibitors 228
Knock sensor 108, 465
Knot, unit 36

L

L-Jetronic 442
L3-Jetronic 443
Ladder-type frame 664
Lambda closed-loop control 443, 482
Lambda sensor 113, 482
Laminar flow 727
Laminated composite materials 175
Laminated Safety Glass (LSG) 698
Laminates 209
Lamp bulbs 687
Lamps 682
Lamps, backup 685
Lamps, clearance 684
Lamps, daytime running 686
Lamps, flood 686
Lamps, fog 681
Lamps, fog warning 685
Lamps, gaseous-discharge 130, 673
Lamps, identification 686
Lamps, licence-plate 686
Lamps, marker 682
Lamps, parking 685
Lamps, side-marker 684
Lamps, signal 682
Lamps, spot 686
Lamps, stop 684
Lamps, stop, high-mounted 684
Lamps, tail 684
Lamps, turn-signal 683
Lamps, stop, primary 684
Lanchester balancing system 383
Laser technology 314
Latency time 163
Lateral area of solids 143
Lateral force, braked wheel 610
Lateral run-out 574
Law of continuity 81
Law of induction 82
Law of quadratic error sum 152
Layout diameter, gears 297
LCD see Liquid crystal display 135
Leakage coefficient, magnetic 81
Leclanché cell 75
LED see Light emitting diode 135
Legal units 11
Lens, headlamp 675
Lever law 47
LH-Jetronic 444
License plates, regulations 821
Light alloy rims 574
Light distribution 671, 673
Light metals 191
Light sources 130

Light transmittance,vehicle windows 699
Light-duty trucks 662
Light-emitting diode (LED) 135
Light/dark cutoff, headlamps 670
Lighting 668...689
Limit fits, ISO system 263
Limits, fatigue 56, 142...151
Limiting field strength 79
Line cross section, hydraulics 727
Linear bus structure (CAN) 776
Linear coefficient of expansion 173
Linear motion, dynamics 324
Liquefied Petroleum Gas (LPG) 231, 490
Liquid crystal display (LCD) 135
Liquid fuels 232
Liquid hydrocarbons 232
Liquid storage, hydrogen 493
Liquids 182
Litronic 673, 674
Load dump 775, 780
Load sensing valves 730,
Load signal 503
Load, permissible 55
Load, pulsating 56
Load-bearing components 653
Load-leveling system 561
Loads, regulations for passenger cars 814
Locating screw 286
Locking devices, threaded fasteners 282
Locking factor 554
Locking nut 285
Locking synchronizer 543
Lockup clutch 541
Logarithmic decrement 40
Logarithms 136, 141
Logical bus states, CAN 777
Long-distance coach, body 666
Long-distance coach, definition 646
Loop scavenging 371
Lorentz force 71, 116
Loudness 65
Loudness level 64
Low beam, headlamps 132, 670, 676
Low-temperature sludge 219
LPG see Liquefied Petroleum Gas 231
Lubricants 218...225
Lubricating greases 224
Lubrication, IC engines 392
Luggage-compartment dimensions 648
Luminance 131
Luminous efficiency 131
Luminous emittance 131
Luminous energy 131
Luminous flux 131, 669
Luminous intensity 131, 669

M

MAN M-system 131
Mach number 36
Machines, electric 123
Magnesium alloy 191
Magnetic field 78, 81...83
Magnetic field strength 78
Magnetic flux 78
Magnetic materials 176
Magnetic steel sheet 176, 194
Magnetic strip 176, 194
Magnetization characteristics 80
Main dimensions, passenger cars 648
Main headlamps, American system 676
Main headlamps, European system 670
Malleable cast iron 185
Manifold-pressure compensator 499
Manipulated variable 165
Manual headlight leveling 680
Manufacturing accuracy 157
Map memory (Travelpilot) 713
Marks of approval, headlamp lens 668
Martensitic structure 252
Materials 174...215
Materials parameters 172
Materials science 168...262
Materials terminology 172
Mathematics 136...143
Matrix 312
Maximum permeability 173
McPherson strut 571
Mean Time To Failure (MTTF) 158
Mean value, vibration/oscillation 40
Measured values, presentation 150
Measuring techniques, EMC 783
Mechanical wiper mechanism 694
Mechanics, basic equations 44
Mechanics, fluids 51
Mechanics, micro 98
Mechatronics 100
Memory, semiconductor 94
Message filtering, CAN 777
Message format, CAN 777
Metal adhesives 309
Metal soaps 219
Metall-hydride tank 493
Metallic coatings 217, 249
Metals 86, 174
Meter, definition 10
Methanol 492
Methylcyclohexanol 493

Microbuses, body 665
Microclimate, 350
Microcomputer 94, 160
Microcontroller 94
Micromechanics 98
Microprocessor 94, 161
MIL specifications, motor oils 223
Mineral oils 219, 235
Minibus, definition 646
Minority carrier 87
Minority carrier, charge 87
Misfire limit 428, 452
Mixed friction 221, 315
Mixing unit, Venturi 491
Mixture formation 353, 430, 478, 493, 512
Mixture formation, SI engine 430, 479, 512
Mixture ignition 446
Mixture, air-fuel 428
Mixture, air-fuel, calorific value 226
Mobile radio 714
Modal analysis 43
Module series, spur and bevel gears 295
Modulus of elasticity 52
Modulus of rigidity, strength 54
Moldings 653
Mole, unit 10
Molybdenum disulphide 219
Moments of inertia, IC engine 48, 52, 59
Moment of inertia of plane areas 59
Moment sensors 111
Moments of inertia 379
MON see Motor Octane Number 227
Monitoring, CAN 778
Mono-Jetronic 436
Mono-piston power unit 376
Monolex tapered-bead seat rim 574
Monolithic integration 92
Monomode fiber 133
Mopeds, regulations 821
MOS transistors 90
MOSFET 90
Motion 44, 330
Motive force 328
Motor cycle, definition 646
Motor Octane Number (MON) 227
Motor-vehicle bulbs 687
Motor-vehicle glass windows 698
Motor-vehicle safety 656
Motor-vehicle specifications 784
Motor-vehicle, definition 646
Motor-vehicle, dynamics 324
Motors, electric 123...127
Motor-driven cycles, noise limits 821
Motor-driven cycles, regulations 821
Motor-vehicle dynamics, power unit 378
Motor-vehicle specifications 784
Motorcycle, definition 646
Motorcycles, regulations 821
Motors, hydraulic 727
Motortesters, diesel engines 511
Motronic 472
MTTF see Mean Time To Failure 158
Muffler, absorption 426, 638
Muffler, reflection 426
Multi-leaf spring 276
Multi-Master Principle, CAN 776
Multi-step transmissions 542
Multifuel engines 367
Multifunction regulator 774
Multigrade oils 219, 223
Multimode fiber 133
Multiplate overrunning clutch, starter 525
Multiple-hole nozzle combustion 363
Multiple-passage intake runners 469
Multiple-purpose truck 646
Multiplex, CAN 776

N

Narrow-band interference source 780
Natural frequency of absorbers 42
Natural oscillation 39
Navigation systems, road 712, 713
Net calorific value 226
Net engine horsepower, specifications 785
Net power 397
Neutral axis 52
Newton's law 11
Newton, unit 10
Newtonian fluids 220
Nitriding 256
Nitrocarburizing 256
No-load speed 499
Noble metals 244
Noise damping, intake 417
Noise reduction 61
Noise reduction, commercial vehicles 667
Noise-source analysis, trucks 667
Nominal power 397
Non-metallic materials 207
Non-positive friction-type transmissions 537
Non-return valves 732
Non-volatile memory 94, 161
Nonconductors 86

Nonferrous metals 190
Normal distribution 151
Normalizing 257
Notch effect 54
Notchback, crosswind response 336
Notched impact strength, laminates 209
Nozzle body 507
Nozzle holder 506
Nozzle holders, standard, diesel engines 507
Nozzle needle 507
Nozzles, hole-type 510
Nozzles, injection, diesel engine 506...510
Nozzles, multi-hole 510
Nozzles, pintle, flat 509
Nozzles, seat-hole 510
Nozzles, throttling-pintle 508
Number of parts, population 155
Number of teeth spanned 294
Number systems 136
Number, octane 227
Number, Reynolds 47
Number, Sommerfeld 268
Numbers, preferred 137
Numbers, useful 136
Nuts, fasteners 283

O

OBD see On-Board Diagnosis 477
Occupant-restraint systems, regulations 816
Octane number 227
Octane rating 227
Octave 61
Octave band spectrum 61
Odometers, regulations 820
Off-board test device 477
Ohm's Law 72, 76
Ohmic resistance 72
Oil control ring 386
Oil coolers 412
Oil filters 393
On-Board Diagnosis (OBD) 477
One-wire interface 163
Opacity measurement, exhaust gas 519
Open Center (OC), hydraulics 730, 734
Open control loop 164
Open-flame soldering 309
Open process, IC engines 352
Open system, load-leveling system 563
Open-circuit potential 243
Open-loop control 164
Open-loop control systems 167
Open-loop controlled system 165
Open-loop operation 340
Opening pressure, nozzle 507
Operating behavior, ISO procedures for evaluating 340
Operating dynamics, commercial vehicles 345
Operating time, energy-storage device 320
Operational amplifier (OP) 101
Operational integrity, passenger cars 652
Optical fibers 133
Optical waveguides 133
Optics, technical 128...135
Oscillating mass 379
Oscillation gyrometer 107
Output power, car radio 705
Output power, hydraulic motor 726
Output power, hydraulic pump 726
Output signals 162
Outside diameter, gears 294, 297
Overall efficiency, IC engines 356
Overall efficiency, reciprocating-piston engine 357
Overlap ratio, gears 294
Overrun fuel cutoff 433, 435
Overrun operation 433
Overrunning clutches, starters 523, 525
Oversteering 338, 341, 587
Overvoltage protection 775
Oxidants 478
Oxidation catalyst 424, 481
Oxides of nitrogen 478
Oxygen-concentration sensor 113

P

P-element, control engineering 166
Painting 250, 654
Paper sizes 20
Paper-base laminate 209
Parallel connection 73, 76
Parallelogram 142
Paramagnetic materials 78
Paramagnets 176
Park-Pilot 709
Parking-brake valve 636
Part-load behavior, IC engines 396
Part-load operation 428
Partial chassis encapsulation 667
Particle compound materials 175
Particle velocity 39, 60
Particulates, exhaust-gas 478
Passenger-car bodies 648...661
Passenger-car combination, definition 646

Passenger car, definitions 646
Passenger-car specifications 784...813
Passenger road train, definition 646
Passenger-car cooling system 412
Passenger-compartment protection, ultrasonic 693
Passing (overtaking) 334
PCI see Program Comparison and Identification 705
Peak factor 41
Peak-to-valley height 265
Peak height , 265
Peltier effect 84
Pendulum motion 45
Penetration, lubricant 219, 221
Perceptibility safety 656
Periodic system of elements 171
Peripheral module 160
Peripheral devices 94
Permanent magnets 176
Permanent permeability 173
Permanent-magnet excitation, motor 123
Permanent-magnet materials 177, 199
Permeability 78, 173
Permissible voltage loss, conductors 757
PES see Poly-Ellipsoid System 672
PES reflectors 673
Phase difference 75, 77
Phon 64
Phonetic alphabets 822
Phosphatizing 248
Photodiode 89
Photometric quantities and units 131
Photovoltaic solar cells 89, 92
Physics, basic 10...135
Physiology of vision 131
Piezoelectric sensor 108, 110
PIN Code see Program Item Number 706
Pinion, starters 523
Pinion-engaging drive, starters 524
Pipe threads 291
Pistons 386
Piston accumulators, hydraulic 567, 737
Piston motors, hydraulic 728
Piston movement, equation 399
Piston pressure, equation 401
Piston pumps 496, 728
Piston rings 386
Piston velocity 399, 404
Pitch, acoustics 65
Pitch diameter, gears 294, 297
Pitch, suspension 561
Pitting corrosion 244
Plain bearings, sinter (PM) metals 192
Planar technology 93
Planetary gear, starters 523
Planetary-gear set, Simpson 543
Planetary-hub reduction axle 552
Plasma polymerization 251
Plastic flow behavior, lubricants 220
Plastics abbreviations 214
Plate-type limited-slip differentials 554
PLD see Programmable Logic Devices 97
Plenum volume, variable-length intake manifold 469
Plunger-and-barrel assembly with control sleeve 502
Ply rating, PR number, tires 578
PN junction 87
Pneumatics, automotive 742
Poisson approximation 156
Poisson distribution 156
Polar substances, lubricants 219
Polarization, electric 71
Polarization, electrolytic 74
Polarization, magnetic 78, 173
Polarization, saturation 78, 79
Poly-Ellipsoid System (PES) 672
Population, engineering statistics 150
Port-closing sensor, diesel engines 500
Positive belt drives 305
Positive-locking transmissions 537
Post-ignition 452
Potential, diffusion 87
Potential, electrical 15, 71
Pour point 219
Powder coating 250
Power density 320
Power factor 75
Power line frequencies, alternating current 75
Power output 361
Power per unit displacement 400
Power piston, Stirling engine 406
Power-assisted steering system 588...591
Power sunroof 723
Power take-off 546
Power transmission, reciprocating-piston engine 376, 378
Power unit, multi-piston 376
Power windows 722
Power, acceleration 331
Power, braking 331, 598
Power, electrical 72, 75
Power, friction 315

Power, mechanical 45, 50
Power, net 397
Power, nominal 397
Power-assisted steering system 588
Power-to-weight ratio, calculation 400
Power-to-weight ratio, definition 785
Powers, mathematics 141
PR number, tire designation 578
Pre-ignition 452
Prechamber system 364
Precipitation hardening treatment 257
Pressure actuator, KE-Jetronic 441
Pressure build-up time, brakes 333, 598
Pressure modulation valve, comm.-vehs. ABS 641
Pressure point, motor vehicles 336
Pressure-reducing valve 732
Pressure regulation, air brakes 633
Pressure-relief valve, hydraulic 731
Pressure sensors 99, 109
Pressure vs. volume work diagram 353
Pressure, unit 14
Pressure-control valve, hydraulic 731
Pressure-wave supercharger 375, 422
Pressurized clinching 311
Prestress, wheel 574
Pretension factor 303
Primary-current regulator, transistorized ignition 459
Primer coat 654
Priority assignments, CAN 777
Prisms 129
Private mobile radio systems 715
Probability, statistics 152, 155
Process audit, quality 144
Production planning 146
Profile peak-to-valley height 265
Program Comparison and Identification (PCI) 705
Program Item Number (PIN) 706
Program Type (PTY-Code) 705
Programmable Logic Devices (PLD) 97
Progression system, carburetor 433
Project specifications manual, quality 144
Projected vehicle cross-sectional area 651
Projection welding 306
PROM, Microcomputer 95
Propagation of sound 60
Properties of gases 184
Properties of liquids 182
Properties of solids 178
Proportional valves 733
Protection against ageing, fuels 228
Protective coatings 249
PS (HP), conversion 14, 30, 31
Psychological glare, lighting 668
PTY Code see Program Type 705
Pulse generator, Hall-type 458
Pulse generator, induction-type 458
Pulse welding 308
Pulse-shaped input signals 160
Pump, accelerator, carburetor 433
Pumps, fuel-injection see Fuel-injection pumps, diesel 494...506
Pump, piston 496
Pump, vane-type 502
Pumps, hydraulic 727
Punch, sheet-metal processing 312
Pyramids, mathematics 143

Q

Qiescent injection process 363
Quadratic equation 140
Quality 144...149
Quality assurance 144
Quality evaluation 144
Quality, antiknock, fuels 227
Quality-test certificate 146
Quantities and units, selected 12
Quantity of electricity, unit 15
Quench and draw 255
Quick solders 308

R

Rack and pinion steering 587
Radial crushing strength 172
Radial force 378
Radial-piston machine, hydraulics 728
Radial run-out, wheel 574
Radial sleeve bearing 268
Radial tires 576, 577
Radial-tooth overrunning clutch (positork) 525
Radian measure 138
Radiator louver 743
Radiator, finned-tube 412
Radiator, forked-pipe 415
Radiator, disk 415
Radio Data System (RDS) 705
Radio information for drivers 704
Radio Paging (RP) 706
Radio Text (RT) 706
Radio-nuclide testing 319
Rain sensor 115
RAM, Microcomputer 95
Ram-pipe supercharging 372
Random measurement error, statistics 157

Random variable, statistics 151
Range, electric vehicles 528
Range, headlamp 668
Rating sound level, noise 64
RDS see Radio Data System 705
Reactance 76
Reaction time, braking 332, 597
Reaction torque, brake analyzers 644
Reactive power 75
Real time, data-processing in vehs. 160
Real-time response 776
Rear hoisting-gear control 735
Rear muffler 427
Rear seating arrangement 648
Rear underride guards 666
Rear-view mirror, regulations 820
Rear-wheel steering for
passenger cars 592
Recessive bit, CAN 777
Recirculating-ball power-steering
system 591
Recirculation cooling 392
Recrystalization annealing 257
Rectification value,
vibration/oscillation 40
Rectifier diode 88
Recycling and environmental
protection 661
Reduction-gear starters 523
Reflection of light 128
Reflection sound-absorber 417
Reflective photometer 519
Reflectors 129, 671, 675
Reflector size 671
Reflector, variable-focus 672
Refraction of light 128
Regenerator, Stirling engine 406
Regional identification, car radio 704
Registration obligation,
motor vehicles 816
Regular cylinder, mathematics 143
Regulations, braking systems 598
Relative permittivity 71
Relaxation, materials 57
Relays, symbols 744
Release time, brakes 598
Reliability 158
Reliability analysis 158
Reliability function, statistics 155
Reliability, automotive
electronic systems 159
Reliability planning 158
Remagnetization losses 80
Remanence 78, 79
Remote frame, CAN 778
Research octane number (RON) 227
Residual austenite 253
Residual gas amount,
gas exchange 368
Residual ripple, EMC 779
Resistance measurement 73
Resistance spot-welding 306
Resistance, braking 323
Resistance, cornering 325
Resistance, flow 121
Resistance, line 73
Resistance, ohmic 72
Resistance, parallel connection 73
Resistance, rolling 324
Resistance, running 323
Resistance, series connection 73
Resistance, thermal 67
Resistivity, electrical 204
Resistors, symbols 744
Resonance 40
Resonator, Helmholtz 417, 427
Response time, brake 333, 598
Retard mechanism 457
Retardation 330, 598
Retarders 546, 630
Reverse state, semiconductor 87
Reynolds number 47
Rheology 220
Rheopexy 220
Rich mixture, SI engines 428
Right-hand rule 82
Rigid axles 570
Rigidity, body 652
Rims, wheel 572...575, 578
Ring gear, IC engine 523
Ring gear, planetary gears 553
Riveting 310
Road train, definition 646
Road-traffic legislation 814
Road-vehicle classification 647
Road-vehicle requirements 320
Road-vehicle systematics 646
Roadster, definition 646
Roll, suspension 561
Roll angle 342
Roll axis 339
Roll bellows, suspension 566
Roll-bar triggering 720
Rollover test 658
Roll-steer angle 342
Roller ring, VE pump 503
Roller-type overrunning clutch,
starter 525
Rolling bearings, loadability 275
Rolling resistance 323, 324

Rollover protection system 720
Rollover sensor 720
ROM, Microcomputer 95
Roman numerals 822
RON see Research Octane Number 227
Root diameter, gears 294, 297
Root stress of tooth, gears 300
Roots blower 419, 484
Rotary engine 408
Rotary engine, eccentric shaft 408
Rotary engine, epitrochoid 408
Rotary engine, peripheral port 409
Rotary-engine, side port 409
Rotating voltage distribution, electronic ignition 450, 463
Rotational frequency, unit 13
Rotocap, valve guide 391
Rotor, charging systems 423
Rotor arm, ignition distributor 456
Roughness 265
Roughness parameters 265
Route and direction recommendations, Travelpilot 713
Route calculations, Travelpilot 713
RP Code see Radio Paging 706
RPM sensor 106
RQ governor 498
RQV governor 498
RS governor 498
RSF governor 498
RSV governor 498
RT see Radio Text 706
Rubber coating 251
Rubber elements, windshield wipers 695
Rubber suspension 567
Rudge hub, wheels 573
Running resistance 323, 324
Russian Alphabet 822
Rust degree scale 247
Rust formation 245

S

S-cam, drum brakes 626
SAE viscosity grades 223
Safety factor, strength 55
Safety glass 698
Safety margin 334
Safety systems, occupant 717...721
Safety, vehicle body 656...661
Safety, active 656
Safety, conditional 656
Safety, drive 656
Safety, exterior 657
Safety, interior 657
Safety, operating 656
Safety, passive 657, 666
Saloon (sedan), definition 646
Salt spray, stresses 350
Sample, statistics 150
Sample and hold 101
Sand, stresses 350
Saturation polarization 78, 79
Scavenge efficiency, gas exchange 368
Scavenging process 371
Scavenging pump 371
Scooter, definition 646
Score depth 265
Score depth, reduced 265
SCS see Stop Control System 617
Seam welding 307
Seat adjustment, electrical 724
Seat belt, three-point 659, 717
Seat belts, regulations 816
Seat position 648
Seat-belt locking 720
Seat-belt tightener system 659, 717
Seat-belt, inertia-reel 659
Seating reference point 648
Seats 655
Seats, regulations 816
Second, unit 10
Secondary retarder 630
Section modulus 52, 59
Sector, mathematics 142
Segment, mathematics 142
Seizure, wear 318
Selectable four-wheel drive 555
Selective camshaft-lobe actuation 370
Self-diagnosis 477
Self-discharge, battery 765
Self-induction 83
Self-locking screw 285
Self-steering angle 345
Self-steering properties, comm. vehs. 345
Self-steering properties, pass. cars 341
Semi-noble metals 244
Semi-rigid axles 570
Semiconductor devices 88...91, 745
Semiconductor memory 94
Semiconductor pressure sensors 110
Semiconductors 86
Semitrailer towing vehicle, definition 646
Sensors, gradient 107
Sensors, acceleration 107
Sensors, bearing-pin 111
Sensors, fiber-optic 103
Sensors, gradient 107
Sensors, Lambda 113
Sensors, needle-travel 502

Sensors, pressure, micromechanical 99
Sensors, rack-travel 500
Sensors 102...115
Sensors, acceleration 107
Sensors, acceleration and vibration 107
Sensors, capacitive ceramic 109
Sensors, ceramic 109
Sensors, classification 102
Sensors, contamination 115
Sensors, differential 105
Sensors, fiber-optic 103
Sensors, force 111
Sensors, half-differential 105
Sensors, Hall 106
Sensors, ignition triggering 106
Sensors, inductive 106
Sensors, integrated 103
Sensors, integration levels 103
Sensors, knock 108
Sensors, miniaturization procedures 103
Sensors, moment 111
Sensors, oxygen-concentration 113
Sensors, piezoelectric 108, 110
Sensors, position 104
Sensors, radar 107
Sensors, rain 115
Sensors, pressure 99,109
Sensors, RPM 106
Sensors, semiconductor pressure 110
Sensors, short-circuiting disc 105
Sensors, short-circuiting ring 104
Sensors, temperature 113, 114
Sensors, thick-film pressure 109
Sensors, thin-film 107
Sensors, velocity 106
Sensors, vibration 107
Sequence valve 732
Series connection, electrical 73, 76
Series of measurement, evaluation 152
Series of metals, electrochemical 243
Series-wound motor, starters 523
Service description codes, tires 579
Service life, expected 158
Service life, gears 299
Service life, rolling bearings 275
Servo drum brake 626
Shear modulus 54
Shearing stress 54
Sheathed-element glow plug 520
SHED test 484
Sheet steel, body materials 653
Sheet-metal processing 312...314
Shift-point control, autom. transmissions 549
Shift-quality control, autom. transmissions 550
Shift programs, drivetrain 549
Shock absorbers 564
Shock-absorber system, bumper 654
Short whip antenna 706
Short-circuit scavenging 371
Shuttle valves, hydraulic 732
SI engines 358...361
SI engines, hydrogen operation 493
SI Units 10
Side force, piston 378
Side impact 658
Siemens, unit 15
Signal processing 162
Signaling and alarm systems 690...693
Signs and symbols, mathematical 136
Silicone fluids 235
Simplex drum brakes 625
Simpson planetary-gear set 543
Sine function 138
Single-action presses 312
Single-circuit braking system 595
Single-component adhesives 309
Single-fuel operation 490
Single-leaf springs 276
Single-pane toughened safety glass (TSG) 698
Single-point fuel injection unit, Multec (Opel) 437
Single-Point Injection (SPI) 436
Single-spark coil 449, 463
Single-tube shock absorbers 564
Single-winding operation, rotary actuator 467
Single-winding rotary actuator 119
Sinter (PM) metals 174, 177, 192, 197
Sinusoidal input, steering angle 343
Skyhook arrangement, shock absorbers 565
Sliding bearings 268
Slip, tire 556, 584
Slip angle, wheel 337, 342, 582, 584
Small units, hydraulics 729
Smart-power IC 97
SMD see Surface-Mounted Devices 97, 98
Smooth running 378
SMT see Surface-Mounting Technology 98
Soft annealing 257
Soft magnetic materials 79, 176, 194
Soft magnets 176
Soft solders 201
Soil resistance 349

Solar cell 91
Solar module 92
Solar radiation, stresses 350
Soldering 308
Soldering materials 201, 308
Solid angle, optics 131
Solid lubricant 218
Solid-body friction 220, 315
Solid-state laser 314
Solids, properties 178
Solution, chemical, definition 172
Sommerfeld number, bearings 268
Sone 65
Soot filter 427, 513
Sound 60
Sound absorber 417
Sound absorption 61
Sound insulation 61
Sound intensity 60, 62
Sound power 60
Sound pressure 60
Sound spiectrum 61
Sound velocity 60
Sounds, assignment 65
Spark, contact break 456
Spark current 449
Spark duration 446
Spark plugs 451...454
Spark plug, center electrode 451
Spark plug, evaluation 453
Spark plug, ground electrode 451
Spark plug, insulator tip 452
Spark plug, ionic current measurement 452
Spark, ignition 446
Spark-advance mechanisms 457
Spark-ignition (Otto) engine 358...361
Sparking rate 455
SPC see Statistical Process Control 148, 154
Speakers, motor vehicle 706
Special bus, definition 646
Special passenger car, definition 646
Special truck, definition 646
Speed droop, governor 499
Speed governing, diesel engines 497...503
Speed reduction,
SI engines 361
Speed, maximum permissible 815
Speed, transmission (electronic data processing) 163
Speedometers, regulations 820
Speeds, critical 339
Sphere, mathematics 143
Spherical sector, mathematics 143
Spherical segment of one base 143
Spherical segment of two bases 143
Spherical triangle, mathematics 140
Spiral filament, glow plug 520
Spiral torsion spring 277
Splash water, stresses 350
Splitter group, transmission 545
Spot lamps 686
Spray water, stresses 350
Spraying, thermal 249
Spring calculation 276...281
Spring steel 188, 280
Springs 276...281, 566
Squish, IC engines 359, 362
Stabilizer, suspension 567
Standard cells (cell-based IC) 96
Standard deviation 150
Standard distance between centers 296
Standard public bus, body 665
Standard thread, metric 289
Standby pressure, diesel engines 494
Star connection 77
Start of frame, CAN 777
Start-locking relay 526
Start-repeating relay 526
Starter batteries see Batteries 763...767
Starter battery, maintenance-free 763
Starter pinion 523
Starters, inertia-drive 524
Starters, reduction-gear 523
Starters, pre-engaged drive 524
Starters, sliding-gear 525
Starters 523...526
Starting device, diesel engines 500
Starting systems 523...526
Starting temperature 758
Starter tooth design 296
State of aggregation, definition 172
Station wagon, definition 646
Statistical evaluation 155
Statistical parameters 151
Statistical Process Control (SPC) 148, 154
Statistics, technical 157
Stator, electric machines 123
Steel 185...188
Steel sheet 185
Steel springs 566
Steering 586...593
Steering behavior 586
Steering box 587
Steering cylinder 589
Steering kinematics 588
Steering roll-radius 588

Steering systems, power-assisted 588...591
Steering systems, regulations 658
Steering systems, muscular energy 588
Steering, hydrostatic 590
Steering-axis inclination 588
Steering-column adjustment 724
Steering-wheel angle 342
Step input, steering angle 342
Step motor, idle-speed actuator 467
Step-index fiber, optics 133
Stepped reflectors 671
Stick-slip, lubrication 218
Stirling engine 406
Stirling engine, displacer 406
Stoichiometric air-fuel ratio 428
Stop Control System (SCS) 617
Stopping distance 332
Stopping time 332
Stored energy welding 308
Straight ahead position, steering behavior 586
Straight gear 294
Strain-gauge resistor 107
Strength analysis, body 660
Strength of materials 52...59
Stress 52, 55, 172
Stress concentration factor 58
Stress corrosion cracking 245
Stress relief 257
Stresses, environmental 350
Stresses, mechanical 52, 55
Stribeck curve 220
Stripline (EMC) 783
Stroke rate, hydraulic cylinder 726
Structural parts, sinter (PM) metals 193
Stub teeth 297
Sulfur in diesel fuels 230
Sun gear, planetary gears 552
Supercharger, centrifugal 418
Supercharger, mechanically driven 418
Supercharger, positive-displacement 374, 418
Supercharger, Roots-type 418, 419
Supercharger, sliding-vane 419
Supercharger, spiral-type 419
Superchargers 418...423
Supercharging/Turbocharging 372
Suppression levels 781
Surface area of solids 143
Surface fatigue 318
Surface hardening 253
Surface hardness 253
Surface-Mounted Devices (SMD), pcb technology 97
Surface-Mounting Technology (SMT), pcb technology 98
Survival probability, statistics 155
Susceptance 77
Susceptibility 176
Suspension 560...567
Suspension linkage 568...571
Suspension systems 561
Suspension, chemical, definition 172
Swept volume, calculation 399, 402
Swirl-chamber system 364
Switches, symbols 744
Symbols and circuit diagrams 744...755
Synchronous drive belts 305
System audit, quality 144
System of units, physical 11
System of units, SI 10
System of units, technical 11
System reliability 159
System-on-chip 93
Systematic measurement error 157

T

Tachograph 710
Tandem brake master cylinder 606
Tangent functions 138
Tapered-bead seat rim, wheels 572, 573
Taylor gauge test 263
TBI see Throttle Body Injection 436
TDC-Code see Transparent Data Channel 706
Technical optics 128...135
Telescopic shock absorbers 564
TEM cell see Transversal Electromagnetic Field 783
Temperature coefficient 173, 204
Temperature entropy diagram 353
Temperature measurement 68
Temperature sensor 113
Temperature, coolant 413
Temperature, stresses 350
Temperature-sensitive starting device 500
Tempomat 467
Tensile strength 55
Tension, strength 52
Tensions, mechanical 52, 55
Terminal designations 748
Tesla, unit 16
Test adapter, universal 476
Test benches, fuel-injection pumps 511
Test cycle, ECE/EC 486, 487
Test cycle, Japanese 488
Test cycle, USA 484...486

Test cycles, exhaust-gas 483...488
514...518
Test equipment 148
Test program, exhaust-gas testing 483
Test pulses, EMC 780
Test units, SI engines 476
Testing, evaporative emissions,
SI engines 483
Testing, exhaust-gas and emissions
483...489, 513...519
Tex, unit 25
Theft-deterrent systems 692
Thermal afterburning 481
Thermal conduction 66
Thermal conductivity 173
Thermal crack-products 478
Thermal radiation 66
Thermal radiator 130
Thermal resistance 67
Thermal spraying 250
Thermo-time switch 439, 443
Thermochemical treatment 255
Thermocouples 84
Thermodynamic cycle 353
Thermodynamics 69
Thermoelectric series 84
Thermoelectromotive force 84
Thermometers 68
Thermoplastics 175, 210
Thermosets 175, 212
Thick-film circuits 97
Thick-film pressure sensor 109
Thin-film circuits 97
Thin-film sensor 107
Third-octave band spectrum 61
Thixotropy 220
Thomson effect 85
Threads, fasteners 289...291
Thread friction 285
Threaded fasteners 282...291
Threaded fasteners, tightening 284
Three-phase alternating current 77
Three-phase machines 124
Throttle Body Injection (TBI) 436
Throttle plate 430, 436
Throttle switch 443
Throttle valve, hydraulic 730
Throttle actuator 434, 437
Throw sequence, crankshaft 383
Thrown body, equations 46
Thyristor-ignition 460
Thyristors 91
Tightening torque 288
Time zones 37
Time, latency 163
Time, real 160
Time, stopping 332
Timing advance, SI engine 447
Timing device, diesel engines 500, 504
Timing gear, cam driving assembly 390
Timing gear, finger follower 390
Timing gear, overhead
bucket-tappet 390
Timing gear, push-rod 390
Timing gear, rocker-arm 390
Timing gear, single rocker arm 390
Tipping resistance 346
Tiptronic gear-shift strategies 550
Tire designation symbols 578, 580
Tire imbalance 574
Tire pressure 579
Tires, tread 581
Tires, bias-ply 576
Tire-pressure monitoring system,
RKS 721
Tires 576...581, 785...813
Tires and tread surfaces,
regulations 816
Tires, aspect ratio 578
Tires, M+S 576
Tires, radial-ply 576
Tires, special high-traction 576
Tires, speed 579
Tires, tubeless 577
Titanium alloy 191
TMC Code see Traffic Message
Channel 706
Toe-in 568, 588
Tolerance of coaxiality 263
Tolerance of form 263
Tolerance of parallelism 263
Tolerance of perpendicularity 263
Tolerance of position 263
Tolerance of run-out 263
Tolerance of symmetry 263
Tolerance of true running 263
Tool steel 186
Tooth systems 292
Tooth thickness 294
Top Dead Center (TDC), piston 368
Toroid bellows 566
Torque 50, 54
Torque control, diesel
fuel-injection pump 499
Torque motor 119
Torque reduction, ASR 467
Torr, conversion 14, 28, 29
Torsion 54
Torsion spring 277
Torsion-bar spring 278, 566

Torus, mathematics 143
Total Acid Number (TAN), lubricants 219
Total braking time 598
Total charge, gas exchange 368
Total contact ratio, cylindrical gears 294
Total conversion range, transmission 541
Total running resistance 324
Total-loss lubrication 392
Toughness, fracture 172
Tour bus, body 666
Tow-away protection, alarm systems 693
Towing vehicle, definition 646
Tox clinching 311
TR rim, wheels 573
Traction control, ASR 467, 556
Tractive force/speed diagram 537
Tractive-force regulation 735
Tractor hydraulics 734...736
Tractor vehicles 663
Trade names, plastics 214
Traffic Message Channel (TMC) 706
Trailer control valve 637
Trailer couplings, regulations 817
Trailer drawbar loads, regulations 817
Trailers, definitions 646
Transcrystalline corrosion 245
Transfer case 555
Transformer 83
Transformer, electrodynamic 117
Transformer, electromagnetic 117
Transistorized ignition 458
Transistors 89...91
Transit-time methods, sensors 105
Transmission, drivetrain 537, 541
Transmission control, electronic 548
Transmission lubricants 224
Transmission of heat 67
Transmission ratios, passenger-cars 785...813
Transmission, influence on fuel consumption 323
Transmissions, automatic 547
Transmissions, continuously variable 551
Transmissions, manually shifted 543
Transmissions, manually shifted, automatic 546
Transmitter initiative, CAN 778
Transparent Data Channel (TDC) 706
Transputers 94
Transversal Electromagnetic Field (TEM cell) 783
Transverse contact ratio, gears 294
Transverse force 52
Transverse link 571
Trapezoid, area 142
Travel Pilot 712
Tread, tires 816
Triac 91
Triangles, equations 140, 142
Tribology 315...319
Trigonometric functions 138
Trilex wheel system 574
Trilok converter 540
Triode thyristors 91
Trip computer 708
Trip recorders 710, 820
Trolley bus, definition 646
Truck assemblies 664
Truck bodies 663
Truck station wagon, definition 646
Trunk radio networks 715
Tubular heating element, glow plug 520
Tuned-intake tube charging 372
Tungsten inert-gas welding 308
Turbine, gas 410...411
Turbine housing, turbocharger 421
Turbine torque, hydrodyn. couplings 539
Turbocharger 374, 420
Turbocharger, rotary-piston 420
Turbulators, radiator 412
Turn signals 690
Turn-signal systems 690
Twin-rotor rotary engine 409
Twin-tube shock absorbers 565
Two-headlamp system 675
Two-stroke process 371
Two-winding operation, idle actuator 466
Two-wire interface 163
Types of spring, suspension 566

U

U-engine 376
Ultrasonic air-flow measurement 112
Ultrasonic passenger-compartment protection 693
Ultrasound 60
Understeering 338, 341, 587
Uniflow scavenging 371
Unit injector 505
Unitized all-steel body 652
Units, conversion 17...38
Units, legal 11
Universal test adapter 476
Urban bus, definition 646

Useful flux, magnetic circuit 81
Useful signal, EMC 782
Useful speed range 396
Utrasound 60

V

V-belt, narrow 303
V-belt, raw edge 303
V-engine 376
Vacuum advance mechanism 457
Vacuum-operated brake booster 606
Valence 74, 168
Valve arrangement 390
Valve guide 391
Valve lift, infinitely-variable 370
Valve seat 391
Valve timing diagram 391
Valve timing gear 390
Valve timing, infinitely-variable 370
Valve, canister-purge 470
Valve, constant-pressure 497
Valve, constant-volume relief 497
Valve, delivery 496
Valve, dust unloading 417
Valve, external filler, LPG 491
Valve, float needle 432
Valve, flow-interrupt, LPG 491
Valve, idle cut-off 432
Valve, regeneration 470
Valve-train assembly 390
Valves, hydraulic 730
Vane-type supply pump 502
Vapor-phase inhibitors 251
Vapor/liquid ratio, fuels 228
Vapour lock 228
Variable camshaft angle 369
Variable-configurationintake manifold 373
Variable-length intake manifold 469
Variable-length intake runners 373
VCI see Volatile Corrosion Inhibitors 251
Vehicle and engine speeds 328
Vehicle bodies, commercial vehicle 662...667
Vehicle bodies, passenger car 648...661
Vehicle cross-sectional area, projected 651
Vehicle drives, electric 527
Vehicle dynamics 324
Vehicle electrical system 758
Vehicle interior heating 700
Vehicle noise limits, regulations 819
Vehicle springs 276
Vehicle-body sheet metal 189
Vehicle-body calculations 660
Velocity sensor 106
Venturi mixing unit 491
Venturi nozzle, muffler 427
Venturi system, exhaust-gas test 484
Vertical stabilizer fins 338
Vibration absorbers, suspension 565
Vibration corrosion cracking 245
Vibration sensor 107
Vibration and oscillation 39...43
Vibrational characteristics, body 652
Visco coupling 414, 555
Viscosity 221, 234
Viscosity index 221
Viscous limited-slip differential 554
Vision, passenger car 650
Visual range 335, 668
Visual signaling systems 690
Volatile Corrosion Inhibitors (VCI) 251
Volatile memories 94
Volatility 228
Voltage drop, permissable 757
Voltage regulators 774
Voltage, magnetic 81
Volume coefficient of expansion 173
Volume of solids 143
Volumetric efficiency 726
Volumetric efficiency 396
VPC see Vapor Phase Inhibitors 251

W

Wafer 92
Wall-film vaporization 362
Wankel engine see rotary engine 408
Warm-up regulator 439
Washing systems, window cleaning 697
Water cooling 412
Water vapor 183
Water, stresses 350
Watt, unit 14
Wave, definition 40
Wavelength 60
Wear, coefficient 318
Wear, types 316
Weber, unit 16
Wedge of water, aquaplaning 329
Wedge, drum brakes 625
Weibull distribution 155
Weight 11
Welding techniques 306
Weston normal cell 75
Wet boiling point, brake fluids 234
Wheatstone bridge circuit 73
Wheel and tow-away protection 693
Wheel brake 608, 624

Wheel centering 574
Wheel cover 573
Wheel imbalance 574
Wheel load 337
Wheel mounting 572, 574
Wheel position, suspension 568
Wheel speed, ABS 610
Wheel suspension, passenger cars 785...813
Wheelbase, passenger cars 786...813
Wheels, commercial vehicles 573
Wheels, passenger cars 572
Whitworth pipe threads 291
Width requirement, commercial vehicle 3
Windings, symbols 745
Window cleaning 694
Windshield wipers, regula
Windshield wipers, oppos
Windshield wipers, single
Windshield wipers, tande
Windshield, glazing 655,
Windshield-wiper systems
Windshields, windows, wi regulations 817
Wipe/wash system, headl
Wiper blades 695
Wiper motor 696, 697
Wiper potentiometer 104
Wiper systems, rear-windo
Wiring diagram, motor veh
Work, acceleration 331
Work, braking 331, 598
Work, electrical 72
Worked penetration 221
Worm and roller steering 587
Worm gears 293

Y

Yard, conversion 17
Yaw-moment build-up delay 613
Yaw-speed progression 347
Yield point, lubricants 218
Yield strength 172

Z

Zener diode, overvoltage protection 775